Gender and Women's Studies in Canada

This map represents Indigenous territories around the time of European contact in what is now Canada. As our book is rooted most firmly in the Canadian context, we wish to begin by acknowledging and honouring Aboriginal peoples who were the original inhabitants of this land.

Gender and Women's Studies in Canada: Critical Terrain
Edited by Margaret Hobbs and Carla Rice

First published in 2013 by
Women's Press, an imprint of Canadian Scholars' Press Inc.
425 Adelaide Street West, Suite 200
Toronto, Ontario
M5V 3C1

www.womenspress.ca

Canadian Scholars' Press Inc./Women's Press gratefully acknowledges financial support for our publishing activities from the Government of Canada through the Canada Book Fund (CBF).

Library and Archives Canada Cataloguing in Publication

Gender and women's studies in Canada : critical terrain / edited by Margaret Hobbs and Carla Rice.

Includes bibliographical references. Issued also in electronic formats.

ISBN 978-0-88961-484-0

1. Feminism—Canada. 2. Women—Canada. 3. Women's studies—Canada. I. Hobbs, Margaret (Margaret Helen) II. Rice, Carla

HQ1181.C3G46 2013   305.420971   C2012-906926-4

Text design by Brad Horning
Cover design by Em Dash
Cover image: Christi Belcourt, *View from the Canoe #2* (2007)

Printed and bound in Canada by Webcom

Canadä

MIX
Paper from
responsible sources
FSC® C004071

Gender and Women's Studies in Canada

Critical Terrain

Edited by
Margaret Hobbs and Carla Rice

Women's Press
Toronto

Dedication

To the prior generations of feminist thinkers and activists
who have made this project possible;

To Carla's faux daughters, Claire Dion Fletcher and Vanessa Dion Fletcher; Marg's nieces
and stepdaughter—Laura Harris, Emily Harris, and Genevieve Sweigard—
and our students whose insight and energy continue to instruct and inspire us;

To the succeeding generations who will carry the struggle, and the vision, forward.

Table of Contents

Part 1: Foundations:
Why Gender and Women's Studies? Why Feminism?

1a: This Is What a Feminist Looks Like

1b: Diversity and Intersectionality

1c: Women's Status, Women's Rights

Part 2: Constructions of Sex and Gender

2a: The Social and Historical Construction of Sexed Bodies

2b: The Making of "Difference" and Inequalities

2c: The Social Construction of Gender

2d: The Social Construction of Sexuality

Part 3: Gendered Identities

3a: Thinking about Difference and Identity

4e: Social Status and Reproductive Rights

4f: Violence against Women

Part 5: Gendering Work, Globalization, and Activism

5a: Women and Global Restructuring

5b: The "New Economy": On (Not) Getting By in North America

5c: Poverty, Homelessness, and Social Welfare in Canada

Part 6: Organizing for Change

6a: Women's Movements in Canada

6b: Transnational Feminism: Challenges and Possibilities

Acknowledgements

First and foremost, Carla would like to thank her tomboy "big sister" and co-conspirator, Marg Hobbs, who taught her how to teach in women's studies and who mentored her in the challenges and pleasures of delivering the first-year course. Marg wants to thank her lipstick fem friend and co-editor, Carla Rice, for her inspiring pedagogy, but mostly for making this project a lot of fun. And thanks to our families and our partners, Gisele Lalonde and Susan Dion, for their love, support, and patience through the long hours and late nights of lively Skype meetings and writing sessions.

We would like to acknowledge the financial assistance of the Frost Centre for Canadian Studies and Indigenous Studies at Trent University. We are grateful to Julia Smith and Claire Dion Fletcher, who worked diligently on some of the special features of this work, and Gisele Lalonde, who helped with the final proofreading. We also want to thank our colleagues in gender and women's studies at Trent, especially Marg McGraw, Colleen O'Manique, Paula Butler, Sedef Arat-Koç, Nan Peacocke, and Karen Sutherland, who have shared with us the joys and challenges of the first-year course. We are grateful to the many guest speakers who have contributed to the vibrancy of the introductory course. We also acknowledge instructors of gender and women's studies classes across Canada who generously provided with us information about their courses and programs/departments.

Finally, we appreciate the support of Canadian Scholars' Press Inc./Women's Press, in particular Susan Silva-Wayne (editor, social work/women's studies), who invited us into this project and gave us invaluable support in the beginning phases, Caley Baker (production editor), who guided us through a complex editing process, and Daniella Balabuk (developmental editor/permissions coordinator), who worked tirelessly in helping to implement our vision for *Gender and Women's Studies in Canada: Critical Terrain*.

Introduction

Mapping the Terrain of Gender and Women's Studies in Canada

Another world is not only possible, she is on her way. Maybe many of us won't be here to greet her, but on a quiet day, if I listen very carefully, I can hear her breathing.
—Arundhati Roy, *War Talk* (2003, p. 75)

The first problem for all of us, men and women, is not to learn, but to unlearn.
—Gloria Steinem, "Women's Liberation 'Aims to Free Men, Too'" (1970, p. 192)

As we thought about this introduction, we were reminded of these two quotes, the first by Arundhati Roy, who describes herself as an "Indian novelist, activist, and world citizen," and the second by American feminist activist and journalist Gloria Steinem. Roy opens us up to the transformative potential of social justice and solidarity by prompting us to hold fast to the belief that another world is possible, that there are alternatives to inequalities that are deepening the new global world order. We have to keep alive visions of gender and economic justice; they can move us, inspire us, sustain us, and galvanize us as thinkers and activists, as global citizens and as members of local communities, working for change. Steinem's words signal that the road ahead is not easy, that it involves a process of critical examination of many of our most taken-for-granted truths and belief systems about the world around us. It is through unlearning as much as learning that we begin to see how inequalities have been created and, hence, how they can be challenged and undone. Unlearning and learning are intertwined in a continual, connected process: the unpacking of prior knowledge and assumptions is important in making space for new versions and visions of social realities.

This volume engages with these practices: unlearning/learning and envisioning change. We aim to offer a broad selection of writings from a range of authors and perspectives to help introduce you to a field that is at the forefront of critical thinking about inequalities and social justice. This introduction provides students with an entry point to consider what women's studies (or gender and women's studies) involves, how it has changed in recent years, and why it continues to be a meaningful and socially relevant area of inquiry. In what follows, we focus on gender and women's studies in the Canadian context, outlining some of its main goals, explaining some current theoretical developments, and highlighting key features of this book. We conclude with some thoughts about the process of critical thinking and how it might apply to your reading of the writings in this book.

What Is Gender and Women's Studies?

As students coming into gender and women's studies introductory classes, you will have different ideas of what to expect. While some of you may have been introduced to women's studies perspectives through a course or extracurricular involvement at high school, or possibly through conversations with family and friends, for many of you this is your first conscious engagement with this field. You likely have many questions: What is this field variously called "women's studies," "women's and gender studies," "gender and women's studies," or other similar names? How does what I learn here differ from and add to what I am studying in my other courses? How relevant is gender and women's studies to my own life and to my future? Will these perspectives be useful to me in the workforce? Will the topics and approaches introduced in this class reflect or revise my understanding of local and global social relations and structures? How might my values and world view be enriched? What is feminism and do I have to be a feminist to take this course?

As you begin this journey, you should know that women's and gender studies is not one thing. It is not one perspective or one analysis but many, expressed differently by scholars and activists whose ideas and approaches differ from one another, shaped by their own backgrounds, interests, training, experience, and understandings of the world. Not surprisingly, then, introductory courses in this field are also diverse. Some professors might choose to introduce you to the field through a few specific themes, perhaps highlighting gendered analyses of popular culture or recent writings from the "third wave" of feminism. Some might engage more with international contexts and others with North America, and some focus mainly on the present while others explore women's historical experiences as well. Most introductory courses, however, aim for a fairly broad fare, taking you through gender and women's studies across a range of themes, issues, and contexts.

Despite the differences in our approaches and perspectives, there is considerable overlap in what instructors in Canadian universities and colleges are trying to accomplish as they introduce you to what has been, and continues to be, a powerfully influential and transformative field. We recently conducted an informal survey of course outlines and website descriptions of introductory gender and women's studies courses across Canada. The following list highlights some commonly shared goals guiding the teaching of entry-level courses in women's studies or gender and women's studies:

- To introduce students to women's/gender studies as a broad, dynamic, interdisciplinary, and global field of inquiry, and to familiarize students with some of the major issues, debates, and approaches in gender and feminist scholarship and activism
- To complicate commonly presumed understandings of concepts such as "women," "sex," "gender," "race," and "disability" by examining how these categories have been "constructed" (or created by society) and how they shape ideas and experiences of human difference
- To analyze and challenge hierarchical and intersecting relations of power influenced by gender, sexuality, class, race, ethnicity, ability, and other categories of difference
- To understand how power relations are embedded in institutions and in everyday, taken-for-granted social relations, practices, and values
- To highlight affinities and differences among women, both within North America and worldwide, and to analyze intersecting social, cultural, political, and economic systems that shape their lives and agency

- To explore the multiple pathways and forms of women's individual and collective resistance to injustice and inequities in the past and the present, and to analyze their creative visions and strategies for change in local and global contexts
- To inspire and empower students to develop their knowledge of feminist scholarship and to engage critically in their communities at local, national, or global levels
- To develop students' skills in critical thinking and analysis, reading, and writing, and to create classroom environments that support learners' respectful debate and disagreement

These goals reflect a vision of women's and gender studies grounded in knowledge that is continually shifting as the field develops and its insights deepen. Feminist scholars in the past and present have explored how ideas about gender work at interpersonal and institutional levels to shape social relations and the lived experiences of diverse women and men. Their explorations of gender, in relation to other social categories of identity and other axes of power, have been transforming the so-called traditional disciplines such as history, philosophy, politics, psychology, and sociology, while also producing new syntheses of knowledge that we call *interdisciplinary* or even *trans-disciplinary*.

When women's studies courses and programs emerged in North America in the 1960s and 1970s, a period of widespread protest against social and economic injustices, they joined other scholars—for example, in Canadian studies, Native studies, and labour studies—who were similarly interested in pressing beyond the limits of the older disciplines. Like these other interdisciplinary fields informed by critiques of social inequalities and visions of social justice, women's studies aimed to understand social relations in order to change them. You will notice from the goals summarized above that gender and women's studies scholarship continues to offer tools, wisdom, and perspectives enabling a critical engagement with the world and its power structures. At the same time, gender and women's studies offers pathways through which we can better understand ourselves, our diverse experiences and identities, and our relationships with others in the wider world.

Current Trends in Gender and Women's Studies

Gender and women's studies courses, and indeed this textbook, have been shaped in important ways by recent debates and new insights emerging from feminist scholarship. The ideas and the tools they suggest also come out of women's and social justice movements, from diversely positioned and especially marginalized people and grassroots communities, locally and globally, at the forefront of feminist thought and action.

Below we describe four of these major trends that together are making gender and women's studies perspectives more relevant than ever before in the critical task of understanding the world in which we live and the major challenges we face as a human community. This list is not exhaustive; there are many other trends shaping the field and the curriculum itself, but we think it is crucial for instructors and students alike to reflect upon and engage with these four distinct, though overlapping, challenges:

1. The concept and practice of intersectionality
2. Gendering and queering women's studies
3. Indigenizing and decolonizing women's studies
4. Globalizing, internationalizing, and transnationalizing women's studies

1. The Concept and Practice of Intersectionality

Intersectionality is a concept and an approach to understanding the lives and experiences of individuals and groups of people in their diversity and complexity. Emerging as a theoretically important and challenging term in feminist scholarship, intersectionality is often used to describe the idea that women and men live multiple layered identities and simultaneously experience oppression and privilege. The Canadian Research Institute for the Advancement of Women, in an article included in this book, explains an intersectional approach as attempting "to understand how multiple forces work together and interact to reinforce conditions of inequality and social exclusion" (CRIAW, 2006, p. 5).

Intersectionality is not a new concept. The term itself was conceived in the early 1990s by African-American feminists and critical race scholars Patricia Hill Collins (1990) and Kimberlé Crenshaw (1994), and the ideas associated with it have since been adapted and developed by feminist scholars, activists, and organizations in Canada and elsewhere. Intersectionality critiques the limitations of perspectives that look narrowly at social relations through a gender lens alone, encouraging a wider view focused on the multiple components of identity and intersecting "axes" of power that constitute individuals' experiences in the world (Karpinski, 2007; Yuval-Davis, 2006). Intersectional theories and methods work, for example, to explore the specific ways in which factors such as gender, sexuality, aboriginality, class, race, disability, geography, refugee and/or immigrant status, size, and age interact to shape people's social positioning. Such differences are also examined in the context of the larger social and political forces and institutions that create unequal access to power and privilege. Colonialism, capitalism, neo-liberalism, the World Trade Organization (WTO), and social welfare policies are all important examples. By examining the complexities and specificities of identities and social locations, intersectionality explores how women and men occupy many different and contradictory positions in social relations of power.

2. Gendering and Queering Women's Studies

Recent developments in gender, queer, and trans theory and activism across North America have placed a spotlight on gender and sexuality as socially created constructs. In response, women's studies, which initially placed women squarely—some say narrowly—in the centre of analysis, is broadening its focus, and engaging more fully with issues and explorations of masculinities, queer and sexuality studies, and "transfeminism." At their heart, gender and queer theory involve critically analyzing the binary (either/or) categories of woman/man and femininity/masculinity by calling into question "the notion of two discrete tidily organized sexes and genders" (Scott-Dixon, 2006, p. 12). This rich theory base has arisen out of gay, lesbian, bisexual, and transsexual (GLBT) studies, itself a fairly new area of academic inquiry that seeks to understand and contextualize gendered and sexed bodies/identities and erotic desires and practices in different times and places (Meem et al., 2010; Stombler et al., 2010). GLTB studies, along with gender studies, has done much to explore sexual diversity, showing how dominant ideas and "norms" about sexuality, sexed bodies, and sexual practices and identities are not rooted naturally in the facts of biology, but are socially constructed in various ways by different societies. Queer theory goes further, aiming not only to interrogate sexuality norms, but also to turn upside down the very idea of "the normal," namely, "everything in the culture that has occupied a position of privilege, power, and normalcy, starting with heterosexuality" (Bacon, 2007, p. 259). Adding another layer of nuance and complexity, transfeminism has emerged at the intersections of feminist and trans ideas as a vibrant gender-inclusive field dedicated to ending the oppression of all gender-crossing and gender-divergent people (Scott-Dixon, 2006).

3. Indigenizing and Decolonizing Women's Studies

The increased attention to decolonization and indigenization in women's studies comes from the proliferation of Indigenous scholarship and activism, and the critique of the historical marginalization of Indigenous perspectives in much North American feminist thought and practice. "Indigenizing" involves the integration of Indigenous knowledge and perspectives into what counts as knowledge. As such, it goes well beyond the additive approach of writing Aboriginal women into existing Western theories, or squeezing their experiences into one or two classes. Instead, the challenge for gender and women's studies teachers and students is to centre aboriginality more fully by weaving it through and across studies of particular themes and issues; by valuing Indigenous knowledge forms; by analyzing colonialism and its continuing legacies for Aboriginal women and their communities; and by understanding the diversity of Indigenous women's lives and perspectives.

The closely related concept of "decolonizing" refers to the anti-colonial project of critiquing Western world views and challenging oppressive power structures that they uphold. According to Maori scholar Linda Tuhiwai Smith (1999), decolonizing, "once viewed as the formal process of handing over the instruments of government, is now recognized as a long-term process involving bureaucratic, cultural, linguistic, and psychological divesting of colonial power," including in the academy (p. 98). For Davis (2010), decolonization of women's studies means displacing white, Western subjectivities from the centre of course texts and topics, and disrupting Eurocentric, First World privilege through an examination of colonial relations from the perspectives of colonized others. Aboriginal feminists, including Andrea Smith (Cherokee) (2005), Emma LaRocque (Métis) (2007), and Joyce Green (Ktunaxa/Cree-Scots Métis) (2007), see such anti-colonial feminist approaches as critical to grasping urgent issues faced by Indigenous women today. For example, Andrea Smith (2005) argues that because sexual violence has been used as a weapon of colonialism to destroy and assimilate Aboriginal peoples into a white, racist, sexist hierarchy, anti-violence and anti-colonial struggles cannot be separated if feminists hope to end violence against *all* women.

4. Globalizing, Internationalizing, and Transnationalizing Women's Studies

These terms themselves, as well as the practices they entail, are the subject of considerable debate. Sometimes they are used interchangeably. Increasingly, however, the language of global feminism, and hence calls for "globalizing" the curriculum, is giving way to the politics of "internationalizing" and/or "transnationalizing." For most, the term "global" in relation to feminism is too reminiscent of the condescension and denial of differences evident in past Western feminists' scholarly and activist approaches to women in the "Third World" (Grewal & Kaplan, 2006; Mohanty, 1991; Shohat, 2001). Internationalization is often employed as a broad umbrella term encompassing various practices and methods, extending feminism's focus beyond the Western world. Such endeavours, however, if not accompanied by a self-reflective critique of the limits of Western world views, can produce knowledge that reinforces, rather than challenges, dominant cultural stereotypes and misunderstandings.

Mohanty, for example, describes three models for internationalizing women's studies. She critiques the "feminist as tourist" approach, which simply adds "Third World" and Indigenous women into existing analytic frameworks, stereotyping them as either hapless victims or roman-tic heroines (2006). The "feminist as explorer" model can be problematic by focusing on women's lives in specific geographic contexts (through courses such as "Women in India," "Third World Women," etc.) without a sustained analysis of structural power relations. Mohanty (2006) instead encourages a third alternate approach, "feminist solidarity," which recognizes differences and hierarchies of power within and across borders while building on affinities and common interests. Increasingly, a transnational lens (as opposed to an international one) is promoted as a richer way to "teach students how to think about gender in a world whose boundaries have changed" (Kaplan & Grewal 2002, p. 79). Transnational approaches emphasize the movement of capital, labour, information, and culture across national borders; they draw out how histories of coloni-zation and, more recently, globalization structure inequalities; and they explore the possibilities for solidarity among women and social movements organizing across geographic boundaries. In a transnationalized women's studies curriculum, Canada and the US can still be examined, but they are not centred (Mohanty in Dua & Trotz, 2002).

These theoretical and political shifts have challenged gender and women's studies to develop more nuanced theories and methods for understanding social relations and differences. Many instructors and students have taken up that challenge by becoming more inclusive of gender and queer theory (see Wilchins, 2004, in this volume); by better integrating Indigenous feminist thought, issues, and activism (see St. Denis, 2007, this volume); by focusing on the gendered genesis and impacts of colo-nization and globalization in Canada and around the world (Mohanty, 2006); and by questioning their own positioning and implicatedness in current conditions (Blyth, 2008; Dion, 2009). Most feminist educators believe that a sustained focus on sexism is still necessary in gender and women's studies classrooms, especially in the face of deepening global gender inequities. At the same time, the theoretical insights offered by gender and queer theory, Indigenous feminism, and transnational fem-inist thought and activism have led many to radically rethink the subject and focus of women's stud-ies. In this book we invite you to engage with new knowledge and methods emerging from the field and contribute to conversations about the challenges we face in our local and global communities.

Features of This Book

Gender and Women's Studies in Canada: Critical Terrain grew out of a familiar annual ritual for many introductory course instructors: the quest to find the perfect text that will engage and inspire students while guiding them skilfully through the dizzying array of concepts, theories, issues, approaches, histories, and contexts that is contemporary feminist and gender scholar-ship. We have a confession: we have never really liked textbooks. As undergraduate students, we had many occasions to throw our textbooks against the wall—once we awoke from the snooze induced by boredom. What, then, are we doing collaborating on our own introductory textbook in gender and women's studies?

Over time, we have come to appreciate how a textbook can help instructors and students navi-gate the dynamic and swiftly changing terrain of gender and women's studies. A text provides students with a concrete tangible work that they can hold in their hands as a guide. At its best, it can provide intellectual glue that makes more readily apparent the themes and flow of the course, as well as the interconnections between topics and the context within which particular pieces should be read. A textbook can include important learning and research aids such as guid-ing questions, relevant websites, and definitions of key terms. Textbooks that include a diversity of feminist authors introduce learners to multiple perspectives and current debates about topics related to women, gender, feminism, and social justice. We believe it is valuable for students, beginning in their first year, to sharpen their analytic skills and develop their own positions in relation to a *multiplicity* of ideas and arguments.

Of course, the perfect text does not, and cannot, exist. Even with a more modest goal in mind, our own attempt at an introductory textbook has proved challenging, and certainly humbling. One of the most difficult parts of the process has been trimming to a reasonable size our initial wish list of wonderful feminist writings. By editing many pieces for length, we have been able to assemble a broadly representative sampling of works. *Critical Terrain* contributes to the growing list of innovative texts on the Canadian market by offering what we hope you will find to be an appealing collection with several unique characteristics and tools for students and instructors. We present below some of the main features of this volume. These were inspired by a wide reading of existing textbooks, an appreciation for both classic insights and new theoretical developments shaping the field, and a recognition of the diversity of readership.

- *Multiplicity of disciplines and fields:* Since women's studies is a multidisciplinary and inter-disciplinary field, we provide writings that give you, as students, exposure to feminist scholarship from across the disciplines as well as within the newer interdisciplinary and trans-disciplinary women's and gender studies stream. Sociology, psychology, history, phi-losophy, Indigenous studies, literature, cultural studies, biology, science studies, Canadian studies, political economy, and anthropology are some of the areas represented in this text.
- *Historical and contemporary contexts:* Many women's studies texts lean heavily on present-day concerns and circumstances. We chose selections that balance contemporary analyses with historical ones. To address broader society's historical amnesia, we aimed for readings that build a strong foundation in the history of women and other marginalized groups (such as Indigenous and racialized people, people with disabilities, and sexual minorities).
- *Diversity of authors:* We think that it is important to feature work by a broad range of authors from various social, economic, and geographic identities and locations. Different viewpoints from diversely located writers can generate critical debate about issues such as the relevance of gender and women's studies, men's relationship to feminism, gendered and racialized beauty ideals, impacts of globalization on women workers, reproductive technologies, and so on. Thus, we highlight the richness of the literature and the diversity of gendered experiences, perspectives, and analyses. We include voices from the margins as well as the centre.
- *Current and classic selections:* While it can be tempting to showcase the newest writing that is stretching the boundaries of feminist ideas and actions, there is great value in revisiting some of the classic works. We have incorporated older and newer selections to honour the powerful contributions of multiple generations of feminist thinkers, to recognize the interconnectedness of the past and the present, and to acknowledge the indebtedness of contemporary insights to the work, knowledge, and struggle of those who came before.
- *Canadian and Aboriginal content:* When we started thinking about this textbook, Amer-ican collections dominated the market, but there are now an increasing number of Canadian-oriented contributions available. We believe that in Canadian gender and women's studies classrooms, there should be some focus on Canada, partly to chal-lenge commonly voiced assumptions that gender and other inequalities exist mainly beyond our borders (over "there"). Consideration of the specificity of issues in Canada

provides you with critical perspectives on the immediate political, social, economic, and geographic context, where you can also begin to untangle the multiple and complex relations of power between "the West and the rest." We have tried to integrate a focus on Indigenous women and colonial histories within Canada and North America, not merely in a few separate sections of the book, but as sustained themes throughout. There is an exciting and growing body of First Nations, Métis, and Inuit women's writing, including work by Indigenous feminists, and incorporating this work across the themes builds breadth and depth of understanding.

- *Global/transnational content:* Although it is useful to emphasize Canadian specificity, we make links to broader global trends and to the diversity of women's experiences within and between different parts of the world. We hope to encourage you to think about the local and the global as mutually constitutive. Analyses of global systems and institutions of power are introduced, and material by and about women in various locations is included. Throughout this volume, we try to avoid the "feminist as tourist model" so aptly critiqued by Mohanty (2006), where women from other countries are merely added into existing Eurocentric frameworks. By foregrounding Canada, we do not take up fully Mohanty's challenge to internationalize women's studies curriculum in accordance with the "feminist solidarity" model that she promotes. Yet our approach still draws on her insights and those of other transnational feminist scholars.

- *Multiple genres and styles:* As instructors, we appreciate materials that vary genres and styles, exposing students to the numerous forms in which feminist ideas are created, sharpening learners' skills at reading across disciplines, and celebrating variety in ways of learning and knowing. In addition to standard scholarly articles, we include reports, news clips, fact sheets, website materials, short fiction, poetry, interviews, and personal narratives. Personal stories and literary works can teach different truths and move audiences in different ways, and often more intimately, than straight scholarly pieces. Popular works by activists or activist organizations ground the material in practice and let students in on strategies and debates from inside the ranks of social justice movements. We hope these works also inspire you to see the relevance of gender and women's studies, and generate ideas for action-oriented praxis.

- *Tools and insights for education and action:* To enhance the learning process, we have added several tools to this volume. Students and teachers will find useful learning aids in the form of text boxes, activist insights, illustrations, charts, lists, fact sheets, graphs, newspaper articles, maps, and activist campaign materials. We have chosen materials and teaching aids with attention to the wide variation in identities, ages, backgrounds, interests, literacy levels, and other academic skills among the student body.

- *Balance of bad news/good news:* Women's and gender studies instructors are well aware that students can be overwhelmed with the "bad news" about gendered and other socially created inequalities. This is particularly evident when we examine indicators such as growing disparities between the wealthy and the poor within and among nations in contemporary neo-liberal times. The optimism that fuelled second-wave feminists is not as accessible for a host of different reasons, yet we want to teach, learn about, and build on signs of hope. Throughout this reader, we highlight diverse examples and case studies of women's resistance in order to dispel lingering myths about women's powerlessness; challenge gendered, classed, racialized, and ablest stereotypes; and convey a sense of the vibrancy of human agency. Since organized and collective activism, as well as individual actions, can create

change, we have included selections that introduce and analyze the limits and possibilities of resistance in its various forms. Many students and instructors yearn to explore and
share ideas about what we can do—as individuals and in groups of our own making and
choosing—to participate in social justice projects.

Critical Thinking for Change

As professors in gender and women's studies for a combined 30-plus years, we believe that a
grounding in the theories, methods, and values of our field is critically important in an historical
moment marked in many ways by pessimism, uncertainty, and austerity. Feminism has made
significant strides toward gender equality, yet women's movements in Canada and around the
world have faced enormous challenges in recent decades—the rise of economic globalization
and the neo-liberal erosion of social welfare, equality rights, and economic security for women,
racialized people, people with disabilities, and the poor are only a few egregious examples of
troubling trends. In 2004, well-known Canadian feminist Judy Rebick commented on some of
these setbacks in Canada:

> The triumph of neo-liberal/neo-conservative politics has dealt a mortal blow to a femi-
> nism that seeks economic and social equality. The gains we have made are threatened by
> the increasing impoverishment of women, even as a few climb the heights of corporate,
> professional and political success; by the shocking degradation of women in interna-
> tional sex slavery; the overwhelming burden of the double day; longer, rather than
> shorter, work times; the rise of racism, militarism and the security state; the monopoly
> of men on power; closer ties, especially military ties, with the United States; and the
> continuing scourge of war and violence against women and children.

Critical problems require critical thinking. The theories, tools, and world views found in women's
and gender studies build our capacities for thinking our way through pressing social problems
and for beginning to imagine more just alternatives. Beyond introducing students to vitally
important content, the field offers vibrant learning opportunities that teach critical thinking for
both personal and social transformation.

But what, then, is *critical thinking*? Feminist theorist and educator bell hooks writes that
"thinking is an action" (2010, p. 7). Thinking is active because it involves asking questions and
seeking answers in order to understand how the world works. hooks argues that students' passion for knowledge often gets undermined when educational institutions value the consumption of information over the teaching of skills needed to think critically. People commonly
assume that being critical means responding negatively and often dismissively to others' ideas.
Critical engagement, however, does not just mean fault-finding. Instead, it involves learning to
think carefully and skilfully to analyze and evaluate the truth, value, and meaning of an idea
or position. It is active and participatory. It is also hard work. Critical thinking is a process of
discerning what is significant about an issue or topic; analyzing and evaluating other people's
thinking about it; questioning the merit and consequences of different positions, including our
own; and working to create new knowledge (hooks, 2010). Critical thinking provides a way to
expand our consciousness and strive for greater understanding across differences. Because of
this, many progressive educators see it as a tool for fostering freedom, democracy, and equality
(Freire, 2000, 2005; hooks, 2010).

Conversation is integral to critical thinking. hooks (2010) insists that it enables students to find their voices, identify the issues that matter to them, discover new ways of seeing and knowing, and better remember the ideas exchanged in the classroom. As students taking gender and women's studies, you have opportunities to engage in many kinds of conversations: with instructors, other students, and, importantly, with the authors of the texts you read. At the same time, like many learners in introductory classes, you may have come to university perplexed about *how* to read assigned texts, listen to lectures, or enter into conversations about what you have read and heard. We must remind ourselves that people engaged in respectful conversation are not passive; rather, participants are alive, open, reflective, and reaching for understanding to deepen, strengthen, and communicate knowledge.

In any learning situation, teachers and students enter a relationship. Lecturers have significant responsibilities, but so too do students. The first is *listening*—again, an active, participatory process. Listening does not mean you stop thinking. Rather, it means striving to make meaning of the speaker's message by working to digest and understand, and from there to analyze and reflect on what they are saying. At the same time, pausing to listen does not mean that you must agree with what is being said. Remember that teaching and learning are processes and that knowledge is always changing and evolving. As listeners, it is your responsibility to acknowledge what you are learning, but also what remains unclear, underdeveloped, or open to question. Careful listening can also lead to well thought-out disagreement and dissent, which are vitally important to critical thinking.

A second set of responsibilities involves *self-reflection*, or examining your responses to others' ideas and questioning how your preconceptions and social positioning may be implicated in your hearing. We each bring our personal histories, identities, social relationships, commitments, values, and politics to our listening. Rather than the common knee-jerk reaction of rejecting new ideas outright, particularly those that challenge dominant thought and the status quo, how can you take seriously unfamiliar ways of thinking? What do your immediate responses to these ideas teach you about yourself and, possibly, your own positionality? Your job is to look for points of connection that can aid in meaning-making while opening yourself to the possibility that the new ideas and vantage points might actually change you. They might take you someplace else, to transport you to new understanding.

A third challenge is *speaking up* and articulating your thoughts, ideas, and positions effectively and respectfully. While speaking in groups can be nerve-racking, finding your voice and figuring out how to use it is a valuable skill whether you continue in academe, pursue a professional degree, or enter the workforce. Both generosity and intellectual rigour are vital to creating an ethical space for sharing ideas and learning from each other. But how can you contribute to creating that space? Before and as you speak, keep reflecting: What is the point of my question or comment? You might also be thinking about your position in relation to the subject under discussion by asking yourself: Who am I in relationship to this topic? What do I bring that can give a unique perspective on this topic? How does my position influence my understanding?

This brings us to the fourth challenge: *critical reading*. The core elements of critical thinking discussed above are also foundational to critical reading. Engagement with written texts similarly demands listening, self-reflection, and even speaking, since you are entering into dialogue with the author. The Academic Skills Centre at our university encourages students to ask questions of the text, to respond to it and to evaluate it—in short, to "make it *mean* something to you" (Academic Skills Centre Handout, http://www.trentu.ca/academicskills/online_StudySkills.php; emphasis ours). Reading requires different approaches to understanding and meaning-making, depending on the type of text you are examining. As you look at each selection in this textbook, it is useful to consider first the genre of the work. Is it a scholarly article? A report by a government or community organization? A newspaper article? A fictional short story? A poem? A personal narrative or an interview? A map, chart, or other kind of illustration? The specific questions you ask as an active reader might vary across genres. At the same time, there are some overarching questions that can guide you in your comprehension and interpretation. Here we outline eight points of entry involving probes intended to facilitate your reading as an active and interactive process.

Questions for Critical Reading

- How and where does this selection fit into the parts and sections of this text and of your course? How does it relate to the main themes examined in this part and section?
- Is the subject matter new to you or do you have some familiarity with it?
- What are the main ideas? How are these ideas presented? How do they relate to what is being addressed in this part of the textbook and in your class?
- If you are reading a scholarly article, what is the central argument or thesis? What information is used as evidence to support the argument? Is the argument persuasive?
- How might this selection relate to key concepts emphasized in this part of the textbook and in your class?
- Is the piece trying to challenge and change dominant thinking about something, deepen and transform your understanding, encourage personal reflection, and/or mobilize you to action?
- Does the piece resonate with your own experiences and/or analyses of the issue or topic? Are there elements that you are questioning? What remains confusing, unclear, or underdeveloped?
- Why is this piece significant? Why do you think it was included as one of your readings?

The Critical Terrain of This Book

We have organized this book into six thematic parts:

Part 1: Foundations: Why Gender and Women's Studies? Why Feminism?
Part 2: Constructions of Sex and Gender
Part 3: Gendered Identities
Part 4: Cultural Representations and Body Politics
Part 5: Gendering Work, Globalization, and Activism
Part 6: Organizing for Change

Within each part, there are between two and six sections that develop the topics and address some key debates in feminist scholarship and activism.

The "critical terrain" signalled in our title has multiple meanings for this volume and for the future of gender and women's studies. Certainly the theoretical trends we have outlined, and that are taken up throughout the book, constitute critical shifts in a field that is continually being re-mapped. Marginalized peoples around the world are facing critical problems requiring critical thought and action by all of us as members of local and global communities. We are at a critical juncture where systems of power and political ideologies are heightening divisions between people, pushing certain groups further to the margins. In this context, feminism offers critical insights and tools for transforming landscapes of inequalities.

As we pass this volume over to you, we hope that you will be informed, engaged, challenged, and inspired by the content and the range of selections. Each piece offers its unique wisdom, and we hope that you will discover your own treasures in these pages. We also hope you will attend to the diversity of voices, issues, identities, and perspectives, taking care to reflect on their meanings and their contributions to feminist critical thought and action. Finally we hope that this textbook facilitates your social justice consciousness as it also fosters your intellectual and creative capacities to appraise and envision different avenues to change. We invite you into the conversation, and like to imagine you discussing, sharing, and debating the ideas with others in various forums and contexts.

Note: Portions of this introduction were adapted from two articles we co-authored: "Rethinking Women's Studies: Curriculum, Pedagogy, and the Introductory Course," published in *Atlantis: A Woman's Studies Journal* (2011a) and "Reading Women's and Gender Studies in Canada: A Review of Recent Introductory Textbooks," published in *Canadian Woman Studies* (2011b).

References

Academic Skills Centre at Trent University. (n.d.). "Reading Critically and Efficiently: Strategies for Study." Retrieved from: http://www.trentu.ca/academicskills/online_StudySkills.php.

Bacon, Jen. (2007). "Teaching Queer Studies at a Normal School." *Journal of Homosexuality, 52*(1), 257–83.

Blyth, Molly. (2008). "'So, What's a White Girl Like Me Doing in a Place Like This?' Re-thinking Pedagogical Practices in an Indigenous Context." *Resources for Feminist Research, 33*(1/2), 63–80.

Canadian Research Institute for the Advancement of Women (CRIAW). (2006). *Intersectional Feminist Frameworks: An Emerging Vision.* Ottawa: Canadian Research Institute for the Advancement of Women.

Collins, Patricia Hill. (1990). *Black Feminist Thought: Knowledge, Consciousness, and the Politics of Empowerment* (1st ed.). Boston: Unwin Hyman.

Crenshaw, Kimberlé. (1994). "Mapping the Margins: Intersectionality, Identity Politics, and Violence against Women of Color." In Martha Fineman & Roxanne Mykitiuk (Eds.), *The Public Nature of Private Violence* (pp. 93–118). New York: Routledge.

Davis, Dawn Rae. (2010). "Unmirroring Pedagogies: Teaching with Intersectional and Transnational Methods in the Women and Gender Studies Classroom." *Feminist Formations, 22*(1), 136–62.

Dion, Susan. (2009). *Braiding Histories: Learning from Aboriginal Peoples' Experiences and Perspectives.* Vancouver: University of British Columbia Press.

Dua, Ena, & Trotz, Alissa (Eds.). (2002). "Transnational Pedagogy: Doing Political Work in Women's Studies. An Interview with Chandra Taldade Mohanty." *Atlantis, 26*(2) (Spring/Summer), 66–77.

Freire, Paulo. (2000). *Pedagogy of the Oppressed: 30th Anniversary Edition.* New York: Continuum.

Freire, Paulo. (2005). *Education for Critical Consciousness.* New York: Continuum.

Green, Joyce. (2007). "Taking Account of Aboriginal Feminism." In Joyce Green (Ed.), *Making Space for Indigenous Feminism* (pp. 20–32). Black Point, NS: Fernwood.

Grewal, Inderpal, & Kaplan, Caren (Eds.). (2006). *An Introduction to Women's Studies: Gender in a Transnational World* (2nd ed.). Boston: McGraw Hill.

Hobbs, Margaret, & Rice, Carla. (2011a). "Rethinking Women's Studies: Curriculum, Pedagogy, and the Introductory Course." *Atlantis, 35*(2), 139–49.

Hobbs, Margaret, & Rice, Carla. (2011b). "Reading Women's and Gender Studies in Canada." *Canadian Woman Studies, 29*(1 & 2), 201–07.

hooks, bell. (2010). *Teaching Critical Thinking: Practical Wisdom.* New York: Routledge.

Kaplan, Caren, & Grewal, Inderpal. (2002). "Transnational Practices and Interdisciplinary Feminist Scholarship: Refiguring Women's and Gender Studies." In Robyn Wiegman (Ed.), *Women's Studies on Its Own: A Next Wave Reader in Institutional Change* (pp. 66–81). London: Duke University Press.

Karpinski, Eva. (2007). "'Copy, Cut, Paste': A Reflection on Some Institutional Constraints of Teaching a Big Intro Course." *Resources for Feminist Research, 32*(3/4), 44–53.

LaRocque, Emma. (2007). "Metis and Feminist: Ethical Reflections on Feminism, Human Rights, and Decolonization." In Joyce Green (Ed.), *Making Space for Indigenous Feminism* (pp. 53–71). Black Point, NS: Fernwood.

Meem, Deborah, Gibson, Michelle, & Alexander, Jonathan (Eds.). (2010). *Finding Out: An Introduction to LGBT Studies.* Thousand Oaks, CA: Sage.

Mohanty, Chandra Talpade. (1991). "'Under Western Eyes': Feminist Scholarship and Colonial Discourses." In Chandra Mohanty, Ann Russo & Loudes Torres (Eds.), *Third World Women and the Politics of Feminism* (pp. 51–80). Bloomington, IN: Indiana University Press.

Mohanty, Chandra Talpade. (2006). "'Under Western Eyes' Revisited: Feminist Solidarity through Anticapitalist Struggles." In Chandra Talpade Mohanty (Ed.), *Feminism without Borders: Decolonizing Theory, Practicing Solidarity* (pp. 221–51). London: Duke University Press.

Rebick, Judy. (2004, March 15). "We've Come Part Way, Baby: A New Opportunity Has Opened for the Women's Movement." Retrieved from: http://rabble.ca/news/weve-come-part-way-baby.

Roy, Arundhati. (2003). *War Talk.* Cambridge: South End Press.

Scott-Dixon, Krista (Ed.). (2006). *Trans/forming Feminisms: Trans-feminist Voices Speak Out.* Toronto: Sumach.

Shohat, Ella. (2001). "Area Studies, Transnationalism, and the Feminist Production of Knowledge." *Signs, 26*(4), 126–72.

Smith, Andrea. (2005). *Conquest: Sexual Violence and American Indian Genocide.* Cambridge, MA: South End Press.

Smith, Linda Tuhiwai. (1999). *Decolonizing Methodologies: Research and Indigenous Peoples.* London: Zed Books.

St. Denis, Verna. (2007). "Feminism Is for Everybody: Aboriginal Women, Feminism, and Diversity." In Joyce Green (Ed.), *Making Space for Indigenous Feminism* (pp. 33–52). Black Point, NS: Fernwood.

Steinem, Gloria. (1970, June 7). "Women's Liberation 'Aims to Free Men, Too.'" *The Washington Post*, p. 192.

Stombler, Mindy, et al. (Eds.). (2010). *Sex Matters: The Sexuality and Society Reader* (3rd ed.). Toronto: Allyn & Bacon.

Wilchins, Riki. (2004). *Queer Theory, Gender Theory.* Los Angeles: Alyson.

Yuval-Davis, Nira. (2006). "Intersectionality and Feminist Politics." *European Journal of Women's Studies, 13*(3), 193–209.

Part 1 Foundations: Why Gender and Women's Studies? Why Feminism?

To be truly visionary we have to root our imagination in our concrete reality while simultaneously imagining possibilities beyond that reality.

—bell hooks, *Feminism Is for Everybody: Passionate Politics* (2000, p. 110)

Part 1 addresses popular misconceptions and stereotypes about feminism, and men's engagements with feminism in contemporary North America. We review some markers of progress and continuing problems in the current status of women in Canada. The concept of "intersectionality" is introduced as a tool to understand women's and men's diverse experiences and relations to systems of power and inequality.

1a: This Is What a Feminist Looks Like

This section introduces you to different ways in which "feminism" has been understood and practised in the past and present. The articles offer multiple definitions of feminism, examine its history and relevance to women's and men's lives, and consider the many myths and stereotypes associated with the term.

1b: Diversity and Intersectionality

Part 1B examines differences among women, in particular differences informed by race, class, geography, histories of colonization and slavery, and embodiment, and introduces the idea of intersectionality to understand/analyze how these shape women's and men's lives.

1c: Women's Status, Women's Rights

In this section, we provide an overview of key markers of progress and problems in the status of women in the Canadian and global contexts. Issues introduced include political representation, income, gendered and racialized labour markets, and women's work in the domestic sphere.

1a This Is What a Feminist Looks Like

Chapter 1

You're a Hardcore Feminist. I Swear.

Jessica Valenti

Jessica Valenti is a well-known American feminist writer, lecturer, and activist. Named one of the Top 100 Inspiring Women in the World by The Guardian, *she is the author of three books, including* The Purity Myth: How America's Obsession with Virginity Is Hurting Young Women, *which has been made into a documentary. Valenti is founder of feminist-ing.com, a feminist online community, for which she has won various awards, including the 2011 Hillman Journalism Prize.*

What's the worst possible thing you can call a woman? Don't hold back, now.

You're probably thinking of words like slut, whore, bitch, cunt (I told you not to hold back!), skank.

Okay, now, what are the worst things you can call a guy? Fag, girl, bitch, pussy. I've even heard the term "mangina."

Notice anything? The worst thing you can call a girl is a girl. The worst thing you can call a guy is a girl. Being a woman is the ultimate insult. Now tell me that's not royally fucked up. Recognizing the screwed nature of this little exercise doesn't necessarily make you a feminist. But it should. Most young women know that something is off. And even if we know that some things are sexist, we're certainly not ready to say we're feminists. It's high time we get past the "I'm not a feminist, but ..." stuff. You know what I'm talking about: "I'm not a feminist or anything, but it is total bullshit that Wal-Mart won't fill my birth control prescription."

Do you think it's fair that a guy will make more money doing the same job as you? Does it piss you off and scare you when you find out about your friends getting raped? Do you ever feel like shit about your body? Do you ever feel like something is wrong with you because you don't fit into this bizarre ideal of what girls are supposed to be like?

Well, my friend, I hate to break it to you, but you're a hardcore feminist. I swear.

Feel-Good Feminism

For some reason, feminism is seen as super anti: anti-men, anti-sex, anti-sexism, anti-everything. And while some of those antis aren't bad things, it's not exactly exciting to get involved in something that's seen as so consistently negative.

The good news is, feminism isn't all about antis. It's progressive and—as cheesy as this sounds—it's about making your life better. As different as we all are, there's one thing most young women have in common: We're all brought up to feel like there's something wrong with us. We're too fat.

We're dumb. We're too smart. We're not ladylike enough—stop *cursing, chewing with your mouth open, speaking your mind.* We're too slutty. We're not slutty enough.

Fuck that.

You're not too fat. You're not too loud. You're not too smart. You're not unladylike. *There is nothing wrong with you.*

I know it sounds simple, but it took me a hell of a long time to understand this. And once I did, damn, did it feel good. Why go through your life believing you're not good enough and that you have to change?

Feminism not only allows you to see through the bullshit that would make you think there's something wrong with you, but also offers ways to make you feel good about yourself and to have self-respect without utilizing any mom-popular sayings, like "Keep your legs together," or boy-popular screamings, like "Show me your tits!"

Really, imagine how nice it would be to realize that all the stuff you've been taught that makes you feel crappy just isn't true. It's like self-help times one hundred.

But all that said, I really do understand the hesitancy surrounding the f-word. My own experience with the exercise that kicked off this chapter—"What's the worst possible thing you can call a woman?"—was presented by a professor on the first day of a women's literature class after she asked how many of us were feminists. Not one person raised a hand. Not even me. My excuse-ridden thinking was, *Oh, there's so many kinds of feminism, how can I say I know what they're all about? Blah, blah, blah, I'm a humanist, blah, blah, blah.* Bullshit. When I think back on it, I knew I was a feminist. I was just too damn freaked out to be the only one raising her hand.

Most young women *are* feminists, but we're too afraid to say it—or even to recognize it. And why not? Feminists are supposed to be ugly. And fat. And hairy! Is it fucked up that people are so concerned about dumb, superficial stuff like this? Of course. Is there anything wrong with being ugly, fat, or hairy? Of course not. But let's be honest: No one wants to be associated with something that is seen as uncool and unattractive. But the thing is, feminists are pretty cool (and attractive!) women.

So let's just get all the bullshit stereotypes and excuses out of the way.

But Feminists Are Ugly!

Yawn. Honestly, this is the most tired stereotype ever. But it's supersmart in its own way. Think about it, ladies. What's the one thing that will undoubtedly make you feel like shit?

Someone calling you ugly.

Back in fifth grade, the love of my life was Douglas Macintyre, who told me I'd be pretty if only I didn't have such a big, ugly nose. I shit you not when I say that for months, every day after school I would stand in front of the three-way mirror in my bathroom, staring at the offending body part and trying to figure out how a nose could go so horribly, horribly wrong.

Ugly stays with you. It's powerful, and that's why the stereotype is so perfect. The easiest way to keep women—especially young women—away from feminism is to threaten them with the ugly stick. It's also the easiest way to dismiss someone and her opinions. ("Oh, don't listen to her—she's just pissed 'cause she's ugly.")

Seems stupid, right? I mean, really, what's with this *na-na-na-boo-boo* kind of argument? Have you ever heard of a Republican saying, "Oh, don't be a Democrat; they're all ugly"? Of course not, because that would be ridiculous. But for some reason, ridiculous is commonplace when it comes to the f-word.

For example, conservative radio host Rush Limbaugh says that feminism was established "to allow unattractive women easier access to the mainstream of society." Okay—have you ever *seen* Rush Limbaugh? Yeah, enough said. Oh, and by the way—I think I'm pretty hot now. So screw you, Douglas Macintyre.

But Things Are Fine the Way They Are!

What do I know? Maybe things are fine for you. Maybe you're lucky and superprivileged and you wake up in the morning to birds chirping and breakfast in bed and all that good stuff. But chances are, that's not the case.

There are plenty of folks who argue that feminism has achieved its goal. The 1998 *Time* magazine article "Is Feminism Dead?" said, "If the women's movement were still useful, it would have something to say; it's dead because it has won."[1]

There's no doubt that women have made progress, but just because we get to vote and have the "right" to work doesn't mean things are peachy keen. Anyone who thinks women have "won," that all is well and good now, should ask why the president of Harvard can say that maybe women are naturally worse at math and then have people actually take him seriously.[2] Or why a teacher can still get fired for being pregnant and unmarried.[3]

Seriously, are things really cool the way they are when so many of us are upchucking our meals and getting raped and beat up and being paid less money than men? And being denied birth control, and being told not to have sex but be sexy, and a hundred other things that make us feel shitty?

Methinks not. It can be better. It has to be.

Feminism Is for Old White Ladies

This one didn't come out of nowhere. The part of the feminist movement that has been most talked about it, most written about, and most paid attention to is the rich-whitey part. For example, back in the '60s and '70s, white middle-class feminists were fighting for the right to work outside the home, despite the fact that plenty of not-so-privileged women were already doing exactly that. Because they had to (more on this later).

Even now, issues of race and class come up in feminism pretty often. But unlike in days of yore, now they're being addressed. Besides, feminism isn't just about the organizations you see at protests, or what you hear about in the news. Feminist actions—particularly the kind spearheaded by younger women—are as diverse as we are. You'll see what I mean when you get to the end of this chapter: Young women are working their asses off for causes they believe in. Which is why this next stereotype is so very annoying.

Feminism Is So Last Week

Every once in a while, there's some big article about feminism being dead—the most famous of which is the aforementioned *Time* piece. And if feminism isn't dead, it's equally often accused of being outdated. Or a failure. Or unnecessary.

But if feminism is dead, then why do people have to keep on trying to kill it? Whether it's in the media, politics, or conservative organizations, there's a big old trend of trying to convince the world that feminism is long gone.

The argument is either that women don't need feminism anymore, or that those crazy radical feminists don't speak for most women. Never mind that recent polls show that most women support feminist goals, like equal pay for equal work, ending violence against women, childcare, women's healthcare, and getting more women in political office. Here comes that "I'm not a feminist, but ..." stuff again!

The obsession with feminism's demise is laughable. And if the powers that be can't convince you that it's dead, that's when the blame game starts. Feminism is the media's favorite punching bag.

The horrors that feminism is supposedly responsible for range from silly contradictions to plainly ludicrous examples. In recent articles, feminism has been blamed for promoting promiscuity;[4] promoting man-hating; the torture at Abu Ghraib; ruining "the family"; the feminization of men; the "failures" of Amnesty International; and even unfairness to Michael Jackson.[5] I'm not kidding. You name it, feminism is the cause.

My all-time favorite accusation: Feminism is responsible for an increase in the number of women criminals. You're going to love this. Wendy Wright of Concerned Women for America—a conservative anti-feminist organization—is quoted in a 2005 article, "Rising Crime among Women Linked to Feminist Agenda," as saying it's pesky feminists who are to blame for the increase of women in prison.[6]

Wright claims that women are committing crimes because feminism has taught them that "women should not be dependent on others" and that "they don't need to be dependent on a husband," which inevitably forces them to "fend for themselves."[7]

Got that, girls? Without a husband to depend on, you'll be selling crack in no time!

For something that is so tired and outdated, feminism certainly seems to be doing a lot of damage, huh?

Obviously there's an awful lot of effort being put into discrediting the f-word—but why all the fuss? If folks didn't see feminism as a threat—and a powerful one—they wouldn't spend so much time putting it down, which is part of what attracted me to feminism in the first place. I wanted to know what all the brouhaha was about.

It's important to remember that all of these stereotypes and scare tactics serve a specific purpose. If you think feminism is all about big fat ugly dykes, or is dead or racist, then you'll stay far the hell away from it.

'Cause don't forget—there are a lot of people benefiting from your feeling like shit about yourself. Think about it: If you don't feel fat, you won't buy firming lotions and diet pills and the like. If you don't feel stupid, you might speak out against all the screwy laws that adversely affect women. It pays—literally—to keep women half there. And god forbid you get involved in anything that would make you wonder why in the world women are having surgery to make their vaginas "prettier."[8] (Sorry, I couldn't help but mention it; it's too freaky not to.)

The solution? Don't fall for it. If feminism isn't for you, fine. But find that out for yourself. I'm betting that you're more likely to be into something that encourages you to recognize that you're already pretty badass than something that insists you're a fat, dumb chick.

Femi-wha?

There are so many stereotypes about feminism, and so many different definitions of it, that what feminism actually is gets insanely confusing—even for women who have been working on women's issues for years. But I always was a fan of the dictionary definition. And I promise this is the only time I'll be quoting the frigging dictionary:

fem·i·nism
1 Belief in the social, political, and economic equality of the sexes.
2 The movement organized around this belief.[9]

Hmm ... don't see anything about man-hating in there. Or hairy legs. Obviously, there are tons of different kinds of feminism and schools of thought, but I'd say the above is enough to get you started. Besides, at the end of the day, feminism is really something you define for yourself.

Sisterhood, My Ass

No matter how clear-cut (or how complex) feminism can be, not all women are feminists by virtue of having ovaries. And that's just fine by me. I realized this in a big way recently. I was quoted in Rebecca Traister's 2005 Salon.com article entitled "The F-Word,"[10] airing my feelings about the word "feminist"—and I got a little pissy. "Part of me gets so angry at younger women who are nervous about feminism because they're afraid that boys won't like them.... Part of me wants to say, 'Yeah, someone's going to call you a lesbian. Someone's going to say you're a fat, ugly dyke. Suck it up.'"[11] My attempt to strongly defend the word "feminism" didn't go over well with a lot of people. One woman actually posted a homophobic rant of a response to Salon.com:

> I'll call myself a feminist when the fat, mannish dykes who do run around calling themselves "Feminist" very loudly and constantly concede that my decision to groom and dress myself as a twenty-first-century professional woman is every bit as valid a choice as their decision to become stereotypical jailhouse bulldaggers. Ovaries only make you female, they do not make you woman, and I am a woman. In other words, I will call myself a feminist when those mannabees are as proud of and joyful in their womanhood as I am in mine.... Until then, fuck off and take your hairy legs with you.[12]

Crazy, right? I didn't need much more than this to realize that feminism isn't for everybody. I never really bought the "We're all sisters" thing anyway. I've met enough racist, classist, homophobic women to know better. Feminism's power isn't in how many women identify with the cause. I'll take quality over quantity any day.

Quality Women

So who are these elusive feminists? Like I've said—you are, even if you don't know it yet. Though I'm hoping by now you're at least slightly convinced. The smartest, coolest women I know are feminists. And they're everywhere. You don't need to be burning bras (actually, this never happened—total myth) or standing on a picket line to be a feminist. Chances are, you've already done stuff that makes you a feminist. You don't have to be a full-time activist to be an awesome feminist.

The work that young women are doing across the country is pretty goddamn impressive. Do they all consider themselves feminists? Probably not. But a lot of the work they're doing is grounded in feminist values. Just a few examples:

A group of high school girls in Allegheny County, Pennsylvania, organized a "girlcott" of

Abercrombie & Fitch when the clothing company came out with a girls' shirt that read: WHO NEEDS BRAINS WHEN YOU HAVE THESE? After the group caused quite a ruckus in the media, A&F pulled the shirt.

Two young women in Brooklyn, Consuela Ruybal and Oraia Reid, used their own money to start an organization called RightRides after a number of young women were raped in their neighborhood. Women can call the service anytime from midnight to 4 AM on the weekends and get a free ride home. Simple, but damn effective. Their motto is: "Because getting home safe should not be a luxury."

The documentary film *The Education of Shelby Knox* was inspired by a high school student in Lubbock, Texas, who took on her town's school board to fight for comprehensive sex education. Shockingly, the abstinence-only brand they were receiving wasn't quite cutting it.

A group of queer women, tired of seeing the art world bypass great women artists, started *riff-RAG* magazine. The magazine features work that slips under the mainstream's radar.

Misty McElroy decided to start Rock 'n' Roll Camp for Girls as part of a class project at Portland State University. She expected about twenty girls to sign up—she ended up getting three hundred. Rock 'n' Roll Camp for Girls teaches young girls to play instruments, deejay, sing, and write songs and ends with a live performance. The camp was so popular in Oregon that there are now rock camps in New York City, Washington, D.C., Nashville, Tennessee, Tucson, Arizona, and various California locations.

This is just a small sampling of the amazing work young women are already doing (and they say we're apathetic!), and it doesn't even touch on all the women's blogs, online and print zines, and community programs that are out there. These women and their work prove that feminism is not only alive and well, but also energized and diverse. Not to mention fun.

You can be a feminist without making it your life's work. It's about finding the cause that works for you, and makes you happy, and doing something about it. (Trust me, getting off your ass can be more fun than you think.) For some women, that means working in women's organizations, fighting against sexist laws. For others, it means volunteering time to teach young girls how to deejay. It doesn't matter what you're doing, so long as you're doing something. Even if it's as simple as speaking up when someone tells a nasty-ass sexist joke.

There's a popular feminist shirt these days that reads: THIS IS WHAT A FEMINIST LOOKS LIKE. Ashley Judd wore one at the 2004 pro-choice March for Women's Lives in Washington, D.C. Margaret Cho wore one on the Spring 2003 cover of *Ms.* magazine. I wear one, too; I love this shirt. Because you never really do know what a feminist looks like. And believe me, we're everywhere.

Notes

1. Ginia Bellafante, "Is Feminism Dead?" *Time* magazine, June 29, 1998.
2. Lawrence Summers is the former president of Harvard University. At a conference about women and minorities in science and engineering while he was still president, Summers theorized that one of the reasons for the lower number of women in the math and science fields was that women don't have the same "natural" or "innate" ability as men.
3. Christine John, a first-year teacher at the Village Adventist Elementary School in Berrien Springs, Michigan, was placed on administrative leave for getting pregnant out of wedlock in 2005. Also in 2005, Michelle McCusker, an unmarried teacher at St. Rose of Lima School in Queens, New York, was fired after she told school officials she was pregnant.

4. Monique Stuart, "Slutty Feminism," *The Washington Times,* January 1, 2006.

5. I'll provide the following articles just to give you a sampling of what's out there: Phyllis Schlafly, "Feminist Dream Becomes Nightmare," Human Events Online, May 18, 2004; Carey Roberts, "Amnesty Stuck on the Shoals of Political Correctness," MensNewsDaily. com, June 4, 2005; David Usher, "Feminism, the WKKK, and the Gender-lynching of Michael Jackson," MensNewsDaily.com, April 21, 2005.

6. Mary Rettig. "CWA Official: Rising Crime among Women Linked to Feminist Agenda," AgapePress, October 27, 2005.

7. Ibid.

8. Vaginal "rejuvenation" is the newest form of plastic surgery by which women can get labiaplasties, vaginal tightening, and liposuction on their labia.

9. *The American Heritage Dictionary.*

10. Rebecca Traister, "The F-Word," Salon.com, July 5, 2005.

11. Ibid.

12. Post in response to Rebecca Traister's "The F-Word." Found online at: www.sabreean. com/?p=10.

Top 10 Feminist Stereotypes

Stop the presses!

I am so sick of being placed into a little box based upon people's inability to think beyond stereotypes.

I understand that people need ways to process information and grouping people by *(perceived)* similar characteristics can be helpful when looking at the world. But the problem is that sometimes people are so focused on their narrow views that they fail to realize that one size does not fit all.

All [insert racial group] are not the same. We do not all have the same interests. We do not all speak the same way. We don't all eat the same foods.

All [insert gender] are not the same. We do not all have the same interests. We do not feel the same way about all issues. We do not all react the same way to the same things.

I think these are somewhat easy to understand—because these types of stereotypes are often discussed. But what about when it comes to things that are slightly more specific?

For the record, let me say that all women who identify as feminists are not the same.

It's tough, though, because when you say you are a feminist, you are trying to convey a certain image. You are trying to express that you feel a certain way about things. But the thing that people seem to forget is that feminist A is not necessarily trying to convey the same thing as feminist B.

Most of the stereotypes about feminism are very negative, so it leads to women throwing out that ever so popular phrase I'm not a feminist, but.... So instead of looking at the issues, women are focused on not being labeled. They can't speak their minds and point out the objectification of women, sexism, and discrimination because they don't want to be labeled as an evil feminist. Therefore complacence runs amok. Or some will speak their minds about these issues but they'll top it off with a "oh, no, I am not a feminist though" as if someone just called them the worst name in the world.

So where is this coming from? It's got to be the negative stereotypes surrounding feminism.

Here's my top ten list of stereotypes about feminists.

10. Feminists hate men
9. Feminists hate the idea of family
8. Feminists are masculine and unattractive
7. Feminists hate God
6. Feminists don't shave

5. Feminists are all pro-choice
4. Feminists can't be stay at home moms
3. Feminists whine about everything
2. Men are not feminists
   and the number one feminist stereotype in my opinion is
1. All people who label themselves as feminist believe in the exact same things.

Source: All Diva Media, "Top 10 Feminist Stereotypes" (2009), retrieved from http://www.alldivamedia.com/blog/2009/05/24/top-10-feminist-stereotypes/

Chapter 2

Excerpts from *Feminism Is for Everybody*

bell hooks

bell hooks is a leading feminist theorist and cultural critic, whose work focuses on the interconnectedness of race, gender, culture, and class. The author of over 30 books, she has been recognized by numerous awards, such as the American Book Awards/Before Columbus Foundation Award, the Writer's Award from the Lila Wallace-Reader's Digest Fund, and the Bank Street College Children's Book of the Year. She has been named one of the most influential American thinkers by Publisher's Weekly *and* The Atlantic Monthly, *and one of the world's top 100 visionaries by* Utne Reader. Ain't I a Woman: Black Women and Feminism, *and* Feminism Is for Everybody *(excerpted here) are among her most well-known books.*

Introduction: Come Closer to Feminism

Everywhere I go I proudly tell folks who want to know who I am and what I do that I am a writer, a feminist theorist, a cultural critic. I tell them I write about movies and popular culture, analyzing the message in the medium. Most people find this exciting and want to know more. Everyone goes to movies, watches television, glances through magazines, and everyone has thoughts about the messages they receive, about the images they look at. It is easy for the diverse public I encounter to understand what I do as a cultural critic, to understand my passion for writing (lots of folks want to write, and do). But feminist theory—that's the place where the questions stop. Instead I tend to hear all about the evil of feminism and the bad feminists: how "they" hate men; how "they" want to go against nature—and god; how "they" are all lesbians; how "they" are taking all the jobs and making the world hard for white men, who do not stand a chance.

When I ask these same folks about the feminist books or magazines they read, when I ask them about the feminist talks they have heard, about the feminist activists they know, they respond by letting me know that everything they know about feminism has come into their lives third hand, that they really have not come close enough to [the] feminist movement to know what really happens, what it's really about. Mostly they think feminism is a bunch of angry women who want to be like men. They do not even think about feminism as being about rights—about women gaining equal rights. When I talk about the feminism I know—up close and personal—they willingly listen, although when our conversations end, they are quick to tell me I am different, not like the "real" feminists who hate men, who are angry.

I assure them I am as real and as radical a feminist as one can be, and if they dare to come closer to feminism they will see it is not how they have imagined it.

*****

I have wanted them to have an answer to the question "What is feminism?" that is rooted neither in fear or fantasy. I have wanted them to have this simple definition to read again and again so they know: "Feminism is a movement to end sexism, sexist exploitation, and oppression." I love this definition, [...] because it so clearly states that the movement is not about being anti-male. It makes it clear that the problem is sexism. And that clarity helps us remember that all of us, female and male, have been socialized from birth on to accept sexist thought and action. As a consequence, females can be just as sexist as men. And while that does not excuse or justify male domination, it does mean that it would be naive and wrongminded for feminist thinkers to see the movement as simplistically being for women against men. To end patriarchy (another way of naming the institutionalized sexism) we need to be clear that we are all participants in perpetuating sexism until we change our minds and hearts, until we let go of sexist thought and action and replace it with feminist thought and action.

Males as a group have and do benefit the most from patriarchy, from the assumption that they are superior to females and should rule over us. But those benefits have come with a price. In return for all the goodies men receive from patriarchy, they are required to dominate women, to exploit and oppress us, using violence if they must to keep patriarchy intact. Most men find it difficult to be patriarchs. Most men are disturbed by hatred and fear of women, by male violence against women, even the men who perpetuate this violence. But they fear letting go of the benefits. They are not certain what will happen to the world they know most intimately if patriarchy changes. So they find it easier to passively support male domination even when they know in their minds and hearts that it is wrong. Again and again men tell me they have no idea what it is feminists want. I believe them. I believe in their capacity to change and grow. And I believe that if they knew more about feminism they would no longer fear it, for they would find in feminist movement the hope of their own release from the bondage of patriarchy.

It is for these men, young and old, and for all of us, that I have written this short handbook, the book I have spent more than 20 years longing for. I had to write it because I kept waiting for it to appear, and it did not. And without it there was no way to address the hordes of people in this nation who are daily bombarded with anti-feminist backlash, who are being told to hate and resist a movement that they know very little about. There should be so many little feminist primers, easy to read pamphlets and books, telling us all about feminism, that this book would be just another passionate voice speaking out on behalf of feminist politics. There should be billboards; ads in magazines; ads on buses, subways, trains; television commercials spreading the word, letting the world know more about feminism. We are not there yet. But this is what we must do to share feminism, to let the movement into everyone's mind and heart. Feminist change has already touched all our lives in a positive way. And yet we lose sight of the positive when all we hear about feminism is negative.

When I began to resist male domination, to rebel against patriarchal thinking (and to oppose the strongest patriarchal voice in my life—my mother's voice), I was still a teenager, suicidal, depressed, uncertain about how I would find meaning in my life and a place for myself. I needed feminism to give me a foundation of equality and justice to stand on. Mama has come around to feminist thinking. She sees me and all her daughters (we are six) living better lives because of feminist politics. She sees the promise and hope in feminist movement. It is that promise and hope that I want to share with you in this book, with everybody.

Imagine living in a world where there is no domination, where females and males are not alike or even always equal, but where a vision of mutuality is the ethos shaping our interaction. Imagine living in a world where we can all be who we are, a world of peace and possibility. Feminist revolution alone will not create such a world; we need to end racism, class elitism, imperialism. But it will make it possible for us to be fully self-actualized females and males able to create beloved community, to live together, realizing our dreams of freedom and justice, living the truth that we are all "created equal." Come closer. See how feminism can touch and change your life and all our lives. Come closer and know firsthand what feminist movement is all about. Come closer and you will see: feminism is for everybody.

Feminist Politics: Where We Stand

Simply put, feminism is a movement to end sexism, sexist exploitation, and oppression. [...]

As all advocates of feminist politics know, most people do not understand sexism, or if they do, they think it is not a problem. Masses of people think that feminism is always and only about women seeking to be equal to men. And a huge majority of these folks think feminism is anti-male. Their misunderstanding of feminist politics reflects the reality that most folks learn about feminism from patriarchal mass media. The feminism they hear about the most is portrayed by women who are primarily committed to gender equality—equal pay for equal work, and sometimes women and men sharing household chores and parenting. They see that these women are usually white and materially privileged. They know from mass media that women's liberation focuses on the freedom to have abortions, to be lesbians, to challenge rape and domestic violence. Among these issues, masses of people agree with the idea of gender equity in the workplace—equal pay for equal work.

Since our society continues to be primarily a "Christian" culture, masses of people continue to believe that god has ordained that women be subordinate to men in the domestic household. Even though masses of women have entered the workforce, even though many families are headed by women who are the sole breadwinners, the vision of domestic life which continues to dominate the nation's imagination is one in which the logic of male domination is intact, whether men are present in the home or not. The wrongminded notion of the feminist movement which implied it was anti-male carried with it the wrongminded assumption that all female space would necessarily be an environment where patriarchy and sexist thinking would be absent. Many women, even those involved in feminist politics, chose to believe this as well.

There was indeed a great deal of anti-male sentiment among early feminist activists who were responding to male domination with anger. It was that anger at injustice that was the impetus for creating a women's liberation movement. Early on most feminist activists (a majority of whom were white) had their consciousness raised about the nature of male domination when they were working in anti-classist and anti-racist settings with men who were telling the world about the importance of freedom while subordinating the women in their ranks. Whether it was white women working on behalf of socialism, black women working on behalf of civil rights and black liberation, or Native American women working for indigenous rights, it was clear that men wanted to lead, and they wanted women to follow. Participating in these radical freedom struggles awakened the spirit of rebellion and resistance in progressive females and led them towards contemporary women's liberation.

As contemporary feminism progressed, as women realized that males were not the only group in our society who supported sexist thinking and behavior—that females could be sexist as well—anti-male sentiment no longer shaped the movement's consciousness. The focus shifted to an all-out effort to create gender justice. But women could not band together to further feminism without confronting our sexist thinking. Sisterhood could not be powerful as long as women were competitively at war with one another. Utopian visions of sisterhood based solely on the awareness of the reality that all women were in some way victimized by male domination were disrupted by discussions of class and race. Discussions of class differences occurred early on in contemporary feminism, preceding discussions of race. Diana Press published revolutionary insights about class divisions between women as early as the mid-'70s in their collection of essays *Class and Feminism*. These discussions did not trivialize the feminist insistence that "sisterhood is powerful," they simply emphasized that we could only become sisters in struggle by confronting the ways women—through sex, class, and race—dominated and exploited other women, and created a political platform that would address these differences.

Even though individual black women were active in the contemporary feminist movement from its inception, they were not the individuals who became the "stars" of the movement, who attracted the attention of mass media. Often individual black women active in the feminist movement were revolutionary feminists (like many white lesbians). They were already at odds with reformist feminists who resolutely wanted to project a vision of the movement as being solely about women gaining equality with men in the existing system. Even before race became a talked about issue in feminist circles it was clear to black women (and to their revolutionary allies in struggle) that they were never going to have equality within the existing white supremacist capitalist patriarchy.

From its earliest inception the feminist movement was polarized. Reformist thinkers chose to emphasize gender equality. Revolutionary thinkers did not want simply to alter the existing system so that women would have more rights. We wanted to transform that system, to bring an end to patriarchy and sexism. Since patriarchal mass media was not interested in the more revolutionary vision, it never received attention in mainstream press. The vision of "women's liberation" which captured and still holds the public imagination was the one representing women as wanting what men had. And this was the vision that was easier to realize. Changes in our nation's economy, economic depression, the loss of jobs, etc., made the climate ripe for our nation's citizens to accept the notion of gender equality in the workforce.

Given the reality of racism, it made sense that white men were more willing to consider women's rights when the granting of those rights could serve the interests of maintaining white supremacy. We can never forget that white women began to assert their need for freedom after civil rights, just at the point when racial discrimination was ending and black people, especially black males, might have attained equality in the workforce with white men. Reformist feminist thinking focusing primarily on equality with men in the workforce overshadowed the original radical foundations of contemporary feminism which called for reform as well as overall restructuring of society so that our nation would be fundamentally anti-sexist.

Most women, especially privileged white women, ceased even to consider revolutionary feminist visions, once they began to gain economic power within the existing social structure. Ironically, revolutionary feminist thinking was most accepted and embraced in academic circles. In those circles the production of revolutionary feminist theory progressed, but more often than not that theory was not made available to the public. It became and remains a privileged discourse available to those among us who are highly literate, well-educated, and usually materially privileged. [...]

While it was in the interest of mainstream white supremacist capitalist patriarchy to suppress visionary feminist thinking which was not anti-male or concerned with getting women the right to be like men, reformist feminists were also eager to silence these forces. Reformist feminism became their route to class mobility. They could break free of male domination in the workforce and be more self-determining in their lifestyles. While sexism did not end, they could maximize their freedom within the existing system. And they could count on there being a lower class of exploited subordinated women to do the dirty work they were refusing to do. By accepting and indeed colluding with the subordination of working-class and poor women, they not only ally themselves with the existing patriarchy and its concomitant sexism, they give themselves the right to lead a double life, one where they are the equals of men in the workforce and at home when they want to be. If they choose lesbianism they have the privilege of being equals with men in the workforce while using class power to create domestic lifestyles where they can choose to have little or no contact with men.

Lifestyle feminism ushered in the notion that there could be as many versions of feminism as there were women. Suddenly the politics was being slowly removed from feminism. And the assumption prevailed that no matter what a woman's politics, be she conservative or liberal, she too could fit feminism into her existing lifestyle. Obviously this way of thinking has made feminism more acceptable because its underlying assumption is that women can be feminists without fundamentally challenging and changing themselves or the culture. [...]

Feminist politics is losing momentum because the feminist movement has lost clear definitions. We have those definitions. Let's reclaim them. Let's share them. Let's start over. Let's have T-shirts and bumper stickers and postcards and hip-hop music, television and radio commercials, ads everywhere and billboards, and all manner of printed material that tells the world about feminism. We can share the simple yet powerful message that feminism is a movement to end sexist oppression. Let's start there. Let the movement begin again.

Chapter 3

Feminism Is for Everybody: Aboriginal Women, Feminism, and Diversity

Verna St. Denis

Verna St. Denis (Cree Métis), associate professor in the College of Education at the University of Saskatchewan, is an award-winning educator and researcher. Her research focuses on the working lives of Aboriginal teachers, critical race theory, and anti-oppressive teacher education. Her publications include co-authorship of Healing Makes Our Hearts Happy: Spirituality and Cultural Transformation among the Kalahari Ju/'hoansi, *and she recently completed a national study of Aboriginal teachers' professional knowledge and experience in Canadian public schools.*

This chapter tells the story about how and why, as an Aboriginal woman and scholar, I have come to re-evaluate my earlier rejection and dismissal of feminism. There was a time when I believed, as others have stated, that organizing women of the world against gender inequality under a banner of universal sisterhood both minimized and erased social, economic and political differences between vastly differently positioned women, particularly Aboriginal women. I could not and would not prioritize gender inequality over the political and economic marginalization of Aboriginal peoples. It has been through the engagement and critique by feminists of colour, as well as the responses of white feminist scholars to those critiques of feminism, that I have come to appreciate the value of feminist theorizing and analyses for both men and women. My own analyses and understandings of inequality have been greatly enriched by both white women's and women of colour's feminist scholarship, and I believe those of us involved in Native studies and Aboriginal education can no longer deny the relevance of this important body of scholarship, analyses and activism.

Ironically, in the mid- to late 1980s, when I was working on my masters degree, while maintaining that feminist theory and analysis were not relevant to Aboriginal women, I relied on the very important scholarship of feminist women in the academy, especially those who critiqued western male scientific approaches to knowledge and research methodologies (Bowles and Klein 1983; Reinharz 1979). My masters thesis (St. Denis 1989, 1992) is an examination of community-based research methodologies, including an exploration of qualitative methodologies, which were becoming increasingly available in the mid-1980s, thanks largely to feminist scholars. Later, as I researched and wrote a paper exploring racialized minority women's critique of feminism (Davis 1981; hooks 1988; Lorde 1984; Moraga and Anzaldua 1983), I came to reconsider my indiscriminate rejection of feminism.

In that exploration I came across Susan Faludi's *Backlash* (1991), and it is because of that book, in combination with reading the writings of women of colour, who, despite their critique of feminism, nonetheless claimed a feminist identity and politics, that I came to rethink my own position. Rather than rejecting feminism altogether, many feminists of colour have focused on contributing to feminist analyses by calling white feminist colleagues to consider multiple forms of discrimination and inequality, such as racism, classism and heterosexism. I came to realize that, just as Faludi claims, the media has had a big influence in shaping public opinion and encouraging misinformation and hostility towards the inequities that feminists were trying to bring attention to. I was especially affected by Faludi's discussion of the politics of making changes to the *Diagnostic Statistical Manual* (DSM), which establishes the standard categories for diagnosing psychiatric illnesses. I both laughed and cried my way through her story of the efforts made by women to change the DSM and to challenge the ways in which psychology and psychiatry often positioned women to blame themselves for the many dire effects of the inequitable conditions of their lives. It was in the midst of working on that paper and trying to understand the critiques of feminism made by women of colour that I came to realize how little I knew about feminism in general, how much misinformation had passed as knowledge and, finally, that I may have some things in common with feminist struggles, especially against the injustices resulting from patriarchal, misogynist and sexist ideologies and practices that have for so long been a foundation in Euro-western societies.

My initial dismissal of feminism was bolstered by what has been a conventional position taken by many Aboriginal and Indigenous women who reject feminism as not only irrelevant but also racist and colonial. Although we, Aboriginal women, may utilize western forms of knowledge, theory and analysis, and even seek legitimization through educational credentials obtained in western institutions, it is still common for Aboriginal women to disapprove of feminism and sometimes, ironically, citing white men to do so (Giroux cited in Grande 2003: 329; McLaren cited in Grande 2003: 331). But I think feminist theory is no more or no less relevant than a wide variety of western social and political theories and analyses, and I now think there is much to be gained by Aboriginal women's and Aboriginal men's exploration of feminist scholarship. In fact, I could not teach the anti-oppressive education university courses I now do without the very important contributions of feminist scholars and educators.

*****

Aboriginal Women's Critique of Feminism

Drawing primarily on the work of Aboriginal scholars and activists (Turpel 1993; Monture-Angus 1995; Monture in Boulton 2003; Tobe 2000; Jaimes with Halsey 1997), I provide here an inventory of some of the reasons why many Aboriginal women reject feminism as not being relevant to their lives and communities. The following list is neither prioritized nor inclusive and many of the reasons overlap. What follows is not a "critique by Aboriginal women" but elements of critique voiced by selected representatives of Aboriginal women. For now I do not specify what form of feminism these critiques are directed towards, nor do I evaluate the positions taken by these scholars, but I develop that analysis later.

First, some Aboriginal women contest the feminist claim that male domination is universal (Jaimes with Halsey 1997; Monture-Angus 1995; Turpel 1993). Insisting that patriarchy is not universal, Turpel explains: "Our communities do not have a history of disentitlement of women from political or productive life" (1993: 180). Monture-Angus also suggests that "[c]urrent thought must recognize that Aboriginal women do not fully share the history of legally sanctioned violence against women with Canadian women" (1995: 175). Both Turpel and Monture-Angus challenge the assumption of universal male domination by referencing historical Aboriginal cultural beliefs and practices that gave high status to women in their societies.

This claim further asserts that there are fundamental differences between Aboriginal and Euro-western cultures in regards to gender relations. Some Aboriginal women claim that Aboriginal cultures do not have a history of unequal gender relations; in fact, it is argued, Aboriginal women occupy or occupied positions of authority, autonomy and high status in their communities. Tobe explains, "We didn't need to fight for our place in our societies because it surrounded us constantly" (2000: 110). Jaimes with Halsey claim, "[W]omen have always formed the backbone of Indigenous nations on the North American continent" (1997: 298). They argue that "family structures centered upon the identities of wives rather than husbands—men joined women's families: ... the position of women was furthered strengthened economically by virtue of their owning all or most property" (Jaimes with Halsey 1997: 304).

Tobe maintains that women in Dine/Navajo culture are valued differently than women in western culture: "Like my mother and other Indian women who grew up in a matrilineal culture, when we cross into the western world, we see how that world values women differently" (Tobe 2000: 107). Tobe explains that the Dine/Navajo culture takes its identity from the female, not the male, through clan membership. As young girls grow into women, their roles in society are determined by age, sex and kinship, which include being groomed for motherhood, which Tobe maintains carries a much different connotation in Dine/Navajo culture than in western culture. Monture-Angus also maintains that

> Aboriginal society is not ordered around the same values, such as sexuality, equality and especially freedom of speech, as Canadian society. Expecting Aboriginal society to be ordered around the same principles as Canadian society ignores the possibility that difference can exist. It also ignores the fact that Aboriginal societies have survived colonization (and that Canadian society colonized). This is a fundamental difference between the two communities. (1995: 176)

Not only is it asserted by these Aboriginal women that there are substantive differences in regards to gender relations between Aboriginal and Euro-western cultures, but also it is claimed that these historical and traditional gender relations have survived colonization.

Second, some Aboriginal women claim that one important difference between Aboriginal and Euro-western cultures is the distinct valorizing of maternalism and motherhood in Aboriginal cultures. For example, Turpel invokes maternalism and motherhood as central to Aboriginal women's authority and status within Aboriginal societies:

> It is commonly known that the future of our nations depends upon the strength of our women ... we must be the hearts of our people.... We do not want to become part of a movement, which seeks equality with men.... Women are at the center. We are the keepers of the culture, the educators, the ones who must instruct the children to respect the Earth, and the ones who ensure that our leaders are remembering and "walking" with their responsibilities demonstrably in mind. (1993: 180–81)

In this belief, Aboriginal women are valorized both as mothers and as caretakers of the nation. In her analysis of Aboriginal women's efforts to change the *Indian Act*, Krosenbrink-Gelissen reports that the Native Women's Association of Canada strategically employed the concept of traditional motherhood in their political struggle for equal rights with Aboriginal men (Krosenbrink-Gelissen 1994). In other words, Native women argued on the basis of a cultural connection between motherhood and nationhood to convince Aboriginal and non-Aboriginal governments that it was not in the interests of Aboriginal peoples to disenfranchise Aboriginal women and their children.

Third, some Aboriginal scholars, citing historical and cultural traditions, claim that the concept of equality is neither relevant nor necessary for Aboriginal women in Aboriginal societies; rather these are concepts imposed by the colonizers, including feminists. Monture-Angus explains that if she were to locate herself within the women's movement, that would mean that she would have to be "willing to accept less than the position accorded to women of my nation historically. Equality is not a high standard in my way of thinking" (Monture-Angus 1995: 179). Monture (cited in Boulton 2003) argues that, given the Mohawk culture and tradition of valuing women and the fact that a gender hierarchy in the traditions of her people is absent, "the idea that a feminist wants equality with men is a strange idea for Mohawk women."

Turpel states, "[E]quality is not an important political or social concept" (1993: 179) in Aboriginal gender relations. As argued by Buffalohead, "We stem from egalitarian cultural traditions. These traditions are concerned less with equality of the sexes and more with the dignity of the individual and their inherent right—whether they are women, men or children—to make their own choices and decisions" (quoted in Jaimes with Halsey 1997: 306).

Fourth, and related to the rejection of gender equality, some Aboriginal women interpret equality as meaning reproducing the Euro-centric patriarchal system. They reject a form of feminism they understand argues for adopting and imitating white male practices, traditions and processes. If the intention of feminism is to achieve equality on the terms set by men, then equality is regarded as a low priority. Aboriginal women do not want equity in a system they do not support. For example, Turpel argues,

> I do not see it as worthwhile and worthy to aspire to, or desire, equal opportunity with white men, or with the system that they have created. The aspirations of white men in the dominant society are simply not our aspirations. We do not want to inherit their objectives and positions or to adopt their worldview. To be perfectly frank, I cannot figure out why non-Aboriginal women would want to do this either. (1993: 184)

Monture-Angus also rejects the idea that "women's oppression will be eradicated when women assume male-defined positions of status and power" (Monture-Angus 1995: 179).

Aboriginal scholars often interpret the feminist call for equality to mean that women are asking for the right for women to be men. For example, Osennontion, a Mohawk woman cited in Turpel, explains that when she hears feminists

> talk about equality, they mean sameness. They appear to want to be the *same* as man. They wanted to be treated the same as man, make the same money as a man ... and, they consider all women, regardless of origin, to be the same, to share the same concerns. I, for one, maintain that Aboriginal women are *different*.... I certainly do not want to be a "man." (1993: 180, emphasis in the original)

Fifth, some Aboriginal women regard it as unnecessary to appeal for the attainment of the same rights as men; rather they appeal for the restoration and reclaiming of cultural traditions and self-government that would allow Aboriginal women to be restored to their once and continuing revered position. They insist that the solution to current problems of gender inequality and violence against Aboriginal women is to assert and reclaim cultural traditions. Part of what this call to tradition accomplishes is the erasure of the larger socio-political context in which Aboriginal women live, including being murdered with impunity. Laura Wittstock, a Seneca leader, maintains, "[T]ribalism, not feminism, is the correct route" for Native women to follow (quoted in Jaimes with Halsey 1997: 319). Clara Sue Kidwell, an Anishinabe-Choctaw scholar, also suggests that "recovery of traditional forms is more than ever called for" (quoted in Jaimes with Halsey 1997: 319). "What we need to be is *more* not less Indian" (Lorelei Means, in Jaimes with Halsey 1997: 317, emphasis in the original). Monture-Angus calls for restoring traditional gender relations: "The relationships among Aboriginal women and Aboriginal men must also be restored and this may require more than just the healing of individuals" (Monture-Angus 1995: 224). She elaborates,

> Striving at all times to re-claim the traditions of my people, the respect and power women once held is the single most important reason why I cannot accept a feminist construction of reality. My ability to re-claim my position in the world as Haudenosaunee woman is preconditioned on the ability of our men to remember the traditions that we have lost. (1995: 179)

Sixth, some Aboriginal women state that gender inequality is neither the only nor the most important form of oppression they face. For example, Janet McCloud disagrees with "many Anglo women [who] try to tell us that our most pressing problem is male supremacy" (quoted in Jaimes with Halsey 1997: 318). Monture-Angus argues that Aboriginal women face multiple forms of discrimination and violence: "Organizing against a single form of violence—men's—is not a luxury I have experienced. The general definition of violence against women is too narrow to capture all of the violence that Aboriginal women face" (Monture-Angus 1995: 171).

Aboriginal women argue that colonization, racism and economic disparity are more pressing concerns than achieving gender equality. As stated by Lorelei Means, "We are *American Indian* women, in that order. We are oppressed, first and foremost as American Indians, as peoples colonized by the United States of America, *not as women*" (quoted in Jaimes with Halsey 1997: 300, emphasis in original). Another American Indian woman, Janet McCloud, a Tulalip activist from Washington State, is quoted as stating,

> *You* join us in liberating *our* land and lives. Lose the privilege *you* acquire at *our* expense by occupying *our* land. Make *that* your first priority for as long as it takes to make it happen. *Then* we'll join you in fixing up whatever's left of the class and gender problems in your society, and our own, if need be. *But*, if you are not willing to do *that*, then don't presume to tell *us* how we should go about our liberation, what priorities and values we should have. (in Jaimes with Halsey 1997: 301, emphasis in the original)

*****

The above reasons form the basis on which some Aboriginal women have rejected feminism as irrelevant. I think it is important to understand and examine these interpretations of feminism as a way to explore and make arguments for the relevance of feminism to Aboriginal women and men.

Reflections

> At the very moment when the Native intellectual is anxiously trying to create a cultural work he fails to realize that he is utilizing techniques and language which are borrowed from the stranger in his country. (Fanon 1968/1963: 223)

I begin my reflections with this quote from Frantz Fanon as one way to acknowledge the extent of the impact and consequences of colonization on Indigenous and Aboriginal people. Some would argue that colonization affected Aboriginal people in varying degrees and scope, and therefore in some places some Aboriginal cultural traditions and practices have remained more or less intact. I argue that the overwhelming majority of Aboriginal people have gone through some degree of socialization into Christianity as well as incorporation into the patriarchal capitalist political economy and education system, and are therefore subject to western ideologies of gender identities and relations. Schools and churches have been described as ideological state apparatuses (Althusser 1971). It is argued that these institutions play a significant role in producing and reproducing ideologies about what it means to be a man or a woman or a family, not through force but through common-sense ideas that are enacted in everyday practices like going to school, courting, getting married and giving birth. Most of us are familiar with how this is done within the boundaries of western traditions and practices, and I argue that we do not stand outside those social and cultural practices. Fanon is also making this point when he comments on the use of the colonizer's language by Indigenous or Aboriginal scholars and activists to make political, poetic and artistic statements (Fanon 1968/1963). This is but one effect of colonization on Aboriginal people. I offer the following reflections about feminism and its relationship to Aboriginal women, while acknowledging that I am both a part of western thinking and practices, as well as separate from them.

*****

Feminist Theory and Practice: Neither Static nor Homogeneous

Just as Aboriginal and Indigenous people are not an homogeneous static monolith, neither are feminists and feminist analyses. Kate Shanley, an American Indian who identifies as a feminist, notes that even she may have in her writing referred to the "women's movement as though it were a single well-defined organization. It is not" (1988: 215). Although feminist scholarship has sometimes been portrayed as an unchanging body of scholarship engaged in male bashing (Jaimes with Halsey 1997), I have found it useful to develop an understanding of the nuanced and complex arguments and analyses that feminists have advanced to challenge gender inequality. Feminist analyses and strategies for overcoming gender oppression have always varied and been debated. An example of the monolithic stereotype is the assumption that feminism is mostly liberal feminism.

I agree with Aboriginal women's claim that equality is not appropriate or relevant in the context of continuing colonization, in which the sovereignty and rights of self-determination of

Aboriginal peoples is denied; in other words, equality is not enough and does little to address colonial relations. However, I find it problematic that feminism is interpreted as a desire by women to be treated like men, and equality is interpreted as advocating "sameness" in treatment. Although there may be a strand of feminism that has advocated same treatment as one way to get access to education, employment and political rights, it is a position that has been contested within and by feminists historically and in the present. For example, radical and cultural feminists have not only rejected male power structures, they have also idealized women's culture. As Freedman explains, radical and cultural feminists have "questioned the liberal feminist goal of integrating women into male power structures" (2002: 87). Radical feminists have also resisted "demeaning images in the media" (99) by seeking to celebrate a positive "women's culture" (88).

*****

Western Patriarchy: A Problem for Us All

I think feminist analyses of western forms of patriarchy are relevant to both Aboriginal women and men, because western patriarchy has impacted all of us. Monture-Angus has argued that Aboriginal societies are not ordered around the same principles and values as Canadian society, that differences do exist and that "Aboriginal societies have survived colonization" (Monture-Angus 1995: 176). On the other hand, Monture-Angus does call for an analysis of patriarchy in the context of colonization: "Understanding how patriarchy operates in Canada without understanding colonization is a meaningless endeavour from the perspective of Aboriginal people" (Monture-Angus 1995: 175). I argue that most if not all Aboriginal people, both men and women, who are living in western societies are inundated from birth until death with western patriarchy and western forms of misogyny. In this view, I am joined by an increasing number of other Aboriginal women who are also claiming that we have not escaped these social and political structures and ideologies at all.

In *Strong Women Stories: Native Vision and Community Survival*, editors Kim Anderson and Bonita Lawrence bring together a refreshing and fuller alternative to discussions about gender relations, feminism and tradition in Aboriginal communities (see St. Denis 2004 for reviews of this book). In this collection, Aboriginal women explore how patriarchy, Christianity and colonialism have affected their lives and how many women must "wrestle with the patriarchal framework of colonialism and ask what it has done to our traditions, including our social and political systems" (Anderson and Lawrence 2003: 5). In one chapter, Fay Blaney, an Aboriginal woman, describes the work of the Aboriginal Women's Action Network, which seeks to educate Aboriginal women about the impact of patriarchy and misogyny in Aboriginal families. She states that the Native Women's Association of Canada acknowledges that "patriarchy is so ingrained in our communities that it is now seen as a 'traditional trait'" (Blaney 2003: 158). Deerchild explains, "[T]hose who question tradition are seen as outsiders to our cultures, or they are seen as people who are misguided about what the teachings mean" (2003: 104).

Anderson and Lawrence challenge doctrinaire notions of traditions as unchanging phenomena. The Aboriginal women authors in the book describe ways in which western and Christian ideologies of gender and gender relations are often incorrectly invoked as Aboriginal tradition and adversely affect women in several ways. For example, in her chapter, Dawn Martin-Hill questions the emergence of the concept of a traditional Indigenous woman whom she identifies as She No Speaks, "a construction born from the tapestry of our colonial landscape," a woman who is encouraged to remain "silent and obedient to male authority" (2003: 108). In a concluding chapter, by Carl Fernandez, a young man reports that in his research one woman observed that "the teachings about womanhood too often focus on what women *can't* do" (2003: 251, emphasis in the original). Rosanna Deerchild also points out that the belief and practice of matriarchy in Aboriginal cultures is often "reduced to an obligatory nod" (2003: 101).

Despite the claims that some Aboriginal women have made about the elevated status Aboriginal women occupy in Aboriginal cultures, Aboriginal women do suffer marginalization and oppression within their own communities now and have done in the past. Emma LaRocque, a Métis scholar, disputes assumptions that Aboriginal women have always occupied high-status positions in Aboriginal cultures. She argues, "We cannot assume that all Aboriginal traditions universally respected and honoured women.... It should not be assumed, even in those original societies that were structured along matriarchal lines, that matriarchies necessarily prevented men from oppressing women. There are indications of male violence and sexism in some Aboriginal societies prior to European contact and certainly after contact" (LaRocque 1996: 14). But even if Aboriginal women were once held in high regard and exercised social, economic and political influence, the effects of colonization and Christianity have certainly brought about change.

Colonization has involved the appropriation of sovereignty, lands, resources and agency, and has included the imposition of western and Christian patriarchy on Aboriginal peoples. Patriarchy is not the only form of oppression experienced by Aboriginal people, but it is certainly a part of that oppression. I agree with Turpel that "[w]e cannot abandon our men; they too have been abused and oppressed by the Canadian state" (1993: 181), but I think understanding how western patriarchy distorts the lives of both men and women is a valuable and significant process in decolonization. We have and can turn to some of the analyses offered by both western and minority feminists, including men who are also concerned with inequitable and unjust gender relations. Certainly the need for education is evident. As Carl Fernandez found, "Most Aboriginal men, particularly the older generation, do not really recognize the ways in which gender inequality affects their community" (2003: 253).

In my anti-racist teaching, I draw on the work of feminists who provide critiques and analyses of how western patriarchy shapes the lives of both men and women, and I think it is something that Aboriginal people can also learn from. For example, I often assign readings from Alan Johnson's book *The Gender Knot: Unraveling Our Patriarchal Legacy*, in which he makes the case that "patriarchy isn't simply about relationships between women and men. It encompasses an entire world organized around principles of control, domination and competition" (1997: 51). Johnson claims,

> Patriarchy encourages men to seek security, status, and other rewards through control; to fear other men's ability to control and harm them; and to identify being in control as both their best defense against loss and humiliation and the surest route to what they need and desire. In this sense, although we usually think of patriarchy in terms of what happens between men and women, it is more about what goes on *among men*. (1997, 26, emphasis in the original)

He argues that our journey out of western patriarchy "begins with seeing how it works and what it does to us, how we participate in it and how we might choose differently" (52). For example, in explaining the high levels of violence against women, Johnson argues that in a patriarchal system, "women's place is to help contain men's resentment over being controlled by *other men* ... men are allowed to dominate women as a kind of compensation for their being subordinated to other men because of social class, race, or other forms of inequality" (37).

There is some merit to this analysis, and I think it offers a partial explanation for the high levels of physical and sexual violence committed by both Aboriginal and non-Aboriginal men against Aboriginal women. "Women's powerful economic, political, social, and religious positions within most tribes are not honoured as they once were, violence against Indigenous women has esca-lated" (Mihesuah 2003: xiv). LaRocque also points out that there is no question that "Aboriginal men have internalized white male devaluation of women" (1994: 74–76).

Furthermore, LaRocque asks important questions about the impact of a sexist and misogynist popular mainstream culture on Aboriginal people: "What happens to Aboriginal males who are exposed not only to pornography but also to the racist/sexist view of the 'Indian' male as a violent 'savage' and the Aboriginal female as a debased sexually loose 'squaw'?" (76). We must be able to draw on the important work that feminists have done in exploring the impact of pornography on gender relations and gendered violence. Aboriginal people are not immune to popular culture, and we must therefore, as LaRocque suggests, explore how "pornography in popular culture is affecting sexual attitudes and behaviour within Aboriginal communities" (76). I remember how disturbing the National Film Board film *This Is Not a Love Story* was for me when I was required to watch it as part of an undergraduate sociology course on crime and deviance. This documen-tary film, produced in the late 1970s, provides a feminist critique of the pornography industry.

Aboriginal people live for the most part in a western capitalistic and patriarchal context; it is that social, economic and political context that irrevocably shapes our lives, and denying this or minimizing these conditions will not change it. Tobe acknowledges this when she states: "When we leave our traditional world and step into the western world, feminism becomes an issue, and we must confront and deal with the same issues that affect all women" (2000: 109). As Kate Shanley argues, "Indian feminists are united with mainstream feminists in outrage against woman and child battering, sexist employment and educational practices, and in many other social concerns" (1988: 215). In regards to these social issues, there is a place in feminist theory and action for dialogue and alliances among diverse women.

Intersection of Race, Class, Nationhood in Feminism

Feminist analysis and activism have evolved over time and have generated new understandings of the effects of the multiple positions women occupy—for example, how social and economic class and racial positioning, sexual identity and disability intersect. There is much in the literature that takes up the contentious relationship between Aboriginal and minority women and feminism. Some of these issues have already been discussed. [...] Aboriginal and minority women have also had to contend with pressure from within Aboriginal and minority communities to reject and deny the relevance of feminist theory and activism. Additionally, Aboriginal and minority women have not always been welcomed within the feminist community. [...]

The denial, inability or resistance on the part of some feminists to address racism is a real issue that affects Aboriginal and minority women within the feminist movement and in the larger society. This issue has been discussed and written about extensively over the past two or three decades. As Freedman and many others have stated, many women of colour have felt excluded from a theory that elevated gender at the expense of race or class identity. In particular, the example of African American women has long provided a critical perspective for white women, alerting them to the integral connections between race and gender (Freedman 2002: 83).

In early-twentieth-century efforts to create an international women's movement, concern was expressed with how those efforts often reproduced colonial relations (Freedman 2002: 105). In a more recent example, Freedman explains that when U.S. feminists arrived in Mexico City in 1975 for the first international conference on women, which launched the United Nations dec laration of the Decade for Women, they encountered criticism from delegates who did not want to discuss gender outside the context of movements for national self-determination (2002: 109). This is similar to the claims that many Aboriginal women have made. It was the non-govern-mental organizations that both worked with women internationally and also attended the inter-national conferences on women beginning in the mid-1970s to the mid-1980s that convinced many western women that world poverty and national liberation were feminist issues because they affected women's lives around the globe (Freedman 2002: 110). Feminism has responded to the multiple and sometimes contradictory positioning of women locally and internationally. As Freedman explains, "Most western feminists have learned that global economic and political justice are prerequisites to securing women's rights" (2002: 3).

Racialized women who claim a feminist politics have provided me with an opening to feminist scholarship. Even though some Aboriginal women maintain that the processes of racialization do not solely define their identity, there are similarities in Aboriginal women's criticisms of feminism and the criticisms made by other racialized and minority women. My own race and gender analy-sis was greatly enhanced by researching the scholarship of these feminists of colour. The concerns raised by Lata Mani, a South Asian feminist scholar, are ones that are shared by other racialized and minority women, including Aboriginal women. Her concern is with "how to argue for women's rights in ways that are not complicit in any way with patriarchal, racist or ethnocentrist formulations of the issues" (1989: 8).

One issue that I have found particularly relevant to Aboriginal and Indigenous women is the claim that one's first loyalty is to one's nation, race or culture, above gender, and that to challenge oppression by one's own community is to betray it. This is a discussion engaged in by racial-ized and Third World women as well. Algerian feminist Marie-Aimee Helie-Lucas explains that women hesitated for years to speak out against unjust laws because they felt "silenced by fears of accusations of betrayal and by the nationalist myth" (Freedman 2002: 104).

Native American women risk being dismissed as "assimilated" if they identify with feminist politics. For example, Jaimes with Halsey argue that those Native women activists who have most openly identified themselves as feminists

> have tended to be among the more assimilated of Indian women activists ... these women are devoted to "civil rights" rather than liberation per se. Native American women who are more genuinely sovereigntist in their outlook have proved far more dubious about the potentials offered by feminist politics and alliances. (1997: 317)

One of the effects of this has been to discourage Aboriginal and Native women from not only writing about feminism, but even from learning about how feminism tries to intervene in sex-ism and misogyny. Mihesuah challenges the belief that Aboriginal and Indigenous women who identify with feminism are being divisive. She writes,

> My position as a Native female who has observed and encountered these relationships is that we are not being divisive; we are being realistic. Misogyny, colorism, ethnocentri-cism, and physical abuse are sad realities among Native people and unless Natives do something about these problems, no one else will. (2003: xiii–viv)

Although earlier scholarship by some Aboriginal women argued that feminism was not compatible with Aboriginal culture and nationhood, more recent Aboriginal women's work disputes those claims. Not unlike other racialized women who argue that feminism is not incompatible with nationalism or religion, "some international feminists have argued for higher education, professional jobs, and an insistence that feminism is compatible with Islam and nationalism" (Freedman 2002: 102). There is a wide range of analysis to be found in feminist scholarship that is potentially relevant and compatible with the needs of Aboriginal women and men and their communities.

Conclusion

> Although Indigenous scholars *do not always agree* with each other, it is critical that we present our opinions and concerns not only to Natives but also to non-Natives. (Mihesuah 2003: xiii, emphasis added)

I want to conclude with the message offered in the above quote, because Aboriginal people are all too familiar with the way in which disagreement within our communities can not only discourage critical debate among ourselves but can be used as a justification by dominant institutions to ignore Aboriginal claims for social justice. Aboriginal people, researchers and scholars must have the freedom to debate and discuss the contradictions and paradoxes that arise in our strategies as we move towards decolonization, including the merits of feminism for Aboriginal people. The diversity of perspectives among Aboriginal peoples in our analyses and strategies for change cannot be used as justification for maintaining the status quo of inequality and marginalization.

I too once maintained that feminism was not relevant to Aboriginal people, and I once thought that to be feminist meant that one had to choose between gender and culture or nation. I no longer hold this view. Increasingly more Aboriginal women are beginning to identify as feminists, or at least with some of the goals of feminism, such as ending violence against women and children. As I have found out in my own use of feminist scholarship, feminism can no longer be dismissed as merely advancing a liberal agenda. Feminist scholarship is very important to my anti-racist teaching, in which I draw upon on a wide range of feminist writing on issues including race, nationhood, class, disability and sexual identity. I have begun encouraging Aboriginal students, both women and men, to take courses in women and gender studies if they have that option in their university programs. We miss an important body of scholarship when we in the Aboriginal community dismiss feminism as irrelevant. This dismissal has the effect of discouraging Aboriginal students from reading feminist scholarship, which is no less relevant than other components of the large body of scholarship we study in any university. As bell hooks (2000) declares, "Feminism Is for Everybody."

References

Althusser, L. 1971. *Lenin and Philosophy, and Other Essays*. Translated from the French by Ben Brewster. London: New Left Books.

Anderson, K., and B. Lawrence (eds.). 2003. *Strong Women Stories: Native Vision and Community Survival*. Toronto: Sumach Press.

Blaney, F. 2003. "Aboriginal Women's Action Network." In Anderson and Lawrence.

Boulton, M. 2003. "Monture Takes Advocacy for Aboriginal Women to National Stage on Person's Day." *On Campus News* 11, 6 (October 31). Available at <http://www.usask.ca/communications/ocn/03-oct-31/news12.shtml> (accessed March 2007).

Bowles, G., and R.D. Klein. 1983. *Theories of Women's Studies*. Routledge and Kegan Paul.

Davis, A. 1981. *Women, Race, and Class*. New York: Random House.

Deerchild, R. 2003. "Tribal Feminism Is a Drum Song." In Anderson and Lawrence.

Faludi, S. 1991. *Backlash: The Undeclared War against American Women*. New York: Crown Publishers.

Fanon, F. 1968/1963. *Wretched of the Earth*. New York: Grove Press.

Fernandez, C. 2003. "Coming Full Circle: A Young Man's Perspective on Building Gender Equity in Aboriginal Communities." In Anderson and Lawrence.

Freedman, E. 2002. *No Turning Back: The History of Feminism and the Future of Women*. New York: Ballantine Books.

Grande, S. 2003. "Whitestream Feminism and the Colonialist Project: A Review of Contemporary Feminist Pedagogy and Praxis." *Educational Theory* 53, 3 (Summer) ProQuest Education Journals.

hooks, b. 1988. *Talking Back: Thinking Feminist, Thinking Black*. Toronto: Between the Lines.

hooks, b. 2000. *Feminism Is for Everybody: Passionate Politics*. Cambridge, MA: South End Press.

Jaimes, A.M., with T. Halsey. 1997. "American Indian Women: At the Center of Indigenous Resistance in Contemporary North American." In A. McClintock, A. Mufti and E. Shohat (eds.), *Dangerous Liaisons: Gender, Nation and Postcolonial Perspectives*. Minneapolis: University of Minnesota Press.

Johnson, A. 1997. *The Gender Knot: Unravelling Our Patriarchal Legacy*. Philadelphia: Temple University Press.

Krosenbrink-Gelissen, L.E. 1994. "Caring Is Indian Women's Business, But Who Takes Care of Them? Canada's Indian Women, the Renewed Indian Act, and Its Implications for Women's Family Responsibilities, Roles and Rights." *Law and Anthropology: International Yearbook for Legal Anthropology* 8.

LaRocque, E. 1994. *Violence in Aboriginal Communities*. Ottawa: National Clearinghouse on Family Violence, Family Violence Prevention Division, Health Programs and Services Branch, Health Canada.

LaRocque, E. 1996. "The Colonization of a Native Woman Scholar." In C. Miller and P. Chuchryk (eds.), *Women of the First Nations: Power, Wisdom and Strength*. Winnipeg: University of Manitoba Press.

Lorde, A. 1984. *Sister Outsider: Essays and Speeches*. Trumansburg, NY: Crossing Press.

Mani, L. 1989. "Multiple Mediations: Feminist Scholarship in the Age of Multinational Reception." *Inscriptions* 5.

Martin-Hill, D. 2003. "She No Speaks and Other Colonial Constructs of 'The Traditional Woman.'" In Anderson and Lawrence.

Mihesuah, D.A. 2003. *Indigenous American Women: Decolonization, Empowerment, Activism*. Lincoln: University of Nebraska Press.

Monture-Angus, P. 1995. *Thunder in My Soul: A Mohawk Woman Speaks*. Halifax: Fernwood Publishing.

Moraga, C., and G. Anzaldua (eds.). 1983. *This Bridge Called My Back: Writings by Radical Women of Color*. Latham, NY: Kitchen Table, Women of Color Press.

Reinharz, S. 1979. *On Becoming a Social Scientist*. New Brunswick, NJ: Transaction Books.

Shanley, K. 1988. "Thoughts on Indian Feminism." In B. Brant (ed.), *A Gathering of Spirit: A Collection by North American Indian Women*. Ithaca: Firebrand Books.

St. Denis, V. 1989. "A Process of Community-Based Participatory Research: A Case Study." Unpublished masters thesis. University of Alaska/Fairbanks, Fairbanks, Alaska.

St. Denis, V. 1992. "Community-Based Participatory Research: Aspects of the Concept Relevance for Practice." *Native Studies Review*, 8, 2.

St. Denis, V. 2004. "Book Review: Strong Women Stories: Native Vision and Community Survival." *Resources for Feminist Research* 31, 1/2.

Tobe, L. 2000. "There Is No Word for Feminism in My Language." *Wicazo Sa Review: A Journal of Native American Studies* Fall.

Turpel, M.E. 1993. "Patriarchy and Paternalism: The Legacy of the Canadian State for First Nations Women." *Canadian Journal of Women and the Law* 6.

Supplement 2

Activist Insight:
Alice Walker (1944–)

Alice Walker is an African-American author, poet, and activist. Born February 9, 1944, Walker grew up in the southern United States, near Eatonton, Georgia. She has published many works of fiction and non-fiction, as well as anthologies and poetry. Walker's 1982 novel The Color Purple *was awarded the National Book Award and the 1983 Pulitzer Prize for Fiction, making her the first African-American woman writer to receive this prestigious literary award. To date, Walker's books have sold more than 15 million copies, and her works have been translated into more than two dozen languages.*

Throughout her literary career, Walker has remained a committed activist, devoting her time to many causes, including the civil rights movement, the women's movement, and, most recently, the movements to end the wars in the Middle East. The excerpt that appears below comes from Walker's first collection of essays, entitled In Search of Our Mothers' Gardens *and published in 1983. In it, Walker uses the term "womanist" for the first time to refer to the experiences of women of colour. This piece remains an important contribution to feminist thought.*

Womanist

1. From *womanish*. (Opp. of "girlish," i.e., frivolous, irresponsible, not serious.) A black feminist or feminist of color. From the black folk expression of mothers to female children, "You acting womanish," i.e., like a woman. Usually referring to outrageous, audacious, courageous, or *willful* behavior. Wanting to know more and in greater depth than is considered "good" for one. Interested in grown-up doings. Acting grown up. Being grown up. Interchangeable with another black folk expression: "You trying to be grown." Responsible. In charge. *Serious.*

2. *Also:* A woman who loves other women, sexually and/or nonsexually. Appreciates and prefers women's culture, women's emotional flexibility (values tears as natural counterbalance of laughter), and women's strength. Sometimes loves individual men, sexually and/or nonsexually. Committed to survival and wholeness of entire people, male *and* female. Not a separatist, except periodically, for health. Traditionally universalist, as in: "Mama, why are we brown, pink, and yellow, and our cousins are white, beige, and black?" Ans.: "Well, you know the colored race is just like a flower garden, with every color flower represented." Traditionally capable, as in: "Mama, I'm walking to Canada and I'm taking you and a bunch of other slaves with me." Reply: "It wouldn't be the first time."

3. Loves music. Loves dance. Loves the moon. *Loves* the Spirit. Loves love and food and roundness. Loves struggle. *Loves* the folk. Loves herself. *Regardless.*
4. Womanist is to feminist as purple to lavender.

Source: Alice Walker, *In Search of Our Mothers' Gardens: Womanist Prose* (San Diego: Harcourt Brace Jovanovich, 1983), x–xii.

Chapter 4

The Historical Case for Feminism

Estelle Freedman

Estelle Freedman is the Edgar E. Robinson professor in U.S. history at Stanford University and a co-founder of the Program in Feminist Studies. Her research areas include the history of women and social reform, including feminism and prison reform, and the history of sexuality. Her book, No Turning Back: The History of Feminism and the Future of Women, *from which the following piece is taken, has been praised as one of the most comprehensive and analytical studies of feminism to date. She is the recipient of an impressive list of teaching and mentorship awards.*

In the past two centuries, a revolution has transformed women's lives. Unlike national revolutions, this social upheaval crosses continents, decades, and ideologies. In place of armed struggle it gradually sows seeds of change, infiltrating our consciousness with the simple premise that women are as capable and valuable as men. To measure the breadth of this ongoing upheaval of old patterns, consider the way feminist movements have transformed law and politics, from divorce reforms in Egypt and sexual harassment cases in Japan and the United States to the nomination of equal numbers of male and female candidates by French political parties. Or note the change in leadership: During the 1990s, 90 percent of the world's nations elected women to national office, and women served as heads of state in more than twenty countries. Just as important, consider the thousands of grassroots organizations such as Women in Law and Development in Africa, the National Black Women's Health Project in the United States, and the Self-Employed Women's Association in India. Women's movements have never been so widespread.

In *No Turning Back* I explain why and how a feminist revolution has occurred. I argue that two related historical transitions have propelled feminist politics. First, the rise of capitalism disrupted older, reciprocal relations within families in ways that initially enhanced men's economic opportunities and defined women as their dependants. Second, new political theories of individual rights and representative government that developed alongside capitalism extended privileges to men only. In response, feminist movements named these disparities as unjust, insisting on the value of women's economic contributions and the justice of political rights for women. In short, the market economies and democratic systems that now dominate the world create both the need for feminism and the means to sustain it.

Feminist politics originated where capitalism, industrial growth, democratic theory, and socialist critiques converged, as they did in Europe and North America after 1800. Women and their male allies began to agitate for equal educational, economic, and political opportunities, a struggle that continues to the present. By 1900 an international women's movement advanced these goals in urban areas of Latin America, the Middle East, and Asia. Since 1970 feminism has spread globally, in both industrialized nations and in the developing regions where agriculture remains an economic mainstay.

Given their specific historical origins, the feminist politics initially forged in Europe and North America have not simply expanded throughout the world. Elsewhere, abundant forms of women's resistance to men's patriarchal authority predated Western democratic theories; they continue to influence feminist movements today. Socialist responses to capitalism invite quite different women's politics than where free markets prevail. Both the term *feminism* and the politics it represents have been continually transformed by the evolving responses of women and men from a variety of cultures. Indeed, women's politics have developed organically in settings so diverse that the plural *feminisms* more accurately describes them.

By the year 2000 these growing international movements to improve women's lives increasingly influenced each other, due in part to the forum provided by the United Nations Decade for Women from 1975 to 1985 and the follow-up conference in Beijing in 1995. While they share the conviction that women deserve full human rights, international feminisms often diverge in their emphases. Only some concentrate solely on women, while others recognize complex links to the politics of race, class, religion, and nationality. Despite these differences, most Western feminists have learned that global economic and political justice are prerequisites to securing women's rights. Women in the developing world have found that transnational feminist movements can help establish strategic international support for their efforts at home.

None of these feminist movements has proceeded without opposition, including formidable backlash in every era in which women have gained public authority. Nonetheless, at the beginning of the twenty-first century the historical conditions that promote feminism can be found in much of the world: Whether through the influence of Western economic and political systems, the refashioning of earlier practices, or both, an impressive array of movements now attempts to empower women. At present, economic globalization, along with international efforts to create stable democratic governments, suggests that new forms of feminism will continue to surface. Because of their flexibility and adaptability, women's political movements, whether explicitly labeled feminist or not, have set much of the world's agenda for the twenty-first century.

The History of a Term

Since I use *feminism* to describe movements whose participants do not necessarily apply that label themselves, I want to acknowledge at the outset the specific historical origins of this term. *Feminism* is a relatively recent word. First coined in France in the 1880s as *féminisme*, it spread through European countries in the 1890s and to North and South America by 1910. The term combined the French word for woman *femme*, and *-isme*, which referred to a social movement or political ideology. At a time when many other "isms" originated, including socialism and communism, *féminisme* connoted that women's issues belonged to the vanguard of change. The term was always controversial, in part because of its association with radicalism and in part because proponents themselves disagreed about the label. Although self-defined *socialist feminists* appeared in Europe as early as 1900, many socialists who supported women's emancipation rejected the label *feminist*. They believed that middle-class demands for suffrage and property rights did not necessarily speak to working women's needs for a living wage and job security. Middle-class women also hesitated to call themselves feminists, especially when the term implied a claim to universal rights as citizens rather than particular rights as mothers.

*****

From its origins through the social upheavals of the 1960s, *feminist* remained a pejorative term among most progressive reformers, suffragists, and socialists around the world. Even as universal adult suffrage gradually extended to women—in England in 1928, in countries such as France, Japan, Mexico, and China by the late 1940s—few politically engaged women called themselves feminists. Within the international women's movement, participants debated whether the term *humanist* rather than *feminist* best applied to them. Nations ruled by communist parties, such as China and later Cuba, officially pronounced the emancipation of women as workers, but their state-sanctioned women's organizations rejected the feminist label and their suppression of oppositional political discourse precluded feminist politics.

A critical turning point in the history of feminisms occurred during the politically tumultuous 1960s. Women's politics revived in the West, at first under the banner of "women's liberation." Although the press quickly derided adherents by calling them "women's libbers," this second wave proved quite tenacious. By this time, both capitalist and socialist economies had drawn millions of women into the paid labor force, and civil rights and anticolonial movements had revived the politics of democratization. In Europe and the United States, millions of women expected to earn wages as well as raise children. The old feminist calls for economic and political equality, and a new emphasis on control over reproduction, resonated deeply across generations, classes, and races.

Western women's movements also significantly expanded their agendas after the 1960s. Along with demands for economic and political rights, women's liberation revived a politics of difference through its critique of interpersonal relations. Women's liberation championed both women's *equality* with men in work and politics and women's *difference* from men within the arenas of reproduction and sexuality. In this way the two competing strains of equality and difference began to converge. Within a decade, the older term *feminist* began to be used to refer to the politics of this new movement, deepening its radical connotation but potentially widening its appeal. At about the same time, the introduction of the term *gender*, rather than *sex*, signaled feminists' growing belief that social practices, and not only biology, have constructed our notions of male and female.

By 1980 an umbrella usage of the term *feminism* took hold in Western cultures. Anyone who challenged prevailing gender relations might now be called a feminist, whether or not they lived long before the coining of the term *feminism*, agreed with all the tenets of women's liberation, or claimed the label. A generation of Western women came of age influenced by feminism to expect equal opportunities. The majority of this generation often proclaimed, "I'm not a feminist, but …," even as they insisted on equal pay, sexual and reproductive choice, parental leave, and political representation. The children they raised, both male and female, grew up influenced by these feminist expectations but not necessarily comfortable with the term. Outside the West, the term *feminism* could still evoke a narrow focus on equal rights. Thus a 1991 essay in the influential Indian women's journal *Manushi*, titled "Why I Do Not Call Myself a Feminist," contrasted Western concerns about women's rights with broader human rights and social justice campaigns that address the needs of both men and women in developing countries.[1]

The term *feminism*, in short, has never been widely popular. Yet the political goals of feminism have survived—despite continuing discomfort with the term, a hostile political climate, and heated internal criticism—largely because feminism has continually redefined itself.

Over the past twenty-five years, for example, activists have amended the term to make it more compatible with their unique perspectives. Self-naming by black feminists, Asian American feminists, Third World feminists, lesbian feminists, male feminists, ecofeminists, Christian feminists, Jewish feminists, Islamic feminists, and others attests to the malleability of the label and to the seemingly contradictory politics it can embrace. To make the movement more racially inclusive, the African American writer Alice Walker once coined *womanist* to refer to a "Black feminist or feminist of color." In the 1990s young women in the United States, such as Walker's daughter, promised to go beyond the second wave of feminism by forging a more racially and sexually diverse movement that emphasized female empowerment rather than male oppression. "I'm not post-feminist," Rebecca Walker explained in 1992, "I'm the Third Wave."[2] Significantly, this generation reclaims rather than rejects the term *feminist*. Internationally as well, more women's organizations incorporate the word, such as the Feminist League in Central Asia, the Center for Feminist Legal Research in New Delhi, and the Working Group toward a Feminist Europe.

By the 1990s the cumulative contributions of working-class women, lesbians, women of color, and activists from the developing world had transformed an initially white, European, middle-class politics into a more diverse and mature feminist movement. Taking into account the range of women's experiences, feminists have increasingly recognized the validity of arguments that once seemed contradictory. Instead of debating whether women are similar to or different from men, most feminists now recognize that both statements are true. Instead of asking which is more important, gender or race, most feminists now acknowledge the indivisibility and interaction of these social categories. Along with demanding the right to work, feminists have redefined work to include caring as well as earning. Along with calling for women's independence, feminists have recognized the interdependence of all people, as well as the interconnection of gender equality with broader social justice movements.

Defining Feminism Today

Given its changing historical meanings, is there any coherence to *feminism* as a term? Can we define it in a way that will embrace its variety of adherents and ideas? For my purposes, a four-part definition contains the critical elements of feminisms, including views that may be shared by those who claim the label as well as many who reject it.

> Feminism is a belief that women and men are inherently of equal worth. Because most societies privilege men as a group, social movements are necessary to achieve equality between women and men, with the understanding that gender always intersects with other social hierarchies.

Each of the four components of this working definition—equal worth, male privilege, social movements, and intersecting hierarchies—requires some clarification. I use "equal worth" rather than *equality* because the latter term often assumes that men's historical experience—whether economic, political, or sexual—is the standard to which women should aspire. The concept of equal worth values traditional female tasks, such as childbearing and child care, as highly as other kinds of work historically performed by men. It also allows us to recognize that women's different experiences can transform, and not simply integrate, political life.

The term *privilege* can refer to formal political rights such as suffrage or the right to hold office, but privilege can also include more personal entitlements, such as the greater social value placed on male children as expressed by strong parental preference for boys across cultures. Privilege also ensues when societies have a sexual double standard that allows male heterosexual autonomy, punishing women but not men who seek non-marital sexual expression.

To refer to feminism in terms of *social movements* may conjure images of people marching in the streets or rallying around political candidates, but it may also mean individual participation, such as enrolling in a women's studies class or engaging in artistic or literary creativity that fosters social change. While women may participate in a variety of social movements—civil rights, ecology, socialism, even fundamentalism—those movements cannot be feminist unless they explicitly address justice for women as a primary concern. Thus human rights or nationalist movements that insist on women's human rights and women's full citizenship may be feminist, while those that overlook or affirm patriarchal authority cannot.

Similarly, feminism must recognize the integral relationship of gender to other forms of *social hierarchy*, especially those based on class, race, sexuality, and culture. Despite the prevalence of hierarchies that privilege men, in every culture some women (such as elites or citizens) enjoy greater opportunities than many other women (such as workers or immigrants). Some women always have higher status than many men. If we ignore these intersecting hierarchies and create a feminism that serves only the interests of women who have more privilege, we reinforce other social inequalities that disadvantage both women and men in the name of improving women's opportunities.

The overlapping identities of women as members of classes, races, and nations raise questions about the usefulness of the category *woman* itself. I use the term but with the recognition that there is no single, universal female identity, for gender has been constructed differently across place and time. Because of historical, social, national, and personal differences, women cannot assume a sisterhood, even though we can find common ground on particular issues. At the same time, feminism cannot deny the significance of gender in a world in which 70 percent of those living in poverty and two-thirds of those who are illiterate are female.

Feminists must continually criticize two kinds of false universals. We must always ask not only "What about women?" (What difference does gender make?) but also "Which women?" (What difference do ideas about race, class, or nationality make?). [...] I believe that we must question both the assumption that the term *man* includes woman as well and the assumption that the term *woman* represents the diversity of female experience.

*****

Why Fear Feminism?

Some readers [...] may be initially uncomfortable with my choice of the word *feminism* to describe diverse women's movements. Ask most people in Europe or the United States if they believe that women should have equal rights, and they will answer in the affirmative, as did 85 percent of Americans in an opinion poll taken in 2000. Ask them if they are feminists, however, and most reject the label; the same year, 29 percent of Americans in another poll claimed it.[3] Ask others what they think of feminists, and you may hear a string of negative associations: radical, man-hating, bra-burning, and worse. Women may be acceptable as equals, but feminists are often seen as frightening, threatening, or simply unnecessary. This hostility to feminists and feminism cannot be dismissed simply by avoiding the terms, for these harsh stereotypes can always be used to discredit women activists, whether they call themselves feminists or not.

The media have contributed to this discomfort by treating feminism as a thing of the past. In the United States, for example, ever since its revival in the 1960s journalists have proclaimed the death of feminism. In 1976 *Harper's* declared a "requiem for the women's movement"; in 1980 the *New York Times* assured readers that the "radical days of feminism are gone"; in 1990 *Newsweek* trumpeted "the failure of feminism." Unconvinced by two decades of obituaries, in 1998 *Time* asked readers to respond online to the question "Is feminism dead?" So ubiquitous is this story that a feminist journalist recently labeled it "False Feminist Death Syndrome."[4] Perhaps these writers notice feminism only during periods of mass public protest and overlook its quieter but more pervasive forms. Or perhaps they are engaging in a form of wishful thinking, for given the power of the media, declaring the death of feminism could become a self-fulfilling prophecy.

If feminism, as I will argue, is so deeply rooted historically and so expansive in the present, why the contradictory claims in the press that it is near death? Why is feminism highly unpopular, even vilified, when first articulated? I suspect that the answers to these questions lie in part in what might be called "fear of feminism." No matter how insightful its politics, feminism feels deeply threatening to many people, both women and men. By providing a powerful critique of the idea of a timeless social hierarchy, in which God or nature preordained women's dependence on men, feminism exposes the historical construction, and potential deconstruction, of categories such as gender, race, and sexuality. Fears that feminism will unleash changes in familiar family, sexual, and racial relationships can produce antifeminist politics among those who wish to conserve older forms of social hierarchy.

Those who do not oppose change may still fear certain connotations of feminism. The recurrent caricatures of feminists as "mannish" reveal an anxiety that feminism is somehow antithetical to femininity, that to embrace its politics is to reject a gender identity that many women and men wish to preserve. For women of color, feminism has often seemed competitive with movements for racial justice. In former colonies and developing countries, suspicion, if not fear, of feminism may result from its association with Western colonialism. In some cultures, feminism connotes a form of rampant individualism associated with the worst features of contemporary Western societies.

Even in countries with strong women's movements, feminism forces all women and men to think about social inequalities and about their own relationships to systems of power. For some, it conjures the fear of losing taken-for-granted privileges; for others, it brings up the pain of acknowledging lack of privilege. Neither is a very pleasant prospect, especially if feminism is presented in the oversimplified language of male oppression and female victimization. Portraying a movement as blaming one group (white men) and denying the resilience of another (all women) will keep it unpopular, even though, as I will argue, feminism at its best offers much more complex interpretations of the dynamics of gender, race, and power. For those of us raised in the United States, a related antipathy sometimes operates, since acknowledging any kind of structural inequality challenges the deeply held myth of equal opportunity. The myth professes that in America anybody can succeed, as if there were no obstacles based on gender, class, or race. To raise questions about fairness implicitly asks whether those who have succeeded are in fact the most deserving. Little wonder they are left fearful of feminism.

Notes

1. Madhu Kishwar, "Why I Do Not Call Myself a Feminist," *Manushi* 61 (1991), 2–8.
2. Alice Walker, *In Search of Our Mothers' Gardens: Womanist Prose* (New York: Harcourt, Brace, Jovanovich, 1983), xi; Rebecca Walker, "Becoming the Third Wave," *Ms.* 2:4 (1992), 39–41.

3. In April 2000 a Gallup poll asked if respondents personally agree or disagree with the goals of the women's rights movement; 45 percent strongly agreed and another 40 percent somewhat agreed. An *NBC News/Wall Street Journal* poll in June 2000 asked "whether you consider yourself a feminist," and 29 percent responded yes.
4. Jennifer Pozner, "False Feminist Death Syndrome," *Sojourner* 23:12 (1998), 2.

1b Diversity and Intersectionality

Chapter 5

Intersectional Feminist Frameworks: A Primer

Canadian Research Institute for the Advancement of Women (CRIAW)

The Canadian Research Institute for the Advancement of Women (CRIAW) provides tools and resources to support researchers and organizations in advancing social justice and equality for all women. CRIAW focuses on generating and promoting urgently needed feminist research, and on making it available for public advocacy and education. Recent projects include Intersectional Feminist Frameworks, which aim to promote inclusiveness in research, and FemNorthNet, which seeks to engage women living in northern communities in research on their experiences and needs due to economic restructuring.

Introduction

While Canada has experienced substantial economic growth over the last decade, poverty continues to persist and grow in Canada. If you're a woman or child, you may be counted among those most affected. One in seven (2.4 million) women live in poverty in this country.[1]

What's worse—if you are an Aboriginal woman, a woman of colour, an immigrant woman, a woman with a disability, a lone mother, or a senior woman, you face an even greater chance of being counted among Canada's poor. In 2003, 38% of lone-parent families headed by mothers had incomes that were less than the after-tax Low Income Cut-Offs. In comparison, only 13% of lone-parent families headed by fathers, and 7% of two-parent families, faced this situation.[2]

These numbers tell us that despite the efforts of many different groups to end poverty and create a more just society, we've made little headway. In fact, poverty is intensifying for those living closest to society's margins.

After years of working towards greater equality for women, CRIAW believes that different approaches are needed to make real social and economic change—approaches that offer diverse contributions, and that work from Intersectional Feminist Frameworks (IFFs).

IFFs offer alternative frameworks to viewing economic and social change that value and bring together the visions, directions, and goals of women from very diverse experiences and different perspectives.

In this document CRIAW hopes to foster interest in IFFs and encourage their use by women's and social justice organizations.

A Case for IFFs

Intersectional Feminist Frameworks (IFFs) aim to foster understanding of the many circumstances that combine with discriminatory social practices to produce and sustain inequality and exclusion. IFFs look at how systems of discrimination, such as colonialism and globalization, can impact the combination of a person's

- social or economic status,
- race,
- class,
- gender,
- sexuality,
- ability,
- geographic location,
- citizenship and nationalities, and/or
- refugee and immigrant status.

Understanding IFFs

While IFFs are not new, many social activists face an ongoing challenge of developing, understanding, and applying these frameworks. However, CRIAW has identified emerging approaches and principles of IFFs that are based on countless conversations and represent many different views.

Some common underlying themes of IFFs include

- using tools for analysis that consider the complexities of women's lives;
- making sure policy analysis is centred on the lives of those most marginalized;
- attempting to think about women's lives in holistic ways when making policies;
- valuing self-reflection in our social justice beliefs so that we are aware of how we are all caught up in systems of power and privilege;
- integrating world views and knowledge that have historically been marginalized;
- understanding that women's varying histories have created many social identities, which place them in different positions of hierarchical power;
- making efforts to challenge binary thinking that sustains inequalities, such as able/disabled, gay/straight, white/black, man/woman, West/East, and North/South; and
- revealing that this binary thinking is a result of unequal power relations.

From these themes it's clear that Intersectional Feminist Frameworks (IFFs) are

- fluid, changing, and continuously negotiated;
- specific to the interaction of a person or group's history, politics, geography, ecology, and culture;
- based upon women's specific locations and situations rather than upon generalizations;
- diverse ways to confront social injustices, which focus on many types of discrimination rather than on just one; and
- locally and globally interconnected.

The Way Forward: Shifting to IFFs

Organizations and individuals who actively engage with IFFs' approaches and principles can be sure to uproot some tensions and challenges, as previously held beliefs and focal points are reexamined. But the adoption of IFFs by policy-makers and activists has the potential to generate equitable and broad-based social and economic change.

IFFs crack open oppressive structures and practices without ranking the fight against one oppression over the fight against another. Putting these types of frameworks in place is urgently needed if we hope to one day see a just society.

Practising IFFs in Social Justice and Policy Work

Today's struggles for equality are being fought from many different levels and perspectives. The following two examples show concrete ways that IFFs could bring about new understandings and strategies for change. The first illustrates the use of IFFs in understanding immigration and refugee policies, while the second takes a look at using IFFs to fight for an end to poverty. [...]

Immigrant and Migrant Women—Viewed through IFFs

Many activists and policy-makers have applied Gender-Based Analysis (GBA) to Canadian immigration policy and procedures to underscore the inequities faced by women applicants. But the reality of women crossing borders is much more complex than this analysis captures.

The following two situations highlight some of the strengths of using IFFs to address Canadian immigration policy and procedures.

I. Broadening the scope of analysis

GBA use in immigration law captures most women's reliance on male spouses because of the way the Canadian immigration classification system is structured. In this gendered dilemma, immigrant and migrant women may face

- difficulty attending English/French language training programs,
- isolation without English language training,
- inadequate or unaffordable child care,
- unemployment, and
- lack of access to a social support network.

While gender plays a significant role, IFFs take note of many other factors of the immigration process to better understand the interlocking impact of racism, sexism, ageism, and discrimination based on language, sexuality, and/or disability upon migrant women. These factors include the

- demand for poorly paid and highly skilled workers in Canada and other Western countries;
- connections between policies on trade, labour, citizenship, education, training, social welfare, health, military, national security, and human rights; and
- historical links between colonialism, nation formation, global economies, and immigration policies.

II. Strengthening domestic worker advocacy

For years domestic worker advocacy groups have tried to challenge and change the government's Live-in Caregiver Program. This program forces foreign domestic workers to live with their employer as a visa condition.

There is sizeable evidence that women are more vulnerable to abuse, exploitation, and isolation as live-in workers. Even with this knowledge, Canada refuses to listen to advocacy groups and end the live-in requirement, and Canadians remain unaware of these workers' mistreatment.

At face value the Live-in Caregiver Program appears

- economically supportive of migrant women,
- sympathetic to poor women migrating to Canada, and
- helpful for privileged women and families in Canada who require extensive child care.

Yet the live-in requirement results in workers being

- vulnerable to extended overtime hours without appropriate compensation, if any;
- unable to take skills training courses;
- unable to establish meaningful networks; [and]
- fearful of reporting any violation on the part of the employer.

IFFs can help build solid support and recognition for domestic workers by viewing gender alongside other forms of oppression that attempt to take away migrant women's power. A review of the Live-in Caregiver Program by advocacy groups and the Canadian government through IFFs would

- expose the role of colonialism and Canada's racist and sexist immigration policies in shaping this program;
- force this issue to become all of society's problem and not only the problem of the women facing the abuse;
- reveal how immigration, employment standards, citizenship, and restrictive labour policies combine to exclude and limit equal treatment of racialized women;
- show how Canada's lack of good-quality, affordable child care spaces mean that affluent Canadian women and their families can meet their child care needs through this program, leading to the exploitation of many migrant women from the South, while lower-income women in Canada, including many women with disabilities, Aboriginal women, racialized women, and women living in rural areas, have few or no child care alternatives; and
- explain the reluctance of governments to address unfair working conditions that are structured into the Live-in Caregiver Program.

Ending Poverty through IFFs

Many anti-poverty campaigns focus their fight upon income gaps created through capitalism. IFFs, however, provide tremendous opportunities for radically re-envisioning such campaigns. For example, IFFs speak to the

- racialization of poverty through slavery, colonization, and labour migration;
- social exclusion of women already pushed to the margins through limited access to housing, child care, education, social services, citizenship, and a living wage; and
- enforcement of poverty through social and economical policies such as the Indian Act and the Immigration and Refugee Protection Act.

As IFFs are used to deal with poverty, social systems that crush the poor become exposed. IFFs make it clear that poverty is not simply about finding and keeping a job, although that is important. It may also be about

- having access to one's culture, religion, and language;
- being part of a supportive community;
- living in decent housing;
- being accepted for who you are no matter what you look like; and
- having access to health, education, and welfare services where your dignity as a human being equal to all others is respected. Fighting poverty is about fighting social injustice across many fronts.

*****

Choosing IFFs

IFFs are beginning to show signs of success for some organizations—particularly those with flexible structures open to change. Recently one community and campus radio station surveyed its ethnic programming to find out which shows provided information and discussion on gay, lesbian, bisexual, and transgendered topics. This survey helped identify the need for expression of issues found within already marginalized groups. Station coordinators demonstrated IFFs' principles by

- challenging programmers to think about who their audience includes,
- thinking about their listeners more holistically by offering more inclusive programming and messages, and
- opening up a self-reflection process for the station's staff and the programmers' social justice beliefs.

How and where social justice and feminist activists begin their analysis depends on the specific conditions of the lives of those with whom they are working. It's important to remember that IFFs

- are flexible and open to shifts and changes in the political, social, economic, and cultural order;
- have multiple points of entry, engagement, and discussion that cannot be determined in advance (i.e., gender may not be the most useful entry point to understand particular issues or situations);
- can inform government policy and organizing strategies for activists in many different areas (i.e., labour, anti-poverty, immigration, environmental issues can be viewed from these frameworks);

- are challenging to adopt—growing pains and tensions are part of the process as previous beliefs are reflected upon; and
- aim to elicit broad-based social and economic change.

As women's movements are now globally connected, an expanded and diverse range of tools and resources for analysis and activism are available to challenge dominant powers. Shifting to IFFs is one way to access the range of marginalized knowledges that are available to social justice activists around the world.

Notes

1. CRIAW, *Women and Poverty Fact Sheet* (3rd ed.) (Ottawa: Canadian Research Institute for the Advancement of Women, 2005).
2. Statistics Canada, *Women in Canada: A Gender-Based Statistical Report* (5th ed.).

Supplement 3

Intersectionality Wheel Diagram

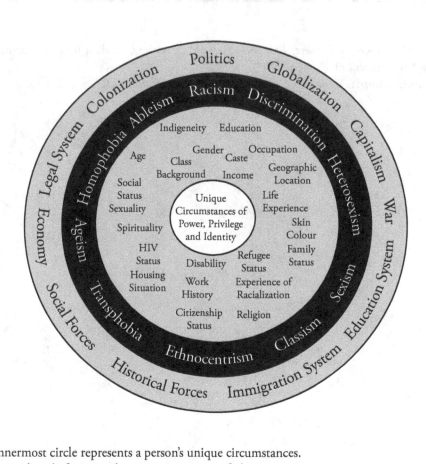

- Innermost circle represents a person's unique circumstances.
- Second circle from inside represents aspects of identity.
- Third circle from inside represents different types of discrimination/isms/attitudes that impact identity.
- Outermost circle represents larger forces and structures that work together to reinforce exclusion.

Note: It is impossible to name every variety of discrimination, identity, or structure. These are just examples to help give you a sense of what intersectionality is.

Source: Joanna Simpson, *Everyone Belongs: A Toolkit for Applying Intersectionality* (Ottawa: Canadian Research Institute for the Advancement of Women, 2009), 5.

Supplement 4

Activist Insight:
Sojourner Truth (1797–1883)

Sojourner Truth, circa 1870, National Portrait Gallery, Smithsonian Institution. Photograph courtesy of Wikimedia Commons.

One critical thematic of feminism that is perennially relevant is the important question of what it means to be a woman under different historical circumstances. Throughout the 1970s and the 1980s, this concern was the subject of major debate as the concept of "global sisterhood" was critiqued for its failure to fully take on board the power relations that divided us.

A century earlier, contestations among feminists involved in anti-slavery struggles and campaigns for women's suffrage also foregrounded similar conflicts. Their memory still resonates with us because the interrelationships between racism, gender, sexuality, and social class were at the heart of these contestations. [The] 19th century political locution *"Ain't I a Woman?"* by fundamentally challenging all ahistoric or essentialist notions of "woman" neatly captures all the main elements of the debate on "intersectionality." We regard the concept of "intersectionality" as signifying the complex, irreducible, varied, and variable effects which ensue when multiple axes of differentiation—economic, political, cultural, psychic, subjective, and experiential—intersect in historically specific contexts. The concept emphasizes that different dimensions of social life cannot be separated out into discrete and pure strands.

The phrase, "Ain't I a Woman?" was first introduced into North American and British feminist lexicon by an enslaved woman, Sojourner Truth (the name she took, instead of her original name, Isabella, when she became a travelling preacher). We know from the biographies of black women such as Sojourner Truth that many of them spoke loud and clear. They would not be caged by the violence of slavery even as they were violently marked by it. Sojourner Truth's 1851 speech at the Women's Rights Convention in Akron, Ohio, very well demonstrates the historical power of a political subject who challenges imperatives of subordination and thereby creates new visions. Sojourner Truth was born into enslavement (to a wealthy Dutch slave-owner living in New York). She campaigned for both the abolition of slavery and for equal rights for women. [Since she was illiterate throughout her life, no formal record of the speech exists and, indeed, two different versions of it are in existence.]

This cutting-edge speech (in all senses of the term) deconstructs every single major truth-claim about gender in a patriarchal slave social formation. More generally, the discourse offers a devastating critique of the socio-political, economic, and cultural processes of "othering" whilst drawing attention to the simultaneous importance of subjectivity—of subjective pain and violence that the inflictors do not often wish to hear about or acknowledge. Simultaneously, the discourse foregrounds the importance of spirituality to this form of political activism when existential grief touches ground with its unconscious and finds affirmation through a belief in the figure of a Jesus who listens. Political identity here is never taken as a given but is performed through rhetoric and narration. Sojourner Truth's identity claims are thus relational, constructed in relation to white women and all men and clearly demonstrate that what we call "identities" are not objects but processes constituted in and through power relations.

It is in this sense of critique, practice, and inspiration that this discourse holds crucial lessons for us today. Part lament, but defiant, articulating razor-sharp politics but with the sensibility of a poet, the discourse performs the analytic moves of a "decolonised mind." It refuses all final closures. We are all in dire need of decolonized open minds today. Furthermore, Sojourner Truth powerfully challenges essentialist thinking that a particular category of woman is essentially this or essentially that (e.g., that women are necessarily weaker than men or that enslaved black women were not real women).

Source: Adapted from Avtar Brah and Ann Phoenix, "Ain't I a Woman? Revisiting Intersectionality," *Journal of International Women's Studies* 5, no. 3 (May 2004): 76–77.

Women's Rights Convention in Akron, Ohio, 1851 Speech by Sojourner Truth

"Well, children, where there is so much racket there must be something out of kilter. I think that 'twixt the negroes of the South and the women of the North, all talking about rights, the white men will be in a fix pretty soon. But what's all this here talking about?

"That man over there says that women need to be helped into carriages and lifted over ditches, and to have the best place everywhere. Nobody ever helps me into carriages, or over mud-puddles, or gives me any best place! And ain't I a woman? Look at me! Look at my arm! I could have ploughed and planted, and gathered into barns, and no man could head me! And ain't I a woman? I could work as much and eat as much as a man—when I could get it—and bear the lash as well! And ain't I a woman? I have borne thirteen children, and seen them most all sold off to slavery, and when I cried out with my mother's grief, none but Jesus heard me! And ain't I a woman?

"Then they talk about this thing in the head; what's this they call it? [Intellect, somebody whispers] ... That's it, honey. What's that got to do with women's rights or negros' rights? If my cup won't hold but a pint, and yours holds a quart, wouldn't you be mean not to let me have my little half measure-full?

"Then that little man in black there, he says women can't have as much rights as men, 'cause Christ wasn't a woman! Where did your Christ come from? Where did your Christ come from? From God and a woman! Man had nothing to do with Him.

"If the first woman God ever made was strong enough to turn the world upside down all alone, these women together ought to be able to turn it right side up again! And now they is asking to do it, the men better let them.

"Obliged to you for hearing me, and now old Sojourner ain't got nothing more to say."

Source: Adapted from Francis Dana Gage, published in 1863, retrieved from http://www.sojournertruth.org/Library/Speeches/Default.htm

Chapter 6

Reformulating the Feminist Perspective: Giving Voice to Women with Disabilities

Neita Kay Israelite and Karen Swartz

Neita Israelite is an associate professor in the Faculty of Education and Graduate Program in critical disability studies at York University. Her research and teaching focus on disability and inclusion, including university experiences of students with disabilities, identity construction of hard-of-hearing adolescents, and transition and adjustment issues.

Karen Swartz is director of York University's Physical, Sensory, and Medical Disability Services, where she supports and advocates on behalf of university students, staff, and faculty living with disabilities. Her research focuses on post-secondary education and disability.

This essay focuses on women with disabilities, a significant and growing segment of Canadian society. According to Statistics Canada (2001), 3.6 million Canadians—12.4% of the population—have disabilities, and more than 50% of them are women. The rate of disability increases with age. Of children from birth to age 14, 3.3% have a disability; amongst working-age adults aged 15 to 64, 9.9% have a disability. This figure rises to 40.5% for Canadians over the age of 65, and more than 50% for those over the age of 75 (Government of Canada, 2002). With more people living longer, and the tendency of women to outlive men, we can expect the number of disabled women to continue to grow.

Persons with disabilities demonstrate relatively high rates of unemployment and low rates of work-related earnings in comparison to those without disabilities. Not surprisingly, women with disabilities have even higher rates of unemployment and lower earnings than their male counterparts (Bunch & Crawford, 1998; Fawcett, 1996). Women with disabilities in Ontario demonstrate exceptionally low rates of workforce participation, and nearly one-third live in poverty.

Despite the growing number of women with disabilities and the challenges they face, disabled women constitute a group that is typically marginalized by the mainstream feminist movement (as well as the masculinist disability movement). As Barbara Cassidy, Robina Lord, and Nancy Mandell point out (1998), feminist analyses of women's oppression tend to take white middle-class women as the norm. Those who differ from this norm with regard to their physical, sensory, or mental status—i.e., women with disabilities—as well as those who differ with regard to factors such as race, class, or ethnicity, are often "left out without anyone noticing they are absent" (Cassidy, Lord, & Mandell, 1998, p. 33).

Our essay begins with an overview of the two major models of disability: the medical model and the social model. Next, we review feminist debates on two critical concerns regarding the social model: (1) its exclusion of the subjective experience of people with disabilities, and (2) its exclusion of discourses on the body and the reality of impairment. Finally, we take up critiques of mainstream feminism by feminist disability theorists.

Throughout this essay, we use personal accounts of women with disabilities to illuminate critical aspects of our discussion. Most of the narratives were collected by second author Karen Swartz (2003) in her participatory qualitative research study of the life transitions of university women with disabilities. These accounts are augmented by narratives of women and girls with disabilities gathered by first author Neita Israelite and her colleagues in several qualitative research projects (Israelite, 2003; Israelite, Karambatsos, Pullan, & Symanzik, 2000; Israelite, Swartz, Huynh, & Tocco, 2004).

The disability field is currently split regarding the use of "disability-first" versus "person-first" terminology (Marks, 1999). Disability-first (i.e., disabled women) is preferred by some women as it acknowledges the community and culture of disabled people and the primacy of disability in their lives; person-first (i.e., women with disabilities) is preferred by other women as it acknowledges the primacy of their personhood. We use both terms in recognition of both points of view.

Models of Disability

Two major theoretical positions inform attitudes and beliefs about disability: the traditional medical model, and the social model.

The Medical Model

The medical model assumes that differences from the norm in terms of physical, sensory, or mental capabilities produce a defective member of society. This model holds that any difficulties people with disabilities experience are due to problems within the individual, and not because of environmental, societal, physical, or attitudinal barriers within the larger society. For instance, it is assumed that women with physical disabilities will have problems with public transit because they cannot climb stairs, that women who are deaf will have parenting problems because they cannot hear their children's voices, and that women with visual impairments will have problems with employment because they cannot read work manuals.

A critical dimension of the medical model is the notion of power. Considering disability as a defect within the individual allows those who are not disabled to take charge. This gives rise to a patriarchal-like set of dynamics in which power is held by, and transferred through, nondisabled people, who are often doctors, allied health professionals, clinicians, or educators. Their professional dominance has led to the medicalization of disability—the extension of the power and influence of medicine such that it "dominates the daily lives and experiences of many disabled people" (French & Swain, 2001, p. 738). One byproduct of this form of social control is labelling, a "medical discourse of diagnosis of impairment" (Swain & Cameron, 1999, p. 77), in which the impairment, nature of the remediation, or the individual's assistive devices become a description of her identity. In a study of attitudes toward university students with disabilities (Israelite et al., 2000), a disabled woman complained about nondisabled peers who identify people with disabilities in terms of their assistive devices:

One of the things that I consistently state when I speak in public is that I am not my machine.... And I'm sure it can be said ... whether that machine happens to be a computer or a wheelchair or a hearing aid. If you can't see the person, then you haven't seen me.

Some disabled people internalize medicalized identities to such an extent that they even refer to themselves in terms of a medical definition rather than "an affirming self-definition" (Marks, 1999, p. 69). In interviews with hard-of-hearing high school students (Israelite, 2003), one young woman with congenital (from birth) hearing loss called herself a "hearing aid" student; another with recently acquired loss said, "Now I am a 'hearing impaired.'"

The Social Model

In contrast to the medical model, the social model views disability as a social identity. It holds that the "problem" of disability is inherent not in the individual, but rather in the social structure. In social model theory, the following distinction is made between impairment and disability:

> Impairment is the functional limitation within the individual caused by physical, mental, or sensory impairment. Disability is the loss or limitation of opportunities to take part in the normal life of a community on an equal level with others due to physical and social barriers. (Barnes, 1991, p. 2)

Therefore, the cause of disability is not impairment per se, but society's failure to provide appropriate services and to adequately ensure that the needs of people with disabilities are fully taken into account. Disability, from this perspective, is constructed as all the things that impose restrictions on people with disabilities, such as individual prejudice, institutional discrimination, inequitable legislation, and restrictive school and work environments. Participants in a study of school-to-work transitions (Israelite et al., 2004) were disabled by a range of restrictions in the workplace. For instance, when a woman with a physical impairment approached a potential place of employment for a job application, she discovered that the human resources building was not wheelchair accessible.

> I went into the human resources building to pick up an application and I couldn't get in because I got stuck. I had to go all the way around to the back and come through, and I just knew that it didn't feel right. If you can't get into the human resources building to get an application, you know, it already discourages you by thinking, "Why would they want me when they wouldn't even let me in?"

Another woman in the study felt that prospective employers seriously underestimated the abilities of disabled people:

> They think, they assume, the job is too big for you. They underestimate you. And they have no faith in you or confidence. And you tell them you can do it successfully ... But generally they'll tell you, "Oh, you can't do it."

The attitudes this woman describes exemplify some of the taken-for-granted or commonly held beliefs that people without disabilities hold about those with disabilities. In our culture, physical, sensory, and mental impairments are often considered to have far-reaching effects on ability. Although such beliefs may be unconscious, they nevertheless strongly influence behaviour and expectations.

Taken-for-granted beliefs play a large part in widespread assumptions of dysfunction regarding the sexuality of disabled women, such as the myth that they are unfit as sexual partners. The women in Karen Swartz's (2003, pp. 21, 22) study, for example, said that, as they were growing up, they got the constant message from nondisabled peers that they were undesirable.

> What I found in high school, a lot of times, was when you try to pursue somebody you're interested in, they wouldn't even look at you twice. There was that perception of, "Oh, you have a disability, part of your body is broken, so therefore you're not a sexual being."

Taken-for-granted beliefs also contribute to marginalization, a process that relegates women who "fall out of the scope of what is currently defined as socially acceptable" (Rauscher & McClintock, 1997, p. 198) to the outer margins of economic and social power and the cultural life of a society, leading to their exclusion from a range of social, cultural, and economic experiences that are part of the everyday lives of non-disabled women. [...]

Since its original conception in Britain more than two decades ago, the social model has had a profound influence on the lives of people with disabilities. At the theoretical level, this model demonstrates "how the previously taken-for-granted, naturalistic category 'disability' is in reality an artificial and exclusionary social construction that penalizes those people who do not conform to mainstream expectations of appearance, behaviour, and/or economic performance" (Tregaskis, 2002, p. 457).

At the personal level, the social model has "liberated individual disabled people from the burden of personal tragedy, the oppression of individual inadequacies" (Morris, 1996, p. 12) by helping them understand that it is an impaired society, not their impaired bodies, that is responsible for the discrimination, marginalization, and exclusion they face.

Feminist Critiques of the Social Model

Although the social model has been beneficial to disabled people in both theory and praxis, it has been criticized for its failure to address the complexity of factors that shape the production of disability. Some prominent feminist debates deal with the exclusion of the subjective experience of people with disabilities from many social model accounts as well as the exclusion of discussions of the body and the reality of impairment.

Subjective Experience and Social Model Theory

Feminists with disabilities such as Susan Wendell (1996), Jenny Morris (1996), and Carol Thomas (1999) have put forward accounts of disability in which personal narratives play an important role. Given the inequitable power differentials that characterize relations between women with and without disabilities, these women emphasize the necessity of foregrounding the individual experiences of disabled women as a vehicle for understanding their collective oppressions (Tregaskis, 2002). Other writers (e.g., Sheldon, 1999) argue that such analyses are too individualized and prioritize subjective experiences of disability over more theoretical explanations. Our position, however, is in line with Carol Thomas, who points out that "by taking the personal experiences of disabled women as their starting point and writing themselves into their own analyses, disabled feminist writers … are thus building upon well-established practices among feminist writers more generally" (1999, p. 70). Giving voice to the personal narratives of women with disabilities is also an important way of increasing the general public's sense of social responsibility while informing and clarifying social model theory.

The Body, Impairment, and Social Model Theory

Recent critiques of the social model focus on the exclusion of discussions of the body and impairment from many social model accounts. Many feminist disability theorists (e.g., Crow, 1996; French, 1994; Morris, 1991; Thomas, 1999; Wendell, 1996) and some masculinist disability theorists (e.g., Abberley, 1987; Hughes, 1999; Hughes & Paterson, 1997; Paterson & Hughes, 1999) take issue with the social model because it neither connects with the embodied experience nor the pain associated with impairment. Some theorists (e.g., Wendell, 1996; French, 1994) argue that the only way for the social model to move forward is to integrate the experience of impairment—the pain and the real limitations—with the experience of disability. Susan Wendell, who has an acquired physical disability, writes that disabled feminists should be discussing "how to live with the suffering body, with that which cannot be noticed without pain, and that which cannot be celebrated without ambivalence" (1996, p. 179). [...]

Sally French, who has a visual impairment, points out that it is her actual lack of visual acuity, and not some barrier created by a sighted society, that prevents her from recognizing people and reading nonverbal cues in social situations (1993).

> While I agree with the basic tenets of [the social] model and consider it to be the most important way forward for disabled people, I believe that some of the most profound problems experienced by people with certain impairments are difficult, if not impossible, to solve by social manipulation. (1993, p. 17)

Social model proponents such as Michael Oliver (1996) point out that the original goal of the social model, when it was proposed more than 20 years ago, was to eradicate what they identify as the "true causes" of disability: societal discrimination and prejudice. The fact that these causes still permeate the lives of women with disabilities is exemplified by their reaction to workplace prejudice and discrimination in our study of school-to-work transitions (Israelite et al., 2004, p. 20):

> "It gets right to the core of your identity. You begin to question, 'What is my role in this world.'"

> "I thought, 'Oh my God, this is what it's like out there. Oh my God, how am I going to find a job?'"

Some disability scholars are calling for an updated version of the social model, one that acknowledges the relevance of bodily experience to the lives of disabled people. They argue that by not incorporating impairment, the social model concedes the body to medicine, thus giving tacit permission for it to be understood in terms of the medical model (Hughes & Paterson, 1997). Bill Hughes and Kevin Paterson (1997) assert that there is a need to wrest control of the impairment discourse from the medical profession and to establish the impaired body as an integral part of what it means to be disabled. This would entail, in part, "tackling the very real repulsion that society feels for the impaired body" (Tregaskis, 2002, p. 464). This repulsion was something that most of the participants in Karen Swartz's (2003, p. 27) study had not only experienced, but also internalized, to a significant extent. One woman explained:

> What you stare at in the mirror is not just something that is going to go away. You're not going to wake up from a dream. This is reality.

Impairment theory provides an explanation that, in keeping with the social model, places the responsibility for "the problem of repulsion" on nondisabled people. Claire Tregaskis (2002) explains that, "in reality, it is the non-disabled gaze which creates abnormality, and that actually it is the gaze that is disfigured, not the [disabled] 'other' who is being gazed at" (p. 463). This point is clearly illustrated in the comments of two women in Karen Swartz's (2003, p. 27) study:

> The only time I saw myself as disabled was when … someone said, "Oh what happened to you?" [I would reply] "Oh what do you mean what happened to me? Oh yeah. Oh God. Oh you're talking about that."

> [You have to] realize what you are feeling isn't you. It is the images that somebody else has transferred on to you.

*****

Disability Theorists Critique Feminist Theory

Many women with disabilities write that they feel marginalized within the feminist movement. Their experience is that mainstream feminist theories tend to privilege "the functional capabilities and social roles characteristic of 'normal' women" (Kittay, Schriempf, Silvers, & Wendell, 2001, p. viii), often not taking women with disabilities into account. Feminist disability scholars share in the marginalization. Carol Thomas cites the cases of Jenny Morris (1991, 1996) and Susan Wendell (1996), both of whom have acquired disabilities. These scholars were accepted as feminist thinkers and writers until they became disabled; after that, they, too, found themselves marginalized from feminist scholarship.

According to feminist scholars Fine and Asch (1988):

> Women with disabilities traditionally have been ignored not only by those concerned about disability but also by those examining women's experiences. Even the feminist scholars to whom we owe great intellectual and political debts have perpetuated this neglect. The popular view of women with disabilities has been one mixed with repugnance. Perceiving disabled women as childlike, helpless, and victimized, nondisabled women have severed them from the sisterhood in an effort to advance more powerful, competent, and appealing female icons. As one feminist academic said to the non-disabled co-author of this essay: "Why study women with disabilities? They reinforce traditional stereotypes of women being dependent, passive and needy." (pp. 3–4)

Several of Karen Swartz's (2003) participants said that during their childhood, doctors, teachers, counselors, and even some family members encouraged them, through both implicit and explicit messages, to be passive and dependent rather than strong and independent. They were dismayed when they got to university to find that such attitudes still predominated. One woman sought out courses in Women's Studies in the hopes of finding answers to her questions about the oppression of disabled women. She was dismayed to find that even a course on the history of women did not address this issue:

> I won't take a women's history course because it doesn't cover disabled women. You can't tell me that disabled women didn't exist.... I think we need to make professors more aware and almost demand that it get put on the curriculum. I mean if they can study women's issues, gay issues, African/American issues. We are part of society and we deserve to be studied. (p. 37)

Feminist disability scholars agree with this student's assessment of university programs and have proposed ways of infusing disability issues into the postsecondary curriculum and making the experience of disabled women more central to teaching and research in Women's Studies (e.g., Garland-Thomson 2002; Linton, 1997). Rosemary Garland-Thomson (2002) argues for the positioning of feminist disability studies as a field of academic study and the inclusion of feminist disability theory as a major subgenre of feminist theory. Garland-Thomson is but one of many feminist scholars calling for the inclusion of the ability/disability binary as a category of analysis alongside gender, race, age, and social class in feminist analyses of oppression.

* * * * *

[...] Disability is a fluid category. Some women are born with disabilities; others acquire them. Some are disabled for some portion of their lives, others for their whole lives. Virtually all women can expect to become disabled if they live long enough. Within the disability movement, masculinist disability scholars have been too slow to acknowledge the gendered nature of disability. Within the feminist movement, nondisabled feminist scholars have been too slow to acknowledge the importance of the disability to identity construction and feminist analyses of oppression. Sadly, what Marion Blackwell-Stratton, Mary Lou Breslin, Arlean Mayerson, and Susan Bailey stated in 1988 still holds true: "For the disabled feminist, neither the disability movement nor the women's movement fully addresses her concerns" (p. 307).

As Garland-Thomson so aptly states:

> Disability—like gender—is a concept that pervades all aspects of culture: its structuring institutions, social identities, cultural practices, political positions, historical communities, and the shared human experience of embodiment.... To understand how disability operates is to understand what it means to be fully human. (2002, p. 4)

References

Abberley, P. (1987). The concept of oppression and the development of a social theory of disability. *Disability, Handicap, and Society*, 2, 5–20.

Barnes, C. (1991). *Disabled People in Britain and Discrimination: A Case for Anti-discrimination Legislation.* London: Hurst.

Blackwell-Stratton, M., Breslin, M., Mayerson, A., & Bailey, S. (1988). Smashing icons: Disabled women and the disability and women's movements. In M. Fine & A. Asch (Eds.), *Women with Disabilities: Essays in Psychology, Culture, and Politics* (pp. 306–332). Philadelphia: Temple University Press.

Bunch, M., & Crawford, C. (1998, June). *Persons with Disabilities: Literature Review of the Factors Affecting Employment and Labor Force Transitions.* Hull: Human Resources Development Canada. Retrieved June 19, 2003 from http://www.hrdc-drhc.gc.ca/sp-ps/arb-dgra/publications/research/disability.shtml.

Cassidy, B., Lord, R., & Mandell, N. (1998). Silenced and forgotten women: Race, poverty, and disability. In N. Mandell (Ed.), *Feminist Issues: Race, Class, and Sexuality* (2nd ed.) (pp. 27–54). Toronto: Prentice-Hall.

Crow, L. (1996). Including all of our lives: Renewing the social model of disability. In J. Morris (Ed.), *Encounters with Strangers: Feminism and Disability* (pp. 206–226). London: Women's Press.

Fawcett, G. (1996). *Living with Disability in Canada: An Economic Portrait.* Hull: Office for Disability Issues, Human Resources Development Canada.

Fine, M., & Asch, A. (Eds.). (1988). *Women with Disabilities: Essays in Psychology, Culture, and Politics.* Philadelphia: Temple University Press.

French, S. (1993). Disability, impairment, or something in between. In J. Swain, V. Finkelstein, S. French, & M. Oliver (Eds.), *Disabling Barriers, Enabling Environments.* Buckingham: Open University Press.

French, S. (1994). *On Equal Terms: Working with Disabled People.* Oxford: Butterworth-Heinemann.

French, S., & Swain, J. (2001). The relationship between disabled people and health and welfare professionals. In G. Albrecht, K. Seelman, & M. Bury (Eds.), *Handbook of Disability Studies* (pp. 734–753). Thousand Oaks: Sage.

Garland-Thomson, R. (2002). Integrating disability theory, transforming feminist theory. *Feminist Disability Studies* [Special issue] [Electronic version]. *NWSA Journal*, 14 (3), 1–32.

Government of Canada. (2002). *Advancing the Inclusion of Persons with Disabilities.* Hull: Human Resources Development Canada. Retrieved March 12, 2004, from www.hrdc-drhc.gc.ca/bcph-odi.

Hughes, B. (1999). The construction of impairment: Modernity and the aesthetic of oppression. *Disability and Society*, 14, 155–172.

Hughes, B., & Paterson, K. (1997). The social model of disability and the disappearing body: Towards a sociology of impairment. *Disability & Society*, 12, 325–340.

Israelite, N. (2003). *Identity Construction of Hard-of-Hearing Adolescents.* Unpublished raw data.

Israelite, N., Karambatsos, S., Pullan, J., & Symanzik, A. (2000, June). *Attitudes of University Students toward Students with Disabilities.* Paper presented at the annual meeting of the Society for Disability Studies, Chicago, IL.

Israelite, N., Swartz, K., Huynh, J., & Tocco, A. (2004). *Postsecondary Students and Graduates with Disabilities: The School-to-Work Transition.* Manuscript submitted for publication.

Kittay, F., Schriempf, A., Silvers, A., & Wendell, S. (2001). Introduction. *Feminism and Disability* [Special issue] [Electronic version]. *Hypatia*, 16 (4), vii–xii.

Linton, S. (1997). *Claiming Disability: Knowledge and Identity.* New York: New York University Press, p. 94.

Marks, D. (1999). *Disability: Controversial Debates and Conversations.* London: Routledge.

Morris, J. (1991). *Pride against Prejudice: Transforming Attitudes to Disability.* London: Women's Press.

Morris, J. (1996). Introduction. In J. Morris (Ed.), *Encounters with Strangers: Feminism and Disability* (pp. 1–16). London: The Women's Press Ltd.

Oliver, M. (1996). *Understanding Disability: From Theory to Practice.* New York: St. Martin's Press.

Paterson, K., & Hughes, B. (1999). Disability studies and phenomenology: The carnal politics of everyday life. *Disability and Society,* 14, 597–610.

Rauscher, L., & McClintock, J. (1997). Ableism curriculum design. In M. Adams, L.A. Bell, & Griffen, P. (Eds.), *Teaching for Diversity and Social Justice* (pp. 198–231). New York: Routledge.

Sheldon, A. (1999). Personal and perplexing: Feminist disability politics evaluated. *Disability and Society,* 14, 643–657.

Swain, J., & Cameron, C. (1999). Unless otherwise stated: Discourses of labeling and coming out. In M. Corker & S. French (Eds.), *Disability Discourse* (pp. 68–78). Buckingham: Open University Press.

Swartz, K. (2003). *Life Transitions of Student with Disabilities Revisited: A Feminist Approach.* Unpublished manuscript. York University, Toronto, Canada.

Thomas, C. (1999). *Female Forms: Experiencing and Understanding Disability.* Buckingham: Open University Press.

Tregaskis, C. (2002). Social model theory: The story so far. *Disability and Society,* 17, 457–470.

Wendell, S. (1996). *The Rejected Body: Feminist Philosophical Reflections on Disability.* New York: Routledge.

Chapter 7

Overview and Introductions:
This Is What a Feminist Looks Like

Shira Tarrant

Shira Tarrant is an associate professor in the Department of Women's, Gender, and Sexuality Studies at California State University, as well as a recognized author, social critic, and expert on gender politics, pop culture, and masculinity. She has recently been awarded the Glidden Professorship at Ohio State University.

Brandon Arber is a feminist. During college, he was the captain of his swim team and an all-around jock. For Brandon, feminism is a moral belief. It's about thinking girls and women shouldn't be raped, abused, discriminated against, or denied health services, especially if they get pregnant. When it comes down to it, he says, feminism is a viable approach to guiding decisions in our personal, political, and public lives. To Brandon, it's just common sense to believe in egalitarian values. It makes sense to care for all people and to bring about a better world.

*****

Derrais Carter graduated from the University of Kansas, where he majored in sociology and African-American studies. When Derrais started college, he fell in love with hip-hop and feminism. In fact, hip-hop is what led Derrais to feminist politics when he started thinking about rap lyrics and what he calls "the battlefield of identity." Being a feminist gave Derrais a platform for changing his life and how he understands his relations with others. "I began to see women as more than a video prop, extra, and eye candy," Derrais writes in his essay "This Is What a Feminist Looks Like." Instead he realized that women are highly misrepresented figures in society whom he had been "conditioned to mistreat and ignore." When Derrais taught a group of high school students one summer, the conversation led to culture, capitalism, and globalization. "By understanding feminism," Derrais says, "we were able to talk about how our 'needs' can exploit women in various other countries. The discussion made all of us think more about how we are all connected."

Still, being a male feminist is a rough road, Derrais says. People are full of race- and gender-based assumptions. "As a black male in college, I was often assumed to be on an athletic scholarship," he explains. "And when I wear my 'This Is What a Feminist Looks Like' T-shirt, people have accused me of trying to get laid." Others have said the same about his job at the campus women's center. "I used to get angry about it. Now I see these comments as mere ignorance and a failure to accept that there are men who truly care about women's issues."

Current feminist perspectives are challenging concepts of gender in fresh, new ways. More men are getting involved in feminist movements led by women. And there are plenty of examples of gender activism initiated by men, such as One in Four and Men Can Stop Rape, programs that work to prevent sexual assault. Colleges and universities are increasingly shifting from women's studies to programs that study gender and sexuality more broadly. At the same time, more guys are becoming interested in feminism. As Julie Bindel reports in the *Guardian,* increasing numbers of men are enrolling in courses with feminist content and perspectives.

*****

What Is Feminism Anyway?

Feminism is a social movement that seeks equality of opportunity for all people, regardless of gender. When there isn't equality of outcome, feminism wants to know why. It is a political perspective that uses gender to critically analyze power—who has it, who doesn't, who abuses it, and why. In their anthology, *The Fire This Time: Young Activists and the New Feminism*, Vivien Labaton and Dawn Lundy Martin define contemporary feminism as a way for women and men to do "social justice work while using a gender lens."

Feminists are committed to addressing problems that happen every day. Some of these issues take place behind the privacy of closed doors; others confront us in the public arena. These problems include things such as domestic violence, rape and sexual assault, racism, homophobia, unequal pay, job segregation, sexual objectification, restrictions on reproductive choices, and unattainable standards of gender, beauty, and behavior. In her article "Can Men Be the Allies of Feminism?" journalist Nighat Gandhi describes feminism as "a philosophy and a movement for ending all forms of oppression, including gender-based oppression."

On an individual level, feminism seeks to make room for all of us to explore who we are, separate from gender constraints. Too often, the social rules and regulations for men and women are restrictive. They don't really describe us well. Feminism questions rigid binary categories or masculinity and femininity, looks at the political consequences of assumptions about gender, and helps us search for better models and greater freedom.

Three core theoretical principles are especially important to understanding what feminism is about. These principles, which involve specific approaches to analyzing social and political issues, also point to why feminism isn't just a movement for women. Gender and power are crucial elements in all people's lives. First, feminists do not see biological sex as determining a person's identity. Second, feminism understands that personal is political. Yet feminism is not *only* personal. It's more than a lifestyle issue or a fashion statement or a strategically placed political tattoo. This points to the third core principle: Feminism is a social and political movement that is concerned about the patterns of domination and the politics of gender, race, class, and sexual orientation.

*****

Biology Is Not Destiny

A central core of feminism is the idea that our biological sex doesn't determine our life goals, emotions, behaviors, and preferences, and it shouldn't determine our opportunities. To convey this idea, innumerable feminist thinkers—Simone de Beauvoir, Ann Oakley, and Christine Delphy among them—have challenged the concept of biological determinism and emphasized the distinction between sex and gender.

"Sex" basically refers to our biology—what's between our legs when we're born. Gender refers to our social class as men and women or—when we don't fit into either of these categories—as transgender or genderqueer. Gender is something that is fluid and learned: We might come into this world with a penis or vagina, but we're not born wanting to fix things with a hammer or carry a purse. We learn gender-appropriate behavior as we go along—or we don't, and we might suffer for it. Gender is taught and reinforced through institutional arrangements that tell us how men and women "should" behave. In other words, gender is about the social construction of masculine, feminine, or genderqueer identity. Gender is not a binary selection but rather a continuum of possibilities.

Gender isn't something we're born with. It's something we perform. And we learn about *doing* gender through friends, school, religion, and family. We are taught to "do" our gender in many ways.

Our parents might tell us to toughen up when we go out for sports. If we're boys, our parents might not worry if we stay out late. If we're girls, we might get in trouble for getting angry. For birthday presents we might get Bratz dolls or skateboards, action figures or video games. Chances are that games with action-adventure names such as *Rogue Trooper* or *Call of Duty* are going to the boys. Even toys for the imagination and upping the smarts are often gender coded. LeapFrog, for example, is a toy that teaches kids vocabulary. Yet the cartridges have gender-based names such as "Disney Princess Stories" and "Thomas the Really Useful Engine." The recommended age for these toys is under ten.

Pop culture is another powerful way that gender is constructed, reinforced, and maintained. Pop culture is a potent institutional source of gender messages because we're exposed to it pretty much all day, every day. Every time we log on to the Internet, surf TV channels, watch YouTube clips, go to the movies, or pass a billboard on the side of the road, we are getting messages about masculinity and femininity, how to do it "correctly," and what happens if we don't.

Take Facebook, MySpace, myYearbook, or whatever the flavor of the day. Social networking sites are full of gender lessons. What this means is that some people might post pics to their sites flashing lots of cleavage. And some might not. It's not that *all* women show skin and *no* men ever do, but for the most part, who does it and who doesn't breaks down along masculine and feminine gender lines.

It's hard to find a MySpace photo of a guy sprawled across his bed in tiny lace panties, coyly licking his lips, but this type of image is ubiquitous among young women. These poses take their cues directly from mainstream pornography, which increasingly infuses our everyday lives and models for gender and relationships. We might want to pay attention to who's wailing the heavy metal and who's uploading sloshy love songs to their sites. Are people using "boy" colors and "girl" colors for the backgrounds on their homepages? These sorts of everyday experiences help create and reinforce our gender- and our sexual-identities. Often we participate in this process without really thinking about it.

Even Internet spam is gendered, with proposals by women to send nude pics and offers to men for penile enhancement products that promise hardness, lasting power, and bigger size. These adjectives construct gendered ideas about masculinity as being strong, hard, and "built." Even what seem to be innocuous ads are actually loaded with gender cues. Take, for example, a 2008 *Martha Stewart Living* magazine ad for grilling spices. The photo shows a man standing over the barbecue with his arms raised high over his head in victory, while the ad copy reads: "Master the Flame. Master the Flavor." Messages such as this create images of the male body as functional, triumphant, in charge. Not that there's anything inherently wrong with these qualities. But because we are so relentlessly bombarded by this limited vision of masculinity through jokes, media, consumer products, and souped-up science that masks underlying politics, these gender messages start to seem normal or "just the way things are." Sometimes we hardly even notice the process, and gender messages become naturalized. In other words, we see gendered messages so often that what are in fact constructed ideologies come to seem natural or essential. Feminism provides critical tools and analytical frameworks that help us notice and that make visible the coded metaphors of gender and sexuality.

With all the pressures of early and ongoing gender socialization, it's no wonder that by the time we're grown up, most nurses, strippers, and kindergarten teachers are still women and most politicians, professors, and firefighters are still men; most stay-at-home parents are women and most CEOs are men; most people with eating disorders are women and most people who use performance-enhancing drugs are men. Gender expectations and assumptions affect all of us—not just women. Fortunately, it looks as if change is on the horizon. We're in the middle of some shifting times when it comes to gender roles and expectations of masculinity and femininity. For now, though, there's still much work to be done.

The Personal Is Political

"The personal is political" is a powerful slogan that was coined during the women's movement of the 1960s and 1970s. It means that what happens in our individual, private lives—at places such as our jobs, clubs, homes, or schools—reflects the power dynamics in broader, public society. As the twentieth-century political scientist Harold Lasswell famously said, politics is the process of who gets what, when, and how. Feminism brings that concept from the public realm into our personal worlds. It recognizes that seemingly personal issues point to larger, institutionalized practices and are therefore legitimately political issues.

Another way to understand this concept is to ask questions such as who gets the goods and resources in society and who bears the burdens? Who sits in positions of power in Fortune 500 companies and who cleans the company offices? Who does the bulk of parenting and who gets paid more on the job? Who is sexually bought and who buys sexual access to bodies? Who is statistically more likely to experience domestic violence and who are the violent offenders? Who gets catcalled on the street? And while we're at it, we can ask who risks their lives in war. Who makes the decisions to go to war in the first place?

These questions point to complicated political and social issues that matter to each of us at the end of the day in deeply personal ways. When we're sitting at home and just want to chill, and we're wondering who's going to watch the kids, or when we're counting how much cash we have to make it until payday, we can look to feminism to help us critically assess the gendered aspects of these experiences.

Gender roles are shifting a bit. But across the board, men still earn about 25 percent more money than women (before we account for race). According to information collected by the U.S. Census Bureau, men spend 50 percent less time grocery shopping than women do. Although men are doing more housework than they used to do, women still shoulder the bulk of it. Diane Swanbrow, of the University of Michigan Institute for Social Research, reports that these days American men do about sixteen hours of housework each week—an increase from the twelve hours a week they did in 1965, but much less than the twenty-seven hours women are clocking each week.

Violence is another gendered aspect of our personal lives. While men and boys make up about 10 percent of victims in all reported rape cases, men are the perpetrators in more than 90 percent of all sexual assaults and all violent crimes. According to the FBI and the U.S. Department of Justice, nearly 99 percent of the offenders in single-victim sexual-assault cases are male and these perpetrators are most likely to be white. Of course, this doesn't mean that more than 90 percent of all men are rapists. And we know that women can commit violent crime as well. What this does mean is that according to current evidence, the vast majority of violence against women (and other men) is perpetrated by men.

This reality connects directly back to the idea that the personal is political. Rape is something that happens to individual women, and it is incredibly personal. Because the risk of sexual assault is far greater for women than for men, this risk keeps many women fearful, restricting their access to some spaces. Rape is sometimes used as a threat or a menacing "joke" toward women who are perceived to be pushing for too much. Rape is something that individual men commit, yet it is supported on a societal level by a culture that encourages men to prove their worth through their physical strength and their sexual power.

During the past several centuries of the women's rights movement, feminism (whether or not it was called by that name at the time) gave women a tool to examine their daily lives to determine how society's sexism was affecting them on a personal level. Women and girls are still asking these questions—and men can, too. It matters who washes the dishes, who takes out the trash, who feels safe walking down the street, and who gets a raise at work. These are political issues. It's all about who gets what, when, and how. Or who doesn't.

Guys have lots of opportunities to examine and make change in everyday issues such as coparenting, pay equity, and consensual sex. Changing diapers might not seem a political act, but it definitely has political meaning. There's certainly nothing wrong with doing domestic, caring work. In fact, feminism is about the right to freely choose our life activities. But if women are doing the majority of the housework and caring for the babies, it means they're doing the unpaid jobs *in addition* to other paid work or it means they're *not* doing something else (such as earning money, writing the great novel, etc.). [...]

Feminism not only resists assumptions that women's place is in the kitchen, but it also questions why only young men have to register for the military draft. It prods us to think about inequity and also about the ways in which institutional and legal structures reinforce binary ideas about gender that try to shove all of us in identity boxes that don't necessarily fit and don't always define us well.

*****

The idea that the personal is political can be a tool to help us explore prevailing ideas about what it means to be a man or a woman in our society and how we internalize these ideas. Understanding how power and domination are both personal and political can also help us incorporate class, race, ethnicity, ability, age, sexuality, religion, and nation of origin—as well as gender—into the feminist equation.

Feminism Is a Social and Political Movement

Feminism is a social and political movement with the goal of ending women's subordination. But it doesn't stop there. The category of woman is amazingly varied, and different women experience gender and gender oppression in different ways depending on class, race, sexual orientation, and more. It's necessary to understand how gender, race, ethnicity, and class are not separate systems of oppression, writes legal scholar Patricia Hill Collins in the journal of feminist philosophy, *Hypatia*. These systems interact with each other and shape how a person experiences power or oppression.

The term intersectionality was introduced by black feminists who argued that white feminists who ignored the interaction of race and gender systems obscured problems uniquely faced by women of color. More to the point, writes political scientist S. L. Weldon, "Black feminists argued that their problems and experiences could not be described as the problems of Black men plus the problems of white women. Black women face many problems as Black women, and their unique perspectives, identities and experiences cannot be derived from examination of the experiences and position of either Black men or white women."

Intersectionality introduces critical perspectives on the complex interrelations of gender, race, class, and sexuality. Feminist theorist bell hooks frames this concept in terms of margin and center; author Gloria Anzaldúa describes experiences as "border" or *mestiza* consciousness; legal scholar Kimberlé Crenshaw uses the term "intersectionality theory." To make a difference, intersectional analysis must go beyond describing individuals' identities. This framework enables us to use a feminist lens for understanding transnational issues such as imperialism, pollution, war, human trafficking, and globalization. Intersectional analysis can be used to work toward the systemic change needed for all people to be able to maximize participation in free societies.

Robert Jensen, author of the antiporn book *Getting Off: Pornography and the End of Masculinity*, also points out that intersectional analysis can help us understand men's lives as well as women's. He argues that living in patriarchal cultures where male domination is the norm doesn't mean that all men have it easy. "Other systems of dominance and oppression," Jensen writes, such as "white supremacy, heterosexism, predatory corporate capitalism—mean that non-white men, gay men, poor and working-class men suffer in various ways. A feminist analysis doesn't preclude us from understanding those problems but in fact helps us see them more clearly."

In a video about her work on cultural criticism and transformation, bell hooks explains that the real issue in feminism is not men or masculinity, but instead patterns of domination. Abuses of power and the constellation of ways they take shape must have our attention, she argues, if we are to be successful in our struggle for collective liberation. What hooks means is that people may experience exploitation as isolated individuals, but to make change we must recognize the structural patterns that replay over and over and affect people in systemic ways. For hooks, social, political, cultural, and economic oppression is based on repeating patterns of "white supremacist, capitalist patriarchy"; she calls this the politics of domination.

The problem isn't men, but men *are* part of the problem. And no matter our gender, we need to be willing to confront the ways in which men participate in systems of domination (while also understanding that feminism isn't about hating men). Otherwise, it's like having conversations about racism without wanting to talk about the ways in which individual white people enact racism. Or it's like saying "gay bashing is bad" without calling out homophobes for their violence.

Feminism's commitment to social and political transformation means making major social, economic, political, and cultural changes in our society. This commitment can take many forms—working for better legislation, breaking glass ceilings in the business world, supporting battered women's shelters, refusing to collude in racist or sexist jokes, or promoting gender equity in pop culture. Making change also means we all have to examine our own place in various systems of domination—how we benefit and how we're held back. Ultimately, feminism is about making a positive difference and being willing to do the hard work of figuring out what this change might look like.

There's Room for Men

One question that often comes up is how feminism is relevant to men. If feminism is a women's movement, then where do men fit in?

The idea that only women can be feminists is based on essentialism—the assumption that men and women possess inherent behavioral traits based on biological sex. Sometimes people think the term "feminist men" is an oxymoron, says sociologist Michael Kimmel. In his essay "Who's Afraid of Men Doing Feminism?" Kimmel explains that essentialism leads us to think that a feminist man is either not a "real" man or he cannot be a real feminist.

But just as being a woman doesn't make someone a feminist, being a man doesn't automatically mean he's not one. The "feminist-equals-woman" equation is a dangerous way of thinking, explains Judith Grant, author of *Fundamental Feminism*. That perspective blurs the point that feminism is about the interpretive lens we're using, not women's experience as women. Anyway, not all women are the same, just like all men aren't the same. Our gender position is always affected by our socioeconomic, racial, national, sexual, and religious identities.

"Feminism is a political way of thinking," explains Matthew Shepherd in *Feminism, Men, and the Study of Masculinity*. "And, like all political thought," Shepherd writes, the attractions of feminism "cut across sex." Being a feminist doesn't require certain plumbing. It requires a certain consciousness. Feminism is about using a particular lens that filters how we understand the world. This lens is analytical and always puts gender front and center. Feminists don't necessarily think that men and women are the same. Instead, they question the assumptions that biology is destiny and that might makes right. Feminists ask why difference comes at such a high price.

Essentialism also reinforces the binary idea that there are only two, opposite genders; in doing so, it limits our understanding of gender politics. Thinking of feminist-as-female excludes transgender, genderqueer, and intersex people, which is inconsistent with the principles of gender justice. According to activist and scholar Susan Stryker, the rise of queer and transgender studies has challenged essentialist-based politics. In her essay "(De)Subjugated Knowledge," Stryker writes that trans studies calls for "new analyses, new strategies and practices, for combating discrimination and injustice based on gender inequality." If we think of feminism as something that women do or believe in, then we conflate feminism with women. This essentializes a political perspective while paradoxically arguing against essentialist foundations.

Feminism benefits from men's participation. When men are involved in gender justice efforts, it maximizes the potential for deep, sustained social change. One practical advantage is that there is strength in numbers and feminism could use more allies. Plus, for the moment, as violence-prevention expert Jackson Katz suggests, men can be heard in ways that women still can't be heard. "Sexist?" Katz asks rhetorically. "Maybe. But effective? Yes."

Men's participation in feminism is not an invitation for male chivalry or for "protecting our women." A protectionist model actually perpetuates the gender stereotypes that are part of the problem, not part of the solution. Getting men involved with feminism means holding men personally and institutionally accountable for the sexist abuse of power, explains Katz. We need more men to challenge other men's sexism or misogyny as it manifests in all sorts of ways. Katz challenges men to move beyond defensive posturing and be willing to call it like it is.

*****

BOX 7.1: You Don't Have to Be Female to Be a Feminist

At times it might seem that feminism is something only women do—or that it's something only women should do. It's not uncommon for domestic violence shelters or rape crisis hotlines, for example, to bar men from volunteering with women. There are compelling arguments for single-sex organizing, for instance, the concern that men's presence may be traumatizing for women who have been recently hurt by men. This fear is legitimate and important. Women-only groups can also play important roles in providing opportunities for women to develop strategies of survival and resistance. Single-sex groups can support women in exploring anger, fear, internalized sexism, and collusion with their own subjugation, giving voice to these issues that matter so deeply.

But there are ways that men can respect the need for some women-only spaces and still get involved in feminist issues. Men work alongside women in feminist groups advocating reproductive freedom. Some feminist issues, such as male violence against women, sexual harassment, and employment inequities, are most effectively solved by stopping the problems before they happen. And men have a central role in preventing physical, emotional, and economic violence.

Single-sex feminist groups for men can help men process, organize, and take action. A few examples include the National Organization for Men against Sexism, the White Ribbon Campaign, which works to end male violence against women, and various men's support programs organized through the Men's Resource Center for Change in Amherst, Massachusetts.

At the same time, single-sex groups are exclusionary and don't serve the needs of gender-queer and transgender people who may not strictly identify as male or female or who may be rejected by single-sex groups. (Such exclusion has been the source of ongoing controversy at the Michigan Womyn's Music Festival, for example, where a woman-born-woman-only policy means that transwomen who were born male are denied entry.)

As with any kind of effective political action, feminism requires coalition building, strategizing, and talking with others who may not always share our perspectives or understand our experience firsthand. That means thinking seriously about men's role in feminism.

Feminism is an inclusive social movement. It's about taking action in the interest of women and also on behalf of all groups that are affected by hegemonic power. Thinking of feminism as a girls-only club would make feminism a political movement with inclusive goals but with exclusive membership. And that doesn't quite make sense.

Joining the Struggle

When punk-rock feminist Chris Crass was hanging out with anarchist political groups in Southern California, his commitment to gender justice went hand in hand with opposing war, feeding homeless people through Food Not Bombs, and supporting students' rights. Chris recognized that ending sexism is key to radical change both within political movements and throughout broader society. For Chris, this continues to mean working with women and men as "allies to each other in the struggle to develop models of anti-racist, class-conscious, pro-queer, feminist manhood that challenges strict binary gender roles and categories." For Grantlin Schafer, being a "comrade in struggle" means working to prevent male violence through his job as an antiviolence educator for a sexual and domestic violence center in Loudoun County, Virginia. These men provide just two examples of the myriad ways men can get involved in feminism.

Nighat Gandhi explains that feminism is about transforming institutions such as the law, the family, the workplace, or marriage to weed out their injustices. Feminists don't necessarily want to destroy these institutions and practices. Many feminists simply want to see them changed into more equitable situations. Men are not excluded from these efforts. In fact, Gandhi says, men should very much feel a part of feminism.

Jackson Katz points out that Americans like to brag how we're "the freest country on earth," yet half of us don't even feel free enough to walk by ourselves at night. Many women aren't even safe in their own homes. By conservative estimates, 20 percent of adolescent girls have been physically or sexually assaulted by a dating partner. Two-thirds of American men responding to a major American public opinion poll in 2000 said that domestic violence is very or fairly common. And 92 percent of people who answered a 2005 national survey said that "family violence is a much bigger problem than people think." And these issues are not unique to the United States.

As Katz points out, it's a mistake to think of sexual assault or domestic violence as "women's issues." Men's violence against women is really more about men than it is about women, Katz explains in *The Macho Paradox: Why Some Men Hurt Women and How All Men Can Help*. What he means is that because men are the "ones committing the vast majority of the violence," it's time for men to face up and do something about it. We live our lives *in relation* to other people, Katz notes. Something that affects women no doubt affects men—and vice versa.

[...] When it comes to issues such as pay inequity or male violence toward women, there's a tremendous amount of work that men can do to stop the problem *before* it even happens! Prevention is the real solution. The most important thing is that we talk with each other as we continue coalition building between women and men and across the political spectrum.

Justice Is a Renewable Resource

Some men steer clear of feminism because they have been taught that it's a movement to take power, resources, authority, and perks from men. The real issue is *not* what men might lose: All of us—women and men alike—actually have a lot to gain from feminism. The problem is that power is often seen as a limited resource. This view of power assumes that if one group gains power, another loses it. Or that if one person achieves resources, it must necessarily happen at someone else's expense.

This scarcity model assumes that there are limited resources in the world and that if I get mine, you can't have yours. For those accustomed to this kind of thinking, the assumption is that if women gain power, men will necessarily lose it. But instead of thinking that equality and justice are finite resources (like fossil fuels), there are other ways to view it. If our power grid is fueled by wind or sun, one person's increase in power doesn't mean that there's less to go around. It is possible that *we* can work cooperatively toward achieving egalitarian conditions. It is possible to think of power as an infinite resource that won't run out when we challenge harmful or limiting gender expectations.

Feminism is about breaking down gender expectations that limit everyone. Feminism holds the potential for each of us to experience a fuller range of possibilities to exist freely in the world and to explore our full humanity while minimizing or eradicating oppression, subjugation, and patterns of domination.

Although equality and gender justice are unlimited resources, feminism does challenge men to change their behavior and to change systems from which they benefit. This requires hard work that some men resist—relinquishing some of the privileges that come with being a man, rethinking sexual pleasure that relies on a woman's denigration, and surrendering unearned authority.

Feminism is a movement for ending gender-based oppression and all forms of related patterns of domination and subjugation in our homes, our communities, and the world. There is a serious and growing movement of men who stand beside women in tackling issues of gender, race, class, sexuality—as well as enormous, complex problems such as war, imperialism, and globalization. These issues are all part of the same package and feminism can be used to address each of them, and more. Sociopolitical issues as seemingly diverse as sexual harassment and the war in Iraq are linked by similar patterns of domination, in which people or groups attempt to obtain power over others. Feminism can offer a new vision of shared power.

Who Me? A Feminist?

Sometimes guys don't get involved with feminist politics because they don't feel welcome. Even walking into a women's studies classroom for the first time can be a challenging experience. Men frequently don't engage with feminism because they think the issues don't involve them. They just can't relate. Or it never occurred to them to get involved in the first place. Not because they're bad men. Maybe it just never crossed their minds.

At the same time, feminist groups that are made up largely of women may intentionally or inadvertently exclude men. Cliques happen anywhere. Politics is no exception. Even social justice and gender politics. It happens. We won't pretend it doesn't.

Men might sometimes feel intimidated by feminism. Or they can believe (or presume) that they are unwelcome to join activist groups. It might feel uncomfortable or strange to stand in a bookstore looking at the feminist titles on the shelves. And sometimes stereotypes about feminists act as barriers that impede men's (and women's) participation.

Stereotypes are a way of labeling people and sticking them in pigeonholes. Stereotypes can be based on a person's race, gender, hair color, sexuality—or even political views. The Guerrilla Girls describe stereotypes as a box that people get jammed into. This box is usually too small to really describe someone.

*****

Stereotypes can take the form of accusatory or dismissive generalizations. These might include sweeping, silly characterizations, such as the notion that all feminists are angry women with hairy legs who burn their bras or don't wear makeup. Other stereotypes are more blatantly hostile, such as calling a feminist a male basher. "Feminazi" is a particularly pernicious stereotype popularized by the reactionary, right-wing media figure Rush Limbaugh. Jackson Katz points out how using this term is effective in silencing people. After all, who wants to be called a Nazi? And what's more, the term is absurd. This word melds "feminism"—a political effort in part concerned with ending male violence—with "Nazi"—a hypermasculinist movement obsessed with male power over women and the genocidal embodiment of violence.

Obviously, stereotypes can hurt. They can limit our sense of self and our belief in what we're capable of doing and achieving. Stereotypes can be really dangerous, especially when people treat us according to their simplified ideas about us. But stereotypes about feminists are also powerful ways of diminishing the strength of a political movement. Nobody likes to be called a wimp or a man-hating dyke. And, no: If a guy says he's a feminist, it doesn't mean he's lying, whipped, or trying to get with a girl. Those are stereotypes, too. Another misperception—assuming that male feminists are gay—melds political preference with sexual orientation and promotes stereotypes about masculinity, sexuality, politics, and feminism.

Stereotypes about feminism have real consequences. If we don't want to be associated with feminism, we risk distancing ourselves from an important source for understanding our lives and for changing inequitable social, economic, and political realities. If we are silenced by stereotypes or jokes, then we aren't standing up to violence and the abuse of power.

Do I Have to Call Myself One?

What's in a name? Does it matter if you call yourself a feminist, a pro-feminist, a feminist ally, or even a member of the Men's Auxiliary? What if you practice your politics and don't want to label yourself?

Debates over terminology are nothing new—and they aren't limited to men. In the 1940s and '50s, for example, there were those who promoted women's rights and who objected to oppressions of all sorts, but who distanced themselves from the term "feminist." Back then there were all sorts of reasons some people shied away from the label. To call oneself a feminist risked evoking images of being militant, racist, a sexual prude, bourgeois, strident, or just plain selfish. Similar assumptions are still made today. Both men *and* women who identify as feminists risk being called what historian Leila Rupp refers to as manhaters and crazies, kooks or queers.

Because there is concern that feminism focuses primarily on white women's issues and uncritically assumes white experience as the norm, some shy away from the term "feminist" because it doesn't go far enough. Thinkers and activists have developed terminology and frameworks to intentionally reflect the matrix of race, class, gender, and ethnicity. Womanism, for example, focuses on how black women experience power, oppression, and status within the social hierarchy. Womanism uses this concept as a base for advocating social change and improved gender politics by providing an option for social and political analysis that makes black women and other women of color central. [...]

Some men who recognize these problems of gender repression, misogyny, sexism, and the politics of domination take a stand by identifying as feminists. Others call themselves pro-feminists, feminist allies, antisexist activists, or even "meninists"—a global group of men who, according to Feminist.com, "believe in and support the feminist principles of women's political, social, and economic equality." These are people who understand that men are not born on Mars and women are not born on Venus but, rather, that *we* are all born on the same planet as equals. Like male feminists, men who are allies actively support gender justice. They "believe that women as a group suffer inequalities and injustices in society, while men as a group receive various forms of power and institutional privilege," writes Australian scholar Michael Flood in his pro-feminist FAQ. These antisexist men resist using the term "feminist" in describing themselves because, while they support gender equity and oppose sexism, they see their role as supporting women who have done feminist work for so long. Pro-feminists want neither to colonize feminism nor to act as if they've got all the answers.

There's no reason to shy away from claiming the term "feminist," though our commitment to sociopolitical improvement may be more important than what we call ourselves. A person can be political without a label and sometimes we might not want to be tied down by a label at all. But particular labels can tell us about a person's politics. And when it comes to the long history of feminist efforts, there have been many men working alongside women in the struggle for gender equality.

References

Anzaldúa, Gloria. *Borderland/La Frontera: The New Mestiza*. San Francisco: Spinsters/Aunt Lute, 1987.

Arber, Brandon. "It's Just Common Sense," in Shira Tarrant, ed., *Men Speak Out: Views on Gender, Sex, and Power*. New York: Routledge, 2008, pp. 163–164.

Bindel, Julie. "The New Feminists." *Guardian*, Tuesday, November 28, 2006, p. 12.

Carter, Derrais. "This Is What a Feminist Looks Like," in Shira Tarrant, ed., *Men Speak Out: Views on Gender, Sex, and Power*. New York: Routledge, 2008, p. 152.

Collins, Patricia Hill. "It's All in the Family: Intersections of Gender, Race, and Nation." *Hypatia: A Journal of Feminist Philosophy*, vol. 13, no. 3 (1998), p. 68.

Crass, Chris, "How Can I Be Sexist? I'm an Anarchist!" in Shira Tarrant, ed., *Men Speak Out: Views on Gender, Sex, and Power*. New York: Routledge, 2008, p. 284.

Crenshaw, Kimberlé. "Demarginalizing the Intersection of Race and Sex: A Black Feminist Critique of Antidiscrimination Doctrine, Feminist Theory, and Antiracist Politics," in Katherine T. Bartlett and Rosanne Kennedy, eds., *Feminist Legal Theory: Readings in Law and Gender*. Boulder, CO: Westview, 1991.

Flood, Michael. "Frequently Asked Questions about Pro-Feminist Men and Pro-Feminist Men's Politics." www.xyonline.net/misc/pffaq.html. Accessed June 23, 2008.

Gandhi, Nighat. "Can Men Be the Allies of Feminism?" www.xyonline.net/Canmenbeallies.shtml. Accessed June 23, 2008.

Grant, Judith. *Fundamental Feminism: Contesting the Core Concepts of Feminist Theory*. New York: Routledge, 1993, p. 109.

Guerrilla Girls. *Bitches, Bimbos, and Ballbreakers: The Guerrilla Girls' Illustrated Guide to Female Stereotypes*. New York: Penguin, 2003, pp. 7–8.

hooks, bell. *bell hooks: Cultural Criticism and Transformation*, Sut Jhally, dir. Northampton, MA: Media Education Foundation, 1997.

hooks, bell. *Feminist Theory: From Margin to Center*. Cambridge, MA: South End, 2000, pp. 68 and 82.

Jensen, Robert. *Getting Off: Pornography and the End of Masculinity*. Cambridge, MA: South End, 2007, pp. 27, 29, and 31.

Katz, Jackson. *The Macho Paradox: Why Some Men Hurt Women and How All Men Can Help*. Naperville, IL: Sourcebooks, 2006, pp. 1–3, 15, and 16.

Kimmel, Michael S. "Who's Afraid of Men Doing Feminism?" in Tom Digby, ed., *Men Doing Feminism (Thinking Gender)*. New York: Routledge, 1998.

Labaton, Vivien, and Dawn Lundy Martin, eds. *The Fire This Time: Young Activists and the New Feminism*. New York: Random House, 2004, p. xxiii.

Lasswell, Harold. *Politics: Who Gets What, When, How*. New York: McGraw-Hill, 1936.

Rupp, Leila J. "The Women's Community in the National Women's Party, 1945 to the 60s." *Signs*, vol. 10, no. 4 (1985), p. 722.

Schafer, Grantlin. "Breaking the Silence One Mile at a Time," in Shira Tarrant, ed., *Men Speak Out: Views on Gender, Sex, and Power*. New York: Routledge, 2008.

Shepherd, Matthew. "Feminism, Men, and the Study of Masculinity: Which Way Now?" in Steven P. Schacht and Doris W. Ewing, eds., *Feminisms and Men: Reconstructing Gender Relations*. New York: New York University, 1998, p. 174.

Stryker, Susan. "(De)Subjugated Knowledge: An Introduction to Transgender Studies," in Susan Stryker and Stephen Whittle, eds., *The Transgender Studies Reader*. New York: Routledge, 2006, p. 7.

Swanbrow, Diane. "Study Finds American Men Doing More Housework." The University Record, March 25, 2002. www.ur.umich.edu/0102/Mar25_02/16.htm. Accessed August 11, 2008.

Weldon, S.L. "Rethinking Intersectionality: Some Conceptual Problems and Solutions for the Comparative Study of Welfare States." Unpublished paper delivered at the 2005 Annual Meeting of the American Political Science Association, Washington, DC, September 1–4, 2005.

Chapter 8

Reality Check: Women in Canada and the Beijing Declaration and Platform for Action 15 Years On

Canadian Feminist Alliance for International Action (FAFIA) and Canadian Labour Congress (CLC)

The Canadian Feminist Alliance for International Action (FAFIA) is an alliance of feminist and equality-seeking organizations committed to making international agreements on women's human rights a reality for women across Canada. FAFIA provides training and resources on women's human rights instruments and helps women to engage in using those instruments to address inequalities in their lives.

The Canadian Labour Congress (CLC) represents a number of Canadian and international unions, provincial federations of labour, and regional labour councils. The CLC advocates for equitable working conditions for all working people in Canada and around the world.

Part One: Overall Achievements and Obstacles

There has been a sharp decrease in institutional and political support by the Government of Canada for the promotion and protection of the human rights of women and girls during the period 2004–2009. This is true of Canadian government policy on women's human rights in the national and the international context. Examples of this shift include:

- the elimination of the phrase "gender equality" from the mandate of Canada's primary institution responsible for gender equality in Canada: Status of Women;
- the closing of 12 of the 16 Status of Women offices, on the principles that women's and men's issues do not need to be separated;[1]
- the reallocation of funding from organizations that support advocacy for women's human rights to organizations that provide front-line services only;
- the elimination of funding to the Court Challenges Program, a program created to provide assistance to court cases related to equality rights guaranteed under Canada's Constitution;
- the elimination in 2006 of the funding agreements that had been negotiated with provinces and territories to provide $5 billion for child care and early learning programs;

- the decrease in levels of financial and human resources specifically committed to gender-equality projects in the Canadian International Development Agency and the Department of Foreign Affairs;[2]
- statements by the Minister of Foreign Affairs indicating a deliberate disengagement from international norms, including international humanitarian law and women's human rights;[3] [and]
- senior policy advisers within the office of the prime minister with strong links to anti-feminist organizations.[4]

Canada's achievements toward women's equality over the past decades have been considerable. For example, women's participation in higher education has increased since the Fourth World Conference on Women was held in 1995. However, from 2004 to 2009, women's achievements in all 12 areas of critical concern outlined in the Beijing Platform for Action have slowed or been turned back. Canada no longer compares favourably against other nations in assessments of gender equality and the gender gap. For example, in the 2004 World Economic Forum Gender Gap Index, Canada was ranked 7th. In the 2009 Gender Gap Index, Canada ranked 25th. In 2009, Canada was ranked 73rd in the UN Gender Disparity Index. Canada has been strongly criticized by several UN human rights bodies on the issues of women's poverty and the endemic violence against Aboriginal women and girls.[5]

As the following report will demonstrate, there has been a systematic erosion of the human rights of women and girls in Canada. The changes to gender architecture, the shifts in policy and programming within the government, and the government's response to the economic crisis have been felt by the most vulnerable women and girls in Canada. The organizations that provide those women and girls with an opportunity to bring their concerns forward have been eliminated or gagged by new funding regulations. Women and girls in Canada call on the international community to condemn the policies that have resulted in the deaths of Aboriginal women, the abandonment of women living in poverty, and the curtailing of the democratic representation of women's needs and interests.

Part Two: Critical Areas of Concern

1. Women and Poverty

Women and girls living in poverty currently rely on welfare incomes so low that the National Council of Welfare called them "cruel" in its 2006 report.[6] The poverty levels and the lack of social assistance to women in Canada have been raised by virtually every United Nations body that reviews Canada's human rights performance, including the CEDAW Committee, the Committee on Economic, Social, and Cultural Rights, the Human Rights Committee, and the Human Rights Council.[7] The United Nations has asked the Government of Canada to establish minimum standards for social assistance, applicable at the federal, provincial, and territorial levels.

The Government of Canada has set no standards. Instead the federal government transfers funds to the provinces and territories and permits them to set social assistance rates so low that they do not fulfill Canada's human rights obligations. The government has not met its obligation under international human rights law to ensure that everyone enjoys equality and an adequate standard of living. The government has not met its obligation under section 36 of the Canadian

Constitution to work with the legislatures and governments of the provinces and territories to provide "essential public services of reasonable quality to all Canadians."

Federal funding for social assistance has been provided through block funding arrangements since 1995.[8] Under the current scheme, provinces and territories receive money ostensibly targeted for social assistance through the Canada Social Transfer (CST). But there are no conditions attached to the transfers that require money from the CST to be spent on social assistance, or that ensure that the receiving provinces and territories will provide benefits at a level adequate to sustain a decent life. There is consequently no accountability at either the federal or provincial level for the violations of women's rights that result when women do not have access to adequate incomes.

The 2009 federal budget provides for an annual 3% increase in the CST through 2011, but does not address the issue of adequacy of social assistance benefits provided by the provinces and territories.[9] According to the Department of Finance, the money provided by the CST is "notionally earmarked" for three spending areas: post-secondary education, child care services, and social assistance programs. Of these, social assistance spending has been allotted the smallest increase in funding from 2007 to 2010.[10] No conditions have been attached to ensure that social assistance is more than "notionally" funded by the CST, or that incomes delivered by the provinces and territories are adequate to meet the needs of the most vulnerable women.

Provinces and territories are not able to address these human rights violations by themselves. Social assistance rates have remained unchanged in seven provinces and territories in the past year, and have risen by only 1–3% in four provinces and territories. For only a few family types in a few jurisdictions do social assistance rates reach the Statistics Canada Low-Income Cut-Offs. Most social assistance incomes in Canada remain well below the poverty line. There is no federal mechanism to ensure that women and girls living in poverty receive support adequate to meet their basic needs.

Cuts to welfare rates and erosion of the value of benefits through inflation have had a harsh impact on women who are in need. Women who are more likely to have to turn to welfare, including single mothers and Aboriginal women, must now rely on welfare incomes so low that the National Council of Welfare chairperson recently called them "shameful and morally unsustainable in a rich country."[11]

Women in Canada have a higher rate of poverty overall than men, and particular groups of women, including single mothers, Aboriginal women, women of colour, immigrant women, women with disabilities, and single women, have shockingly high rates of poverty. *Women in Canada* shows rates of poverty for Aboriginal women—including First Nations, Métis, and Inuit women at 36%, for women of colour at 29%, for immigrant women at 23%, rising to 35% for those who arrived in Canada between 1991 and 2000, and for women with disabilities at 26%.[12] Single mothers had an after-tax poverty rate of 35.6% in 2004,[13] while single women over 65 had a poverty rate of 17%.[14]

In summary, by the government's own admission, there is no accountability for expenditure of the funds transferred by the federal government to the provinces and territories through the CST; there is no documentation of any gender-based analysis conducted by the three central agencies of the Government of Canada. If there has been any impact assessment of social programs related to women's human rights, there is no proof, no public record, and no positive result. Most importantly, most welfare incomes across the country remain inadequate to meet the basic needs of Canada's poorest women and men.

2. Women and Education and Training

2.1 Aboriginal women and education

The female Aboriginal population is growing at a rate of four times that of the non-Aboriginal female population of Canada, according to Statistics Canada. It is relatively young, with twice as many Aboriginal girls and women of school age than non-Aboriginal females. Yet, some 40 percent of Aboriginal women over age 25 have not completed high school. Less than half as many Aboriginal women complete a university education as their non-Aboriginal peers.

Funding for the education of children on reserves is capped at a rate well below the average for spending on children's education elsewhere in Canada.[15]

As stated in the First Nations Child and Family Caring Society of Canada report to the Senate Human Rights Committee: "The Auditor General of Canada (2004) found elementary and secondary funding on reserves to be inequitable. The Assembly of First Nations estimates that at the current rate of federal investment it will take 28 years to achieve equity with non-Aboriginal education systems. There are also severe shortages of schools on reserves with 53 First Nations communities not having schools, and schools in many other communities are in need of substantial renovations or expansion. Only three out of ten First Nations children on reserves graduate from high school."

2.2 Women and higher education

Women have made significant gains in access to higher education. Notably, women now make up more than half of all students enrolled in undergraduate programs in Canadian universities. The representation of women in programs in medicine and law has increased dramatically since the time of the Fourth World Conference on Women in 1995. However, women are still underrepresented in the Natural Sciences and Engineering.

Hiring and promotion within academic institutions have not kept pace with women's enrolment. Men with doctorates are still twice as likely to hold the position of full professor as are women with doctorates.[16] Female faculty who have children see significant decreases in their rates of promotion compared to male faculty who have children (who see no decrease).[17] Moreover, women working in academia experience the same wage gap that women working in other fields experience—earning 79 cents on every dollar their male peers earn (only slightly better than the overall wage gap, which stands at 70.5%).[18]

3. Violence against Women

3.1 Violence against Aboriginal women and girls

On March 31, 2009, the Native Women's Association of Canada (NWAC) issued its second report from the Sisters in Spirit project,[19] which documents the disappearances and murders of 520 Aboriginal women and girls over the last 30 years. Of the 520 cases:

- 43% of disappearances and 50% of murders occurred during or since 2000;
- 24% are cases of missing women and girls;
- 67% are cases of murder (homicide or negligence causing death);

- 52% of murder cases have been cleared by charges or suicide;
- 43% remain open (no one charged);
- 26% of cases are in British Columbia, 17% in Alberta, 14% in Manitoba, 12% in Saskatchewan;
- 52% are women and girls under 30; and
- the majority of women were mothers.[20]

The Native Women's Association of Canada points out that their documented number "likely does not reflect the actual number of missing and murdered Aboriginal women and girls in Canada." They have included only cases in the public domain, that is, cases that have been: (1) reported to police/media; (2) acknowledged by police/media; and (3) publicized by police/ media.[21]

Walk 4 Justice has carried out a walk across Canada each summer for the last four years to talk with Aboriginal families and communities about missing women. From anecdotal evidence, Walk 4 Justice believes that there are many more cases of missing and murdered Aboriginal women and girls that have gone undocumented by police or media. Most informed observers and non-governmental organizations that work on this issue agree that the count of missing and murdered Aboriginal women and girls is likely much higher.

The disappearances and murders of Aboriginal women and girls are not a phenomenon of the past. As the Sisters in Spirit documented cases show, 43% of the disappearances and 50% of the murders have occurred since 2000. Six Aboriginal girls have gone missing in Manitoba just over the last year, and two young Aboriginal women, Cherisse Houle, 17, and Hillary Angel Wilson, 18, were found murdered in August, in Winnipeg.[22] The disappearances and murders continue.

Two facets of this problem have been identified by Aboriginal women, families of the missing and murdered Aboriginal women and girls, and non-governmental organizations, including the Native Women's Association of Canada, the Assembly of First Nations Women's Council, Pauktuutit Inuit Women's Association, Amnesty International, the Canadian Feminist Alliance for International Action, the Aboriginal Women's Action Network, and the B.C. CEDAW Group. These two facets are:

1. the failure of police to protect Aboriginal women and girls and to investigate promptly and thoroughly when they are missing or murdered; and
2. the social and economic conditions in which many Aboriginal women and girls live.

Police Failure: Despite the overwhelming evidence of high levels of violence against Aboriginal women and girls, Canadian police forces have been slow, if not reluctant, to take this violence seriously. There are multiple reports in the media and in the reports from the Native Women's Association of Canada of the negative experiences that families, communities, and friends of missing Aboriginal women and girls have had with police. From police personnel, NWAC reports that families have experienced "a lack of responsiveness, disrespect, confusing or incorrect information, poor adherence to policies and protocols, and an overall discounting of family information."[23] Many family members or friends who report the disappearance of an Aboriginal woman or girl have been brushed off with justifications that stereotyped and discounted the women, such as, "she has a transient life style" or "she'll come back when she wants to." Many of the cases did not receive timely or thorough investigation.[24] Beverly Jacobs, then president of the Native Women's Association of Canada, said to the media when presenting Sisters in Spirit's second report, "[I]t's as if society is prepared to disregard the missing women as 'garbage.'"[25]

Racialized Violence: The racism and sexism inherent in the high rates of violence against Aboriginal women have been widely acknowledged.[26] Racism and sexism affect the attitudes of violent men who view Aboriginal women and girls as socially unprotected targets because of the depth of discrimination against them. Racism and sexism also affect how seriously the police take their disappearances and murders, and the treatment their families receive. Racism and sexism are also root causes of the disadvantaged social and economic conditions of Aboriginal women and girls and are manifest in the long-standing failure of the Government of Canada to correct these conditions. The failure by all levels of government in Canada to fulfill the social and economic rights of Aboriginal women and girls to an adequate standard of living, including adequate food, clothing, and housing, directly violates their rights to security of the person and to life.[27]

Conditions for Aboriginal women and girls will not change until strategic and coordinated policies are put in place by the Government of Canada, working in co-operation with provincial and territorial governments, to address and reverse the specific disadvantages of Aboriginal women and girls. Further, conditions will not change until adequate resources are allocated, over a sustained period, to support systemic change.

3.2 Violence against women in northern communities

Violence against women and girls in northern Canadian communities is acute. Rates of violence against women in the North are consistently higher than for southern Canadian populations.[28] Pauktuutit reports that in Nunavut "it is estimated that only 29% of spousal abuse cases are reported. Nunavut has 6.5 times the national reported spousal abuse rate—the highest in Canada."[29] Access to services, including medical care, counselling, and shelters, is significantly lower than in the South of the country.[30] Several interlocking factors contribute to the crisis: remote locations; lack of access to health care and social services; lack of housing; the legacy of residential schools and other forms of institutionalized abuse of Inuit, Métis, and First Nations populations; lack of economic opportunities; and climate change.

Higher rates of child apprehension, the legacy of residential schools, and racial discrimination against Inuit, Métis, and First Nations mothers contribute to the unwillingness or inability of women to leave violent relationships because in doing so, they may lose custody of their children. Exposure to domestic violence, direct experience of violence, and the lack of economic and social resources additionally contribute to high rates of suicide, particularly among young people.[31]

There is a long-standing and widespread lack of housing in northern communities. Where housing is available, renting practices are often racially discriminatory.[32] Overcrowding and lack of adequate and secure housing in communities that are subject to extreme weather conditions contribute to violence against women and girls.[33]

In 2006, the federal government unilaterally reneged the funding agreements to the First Nations communities that had been negotiated in the Kelowna Accord. This Accord would have provided $5 billion to help reserves across Canada provide much-needed housing and social and economic services and programs. The cancellation of the Kelowna Accord has exacerbated the economic and social vulnerability of women living on reserves, particularly in northern communities, by denying them much-needed services and housing.

3.3 Violence against women across Canadian communities

Although there are some signs that some forms of violence against women are decreasing, for many groups of women, violence against women remains endemic. One in two women in Canada will experience violence during her lifetime. Women are far more likely than men to be victims of sexual violence, family violence, and intimate-partner violence.

According to the Government of Canada's Statistics Agency (Statistics Canada), rates of sexual violence in Canada have been stable. However, rates of reporting crimes of sexual violence to police are decreasing.[34]

Rates of spousal violence and spousal homicide committed against women have decreased by 15% in the past decade.[35] However, women are still four times as likely to be killed by their spouse as are men.[36] Eighty-three percent of victims of spousal violence are female, and estimates suggest that as many as 70% of incidents of spousal violence are never reported.[37]

Rates of firearms-related spousal homicides have decreased in the past decade in Canada.[38] However, one of the most significant factors in this decrease is the gun registry. The gun registry was created as a response to the Montréal Massacre, where 14 young women were killed by Marc Lépine in the name of "fighting feminism." The Royal Canadian Mounted Police have cited the gun registry as a "key to the safety of both police officers and the public."[39] The long-gun registry is now likely to be eliminated and all records of existing gun registrations excised as a result of legislation tabled in the Canadian Parliament.

As described in detail above, levels of violence against women vary significantly across different groups and regions, with Aboriginal women being disproportionately subject to violence. Other groups who are disproportionately subject to violence include: women with disabilities, criminalized and imprisoned women, single women over 65, and women living in poverty.

In all instances, violence against women is under-reported. It is, therefore, a matter of urgency to ensure that data on violence against women are collected consistently by both governmental and non-governmental organizations. Many of these organizations are receiving decreasing or inconsistent levels of support. Projects such as Sisters in Spirit represent a unique tool for assessing and understanding violence against women, which, in turn, provides a basis for better policy and programming efforts to eliminate violence against women.

*****

4. Women and the Economy

4.1 Labour force participation and income

In Canada, as in all advanced industrial countries, there is still very marked occupational segregation between women and men. Men and women hold very different kinds of jobs, working in almost parallel occupational worlds. Jobs where women predominate still tend to be lower paid than jobs where men predominate, even though the educational and skill requirements may differ very little.

Traditionally, men were relatively concentrated in blue-collar industrial occupations, in white-collar management jobs, and in the professions, while women were relatively concentrated in low-level, "pink-collar" clerical and administrative jobs in offices, and in sales and services occupations. This division has broken down over time as women have entered professional and managerial jobs in increasing numbers. But women in better-paid occupations are mainly to be found in only a relatively few occupational groups, notably in health, education, and social services in the broader public sector. Women are much more likely than men to work in the public sector, defined as working directly for government or in almost entirely government-funded bodies, such as schools, universities, and hospitals.

One in four women employees (28.6%) worked in public services in 2006, compared to just less than one in five men (17.3%). The better-paid professional and managerial jobs in the business sector and, indeed, many of the higher-level jobs in the public sector are still held mainly by men. In 2006, four in 10 men (39.7%) were still in blue-collar jobs.[40] While by no means all well paid, these kinds of jobs do tend to command above-average pay, and are often unionized. In 2006, by contrast, just 7.7% of women were employed in these blue-collar jobs, one-fifth the proportion of men.[41] This small minority of women are mainly to be found in relatively low-paid manufacturing jobs in sectors like clothing. By contrast, one-quarter of women (24.1%) are still in non-professional office jobs—that is, in clerical, administrative, and secretarial jobs—compared to just 7.1% of men.[42] Many of these jobs are quite skilled, but they tend to pay less than skilled blue-collar jobs.

Both men and women work in low-paid, often part-time, sales and service jobs. But, more women are employed in these lower-end jobs than are men, explaining why women are much more likely to be low-paid than men. More than one in four women (28.6%) worked in these occupations in 2006 compared to one in five men (19.3%), and the men who work in these kinds of jobs tend to be younger workers.[43]

Turning to professional occupations, which require formal post-secondary education and qualifications, women now hold a significant edge over men. Almost one in three women (32.5%) work in these kinds of jobs, a much higher proportion than for men (22.9%). But, women are significantly more likely to work in professional jobs in public and social services: in health care, social services, government, and teaching. In 2006, women accounted for 55.9% of all professional jobs, but 87.4% of jobs in nursing, therapy, and other health-related professional jobs; 71.3% of professional social sciences and religion jobs (most in public and not-for-profit social services); and 63.9% of teaching jobs.[44] Of the 32.5% of all women who are professionals, two in three are employed in these predominantly public sector/female-dominated occupations. By contrast, the majority of professional men are to be found in business/finance and natural sciences/engineering/mathematics occupations in the private sector (where women account for just 22.0% of employment), and still account for about half of all professional jobs in business and finance.[45]

Men also still hold a big lead in management jobs. More than one in 10 men (11.0%) are in management jobs compared to 7.1% of women.[46] Moreover, men hold double the proportion of senior management jobs, which make up 0.8% of all men's jobs compared to just 0.3% of all women's jobs. These positions predominate in the top 1% of the workforce, whose share of all earnings exploded in the 1990s.

To summarize, the majority of women still work in the traditional and relatively badly paid clerical, sales, and services categories, and very few women work in the blue-collar occupations. A high and rising proportion of women work in professional occupations requiring higher levels of education and providing better levels of pay, but are still relatively concentrated in public and social services.

The report of the federal government's Pay Equity Task Force further details the fact that women are still highly concentrated in a small number of traditionally female occupational categories— health care, teaching, clerical, administrative, and sales and services jobs, and overwhelmingly predominate in the very lowest-paid occupations, such as child care workers, cashiers, and food services workers.[47]

Women are still greatly under-represented in most of the very highest-paying professions, from specialist physicians, to senior private-sector managers, to corporate lawyers and security dealers. Even in the public sector, where women predominate, men are much more likely to hold senior management jobs. In the federal public service, men are more than twice as likely to be senior managers.[48] These differences persist despite employment equity policies, which were intended to increase the proportion of women in management jobs in the federal public service.

4.2 The gender wage gap

The Government of Canada report claims that "Canada continues to close the gender gap in earnings."[49] This is, unfortunately, not the case. One striking development in Canada over the past decade has been that the gender pay gap has, after many years of gradual progress, remained more or less stuck. Continued economic inequality between women and men, despite the fact that formal educational qualifications of at least younger women now exceed those of men, tells us that women still face discrimination and barriers, and that real equality of opportunity does not yet exist. As a result, many women remain economically dependent upon the earnings of men to sustain a decent family income, and many are especially vulnerable to low income and poverty.

While the Government of Canada has chosen to measure the gender wage gap using a "dollar per hour" comparison, the most commonly cited indicator of the gender wage gap is annual earnings of full-time, full-year workers, i.e., of workers in full-time jobs who work all year. The annual earnings indicator combines the impact of lower hourly wages with fewer weeks and hours worked over the year.

By this measure, women earned just 70.5% as much as men in 2005.[50] The situation is even worse for women of colour, who earn only 64% as much as men and for Aboriginal women, who earn an appalling 46% as much as men working full-time, full year. If we look at all workers—including part-time and part-year workers—the gap is even greater, with women earning just 64.0% as much as men. The gender wage gap for workers with a university degree closed steadily until the mid-1990s, and then suddenly rose again in 1997. It has remained stuck at between 66% and 68% since that time. In short, the long trend toward greater economic equality of women and men has drawn to a close over the past decade.

The failure of the gender wage gap to continue to close is particularly surprising in view of the fact that the educational attainment of women, especially younger women, has continued to improve compared to that of men. By age 25–44, half (49.0%) of women in 2001 had a post-secondary qualification, compared to just 40.1% of men, with women accounting for the majority of university graduates and almost 60% of those with a community college qualification. Yet, the annual earnings gap has continued to widen, not least among those with a university education.

In terms of the dollar-per-hour comparison preferred by the Government of Canada, there continues to be pure gender gap per hour worked. Women earned an average of $17.96 per hour compared to $21.43 for men in 2006, meaning that women earned, on average, 83.8% of the male hourly wage. As indicated, the wage gap tended to be greatest in the male-dominated blue-collar occupations, and in the low-paid sales and service sector. Overall, women earned significantly less than men in lower-paid occupations. By contrast, the wage gap is smaller in better-paid occupations, especially in health occupations.

The impact of these wage differences between occupations and wage gaps within occupations is amplified by the fact that women are disproportionately overrepresented in low-wage occupations. There is a higher proportion of women than men in all earnings brackets until an income level of $35,000 to $40,000 is reached. At an annual earnings level of $60,000 and more, men predominate in a proportion of about 2.5 to 1. Almost one in five men earned more than $60,000 in 2005, compared to well under one in ten women. At the very top of the income spectrum, men overwhelmingly dominate. In 2004, the top 5% of Canadian tax-filers earned $89,000 or more. Of this top group, 76% were men, rising to 79% in the elite top 1% group earning more than $181,000.

The gender wage gap exists in all OECD countries, with the median hourly pay of women full-time workers averaging 18% less than that of men. The gender pay gap in Canada measured by this key international indicator is, however, well above average, with women earning 23% less than men in full-time jobs. The Canadian gender pay gap is now the fifth greatest among 22 OECD countries, somewhat greater than in the United States.

*****

5. Women and Politics

Women's political representation in Canada has remained fairly stagnant over the last five years, barely showing any traces of improvement. According to data compiled by the Inter-Parliamentary Union, Canada's ranking in the world has just recently slipped to 49th from 47th regarding women's representation in Parliament. This ranking places Canada behind many European countries and a significant number of developing countries. Women account for only 22.1% of Canadian Parliament, even though they comprise 50.4% of the population. The United Nations has stipulated that in order for public policy to be significantly reflective of women, women's political representation in the lower house of a Parliament must be no less than 30%, also known as critical mass.

Although Canada's current Parliament boasts the highest level of women's representation in Canadian history at 22.1%, this increase is a remarkably modest one. Following the 2006 election, women's representation in Parliament stood at 20.8%, but in 2004 it was higher, standing at 21.1%. Representation of women in the 2006 election more closely resembled elections from 1997 and 2003, at 20.6%. These small fluctuations show that the representation of women in Parliament has not moved consistently or significantly forward. This said, women presently have a greater presence in the federal cabinet than they did following the 2006 election. Out of 38 ministerial positions, 11 cabinet ministers are women, amounting to 28.9%. There were seven women in the federal cabinet as of 2007 and six as of 2006.

The Beijing Declaration places emphasis on women's equal rights, opportunities, access, and participation. Full equality cannot be met without women's equal access to positions of power and the decision-making processes. Women's advancement in Canadian federal politics is not necessarily going backwards, but not adequately moving forward either. Canada is a country that prides itself on its Charter of Rights and Freedoms and its dedication to human rights. For a country that is both economically and politically advanced, the persistent gaps between women's and men's parliamentary representation need to close.

Part Three: Gender Architecture in Canada

In its report on Canada's implementation of the Beijing Declaration and Platform of Action, the Government of Canada presents the Status of Women Canada (SWC) as a successful institutional mechanism ("main co-ordinating agency") for advancing women's rights in Canada. In reality, however, the current government has made several changes to Status of Women that have significantly undermined the ability of the organization to achieve this objective.

Between 2006 and 2008, the word "equality" was removed from the mandate of Status of Women Canada, 43% of the budget of SWC was cut, 12 out of 16 regional offices were closed, and approximately 50% of its staff were laid off, despite a national outcry from women's organizations, unions, opposition members of Parliament, academics, and other community members and leaders.

At the same time, the Status of Women Independent Policy Research Fund was cancelled and the criteria for funding from SWC were changed to preclude support for advocacy or lobbying for law reform. This meant that important national women's rights organizations dedicated to advocacy, law reform, and systemic change, such as the National Association of Women and the Law (which published influential research reports and submissions, including on pay equity, family law, criminal law, and other areas) lost all of their funding.

In 2008, the word "equality" was officially returned to the SWC's mandate, but without any corresponding substantive commitment to achieving women's equality through this institutional mechanism. The ban on funding for women's organizations that engage in advocacy or lobbying for law reform remains in place, thus shutting out funding for research and other efforts to achieve systemic change. According to the federal government, total funding for SWC has increased, but these funds are largely directed to organizations that provide direct service delivery.

The 2006–2008 cuts to SWC contributed to a climate of financial insecurity and fear for women's organizations and civil society. Women's organizations have been threatened with the withholding or cancellation of funding if their positions are critical of the performance of the current government. This is part of a general trend with respect to the funding of non-governmental organizations.[51]

In May 2006, the all-party House of Commons Standing Committee on the Status of Women (SCSW) issued a study on gender-based analysis in federal departments, which found that gender-based analysis processes were weak, inconsistent across government departments, and, in some cases, perfunctory.[52]

Following this study, the Committee recommended that the Government of Canada

- develop legislation immediately that would ensure the systematic application of gender-based analysis to all federal policy and program activities; and
- establish a secretariat in the Privy Council Office with responsibility for ensuring the development and implementation of effective gender equality legislation.[53]

The Government of Canada refused to implement the Committee's recommendations, preferring to maintain the status quo of uncoordinated departmental efforts.

In 2008, the SCSW again recommended that the Government of Canada introduce legislation by April 2009 to promote gender equality, to set out the GBA and gender budgeting obligations of federal departments and agencies, and to create the Office of the Commissioner for Gender Equality.

The Committee also recommended that "the Auditor General of Canada regularly conduct audits to review Canada's implementation of gender-based analysis in the federal government; and, that such audits take into account all of the elements of Canada's framework for equality, including the *Convention on the Elimination of All Forms of Discrimination against Women*, and other international treaties to which Canada is a signatory."[54]

In the spring of 2009, the auditor general of Canada, Sheila Fraser, confirmed that there is no government-wide policy requiring that departments and agencies perform gender-based analysis. She also found that few of the departments that do perform gender-based analysis can provide evidence that these analyses are used in designing public policy.[55]

In October 2009, the auditor general's Spring Report was considered by the House of Commons Public Accounts Committee. Ms. Fraser testified that she was astonished that the government's central agencies—the Privy Council Office, the Finance Department, and the Treasury Board—could provide no proof that they subject their advice regarding resource allocations and programming to any assessment of impacts on women. The Treasury Board secretary, Michelle Auray, explained that the gender "challenge" function is conducted verbally. "We do not document."[56]

By the government's own admission, there is no accountability for expenditure of the funds transferred by the Government of Canada to the provinces and territories through the CST, which are only "notionally" earmarked for social assistance; there is no documentation of any gender-based analysis conducted by the three central agencies of the Government of Canada. If there has been any impact assessment of social programs related to women's human rights, there is no proof, no public record, and no positive result.

With the current restrictions on its funding and mandate of Status of Women Canada and the lack of a comprehensive government-wide action plan on gender equality, Canada has little institutional capacity to protect and advance women's rights.

Part Four: Key Challenges and Plans for the Future

Women and girls in Canada are facing an array of social, economic, and structural challenges. Many women and girls across Canada are struggling to realize their potential while facing the multiple pressures of poverty, violence, and isolation. We acknowledge their strength and courage. Canadian civil society will continue to work with the Government of Canada and international human rights bodies to ensure that Canada meets its commitments to those women and girls. We look forward to seeing progress toward the full and equal realization of their human rights by all Canadians.

Notes

1. "Tories Shutting Status of Women Offices." *CBC News*, November 30, 2006, http://www.cbc.ca/canada/story/2006/11/29/status-women.html#ixzz0egDF7BLH

2. "Strengthening Canada's International Leadership in the Promotion of Gender Equality: A Civil Society Response to the Evaluation of the Implementation of CIDA's 1999 Policy on Gender Equality." Informal CSO Working Group on Women's Rights, September 2009, http://www/ccic.ca/e/docs/002_gender_cida_analysis_cso_response.pdf; see also "Proceedings of the Standing Senate Committee on Human Rights; Second Session, Fortieth Parliament, 2009," September 14, 2009.

3. Michelle Collins, "'Gender Equality,' 'Child Soldiers,' and 'Humanitarian Law' Are Axed from Foreign Policy Language." *Embassy*, July 29, 2009, http://www.embassymag.ca/page/view/foreignpolicy-7-29-2009

4. Cynthia Münster, "Harper Government More Connected to 'Organized Anti-feminism' Than Previous Conservative or Liberal Parties." *The Hill Times*, August 10, 2009, http://www.thehilltimes.ca/page/view/qa_bashevkin-8-10-2009; Sylvia Bashevkin, *Women, Power, Politics: The Hidden Story of Canada's Unfinished Democracy* (Toronto: Oxford University Press Canada, 2009).

5. Committee on Economic, Social, and Cultural Rights, Concluding Observations of the Committee on Economic, Social, and Cultural Rights: Canada, May 19, 2006, E/C.12/CAN/CO/5; Human Rights Committee, Concluding Observations of the Human Rights Committee, April 20, 2006, CCPR/C/CAN/CO/5; Human Rights Council, Universal Periodic Review, Report of the Working Group: Canada, March 3, 2009, A/HRC/11/17; Concluding Observations of the Committee on the Elimination of Discrimination against Women: Canada, CEDAW/C/CAN/CO/7, November 7, 2008.

6. National Council of Welfare, "Staggering Losses in Welfare Incomes," August 24, 2006, http://www.ncwcnbes.net/documents/researchpublications/ResearchProjects/WelfareIncomes/2005Report_Summer2006/PressReleaseENG.pdf

7. Committee on Economic, Social, and Cultural Rights, Concluding Observations of the Committee on Economic, Social, and Cultural Rights: Canada, May 19, 2006, E/C.12/CAN/CO/5 at paras. 15, 44, 52, 53; Human Rights Committee, Concluding Observations of the Human Rights Committee, April 20, 2006, CCPR/C/CAN/CO/5, at para. 24; Human Rights Council, Universal Periodic Review, Report of the Working Group: Canada, March 3, 2009, A/HRC/11/17, at para. 45.

8. Department of Finance Canada, "Canada Social Transfer," http://www.fin.gc.ca/fedprov/his-eng.asp

9. Department of Finance Canada, "Canada's Economic Action Plan: Budget 2009," http://www.budget.gc.ca/2009/pdf/budget-planbugetaire-eng.pdf, p. 189.

10. Department of Finance Canada, "Canada Social Transfer," http://www.fin.gc.ca/fedprov/cst-eng.asp

11. National Council of Welfare, "Staggering Losses in Welfare Incomes," http://ncwcnbes.net/documents/researchpublications/ResearchProjects/WelfareIncomes/2005Report_Summer2006/PressReleaseENG.pdf

12. Statistics Canada, *Women in Canada: A Gender-Based Statistical Report (2005)*, http://www.statcan.ca/english/freepub/89-503-XIE/0010589-503-XIE.pdf

13. National Council of Welfare, *Poverty by Selected Family Types, 2004*, http://www.ncwcnbes.net/documents/researchpublications/ResearchProjects/PovertyProfile/2004/PovertyRates-FamiliesENG.pdf

14. National Council of Welfare, *Poverty for Unattached Individuals by Sex and Age*, http://www.ncwcnbes.net/documents/researchpublications/ResearchProjects/PovertyProfile/2004/PovertyRates-IndividualsENG.pdf

15. Cindy Blackstock, "First Nations Child and Family Caring Society of Canada: Federal Government Under-funding of Children's Services on Reserves as a Risk Factor for Disadvantage Including Sexual Exploitation," Senate Committee on Human Rights, October 26, 2009.

16. Deborah Sussman and Lahouaria Yssaad, "The Rising Profile of Women Academics," *Perspectives*, Statistics Canada, 2005.

17. Ibid.
18. Ibid.
19. Native Women's Association of Canada, *Voices of Our Sisters in Spirit: A Report to Families and Communities*, 2nd ed., March 2009, http://www.nwac-hq.org/en/documents/NWAC_VoicesofOurSistersInSpiritII_March2009FINAL.pdf
20. Ibid., pp. 88–93.
21. Ibid., p. 6.
22. CBC News-Manitoba, "Unsolved Murders of Women under Review by Winnipeg Police," August 25, 2009, http://www.cbc.ca/canada/manitoba/story/2009/08/25/mb-missing-women-review-manitoba.html
23. NWAC, *Voices*, supra note 20 at 96.
24. See *Voices*; supra note 20. See also Amnesty International, *Stolen Sisters: Discrimination and Violence against Indigenous Women in Canada*, 2004, at 2 and 23–33, http://www.amnesty.ca/campaigns/resources/amr2000304.pdf; and Amnesty International, *No More Stolen Sisters: The Need for a Comprehensive Response to Discrimination and Violence against Aboriginal Women*, September 2009, at 1, http://www.amnesty.org/en/library/info/AMR20/012/2009/en
25. Winnipeg Free Press, Mia Rabson, "Feds Urged to Stem Tragedies," May 1, 2009, http://www.winnipegfreepress.com/local/feds-urged-to-stem-tragedies-44125677.html
26. See Manitoba Justice Inquiry, 1991, re: the death of Helen Betty Osborne, http://www.ajic.mb.ca/volume11/toc.html; see also *No More Stolen Sisters*, supra note 25 at 5–6. See also statement from Minister for Status of Women, the Honourable Helena Guergis, quoted below.
27. These rights are set out in articles 6 and 9 of the *International Covenant on Civil and Political Rights*, which Canada ratified in 1976, as well as in Section 7 of the *Canadian Charter of Rights and Freedoms*.
28. *Family Violence in Canada: A Statistical Profile*, Statistics Canada, Government of Canada, 2009.
29. "Family Violence in the Canadian Arctic," Pauktuutit, 2009.
30. Ibid. See also "Violence against Women in the NWT," Department of Labrador and Aboriginal Affairs, 2007; "Family Violence in the Canadian Arctic," Pauktuutit, 2009.
31. "Acting on What We Know: Preventing Youth Suicide in First Nations," Suicide Prevention Advisory Group, Health Canada, [undated].
32. "Rights North: Housing and Human Rights in Northern Ontario," Centre for Equality Rights in Accommodation, 2009, http://www.equalityrights.org/cera/docs/Rights%20North%20Public%20Report.pdf; *The Little Voices of Nunavut: A Study of Women's Homelessness North of 60 Territorial Report*, Qulliit Nunavut Status of Women Council, 2007, http://www.qnsw.ca/projects/documents/Nunavut-FinalFinalReport.pdf
33. Ibid. See also "Family Violence in the Canadian Arctic," Pauktuutit, 2009.
34. *Sexual Assault in Canada 2004 and 2007*, Statistics Canada and Canadian Centre for Justice Statistics, Government of Canada, 2008.
35. *Family Violence in Canada: A Statistical Profile*, Statistics Canada, Government of Canada, 2009.
36. Ibid.
37. Ibid.
38. Ibid.

39. *Commissioner of Firearms: 2007 Report*, Minister of Public Works and Government Services Canada, 2008.

40. *Women in Canada: Work Chapter Updates*, Statistics Canada, Government of Canada, 2007, http://www.statcan.gc.ca/pub/89f0133x/89f0133x2006000-eng.pdf

41. Ibid.

42. Ibid.

43. Ibid.

44. Ibid.

45. Ibid.

46. Ibid.

47. *Pay Equity: A New Approach to a Fundamental Right*, Pay Equity Task Force, Government of Canada, 2004, http://www.justice.gc.ca/en/payeqsal/docs/PETF_final_report.pdf

48. Katarzyna Nack, *Female Employment in the Core (Federal) Public Administration*, Statistics Canada, Government of Canada, 2007, http://www.statcan.gc.ca/pub/11-621-m/11-621-m2007061-eng.pdf

49. "Canada's Response to the Questionnaire on Implementation of the Beijing Declaration and Platform for Action (1995) and The Outcome of the Twenty-third Special Session of the General Assembly (2000)," Government of Canada, 2009, http://www.unece.org/gender/documents/Beijing+15/Canada.pdf

50. *Income Trends in Canada*, Statistics Canada, Government of Canada, 2007; Canadian Labour Force Survey, Statistics Canada, Government of Canada, 2007.

51. Laura Payton, "KAIROS Funding Cuts Chill Community," *Embassy*, December 9, 2009, http://www.embassymag.ca/page/view/kairos-12-9-2009; "Rights and Democracy Anger," *Embassy*, January 13, 2010, http://www.embassymag.ca/page/view/edit-01-13-2010

52. *Towards Responsive Gender Budgeting: Rising to the Challenge of Gender Equality*, Report of the Standing Committee on the Status of Women, June 2008, 39th Parliament, 2nd session, http://www2.parl.gc.ca/content/hoc/Committee/392/FEWO/Reports/RP3551119/feworplle.pdf

53. Standing Committee on the Status of Women, Second Report, 39th Parliament, Session 1, http://www.2parl.gc.ca/HousePublications/Publication.aspx? DocId=2216072&Language=E&Mode=1&Parl=39&Ses=1

54. Standing Committee on the Status of Women, Ninth Report, 39th Parliament, Session 2, http://www.2parl.gc.ca/HousePublications/Publication.aspx?DocID=3431733&Language=E&Mode=1&Parl=39&Ses=2

55. Spring Report of the Auditor General of Canada, Chapter 1, Gender-Based Analysis, http://www.oag-bvg.gc.ca/internet/English/parl_oag_200905_01_e_32514.html#hd3a

56. Cynthia Münster, "Treasury Board Won't Commit to Documenting GBA," *The Hill Times*, Ottawa, October 26, 2009, at 34, http://www.thehilltimes.ca/page/view/civil_circles-10-26-2009

Supplement 5

Race and Income Inequality in Canada: A Troubling Trend

Recent studies demonstrate drastic income disparities that continue to exist between racialized and non-racialized Canadians. As these studies illustrate, even when controlling for such other factors as location, education, and language, racialized and Aboriginal Canadians consistently earn less than non-racialized, non-Aboriginal Canadians.

Ontario's Growing Gap
Sheila Block

The income gap between the rich and the rest of Ontario families has gotten worse, not better, over the past generation.

This study looks at 2006 Census data to describe the labour market experience of racialized Ontarians. It relies on Census data for Ontarians who self-describe as "visible minority," since Census terminology has not been updated to reflect the concept of racialization.

The Census findings show a striking difference between racialized and non-racialized Ontarians. Racialized Ontarians are far more likely to live in poverty, to face barriers to Ontario's workplaces, and even when they get a job, they are more likely to earn less than the rest of Ontarians.

Among the core findings:

Racialized Ontarians want work, but have trouble finding it. While a larger share of racialized workers in Ontario were looking for work, fewer of them found jobs compared to the rest of Ontarians. Higher unemployment rates cut across the majority of racialized groups, accounting for 90 per cent of the racialized population. In 2005, long before the Great Recession wreaked havoc on Canada's employment scene, the unemployment rate for racialized workers in Ontario was high—8.7 per cent—compared to the 5.8 unemployment rate for the rest of Ontarians.

Racialized Ontarians are paid less. Sexism and racial discrimination pack a double wallop for racialized women in Ontario, seriously hampering their earnings. They made 53.4 cents for every dollar non-racialized men made in 2005. Racialized men in Ontario made 73.6 cents for every dollar that non-racialized men made. Racialized women made 84.7 cents for every dollar that non-racialized women made.

Controlling for age, immigration status, and education doesn't eliminate the gap. First-generation racialized Ontarians ages 25–44 who have a university education earn less than non-racialized immigrants of the same age and educational attainment. The gap is widest for first-generation immigrants: racialized women make 47 cents for every dollar that male, non-racialized immigrants make. For second-generation [racialized Ontarians], that gap persists at 54 cents.

These labour market experiences result in much higher poverty rates for racialized Ontarians. While 6 per cent of non-racialized families lived in poverty in 2005, more than three times the share of racialized families, 18.7 per cent, lived in poverty.

The findings show the employment and earnings gap between racialized Ontarians and the rest of the population remains stubbornly high—despite strong economic performance that Ontario enjoyed when this Census data was collected. It points to an overwhelming need for government to step in with policies to help break down racial and gender barriers in Ontario's labour market.

Source: Excerpted from Sheila Block, *Ontario's Growing Gap: The Role of Race and Gender* (Ottawa: Canadian Centre for Policy Alternatives, 2010), 3–4 and 7–8.

The Income Gap between Aboriginal Peoples and the Rest of Canada
Daniel Wilson and David Macdonald

- In 2006, the median income for Aboriginal peoples was $18,962—30% lower than the $27,097 median income for the rest of Canadians. Income inequality persists no matter where Aboriginal peoples live in Canada.
- Income inequality persists despite rapid increases in educational attainment for Aboriginal peoples over the past 10 years, with one exception. Aboriginal peoples with university degrees have overcome much of the income gap between them and the rest of Canadians.
- Below the bachelor's degree level, Aboriginal peoples consistently make far less than the rest of Canadians with the same level of education.
- Despite new strides made by Aboriginal women attaining university degrees, there has been a limited reduction in income disparity between Aboriginal peoples and the rest of Canadians in the past 10 years.
- The situation demands new approaches and solutions that come from Aboriginal peoples themselves. The market alone will not resolve the income differences between Aboriginal peoples and the rest of Canadians. Higher educational attainment alone is not the silver bullet. A more comprehensive approach to the problem is needed. It starts by acknowledging the legacy of colonialism [that] lies at the heart of income disparities for Aboriginal peoples.

Median Income by Gender and Identity (2006)

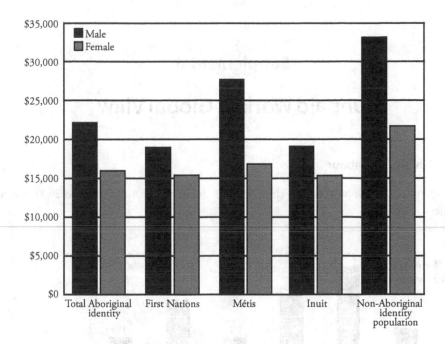

Source: Adapted from Daniel Wilson and David Macdonald, *The Income Gap between Aboriginal Peoples and the Rest of Canada* (Ottawa: Canadian Centre for Policy Alternatives, 2010), 3–5 and 21.

Supplement 6

Unpaid Work: A Global View

Gender Division of Labour

Hours spent each week on cooking, cleaning, and childcare, most recent since 2000, selected countries

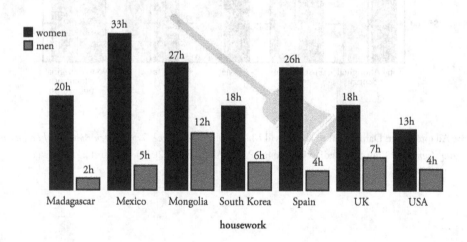

■ women
■ men

housework

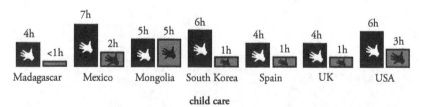

women
men

child care

Water Carriers

Average hours per week spent fetching water, 1998–2005

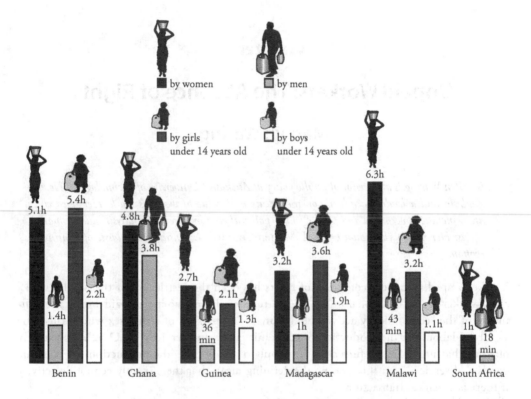

Source: Excerpted from Joni Seager, "Plate 25 (Unpaid Work)," *The Penguin Atlas of Women in the World*, 4th ed. (New York: Penguin Books, 2009), 70–71.

Chapter 9

Unpaid Workers: The Absence of Rights

Marilyn Waring

Marilyn Waring is a professor of public policy at Auckland University of Technology in New Zealand and a leading academic on the nature and value of women's work. Her research areas include governance and public policy, political economy, gender analysis, and human rights. Her most well-known book, If Women Counted, *is considered a classic of feminist economics.*

The key impediment to recognition of rights has been the restriction of the words "work" and "worker" in international human rights texts to those who are in paid work. The definition of the "economically active population" is "all persons of either sex who furnish the supply of labour for the production of economic goods and services" (ILO 32). It's patently obvious that unpaid work furnishes the supply of labour for "the production of economic goods and services," yet those doing the defining mean that there is only economic activity if there is a market transaction.

Unpaid work is the predominant form of labour in four sectors: subsistence production; the household economy, which includes unpaid productive, reproductive, and service work; the informal sector; and in voluntary and community work. The informal sector includes large numbers of people who are marginal to the "modern economy" and often invisible. Lourdes Benería speaks of its "clandestine character ... often involving activities that are bordering on the illegal" and "its unstable, precarious and unregulated nature" (290–291). But it's not all like that: a lot of the regular "babysitting" arrangements people make in their communities fall into this category.

The United Nations Systems of National Accounts (SNA) rules of 1993 expanded the boundary of production so that the accounts should include subsistence and informal sector work. It recommended that all production of *goods* in households for their own consumption be included, but it still excluded own-account production of *services*. This means that (subsistence) agriculture and non-market production of goods for household consumption now fall inside the production boundary as recommended by the SNA, but that household work (including meal preparation), child and elderly care, and other family-related services are still excluded. This leads to the remarkable feats accomplished with one bucket of water: wash the dishes, wash the child, cook the rice—not production. Use the same water to spray the corn and wash the pig—this is productive. The boundary has effectively shifted only theoretically, and not in practice, and the demarcations are increasingly blurred.

In this article I would like to focus on those in the unpaid, or underpaid, or differently paid full-time caregiving role, and the ways in which legulations and regulations continue to compromise their rights.

The UK Census 2001 was the first to include a question on health, disability, and the provision of care. It showed more than a million people working more than 50 hours a week unpaid to care for family members, friends, neighbours, or others because of long-term physical or mental ill health or disability, or problems related to old age. More than 175,000 children under 18 were acting as caregivers, of which 13,000 were providing more than 50 hours [of] care a week! Let's reflect on the question of the rights of these workers, and imagine the compromised rights of these children—to leisure, to education, to full enjoyment of life.

Who Does the Bulk of Unpaid Work?

Since I finished the first edition of *Counting for Nothing* in 1988 (Waring), there have been some extraordinary changes in the economic environment in which we live. Changes in technology, in women's paid labour force participation, in government provision of social services, and the impact of structural adjustment policies and globalization agreements are all of enormous significance. So just how resistant and entrenched have the patriarchal rules around unpaid work been?

Michael Bittman writes that "Finland represents an instance of a country that combines a high level of expenditure on the public provision of social services and a remarkably high proportion of the female population in full-time employment." Yet women spend 25.78 hours and men spend 15.17 hours a week in unpaid work (Bittman 37). In a situation where the majority of women are in full-time as opposed to part-time paid employment, men in Finland seldom take parental leave. There are major divisions of labour by gender in the paid work force, more so than anywhere else in Europe. Women are paid on average 80 per cent of the male wage for full-time work. Men still occupy most managerial positions in the public and private sectors, and only 2 per cent of the top managers in big enterprises are women (*CEDAW Finland Fourth Country Report*). Bittman also reports that almost regardless of their position at any time in their life, Finnish men's weekly hours of unpaid work tend to be a fixed quantity, while the amount of time women spend in unpaid work varies.

> A reduction in men's paid work hours generally results in greater leisure time, so that men literally can choose between (paid) work and leisure. The best predictors of the hours men make available for leisure are the hours they must commit to paid work. For women, however, it is statistically more likely to be a choice between paid and unpaid work. (28)

In Australia the gap between men's and women's average time spent in unpaid work has decreased, but because of a sharp reduction in women's hours of work in the kitchen, and in laundry, ironing, and clothes care, rather than because of any large change in men's hours. The major reason for the change was attributable to increased reliance on market substitutes for women's domestic labour (Bittman 27). Women have also increased their activity in home maintenance and car care.

> While men have increased the hours they devote to child care, their share of this responsibility has not grown because women's time spent in child care has increased at the same rate. Parents have been devoting an ever increasing amount of time to primary face-to-face child care despite falling family size. (Bittman 30)

In New Zealand, 60 per cent of men's work is paid, but almost 70 per cent of women's work is unpaid. The New Zealand time use survey of 1998–1999 demonstrated how economically valuable the contribution of this work is to the nation's economy. "In a year, the time spent by men and women on unpaid work in New Zealand as a primary activity equates, at 40 hours per week, to two million full-time jobs. This compares with the equivalent of 1.7 million full-time jobs in time spent in labour force activity" (*Around the Clock: Findings from the New Zealand Time Use Survey 1998–99* 17–18).

A combination of the most advanced collection of national data on unpaid work by Statistics Canada, and the use of this data by advocates and scholars, make it possible to track the effects of unpaid work on the lives of men and women in Canada.

The *Canada Year Book 2001* reported that in 1998 women spent 15.2 hours on unpaid housework (not counting childcare) per week compared with 8.3 hours for men. Mothers ages 25–44 who were working full-time also spent nearly 35 hours a week at unpaid work (Statistics Canada 2001).

Data from the 1995 Statistics Canada General Social Survey reveal that between married couples, few husbands take over their wives' unpaid work responsibilities when wives' paid work hours increase (cited in Phipps, Burton, and Osberg 2). At the same time there's a market premium rather than a penalty associated with being a father (the ratio of income for fathers who worked full-time in the paid labour market to men who had never had children was 133.6 per cent in 1996) (Phipps et al. 412). My own suspicion is that this is a marriage premium rather than a child premium.

Any woman who has ever had a child earns less than women who have never had children. For example, in 1996 mothers in Canada (ages 24 to 54) who worked full-time in the paid labour market received 87.3 per cent of the income received by women who had never had children (Phipps, Burton, and Lethbridge 412). Research results suggest a "human capital depreciation" for each year of absence from the paid labour market. The magnitude of the depreciation is substantial (what is lost in one year out is equal to about 37 per cent of what is gained by one year in) (Phipps et al. 420). For women, the finding of a child penalty is consistent regardless of whether or not we control for marital history. Thus, the "child penalty" is not actually a "marriage penalty" for women, though the "child premium" may be a "marriage premium" for men (Phipps et al. 416–417).

Canada's method of assessing the value of unpaid activities is one of the more conservative approaches, but even that gives a result of the value of unpaid work being one third of Canada's Gross Domestic Product (GDP).

What does that mean? If you take a look at the monthly GDP figures for Canada in March 2004, unpaid work was equal to the total production from agriculture, forestry, fishing, hunting, mining and oil and gas extraction, manufacturing, and the construction industries utilities—and at that point it was still $20 million short.

Have We Ever Made Progress?

In reviewing where the feminist movement needs to go with respect to unpaid work, it's important to ask if we ever made some headway in achieving recognition of unpaid work and the rights of the workers in that sector. In 1975, when I was elected to the New Zealand parliament, our issues and situation were very different. In a country that had gained full suffrage in 1893, I was only the thirteenth woman elected. There were no women Cabinet Ministers, no women judges, no women editors of major daily newspapers, or jockeys or firefighters or

Air New Zealand pilots. There were no rape amendments, no matrimonial property changes, no domestic protection legislation, no reproductive freedom, no Human Rights Commission, little formal quality childcare provision for working parents, no parental leave, and an even larger pay gap between men and women.

But there was a consciousness about unpaid work. In a formal international context the first references on unpaid work were at the first United Nations World Conference for Women held in Mexico City in 1975. I was on the floor in the New Zealand delegation in Copenhagen to extend those paragraphs and references continued in other major UN conferences in Nairobi (1985), Beijing (1995), Copenhagen (1995), Vienna (1993), and Rio de Janeiro (1992). Through publications such as the United Nations Development Program's *Human Development Reports* and *The World's Women*,[1] commentary and statistics and research kept up the pressure.

But the ideology of the New Right swept through our national and international movement post Nairobi. The women's movement was caught between Structural Adjustment Policies and the World Trade Organization agendas. The market ruled our economic lives and the energy required for activism in the face of its power dominated the movement's activities. The feminist response and focus was to allow itself to be restricted to activity and energy around that debate—fostered in part by the old left approach about exploitation of women only happening in the market.

Isabella Bakker has written that "researchers have argued that gender-neutral macro-economic policy will only address women's needs and experiences to the extent to which they conform to male norms" (1). And feminist advocates were overwhelmingly co-opted to work primarily on analysis and criticism of the dominating economic paradigms in their political and academic work too, and far from proposing alternatives, addressed women's needs and experiences in the realms in which women conformed to male norms, and could be measured against them. There have been a number of exceptions to this framework in Canada: Carol Lees, Evelyn Drescher, Beverly Smith, Meg Luxton, Isabella Bakker, Shelley Phipps, Lynn Lethbridge, Peter Burton, Ron Coleman, Mark Anielski, and others.

I don't want to set up an either/or or dichotomous debate here: we have always needed both/and approaches to the issues of women in paid and unpaid work, but that has simply disappeared. For feminists actively concerned with the both/and approach, this has made us very wary of the kind of support we attract. In Canada, Meg Luxton wrote:

> The absence of much of the feminist movement from these debates was reflected in the discussion about whether or not unpaid work would be included in the 1996 Canadian census. With the notable exception of Mothers Are Women (MAW) and the Work is Work is Work coalition, the women's groups lobbying for its inclusion were non-feminist or explicitly antifeminist and represented women who were primarily homemakers themselves, or whose political activities focused on what they call "the family." (436)

Statistics Canada Reported This Advocacy as Follows

> Proponents for inclusion indicated that recognizing unpaid work promotes the status of those who choose to stay at home to look after young children, seniors or other family members. (Luxton 436)

Note the use of the word "choose," which is of key importance to issues raised a little later in the paper. But, in addition, Luxton focused attention on the double work situation of significant numbers of the paid work force:

Missing was any recognition that most women, including those with paid employment, do domestic labour and would benefit from having its (and therefore their) status promoted. A bias in favour of women "who choose to stay at home" could have serious implications for policy development. (436)

The consultation for the 2006 Canadian Census resulted in 42 comments on unpaid work. Fifty-five per cent of these asked for the question to be removed or asked only every ten years. Among the reasons given were that there was no widespread need for unpaid work data. The estimates were not reliable enough because "some respondents might confuse family and friendship support with a broad range of volunteer activities" (Statistics Canada 2004: chapter 14). (So that means it's not work?)

So many of the key policy agenda items for the feminist movement have just made it easier for women to do two jobs more effectively, becoming the cohort group who work the most hours of any in the nation's economy. For example, when social policy suggests "family-friendly" alternatives, from childcare to flex-time to family leave, the implementation of these policies is often skewed by patriarchy and the marketplace. Since women's market wages are, on average, lower than men's, and women's traditional role has been that of caregiver, the burden of using family-friendly policies is often shifted, as an implicit cost, to women, further restricting their labour market options. Almost all the recent CEDAW reports from the Scandinavian countries reflect this position.[2] In addition, wherever there are policy provisions for unpaid leave, or parental leave at a reduced salary, it is clearly biased in favour of high-income, dual-earner families who can more easily absorb a cessation [of] one member's income; in Canada, up to 12 months' combination of paid maternity and parental leave are available.

In Canada a range of policies discriminate against the unpaid worker and alternative arrangements. The childcare expense deduction under the *Income Tax Act* is restricted to receipted daycare or nanny care and excludes recognition of market costs and social capital benefits of other forms of care of children. Unpaid caregivers are ineligible to contribute to their own registered retirement savings or pensions under the Canada Pension Plan. New mothers who are self-employed, or unpaid caregivers are ineligible for maternity benefits under the *Employment Insurance Act*. Unpaid caregivers in the home are also excluded from parental benefits under the *Employment Insurance Act* (Smith).

The policies of most OECD-member countries to try and persuade men to accept an equal share of unpaid work rely on round-about ("soft") measures such as education and information. An additional disadvantage of this strategy is the presupposed presence of someone with whom to share your household chores. Lone mothers and singles of all ages and sexes lack a "sharing partner" (Swiebel 17).

Specific Cases

*****

In Ontario, Canada, the situation is variable, but let me present one example. If I was extremely ill or lived with a severe disability and I was not being cared for by an immediate family member, I would be able to gather receipts for full-time attendant care, for supervision if I was residing in a home with a prolonged impairment, and for sign language interpreter fees if I was deaf. The attendant care component would cover health care, meal preparation, housekeeping, laundry, a transportation driver, and security services where applicable. Now when my mother or father or my sister or brother or my daughter or son are doing this work full-time for months, if not years, they are allowed to deduct reasonable expenses associated with the cost of training required to care for me. They might get a disability credit, as a caregiver, which varies according to whether I am under 18 years of age and which can be claimed with other expenses to a maximum of $5,808. If the family income of my caregiver was less than $33,487 in 2003, he or she might have received another $1,600. Then, there are also personal tax credits for caregivers of relatives over 17 years of age of up to $587. This is an extraordinary exploitation (Ontario Government).

But, a recent ruling on a case tried in British Columbia this past summer will have significant implications for the unpaid work of family members providing care for relatives that are severely disabled. On June 29, 2004, the B.C. Human Rights Tribunal ruled that the Ministry of Health had discriminated against a 34-year-old woman with severe cerebral palsy by denying her the right to pay her father as her caregiver (*C & P Hutchison v. HMTQ*). Phillip Hutchinson, who is 73 years old, had been caring for his daughter Cheryl since she was 13. Cheryl Hutchinson suffers from cerebral palsy and requires 24-hour attendant care. She receives services under B.C.'s Choices in Supports for Independent Living (CSIL) program, an individualized funding program that allows people with disabilities to arrange their own caregiving according to their needs and to hire the caregiver of their choice. However, the CSIL program prohibits people with severe disabilities from hiring relatives as personal care attendants. Ms. Hutchison challenged that policy, arguing that she could not find a reliable caregiver to meet her most intimate needs that she trusted as much as her own father. The government was ordered to pay Mr. Hutchison $105,000 in wage loss for the services he provided (British Columbia Association for Community Living). The provincial government has, however, filed an appeal of the decision, and it will be interesting to watch what happens.

The introductory speech to Parliament of Chris Bentley, Ontario Minister of Labour, in moving the *Employment Standards Amendment Act* (Family Medical Leave) 2004 on April 13, 2004, is revealing in terms of the motivations for enactment of such legislation. The bill is intended to provide up to eight weeks of job-protected, unpaid time off work for those taking care of seriously ill family members. He said:

> It is clear that an aging population and significantly increasing workplace demands have contributed to growing levels of employee stress due to work-family conflict.... A recent Ipsos-Reid poll found that almost 32 per cent of Canadian adults were now responsible for the care of older relatives.... Most of our work life schedules do not include the additional time to provide the necessary care and support for seriously ill dependents [*sic*].

(I love it when men use "we" in situations in which they would never find themselves!)

> ... Employees making the impossible choice are less productive. They are often forced by circumstance into unplanned absences. When employees are forced to quit their job, the employees lose their skills, training and experience as well as their work. The costs to business are massive.

And finally, "the availability of Family Medical leave will support our existing health services. In some cases, it might reduce the demand on these services." At last came the admission that the unpaid work is relieving expenditure by the state.

Unlike some of the other supposedly women-friendly leave policies in Canada, this applies to all employees, including those working part-time. Seniority and credit for length of service and length of employment will count as if they had been at work. Employer contributions to the premiums for pension plans, life and extended health insurance plans, accidental death plans, and dental plans will have to be kept up. But for those in the full-time unpaid workforce in the same circumstances, there is nothing.

Rights Questions

These cases raise questions about many more potential complaints for lack of access to fundamental human rights. What of the family members who care full-time for someone who does not fit into the current operative definition of "disability" for the sake of a benefit? Should rights extend only to those full-time caregivers whose work continues for years and years without ceasing? Is there some time consideration, which would mean that a parent stopping work to care for a child accident victim or terminally ill parent for six to nine months is in a different category from one who undertakes caring for five years?[3] What about grandparents who are full-time caregivers for grandchildren, in a situation where the child might otherwise be placed in foster care?[4] Do we think that their capability and freedom to function effectively might be compromised? Do we think that the payment differential between their eligibility for assistance and that of foster parents might be discriminatory? Do we think that the rights of children who work long hours in unpaid work might be losing out on access and opportunities—to education, to leisure and enjoyment of life? Should day care subsidies flow to institutions, or with the child to the person who carries out the care? Unpaid caregiving of the sick is a critical part of the healthcare system, which compromises the well-being of the caregiver, who is then further penalized by the system in terms of loss of earnings, or no recognition at all.

Canadian research has found evidence that women in dual-earner households are more time-stressed than men, apparently as a result of the continued gendered division of housework, despite high levels of paid work by wives (Phipps, Burton, and Osberg 1).

In respect of a right to leisure, having a pre-school-aged child in the household is important for men. A pre-schooler in the family reduces a husband's satisfaction with time for self by a small amount (about seven percentage points); *any* child in the family reduces a wife's satisfaction with personal time by a much larger amount (almost 20 percentage points). For women, there is no difference between having a pre-schooler and having an elementary-school-aged child; having any children is the key variable. The researchers note that for men, making "leisure time for one's spouse is a poor substitute for having such time for oneself" (Phipps, Burton, and Osberg 18).

> Women's opportunities to take an equal part in civil and political life is [*sic*] compromised. In bolstering ... civil society ... strategies of increased civic participation and engagement rest on sufficient leisure time. [This is not possible when] women's unpaid work is intensifying not easing. (Bakker 17)

In terms of a rights-based approach to those in the unpaid workforce, and, for example, for those in the unpaid or underpaid or differently paid full-time caregiving role, we have to ask: To what extent does the discrimination and different treatment of family members in long-term caregiving (in terms of the legislation and regulations surrounding this) compromise or inhibit their capacity to participate effectively in political or community life, to attain the highest possible standard of physical and mental health, to exercise their right to opportunities of lifelong education, to enjoy safe and healthy working conditions, and so on? It's time the rights debate encompassed and included (again) the exploited, unpaid work of women.

Notes

1. These reports can be accessed on the United Nations Development Program website: http://hdr.undp.org/reports/view reports.cfm?type= 1.
2. CEDAW Country Reports are available online: http://www.un.org/womenwatch/daw/cedaw/reports.htm
3. The Federal Government of Canada has now introduced a compassionate leave policy which allows those paid workers who have put in at least 600 paid hours and who have a doctor's certificate to prove their relative is dying the chance to spend six months at home caring for that person on partial salary. Of course the unpaid full-time caregiver remains unpaid.
4. Under s.3 of the *Children, Young Person's and Their Families Act* 1989, payments received by people in receipt of a social security benefit and providing foster care under the *Act* have all payments disregarded as income for benefit abatement purposes, but no one has been able to tell me what the position is in respect of superannuation.

References

Around the Clock: Findings from the New Zealand Time Use Survey 1998–99. Auckland: Statistics New Zealand, 2001.

Bakker, Isabella. *Unpaid Work and Macroeconomics: New Discussions, New Tools for Action.* Ottawa: Status of Women Canada's Policy Research Fund, 1998.

Benería, Lourdes. "The Enduring Debate over Unpaid Labour." *International Labour Review* 138 (3) (1999): 290–291.

Bittman, Michael. "Parenthood without Penalty: Time Use and Public Policy in Australia and Finland." *Feminist Economics* 5 (3) (1999): 27–42.

British Columbia Association for Community Living. Online: http://www.bcacl.org /issues/family/updates.shtml

CEDAW Finland Fourth Country Report. CEDAW/FIN/4. Online: http://daccess-ods.un.org/TMP/5854976.html

International Labour Organization (ILO). *International Recommendations on Labour Statistics.* Geneva: ILO, 1976.

Luxton, Meg. "The UN, Women, and Household Labour: Measuring and Valuing Unpaid Work." *Women's Studies International Forum* 20 (3) (1997): 431–439.

Ontario Government. Disability Tax Credit. Online: http://www.children.gov.on.ca/CS/en/programs/SpecialNeeds/disabilityTaxCredit.htm

Phipps, Shelley, Peter Burton, and Lynn Lethbridge. "In and out Labour Market: Long-term Income Consequences of Child-Related Interruptions to Women's Paid Work." *Canadian Journal of Economics* 34 (2) (2001): 411–429.

Phipps, Shelley, Peter Burton, and Lars Osberg. "Time as a Source of Inequality within Marriage: Are Husbands More Satisfied with Time for Themselves Than Wives?" *Feminist Economics* 7 (2) (2001): 1–21.

Smith, Beverly. Personal communication, June 21, 2004.

Statistics Canada. *Canada Year Book 2001*. Ottawa: Statistics Canada, 2001. Catalogue no.
    11-402-XPE.

Statistics Canada. *2006 Census Content Consultation Report*. Ottawa, 2004. Catalogue no.
    92-130-X1E. Online: http://www12.statcan.*ca*/English/census06/products/referen*ce*/consult
    ation/contentreport-unpaidwork.htm

Swiebel, Joke. *Unpaid Work and Policy-Making: Towards a Broader Perspective of Work and Employ-
    ment*. Discussion paper no.4, ST/ESA/DP.4.DESA. New York: United Nations, 1999.

System of National Accounts. New York: United Nations, 1993.

UK Census 2001. Online: http://www.statistics.gov.uk/census2001/default.asp

Waring, Marilyn. *Counting for Nothing: What Men Value and What Women Are Worth*. Welling-
    ton: Allen and Unwin, 1988. [Published under the title *If Women Counted* in the UK and the
    US.]

Chapter 10

Don't Blame Mother: Then and Now

Paula Caplan

Paula Caplan is a clinical and research psychologist, an author, a playwright, and a mental health activist. A trailblazer and leading expert in her field, her research and publications have focused on bias in psychiatric diagnoses, women's mental health issues, and women and mother blaming in psychological research and practice. She is a research associate at the DuBois Institute, Harvard University, and a fellow at the Women and Public Policy Program of the Kennedy School of Government at Harvard.

This chapter is about the practice of mother blame, from the time leading up to my writing *Don't blame mother: Mending the mother–daughter relationship*[1] to the present. First I shall explain what motivated me to write the book beginning in the mid-1980s, [and] then I shall discuss how much of what was relevant then remains relevant today. […]

I became interested in mother blaming when I was working in a clinic where we were evaluating families. I noticed that no matter what was wrong, no matter what the reason for the family's coming to the clinic, it turned out that the mother was always assumed to be responsible for the problem. And if, in the assessment interview, she sat right next to the child, my colleagues would say afterward, "Did you see how she sat right next to the child? She is smothering and overcontrolling and too close and enmeshed and symbiotically fused with the child." But if she did not sit right next to the child, she was called cold and rejecting—and, if the child was a boy, castrating.

So my interest in mother blaming began because it seemed that there was nothing that a mother could do that was right, and it was particularly interesting and painful to me because I myself was a mother.

In 1986, when I received tenure and considered what I most wanted to teach, one of the two courses I created was about mothers. I wasn't aware at the time of any other course about mothers, so I started trying to design the course and talking to people about it. Often, both men and women would laugh and say, "What are you going to talk about for a whole semester?" or just, "Hah! A course about mothers?" You may remember a similar reaction people had ten years earlier to "Oh! You're going to have a course about women?"

Teaching that course to graduate students at the University of Toronto's Ontario Institute for Studies in Education led to my writing *Don't blame mother*. In the book, I describe aspects of girls' and women's socialization that create or exacerbate problems between mothers and daughters, as well as methods that mothers and daughters have found helpful in repairing rifts between them. (I did not believe and still do not believe that the mother–daughter relationship is more fraught with problems than the mother–son relationship, or the relationships between fathers and their children of either sex. However, as a feminist I was primarily concerned with the kinds of socially created—and, therefore, hopefully surmountable—barriers between women.) In addressing the question "To what extent is the content of *Don't blame mother* applicable today?" I find it depressing that most of the basic principles that concerned me as I wrote the book still apply today. I shall return to this point later.

After my experience in the clinical setting described earlier, I did some research with Ian Hall-McCorquodale,[2] looking at articles in clinical journals written by psychoanalysts, psychiatrists, social workers, psychologists, behavior therapists, and clinicians of all stripes. We found that mothers were blamed for virtually every kind of psychological or emotional problem that ever brought any patient to see a therapist. We were also disappointed to find that the sex of the person who was writing the paper did not determine the presence or absence of mother blaming, and, even more depressingly, that it didn't get better as the years passed after the resurgence of the women's movement during the 1970s. With respect to mother blame, so many therapists still seemed to be buried under their rocks.

When I began to bring up this subject of mother blame I pointed out that there are myths about mothers that allow us to take anything a mother might do and turn it into evidence of something "bad" about her. Important work that a mother does goes largely unnoticed, except when she doesn't do it, as when she is sick and can't make dinner. I would point out that nobody I knew of was likely to say to their mother, "That was a great week's work of dusting you did," or "That was a week of delicious and nourishing meals that you prepared." When I would say this, people would laugh—and still do, in fact.

So we have to ask, "Why does this make us laugh? Would you laugh if I said, 'Dad, the lawn looks great now that you have mowed it'?" Nobody laughs at that. Why? Because we laugh at the unexpected. It is so unimaginable to us that anyone would express appreciation for, or a sense of valuing of, the work that mothers do as mothers and housekeepers and cooks and chauffeurs. So I used to talk about that.

As observed in a review of *The time bind: When work becomes home and home becomes work*,[3] Arlie Hochschild points out that women increasingly spend time at paid work because they feel appreciated there. She says that even for relatively uninteresting work, such as factory work, women find work to be a greater source of self-esteem than home life. This was something that had concerned me years ago, because it seemed to me that, as in that story about no one thanking you for dusting, even if you work at a really boring, miserable job, every week or two somebody hands you a paycheque. The cheque might not be much, but it communicates the notion that somebody puts some value on the work that you do. And it's still no better in terms of mothering.

At the heart of *Don't blame mother* are mother myths I call the "Good Mother Myths" and mother myths I call the "Bad Mother Myths." The Good Mother Myths set standards that no human being could ever match, such as that mothers are always, naturally, one hundred percent nurturant. We have a double standard. We don't have that kind of expectation of fathers. So, when, one percent of the time, mothers don't do what we wish they would do, we feel betrayed, because the myth is that they naturally are able to and, in fact, are desperate to be nurturant all the time. But when our fathers do anything nurturant, we feel that it is wonderful that Daddy did something like that. (Naturally, the answer is not to stop appreciating what fathers do but rather to be ready to give mothers equal credit when they are nurturant.)

The Bad Mother Myths allow us to take mothers' neutral or bad behavior—because mothers are human, so we do some bad things—or even mothers' good behavior, and transform it into further proof that mothers are bad. One example that disturbs me the most is the myth that mother–daughter closeness is sick, that it is a form of psychopathology. When *Don't blame mother* was first published, and I was doing media interviews, every woman interviewer would confess, with the microphone turned off, that she talked to her mother every day. I would ask her, "How do you feel afterward?" and the woman would reply, "Oh, great. My mother has a great sense of humor, and we are great friends, and we give each other advice." I would then ask her, "Do you have a partner?" "Yes." "Do you talk to them every day?" "Yes." "Does that embarrass you?" "No." And I would ask, "Well, then, why did you confess that you talk to your mother every day?" These women would reply that they worried that the daily talks with their mothers were signs that they hadn't "individuated" or "achieved autonomy" from their mothers, and if they had been in therapy they would say, "I know it means we're enmeshed or symbiotically fused." My point here is that anything associated with mothers becomes devalued and pathologized.

If you look at the myths about mothers, you find that some of them are mutually exclusive.[4] One of the Bad Mother Myths is that mothers are an endless drain on our energy: just on the basis of strict physics principles alone, you cannot be constantly putting out force (nurturance), while constantly taking in force and energy as you are draining it from others. Another set of mutually exclusive myths involves the Good Mother Myth, according to which mothers naturally, perhaps for hormonal reasons, know everything they need to know about mothering, and the Bad Mother Myth, according to which mothers cannot raise emotionally healthy children without the advice of lots of experts.

I believe that these mutually exclusive myths continue to coexist because every society needs scapegoated groups if the people in power want to maintain their power. What happens if I'm in the powerful group and some member of the scapegoated group does something good? Somebody might get the idea that the scapegoated people are not as bad as I portray them to be, and if that's the case, maybe I don't deserve to have all of the power I have. So I have to make sure there is a myth for every occasion, so that no matter what the members of that scapegoated group might do, I can transform it into further proof that they are wrong, bad, or pathological, and deserve to continue to have no power and be scapegoated.[5] That is the powerful function that these myths serve, and that is why we need to keep questioning them.

This power hierarchy still exists, and the women's movement hasn't been able to change it yet. I think it hasn't changed partly because we often substitute the word *mother* for *woman*. For instance, people at a party may stop you when you tell a "joke" that is woman-hating, but if you change the word *woman* to *mother*, you can still get away with the comment. You are much less likely to have someone interrupt you to say, "I don't think that's funny, and I don't want you to go on like that."

What the women's movement can do is to make the repeated exposure of mother myths—the placing of them front and center—a priority. Anti-feminist backlash makes all feminist efforts more difficult, of course. But until we recognize the need for what we might call "the Norma Rae-ing of mothers' struggles," the need to reveal mothers' oppression and its systemic nature, few women of any ethnic or racialized group or class or sexual orientation (and certainly not women with disabilities or women who don't weigh the "right" amount) will be free. Why? Because we all had mothers, and so we're connected with what is done to, what is said about mothers. Because we have all been subjected as women to strong pressure to prove we are unlike our mothers. You'll often hear women say, "My greatest fear is that I will be like my mother." What I find that these women usually mean if you explore that statement is, "I don't want to be treated the way she has been treated. I don't want to be demeaned and undervalued the way she is." At the same time as we are taught to not want to be like our mothers, we are taught—sometimes subliminally—that we should want to be like our mothers, when they are passive, pliable, and ashamed of themselves. And no one is free until the truths about mothers are highlighted, because all women, and especially as we age,[6] are expected to be motherly, motherlike, as in being self-denying and serving others.

No, it's not getting any better—not socially and not in the research arena. A recent issue of the *American Journal of Orthopsychiatry* includes a longitudinal report on "Preschool antecedents of adolescent assaultive behavior."[7] The researchers studied children from preschool through adolescence in an attempt to discern the determinants of adolescents' assaultive behavior. How did they look at the alleged determinants? Among other things, they observed what they call early in their article "parental interactions" with the young children. That really meant "mothers' interactions," even though eighty-six percent of the children in their study had both a male and a female parent in the home. When they looked at how mothers interact with children, and then later on looked at which children become assaultive, it is not surprising that they concluded that it was the children's negative interactions with their mothers that led to their assaultive behavior.

The methodology you choose can go far to determine the results that you get. I believe that there are at least two major methodological problems evident in this study. One problem is not looking at the fathers or the society in which the children live, and what the determinants of their assaultive behavior might be. The second is a cause–effect problem. People who are assaultive when they are teenagers, for reasons that may have had nothing to do with their mothers, might have been difficult to handle as children, and thus their mothers' interactions with them would have been observed to be relatively "negative." For example, their mothers might have had to do more of the disciplining of them, more of the saying "no." That is just one example of the persistence of the practice of mother blame in "scholarly" journals.

Mother blame also persists on a grand scale in the arena of the diagnosis of mental illness. My book, *They say you're crazy: How the world's most powerful psychiatrists decide who's normal*,[8] is an exposé of the *Diagnostic and statistical manual of mental disorders*[9] (also called the DSM). The DSM is the "Bible" of mental health professionals that lists 374 supposedly different mental disorders. It is marketed as "science," but the way it is put together is far from scientific, and pieces of relevant scientific research are often ignored or distorted. I became involved in learning about the DSM in 1985 because I was concerned about a new category the American Psychiatric Association was proposing to include in the DSM called "Self-Defeating Personality Disorder." This new category might be described as "the Good Wife, or Good Mother Syndrome." It included criteria such as not putting other people's needs ahead of one's own, feeling unappreciated, and choosing less desirable options for their lives when clearly better ones are available. But this is what society still thinks we are supposed to do as a mother and as a "good" woman. Once involved, I was horrified when I learned about the way that the DSM's authors decide who is "normal." I ended up calling their process "Diagnosisgate" because of the similarities to Watergate in terms of lies, cover-ups, and distortions of what the research literature shows.[10]

This "Self-Defeating Personality Disorder" is a real catch-22 for women. If women act in those ways, they supposedly have this mental disorder, but if they do not act in those ways, they are rejected and pathologized for not being real women, not being "good" women.[11] [...]

*****

I hope that this sampling of the recent history of mother blame makes it clear that, despite some gains that feminists have made, there are still miles to go before we can relax in the knowledge that mother blame has been eradicated. For this reason, I suggest that we join together in declaring that women don't speak enough and don't speak up enough, certainly not in defense of mothers. Let us vow that at every possible opportunity we will protest, we will educate, even interrupt—as we would a sexist or a racist "joke"—when anyone in any setting utters or implies any of the dangerous myths about mothers.

Notes

1. Paula Caplan, *Don't blame mother: Mending the mother–daughter relationship* (New York: Routledge, 2000).
2. Paula Caplan and Ian Hall-McCorquodale, "Mother-blaming in major clinical journals," *American Journal of Orthopsychiatry* 55 (1985): 345–53; Paula Caplan and Ian Hall-McCorquodale, "The scapegoating of mothers: A call for change," *American Journal of Orthopsychiatry* 55 (1985): 610–13.
3. Arlie Hochschild, "A review of sex role research," in *Changing women in a changing society*, ed. Joan Huber (Chicago: University of Chicago Press, 1973), 249–67.
4. Caplan, *Don't blame mother.*
5. Ibid.
6. Rachel Josefowitz Siegel, "Old women as mother figures," in *Woman-defined motherhood*, ed. Jane Price and Ellen Cole (New York: Harrington Park, 1990), 89–97.
7. Roy C. Herrenkohl, Brenda P. Egolf, and Ellen C. Herrenkohl, "Preschool antecedents of adolescent assaultive behavior: A longitudinal study," *American Journal of Orthopsychiatry* 67 (1997): 422–32.
8. Paula Caplan, *They say you're crazy: How the world's most powerful psychiatrists decide who's normal* (Reading, Mass.: Addison-Wesley, 1995).
9. American Psychiatric Association, *Diagnostic and statistical manual of mental disorders IV* (Washington, D.C.: American Psychiatric Association, 1994).
10. Caplan, *They say you're crazy.*
11. For apparently political reasons, Self-Defeating Personality Disorder was removed from the most recent edition of the DSM, but that has not kept it from being used.

Part 2 Constructions of Sex and Gender

One is not born, but rather becomes, a woman.
        —Simone de Beauvoir, *The Second Sex* (1974, p. 301)

[Woman] is a term in process, a becoming, a constructing that cannot rightfully be said to originate or end.
        —Judith Butler, *Gender Trouble* (1990, p. 33)

Part 2 explores the role of Western science and culture in making social differences and hierarchies based on categories such as sex, gender, race, ability, class, and sexuality. We highlight concepts like "essentialism" and "social constructionism," examine feminist critiques of and contributions to science, and trace scientific and social constructions of differences across time and place.

2a: The Social and Historical Construction of Sexed Bodies

In the first section, we introduce feminist and critical theory that challenges Western culture's taken-for-granted and deeply held ideas about sexed bodies. We call into question sexual binaries of male and female bodies, and invite you to consider alternative ways of conceptualizing sex differences.

2b: The Making of "Difference" and Inequalities

We are particularly interested in this section in examining feminist critiques of Western science and its role in constructing dualist thinking and hierarchical categories of difference based on ideas about sex, race, and disability. We see some of the ways in which inequalities among groups of people have been constructed, maintained, justified, and resisted. You are also introduced to new ways of thinking about the relationship of biology and culture as interactive.

2c: The Social Construction of Gender

Here we explore the social construction of our gendered identities through language and everyday practices. We also introduce important insights from contemporary studies on masculinity and men's political involvement in feminism, and take up key concepts in queer theory, such as transgender, which challenge the narrow rigidity of dominant constructions of masculinity and femininity.

2d: The Social Construction of Sexuality

We examine in this section how social constructionist theory has been applied to historical and contemporary studies of sexuality within Canadian and global contexts. We invite you to assess critically the "naturalness" of heterosexuality, heterosexism, and homophobia, as well as the ethics of scientific research on sexual orientation.

2a The Social and Historical Construction of Sexed Bodies

Supplement 7

Sex = Gender?

The English-language distinction between the words "sex" and "gender" was first developed in the 1950s and 1960s by British and American psychiatrists and other medical personnel working with intersex and transsexual patients.[1] Since then, the term "gender" has been increasingly used to distinguish between sex as biological and gender as socially and culturally constructed. Feminists have used this terminology to argue against the "biology is destiny" line, and gender and development approaches have widely adopted this system of analysis.

"Sex marks the distinction between women and men as a result of their biological, physical, and genetic differences.... Gender roles are set by convention and other social, economic, political and cultural forces."

—One World Action Glossary,
http://owa.netxtra.net/indepth/project.jsp?project=206

From this perspective, sex is fixed and based in nature; gender is fluid and based in culture.[2] This distinction constitutes progress compared with "biology is destiny." However, it ignores the existence of people who do not fit neatly into the biological or social categories of women and men, such as intersex, transgender, transsexual people, and hijras.[3] Furthermore, for many people the sex categories of female and male are neither fixed nor universal, but vary over time and across cultures. Accordingly, sex, like gender, is seen as a social and cultural construct.

Gender and Sex: A Sample of Definitions

"Gender refers to the array of socially constructed roles and relationships, personality traits, attitudes, behaviours, values, relative power and influence that society ascribes to the two sexes on a differential basis. *Whereas biological sex is determined by genetic and anatomical characteristics, gender is an acquired identity* that is learned, changes over time, and varies widely within and across cultures. Gender is relational and refers not simply to women or men but to the relationship between them."

—INSTRAW, *Glossary of Gender-Related Terms and Concepts*,
http://www.uninstraw.org/en/index.php?option=content&task=view&id=37&Itemid=76

"*Gender refers to the economic, social and cultural attributes and opportunities* associated with being male or female at a particular point in time."

—World Health Organization, 2001,
Transforming Health Systems: Gender and Rights in Reproductive Health,
http://www.who.int/reproductive-health/gender/glossary.html

"*Sex refers to the biological characteristics that define humans as female or male.* While these sets of biological characteristics are not mutually exclusive, as there are individuals who possess both, they tend to differentiate humans as males and females."

—World Health Organization, 2002,
Gender and Reproductive Rights: Working Definitions,
http://www.who.int/reproductive-health/gender/sexual_health.html#1

"*(Sex) in human beings is not a purely dichotomous variable.* It is not an evenly continuous one either … *a fair number of human beings are markedly intersexual*, a number of them to the point where both sorts of external genitalia appear, or where developed breasts occur in an individual with male genitalia, and so on."

—Clifford Geertz,
Local Knowledge: Further Essays in Interpretive Anthropology
(New York: Basic Books, 1983), p. 81

"If the immutable character of sex is contested, *perhaps this construct called 'sex' is as culturally constructed as gender*; indeed, perhaps it was always already gender, with the consequence that the distinction between sex and gender turns out to be no distinction at all."

—Judith Butler,
Gender Trouble: Feminism and the Subversion of Identity
(New York & London: Routledge, 1990),
Chapter 1: Subjects of Sex/Gender/Desire, p. 346

"Gender is not what culture created out of my body's sex; rather; *sex is what culture makes when it genders my body.*"

—Wilchins, transgender activist,
quoted in Surya Monro,
Gender Politics: Citizenship, Activism, and Sexual Diversity
(London: Pluto Press, 2006), p. 30

"*Gender categorisation can be best described as a large machine with lots of pins that dig into the sense of self and tear the mind to pieces.* And in my situation, having been 'surgically treated' as a child … I see a lot of malice behind it."

—Salamacis, quoted in Surya Munro,
Gender Politics: Citizenship, Activism, and Sexual Diversity
(London: Pluto Press, 2006), p. 47

"*We believe it is indispensable to deconstruct the binary sex/gender system* that shapes the Western world so absolutely that in most cases it goes unnoticed. For 'other sexualities to be possible' it is indispensable and urgent that we stop governing ourselves by the absurd notion that only two possible body types exist, male and female, with only two genders inextricably linked to them, man and woman. We make trans and intersex issues our priority because their presence, activism, and theoretical contributions show us the path to a new paradigm that will allow as many bodies, sexualities, and identities to exist as those living in this world might wish to have, with each one of them respected, desired, celebrated."

—International Gay and Lesbian Human Rights Commission [IGLHRC], 2005,
Institutional Memoir of the 2005 Institute for Trans and Intersex Activist Training, p. 8,
http://www.iglhrc.org/files/iglhrc/LAC/ITIAT-Aug06-E.pdf

Notes

1. T. Moi, *Sex, Gender, and the Body* (New York: Oxford University Press, 2005).
2. J. Goldstein, *War and Gender* (Cambridge: Cambridge University Press, 2003), p. 2.
3. Intersex people are born with some combination of male and female characteristics. Transsexual people are born with the body of one sex, but feel they belong to the "opposite" sex. Transgender are those who feel they are neither male nor female, but somewhere in between. Hijras are a South Asian transgender population.

Source: Emily Esplen and Susie Jolly, "Gender and Sex: A sample of definitions," BRIDGE Development/Gender website (2006), retrieved from http://www.bridge.ids.ac.uk

Chapter 11

Introduction to *Beyond the Natural Body*

Nelly Oudshoorn

Nelly Oudshoorn is professor of technology dynamics and health care at the University of Twente in the Netherlands, where she researches medical technology, and information and communication technology. Her scholarly works looking at the development of the "male pill" and the naming of "sex" hormones uncover some of the ways that science is implicated in creating and maintaining sex differences.

*****

What about sex and the body? [...] During the second wave of feminism that started in the 1970s, (fe)male bodies were of central concern in many debates, although in a rather peculiar way. Feminist biologists, like myself, were certain that biological determinism had to be rejected. We knew that nature does not determine what we mean when we use terms such as woman, body, femininity. We chose this position to contest those opponents of feminism who suggested that social inequality between women and men is primarily rooted in biological sex differences. According to this opinion, social changes demanded by feminists are wishful thinking because biology, rather than society, sets constraints on the behavior and abilities of women. Biology is destiny, and feminists simply have to accept this reality.

*****

Feminist biologists and historians of science did not hesitate to make [a] crucial move in exposing the myth of the natural body. Ruth Bleier, Ruth Hubbard, Evelyn Fox Keller and Helen Longino suggested that anatomical, endocrinological or immunological "facts" are anything but self-evident.[1] From these feminist scholars I adopted the intellectually challenging and politically relevant notion that there does not exist an unmediated natural truth of the body. Our perceptions and interpretations of the body are mediated through language and, in our society, the biomedical sciences function as a major provider of this language.[2] This view of the body is linked to a critical reappraisal of the status of biomedical knowledge. If understanding the body is mediated by language, scientists are bound by language as well. Consequently, the assumption that the biomedical sciences are the providers of objective knowledge about the "true nature" of the body could be ejected. This really changed my view of science and the world. What is science all about if scientists are not discovering reality? In search of an answer to this question I was inspired by the literature of the emerging field of social studies of science that introduced the powerful idea that scientific facts are not objectively given, but collectively created.[3] This implies a totally different perspective on what scientists are doing: scientists are actively constructing reality, rather than discovering reality. For the debate about the body, this means that the naturalistic reality of the body as such does not exist; it is created by scientists as the object of scientific investigation (Duden 1991: 22). The social constructivist approach opened up a whole new line of research exposing the multiple ways in which the biomedical sciences as discursive technologies (re)construct and reflect our understanding of the body.[4] The body, in all its complexities, thus achieved an important position on the feminist research agenda.

*****

Sex and the Body

In these biomedical discourses, the construction of the body as something with a sex has been a central theme all through the centuries. The myriad ways in which scientists have understood sex provide many illuminating counter-moves to the argument that sex is an unequivocal, ahistorical attribute of the body that once unveiled by science is valid everywhere and within every context. Early medical texts in particular challenge our present-day perceptions of male and female bodies. For our postmodern minds it is hard to imagine that for two thousand years, male and female bodies were not conceptualized in terms of differences. Medical texts from the ancient Greeks until the late eighteenth century described male and female bodies as fundamentally similar. Women had even the same genitals as men, with one difference: "theirs are inside the body and not outside it." In this approach, characterized by Thomas Laqueur as the "one-sex model," the female body was understood as a "male turned inside herself," not a different sex, but a lesser version of the male body (Laqueur 1990). Medical textbooks of this period show drawings of the female genitals that stress their resemblance to male genitalia so vividly that one could believe them to be representations of the male penis. For thousands of years the "one-sex model" dominated biomedical discourse, even to such an extent that medical texts lacked a specific anatomical nomenclature for female reproductive organs. The ovary, for instance, did not have a name of its own but was described as the female testicle, thus referring again to the male organ. The language we are now familiar with, such as vagina and clitoris, simply did not exist (Laqueur 1990: 5, 96).

This emphasis on similarities rather than differences is also present in the texts of anatomists who studied parts of the body other than the reproductive organs. For Vesalius, the father of anatomy, "sex was only skin deep, limited to differences in the outline of the body and the organs of reproduction. In his view, all other organs were interchangeable between the sexes" (Schiebinger 1989: 189). In his beautiful drawings of the skeleton in *Epitome*, an anatomical atlas that appeared in 1543, Vesalius did not give sex to the bony structure of the body (Schiebinger 1989: 182). This (as we would now perceive it) "indifference" of medical scientists to bodily differences between the sexes does not seem to be a consequence of ignorance of the female body. Since the fourteenth century, the dissection of women's bodies was part of anatomical practice (Schiebinger 1989: 182). According to Laqueur, the stress on similarities, representing the female body as just a gradation of one basic male type, was inextricably intertwined with patriarchal thinking, reflecting the values of an overwhelmingly male public world in which "man is the measure of all things, and woman does not exist as an ontologically distinct category" (Laqueur 1990: 62).

It was only in the eighteenth century that biomedical discourse first included a concept of sex that is more familiar to our present-day interpretations of the male and the female body. The long-established tradition that emphasized bodily similarities over differences began to be heavily criticized. In the mid-eighteenth century, anatomists increasingly focused on bodily differences between the sexes, and argued that sex was not restricted to the reproductive organs, or as one physician put it: "the essence of sex is not confined to a single organ but extends, through more or less perceptible nuances, into every part" (Schiebinger 1989: 189). The first part of the body to become sexualized was the skeleton. If sex differences could be found in "the hardest part of the body," it would be likely that sex penetrated "every muscle, vein, and organ attached to and molded by the skeleton" (Schiebinger 1989: 191). In the 1750s, the first female skeletons appeared in medical textbooks. Londa Schiebinger has described how anatomists paid special attention to those parts of the skeleton that would become socially signifi-cant, amongst which was the skull. The depiction of the female skull was used to prove that women's intellectual capacities were inferior to those of men (Schiebinger 1986). The history of medicine in this period contains many illustrations of similar reflections of the social role of women in the representa-tion of the human body. Anatomists of more recent centuries "mended nature to fit emerging ideals of masculinity and femininity" (Schiebinger 1989: 203).[5] In nineteenth-century cellular physiology the medical gaze shifted from the bones to the cells. Physiological "facts" were used to explain the passive nature of women. The biomedical sciences thus functioned as an arbiter in socio-political debates about women's rights and abilities (Laqueur 1990: 6, 215). By the late nineteenth century medical sci-entists had extended this sexualization to every imaginable part of the body: bones, blood vessels, cells, hair and brains (Schiebinger 1989: 189). Only the eye seems to have no sex (Honegger 1991: 176). Biomedical discourse thus shows a clear shift in focus from similarities to differences.[6] The female and the male body now became conceptualized in terms of opposite bodies with "incommensurably dif-ferent organs, functions, and feelings" (Laqueur 1990: viii).

Following this shift, the female body became the medical object *par excellence* (Foucault 1976), emphasizing woman's unique sexual character. Medical scientists now started to identify the "essential features that belong to her, that serve to distinguish her, that make her what she is" (Laqueur 1990: 5). The medical literature of this period shows a radical naturalization of femi-ninity in which scientists reduced woman to one specific organ. In the eighteenth and nineteenth centuries scientists set out to localize the "essence" of femininity in different places in the body. Until the mid-nineteenth century, scientists considered the uterus as the seat of femininity. This conceptualization is reflected in the statement of the German poet and naturalist Johann Wolf-gang von Goethe (1749–1832): Der Hauptpunkt der ganzen weiblichen Existenz ist die Gebaer-mutter (The main point [or the essence] of the entire female existence is the womb) (Medvei 1983: 213).

In the middle of the nineteenth century, medical attention began to shift from the uterus to the ovaries, which came to be regarded as largely autonomous control centers of reproduction in the female animal, while in humans they were thought to be the "essence" of femininity itself (Gal-lagher and Laqueur 1987: 27). In 1848, Virchow (1817–1885), often portrayed as the founding father of physiology, characterized the function of the ovaries:

> It has been completely wrong to regard the uterus as the characteristic organ.... The womb, as part of the sexual canal, of the whole apparatus of reproduction, is merely an organ of secondary importance. Remove the ovary, and we shall have before us a mas-culine woman, an ugly half-form with the coarse harsh form, the heavy bone formation, the moustache, the rough voice, the flat chest, the sour and egoistic mentality and the distorted outlook ... in short, all that we admire and respect in woman as womanly, is merely dependent on her ovaries. (Medvei 1983: 215)

The search for the female organ *par excellence* was not just a theoretical endeavor. The place in the body where the "essence" of femininity was located became the object of surgical interventions. The ovaries, perceived as the "organs of crises," became the paradigmatic object of the medical specialty of gynecology that was established in the late nineteenth century (Honegger 1991: 209, 211). The medical attention given to the ovaries resulted in the widespread practice of surgical operations for removal of the ovaries in many European countries, as well as in the United States. In the 1870s and 1880s, thousands of women were subjected to this drastic procedure for the treatment of menstrual irregularities and various neuroses (Corner 1965: 4).

Early in the twentieth century, the "essence" of femininity came to be located not in an organ but in chemical substances: sex hormones. The new field of sex endocrinology introduced the concept of "female" and "male" sex hormones as chemical messengers of femininity and masculinity. This hormonally constructed concept of the body has developed into one of the dominant modes of thinking about the biological roots of sex differences. Many types of behaviour, roles, functions and characteristics considered as typically male or female in western culture have been ascribed to hormones.[7] In this process, the female body, but not the male body, has become increasingly portrayed as a body completely controlled by hormones. At this moment, the hormones estrogen and progesterone are the most widely used drugs in the history of medicine. These substances are a popular means of controlling fertility and are used for numerous other purposes: as menstruation regulators or abortifacients, in pregnancy tests and as specific medications for female menopause. Hormones are produced by pharmaceutical companies and delivered to women through a worldwide distribution network, including Third World countries (Wolffers et al. 1989: 27). This was not so a century ago. Our grandmothers did not know of any hormones: estrogen and progesterone as such did not exist in the nineteenth century. The concept of hormones was coined in 1905, and it took two decades before pharmaceutical companies began the mass production of hormones. Nowadays millions of women take hormonal pills and many of us have adopted the hormonal model to explain our bodies.

*****

Feminist studies have pointed out that cultural stereotypes about women and men play an important role in shaping scientific theories. The major question that emerges then is: To what extent do scientists use cultural notions as resources in their research practice?

*****

Notes

1. Bleier (1984, 1986); Hubbard (1981); Hubbard et al. (1982); Keller (1982, 1984); Longino (1990); Longino and Doell (1983). In contrast to feminist sociologists, feminist biologists considered the body as relevant for the feminist research agenda. Actually, feminist biologists have adopted this position from the beginning of the debate about sex and gender. My account of the history of feminist studies should therefore not be read as a story of continuity and progress. There have been, and still are, many different positions in this debate about sex, gender and the body.

2. There is, of course, the important question of the extent to which women adopt biomedical knowledge in understanding of their bodies. In *Woman beneath the Skin: A Doctor's Patients in Eighteenth-Century Germany*, Barbara Duden argues that body perception has two very different histories dealing with two different traditions: the tradition of the oral culture and the written medical tradition. Duden suggests that the woman's body should be understood in terms of a "fragile synthesis" of these two traditions (Duden 1991c: 35, 182). In *The Woman in the Body*, Emily Martin concludes that all women are affected in one way or another by biomedical views of physical life events such as menstruation, menopause and childbirth. She showed important differences in the extent to which women accept or resist this knowledge. Middle-class women in the USA (black or white) readily inclined toward the medical view of their bodies, explaining reproductive processes in terms of "internal organs, structures, and functions" (Martin 1987: 105). Working-class women, on the other hand, seem to share an absolute resistance to this medical view, and explain their bodies in terms of what a woman sees or feels or the significance it has in her life (Martin 1987: 109).

3. See, among other, Bijker and Law (1992); Bijker et al. (1987); Gilbert and Mulkay (1984); Latour (1987); Latour and Woolgar (1979).

4. See, for example, Bell (1987); Birke (1986); Bleier (1984, 1986); Clarke (1990); Fausto-Sterling (1985); Haraway (1981, 1989); Honegger (1991); Hubbard (1981); Hubbard et al. (1982); Jacobus et al. (1990); Jordanova (1980, 1989); Laqueur (1990); Longino (1990); Longino and Doell (1983); Mol (1988); Sayers (1982); Schiebinger (1986, 1989); Wijngaard (1991a, 1991b).

5. Ludmilla Jordonova gave another striking example in her analysis of the representation of the female and the male body in the wax models used for making anatomical drawings in the biomedical sciences in France and Britain in the eighteenth and nineteenth centuries. She described how these wax models depict male figures as active agents and females as the passive objects of sexual desire. The female figures, or "Venuses," lie on the velvet or silk cushions, whereas male figures are usually upright, and often in positions of motion, thus reflecting the cultural stereotypes of the active male and the passive female (Jordanova 1980: 54).

6. This shift seems to have been caused by epistemological and socio-political changes rather than by scientific progress. In *Making Sex*, Thomas Laqueur described this shift in the context of changes in the political climate. The French Revolution and new liberal claims in the seventeenth century led to new ideals about the social relationships between men and women, in which the complementarity between the sexes was emphasized. This theory of complementarity "taught that men and women are not physical and moral equals but complementary opposites." Women now became viewed as "fundamentally different from, and thus incomparable to, men" (Laqueur 1990: 32, 216, 217). The theory of sexual complementarity was meant to keep women out of competition with men, designing separate spheres for men and women. In this theory, which came to be known as the "doctrine of the two spheres," the sexes were expected to complement, rather than compete with, each other. The shift from studying similarities to differences was not caused by new scientific findings; on the contrary, Laqueur described how scientific literature provided many new discoveries which could have strengthened the one-sex model. The new field of embryology, for instance, claimed that reproductive organs "begin from one and the same embryonic structure," offering support to the earlier belief in the similarity between male and female reproductive systems (Laqueur 1990: 169). However, Laqueur does not present a simple

causal model for scientific and political changes: "these social and political changes are not, in themselves, explanations for the reinterpretation of bodies … none of these things caused the making of a new sex body. Instead, the remaking of the body is itself intrinsic to each of these developments" (Laqueur 1990: 11).

7. See Briscoe (1978); Fausto-Sterling (1985); Fried (1982); Messent (1976); Money and Ehrhardt (1972); Rogers (1976).

References

Bell, S.E. (1987) "Changing Ideas: The Medicalization of Menopause," *Social Science and Medicine* 24: 535–542.

Bijker, W.E., Hughes, T.P., Pinch, T.J. (eds) (1987) *The Social Construction of Technological Systems: New Directions in the Sociology and History of Technology*. Cambridge, Mass.: MIT Press.

Bijker, W.E., Law, J. (1992) *Shaping Technology—Building Society*. Cambridge, Mass.: MIT Press.

Birke, L. (1986) *Women, Feminism and Biology: The Feminist Challenge*. Brighton, Sussex: Harvester.

Bleier, R. (1984) *Science and Gender: A Critique of Biology and Its Theories on Women*. New York: Pergamon.

Bleier, R. (ed.) (1986) *Feminist Approaches to Science*. New York: Pergamon.

Briscoe, A.M. (1978) "Hormones and Gender," in E. Tobach, B. Rosoff (eds), *Genes and Gender*. New York: Gordian.

Clarke A.E. (1990) "Women's Health over the Life Cycle," in R. Apple (ed.), *The History of Women, Health and Medicine in America: An Encyclopedic Handbook*. New York: Garland.

Corner, G.W. (1965) "The Early History of Oestrogenic Hormones," *Proceedings of the Society of Endocrinology* 33: 3–18.

Duden, B. (1991) *The Woman beneath the Skin: A Doctor's Patients in Eighteenth-Century Germany*. Cambridge, Mass., and London: Harvard University Press.

Fausto-Sterling, A. (1985) *Myths of Gender: Biological Theories about Women and Men*. New York: Basic Books.

Foucault, M. (1976) *Histoire de la sexualité, 1: La Volonté de savoir*. Paris: Gallimard.

Fried, B. (1982) "Boys Will Be Boys: The Language of Sex and Gender," in R. Hubbard, M.S. Henefin, B. Fried (eds), *Biological Woman: The Convenient Myth*. Cambridge: Schenkman.

Gallagher, C., Laqueur T., (eds) (1987) *The Making of the Modern Body: Sexuality and Society in the Nineteenth Century*. Berkeley, Los Angeles and London: University of California Press.

Gilbert, G.N., Mulkay, M. (1984) *Opening Pandora's Box: A Sociological Analysis of Scientific Discourse*. Cambridge: Cambridge University Press.

Haraway, D. (1981) "In the Beginning Was the Word: The Genesis of Biological Theory," in D. Haraway, *Simians, Cyborgs and Women: The Reinvention of Women*. New York: Routledge.

Haraway, D. (1989) "The Biopolitics of Postmodern Bodies: Determinants of Self in Immune System Discourse," *Differences* 1: 3–43.

Honegger, C. (1991) *Die Ordnung der Geslechter Die Wissenschaften vom Menschen und das Weib*. Frankfurt and New York: Campus Verlag.

Hubbard, R. (1981) "The Emperor Doesn't Wear Any Clothes: The Impact of Feminism on Biology," in D. Spender (ed.), *Men's Studies Modified: The Impact of Feminism on the Academic Disciplines*. Oxford and New York: Pergamon.

Hubbard, R., Henifin, M.S., Fried, B. (eds) (1982) *Biological Woman: The Convenient Myth.* Cambridge, Mass.: Schenkman.

Jacobus, M., Keller, E.F., Shuttleworth, S. (eds) (1990) *Body/Politics: Women and the Discourses of Science.* New York and London: Routledge.

Jordanova, L. (1980) "Natural Facts: A Historical Perspective on Science and Sexuality," in C. MacCormack, M. Strathern (eds) *Nature, Culture and Gender.* New York: Cambridge University Press.

Jordanova, L. (1989) *Sexual Visions: Images of Gender in Science and Medicine between the Eighteenth and Twentieth Centuries.* New York and London: Harvester Wheatsheaf.

Keller, E. Fox (1982) "Feminism and Science," *Signs: Journal of Women in Culture and Society* 7 (1): 589–595.

Keller, E. Fox (1984) *Reflections on Gender and Science.* New Haven, Conn: Yale University Press.

Laqueur, T. (1990) *Making Sex: Body and Gender from the Greeks to Freud.* Cambridge, Mass. and London: Harvard University Press.

Latour, B. (1987) *Science in Action: How to Follow Scientists and Engineers through Society.* Milton Keynes: Open University Press.

Latour, B., Woolgar, S. (1979) *Laboratory Life: The Social Construction of Scientific Facts.* Beverly Hills, Calif. and London: Sage.

Longino, H. (1990) *Science as Social Knowledge: Value and Objectivity in Scientific Inquiry.* Princeton, N.J. and Oxford: Princeton University Press.

Longino, H., Doell, R. (1983) "Body, Bias and Behavior: A Comparative Analysis of Reasoning in Two Areas of Biological Science," *Signs: Journal of Women in Culture and Society* 9 (2): 20–227.

Martin, E. (1987) *The Woman in the Body: A Cultural Analysis of Reproduction.* Boston, Mass.: Beacon.

Medvei, V.C (1983) *A History of Endocrinology.* The Hague: MTP Press.

Messent, P.R. (1976) "Female Hormones and Behavior," in B. Lloyd, J. Archer (eds), *Exploring Sex Differences.* London and New York: Academic Press.

Mol, A. (1988) "Baarmoeder, pigment en pyramiden," *Tijdschrift voor Vrouwenstudies* 9 (3): 276–90.

Money, J., Ehrhardt, A. (1972) *Man and Woman, Boy and Girl.* Baltimore, Md.: Johns Hopkins University Press.

Rogers, L. (1976) "Male Hormones and Behaviour," B. Lloyd, J. Archer (eds), *Exploring Sex Differences.* London and New York: Academic Press.

Sayers, J. (1982) *Biological Politics: Feminist and Anti-feminist Perspectives.* New York: Tavistock.

Schiebinger, L. (1986) "Skeletons in the Closet: The First Illustrations of the Female Skeleton in the Nineteenth-Century Anatomy," *Representations* 14: 42–83.

Schiebinger, L. (1989) *The Mind Has No Sex? Women in the Origins of Modern Science.* Cambridge, Mass. and London: Harvard University Press.

Wijngaard, M. van den (1991a) "Acceptance of Scientific Theories and Images of Masculinity and Femininity," *Journal of the History of Biology* 24 (1): 19–49.

Wijngaard, M. van den (1991b) "Reinventing the Sexes: Feminism and Biomedical Construction of Femininity and Masculinity, 1959–1985," Thesis, University of Amsterdam.

Wolffers, I., Hardon, A., Janssen, J. (1989) *Marketing Fertility: Women, Menstruation and the Pharmaceutical Industry.* Amsterdam: Wemos.

Chapter 12

The Egg and the Sperm:
How Science Has Constructed a Romance
Based on Stereotypical Male–Female Roles

Emily Martin

*Emily Martin, a professor of anthropology at New York University, focuses her research on
the anthropology of science and medicine, emotion and rationality, and history of psychiatry
and psychology. She analyzes science from a feminist perspective by investigating the ways
that scientific literature is gender-biased, and how this bias becomes entrenched in language.
She has published a number of books on this topic, including her classic* The Women in the
Body: A Cultural Analysis of Reproduction.

*****

As an anthropologist, I am intrigued by the possibility that culture shapes how biological scientists describe what they discover about the natural world. [...] In the course of my research
I realized that the picture of egg and sperm drawn in popular as well as scientific accounts of
reproductive biology relies on stereotypes central to our cultural definitions of male and female.
The stereotypes imply not only that female biological processes are less worthy than their male
counterparts, but also that women are less worthy than men. Part of my goal in writing this
article is to shine a bright light on the gender stereotypes hidden within the scientific language of
biology. Exposed in such a light, I hope they will lose much of their power to harm us.

Egg and Sperm: A Scientific Fairy Tale

At a fundamental level, all major scientific textbooks depict male and female reproductive
organs as systems for the production of valuable substances, such as eggs and sperm. In the
case of women, the monthly cycle is described as being designed to produce eggs and prepare a suitable place for them to be fertilized and grown—all to the end of making babies.
But the enthusiasm ends there. By extolling the female cycle as a productive enterprise,
menstruation must necessarily be viewed as a failure. Medical texts describe menstruation as
the "debris" of the uterine lining, the result of necrosis, or death of tissue. The descriptions
imply that a system has gone awry, making products of no use, not to specification, unsal-
able, wasted, scrap. An illustration in a widely used medical text shows menstruation as a

chaotic disintegration of form, complementing the many texts that describe it as "ceasing," "dying," "losing," "denuding," "expelling."[1]

Male reproductive physiology is evaluated quite differently. One of the texts that sees menstruation as failed production employs a sort of breathless prose when it describes the maturation of sperm: "The mechanisms which guide the remarkable cellular transformation from spermatid to mature sperm remain uncertain.... Perhaps the most amazing characteristic of spermatogenesis is its sheer magnitude: the normal human male may manufacture several hundred million sperm per day."[2] In the classic text *Medical Physiology*, edited by Vernon Mountcastle, the male/female, productive/destructive comparison is more explicit: "Whereas the female *sheds* only a single gamete each month, the seminiferous tubules *produce* hundreds of millions of sperm each day" (emphasis mine).[3] The female author of another text marvels at the length of the microscopic seminiferous tubules, which, if uncoiled and placed end to end, "would span almost one-third of a mile!" She writes, "In an adult male these structures produce millions of sperm cells each day." Later she asks, "How is this feat accomplished?"[4] None of these texts expresses such intense enthusiasm for any female processes. It is surely no accident that the "remarkable" process of making sperm involves precisely what, in the medical view, menstruation does not: production of something deemed valuable.

One could argue that menstruation and spermatogenesis are not analogous processes and, therefore, should not be expected to elicit the same kind of response. The proper female analogy to spermatogenesis, biologically, is ovulation. Yet ovulation does not merit enthusiasm in these texts either. Textbook descriptions stress that all of the ovarian follicles containing ova are already present at birth. Far from being *produced*, as sperm are, they merely sit on the shelf, slowly degenerating and aging like overstocked inventory: "At birth, normal human ovaries contain an estimated one million follicles [each], and no new ones appear after birth. Thus, in marked contrast to the male, the newborn female already has all the germ cells she will ever have. Only a few, perhaps 400, are destined to reach full maturity during her active productive life. All the others degenerate at some point in their development so that few, if any, remain by the time she reaches menopause at approximately 50 years of age."[5] Note the "marked contrast" that this description sets up between male and female: the male, who continuously produces fresh germ cells, and the female, who has stockpiled germ cells by birth and is faced with their degeneration.

Nor are the female organs spared such vivid descriptions. One scientist writes in a newspaper article that a woman's ovaries become old and worn out from ripening eggs every month, even though the woman herself is still relatively young: "When you look through a laparoscope ... at an ovary that has been through hundreds of cycles, even in a superbly healthy American female, you see a scarred, battered organ."[6]

To avoid the negative connotations that some people associate with the female reproductive system, scientists could begin to describe male and female processes as homologous. They might credit females with "producing" mature ova one at a time, as they're needed each month, and describe males as having to face problems of degenerating germ cells. This degeneration would occur throughout life among spermatogonia, the undifferentiated germ cells in the testes that are the long-lived, dormant precursors of sperm.

But the texts have an almost dogged insistence on casting female processes in a negative light. The texts celebrate sperm production because it is continuous from puberty to senescence, while they portray egg production as inferior because it is finished at birth. This makes the female seem unproductive, but some texts will also insist that it is she who is wasteful. In a section heading for *Molecular Biology of the Cell*, a best-selling text, we are told that "Oogenesis is wasteful." The text goes on to emphasize that of the seven million oogonia, or egg germ cells, in the female embryo, most degenerate in the ovary. Of those that do go on to become oocytes, or eggs, many also degenerate, so that at birth only two million eggs remain in the ovaries. Degeneration continues throughout a woman's life: by puberty 300,000 eggs remain, and only a few are present by menopause. "During the 40 or so years of a woman's reproductive life, only 400 to 500 eggs will have been released," the authors write. "All the rest will have degenerated. It is still a mystery why so many eggs are formed only to die in the ovaries."[7]

The real mystery is why the male's vast production of sperm is not seen as wasteful. Assuming that a man "produces" 100 million sperm per day (a conservative estimate) during an average reproductive life of sixty years, he would produce well over two trillion sperm in his lifetime. Assuming that a woman "ripens" one egg per lunar month, or thirteen per year, over the course of her forty-year reproductive life, she would total five hundred eggs in her lifetime. But the word "waste" implies an excess, too much produced. Assuming two or three offspring, for every baby a woman produces, she wastes only around two hundred eggs. For every baby a man produces, he wastes more than one trillion sperm.

How is it that positive images are denied to the bodies of women? A look at language—in this case, scientific language—provides the first clue. Take the egg and the sperm.[8] It is remarkable how "femininely" the egg behaves and how "masculinely" the sperm.[9] The egg is seen as large and passive.[10] It does not *move* or *journey*, but passively "is transported," "is swept,"[11] or even "drifts"[12] along the fallopian tube. In utter contrast, sperm are small, "streamlined,"[13] and invariably active. They "deliver" their genes to the egg, "activate the developmental program of the egg,"[14] and have a "velocity" that is often remarked upon.[15] Their tails are "strong" and efficiently powered.[16] Together with the forces of ejaculation, they can "propel the semen into the deepest recesses of the vagina."[17] For this they need "energy," "fuel,"[18] so that with a "whiplashlike motion and strong lurches"[19] they can "burrow through the egg coat"[20] and "penetrate" it.[21]

At its extreme, the age-old relationship of the egg and the sperm takes on a royal or religious patina. The egg coat, its protective barrier, is sometimes called its "vestments," a term usually reserved for sacred, religious dress. The egg is said to have a "corona,"[22] a crown, and to be accompanied by "attendant cells."[23] It is holy, set apart and above, the queen to the sperm's king. The egg is also passive, which means it must depend on sperm for rescue. Gerald Schatten and Helen Schatten liken the egg's role to that of Sleeping Beauty: "a dormant bride awaiting her mate's magic kiss, which instills the spirit that brings her to life."[24] Sperm, by contrast, have a "mission,"[25] which is to "move through the female genital tract in quest of the ovum."[26] One popular account has it that the sperm carry out a "perilous journey" into the "warm darkness," where some fall away "exhausted." "Survivors" "assault" the egg, the successful candidates "surrounding the prize."[27] Part of the urgency of this journey, in more scientific terms, is that "once released from the supportive environment of the ovary, an egg will die within hours unless rescued by a sperm."[28] The wording stresses the fragility and dependency of the egg, even though the same text acknowledges elsewhere that sperm also live for only a few hours.[29]

*****

Social Implications: Thinking Beyond

Can we envision a less stereotypical view? Biology itself provides another model that could be applied to the egg and the sperm. The cybernetic model—with its feedback loops, flexible adaptation to change, coordination of the parts within a whole, evolution over time, and changing response to the environment—is common in genetics, endocrinology, and ecology and has a growing influence in medicine in general.[30] This model has the potential to shift our imagery from the negative, in which the female reproductive system is castigated both for not producing eggs after birth and for producing (and thus wasting) too many eggs overall, to something more positive. The female reproductive system could be seen as responding to the environment (pregnancy or menopause), adjusting to monthly changes (menstruation), and flexibly changing from reproductivity after puberty to nonreproductivity later in life. The sperm and egg's interaction could also be described in cybernetic terms. J.F. Hartman's research in reproductive biology demonstrated fifteen years ago that if an egg is killed by being pricked with a needle, live sperm cannot get through the zona.[31] Clearly, this evidence shows that the egg and sperm *do* interact on more mutual terms, making biology's refusal to portray them that way all the more disturbing.

We would do well to be aware, however, that cybernetic imagery is hardly neutral. In the past, cybernetic models have played an important part in the imposition of social control. These models inherently provide a way of thinking about a "field" of interacting components. Once the field can be seen, it can become the object of new forms of knowledge, which in turn can allow new forms of social control to be exerted over the components of the field. During the 1950s, for example, medicine began to recognize the psychosocial *environment* of the patient: the patient's family and its psychodynamics. Professions such as social work began to focus on this new environment, and the resulting knowledge became one way to further control the patient. Patients began to be seen not as isolated, individual bodies, but as psychosocial entities located in an "ecological" system: management of "the patient's psychology was a new entrée to patient control."[32]

The models that biologists use to describe their data can have important social effects. During the nineteenth century, the social and natural sciences strongly influenced each other: the social ideas of Malthus about how to avoid the natural increase of the poor inspired Darwin's *Origin of Species*.[33] Once the *Origin* stood as a description of the natural world, complete with competition and market struggles, it could be reimported into social science as social Darwinism, in order to justify the social order of the time. What we are seeing now is similar: the importation of cultural ideas about passive females and heroic males into the "personalities" of gametes. This amounts to the "implanting of social imagery on representations of nature so as to lay a firm basis for reimporting exactly that same imagery as natural explanations of social phenomena."[34]

Further research would show us exactly what social effects are being wrought from the biological imagery of egg and sperm. At the very least, the imagery keeps alive some of the hoariest old stereotypes about weak damsels in distress and their strong male rescuers. That these stereotypes are now being written in at the level of the *cell* constitutes a powerful move to make them seem so natural as to be beyond alteration.

The stereotypical imagery might also encourage people to imagine that what results from the interaction of egg and sperm—a fertilized egg—is the result of deliberate "human" action at the cellular level. Whatever the intentions of the human couple, in this microscopic "culture" a cellular "bride" (or femme fatale) and a cellular "groom" (her victim) make a cellular baby. Rosalind Petchesky points out that through visual representations such as sonograms, we are given "*images* of younger and younger, and tinier and tinier, fetuses being 'saved.'" This leads to "the point of visibility being 'pushed back' *indefinitely.*"[35] Endowing egg and sperm with intentional action, a key aspect of personhood in our culture, lays the foundation for the point of viability being pushed back to the moment of fertilization. This will likely lead to greater acceptance of technological developments and new forms of scrutiny and manipulation, for the benefit of these inner "persons": court-ordered restrictions on a pregnant woman's activities in order to protect her fetus, fetal surgery, amniocentesis, and rescinding of abortion rights, to name but a few examples.[36]

Even if we succeed in substituting more egalitarian, interactive metaphors to describe the activities of egg and sperm, and manage to avoid the pitfalls of cybernetic models, we would still be guilty of endowing cellular entities with personhood. More crucial, then, than what *kinds* of personalities we bestow on cells is the very fact that we are doing it at all. This process could ultimately have the most disturbing social consequences.

One clear feminist challenge is to wake up sleeping metaphors in science, particularly those involved in descriptions of the egg and the sperm. Although the literary convention is to call such metaphors "dead," they are not so much dead as sleeping, hidden within the scientific content of texts—and all the more powerful for it.[37] Waking up such metaphors, by becoming aware of when we are projecting cultural imagery onto what we study, will improve our ability to investigate and understand nature. Waking up such metaphors, by becoming aware of their implications, will rob them of their power to naturalize our social conventions about gender.

Notes

1. Arthur C. Guyton, *Physiology of the Human Body*, 6th ed. (Philadelphia: Saunders College Publishing, 1984), 624.
2. Arthur J. Vander, James H. Sherman, and Dorothy S. Luciano, *Human Physiology: The Mechanisms of Body Function*, 3d ed. (New York: McGraw Hill, 1980), 483–84.
3. Vernon B. Mountcastle, *Medical Physiology*, 14th ed. (London: Mosby, 1980), 2:1624.
4. Eldra Pearl Solomon, *Human Anatomy and Physiology* (New York: CBS College Publishing, 1983), 678.
5. Vander, Sherman, and Luciano (n. 2 above), 568.
6. Melvin Kanner, "Childbearing and Age," *New York Times Magazine* (December 27, 1987), 22–23, esp. 22.
7. Bruce Alberts et al., *Molecular Biology of the Cell* (New York: Garland, 1983), 795.
8. For a newspaper report, see Malcolm W. Browne, "Some Thoughts on Self Sacrifice," *New York Times* (July 5, 1988), C6. For a literary rendition, see John Barth, "Night-Sea Journey," in his *Lost in the Funhouse* (Garden City, N.Y.: Doubleday, 1968), 3–13.
9. Carol Delaney, "The Meaning of Paternity and the Virgin Birth Debate," *Man* 21, no. 3 (September 1986): 494–513.
10. Erik H. Erikson, "Inner and Outer Space: Reflections on Womanhood," *Daedalus* 93, no. 2 (Spring 1964): 582–606, esp. 591.
11. Guyton (n. 1 above), 619; and Mountcastle (n. 3 above), 1609.
12. Jonathan Miller and David Pelham, *The Facts of Life* (New York: Viking Penguin, 1984), 5.
13. Alberts et al. (n. 7 above), 796.
14. Ibid., 796.
15. See, e.g., William F. Ganong, *Review of Medical Physiology*, 7th ed. (Los Altos, Calif.: Lange Medical Publications, 1975), 322.
16. Alberts et al., 796.
17. Guyton, 615.
18. Solomon (n. 4 above), 683.
19. Vander, Sherman, and Luciano, 4th ed. (1985), 580.

20. Alberts et al., 796.

21. All biology texts quoted above use the word "penetrate."

22. Solomon, 700.

23. A. Beldecos et al., "The Importance of Feminist Critique for Contemporary Cell Biology," *Hypatia* 3, no. 1 (Spring 1988): 61–76.

24. Gerald Schatten and Helen Schatten, "The Energetic Egg," *Medical World News* 23 (January 23, 1984): 51–53, esp. 51.

25. Alberts et al., 796.

26. Guyton, 613.

27. Miller and Pelham (n. 12 above), 7.

28. Alberts et al., 804.

29. Ibid., 801.

30. William Ray Arney and Bernard Bergen, *Medicine and the Management of Living* (Chicago: University of Chicago Press, 1984).

31. J.F. Hartman, R.B. Gwatkin, and C.F. Hutchison, "Early Contact Interactions between Mammalian Gametes *In Vitro*," *Proceedings of the National Academy of Sciences (U.S.)* 69, no. 10 (1972): 2767–69.

32. Arney and Bergen, 68.

33. Ruth Hubbard, "Have Only Men Evolved?", 51–52, in *Discovering Reality: Feminist Perspectives on Epistemology, Metaphysics, Methodology, and Philosophy of Science*, ed. Sandra Harding and Merrill B. Hintikka (Dordrecht: Reidel, 1983).

34. David Harvey, personal communication, November 1989.

35. Rosalind Petchesky, "Fetal Images: The Power of Visual Culture in the Politics of Reproduction," *Feminist Studies* 13, no. 2 (Summer 1987): 263–92, esp. 272.

36. Rita Arditti, Renate Klein, and Shelley Minden, *Test-Tube Women* (London: Pandora, 1984); Ellen Goodman, "Whose Right to Life?" *Baltimore Sun* (November 17, 1987); Tamar Lewin, "Courts Acting to Force Care of the Unborn," *New York Times* (November 23, 1987), A1 and B10; Susan Irwin and Brigitte Jordan, "Knowledge, Practice, and Power: Court Ordered Cesarean Sections," *Medical Anthropology Quarterly* 1, no. 3 (September 1987): 319–34.

37. Thanks to Elizabeth Fee and David Spain, who in February 1989 and April 1989, respectively, made points related to this.

Where's the Rulebook for Sex Verification?

Alice Dreger

Alice Dreger is a noted historian, writer, and patient advocate. She is a professor of clinical medical humanities and bioethics at Northwestern University's Feinberg School of Medicine. Through her publications and years of association with the Intersex Society of North America (ISNA), she has played a central role in policy development and advocacy for intersex rights and medical reform.

The only thing we know for sure about Caster Semenya, the world-champion runner from South Africa, is that she will live the rest of her life under a cloud of suspicion after track and field's governing body announced it was investigating her sex.

The IAAF's process for determining whether Caster Semenya [...] is a woman will involve at least a geneticist, an endocrinologist, a gynecologist and a psychologist.

Why? Because the track organization, the IAAF, has not sorted out the rules for sex typing and is relying on unstated, shifting standards.

To be fair, the biology of sex is a lot more complicated than the average fan believes. Many think you can simply look at a person's "sex chromosomes." If the person has XY chromosomes, you declare him a man. If XX, she's a woman. Right?

Wrong. A little biology: On the Y chromosome, a gene called SRY usually makes a fetus grow as a male. It turns out, though, that SRY can show up on an X, turning an XX fetus essentially male. And if the SRY gene does not work on the Y, the fetus develops essentially female.

Even an XY fetus with a functioning SRY can essentially develop female. In the case of Androgen Insensitivity Syndrome, the ability of cells to "hear" the masculinizing hormones known as androgens is lacking. That means the genitals and the rest of the external body look female-typical, except that these women lack body hair (which depends on androgen-sensitivity).

Women with complete Androgen Insensitivity Syndrome are less "masculinized" in their muscles and brains than the average woman, because the average woman makes and "hears" some androgens. Want to tell women with Androgen Insensitivity Syndrome they have to compete as men, just because they have a Y chromosome? That makes no sense.

So, some say, just look at genitals. Forget the genes—pull down the jeans! The IAAF asks drug testers to do this. But because male and female genitals start from the same stuff, a person can have something between a penis and a clitoris, and still legitimately be thought of as a man or a woman.

Moreover, a person can look male-typical on the outside but be female-typical on the inside, or vice versa. A few years ago, I got a call from Matthew, a 19-year-old who was born looking obviously male, was raised a boy, and had a girlfriend and a male-typical life. Then he found out, by way of some medical problems, that he had ovaries and a uterus.

Matthew had an extreme form of Congenital Adrenal Hyperplasia. His adrenal glands made so many androgens, even though he had XX chromosomes and ovaries, that his body developed to look male-typical. In fact, his body is mostly male-typical, including his muscle development and his self identity.

OK, you say, if chromosomes and genitals do not work, how about hormones? We might assume that it is hormones that really matter in terms of whether someone has an athletic advantage.

Well, women and men make the same hormones, just in different quantities, on average. The average man has more androgens than the average woman. But to state the obvious, the average female athlete is not the average woman. In some sports, she is likely to have naturally high levels of androgens. That is probably part of why she has succeeded athletically.

By the way, that is also why she is often flat-chested, boyish looking and may have a bigger-than-average clitoris. High levels of androgens can do all that.

Sure, in certain sports, a woman with naturally high levels of androgens has an advantage. But is it an unfair advantage? I don't think so. Some men naturally have higher levels of androgens than other men. Is that unfair?

Consider an analogy: Men on average are taller than women. But do we stop women from competing if a male-typical height gives them an advantage over shorter women? Can we imagine a Michele Phelps or a Patricia Ewing being told, "You're too tall to compete as a woman"? So why would we want to tell some women, "You naturally have too high a level of androgens to compete as a woman"? There seems to be nothing wrong with this kind of natural advantage.

So where do we draw the line between men and women in athletics? I don't know. The fact is, sex is messy. This is demonstrated in the IAAF's process for determining whether Semenya is in fact a woman. The organization has called upon a geneticist, an endocrinologist, a gynecologist, a psychologist and so forth.

Sex is so messy that in the end, these doctors are not going to be able to run a test that will answer the question. Science can and will inform their decision, but they are going to have to decide which of the dozens of characteristics of sex matter to them.

Their decision will be like the consensus regarding how many points are awarded for a touchdown and a field goal—it will be a sporting decision, not a natural one, about how we choose to play the game of sex.

These officials should—finally—come up with a clear set of rules for sex typing, one open to scientific review, one that will allow athletes like Semenya, in the privacy of their doctors' offices, to find out, before publicly competing, whether they will be allowed to win in the crazy sport of sex. I bet that's a sport no one ever told Semenya she would have to play.

Source: Alice Dreger, "Where's the Rulebook for Sex Verification?" *New York Times*, August 21, 2009, retrieved from http://www.nytimes.com/2009/08/22/sports/22runner.html

Chapter 13

Dueling Dualisms

Anne Fausto-Sterling

Anne Fausto-Sterling is the Nancy Duke Lewis professor of biology and gender studies in the Department of Molecular and Cell Biology and Biochemistry at Brown University. One of the world's leading researchers on the development of sexual identity and the biology of gender, her trail-breaking works on gender and sexuality include Myths of Gender *and* Sexing the Body: Gender Politics and the Construction of Sexuality *(excerpted below).*

Male or Female?

In the rush and excitement of leaving for the 1988 Olympics, Maria Patiño, Spain's top woman hurdler, forgot the requisite doctor's certificate stating, for the benefit of Olympic officials, what seemed patently obvious to anyone who looked at her: she was female. But the International Olympic Committee (IOC) had anticipated the possibility that some competitors would forget their certificates of femininity. Patiño had only to report to the "femininity control head office,"[1] scrape some cells off the side of her cheek, and all would be in order—or so she thought.

A few hours after the cheek scraping she got a call. Something was wrong. She went for a second examination, but the doctors were mum. Then, as she rode to the Olympic stadium to start her first race, track officials broke the news: she had failed the sex test. She may have looked like a woman, had a woman's strength, and never had reason to suspect that she wasn't a woman, but the examinations revealed that Patiño's cells sported a Y chromosome, and that her labia hid testes within. Furthermore, she had neither ovaries nor a uterus. According to the IOC's definition, Patiño was not a woman. She was barred from competing on Spain's Olympic team.

Spanish athletic officials told Patiño to fake an injury and withdraw without publicizing the embarrassing facts. When she refused, the European press heard about it and the secret was out. Within months after returning to Spain, Patiño's life fell apart. Spanish officials stripped her of past titles and barred her from further competition. Her boyfriend deserted her. She was evicted from the national athletic residence, her scholarship was revoked, and suddenly she had to struggle to make a living. The national press had a field day at her expense. As she later said, "I was erased from the map, as if I had never existed. I gave twelve years to sports."[2]

Down but not out, Patiño spent thousands of dollars consulting doctors about her situation. They explained that she had been born with a condition called *androgen insensitivity*. This meant that, although she had a Y chromosome and her testes made plenty of testosterone, her cells couldn't detect this masculinizing hormone. As a result, her body had never developed male characteristics. But at puberty her testes produced estrogen (as do the testes of all men), which, because of her body's inability to respond to its testosterone, caused her breasts to grow, her waist to narrow, and her hips to widen. Despite a Y chromosome and testes, she had grown up as a female and developed a female form.

Patiño resolved to fight the IOC ruling. "I knew I was a woman," she insisted to one reporter, "in the eyes of medicine, God and most of all, in my own eyes."[3] [...] After two and a half years the International Amateur Athletic Federation (IAAF) reinstated her, and by 1992 Patiño had rejoined the Spanish Olympic squad, going down in history as the first woman ever to challenge sex testing for female athletes. Despite the IAAF's flexibility, however, the IOC has remained adamant: even if looking for a Y chromosome wasn't the most scientific approach to sex testing, testing *must* be done.

*****

Sex or Gender?

Until 1968 female Olympic competitors were often asked to parade naked in front of a board of examiners. Breasts and a vagina were all one needed to certify one's femininity. But many women complained that this procedure was degrading. Partly because such complaints mounted, the IOC decided to make use of the modern "scientific" chromosome test. The problem, though, is that this test, and the more sophisticated polymerase chain reaction to detect small regions of DNA associated with testes development that the IOC uses today, cannot do the work the IOC wants it to do. A body's sex is simply too complex. There is no either/or. Rather, there are shades of difference. [...] One of the major claims I make [...] is that labeling someone a man or a woman is a social decision. We may use scientific knowledge to help us make the decision, but only our beliefs about gender—not science—can define our sex. Furthermore, our beliefs about gender affect what kinds of knowledge scientists produce about sex in the first place.

Over the last few decades, the relation between *social expression* of masculinity and femininity and their *physical underpinnings* has been hotly debated in scientific and social arenas. In 1972 the sexologists John Money and Anke Ehrhardt popularized the idea that sex and gender are separate categories. *Sex*, they argued, refers to physical attributes and is anatomically and physiologically determined. *Gender* they saw as a psychological transformation of the self—the internal conviction that one is either male or female (gender identity) and the behavioral expressions of that conviction.[4]

Meanwhile, the second-wave feminists of the 1970s also argued that sex is distinct from gender—that social institutions, themselves designed to perpetuate gender inequality, produce most of the differences between men and women.[5] Feminists argued that although men's and women's bodies serve different reproductive functions, few other sex differences come with the territory, unchangeable by life's vicissitudes. If girls couldn't learn math as easily as boys, the problem wasn't built into their brains. The difficulty resulted from gender norms—different expectations and opportunities for boys and girls. Having a penis rather than a vagina is a sex difference. Boys performing better than girls on math exams is a gender difference. Presumably, the latter could be changed even if the former could not.

Money, Ehrhardt, and feminists set the terms so that *sex* represented the body's anatomy and physiological workings and *gender* represented social forces that molded behavior. Feminists did not question the realm of physical sex; it was the psychological and cultural meanings of these differences—gender—that was at issue. But feminist definitions of sex and gender left open the possibility that male/female differences in cognitive function and behavior could *result* from sex differences, and thus, in some circles, the matter of sex versus gender became a debate about how "hardwired" intelligence and a variety of behaviors are in the brain, while in others there seemed no choice but to ignore many of the findings of contemporary neurobiology.

In ceding the territory of physical sex, feminists left themselves open to renewed attack on the grounds of biological difference. Indeed, feminism has encountered massive resistance from the domains of biology, medicine, and significant components of social science. Despite many positive social changes, the 1970s optimism that women would achieve full economic and social equality once gender inequity was addressed in the social sphere has faded in the face of a seemingly recalcitrant inequality.[6] All of which has prompted feminist scholars, on the one hand, to question the notion of sex itself,[7] while on the other to deepen their inquiry into what we might mean by words such as *gender*, *culture*, and *experience*. The anthropologist Henrietta A. Moore, for example, argues against reducing accounts of gender, culture, and experience to their "linguistic and cognitive elements." [...] I argue, as does Moore, that "what is at issue is the embodied nature of identities and experience. Experience ... is not individual and fixed, but irredeemably social and processual."[8]

Our bodies are too complex to provide clear cut answers about sexual difference. The more we look for a simple physical basis for "sex," the more it becomes clear that "sex" is not a pure physical category. What bodily signals and functions we define as male or female come already entangled in our ideas about gender. Consider the problem facing the International Olympic Committee. Committee members want to decide definitively who is male and female. But how? [...] Could the IOC use muscle strength as some measure of sex? In some cases. But the strength of men and women, especially highly trained athletes, overlap. [...] And although Maria Patiño fit a commonsense definition of femininity in terms of looks and strength, she also had testes and a Y chromosome. But why should these be the deciding factors?

The IOC may use chromosome or DNA tests or inspection of the breasts and genitals to ascertain the sex of a competitor, but doctors faced with uncertainty about a child's sex use different criteria. They focus primarily on reproductive abilities (in the case of a potential girl) or penis size (in the case of a prospective boy). If a child is born with two X chromosomes, oviducts, ovaries, and a uterus on the inside, but a penis and scrotum on the outside, for instance, is the child a boy or a girl? Most doctors declare the child a girl, despite the penis, because of her potential to give birth, and intervene using surgery and hormones to carry out the decision. Choosing which criteria to use in determining sex, and choosing to make the determination at all, are social decisions for which scientists can offer no absolute guidelines.

Real or Constructed?

I enter the debates about sex and gender as a biologist and a social activist. Daily, my life weaves in and out of a web of conflict over the politics of sexuality and the making and using of knowledge about the biology of human behavior. [...] Truths about human sexuality created by scholars in general and by biologists in particular are one component of political, social, and moral struggles about our cultures and economies. At the same time, components of our political, social, and moral struggles become, quite literally, embodied, incorporated into our very physiological being. My intent is to show how these mutually dependent claims work, in part by addressing such issues as how—through their daily lives, experiments, and medical practices— scientists create truths about sexuality; how our bodies incorporate and confirm these truths; and how these truths, sculpted by the social milieu in which biologists practice their trade, in turn refashion our cultural environment.

My take on the problem is idiosyncratic, and for good reason. Intellectually, I inhabit three seemingly incompatible worlds. In my home department I interact with molecular biologists, scientists who examine living beings from the perspective of the molecules from which they are built. They describe a microscopic world in which cause and effect remain mostly inside a single cell. Molecular biologists rarely think about interacting organs within an individual body, and even less about how a body bounded by skin interacts with the world on the other side of the skin. Their vision of what makes an organism tick is decidedly bottom up, small to large, inside to outside.

I also interact with a virtual community—a group of scholars drawn together by a common interest in sexuality—and connected by something called a listserve. On a listserve, one can pose questions, think out loud, comment on relevant news items, argue about theories of human sexuality, and report the latest research findings. The comments are read by a group of people hooked together via electronic mail. My listserve (which I call "Loveweb") consists of a diverse group of scholars—psychologists, animal behaviorists, hormone biologists, sociologists, anthropologists, and philosophers. Although many points of view coexist in this group, the vocal majority favor body-based, biological explanations of human sexual behavior. [...]

Unlike molecular biologists and Loveweb members, feminist theorists view the body not as essence, but as a bare scaffolding on which discourse and performance build a completely acculturated being. Feminist theorists write persuasively and often imaginatively about the processes by which culture molds and effectively creates the body. Furthermore, they have an eye on politics (writ large), which neither molecular biologists nor Loveweb participants have. Most feminist scholars concern themselves with real-world power relationships. They have often come to their theoretical work because they want to understand (and change) social, political, and economic inequality. Unlike the inhabitants of my other two worlds, feminist theorists reject what Donna Haraway, a leading feminist theoretician, calls "the God-trick"—producing knowledge from above, from a place that denies the individual scholar's location in a real and troubled world. Instead, they understand that all scholarship adds threads to a web that positions racialized bodies, sexes, genders, and preferences in relationship to one another. New or differently spun threads change our relationships, change how we are in the world.

Traveling among these varied intellectual worlds produces more than a little discomfort. When I lurk on Loveweb, I put up with gratuitous feminist-bashing aimed at some mythic feminist who derides biology and seems to have a patently stupid view of how the world works. When I attend feminist conferences, people howl in disbelief at the ideas debated on Loveweb. And the molecular biologists don't think much of either of the other worlds. The questions asked by feminists and Loveweb participants seem too complicated; studying sex in bacteria or yeast is the only way to go.

To my molecular biology, Loveweb, and feminist colleagues, then, I say the following: as a biologist, I believe in the material world. As a scientist, I believe in building specific knowledge by conducting experiments. But as a feminist Witness (in the Quaker sense of the word) and in recent years as a historian, I also believe that what we call "facts" about the living world are not universal truths. Rather, as Haraway writes, they "are rooted in specific histories, practices, languages and peoples."[9] Ever since the field of biology emerged in the United States and Europe at the start of the nineteenth century, it has been bound up in debates over sexual, racial, and national politics. And as our social viewpoints have shifted, so has the science of the body.

Many historians mark the seventeenth and eighteenth centuries as periods of great change in our concepts of sex and sexuality.[10] During this period a notion of legal equality replaced the feudal exercise of arbitrary and violent power given by divine right. As the historian Michel Foucault saw it, society still required some form of discipline. A growing capitalism needed new methods to control the "insertion of bodies into the machinery of production and the adjustment of the phenomena of population to economic processes."[11] Foucault divided this power over living bodies (*bio-power*) into two forms. The first centered on the individual body. The role of many science professionals (including the so-called human sciences—psychology, sociology, and economics) became to optimize and standardize the body's function.[12] In Europe and North America, Foucault's standardized body has, traditionally, been male and Caucasian. And although this book focuses on gender, I regularly discuss the ways in which the ideas of both race and gender emerge from underlying assumptions about the body's physical nature. Understanding how race and gender work—together and independently—helps us learn more about how the social becomes embodied.

Foucault's second form of bio-power—"*a biopolitics of the population*"[13]—emerged during the early nineteenth century as pioneer social scientists began to develop the survey and statistical methods needed to supervise and manage "births and mortality, the level of health, life expectancy and longevity."[14] For Foucault, "discipline" had a double meaning. On the one hand, it implied a form of control or punishment; on the other, it referred to an academic body of knowledge—the discipline of history or biology. The disciplinary knowledge developed in the fields of embryology, endocrinology, surgery, psychology, and biochemistry have encouraged physicians to attempt to control the very gender of the body—including "its capacities, gestures, movements, location and behaviors."[15]

By helping the normal take precedence over the natural, physicians have also contributed to populational biopolitics. We have become, Foucault writes, "a society of normalization."[16] One important mid-twentieth-century sexologist went so far as to name the male and female models in his anatomy text Norma and Normman [*sic*].[17] Today we see the notion of pathology applied in many settings—from the sick, diseased, or different body, to the single-parent family in the urban ghetto. But imposing a gender norm is socially, not scientifically, driven. The lack of research into the normal distributions of genital anatomy, as well as many surgeons' lack of interest in using such data when they do exist [...], clearly illustrate this claim. From the viewpoint of medical practitioners, progress in the handling of intersexuality involves maintaining the normal. Accordingly, there *ought* to be only two boxes: male and female. The knowledge developed by the medical disciplines empowers doctors to maintain a mythology of the normal by changing the intersexual body to fit, as nearly as possible, into one or the other cubbyhole.

One person's medical progress, however, can be another's discipline and control. Intersexuals such as Maria Patiño have unruly—even heretical—bodies. They do not fall naturally into a binary classification; only a surgical shoehorn can put them there. But why should we care if a "woman" (defined as having breasts, a vagina, uterus, ovaries, and menstruation) has a "clitoris" large enough to penetrate the vagina of another woman? Why should we care if there are individuals whose "natural biological equipment" enables them to have sex "naturally" with both men and women? Why must we amputate or surgically hide that "offending shaft" found on an especially large clitoris? The answer: to maintain gender divisions, we must control those bodies that are so unruly as to blur the borders. Since intersexuals quite literally embody both sexes, they weaken claims about sexual difference.

*****

[…] Euro-American ways of understanding how the world works depend heavily on the use of dualisms—pairs of opposing concepts, objects, or belief systems.

*****

Why worry about using dualisms to parse the world? I agree with the philosopher Val Plumwood, who argues that their use makes invisible the interdependencies of each pair. This relationship enables sets of pairs to map onto each other. Consider an extract of Plumwood's list:

Reason	Nature
Male	Female
Mind	Body
Master	Slave
Freedom	Necessity (nature)
Human	Nature (nonhuman)
Civilized	Primitive
Production	Reproduction
Self	Other

In everyday use, the sets of associations on each side of the list often run together. "Culture," Plumwood writes, accumulates these dualisms as a store of weapons "which can be mined, refined and redeployed. Old oppressions stored as dualisms facilitate and break the path for new ones."[18] For this reason, even though my focus is on gender, I do not hesitate to point out occasions in which the constructs and ideology of race intersect with those of gender.

Ultimately, the sex/gender dualism limits feminist analysis. The term *gender*, placed in a dichotomy, necessarily excludes biology. As the feminist theorist Elizabeth Wilson writes: "Feminist critiques of the stomach or hormonal structure … have been rendered unthinkable."[19] […] Such critiques remain unthinkable because of the real/constructed divide (sometimes formulated as a division between nature and culture), in which many map the knowledge of the real onto the domain of science (equating the constructed with the cultural). Dichotomous formulations from feminists and nonfeminists alike conspire to make a sociocultural analysis of the body seem impossible.

Some feminist theorists, especially during the last decade, have tried—with varying degrees of success—to create a nondualistic account of the body. Judith Butler, for example, tries to reclaim the material body for feminist thought. Why, she wonders, has the idea of materiality come to signify that which is irreducible, that which can support construction but cannot itself be constructed?[20] We have, Butler says (and I agree), to talk about the material body. There *are* hormones, genes, prostates, uteri, and other body parts and physiologies that we use to differentiate male from female, that become part of the ground from which varieties of sexual experience and desire emerge. Furthermore, variations in each of these aspects of physiology profoundly affect an individual's experience of gender and sexuality. But every time we try to return to the body as something that exists prior to socialization, prior to discourse about male and female, Butler writes, "we discover that matter is fully sedimented with discourses on sex and sexuality that prefigure and constrain the uses to which that term can be put."[21]

Western notions of matter and bodily materiality, Butler argues, have been constructed through a "gendered matrix." That classical philosophers associated femininity with materiality can be seen in the origins of the word itself. "Matter" [is] derived from *mater* and *matrix*, referring to the womb and problems of reproduction. In both Greek and Latin, according to Butler, matter was not understood to be a blank slate awaiting the application of external meaning. "The matrix is a ... formative principle which inaugurates and informs a development of some organism or object ... for Aristotle, 'matter is potentiality, form actuality.' ... In reproduction women are said to contribute the matter, men the form."[22] As Butler notes, the title of her book, *Bodies That Matter*, is a well thought-out pun. To be material is to speak about the process of materialization. And if viewpoints about sex and sexuality are already embedded in our philosophical concepts of how matter forms into bodies, the matter of bodies cannot form a neutral, pre-existing ground from which to understand the origin of sexual difference.

Since matter already contains notions of gender and sexuality, it cannot be a neutral recourse on which to build "scientific" or "objective" theories of sexual development and differentiation. At the same time, we have to acknowledge and use aspects of materiality "that pertain to the body." "The domains of biology, anatomy, physiology, hormonal and chemical composition, illness, age, weight, metabolism, life and death" cannot "be denied."[23] The critical theorist Bernice Hausman concretizes this point in her discussion of surgical technologies available for creating male-to-female versus female-to-male transsexual bodies. "The differences," she writes, "between vagina and penis are not merely ideological. Any attempt to engage and decode the semiotics of sex ... must acknowledge that these physiological signifiers have functions in the real that will escape ... their function in the symbolic system."[24]

To talk about human sexuality requires a notion of the material. Yet the idea of the material comes to us already tainted, containing within it pre-existing ideas about sexual difference. Butler suggests that we look at the body as a system that simultaneously produces and is produced by social meanings, just as any biological organism always results from the combined and simultaneous actions of nature and nurture.

Unlike Butler, the feminist philosopher Elizabeth Grosz allows some biological processes a status that pre-exists their meaning. She believes that biological instincts or drives provide a kind of raw material for the development of sexuality. But raw materials are never enough. They must be provided with a set of meanings, "a network of desires"[25] that organize the meaning and consciousness of the child's bodily functions. This claim becomes clear if one follows the stories of so-called wild children raised without human constraints or the inculcation of meaning. Such children acquire neither language nor sexual drive. While their bodies provided the raw materials, without a human social setting the clay could not be molded into recognizable psychic form. Without human sociality, human sexuality cannot develop. Grosz tries to understand how human sociality and meaning that clearly originate outside the body end up incorporated into its physiological demeanor and both unconscious and conscious behaviors.

Some concrete examples will help illustrate. A tiny gray-haired woman, well into her ninth decade, peers into the mirror at her wrinkled face. "Who is that woman?" she wonders. Her mind's image of her body does not synchronize with the mirror's reflection. Her daughter, now in her mid-fifties, tries to remember that unless she thinks about using her leg muscles instead of her knee joint, going up and down the stairs will be painful. (Eventually she will acquire a new kinesic habit and dispense with conscious thought about the matter.) Both women are readjusting the visual and kinesic components of their body image, formed on the basis of past information, but always a bit out of date with the current physical body. How do such readjustments occur, and how do our earliest body images form in the first place? Here we need the concept of the psyche, a place where two-way translations between the mind and the body take place—a United Nations, as it were, of bodies and experiences.

Figure 13.1: Möbius Strip

Source: Courtesy of John Harrison.

In *Volatile Bodies*, Elizabeth Grosz considers how the body and the mind come into being together. To facilitate her project, she invokes the image of a Möbius strip as a metaphor for the psyche. The Möbius strip is a topological puzzle (Figure 13.1), a flat ribbon twisted once and then attached end to end to form a circular twisted surface. One can trace the surface, for example, by imagining an ant walking along it. At the beginning of the circular journey, the ant is clearly on the outside. But as it traverses the twisted ribbon, without ever lifting its legs from the plane, it ends up on the inside surface. Grosz proposes that we think of the body—the brain, muscles, sex organs, hormones, and more—as composing the inside of the Möbius strip. Culture and experience would constitute the outside surface. But, as the image suggests, the inside and outside are continuous and one can move from one to the other without ever lifting one's feet off the ground.

As Grosz recounts, psychoanalysts and phenomenologists describe the body in terms of feelings.[26] The mind translates physiology into an interior sense of self. Oral sexuality, for example, is a physical feeling that a child and later an adult translates into psychosexual meaning. This translation takes place on the inside of the Möbius surface. But as one traces the surface toward the outside, one begins to speak in terms of connections to other bodies and objects—things that are clearly not-self. Grosz writes, "Instead of describing the oral drive in terms of what it feels like … orality can be understood in terms of what it does: creating linkages. The child's lips, for example, form connections … with the breast or bottle, possibly accompanied by the hand in conjunction with an ear, each system in perpetual motion and in mutual interrelation."[27]

Continuing with the Möbius analogy, Grosz envisions that bodies create psyches by using the libido as a marker pen to trace a path from biological processes to an interior structure of desire. It falls to a different arena of scholarship to study the "outside" of the strip, a more obviously social surface marked by "pedagogical, juridical, medical, and economic texts, laws, and practices" in order to "carve out a social subject … capable of labor, or production and manipulation, a subject capable of acting as a subject."[28] Thus Grosz also rejects a nature versus nurture model of human development. While acknowledging that we do not understand the range and limits of the body's pliability, she insists that we cannot merely "subtract the environment, culture, history" and end up with "nature or biology."

Beyond Dualisms

Grosz postulates innate drives that become organized by physical experience into somatic feelings, which translate into what we call emotions. Taking the innate at face value, however, still leaves us with an unexplained residue of nature. Humans are biological and thus in some sense natural beings *and* social and in some sense artificial—or, if you will, constructed entities. Can we devise a way of seeing ourselves, as we develop from fertilization to old age, as simultaneously natural and unnatural? During the past decade an exciting vision has emerged that I have loosely grouped under the rubric of developmental systems theory, or DST. What do we gain by choosing DST as an analytic framework?

Developmental systems theorists deny that there are fundamentally two kinds of processes: one guided by genes, hormones, and brain cells (that is, nature), the other by the environment, experience, learning, or inchoate social forces (that is, nurture). The pioneer systems theorist, philosopher Susan Oyama, promises that DST "gives more clarity, more coherence, more consistency and a different way to interpret data; in addition it offers the means for synthesizing the concepts and methods ... of groups that have been working at cross-purposes, or at least talking past each other for decades." Nevertheless, developmental systems theory is no magic bullet. Many will resist its insights because, as Oyama explains, "it gives less ... guidance on fundamental truth" and "fewer conclusions about what is inherently desirable, healthy, natural or inevitable."[29]

How, specifically, can DST help us break away from dualistic thought processes? Consider an example described by systems theorist Peter Taylor: a goat born with no front legs. During its lifetime it managed to hop around on it hind limbs. An anatomist who studied the goat after it died found that it had an S-shaped spine (as do humans), "thickened bones, modified muscle insertions, and other correlates of moving on two legs."[30] This (and every goat's) skeletal system developed as part of its manner of walking. Neither its genes nor its environment determined its anatomy. Only the ensemble had such power. Many developmental physiologists recognize this principle. As one biologist writes, "enstructuring occurs during the enactment of individual life histories."[31]

A few years ago, when the neuroscientist Simon LeVay reported that the brain structures of gay and heterosexual men differed (and that this mirrored a more general sex difference between straight men and women), he became the center of a firestorm.[32] Although an instant hero among many gay males, he was at odds with a rather mixed group. On the one hand, feminists such as myself disliked his unquestioning use of gender dichotomies, which have in the past never worked to further equality for women. On the other, members of the Christian right hated his work because they believe that homosexuality is a sin that individuals can choose to reject. LeVay's, and later geneticist Dean Hamer's, work suggested to them that homosexuality was inborn or innate.[33] The language of the public debate soon became polarized. Each side contrasted words such as *generic, biological, inborn, innate,* and *unchanging* with *environmental, acquired, constructed,* and *choice.*

The ease with which such debates evoke the nature/nurture divide is a consequence of the poverty of a nonsystems approach. Politically, the nature/nurture framework holds enormous dangers. Although some hope that a belief in the nature side of things will lead to greater tolerance, past history suggests that the opposite is also possible. Even the scientific architects of the nature argument recognize the dangers. In an extraordinary passage in the pages of *Science,* Dean Hamer and his collaborators indicated their concern: "It would be fundamentally unethical to use such information to try to assess or alter a person's current or future sexual orientation. Rather, scientists, educators, policy-makers and the public should work together to ensure that such research is used to benefit all members of society."[34]

The feminist psychologist and critical theorist Elisabeth Wilson uses the hubbub over LeVay's work to make some important points about systems theory. Many feminist, queer, and critical theorists work by deliberately displacing biology, hence opening the body to social and cultural shaping. This, however, is the wrong move to make. Wilson writes: "What may be politically and critically contentious in LeVay's hypothesis is not the conjunction neurology-sexuality per se, but the particular manner in which such a conjunction is enacted."[35] An effective political response, she continues, doesn't have to separate the study of sexuality from the neurosciences. Instead, Wilson, who wants us to develop a theory of mind and body—an account of psyche that joins libido to body—suggests that feminists incorporate into their worldview an account of how the brain works that is, broadly speaking, called connectionism.

The old-fashioned approach to understanding the brain was anatomical. Function could be located in particular parts of the brain. Ultimately function and anatomy were one. [...] Many scientists [still] believe that a structural difference represents the brain location for measured behavioral differences. In contrast, connectionist models argue that function emerges from the complexity and strength of many neural connections acting at once. The system has some important characteristics: the responses are often nonlinear, the networks can be "trained" to respond in particular ways, the nature of the response is not easily predictable, and information is not located anywhere—rather, it is the net result of the many different connections and their differing strengths.

The tenets of some connectionist theory provide interesting starting points for understanding human sexual development. Because connectionist networks, for example, are usually nonlinear, small changes can produce large effects. One implication for studying sexuality: we could easily be looking in the wrong places and on the wrong scale for aspects of the environment that shape human development. Furthermore, a single behavior may have many underlying causes, events that happen at different times in development. I suspect that our labels of homosexual, heterosexual, bisexual, and transgender are really not good categories at all, and are best understood only in terms of unique developmental events affecting particular individuals. Thus, I agree with those connectionists who argue that "the developmental process itself lies at the heart of knowledge acquisition. Development is a process of emergence."[36]

In most public and most scientific discussions, sex and nature are thought to be real, while gender and culture are seen as constructed. But these are false dichotomies.

*****

Notes

We have cut extensively the notes and references, which were lengthy in the original.

1. Hanley 1983.
2. Quoted in Carlson 1991, p. 27.
3. Ibid. The technical name for Patiño's condition is Androgen Insensitivity Syndrome. It is one of a number of conditions that leads to bodies having mixtures of male and female parts. Today we call such bodies *intersexes*.
4. [...] Money and Ehrhardt 1972, p. 4. [...]
5. See, for example, Rubin 1975. Rubin also questions the biological basis of homosexuality and heterosexuality. Note that feminist definitions of gender applied to institutions as well as personal or psychological differences.
6. For a discussion of this recalcitrance in terms of gender schema in adulthood, see Valian 1998a, 1998b.
7. [...] Feinberg 1996; Kessler and McKenna 1978; Haraway 1989, 1997; Hausman 1995; Rothblatt 1995; Burke 1996; and Dreger 1998. [...]

8. Moore 1994, pp. 2–3.

9. Haraway 1997, p. 217. See also Foucault 1970; Gould 1981, Schiebinger 1993a, 1993b.

10. During this time, Foucault maintains, the change from Feudalism to Capitalism required a new concept of the body. Feudal lords applied their power directly. Peasants and serfs obeyed because God and their sovereign told them to (except, of course, when they revolted, as they did from time to time). The punishment for disobedience was, to the modern eye, violent and brutal: drawing and quartering. For a stunning description of this brutality, see the opening chapters of Foucault 1979.

11. Foucault 1978, p. 141.

12. These efforts created "an *anatomo-politics of the human body*" (Foucault 1978, p. 139; emphasis in the original).

13. Foucault 1978, p. 139; emphasis in the original.

14. Ibid. [...]

15. Sawicki 1991, p. 67. [...]

16. Foucault 1980, p. 107.

17. Quoted in Moore and Clarke 1995, p. 271.

18. Plumwood 1993, p. 43. Plumwood also argues that dualisms "result from a certain kind of denied dependency on a subordinated other." The denial, combined with a relationship of domination and subordination, shape the identity of each side of the dualism (ibid., p. 41). [...]

19. Wilson 1998, p. 55.

20. In her words she "wants to ask how and why 'materiality' has become a sign of irreducibility, that is, how is it that the materiality of sex is understood as that which only bears cultural constructions and, therefore, cannot be a construction" (Butler 1993, p. 28).

21. Ibid., p. 29.

22. Ibid., p. 31.

23. Ibid., p. 66.

24. Hausman 1995, p. 69.

25. Grosz 1994, p. 55.

26. Phenomenology is a field that studies the body as an active participant in the creation of self. [...]

27. Grosz 1994, p. 116.

28. Ibid., p. 117. [...]

29. Oyama 1985, p. 9. The revised and expanded edition of Oyama's book is due out in the year 2000 (Duke University Press).

30. Taylor 1998, p. 24.

31. Ho 1989, p. 34. [...]

32. LeVay's results still await confirmation and in the meantime have been subject to intense scrutiny (LeVay 1991). See Fausto-Sterling 1992a and 1992b; Byne and Parsons 1993; and Byne 1995. [...]

33. [...] Hamer et al. 1993.

34. Extraordinary, because it is not customary to use a strictly scientific report to discuss the potential social implications of one's work. Hamer et al. 1993, p. 326.

35. Wilson 1998, p. 203.

36. Elman et al. 1996, p. 359. See also Fischer 1990.

References

Burke, P. 1996. *Gender shock: Exploding the myth of male and female.* New York: Doubleday.

Butler, J. 1993. *Bodies that matter: On the discursive limits of sex.* New York: Routledge.

Byne, W. 1995. Science and belief: Psychological research on sexual orientation. *Journal of Homosexuality* 28(3–4): 303–44.

Byne, W., and B. Parsons. 1993. Human sexual orientation: The biological theories reappraised. *Archives of General Psychiatry* 50 (March): 228–39.

Carlson, A. 1991. When is a woman not a woman? *Women's Sports and Fitness* 13: 24–29.

Dreger, A.D. 1998. *Hermaphrodites and the medical invention of sex.* Cambridge: Harvard University Press.

Elman, J.L., E.A. Bates, et al. 1996. *Rethinking innateness: A connectionist perspective on development.* Cambridge: MIT Press.

Fausto-Sterling, A. 1992a. Why do we know so little about human sex? *Discover* 13: 6, 28–30.

Fausto-Sterling, A. 1992b. *Myths of gender: Biological theories about women and men.* New York: Basic Books.

Feinberg, L. 1996. *Transgender warriors.* Boston: Beacon Press.

Fischer, R. 1990. Why the mind is not in the head but in the society's connectionist network? *Diogenes* 151 (Fall): 1–28.

Foucault, M. 1978. *This history of sexuality.* New York: Pantheon.

Foucault, M. 1980. Two lectures. In *Power/knowledge: Selected interviews and other writings 1972–1977 by Michel Foucault,* ed. C. Gordon. New York: Pantheon, pp. 78–108.

Grosz, E. 1994. *Volatile bodies: Towards a corporeal feminism.* Bloomington: Indiana University Press.

Hamer, D., S. Hu, et al. 1993. Linkage between DNA markers on the X chromosome and male sexual orientation. *Science* 261: 321–25.

Hanley, D.F. 1983. Drug and sex testing: Regulations for the international competition. *Clinics in Sports Medicine* 2: 13–17.

Haraway, D. 1989. *Primate visions.* New York: Routledge.

Haraway, D. 1997. *Modest_Witness@Second_Millennium.FemaleMan_Meets_OncoMouse*™ New York: Routledge.

Hausman, B.L. 1995. *Changing sex: Transsexualism, technology, and the idea of gender in the 20th century.* Durham, NC: Duke University Press.

Ho, M.W. 1989. A structuralism of process: Towards a post-Darwinian rational morphology. In *Dynamic Structures in Biology,* ed. B. Goodwin, A. Sibatani, and G. Webster. Edinburgh: Edinburgh University Press, pp. 31–48.

Kessler, S.J., and W. McKenna. 1978. *Gender: An ethnomethodological approach.* New York: Wiley.

LeVay, S. 1991. A difference in hypothalamic structure between heterosexual and homosexual men. *Science* 253: 1034–37.

Money, J., and A.A. Ehrhardt. 1972. *Man and women, boy and girl.* Baltimore: Johns Hopkins University Press.

Moore, H.L. 1994. *A passion for difference: Essays in anthropology and gender.* Bloomington: Indiana University Press.

Moore, L.J., and A.E. Clarke. 1995. Clitoral conventions and transgressions: Graphic representations in anatomy texts, C1900–1991. *Feminist Studies* 21(2): 255–301.

Oyama, S. 1985. *The ontogeny of information.* Cambridge, UK: Cambridge University Press.

Plumwood, V. 1993. *Feminism and the mastery of nature.* New York: Routledge.

Rothblatt, M. 1995. *The apartheid of sex: A manifesto on the freedom of gender.* New York: Crown.

Rubin, G. 1975. The traffic in women: Notes on the "political economy" of sex. In *Toward an anthropology of women*, ed. R.R. Reiter. New York: Monthly Review Press, 157–210.

Sawicki, J. 1991. *Disciplining Foucault.* New York: Routledge.

Schiebinger, L. 1993a. Why mammals are called mammals: Gender politics in eighteenth-century natural history. *American Historical Review* 98(2): 382–411.

Schiebinger, L. 1993b. *Nature's body: Gender in the making of modern science.* Boston: Beacon Press.

Taylor, P.J. 1998. Natural selection: A heavy hand in biological and social thought. *Science as Culture* 7(1): 5–32.

Valian, V. 1998a. Running in place. *The Science* (January/February): 18–23.

Valian, V. 1998b. *Why so slow? The advancement of women.* Cambridge: MIT Press.

Wilson, E. 1998. *Neural geographies: Feminism and the microstructure of cognition.* New York: Routledge.

Defining Genitals:
Who Will Make Room for the Intersexed?

Kate Haas

Between 1.7 and 4% of the world population is born with intersex conditions, having primary and secondary sexual characteristics that are neither clearly male nor female.[1] The current recommended treatment for an infant born with an intersex condition is genital reconstruction surgery to render the child as clearly sexed either male or female.[2] Every day in the United States, five children are subjected to genital reconstruction surgery that may leave them with permanent physical and emotional scars.[3] Despite efforts by intersexed people to educate the medical community about their rejection of infant genital reconstruction surgery, the American medical community has not yet accepted the fact that differences in genital size and shape do not necessarily require surgical correction.[4]

Size Does Matter

The size of an infant's genitals is important to physicians who "manage" the sex assignment of intersexed infants. In her book entitled *Lessons from the Intersexed*, Suzanne Kessler explores how physicians use size to determine the appropriateness of genitals.

Ranges of Medically Acceptable Infant Clitoral and Penile Lengths

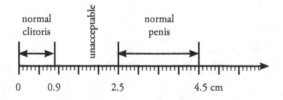

How big must a clitoris be before physicians decide it is too large? ... In spite of there being a table of standards, physicians are more likely to refer to the average clitoris in food terminology, such as a pea or a small bean. In general, medical standards do not allow clitorises larger than .9 centimeters (about 3/8 of an inch). [...]

When is a penis too small? In general, medical standards permit infant penises as small as 2.5 centimeters (about one inch) to mark maleness, but usually not smaller. [Boys with penises smaller than 2.5 centimeters may be reassigned as girls based on the assumption that] a male infant needs a penis of a certain size in order to be accepted by family and peers. [The figure shown here] indicates standard clitoral and penile lengths for infants, revealing intermediate areas of phallic length that neither females nor males are permitted to have.

Notes

1. Anne Fausto-Sterling, *Sexing the Body: Gender Politics and the Construction of Sexuality* 51 (2000) (reporting that 1.7% of the population may be intersexed); Julie A. Greenberg, *Defining Male and Female Intersexuality and the Collision between Law and Biology*, 41 Ariz. L. Rev. 265, 267 (1999) (reporting that Johns Hopkins sex researcher John Money estimates the number of people born with ambiguous genitals at 4%). Historically, people with intersex conditions were referred to as "hermaphrodites" but this word has been rejected as embodying many of the misperceptions and mistreatment of intersexed people. Raven Kaldera, *American Boyz Intersexuality Flyer*, at http://www.amboyz.org/intersection/flyerprint. html (last visited Mar. 27, 2004).

2. Hazel Glenn Beh & Milton Diamond, *An Emerging Ethical and Medical Dilemma: Should Physicians Perform Sex Assignment Surgery on Infants with Ambiguous Genitalia?* 7 Mich. J. Gender & L. 1, 3 (2000); Fausto-Sterling, *supra* note 1, at 45; *see infra* note 4.

3. Emi Koyama, *Suggested Guidelines for Non-Intersex Individuals Writing about Intersexuality and Intersex People*, at http://isna.org/faq/writing-guidelines.html (last visited Mar. 27, 2004). *But see* Beh & Diamond, *supra* note 2, at 17 (estimating the number of sex reassignments in the United States at 100 to 200 annually).

4. Kishka-Kamari Ford, *"First Do No Harm"—The Fiction of Legal Parental Consent to Genital-Normalizing Surgery on Intersexed Infants*, 19 Yale L. & Pol'y Rev. 469, 471 (2001).

Sources: Kate Haas, "Who Will Make Room for the Intersexed?" *American Journal of Law & Medicine* 30 (2004): 41–68; Suzanne J. Kessler, *Lessons from the Intersexed* (New Brunswick, NJ: Rutgers University Press, 1998), reprinted in *Sex Matters for College Students: FAQs in Human Sexuality*, Sandra L. Caron (Upper Saddle River, NJ: Pearson Prentice Hall, 2007), 23.

Chapter 14

Women's Brains

Stephen Gould

Stephen Gould was a highly influential paleontologist, evolutionary biologist, and an award-winning popular science writer. Among the best-known scientists of his generation, he held the position of Alexander Agassiz Professor of Zoology at Harvard University and was curator for paleontology at Harvard's Museum of Comparative Zoology. Gould also wrote numerous widely read books, as well as regularly contributed essays to Natural History Magazine *that uncovered and critiqued scientific sexism and racism in research.*

In the prelude to *Middlemarch*, George Eliot lamented the unfulfilled lives of talented women:

> Some have felt that these blundering lives are due to the inconvenient indefiniteness with which the Supreme Power has fashioned the natures of women; if there were one level of feminine incompetence as strict as the ability to count three and no more, the social lot of women might be treated with scientific certitude.

Eliot goes on to discount the idea of innate limitation, but while she wrote in 1872, the leaders of European anthropometry were trying to measure "with scientific certitude" the inferiority of women. Anthropometry, or measurement of the human body, is not so fashionable a field these days, but it dominated the human sciences for much of the nineteenth century and remained popular until intelligence testing replaced skull measurement as a favored device for making invidious comparisons among races, classes, and sexes. Craniometry, or measurement of the skull, commanded the most attention and respect. Its unquestioned leader, Paul Broca (1824–80), professor of clinical surgery at the Faculty of Medicine in Paris, gathered a school of disciples and imitators around himself. Their work, so meticulous and apparently irrefutable, exerted great influence and won high esteem as a jewel of nineteenth-century science.

Broca's work seemed particularly invulnerable to refutation. Had he not measured with the most scrupulous care and accuracy? (Indeed, he had. I have the greatest respect for Broca's meticulous procedure. His numbers are sound. But science is an inferential exercise, not a catalog of facts. Numbers, by themselves, specify nothing. All depends upon what you do with them.) Broca depicted himself as an apostle of objectivity, a man who bowed before facts and cast aside superstition and sentimentality. He declared that "there is no faith, however respectable, no interest, however legitimate, which must not accommodate itself to the progress of human knowledge and bend before truth." Women, like it or not, had smaller brains than men and, therefore, could not equal them in intelligence. This fact, Broca argued, may reinforce a common prejudice in male society, but it is also a scientific truth. L. Manouvrier, [a contemporary of Broca], rejected the inferiority of women and wrote with feeling about the burden imposed upon them by Broca's numbers:

> Women displayed their talents and their diplomas. They also invoked philosophical authorities. But they were opposed by *numbers* unknown to Condorcet or to John Stuart Mill. These numbers fell upon poor women like a sledge hammer, and they were accompanied by commentaries and sarcasms more ferocious than the most misogynist imprecations of certain church fathers. The theologians had asked if women had a soul. Several centuries later, some scientists were ready to refuse them a human intelligence.

Broca's argument rested upon two sets of data: the larger brains of men in modern societies, and a supposed increase in male superiority through time. His most extensive data came from autopsies performed personally in four Parisian hospitals. For 292 male brains, he calculated an average weight of 1,325 grams; 140 female brains averaged 1,144 grams for a difference of 181 grams, or 14 percent of the male weight. Broca understood, of course, that part of this difference could be attributed to the greater height of males. Yet he made no attempt to measure the effect of size alone and actually stated that it cannot account for the entire difference because we know, a priori, that women are not as intelligent as men (a premise that the data were supposed to test, not rest upon):

> We might ask if the small size of the female brain depends exclusively upon the small size of her body. Tiedemann has proposed this explanation. But we must not forget that women are, on the average, a little less intelligent than men, a difference which we should not exaggerate but which is, nonetheless, real. We are therefore permitted to suppose that the relatively small size of the female brain depends in part upon her physical inferiority and in part upon her intellectual inferiority.

In 1873, the year after Eliot published *Middlemarch*, Broca measured the cranial capacities of prehistoric skulls from L'Homme Mort cave. Here he found a difference of only 99.5 cubic centimeters between males and females, while modern populations range from 129.5 to 220.7. Topinard, Broca's chief disciple, explained the increasing discrepancy through time as a result of differing evolutionary pressures upon dominant men and passive women:

> The man who fights for two or more in the struggle for existence, who has all the responsibility and the cares of tomorrow, who is constantly active in combating the environment and human rivals, needs more brain than the woman whom he must protect and nourish, the sedentary woman, lacking any interior occupations, whose role is to raise children, love, and be passive.

In 1879, Gustave Le Bon, chief misogynist of Broca's school, used these data to publish what must be the most vicious attack upon women in modern scientific literature (no one can top Aristotle). I do not claim his views were representative of Broca's school, but they were published in France's most respected anthropological journal. Le Bon concluded:

In the most intelligent races, as among the Parisians, there are a large number of women whose brains are closer in size to those of gorillas than to the most developed male brains. This inferiority is so obvious that no one can contest it for a moment; only its degree is worth discussion. All psychologists who have studied the intelligence of women, as well as poets and novelists, recognize today that they represent the most inferior forms of human evolution and that they are closer to children and savages than to an adult, civilized man. They excel in fickleness, inconstancy, absence of thought and logic, and incapacity to reason. Without doubt there exist some distinguished women, very superior to the average man, but they are as exceptional as the birth of any monstrosity, as, for example, of a gorilla with two heads; consequently, we may neglect them entirely.

Nor did Le Bon shrink from the social implications of his views. He was horrified by the proposal of some American reformers to grant women higher education on the same basis as men:

A desire to give them the same education, and, as a consequence, to propose the same goals for them, is a dangerous chimera.... The day when, misunderstanding the inferior occupations which nature has given her, women leave the home and take part in our battles; on this day a social revolution will begin, and everything that maintains the sacred ties of the family will disappear.

Sound familiar?[1]

I have reexamined Broca's data, the basis for all this derivative pronouncement, and I find his numbers sound but his interpretation ill-founded, to say the least. The data supporting his claim for increased difference through time can be easily dismissed. Broca based his contention on the samples from L'Homme Mort alone—only seven male and six female skulls in all. Never have so little data yielded such far-ranging conclusions.

In 1888, Topinard published Broca's more extensive data on the Parisian hospitals. Since Broca recorded height and age as well as brain size, we may use modern statistics to remove their effect. Brain weight decreases with age, and Broca's women were, on average, considerably older than his men. Brain weight increases with height, and his average man was almost half a foot taller than his average woman. I used multiple regression, a technique that allowed me to assess simultaneously the influence of height and age upon brain size. In an analysis of the data for women, I found that, at average male height and age, a woman's brain would weigh 1,212 grams. Correction for height and age reduces Broca's measured difference of 181 grams by more than a third, to 113 grams.

I don't know what to make of this remaining difference because I cannot assess other factors known to influence brain size in a major way. Cause of death has an important effect: degenerative disease often entails a substantial diminution of brain size. (This effect is separate from the decrease attributed to age alone.) Eugene Schreider, also working with Broca's data, found that men killed in accidents had brains weighing, on average, 60 grams more than men dying of infectious diseases. The best modern data I can find (from American hospitals) records a full 100-gram difference between death by degenerative arteriosclerosis and by violence or accident. Since so many of Broca's subjects were very elderly women, we may assume that lengthy degenerative disease was more common among them than among the men.

More importantly, modern students of brain size still have not agreed on a proper measure for eliminating the powerful effect of body size. Height is partly adequate, but men and women of the same height do not share the same body build. Weight is even worse than height, because most of its variation reflects nutrition rather than intrinsic size—fat versus skinny exerts little influence upon the brain. Manouvrier took up this subject in the 1880s and argued that muscular mass and force should be used. He tried to measure this elusive property in various ways and found a marked difference in favor of men, even in men and women of the same height. When he corrected for what he called "sexual mass," women actually came out slightly ahead in brain size.

Thus, the corrected 113-gram difference is surely too large; the true figure is probably close to zero and may as well favor women as men. And 113 grams, by the way, is exactly the average difference between a 5-foot 4-inch and a 6-foot 4-inch male in Broca's data. We would not (especially us short folks) want to ascribe greater intelligence to tall men. In short, who knows what to do with Broca's data? They certainly don't permit any confident claim that men have bigger brains than women.

To appreciate the social role of Broca and his school, we must recognize that his statements about the brains of women do not reflect an isolated prejudice toward a single disadvantaged group. They must be weighed in the context of a general theory that supported contemporary social distinctions as biologically ordained. Women, blacks, and poor people suffered the same disparagement, but women bore the brunt of Broca's argument because he had easier access to data on women's brains. Women were singularly denigrated but they also stood as surrogates for other disenfranchised groups. As one of Broca's disciples wrote in 1881: "Men of the black races have a brain scarcely heavier than that of white women." This juxtaposition extended into many other realms of anthropological argument, particularly to claims that, anatomically and emotionally, both women and blacks were like white children—and that white children, by the theory of recapitulation, represented an ancestral (primitive) adult stage of human evolution. I do not regard as empty rhetoric the claim that women's battles are for all of us.

Maria Montessori did not confine her activities to educational reform for young children. She lectured on anthropology for several years at the University of Rome, and wrote an influential book entitled *Pedagogical Anthropology* (English edition, 1913). Montessori was no egalitarian. She supported most of Broca's work and the theory of innate criminality proposed by her compatriot Cesare Lombroso. She measured the circumference of children's heads in her schools and inferred that the best prospects had bigger brains. But she had no use for Broca's conclusions about women. She discussed Manouvrier's work at length and made much of his tentative claim that women, after proper correction of the data, had slightly larger brains than men. Women, she concluded, were intellectually superior, but men had prevailed heretofore by dint of physical force. Since technology has abolished force as an instrument of power, the era of women may soon be upon us: "In such an epoch there will really be superior human beings, there will really be men strong in morality and in sentiment. Perhaps in this way the reign of women is approaching, when the enigma of her anthropological superiority will be deciphered. Woman was always the custodian of human sentiment, morality and honor."

This represents one possible antidote to "scientific" claims for the constitutional inferiority of certain groups. One may affirm the validity of biological distinctions but argue that the data have been misinterpreted by prejudiced men with a stake in the outcome, and that disadvantaged groups are truly superior. In recent years, Elaine Morgan has followed this strategy in her *Descent of Woman*, a speculative reconstruction of human prehistory from the woman's point of view— and as farcical as more famous tall tales by and for men.

I prefer another strategy. Montessori and Morgan followed Broca's philosophy to reach a more congenial conclusion. I would rather label the whole enterprise of setting a biological value upon groups for what it is: irrelevant and highly injurious. George Eliot well appreciated the special tragedy that biological labeling imposed upon members of disadvantaged groups. She expressed it for people like herself—women of extraordinary talent. I would apply it more widely—not only to those whose dreams are flouted but also to those who never realize that they may dream—but I cannot match her prose. In conclusion, then, the rest of Eliot's prelude to *Middlemarch*:

> The limits of variation are really much wider than anyone would imagine from the sameness of women's coiffure and the favorite love stories in prose and verse. Here and there a cygnet is reared uneasily among the ducklings in the brown pond, and never finds the living stream in fellowship with its own oary-footed kind. Here and there is born a Saint Theresa, foundress of nothing, whose loving heartbeats and sobs after an unattained goodness tremble off and are dispersed among hindrances instead of centering in some long recognizable deed.

Note

1. When I wrote this essay, I assumed that Le Bon was a marginal, if colorful, figure. I have since learned that he was a leading scientist, one of the founders of social psychology, and best known for a seminal study on crowd behavior, still cited today (*La psychologie des foules*, 1895), and for his work on unconscious motivation.

Chapter 15

Freaks and Queers

Eli Clare

Eli Clare is a writer, speaker, activist, teacher, and poet. His areas of expertise and activism are disability, queer, and trans rights and integrating ableism into feminist understandings of oppression. Exile and Pride, *from which the following selection is taken, has established Clare as one of the leading writers on the intersections of queerness and disability. He has also published a collection of poetry,* The Marrow's Telling: Words in Motion.

Freak Show

The history of freakdom extends far back into western civilization. The court jester, the pet dwarf, the exhibition of humans in Renaissance England, the myths of giants, minotaurs, and monsters all point to this long history, which reached a pinnacle in the mid-1800s to mid-1900s. During that century, freaks were big entertainment and big business. Freak shows populated the United States, and people flocked to the circus, the carnival, the storefront dime museum. They came to gawk at "freaks," "savages," and "geeks." They came to be educated and entertained, titillated and repulsed. They came to have their ideas of normal and abnormal, superior and inferior, their sense of self, confirmed and strengthened. And gawk they did. But who were they gawking at? This is where I want to start.

Whatever these paying customers—*rubes* in circus lingo—believed, they were not staring at freaks of nature. Rather, the freak show tells the story of an elaborate and calculated social construction that utilized performance and fabrication as well as deeply held cultural beliefs. At the center of this construction is the showman, who, using costuming, staging, elaborate fictional histories, marketing, and choreography, turned people from four groups into freaks. First, disabled people, both white people and people of color, became Armless Wonders, Frog Men, Giants, Midgets, Pinheads, Camel Girls, Wild Men of Borneo, and the like. Second, nondisabled people of color—bought, persuaded, forced, and kidnapped to the United States from colonized countries all over the world—became Cannibals and Savages. Third, nondisabled people of color from the United States became Natives from the Exotic Wilds. And fourth, nondisabled people with visible differences—bearded women, fat women, very thin men, people covered with tattoos, intersex people—became wondrous and horrifying exhibits. Cultural critic and disability theorist Rosemarie Garland Thomson argues that the differences among these sometimes overlapping groups of people melded together:

> Perhaps the freak show's most remarkable effect was to eradicate distinctions among a wide variety of bodies, conflating them under a single sign of the freak-as-other....

[A]ll the bodily characteristics that seemed different or threatening to the dominant order merged into a kind of motley chorus line of physical difference on the freak show stage.... [A] nondisabled person of color billed as the "Fiji Cannibal" was equivalent to a physically disabled Euro-American called the "Legless Wonder."[1]

In the eyes of many rubes, particularly white and/or nondisabled folks, the freak show probably was one big melting pot of difference and otherness. At the same time, the differences among the various groups of people who worked as freaks remain important to understanding the freak show in its entirety. But whatever the differences, all four groups held one thing in common: nature did not make them into freaks. The freak show did, carefully constructing an exaggerated divide between "normal" and Other, sustained in turn by rubes willing to pay good money to stare.

Hiram and Barney Davis performed wildly for their audiences, snapping, snarling, talking gibberish from stage. The handbill sold in conjunction with their display described in lengthy, imagined detail "What We Know About Waino and Plutano, the Wild Men of Borneo." In reality Hiram and Barney were white, cognitively disabled brothers from an immigrant farm family who lived in Ohio. Their mother, after many offers which she refused, finally sold them to a persistent showman for a wash pan full of gold and silver. Off-stage Hiram and Barney were quiet, unassuming men. In one photo they stand flanking their manager Hanford Lyman. Their hair falls past their shoulders; they sport neatly trimmed goatees; Hiram folds his hands in front of him; Barney cocks his hands on his hips; they look mildly and directly into the camera.

Ann Thompson, a white woman born without arms, posed as "The Armless Wonder." From stage she signed and sold photographs as souvenirs, writing with her toes sayings like, "So you perceive it's really true, when hands are lacking, toes will do," or more piously, "Indolence and ease are the rust of the mind." In her autobiography, which she hawked along with her photos and trinkets, Ann presented herself as a respectable, religious lady. In one photo, she sits beside her husband and son, all of them wearing formal Victorian clothing.

William Johnson, a cognitively disabled African American man from New Jersey, became the "What Is It?" the "missing link," the "Monkey Man." He wore hairy ape-like costumes, shaved his head bald except for a little tuft at the very top, and posed in front of a jungle backdrop. The showmen at P. T. Barnum's American Museum in New York City described William as "a most singular animal, which though it has many of the features and characteristics of both the human and the brute, is not, apparently, either, but in appearance, a mixture of both—the connecting link between humanity and brute creation."[2] Although the way in which he came to the freak show is unknown—Barnum may have bought him at a young age and coerced him into performing at first—William died in his 80s at home, a rich and well-liked man, referred to, by his co-workers, as the "dean of freaks."

Charles Stratton, a working-class short person—*dwarf* in medical terminology—from Connecticut worked the freak show as General Tom Thumb. He played the role of a European aristocrat, complete with resplendent suits, a miniature carriage pulled by ponies, and meetings with rich and famous people around the world, becoming in the process a rich man himself. When Charles and Mercy Lavinia Warren Bump, a short woman who also worked the freak show, fell in love and decided to get married, P. T. Barnum set out, in an extravagant example of showmanship, to turn their wedding into a huge media spectacle. He was successful; 2,000 people attended the event, and the *New York Times* ran a full-page story, headlined "Loving Lilliputians." Charles and Mercy played their roles and used the publicity to springboard another European tour.

Two Congolese men and thirteen Congolese women, wearing large, heavy jewelry in their pierced lips, were bought by circus agent Ludwig Bergonnier and shipped from Africa to the United States. The poster advertising their display in the Ringling Brothers Circus freak show proclaimed them "Genuine Monster-Mouthed Ubangi Savages World's Most Weird Living Humans from Africa's Darkest Depths." The women were forced to wear only gunny sack skirts; the men, given only loincloths, carried spears. Ubangi was a name randomly pulled off a map of Africa and had no relationship to where these women and men had actually lived. Their real names and actual homeland are unknown.

The Davis brothers, Thompson, Johnson, Stratton, the now unknown African men and women did not slide into the world as infant freaks. They were made freaks, socially constructed for the purposes of entertainment and profit. This construction depended not only upon the showmanship of the "freaks" and their managers. It also capitalized on the eagerness of rubes to gawk at freaks and on the ableism and racism, which made the transitions from disabled white person, disabled person of color, nondisabled person of color, to freak even possible. Without this pair of oppressive ideologies, the attendant fear and hatred of all disabled people and all people of color, and the desire to create an Other against whom one could gauge her/his normality, who could ever believe for even one farcical moment that William Johnson was Darwin's missing link; Barney Davis, a wild man from Borneo; Ann Thompson, an armless wonder?

Ann, in that photo of you with your husband and son, you sit on a rug decorated with crosses, a rug you crocheted. The showmen made a big deal of your dexterity. But did you learn to crochet as a freak show stunt? Or did you, like so many women of your time, sew and knit, embroider and crochet, simply as a necessity and a pastime?

Within this context of ableism and racism, the people who worked the freak show did not live only as victims. Many of the "freaks" themselves—particularly those who were not cognitively disabled or brought to the United States from Africa, Asia, South and Central America, the Pacific islands, and the Caribbean—controlled their own acts and displays, working alongside their managers to shape profitable shows. Many of them made decent livings; some, like Charles Stratton, Mercy Lavinia Warren Bump, and William Johnson, even became wealthy. When P. T. Barnum lost all his money in a bad business deal, Stratton came out of semi-retirement and rescued him by agreeing to go on yet another lucrative European tour. Others, like the Hilton sisters, conjoined twins who worked in the mid-1900s, became their own managers, or, like Bump and her Lilliputian Opera Company, formed their own performing groups, which were employed by dime museums and traveling vaudeville companies. In other words, white, nondisabled freak show owners and managers didn't only exploit "their freaks." The two groups also colluded together to dupe the audience, to make a buck off the rube's gullibility. Within the subculture of the freak show, rubes were understood as exploited victims—explicitly lied to, charged outrageous sums for mere trinkets, pickpocketed, or merely given incorrect change at the ticket counter.

Charles, there is a picture of you, taken during a visit with the Queen of England. You have a miniature sword drawn and are staging a fight with a poodle. Your wife, Mercy, writes of embarrassment and outrage. Of presidential candidate Stephen Douglas, she remembers: "He expressed great pleasure at again seeing me, and as I stood before him he took my hand and, drawing me toward him, stooped to kiss me. I instinctively drew back, feeling my face suffused with blushes. It seemed impossible to make people at first understand that I was not a child."[3] *Did you share her embarrassment and outrage as you faced that poodle? Or did you and Barnum laugh long and hard as you concocted your stunts?*

The questions about exploitation are complicated; simple answers collapse easily. Robert Bogdan, in his history *Freak Show*, excerpts a letter he received from freak show manager Ward Hall: "I exhibited freaks and exploited them for years. Now you are going to exploit them. The difference between authors and the news media, and the freak show operators is that we paid them." Bogdan comments, "[Hall's] use of the word *exploit* was playful. He does not think he exploited them. He had a business relationship, complete with contract, with his troupe of human oddities. His livelihood depended on them, as theirs did on him. He had no pretensions of doing good...."[4] Although Bogdan chronicles the social construction of freaks in amazing detail and refuses to situate the people who worked the freak shows as passive victims, I believe he is reaching toward a simple answer to the question of exploitation.

Hall's exploitation of people who worked as freaks may not have revolved around ableism and racism. Maybe he wasn't acting out of fear and hatred of disabled people and people of color, out of his internal psychological sense and the external legislated reality of privilege. And then again, maybe he was. But most certainly, like all the people who profited from the freak show, he used ableism and racism to his benefit. This use of oppression by white, nondisabled businessmen is common, fraught, and ultimately unacceptable. In his letter, Hall explicitly casts himself as a boss exploiting his workers, placing the freak show within the context of capitalism. Bogdan defends Hall in a backhanded way when he writes: "[Hall] had no pretensions of doing good." But since when do bosses in most profit-making business have real pretensions of doing good by their workers? Doing good may be a byproduct of making profit, but only a byproduct. Is Hall any less exploitative because he was acting as a boss rather than, or in addition to, a racist white person and an ableist nondisabled person?

Any estimation of exploitation in the freak show needs to also include Hall and "his troupe of human oddities" colluding together to exploit the rube. Sometimes this exploitation carried with it a sense of absurdity, a sense that the rubes would believe anything, that they were simple, gullible fools. Other times this exploitation was pure thievery, the sideshow creating situations in which it was easy to steal the rube's money. But to cast the audience only as victim neglects the very real ways in which the freak show bolstered white people's and nondisabled people's sense of superiority and well-being. The social construction of freaks always relied upon the perceived gap between a rube's normality and a freak's abnormality. Unsurprisingly, normality was defined exclusively in terms of whiteness and able-bodiedness.

The complexities of exploitation pile up, layer upon layer. White people and nondisabled people used racism and ableism to turn a profit. The freak show managers and owners were bosses and as such had power over their workers, the people who worked as freaks. Boss and worker together consciously manipulated their audience. That same audience willingly used lies to strengthen its own self-image. Given this maze of relationships, I have trouble accepting the assessment that exploitation in the freak show, if it existed at all, wasn't truly serious. Rather, I believe it exerted influence in many directions.

Working as a freak never meant working in a respectful, liberating environment, but then disabled people had no truly respectful and liberating options available to them in the mid-1800s. They could beg in the streets. They could survive in almshouses, where, as reformer Dorothea Dix put it, mentally ill people and developmentally disabled people lived "in cages, closets, cellars, stalls, pens! Chained naked, beaten with rods, and lashed into obedience."[5] They could live behind closed doors with their families. Consider William Johnson. As a Black, cognitively disabled man who apparently had no surviving family, he had few options. P. T. Barnum found William's counterpart, the woman displayed as the female "What Is It?," abandoned in an outhouse, covered with shit, left to die. In a world such as this, where the freak show existed alongside the street, the almshouse, the outhouse, William's position as the "dean of freaks," although dehumanizing in a number of ways, doesn't look so bad.

William, late after the exhibits had closed, the rubes gone home, did you and your friends gather backstage to party, passing a bottle of whiskey round and round? Did you entertain some more, pull out your fiddle and play silly squeaky songs? Or did you sit back and listen to one joke after another until you were breathless with laughter?

In many ways working as a freak was similar to working as a prostitute. Cultural worker and working-class scholar Joe Kadi writes, "Left-wing working-class analysis ... situates prostitution within the context of capitalism (one more *really* lousy job), celebrates the women who survive, thumbs its nose at the moralistic middle-class attitudes that condemn without understanding, and relays the women's stories and perspectives."[6] This same theoretical and political framework can be used to examine the job of freak. Clearly, working as a freak meant working a lousy job, many times the *only* job available, in a hostile ableist and racist world. Sometimes the job was lousier than others. The African women and men who performed as "Ubangi savages" made a nickel on every photograph they sold, nothing else; whereas their manager, Ludwig Bergonnier, made $1,500 a week renting "his display" to the Ringling Brothers Circus. In contrast, Charles Stratton became rich, owning a horse farm and a yacht. Still others, like William Johnson, found community among the people who worked the freak show.

You who ended up in the history books named only "Ubangi Savages," no names of your own: night after night, you paraded around the circus tent, air sticky against your bare skin, burlap prickly against your covered skin. Did you come to hate Bergonnier?

What did the people who worked as freaks think of their jobs, their lives? I want to hear their stories, but like the stories of other marginalized people, they were most often never told, but rather eaten up, thrown away, lost in the daily grind of survival. Some of these people didn't read or write, due to their particular disabilities or to the material/social circumstances of their lives. Or, as in the case of many of the people brought here from other countries, they didn't speak English and/or didn't come from cultures that passed stories through the written word. A few people who worked the freak show did write autobiographies, but these pamphlets or books were mostly part of the whole production, sold alongside the handbills and photos. These stories ended up being part of the showmen's hyperbole. So, in order to reconstruct, celebrate, and understand the lives of the people who worked the freak show, I rely on historians, like Robert Bogdan, who have sifted through thousands of handbills, posters, newspaper articles, and promotional garbage used to create The Armless Wonder, The Wild Men of Borneo. In large part, I will never truly know their lives but can only use my imagination, political sensibilities, and intuition to fill the holes between the outrageous headlines in the *New York Times* and other newspapers and the outrageous handbills sold at the carnival.

The historians who moralize about the freak show frustrate me. These academics will take a detail, like the fact that Hiram and Barney Davis's mother sold her sons to a showman, and use it to demonstrate just how despicable showmen could be and how oppressive the freak show was. The disturbing fact that many of the people who worked as freaks—disabled people from the United States[7] as well as people from colonized countries—were sold into the business needs to be examined. The question, why were they sold, has to be asked. Certainly, in many cases, the answer must revolve around fear and hatred, undiluted ableism and racism, imperialism, and capitalism. But consider Hiram and Barney. They were sold for a wash pan full of gold and silver. What did that wash pan mean to their mother, Catherine Davis? My sources suggest, although don't explicitly state, that the Davises were a *poor* immigrant farm family. Did that gold and silver mean economic survival to Catherine Davis? What happened to working-class and poor disabled people who needed care but whose families could not provide it? The options did not abound: the almshouse, the street, the freak show. Rather than moralize and condemn, I want freak show historians to examine the whole context, including racism, ableism, and classism, and begin to build a complex understanding of exploitation. Like the women Joe Kadi refers to in his analysis of prostitution, the people who worked as freaks—especially those who had some control over their own display—grasped an exploitative situation in an exploitative world and, as often as possible, turned it to their benefit.

At the same time, the people who had the least power in the freak show—people from colonized countries and cognitively disabled people—underscore just how exploitative this institution could be. Many of the people of color brought to the United States died bleak deaths of pneumonia, pleurisy, or tuberculosis. They died on the long ship rides. They died wanting desperately to return to their home countries. They did not want to be part of the freak show; they never came to like the freak show; they didn't become showmen and -women in their own right. Instead, the circus, the dime museum, the vaudeville act, the natural history museum were simply sites of imperialist atrocity. Likewise, cognitively disabled people most frequently had no control over their displays. Some lacked the abilities to say yes or no to their own exhibition; others were simply trapped by unscrupulous managers, who typically were also their legal guardians. Although some cognitively disabled people had what appear to be good and happy relationships with their managers, the dual role of showman and legal guardian is a setup for exploitation.

The display of both groups of people capitalized on the theory of the time that nondisabled people of color and cognitively disabled people embodied the missing link between primates and humans. Eminent zoologist Baron Georges Cuvier wrote in the early 1800s:

> The negro race is confined to the south of Mount Atlas. Its characteristics are, black complexion, woolly hair, compressed cranium, and flattish nose. In the prominence of the lower part of the face, and the thickness of the lips, it manifestly approaches the monkey tribe.[8]

Much the same was believed about cognitively disabled people. Following the same train of thought as Cuvier, German scientist Carl Vogt wrote in 1867 even more explicitly about evolutionary theory:

> Microcephalics [people with a type of cognitive disability medically known as microcephalia] must necessarily represent an earlier developmental state of the human being … they reveal to us one of the milestones which the human passed by during the course of his historical evolution.[9]

The racism and ableism imbedded in these theories intersect intensely in the exhibition of cognitively disabled people of color. Consider the story of two cognitively disabled siblings kidnapped as children from San Salvador. Called "Maximo" and "Bartola," they were declared to be from "a long-lost race of Aztecs." Scientists and anthropologists studied them; showmen displayed them. Both groups helped create and defend the "long-lost race" fabrication, anthropologists to substantiate their theories, showmen to make money, each feeding off the other. They used a variety of observations as their proof. They emphasized physical attributes associated with being disabled by microcephalia, particularly short stature and a slightly sloping skull. They took note of "Maximo's" and "Bartola's" dark skin and thick black hair. They made much of their subjects' language use and food preferences, citing the cultural differences between "civilized" white people and "barbaric" people of color. They exaggerated the specific cognitive impairments of "Maximo" and "Bartola." In short, these white, nondisabled men totally intertwined race and disability; racism and ableism, to create "their freaks."

In one set of photos, "Maximo" and "Bartola" are stripped naked, posed against a blank wall. I imagine scientists measuring the diameter of their skulls, the length of their legs, taking notes about their skin color and speech patterns, then snapping these pictures to add to their documentation. A second set of photos has them sitting against a stone wall. "Maximo" wears striped pants and a shirt with a big sun on its front. "Bartola's" dress has a zig-zag design woven through it. Their hair is teased into big, wild afros. "Maximo" looks dazedly beyond the camera; "Bartola" looks down. I imagine showmen carefully arranging their props, calculating their profits. There are no complex or ambiguous answers here to the questions of power, control, and exploitation.

During the freak show's heyday, today's dominant model of disability—the medical model—did not yet exist. This model defines disability as a personal problem, curable and/or treatable by the medical establishment, which in turn has led to the wholesale medicalization of disabled people. As theorist Michael Oliver puts it:

> Doctors are centrally involved in the lives of disabled people from the determination of whether a foetus is handicapped or not through to the deaths of old people from a variety of disabling conditions. Some of these involvements are, of course, entirely appropriate, as in the diagnosis of impairment, the stabilisation of medical condition after trauma, the treatment of illness occurring independent of disability, and the provision of physical rehabilitation. But doctors are also involved in assessing driving ability, prescribing wheelchairs, determining the allocation of financial benefits, selecting educational provision and measuring work capabilities and potential; in none of these cases is it immediately obvious that medical training and qualifications make doctors the most appropriate persons to be so involved.[10]

In the centuries before medicalization, before the 1930s and '40s when disability became a pathology and the exclusive domain of doctors and hospitals, the Christian western world had encoded disability with many different meanings. Disabled people had sinned. We lacked moral strength. We were the spawn of the devil or the product of god's will. Our bodies/minds reflected events that happened during our mothers' pregnancies.

At the time of the freak show, disabled people were, in the minds of nondisabled people, extraordinary creatures, not entirely human, about whom everyone—"professional" people and the general public alike—was curious. Doctors routinely robbed the graves of "giants" in order to measure their skeletons and place them in museums. Scientists described disabled people in terms like "female, belonging to the monocephalic, ileadelphic class of monsters by fusion,"[11] language that came from the "science" of teratology, the centuries-old study of monsters. Anthropologists studied disabled people with an eye toward evolutionary theory. Rubes paid good money to gawk.

Hiram, did you ever stop mid-performance, stop up there on your dime museum platform and stare back, turning your mild and direct gaze back on the rubes, gawking at the gawkers, entertained by your own audience?

At the same time, there were signs of the move toward medicalization. Many people who worked as freaks were examined by doctors. Often handbills included the testimony of a doctor who verified the "authenticity" of the "freak" and sometimes explained the causes of his or her "freakishness." Tellingly doctors performed this role, rather than anthropologists, priests, or philosophers. But for the century in which the freak show flourished, disability was not yet inextricably linked to pathology, and without pathology, pity and tragedy did not shadow disability to the same extent they do today.

Consequently, the freak show fed upon neither of these, relying instead on voyeurism. The "armless wonder" played the fiddle on stage; the "giant" lived as royalty; the "savage" roared and screamed. These performances didn't create freaks as pitiful or tragic but as curious, odd, surprising, horrifying, wondrous. Freaks were not supercrips. They did not *overcome* disability; they *flaunted* it. Nor were freaks poster children, the modern-day objects of pity, used to raise money on the telethon stage. Instead, the freaks performed, and the rubes gawked. In a culture that paired disability and curiosity, voyeurism was morally acceptable. Thus, people flocked without shame or compunction to see the "freaks," primed by cultural beliefs about disability to be duped by the lies and fabrications created at the freak show.

In the same way, cultural beliefs about race—notions about the "wild savage," the "noble savage," and an eagerness to see both—made the exhibition of nondisabled people of color at the freak show and other venues extraordinarily profitable. Take, for example, the display of Filipino people at the 1904 World's Fair in St. Louis. The exhibit was billed as the "Igorot Village," complete with mostly naked women and men dancing wildly and eating dog stew. One among many "anthropological" displays at the Fair, the Village, as a near perfect representation of the "wild savage," attracted by far the most Fair-goers and media attention. Christopher Vaughan, in his article "Ogling Igorots," writes:

> The "civilized" Visayans, despite offering hourly theatrical and orchestral performances—concluding with "The Star Spangled Banner," sung in English by the entire village—went relatively ignored in comparison with the Igorots…. Gate receipts at the Igorot concession nearly quadrupled the total for the Visayans and tripled that of the colorful Moros.[12]

It was all too easy for white people to gawk at people of color, using the image of dog-eating savages from far-away "uncivilized" islands both to create and strengthen their sense of white identity and white superiority.

During this same period of time, imperialism had intensified to a fevered pitch, both abroad in places like the Philippines and at home as white people continued to subjugate and destroy Native peoples and cultures. By the time of the 1904 World's Fair, the United States had won the Spanish-American War and gained control over the Philippines. In explaining his decision to solidify the United States' colonial rule there, President McKinley referred to "our civilizing mission." What better way to justify that mission than to display Filipino people as "uncivilized savages"?

This interplay between politics and the freak show also occurred on the national level. For instance, the missing-link evolutionary theory, used so profitably by showmen, supported slavery before Emancipation and the suppression of civil rights after. But the freak show didn't only *use* this ideology. The display of Black and white cognitively disabled people and nondisabled people of color as the "missing link" and the "What Is It?" actually bolstered the theory. The scientists and politicians could point to William Johnson and say, "See, here is living proof. Look at this creature." In doing so, they were reaffirming the less-than-human status of people of color and rationalizing much of their social and political policy. Simply put, the freak show both fed upon and gave fuel to imperialism, domestic racist politics, and the cultural beliefs about "wild savages" and white superiority.

The decline of the freak show in the early decades of the 20th century coincided with the medicalization of disability. As pity, tragedy, and medical diagnosis/treatment entered the picture, the novelty and mystery of disability dissipated. Explicit voyeurism stopped being socially acceptable except when controlled by the medical establishment. And later in the 20th century, as colonized people of color fought back successfully against their colonizers and as legal segregation in the United States ended and civil rights started to take hold, the exhibition of people of color also became, at least ostensibly, unacceptable. Along with these changes came a scorn for the freak show as an oppressive institution from the bad old days. But I'm not so sure the freak show is all that dead.

Consider Coco Fusco and Guillermo Gomez-Peña's performance piece "The Couple in the Cage," created in 1992 as part of the "500 Years of Resistance" celebration.[13] Fusco and Gomez-Peña costumed themselves in everything from false leopard skins to mirrored sunglasses and posed as native people from a newly discovered tribe. They toured natural history museums, art galleries, and street corners in a cage, performing the script of exotic and noble "savages." In the long tradition of showmen and -women, they even invented an island in the Gulf of Mexico from which they supposedly came and, as they toured, didn't let on to their ruse. Fusco and Gomez-Peña expected their audiences to immediately recognize the parody. Instead, as documented in a video shot at the scene of several performances,[14] many people apparently took the ruse seriously. Some people expressed shock and disgust. Others, particularly white people, expounded on their theories about why Fusco paced back and forth, why Gomez-Peña grunted, staring out at the audience. Still others paid 50 cents for Polaroid pictures of the "savages" posed at their bars. Whether these people were serious, whether they all left the performance sites still duped, whether they truly believed their own theories, is not clear. But at least to some extent, it appears that "The Couple in the Cage" easily replicated the relationship between rube and freak—even as there are significant differences between this performance art piece and the freak show—suggesting that the old images of race, rather than being dead, live painfully close to the surface.

The scorn for the freak show also assumes that the bad old days were really awful, but I'm not so sure that they were in actuality all that bad for some of the "freaks." Listen to the stories Robert Waldow and Violet and Daisy Hilton tell. All of them lived during the freak show's decline as medicalization took hold.

Robert Waldow, a tall man born in the 1920s, resisted becoming a giant, a freak. He wanted to be a lawyer, but unable to get the necessary education, he turned to shoe advertising. And later, after being pursued for years by showmen, he worked for the circus, earning a large salary and refusing to participate in the hype that would have made him appear taller than he really was. At the same time, doctors also pursued Robert, reporting him to be the tallest man in the world—this being medical hype, not circus hype. They refused to leave him alone. In 1936 a Dr. Charles Humberd showed up uninvited at the Waldows' home. Robert refused a physical exam and wouldn't cooperate with the interview. Humberd left disgruntled and the next year, unbeknownst to the Waldows, published an article in the *Journal of the American Medical Association* called, "Giantism: A Case Study," in which Robert became a case study of a "preacromegalic giant." Because of the article, which cast him as a surly brute, Robert and his family were deluged with unwelcome attention from the media, the general public, and the medical establishment. In the biography *The Gentleman Giant*, Waldow's father reveals that Robert was far more disturbed and angered by his dealings with doctors than with showmen.

Conjoined twins Daisy and Violet Hilton echo this reaction. These women worked the circus, carnival, and vaudeville circuits from the time they could talk. Early on, their abusive guardians controlled and managed the show. They would lock Daisy and Violet away for days at a time to ensure that no one but rubes paying good money could see them. Later, after a court order freed the sisters, they performed on their own. The cover of one publicity pamphlet has Daisy playing the saxophone, Violet, the piano, and both of them smiling cheerfully at the viewer. Much of their lives they spent fighting poverty as the freak show's popularity waned. And yet in their autobiography, they write about "loath[ing] the very tone of the medical man's voice" and fearing that their guardians would "stop showing us on stage and let the doctors have us to punch and pinch and take our picture always."[15] Try telling Robert Waldow and the Hilton sisters how enlightened today's medical model of disability is, how much more progressive it is than the freak show, how bad the bad old days were. Try telling Coco Fusco and Guillermo Gomez-Peña that the freak show is truly dead.

The end of the freak show meant the end of a particular kind of employment for the people who had worked as freaks. For nondisabled people of color from the United States, employment by the 1930s didn't hinge heavily on the freak show, and so its decline didn't have a huge impact. And for people from Africa, Asia, South and Central America, the Pacific islands, and the Caribbean, the decline meant only that white people had one less reason to come kidnap and buy people away from their homes. But for disabled people—both people of color and white people—the end of the freak show almost guaranteed unemployment, disability often being codified into law as the inability to work.

In the '30s when Franklin Roosevelt's work programs employed many people, the federal government explicitly deemed disabled people unable to work, stamping their work applications "P. H. Physically handicapped. Substandard. Unemployable," sending them home with small monthly checks. The League of the Physically Handicapped protested in Washington, DC, occupying the Work Progress Administration's offices, chanting, "We want jobs, not tin cups."[16] In this climate, as freak show jobs disappeared, many disabled people faced a world devoid of employment opportunities.

Listen, for instance, to Otis Jordan, a disabled African American man who works the Sutton Sideshow, one of the only remaining freak shows in the country, as "Otis the Frog Man." In 1984, his exhibit was banned from the New York State Fair when someone lodged a complaint about the indignities of displaying disabled people. Otis responded, "Hell, what does she [the woman who made the complaint] want from me—to be on welfare?"[17] Working as a freak may have been a lousy job, but nonetheless it was a job.

Pride

Now with this history in hand, can I explain why the word *freak* unsettles me, why I have not embraced this piece of disability history, this story of disabled people who earned their livings by flaunting their disabilities, this heritage of resistance, an in-your-face resistance similar to "We're here, we're queer, get used to it"? Why doesn't the word *freak* connect me easily and directly to subversion? The answer I think lies in the transition from freak show to doctor's office, from curiosity to pity, from entertainment to pathology. The end of the freak show didn't mean the end of our display or the end of voyeurism. We simply traded one kind of freakdom for another.

Take, for instance, public stripping, the medical practice of stripping disabled children to their underwear and examining them in front of large groups of doctors, medical students, physical therapists, and rehabilitation specialists. They have the child walk back and forth. They squeeze her muscles. They watch his gait, muscle tension, footfall, back curvature. They take notes and talk among themselves about what surgeries and therapies they might recommend. Since the invention of video cameras, they tape the sessions. They justify public stripping by saying it's a training tool for students, a way for a team of professionals to pool knowledge.[18] This isn't a medical practice of decades gone by. As recently as 1996, disability activist Lisa Blumberg reported in *The Disability Rag* that "specialty" clinics (cerebral palsy clinics, spina bifida clinics, muscular dystrophy clinics, etc.) at a variety of teaching hospitals regularly schedule group—rather than private—examinations and conduct surgery screenings in hospital amphitheaters.[19] Excuse me, but isn't public stripping exactly what scientists and anthropologists did to "Maximo" and "Bartola" a century ago? Tell me, what is the difference between the freak show and public stripping? Which is more degrading? Which takes more control away from disabled people? Which lets a large group of nondisabled people gawk unabashedly for free?

Today's freakdom happens in hospitals and doctors' offices. It happens during telethons as people fork over money out of pity, the tragic stories milked until they're dry. It happens in nursing homes where severely disabled people are often forced to live against their wills. It happens on street corners and at bus stops, on playgrounds and in restaurants. It happens when nondisabled people stare, trying to be covert, smacking their children to teach them how to pretend not to stare. A character in the play *P.H. *reaks: The Hidden History of People with Disabilities* juxtaposes the voyeurism of the freak show with the voyeurism of everyday life, saying:

> We're always on display. You think if I walked down the street of your stinking little nowhere town people wouldn't stare at me? Damn right they would, and tell their neighbors and friends and talk about me over dinners and picnics and PTA meetings. Well, if they want to do that, they're going to have to pay me for that privilege. You want to stare at me, fine, it's 25 cents, cash on the barrel. You want a picture, that's another quarter. My life story. Pay me. You think I'm being exploited? You pay to go to a baseball game, don't you?[20]

Today's freakdom happens all the time, and we're not even paid for it. In fact disabled people have, as a group, an astounding unemployment rate of 71 percent.[21] When we do work we make 64 cents to a nondisabled worker's dollar.[22]

We don't control today's freakdom, unlike the earlier freak show freakdom, which sometimes we did. The presentation of disability today has been shaped entirely by the medical establishment and the charity industry. That is, until the disability rights movement came along. This civil rights and liberation movement established Centers for Independent Living all over the country, working to redefine the concept of independence. These centers offer support and advocacy, helping folks find accessible housing and personal attendants, funding for adaptive equipment and job training. Independent living advocates measure independence not by how many tasks one can do without assistance, but by how much control a disabled person has over his/her life and by the quality of that life.

The movement founded direct-action, rabble-rousing groups, like ADAPT[23] and Not Dead Yet,[24] that disrupt nursing home industry conventions, blockade non-accessible public transportation, occupy the offices of politicians committed to the status quo, and protest outside courtrooms. Disabled people have a history of direct-action protest, beginning with the League of the Physically Handicapped's WPA protest. In 1977, disabled people occupied the HEW (Department of Health, Education, and Welfare) offices in San Francisco for 25 days, successfully pressuring politicians into signing Section 504 of the Rehabilitation Act, the first civil rights legislation in the United States for disabled people.[25] And today, ADAPT is rabble-rousing hard, both on the streets and in Congress, to pass legislation that would make it more possible for people with significant disabilities to live in homes of their own choosing, rather than nursing homes.

The movement is creating a strong, politicized disability culture with a growing body of literature, performances, humor, theory, and political savvy. We have theater, dance, poetry, anthologies, fiction, magazines, art exhibits, film festivals, analysis and criticism written by disabled folks, conferences, and a fledgling academic discipline called disability studies. At the same time, there are disabled people working to crossover into mainstream culture, working to become models photographed for the big-name fashion magazines, actors in soap operas, sitcoms, and Hollywood movies, recognized artists, writers, and journalists.

The movement lobbied hard for laws to end separate and unequal education, for comprehensive civil rights legislation. The 1990 Americans with Disabilities Act (ADA) did not spring from George H. W. Bush's head, fully formed and shaped by his goodwill and understanding of disability issues. Rather, lawyers schooled in disability rights and disabled White House appointees with a stake in disability politics crafted the bill, disability lobbyists educated and lobbied hard, and grassroots disability activists mobilized to get the ADA passed. In short the disability rights movement founded in the same storm of social change as women's liberation and gay/lesbian liberation, riding on the energy and framework created by the Black civil rights movement, came along and is undoing internalized oppression, making community, creating a culture and sense of identity, and organizing to change the status quo.

These forces are taking freakdom back, declaring that disabled people will be at the center of defining disability, defining our lives, defining who we are and who we want to be. We are declaring that doctors and their pathology, rubes and their money, anthropologists and their theories, gawkers and their so-called innocuous intentions, bullies and their violence, showmen and their hype, Jerry Lewis and his telethon, government bureaucrats and their rules will no longer define us. To arrive as a self-defined people, disabled people, like other marginalized people, need a strong sense of identity. We need to know our history, come to understand which pieces of that history we want to make our own, and develop a self-image full of pride. The women and men who worked the freak show, the freaks who knew how to flaunt their disabilities—the tall man who wore a top hat to add a few inches to his height, the fat woman who refused to diet, the bearded woman who not only refused to shave, but grew her beard longer and longer, the cognitively disabled person who said, "I know you think I look like an ape. Here let me accentuate that look"—can certainly teach us a thing or two about identity and pride.

Pride is not an inessential thing. Without pride, disabled people are much more likely to accept unquestioningly the daily material conditions of ableism: unemployment, poverty, segregated and substandard education, years spent locked up in nursing homes, violence perpetrated by caregivers, lack of access. Without pride, individual and collective resistance to oppression becomes nearly impossible. But disability pride is no easy thing to come by. Disability has been soaked in shame, dressed in silence, rooted in isolation.

In 1969 in the backwoods of Oregon, I entered the "regular" first grade after a long struggle with the school officials who wanted me in "special education," a battle won only because I had scored well on an IQ test, my father knew the principal, and the first grade teacher, who lived upriver from us, liked my family and advocated for me. I became the first disabled kid to be mainstreamed in the district. Eight years later, the first laws requiring public education for disabled kids, Individuals with Disabilities Education Act (IDEA) and Section 504, were signed. By the mid-1980s, mainstreaming wasn't a rare occurrence, even in small, rural schools, but in 1969 I was a first.

No one—neither my family nor my teachers—knew how to acknowledge and meet my particular disability-related needs while letting me live a rather ordinary, rough-and-tumble childhood. They simply had no experience with a smart, gimpy six-year-old who learned to read quickly but had a hard time with the physical act of writing, who knew all the answers but whose speech was hard to understand. In an effort to resolve this tension, everyone ignored my disability and disability-related needs as much as possible. When I had trouble handling a glass of water, tying my shoes, picking up coins, screws, paper clips, writing my name on the blackboard, no one asked if I needed help. When I couldn't finish an assignment in the allotted time, teachers insisted I turn it in unfinished. When my classmates taunted me with *retard, monkey, defect*, no one comforted me. I rapidly became the class outcast, and the adults left me to fend for myself. I took as much distance as I could from the kids in "special ed." I was determined not to be one of them. I wanted to be "normal," to pass as nondisabled, even though my shaky hands and slurred speech were impossible to ignore.

Certainly I wasn't the only disabled person I knew. In Port Orford, many of the men had work-related disabilities: missing fingers, arms, and legs, broken backs, serious nerve damage. A good friend of my parents had diabetes. A neighbor girl, seven or eight years younger than me, had CP much like mine. My best friend's brother had a significant cognitive disability. And yet I knew no one with a disability, none of us willing to talk, each of us hiding as best we could.

No single person underlines this ironic isolation better than Mary Walls, who joined my class in the fourth grade. She wore hearing aids in both ears and split her days between the "regular" and the "special ed" classrooms. We shared a speech therapist. I wish we had grown to be friends, but rather we became enemies, Mary calling me names and me chasing her down. I understand now that Mary lived by trying to read lips, and my lips, because of the way CP affects my speech, are nearly impossible to read. She probably taunted me out of frustration, and I chased her down, as I did none of my other bullies, because I could. I understand now about horizontal hostility: gay men and lesbians disliking bisexual people, transsexual women looking down on drag queens, working-class people fighting with poor people. Marginalized people from many communities create their own internal tensions and hostilities, and disabled people are no exception. I didn't have a disabled friend until I was in my mid-20s, and still today most of my close friends, the people I call "chosen family," are nondisabled. Often I feel like an impostor as I write about disability, feel that I'm not disabled enough, not grounded deeply enough in [the] disability community, to put these words on paper. *This* is the legacy for me of shame, silence, and isolation.

Pride works in direct opposition to internalized oppression. The latter provides fertile ground for shame, denial, self-hatred, and fear. The former encourages anger, strength, and joy. To transform self-hatred into pride is a fundamental act of resistance. In many communities, language becomes one of the arenas for this transformation. Sometimes the words of hatred and violence can be neutralized or even turned into the words of pride. To stare down the bully calling *cripple*, the basher swinging the word *queer* like a baseball bat, to say "Yeah, you're right. I'm queer, I'm a crip. So what?" undercuts the power of those who want us dead.

*****

Whatever we name ourselves, however we end up shattering our self-hatred, shame, silence, and isolation, the goal is the same: to end our daily material oppression.

Notes

1. Rosemarie Garland Thomson, *Extraordinary Bodies: Figuring Physical Disability in American Culture and Literature* (New York: Columbia University Press, 1997), 62–63.
2. Robert Bogdan, *Freak Show: Presenting Human Oddities for Amusement and Profit* (Chicago: University of Chicago Press, 1988), 136.
3. Quoted in Lori Merish, "Cuteness and Commodity Aesthetics: Tom Thumb and Shirley Temple" in *Freakery: Cultural Spectacles of the Extraordinary Body*, ed. Rosemarie Garland Thompson (New York: New York University Press, 1996), 190.
4. Bogdan, *Freak Show*, 268.
5. Quoted in Joseph Shapiro, *No Pity: How the Disability Rights Movement is Changing America* (New York: Times Books, 1993), 59.
6. Joanna Kadi, *Thinking Class: Sketches from a Cultural Worker* (Boston: South End Press, 1996), 103.
7. For instance, before the end of slavery, enslaved children born disabled were often sold to showmen, sometimes for large sums of money. Conjoined twins Millie and Christina McCoy, born into slavery in 1852, brought their enslaver $30,000.
8. Quoted in Beruth Lindfors, "Circus Africans," *Journal of American Culture* 6.2 (1983): 9.
9. Quoted in Nigel Rothfels, "Aztecs, Aborigines, and Ape-People: Science and Freaks in Germany, 1850–1900" in *Freakery*, 158.
10. Michael Oliver, *The Politics of Disablement* (New York: St. Martin's Press, 1990), 48.
11. Bogdan, *Freak Show*, 230.
12. Christopher Vaughan, "Ogling Igorots" in *Freakery*, 222.
13. This year-long celebration, marking the 500th-year anniversary of Christopher Columbus's arrival in the Americas, focused on people of color's ongoing resistance to racism, imperialism, and genocide.
14. *The Couple in the Cage: A Guatinaui Odyssey*, prod. and dir. Coco Fusco and Paula Heredia, 31 min., sd., col. with b&w sequences, 4 3/4 cm (Chicago: Authentic Documentary Productions/Video Data Bank, 1993), videodisc/DVD.
15. Quoted in Bogdan, *Freak Show*, 173.
16. Shapiro, *No Pity*, 63–64.
17. Bogdan, *Freak Show*, 280.
18. Lisa Blumberg, "Public Stripping" in *The Ragged Edge: The Disability Experience from the Pages of the First Fifteen Years of The Disability Rag*, ed. Barrett Shaw (Louisville: Avocado Press, 1994), 73–77.
19. Lisa Blumberg, "Public Stripping Revisited," *The Disability Rag* 17.3 (1996): 18–21.

20. Doris Baizley and Victoria Ann Lewis, *P.H.*reaks: The Hidden History of People with Disabilities* from *Beyond Victims and Villains*, ed. Victoria Ann Lewis (New York: Theatre Communications Group, 2006), 78–79.
21. Disability Rights Nation, "'Nearly Half of Us Don't Know About the ADA,' Says New Harris Poll," *Ragged Edge* 19.5 (1998): 5.
22. Shapiro, *No Pity*, 28.
23. ADAPT (American Disabled for Attendant Programs Today) can be reached at 1640 E. Second St., Suite 100, Austin, TX 78702. Telephone: (512) 442-0252. www.adapt.org | adapt@adapt.org.
24. Not Dead Yet can be reached at 497 State St., Rochester, NY 14608-1642. Contact: Diane Coleman, telephone: (585) 697-1640. www.notdeadyet.org | ndycoleman@aol.com.
25. Shapiro, *No Pity*, 66–70.

Supplement 10

Ten Things Everyone Should Know About Race

Robin D. G. Kelley

Robin D. G. Kelley is professor of American studies and ethnicity and history at the University of Southern California. His diverse research interests include the history of the radical movements in the US, the African diaspora, and Africa, contemporary urban and poverty studies, music and visual culture, colonialism/imperialism, and constructions of race, among other topics. He has published several books that focus on African-American history and culture and on race relations.

Our eyes tell us that people look different. No one has trouble distinguishing a Czech from a Chinese, but what do those differences mean? Are they biological? Has race always been with us? How does race affect people today?

There's less—and more—to race than meets the eye:

1. *Race is a modern idea.* Ancient societies, like the Greeks, did not divide people according to physical distinctions, but according to religion, status, class, even language. The English language didn't even have the word "race" until it turned up in a 1508 poem by William Dunbar referring to a line of kings.

2. *Race has no genetic basis.* Not one characteristic, trait, or even gene distinguishes all the members of one so-called race from all the members of another so-called race.

3. *Human subspecies don't exist.* Unlike many animals, modern humans simply haven't been around long enough or isolated enough to evolve into separate subspecies or races. Despite surface appearances, we are one of the most genetically similar of all species.

4. *Skin color really is only skin deep.* Most traits are inherited independently from one another. The genes influencing skin color have nothing to do with the genes influencing hair form, eye shape, blood type, musical talent, athletic ability or forms of intelligence. Knowing someone's skin color doesn't necessarily tell you anything else about him or her.

5. *Most variation is within, not between, "races."* Of the small amount of total human variation, 85% exists within any local population, be they Italians, Kurds, Koreans, or Cherokees. About 94% can be found within any continent. That means two random Koreans may be as genetically different as a Korean and an Italian.

6. *Slavery predates race.* Throughout much of human history, societies have enslaved others, often as a result of conquest or war, even debt, but not because of physical characteristics or a belief in natural inferiority. Due to a unique set of historical circumstances, ours was the first slave system where all the slaves shared similar physical characteristics.

7. *Race and freedom evolved together.* The U.S. was founded on the radical new principle that "All men are created equal." But our early economy was based largely on slavery. How could this anomaly be rationalized? The new idea of race helped explain why some people could be denied the rights and freedoms that others took for granted.

8. *Race justified social inequalities as natural.* As the race idea evolved, white superiority became "common sense" in America. It justified not only slavery but also the extermination of Indians, exclusion of Asian immigrants, and the taking of Mexican lands by a nation that professed a belief in democracy. Racial practices were institutionalized within American government, laws, and society.

9. *Race isn't biological, but racism is still real.* Race is a powerful social idea that gives people different access to opportunities and resources. Our government and social institutions have created advantages that disproportionately channel wealth, power, and resources to white people. This affects everyone, whether we are aware of it or not.

10. *Colorblindness will not end racism.* Pretending race doesn't exist is not the same as creating equality. Race is more than stereotypes and individual prejudice. To combat racism, we need to identify and remedy social policies and institutional practices that advantage some groups at the expense of others.

Source: Public Broadcasting Service (PBS), "RACE—The Power of an Illusion: Background Readings: Ten Things Everyone Should Know about Race" (2003), retrieved from http://www.pbs.org/race/000_ About/002_04-background-01-x.htm

Supplement 11

Racism in Canada: A Timeline

1608   The French introduce Black slavery into Canada.

1613   French and English practise genocide and attempt to exterminate the Beothuck people from Newfoundland.

1709   Proclamation makes slavery legal in French Canada.

1763   European settlers exploit, kill, and infect Indigenous peoples with tuberculosis and smallpox in order to obtain Indigenous land. For instance, Lord Jeffrey Amherst practises germ warfare by giving out smallpox-infected blankets.

1763   Through the Treaty of Paris, France cedes Canada to Britain. One effect of this transfer in power is the legal strengthening of slavery in Canada.

1784   Race riot in Shelburne and Birchtown, Nova Scotia. A mob destroys Black people's property and drives Blacks out of the townships.

1875   Chinese Canadians are disenfranchised.

1876   Canada passes the Indian Act as one tool to eradicate Indigenous culture and expropriate land and resources for profit and settlement.

1880s–1996 Government/church-run residential schools are established. Indigenous children are taken from parents to be "civilized and educated" and "to kill the Indian in the child."

1885   In response to white Canada's racist fears of Chinese immigration, the federal government passes the Chinese Immigration Act, which introduced the Head Tax.

1900s   Federal government officials engage in a campaign to discourage Black American applicants from settlement and reject them on the basis of medical or other grounds. The Ontario legislature establishes segregated schools for Black people (in place until 1964). Black people are refused service and segregated in restaurants, theatres, and recreational facilities.

1907   The Asiatic Exclusion League forms with the goal of restricting Asian admission to Canada. The League carries out a major demonstration, which culminates in the worst race riot in the history of British Columbia.

1910   The Canadian Immigration Act creates a list of preferred and non-preferred countries, with British and white European immigrants on the "preferred" list and the rest of the world, made up largely of people of colour, on the "non-preferred" list.

1923   The Chinese Exclusion Act bans Chinese immigration until 1947.

1942   Canada closes its doors to Jewish refugees fleeing Hitler's Final Solution. Of all the Western countries, Canada admits the fewest Jewish refugees.

1942–1947   The federal government force[s] Japanese Canadians into internment camps and confiscate[s] their property.

1955   Canadian Domestic Workers Program is established to deal with the chronic shortage of Canadian workers prepared to accept low wages and undesirable working conditions as domestic servants. The program initially targets Black women from the Caribbean, and later women from the Philippines.

1964–1970   Africville, a Black settlement near Halifax, Nova Scotia, is demolished and its residents are forced to relocate. Vancouver City Council destroys Hogan's Alley, Vancouver's Black community, with the construction of the Georgia Street Viaduct.

1995   As part of the federal budget, the government imposes the Right of Landing Fee, widely known as the Head Tax. The fee of $975 applies to all adults, including refugees, becoming permanent residents. In 2000, the government rescinds the fee for refugees, but maintains it for immigrants.

2002   The Immigration and Refugee Protection Act comes into force in 2002 as a "security" measure in the wake of the September 11, 2001 attacks. The Act erodes basic rights in Canada, with some of the worst impacts being experienced by refugees and immigrants.

Source: Adapted from Vancouver Status of Women, "History in Our Faces on Occupied Land" (2008), retrieved from http://www.anti-racism.ca/content/history-our-faces-occupied-land-race-relations-timeline

Chapter 16

X: A Fabulous Child's Story

Lois Gould

Lois Gould was as an acclaimed American writer, known for her novels, memoirs, and other works about women's lives. Her only children's story, "X: A Fabulous Child's Story," was first published in Ms. Magazine *in 1972. She wrote a column for the* New York Times, *and served as editor of the* Ladies Home Journal *and other national magazines.*

Once upon a time, a baby named X was born. This baby was named X so that nobody could tell whether it was a boy or a girl. Its parents could tell, of course, but they couldn't tell anybody else. They couldn't even tell Baby X, at first.

You see, it was all part of a very important Secret Scientific Xperiment, known officially as Project Baby X. The smartest scientists had set up this Xperiment at a cost of Xactly 23 billion dollars and 72 cents, which might seem like a lot for just one baby, even a very important Xperimental baby. But when you remember the prices of things like strained carrots and stuffed bunnies, and popcorn for the movies and booster shots for camp, let alone twenty-eight shiny quarters from the tooth fairy, you begin to see how it adds up.

Also, long before Baby X was born, all those scientists had to be paid to work out the details of the Xperiment, and to write the *Official Instruction Manual* for Baby X's parents and, most important of all, to find the right set of parents to bring up Baby X. These parents had to be selected very carefully. Thousands of volunteers had to take thousands of tests and answer thousands of tricky questions. Almost everybody failed because, it turned out, almost everybody really wanted either a baby boy or a baby girl, and not Baby X at all. Also, almost everybody was afraid that a Baby X would be a lot more trouble than a boy or a girl. (They were probably right, the scientists admitted, but Baby X needed parents who wouldn't mind the Xtra trouble.)

There were families with grandparents named Milton and Agatha, who didn't see why the baby couldn't be named Milton or Agatha instead of X, even if it *was* an X. There were families with aunts who insisted on knitting tiny dresses and uncles who insisted on sending tiny baseball mitts. Worst of all, there were families that already had other children who couldn't be trusted to keep the secret. Certainly not if they knew the secret was worth 23 billion dollars and 72 cents—and all you had to do was take one little peek at Baby X in the bathtub to know if it was a boy or a girl.

But, finally, the scientists found the Joneses, who really wanted to raise an X more than any other kind of baby—no matter how much trouble it would be. Ms. and Mr. Jones had to promise they would take equal turns caring for X, and feeding it, and singing it lullabies. And they had to promise never to hire any babysitters. The government scientists knew perfectly well that a babysitter would probably peek at X in the bathtub, too.

The day the Joneses brought their baby home, lots of friends and relatives came over to see it. None of them knew about the secret Xperiment, though. So the first thing they asked was what kind of a baby X was. When the Joneses smiled and said, "It's an X!" nobody knew what to say. They couldn't say, "Look at her cute little dimples!" And they couldn't say, "Look at his husky little biceps!" And they couldn't even say just plain "kitchycoo." In fact, they all thought the Joneses were playing some kind of rude joke.

But, of course, the Joneses were not joking. "It's an X" was absolutely all they would say. And that made the friends and relatives very angry. The relatives all felt embarrassed about having an X in the family. "People will think there's something wrong with it!" some of them whispered. "There *is* something wrong with it!" others whispered back.

"Nonsense!" the Joneses told them all cheerfully. "What could possibly be wrong with this perfectly adorable X?" Nobody could answer that, except Baby X, who had just finished its bottle. Baby X's answer was a loud, satisfied burp.

Clearly, nothing at all was wrong. Nevertheless, none of the relatives felt comfortable about buying a present for a Baby X. The cousins who sent the baby a tiny football helmet would not come and visit any more. And the neighbors who sent a pink-flowered romper suit pulled their shades down when the Joneses passed their house.

The *Official Instruction Manual* had warned the new parents that this would happen, so they didn't fret about it. Besides, they were too busy with baby X and the hundreds of different Xercises for treating it properly. Ms. and Mr. Jones had to be Xtra careful about how they played with little X. They knew that if they kept bouncing it up in the air and saying how *strong* and *active* it was, they'd be treating it more like a boy than an X. But if all they did was cuddle it and kiss it and tell it how *sweet* and *dainty* it was, they'd be treating it more like a girl than an X.

On page 1,654 of the *Official Instruction Manual,* the scientists prescribed: "plenty of bouncing and plenty of cuddling, *both*. X ought to be strong and sweet and active. Forget about *dainty* altogether."

Meanwhile, the Joneses were worrying about other problems. Toys, for instance. And clothes. On his first shopping trip, Mr. Jones told the store clerk, "I need some clothes and toys for my new baby." The clerk smiled and said, "Well, now, is it a boy or a girl?" "It's an X," Mr. Jones said, smiling back. But the clerk got all red in the face and said huffily, "In that case, I'm afraid I can't help you, sir." So Mr. Jones wandered helplessly up and down the aisles trying to find what X needed. But everything in the store was piled up in sections marked "Boys" or "Girls." There were "Boys' Pajamas" and "Girls' Underwear" and "Boys' Fire Engines" and "Girls' Housekeeping Sets." Mr. Jones went home without buying anything for X. That night he and Ms. Jones consulted page 2,326 of the *Official Instruction Manual.* "Buy plenty of everything!" it said firmly.

So they bought plenty of sturdy blue pajamas in the Boys' Department and cheerful flowered underwear in the Girls' Department. And they bought all kinds of toys. A boy doll that made pee-pee and cried, "Pa-pa." And a girl doll that talked in three languages and said, "I am the Pres-i-dent of Gen-er-al Mo-tors." They also bought a storybook about a brave princess who rescued a handsome prince from his ivory tower, and another one about a sister and brother who grew up to be a baseball star and a ballet star, and you had to guess which was which.

The head scientists of Project Baby X checked all their purchases and told them to keep up the good work. They also reminded the Joneses to see page 4,629 of the *Manual*, where it said, "Never make Baby X feel *embarrassed* or *ashamed* about what it wants to play with. And if X gets dirty climbing rocks, never say 'Nice little Xes don't get dirty climbing rocks.'"

Likewise, it said, "If X falls down and cries, never say 'Brave little Xes don't cry.' Because, of course, nice little Xes *do* get dirty, and brave little Xes *do* cry. No matter how dirty X gets, or how hard it cries, don't worry. It's all part of the Xperiment."

Whenever the Joneses pushed Baby X's stroller in the park, smiling strangers would come over and coo: "Is that a boy or a girl?" The Joneses would smile back and say, "It's an X." The strangers would stop smiling then, and often snarl something nasty—as if the Joneses had snarled at *them*.

By the time X grew big enough to play with other children, the Joneses' troubles had grown bigger, too. Once a little girl grabbed X's shovel in the sandbox, and zonked X on the head with it. "Now, now, Tracy," the little girl's mother began to scold, "little girls mustn't hit" and she turned to ask X, "Are you a little boy or little girl, dear?"

Mr. Jones, who was sitting near the sandbox, held his breath and crossed his fingers.

X smiled politely at the lady, even though X's head had never been zonked so hard in its life. "I'm a little X," X replied.

"You're a *what?*" the lady exclaimed angrily. "You're a little b-r-a-t, you mean!"

"But little girls mustn't hit little Xes, either!" said X, retrieving the shovel with another polite smile. "What good does hitting do, anyway?"

X's father, who was still holding his breath, finally let it out, uncrossed his fingers, and grinned back at X.

And at their next secret Project Baby X meeting, the scientists grinned, too. Baby X was doing fine.

But then it was time for X to start school. The Joneses were really worried about this, because school was even more full of rules for boys and girls, and there were no rules for Xes. The teacher would tell boys to form one line, and girls to form another line. There would be boys' games and girls' games, and boys' secrets and girls' secrets. The school library would have a list of recommended books for girls, and a different list of recommended books for boys. There would even be a bathroom marked BOYS and another one marked GIRLS. Pretty soon boys and girls would hardly talk to each other. What would happen to poor little X?

The Joneses spent weeks consulting their *Instruction Manual* (there were 249 1/2 pages of advice under "First Day of School"), and attending urgent special conferences with the smart scientists of Project Baby X.

The scientists had to make sure that X's mother had taught X how to throw and catch a ball properly, and that X's father had been sure to teach X what to serve at a doll's tea party. X had to know how to shoot marbles and how to jump rope and, most of all, what to say when the Other Children asked whether X was a Boy or a Girl.

Finally, X was ready. The Joneses helped X button on a nice new pair of red-and-white checked overalls, and sharpened six pencils for X's nice new pencilbox, and marked X's name clearly on all the books in its nice new bookbag. X brushed its teeth and combed its hair, which just about covered its ears, and remembered to put a napkin in its lunchbox.

The Joneses had asked X's teacher if the class could line up alphabetically, instead of forming separate lines for boys and girls. And they had asked if X could use the principal's bathroom, because it wasn't marked anything except BATHROOM. X's teacher promised to take care of all those problems. But nobody could help X with the biggest problem of all—Other Children.

Nobody in X's class had ever known an X before. What would they think? How would X make friends?

You couldn't tell what X was by studying its clothes—overalls don't even button right-to-left, like girls' clothes, or left-to-right, like boys' clothes. And you couldn't guess whether X had a girl's short haircut or a boy's long haircut. And it was very hard to tell by the games X liked to play. Either X played ball very well for a girl, or else X played house very well for a boy.

Some of the children tried to find out by asking X tricky questions, like "Who's your favorite sports star?" That was easy. X had two favorite sports stars: a girl jockey named Robyn Smith and a boy archery champion named Robin Hood. Then they asked, "What's your favorite TV program?" And that was even easier. X's favorite TV program was "Lassie," which stars a girl dog played by a boy dog.

When X said that its favorite toy was a doll, everyone decided that X must be a girl. But then X said that the doll was really a robot, and that X had computerized it, and that it was programmed to bake fudge brownies and then clean up the kitchen. After X told them that, the other children gave up guessing what X was. All they knew was they'd sure like to see X's doll.

After school, X wanted to play with the other children. "How about shooting some baskets in the gym?" X asked the girls. But all they did was make faces and giggle behind X's back.

"How about weaving some baskets in the arts and crafts room?" X asked the boys. But they all made faces and giggled behind X's back, too.

That night, Ms. and Mr. Jones asked X how things had gone at school. X told them sadly that the lessons were okay, but otherwise school was a terrible place for an X. It seemed as if Other Children would never want an X for a friend.

Once more, the Joneses reached for their *Instruction Manual.* Under "Other Children," they found the following message: "What did you Xpect? *Other Children* have to obey all the silly boy-girl rules, because their parents taught them to. Lucky X—you don't have to stick to the rules at all! All you have to do is be yourself. P.S. We're not saying it'll be easy."

X liked being itself. But X cried a lot that night, partly because it felt afraid. So X's father held X tight, and cuddled it, and couldn't help crying a little, too. And X's mother cheered them both up by reading an Xciting story about an enchanted prince called Sleeping Handsome, who woke up when Princess Charming kissed him.

The next morning, they all felt much better, and little X went back to school with a brave smile and a clean pair of red-and-white checked overalls.

There was a seven-letter-word spelling bee in class that day. And a seven-lap boys' relay race in the gym. And a seven-layer-cake baking contest in the girls' kitchen corner. X won the spelling bee. X also won the relay race. And X almost won the baking contest, except it forgot to light the oven. Which only proves that nobody's perfect.

One of the Other Children noticed something else, too. He said: "Winning or losing doesn't seem to count to X. X seems to have fun being good at boys' skills *and* girls' skills."

"Come to think of it," said another one of the Other Children, "maybe X is having twice as much fun as we are!"

So after school that day, the girl who beat X at the baking contest gave X a big slice of her prizewinning cake. And the boy X beat in the relay race asked X to race him home.

From then on, some really funny things began to happen. Susie, who sat next to X in class, suddenly refused to wear pink dresses to school any more. She insisted on wearing red-and-white checked overalls—just like X's. Overalls, she told her parents, were much better for climbing monkey bars.

Then Jim, the class football nut, started wheeling his little sister's doll carriage around the football field. He'd put on his entire football uniform, except for the helmet. Then he'd put the helmet in the carriage, lovingly tucked under an old set of shoulder pads. Then he'd start jogging around the field, pushing the carriage and singing "Rockabye Baby" to his football helmet. He told his family that X did the same thing, so it must be okay. After all, X was now the team's star quarterback.

Susie's parents were horrified by her behavior, and Jim's parents were worried sick about his. But the worst came when the twins, Joe and Peggy, decided to share everything with each other. Peggy used Joe's hockey skates, and his microscope, and took half his newspaper route. Joe used Peggy's needlepoint kit, and her cookbooks, and took two of her three babysitting jobs. Peggy started running the lawn mower, and Joe started running the vacuum cleaner.

Their parents weren't one bit pleased with Peggy's wonderful biology experiments, or with Joe's terrific needlepoint pillows. They didn't care that Peggy mowed the lawn better, and that Joe vacuumed the carpet better. In fact, they were furious. It's all that little X's fault, they agreed. Just because X doesn't know what it is, or what it's supposed to be, it wants to get everybody *else* mixed up, too!

Peggy and Joe were forbidden to play with X anymore. So was Susie, and then Jim, and then *all* the Other Children. But it was too late; the Other Children stayed mixed up and happy and free, and refused to go back to the way they'd been before X.

Finally, Joe and Peggy's parents decided to call an emergency meeting of the school's Parents' Association, to discuss "The X Problem." They sent a report to the principal stating that X was a "disruptive influence." They demanded immediate action. The Joneses, they said, should be *forced* to tell whether X was a boy or a girl. And then X should be *forced* to behave like whichever it was. If the Joneses refused to tell, the Parents' Association said, then X must take an Xamination. The school psychiatrist must Xamine it physically and mentally, and issue a full report. If X's test showed it was a boy, it would have to obey all the boys' rules. If it proved to be a girl, X would have to obey all the girls' rules.

And if X turned out to be some kind of mixed-up misfit, then X should be Xpelled from the school. Immediately!

The principal was very upset. Disruptive influence? Mixed-up misfit? But X was an Xcellent student. All the teachers said it was a delight to have X in their classes. X was president of the student council. X had won first prize in the talent show, and second prize in the art show, and honorable mention in the science fair, and six athletic events on field day, including the potato race.

Nevertheless, insisted the Parents' Association, X is a Problem Child. X is the Biggest Problem Child we have ever seen!

So the principal reluctantly notified X's parents that numerous complaints about X's behavior had come to the school's attention. And that after the psychiatrist's Xamination, the school would decide what to do about X.

The Joneses reported this at once to the scientists, who referred them to page 85,759 of the *Instruction Manual.* "Sooner or later," it said, "X will have to be Xamined by a psychiatrist. This may be the only way any of us will know for sure whether X is mixed up—or whether everyone else is."

The night before X was to be Xamined, the Joneses tried not to let X see how worried they were. "What if—?" Mr. Jones would say. And Ms. Jones would reply, "No use worrying." Then a few minutes later, Ms. Jones would say, "What if—?" and Mr. Jones would reply, "No use worrying."

X just smiled at them both, and hugged them hard and didn't say much of anything. X was thinking, What if—? And then X thought: No use worrying.

At Xactly nine o'clock the next day, X reported to the school psychiatrist's office. The principal, along with a committee from the Parents' Association, X's teacher, X's classmates, and Ms. and

Mr. Jones, waited in the hall outside. Nobody knew the details of the tests X was to be given, but everybody knew they'd be *very* hard, and that they'd reveal Xactly what everyone wanted to know about X, but were afraid to ask.

It was terribly quiet in the hall. Almost spooky. Once in a while, they would hear a strange noise inside the room. There were buzzes. And a beep or two. And several bells. An occasional light would flash under the door. The Joneses thought it was a white light, but the principal thought it was blue. Two or three children swore it was either yellow or green. And the Parents' Committee missed it completely.

Through it all, you could hear the psychiatrist's low voice, asking hundreds of questions, and X's higher voice, answering hundreds of answers.

The whole thing took so long that everyone knew it must be the most complete Xamination anyone had ever had to take. Poor X, the Joneses thought. Serves X right, the Parents' Committee thought. I wouldn't like to be in X's overalls right now, the children thought.

At last, the door opened. Everyone crowded around to hear the results. X didn't look any different; in fact, X was smiling. But the psychiatrist looked terrible. He looked as if he was crying! "What happened?" everyone began shouting. Had X done something disgraceful? "I wouldn't be a bit surprised!" muttered Peggy and Joe's parents. "Did X flunk the *whole* test?" cried Susie's parents. "Or just the most important part?" yelled Jim's parents.

"Oh, dear," sighed Mr. Jones.

"Oh, dear," sighed Ms. Jones.

"*Sssh,*" ssshed the principal. "The psychiatrist is trying to speak."

Wiping his eyes and clearing his throat, the psychiatrist began, in a hoarse whisper. "In my opinion," he whispered—you could tell he must be very upset—"in my opinion, young X here—"

"Yes? Yes?" shouted a parent impatiently.

"*Sssh!*" ssshed the principal.

"Young *Sssh* here, I mean young X," said the doctor, frowning, "is just about—"

"Just about *what?* Let's have it!" shouted another parent.

"… just about the *least* mixed-up child I've ever Xamined!" said the psychiatrist.

"Yay for X!" yelled one of the children. And then the others began yelling, too. Clapping and cheering and jumping up and down.

"*SSSH!*" SSShed the principal, but nobody did.

The Parents' Committee was angry and bewildered. How *could* X have passed the whole Xamination? Didn't X have an *identity* problem? Wasn't X mixed up at *all?* Wasn't X *any* kind of a misfit? How could it *not* be, when it didn't even *know* what it was? And why was the psychiatrist crying?

Actually, he had stopped crying and was smiling politely through his tears. "Don't you see?" he said. "I'm crying because it's wonderful! X has absolutely no identity problem! X isn't one bit mixed up! As for being a misfit—ridiculous! X knows perfectly well what it is! Don't you, X?" The doctor winked. X winked back.

"But what *is* X?" shrieked Peggy and Joe's parents. "*We* still want to know what it is!"

"Ah, yes," said the doctor, winking again. "Well, don't worry. You'll all know one of these days. And you won't need me to tell you."

"What? What does he mean?" some of the parents grumbled suspiciously.

Susie and Peggy and Joe all answered at once. "He means that by the time X's sex matters, it won't be a secret anymore!"

With that, the doctor began to push through the crowd toward X's parents. "How do you do," he said, somewhat stiffly. And then he reached out to hug them both. "If I ever have an X of my own," he whispered, "I sure hope you'll lend me your instruction manual."

Needless to say, the Joneses were very happy. The Project Baby X scientists were rather pleased, too. So were Susie, Jim, Peggy, Joe, and all the Other Children. The Parents' Association wasn't, but they had promised to accept the psychiatrist's report, and not make any more trouble. They even invited Ms. and Mr. Jones to become honorary members, which they did.

Later that day, all X's friends put on their red-and-white checked overalls and went over to see X. They found X in the back yard, playing with a very tiny baby that none of them had ever seen before. The baby was wearing very tiny red-and-white checked overalls.

"How do you like our new baby?" X asked the Other Children proudly.

"It's got cute dimples," said Jim.

"It's got husky biceps, too," said Susie.

"What kind of baby is it?" asked Joe and Peggy.

X frowned at them. "Can't you tell?" Then X broke into a big, mischievous grin. "It's a Y!"

Supplement 12

Understanding Masculinities:
The Work of Raewyn Connell

Raewyn Connell holds a university chair at the University of Sydney in Australia. Widely known for her studies on masculinity, she was one of the founders of this research field. She has written or co-written 22 books and over 150 research papers on masculinity, class, and other equity issues, and her work is translated into 15 languages. Connell is a transsexual woman, making a formal transition later in life. Most of her earlier work was published under the name R.W. Connell. Below are some of her key insights about the workings of masculinity.

- *Multiple Masculinities.* Historians and anthropologists have shown that there is no one pattern of masculinity that is found everywhere. Different cultures and different periods of history construct masculinity differently. Equally important, more than one kind of masculinity can be found within a given cultural setting. Within any workplace, neighbourhood or peer group, there are likely to be different understandings of masculinity and different ways of "doing" masculinity.
- *Hierarchy of Masculinities.* Different masculinities do not sit side-by-side like dishes in a smorgasbord; there are definite relations between them. Typically, some masculinities are more honoured than others. Some may be actively dishonoured, for example, homosexual masculinities in modern western culture. Some are socially marginalized, for example, the masculinities of disempowered ethnic minorities. Some are exemplary, taken as symbolizing admired traits, for example, the masculinities of sporting heroes.
- *Hegemonic Masculinity.* The form of masculinity that is culturally dominant in a given setting is called "hegemonic masculinity." "Hegemonic" signifies a position of cultural authority and leadership, not total dominance; other forms of masculinity persist alongside. The hegemonic form need not be the most common form of masculinity. Hegemonic masculinity is, however, highly visible. It is likely to be what casual commentators have noticed when they speak of "the male role." Hegemonic masculinity is hegemonic not just in relation to other masculinities, but in relation to the gender order as a whole. It is an expression of the privilege men collectively have over women. The hierarchy of masculinities is an expression of the unequal shares in that privilege held by different groups of men.
- *Active Construction of Masculinities.* Masculinities do not exist prior to social behaviour, either as bodily states or fixed personalities. Rather, masculinities come into existence as people act. They are accomplished in everyday conduct or organizational life, as patterns of social practice. In other words, we "do gender" in everyday life. However, masculinities

are far from settled. From bodybuilders in the gym, to managers in the boardroom, to boys in the elementary school playground, a great deal of effort goes into the making of conventional, as well as non-conventional, masculinities. Recent research on homosexual men shows that for men too, identity and relationships involve a complex and sustained effort of construction.

- *Dynamics of Masculinities*. Since different masculinities exist in different cultures and historical epochs, we can deduce that masculinities are able to change. Masculine identities are not fixed but are dynamic; particular masculinities are composed, de-composed, contested and replaced. Sometimes this process of contestation and change finds spectacular public expression in large-scale rallies or demonstrations. More often it is local and limited. Sometimes it becomes conscious and deliberate; at other times it is non-conscious.

Source: Adapted from R.W. Connell, "Understanding Men: Gender, Sociology, and the New International Research on Masculinities," *Social Thought and Research*, 24, no. 1 & 2 (2001): 13–32.

Chapter 17

"No Way My Boys Are Going to Be Like That!" Parents' Responses to Children's Gender Nonconformity

Emily W. Kane

Emily W. Kane is the Whitehouse Professor of Sociology at Bates College in Maine. Her research interests include inequalities of race, class, gender and sexuality, gender and family, and community-based research. Some of her recent publications investigate parents' preferences for sons and daughters, parental monitoring of child's gender conformity, and public opinion toward feminism.

Parents begin gendering their children from their very first awareness of those children, whether in pregnancy or while awaiting adoption. Children themselves become active participants in this gendering process by the time they are conscious of the social relevance of gender, typically before the age of two. I address one aspect of this process of parents doing gender, both for and with their children, by exploring how parents respond to gender nonconformity among preschool-aged children. As West and Zimmerman (1987, 136) note, "to 'do' gender is not always to live up to normative conceptions of femininity or masculinity; it is to engage in behavior *at the risk of gender assessment*." I argue that many parents make efforts to stray from and thus expand normative conceptions of gender. But for their sons in particular, they balance this effort with conscious attention to producing a masculinity approximating hegemonic ideals. This balancing act is evident across many parents I interviewed regardless of gender, race/ethnicity, social class, sexual orientation, and partnership status. But I also argue that within that broader pattern are notable variations. Heterosexual fathers play a particularly central role in accomplishing their sons' masculinity and, in the process, reinforce their own as well. Their expressed motivations for that accomplishment work often involve personal endorsement of hegemonic masculinity. Heterosexual mothers and gay parents, on the other hand, are more likely to report motivations that invoke accountability to others for crafting their sons' masculinity in accordance with hegemonic ideals.

*****

Responses to Gender Nonconformity

Mothers and fathers, across a variety of social locations, often celebrated what they perceived as gender nonconformity on the part of their young daughters. They reported enjoying dressing their daughters in sports-themed clothing, as well as buying them toy cars, trucks, trains, and building toys. Some described their efforts to encourage, and pleased reactions to, what they considered traditionally male activities such as t-ball, football, fishing, and learning to use tools. Several noted that they make an effort to encourage their young daughters to aspire to tradition-ally male occupations and commented favorably on their daughters as "tomboyish," "rough and tumble," and "competitive athletically." These positive responses were combined with very little in the way of any negative response. [...]

A few parents combined these positive responses with vague and general negative responses. But these were rare and expressed with little sense of concern, as in the case of an African American, low-income, heterosexual mother who offered positive responses but also noted limits regarding her daughter: "I wouldn't want her to be too boyish, because she's a girl." In addition, no parents expressed only negative responses. These various patterns suggest that parents made little effort to accomplish their daughters' gender in accordance with any particular conception of femininity, nor did they express any notable sense of accountability to such a conception. Instead, parental responses may suggest a different kind of gendered phenomenon closely linked to the pattern evident in responses toward sons: a devaluing of traditionally feminine pursuits and qualities. Although many parents of daughters reported positive responses to what they consider typical interests and behaviors for a girl, most also celebrated the addition of atypical pursuits to their daughters' lives, and very few noted any negative response to such additions.

It is clear in the literature that there are substantial gendered constraints placed on young girls, and any devaluation of the feminine is potentially such a constraint. But the particular constraint of negative responses by parents to perceived gender nonconformity was not evident in my inter-view results. It is possible that negative response from parents to perceived departures from tra-ditional femininity would be more notable as girls reach adolescence. Pipher (1998, 286) argues that parents of young girls resist gender stereotypes for their daughters but that "the time to really worry is early adolescence. That's when the gender roles get set in cement, and that's when girls need tremendous support in resisting cultural definitions of femininity." Thorne (1994, 170) invokes a similar possibility, claiming that girls are given more gender leeway than boys in earlier childhood, "but the leeway begins to tighten as girls approach adolescence and move into the heterosexualized gender system of teens and adults." The question of whether negative parental responses might be less gender differentiated in adolescence cannot be addressed with my inter-view data and remains instead an intriguing question for future research.

In stark contrast to the lack of negative response for daughters, 23 of 31 parents of sons expressed at least some negative responses, and 6 of these offered only negative responses regard-ing what they perceived as gender nonconformity. Of 31 parents, 25 did indicate positive responses as well, but unlike references to their daughters, they tended to balance those positive feelings and actions about sons with negative ones as well.[1] The most common combination was to indicate both positive and negative responses.

Domestic Skills, Nurturance, and Empathy

Parents accepted, and often even celebrated, their sons' acquisition of domestic abilities and an orientation toward nurturance and empathy. Of the 25 parents of sons who offered positive/neutral responses, 21 did so in reference to domestic skills, nurturance, and/or empathy. For example, they reported allowing or encouraging traditionally girl toys such as dolls, doll houses, kitchen centers, and tea sets, with that response often revolving around a desire to encourage domestic competence, nurturance, emotional openness, empathy, and nonviolence as attributes they considered nontraditional but positive for boys. These parents were reporting actions and sentiments oriented toward accomplishing gender in what they considered a less conventional manner. One white, low-income, heterosexual mother taught her son to cook, asserting that "I want my son to know how to do more than boil water, I want him to know how to take care of himself." Another mother, this one a white, working-class, heterosexual parent, noted that she makes a point of talking to her sons about emotions: "I try to instill a sense of empathy in my sons and try to get them to see how other people would feel." And a white, middle-class, heterosexual father emphasized domestic competence when he noted that it does not bother him for his son to play with dolls at his cousin's house: "How then are they going to learn to take care of their children if they don't?" This positive response to domestic activities is consistent with recent literature on parental coding of toys as masculine, feminine, or neutral, which indicates that parents are increasingly coding kitchens and in some cases dolls as neutral rather than exclusively feminine (Wood, Desmarais, and Gugula 2002).

In my study, mothers and fathers expressed these kinds of efforts to accomplish gender differently for their sons with similar frequency, but mothers tended to express them with greater certainty, while fathers were less enthusiastic and more likely to include caveats. For example, this mother described her purchase of a variety of domestic toys for her three-year-old son without ambivalence: "One of the first big toys [I got him] was the kitchen center.... We cook, he has an apron he wears.... He's got his Dirt Devil vacuum and he's got his baby [doll]. And he's got all the stuff to feed her and a highchair" (white, low-income, heterosexual mother).

Some mothers reported allowing domestic toys but with less enthusiasm, such as a white, low-income, heterosexual mother who said, regarding her three-year-old son, "He had been curious about dolls and I just said, you know, usually girls play with dolls, but it's okay for you to do it too." But this kind of caution or lack of enthusiasm, even in a response coded as positive or neutral due to its allowance of gender-atypical behavior, was more evident among fathers, as the following quote illustrates: "Occasionally, if he's not doing something, I'll encourage him to maybe play with his tea cups, you know, occasionally. But I like playing with his blocks better anyway" (white, middle-class, heterosexual father).

Thus, evident among both mothers and fathers, but with greater conviction for mothers, was widespread support among parents for working to "undo" gender at the level of some of their sons' skills and values. However, this acceptance was tempered for many parents by negative responses to any interest in what I will refer to as iconic feminine items, attributes, or activities, as well as parental concern about homosexuality.

Icons of Femininity

A range of activities and attributes considered atypical for boys were met with negative responses, and for a few parents (3 of 31 parents of sons) this even included the kind of domestic toys and nurturance noted above. But more common were negative responses to items, activities, or attributes that could be considered icons of femininity. This was strikingly consistent with Kimmel's (1994, 119) previously noted claim that the "notion of anti-femininity lies at the heart of contemporary and historical constructions of manhood," and it bears highlighting that this was evident among parents of very young children. Parents of sons reported negative responses to their sons' wearing pink or frilly clothing; wearing skirts, dresses, or tights; and playing dress up in any kind of feminine attire. Nail polish elicited concern from a number of parents too, as they reported young sons wanting to have their fingernails or toenails polished. Dance, especially ballet, and Barbie dolls were also among the traditionally female activities often noted negatively by parents of sons. Of the 31 parents of sons, 23 mentioned negative reactions to at least one of these icons.

*****

Playing with nail polish and makeup, although tolerated by some parents, more often evoked negative responses like this one, from a white, upper-middle-class, gay father, speaking about his four-year-old son's use of nail polish: "He put nail polish on himself one time, and I said 'No, you can't do that, little girls put nail polish on, little boys don't.'"

Barbie dolls are an especially interesting example in that many parents reported positive responses to baby dolls, viewing these as encouraging nurturance and helping to prepare sons for fatherhood. Barbie, on the other hand, an icon of femininity, struck many parents of sons as more problematic. Barbie was often mentioned when parents were asked whether their child had ever requested an item or activity more commonly associated with the other gender. Four parents—three mothers and one father—indicated that they had purchased a Barbie at their son's request, but more often parents of sons noted that they would avoid letting their son have or play with Barbie dolls. Sometimes this negative response was categorical, as in the quote above in which a mother of a three-year-old son noted that "there's not many toys I wouldn't get him, except Barbie." A father offers a similar negative reaction to Barbie in relation to his two young sons: "If they asked for a Barbie doll, I would probably say no, you don't want [that], girls play with [that], boys play with trucks" (white, middle-class, heterosexual father).

*****

Along with material markers of femininity, many parents expressed concern about excessive emotionality (especially frequent crying) and passivity in their sons. For example, a white, upper-middle-class, heterosexual father, concerned about public crying, said about his five-year-old son, "I don't want him to be a sissy.... I want to see him strong, proud, not crying like a sissy." Another father expressed his frustration with his four-year-old son's crying over what the father views as minor injuries and indicated action to discourage those tears: "Sometimes I get so annoyed, you know, he comes [crying], and I say, 'you're not hurt, you don't even know what hurt is yet,' and I'm like 'geez, sometimes you are such a little wean,' you know?" (white, middle-class, heterosexual father).

*****

Taken together, these various examples indicate clearly the work many parents are doing to accomplish gender with and for their sons in a manner that distances those sons from any association with femininity. This work was not evident among all parents of sons. But for most parents, across racial, class, and sexual orientation categories, it was indeed evident.

Homosexuality

Along with these icons of feminine gender performance, and arguably directly linked to them, is the other clear theme evident among some parents' negative responses to perceived gender nonconformity on the part of their sons: fear that a son either would be or would be perceived as gay. Spontaneous connections of gender nonconformity and sexual orientation were not evident in parents' comments about daughters, nor among gay and lesbian parents, but arose for 7 of the 27 heterosexual parents who were discussing sons. [...]

*****

The fact that the connection between gender performance and sexual orientation was not raised for daughters, and that fear of homosexuality was not spontaneously mentioned by parents of daughters whether in connection to gender performance or not, suggests how closely gender conformity and heterosexuality are linked within hegemonic constructions of masculinity. Such connections might arise more by adolescence in relation to daughters, as I noted previously regarding other aspects of parental responses to gender nonconformity. But for sons, even among parents of very young children, heteronormativity appears to play a role in shaping parental responses to gender nonconformity, a connection that literature on older children and adults indicates is made more for males than females (Antill 1987; Hill 1999; Kite and Deaux 1987; Sandnabba and Ahlberg 1999). Martin's (2005) recent analysis also documents the importance of heteronormativity in the advice offered to parents by experts. She concludes that expert authors of child-rearing books and Web sites are increasingly supportive of gender-neutral child rearing. But especially for sons, that expert support is limited by implicit and even explicit invocations of homosexuality as a risk to be managed. [...] Given the connections between male heterosexuality and the rejection of femininity noted previously as evident in theories of hegemonic masculinity, the tendency for parents to associate gender performance and sexual orientation for sons more than daughters may also reflect a more general devaluation of femininity.

Mothers versus Fathers in the Accomplishment of Masculinity

[...] Although both mothers and fathers were equally likely to express a combination of positive and negative responses to their sons' perceived gender nonconformity, with domestic skills and empathy accepted and icons of femininity rejected, the acceptance was more pointed for mothers, and the rejection was more pointed for fathers. More fathers (11 of 14) than mothers (12 of 17) of sons indicated negative reactions to at least one of the icons discussed. Fathers also indicated more categorically negative responses: 7 of the 14 fathers but only 2 of the 17 mothers reported simply saying "no" to requests for things such as Barbie dolls, tea sets, nail polish, or ballet lessons, whether actual requests or hypothetical ones. Although fewer parents referred to excessive emotionality and passivity as concerns, the 6 parents of sons who did so included 4 fathers and 2 mothers, and here too, the quotes indicate a more categorical rejection by fathers.

Another indication of more careful policing of icons of femininity by fathers is evident in comments that placed age limitations on the acceptability of such icons. Four fathers (but no mothers) commented with acceptance on activities or interests that they consider atypical for boys but went on to note that these would bother them if they continued well past the preschool age range. The following quote from a father is typical of these responses. After noting that his four-year-old son sometimes asks for toys he thinks of as "girl toys," he went on to say, "I don't think it will ruin his life at this age but ... if he was 12 and asking for it, you know, My Little Pony or Barbies, then I think I'd really worry" (white, middle-class, heterosexual father). While comments like this one were not coded as negative responses, since they involved acceptance, I mention them here as they are consistent with the tendency for fathers to express particular concern about their sons' involvement with icons of femininity.

Three of 15 heterosexual mothers and 4 of 12 heterosexual fathers of sons responded negatively to the possibility of their son's being, or being perceived as, gay. These numbers are too small to make conclusive claims comparing mothers and fathers. But this pattern is suggestive of another arena in which fathers—especially heterosexual fathers—may stand out, especially taken together with another pattern. Implicit in the quotes offered above related to homosexuality is a suggestion that heterosexual fathers may feel particularly responsible for crafting their sons' heterosexual orientation. In addition, in comparison to mothers, their comments are less likely to refer to fears for how their son might be treated by others if he were gay and more likely to refer to the personal disappointment they anticipate in this hypothetical scenario. I return to consideration of these patterns in my discussion of accountability below.

Parental Motivations for the Accomplishment of Masculinity

The analysis I have offered thus far documents that parents are aware of their role in accomplishing gender with and for their sons. Although some parents did speak of their sons as entirely "boyish" and "born that way," many reported efforts to craft a hegemonic masculinity. Most parents expressed a very conscious awareness of normative conceptions of masculinity (whether explicitly or implicitly). Many, especially heterosexual mothers and gay parents, expressed a sense that they felt accountable to others in terms of whether their sons live up to those conceptions. In numerous ways, these parents indicated their awareness that their sons' behavior was at risk of gender assessment, an awareness rarely noted with regard to daughters. Parents varied in terms of their expressed motivations for crafting their sons' masculinity, ranging from a sense of measuring their sons against their own preferences for normative masculinity (more common among heterosexual fathers) to concerns about accountability to gender assessment by peers, other adults, and society in general (more common among heterosexual mothers and gay parents, whether mothers or fathers).

*****

Conclusion

The interviews analyzed here, with New England parents of preschool-aged children from a diverse array of backgrounds, indicate a considerable endorsement by parents of what they perceive as gender nonconformity among both their sons and their daughters. This pattern at first appears encouraging in terms of the prospects for a world less constrained by gendered expectations for children. Many parents respond positively to the idea of their children's experiencing a greater range of opportunities, emotions, and interests than those narrowly defined by gendered stereotypes, with mothers especially likely to do so. However, for sons, this positive response is primarily limited to a few attributes and abilities, namely, domestic skills, nurturance, and empathy. And it is constrained by a clear recognition of normative conceptions of masculinity (Connell 1987, 1995). Most parents made efforts to accomplish, and either endorsed or felt accountable to, an ideal of masculinity that was defined by limited emotionality, activity rather than passivity, and rejection of material markers of femininity. Work to accomplish this type of masculinity was reported especially often by heterosexual fathers; accountability to approximate hegemonic masculinity was reported especially often by heterosexual mothers, lesbian mothers, and gay fathers. Some heterosexual parents also invoked sexual orientation as part of this conception of masculinity, commenting with concern on the possibility that their son might be gay or might be perceived as such. No similar pattern of well-defined normative expectations or accountability animated responses regarding daughters, although positive responses to pursuits parents viewed as more typically masculine may well reflect the same underlying devaluation of femininity evident in negative responses to gender nonconformity among sons.

In the broader study from which this particular analysis was drawn, many parents invoked biology in explaining their children's gendered tendencies. Clearly, the role of biological explanations in parents' thinking about gender merits additional investigation. But one of the things that was most striking to me in the analyses presented here is how frequently parents indicated that they took action to craft an appropriate gender performance with and for their preschool-aged sons, viewing masculinity as something they needed to work on to accomplish. [...]

[...] I began this project expecting that parents accept with little question ideologies that naturalize gender difference. Instead, the results I have presented here demonstrate that parents are often consciously aware of gender as something that they must shape and construct, at least for their sons. This argument extends the literature on the routine accomplishment of gender in childhood by introducing evidence of conscious effort and awareness by parents as part of that accomplishment. This awareness also has implications for efforts to reduce gendered constraints on children. Recognition that parents are sometimes consciously crafting their children's gender suggests the possibility that they could be encouraged to shift that conscious effort in less gendered directions.

In addition to documenting this parental awareness, I am also able to extend the literature by documenting the content toward which parents' accomplishment work is oriented. The version of hegemonic masculinity I have argued underlies parents' responses is one that includes both change and stability. Parental openness to domestic skills, nurturance, and empathy as desirable qualities in their sons likely represents social change, and the kind of agency in the accomplishment of gender to which Fenstermaker and West (2002) refer. As Connell (1995) notes, hegemonic masculinity is historically variable in its specific content, and the evidence presented in this article suggests that some broadening of that content is occurring. But the clear limits evident within that broadening suggest the stability and power of hegemonic conceptions of masculinity. The parental boundary maintenance work evident for sons represents a crucial obstacle limiting boys' options, separating boys from girls, devaluing activities marked as feminine for both boys and girls, and thus bolstering gender inequality and heteronormativity.

Finally, along with documenting conscious awareness by parents and the content toward which their accomplishment work is oriented, my analysis also contributes to the literature by illuminating the process motivating parental gender accomplishment. The heterosexual world in general, and heterosexual fathers in particular, play a central role in that process. This is evident in the direct endorsement of hegemonic masculinity many heterosexual fathers expressed and in the accountability to others (presumably heterosexual others) many heterosexual mothers, lesbian mothers, and gay fathers expressed. Scholarly investigations of the routine production of gender in childhood, therefore, need to pay careful attention to the role of heterosexual fathers as enforcers of gender boundaries and to the role of accountability in the process of accomplishing gender. At the same time, practical efforts to loosen gendered constraints on young children by expanding their parents' normative conceptions of gender need to be aimed at parents in general and especially need to reach heterosexual fathers in particular. The concern and even fear many parents—especially heterosexual mothers, lesbian mothers, and gay fathers—expressed about how their young sons might be treated if they fail to live up to hegemonic conceptions of masculinity represent a motivation for the traditional accomplishment of gender. But those reactions could also serve as a motivation to broaden normative conceptions of masculinity and challenge the devaluation of femininity, an effort that will require participation by heterosexual fathers to succeed.

Note

1. One explanation for the paucity of negative responses could be that a broader range of actions, objects, and attributes are considered appropriate for girls than for boys. But this seems unlikely given that a similar number of parents offered positive or neutral comments about sons and daughters, indicating that they were equally likely to identify a range of actions, attributes, and objects as atypical for each gender.

References

Antill, John K. 1987. Parents' beliefs and values about sex roles, sex differences, and sexuality. *Review of Personality and Social Psychology* 7:294–328.

Connell, R.W. 1987. *Gender and power*. Stanford, CA: Stanford University Press.

———. 1995. *Masculinities*. Berkeley: University of California Press.

Fenstermaker, Sarah, and Candace West, eds. 2002. *Doing gender, doing difference*. New York: Routledge.

Hill, Shirley A. 1999. *African American children*. Thousand Oaks, CA: Sage.

Kimmel, Michael S. 1994. Masculinity as homophobia. In *Theorizing masculinities*, edited by Harry Brod. Thousand Oaks, CA: Sage.

Kite, Mary E., and Kay Deaux. 1987. Gender belief systems: Homosexuality and the implicit inversion theory. *Psychology of Women Quarterly* 11:83–96.

Martin, Karin A. 2005. William wants a doll, can he have one? Feminists, child care advisors, and gender-neutral child rearing. *Gender & Society* 20:1–2.

Pipher, Mary. 1998. *Reviving Ophelia*. New York: Ballantine Books.

Sandnabba, N. Kenneth, and Christian Ahlberg. 1999. Parents' attitudes and expectations about children's cross-gender behavior. *Sex Roles* 40:249–63.

Thorne, Barrie. 1994. *Gender play*. New Brunswick, NJ: Rutgers University Press.

West, Candace, and Sarah Fenstermaker. 1993. Power, inequality, and the accomplishment of gender. In *Theory on gender/feminism on theory*, edited by Paula England. New York: Aldine de Gruyter.

West, Candace, and Don Zimmerman. 1987. Doing gender. *Gender & Society* 1:124–51.

Wood, Eileen, Serge Desmarais, and Sara Gugula. 2002. The impact of parenting experience on gender stereotyped toy play of children. *Sex Roles* 47:39–49.

Supplement 13

Guide to Intersex and Trans Terminologies

Survivor Project

Survivor Project is a non-profit organization committed to addressing the needs of intersex and trans survivors of domestic and sexual violence through caring action, education, and expanding access to resources and to opportunities for action. The project provides presentations, consultation, and referrals to many anti-violence organizations and universities across the US, as well as collects and disseminates information about issues faced by intersex and trans survivors of domestic and sexual violence.

Intersex people naturally (that is, without any medical intervention) develop primary or secondary sex characteristics that do not fit neatly into society's definitions of male or female. Many visibly intersex people are mutilated in infancy and early childhood by doctors to make their sex characteristics conform to their idea of what normal bodies should look like. Intersex people are relatively common, although the society's denial of their existence has allowed very little room for intersexuality to be discussed publicly.

Trans people break away from one or more of society's expectations around sex and gender. These expectations include that everyone is either a man or a woman, that one's gender is fixed, that gender is rooted in their physiological sex, and that our behaviors are linked to our gender. Survivor Project uses "trans" as a very broad umbrella term.

Transsexual people perceive themselves as members of gender or sex that is different from the one they were assigned at birth. Many transsexual people pursue hormone and/or surgical interventions to make it easier to live as members of the gender or sex they identify as.

The term *transgender* is used in so many different ways that it is almost impossible to define it. Some use it to refer to people whose behavior or expression do[es] not match with their gender. Some use it to describe a gender outside of man/woman binary. Some use it to describe the condition of having no gender or multiple genders. Other possibilities include people who perform genders or deliberately play within/on gender as well as being gender-deviant in other ways.

Respectful Languages

Here is some additional advice about certain "hot button" languages that you might want to think twice before using.

"Hermaphrodite": An old medical term describing intersex people. Many intersex activists reject this word due to the stigmatization arising from its mythical roots and the abuse that medical professionals inflicted on them under this label.

"Ambiguous genitalia": Many intersex activists contest the use of this phrase to describe their bodies because the ambiguity is with the society's definition of male and female rather than their bodies.

"Berdache": Used by Western colonialists to refer to Native American genders that they could not neatly classify into the Eurocentric binary system of gender and sex. The contemporary language that is accepted by Native American people who identify with these genders is "two-spirit."

Bottom Line

- These definitions are not fixed or universally accepted. They are presented to you for the purpose of communication, and should not be considered an authoritative source.
- We need to respect the rights of intersex and trans people to define themselves. Do not categorize people based on these definitions, but rather ask them how they identify and address them accordingly.
- Use pronouns preferred by intersex or trans people. Do not ever call them "it" or "he-she" unless they actually identify themselves as such.
- It is generally considered rude to ask someone about the shape of their genitalia, and this is true even when you are speaking to an intersex or trans person. Do not ask their medical diagnosis or surgical status merely out of curiosity.
- Do not make assumptions based on appearance, voice, etc. Do not assume that someone is intersex, trans, both or neither from external cues.
- Do not assume that "trans women" are male-to-female transsexuals (or "trans men" are female-to-male transsexuals), because there are many ways to be trans other than being transsexual. Someone who was assigned as female at birth and still identifies as a woman may call herself a "trans woman" if she does not fit into the society's definition of femininity.
- Intersex people and FtM trans people are often underrepresented in the discussion about intersex and trans issues. Do not let MtF trans people speak for others, and pay an extra effort to listen to intersex people and FtM trans people.
- Intersex and trans people, like any other groups, come from diverse backgrounds. Make sure that you are not just listening to the most privileged within intersex and trans communities. Avoid reinforcing racism, classism and other oppressions within these communities.

Source: Adapted from Survivor Project, "Guide to Intersex & Trans Terminologies" (2003), retrieved from http://www.survivorproject.org/basic.html

Chapter 18

Transgender Rights

Riki Wilchins

Riki Wilchins is a leader in transgender rights and advocacy and founder of the Gender Public Advocacy Coalition (GenderPAC), one of the first transgender advocacy groups in North America. A well-known author on gender theory, she also uses stand-up comedy to educate audiences. In addition to the book excerpted here, Queer Theory/Gender Theory: An Instant Primer, *her publications include* Read My Lips: Sexual Subversion and the End of Gender *and* GenderQueer: Voices from Beyond the Sexual Binary. *She was selected by* Time Magazine *as one of "100 Civic Innovators for the 21st Century."*

Women's and gay rights advocates made phenomenal mainstream progress in the 1970s and 1980s, in part by detouring around some of the more difficult aspects of gender rights. But in the 1990s, gender advocacy received an incredible infusion of energy from two sources: the unexpected rise of an energetic transgender rights movement, and the amazing conquest of academia by post-modernism, particularly queer theory. Both movements would make enormous strides in the struggle for gender rights, and both would pull up short of the goal for very different reasons.

Transcending gender stereotypes had always been a subtext for gay rights. [...] In many ways, gender defined what most Americans thought of when they said "queer." If it is true that queers who transcended gender norms were not well-served by two movements that wanted to focus only on sex and sexual orientation, it was also true that the tremendous political success of both movements held out hope for a better day.

Genderqueer gays and feminists undertook major movement roles, often remaining quietly behind the scenes and hoping for better days. But in the early 1990s that equation began to break down in unexpected ways. A lesbian feminist friend, responding tartly to some new and loud demands for the inclusion of transgender people, remarked to me, "Where were all these transgender people in the '70s and '80s?"

I replied, "Oh, they were here. They were just still *gay*."

Transgender people had always been around, living under the broad umbrella of the gay community. But as gayness and gender became separated, a new term was needed—*transgender*.

In many communities of color, transpeople still simply called themselves *gay*—which makes sense, since white American culture tends to be one of the few that splits sexual orientation from gender. In fact, in many countries, the word *transgender* is hardly used, as is also the case in some communities in the United States. As queer ethnographer David Valentine notes, a black femme-queen who "walks the balls" as part of the New York house culture (and who takes hormones and has breast implants) is more likely to describe herself as gay or queer than transgender.

But gay rights advocates had left cross-dressers, transsexuals, drag queens, intersexuals, and stone butches with battles left to fight. They could love being queer, but could they look and act queer? The answer was still no.

The groundwork for the coming "transgender revolution" was laid by the community's quietest members—cross-dressers. An immense social network of cross-dressers had been forming since Virginia Prince's efforts in the 1960s. Thinking that perhaps what she did was not a perversion, she placed a small ad in an out-of-the-way publication to invite others to join her anonymously in a hotel room.

Twelve men showed up, each carrying a bag or suitcase with women's clothing. There, almost frantic with shame, anxiety, and fear, they all agreed to put on their clothes in front of one another. As a friend put it, "Virginia Prince made it possible for two cross-dressers to look one another in the eye."

By the 1970s, there was at least one major cross-dressing convention each year where men could go for a whole weekend and be themselves, dress openly, and—as long as they didn't leave the grounds—pretend that they were normal and society was tolerant. By the 1990s, there were one or two major conventions a month. And transsexuals began to show up in increasing numbers.

For transsexuals in the 1970s and 1980s, the most important thing in the world was passing. If you couldn't pass, you couldn't live, and that's still too often true today. Buying groceries, using a lavatory, seeing a movie, or going to class were all incredibly difficult if you were obviously transgender. Finding a date or a mate was practically impossible. It was enough to make you feel like a complete closeted freak—a certain recipe for self-loathing.

As hospitals backed out of the sex-reassignment business, private doctors around the country took it over. It became more democratic: cheaper and easier to get. By the end of the 1990s, postoperative transsexuals probably numbered more than 50,000.

Surrounded by scores of transsexuals and hundreds of cross-dressers at conventions, it was impossible for differently gendered people to feel the same shame. And it was impossible for them not to want to take this strange feeling of being open and unafraid and make it a daily thing. Transsexuals and cross-dressers began to see themselves less as social problems and more as the next oppressed minority. It was a powerful moment of political recognition.

The emergence of the internet and e-mail enabled transgender people to communicate privately and cheaply and to build more elaborate social networks.

*****

For the first time, transsexuals became conscious of themselves not as just a social minority, but as a political minority. Enthusiasm for activism, even protest, began to develop. For the first time, there were street actions by transsexual groups such as Transgender Nation and Transexual Menace.

The murder of Brandon Teena (memorialized in the movie *Boys Don't Cry* and *The Brandon Teena Story*) radicalized many transsexual activists and provided a rallying cry. On the opening day of the trial of Brandon's murderers, 40 people—most of them strangers—flew to Nebraska from around the country to hold a vigil in front of the courthouse. Most of them wore Transexual Menace T-shirts. It was a cultural clash across any number of boundaries. Townspeople saw weirdos—outside agitators—who weren't welcome. School kids came by to gawk. The sheriff's office, largely responsible for Brandon's death in the first place, tried hard to accommodate and protect us.

*****

By 1996, gay newspapers finally began covering transsexual protests, hate crimes, and police violence—topics the press had previously ignored. By 2002, a National Day of Remembrance (which had originated with a 1998 vigil in San Francisco) for such victims was being held in cities around the country. This was the birth of real awareness of the need for a gender rights movement, and the seeds were sown for what would later become GenderPAC.

The push by gay organizations to add the "T" to "LGB" was on for real. An energetic and often rancorous debate over the inclusion of transgender people broke out across the US virtually overnight. Change began to happen very fast. Within two years, LLEGO (the national Latina/o gay group) and the National Gay and Lesbian Task Force both added transgender to their mission statements. A furious battle broke out between transgender activists and the Human Rights Campaign over the inclusion of gender protections in the Employment Non-Discrimination Act (ENDA).

The first National Gender Lobby Day was held on Capitol Hill. American Airlines became the first major corporation to add gender identity to its Equal Employment Opportunity (EEO) policies. Cities and municipalities began passing local ordinances adding gender expression and identity to their nondiscrimination protections. Within seven years, almost every major and regional gay group identified itself or its mission as "lesbian, gay, bisexual, *and transgender.*"

*****

Yet the embrace of "T" by LGB groups remains far from complete. For one thing, although transsexuals have been historically sheltered in the gay community and have made incredible contributions to the cause of gay rights, the relationship between gender identity and sexual orientation remains murky for many gays and lesbians. Transsexual activists have often addressed this by calling attention to butches, drag queens, and effeminate gay men and pointing out that "It's all about gender, honey."

Yet, because most drag and butch people still identify as gay rather than transgender, some LGB activists remain sympathetic but unconvinced. While they include transsexuals in the scope of their activism, they still see gender identity and sexual orientation as two different, if related, problems.

In addition, the term *transgender* is still burdened with its share of hurdles. It arose in the mid 1990s as a way to distinguish people who cross sexes by changing their bodies (transsexual) from people who cross genders by changing their clothing, behavior, and grooming (transgender).

Within a few years, *transgender* became an umbrella term for *anyone* who crossed gender lines. But (in my own simplistic binary) there is a strong and a weak version of this solution. The strong version includes practically everyone, since almost every person rubs up against narrow gender roles at some point in their lives. In the weak version, transgender not only includes transsexuals and cross-dressers, but also butch/femmes, "aggressive" women, drag queens and kings, effeminate gay men, intersexuals, and so on. The idea is that all people who are *visibly queer* face common political problems and make natural allies.

The challenges are many. For one thing, subgroups such as drag people, effeminate gay men, and stone butches do not perceive themselves as political minorities. They tend to be underorganized and underrepresented politically. Second, for most people, crossing gender lines is still a source of shame, and not something to be claimed, especially as a basis for identity. Witness my room full of gay men who were abashed by the notion that any of them are bottoms. It's hard to rally people to a cause with which they're embarrassed to be associated.

Obviously, most people still don't grasp gender as a valid civil rights issue like sexual orientation, race, or sex.

*****

At the same time, *transgender rights* have increasingly come to mean *transsexual rights*. Much of the remaining advocacy in the transcommunity has focused on hate crimes against transsexuals, access to hormones and surgery, name-change laws, insurance reimbursement, and changes to birth certificates. These are all important and often neglected problems. But they are of interest mostly to people who want to change sexes.

Most of the people who might call themselves *transgender* have so far failed to claim the identity, and it's unclear that they will ever do so. It is also debatable whether such people are really included in this new movement, or simply added on as an afterthought. The great "silent majority" of those who do call themselves transgender continues to be cross-dressers, and they are seldom heard from. There may be 100,000 or so transsexuals in the United States, but there are undoubtedly several million cross-dressers, many of whom are married middle-class fathers and grandfathers.

Many cross-dressers have a sophisticated appreciation of advocacy politics, are aware of transgender activism, and have the financial means to participate at a high level. Moreover, they are an underserved community who are bitterly oppressed for something as simple as claiming their feminine feelings and enjoying wearing feminine clothing—something my mom has done for years without noticeable harm.

Cross-dressers should be an enormous source of strength and support for a transgender movement. Yet they are not. For one thing, nearly everyone, even those belonging to other minorities, still considers a man in a dress to be a joke. Even many transsexuals look down on cross-dressers because what they do is seen as a choice. As one transsexual said, "I do this 24/7. I can't take off who I am and hang it in the closet on weekdays when it becomes inconvenient."

Yet a man who wears a dress in public—unless he passes really well—is almost certain to be verbally or even physically assaulted. He may lose his job and—if he does not confine his cross-dressing to weekends at distant conferences—his wife and family too. Which is to say, we can make all the jokes we want, but it still takes a real man to wear a dress.

*****

The upshot [of] this, even with the rise of transgender activism and its growing success, is that gender rights remains a contested frontier. This is strange at a time when *The New York Times* reports that nearly one in seven new cases filed at the Equal Employment Opportunity Commission (EEOC) is male-on-male gender harassment: men calling each other "bitch," "she," or "honey," simulated sex acts, limp-wristed imitations of effeminacy, or sexual menacing. In short, grown men continue to use all the nasty tricks boys learn in high school to humiliate the geeky kid who likes math more than football or girls.

Feminists remain largely unsure what to make of transgender people. FTM transsexuals are simply confusing—they seem to be women who've given up the battle against patriarchy and joined the other side. And while imitation may be the sincerest form of flattery, many feminists suspect that MTF transsexuals and cross-dressers are merely pretending to be women—enacting a parody of sexism's worst excesses in makeup, high heels, and inevitably prodigious breasts.

As for LGB groups, adding the T to your mission statement or political efforts is now considered de rigueur—LGBT is here to stay. [...]

Yet in embracing the "T," gays, lesbians, and bisexuals still confine issues of gender to the transgender community. This combines the political correctness of the inclusion of transgender people with practical separation from the social and political embarrassments of gender issues. "Gender issues are something *those people over there* have. We're doing the right thing by including them, but it's not a problem *any of us* have."

*****

If it sounds like I'm disappointed, I am. It was second-class treatment from the gay and feminist movements that propelled many of us to start a separate transgender activism. Now even the transgender movement is creating its own class of politically marginalized people. At one time, we gratefully welcomed anyone who wanted to identify as *transgender*, which seems to me the way it should be. But with new legitimacy came a strengthening sense of identity. [...]

I began to hear the stories of people being told they weren't "really" transgender because they didn't want to take hormones or have surgery. It would have once seemed unbelievable, but *transgender*—that grand experimental umbrella for all the other misfits—has become yet another identity with its own boundaries, hierarchies, and norms.

The new reverse-hierarchy is forming around who is *most transgressive* and therefore *least privileged*. As one friend put it, "Transsexuals should come first, because they're the most oppressed."

*****

Transsexuals face a unique array of institutional inequities in medicine, legal identity, insurance, child custody laws, and sex-change laws. It may be that transsexuals are such a singular case that it will take a movement focused solely on their needs to get the job done. As anyone can attest who has sat through the story of Brandon Teena in *Boys Don't Cry*, that would be no small achievement.

At the same time, it's important to bear in mind what [...] Seth Goldman once wrote in a passionate—if tormented—e-mail:

> Whether in my philosophy of race and gender course at school, in queer circles where transgender issues are trendy or, in the large number of media outlets now covering gay rights, sexual harassment, and women's issues, I'm getting more and more angry that no one will ever say those two words: "gender stereotypes." [...] It's frustrating because I constantly feel that wall in almost everyone's head—whether they're gay or straight, trans or feminist, elder or youth—to seeing the larger gender paradigm that includes them all.

Supplement 14

Activist Insight: Men and Feminism

The White Ribbon Campaign

What is the White Ribbon Campaign (WRC)?
The White Ribbon Campaign (WRC) is the largest effort in the world of men working to end violence against women (VAW). In over sixty countries, campaigns are led by both men and women, even though the focus is on educating men and boys. In some countries it is a general public education effort focused on ending violence against women.

How did the WRC get started?
In 1991, a handful of men in Canada decided they had a responsibility to urge men to speak out about violence against women. Wearing a white ribbon would be a symbol of men's opposition to violence against women.

What does it mean to wear a white ribbon?
Wearing a white ribbon is a personal *pledge to never commit, condone or remain silent about violence against women and girls*. Wearing a white ribbon is a way of saying, "Our future has no violence against women."

What is the goal of WRC? How is this accomplished?
The main goal of WRC is ending violence against women in all its forms. We accomplish this in five ways:

- Challenging everyone to speak out, and think about their own beliefs, language and actions.
- Educating young people, especially young men and boys, on the issue through the educational resources we produce.
- Raising public awareness of the issue.
- Working in partnership with women's organizations, the corporate sector, the media and other partners to create a future with no violence against women.
- Supporting White Ribbon Campaigns with our experience, resources and networks.

Does this mean you think that men are bad?
We do not think that men are naturally violent and we don't think that men are bad; however, we do think all men have roles and responsibilities in ending violence against women. The majority of men are not physically violent. Researchers tell us many past cultures had little or no violence.

At the same time, we do think that some men have learned to express their anger or insecurity through violence. Far too many men have come to believe that violence against a woman, child or another man is an acceptable way to control another person, especially an intimate partner.

By remaining silent about these things, we allow other men to poison our work, schools and homes. The good news is that more and more men and boys want to make a difference. Caring men are tired of the sexism that hurts the women around them. Caring men are also concerned with the impact of this violence on the lives of men and boys.

Source: Excerpted from the White Ribbon Campaign, "The Campaign," retrieved from: http://www.whiteribbon.ca/about_us/

Source: Men Can Stop Rape (2008), retrieved from http://www.mystrength.org/8.0.html

Chapter 19

Becoming 100 Percent Straight

Michael A. Messner

Michael A. Messner is professor of sociology and gender studies at the University of Southern California. His research areas include men and masculinity, gender relations and the gendered division of labour in organized sports and athletics, and gender-based violence. He is the author of a dozen books, including a recently published intergenerational study of masculinity called King of the Wild Suburb: A Memoir of Fathers, Sons, and Guns. *Along with Cheryl Cooky of Purdue University, he recently finished an update of a longitudinal study of gender in televised sports news and highlights shows.*

In 1995, as part of my job as the president of the North American Society for the Sociology of Sport, I needed to prepare an hour-long presidential address for the annual meeting of some 200 people. This presented a challenge to me: how might I say something to my colleagues that was interesting, at least somewhat original, and above all, not boring. Students may think that their professors are especially dull in the classroom but, believe me, we are usually much worse at professional meetings. For some reason, many of us who are able to speak to our classroom students in a relaxed manner, using relatively jargon-free language, seem to become robots, dryly reading our papers—packed with impressively unclear jargon—to our yawning colleagues.

Since I desperately wanted to avoid putting 200 sport studies scholars to sleep, I decided to deliver a talk which I entitled "Studying Up on Sex." The title, which certainly did get my colleagues' attention, was intended as a play on words, a double entendre. "Studying up" has one generally recognizable colloquial meaning, but in sociology it has another. It refers to studying "up" in the power structure. Sociologists have perhaps most often studied "down"—studying the poor, the blue- or pink-collar workers, the "nuts, sluts and perverts," the incarcerated. The idea of "studying up" rarely occurs to sociologists unless and until we live in a time when those who are "down" have organized movements that challenge the institutional privileges of elites. For example, in the wake of labor movements, some sociologists like C. Wright Mills studied up on corporate elites. Recently, in the wake of racial and ethnic civil rights movements, some scholars like Ruth Frankenberg have begun to study the social meanings of "whiteness." Much of my research, inspired by feminism, has involved a studying up on the social construction of masculinity in sport. Studying up, in these cases, has raised some fascinating new and important questions about the workings of power in society.

However, I realized that when it comes to understanding the social and interpersonal dynamics of sexual orientation in sport we have barely begun to scratch the surface of a very complex issue. Although sport studies have benefited from the work of scholars such as Helen Lenskyj (1986, 1997),

Brian Pronger (1990) and others who have delineated the experiences of lesbians and gay men in sports, there has been very little extension of their insights into a consideration of the social construction of heterosexuality in sport. In sport, just as in the larger society, we seem obsessed with asking "How do people become gay?" Imbedded in the question is the assumption that people who identify as heterosexual, or "straight" require no explanation, since they are simply acting out the "natural" or "normal" sexual orientation. We seem to be saying that the "sexual deviants" require explanation, while the experience of heterosexuals, because we are considered normal, seems to require no critical examination or discussion. But I knew that a closer look at the development of sexual orientation or sexual identity reveals an extremely complex process. I decided to challenge myself and my colleagues by arguing that although we have begun to "study up" on corporate elites in sport, on whiteness, on masculinity, it is now time to extend that by studying up on heterosexuality.

But in the absence of systematic research on this topic, where could I start? How could I explore, raise questions about, and begin to illuminate the social construction of heterosexuality for my colleagues? Fortunately, for the previous two years I have been working with a group of five men (three of whom identified as heterosexual, two as gay) mutually to explore our own biographies in terms of the earlier bodily experiences that helped to shape our gender and sexual identities. We modeled our project after that of a German group of feminist women, led by Frigga Haug who created a research method which they call "memory work." In short, the women would mutually choose a body part, such as "hair," and each would then write a short story based on a particularly salient childhood memory that related to their hair (for example, being forced by parents to cut one's hair, deciding to straighten one's curly hair in order to look more like other girls, etc.). Then the group would read all of the stories and discuss them one by one in the hope of gaining more general understanding of, and raising new questions about, the social construction of "femininity." What resulted from this project was a fascinating book called *Female Sexualization* (Haug 1987), which my men's group used as the inspiration for our project.

As a research method, memory work is anything but conventional. Many sociologists would argue that this is not really a "research method" at all. The information that emerges from the project cannot be used very confidently as a generalizable "truth," and in this sort of project the researcher is simultaneously part of what is being studied. How, my more scientifically oriented colleagues might ask, is the researcher to maintain his or her objectivity? My answer is that in this kind of project objectivity is not the point. In fact, the strength of this sort of research is the depth of understanding that might be gained through a systematic group analysis of one's experience, one's subjective orientation to social processes. A clear understanding of the subjective aspect of social life—one's bodily feelings, emotions, and reaction to others—is an invaluable window that allows us to see and ask new sociological questions about group interaction and social structure. In short, group memory work can provide an important, productive, and fascinating insight on social reality, though not a complete (or completely reliable) picture.

As I pondered the lack of existing research on the social construction of heterosexuality in sport, I decided to draw on one of my own stories from my memory work in the men's group. Some of my most salient memories of embodiment are sports memories. I grew up as the son of a high school coach, and I eventually played point guard on my dad's team. In what follows, I juxtapose my story with that of a gay former Olympic athlete, Tom Waddell, whom I had interviewed several years earlier for a book on the lives of male athletes (Messner 1994).

Many years ago I read some psychological studies that argued that even for self-identified heterosexuals it is a natural part of their development to have gone through "bisexual" or even "homosexual" stages of life. When I read this, it seemed theoretically reasonable, but did not ring true in my experience. I have always been, I told myself, 100 percent heterosexual! The group process of analyzing my own autobiographical stories challenged the concept I had developed of myself, and also shed light on the way in which the institutional context of sport provided a context for the development of my definition of myself as "100 percent straight." Here is one of the stories.

When I was in the 9th grade, I played on a "D" basketball team, set up especially for the smallest of high school boys. Indeed, though I was pudgy with baby fat, I was a short 5'2", still pre-pubescent with no facial hair and a high voice that I artificially tried to lower. The first day of practice, I was immediately attracted to a boy I'll call Timmy, because he looked like the boy who played in the *Lassie* TV show. Timmy was short, with a high voice, like me. And like me, he had no facial hair yet. Unlike me, he was very skinny. I liked Timmy right away, and soon we were together a lot. I noticed things about him that I didn't notice about other boys: he said some words a certain way, and it gave me pleasure to try to talk like him. I remember liking the way the light hit his boyish, nearly hairless body. I thought about him when we weren't together. He was in the school band, and at the football games, I'd squint to see where he was in the mass of uniforms. In short, though I wasn't conscious of it at the time, I was infatuated with Timmy—I had a crush on him. Later that basketball season, I decided—for no reason that I could really articulate then—that I hated Timmy. I aggressively rejected him, began to make fun of him around other boys. He was, we all agreed, a geek. He was a faggot.

Three years later, Timmy and I were both on the varsity basketball team, but had hardly spoken a word to each other since we were freshmen. Both of us now had lower voices, had grown to around 6 feet tall, and we both shaved, at least a bit. But Timmy was a skinny, somewhat stigmatized reserve on the team, while I was the team captain and starting point guard. But I wasn't so happy or secure about this. I'd always dreamed of dominating games, of being the hero. Halfway through my senior season, however, it became clear that I was not a star, and I figured I knew why. I was not aggressive enough.

I had always liked the beauty of the fast break, the perfectly executed pick and roll play between two players, and especially the long twenty-foot shot that touched nothing but the bottom of the net. But I hated and feared the sometimes brutal contact under the basket. In fact, I stayed away from the rough fights for rebounds and was mostly a perimeter player, relying on my long shots or my passes to more aggressive teammates under the basket. But now it became apparent to me that time was running out in my quest for greatness: I needed to change my game, and fast. I decided one day before practice that I was gonna get aggressive. While practising one of our standard plays, I passed the ball to a teammate, and then ran to the spot at which I was to set a pick on a defender. I knew that one could sometimes get away with setting a face-up screen on a player, and then as he makes contact with you, roll your back to him and plant your elbow hard in his stomach. The beauty of this move is that your own body "roll" makes the elbow look like an accident. So I decided to try this move. I approached the defensive player, Timmy, rolled, and planted my elbow deeply into his solar plexus. Air exploded audibly from Timmy's mouth, and he crumbled to the floor momentarily.

Play went on as though nothing had happened, but I felt bad about it. Rather than making me feel better, it made me feel guilty and weak. I had to admit to myself why I'd chosen Timmy as the target against whom to test out my new aggression. He was the skinniest and weakest player on the team.

At the time, I hardly thought about these incidents, other than to try to brush them off as incidents that made me feel extremely uncomfortable. Years later, I can now interrogate this as a sexual story, and as a gender story unfolding within the context of the heterosexualized and masculinized institution of sport. Examining my story in light of research conducted by Alfred Kinsey a half-century ago, I can recognize in myself what Kinsey saw as a very common fluidity and changeability of sexual desire over the life course. Put simply, Kinsey found that large numbers of adult, "heterosexual" men had previously, as adolescents and young adults, experienced sexual desire for males. A surprisingly large number of these men had experienced sexual contact to the point of orgasm with other males during adolescence or early adulthood. Similarly, my story invited me to consider what is commonly called the "Freudian theory of bisexuality." Sigmund Freud shocked the post-Victorian world by suggesting that all people go through a stage, early in life, when they are attracted to people of the same sex.[1] Adult experiences, Freud argued, eventually led most people to shift their sexual desire to what he called an appropriate "love object"—a person of the opposite sex. I also considered my experience in light of what lesbian feminist author Adrienne Rich called the institution of compulsory heterosexuality. Perhaps the extremely high levels of homophobia that are often endemic in boys' and men's organized sports led me to deny and repress my own homoerotic desire through a direct and overt rejection of Timmy, through homophobic banter with male peers, and the resultant stigmatization of the feminized Timmy. Eventually I considered my experience in the light of what radical theorist Herbert Marcuse called the sublimation of homoerotic desire into an aggressive, violent act as serving to construct a clear line of demarcation between self and other. Sublimation, according to Marcuse, involves the driving underground, into the unconscious, of sexual desires that might appear dangerous due to their socially stigmatized status. But sublimation involves more than simple repression into the unconscious. It involves a transformation of sexual desire into something else—often into aggressive and violent acting out toward others. These acts clarify the boundaries between oneself and others and therefore lessen any anxieties that might be attached to the repressed homoerotic desire.

Importantly, in our analysis of my story, the memory group went beyond simply discussing the events in psychological terms. The story did perhaps suggest some deep psychological processes at work, but it also revealed the importance of social context—in this case, the context of the athletic team. In short, my rejection of Timmy and the joining with teammates to stigmatize him in 9th grade stands as an example of what sociologist R. W. Connell calls a moment of engagement with hegemonic masculinity, where I actively took up the male group's task of constructing heterosexual/masculine identities in the context of sport. The elbow in Timmy's gut three years later can be seen as a punctuation mark that occurred precisely because of my fears that I might be failing in this goal.

It is helpful, I think, to compare my story with gay and lesbian "coming out" stories in sport. Though we have a few lesbian and bisexual coming out stories among women athletes, there are very few from gay males. Tom Waddell, who as a closeted gay man finished sixth in the decathlon in the 1968 Olympics, later came out and started the Gay Games, an athletic and cultural festival that draws tens of thousands of people every four years. When I interviewed Tom Waddell over a decade ago about his sexual identity and athletic career, he made it quite clear that for many years sports was his closet:

> When I was a kid, I was tall for my age, and was very thin and very strong. And I was usu-
> ally faster than most other people. But I discovered rather early that I liked gymnastics and

> I liked dance. I was very interested in being a ballet dancer … [but] something became obvious to me right away—that male ballet dancers were effeminate, that they were what most people would call faggots. And I thought I just couldn't handle that … I was totally closeted and very concerned about being male. This was the fifties, a terrible time to live, and everything was stacked against me. Anyway, I realized that I had to do something to protect my image of myself as a male—because at that time homosexuals were thought of primarily as men who wanted to be women. And so I threw myself into athletics—I played football, gymnastics, track and field … I was a jock—that's how I was viewed, and I was comfortable with that.

Tom Waddell was fully conscious of entering sports and constructing a masculine/heterosexual athletic identity precisely because he feared being revealed as gay. It was clear to him, in the context of the 1950s, that being known as gay would undercut his claims to the status of manhood. Thus, though he described the athletic closet as "hot and stifling," he remained there until several years after his athletic retirement. He even knowingly played along with locker room discussions about sex and women as part of his "cover."

> I wanted to be viewed as male, otherwise I would be a dancer today. I wanted the male, macho image of an athlete. So I was protected by a very hard shell. I was clearly aware of what I was doing … I often felt compelled to go along with a lot of locker room garbage because I wanted that image—and I know a lot of others who did too.

Like my story, Waddell's points to the importance of the athletic institution as a context in which peers mutually construct and reconstruct narrow definitions of masculinity. Heterosexuality is considered to be a rock-solid foundation of this concept of masculinity. But unlike my story, Waddell's may invoke a dramaturgical analysis.[2] He seemed to be consciously "acting" to control and regulate others' perceptions of him by constructing a public "front stage" persona that differed radically from what he believed to be his "true" inner self. My story, in contrast, suggests a deeper, less consciously strategic repression of my homoerotic attraction. Most likely, I was aware on some level of the dangers of such feelings, and was escaping the risks, disgrace, and rejection that would likely result from being different. For Waddell, the decision to construct his identity largely within sport was to step into a fiercely heterosexual/masculine closet that would hide what he saw as his "true" identity. In contrast, I was not so much stepping into a "closet" that would hide my identity; rather, I was stepping out into an entire world of heterosexual privilege. My story also suggests how a threat to the promised privileges of hegemonic masculinity—my failure as an athlete—might trigger a momentary sexual panic that can lay bare the constructedness, indeed, the instability of the heterosexual masculine identity.

In either case, Waddell's or mine, we can see how, as young male athletes, heterosexuality and masculinity was not something we "were," but something we were doing. It is significant, I think, that although each of us was "doing heterosexuality," neither of us was actually "having sex" with women (though one of us desperately wanted to). This underscores a point made by some recent theorists that heterosexuality should not be thought of simply as sexual acts between women and men. Rather, heterosexuality is a constructed identity, a performance, and an institution that is not necessarily linked to sexual acts. Though for one of us it was more conscious than for the other, we were both "doing heterosexuality" as an ongoing practice through which we sought to do two things:

- avoid stigma, embarrassment, ostracism, or perhaps worse if we were even suspected of being gay;
- link ourselves into systems of power, status, and privilege that appear to be the birthright of "real men" (i.e., males who are able to compete successfully with other males in sport, work, and sexual relations with women).

In other words, each of us actively scripted our own sexual and gender performances, but these scripts were constructed within the constraints of a socially organized (institutionalized) system of power and pleasure.

Questions for Future Research

As I prepared to tell this sexual story publicly to my colleagues at the sport studies conference, I felt extremely nervous. Part of the nervousness was due to the fact that I knew some of them would object to my claim that telling personal stories can be a source of sociological insights. But a larger part of the reason for my nervousness was due to the fact that I was revealing something very personal about my sexuality in such a public way. Most of us are not accustomed to doing this, especially in the context of a professional conference. But I had learned long ago, especially from feminist women scholars, and from gay and lesbian scholars, that biography is linked to history. Part of "normal" academic discourse has been to hide "the personal" (including the fact that the researchers are themselves people with values, feelings, and, yes, biases) behind [a] carefully constructed facade of "objectivity." Rather than trying to hide or be ashamed of one's subjective experience of the world, I was challenging myself to draw on my experience of the world as a resource. Not that I should trust my experience as the final word on "reality." White, heterosexual males like me have made the mistake for centuries of calling their own experience "objectivity," and then punishing anyone who does not share their world view by casting them as "deviant." Instead, I hope to use my experience as an example of how those of us who are in dominant sexual/racial/gender/class categories can get a new perspective on the "constructed-ness" of our identities by juxtaposing our subjective experiences against the recently emerging world views of gay men and lesbians, women, and people of color.

Finally, I want to stress that in juxtaposition neither my own nor Tom Waddell's story sheds much light on the question of why some individuals "become gay" while others "become" heterosexual or bisexual. Instead, I should like to suggest that this is a dead-end question, and that there are far more important and interesting questions to be asked:

- How has heterosexuality, as an institution and as an enforced group practice, constrained and limited all of us—gay, straight, and bi?
- How has the institution of sport been an especially salient institution for the social construction of heterosexual masculinity?
- Why is it that when men play sports they are almost always automatically granted masculine status, and thus assumed to be heterosexual, while when women play sports, questions are raised about their "femininity" and sexual orientation?

These kinds of questions aim us toward an analysis of the workings of power within institutions—including the ways that these workings of power shape and constrain our identities and relationships—and point us toward imagining alternative social arrangements that are less constraining for everyone.

Notes

1. The fluidity and changeability of sexual desire over the life course is now more obvious in evidence from prison and military populations, and single-sex boarding schools. The theory of bisexuality is evident, for example, in childhood crushes on same-sex primary school-teachers.
2. Dramaturgical analysis, associated with Erving Goffman, uses the theater and performance to develop an analogy with everyday life.

References

Haug, Frigga (1987) *Female Sexualization: A Collective Work of Memory.* London: Verso.

Lenskyj, Helen (1986) *Out of Bounds: Women, Sport and Sexuality.* Toronto: Women's Press.

Lenskyj, Helen (1997) "No fear? Lesbians in sport and physical education." *Women in Sport and Physical Activity Journal* 6(2): 7–22.

Messner, Michael A. (1994) "Gay athletes and the Gay Games: In interview with Tom Waddell," in M.A. Messner and D.F. Sabo (eds) *Sex, Violence and Power in Sports: Rethinking Masculinity.* Freedom, CA: The Crossing Press, pp. 113–19.

Pronger, Brian (1990) *The Arena of Masculinity: Sports, Homosexuality and the Meaning of Sex.* New York: St. Martin's Press.

The Heterosexual Questionnaire

Martin Rochlin

Martin Rochlin was a scholar, an activist, and a pioneer in the field of gay-affirmative psychotherapy. Through his clinical practice, mentorship of students, professional presentations, and public appearances, he promoted the rights of sexual minorities. Rochlin was a leader in the campaign that resulted in the removal of homosexuality from the list of mental disorders in the Diagnostic and Statistical Manual of Mental Disorders. *The American Psychological Association (APA) awarded him the Distinguished Professional Contribution Award, and he was honoured as a fellow of the APA. His heterosexual questionnaire, originally published in 1972, is still widely reprinted in textbooks and anthologies in gender and women's studies and sociology.*

1. What do you think caused your heterosexuality?
2. When and how did you decide that you were a heterosexual?
3. Is it possible that your heterosexuality is just a phase you may grow out of?
4. Is it possible that your heterosexuality stems from a neurotic fear of others of the same sex?
5. If you have never slept with a person of the same sex, is it possible that all you need is a good gay lover?
6. Do your parents know that you are straight? Do your friends and/or roommate(s) know? How did they react?
7. Why do you insist on flaunting your heterosexuality? Can't you just be who you are and keep it quiet?
8. Why do heterosexuals place so much emphasis on sex?
9. Why do heterosexuals feel compelled to seduce others into their lifestyles?
10. A disproportionate majority of child molesters are heterosexual. Do you consider it safe to expose children to heterosexual teachers?
11. Just what do men and women *do* in bed together? How can they truly know how to please each other, being so anatomically different?
12. With all the societal support marriage receives, the divorce rate is spiraling. Why are there so few stable relationships among heterosexuals?
13. Statistics show that lesbians have the lowest incidence of sexually transmitted diseases. Is it really safe for a woman to maintain a heterosexual lifestyle and run the risk of disease and pregnancy?
14. How can you become a whole person if you limit yourself to compulsive, exclusive heterosexuality?

15. Considering the menace of overpopulation, how could the human race survive if everyone were heterosexual?

16. Could you trust a heterosexual therapist to be objective? Don't you feel s/he might be inclined to influence you in the direction of her/his own leanings?

17. There seem to be very few happy heterosexuals. Techniques have been developed that might enable you to change if you really want to. Have you considered trying aversion therapy?

18. Would you want your child to be heterosexual, knowing the problems that s/he would face?

Source: Martin Rochlin, "The Language of Sex: The Heterosexual Questionnaire," in *Gender in the 1990s: Images, Realities, and Issues*, ed. E.D. Nelson and B.W. Robinson (Toronto: Nelson Canada, 1995), 38–39.

Chapter 20

The Ethics of Genetic Research
on Sexual Orientation

Udo Schüklenk, Edward Stein,
Jacinta Kerin, and William Byne

Udo Schüklenk is the Ontario research chair in bioethics in the Department of Philosophy at Queen's University. A leading expert in the field of bioethics (the study of ethics in health care), he has authored or co-authored a number of books and over 100 academic papers. His research interests include ethical and other issues in drug development and marketing, infectious disease control and public health issues, and other ethical and policy issues in the context of public and international health.

Edward Stein is vice dean, professor of law, and director of the program in family law, policy, and bioethics at the Cardozo School of Law in New York City. He is the author of The Mismeasure of Desire: The Science, Theory, and Ethics of Sexual Orientation *and editor of* Forms of Desire: Sexual Orientation and the Social Constructionist Controversy.

Jacinta Kerin completed her PhD in bioethics at Monash University in 2004. Her research concerns focus on the philosophy of science, ethics, and feminism.

William Byne is director of the Laboratory of Neuroanatomy and Morphometrics at Mount Sinai School of Medicine in New York City and sits on the editorial board of the Journal of Gay and Lesbian Psychotherapy.

Research on the origins of sexual orientation has received much public attention in recent years, especially findings consistent with the notion of relatively simple links between genes and sexual orientation.

*****

Ethical Concerns

We have several ethical concerns about genetic research on sexual orientation. Underlying these concerns is the fact that even in our contemporary societies, lesbians, gay men, and bisexuals are subject to widespread discrimination and social disapprobation. Against this background, we are concerned about the particularly gruesome history of the use of such research. Many homosexual people have been forced to undergo "treatments" to change their sexual orientation, while others have "chosen" to undergo them in order to escape societal homophobia. All too often, scientifically questionable "therapeutic" approaches destroyed the lives of perfectly healthy people. "Conversion therapies" have included electroshock treatment, hormonal therapies, genital mutilation, and brain surgery.[1] We are concerned about the negative ramifications of biological research on sexual orientation, especially in homophobic societies. In Germany, some scholars have warned of the potential for abuse of such genetic research, while others have called for a moratorium on such research to prevent the possible abuse of its results in homophobic societies. These warnings should be taken seriously.

We are concerned that people conducting research on sexual orientation work within homophobic frameworks, despite their occasional claims to the contrary. A prime example is the German obstetrician Günter Dörner, whose descriptions of homosexuality ill-conceal his heterosexism. Dörner writes about homosexuality as a "dysfunction" or "disease" based on "abnormal brain development." He postulates that it can be prevented by "*optimizing*" natural conditions or by "*correcting* abnormal hormonal concentrations prenatally" (emphasis added).[2] Another example is provided by psychoanalyst Richard Friedman, who engages in speculation about nongay outcome given proper therapeutic intervention.[3] Research influenced by homophobia is likely to result in significantly biased accounts of human sexuality; further, such work is more likely to strengthen and perpetuate the homophobic attitudes on which it is based.

Sexual Orientation Research Is Not Value Neutral

Furthermore, we question whether those who research sexual orientation can ever conduct their work in a value-neutral manner. One might think that the majority of American sex researchers treat homosexuality not as a disease, but rather as a variation analogous to a neutral polymorphism. To consider whether or not this is the case, one must look at the context in which interest in sexual orientation arises. Homophobia still exists to some degree in all societies within which sexual orientation research is conducted. The cultures in which scientists live and work influence both the questions they ask and the hypotheses they imagine and explore. Given this, we believe it is unlikely that the sexual orientation research of any scientist (even one who is homosexual) will escape some taint of homophobia.

*****

We are not claiming that all researchers are homophobic to some degree whether or not they are aware of it. Nor are we talking about the implicit or explicit intentions of individual sexual orientation researchers. Rather we are seeking to highlight that the very motivation for seeking the "origin" of homosexuality has its source within social frameworks that are pervasively homophobic. Recognition that scientific projects are constituted by, and to some degree complicit in, social structures does not necessarily entail that all such science should cease. At the very least, however, it follows that sexual orientation research and its use should be subject to critique. Such a critique will call into question the claim that, by treating homosexuality as a mere variation of human behavior, researchers are conducting neutral investigations into sexual orientation.

*****

Normativity of Naturalness and Normality. Why is there a dispute as to whether homosexuality is natural or normal? We suggest it is because many people seem to think that nature has a prescriptive normative force such that what is deemed natural or normal is necessarily good and therefore *ought* to be. Everything that falls outside these terms is constructed as unnatural and abnormal, and it has been argued that this constitutes sufficient reason to consider homosexuality worth avoiding.[4] Arguments that appeal to "normality" to provide us with moral guidelines also risk committing the naturalistic fallacy. The naturalistic fallacy is committed when one mistakenly deduces from the way things are to the way they ought to be. For instance, Dean Hamer and colleagues commit this error in their *Science* article when they state that "it would be fundamentally unethical to use such information to try to assess or alter a person's current or future sexual orientation, either heterosexual or homosexual, or other normal attributes of human behavior."[5] Hamer and colleagues believe that there is a major genetic factor contributing to sexual orientation. From this they think it follows that homosexuality is normal, and thus worthy of preservation. Thus they believe that genetics can tell us what is normal, and that the content of what is normal tells us what ought to be. This is a typical example of a naturalistic fallacy.

Normality can be defined in a number of ways, but none of them direct us in the making of moral judgments. First, normality can be reasonably defined in a *descriptive* sense as a statistical average. Appeals to what is usual, regular, and/or conforming to existing standards ultimately collapse into statistical statements. For an ethical evaluation of homosexuality, it is irrelevant whether homosexuality is normal or abnormal in this sense. All sorts of human traits and behaviors are abnormal in a statistical sense, but this is not a sufficient justification for a negative ethical judgment about them.

Second, "normality" might be defined in a functional sense, where what is normal is something that has served an adaptive function from an evolutionary perspective. This definition of normality can be found in sociobiology, which seeks biological explanations for social behavior. There are a number of serious problems with the sociobiological project.[6] For the purposes of this argument, however, suffice it to say that even if sociobiology could establish that certain behavioral traits were the direct result of biological evolution, no moral assessment of these traits would follow. To illustrate our point, suppose any trait that can be reasonably believed to have served an adaptive function at some evolutionary stage is normal. Some questions arise that exemplify the problems with deriving normative conclusions from descriptive science. Are traits that are perpetuated simply through linkage to selectively advantageous loci less "normal" than those for which selection was direct? Given that social contexts now exert "selective pressure" in a way that nature once did, how are we to decide which traits are to be intentionally fostered?

*****

U.S.-Specific Arguments. In the United States, several scholars and lesbian and gay activists have argued that establishing a genetic basis for sexual orientation will help make the case for lesbian and gay rights. The idea is that scientific research will show that people do not choose their sexual orientations and therefore they should not be punished or discriminated against in virtue of them. This general argument is flawed in several ways.[7] First, we do not need to show that a trait is genetically determined to argue that it is not amenable to change at will. This is clearly shown by the failure rates of conversion "therapies."[8] These failures establish that sexual orientation is resistant to change, but they do not say anything about its ontogeny or etiology. Sexual orientation can be unchangeable without being genetically determined. There is strong observational evidence to support the claim that sexual orientation is difficult to change, but this evidence is perfectly compatible with nongenetic accounts of the origins of sexual orientations. More importantly, we should not embrace arguments that seek to legitimate homosexuality by denying that there is any choice in sexual preference because the implicit premise of such arguments is that if there *was* a choice, then homosexuals would be blameworthy.

Relatedly, arguments for lesbian and gay rights based on scientific evidence run the risk of leading to impoverished forms of lesbian and gay rights. Regardless of what causes homosexuality, a person has to decide to publicly identify as a lesbian, to engage in sexual acts with another woman, to raise children with her same-sex lover, or to be active in the lesbian and gay community. It is when people make such decisions that they are likely to face discrimination, arrest, or physical violence. It is decisions like these that need legal protection. An argument for lesbian and gay rights based on genetic evidence is impotent with respect to protecting such decisions because it focuses exclusively on the very aspects of sexuality that might not involve choices.

Another version of this argument focuses on the specifics of U.S. law. According to this version, scientific evidence will establish the immutability of sexual orientation, which, according to one current interpretation of the Equal Protection Clause of the Fourteenth Amendment of the U.S. Constitution, is one of three criteria required of a classification if it is to evoke heightened judicial scrutiny. While this line of argument has serious internal problems,[9] such an argument, like a good deal of American bioethical reasoning, has limited or no relevance to the global context. Since the results of the scientific research are not confined within American borders, justifications that go beyond U.S. legislation are required.

The same sort of problem occurs in other defenses of sexual orientation research that discuss possible ramifications in U.S.-specific legislative terms. For instance, Timothy Murphy claims that, even if a genetic probe predictive of sexual orientation were available, mandatory testing would be unlikely.[10] He bases this claim on the fact that in some states employment and housing discrimination against homosexual people is illegal. In many countries, however, the political climate is vastly different, and legal anti-gay discrimination is widespread. And there is evidence that scientific research would be used in a manner that discriminates against homosexuals.[11] [For example,] in Singapore, homosexual sex acts are a criminal offense. The Singapore Penal Code sections 377 and 377A threaten sentences ranging from two years to life imprisonment for homosexual people engaging in same-sex acts. Not coincidentally, in light of our concerns, a National University of Singapore psychiatrist recently implied that "pre-symptomatic testing for homosexuality should be offered in the absence of treatment,"[12] thereby accepting the idea that homosexuality is something in need of a cure.

Genetic Screening. Several attempts to defend sexual orientation research against ethical concerns related to the selective abortion of "pre-homosexual" fetuses have been made. It has been claimed that this sort of genetic screening will not become commonplace because "diagnostic genetic testing is at present the exception rather than the rule."[13] While this may indeed be true in the U.S., it has far more to do with the types of tests currently offered than with a reluctance on the part of either the medical profession or the reproducing public to partake of such technology. For example, the types of tests available are diagnostic for diseases and are offered on the basis of family history or specific risk factors. The possibility of tests that are supposed to be (however vaguely) predictive of behavioral traits opens genetic technology to a far greater population, especially when the traits in question are undesired by a largely prejudiced society.

Furthermore, it has been claimed that the medical profession would not advocate such a test that does not serve "important state interests" (p. 341). This argument not only ignores the existence of homophobia among individuals within medicine,[14] it assumes also that public demand for genetic testing varies predominantly according to medical advice. However, should such a test become available, the media hype surrounding its market arrival would render its existence common knowledge, which, coupled with homophobic bias, would create a demand for the test irrespective of its accuracy and of any kind of state interest. Furthermore, this argument ignores the fact that genetic screening for a socially undesirable characteristic has already been greeted with great public demand in countries such as India, where abortion on the basis of female sex is commonplace, irrespective of its legality.[15] Techniques to select the sexual orientation of children, if made available, might well be widely utilized.[16]

*****

The Value of Knowing the Truth. Finally, various scholars appeal to the value of the truth to defend research on sexual orientation in the face of ethical concerns. Scientific research does, however, have its costs and not every research program is of equal importance. Even granting that, in general, knowledge is better than ignorance, not all risks for the sake of knowledge are worth taking. With respect to sexual orientation, historically, almost every hypothesis about the causes of homosexuality led to attempts to "cure" healthy people. History indicates that current genetic research is likely to have negative effects on lesbians and gay men, particularly those living in homophobic societies.[17]

A Global Perspective

Homosexual people have in the past suffered greatly from societal discrimination. Historically, the results of biological research on sexual orientation have been used against them. We have analyzed the arguments offered by well-intentioned defenders of such work and concluded that none survive philosophical scrutiny. It is true that in some countries in Scandinavia, North America, and most parts of Western Europe, the legal situation of homosexual people has improved, but an adequate ethical analysis of the implications of genetic inquiry into the causes of sexual orientation must operate from a global perspective. Sexual orientation researchers should be aware that their work may harm homosexuals in countries other than their own. It is difficult to imagine any good that could come of genetic research on sexual orientation in homophobic societies. Such work faces serious ethical concerns so long as homophobic societies continue to exist. Insofar as socially responsible genetic research on sexual orientation is possible, it must begin with the awareness that it will not be a cure for homophobia and that the ethical status of lesbians and gay men does not in any way hinge on its results.

Notes

1. Jonathan Ned Katz, *Gay American History* (New York: Thomas Crowell, 1976), pp. 197–422.
2. Günter Dörner, "Hormone-Dependent Brain Development and Neuroendocrine Prophylaxis," *Experimental and Clinical Endocrinology* 94 (1989): 4–22.
3. Richard C. Friedman, *Male Homosexuality: A Contemporary Psychoanalytic Perspective* (New Haven: Yale University Press, 1988), p. 20.

4. Michael Levin, "Why Homosexuality Is Abnormal," *Monist* 67 (1984): 251–83.

5. Dean Hamer et al., "A Linkage between DNA Markers on the X Chromosome and Male Sexual Orientation," *Science* 261 (1993): 326.

6. Philip Kitcher, *Vaulting Ambition: Sociobiology and the Quest for Human Nature* (Cambridge, Mass.: MIT Press, 1985).

7. Edward Stein, "The Relevance of Scientific Research Concerning Sexual Orientation to Lesbian and Gay Rights," *Journal of Homosexuality* 27 (1994): 269–308.

8. Charles Silverstein, "Psychological and Medical Treatments of Homosexuality," in *Homosexuality: Research Implications for Public Policy*, ed. J.C. Gonsiorek and J.D. Weinrich (Newbury Park, Calif.: Sage, 1991), pp. 101–14.

9. Janet Halley, "Sexual Orientation and the Politics of Biology: A Critique of the New Argument from Immutability," *Stanford Law Review* 46 (1994): 503–68.

10. Timothy Murphy, "Abortion and the Ethics of Genetic Sexual Orientation Research," *Cambridge Quarterly of Healthcare Ethics* 4 (1995): 341.

11. Paul Billings, "Genetic Discrimination and Behavioural Genetics: The Analysis of Sexual Orientation," in *Intractable Neurological Disorders, Human Genome, Research, and Society*, ed. Norio Fujiki and Darryl Macer (Christchurch and Tsukuba: Eubios Ethics Institute, 1993), p. 37; Paul Billings, "International Aspects of Genetic Discrimination," in *Human Genome Research and Society*, ed. Norio Fujiki and Darryl Macer (Christchurch and Tsukuba: Eubios Ethics Institute, 1992), pp. 114–17.

12. L.C.C. Lim, "Present Controversies in the Genetics of Male Homosexuality," *Annals of the Academy of Medicine Singapore* 24 (1995): 759–62.

13. Murphy, "Abortion and the Ethics of Genetic Sexual Orientation Research," p. 341.

14. Kevin Speight, "Homophobia Is a Health Issue," *Health Care Analysis* 3 (1995): 143–48.

15. Kusum, "The Use of Prenatal Diagnostic Techniques for Sex Selection: The Indian Scene," *Bioethics* 7 (1993): 149–65.

16. Richard Posner, *Sex and Reason* (Cambridge, Mass.: Harvard University Press, 1992), p. 308.

17. For further elaborations on this argument, see Edward Stein, Udo Schuklenk, and Jacinta Kerin, "Scientific Research on Sexual Orientation," in *Encyclopedia of Applied Ethics*, ed. Ruth Chadwick (San Diego: Academic Press, 1997).

Supplement 16

Activist Insight:
Homophobia and Heterosexism

Below are two definitions by noted American feminists Suzanne Pharr and Audre Lorde. Pharr is a long-time activist and organizer for social and economic justice movements, and is also the author of Homophobia: A Weapon of Sexism. *Lorde was a writer, poet, and activist, and a key figure in the black feminist and lesbian movements of the 1970s and 1980s.*

Pharr and Lorde each define homophobia and heterosexism in a different way. What does each writer contribute to your understanding of these concepts?

Homophobia: A Weapon of Sexism, Suzanne Pharr
Homophobia works effectively as a weapon of sexism because it is joined with a powerful arm, heterosexism. Heterosexism creates the climate for homophobia with its assumption that the world is and must be heterosexual and its display of power and privilege as the norm. Heterosexism is the systemic display of homophobia in the institutions of society. Heterosexism and homophobia work together to enforce compulsory heterosexuality and that bastion of patriarchal power, the nuclear family. The central focus of the rightwing attack against women's liberation is that women's equality, women's self-determination, women's control of our own bodies and lives will damage what they see as the crucial societal institution, the nuclear family.

Scratching the Surface, Audre Lorde
Heterosexism: The belief in the inherent superiority of one pattern of loving and thereby its right to dominance.

Homophobia: The fear of feelings of love for members of one's own sex and therefore the hatred of those feelings in others.

How Do You Recognize Homophobia in Yourself and Others?

The Campaign to End Homophobia, Cooper Thompson and Barbara Zoloth
There are four distinct but interrelated types of homophobia: personal, interpersonal, institutional, and cultural.

Personal homophobia is prejudice based on a personal belief that lesbian, gay, and bisexual people are sinful, immoral, sick, inferior to heterosexuals, or incomplete women and men.
Personal homophobia is experienced as a feeling of fear, discomfort, dislike, hatred, or disgust with same-sex sexuality. Anyone, regardless of their sexual orientation or preference, can

experience personal homophobia; when this happens with lesbian, gay, and bisexual people, it is called *internalized homophobia*.

Interpersonal homophobia is individual behavior based on personal homophobia. This hatred or dislike may be expressed by name-calling, telling "jokes," verbal and physical harassment, and other individual acts of discrimination.

Interpersonal homophobia, in its extreme, results in lesbians, gays, and bisexuals being physically assaulted for no other reason than their assailants' homophobia. Most people act out their fears of lesbian, gay, and bisexual people in non-violent, more commonplace ways. Relatives often shun their lesbian, gay, and bisexual family members; co-workers are distant and cold to lesbian, gay, and bisexual colleagues; heterosexual friends aren't interested in hearing about their lesbian, gay, and bisexual friends' relationships.

Institutional homophobia refers to the many ways in which government, businesses, churches, and other institutions and organizations discriminate against people on the basis of sexual orientation. Institutional homophobia is also called *heterosexism*.

Institutional homophobia is reflected in religious organizations which have stated or implicit policies against lesbians, gays, and bisexuals leading services; agencies which refuse to allocate resources to services to lesbian, gay, and bisexual people; and governments which fail to insure the rights of all citizens, regardless of their sexual orientation.

Cultural homophobia refers to social standards and norms which dictate that being heterosexual is better or more moral than being lesbian, gay, or bisexual, and that everyone is or should be heterosexual. Cultural homophobia is also called *heterosexism*.

Cultural homophobia is spelled out each day in television shows and print advertisements where virtually every character is heterosexual, every erotic relationship involves a female and a male, and every "normal" child is presumed to be attracted to and will eventually marry someone of the other sex. In the few cases where lesbians, gays, or bisexual are portrayed, they are usually unhappy, stereotyped, engaged in self-destructive behaviors, or ambivalent about their sexual orientation.

Can Homophobia Be Cured?

Dealing constructively with homophobia first requires an acknowledgement of its pervasive existence. We cannot easily eradicate our homophobic feelings, but if we are willing to acknowledge that we are all homophobic, then we can begin to take responsibility for our choices and change our behaviors.

In addition to assuming the ever presence of homophobia, we can do the following:

Identify homophobia, not homosexuality, as the problem to be addressed. In conversations with friends and colleagues, speak out about homophobia. For many people, the only time they talk about lesbian, gay, and bisexual people is in the context of homophobic "jokes."

Think about the similarities and differences between homophobia and other forms of oppression. Use what you know about racism, sexism, classism, etc., to better understand homophobia and to look for ways to respond to homophobia.

Listen to the experiences of lesbian, gay, and bisexual people and assume that their experience with oppression is valid. Similarly, assume that the ways in which lesbian, gay, and bisexual people experience the world are different from the ways in which heterosexuals experience the world.

Actively support anti-discrimination efforts, as well as campaigns to stop homophobic prejudice and violence.

Sources: Suzanne Pharr, *Homophobia: A Weapon of Sexism* (Inverness, CA: Chardon Press, 1988), 16; Audre Lorde, "Scratching the Surface: Some Notes on Barriers to Women and Loving," in *Sister Outsider: Essays and Speeches* (Freedom, CA: The Crossing Press, 1984), 45, originally published in *The Black Scholar* 9, no. 7 (1978): 31–35; Cooper Thompson and Barbara Zoloth, "The Campaign to End Homophobia: Homophobia Pamphlet," Campaign to End Homophobia (1990), retrieved from http://www.endhomophobia.org/homophobia.htm

Chapter 21

Loving Women in the Modern World

Leila J. Rupp

Leila J. Rupp is associate dean (Division of Social Sciences) and professor in the Depart-ment of Feminist Studies at the University of California, Santa Barbara. An historian by training, she was editor of the Journal of Women's History *for many years. She researches and publishes widely in the areas of women's movements, sexualities, and comparative and transnational women's history. Recently, she authored* Sapphistries: A Global History of Love between Women, *and co-edited the 9th edition of* Feminist Frontiers, *a widely used anthology of feminist writings.*

What does it mean to be a "lesbian" in the modern world? In the 21st century it means loving women, desiring women, forming relationships with women, engaging in sexual behaviour with women, claiming an identity as a lesbian, and perhaps forming communities with other lesbians, although not all of these are necessary to the definition. But what do we make of women who loved, desired, formed relationships with and had sex with women before the concept and iden-tity of "lesbian" were available? What do we make of such women in cultures that have different categories of gender and sexual behaviour? We might call them "lesbian-like" or talk of same-sex love, desire or sexual acts.[1] What is crucial is that we contemplate, as best we can, the ways in which women in the past and in different parts of the world negotiated and understood their desire, love and self-conceptions.

I explore here different patterns of loving women in various parts of the world, from around the beginning of the 19th century up to the present. It is impossible, of course, to be compre-hensive, since research on many societies remains sketchy or is entirely lacking. Nor is there space to do justice to more than a few places. But my aim is to give a sense of women's lives with other women before, during and after the "discovery," naming and claiming of lesbian identity. Although lesbianism is often dismissed in societies subject to Western imperialism as an imported perversion (and in Western societies traditionally attributed to those of "other" races, classes or nations), women all around the world have found many ways of loving other women.

The story of loving women in the modern world is a tale of women who dressed and passed as men and who married women, of female-husbands and manly women, of romantic friends who made lives together, of trysts in domestic spaces, of secretive and not-so-secretive communities, of sapphists and female inverts and marriage-resisters and bulldaggers and butches and fems and les-bians. Yet it is not simply a tale of women with same-sex desires freeing and naming themselves as the modern world came into being. What history teaches us is how differently sexuality has been conceived and practised in the past and in various societies, and how mistaken we are to think solely in terms of progress. As a way of disrupting a narrative of progress, I have approached the history of loving women thematically, looking first at marrying women, then desiring women, and finally at women claiming diverse identities.

Marrying Women

One of the most persistent patterns of what may or may not accurately be called female same-sex sexuality is the case of women crossing the gender line to live as men and to marry women. What we do not know in such cases is whether women became men solely for the economic and social freedom that male dress and employment provided, whether a sexual motivation figured in their decisions, or whether they conceived of themselves as something akin to transgendered, even if no such concept existed. We are particularly in the dark about the motives of their wives. What we do know is that such gender-crossing and marriage to women existed in a number of contexts.

Consider the story of Edward De Lacy Evans, born a woman, who lived as a man for twenty-three years in Victoria, Australia.[2] The case came to light in 1879 when he was forcibly stripped for a bath, having just arrived at Kew Asylum in Melbourne. Evans had emigrated to Australia from Ireland in 1856 as Ellen Tremaye, but after working for a short time as a domestic servant began dressing as a man and married one of his shipmates. He went to work as a miner and, when his first wife left him for another man, explaining that Evans was actually a woman, he married a young Irishwoman. When she died, he married a third young woman, who bore a child after being impregnated by her sister's husband. Although Evans claimed the child as his own, it was the birth, it seems, that sent Evans to the asylum.

What grabbed public interest was not the masquerade itself but the three marriages. Newspaper stories reported Evans's interest in women on board ship, and one journalist concluded that "the woman must have been mad on the subject of sex from the time she left Ireland."[3] The fact that Evans had been committed may have explained his sexual deviance, but how was one to account for his wives? It was difficult to ignore the fact that his third wife had borne a child, so therefore must have engaged in sexual intercourse with a man. Although she claimed not to know either that Evans was a woman or how she became pregnant, her speculation that Evans had one night substituted a real man for himself suggested that she and Evans did indeed regularly have sex. One newspaper story reported that his wives did not expose him because they were "nymphomaniacs," suggesting knowledge of the emerging medical literature that linked excessive heterosexual desire and prostitution with female same-sex sexuality. When Evans's wife eventually named her brother-in-law as the father of the child in a bid for support, Evans testified in court that he had witnessed the two in bed together, but that it was so painful he could barely speak of it.

Evans's story, like so many tales of women who became men and married women, leaves us uncertain what to think.[4] Clearly there was more here at stake than occupational mobility. That Evans loved and desired women seems evident, but did he think of himself as male? Did his wives? What was crucial to the public commentary was the insistence that gender transgression was a sign of mental illness, and in fact the doctors proclaimed Evans cured only when he donned female clothing.

In other cultures in other parts of the world, "manly women" might marry women without the need for deception. The crucial difference was societal acceptance of gender-crossing or the existence of a third (or more) category of gender. In some Native American cultures, what are called "two-spirit" manly females are conceptualized as a mixture of the masculine and feminine, a gender apart from either women, men or womanly men. The two-spirit role has to do with spirituality, occupation, personality and gender more than sexuality, so when sex does take place between a manly woman and another woman, it may technically be "same-sex sex"—because the bodies involved are physiologically alike—but in fact the sex is more accurately conceptualized as cross-gender.[5] Among the Mohaves, *hwames* are women who take on male roles and who are able to marry women and serve as fathers of children borne by their wives.

*****

Native American societies were not the only ones that conceptualized multiple genders and allowed same-sex but cross-gender relationships, nor were they the only social group in which two biological women might marry one another. In more than thirty African groups woman–woman marriage has been, and in some cases still is, a possibility. As among the Mohaves, a female husband could be the father of children born to her wife from a union with a biological male. In that sense, she is a "social male." In at least some cases, such a role involved male dress and occupations, as for third-gender Native Americans. In Nigeria in the 1990s, an elderly Ohagia Igbo *dike-nwami* ("brave-woman") by the name of Nne Uko told an ethnographer that she "was interested in manly activities" and felt that she was "meant to be a man."[6] Although she was divorced from a husband, she farmed and hunted, joined men's societies and married two women who gave birth to children biologically fathered by her brother. The fundamental reason for the existence of such marriages is economic and familial: if a woman cannot conceive, she can continue her family line by taking a wife who will bear children. Women might choose a female husband for a number of reasons, including the possibility of greater sexual freedom, more companionship, less quarrelling and physical violence, distaste for men, more input in household decisions or more bridewealth.[7] We know little or nothing about the emotional and sexual aspects of having a female husband, although scholars tend to insist that sex is not a part of such marriages. One ethnographer who spent two years studying the Bangwa of Cameroon in the 1970s suggested the presence of at least an emotional component when he described his best woman informant's relationship with one of her wives, commenting on "their obvious satisfaction in each other's company."[8]

A quite different kind of marriage from one in which a partner passed as a man or became a social male developed in the Euro-American world in the late 18th and early 19th centuries. As an ideology of sexual difference between women and men took hold among the urban middle classes, the phenomenon known as "romantic friendship" flourished. Women, assigned the domestic sphere of the home and assumed to be emotional and asexual, developed strong and passionate ties to other women that thrived in addition to or alongside marriage to men. When romantic friends in certain privileged circumstances chose not to marry as expected, they sometimes formed marriage-like relationships that became known in the United States, because of their prevalence in the north-east, as "Boston marriages."

No doubt the most famous marriage between romantic friends was that of Eleanor Butler and Sarah Ponsonby, who ran away together from their aristocratic Irish homes in 1778 when they were thirty-nine and twenty-three respectively. Although Butler, the elder of the pair, dressed and behaved in a masculine manner, they lived respectably, if eccentrically and not without occasional criticism, in a rural retreat in Wales for fifty-one years. As the "Ladies of Llangollen" they came to embody romantic friendship and the possibility of marriage, in practice if not in name, between two women. They called each other "my Better Half," "my Sweet Love" and "my Beloved."[9] Visitors flocked to their home, newspaper accounts described their house and garden, and other women who loved women viewed them as icons of female love. Anne Lister, a member of the

Yorkshire gentry who was quite forthright about her love and lust for women, visited the Ladies in 1822 and felt a connection. She concluded that the long marriage between the two women must have been held together by "something more tender still than friendship."[10] When Butler died, leaving Ponsonby almost penniless, friends managed to arrange for Butler's pension to be paid to her—in effect a recognition that they had been married.

*****

The Ladies of Llangollen [...] lived in [a society] that did not have a category for women who married women. Their relationship [was] nonetheless accepted, or at least tolerated, because of class privilege and because of ignorance, wilful or otherwise, that sexual relationships formed part of the arrangement. In 19th-century England and Wales, as throughout Europe and the United States, romantic friendships crossed the boundaries of respectability if there was too much gender transgression or suspicion of sexual activity beyond kissing and cuddling, as we shall see. But by the end of the 19th century, as the science of sexology began to describe and categorize masculine women and women with same-sex desires as "inverts" or "perverts," everything began to change.

Consider the case of Alice Mitchell and Freda Ward in late 19th-century Memphis, Tennessee. Mitchell, a middle-class white nineteen-year-old, fell in love with her seventeen-year-old friend Freda Ward (known as 'Fred') and hatched a plot to dress as a man, run away with her and marry her. To this point their attachment seemed, to their families, to fit the familiar pattern of romantic friendship. Then Ward's family uncovered the plot and sent back Mitchell's engagement ring and other tokens of their love, forbidding them to see each other. Even worse from Mitchell's perspective, Ward began to be courted by a man. Early on in their plans to run away, Mitchell had said that she would kill Ward if she backed out of her promise to marry her, and she acted on this threat by slashing Ward's throat on the streets of Memphis in 1892. The case attracted attention from doctors and the popular press not only because of its drama, but also because it seemed to fit so perfectly the newly emerging theory of gender inversion and sexual deviance as inextricably linked. That is, Alice Mitchell became the embodiment of the "invert" or "lesbian" in American medical and popular discourse.[11] Her family's strategy for the defence was to have her declared insane, and she died in an asylum.

Across the Atlantic, at about the same time, the Hungarian count Sandor Vay was accused by his father-in-law not only of forgery, but also of fraud, since he "was only a woman, walking around in masculine clothes."[12] Unlike Mitchell, Vay was a "passing woman" who was raised as a boy, had affairs with women and worked as a journalist and writer. His father-in-law testified that one could see the shape of (rather large) male equipment between Vay's legs, and Vay's wife reported that she had given herself to him and had had no idea prior to his arrest that he was not biologically a man. Yet other witnesses testified that they knew the count to be a woman. The doctor who reported on the case to the court was himself confused, finding it difficult to deal with the masculine countess as a lady and much "easier, natural, and more correct" to think of Sandor as "a jovial, somewhat boyish student."[13] At this point the medical authorities proceeded from the story of a passing woman to a diagnosis of inversion and mental illness. As in the case of Alice Mitchell, the emerging ideas of the sexologists concerning gender inversion and same-sex sexual desire came to the fore. Sandor Vay was to Hungary, and to Europe more generally, what Alice Mitchell was to the United States: the embodiment of a sexual invert.

Once women who passed as men became defined in Euro-American cultures as sexual inverts and subsequently as mannish lesbians, marriages between women—whether passing women, manly women, social males, female husbands or romantic friends—had the potential to take on an air of sexual deviance. Nevertheless, some women continued to cross the gender line secretly, to live their lives as men and to marry women. Billy Tipton, a US jazz musician, originally invented himself as a man in order to earn a living during the Depression, but in 1989, when he died, his secret was revealed. He had been married several times and had adopted sons, and none of his immediate family—including his wives—knew that he had been born a woman.[14]

In the contemporary world, women in a few places can actually marry. In Belgium, Canada, Denmark, The Netherlands, Sweden and, in the United States, Massachusetts, lesbian marriages are taking place. Even in India, a society that does not condone same-sex relations, the fact that the Hindu Marriage Act allows diverse communities to define marriage means that some same-sex couples are able get married.[15] In the 1990s in a very poor rural region of India, Geeta, a woman from a *dalit* or "untouchable" family who was married to an abusive husband, met Manju, an older woman whose masculinity had won her a great deal of respect and power in her village. They came to know each other at a residential school run by a women's organization devoted to equality and empowerment, and they fell in love. As Geeta put it, "I do not know what happened to me when I met Manju but I forgot my man. I forgot that I had been married. We were so attracted to each other that we immediately felt like husband and wife."[16] Geeta accepted Manju as her husband at a Shiva temple, Manju's family accepted Geeta as a daughter-in-law, and Manju became both a second mother and a father to Geeta's daughter.

Marriage between women, then, has a long and complicated history. Many of the stories of women who married other women involve gender transgression, whether secret or open. Some take place in societies that recognize more than two genders or, for a variety of reasons, accept the idea of women as social males. There are many reasons why women might choose to cross the gender line or identify with a third or fourth gender, sexual desire for other women being only one. We know even less about why women might choose to marry female husbands. But what is clear is that women in various places in modern history have chosen to live their lives with other women.

Desiring Women

What do we know of women's sexual activities with one another, much less of their desires? This is a question not only of evidence, but also of interpretation. What counts as "sex"? Kissing, hugging, cuddling? And what about acts that seem clearly sexual from a contemporary Western perspective but might have little to do with erotic desire in other contexts? These are tricky questions. What we do know is that, despite all the obstacles, some record of women's same-sex desires has survived.

Let us begin with romantic friendship in the 18th-and 19th-century Western world, since one of the central debates in the history of sexuality hinges on the question of whether or not these passionate, intense, loving and physically affectionate relationships included sex, by which we presumably mean the involvement of genitals and/or sexual desire and/or sexual gratification. Certainly some of what romantic friends wrote to each other sounds like declarations of desire. There is Alice Baldy, a white woman from the US state of Georgia, writing in 1870 to her beloved, Josie Varner: "Do you know that if you only touch me, or speak to me there is not a nerve or fibre in my body that does not respond with a thrill of delight?"[17] Or 19th-century Czech writer Božena Němcová writing to Sofie Rottová, a fellow author: "Believe me, sometimes I dream that your eyes are right in front of me, I am drowning in them, and they have the same sweet expression as they did when they used to ask: 'Božena, what's wrong? Božena, I love you.'"[18] Or African-American poet Angelina

Weld Grimké writing in 1896 to her school friend Mamie Burrell: "Oh Mamie if you only knew how my heart beats when I think of you and it yearns and pants to gaze, if only for one second upon your lovely face."[19] Are these expressions of physical desire? Formulaic expressions of friendship? Or sometimes the former, sometimes the latter and sometimes both?

One of the cases that most troubles our understanding of the relationship between romantic friendship and sexual desire is that of Scottish schoolteachers Jane Pirie and Marianne Woods. In the early 19th century, Pirie and Woods fulfilled a dream by establishing a school together in Edinburgh. Then their plans all came crashing down one day when one of their students, Jane Cumming, born of a liaison between an Indian woman and an aristocratic Scottish man serving the empire in the East, reported shocking behaviour to her grandmother. According to Jane Cumming, the two teachers visited each other in bed, lay one on top of the other, kissed and shook the bed. Furthermore, Cumming reported that Jane Pirie said one night, "You are in the wrong place," and Marianne Woods replied "I know," and asserted that she was doing it "for fun." Another night, said Cumming, Pirie had whispered, "Oh, do it, darling." And she described a noise she heard as similar to "putting one's finger into the neck of a wet bottle."[20]

One can only imagine the reactions of the judges in the case, forced to make an impossible choice between believing that respectable Scottish schoolteachers might engage in sexual behaviour or believing that decent schoolgirls could make up such tales. As one judge put it, making clear the acceptability of normal romantic friendship, "Are we to say that every woman who has formed an intimate friendship and has slept in the same bed with another is guilty? Where is the innocent woman in Scotland?"[21] Ultimately, they had to decide whether Pirie and Woods kissed, caressed and fondled "more than could have resulted from ordinary female friendship," suggesting a line between affectionate behaviour and sexuality that could be crossed.[22] The only way out of the dilemma was provided by Jane Cumming's heritage and childhood in India, where surely, many of the judges decided, she must have learned not only about sex, but also about sexual relations between women—something no respectable Scottish schoolgirl would be able to imagine.

*****

In describing and defining lesbianism, sexologists have left us some of the first detailed and reliable records of female same-sex sexual behaviour. Despite the filter of the doctors' own intentions and interpretations, women's voices do sometimes break through. In one famous US study of "sex variants" in New York in the 1930s, women described their sex lives and bragged about their ability to satisfy their lovers. Perhaps playing with both traditional notions about lesbians and the experts' belief in the hypersexuality of black women, a number of African-American subjects boasted of their sexual technique: "I insert my clitoris in the vagina just like the penis of a man.... Women enjoy it so much they leave their husbands."[23] Far more reliable are oral histories collected by historians sympathetic to their narrators. In the working-class lesbian bar culture of 1940s and 1950s Buffalo, New York, white, black and Native American butches saw their role as pleasuring their fems, primarily through tribadism or what they called "friction."[24] Oral sex became more acceptable in the 1950s at the same time that the idea of the "untouchable" or "stone butch"—the "doer" who did not let her lover make love to her—became more firmly entrenched. As one stone butch from the 1950s put it, "I wanted to satisfy them, and I wanted to make love—I love to make love. I still say that's the greatest thing in the world."[25]

These varied sources from different places provide evidence of kissing, the caressing of breasts, tribadism, manual stimulation, the use of dildoes, and oral sex. Sex practices change over time and vary in different cultures. But what all this evidence makes clear is that there is a long history of women desiring other women and acting on that desire. How women thought about what they did with each other, both before and after "lesbian" became a possible identity, we know less about. Yet women who loved women did, in different contexts, come to define identities that were based on their love and desire.

Claiming an Identity

The story of the emergence of lesbian identity has both geographical and chronological limitations, but the notion of love, sexual desire or sexual activity making one a kind of person has more fluid boundaries. That is, the term "lesbian" has a relatively recent origin in Western culture, but there were other words or concepts that women applied to themselves to describe their desires and actions. Before the invention of the term "homosexuality" in 1869, Anne Lister saw her love and desire for women as a defining characteristic. She knew the term "Saffic," considered her attraction to women natural, and proclaimed proudly that "I love, & only love, the fairer sex & thus beloved by them in turn, my heart revolts from any other love than theirs."[26]

At the same time we need to remember that there have always been, and still are, women who love and desire other women but do not see that as defining their identities in any way. In Lesotho, for example, a small, poor country entirely enclosed by South Africa, women love other women and engage in activities that seem to a modern Western sensibility to be sexual; yet they neither identify as a particular category of "sexual being" nor even define what they do as "sex," which in Lesotho requires a penis.[27] As in much of the rest of the world, women must expect to marry and bear children. But boarding-school girls pair up as "Mummy" and "Baby" and kiss, rub each other's bodies, sometimes have genital contact, and jealously guard their relationships. Older women greet each other with long "French" kisses, fondle one another and engage in tribadism and cunnilingus, all of which they describe as "loving each other," "staying together nicely," "holding each other" or "having a nice time together," but not as sex.[28] And they are not lesbians.

In other cultures, women may engage in actions that provide an identity, but not one that corresponds to the concept "lesbian." At the end of the 19th century in Canton, a Chinese silk-producing area, women organized "sworn sisterhoods" (*zishu*) and identified as "marriage-resisters" (*dushen zhyyi nüzi*, literally "women believing in remaining single").[29] Although there were economic and cultural reasons behind their decision, commentators at the time attributed the phenomenon in part to the fact that women "acquired intimate friends with whom they practiced homosexual love."[30]

Once the sexologists had undertaken the process of naming and defining the kind of people who loved others of the same sex, what did such definitions mean to women who loved other women? For some, the medicalization of same-sex love brought unwanted attention and shame; for others, self-understanding and an identity. Jeannette Marks, a professor of English at Mount Holyoke College, Massachusetts, who lived in an intimate relationship with Mary Woolley, the college's president from 1901 to 1937, was one who worried that others might see her as a lesbian. [...]

On the other hand, the concept of lesbianism as a defining characteristic allowed some women to embrace their own sexuality more fully. British feminist Frances Wilder expressed her gratitude to homosexual sexologist Edward Carpenter, whose work made her realize that she "was more closely related to the intermediate sex than I had hitherto imagined."[31] In *The Well of Loneliness*, Radclyffe Hall had her famous character Stephen discover her true nature when she finds a copy of Richard von Krafft-Ebing's monumental work *Psychopathia Sexualis*, Hall hoped that her novel would help young women like herself come to terms with their desires, as well as elicit sympathy from heterosexual readers.[32]

But it would be a mistake to assume that the experts defined lesbian identity independently, leaving women-loving women either to reject or embrace what was offered them. For the sexologists fashioned their analyses from what they saw around them, including the cases of women such as Alice Mitchell and Sandor Vay. And in the early 20th century a self-fashioning of the modern lesbian was taking place in communities where women with same-sex desires found others like themselves.

In Paris, the salon of the American Natalie Clifford Barney was the heart of one such lesbian community from the 1890s to the 1930s. A wealthy heiress, Barney wasted no time agonizing over the conclusions of the sexologists. Secure in her sexual desire for women, feminine in her self-presentation and protected by class privilege, Barney flourished in an environment in which homosexuality was celebrated among the elite. In her salon, she gathered around her a coterie of writers, artists and lovers whose works celebrated lesbianism. And she eschewed shame: "Albinos aren't reproached for having pink eyes and whitish hair, why should they [society] hold it against me for being a lesbian? It's a question of nature: my queerness isn't a vice, isn't 'deliberate,' and harms no one."[33] Flamboyant and self-confident, Barney had no qualms about flaunting her non-monogamous lesbianism.

Berlin, too, was home in the 1920s to a vibrant lesbian world. Until the Nazi rise to power, an astonishing number of lesbian clubs, bars, balls, groups, circles and publications catered to women who loved women, and cabaret acts openly represented lesbian love.[34] The periodical *Die Freundin* ("The Girlfriend"), published in Berlin from 1924 to 1933, directed its stories and articles to women described as "same-sex loving" (*gleichgeschlechtlichliebend*), "homosexual" (*homosexuell*), "homoerotic" (*homoerotisch*) or "lesbian" (*lesbisch*).[35] The transnational aspects of lesbian culture among elites is evident in the title of another periodical published in Berlin in the 1930s. *Garçonne* (the French for "boy" with an added feminine ending, meaning also an "emancipated woman") catered to a lesbian and male transvestite audience.[36] Both periodicals featured photographs and illustrations of a variety of lesbians: some cross-dressed, some in butch–fem couples, some entirely feminine.

New York was also home to commercial and private venues that catered to a crowd with same-sex desires, and not just to elite women. By the 1920s, two neighbourhoods—Greenwich Village and Harlem—had established reputations as welcoming places for lesbians as well as gay men. Like Paris and Berlin, both districts were also artistic and bohemian centres. The Harlem Renaissance in particular spread word of lesbian love through literature, art and the blues. Lucille Bogan, in "B.D. Women Blues," sang of "bulldagger" women, and in fact many of the great women blues singers were themselves lesbian or bisexual. Mabel Hampton, a black performer who in her teens lived in Harlem, described private parties where women who desired women might meet: "The bulldykers used to come and bring their women with them, you know."[37]

Such vibrant lesbian communities were the exception rather than the rule, however, for in much of the world the idea that women should live independently of men remained unthinkable. But even where the conditions for such lesbian communities were lacking, the language of same-sex love began to enter the vernacular. In Republican China, indigenous developments—such as the emergence of marriage resistance, the widespread existence of same-sex love relations in sex-segregated schools, and changes in gender roles accompanying urbanization—combined with the translation of the work of Western sexologists and drew attention to the new concept of "same-sex love" (*tongxing ai*) that had migrated from Japan.[38] A number of women writers from the progressive May Fourth movement wrote about love between women, often telling of relationships between women in school. One such author, Lu Yin, in *Lishi's Diary* (1923) tells the story of a woman who does not wish to marry and whose feelings for her school friend Yuanqing change from "ordinary friendship" to "same-sex romantic love." They make plans to live together, and Lishi that night dreams that they are rowing a boat in the moonlight. Then Yuanqing's mother forces her to move away and plans to marry her off to her cousin. Yuanqing writes to Lishi, "Ah, Lishi! Why didn't you plan ahead! Why didn't you dress up in men's clothes, put on a man's hat, act like a roan, and visit my parents to ask for my hand?"[39] In the end, Yuanqing repudiates their dream and Lishi dies of melancholia. Lu Yin herself married twice, but her writings suggest that she struggled with lesbian desire. She described her urge to dress as a man and visit a brothel, although she feared that if anyone found out, they would have "dreadful suspicions" about her.[40]

*****

In the 1960s and 1970s, in conjunction with movements for social justice that were appearing around the world, women who identified as lesbians began to speak out and organize public protests, even in places where that put them in a great deal of danger. When the United Nations–sponsored first International Women's Year Conference came to Mexico City in 1975, the press attacked the lesbian presence as imported and alien to Mexican culture, but four years later a group of lesbians promoted their cause publicly at the first World Sexology Congress.[41] In South Africa, groups such as Sunday's Women in Durban, the GLOW (Gay and Lesbian Organization of the Witwatersrand), Lesbian Forum in Soweto-Johannesburg, and Lesbians in Love and Compromising Situations (LILACS) in Cape Town emerged during the 1980s.[42] Lesbians with sufficient class or organizational privilege connect at international feminist and gay/lesbian conferences such as those sponsored by the International Lesbian and Gay Association. The Asian Lesbian Network brings together lesbians from ten Asian countries and Asian lesbians living outside Asia, and the Encuentros de Lesbianas Feministas are conferences for lesbians in Latin America and the Caribbean.[43]

Claiming an identity—as Saffic or lesbian; as a marriage-resister, a *garçonne* or a bulldagger; as *bombero* (literally "firefighter," for butch) or *mucama* ("housemaid," for fem) in Argentina, or as *chapatbaz* (women who engage in tribadism) in Urdu—requires one to have a concept of a particular kind of person with which one can relate, a notion that there are others like oneself with whom one might build a community. Although identity is important to the construction of the modern lesbian, we must remember that there are still women all around the globe who are crossing the gender line, loving women and engaging in sexual relations without thinking of themselves as lesbians.

Loving Women

What does it mean to love women in the modern world? As all of these manifestations of relationships between women make clear, there are many and various ways in which women love other women. Some cross the gender line to marry their lovers. [...] And others, in different ways, celebrated their love, claimed an identity and joined together to make the world a more hospitable place for loving women.

Notes

1. Judith M. Bennett, "'Lesbian-Like' and the Social History of Lesbianisms," *Journal of the History of Sexuality*, vol. 9, no. 1–2 (2000), pp. 1–24; Leila J. Rupp, "Toward a Global History of Same-Sex Sexuality," *Journal of the History of Sexuality*, vol. 10, no. 2 (2001), pp. 287–302.

2. Lucy Chesser, "'A Woman Who Married Three Wives': Management of Disruptive Knowledge in the 1879 Australian Case of Edward De Lacy Evans," *Journal of Women's History*, vol. 9, no. 4 (1998), pp. 53–77.

3. Ibid., p. 60.

4. See Rudolf Dekker and Lott van de Pol, *The Tradition of Female Transvestism in Early Modern Europe* (London 1989), and Julie Wheelwright, *Amazons and Military Maids: Women Who Dressed as Men in Pursuit of Life, Liberty and Happiness* (London 1989).

5. See Sabine Lang, "Various Kinds of Two-Spirit People: Gender Variance and Homosexuality in Native American Communities," in Sue-Ellen Jacobs, Wesley Thomas and Sabine Lang (eds.), *Two-Spirit People* (Urbana, IL 1997), pp. 100–118; and Walter L. Williams, *The Spirit and the Flesh: Sexual Diversity in American Indian Culture* (Boston, MA 1986).

6. Quoted in Joseph M. Carrier and Stephen O. Murray, "Woman–Woman Marriage in Africa," in Stephen O. Murray and Will Roscoe (eds.), *Boy-Wives and Female Husbands: Studies in African Homosexualities* (New York 1998), p. 259.

7. See Carrier and Murray, *Boy-Wives*.

8. Quoted in Carrier and Murray, *Boy-Wives*, p. 263.

9. Quoted in Martha Vicinus, *Intimate Friends: Women Who Loved Women, 1778–1928* (Chicago 2004), p. 9.

10. Ibid., p. 45.

11. See Lisa Duggan, *Sapphic Slashers: Sex, Violence and American Modernity* (Durham, NC 2000).

12. Quoted in Geertje Mak, "Sandor/Sarolta Vay: From Passing Woman to Invert," *Journal of Women's History*, vol. 16, no. 1 (2004), p. 54.

13. Ibid., p. 61.

14. See Diane Wood Middlebrook, *Suits Me: The Double Life of Billy Tipton* (New York 1998).

15. Ruth Vanita, "CLAGS Reports," *Centre for Lesbian and Gay Studies News*, vol. 14, no. 2 (2004), p. 14.

16. Quoted in Amanda Lock Swarr and Richa Nagar, "Dismantling Assumptions: Interrogating 'Lesbian' Struggles for Identity and Survival in India and South Africa," *Signs: Journal of Women in Culture and Society*, vol. 29 (2004), p. 500.

17. Quoted in Elizabeth W. Knowlton, "'Only a Woman Like Yourself': Rebecca Alice Baldy, Dutiful Daughter, Stalwart Sister and Lesbian Lover of Nineteenth-Century Georgia," in John Howard (ed.), *Carryin' on in the Lesbian and Gay South* (New York 1997), p. 48.

18. Quoted in Dasa Francikova, "Female Friends in Nineteenth-Century Bohemia: Troubles with Affectionate Writing and 'Patriotic Relationships,'" *Journal of Women's History*, vol. 12, no. 3 (2000), pp. 23–28, quotation on p. 24.

19. Quoted in Gloria T. Hull, *Color, Sex and Poetry: Three Women Writers of the Harlem Renaissance* (Bloomington, IN 1987), p. 139.

20. Quoted in Lillian Faderman, *Scotch Verdict* (New York 1983), p. 147.

21. Ibid., p. 281.

22. Ibid., p. 82.
23. Quoted in Jennifer Terry, *An American Obsession: Science, Medicine and Homosexuality in Modern Society* (Chicago 1999), p. 242.
24. See Elizabeth Lapovsky Kennedy and Madeline D. Davis, *Boots of Leather, Slippers of Gold: The History of a Lesbian Community* (New York 1993).
25. Ibid., p. 204.
26. Anne Lister, *I Know My Own Heart: The Diaries of Anne Lister (1797–1810)*, ed. Helena Whitbread (London 1988), p. 145.
27. Kendall, "'When a Woman Loves a Woman' in Lesotho: Love, Sex, and the (Western) Construction of Homophobia," in Stephen O. Murray and Will Roscoe (eds.), *Boy-Wives and Female Husbands: Studies in African Homosexualities* (New York 1998), pp. 223–41.
28. Ibid., p. 233. On boarding-school relationships, Kendall cites Judith Gay, "Mummies and Babies and Friends and Lovers in Lesotho," *Journal of Homosexuality*, vol. 11, no. 3–4 (1985), pp. 97–116.
29. See Tze-Ian D. Sang, *The Emerging Lesbian: Female Same-Sex Desire in Modern China* (Chicago 2003), pp. 52, 377.
30. Ibid., p. 52.
31. Quoted in Carroll Smith-Rosenberg, "Discourses of Sexuality and Subjectivity: The New Woman, 1870–1936," in Martin Bauml Duberman, Martha Vicinus and George Chauncey (eds.), *Hidden from History: Reclaiming the Gay and Lesbian Past* (New York 1989), p. 275.
32. See Vicinus, *Intimate Friends*, p. 217.
33. Ibid., pp. 189–90.
34. See the articles in *Eldorado: Homosexualle Frauen und Männer in Berlin 1850–1950*, exh. cat., Berlin, Schwules Museum (Berlin 1984).
35. Katharine Vogel, "Zum Selbstverständnis lesbischer Frauen in der Weimarer Republik," in *Eldorado*, pp. 162–68.
36. Quoted in Petra Shlierkamp, "Die Garçonne," in *Eldorado*, p. 173.
37. Joan Nestle, "Excerpts from the Oral History of Mabel Hampton," *Signs: Journal of Women in Culture and Society*, vol. 18 (1993), p. 933.
38. See Sang, *The Emerging Lesbian*.
39. Ibid., p. 139.
40. Ibid., p. 144.
41. Claudia Hinojosa, "Mexico," in Bonnie Zimmerman (ed.), *Lesbian Histories and Cultures* (New York 2000), pp. 494–96.
42. Ian Barnard, "South Africa," in Zimmerman, *Lesbian Histories and Cultures*, pp. 721–22.
43. Julie Dorf, "International Organizations," in Zimmerman, *Lesbian Histories and Cultures*, pp. 398–400.

Chapter 22

Man-Royals and Sodomites: Some Thoughts on the Invisibility of Afro-Caribbean Lesbians

Makeda Silvera

Makeda Silvera is a Caribbean Canadian writer, activist, and scholar. As co-founder and managing editor of Sister Vision: Black Women and Women of Colour Press, she has worked tirelessly to promote the development and publishing of writing by women of colour. She is the author of the critically acclaimed novel The Heart Does Not Bend, *and the editor of the groundbreaking anthology* Piece of My Heart: A Lesbian of Colour Anthology, *from which the following excerpt is taken.*

I will begin with some personal images and voices about woman-loving. These have provided a ground for my search for cultural reflections of my identity as a Black woman artist within the Afro-Caribbean community of Toronto. Although I focus here on my own experience (specifically, Jamaican), I am aware of similarities with the experience of other Third World women of colour whose history and culture has been subjected to colonisation and imperialism.

I spent the first thirteen years of my life in Jamaica among strong women. My great-grandmother, my grandmother, and grand-aunts were major influences in my life. There are also men whom I remember with fondness—my grandmother's "man friend" G., my Uncle Bertie, his friend Paul, Mr. Minott, Uncle B., and Uncle Freddy. And there were men like Mr. Eden who terrified me because of stories about his "walking" fingers and his liking for girls under age fourteen.

I lived in a four-bedroom house with my grandmother, Uncle Bertie, and two female tenants. On the same piece of land, my grandmother had other tenants, mostly women and lots of children. The big verandah of our house played a vital role in the social life of this community. It was on the verandah that I received my first education on "Black women's strength"—not only from their strength, but also from the daily humiliations they bore at work and in relationships. European experience coined the term "feminism," but the term "Black women's strength" reaches beyond Eurocentric definitions to describe what is the cultural continuity of my own struggles.

The verandah. My grandmother sat on the verandah in the evenings after all the chores were done to read the newspaper. People—mostly women—gathered there to discuss "life." Life covered every conceivable topic—economic, local, political, social, and sexual; the high price of salt-fish, the scarcity of flour, the nice piece of yellow yam bought at Coronation market, Mr. Lam, the shop-keeper who was taking "liberty" with Miss Inez, the fights women had with their menfolk, work, suspicions of Miss Iris and Punsie carrying on something between them, the cost of school books.

My grandmother usually had lots of advice to pass on to the women on the verandah, all grounded in the Bible. Granny believed in Jesus, in good and evil, and in repentance. She was also a practical and sociable woman. Her faith didn't interfere with her perception of what it meant to be a poor Black woman; neither did it interfere with our Friday night visits to my Aunt Marie's bar. I remember sitting outside on the piazza with my grandmother, two grand-aunts, and three or four of their women friends. I liked their flashy smiles and I was fascinated by their independence, ease, and their laughter. I loved their names—Cherry Rose, Blossom, Jonesie, Poinsietta, Ivory, Pearl, Iris, Bloom, Dahlia, Babes. Whenever the conversation came around to some "big 'oman talk,"—who was sleeping with whom or whose daughter just got "fallen," I was sent off to get a glass of water for an adult, or a bottle of Kola champagne. Every Friday night I drank as much as half a dozen bottles of Kola champagne, but I still managed to hear snippets of words, tail ends of conversations about women together.

In Jamaica, the words used to describe many of these women would be "Man-Royal" and/or "Sodomite." Dread words. So dread that women dare not use these words to name themselves. They were names given to women by men to describe aspects of our lives that men neither under-stood nor approved.

I heard "sodomite" whispered a lot during my primary school years, and tales of women secretly having sex, joining at the genitals, and being taken to the hospital to be "cut" apart were told in the school yard. Invariably, one of the women would die. Every five to ten years the same story would surface. At times, it would even be published in the newspapers. Such stories always generated much talking and speculation from "Bwoy dem kinda gal naasti sah!" to some wise old woman saying, "But dis caan happen, after two shutpan caan join"—meaning identical objects cannot go into the other. The act of loving someone of the same sex was sinful, abnormal—some-thing to hide. Even today, it isn't unusual or uncommon to be asked, "So how do two 'omen do it? … What unnu use for a penis? … Who is the man and who is the 'oman?" It's inconceivable that women can have intimate relationships that are whole, that are not lacking because of the absence of a man. It's assumed that women in such relationships must be imitating men.

The word "sodomite" derives from the Old Testament. Its common use to describe lesbians (or any strong independent woman) is peculiar to Jamaica—a culture historically and strongly grounded in the Bible. Although Christian values have dominated the world, their effect in slave colonies is particular. Our foreparents gained access to literacy through the Bible when they were being indoctrinated by missionaries. It provided powerful and ancient stories of strength, endurance, and hope, which reflected their own fight against oppression. This book has been so powerful that it continues to bind our lives with its racism and misogyny. Thus, the importance the Bible plays in Afro-Caribbean culture must be recognized in order to understand the historical and political context for the invisibility of lesbians. The wrath of God "rained down burning sulphur on Sodom and Gomorrah" (Genesis 19:23). How could a Caribbean woman claim the name?

When, thousand of miles away and fifteen years after my school days, my grandmother was confronted with my love for a woman, her reaction was determined by her Christian faith and by this dread word sodomite—its meaning, its implication, its history.

And when, Bible in hand, my grandmother responded to my love by sitting me down, at the age of twenty-seven, to quote Genesis, it was within the context of this tradition, this politic. When she pointed out that "this was a white people ting," or "a ting only people with mixed blood was involved in" (to explain or include my love with a woman of mixed race), it was strong denial of many ordinary Black working-class women she knew.

It was finally through my conversations with my grandmother, my mother, and my mother's friend five years later that I began to realize the scope of this denial, which was intended to dissuade and protect me. She knew too well that any woman who took a woman lover was attempting to walk on fire—entering a "no man's land." I began to see how commonplace the act of loving women really was in working-class communities. I realized, too, just how heavily shame and silence weighed down this act.

A conversation with a friend of my mother:
Well, when I growing up we didn't hear much 'bout woman and woman. They weren't "suspect." There was much more talk about "batty man business" when I was a teenager in the 1950s.

I remember one story about a man who was "suspect" and that every night when he was coming home, a group of guys use to lay wait him and stone him so viciously that he had to run for his life. Dem time, he was safe only in the day.

Now with women, nobody really suspected. I grew up in the country and I grew up seeing women holding hands, hugging up, sleeping together in one bed, and there was no question. Some of this was based purely on emotional friendship, but I also knew of cases where the women were dealing but no one really suspected. Close people around knew, but not everyone. It wasn't a thing that you would go out and broadcast. It would be something just between the two people.

Also one important thing is that the women who were involved carried on with life just the same, no big political statements were made. These women still went to church, still got baptized, still went on pilgrimage, and I am thinking about one particular woman named Aunt Vie, a very strong woman, strong-willed and everything, they used to call her "man-royal" behind her back, but one ever dare to meddle with her.

Things are different now in Jamaica. Now all you have to do is not respond to a man's call to you and dem call you sodomite or lesbian. I guess it was different back then forty years ago because it was harder for anybody to really conceive of two women sleeping and being sexual. But I do remember when you were "suspect," people would talk about you. You were definitely classed as "different," "not normal," a bit "crazy." But women never really got stoned like the men.

What I remember is that if you were a single woman alone or two single women living together and a few people suspected this ... and when I say a few people I mean like a few guys, sometimes other crimes were committed against the women. Some very violent, some very subtle. Battery was common, especially in Kingston. A group of men would suspect a woman or have it out for her because she was a "sodomite" or because she act "man-royal" and so the men would organize and gang rape whichever woman was "suspect." Sometimes it was reported in the newspapers, other times it wasn't—but when you live in a little community, you don't need a newspaper to tell you what's going on. You know by word of mouth and those stories were frequent. Sometimes you also knew the men who did the battery.

Other subtle forms of this was "scorning" the women. Meaning that you didn't eat anything from them, especially a cooked meal. It was almost as if those accused of being "man-royal" or "sodomite" could contaminate.

A conversation with my grandmother:
I am only telling you this so that you can understand that this is not a profession to be proud of and to get involved in. Everybody should be curious and I know you born with that, ever since you growing up as a child and I can't fight against that, because that is how everybody get to know what's in the world. I am only telling you this because when you were a teenager, you always say

you want to experience everything and make up your mind on your own. You didn't like people telling you what was wrong and right. That always use to scare me.

Experience is good, yes. But it have to be balanced, you have to know when you have too much experience in one area. I am telling you this because I think you have enough experience in this to decide now to go back to the normal way. You have two children. Do you want them to grow up knowing this is the life you have taken? But this is for you to decide....

Yes, there was a lot of women involved with women in Jamaica. I knew a lot of them when I was growing up in the country in the 1920s. I didn't really associate with them. Mind you, I was not rude to them. My mother wouldn't stand for any rudeness from any of her children to adults.

I remember a woman we use to call Miss Bibi. She live next to us; her husband was a fisherman, I think he drowned before I was born. She had a little wooden house that back onto the sea, the same as our house. She was quiet, always reading. That I remember about her because she use to go to the little public library at least four days out of the week. And she could talk. Anything you want to know, just ask Miss Bibi and she could tell you. She was a mulatto woman, but poor. Anytime I had any school work that I didn't understand, I use to ask her. The one thing I remember, though, we wasn't allowed in her house by my mother, so I use to talk to her outside, but she didn't seem to mind that. Some people use to think she was mad because she spent so much time alone. But I didn't think that because anything she help me with, I got a good mark on it in school.

She was colourful in her own way, but quiet, always alone, except when her friend come and visit her once a year for two weeks. Them times I didn't see Miss Bibi much because my mother told me I couldn't go and visit her. Sometimes I would see her in the market exchanging and bartering fresh fish for vegetables and fruits. I used to see her friend too. She was a jet Black woman, always had her hair tied in bright coloured cloth and she always had on big gold earrings. People use to say she live on the other side of the island with her husband and children and she came to Port Maria once a year to visit Miss Bibi.

My mother and father were great storytellers and I learnt that from them, but is from Miss Bibi that I think I learnt to love reading so much as a child. It wasn't until I move to Kingston that I notice other women like Miss Bibi....

Let me tell you about Jones. Do you remember her? Well she was the woman who live the next yard over from us. She is the one who really turn me against people like that, why I fear so much for you to be involved in this ting. She was very loud. Very show-off. Always dressed in pants and man-shirt that she borrowed from her husband. Sometimes she use to invite me over to her house, but I didn't go. She always had her hair in a bob hair cut, always barefoot and tending to her garden and her fruit trees. She tried to get me involved in that kind of life, but I said no. At the time I remember I needed some money to borrow and she lent me, later she told me I didn't have to pay her back, but to come over to her house and see the thing she had that was sweeter than what any man could offer me. I told her no and eventually paid her back the money.

We still continued to talk. It was hard not to like Jonesie—that's what everybody called her. She was open and easy to talk to. But still there was a fear in me about her. To me it seem like she was in a dead end with nowhere to go. I don't want that for you.

I left my grandmother's house that day feeling anger and sadness for Miss Jones—maybe for myself, who knows. I was feeling boxed in. I had said nothing. I'd only listened quietly.

In bed that night, I thought about Miss Jones. I cried for her (for me) silently. I remember her, a mannish looking Indian woman, with flashy gold teeth, a Craven A cigarette always between them.

She was always nice to me as a child. She had the sweetest, juiciest Julie, Bombay and East Indian mangoes on the street. She always gave me mangoes over the fence. I remember the dogs in her yard and the sign on her gate. "Beware of bad dogs." I never went into her house, though I was always curious.

I vaguely remember her pants and shirts, though I never thought anything of them until my grandmother pointed them out. Neither did I recall that dreaded word being used to describe her, although everyone on the street knew about her.

A conversation with my mother:

Yes I remember Miss Jones. She smoke a lot, drank a lot. In fact, she was an alcoholic. When I was in my teens she use to come over to our house—always on the verandah. I can't remember her sitting down—seems she was always standing up, smoking, drinking, and reminiscing. She constantly talked about the past, about her life and it was always on the verandah. And it was always women: young women she knew when she was a young woman, the fun they had together, and how good she would make love to a woman. She would say to whoever was listening on the verandah, "Dem girls I use to have sex with was shapely. You shoulda know me when I was younger, pretty, and shapely just like the 'oman dem I use to have as my 'oman."

People use to tease her on the street, but not about being a lesbian or calling her sodomite. People use to tease her when she was drunk, because she would leave the rumshop and stagger down the avenue to her house.

I remember the women she use to carry home, usually in the daytime. A lot of women from downtown, higglers and fishwomen. She use to boast about knowing all kinds of women from Coronation market and her familiarity with them. She had a husband who lived with her and that served as her greatest protection against other men taking steps with her. Not that anybody could easily take advantage of Miss Jones, she could stand up for herself. But having a husband did help. He was a very quiet, insular man. He didn't talk to anyone on the street. He had no friends so it wasn't easy for anyone to come up to him and gossip about his wife.

No one could go to her house without being invited, but I wouldn't say she was a private person. She was a loner. She went to the rumshops alone, she drank alone, she staggered home alone. The only time I ever saw her with somebody were the times when she went off to the Coronation market or some other place downtown to find a woman and bring her home. The only times I remember her engaging in conversation with anybody was when she came over on the verandah to talk about her women and what they did in bed. That was all she let out about herself. There was nothing about how she was feeling, whether she was sad or depressed, lonely, happy. Nothing. She seemed to cover up all that with her loudness and her vulgarness and her constant threat—which was all it was—to beat up anybody who troubled her or teased her when she was coming home from the rumshop.

Now Cherry Rose—do you remember her? She was a good friend of Aunt Marie and of Mama's. She was also a sodomite. She was loud too, but different from Miss Jones. She was much more outgoing. She was a barmaid and had lots of friends—both men and women. She also had the kind of personality that attracted people—very vivacious, always laughing, talking, and touching. She didn't have any children, but Gem did.

Do you remember Miss Gem? Well she had children and she was also a barmaid. She also had lots of friends. She also had a man friend name Mickey, but that didn't matter because some women had their men and still had women they carried on with. The men usually didn't know what was going on, and seeing as these men just come and go and usually on their own time, they weren't around every day and night.

Miss Pearl was another one that was in that kind of thing. She was a dressmaker, she use to sew really good. Where Gem was light complexion, she was a very black Black woman with deep dimples. Where Gem was a bit plump, Pearl was slim, but with big breast and a big bottom. They were both pretty women.

I don't remember hearing that word sodomite a lot about them. It was whispered sometimes behind their backs, but never in front of them. And they were so alive and talkative that people were always around them.

The one woman I almost forgot was Miss Opal, a very quiet woman. She use to be friends with Miss Olive and was always out at her bar sitting down. I can't remember much about her except she didn't drink like Miss Jones and she wasn't vulgar. She was soft spoken, a half-Chinese woman. Her mother was born in Hong Kong and her father was a Black man. She could really bake. She use to supply shops with cakes and other pastries.

So there were many of those kind of women around. But it wasn't broadcast.

I remembered them. Not as lesbians or sodomites or man-royals, but as women that I liked. Women whom I admired. Strong women, some colourful, some quiet.

I loved Cherry Rose's style. I loved her loudness, the way she challenged men in arguments, the bold way she laughed in their faces, the jingle of her gold bracelets. Her colourful and stylish way of dressing. She was full of wit; words came alive in her mouth.

Miss Gem: I remember her big double iron bed. That was where Paula and Lorraine (her daughters, my own age) and I spent a whole week together when we had chicken pox. My grandmother took me there to stay for the company. It was fun. Miss Gem lived right above her bar and so at any time we could look through the window and onto the piazza and street, which was bursting with energy and life. She was a very warm woman, patient and caring. Every day she would make soup for us and tell us stories. Later on in the evening she would bring us Kola champagne.

Miss Pearl sewed dresses for me. She hardly ever used her tape measure—she could just take one look at you and make you a dress fit for a queen. What is she doing now, I asked myself? And Miss Opal, with her calm and quiet, where is she—still baking?

What stories could these lesbians have told us? I, an Afro-Caribbean woman living in Canada, come with this baggage—their silenced stories. My grandmother and mother know the truth, but silence still surrounds us. The truth remains a secret to the rest of the family and friends, and I must decide whether to continue to sew this cloth of denial or break free, creating and becoming the artist that I am, bring alive the voice and images of Cherry Rose, Miss Gem, Miss Jones, Opal, Pearl, and others....

There is more at risk for us than for white women. Through three hundred years of history we have carried memories and the scars of racism and violence with us. We are the sister, daughter, mothers of a people enslaved by colonialists and imperialists. Under slavery, production, and reproduction were inextricably linked. Reproduction served not only to increase the labour force of slave owners but also, by "domesticating" the enslaved, facilitated the process of social conditions by focusing on those aspects of life in which they could express their own desires. Sex was an area in which to articulate one's humanity, but, because it was tied to attempts "to define oneself as human," gender roles, as well as the act of sex, became badges of status. To be male was to be the stud, the procreator; to be female was to be fecund, and one's femininity was measured by the ability to attract and hold a man, and to bear children. In this way, slavery and the post-emancipated colonial order defined the structures of patriarchy and heterosexuality as necessary for social mobility and acceptance.

Socio-economic conditions and the quest for a better life has seen steady migration from Jamaica and the rest of the Caribbean to the U.S., Britain, and Canada. Upon my arrival, I became part of the so-called "visible minorities" encompassing Blacks, Asians, and Native North Americans in Canada. I live with a legacy of continued racism and prejudice. We confront this daily, both as individuals and as organized political groups. Yet for those of us who are lesbians, there is another struggle: the struggle for acceptance and positive self-definition within our own communities. Too often, we have had to sacrifice our love for women in political meetings that have been dominated by the "we are the world" attitude of heterosexual ideology. We have had to hide too often that part of our identity which contributes profoundly to make up the whole.

Many lesbians have worked, like me, in the struggles of Black people since the 1960s. We have been on marches every time one of us gets murdered by the police. We have been at sit-ins and vigils. We have flyered, postered, we have cooked and baked for the struggle. We have tended to the youths. And we have all at one time or another given support to men in our community, all the time painfully holding onto, obscuring, our secret lives. When we do walk out of the closet (or are thrown out), the "ideologues" of the Black communities say "Yes, she was a radical sistren, but I don't know what happen, she just went the wrong way." What is implicit in this is that one cannot be a lesbian and continue to do political work, and not surprisingly, it follows that a Black lesbian/artist cannot create using the art forms of our culture. For example, when a heterosexual male friend came to my house, I put on a dub poetry tape. He asked, "Are you sure that sistren is a lesbian?"

"Why?" I ask.

"Because this poem sound wicked; it have lots of rhythm; it sounds cultural."

Another time, another man commented on my work, "That book you wrote on domestic workers is really a fine piece of work. I didn't know you were that informed about the economic politics of the Caribbean and Canada." What are we to assume from this? That Afro-Caribbean lesbians have no Caribbean culture? That they lose their community politics when they sleep with women? Or that Afro-Caribbean culture is a heterosexual commodity?

The presence of an "out" Afro-Caribbean lesbian in our community is dealt with by suspicion and fear from both men and our heterosexual Black sisters. It brings into question the assumption of heterosexuality as the only "normal" way. It forces them to acknowledge something that has always been covered up. It forces them to look at women differently and brings into question the traditional Black female role. Negative response from our heterosexual Black sister, though more painful, is, to a certain extent, understandable because we have no race privilege and very, very few of us have class privilege. The one privilege within our group is heterosexual. We have all suffered at the hands of this racist system at one time or another and to many heterosexual Black women it is inconceivable, almost frightening, that one could turn her back on credibility in our community and the society at large by being lesbian. These women are also afraid that they will be labelled "lesbian" by association. It is that fear, that homophobia, which keeps Black women isolated.

The Toronto Black community has not dealt with sexism. It has not been pushed to do so. Neither has it given a thought to its heterosexism. In 1988, my grandmother's fear is very real, very alive. One takes a chance when one writes about being an Afro-Caribbean lesbian. There is the fear that one might not live to write more. There is the danger of being physically "disciplined" for speaking as a woman-identified woman.

And what of our white lesbian sisters and their community? They have learnt well from the civil rights movement about organizing, and with race and some class privilege, they have built a predominantly white lesbian (and gay) movement—a pre-condition for a significant body of work by a writer or artist. They have demanded and received recognition from politicians (no matter how little). But this recognition has not been extended to Third World lesbians of colour—neither from politicians nor from white lesbian (and gay) organizations. The white lesbian organizations/groups have barely (some not at all) begun to deal with or acknowledge their own racism, prejudice, and biases—all learned from a system which feeds on their ignorance and grows stronger from its institutionalized racism. Too often white women focus only on their oppression as lesbians, ignoring the more complex oppression of non-white women who are also lesbians. We remain outsiders in these groups, without images or political voices that echo our own. We know too clearly that, as non-white lesbians in this country, we are politically and socially at the very bottom of the heap. Denial of such differences robs us of true visibility. We must identify and define these differences, and challenge the movements and groups that are not accessible to non-whites—challenge groups that are not accountable.

But where does this leave us as Afro-Caribbean lesbians, as part of this "visible minority" community? As Afro-Caribbean women we are still at the stage where we have to imagine and discover our existence, past and present. As lesbians, we are even more marginalized, less visible. The absence of a national Black lesbian and gay movement through which to begin to name ourselves is disheartening. We have no political organization to support us and through which we could demand respect from our communities. We need such an organization to represent our interests, both in coalition building with other lesbian/gay organizations, and in the struggles which shape our future—through which we hope to transform the social, political, and economic systems of oppression as they affect all peoples.

Though not yet on a large scale, lesbians and gays of Caribbean descent are beginning to seek each other out—are slowly organizing. Younger lesbians and gays of colour are beginning to challenge and force their parents and the Black community to deal with their sexuality. They have formed groups, "Zami for Black and Caribbean Gays and Lesbians" and "Lesbians of Colour," to name two.

The need to make connections with other Caribbean and Third World people of colour who are lesbian and gay is urgent. This is where we can begin to build that other half of our community, to create wholeness through our art. This is where we will find the support and strength to struggle, to share our histories, and to record these histories in books, documentaries, film, sound, and art. We will create a rhythm that is uniquely ours—proud, powerful, and gay, naming ourselves, and taking our space within the larger history of Afro-Caribbean peoples.

Part 3 Gendered Identities

Movements begin when people refuse to live divided lives.
—Parker J. Palmer, quoted in *The Cultural Creatives: How 50 Million People Are Changing the World* (1991, p. 20)

This part of the book examines gendered identities, systemic inequalities, and the power of stereotypes. We emphasize some of the main institutions in societies that shape gendered social relations through, for example, the family, the community, the educational system, and the state. The main focus is on the practices and legacies of colonization and imperialism.

3a: Thinking about Difference and Identity

We introduce here some basic concepts for understanding constructions of difference and identity in the contemporary social world. These include critical writings on identity, difference, stereotyping, white privilege, and culture. We use women's experiences of racism and racialized girls' struggles for belonging as two North American case studies that illustrate the significance of race to women's lives.

3b: Histories and Legacies of Colonialism and Imperialism

In this section, we take up histories and legacies of slavery, colonization, and imperialism, nationally and transnationally. We introduce readers to "difficult knowledge" about the histories of slavery and colonization in Canada and the implicatedness of white women in colonialism and imperialism. We examine legacies of racism and colonialism today by exploring how race and gender interact in diverse women's lives. This section and the next also work together to ground and elaborate our analysis of colonization by examining its specific operations and consequences for one group in particular: Indigenous women within a Canadian context.

3c: Aboriginal Women: Agency, Creativity, and Strength

We turn in our third section to examining Aboriginal women's individual and collective strategies for survival and resistance in North America in the past and present. Highlighted are women's involvements in political activism, community leadership, artistic expression (including performance and poetry), and various strategies employed to negotiate and challenge colonial imagery and institutions.

Chapter 23

Stereotyping as a Signifying Practice

Stuart Hall

Stuart Hall is a leading cultural theorist and sociologist, and one of the founding figures of British cultural studies. Hall became director of the Centre for Contemporary Cultural Studies at Birmingham University in England, where he played an instrumental role in expanding the scope of cultural studies to include an analysis of race and gender. After he left the centre he became a professor of sociology at the Open University, where he is now professor emeritus. The British newspaper The Observer *has called him "one of the country's leading cultural theorists."*

[...] We need to reflect on how a racialized regime of representation actually works. Essentially, this involves examining more deeply the set of representational practices known as *stereotyping*. [...] Stereotyping reduces people to a few, simple, essential characteristics, which are represented as fixed by Nature. Here, we examine four further aspects: (a) the construction of "otherness" and exclusion; (b) stereotyping and power; (c) the role of fantasy; and (d) fetishism.

Stereotyping as a signifying practice is central to the representation of racial difference. But what is a stereotype? How does it actually work? In his essay on "Stereotyping," Richard Dyer (1977) makes an important distinction between *typing* and *stereotyping*. He argues that, without the use of *types*, it would be difficult, if not impossible, to make sense of the world. We understand the world by referring individual objects, people, or events in our heads to the general classificatory schemes into which—according to our culture—they fit. Thus we "decode" a flat object on legs on which we place things as a "table." We may never have seen that kind of "table" before, but we have a general concept or category of "table" in our heads, into which we "fit" the particular objects we perceive or encounter. In other words, we understand "the particular" in terms of its "type." We deploy what Alfred Schutz called *typifications*. In this sense, "typing" is essential to the production of meaning.

Richard Dyer argues that we are always "making sense" of things in terms of some wider categories. Thus, for example, we come to "know" something about a person by thinking of the *roles* which he or she performs: is he/she a parent, a child, a worker, a lover, boss, or an old age pensioner? We assign him/her to the *membership* of different groups, according to class, gender, age group, nationality, "race," linguistic group, sexual preference, and so on. We order him/her in terms of *personality type*—is he/she a happy, serious, depressed, scatter-brained, over-active kind of person? Our picture of who the person "is" is built up out of the information we accumulate from positioning him/her within these different orders of typification. In broad terms, then, "a *type* is any simple, vivid, memorable, easily grasped and widely recognized characterization in which a few traits are foregrounded and change or 'development' is kept to a minimum" (Dyer, 1977, p. 28).

What, then, is the difference between a *type* and a *stereotype? Stereotypes* get hold of the few "simple, vivid, memorable, easily grasped and widely recognized" characteristics about a person, *reduce* everything about the person to those traits, *exaggerate* and *simplify* them, and *fix* them without change or development to eternity. This is the process we described earlier. So the first point is—*stereotyping reduces, essentializes, naturalizes, and fixes "difference."*

Secondly, *stereotyping deploys a strategy of "splitting."* It divides the normal and the acceptable from the abnormal and the unacceptable. It then *excludes* or *expels* everything which does not fit, which is different. Dyer argues that "a system of social- and stereo-types refers to what is, as it were, within and beyond the pale of normalcy [i.e., behaviour which is accepted as "normal" in any culture]. Types are instances which indicate those who live by the rules of society (social types) and those who the rules are designed to exclude (stereotypes). For this reason, stereotypes are also more rigid than social types ... [B]oundaries ... must be clearly delineated and so stereotypes, one of the mechanisms of boundary maintenance, are characteristically fixed, clear-cut, unalterable" (ibid., p. 29). So, *another feature of stereotyping is its practice of "closure" and exclusion. It symbolically fixes boundaries, and excludes everything which does not belong.*

Stereotyping, in other words, is part of the maintenance of social and symbolic order. It sets up a symbolic frontier between the "normal" and the "deviant," the "normal" and the "pathological," the "acceptable" and the "unacceptable," what "belongs" and what does not or is "Other," between "insiders" and "outsiders," Us and Them. It facilitates the "binding" or bonding together of all of Us who are "normal" into one "imagined community"; and it sends into symbolic exile all of Them—"the Others"—who are in some way different—"beyond the pale." Mary Douglas (1966), for example, argued that whatever is "out of place" is considered as polluted, dangerous, taboo. Negative feelings cluster around it. It must be symbolically excluded if the "purity" of the culture is to be restored. The feminist theorist, Julia Kristeva, calls such expelled or excluded groups "abjected" (from the Latin meaning, literally, "thrown out") (Kristeva, 1982).

The third point is that *stereotyping tends to occur where there are gross inequalities of power.* Power is usually directed against the subordinate or excluded group. One aspect of this power, according to Dyer, is *ethnocentrism*—"the application of the norms of one's own culture to that of others" (Brown, 1965, p. 183). Again, remember Derrida's argument that, between binary oppositions like Us/Them, "we are not dealing with ... peaceful coexistence ... but rather with a violent hierarchy. One of the two terms governs ... the other or has the upper hand" (1972, p. 41).

In short, stereotyping is what Foucault called a "power/knowledge" sort of game. It classifies people according to a norm and constructs the excluded "other." Interestingly, it is also what Gramsci would have called an aspect of the struggle for hegemony. As Dyer observes, "The establishment of normalcy (i.e., what is accepted as 'normal') through social- and stereo-types is one aspect of the habit of ruling groups ... to attempt to fashion the whole of society according to their own world view, value system, sensibility and ideology. So right is this world view for the ruling groups that they make it appear (as it *does* appear to them) as 'natural' and 'inevitable'— and for everyone—and, in so far as they succeed, they establish their hegemony" (Dyer, 1977, p. 30). Hegemony is a form of power based on leadership by a group in many fields of activity at once, so that its ascendancy commands widespread consent and appears natural and inevitable.

*****

References

Brown, R. (1965) *Social Psychology*. London/New York, Macmillan.
Derrida, J. (1972) *Positions*. Chicago, IL, University of Chicago Press.
Douglas, M. (1966) *Purity and Danger*. London, Routledge & Kegan Paul.
Dyer, R. (ed.) (1977) *Gays and Film*. London, British Film Institute.
Kristeva, J. (1982) *Powers of Horror*. New York, Columbia University Press.

Chapter 24

Undoing the "Package Picture" of Cultures

Uma Narayan

Uma Narayan is the Andrew W. Mellon professor in the humanities and chair of philosophy at Vassar College in the United States. Her research and teaching areas include contemporary moral issues, feminist theory, and global feminisms. She is co-editor of a number of anthologies and the author of Dislocating Cultures: Identities, Traditions and Third World Feminism. *Narayan's work is especially influential for challenging the common misconception that feminism is solely a Western notion.*

Many feminists of color have demonstrated the need to take into account differences among women to avoid hegemonic gender-essentialist analyses that represent the problems and interests of privileged women as paradigmatic. As feminist agendas become global, there is growing feminist concern to consider national and cultural differences among women. However, in attempting to take seriously these cultural differences, many feminists risk replacing gender-essentialist analyses with culturally essentialist analyses that replicate problematic colonialist notions about the cultural differences between "Western culture" and "non-Western cultures" and the women who inhabit them (Narayan 1998). Seemingly universal essentialist generalizations about "all women" are replaced by culture-specific essentialist generalizations that depend on totalizing categories such as "Western culture," "non-Western cultures," "Indian women," and "Muslim women." The picture of the "cultures" attributed to these groups of women remains fundamentally essentialist, depicting as homogeneous groups of heterogeneous peoples whose values, ways of life, and political commitments are internally divergent.

I believe that many contemporary feminists are attuned to the problem of imposing Sameness on Other women but fail to register that certain scripts of Difference can be no less problematic. Cultural imperialism in colonial times denied rather than affirmed that one's Others were "just like oneself," insisting on the colonized Others' difference from and inferiority to the Western subject. Insistence on sharp contrasts between "Western culture" and "Other cultures" and on the superiority of Western culture functioned as justifications for colonialism. However, this self-portrait of Western culture had only a faint resemblance to the political and cultural values that actually pervaded life in Western societies. Thus, liberty and equality could be represented as paradigmatic Western values at the very moment when Western nations were engaged in slavery, colonization, and the denial of liberty and equality to large segments of Western subjects, including women.

Anticolonial nationalist movements added to the perpetuation of essentialist notions of national culture by embracing, and trying to revalue, the imputed facets of their own culture embedded in the colonialists' stereotypes. Thus, while the British imputed "spiritualism" to Indian culture to suggest lack of readiness for the worldly project of self-rule, many Indian nationalists embraced this definition to make the anticolonialist and nationalist argument that their culture was distinctive from and superior to that of the West. Thus, sharply contrasting pictures of Western culture and of various colonized national cultures came to be reiterated by both colonizers and colonized.

Prevalent essentialist modes of thinking about cultures depend on a problematic picture of what various cultures are like, or on what I call the "Package Picture of Cultures." This view understands cultures on the model of neatly wrapped packages, sealed off from each other, possessing sharply defined edges or contours, and having distinctive contents that differ from those of other "cultural packages." I believe that these packages are more badly wrapped and their contents more jumbled than is often assumed and that there is a variety of political agendas that determine who and what are assigned places inside and outside a particular cultural package.

The essentialist Package Picture of Cultures represents cultures as if they were entities that exist neatly distinct and separate in the world, independent of our projects of distinguishing among them, obscuring the reality that boundaries between them are human constructs, underdetermined by existing variations in worldviews and ways of life. It eclipses the reality that the labels currently used to demarcate particular cultures themselves have a historical provenance and that what they individuate as one culture often changes over time. For example, while a prevailing picture of Western culture has it beginning in ancient Greece and perhaps culminating in the contemporary United States, a historical perspective would register that the ancient Greeks did not define themselves as part of "Western culture" and that "American culture" was initially distinguished from "European culture" rather than assimilated to it under the rubric "Western culture." The *Shorter Oxford English Dictionary* indicates that the use of the term "Western" to refer to Europe in distinction to "Eastern" or "Oriental" began around 1600, testimony to its colonial origins. Similarly, "Indian culture" is a label connected to the historical unification of an assortment of political territories into "British India," a term that enabled the nationalist challenge to colonialism to emerge as "Indian." Labels that pick out particular cultures are not simple descriptions that single out already distinct entities; rather, they are arbitrary and shifting designations connected to political projects that, for different reasons, insist on the distinctness of one culture from another.

The Package Picture of Cultures also assumes that the assignment of individuals to specific cultures is an obvious and uncontroversial matter. Under the influence of this picture, many of us assume that we know as a simple matter of fact to what "culture" we and others belong. I invite readers who think that they are members of Western culture or American culture to ask themselves what they have in common with the millions of people who would be assigned to the same cultural package. Do I share a common culture with every other Indian woman, and, if so, what are the constituent elements that make us members of the same culture? What is *my* relationship to Western culture? Critical reflection on such questions suggests that the assignment of individuals to particular cultures is more complicated than assumed and that it is affected by numerous, often incompatible, political projects of cultural classification.

The Package Picture of Cultures mistakenly sees the centrality of particular values, traditions, or practices to any particular culture as a given and thus eclipses the historical and political processes by which particular values or practices have come to be deemed central components of a particular culture. It also obscures how projects of cultural preservation themselves change over time. Dominant members of a culture often willingly discard what were previously regarded as important cultural practices but resist and protest other cultural changes, often those pertaining to the welfare of women. For instance, Olayinka Koso-Thomas's work reveals that in Sierra Leone virtually all the elaborate initiation rites and training that were traditional preliminaries to female circumcision have been given up because people no longer have the time, money, or social infrastructure for them. However, the rite of excision, abstracted from the whole context of practices in which it used to be embedded, is still seen as a crucial component of "preserving tradition" (Koso-Thomas 1987, 23). Feminists need to be alert to such synecdochic moves, whereby parts of a practice come to stand in for the whole, because such substitutions conceal important dimensions of social change.

Feminist engagement with cultural practices should be attentive to a process that I call "selective labeling," whereby those with social power conveniently designate certain changes in values and practices as consonant with cultural preservation and others as cultural loss or betrayal. Selective labeling allows changes approved by socially dominant groups to appear consonant with the preservation of essential values or core practices of a culture, while depicting changes that challenge the status quo as threats to that culture. The Package Picture of Cultures poses serious problems for feminist agendas in third-world contexts, since it often depicts culturally dominant norms of femininity, along with practices that adversely affect women, as central components of cultural identity and casts feminist challenges to norms and practices affecting women as cultural betrayals (Narayan 1997).

Giving up the Package Picture's view of cultural contexts as homogeneous helps us see that sharp differences in values often exist among those described as members of the same culture while among those described as "members of different cultures" there are often strong affinities in values, opening up liberating possibilities with respect to cross-cultural feminist judgments. For instance, the values and judgments of a Western feminist may diverge greatly from those of politically conservative members of her "package," while they might converge quite strongly with those of an Indian feminist counterpart. A Western feminist accused of imposing Western values in her negative judgment of an Indian cultural practice could, for instance, point out that her judgments correspond closely to those of some Indian feminists. Making this assertion does require her to be informed about Indian feminists' analyses of the practice and to use her critical judgment when such analyses disagree, as sometimes happens. Feminists can avoid the Package Picture of Cultures by attending to the historical variations and ongoing changes in cultural practices, to the wide range of attitudes toward those practices manifested by different members of a culture, and to the political negotiations that help to change the meanings and significances of these practices. Such attention would facilitate informed and astute feminist engagement with women's issues in national contexts different from their own.

References

Koso-Thomas, Olayinka. 1987. *The Circumcision of Women*. New York: Zed.

Narayan, Uma. 1997. *Dislocating Cultures: Identities, Traditions, and Third World Feminism*. New York: Routledge.

Narayan, Uma. 1998. "Essence of Culture and a Sense of History." *Hypatia* 13(2):86–106.

Chapter 25

Women's Experience of Racism:
How Race and Gender Interact

Canadian Research Institute
for the Advancement of Women (CRIAW)

The Canadian Research Institute for the Advancement of Women (CRIAW) provides tools and resources to support researchers and organizations in advancing social justice and equality for all women. CRIAW focuses on generating and promoting urgently needed feminist research, and on making it available for public advocacy and education. Recent projects include Intersectional Feminist Frameworks, which aims to promote inclusiveness in research, and FemNorthNet, which seeks to engage women living in northern communities in research on their experiences and needs due to economic restructuring.

The purpose of this fact sheet is to provide easy-to-understand statistical information and research on how women experience racism, and to provide suggestions for resources and action. We hope it will serve as a basic introduction for people with no knowledge of how race and gender affect women's lives. [...]

Anti-racism does not mean pretending that race doesn't exist. It means recognizing racism; effectively and constructively challenging racism in yourself and others; and eliminating racism embedded in public policy, workplaces, and every other area of life.

Jobs/Income

Racism and sexism combine to produce more economic inequalities for racialized women than for either white women or racialized men. Average annual income for 1995/96[1]:

$31,117: All Canadian men
$23,600: Visible minority men
$19,208: All Canadian women
$18,200: Aboriginal men
$16,600: Visible minority women
$13,300: Aboriginal women

Over half or nearly half of some racialized groups of women in Canada are living in poverty: 52% of women of Arab/West Asian (Middle Eastern) ancestry, 51% of women of Latin American ancestry, 47% of Black women, and 43% of Aboriginal women live in poverty. In the case of the first two groups, recent immigration may be a factor. Racialized immigrant women face more roadblocks to employment in Canada. More often than not, foreign university degrees and qualifications and foreign work experience are not recognized because Canada has inadequate systems to judge academic equivalencies.[2] Although governments invest in English or French as a second language programs, existing programs are inadequate to meet the need. Many women in particular are not receiving enough language training to integrate themselves as full participants in Canadian society. Racism is a major barrier to employment: Many employers and managers

---

BOX 25.1: What the Words Mean

Aboriginal or indigenous peoples: "Native" peoples, including First Nations, Inuit, Métis, and status and non-status Indians.

Visible minority, racial minority, women/people of colour: "Visible minority" tends to be used by the Canadian government, and will be used in this fact sheet when reporting statistics collected by the federal government. These terms do not include Aboriginal peoples.
Some people are now using the term "racialized" to refer to this group, to show that "race is socially constructed." For example, in Canada "Irish" and "French Canadians" used to be considered races. There were signs saying "No Irish allowed" and Irish people were discriminated against in employment. Racist hatred has nothing to do with the target groups and everything to do with how dominant groups in a society identify non-dominant groups for discrimination.

Racialized: This word has been used in different ways by different people. In this fact sheet, "racialized" will refer to anyone who experiences racism because of his or her race, skin colour, ethnic background, accent, culture, or religion. In this fact sheet, "racialized" includes people of colour, Aboriginal peoples, and ethnic, linguistic, religious, or cultural minorities who are targets of racism. When terms such as "women of colour" are used, it refers only to that group, as Canadian statistics are often collected separately for "visible minority," "Aboriginal," and "immigrant" groups. Racialized women have different cultures, histories, religions, family norms, life experiences, and are subject to different stereotypes. What they have in common is they are *racialized*—that is, they are subject to racism and made to feel different because of their racial/ethnic background.

Immigrant: An immigrant is someone who moves to Canada with the intention of staying permanently. Immigrants come from all over the world: Asia, Africa, Europe, North or South America, or Oceania. Immigrants can be white or people of colour, speak English, French, or another language as a mother tongue.

Refugee: Refugees move to Canada under a special category ("refugee") because they are fleeing persecution or war in their own countries.

make assumptions about work habits, suitability of certain types of work, and ability to "fit in" on the basis of skin colour, or assume that someone who speaks English or French with a different accent is stupid.[3] In the case of Black women and Aboriginal women, long-standing policies and practices of racism and marginalization keep almost half (over 40%) of these groups of women living in poverty, compared with 19% of women who are not visible minorities.[4] In 1996, 17% of visible minority women in Canada had a university degree compared to 12% of Canadian women who did not belong to a visible minority group. Nevertheless, 15% of visible minority women were unemployed, compared with 9% of non-visible minority women.[5]

Housing

Racial discrimination in housing is well documented. Jamaican and Somali immigrants had particular difficulties in finding rental housing because of some landlords' perceptions of these groups.[6] Race is also a barrier to home ownership. Two studies of Black and white people in Toronto (matched for income and family characteristics) found a lower rate of home ownership among Black people.[7] There is also a racist perception that Chinese immigrants in British Columbia's Lower Mainland, for example, are "taking over," particularly certain suburbs like Richmond.[8] No one seems to feel that white people have "taken over" certain communities, even though all white people in Canada are immigrants or the descendants of immigrants. Research has shown that racialized immigrant women can experience extreme forms of discrimination when finding housing, especially if they are single parents. They are very vulnerable to abuse by landlords.[9]

BOX 25.2: What Racism Affects

Racism affects

- housing
- jobs
- self-esteem
- health
- and every aspect of your life

If you are subject to racism, it may cost you money, a place to live, a job, your self-respect, your health, or your life. Women who experience racism may live through it in a different way from men, and from each other.

Access to Justice

For racialized women, gender-based violence is not the only type of violence they experience: race and gender combine to increase their likelihood of being assaulted. For example, First Nations woman Helen Betty Osbourne was brutally gang-raped, tortured, and killed by a group of white men, and the white townsfolk kept a conspiracy of silence about her rapists and murderers. Because of the documented racism of Canada's police forces, criminal justice system, and jails,[10] racialized women may be reluctant to call police in cases of domestic assault out of loyalty to their family and community, or because they do not wish to fuel racist stereotypes about their community or to subject themselves or family members to a racist system. Refugees from places in which police forces, the military, and the government were involved in violence against civilians, including organized or systemic rape of women, may have no trust in systems of authority.[11] Aboriginal women are subject to racism in the courts, and are overrepresented in Canadian jails, which is a soul-destroying experience. Aboriginal women make up over 20% of Canada's female prison population, but only 2% of the female population of Canada.[12] In Canada, you are more likely to be sent to jail if you are poor or racialized.[13] Programs in jail are often not appropriate for racialized women.[14]

BOX 25.3: More Words and Ideas

Overt racism: Racism can be overt, such as calling people names, beating them up, excluding them on the basis of race or ethnicity. Some companies ask employment agencies for white candidates only.

Covert, subtle, or "polite" racism: Lets you know you are different, that the most salient characteristic about you is your race, rather than your personality, your achievements as an individual, or anything else.

Structural racism: Not all racism is as obvious as beating someone up or even secretly excluding someone while being polite to his or her face. Racism can be structural (it's a part of every aspect of society). Sometimes structural racism in hiring is not conscious or deliberate: People tend to hire those they know, people like themselves, or they advertise the job among their own networks. When the majority of people in decision-making positions are white men, they tend to hire other white men. Employment equity programs are supposed to get companies and government departments to expand their networks, to ensure that racialized communities hear about job opportunities, to give them a fair chance, and to introduce anti-discrimination policies and workshops in the workplace.

Health

Racism itself can cause illness. When people are overtly racist, it translates into poorer health for the targets of racism.[15] Structural racism can also cause illness and death. Language and cultural barriers mean less access to life-saving medical procedures.[16] Structural racism leading to less income and social status has a direct impact on health.[17] Another example of structural racism is using standards developed in research using white men to measure health and health risks when these standards may not be the same for women, racialized people, and particularly racialized women.

Some women refugees in Canada have experienced rape during wartime and have seen their children and other family members tortured and killed. This has particular physical and mental health consequences. Some women have been subject to female genital mutilation, which may also pose health problems and isolate them from health care providers and from women outside their communities.[18]

Women tend to be the health guardians of their families, and sacrifice paid work and personal happiness to care for sick relatives. Greater vulnerability to illness and less access to health care and home care services for racialized communities[19] mean more unpaid health care work for racialized women, which can have an impact on their own health.

BOX 25.4: "But All That Is in the Past. Why Can't We Forget about It?"

It's obviously not in the past. Take a look at the statistics about how racism affects access to housing, jobs, health, justice, and citizenship. The past also shapes people's experiences in the present. For example, for over 100 years, a Canadian government policy to assimilate Aboriginal peoples by taking children away from their families to residential schools—where they were punished for speaking their language, practising their own cultural and religious traditions, and where they were often the victims of physical and sexual abuse—left generations of Aboriginal peoples without parenting skills, without self-esteem, and feeling ashamed of who they were and hopeless about the future. Survivors of residential schools are still trying to heal from the damage.

Racialized Sexuality

Racialized women are often sexualized in racist ways. This is one of the ways racism and sexism can combine. For women of colour, sexual harassment can be racialized. A man might sexually harass a woman of colour by making racist comments or assumptions about her sexuality. Women of Asian origin are often stereotyped as exotic and obedient. Black women are stereotyped as highly sexual and available.[20] It is possible that women of colour face more sexual harassment and may be more vulnerable to sexual assault because of racist stereotypes. In addition, if they are harassed or assaulted, racist stereotypes on the part of the police and the courts mean they may have less access to justice. Racialized women who are lesbian, bisexual, or transgendered face homophobia and racism from mainstream society; marginalization from their own communities; and racism, exclusion, and stereotyping from movements seeking gay, lesbian, bisexual, and transgendered rights.

BOX 25.5: "Why Can't Women Just Join Together as a Sisterhood Instead of Bringing up Things That Divide Us?"

Kalwant Bhopal says that the idea of sisterhood implies that all women experience the same oppression, but solidarity implies an understanding that the struggles of all women are different, but interconnected. Métis anti-racist, feminist activist educator Jean Fyre Graveline discusses the myths that "skin colour doesn't matter," "we are all equal," "we all have equal opportunity to succeed." She draws on Aboriginal healing methods to show that we are all interconnected, but we must recognize that people have different privileges that affect how people work together. To build a strong women's movement and a strong society, we must face head-on the challenges of racism and how it interacts with many other factors to produce our different life experiences.

Schools

School curricula tend to erase the contributions of racialized women in building Canada. For example, many Canadians still believe that Canada is made of "two founding peoples" (English and French), and do not learn about the 10,000-year history of Aboriginal women and men on this land, Canada's own history of slavery prior to 1833 and the particular suffering of Black women slaves, the interaction of racism and sexism in Canada's old law banning men of Asian origin from employing white women, the trafficking of Aboriginal women as prostitutes by white male Indian agents, a law (which lasted until 1946) that banned women of Chinese origin from becoming citizens, or the fact that Aboriginal women and men did not receive the federal vote until 1960, 42 years after the full federal vote was granted to white women. When they learn about the contributions of racialized people to Canada, it tends to be about those of racialized men. In addition, teachers may treat racialized students differently, sometimes without realizing they are doing so. Some racialized students do not do well at school because of their teachers' racist low expectations of them.[21] Both sexist and racist expectations of teachers and guidance counsellors can have a profound effect on the lives of racialized girls. A study found that young Canadian-born Black francophone and anglophone women and men living in Montreal also experienced racial confrontations and harassment by fellow students in English and French elementary and high schools.[22]

Media

The media portrayal of white women still leaves a lot to be desired, but the media portrayal of racialized women is worse. Apart from a small minority of racialized women who appear to be confident, whole people, racialized people in general and racialized women in particular are underrepresented in Canadian television drama and news media relative to their proportion in the Canadian population, and where racialized women do appear, they are often relegated to stereotypical positions.[23]

Self-Esteem

Racism can create feelings of powerlessness and low self-esteem,[24] which have an impact on health, happiness, and life chances.

Citizenship and Immigration

Canada claims to have a non-racist, non-sexist immigration system. Why, then, is there an over-representation of Canadian overseas immigration offices in the United States and Europe, when most of Canada's immigrants now come from Asia?[25] Canada's immigration system divides people into classes: If you have enough money, you can buy your way in under the investor class. Canada judges independent-class immigrants according to a point system, which gives points for education and for speaking one of Canada's official languages, for example. This discriminates against women because "women have been denied access to education, training and employment opportunities. As a result, most women entering Canada are unable to qualify as independent immigrants."[26] Most women enter Canada as sponsored immigrants, which means that they are financially dependent on their sponsors, usually their husbands, for a period of 10 years. It means they do not qualify for many social services or programs. It gives husbands and other sponsors a huge amount of power over women, who can be abused and threatened with deportation if they complain. Many women do not know their rights.

BOX 25.6: "What about Reverse Racism?"

"Reverse racism" is a term mainly used by people to justify their own racism. Some people defend white privilege by saying, "Well, such-and-such a group is racist too." The big difference is because white people, particularly white men, are overrepresented in positions of power relative to their proportion in the population, white racism against other groups often means lost job opportunities, particularly for racialized women. There are so few racialized women in positions of power that if some of them dislike white men, it has no real effect on white men. Quite frankly, after experiencing the horrible effects of racism, the onus is not on racialized women to embrace and trust white people, but on white people to stop being racist. "Reverse racism" is also used to describe employment equity programs by people who believe such programs are "race-based, gender-based hiring systems." What these people do not want to acknowledge is that in the absence of employment equity systems, there is often an unwritten race-based, gender-based hiring system that favours white men, which is why white men are overrepresented in decision-making positions. [...] Employment equity is not an attack on white men. It is a mechanism to ensure that everyone has a fair chance.

Domestic Workers

Some advocates refer to the federal government's immigration Live-in Caregiver Program as "a form of slavery." Women from other countries and regions, particularly the Philippines and the Caribbean, come to Canada because of a lack of economic alternatives in their own countries, in order to send money back to support their children and other relatives. This obligation and lack of choices makes them very vulnerable to abuse of all kinds. Women who come to Canada under the Live-in Caregiver Program must live in their employer's home (which increases their vulnerability to sexual assault, eliminates privacy, and means they are on call 24 hours a day and are usually not paid for overtime). They can work only for the employer who is listed on the Employment Authorization (EA) form and cannot take other work. They can stay in Canada only until the date specified on the EA. They are frequently unaware of their rights, and employers have threatened them with deportation and other measures to ensure their silence about abusive working conditions.[27]

BOX 25.7: Racism Hurts the Country and the World

White people unknowingly experience immediate benefits of racism, such as access to housing and jobs because racialized candidates have been turned down. However, in the end, racism destroys community and individual well-being. Hatred, suspicion, lack of trust, putting up barriers between oneself and others, [...] or seeing someone [negatively because of his or her race create] conflicts and problems in the country and [elsewhere] in the world. Racial discrimination is also a terrible waste of human resources, which hurts our economy as a whole.

Hate Crimes

In Toronto there are about 300 overt acts of racism every year, involving mainly vandalism and assault, particularly against Jewish and Black people. However, these statistics are from before September 11, [2001,] after which there was a huge increase in vandalism and assault of Muslims and people who looked like they might be of Arab origin, as well as bombings and vandalism of Muslim, Jewish, and Hindu places of worship.[28] Hate crimes, in terms of being beaten because of your race, ethnicity, or religion, can lead to injury, permanent disability, or death. Hate crimes involving vandalism of places of worship or other buildings or objects identified with a group can leave the community fearful and feeling excluded from society. Women may have particular safety concerns as the targets of sexual as well as physical assault.

BOX 25.8: "What about So-and-So Who's in a Position of Power? Doesn't That Mean All Racialized Women Can Make It If They Work Hard Enough?"

A few token racialized women in positions of power does not mean that things are fine for all racialized women, or that racism and sexism do not exist. Many racialized women have worked very hard to get where they are, and many have worked very hard and not reached their goals because of racist attitudes and structures.

Assumptions That Reflect Gendered Racism

Assumptions That All People of Colour Are Immigrants

White women who emigrate from the United States or other primarily English- or French-speaking countries are often not viewed as immigrants, but as Canadians who were born elsewhere. Women of colour who were born in Canada are often viewed as immigrants, even though they are not. They are asked, "Where are you from?" If they answer, "Edmonton," they are then asked, "No, where are you really from?" They are made to feel like foreigners in their own country.

Assumptions That Racialized Women Are Not Feminists

Some people assume that women may have certain beliefs and outlooks depending on their racial, ethnic, or religious background. Women of South Asian ancestry (including India and Pakistan) are often assumed to want to have only sons. Muslim women who wear the *hijab* (head scarf) are often assumed not to be feminists or to be subservient to men. The only way to know what a woman believes is by asking her.

Resistance to Acknowledging Racism

Most Canadians know that to be racist is a bad thing, so they deny being racist. However, many Canadians continue to hold stereotypes that benefit white people and hurt everyone else in very real ways. Some people think racism is about only a few isolated incidents perpetrated by a few ignorant individuals. However, there have recently been a number of disturbing comments by people with decision-making power over others, such as these examples from early 2002 alone:

- Ontario Finance Minister Jim Flaherty suggested in January 2002 that Aboriginal peoples were not "real people."[29] Flaherty held the purse strings for every initiative in Ontario, and came in second in the leadership race to become premier of Ontario.
- Saskatchewan Member of Parliament Roy Bailey publicly stated in January 2002 that Dr. Rey Pagtakhan, the new minister for veterans' affairs, was unsuited for the job because he is "Asiatic."[30]
- PEI Member of the Legislative Assembly Wilbur MacDonald said in an April 2002 speech that "the white human race is on a fast track which will destroy us ... we're not at the present time keeping up with the numbers of people who are in our society.... England, for example, is being taken over by British West Indies people, France is being taken over by another group of people. It won't be long in the United States ... [that] Spanish people will be taking over.... We're going to deteriorate in our population too...."[31]

Internalized Racism

Racialized people can also be racist, both in terms of accepting mainstream views about other racial, ethnic, and cultural groups, and in terms of believing the repeated racist messages they have heard all their lives. We all have a voice in our head that repeats messages about good and bad, right and wrong—messages we internalized when we were growing up. When someone has grown up with racism, that voice repeats the racist messages throughout life about not being good enough. It can also harm that person's relationships with people within his or her community. One example of this is in Beatrice Culleton's book, *In Search of April Raintree*, in which two Métis sisters grow up in separate foster homes. One can "pass for white" and the other has darker skin. The lighter-skinned sister, despite her lighter skin, grew up being called "half-breed," "dirty Indian," etc., and was mistreated by her white foster family, while the darker-skinned sister grew up in a Métis-positive home. The lighter-skinned sister is ashamed to be seen with her darker-skinned sister, and renounces her heritage and wants to "live like a white person." This is internalized racism, and it has an effect on the relationship between the sisters. It is when even some small part of you believes the racist garbage you have heard. It can affect how you live your life. Developing high self-esteem and modelling this for others is a powerful act of resistance.

Race Interacts with Many Other Factors

Race can interact with class, income, occupation, social status, language, physical appearance, culture, religion, ability, sexual orientation, age, immigration status, Indian status, personal background, and experience. To find out how, check out our website: www.criaw-icref.ca/womensexperienceofracismHowraceandgenderinteract%20

Action

To find out more about what governments, workplaces, organizations, and individuals can do, check out the full version of this fact sheet on our website. (A revised version of this factsheet is in preparation and will be available in 2012 from CRIAW-ICREF at http://criaw-icref.ca.)

Notes

1. The averages for all men and all women in Canada are 1995 data from the 1996 Census, reported in Statistics Canada, 1996 Census: Sources of Income, Earnings, and Total Income, and Family Income, *The Daily*, May 12, 1998. The other data are from Statistics Canada, *Women in Canada 2000: A Gender-Based Statistical Report* (Ottawa: Minister of Industry, 2000).

2. National Organization of Immigrant and Visible Minority Women of Canada, *A Survey of Immigrant and Visible Minority Women on the Issue of Recognition of Foreign Credentials* (Ottawa: NOIVMC, 1996).

3. West Coast Domestic Workers Association website: www.vcn.bc.ca/wcdwa/eng_1.htm.

4. Statistics Canada, *Women in Canada 2000: A Gender-Based Statistical Report* (Ottawa: Minister of Industry, 2000), p. 246.

5. Statistics Canada, *Women in Canada 2000*, pp. 224, 226.

6. Kenneth Dion, Immigrants' Perceptions of Housing Discrimination in Toronto: The Housing New Canadians Project, *The Journal of Social Issues*, volume 57, number 3 (Fall 2001): pp. 523–39.

7. Joe T. Darden and Sameh M. Kamel, Black and White Differences in Homeownership Rates in the Toronto Census Metropolitan Area: Does Race Matter? *The Review of Black Political Economy*, volume 28, number 2 (Fall 2000): 53–76; Andrejs Skaburskis, Race and Tenure in Toronto, *Urban Studies*, volume 33 (March 1996): 223–52.

8. Brian K. Ray, Greg Halseth, and Benjamin Johnson, The Changing "Face" of the Suburbs: Issues of Ethnicity and Residential Change in Suburban Vancouver, *International Journal of Urban and Regional Research*, volume 21 (March 1997): 75–99.

9. Sylvia Novac, Immigrant Enclaves and Residential Segregation: Voices of Racialized Refugee and Immigrant Women, *Canadian Woman Studies*, volume 19, number 3 (Fall 1999): 88–93.

10. Commission on Systemic Racism in the Ontario Criminal Justice System, *Report of the Commission on Systemic Racism in the Ontario Criminal Justice System* (Toronto: Queen's Printer for Ontario); Jean Charles Coutu, *La Justice pour et par les autochtones* (Québec: Ministre de la Justice du Québec, 1995); A. Currie and George Kiefl, *Ethnocultural Groups and the Justice System in Canada: A Review of the Issues* (Ottawa: Department of Justice Canada, 1994); Commission on Systemic Racism in the Ontario Criminal Justice System, *Racism behind Bars: The Treatment of Black and Other Racial Minority Prisoners in Ontario Prisons* (Toronto: Queen's Printer for Ontario, 1994); Urban Alliance on Race Relations, *Race and the Canadian Justice System: An Annotated Bibliography* (Toronto: Urban Alliance on Race Relations, 1995); the Hon. Louise Arbour, *Commission of Inquiry into Certain Events at the Prison for Women in Kingston* (Ottawa: Public Works and Government Services, 1996).

11. Amnesty International, *Women's Rights Are Human Rights: Resources for Information and Action* (Ottawa: Amnesty International Canada, 2002): www.amnesty.ca/women/index.html.

12. Statistics Canada, *Women in Canada 2000*, p. 177.

13. Canadian Association of Elizabeth Fry Societies, *Factsheet: Justice and the Poor* (Ottawa: CAEFS, no date): www.elizabethfry.ca/eweek02/factsht.htm#justice; Elizabeth Comack, Vanessa Chopyk, and Linda Wood, *Mean Streets? The Social Locations, Gender Dynamics, and Patterns of Violent Crime in Winnipeg* (Ottawa: Centre for Policy Alternatives, December 2000).

14. Kelly Blanchette, *Risk and Need among Federally Sentenced Female Offenders: A Comparison of Minimum, Medium, and Maximum Security Inmates* (Ottawa: Research Division, Correctional Service of Canada, 1997); Barbara Bloom, Gender-Responsive Programming for Women Offenders: Guiding Principles and Practices, *Forum on Corrections Research*, volume 11, number 3 (2000): 22–27; Canadian Association of Elizabeth Fry Societies (CAEFS), *Position of the Canadian Association of Elizabeth Fry Societies (CAEFS) Regarding the Classification and Carceral Placement of Women Classified as Maximum Security Prisoners* (Ottawa: CAEFS, 1997); Kim Pate, *Complaint Regarding the Discriminatory Treatment of Federally Sentenced Women by the Government of Canada* (Ottawa: Canadian Association of Elizabeth Fry Societies, 2001): www.elizabethfry.ca/complain.htm.

15. See Nancy Krieger and Stephen Sidney, Racial Discrimination and Blood Pressure: The CARDIA Study of Young Black and White Adults, *American Journal of Public Health*, volume 86, number 19 (October 1996): 1370–78; Wornie L. Reed, Suffer the Children: Some Effects of Racism on the Health of Black Infants, in Peter Conrad and Rochelle Kern (Eds.), *The Sociology of Health and Illness: Critical Perspectives* (New York: St. Martin's Press, 1994), pp. 314–27, quoted in Boston Women's Health Book Collective, *Our Bodies, Ourselves for the New Century* (New York: Touchstone, 1998), p. 683.

16. T. Gregory Hislop, Chong The, Agnes Lai, Tove Lobo, and Victoria M. Taylor, Cervical Cancer Screening in BC Chinese Women, *BC Medical Journal*, volume 42, number 10 (December 2000): 456–60.

17. Income is the primary determinant of health, beyond smoking, "lifestyle choices," and genetic endowment: see Andrew Haines and Richard Smith, Working Together to Reduce Poverty's Damage, *British Medical Journal*, volume 317 (February 22, 1997): 529; Dennis Raphael, Health Inequalities in Canada: Current Discourses and Implications for Public Health Action, *Critical Public Health*, volume 10, number 2 (2000): 193–216; Pat Armstrong, Hugh Armstrong, and David Coburn, *Unhealthy Times: Political Economy Perspectives on Health and Care* (Oxford: Oxford University Press, 2001); Dennis Raphael, Health Effects of Economic Inequality, *Canadian Review of Social Policy*, volume 44 (1999): 25–40; J.A. Auerbach and B.K. Krimgold, *Income, Socioeconomic status, and Health: Exploring the Relationships* (Washington, DC: National Policy Association, 2001); I. Kawachi, B.P. Kennedy, and R.G. Wilkinson (Eds.), *Income Inequality and Health* (New York: New Press, 1999); R.G. Wilkinson and M. Marmot (Eds.), *Social Determinants of Health: The Solid Facts* (Copenhagen: World Health Organization, 1998): www.who.dk/healthy-cities; D. Acheson, *Independent Inquiry into Inequalities in Health* (London, UK: Stationary Office, 1998): www.official-documents.co.uk/document/doh/ih/contents.htm; David Ross and P. Roberts, *Income and Child Well-being: A New Perspective on the Poverty Debate* (Ottawa: Canadian Council on Social Development, 1999); Monica Townson, *Health and Wealth* (Ottawa: Canadian Centre for Policy Alternatives, 1999); US Department of Health and Human Services, *Socioeconomic Status and Health Chartbook in Health, United States, 1998*: www.cdc.gov/nchs/products/pubs/pubd/hus/2010/98chtbk.htm; M. Bartley, D. Blane, and S. Montgomery, Health and the Life Course: Why Safety Nets Matter, *British Medical Journal*, volume 314 (1997): 1194–96; D. Coburn, Income Inequality, Lowered Social Cohesion, and the Poorer Health Status of Populations: The Role of Neoliberalism, *Social Science and Medicine*, volume 51 (2000): 135–46; J.W. Lynch, G. Davey Smith, G.A. Kaplan, and J.S. House, Income Inequality and Mortality: Importance to Health of Individual Income, Psychosocial Environment, or Material Conditions, *British Medical Journal*, volume 320 (2000): 1200–4.

18. Canadian Women's Health Network, *Female Genital Mutilation and Health Care: Current Situation and Legal Status Recommendations to Improve the Health Care of Affected Women* (Ottawa: Health Canada Women's Health Bureau, 2000): www.cwhn.ca/resources/fgm.

19. Mary Ann Mulvihill, Louise Mailloux, and Wendy Atkin, *Advancing Policy and Research Responses to Immigrant and Refugee Women's Health in Canada* (Ottawa: Centres of Excellence for Women's Health, Health Canada, 2001): www.cewh-cesf.ca/resources/im-ref_health/im_ref_health.pdf.

20. Philomena Essed, *Towards a Methodology to Identify Converging Forms of Everyday Discrimination* (New York: United Nations, no date), quoted in Canadian Feminist Alliance for International Action (FAFIA), *Report on Canada's Compliance with the International Convention on the Elimination of All Forms of Racial Discrimination in Response to Canada's 13th and 14th Reports to the Committee in the Elimination of All Forms of Racial Discrimination*, FAFIA Think Tank Paper no. 3 (Ottawa: FAFIA, August 2001).

21. See Canadian Race Relations Foundation, *Racism in Our Schools: What to Know about It; How to Fight It* (Toronto, CRRF, 2000): www.crr.ca/en/MediaCentre/FactSheets/FACTJune2000.pdf.

22. Micheline Labelle, Daniel Salée, and Yolande Frenette, *Civic Incorporation or Exclusion? Representation of Citizenship among Second-Generation Youth of Jamaican and Haitian Origin in Montreal* (Montréal: Centre de recherche sur l'immigration, l'ethnicité et la citoyenneté (CRIEC)): www.unites.uqam.ca/criec.

23. MediaWatch, *Front and Centre: Minority Representation on Television* (Toronto: MediaWatch, no date), data collected in 1993: www.mediawatch.ca/research/front.

24. Josephine Enang, Mothering at the Margins: An African-Canadian Immigrant Woman's Experience, *Canadian Women's Health Network* (Spring 2001): 7–8: www.cwhn.ca.

25. Applicants who immigrate to Canada must submit their applications to the Canadian embassy, consulate, or commission nearest them. There are six such offices in the United States alone, whereas many Asian countries do not have even one, and India, one of the largest countries in the world, has only one for the whole country. See Citizenship and Immigration Canada, *Immigration Processing Missions Abroad*: www.cic.gc.ca/english/info/emission.html.

26. Judy Vashti Persad and Véronica Moreno, *Community Development with Immigrant Women: A Resource Kit for Community Educating and Organizing* (Toronto: Cross Cultural Communication Centre, 1990), p. 21.

27. West Coast Domestic Workers Association website: www.vcn.bc.ca/wcdwa/eng_1.htm: The West Coast Domestic Worker's Association (WCDWA) is an independent organization formed and run by domestic workers and their supporters to help nannies and caregivers with employment rights and immigration issues. The majority of our members are—or were—domestic workers like you and come from many different places around the world including the Philippines and other South Asian countries, Eastern and Western Europe, Australia and New Zealand, Latin America and Canada.

28. Canadian Human Rights Commission, *Annual Report 2001* (Ottawa: CHRC, 2002).

29. Canadian Race Relations Foundation, "Flaherty: Enough Is Enough: Says the Executive Director of the CRRF," News release (Toronto: CRRF, January 22, 2002).
30. Canadian Race Relations Foundation, "'Asiatic' Remark Inappropriate: A Statement from the Executive Director," News release (Toronto: CRRF, January 2002).

31. Wilbur MacDonald speaking in the PEI legislature, *Hansard*, Prince Edward Island Legislative Assembly, Third session of the 61st General Assembly, April 19, 2002: www.gov.pe.ca/leg/hansard/2002spring.

Chapter 26

The Hall of Shame:
Lies, Masks, and Respectful Femininity

Amita Handa

Amita Handa is a scholar, author, and DJ. She has an MA in women's studies and a PhD in sociology, and has produced cutting-edge Canadian research focusing on issues of cultural conflict among second-generation South Asian youth. Handa is a student equity adviser for the Toronto District School Board and a well-known DJ with a popular radio show, Masala Mixx. *Her book,* The Hall of Shame, *from which we have drawn the following selection, has been described as "an articulate and richly textured account of South Asian girls' attempts to 'fit in' without abandoning their diasporic roots."*

In my interviews with young South Asian women it became apparent that parental and community regulation of women's sexuality was tied into protecting young women from the ills of Western society. All the women in my study knew how they had to behave in order to be accepted as "good" daughters and community members. They were all concerned about their sexual reputations in one way or another and were very aware that their behaviour has an impact on how their family is viewed by the rest of the community. In their experience, their reputation, and the resulting family reputation, was closely monitored by community members: relatives, family friends, and acquaintances. What struck me as familiar and noteworthy were the lengths to which the women would go to protect their reputations, and the extent to which their lives were experienced as fragmented. This fragmentation meant that the codes of femininity they observed outside the home were completely different to those observed within the family and community. Our good reputations were always ultimately based on our sexual reputations, although much of the discourse around reputation was embedded in taken-for-granted notions of feminine codes of behaviour; hence its sexual subtext was often implicit.

Mis-Uses of the Body

The debates involving women in colonial India are not only a historical example of how women come to represent and maintain cultural boundaries but the illustration of a process of contestation over cultural difference. There are continuities between this earlier period of colonialism and nationalism and the present diasporic context. [...] Specifically, there are parallels between colonial racism and Canadian racism, and the South Asian diaspora mirrors, in significant ways, the Indian nation-state. In the diasporic context young women continue to mark boundaries of cultural difference. These boundaries are maintained through notions of femininity that regulate the body in how it is adorned, what it consumes, and where it goes (meaning women can go [to] only certain places at certain times).

Leslie Roman has argued that the body is a primary site on which notions of femininity are constructed.[1] She shows how bodily consumption and adornment are tied into sexual reputation, and how control of the body is an expression of social control. As a mechanism of social control, "dirtiness" is linked not only to health but also to prevailing cultural norms around order and propriety. Individuals who transgress these are seen as vulgar and bad.[2] Roman applies this theoretical framework to her study of girls in a Catholic high school. She points out that for women, smoking is associated with "low" behaviour, such as alcoholism, and "provocative" dress. It suggests a "looser construction of the body; a body freed to its desires, so to speak, as well as a rejection of the 'little girl,' the niceness, the willingness to get along, the softness," that often characterizes dominant notions of femininity.[3] Roman found that the "'price' of freedom of the body—freedom to be at ease in public arenas, to wear comfortable and casual clothes, to smoke cigarettes—was the loss of a good reputation."

For the young women I interviewed, maintaining a notion of difference from white Canadians is also contingent on notions of appropriate femininity. Like most girls, South Asian teenagers face community sanctions if their conduct does not conform to expected feminine behaviour. Regulations and sanctions are strategies of identification and a means by which community is imagined and produced. It is through the sanctioning of those who transgress the boundaries that communities are constituted as bounded entities. By observing specific norms of conduct, "we" come to feel identity with each other and see ourselves as different from "others."

Most of the women I spoke with defined normative feminine behaviour by things they were not supposed to do: drinking, smoking, doing drugs, and dating boys. What they were expected to do included studying hard, going to family and community gatherings, and helping with domestic duties. For South Asian women, negotiating their femininities doesn't just affect their sexual reputations—it also indicates their degree of allegiance to an ethnic collectivity. The danger of engaging in immoral activities is associated with the outside world. Nina explained that much of her life outside the home was hidden from her parents and that they did not understand or accept many of the things that she wanted to do: "Indian girls are not supposed to drink or smoke or go out, you know. My parents think, well you know, if you go out so much, if you're going to clubs and stuff, it looks so bad on you. Like I know friends whose parents think, well you know, if you go to a club nobody's going to marry you, because you're always going out all the time and you're doing this and that."

Nina shows how the East/West dualism is embedded in codes of feminine behaviour that regulate drinking, smoking, and social (potentially sexual) affiliations. A woman's failure to comply with these codes brands her with an unscrupulous sexual reputation and will eventually inhibit her marriageability. Nina explains how restrictions on freedom of movement and bodily expression are synonymous with being South Asian. Her ethnic identity depends on complying with these restrictions around femininity. Notions of South Asian-ness and femininity are integral to each other, so that transgressing the norms of one category simultaneously destabilizes the other. Later, Nina said about her friends: "They're aware that I am Indian 'cause they, I mean, I feel like I constantly have to explain to them why I am Indian, because of the way my parents are. I have to explain that I can't do this with you, I can't do this with you. Why? Because my parents are Indian and that's why I can't." Here, the restriction of social activities by parents becomes part of what actually defines being South Asian.

*****

Geography of Gender

As mentioned previously, the boundary of ethnicity is often dependent on gender. Characteristics that have become associated with gender serve to carve out ethnic identity and what most often distinguishes one ethnic collective from another are "rules relating to sexuality, marriage and family … and a *true* member will perform these roles properly" (my emphasis).[4] Gender and ethnicity work together in establishing definitions of identity, and notions of cultural authenticity help to maintain regulations around "appropriate" femininity. This became apparent during the course of these conversations.

My interviews often began with an exploration of school environments, and I used these discussions to explore the young women's sense of ethnic identity vis-à-vis their sense of belonging in relation to other cultural groups. In all of the interviews it was often implicit that they had to be different from "Canadian women," by which they meant white women. I observed the contest between East and West in the various discourses that construct white and South Asian women's sexualities in contrast with one another. I spoke with Salimah, for example, about the various cultural groups in her school, and we began to tease out some of the ways in which South Asian women were located differently from white women in relation to sexuality. In a discussion of stereotypical representations, Salimah said: "Okay, when I see white girls, I can generalize here, most white girls are more giving, like fast sexually, you know. Even though Indian girls aren't [fast], well not all, but I'm just saying they're taught not to be. But I don't think that's enforced in, in you know, white families. I know of this one girl whose mother bought her the pill. That would never happen in an Indian family."

The East/West dualism operates as an organizing category in her talk and she points to the oppositional relationship between brown and white women. Here, brown/white stands in for East/West. Part of what differentiates South Asian and white girls are codes around sexual behaviour and family acceptance of (heterosexual) sexuality: Salimah shows that in order to be seen as good girls, young South Asian women must conform to sexual norms that are not associated with what white girls do.

Within modernity, unresolved fears about modern social progress, anxieties about social change, and the possibility that unregulated freedom could cause moral and social disintegration have been projected onto both youth and women. We have also seen how the West has become synonymous with modernity, while the East is associated with tradition or premodernity. The young women in my study suggest that fears about modern change are manifested in fears about westernization. Within South Asian communities, in the sexualized discourse of East as pure and West as temptress, women are often positioned as sexual by the mere fact of living in the modern West. Salimah talked about how diasporic sexuality is viewed by those "back home."

> […] [There's] definitely a double standard. 'Cause I want to meet a really nice sweet guy kind of thing, but once you get them, *they don't want the modern girl, they don't want that girl who could be smart or anything.* They want that girl who's going to do everything for them, who's going to be that typical Indian girl. You know, and that's not what Canada's producing at the moment, I'm not lying. That's another thing, the Pakistani cricket team was here and one of the guys met this girl and phoned her and said, "Oh I want to get with you" and this and that. And she's like, "What do you think I am? *Just 'cause I'm from Canada I'm a slut? Just 'cause I'm from Canada, I'm not your typical one,* so you can turn around and do anything with me?" That's what a lot of Indian girls are

getting slack for, just 'cause they're from Canada, they're modernized, and they're not what people want them to be. (my emphasis)

Salimah begins by commenting on how men are threatened by women's independence and popularity. For her, the typical Pakistani girl fits modern colonial notions of South Asian womanhood: servitude, docility, and chastity. A typical Canadian woman, on the other hand, is seen as sexually active and associated with modernity. Modern is defined as both intelligent and sexually promiscuous. There is also a subtext of cultural authenticity; living in Canada makes one less Pakistani than living "back home."

[...] Salimah's comments indicate that the discourse around sexuality is not just about the relationship between white and brown. Even within the category of "brown" some forms of sexual behaviour are seen as more authentic than others. Let us refer back to Yuval-Davis's claim about the boundaries of ethnic identity being dependent on gender. From Salimah's account we can see that the definition of South Asian is contingent on the degree to which it is associated with the non-West. The non-West is not defined just geographically, however; it is also contingent upon certain sexual codes, whereby women become the territory upon which East is constructed as pure and West as degenerate. This moral discourse views the modern/West as a sexual threat to notions of South Asian femininity and thereby constructs women on a modern terrain as sexually available to men. Salimah's passage maps out Canada as a modern terrain. This terrain is gendered and thus a South Asian girl's mere residency in the modern positions her as a sexual object.

Most of the young women I interviewed commented on how their parents often referenced "back home" as a standard of measure. [...] Alka shows how the myth of "back home" works in regulating young women's sexualities. She addresses this myth in relation to upper-class youth culture in India:

I went to boarding school in India for six months.... And I go back there every year and I know. I mean, [...] girls go out left, right, and centre. Where they go out? To clubs and you name it. The only happening thing right now is big clubs and nice hotels and whatever. They go out for coffee, they come home late nights, even. I'm talking about even in the most decent homes they go out, they go out guys and girls. I mean you should see New Year's, it's a blast there.... But the really funny thing is that when I go back it's like freedom like you wouldn't believe. I get freedom like you wouldn't believe and I enjoy it. That's why I like India a lot, 'cause I get freedom like you wouldn't....

Alka explodes the "back home" myth by revealing that the worst fears about women and the West are actually occurring in the East. The strictness and sexual propriety associated with the homeland are displaced by her account of experiencing more freedom in India itself than she does here in the Toronto diasporic community. Why, then, maintain the fantasy? Because this myth serves as a means to hold on to a notion of protection, purity, and propriety associated with the East. This protection from modernity may be all the way back home, but it serves as a distant standard to aspire to. This myth also justifies the regulation and protection of women on diasporic terrain by giving permission for the reproduction of "Indian" (from India) in Canada.

White Lies, Brown Parents

All of the girls I interviewed admitted that they lied to their parents. While most teenagers do not share everything with their parents, I was struck by how instrumental lying is in maintaining the next-to-impossible status of the good South Asian girl. Salimah told me she "had to lie," although she had mixed feelings about it. She explained that her parents viewed her as an innocent, good daughter and that it was very important for her to maintain this image: "I lie to my parents a lot, and if I started thinking that I feel bad about lying then there wouldn't be much to my life. It's kind of like living, doing what you have to do. I do feel bad about lying, but I want to keep my parents happy. If I didn't lie I wouldn't get anywhere. And I do feel bad about lying that much but I'd feel more bad if … I want to keep my parents happy. I really do. I really look for their approval."

I recall learning about concealment as central to ideas of respect in my own family, when I found a pack of Du Maurier cigarettes in my older brother's room. He was smoking but hiding it from my parents. Later that evening, my father lit up a cigar with some friends, a habit he indulged in occasionally. My grandparents were not at home. He was smoking but hiding it from his parents. The next day, I saw my grandfather come inside from an afternoon walk, and I detected the smell of bidis (Indian cigarettes) on his breath. He realized that his secret had been found out. "Shhh, please don't tell anyone," he said. He was smoking but hiding it from everyone! Over time I realized: it was not that nobody knew about each other's smoking, but that not openly engaging in a behaviour that was deemed negative was enmeshed in notions of respect.

For the women I interviewed, lying is used not only to negotiate freedom, but also to uphold the good girl image in the eyes of their parents and the larger South Asian community. Even when family members are aware that their daughters are engaged in activities deemed inappropriate by family and community members, they participate in maintaining the lie. To speak about these activities honestly is considered to be disrespectful. In addition to upholding the image of goodness for family and community, however, with their peers the girls had to negotiate another set of expectations. With friends, they often lied about lying, because they found those who were able to participate more freely in the social world often did not understand the necessity for masking. Lying, it seemed, conformed only too well to the stereotype of the South Asian girl. For example, Nina explained that she could not be open with her white friends about the extent to which she lied to her parents:

> It is easier to turn to them [South Asian friends] than to my other friends sometimes, when they don't understand and I, I feel like I'm being put down, like my own character is being put down.… They go, "Why can't you argue with your parents?" And I tell them that I try to. But I feel like they're putting me down.… They go, "But why don't you be stronger?" and they don't realize that I'm trying to be really, really strong and they don't understand that and I get really defensive.… They go, "Oh but if I was your parents' daughter, they would die, they wouldn't last," and I go, "If you were my parents' daughter then you wouldn't be like the way you are now."

In relation to her friends, lying represents not being rebellious enough. Acquiescing to authority is equivalent to docility and does not measure up to the carefree, heroic rebellious image of the westernized teenager. And yet for Nina in relation to her parents, telling the truth risks the loss of a good reputation.

Although most girls crossed over the boundaries of proper femininity, many of them did not feel that they were "bad" girls. Yet they knew that in the eyes of their parents they would be seen as disobedient or immoral and therefore un-Indian. Defining South Asian femininity as synonymous with the restrictions around self-determination that I have spoken about leaves very little room for a self-definition that describes the reality of the young women's lived experiences. I found that young women were able to negotiate their freedom and sexual reputations through the use of clothing. Lying, in this case, takes the form of masking and manipulating femininity. Salimah described her relationship to clothing:

> They [parents] don't mind me wearing normal clothes and everything. The only thing they don't like is ripped jeans, anything that is tight. I'm not allowed to wear shorts, all that kind of stuff. One story, it was in the summer, I was in shorts and all of a sudden I see my dad at the end of the driveway and I started waving to my dad [instinctively] and he started driving by and then I realized. So I jumped into a bush and I changed and my friend's just watching me and watching my dad driving by, and I changed in the bush, in the mud and everything, and I got up and she said, "Ahh, he's gone," and I'm like, "Oh shit, oh well" [laughter].[5]

In her study of working-class girls in England, Susan Lees showed that young women walk a tightrope in order to negotiate their reputations.[6] She argues that both "good" girls and "bad" girls stake out their femininity through clothing. Good girls must negotiate the next-to-impossible line between adhering to the ideals of beauty and attractiveness and appearing too sexual. In my conversation with Tina and Pam [...] they pointed to how dress conveys certain meanings around traditional and modern, good girls and bad girls:

> *Tina:* Well okay, you have your modern Indian girl and the traditional.... Okay, if you see like the traditional Indian girl, they're more like, okay, study well, do what your parents say, and there's lots of them. I'm talking the traditional Indian girl.
> *Pam:* Okay there's this girl.... We went to Square One one day, I saw her walking into the mall with her father, plain face okay? When we saw her in the mall later on, she left her father and she was wearing bright red lipstick and makeup and everything, and I bet she like washes her face by the time she goes and sees her dad again, and goes home like nothing happened. And I see this girl go to dances and ...
> *Tina:* Ahh, she's pretty, ahh, promiscuous.

The sisters indicate how girls manipulate their femininity through fashion in order to suit the dictates of a particular context. For the girl they discuss, the mall represents a public space where she negotiates contradictory codes of femininity. Her dilemma is similar to Salimah's description of changing clothes in the bushes. The fear of getting caught by her father translates into getting caught for wearing clothes that transgress the boundaries of appropriate femininity. The trouble is, of course, that appropriate femininity is defined differently in other social spaces, to which these young women also wish to belong.

****

While lying helps young women gain more freedom, it also helps them negotiate their reputations. Lying gives them some control over their reputations at home and school. While the emotional cost of "living lies" is extremely high for these young women, for most of them honesty is too high a price to pay. It carries the risk of exclusion from the definition of "South Asian." Walking this tightrope of upholding community identity in a white dominant context brings with it a tremendous amount of emotional stress. Constantly masking or hiding parts of the self which are not accepted either by the world of peers or parents has a serious negative effect on self-esteem and self-worth. It is seldom that all the parts of the self can be celebrated, approved of, and accepted.

Defiance of adulthood is manifested for youth in terms of challenging and defying authority. For young women this takes place on the sexual terrain; manipulating their femininities and transgressing expected codes of behaviour. In its narrative of womanhood, the South Asian community draws on nationalist constructions of femininity that are in direct opposition to discourses around teens in the West. While white girls may defy social norms around growing up through dress and "sexual deviance," (i.e., sexual expression) for South Asian girls, rebellion against the responsible adult citizen narrative is also seen as a defiance of cultural identity and a disloyalty to ethnic membership. South Asian girls in Canada have to negotiate contradictory messages about their sexuality. On the one hand, they "get slack" because they are modernized; not being "typical" makes them open to assumptions about their sexual availability. On the other hand, being South Asian in Canada automatically sets them up as sexually unavailable in relation to dominant white culture. According to the latter, the typical South Asian girl is a patriarchal construction of docility and passivity. Her subjectivity is depersonalized and disregarded by a discursive construction that locates her as a victim within a cultural problematic only. While these narratives regulate and limit the lives of young South Asian women, I would like to place them within the wider context of Canadian racism. An allegiance to certain authentic notions of tradition and culture is also a means by which to articulate a standpoint against a racist and assimilationist white Canadian society. In this sense diaspora is a complex and overlapping space: it disrupts some normative categories while simultaneously reproducing others. In the context of negative or absent representations, notions of South Asian cultural authenticity also serve as a powerful site of resistance.

*****

Notes

1. Leslie Roman, "Intimacy, Labour, and Class."
2. M. Douglas, *Purity and Danger*.
3. Roman, "Intimacy, Labour, and Class," pp. 134, 136.
4. Floya Anthias and Nira Yuval-Davis, Introduction to *Woman-Nation-State*, p. 102.
5. The regulation of women's bodies through social sanctions and controls, such as the bodily controls that Leslie Roman speaks about (in "Intimacy, Labour, and Class"), has been documented in both sociological as well as anthropological research. See S. Ardener, "Introduction: The Nature of Women in Society"; S. Ortner and H. Whitehead, "Introduction: Accounting for Sexual Meanings," pp. 1–28; E.M. Schur, *Labelling Women Deviant*; C. Smart and B. Smart, *Women, Sexuality, and Social Control*. Feminist scholars have also illustrated that women who challenge the norms of appropriate feminine behaviour are often open to social disapproval through the "sexualization" of their behaviour. For example, L.S. Smith has argued that girls who transcend the norms of femininity through delinquent behaviour are portrayed by adults in the legal system as sexually promiscuous (1978, pp. 74–86).
6. Susan Lees, *Losing Out: Sexuality and Adolescent Girls*.

References

Anthias, F. and N. Yuval-Davis. Introduction to *Woman-Nation-State*. Ed. F. Anthias and N. Yuval-Davis. London: Macmillan, 1989.

Ardener, S. "Introduction: The Nature of Women in Society." *Defining Females*. Ed. S. Ardener. New York: Wiley, 1978.

Douglas, M. *Purity and Danger*. London: Routledge, 1984.

Lees, S. *Losing Out: Sexuality and Adolescent Girls*. London: Hutchinson, 1986.

Ortner, S. and H. Whitehead. "Introduction: Accounting for Sexual Meanings." *Sexual Meanings*. Ed. S. Ortner and H. Whitehead. Cambridge: Cambridge University Press, 1981, pp. 1–28.

Roman, L.G. "Intimacy, Labour, and Class: Ideologies of Feminine Sexuality in the Punk Slam Dance." *Becoming Feminine: The Politics of Popular Culture*. Ed. L.G. Roman, L.K. Christian-Smith, with E. Ellsworth. London: The Falmer Press, 1988.

Schur, E.M. *Labelling Women Deviant*. Philadelphia: Temple University Press, 1984.

Smart, C. and B. Smart. *Women, Sexuality and Social Control*. London: Routledge, 1978.

Smith, L.S. "Sexist Assumptions and Female Delinquency: An Empirical Investigation." *Women, Sexuality, and Social Control*. Ed. B. Smart and C. Smart. London: Routledge, 1978, 74–86.

3b Histories and Legacies of Colonialism and Imperialism

Chapter 27

The Secret of Slavery in Canada

Afua Cooper

Afua Cooper is a scholar, author, and poet. She holds the James Robinson Johnston chair in Black Canadian studies at Dalhousie University. She is a leading authority on Black Canadian history and slavery. The following selection is from her national bestseller, The Hanging of Angelique: The Untold Story of Canadian Slavery and the Burning of Old Montreal, *which was a finalist for the Governor General's Literary Awards. She has also published five books of poetry and two historical novels, and she has curated exhibits on African-Canadian history and the transatlantic slave trade.*

Slavery is Canada's best-kept secret, locked within the national closet. And because it is a secret it is written out of official history. But slavery was an institutionalized practice for over two hundred years. Canada also engaged in the nefarious business of slaving. Stephen Behrendt, a historian and demographer of slavery, reveals that the shipyards of several of the older Canadian colonies constructed ships for use in the British slave trade.[1] Canada might not have been a slave society—that is, a society whose economy was based on slavery—but it was a society with slaves. It shared this feature with virtually all other New World societies. Contrary to popular belief, slavery was common in Canada.

The reluctance to discuss and accept Canada as a place where slavery was institutionalized for 206 years is understandable. In North America, we associate the word "slavery" with the United States, not Canada, because the American economy, especially the southern portion, was fuelled by the labour of millions of African slave captives. In the story of North American slavery, we associate Canada with "freedom" or "refuge," because during the nineteenth century, especially between 1830 and 1860, the period known as the Underground Railroad era, thousands of American runaway slaves escaped to and found refuge in the British territories to the north. Therefore, the image of Canada as "freedom's land" has lodged itself in the national psyche and become part of our national identity. One result is the assumption that Canada is different from and morally superior to that "slave-holding republic," the United States.

When most people think of slavery, they see a huge cotton or sugar cane plantation worked by hundreds of slaves, with blood dripping down their backs as they endure constant whipping from the slave-drivers. The slaveholder (usually a male) sits on the verandah of his mansion, fanned by docile young slaves. This lurid image is drawn from a southern United States or Caribbean version of slavery, and most people cannot associate it with Canada's early history. Yet the White settlers who colonized Canada during both the French and English periods were indeed slaveholders.

Scholars have painted a pristine picture of Canada's past. It is difficult to find a scholarly or popular publication on the country's past in which images, stories, and analyses of slave life are depicted. We read numerous accounts of pioneer life without learning that some of these pioneers were enslaved people who, like the free White pioneers, built roads and highways, constructed homesteads, fought off bears, caught beavers, established farms from forests, and helped in the defence of the young country.[2] People of African descent, free and enslaved, have vanished from national narratives. It is possible to complete a graduate degree in Canadian studies and not know that slavery existed in Canada.

A useful definition of slavery is the robbery of one's freedom and labour by another, usually more powerful person. Violence and coercion are used to carry out the theft and to keep the slave captive in the condition of bondage and servitude. This definition applies to slavery in Canada. Laws were enacted and institutions created to rob persons of their freedom and labour and keep them in perpetual servitude. In the earliest era of colonial rule in Canada, both Aboriginal peoples and Africans and their descendants were enslaved (Aboriginal slaves were colloquially termed *Panis*). From 1628 to 1833, slavery was a legal and acceptable institution in both French and British Canada and was vigorously practised.

The colonists in New France wanted slaves, especially Black slaves. In all European New World settlements, large percentages of the Native populations were exterminated through genocide, the harsh conditions of slavery, and the arrival of new diseases in their midst. In enslavement, the Native populations declined rapidly, which gave Europeans the notion that Natives could not withstand slavery. In the belief that Blacks were sturdier people, Europeans began to bring African captives into the colonies to work as slaves. On the whole, Blacks appeared somewhat better able to withstand the physical demands of slavery: they lived a little longer than the Native people. Canada's political and administrative leaders—suave, urbane, and educated men, some of whom spent time in the tropical colonies—knew this. They therefore used their power and influence to bring Black slaves into the country.

*****

As French colonists settled in Canada and expanded their colonizing ventures, it became clear that the available labour force could not meet the demands created by a burgeoning economy. Thus, New France began its colonial life with a chronic labour shortage. Even though a system of indentureship had been set in place, with contract labourers coming from France to serve out an indenture, it did not solve the problem. Seeing the prosperity of their New England neighbours, a prosperity based on slave labour, *les Canadiens* hit on the idea that slavery was exactly what their colony needed.

*****

[...] By 1690, New France had a population of 12,000. But it was not enough. The labour shortage continued. In 1688, bowing to pressure from the settlers, the governor, Marquis de Denonville, and the intendant, Jean Bochart de Champigny, wrote to Louis XIV, requesting permission to introduce Black slaves into the colony. [...]

The following year the king gave his consent, though he expressed doubts about the effects of the severe Canadian climate on slaves from the tropics. Despite his concerns, enslaved Africans were brought into the colony. Further royal consent was given in 1701, and slavery began to take root. [...]

*****

With or without help from the Crown, New France's colonists were able, with varying degrees of success, to obtain enslaved Africans. One method available to the French was the use of Native allies. The Abenaki and sometimes the Iroquois captured Black slaves from the English to the south and sold them to the French settlers in Canada. However, there were also legal transactions between the French and the English: French colonists bought Black slaves from New York, New England, the Carolinas, and other American colonies. Enslaved Africans also came to New France from the West Indies, from Africa, and from Europe.

In Montréal, which eventually would have the largest slave population in the colony, the first Black person recorded as a slave in the register of the church of Notre-Dame is simply named "Louis." It is noted that he was a native of Madagascar and was twenty-six at the time of his baptism on May 24, 1692. Louis Lecomte-Dupre owned Louis, the slave. On the same day, another slave, Pierre Célestin, age twenty-four, was baptized as well. Also a native of Madagascar, his owner was Pierre Leber. It would seem that both of these slaves received the first names of their owners.[3]

*****

The French empire in the West Indies was built on sugar production and the labour of enslaved Africans. The Code Noir, a French legal code, regulated slavery in the West Indies. Though it was never made law in Canada, New France's slaveholders applied the Code Noir when they thought it necessary. [...] Under the Code Noir, slaves were declared "movable," that is, personal property, in the same category as livestock, furniture, and trade goods. The Code Noir regulated other aspects of slave life, such as relations between master and slave, the status of slave children, slave marriages, and so forth.[4]

*****

Imperial edicts and local laws also consolidated, regularized, and protected slavery in New France and enshrined the rights of colonists to own slaves. In 1701, Louis XIV gave his full consent to Black slavery in Canada, authorizing "its colonists to own slaves ... in full proprietorship."[5] This consent was merely academic, because Canadians had already been doing so. [...]

*****

Black slavery in Canada was patriarchal, meaning that the male slaveholder was the head of an extended family that included people he was related to by marriage and blood (his wife and children) and enslaved persons. Slaves often lived in the same houses as their owners, ate the same food, were baptized by their owners, and had owners or their close relatives as godparents, and sometimes they received the name of the owner's family.

The paternalistic nature of slavery in New France had much to do with the scarcity of labour in a growing colony: slaves were a valuable resource. Yet the economy, largely based on the fur trade, did not demand large gangs of labourers in the way that an agriculturally based economy would have. True, in Canada, agriculture was an important secondary economic activity, and many of the White colonists were farmers who did use slaves as farm labourers. Canada's economic model made for a form of slavery that was, to some degree, different from the slavery seen across the southern United States. It was more in line with the type of slavery found in colonial New England and New York.

Slaves in Canada engaged in a variety of occupations—from rat catcher to hangman—but most worked as house servants, as farm labourers, or in skilled occupations. In New France, and later in British Canada, slaves were owned by a variety of individuals and corporations. The Church, the nobility, merchants, lawyers, government officials, gentry, soldiers, seigneurs, tavern-keepers, farmers, business people, and artisans all held slaves. The merchant elite, as a group, held the largest number of enslaved people.

[…] The majority of this population lived in the three main centres of the colony: Montréal, Trois-Rivières, and the capital, Québec. This made slavery in New France a more or less urban phenomenon. By the end of the French period, in 1760, seventy-seven percent of all enslaved people lived in urban areas, with fifty-two percent of this group residing in Montréal alone.[6] Living in cities, the enslaved had some mobility and so became acquainted with the geography of their locale. This knowledge, in many instances, accounted for their frequent escapes.

Generally speaking, the kind of work enslaved people did ensured close proximity to their owners. Even if relationships between owners and slaves were hostile, the two parties nonetheless maintained physical domestic closeness. Enslaved people could legally marry, with the permission of their owners, and upon death were usually given a Christian burial. New France's slaves also had certain rights typically reserved for free persons in the rest of the New World. For example, they could serve as witnesses at religious functions and could petition against free persons.[7]

*****

Enslaved Africans were hired out, […] and they were also sold and bought. On September 25, 1743, Charles Réaume drew up a contract in the office of a Québec notary to sell five enslaved Africans to Louis Cureux. […]

The entire slave party was sold for 3,000 livres.

The French colonists and rulers also gave away slave children as gifts:

> In July, 1748, Jean-Pierre Roma, Commandant for the King at the Island of St. Jean [Prince Edward Island] … on his passage to Québec, made a singular Gift to his friend, Fleury de la Gorgendière…. He gave him a mulatto Girl, five months old and named Marie.
>
> The child was born at Québec, February 20, 1848; she was baptized the following day, and her godfather and godmother were M. Perrault, a merchant, and Marie-Anne Roma, daughter of Commandant Roma.
>
> The gift made to M. Fleury de la Gorgendière is explained by the fact that the mother of the child, the slave of Roma, died in giving it birth. Roma, not being able to charge himself with raising the orphan, preferred to give it to M. Fleury de la Gorgendière.
>
> The deed is drawn up by the Notary, Jean-Claude Panet, July 15, 1748; and it is the stipulation that in case of the death of Fleury and his wife, the mulatto will return to Mlle [Mademoiselle] Roma (her godmother). If she cannot take her, it is stipulated that she will receive her freedom.[8]

This sad story hides as much as it reveals. The slave mother died giving birth to her child, and her owner gave the baby away because he felt he could not raise her himself. The child, described as a mulatto, was called an "orphan." But for a child to be created, a father had to be involved.

Who was the child's father? Was it Roma himself? Was that why he felt so obliged to find a home for the child, and why he gave her away to his trusted friend instead of selling her? A veil of semi-protectiveness was drawn around the slave baby. Not only was she given to someone whom Roma believed would care for her, but Roma's daughter was the baby's godmother and a stand-in parent if that became necessary. The baby's mother remained nameless, but we know a few things about her: she was a Black woman; she was Roma's slave; and she died in childbirth.

Enslaved Africans in Canada reacted to slavery in much the same way that slaves did in other New World societies and took steps to wreak revenge on their owners. They ran away, talked back, broke tools, were disobedient, threatened their owners, organized slave uprisings, and in two cases allegedly set major fires that devastated colonial towns.

Slaves also died young. The average age of death for Panis was 17.7 years, and for Blacks, 25.2. Only a few Blacks lived to be 80.[9]

During the French period, enslaved Panis [Aboriginal slaves] were more numerous than enslaved Africans because Panis were easier to obtain. This situation would be reversed with the Conquest of Canada.

In 1760, at the end of the Seven Years War between Britain and France, Britain conquered Canada. Three years later, by the Treaty of Paris, France ceded Canada to Britain. New France ceased to be, and the Canadian territory seized by the British was renamed and transformed into the colony of Québec. By the time of the conquest, over 1,500 Black slaves had landed in Canada.

With the 47th article of the treaty of capitulation, signed between the victorious British and the defeated French, the British confirmed the rights of the French colonists to own and retain their slaves. [...]

*****

With its successes in the Seven Years War, Britain became the strongest power in the world. By this time, it was also the most powerful slave trading nation. [...] By the time of the Conquest of Canada, Britain had transported hundreds of thousands of captive Africans to the New World in numerous slave ships. Britain also had a large slave empire centred in the West Indies and the United States, with slave colonies in southern India and south Africa.

If the enslaved Canadian Blacks and Panis thought the Conquest would deliver a chance for freedom, they were wrong. The British conquest led to the intensification of slavery in Canada. Britain had the resources to pump slaves into Canada; however, no large-scale shipments of slaves were required to provide the Canadian colonists with slave labour. With Canada now a British possession, land-hungry British-American colonists to the south began migrating in large numbers to the new territory. The post-Conquest immigrants brought their Black slave labourers with them, thus increasing the slave population in Canada.

The British preferred Black slaves to enslaved Panis, and, having the resources, ensured that more Black bondspeople would enter the colony. As a result, under the British regime, Black enslaved labourers became more numerous than Panis. Consequently, enslavement gradually became identified solely with Africans.

*****

The British conquerors introduced the printing press and the newspaper to the newly acquired territory. From these papers we learn that slaves in the new dispensation, as in the old regime, continued to run away. Throughout the colonial period, English language newspapers regularly announced slave flight. These advertisements give us insight into the enslaved people, their condition, and their responses to slavery. [...]

*****

[One] runaway was the slave woman Cash.

Quebec Gazette, October 19, 1769

On Sunday morning ... a Negro wench named Cash, twenty-six years old ... speaks English and French very fluently, carried with her a considerable quantity of linen and other valuable effects not her own; and as she has also taken with her a large bundle of wearing apparel belonging to herself, consisting of a black satin cloak, caps, bonnets, ruffles, ribbons, six or seven petticoats, a pair of old stays, and many other articles of value which cannot be ascertained, it is likely that she may change her dress.

Cash absconded with a large portion of her owner's wardrobe and must have thought of using these clothes as a means of disguise. Or, quite likely, she felt that her owner owed her all that she took.

From these ads, we learn that many slaves were bilingual, sometimes multi-lingual. We often learn of a slave's knowledge of skills and trades. For example, one Pompey was noted to be a sailor. And we get a description of the kind of clothes the runaways wore.

Where would slaves run? Slave runaways could take refuge with sympathetic Natives in the Upper Country or disappear into some frontier communities. Escaping to land held by a foreign power was another possibility, as was escaping via ship to the West Indies or Florida. But it is likely that slaves like Cash and others who came with their owners from places such as New England and New York were running *back* to these places—places they knew and where they may have had relatives. When going back to the thirteen colonies, escapees traversed a reverse Underground Railroad.

*****

Marronage, the act of running away, could be either temporary or permanent. With temporary (or *petit*) *marronage*, enslaved persons ran away for a few days or weeks because they were upset and angry with their owners. However, they intended to go back. Temporary *marronage* was a weapon enslaved Africans used to show their owners that they did not have to "put up with it." It also showed that slaveholders did not have complete ownership over the bodies of their slave property. Permanent *marronage* meant that the captives escaped and lived in freedom in hard-to-reach places such as forests, wildernesses, swamps, and mountain strongholds.[10]

Newspapers in the colony of Québec were not the only ones that broadcasted the flight of slaves. In the forty years after the Conquest, and in the early years of the nineteenth century, ads for runaway and missing slaves also graced the pages of colonial newspapers in New Brunswick, Nova Scotia, and Upper Canada.

The sale of slaves was another feature of life in Canada. The value of slave property depended on physical health (acquired immunity from smallpox was an asset), special aptitudes, age, and sex, among other factors. Olivier Le Jeune was sold for 50 livres in 1628. Marie-Joseph Angélique was sold for a barrel of gunpowder. In 1738, in Montréal, Catherine Raimbault sold two of her Black male slaves, Laramee, aged thirty, and Charles, aged ten, for 200 and 570 livres respectively.

That a ten-year-old child fetched more than a thirty-year-old man is not strange, given that slaves died so young in the colony. The seller and purchaser probably knew that Laramee did not have long to live, while the boy could potentially render fifteen more years of service.

In the post-Conquest period, a woman skilled in housework could fetch between £30 and £50. The woman described in this ad would likely have commanded a good price:

Quebec Gazette, February 23, 1769

Mr. Prenties has to sell a negro woman, aged 25 years, with a mulatto male child, 9 months old. She was formerly the property of General Murray; she can be well recommended for a good house servant; handles milk well and makes butter to perfection.

*****

[Such ads] reveal, certainly, that slaves were seen as chattel, like horses or harnesses. They also tell us that women's primary occupation was that of domestic. Black women laboured in the homes of their owners doing all manner of housework, including child care. The image of the Black woman who "understands thoroughly every kind of housework," the tireless domestic, has persisted throughout the centuries. [...]

Sale of slaves was usually a transaction between two parties, but sometimes slaves were sold publicly. The same Mr. Prenties who advertised in February 1769 was not successful in selling his slaves. Six months later, he chose to do so at a public market. "To be sold at public vendue ... a negro woman aged 25, with a mulatto child, male...."[11]

Slave ads pertaining to women and children often indicate that children were sold with their mothers. Some of these children are described as mulattoes, the fathers of whom are "unknown." The relatively large mulatto population at the time of the Conquest reveals that White men often sired the children of Black women, most of whom were enslaved women. This fact must be placed in the context of the power relationships in slave societies. White men owned Black women's bodies and what came out of those bodies. Black women were regularly subjected to sexual assaults by their owners and other White men. If the women were impregnated and had children, these children inherited the status of their mothers and were enslaved. It mattered little that the children's fathers were White men, sometimes very prominent White men; what mattered was that their mothers were enslaved and Black. One of the most dehumanizing aspects of slavery was the loss of control that Black people, especially women, experienced over their bodies.[12]

One commentator on Canadian slavery makes light of the sexual abuse that Black women faced when he casts them as seducers whose charms (hapless) White men cannot resist.[13] Slaveholders who sexually abused Black women, kept them as concubines, and impregnated them may have subscribed to this sentiment. It is a common attitude of those in power. Refusing to take responsibility for their offence, they blame the victim.

The American Revolutionary War (1776–1783) produced a further expansion of slavery in Canada. Many Americans who remained loyal to the Crown fled to Canada, with their enslaved chattel, on the heel of British defeat by the American forces. At least 35,000 of these Loyalists fled to Nova Scotia. Five thousand were Black, both slave and free; however, the majority were free. The expansion of Nova Scotia's population led, in 1784, to the province being divided to create New Brunswick. This new province got its share of free and enslaved Black Loyalists. Likewise, some Black Loyalists made it into Prince Edward Island.

About 10,000 Loyalists—White, Black, and Native—came to the province of Québec. However, unlike in the Maritime provinces, most of the Québec Black Loyalists were enslaved. They came with their White owners from New York, New England, Virginia, the Carolinas, and other parts of the thirteen colonies. Some of the enslaved Blacks were also in the parties of members of the Iroquois Confederacy.

*****

In Upper Canada and Québec (renamed Lower Canada after 1791), though many Blacks were free people, the majority were enslaved. The enslaved population, brought to Canada mainly by White Loyalists (members of the Mohawk elite also held Black slaves), came with a variety of skills, which they used in the founding and development of the colonies. Slaves worked as millwrights, blacksmiths, coopers, printers, and tinsmiths. They felled trees, made roads, opened highways, and worked as domestics, nannies, and farm labourers. James Walker insists that "we cannot understand early pioneer history unless we acknowledge that slavery existed...."[14] By 1793, it is estimated that there were five hundred slaves in Upper Canada.

Like many of the families of the old French regime, most of Upper Canada's leading families, including many of the province's founding fathers and mothers, were slaveholders. [...]

*****

Peter Russell, a member of the Executive Council and future provincial administrator, held at least five slaves, four of whom comprised one family: a woman named Peggy and her three children. Peggy and her family lived with Russell and big sister Elizabeth in their town home in York (now part of Toronto).[15]

*****

Peggy, the mother of three children, Milly, Amy, and Jupiter, and the wife of a free Black man named Pompadour, was a disobedient and recalcitrant slave who bucked the Russells' authority by talking back to them and running away whenever she felt like it. On more than one occasion, her master had her confined to the town's jail. Jupiter, her son, was also a runaway and "disobedient"; he too was lodged in jail for his rudeness and "saucy ways." Peter Russell determined to get Peggy off his hands by selling her to another member of the colonial elite, slaveholder Matthew Elliott then living in Sandwich. [...]

*****

Peter Russell, an Anglo-Irish man, accepted the institution of slavery in Upper Canada even though in Britain itself slavery was on the decline. He behaved like a typical American slaveholder: he separated families if he saw fit, he punished and imprisoned his slaves, and when they would not "obey" he sold them. He was not going to put Peggy on the auction block; rather, he was selling her through a more "genteel" method. Nevertheless, the result would be the same: Peggy would be separated from her husband and children.

Yet, contrary to a once-popular belief that slave masters had "absolute authority" over their slaves, Russell was not in total control. If conditions were not to their liking, slaves often tried in subtle and not so subtle ways to live within the bounds of the institution on their own terms, to change the frame of reference. Peggy was doing just that when she left the Russell household to live "at large."

Peggy's way of dealing with her enslavement paralleled that of enslaved people throughout the Americas and Canada. [...] Peggy may not have tried to make a permanent bid for her freedom because she had young children and wanted to remain with her family. What Peggy engaged in was *petit marronage*, running away temporarily to protest one's enslavement, or taking a vacation of sorts to escape the vagaries of slave life.

*****

Even though York was a small town, others would employ and harbour Peggy while knowing she belonged to someone else. Because there was a labour shortage, Peggy could find sympathizers who would take her in. Who knows what was going on in the Russell household that led Peggy to run from it. Was she sexually abused by either owner? It seems that her relationship with Elizabeth Russell, in particular, was strained. Peter Russell, in his letter to Elliott, said that Peggy showed a "disposition at times to be very troublesome," revealing that Peggy was an incorrigible slave. She would not behave.

*****

By 1806, Peter Russell, who by this time was no longer the provincial administrator, was at the point of desperation. He wanted to rid himself of Peggy and her son, Jupiter. He advertised in the *York Gazette*:

February 19, 1806, To Be Sold:

A Black woman named Peggy, aged forty years, and a Black boy, her son, named Jupiter, aged about fifteen years, both of them the property of the subscriber. The woman is a tolerable cook and washerwoman, and perfectly understands making soap and candles. The boy is tall and strong for his age, and has been employed in the country business, but brought up principally as a house servant. They are each of them servants for life. The price of the woman is one hundred and fifty dollars. For the boy two hundred dollars, payable in three years, with interest from the day of sale, and to be secured by bond, &c. But one-fourth less will be taken for ready money.

If the Russells seem to have been "reluctant" masters, Peggy and her family were "irresolute" slaves. What is quite clear is that Peggy and her family pushed and pulled at slavery and sought to effect their freedom or gain concessions. [...]

Common people also bought, held, and sold slaves. In the *Niagara Herald*, on January 2, 1802, we find "for sale, a negro slave, 18 years of age, stout and healthy, has had the smallpox and is capable of service either in the house or out of doors." In the same paper, on January 18: "For sale, negro man and woman, the property of Mrs. Widow Clement. They have been bred to the work of the farm; will be sold on highly advantageous terms for cash or lands. Apply to Mrs. Clement."

Colonists could also place ads when they wished to buy slaves. The *Niagara Gazette* and *Oracle* of January 11, 1797, ran the following: "Wanted to purchase, a negro girl from seven to twelve years of age of good disposition. For full particulars, apply to ... W.J. Cooke, West Niagara."

How were enslaved people treated? Some masters baptized their slaves, married them, and remembered them in their wills. One salient example of a "good and paternalistic master" is Robert I.D. Gray. He apparently treated his slave family well, and provided generously for them in his will, manumitting them and setting up a trust fund for them. Yet not even he could free the slaves while he lived. They had to wait until he died, and therefore had no further use of their time and labour, to get their freedom. Another slaveholder, Isaac Bennett, made provision in his will for the education and freedom of his two slave boys. But, for every humane master, there was a brutal one to match. [...]

*****

Black people, then, throughout the length and breadth of British North America, were owned, bought, and sold by White colonists. The lives of the Black enslaved people and their offspring were regulated and circumscribed by those who owned them and the legal resources they could access. Slavery was as Canadian as it was American or West Indian. It is important to note, though, that in this period of the mid- to late eighteenth century, there were also free Black communities in British North America. In Nova Scotia and New Brunswick, Black people of Loyalist origin built free villages and towns in such places as Preston, Shelburne, Birchtown, and Saint John. In fact, these and others became the first free Black communities in North America. However, the residents of these communities faced extreme hostility from Whites. [...]

Slavery did not remain unchallenged. And the enslaved were always the first to challenge the conditions of their servitude. We have seen that they ran away and performed other hostile acts against their owners. However, the first official challenge to slavery came from the top down and occurred in the colony of Upper Canada. Colonel John Graves Simcoe, veteran of the Revolutionary War, arrived in Canada in 1792 to take up the post of lieutenant governor of the new province of Upper Canada. Simcoe had been a member of the British Parliament and supported antislavery measures in its House. On arriving in Canada (he came by way of Montréal), Simcoe realized the extent of slaveholding among the White population and is reputed to have said that, under his governorship, he would not discriminate "between the natives of Africa, America, or Europe."[16] On reaching Upper Canada, Simcoe was determined to abolish slavery.

He had his chance in March 1793, when he heard of the case of Chloe Cooley, a slave woman who was manhandled, tied up with ropes, and thrown in a boat by her owner, William Vrooman of Queenston in the Niagara district. Vrooman then rowed the boat to the New York side of the Niagara River and sold his slave to someone on the American side. Eyewitnesses related that Cooley "screamed violently and made resistance."[17] Simcoe decided to prosecute Vrooman, but his chief justice told him he did not have a leg to stand on, since slavery was legal in the British empire and Vrooman was well within his rights to dispose of his slave in any manner he wished. Simcoe then decided to prosecute Vrooman for disturbing the peace.

Later, Simcoe gathered enough support in the legislative and executive councils and the assembly to push for a bill on the immediate abolition of slavery in the province. But it was not to be. The slaveholders inside his parliament and those outside were outraged at his audacity and fought him. They claimed that slave labour was essential for the economic life of the colony and that Simcoe would ruin them if he abolished slavery. [...] So Simcoe backed off, and he and his advisers worked out a compromise. In July 1793, "An act to prevent the further introduction of slaves and to limit the term of contracts for servitude within this province" was pushed through the legislature.[18] The title of the act tells us that it was a compromise indeed. Nothing was said about abolition, because that was not the act's intent. The act did not free a single slave.

It did accomplish other things. First, it confirmed that current slaves would remain slaves. Slaveholders had pushed for this, and they got it. Now they could breathe a sigh of relief. Second, the act banned the introduction of new slaves. Third, the children of current slaves would gain their freedom upon reaching twenty-five, and if they had children before they reached that magic number, their children would be automatically free.

Interestingly, the act did not prevent the sale of slaves across international borders. Many slaveholders saw this loophole and, like Vrooman, sold their slaves into New York.

Upper Canadian slaves who were hoping to be freed by Simcoe's bill had to look for their freedom elsewhere. In 1787, the Northwest Territory (Michigan, Indiana, Ohio, Illinois, Wisconsin, and part of Minnesota) issued an ordinance prohibiting slavery. Vermont and other parts of New England had also abolished slavery by this date. And, in 1799, New York made provisions for the gradual abolition of slavery. As a result, many Upper Canadian enslaved Blacks escaped into these free territories.[19] So numerous were some of these former Canadians in American cities that, in Detroit, for example, a group of former Upper Canadian slaves formed a militia in 1806 for the defence of the city against the Canadians. They also fought against Canada in the War of 1812.

If Simcoe's bill had a redeeming feature, it was the article that prohibited the importation of new slaves into the province. This meant, in effect, that slavery would decline, as it could not be expanded through importation. Perhaps, more important, it also meant that any foreign slaves would be immediately freed upon reaching the soil of Upper Canada. That was what began the Underground Railroad for enslaved Americans. By the War of 1812, they had heard of this novel situation and many began making the trek northward. The paradox is inescapable: at the same time, many Upper Canadian slaves were making the trek southward to freedom in Michigan and New England.

*****

In the other provinces, there was some movement against slavery. A few legislators in Lower Canada tried to copy Simcoe's bill, but they were roundly defeated by the slaveholding interests in the House. One such pro-slavery legislator, a slaveholder himself, was none other than Québec nationalist Joseph Papineau. It would be the courts in Lower Canada, not the government, that would move against slavery. Some Québec slaves took their masters to court, claiming that their masters were holding them illegally. In 1797, the courts began to rule in favour of the enslaved. In some instances in Nova Scotia and New Brunswick, local courts also freed some slaves who petitioned for their freedom. The slaveholders of Prince Edward Island, on the other hand, held fast to their right to own enslaved property. Slaves there did not even bother to present their case in court. Gradually, over time, slavery declined in the five colonies that made up British North America. It would eventually come to an end in 1834, when the British Parliament outlawed and abolished it in all its territories.

Though the story of slavery in Canada has been silenced, those who owned slaves and those whose actions impinged directly on the lives of the enslaved did not adopt a secretive pose in their dealings with their slave property. Government officials deliberated slavery as a public issue. Various statutes and acts concerning Black enslavement came from the imperial and provincial parliaments. The courts also documented the presence of slaves and their concerns. Further, census takers counted enslaved Blacks among the general population. In fact, in the years following the Revolutionary War, there were at least two censuses done to count the number of slaves in the populations of Upper and Lower Canada.[20] As important, enslaved people bore witness to their own presence through flight and other subversive actions.

*****

Notes

1. Stephen D. Behrendt, *The Atlantic Slave Trade* [CD ROM] (Cambridge, UK: Cambridge University Press, 1999). This database has information on over 30,000 slave ships used in the British trade.

2. James Walker, a historian at the University of Waterloo, discusses how Black history is missing from pioneer history. See James Walker, *A History of Blacks in Canada* (Hull, Québec: Ministry of State for Multiculturalism, 1980), 1–7.

3. O.M.H. Lapalice, "Les Esclaves noir à Montréal sous l'ancien régime," *Canadian and Numismatic Journal* 12 (1915): 139.

4. William Riddell, "The Code Noir," *Journal of Negro History* 10, no. 3 (1925): 321–28.

5. Robin W. Winks, *The Blacks in Canada: A History* (Montréal: McGill-Queen's University Press, 1997), 1.

6. Ibid., 9. See also Marcel Trudel, *L'esclavage au Canada Français: Histoire et conditions de l'esclavage* (Québec: Les Presses Universitaire Laval, 1960), 130. On demography, see Kenneth Donovan, "Slaves and Their Owners in Ile Royale," *Acadiensis* xxv, no. 1 (Autumn 1995, pp. 3–32), 3.

7. See Winks, *The Blacks in Canada*, 11.

8. William Riddell, "An Early Canadian Slavery Transaction," *Journal of Negro History* 13, no. 2 (1928): 207. The translation is Riddell's. The original is in French and is taken from Pierre Georges Roy, *Le bulletin des recherches historiques* 33, no. 8: 584.

9. Winks, *The Blacks in Canada*, 10.

10. See Bernard Moitt, "Women and Resistance," in *Women and Slavery in the French Antilles, 1635–1848* (Bloomington: Indiana University Press, 2001), 125–50.

11. Hurbert Neilson, "Slavery in Old Canada, before and after the Conquest," *Transactions of the Literary and Historical Society of Quebec* 2, no. 26 (1906): 35.

12. See Dorothy Roberts, *Killing the Black Body: Race, Reproduction, and the Meaning of Liberty* (New York: Vintage Books, 1999), 23–25; Maureen Elgersman, *Unyielding Spirits: Black Women and Slavery in Early Canada and Jamaica* (New York: Garland Publishing, 1999), 21–38.

13. Trudel, *L'eslavage au Canada Français*, 258.

14. Walker, *A History of Blacks in Canada*, 6.

15. The Russells wrote about their slave woman Peggy and her family. Much of Peggy's story is contained in the Russell Papers, a portion of which is Elizabeth Russell's diary, housed at the Baldwin Room, Toronto Public Library. Sections of Elizabeth's diary are reprinted in Edith Firth, *Town of York, 1791–1815* (Toronto: Champlain Society, 1962).

16. Winks, *The Blacks in Canada*, 96.

17. Peter Martin, a free Black man, and William Grisley, a White man, witnessed Vrooman binding and disposing of Chloe Cooley. Martin and Grisley related the matter to Simcoe and some members of his Executive Council. See E.A. Cruikshank, ed., *The Correspondence of Lieut. Governor John Graves Simcoe* [hereafter cited as Simcoe Papers], vol. 1 (Toronto: Ontario Historical Society, 1923–31), 304.

18. For the complete "Act to Prevent Further Introduction of Slaves …," see Nancy Power and Michael Butler, *Slavery and Freedom in Niagara* (Niagara-on-the-Lake: Niagara Historical Society, 1993), Appendix A. The act can also be viewed in *Statutes of Ontario, 1791–1840*, or on the Archives of Ontario Black history website.

19. William Riddell, "The Slave in Canada," *The Journal of Negro History* 3 (July 1920): 324. Henry Lewis, a former slave of William Jarvis, escaped to Schenectady, New York, and wrote to his ex-owner, offering to buy himself. See Henry Lewis to William Jarvis, 3 May 1798, Jarvis Papers, Toronto Public Library.

20. Two censuses of slaves in the Niagara district of Upper Canada were carried out in 1783. The Lower Canadian census was done in 1784. See Winks, *The Blacks in Canada*, 35; Power and Butler, *Slavery and Freedom*, 13–15.

Chapter 28

Black Women Rage

Wendy Brathwaite

Wendy (Motion) Brathwaite is a poet, performer, and award-winning spoken word/hip hop artist. Her work addresses some of the difficult realities of African-Canadian life in Greater Toronto, including racism, marginalization, gender inequalities, and Black motherhood. She is the author of two published works of poetry, Motion in Poetry *and* 40 dayz, *a children's book entitled* WORDZ, *and the play* Aneemah's Spot.

Black Woman rage makes us take to the stages
Up front at rallies
Leading black families
Black woman rage is a thing of beauty
Doing our duty,
making our roles
Suffering in silence, giving the bad eye
Calling on God,
dealing with spirits
Jah-Jah takes over as riddims move hips
Cusses come from full brown female lips
Black woman rage is a sight to behold
Working the fields
suns beat on bent backs
Black songs rise with density of deep sound
Deep pasts seep to all who have the ear—
Can you understand the meaning
of Rage ... Black ... Woman ... Song?
Sad, true, throaty, tired
Awakened
As we stretch to the heights of creation
Leggo our hand in the offending face
Stay in our place? What place?
When we just be all over ...
Never removed as we feed the masses
with milk, poems and minds
Full breasts and asses

Queen Nzinga looks on
as we swing our small axes
through the forests of fearsome shadows
that mean us no good
We learn to run from home-grown licks
Give 2 snaps up
and stand akimbo
as only Raging Black Women could.
We beat the drums to call on the sisters
to pass on the secrets that only mothers know.
two hundred and forty days of
two heart-beats, two sighs,
two souls, two-fold life-form multiply
with the powers of Yin and Yang
One moment kisses to heal the sting of her strong hand
Raging. Woman Black—
back to the basics of the Motherland …
Speak your story, speak
sister songs
and weep if you will
at the rage that kept us frozen, still
under humping weights
that pinned us in darkened places
Rage that kept us from killing our rapists
In order to maintain we paralyzed ourselves instead
They left us for dead
They *thought* we were
dead
But we don't die,
we …
grow, laugh, spread, cry
Daughters of the cotton and cane
cannot wither and die.

Chapter 29

The Construction of a Negative Identity

Kim Anderson

Kim Anderson (Cree Métis) is an assistant professor of Indigenous studies at Wilfrid Laurier University and adjunct faculty at the Department of History at the University of Guelph in Ontario. She is most well known for her book, A Recognition of Being: Reconstructing Native Womanhood, *which was recently followed by* Life Stages and Native Women: Memory, Teachings, and Story Medicine. *As part of her ongoing commitment to rebuilding culture-based identities, Anderson's current research explores Indigenous masculinities.*

Drunken squaw.
Dirty Indian.
Easy.
Lazy.

Every Canadian knows these words to commonly describe and identify Aboriginal women. Many Canadians are fooled by this construction of Native womanhood. This imagery is so ingrained in the North American consciousness that even Native people have, in dark times, internalized these beliefs about their grandmothers, their aunties, their daughters, and themselves.

Perhaps people begin to see alcohol abuse, sexual dysfunction, and poverty through the lens of these stereotypes. There are many people in our communities who are still using alcohol to drown the shame and confusion that festers within such negative definitions of their ancestry. We have a lot of family and sexual dysfunction because of the imposition of Christianity, western morality, and abuses endured in the residential school system. Yet, when we consider our lived experience, the drunken, easy squaw is not a character that Aboriginal people know. I would not describe my Native female relations as lazy and dirty. I don't know any squaws. So where did these images come from? How did they become so widespread, and how do they affect the day-to-day living of contemporary Native women?

As I began to explore these questions, I discovered how this negative understanding of Native womanhood was constructed. The dirty, easy squaw was invented long before poverty, abuse, and oppression beset our peoples. She was invented and then reinforced because she proved useful to the colonizer. The "uncivilized" squaw justified taking over Indian land. She eased the conscience of those who wished to sexually abuse without consequence. She was handy to greedy consumers. Dirty and lazy, she excused those who removed her children and paved the way for assimilation into mainstream culture. She allowed for the righteous position of those who participated in the eradication of Native culture, language, and tradition.

To me, these images are like a disease that has spread through both the Native and the non-Native mindset. In tracing this development, I hope to highlight a renewed understanding of Native womanhood that will help us to recover our strength, self-esteem, and dignity.

Roots of a Negative Female Image

In both western and Indigenous frameworks, Native women have historically been equated with the land. The Euro-constructed image of Native women, therefore, mirrors western attitudes towards the earth. Sadly, this relationship has typically developed within the context of control, conquest, possession, and exploitation. The Euro-Canadian image of Native women has been constructed within this context and has evolved along with the evolving relationship of European people to this continent.

When they first arrived on Turtle Island in the sixteenth century, Europeans produced images of Native womanhood to symbolize the magnificent richness and beauty they encountered. This was the phase of the great mother, the Indian Queen. Cherokee scholar Rayna Green describes the personification of "America" typical to this period (1575–1765):

> Draped in leaves, feathers, and animal skins, as well as in heavy jewelry, she appeared aggressive, militant, and armed with spears and arrows. Often she rode on an armadillo, and stood with her foot on the slain body of an animal or human enemy. She was the familiar mother-goddess figure—full bodied, powerful, nurturing but dangerous—embodying the wealth and danger of the New World.[1]

"Exotic, powerful, dangerous and beautiful," this Native female symbol represented both "American liberty and European virtue,"[2] but as the European settler became more familiar with the land, the queen was demoted. Colonial claims to the land would only work if the queen became more accessible, less powerful, and within the grasp of the white man. Out of this need, the "Indian princess" was born. The queen was transformed from a mother-goddess figure to a girlish-sexual figure, for who can own mother or dominate the gods?

"Indian princess" imagery constructed Indigenous women as the virgin frontier, the pure border waiting to be crossed.[3] The enormous popularity of the princess lay within her erotic appeal to the covetous European male wishing to lay claim to the "new" territory. This equation of the Indigenous woman with virgin land, open for consumption, created a Native female archetype, which, as Elizabeth Cook-Lynn has pointed out, could then be "used for the colonizer's pleasure and profit."[4]

The erotic image of Native female as "new" territory in the American narrative persists to this day. You need only to glance at posters of Walt Disney's *Pocahontas* to be confronted with a contemporary example of this archetype. We see a voluptuous yet innocent looking Native (but not too Native) "girl," who will soon become involved with an adventurous young white male. As Emma LaRocque points out, Disney's *Pocahontas* combines a lot of the overarching stereotypes about Native people. LaRocque sees a Pocahontas who is "so oversexualized, kind of crouching around, slithering around on the rocks," part noble savage, part princess, part loose squaw. This archetype has been perpetrated again and again throughout North American his-story. It has been promoted through other popular his-storical characters like Sacajewea, the Shoshone woman who led "explorers" Lewis and Clarke into the interior of the North American continent. In Spanish colonial history, there is la Malinche, the Aztec woman who birthed the mestizo children of Cortez and interpreted for Spanish troops.

It is possible to interpret characters like Pocahontas, Sacajewea, and la Malinche as strong Indigenous leaders,[5] but the mainstream interpretation of these mythic characters is quite the opposite: Native women (and, by association, the land) are "easy, available and willing" for the white man.[6] This mythology ensures that the "good" Native woman who willingly works with white men is rewarded with folk hero or "princess status."[7] Racism dictates that the women of these celebrated liaisons are elevated above the ordinary Indigenous female status; they must be some kind of royalty. The ultimate "reward" for the Indian princess is marriage to a white man, providing her the ability to transcend into his world.

What, then, of the Native woman who does not comply with the colonizer?

As with other colonial his-stories, once Indigenous peoples began to resist colonization, the archetypes changed. Indigenous women worldwide became symbols of the troublesome colonies, and in the Americas the squaw emerged. Carol Douglas Sparks has traced the princess-to-squaw devolution in colonizer accounts of the Navajo.[8] The virgin-princess, so commonly found in white male adventurer records of the nineteenth century, is soon transformed. While the princess held erotic appeal for the covetous imperial male wishing to claim the "new" territory, the squaw drudge justified the conquest of an uncivilized terrain:

> … Americans found squaw drudges far more comfortable than these outspoken and pow-
> erful women, whose presence defied colonial rationalizations. Not only could the squaw
> be pitied, but her very existence justified American intrusion into her land and society.[9]

In her book, *Capturing Women: The Manipulation of Cultural Imagery in Canada's Prairie West*, Sarah Carter demonstrates how both the Canadian state and the national press deliberately promoted "dirty squaw" imagery in the late 1800s.[10] At the time of settler invasion in western Canada, "dirty squaw" fiction was useful for a number of reasons. The uncivilized squaw provided a backdrop for the repressive measures against the Native population of the time. Like the men who were depicted as savage warriors, the women were reported to be "violent instigators of atrocities" (against whites),[11] thereby justifying colonial violence against Indigenous peoples. The image of the Native woman as the beast of burden in her society was drawn up to demonstrate the superiority of European womanhood and femininity (after all, women did not "labour"), and the necessity for replacing Native womanhood with European womanhood. This distortion of Native women's physical labour and contribution to their community is at the root of the long-standing "squaw-drudge" image. Rather than being seen as significant players in the economic structure of society, Native women were framed as drudges and beasts of burden.

As Native people moved off the land, and women lost their status and role as producers within the economic structure of their societies, they were cast as lazy and slovenly. Women were no longer able to provide for their families because they had lost the means to produce primary goods, such as clothing and food. They became dependent upon purchased goods and an economy in which they held no power. The dirty squaw emerged, conveniently taking the blame for the increasing poverty on reserve and deflecting attention from government and public complicity in the devastation of Indigenous peoples. If Native women were constructed as "squaws," dirty, lazy, and slovenly, it was easier to cover up the reality of Native women who were merely struggling with the increasingly inhumane conditions on reserve:

> In the unofficial and unpublished reports of reserve life … it was widely recognized
> that problems with reserve housing and health had little to do with the preferences,

temperament, or poor housekeeping abilities of the women. Because of their poverty, the people were confined in one-room shacks, which were poorly ventilated and were impossible to keep clean because they had dirt floors and were plastered with mud and hay. One inspector of the agencies noted in 1891 that the women did not have soap, towels, wash basins, or wash pails, nor did they have any means of acquiring them. Similarly, it was frequently noted that the women were short of basic clothing and had no textiles or yarn to work with. Yet in official public statements, the tendency was to ascribe blame to the women rather than drawing attention to conditions that would injure the reputation of government administration.[12]

Similarly, if Native women were portrayed as poor parents, it was then excusable for the state to remove Native children and place them in residential schools and foster homes.

Native female sexuality was also transformed into the "squaw" who was "lewd and licentious" and morally reprehensible. This representation was projected onto Native women to excuse the mistreatment they endured from white settler males. Within the context of late-nineteenth-century morality, it was easier to blame Native women than to challenge the behaviour of the heroes on the frontier. The narrative espousing how "easy" Native women were was developed to cover up the fact that white males were involved in unmarried sexual activity and that state officials were perpetrators of sexual assault. This tactic is common in rape cases and is well entrenched in the western consciousness: blame women for the sexual deviance of certain men. As part of the Native woman-blaming campaign, the *Toronto Daily Mail* of February 2, 1886, railed, "The character of the men of this country has been assailed."[13]

The squalor of the media-driven uncivilized easy squaw was further intended to guard against interracial marriages, thus protecting racial "purity" in the new country: "There were fears that the Anglo-Celts might be overrun by more fertile, darker and lower people, who were believed to be unable to control their sexual desires."[14] The moral reform movement of the late 1880s in the West embraced images of the dirty squaw in an effort to keep the races segregated and to keep the white race pure.

The dirty, dark squaw not only justified the deplorable treatment of Aboriginal peoples, she also created a gauge against which white femininity could be measured and defined. Where Native women were powerful physical workers, white women were encouraged to be weak and frail. The Native woman thus was re-invented as a drudge. Where Native women had sexual liberty, white women were restricted from pleasure. The Native woman had then to be perceived as easy. Where Native women resisted the increasing restrictions and poverty of reserves, white women were expected to be models of domesticity, industriousness, and obedience. The Native woman had to be reconstructed as deficient in order to prop up the image of the white woman:

> The particular identity of white women depended for its articulation on a sense of difference from Indigenous women. What it meant to be a white woman was rooted in a series of negative assumptions about the malign influence of Aboriginal women. The meanings of and different ways of being female were constantly referred to each other, with Aboriginal women always appearing deficient.[15]

Since contact with the European, Native women have been trapped within a western dichotomous worldview, where everything is either good or bad; dark or light; pure or corrupt. The Euro-constructed Indigenous woman with her dark ways, her squalor, and corruption makes the construction of whiteness all the more attractive. In the absence of white women, Native women can represent both characters: the "Indian princess," bathed in a sublime light (and well on her way to becoming white), or the "easy squaw," hunched and wallowing in her darkness. In terms of female identity, the Native woman must endure the western framework of virgin-whore, which was translated to princess-squaw and slapped on top of the complex understanding of Native womanhood that had existed for tens of thousands of years. This his-story continues to interfere with the lives of contemporary Native women.

Ghosts of the Squaw and the Princess

The majority of Native women will tell you that, at some point in their experience, they have been called a "squaw." Depending on the degree of overt racism in their environment, this will happen to a greater or lesser extent. Sometimes it is applied in the context of "friendly" joking; often in the form of a violent assault. Whatever the context, the "squaw" label has been applied to Native women right across North America; there are accounts from women of nations as wide-spread as the Mi'kmaq (Rita Joe) and the Pawnee/Otoe (Anna Lee Walters).[16]

Native girls begin to hear racial/sexual slurs from an early age, often before they even under-stand the terms themselves. Ojibway professor Shirley Williams says she remembers hearing white boys singing, "Squaws along the Yukon aren't good enough for me." The boys would follow up with, "Would two dollars be enough?" playing on the myth that Native women are "easy." Williams states that she thought "squaw" must be an English word "because it sounded like something dirty." Laverne Gervais-Contois, a woman of Ojibway, Cree, and Sioux heritage, recalls the slurs she heard while growing up in Winnipeg. Typically, the images were (and are) steeped with degrading sexual innuendo. She recalls hearing Native women referred to as "dark coffee," which was implicitly sexual, as the boys would say, "Dark coffee is good if you like it good and strong."

When negative images of Native women are so ingrained in the Canadian consciousness that even children participate in using them, it is easy to see how Native women might begin to think of themselves as "easy squaws." Janice Acoose describes how these negative images affected her consciousness:

> I learned to passively accept and internalize the easy squaw, Indian-whore, dirty Indian, and drunken Indian stereotypes that subsequently imprisoned me, and all Indigenous peoples, regardless of our historic, economic, cultural, spiritual, political, and geographi-cal differences ... I shamefully turned away from my history and cultural roots, becoming, to a certain extent, what was encouraged by the ideological collusiveness of textbooks, and the ignorant comments and peer pressure from non-Indigenous students.[17]

Many Native female writers—including Joanne Arnott, Beth Brant, Maria Campbell, Janet Campbell Hale, Beatrice Culleton, Paula Gunn Allen, Lee Maracle, and Anna Lee Walters[18]— have provided accounts of how they or other Native women have fostered destructive and hateful attitudes towards themselves. This self-hatred is rooted in internalized racism that comes from the negative self-concepts of racist stereotypes. Internalized racism spreads like a disease through Native communities.[19] It makes us doubt the validity of the existence of our people, and thus ourselves. This results in self-destructive behaviours, including addictions and involvement in violent relationships.

Less destructive and overt but equally as false is the princess. This is a stereotype that I am more familiar with in my personal experience. My class, age, and stature likely play into this interpretation of my being. The fact that I am half-white also helps. Remember, the Indian princess is well on her way to becoming white, so it follows that those of us who are more assimilated qualify for this racist nobility. Mixed-bloods have "exotic" appeal because we look "different," yet we are accessible to white people.

No one would ever call you a princess, but you can see it in their approach. Sometimes people glow all over you about your heritage; others want to use you as some kind of showpiece. It is a sexualized identity, which, in my case, has, for example, resulted in the humiliating experience of being called "my little Indian" as a measure of affection. I have felt stalked by Canadian and European men because of my Indianness, which, to them, was a "bonus" to whatever interest they had in me as a female.

When I read bell hooks for the first time, I felt a wash of relief to discover that I hadn't been imagining this syndrome; that, in fact, several people have written about it. As I discussed earlier, hooks provided me a name for it: "eating the Other." In an essay so named, she explains how it has become fashionable to "enjoy racial difference." She demonstrates, for instance, how advertising has picked up on this desire, and has used people of colour to sell products.[20]

People with a desire for "eating the Other" do not see themselves operating within a racist framework; rather, they think they are progressive in their desire to make contact. hooks suggests that relations of this nature may further be used to assuage guilt and "take the form of a defiant gesture where one denies accountability and historical connection."[21] People need to believe that their desire to befriend an Indian or to sleep with a woman of colour is proof that we have all transcended the racism that plagues the Americas, and that in so doing we are tucking our racism safely in the past. But what is implied in this type of contact? What narratives are we replaying?

I see Pocahontas looming in the background. There is a desire to cross some kind of frontier, to be transformed by the experience and, finally, to take possession. hooks relates her experience of hearing some white college boys talk about how many Black, Aboriginal, and Asian women they could "fuck" before graduation. To these boys, sex with the Other represents a rite of passage into a more "worldly" state. Whether overtly stated or covertly desired, transformation through contact with the "exotic" is played out in the forum of certain white-dark sexual relations. These attitudes reinforce colonial power relations, where the dark, earthly, and sensual paradise is there for the enjoyment of the white newcomer.

Whether princess or squaw, Native femininity is sexualized. This understanding finds its way into our lives and our communities. Sometimes, it means constantly having to fend off the advances of people with an appetite for the "Other." It may involve a continual struggle to resist crass, sexualized interpretations of one's being, as in the experience of these (anonymous) women:

> I can't stand at night in any place by myself because all the men think that I am trying to pick them up. I am telling you, it doesn't matter where I am ... They think that all the Native women in the world, we are there just to [have sex with them]. All the time—it doesn't matter where—poor area, rich area, it doesn't matter.[22]

> I found that I was constantly, throughout my life, pestered by men who were drunk, alcoholics, feeling like they had a chance with me. I found this really insulting. I mean, I may not be rich, but I'm well educated, I'm hard-working, I'm not an alcoholic—you know, to me I've got a lot of positive things going for me, and I feel that I should have

men who are at least my equal coming after me. And I've found throughout my life that I have not had that. I have them coming up for one-night stands. They don't want a relationship with me, they just want sex. And this is quite upsetting.[23]

This sexualized understanding of Native women can be seen in our communities, where, as Lee Maracle has observed, "it is nearly impossible for Native men to cherish the femininity of Native women. They have grown up in a world in which there is no such thing as dark-skinned femininity. There is only dark-skinned sensuality."[24]

In terms of overt violence, Plains Cree/Métis professor Emma LaRocque asserts that "the dehumanizing portrayal of the squaw and the over-sexualization of Native females such as Disney's Pocahontas surely render all Native female persons vulnerable."[25] After telling me, "Since childhood, I have had to walk through a maze of racist and sexist assaults on me," she told me a story that offered a striking image of the perceived worthlessness of Native female existence as it has too often been understood by the dominant society:

> My first experience of when I was conscious of this kind of assault happened when I was about ten years old. I was sitting in a café in my home town, reading a comic book, as I was wont to do. Minding my own business. I don't know where my parents were, but I just remember a big, fat, red-faced white guy coming in. Leering at me. I don't even think I could identify what that look was, because I had been so safe at home and in my community. I had never been attacked, and I didn't know what on earth that was. This guy, he throws a quarter. I still remember, and I still see that quarter rolling right past my coke bottle. He threw a quarter and he said, "Want to go for a ride, little squaw?"

LaRocque acknowledges the danger she was in at that moment, and how racist stereotypes endanger Native girls and women: "To this day, I am profoundly grateful he did nothing else. He could have just picked me up and taken me away. Nobody would have known the difference." She asks, "Where do these men get off on attacking little children, teenagers, regular aged women and grandmothers? It has to come from some conditioning, some horrendous sociological, racist and sexist conditioning, to be so inhumane to your co-human beings. It is really stunning."

Negative images of Native women, whether in historical accounts, anecdotes, jokes, movies, or Canadian literature,[26] are at the root of stories like that of Helen Betty Osbourne, a sixteen-year-old Native woman who was picked up by four white men and brutally raped and murdered in The Pas, Manitoba, in 1972. This story remains fixed in the consciousness of many Native women, as it demonstrates how mainstream society interprets violence against Native women, especially when it is committed by whites. In my conversation with Gertie Beaucage (Ojibway), she pointed out that Osbourne was killed because she was expected to be "easy," and yet she resisted the sexual assault of the white men who attacked her. As Emma LaRocque has further pointed out, "In the minds of 'good boys who did bad things,' it is not the place of 'squaws' to resist white power, especially power snakily connected to the male ego."[27]

The Osbourne case eventually received a moderate amount of publicity because of the injustices it represented. There are, however, many more Native women's tales that would reveal the minimal worth placed on Native female lives. In our conversations, Lee Maracle (Sto:lo) and Catherine Martin (Mi'kmaw) have demonstrated to me that the notion that Native women are there for the sexual taking has been acted out from one side of the continent to the other. Maracle recalls her childhood on the West Coast:

In my village, every single weekend … men came into the village, picked up little children, took them to the gravel pit, raped them—sometimes killed them—and were never prosecuted. I personally was chased in automobiles by white men. And when I went to swear out a complaint, they said it was in my imagination. I had charged a white man with assault, and I was called not a credible witness. Those things happen in our personal lives.

Maracle attributes this to the "permission that white society gave to white men to enter our communities, murder, pillage, rape and plunder us at will, right up until 1963."

A Mi'kmaw from Nova Scotia, Catherine Martin recalls, "In my grandmother's time, during the war, during the time when the Indian Agent had total rule, atrocities happened to our women. I know that." This was a time when, in the absence of Indian men, women were even more subject to attack. But Martin knows that racist ideology was at work:

Our women were raped. They weren't just raped back in cowboy and Indian days, they are still raped. But that myth or misperception about our women [being easy] is in the minds of the mainstream society, which is why our women end up being attacked and raped. The fact that we have been raped tends to make them think that we are easy. It is a way to excuse the rapist, or to ignore the race issue.

Hereditary Wit'suwet'en Chief Theresa Tait lives in central British Columbia. When I spoke with her about this issue, she told me that in the last decade there have been at least five Aboriginal women who have been killed in her local area. There is little investigation and next to no media coverage about these incidents. Tait contrasts the lack of attention to violence against Aboriginal females with cases involving white women who go missing in Vancouver: "There, you have the media, you have everybody on side."

Native women seeking justice against the violence in their lives are overshadowed by the image of the squaw. In her study of how race figures into sexual abuse trials, Sherene Razack notes that Aboriginal women are treated as "inherently rapeable" because of assumptions made about Native female promiscuity and the insistence that a rape victim who has passed out because of alcohol is considered to have suffered less of a violation.[28] A Native woman who is drunk is deemed particularly unworthy of human treatment, and Native women who are involved in abusive relationships may not feel comfortable calling police in the case of domestic violence because they may be seen "at fault," or deserving of the abuse.[29]

The construction of a negative identity can rule a Native woman's experience, as these women have described. The triangle of oppression, developed by the Doris Marshall Institute,[30] is a useful tool for analysing how the oppression functions:

Each point of the triangle supports the others to maintain the oppression of Native women. If Native women are constructed as "easy squaws" and are locked into this imagery through the behaviour of individuals, they will continue to be rendered worthless in public institutions such as courtrooms or hospitals. If we treat Native women as easy or drunken squaws in the court system, we feed negative stereotypes that will further enable individuals to abuse Native females, and so on. Negative Native female images are part of a vicious cycle that deeply influences the lives of contemporary Native women. We need to get rid of the images, the systems that support them, and the abusive practices carried out by individuals.

Figure 29.1: The Triangle of Oppression

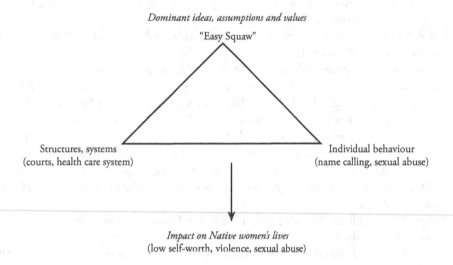

Dominant ideas, assumptions and values
"Easy Squaw"

Structures, systems
(courts, health care system)

Individual behaviour
(name calling, sexual abuse)

Impact on Native women's lives
(low self-worth, violence, sexual abuse)

Notes

1. Rayna Green, "The Pocahontas Perplex: The Image of the Indian Woman in American Culture," *Sweetgrass* (July–August 1984), 19.
2. Ibid.
3. This was a typical application of Indigenous women in other colonial contexts as explained in Ann McClintock, *Imperial Leather: Race, Gender, and Sexuality in the Colonial Context* (New York: Routledge, 1995).
4. Elizabeth Cook-Lynn, *Why I Can't Read Wallace Stegner and Other Essays* (Madison: University of Wisconsin Press, 1996), 145.
5. Beth Brant, *Writing as Witness: Essay and Talk* (Toronto: Women's Press, 1984), 83–103; Clara Sue Kidwell, "Indian Women as Cultural Mediators," *Ethnohistory* 39, no. 2 (Spring 1992), 97–107.
6. Cook-Lynn, *Why I Can't Read Wallace Stegner and Other Essays*, 106.
7. Green, "The Pocahontas Perplex," 20.
8. Carol Douglas Sparks, "The Land Incarnate: Navajo Women and the Dialogue of Colonialism," in Nancy Shoemaker, ed., *Negotiators of Change: Historical Perspectives on Native American Women* (New York: Routledge), 135–156.
9. Ibid., 147.
10. Sarah Carter, *Capturing Women: The Manipulation of Cultural Imagery in Canada's Prairie West* (Montreal: McGill-Queen's University Press, 1997), 158–193.
11. Ibid., 160.
12. Ibid., 162.
13. Ibid., 183.
14. Ibid., 191.

15. Ibid., 205.
16. Rita Joe, *Song of Rita Joe: Autobiography of a Mi'kmaq Poet* (Charlottetown, PEI: Ragweed Press, 1996), 62; Anna Lee Walters, *Talking Indian: Reflections on Survival and Writing* (Ithaca, NY: Firebrand Books, 1992), 211.
17. Janice Acoose, *Iskwewak. Kah'Ki Yaw Ni Wahkomakanak: Neither Indian Princesses nor Easy Squaws* (Toronto: Women's Press, 1995), 29.
18. Joanne Arnott, *Breasting the Waves: On Writing and Healing* (Vancouver: Press Gang, 1995), 76; Brant, *Writing as Witness*, 13, 119–120; Maria Campbell, *Halfbreed* (Toronto: McClelland and Stewart Limited, 1973), 47, 90; Janet Campbell Hale, *Bloodlines: Odyssey of a Native Daughter* (New York: HarperPerennial, 1993), 139–140; Beatrice Culleton, *In Search of April Raintree* (Winnipeg: Pemmican Publications, 1983); Paula Gunn Allen, *The Sacred Hoop: Recovering the Feminine in American Indian Tradition* (Boston: Beacon Press, 1986), 48–49; Lee Maracle, *I Am Woman* (Vancouver: Press Gang Publishers, 1996), 14–19; Anna Lee Walters, *Talking Indian: Reflections on Survival and Writing* (Ithaca, NY: Firebrand Books, 1992), 52.
19. Barbara Helen-Hill, *Shaking the Rattle: Healing the Trauma of Colonization* (Penticton, BC: Theytus Books, 1995).
20. bell hooks, *Black Looks: Race and Representation* (Toronto: Between the Lines Press, 1992), 21–39.
21. Ibid., 25.
22. Quoted in Bonita Lawrence, "'Real' Indians and Others: Mixed-Race Urban Native People, *The Indian Act*, and the Rebuilding of Indigenous Nations" (PhD thesis, Ontario Institute for Studies in Education of the University of Toronto, 1999), 261–262.
23. Ibid.
24. Maracle, *I Am Woman*, 56.
25. Emma LaRocque, "The Colonization of a Native Woman Scholar," in Patricia Chuchryk and Christine Miller, eds., *Women of the First Nations: Power, Wisdom, and Strength* (Winnipeg: The University of Manitoba Press, 1996), 12.
26. See Acoose, *Iskwewak*.
27. Emma LaRocque, "Tides, Towns, and Trains," in Joan Turner, ed., *Living the Changes* (Winnipeg: University of Manitoba Press, 1990), 87.
28. Sherene Razack, *Looking White People in the Eye: Gender, Race, and Culture in Courtrooms and Classrooms* (Toronto: University of Toronto Press, 1998), 68–72.
29. Anne McGillivary and Brenda Comaskey, *Black Eyes All of the Time: Intimate Violence, Aboriginal Women, and the Justice System* (Toronto: University of Toronto Press, 1999), 100.
30. Rick Arnold, Bev Burke, Carl James, D'Arcy Martin, and Barb Thomas, *Educating for a Change* (Toronto: Between the Lines and the Doris Marshall Institute for Education and Action, 1991), 91–92.

References

Acoose, Janice (Nehiowe-Métis/Nahkawe). *Iskwewak. Kah'Ki Yaw Ni Wahkomakanak: Neither Indian Princesses nor Easy Squaws*. Toronto: Women's Press, 1995.
Allen, Paula Gunn (Laguna Pueblo/Lakota Sioux). *The Sacred Hoop: Recovering the Feminine in American Indian Tradition*. Boston: Beacon Press, 1986.

Arnold, Rick, Bev Burke, Carl James, D'Arcy Martin, and Barb Thomas. *Educating for Change*. Toronto: Between the Lines and the Doris Marshall Institute for Education and Action, 1991.

Arnott, Joanne (Métis). *Breasting the Waves: On Writing and Healing*. Vancouver: Press Gang Publishers, 1995.

Brant, Beth (Mohawk). *Writing as Witness: Essay and Talk*. Toronto: Women's Press, 1994.

Campbell, Maria (Cree/Métis). *Halfbreed*. Toronto: McClelland and Stewart, 1973.

Campbell Hale, Janet (Coeur d'Alene). *Bloodlines: Odyssey of a Native Daughter*. New York: Harper Perennial, 1993.

Carter, Sarah. *Capturing Women: The Manipulation of Cultural Imagery in Canada's Prairie West*. Montreal: McGill-Queen's University Press, 1997.

Cook-Lynn, Elizabeth (Sioux). *Why I Can't Read Wallace Stegner and Other Essays*. Madison: University of Wisconsin Press, 1996.

Culleton, Beatrice (Métis). *In Search of April Raintree*. Winnipeg: Pemmican Publications, 1983.

Douglas Sparks, Carol. "The Land Incarnate: Navajo Women and the Dialogue of Colonialism." In *Negotiators of Change: Historical Perspectives on Native American Women*, edited by Nancy Shoemaker. New York: Routledge, 1994.

Green, Rayna (Cherokee). "The Pocahontas Perplex: The Image of the Indian Woman in American Culture." *Sweetgrass* (July–August 1984): 17–23.

Helen-Hill, Barbara. *Shaking the Rattle: Healing the Trauma of Colonization*. Penticton, BC: Theytus Books, 1995.

hooks, bell. *Black Looks: Race and Representation*. Toronto: Between the Lines Press, 1992.

Joe, Rita (Mi'kmaw). *Song of Rita Joe: Autobiography of a Mi'kmaq Poet*. Charlottetown, PEI: Ragweed Press, 1996.

Kidwell, Clara Sue (Chippewa/Choctaw). "Indian Women as Cultural Mediators." *Ethnohistory* 39, no. 2 (1992): 97–107.

LaRocque, Emma (Plains Cree/Métis). "Tides, Towns, and Trains." In *Living the Changes*, edited by Joan Turner. Winnipeg: University of Manitoba Press, 1990.

LaRocque, Emma (Plains Cree/Métis). "The Colonization of a Native Woman Scholar." In *Women of the First Nations: Power, Wisdom, and Strength*, edited by Patricia Chuchryk and Christine Miller. Winnipeg: The University of Manitoba Press, 1996.

Lawrence, Bonita (Mi'kmaw). "'Real' Indians and Others: Mixed-Race Urban Native People, the *Indian Act*, and the Rebuilding of Indigenous Nations." PhD thesis, Ontario Institute for Studies in Education of the University of Toronto, 1999.

Maracle, Lee (Sto:lo/Métis). *I Am Woman*. Vancouver: Press Gang Publishers, 1996.

McClintock, Ann. *Imperial Leather: Race, Gender, and Sexuality in the Colonial Context*. New York: Routledge, 1995.

McGillivary, Anne, and Brenda Comaskey. *Black Eyes All of the Time: Intimate Violence, Aboriginal Women, and the Justice System*. Toronto: University of Toronto Press, 1999.

Razack, Sherene. *Looking White People in the Eye: Gender, Race, and Culture in Courtrooms and Classrooms*. Toronto: University of Toronto Press, 1998.

Shoemaker, Nancy, ed. *Negotiators of Change: Historical Perspectives on Native American Women*. New York: Routledge, 1995.

Walters, Anna Lee (Pawnee/Otoe). *Talking Indian: Reflections on Survival and Writing*. Ithaca, NY: Firebrand Books, 1992.

Williams, Shirley (Ojibway/Odawa). "Women's Role in Ojibway Spirituality." *Journal of Canadian Native Studies* 27, no. 3 (1992): 100–104.

Supplement 17

Colonization and the Indian Act

The Indian Act is a Canadian federal law that governs in matters pertaining to Indian status, bands, and Indian reserves. Throughout history it has been highly invasive and paternalistic, as it authorizes the Canadian federal government to regulate and administer in the affairs and day-to-day lives of registered Indians and reserve communities. This authority has ranged from overarching political control, such as imposing governing structures on Aboriginal communities in the form of band councils, to control over the rights of Indians to practise their culture and traditions. The Indian Act has also enabled the government to determine the land base of these groups in the form of reserves, and even to define who qualifies for Indian status. While the Indian Act has undergone numerous amendments since it was first passed in 1876, today it largely retains its original form. The Indian Act is a part of a long history of assimilation policies that were intended to terminate the cultural, social, economic, and political distinctiveness of Aboriginal peoples by absorbing them into mainstream Canadian life and values.

The Indian Act has been highly criticized for its gender bias as another means of terminating one's Indian status, thus excluding women from their Aboriginal rights. Legislation stated that a status Indian woman who married a non-Indian man would cease to be an Indian. She would lose her status, and with it, she would lose treaty benefits, health benefits, the right to live on her reserve, the right to inherit her family property, and even the right to be buried on the reserve with her ancestors. However, if an Indian man married a non-status woman, he would keep all his rights. Even if an Indian woman married another Indian man, she would cease to be a member of her own band and become a member of his. If a woman was widowed, or abandoned by her husband, she would become enfranchised and lose status altogether. Alternatively, if a non-Native woman married an Indian man, she would acquire status. In all these situations, a woman's status was entirely dependent on her husband.

Source: Excerpted from Indigenous Foundations retrieved from: http://indigenousfoundations.arts.ubc.ca/home/government-policy/the-indian-act.html

Excerpts from the Indian Act of Canada
Edited by Pamela J. Downe

> *Pamela J. Downe is a medical anthropologist and professor in the Department of Archaeology and Anthropology at the University of Saskatchewan. Her research focuses on how illness, injury, and risk are connected to cultural ideas of contagion and communicability. With a strong commitment to engaged anthropology, she has explored the intersections between HIV/AIDS and violence, maternal health in relation to HIV and other infections, and government responses to emerging health conditions, both internationally and in Canada.*

1. The Indian Act, 1876

Terms

3. The following terms contained in this Act shall be held to have the meaning hereinafter assigned to them ... :

1) The term "band" means any tribe, band or body of Indians who own or are interested in a reserve or in Indian lands in common, of which the legal title is vested in the Crown ...

3) The term "Indian" means

First. Any person of Indian blood reputed to belong to a particular band;

Second. Any legitimate child of such person;

Thirdly. Any woman who is or was lawfully married to such person.

(a) Provided that any illegitimate child, unless having shared with the consent of the band in the distribution of moneys of such band for a period exceeding two years, may, at any time, be excluded from the membership thereof by the band, if ... sanctioned by the Superintendent-General: ...

(c) Provided that any Indian woman marrying any other than an Indian or non-treaty Indian shall cease to be an Indian in any respect within the meaning of this Act....

(d) Provided that any Indian woman marrying an Indian of any other band shall cease to be a member of the band to which she formerly belonged, and become a member of the band ... of which her husband is a member:

(e) Provided also that no half-breed in Manitoba who has shared in the distribution of half-breed lands shall be accounted an Indian; and that no half-breed head of family (Except the widow of an Indian, or a half-breed who has already been admitted into a treaty), shall ... be accounted an Indian, or entitled to be admitted into any Indian treaty....

5) The term "reserve" means any tract or tracts of land set apart by treaty or otherwise for the use of, benefit of or granted to a particular band of Indians, of which the legal title is the Crown's, but which is unsurrendered, and includes all the trees, wood, timber, soil, stone, minerals, metals or other valuables thereon or therein....

Protection of Reserves

11. No person ... other than an Indian of the band, shall settle, reside or hunt upon, occupy or use any land or marsh, or shall settle, reside upon or occupy any road, or allowance for roads running through any reserve belonging to ... such a band; ...

Privileges of Indians

64. No Indian or non-treaty Indian shall be liable to be taxed for any real or personal property, unless he holds real estate under lease or in fee simple, or personal property, outside of the reserve or special reserve, in which case he shall be liable to be taxed for such real or personal property at the same rate as other persons in the locality in which it is situated....

Disabilities and Penalties

72. The Superintendent-General shall have the power to stop the payment of the annuity and interest money of any Indian who may be proved, to the satisfaction of the Superintendent-

General, to have been guilty of deserting his family, and the said Superintendent-General may apply the same towards the support of any family, woman or child so deserted; also to stop the payment of the annuity and interest money of any woman having no children, who deserts her husband and lives immorally with another man....

Enfranchisement

86. Whenever any Indian man, or unmarried woman, of the full age of twenty-one years, obtains the consent of the band of which he or she is a member to become enfranchised ... the local agent shall report ... the name of the applicant to the Superintendent-General; whereupon the Superintendent-General ... shall authorize some competent person to report whether the applicant is an Indian who, from the degree of civilization to which he attained, and the character for integrity, morality, and sobriety which he bears, appears to be qualified to be [enfranchised]:
  (I) Any Indian who may be admitted to the degree of Doctor of Medicine, or to any other degree by any University of Learning, or who may be admitted in any Province of the Dominion to practice law ... or who may enter Holy Orders or who may be licensed by any denomination of Christians as a Minister of the Gospel, shall *ipso facto* become and be enfranchised under this Act.

Assented to 12 April 1876

2. The Indian Act, 1970

Administration

3. (I) This Act shall be administered by the Minister of Indian Affairs and Northern Development, who shall be the superintendent-general of Indian affairs....

Definition and Registration of Indians

5. An Indian Register shall be maintained in the Department [of Indian Affairs], which shall consist of Band Lists and General Lists and in which shall be recorded the name of every person who is entitled to be registered as an Indian....

11. Subject to section 12, a person is entitled to be registered if that person
  (a) [is] entitled to hold, use or enjoy the lands and other immovable property belonging to the various tribes, bands or bodies of Indians in Canada;
  (b) is a member of a band ...
  (c) is a male person who is a direct descendant in the male line of a male person described in paragraph (a) or (b);
  (d) is the legitimate child of
      (i) a male person described in paragraph (a) or (b), or
      (ii) a person described in paragraph (c);
  (e) is the illegitimate child of a female person described in paragraph (a), (b) or (d); or
  (f) is the wife or widow of a person who is entitled to be registered by virtue of paragraph (a), (b), (c), (d), or (e)....

12. (I) The following persons are not entitled to be registered ... :
  (a)   a person who
        (i) has received or has been allotted half-breed lands or money scrip,
        (ii) is a descendant of a person described in subparagraph (i),
        (iii) is enfranchised....
  (b)   a woman who married a person who is not an Indian, unless that woman is subsequently
        the wife or widow of a person described in section 11....

14. A woman who is a member of a band ceases to be a member of that band if she marries a person who is not a member of that band, but if she marries a member of another band, she thereupon becomes a member of the band of which her husband is a member.

Enfranchisement

[Previous sections pertaining to enfranchisement are replaced by sections 109–112.]

109. (I) On the report of the Minister that an Indian has applied for enfranchisement and that in his opinion the Indian
  (a)   is of the full age of twenty-one years,
  (b)   is capable of assuming duties and responsibilities of citizenship, and
  (c)   when enfranchised, will be capable of supporting himself and his dependents [sic], the
Governor in Council may by order declare that the Indian and his wife and minor unmarried children are enfranchised....

(2) On the report of the Minister that an Indian woman married a person who is not an Indian, the Governor in Council may by order declare that the woman is enfranchised as of the date of her marriage and, on the recommendation of the Minister may by order declare that all or any of her children are enfranchised as of the date of the marriage or such other date as the order may specify....

3. Bill C-31: An Act to Amend the Indian Act, 1985

Clause 4. This amendment would substitute for the existing scheme of band membership....
    It would also eliminate provisions relating to entitlement to registration that discriminate on the basis of sex and would replace them with non-discriminatory rules for determining entitlement. As well, it would eliminate the distinction between "legitimate" and "illegitimate" children and provide for the reinstatement of persons who have lost their entitlement to registration under discriminatory provisions or, in certain cases, through enfranchisement.
    The proposed sections 5 to 7 would deal with registration in the Indian Register, sections 6 and 7 replacing the present sections 11 and 12....

6. (I) Subject to section 7, a person is entitled to be registered if ...
  (c)   the name of that person was omitted or deleted from the Indian Register, or from a band list ... under subparagraph ... 12(1)(b), subsection 12(2) or subsection 109(2) ... or under any former provision of this Act relating to the same subject matter as any of those provisions....

Clause 12: The amendment to subsection 68(1) and the repeal of subsection 68(2) [based on section 72 in the 1876 Indian Act] would establish the same rule for male and female Indians with respect to support payments in circumstances such as desertion. The repeal of subsection 68(3) would remove a special rule for "illegitimate" children....

Clause 14: The repeal of section 109 to 113 would remove the concept of enfranchisement from the Indian Act.

Source: Gendered Intersections: An Introduction to Women's and Gender Studies, eds. Lesley Biggs and Pamela J. Downe (Halifax, NS: Fernwood, 2005), 103–106.

Chapter 30

Regulating Native Identity by Gender

Bonita Lawrence

Bonita Lawrence (Mi'kmaw) is an associate professor in the Department of Equity Studies at York University. Her research focuses primarily on urban, non-status, and Métis identities, federally unrecognized Aboriginal communities, Aboriginal peoples and the criminal justice system, and Indigenous nationhood and justice. Her well-known book, Real Indians and Others: Mixed-Blood Urban Native Peoples and Indigenous Nationhood, *from which the following chapter is taken, explores many of these themes. She is a founding member of the undergraduate program in Indigenous studies and of the upcoming graduate program in Indigenous thought.*

*****

In Canada a history of gender discrimination in the Indian Act has created an ongoing conflict within Native organizations and reserve communities around notions of individual and collective rights, organized along lines of gender. It is crucially important, then, to understand the central role that the subordination of Native women has played in the colonization process, in order to begin to see the violation of Native women's rights through loss of Indian status, not as the problems faced by individuals, but as a *collective* sovereignty issue.

Gendering Indianness in the Colonial Encounter

The nation-building process in Canada began to accelerate between 1781 and 1830, in what is now Southern Ontario, when the British began to realize the necessity of bringing in settlers on the lands where previously they had engaged in the fur trade, to secure the territory they claimed against the threat of American expansion. Settlement of the area was only made possible as individual Anishinaabe (Ojibway) bands were gradually induced to cede, in small packages, the land immediately north of Lake Ontario and Lake Erie to the British. Many of these land surrenders were framed as peace treaties, to ensure that the British would be allies to the Ojibway against the possible northern encroachment of American settler violence; on this basis, only male leaders or representatives were asked to participate in treaty negotiation and the signing away of land (Schmalz 1991, 120–22).

In negotiating only with men, the British deliberately cut out the stabilizing presence of older women and the general authority that was given to their voices in major decisions concerning the land. As Kim Anderson has written, traditional Native societies were often matrilineal in very balanced ways (2000, 66–68). Even in societies where men made the decisions about which lands to hunt on each year, clans organized along the female line frequently controlled land inheritance. To bypass older women in traditional societies effectively removed from the treaty process the people centrally responsible for regulating land access.

Moreover the British were confident in their knowledge that, as Major Gladwin articulated, "The free sale of rum will destroy them more effectively than fire and sword" (Schmalz 1991, 82). The "chemical warfare" of alcohol, deliberately introduced north of the Great Lakes after the Pontiac uprising of 1763, had an immediate and devastating effect on Ojibway communities in the Toronto and southwestern Ontario region, whose social disintegration and their resulting dependency on the British were devastating (Schmalz 1991, 87). In such circumstances, as the abilities of the men to make good choices for the future were increasingly destabilized by alcohol, it was frequently the women whose decision-making capabilities became crucial for the survival of the society as a whole. The fact that the women invariably spoke with the future of the children always in mind meant that "choices" being forced on the men, such as surrendering the lands they could no longer hunt or trap on in exchange for the promise of assistance in the transition to farming (or later, of jobs in resource development), were most strenuously resisted by the women, who saw holding on to the land base as the only way in which the social fabric of the society to nurture the next generation would survive at all.

Finally, as Kathleen Jamieson has noted, most of the early land treaties and Indian legislation were premised on the Indigenous peoples the English were most familiar with—the Anishinaabe (Ojibway) and Haudenosaunee (Iroquois) peoples. Especially in Haudenosaunee society, female-led clans held the collective land base for all of the nations of the confederacy. Removing women, then, was the key to privatizing the land base. For all of these reasons, a central aspect of the colonization process in Canada would be to break the power of Indigenous women within their nations (Jamieson 1978, 13).

It is also important to take into account not only the concerns of British colonial administrators, for whom Indian administration was but another post of the empire, but the fears of the growing body of white settlers, where colonial anxieties about white identity and who would control settler societies were rampant. As Ann Stoler has noted, the European settlements that developed on other people's lands have generally been obsessed with ways of maintaining colonial control and of rigidly asserting differences between Europeans and Native peoples to maintain white social solidarity and cohesion (Stoler 1991, 53). Colonial societies have had to invent themselves as new groupings of individuals with no organic link to one another, in settings that are often radically different from their places of origin. They have had to invent the social institutions that will then define them as a society—and they have to be capable of rationalizing or justifying their existence on other people's lands and the brutality through which their presence is maintained. The very existence of white settler societies is therefore predicated on maintaining racial apartheid, on emphasizing racial difference, both white superiority and Native inferiority.

This flies in the face of the actual origins of many white settlements in Canada—which frequently began with displaced and often marginal white men, whose success with the fur trade or settlement, and often their very survival, depended on their ability to insinuate themselves into Indigenous societies through intermarriage. The early days of European–Native contact frequently involved negotiated alliances with local Indigenous communities, often cemented through marriage. [...]

Meanwhile the entire structure of the fur trade, in both eastern and western Canada, involved "country marriages" between European men and the Native women that the traders depended on so heavily for their survival—and a growing reliance on the mixed-blood children of these marriages to fill specific niches in the fur trade—which meant that, as time went on, the boundaries between who should be considered European and who should be considered Native (and by what means) have not always been clear. By the mid-nineteenth century, the presence of numerous mixed-blood communities in the Great Lakes area made it difficult for Anglo settlers to maintain clear boundaries between colonizers and colonized.[1] Social control was predicated on legally identifying who was white, who was Indian, and which children were legitimate progeny—citizens rather than subjugated Natives (Stoler 1991, 53). [...]

Moreover, fur trade society in western Canada, in the years before the 1885 Rebellion, was in many respects highly bicultural. Many settlements consisted primarily of white men married to Cree women, raising Cree families. While the language spoken in public was English, the language spoken in many of the homes was Cree. Clearly, if a white settler society modeled on British values was to be established, white women had to take the place of Native women, and Native women had to be driven out of the place they had occupied in fur trade society, a process that would continue through successive waves of white settlement, from the Great Lakes westward across the continent. The displacement of Native women from white society, and the replacement of the bicultural white society that their marriages to white men created to an openly white supremacist society populated by all-white families, was accomplished largely through the introduction of punitive laws in the Indian Act concerning prostitution and intoxication off-reserve. These laws targeted Aboriginal women as responsible for the spread of venereal disease among the police and officials in western Canada and therefore increasingly classified urban Aboriginal women as prostitutes within the criminal code after 1892 (Carter 1997, 187).

*****

Gender Discrimination in the Indian Act

Many of the legal disabilities for women in the Indian Act have existed as much by omission as by explicit statement through the use of the constant masculine term in the legislation, even though a separate legal regime has existed for Indian women with respect to marriage, childbirth, regulation of sexual conduct, exclusion from the right to vote or otherwise partake in band business, and rights to inherit and for a widow to administer her husband's estate. Because of the constant use of the masculine pronoun, confusion has existed at times in various communities as to whether Native women actually have any of the rights pertaining to men in much of the Indian Act legislation (Jamieson 1978, 56). Finally, definitions of Indianness have been asserted in such a patriarchal manner as to be fraught with discriminatory consequences for Indian women.

[...] Legislation in 1850 first defined Indianness in gendered terms, so that Indian status depended either on Indian descent or marriage to a male Indian. With the Gradual Enfranchisement Act of 1869, not only were wives removed from inheritance rights and automatically enfranchised with their husbands, but Section 6 began a process of escalating gender discrimination that would not be definitively changed until 1985. With this section, for the first time, Indian women were declared "no longer Indian" if they married anybody who lacked Indian status. On marrying an Indian from another "tribe, band, or body," she and her children now belonged to her husband's tribe only (Jamieson 1978, 29–30).

Prior to 1951 some recognition on a local basis was given to the needs of Indian women who were deserted or widowed. Indian women who lost their status were no longer legally Indian and no longer formal band members, but they were not considered to have the full rights that enfranchised women had. These women were often issued informal identity cards, known as "red tickets," which identified them as entitled to shares in treaty monies and recognized on an informal basis their band membership, to the extent that some of them were even able to live on the reserve. It was not until 1951 that women who lost their Indian status were also compulsorily enfranchised. This meant that they not only lost band membership, reserve residency, or any property they might have held on the reserve, but also access to any treaty monies or band assets (RCAP 1996, 19:301–02).

Section 6, governing loss of status, was only one of the many aspects of the 1869 legislation that limited the power of Native women in their societies. Particularly in the context of matrilineal practices, this act ripped huge holes in the fabric of Native life. The clan system of the Iroquois was disrupted in particularly cruel ways. Not only was the matrilineal basis of the society (and therefore its framework of land tenure) threatened by legislation that forced Native women to become members of their husbands' communities, but the manner in which white women received the Indian status of their husbands resulted in the births of generations of clanless individuals within reserve communities, since clan inheritance passed through the mother. Finally, in addition to these processes, which subverted and bypassed the power of Native women in matrilineal societies and opened up their lands for privatization, Native women were formally denied any political role in the governance of their societies. For example, when the 1869 legislation divided reserves into individual lots, married women could not inherit any portion of their husband's lots, and they lost their own allocations if they married non-Natives. After 1884 widows were allowed to inherit one-third of their husband's lot—if a widow was living with her husband at his time of death and was determined by the Indian agent to be "of good moral character" (RCAP 1996, 4:28–29). Meanwhile, in 1876, the Indian Act prevented Native women from voting in any decisions about surrender of reserve lands. The many ways in which Native women were rendered marginal in their communities by patriarchal colonial laws not only made it more difficult for them to challenge the tremendous disempowerment that loss of status represented—it made land theft much easier.

From the perspective of the colonial administration, the 1869 legislation had two primary goals—to remove as many individuals as possible from Indianness and, as part of this process, to enforce Indianness as being solely a state of "racial purity" by removing those children designated as "half-breed" from Indian communities. At the same time, however, if reserve residents were to grow increasingly mixed-blooded, it would facilitate their enfranchisement, as individuals who were "too civilized" to be Indians. In this respect it is, of course, important to note that when white women married Native men, they also produced "half-breed" children, who nevertheless were allowed to stay in Native communities as Indians. Because of patriarchal notions that children were solely the products of their fathers, these children were not recognized by colonial administrators as half-breed. However, communities where there was a great deal of such intermarriage were often reported of approvingly, as when glowing comments were made about Caughnawaga (Kahnawake) in the 1830's that "there is scarcely a pure blooded Indian in the settlement" (Jamieson 1978, 23).

It is clear from the government debates at the time that this legislation was also aimed at undermining the collective nature of Native societies, where lands, monies, and other resources were shared in common. By restricting reserves only to those who were granted location tickets, by externalizing the Indian women who married white men and their children, and by forcing exogamy on Native women (where the custom in many communities was that Native men would join their wives' extended family, who controlled the land along clan lines), most of the collective aspects of Native society were to be subverted or suppressed.

In 1874, legislation altered and elaborated upon the definition of the term *Indian*, making Indian descent solely flowing from the male line. With this act, the status of the illegitimate children of Native women was also continuously subject to changing standards at the whim of the superintendent of Indian Affairs, depending on whether the father was known to be Native or not. The superintendant was also given the power to stop the payment of annuities and interest to any woman having no children, who deserted her husband, and "lived immorally with another man" (Jamieson 1978, 45). Other legislation criminalized Indian women further, targeting them as prostitutes and providing them with penalties of one hundred dollars and up to six months in jail. [...]

The 1920's legislation that evicted or jailed Native "squatters" on band lands had severe implications for women who lost their status and were increasingly rendered homeless, especially if their husbands were not white but were, rather, nonstatus Indians or Métis, or if their marriages to white men failed, or they were widowed (Jamieson 1978, 51). [...]

While the 1951 Indian Act represents a lessening of colonial control for Indian men, it actually heightened colonial regulation for Indian women in general and especially for those women who married non-Natives. The membership section became even more elaborate, couched in almost unreadable bureaucratic language, which spelled out not only who was entitled to be registered as an Indian but who was not. The male line of descent was further emphasized as the major criterion for inclusion—in fact mention of "Indian blood" was altogether removed. The areas of the act that dictated who was not an Indian included Section 12(I)(b), which removed the status of any woman who married a non-Indian (which included American Indians and nonstatus Native men from Canada), and Section 12(I)(a)(iv), also known as the "double-mother" clause, which removed the status of any individual whose mother *and* paternal grandmother lacked Indian status prior to their marriages to Indian men. [...]

The major change for Native women who "married out" was that from the date of their marriages they were not only automatically deprived of their Indian status and band rights, but by order of the governor-in-council they were declared enfranchised. Enfranchisement for these Indian women, however, did not involve the same conditions as those that had been experienced by Indian men and their families either through voluntary or involuntary enfranchisement. Individuals who enfranchised, voluntarily or involuntarily, had to have sufficient resources to survive off-reserve. No such condition was considered necessary for Indian women compulsorily enfranchised, since they were assumed to be, effectively, "wards" of their husband. [...]

The financial losses experienced by Native women due to loss of status have been considerable. When enfranchised, the women were entitled to receive a per capita share of band capital and revenue, as well as the equivalent of twenty years' treaty money. Since the treaty money is either four or five dollars a year, depending on the treaty, the women were therefore entitled to receive either eighty or one hundred dollars. However, during the interval when large numbers of women were being enfranchised and "paid off," most Native communities had relatively few assets and revenue available to provide meaningful shares to the women. Many of those bands subsequently received significant monies from resource development, to which the enfranchised women and their children never had access.

Another series of financial losses that Native women experienced when they lost their Indian status included the lack of access to postsecondary-education funding, free day-care provisions in some communities, funding for school supplies and social schooling programs, housing policies that enabled on-reserve Indians to buy houses with assistance from the Central Mortgage and Housing Corporation and Indian Affairs, loans and grants from the Indian Economic Development

Fund, health benefits, exemption from taxation and from provincial sales tax, hunting, fishing, animal grazing and trapping rights, cash distributions from sales of band assets, and the ability to be employed in the United States without a visa and to cross the border without restrictions (Jamieson 1978, 70–71). Finally, Indian women were generally denied access to personal property willed to them, evicted from their homes, often with small children and no money (especially when widowed or separated), and generally faced hostile band councils and indifferent Indian Affairs bureaucrats (Jamieson 1978, 72).

However, it is the personal and cultural losses of losing status that Indian women have most frequently spoken about. Some of the costs have included being unable to participate with family and relatives in the life of their former communities, being rejected by their communities, being culturally different and often socially rejected within white society, being unable to access cultural programs for their children, and finally not even being able to be buried with other family members on the reserve. The extent of penalties and lack of compensation for losses suffered has made the forcible enfranchisement of Indian women "retribution, not restitution," what Justice Bora Laskin, in his dissenting opinion in *Lavell and Bedard*, termed "statutory banishment" (Jamieson 1978, 72).

Finally, in terms of Native empowerment generally, it is important to note that this "bleeding off" of Native women and their children from their communities was in place for 116 years, from 1869 until 1985. The phenomenal cultural implication hidden in this legislation is the sheer numbers of Native people lost to their communities. Some sources have estimated that by far the majority of the twenty-five thousand Indians who lost status and were externalized from their communities between 1876 and 1985 (Holmes 1987, 8) did so because of ongoing gender discrimination in the Indian Act.[2] But it is not simply a matter of twenty-five thousand individuals. If one takes into account the fact that for every individual who lost status and had to leave her community, all of her descendants (many of them the products of nonstatus Indian fathers and Indian mothers) also lost status and for the most part were permanently alienated from Native culture, the numbers of individuals who ultimately were removed from Indian status and lost to their nations may, at the most conservative estimates, number between one and two million.

By comparison, in 1985, when Bill C-31 was passed, there were only 350,000 status Indians still listed on the Department of Indian Affairs' Indian register (Holmes 1987, 54). In comparing the potential numbers of people lost to their Native communities because of loss of status with the numbers of individuals still considered Indian in 1985, the scale of cultural genocide caused by gender discrimination becomes visible. Because Bill C-31 allowed the most recent generation of individuals who had lost status to regain it, along with their children, approximately one hundred thousand individuals had regained their status by 1995 (Switzer 1997, 2). But the damage caused, demographically and culturally, by the loss of status of so many Native women for a century prior to 1985, whose grandchildren and great-grandchildren are no longer recognized—and in many cases no longer identify—as Indian, remain incalculable.

The Struggle to Change the Indian Act

Given the accelerating gender discrimination in the Indian Act created by the modifications of 1951, Mohawk women in the 1960s created an organization known as Indian Rights for Indian Women, which attempted to address the disempowerment of Indian women, particularly with respect to loss of status. In 1971 Jeannette Corbiere Lavell and Yvonne Bedard, two Indian women who had lost status through their marriages, challenged the discriminatory sections of the Indian Act in the Canadian courts. [...]

[...] Lavell challenged the deletion of her name from her band list, while Bedard, in a separate case, challenged the fact that her reserve was evicting her and her children from the house which her mother had willed to her, even though she was no longer married to her husband. Both women lost at the federal court level, but were successful at winning appeals, and their cases were heard together in the Supreme Court. Their argument was based on the fact that the Indian Act discriminated against them on the basis of race and sex, and that the Bill of Rights should therefore override the discriminatory sections of the Indian Act with respect to membership. [...]

In 1973 the Supreme Court, by a five-to-four decision, ruled against Lavell and Bedard. Among other reasons, the decision noted that since not all Indians were discriminated against, only Indian women who married non-Indians, then racial discrimination could not be said to exist; and since enfranchised Indian women gained the citizenship rights that made them equal (in law) to white women, then gender discrimination could not be said to exist. While this judgment clarified none of the issues, it did assert that the Bill of Rights could not take precedence over the Indian Act. Because of this decision, the Indian Act was exempt from the application of the Canadian Human Rights Act in 1977 (Holmes 1987, 5).

The Maliseet community of Tobique was the next focus of resistance. The women at Tobique began their struggle over the issue of homelessness—the manner in which their band council interpreted Indian Act legislation to suggest that Indian women had no right to own property on the reserve. As the women addressed the problems they faced, their struggle slowly broadened until their primary goal became changing the Indian Act (Silman 1987, 119–72). Since the decision in *Lavell and Bedard* had foreclosed any possibility of justice within Canada, the Tobique women decided to support Sandra Lovelace in an appeal to the United Nations Human Rights Committee. Lovelace argued that Section 12(I)(b) of the Indian Act was in violation of Article 27 of the International Covenant on Civil and Political Rights, which provides for the rights of individuals who belong to minorities to enjoy their culture, practice their religion, and use their language in community with others from the group (Beyefsky 1982, 244–66). In 1981 the United Nations determined that Sandra Lovelace had been denied her cultural rights under Article 27 because she was barred from living in her community. Canada, embarrassed at the international level, at this point stated its intention to amend the discriminatory sections of the Indian Act. After some degree of consultation and proposed changes, Bill C-31, An Act to Amend the Indian Act, was passed in 1985.[3]

The violence and resistance that Native women struggling for their rights faced from male-dominated band councils and political organizations during this interval cannot be ignored.[4] For example, when Mary Two Axe Early and sixty other Native women from Kahnawake (then known as the Caughnawaga band) chose to focus international attention on their plight by bringing their organization, Indian Rights for Indian Women, to the International Women's Year conference in Mexico City in 1975, they were all served with eviction notices in their absence by their band council (Jamieson 1979, 170). Meanwhile when the Tobique women, protesting homelessness in their communities, occupied the band office in order to have a roof over their heads and draw attention to their plight, they were threatened with arrest by the band administration, physically beaten up in the streets, and had to endure numerous threats against their families from other community members.[5]

It has been the children of Native mothers and white, nonstatus Indian, or Métis fathers who have been forced to become urban Indians and who, in their Native communities of origin, are currently being regarded as outsiders because they *have* been labeled as "not Indian." Gender has thus been crucial in determining not only who has been able to stay in Native communities but who has been called mixed-blood and externalized as such. In this respect, gender discrimination in the Indian Act has shaped what we think about who is Native, who is mixed-blood, and who is entitled access to Indian land. These beliefs are only rendered more powerful by the strongly protectionist attitudes toward preserving Native culture as it is lived on reserves at present, where outsiders may be seen as profoundly threatening to community identity.

This history has even deeper repercussions, however, for Native communities today. Because the subordination of Indigenous women has been a central nexus through which colonizers have sought to destroy Indigenous societies, contemporary gender divisions created by the colonizer continue to subvert sovereignty struggles in crucial ways. And yet, almost inevitably, when issues of particular concern to Native women arise, they are framed as "individual rights," while in many cases, those who oppose Native women's rights are held to represent "the collective." In a context where a return to traditional collective ways is viewed as essential to surviving the ravages of colonization, Native women are routinely asked to separate their womanness from their Nativeness, as if violations of Native women's rights are not violations of Native rights.

Notes

1. Recent research has documented the presence of mixed-blood communities at no fewer than fifty-three locations in the Great Lakes region between 1763 and 1830 (RCAP 1996, I:150).

2. These figures include both those individuals who were enfranchised and those who lost their status because of gender discrimination in the Indian Act. However, the numbers of individuals who lost status due to enfranchisement only reached significant levels for a few years during the 1920s and 1930s, and the policy was ended for everybody but women marrying non-Natives in 1951. By comparison, for over a century, the majority of individuals who lost status were Indian women who married out.

3. In April 1985 the Charter of Rights and Freedoms came into effect. The identity legislation within the 1951 Indian Act was in violation of Section 15(1), which prohibited discrimination on the basis of race and gender, as well as other particularities. Because of this, when Bill C-31 came into effect on 28 June 1985, its amendments to the 1951 act came into legal effect retroactively back to 17 April 1985, the date that the charter came into effect (Gilbert 1996, 129).

4. At the time of *Lavell and Bedard*, there were no women on the National Indian Brotherhood executive council, and the Association of Iroquois and Allied Indians, which first enlisted the help of the solicitor general and turned the tide against Lavell, represented twenty thousand Indian men (Jamieson 1978, 91).

5. The American Indian Movement, with long experience in defending traditional and grassroots Native people against "puppet" Indian governments, offered their assistance to the Tobique women. The women declined, however, for fear that the situation would escalate still further if AIM entered the reserve to support them (Silman 1987, 129–30).

References

Anderson, Kim. 2000. *A Recognition of Being: Reconstructing Native Womanhood.* Toronto: Second Story Press.

Beyefsky, Anne F. 1982. The Human Rights Committee and the Case of Sandra Lovelace. In *The Canadian Yearbook of International Law*, Vol. 20.

Carter, Sarah. 1997. *Capturing Women: The Manipulation of Cultural Imagery in Canada's Prairie West*. Kingston and Montreal: McGill-Queen's University Press.

Gilbert, Larry. 1996. *Entitlement to Indian Status and Membership Codes in Canada*. Toronto: Thompson Canada Ltd.

Holmes, Joan. 1987. *Bill C-31—Equality or Disparity? The Effects of the New Indian Act on Native Women*. Background Paper. Canadian Advisory Council on the Status of Women.

Jamieson, Kathleen. 1978. *Indian Women and the Law in Canada: Citizens Minus*. Canadian Advisory Council on the Status of Women and Indian Rights for Indian Women.

Jamieson, Kathleen. 1979. Multiple Jeopardy: The Evolution of a Native Women's Movement. *Atlantis* 4, no. 2:157–76.

Royal Commission on Aboriginal Peoples (RCAP). 1996. *For Seven Generations: Report of the Royal Commission on Aboriginal Peoples*, Vols. 1–5. Ottawa: Government of Canada.

Schmalz, Peter S. 1991. *The Ojibwa of Southern Ontario*. Toronto: University of Toronto Press.

Silman, Janet. 1987. *Enough Is Enough: Aboriginal Women Speak out*, as told to Janet Silman. Toronto: The Women's Press.

Stoler, Ann. 1991. Carnal Knowledge and Imperial Power: Gender, Race, and Morality in Colonial Asia. In *Gender at the Crossroads: Feminist Anthropology in the Post-modern Era*, edited by Micaela di Leonardo. Berkeley: University of California Press.

Switzer, Maurice. 1997. Time to Stand up and Be Counted. *The First Perspective* (December): 2.

Supplement 18

Colonization and Residential Schools

What Is a Residential School?

In the 19th century, the Canadian government believed it was responsible for educating and caring for the country's Aboriginal peoples. It thought their best chance for success was to learn English and adopt Christianity and Canadian customs. Ideally, they would pass their adopted lifestyle on to their children, and Native traditions would diminish, or be completely abolished in a few generations.

The Canadian government developed a policy called "aggressive assimilation" to be taught at Church-run, government-funded industrial schools, later called residential schools. The government felt children were easier to mould than adults, and the concept of a boarding school was the best way to prepare them for life in mainstream society.

Residential schools were federally run under the Department of Indian Affairs. Attendance was mandatory. Agents were employed by the government to ensure that all Native children attended.

How Many Residential Schools and Students Were There?

Initially, about 1,100 students attended 69 schools across the country. In 1931, at the peak of the residential school system, there were about 80 schools operating in Canada. There was a total of about 130 schools in every territory and province except Newfoundland, Prince Edward Island and New Brunswick from the earliest in the 19th century to the last, which closed in 1996.

In all, about 150,000 Aboriginal, Inuit, and Métis children were removed from their communities and forced to attend the schools.

What Went Wrong?

Residential schools were established with the assumption that Aboriginal culture was unable to adapt to a rapidly modernizing society. It was believed that Native children could be successful if they assimilated into mainstream Canadian society by adopting Christianity and speaking English or French. Students were discouraged from speaking their first language or practising Native traditions. If they were caught, they would experience severe punishment.

Throughout the years, students lived in substandard conditions and endured physical and emotional abuse. There are also many allegations of sexual abuse. Students at residential schools rarely had opportunities to see examples of normal family life. They were in school 10 months a year, away from their parents. All correspondence from the children was written in English, which many parents couldn't read. Brothers and sisters at the same school rarely saw each other as all activities were segregated by gender.

When students returned to the reserve, they often found they didn't belong. They didn't have the skills to help their parents, and became ashamed of their Native heritage. The skills taught at the schools were generally substandard; many found it hard to function in an urban setting. The aims of assimilation meant devastation for those who were subjected to years of mistreatment.

When Did the Calls for Victim Compensation Begin?

In 1990, Phil Fontaine, then leader of the Association of Manitoba Chiefs, called for the churches involved to acknowledge the physical, emotional, and sexual abuse endured by students at the schools. A year later, the government convened a Royal Commission on Aboriginal Peoples. Many people told the commission about their residential school experiences, and its 1996 report recommended a separate public inquiry into residential schools. That recommendation was never followed.

Over the years, the government worked with the Anglican, Catholic, United, and Presbyterian churches, which ran residential schools, to design a plan to compensate the former students.

In 2007, two years after it was first announced, the federal government formalized a $1.9 billion compensation package for those who were forced to attend residential schools.

Under the Federal Compensation Package, What Will Former Students Receive?

Compensation, called Common Experience Payments, was made available to all residential schools students who were alive as of May 30, 2005. Former residential school students were eligible for $10,000 for the first year or part of a year they attended school, plus $3,000 for each subsequent year. Any money remaining from the $1.9 billion package will be given to foundations that support the learning needs of Aboriginal students. As of April 15, 2010, $1.55 billion had been paid, representing 75,800 cases.

Acceptance of the Common Experience Payment releases the government and churches from all further liability relating to the residential school experience, except in cases of sexual abuse and serious incidents of physical abuse.

The settlement also promised a Truth and Reconciliation Commission to examine the legacy of the residential schools. The commission was established on June 1, 2008. Prime Minister Stephen Harper delivered an official apology to residential school students in Parliament on June 11, 2008.

Sources: Excerpted from CBC News, "A History of Residential Schools in Canada," (May 16, 2008 updated June 14, 2010), retrieved from http://www.cbc.ca/news/canada/story/2008/05/16/f-faqs-residential-schools.html; Truth and Reconciliation Commission of Canada, "Residential Schools of Canada Map."

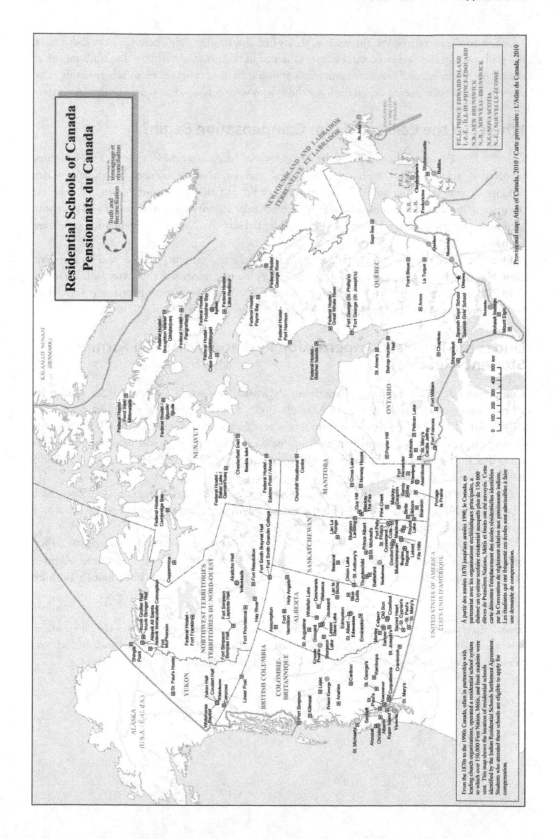

Alberta

Residential Schools / Pensionnats	Location / Emplacement	Church / Église
Assumption (Hay Lakes)	Assumption	C
Blue Quills (Saddle Lake, Sacred Heart, Lac la Biche)	Lac la Biche, 1891-98; Saddle Lake, 1898-1931; St. Paul, 1931	C
Crowfoot (Blackfoot, St. Joseph's, St. Trinité)	Cluny	C
Desmarais (St. Martins, Wabiscaw Lake, Wabasca)	Desmarais-Wabasca	C
Edmonton (Red Deer Industrial, St. Albert)	St. Albert	U
Ermineskin	Hobbema	C
Fort Vermilion (St. Henry's)	Fort Vermilion	C
Grouard (St. Bernard's, Lesser Slave Lake Roman Catholic)	Grouard	C
Holy Angels (Fort Chipewyan, École des Saints-Anges)	Fort Chipewyan	C
Joussard (St. Bruno's)	Joussard	C
Lac la Biche (Notre Dame des Victoires, Blue Quills)	Lac La Biche	C
Lesser Slave Lake (St. Peter's)	Lesser Slave Lake	A
Morley (Stony/Stoney)	Morley	U
Old Sun (Blackfoot)	Gleichen	A
Sacred Heart (Peigan, Brocket)	Brocket	C
St. Albert (Youville)	Youville	C
St. Augustine (Smoky River)	Peace River	C
St. Cyprian's (Victoria Home, Peigan)	Brocket	A
St. Joseph's (High River, Dunbow)	High River	C
St. Mary's (Blood, Immaculate Conception)	Cardston	C
St. Paul's (Blood)	Cardston	A
Sarcee (St. Barnabas)	Sarcee Junction, Tsuu T'ina	A

British Columbia / Colombie-Britannique

Residential Schools / Pensionnats	Location / Emplacement	Church / Église
Ahousat	Ahousat	U
Alberni	Port Alberni	U
Anahim (Anahim Lake)	Anahim Lake	N
Cariboo (St. Joseph's, William's Lake)	Williams Lake	C
Christie (Clayoquot, Kakawis)	Tofino	C
Coqualeetza	Chilliwack	U
Cranbrook (St. Eugene's, Kootenay)	Cranbrook	C
Kamloops	Kamloops	C
Kitimaat	Kitimaat	U
Kuper Island	Kuper Island	C
Lejac (Fraser Lake)	Fraser Lake	C
Lower Post	Lower Post	C
Port Simpson (Crosby Home for Girls)	Port Simpson	A
St. George's (Lytton)	Lytton	A
St. Mary's (Mission)	Mission	C
St. Michael's (Alert Bay Girls' Home, Alert Bay Boys' Home)	Alert Bay	A
St. Paul's (Squamish, North Vancouver)	North Vancouver	C
Sechelt	Sechelt	C

Manitoba

Residential Schools / Pensionnats	Location / Emplacement	Church / Église
Assiniboia (Winnipeg)	Winnipeg	C
Birtle	Birtle	P
Brandon	Brandon	U/C
Churchill Vocational Centre	Churchill	N
Cross Lake (St. Joseph's, Norway House, Jack River, Annex, Notre Dame Hostel)	Cross Lake	C
Elkhorn (Washakada)	Elkhorn	A
Fort Alexander (Pine Falls)	Pine Falls	C

Manitoba (continued / suite)

Residential Schools / Pensionnats	Location / Emplacement	Church / Église
Guy Hill (Clearwater, The Pas, Sturgeon Landing (SK))	Clearwater Lake	C
Mackay – Dauphin	Dauphin	A
Mackay – The Pas	The Pas	A
Norway House	Norway House	U
Pine Creek (Camperville)	Camperville	C
Portage la Prairie	Portage la Prairie	U
Sandy Bay	Sandy Bay Reserve	C

Northwest Territories / Territoires du Nord-Ouest

Residential Schools / Pensionnats	Location / Emplacement	Church / Église
Akaitcho Hall (Yellowknife)	Yellowknife	N
Aklavik - Immaculate Conception	Aklavik	C
Aklavik (All Saints)	Aklavik	A
Federal Hostel - Fort Franklin	Déline	N
Fort McPherson (Fleming Hall)	Fort McPherson	A
Fort Providence (Sacred Heart)	Fort Providence	C
Fort Resolution (St. Joseph's)	Fort Resolution	C
Fort Simpson - Bompas Hall (Koe Go Cho)	Fort Simpson	A
Fort Simpson - Lapointe Hall (Deh Cho Hall, Koe Go Cho)	Fort Simpson	C
Fort Smith - Breynat Hall	Fort Smith	C
Fort Smith - Grandin College	Fort Smith	C
Hay River (St. Peter's)	Hay River	A
Inuvik - Grollier Hall	Inuvik	C
Inuvik - Stringer Hall	Inuvik	A

Nova Scotia / Nouvelle-Écosse

Residential Schools / Pensionnats	Location / Emplacement	Church / Église
Shubenacadie	Shubenacadie	C

Nunavut

Residential Schools / Pensionnats	Location / Emplacement	Church / Église
Chesterfield Inlet (Joseph Bernier, Turquell Hall)	Chesterfield Inlet	C
Coppermine (Tent Hostel)	Coppermine	A
Federal Hostel - Baker Lake/Qamani'tuaq	Qamani'tuaq	N
Federal Hostel - Belcher Islands	South Camp, Flaherty Island	N

Ontario

Residential Schools / Pensionnats	Location / Emplacement	Church / Église
Bishop Horden Hall (Moose Fort, Moose Factory)	Moose Factory Island	A
Cecilia Jeffrey (Kenora, Shoal Lake)	Kenora	P
Chapleau (St. Joseph's, St. John's)	Chapleau	A
Fort Frances (St. Margaret's)	Fort Frances	C
Fort William (St. Joseph's)	Fort William	C
McIntosh (Kenora)	McIntosh	C
Mohawk Institute	Brantford	A
Mount Elgin (Muncey, St. Thomas)	Muncey	U
Pelican Lake (Pelican Falls)	Sioux Lookout	A
Poplar Hill	Poplar Hill	M
St. Anne's (Fort Albany)	Fort Albany	C
St. Mary's (Kenora, St. Anthony's)	Kenora	C
Shingwauk	Sault Ste. Marie	A
Spanish Boys' School (Charles Garnier, St. Joseph's, Wikwemikong Industrial)	Spanish	C
Spanish Girls' School (St. Joseph's, St. Peter's, St. Anne's, Wikwemikong Industrial)	Spanish	C

Québec

Residential Schools / Pensionnats	Location / Emplacement	Church / Église
Amos (St. Marc-de-Figuery)	Amos	C
Fort George (St. Philip's)	Fort George	A
Fort George (St. Joseph's Mission, Residence Couture, Sainte-Thérèse-de-l'Enfant-Jésus)	Fort George	C
Federal Hostel - George River	Kangirsualujjuaq	N
Federal Hostel - Great Whale River (Poste-de-la-Baleine, Kuujjuarapik)	Kuujjuaraapik	N
Federal Hostel - Payne Bay (Bellin)	Kangirsuk	N
Federal Hostel - Port Harrison (Inoucdjouac, Innuucdouac)	Inukjuak	C
La Tuque	La Tuque	A
Point Bleue	Pointe-Bleue	C
Sept-Îles (Seven Islands, Notre Dame, Maliotenam)	Sept-Îles	C

Saskatchewan

Residential Schools / Pensionnats	Location / Emplacement	Church / Église
Battleford	Battleford	A
Beauval (Lac la Plonge)	Beauval	C
Cote Improved Federal Day School	Kamsack	U
Crowstand	Kamsack	P
File Hills	Balcarres	U
Fort Pelly	Fort Pelly	C
Gordon	Punnichy	A
Lac La Ronge (see/voir Prince Albert)	Lac La Ronge	A
Lebret (Qu'Appelle, Whitecalf, St. Paul's High School)	Lebret	C
Marieval (Cowessess, Crooked Lake)	Grayson	C
Muscowequan (Lestock, Touchwood)	Lestock	C
Onion Lake (see/voir Prince Albert)	Onion Lake	A
Prince Albert (Onion Lake, St. Alban's, All Saints, S. Barnabas, Lac La Ronge)	Prince Albert	A
Regina	Regina	P
Round Lake	Broadview	U
St. Anthony's (Onion Lake, Sacred Heart)	Onion Lake	C
St. Michael's (Duck Lake)	Duck Lake	C
St. Philip's	Kamsack	C
Sturgeon Landing (Guy Hill, Manitoba)	Sturgeon Landing	C
Thunderchild (Delmas, St. Henri)	Delmas	C

Yukon

Residential Schools / Pensionnats	Location / Emplacement	Church / Église
Carcross (Chooutla)	Carcross	A
Coudert Hall (Whitehorse Hostel/Student Residence, Yukon Hall)	Whitehorse	C
St. Paul's Hostel (Dawson City)	Dawson	A
Shingle Point (St. John's)	Shingle Point	A
Whitehorse Baptist (Lee Mission)	Whitehorse	B
Yukon Hall (Whitehorse/Protestant Hostel)	Whitehorse	N

Church / Église

A = Anglican / Anglicane
B = Baptist / Baptiste
C = Catholic / Catholique
M = Mennonite / Mennonite
N = Non-denominational / Non-confessionnelle
P = Presbyterian / Presbytérienne
U = United / Unie

3c Aboriginal Women: Agency, Creativity, and Strength

Chapter 31

The Cattle Thief

Pauline E. Johnson

Pauline E. Johnson (Tekahionwake) was a popular late 19th-century Canadian writer, poet, and performer. The daughter of a Mohawk father and an English mother, her poems and performances before largely Euro-Canadian audiences highlighted the intersection of her two heritages. Feminist and Indigenous scholars have recently reconsidered Johnson's writings and performance career, re-evaluating her as a complex and contradictory figure who engaged with and resisted dominant ideas about race, gender, Aboriginal rights, and Canada.

THEY were coming across the prairie, they were galloping hard and fast;
For the eyes of those desperate riders had sighted their man at last—
Sighted him off to Eastward, where the Cree encampment lay,
Where the cotton woods fringed the river, miles and miles away.
Mistake him? Never! Mistake him? the famous Eagle Chief!
That terror to all the settlers, that desperate Cattle Thief—
That monstrous, fearless Indian, who lorded it over the plain,
Who thieved and raided, and scouted, who rode like a hurricane!
But they've tracked him across the prairie; they've followed him hard and fast;
For those desperate English settlers have sighted their man at last.

Up they wheeled to the tepees, all their British blood aflame,
Bent on bullets and bloodshed, bent on bringing down their game;
But they searched in vain for the Cattle Thief: that lion had left his lair,
And they cursed like a troop of demons—for the women alone were there.
"The sneaking Indian coward," they hissed; "he hides while yet he can;
He'll come in the night for cattle, but he's scared to face a *man*."
"Never!" and up from the cotton woods rang the voice of Eagle Chief;
And right out into the open stepped, unarmed, the Cattle Thief.
Was that the game they had coveted? Scarce fifty years had rolled
Over that fleshless, hungry frame, starved to the bone and old;
Over that wrinkled, tawny skin, unfed by the warmth of blood.
Over those hungry, hollow eyes that glared for the sight of food.

He turned, like a hunted lion: "I know not fear," said he;
And the words outleapt from his shrunken lips in the language of the Cree.
"I'll fight you, white-skins, one by one, till I kill you *all*," he said;
But the threat was scarcely uttered, ere a dozen balls of lead
Whizzed through the air about him like a shower of metal rain,
And the gaunt old Indian Cattle Thief dropped dead on the open plain.
And that band of cursing settlers gave one triumphant yell,
And rushed like a pack of demons on the body that writhed and fell.
"Cut the fiend up into inches, throw his carcass on the plain;
Let the wolves eat the cursed Indian, he'd have treated us the same."
A dozen hands responded, a dozen knives gleamed high,
But the first stroke was arrested by a woman's strange, wild cry.
And out into the open, with a courage past belief,
She dashed, and spread her blanket o'er the corpse of the Cattle Thief;
And the words outleapt from her shrunken lips in the language of the Cree,
"If you mean to touch that body, you must cut your way through *me*."
And that band of cursing settlers dropped backward one by one,
For they knew that an Indian woman roused, was a woman to let alone.
And then she raved in a frenzy that they scarcely understood,
Raved of the wrongs she had suffered since her earliest babyhood:
"Stand back, stand back, you white-skins, touch that dead man to your shame;
You have stolen my father's spirit, but his body I only claim.
You have killed him, but you shall not dare to touch him now he's dead.
You have cursed, and called him a Cattle Thief, though you robbed him first
      of bread—
Robbed him and robbed my people—look there, at that shrunken face,
Starved with a hollow hunger, we owe to you and your race.
What have you left to us of land, what have you left of game,
What have you brought but evil, and curses since you came?
How have you paid us for our game? how paid us for our land?
By a *book*, to save our souls from the sins *you* brought in your other hand.
Go back with your new religion, we never have understood
Your robbing an Indian's *body*, and mocking his *soul* with food.
Go back with your new religion, and find—if find you can—
The *honest* man you have ever made from out a *starving* man.
You say your cattle are not ours, your meat is not our meat;
When *you* pay for the land you live in, *we'll* pay for the meat we eat.
Give back our land and our country, give back our herds of game;
Give back the furs and the forests that were ours before you came;
Give back the peace and the plenty. Then come with your new belief,
And blame, if you dare, the hunger that *drove* him to be a thief."

Chapter 32

I Am Not Your Princess

Chrystos

Chrystos (Menominee) is an Aboriginal poet, artist, and activist. She writes on a range of themes, from extremely personal poems that deal with difficult family relations, love, and lust, to political pieces that speak out against the forced invisibility of Aboriginal peoples. Her work has been published in numerous anthologies such as This Bridge Called My Back: Writings by Radical Women of Color *and* Living the Spirit: A Gay American Indian Anthology.

Preface

Because there are so many myths & misconceptions about Native people, it is important to clarify myself to the reader who does not know me. I was not born on the reservation, but in San Francisco, part of a group called "Urban Indians" by the government. I grew up around Black, Latin, Asian & white people & am shaped by that experience, as well as by what my father taught me. He had been taught to be ashamed & has never spoken our language to me. Much of the fury which erupts from my work is a result of seeing the pain that white culture has caused my father. It continues to give pain to all of us. I am not the "Voice" of Native women, nor representative of Native women in general. I am not a "Spiritual Leader," although many white women have tried to push me into that role. While I am deeply spiritual, to share this with strangers would be a violation. Our rituals, stories & religious practices have been stolen & abused, as has our land. I don't publish work which would encourage this—so you will find no creation myths here. My purpose is to make it as clear & as inescapable as possible, what the actual, material conditions of our lives are. Hunger, infant mortality, forced sterilization, treaty violations, the plague of alcohol & drugs, ridiculous jail terms, denial of civil rights, radiation poisoning, land theft, endless contrived legal battles which drain our wills, corrupt "tribal" governments, harassment & death at the hands of the BIA & FBI are the realities we face. Don't admire what you perceive as our stoicism or spirituality—work for our lives to continue in our own Ways. Despite the books which still appear, even in radical bookstores, we are not Vanishing Americans.

I Am Not Your Princess

Sandpaper between two cultures which tear
one another apart I'm not
a means by which you can reach spiritual understanding or even
learn to do beadwork

I'm only willing to tell you how to make fry bread
1 cup flour, spoon of salt, spoon of baking powder
Stir   Add milk or water or beer until it holds together
Slap each piece into rounds   Let rest
Fry in hot grease until golden
This is Indian food
only if you know that Indian is a government word
which has nothing to do with our names for ourselves
I won't chant for you
I admit no spirituality to you
I will not sweat with you or ease your guilt with fine turtle tales
I will not wear dancing clothes to read poetry or
explain hardly anything at all
I don't think your attempts to understand us are going to work so
I'd rather you left us in whatever peace we can still
scramble up   after all you continue to do
If you send me one more damn flyer about how to heal myself
for $300 with special feminist counseling
I'll probably set fire to something
If you tell me one more time that I'm wise I'll throw up on you
Look at me
See my confusion   loneliness   fear   worrying about all our
struggles to keep   what little is left for us
Look at my heart   not your fantasies   Please don't ever
again tell me about your Cherokee great-great grandmother
Don't assume I know every other Native Activist
in the world personally   That I even know names of all the tribes
or can pronounce names I've never heard
or that I'm expert at the peyote stitch
If   you ever
again tell me
how strong I am
I'll lay down on the ground & moan so you'll see
at last   my human weakness   like your own
I'm not strong   I'm scraped
I'm blessed with life while so many I've known are dead
I have work to do   dishes to wash   a house to clean
There is no magic
See my simple cracked hands which have washed the same things
you wash   See my eyes dark with fear in a house by myself
late at night   See that to pity me or to adore me
are the same
1 cup flour, spoon or salt, spoon of baking powder, liquid to hold
Remember this is only my recipe   There are many others
Let me rest
here
at least

Chapter 33

"You Can't Change the Indian Act?"

Shirley Bear with the Tobique Women's Group

Shirley Bear (Maliseet) is a multimedia artist, writer, activist, and First Nation herbalist and Elder. Born on the Tobique First Nation in New Brunswick, she has been a long-time advocate for the rights of Indigenous women, and she has played a crucial role in promoting Aboriginal arts and artists in Canada. She has served as cultural adviser at the British Columbia Institute of Technology, education adviser at the Emily Carr Institute of Art and Design, and as resident Elder for the First Nations House of Learning at the University of British Columbia. Shirley Bear is the recipient of the New Brunswick Arts Board's Excellence in the Arts Award, and she was recently named to the Order of Canada.

In Canada, the Indian Act is federal legislation that governs the day-to-day lives of more than 350,000 Aboriginal peoples of whom there are approximately 200,000 residing on "Indian reserves." The Indian Act, legislated in 1869, explicitly defines Canada's original inhabitants, not by blood or familial association, but by marriage. Until 1985, "Indian status" was determined by a patrilineal system; that is, by a person's relationship to "a male person who is a direct descendant in the male line of a male person...." When a woman born of "Indian status" married a non-status man, even a non-status Native or Métis man, she lost her original status and was never able to regain it even if she was divorced or widowed. Along with losing her status, a woman lost her band membership, her property, inheritance, burial, medical, educational, and voting rights on the reserve. However, when a non-status female married a status male, "Indian status" was conferred upon her.

A section of the offending pre-1985 Indian Act reads:

> Persons not entitled to be registered
> 12 (1) The following persons are not entitled to be registered, namely:
> (b) a woman who married a person who is not an Indian, unless that woman is subsequently the wife or widow of a person described in section 11.

In June 1985, the Canadian Parliament passed C-31, ending more than 100 years of legislated sexual discrimination against Native Indian women. The passage of legislation to amend the Indian Act marked the culmination of a long campaign by Native women to regain their full Indian status, rights, and identity. This chapter is the story of an extraordinary group of women from Tobique Reserve in New Brunswick who have been in the forefront of that struggle.

These women are uniquely diverse ideologically, psychologically, and functionally. This is a fairly small group of individuals who came together through their awareness of the injustices toward women (in particular, Aboriginal women) in Canada. *Enough Is Enough: Aboriginal Women Speak out* (1987), compiled and introduced by Janet Silman of Winnipeg, chronicles via a series of personal interviews the events that led up to the now controversial Bill C-31.

My involvement with the Tobique Women's Group started with my activities on the Big Cove Reserve involving the unjust treatment of single mothers and housing. In late 1980, members of the Tobique Women's Group invited me to participate in a meeting of Aboriginal women interested in establishing a political body that would represent the Aboriginal women of New Brunswick. A provincial conference at Fredericton created a reorganized Native Women's Council, which remained a daughter organization of the National Native Indian Women's Association of Canada. The women, whose stories are told in *Enough Is Enough*, grew up on the Tobique Reserve, a community located between the St. John and Tobique rivers in New Brunswick. The community is better known to its residents as Negoot Gook.

In this chapter I wish to share with the reader my perceptions of who we are and how we developed into "political activists" as we were later known. This will be done in conjunction with excerpts from *Enough Is Enough: Aboriginal Women Speak Out*.

Activism, social or political, starts when one understands that her deprivation of power stems from an injustice toward her. This growing awareness may take many years to develop, as it did for a small group of women from the Tobique Indian Reserve (Negoot Gook).

Early Recollections

Ida Paul is the eldest of the women featured in *Enough Is Enough*. Her earliest memories recount:

> My father was working in the woods where the men would be gone for two or three months in the winter trapping for furs. When my mother died, they couldn't reach him, and when he got back she was already buried. I was four and my sister Lilly was two. Later my father came back and gave me away to an Indian man and his French wife in Edmundston and Lilly went to a family in Old Town, Maine. We couldn't go to school in the winter time—no shoes. When I was fourteen my grandmother said to me, "Now that you are fourteen, you have to go out and earn your own living." I'd go from one place to another, staying with different people—for a while here, for a while there. I stayed with Madeline for a time, but her husband would say, "I've got kids of my own to feed. I can't afford to keep you." He went down to McPhail's store (McPhail was the Indian agent and owned the store) and asked him for some money for my keep, but McPhail refused, saying, "No, she's got a father. He has to look after her." I met Frank about that time and married him when I was seventeen.

Lilly Harris, Ida Paul's sister, also remembers the hard times as a child without a home. Lilly, unlike her sister, became actively political with the women of the Tobique. Lilly recalls:

> My mother died when I was two so I stayed with my grandmother and shifted around, sometimes with my older sisters. I went to school till about the fourth grade, but couldn't go to school in winter time—no shoes. One day my girl friend's father left the mother and the children. The mother got some help from the Indian agent, so that my little friend got a pair of rubber boots. She told me to go down and ask the Indian agent. She said, "He gave me a pair so I can go to school. You go down and ask him."

I went down early in the morning and sat there. I sat there all day while he was seeing everybody else. I asked him, "I can't go to school. I need a pair of rubbers," and he said, "You've got a father. Let him buy you shoes." So after all that the Indian agent wouldn't give me no shoes. When I was fourteen I left. It was especially hard for orphaned children and for women who didn't have husbands.

Eva (Gookum) Saulis—Gookum, meaning aunt, is the name she's known by in the whole community—grew up in what she calls good old times. Gookum's mother and father had a small farm on the Tobique Reserve. Gookum recalls:

I had nine brothers in all; I was the only girl. The old times were good for my mother, good for us too. By the time I was born, everybody was Roman Catholic. There must have been Indian celebration days and stories, of course, but the priests were so against anything traditional, I think they tried to break all those traditions. When people say, "The missionaries christianized the Indians," that means that they tried to take their language, their traditions, their legends, everything. When the missionaries came they told us to bow our heads and pray. When we looked up, our land was gone.

Mavis Goeres grew up on the Tobique Reserve in the 1930s and 1940s and she remembers:

At a very early age my brother quit school and went out working in the woods with my father. They'd be gone all winter long. I don't remember our family ever having a hard time. We had a lot of fun growing up here. We made our own fun and there wasn't any drinking or drugs involved. When I was fifteen years old, I went away to pick potatoes. I was in the eleventh grade and I met a man and got married.

Juanita Perley was the first woman to actively challenge the Reserve administration by taking over a public building. Juanita recalls some early memories and impressions:

The reserve was a really beautiful place to live, for children growing up especially. When people went shopping, they never got money to buy the groceries; the Indian agent would write up a purchase order at his own store—McPhail's store. They'd be making fun of the Indian people that came in—they called us "gimmes"—like "gimme this," "gimme that." I always resented the way the white people treated us and even today resent it—I don't like them one bit, and I don't care if that is printed in the book either!

Glenna Perley is considered by the Tobique Women's Group to be their strength and sustaining courage and is also very respected within the larger community. Her mother died when she was quite young and she recalls living with her grandmother:

When I was living with my grandmother, she would talk to me a lot about religion—but, even though she was a good Catholic, it was her Indian religion she would talk about. Without the ways my grandmother taught me, maybe I would have turned to drinking, but I know I'm strong and that's why, I guess.

Caroline Ennis has devoted a large portion of her time since 1977 to right the unjust attitudes and practices toward women, in particular toward Aboriginal women in Canada. When Glenna asked her to arrange media coverage of the first housing protest on the Tobique Reserve, Caroline's first recollections are about injustices toward her mother:

> I don't remember much about my father but I know my mother left him because he used to drink and beat her up. Tobique was a nice place for kids to grow up in. You made your own fun. I didn't feel poor because everybody else around here was poor too.

In 1977, Sandra Lovelace-Sappier, as a woman who had lost her Indian status through the discriminatory clause, 12 (1)(b), of the Indian Act, agreed to take her case to the United Nations Human Rights Committee. Of her early life Sandra remembers:

> We were really poor because my mom brought us four girls up by herself. At first we went to school on the reserve. The nuns taught us and we couldn't talk Indian. They used to tell us we were dirty. They made us ashamed we were Indians. After grade six we went to school down town and there was a lot of "Go back where you came from." The white kids would make fun of us, put us down because we were Indians, so I quit school about grade eight. I figured if this is what the world is like, I don't want to be around white people. I left home at about seventeen, went with a bunch of girls to work at a potato factory in Maine.

Karen Perley, Sandra's sister, is a committed person in community activities. Karen recalls:

> I grew up without my father being around. In this little school on the reserve, the nuns used to show preference to the light-skinned kids. I was really religious and I used to pray every morning, every night and sometimes in the afternoon. I would pray that I would wake up the next morning and have blue eyes. In 1966, when Carl and I left for California, I was fifteen.

A child of the sixties, during the "hippie" movement, Bet-te Paul is a single mother of two, by choice. Her commitment to the Aboriginal peoples is definitely radical by any standards. She doesn't recall much about her early life on the reserve.

Joyce (YC) Sappier, Bet-te's mother, grew up with her grandmother and was one of the original occupiers of the public buildings at the Tobique Reserve in 1977.

Cheryl Bear is the youngest member of the Tobique Women's Group, but a seasoned woman activist. Cheryl has a strong sense of her rights as a person. She has lived through very difficult relationships. She says of her early life:

> I enjoyed growing up on the reserve—I had a good childhood. I was raised by my grandparents. I was spoiled, I guess, to put it bluntly. I quit school in grade eight. I regret quitting school almost every day now—got married when I was fifteen.

My early memories on the Tobique Reserve include the freedom of movement we had. Children spent much time in creative play without the worries of physical harm. Being a typically dark-skinned person, I also recall the different treatment I received from our grade school teachers, the nuns. Growing up, we all knew that we were different from the time we started school. Some of us were painfully aware that the difference was also something to be ashamed of. We didn't realize that this was in violation of our rights, or that it was wrong for the religious who were our teachers to exercise these types of practices and attitudes. We didn't know what it was called; we just knew that it didn't feel good.

The women grew up experiencing different levels of consciousness, but each one was starting to internalize and intellectualize the various forms of injustices that they were either experiencing or living. From as early as 1950, some women were returning to their original home communities only to realize for the first time that they did not belong. We may have been told previously that we were no longer Indian, but that had no impact on us until our return. I returned in 1960 after a marriage breakup and my father said that they could not afford to feed me and my two children because we were not Indian or even belonged in Tobique. Because there was no employment on the reserve, we were forced to move out.

The Law Is the Law

The attitudes at the time that the Tobique Women's Group came together in the early 1970s reflected the subordination of the Aboriginal peoples. The law was the law, i.e., the Indian Act was considered to be the final arbiter of all matters among Aboriginal peoples, and between Aboriginal peoples and government bureaucracy. One exception to this attitude has always been the Six Nations Confederacy, consisting of the Oneida, Tuscarora, Mohawk, Seneca, Cayuga, and Onondaga. They always knew they were sovereign and this has been reflected in their treatment of Six Nations women.

The activism of the Tobique Women's Group was preceded by the actions of other Aboriginal women. Mary Two Axe Early was the first Aboriginal woman to speak out publicly against the section of the Indian Act that stripped women of their rights if they married non-status men. In the 1950s, after marrying a non-status man, she moved back to the Mohawk Reserve in Quebec that had been her birthplace. She was not refused the right to reside in the community of her birth, since, in accordance with Mohawk culture, the community has always been matrilineal. However, Section 12 (1)(b) did prevent her from having access to financial support; it would also have prevented her from being buried in the community of her birth. In the seventies, other Native women began to organize across Canada, with the offending section of the Indian Act being one of the major issues they raised. In 1973 the Supreme Court of Canada heard the cases of Jeanette Lavell and Yvonne Bedard against Section 12 (1)(b). In a five-to-four decision, the court ruled that the Indian Act was *exempt* from the Canadian Bill of Rights.

Organizations such as the National Indian Brotherhood (formed in the 1950s to represent status Indians, socially and politically) mounted a lobbying campaign against Lavall and Bedard. Their argument was that it was necessary for the Indian Act to be kept intact for use as a bargaining lever with the federal government and that any tampering—such as amending Section 12 (1) (b)—would play into the government's 1969 White Paper plan of doing away with special Indian status and assimilating Indians into the mainstream of Canada. It was against this historical background that the women of Tobique began their activism.

An Issue of Housing

In 1976, Juanita Perley's husband threw her and their 10 children out of their home and won the legal argument that she had no right to their house. The house was in his name only and only he had any legal right to it. But Juanita, a woman of petite stature, was not going to put up with any nonsense and, more importantly, was not going to see her family be broken up like this and forced to live in the streets. So she occupied a public building. Juanita recounts:

> It was Labour Day weekend when we first got thrown out. When I moved all of the kids up to the band office the RCMP showed up. It was the first time here that anyone had occupied a public building. The police said that I was going to be arrested for breaking and entering. He said, "I'm going to charge you with B and E." I replied, "What's that, bacon and eggs?"

When Cheryl Bear's marriage broke down, she was in need of housing so she moved into the next available house and found that it had been destined for someone else—but she remained strong and stayed. Cheryl's grandfather was encouraging and gave her the spiritual strength needed to maintain her decision.

In 1977, Glenna Perley and Gookum Saulis would no longer put up with housing conditions and the unjust treatment toward women and children in Negoot Gook. They organized women to protest against inadequate housing by occupying the Tobique (Negoot Gook) band office. What started out to be an issue of poor housing for women was soon usurped by the media to be an issue of status. One headline in the *Telegraph-Journal* in 1977 read "Women Occupy Band Office—Want Indian Act Changes."

The women in the book identify in their stories where the change began to take place from the Tobique women's original concerns about housing to the media emphasis on the status issue.

Caroline Ennis: "It was status women who were having trouble with housing. When I got involved in the demonstrations and lobbying, it wasn't for the non-status thing; it was purely a women's thing."

Juanita Perley: "This business about women getting kicked out of their homes, it goes way back."

Cheryl Bear: "See, the woman was supposed to move out with the kids, and it was the man's house."

Karen recalls her mother's situation: "My mother had tried to get some help with the house. She said, 'The men are getting helped more than the women are.'"

The women who had lost their status were moving back to the Tobique Reserve after marriage breakups or becoming widowed, and were experiencing difficulties finding housing for themselves and their children. Four of the women tell about their feelings and sudden awareness of their non-status positions:

Lilly Harris: "When we were growing up, nobody talked about status and non-status. When I married I lost my status, but I didn't know it at the time. I didn't find out until I moved back in the mid-1970s."

Mavis Goeres: "I find out that white women are Indians now, but I'm not! Here, when I came back, men could kick their wife and children out because the Indian Act made the man sole owner of the house."

Joyce Sappier: "No, I never knew I'd lost it because I didn't sell my rights."

Sandra Lovelace-Sappier: "I had gone to the band office before and asked for a house for myself and my child. I'd had to pitch a tent because I couldn't find a place to stay. They'd told me I had no rights, that I was non-status. That was when Dan and Caroline Ennis approached me about taking my case to the United Nations."

The Occupation of the Band Office

In late August women from the Tobique Reserve demonstrated in front of the band office over housing. A demonstration was also staged in front of the Indian Affairs office in Fredericton, NB. At the end of August women of the Tobique began to occupy the band office.

There were frightening instances of verbal and physical harassment toward the women who were protesting, and their children. Some members of the Tobique Reserve took the women's action as a personal affront against them and their chief and his supporters; this resulted in a counterattack. In early September the women were served with an injunction from the chief and council ordering them out of the band office, but they disregarded it. In mid-September the band administration moved all of their equipment and files out of the band office, but the women remained. An election was called on October 3, 1977, and a new chief was declared who supported the women's issue. (Unfortunately, he was pressured to resign within a year.) On October 4, 1977, fire was set to the band office. Fortunately, no one was hurt and the women started to move out gradually, although there had been no adequate resolution to the question of adequate housing. The women recall experiences related to the occupation:

Bet-te: "We didn't really move in; we were just going to sit there until we got a meeting with the chief and council. That's actually how the occupation got started."

Glenna: "Really, we went in mainly to try and talk to the chief."

Karen: "The chief treated us like we were invisible, like he couldn't see us. A lot of reserve residents cooked meals and sent them over."

Glenna: "Then they wanted to put us in jail."

Caroline: "The situation got more volatile as the occupation continued."

Bet-te: "We were, 'the shit disturbers, radicals, whitewashed, women's lib' … we were just women who needed decent homes."

Joyce: "I got evicted because I believed so strongly in what the women were fighting for."

Bet-te: "That's around the time the violence really started. The occupation wasn't only hard on us; it was hard on the other reserve residents, too. When it really got bad, we had guns in the band office."

Glenna: "In interviews (during the occupation), that's when I realized non-status was the main problem I was talking about."

The women discussed the actual violence that they and their children experienced during the three-month occupation. All the while they sought help from other political organizations and received very little response from the Native Indian groups or from the Department of Indian Affairs. The main help came from some reserve residents, namely the elders, and non-Indian women's groups.

On December 29, 1977, Sandra Lovelace (Sappier) filed a complaint against Canada with the United Nations Human Rights Committee in Geneva, Switzerland. For the next four years the main focus was on the discriminatory clause, Section 12 (1)(b), of the Indian Act, which dictates a Native woman's loss of Indian status should she marry a non-status man. And, in 1981, the United Nations Human Rights Committee found Canada in breach of the International Covenant on Civil and Political Rights over sexual discrimination.

The 100-Mile Walk

In the meantime, the women never let up on the lobbying momentum. The housing problem did not lessen because the band administration had gone through more changes, only to find itself with the same leadership that had precipitated the original band office occupations. But by now the women were aware of the power of the political lobby outside of their own community.

In July 1979, the women who had occupied the Tobique band office saw that the situation was not getting any better, so they decided to organize a 100-mile walk from Oka, Quebec (outskirts of Montreal), to Ottawa. This walk by women and children attracted national attention. Native peoples from British Columbia, the Yukon, Northwest Territories, Ontario, and Quebec joined the 100-mile march. During the walk, the participants became more vocal about the non-status issue. Sandra Lovelace, who participated in the walk, gave a number of interviews to the press, and the issue of the discriminatory Indian Act Clause 12 (1)(b) received cross-country coverage to the exclusion of the many other concerns of the walkers. The issues that had inspired the walk were not restricted to the sexual discrimination of 12 (1)(b), but included living conditions on the reserves, housing, and distribution of resources. The walk received so much attention that government officials had to take notice and start addressing the issues that the women were talking about. The number of walkers grew from 50 to more than 200 by the time they reached Parliament Hill in Ottawa. Publicity from the walk precipitated a meeting with Prime Minister Joe Clark, his wife Maureen McTeer, and a number of Cabinet ministers. The women were assured that the government would be making moves to change the Indian Act. Some of the women described their feelings as they made the historic 100-mile walk to Ottawa:

Caroline: "We wanted to raise public consciousness about Native women's problems, and mainly the walk was over housing. I know the RCMP kept an eye on us during the walk, too, ... but really, what threat could we be to the country anyway?"

Sandra: "When we started out on the walk, getting on the bus here on the reserve, you should have seen the men. They were standing outside laughing at us, saying, 'You fools, what are you going to accomplish?'"

Lilly: "Oh, it was hot, but most people walked all of the way. I was 62 when we made the walk. I think I was the oldest walker."

Caroline: "I'll never forget that hectic first morning at breakfast. We filled the whole restaurant. We had thought we could stay overnight at the Catholic school or some kind of retreat house where they had all kinds of room, but the priest wouldn't let us. We got denied help from the Catholic priests along the route."

Glenna: "When we passed this one reserve, people had sandwiches for us. They knew we would be walking by there around noon hour, so all these women got together and had lunches out along the road. I'll never forget that."

Karen: "We had meetings and meetings. Walking during the day and meetings at night. We'd have meetings to decide whether we should have a meeting."

Caroline: "We got more and more media coverage as we went along."

Karen: "We told people a lot about housing, of course. Then reporters started asking Sandra about 12 (1)(b) and sexual discrimination in the Indian Act."

Sandra: "It all happened on the walk."

Karen: "The last day of the walk before arriving in Ottawa, the women from the NIB (National Indian Brotherhood) offices came and joined us. They were all in their high heels, fancy clothes, the kind of fancy tee-shirts the NIB used to give out, nail polish on their fingers. And here we were, grubby and sweaty."

Sandra: "We really didn't think anybody would listen to us, or that we would accomplish anything. Just getting there was emotional."

Lilly: "There was a big rally when we got to Parliament Hill, speeches, television cameras. People had hot dogs and hamburgers, cold drinks for us."

Gookum: "I looked back to see all them women come walking up. They looked so determined."

Bet-te: "I got chills seeing that."

Gookum: "I felt like crying."

Karen: "Oh jeez, it was so emotional—tears coming down our eyes, crying. I hadn't realized that we had made such an impact, but we did. I'd thought, here we are walking all this way and nobody cares, but they did!"

The positive outcomes of the walk were that $300,000 extra housing money was allotted to Tobique Reserve, and the Native Women's Association of Canada received a major increase in funding. But the women had to continue their lobbying after the walk. Unfortunately, Joe Clark's Conservative government was defeated shortly after the walk by the Liberal government of Pierre Trudeau, and no action was taken to change the Indian Act. The Tobique women believe that at no point during Trudeau's term of office did he show any interest in the plight of Native women or a willingness to consider changes in the Indian Act.

The women had continuing problems when they returned to the reserve. Only a fraction of the $300,000 allotted for housing as a result of the Walk was used for housing for single women and their children. Women in desperate need of housing were not getting it and women were still having difficulty getting the other material resources they needed to survive. In spite of efforts to directly pressure the band administration, and another brief occupation of the band office, only token gestures were made by the band council to meet women's needs.

Lobbying to Change the Indian Act

Taking the case of non-status women to the United Nations had initially been a strategy to put pressure on the Canadian government in order to make officials address the concerns Native women were raising. The Tobique women's strategy of going to the United Nations did exert tremendous pressure on the federal government to change the Indian Act.

On December 29, 1977, the complaint of Sandra Lovelace against the Canadian government was communicated to the Human Rights Committee in Geneva, Switzerland. Because of delays by the Canadian government in responding to the Human Rights Committee's request for information, the final verdict was not made until July 30, 1981. The UN Human Rights Committee ruled in Sandra Lovelace's favour, finding Canada in breach of the International Covenant because the Indian Act denied Sandra the legal right to live in the community of her birth.

The final ruling put additional pressure on the federal government to amend the Indian Act by "embarrassing" Canada—tarnishing the country's image—in the international community. Although the lobbying campaign to amend 12 (1)(b) of the Indian Act seemed on the verge of victory, four more years of concentrated lobbying actually were necessary. During those subsequent years, Tobique women became seasoned lobbyists with an issue that had become a "political football."

The women became involved in a variety of activities that allowed them to exert influence. For example, Sandra Lovelace attended the 1981 UN Convention as a Canadian delegate, where she spoke about the condition of Indian women in Canada. Caroline Ennis became a member of NAC, where her activities strengthened the support of NAC and its member women's groups for the Native women's cause.

My appointment to the New Brunswick Advisory Council on the Status of Women gave us the influence we needed on the provincial level. It also enabled us to take active participation at the five annual First Ministers' conferences on constitutional Aboriginal matters because the Province of New Brunswick was willing to assert support on sexual equality.

The Tobique Women's Group has always supported that we, as Aboriginal peoples, should hold a special status in Canada, but we did not wish to see it entrenched in the Canadian Constitution, which was repatriated in 1982 without any guarantee that it would apply equally to men and women. It is necessary for this to happen as there is already evidence of continuing discriminatory treatment toward women. It is necessary to have some judicial recourse because Indians negotiating for self-government for Indian communities are making their own membership laws. The same sexual discrimination will happen as in the case of Sandra Lovelace, where women will be denied residence in their mother's and grandmother's birthplaces.

The lobbying continued with the development of a pamphlet identifying the offending law and explaining in detail how it affected women in Indian communities for more than 100 years. This is when I became totally committed and involved. It took several political lobbying trips to Ottawa and several more conferences to inform the people of Canada that this offending law had to be eliminated.

Reinstatement

By 1985, when Canada passed legislation to eliminate sexual discrimination from the Indian Act, the women of Tobique had seen how their power was being evidenced within the community. In 1982, it was largely their efforts that finally changed the band administration, by electing a chief who understood the issue of sexual discrimination, and who had given his assurance to change similar practices within his administration. The women started seeing a better situation for themselves. When the Indian Act changes came about through Bill C-31, the Tobique Reserve was ready and they hired women who had been in the lobby to change the Indian Act to develop policies to implement the new law.

The first thing was to reinstate to band membership of the Tobique Band all the women who had lost their status through 12 (1)(b) and subsequently all the first-generation children.

There was never any fear that we could not accommodate at the Tobique Reserve the number of people being reinstated, or what it would mean in terms of the services we would have to provide. Public statements accompanying the information on Bill C-31 were explicit in their assurances that the Indian reserves would not suffer any hardships from the possible influx of reinstated band members. The impact of Bill C-31 on the Tobique Reserve does not follow the same pattern as most other Indian reserves.

By the time the government was trying to determine how much money would be allocated for services to the total population increases, the Tobique Reserve already had a large number of non-status residents who were receiving health and welfare benefits. There were also a small number of people receiving education benefits. Concerning the Tobique Reserve, the Indian Affairs department of the federal government assessed the number of people reinstated against the total required increase of funds, but the actual funding that finally came through was inadequate.

Furthermore, the increase in residency was higher than we anticipated because Tobique had an open-door policy for reinstatement. The Tobique Women's Group would never regress in their political demands and activities. We addressed the injustices and demanded retribution. The issues that we lobbied for were rectified and we celebrated.

The comic but sad situation that has developed and is causing such confusion within our communities arises from the fact that the policy developers of the Canadian government, along with the intervention of Aboriginal political representatives, produced a compromising Bill C-31. The Tobique Women's Group specifically addressed the reinstatement of the offended women and their first-generation children. We did not lobby for the war veterans who had lost their status, nor for people who, for other reasons, wanted to enter the Canadian mainstream system. Confusion developed when other lobbying groups saw the momentum we created and insisted on being heard. The resulting Bill C-31 is a weak attempt by the government to appease all factions.

The underlying currents of dissatisfaction toward Indian community leaders, because they cannot meet the demand for proper and satisfying services to every band member, are causing an unhealthy social and psychological backlash in the communities.

Some of the following problems are causing hardships:

- The federal government has not lived up to its promised financial support.
- There is an existing housing shortage.
- Indian Act policies do not allow for an economic foundation to flourish and encourage a comfortable economic growth.

- The higher standards of education demanded by residents of the reserve are not being realized as a result of cutbacks and, in some instances, denials.
- Population has increased by 33 percent resulting from reinstatements.

It's a constant day-to-day negotiation between the reserve administration officers and the Department of Indian Affairs bureaucracy just to make sure that band members on the Tobique Reserve are not hungry, cold, or uneducated. Misinterpretations of the bill are delaying real progress. Too much energy is being wasted on this process. To the Tobique Women's Group, Bill C-31 meant only the beginning of a real growth of our community.

Many of the women whom we grew up with have returned, either alone, widowed, divorced, or with their retired husbands. In some cases, their children have decided to return and make their lives at their mother's birthplace. In any case, each person who has returned has brought a new viewpoint, a new energy, and a new confidence and pride in who he or she is. The grandmothers of this community express the joy that they feel for the return of their daughters who, through no fault of their own, were treated with such disrespect under and over the Canadian law. The book *Enough Is Enough: Aboriginal Women Speak Out* is about struggles; it's about lives and the political progression of this small group of very brave women who cared—and still care—as they continue to be involved in the community.

As of this writing, two of the women—Ida Paul and Lilly Harris—have since passed away. They encouraged us with their humour, common sense, and total support through the arduous journeys to Ottawa, fundraising, and the battles with band administrations. They are fondly remembered by the group and will continue to remain in our memories through these personal accounts.

The impact of Bill C-31 is being felt throughout Canada in different ways. In 1987, the federal government issued a report on the impact of Bill C-31 that did not involve input by the First Nations. After extensive lobbying from the three national political groups—the Assembly of First Nations, the Native Indian Women's Association of Canada, and the Native Council of Canada—an inquiry was developed that established consultation between these three groups and the federal government. The first phase has been realized, and some of the points that have been identified in presentations to the inquiry are the following:

- Bill C-31 has not improved the lives of Indian people, but has simply created more problems, tensions, and splits in communities.
- DIAND registration process has caused hardship for registrants.
- Many off-reserve registrants believe that all Indians should enjoy the same rights despite their place of residence.
- Insufficient information has been provided regarding the registration process and there is a lack of consistency in processing applications.
- Many registrants indicated that, once registered, they are given no further information as to eligibility for services, etc.... Regional organizations felt that they should receive funding to address this informational need of reinstated people.
- Presenters from bands and tribal councils felt that the federal government has not lived up to its promise to implement Bill C-31 with adequate lands and resources.
- Band and tribal council presenters indicated an increased pressure on program and service delivery coupled with inadequate resources to meet higher demands for these programs and services.

- Band and tribal councils noted that band staff and councils are not receiving adequate resources to deal with the range of issues brought forward by Bill C-31.
- Some presenters argued that the social, political, and cultural fabric of First Nations communities have been weakened by Bill C-31, while others felt that Bill C-31 has strengthened the community fabric.
- Organizations stated that, despite Bill C-31, discrimination continues to exist.

This, of course, is only a summary of the positions put forward to date. The inquiry is hearing from small groups, band administrations, provincial organizations, individuals across the country, and those who have been affected by Bill C-31. Extensive reports will be available from the national offices of these three political organizations—The Assembly of First Nations, the Native Indian Women's Association of Canada, and the Native Council of Canada—in Ottawa.

The realities of reserve life still reflect colonial influences. The Indian Act perpetuates those attitudes. This is a document that requires massive revision. It does not protect or enhance our original cultures.

Our land base is painfully small and meagrely supports its residents. Some of our reserves have to accommodate 180 families, a school, a church, and possibly a small administration office on a piece of land that is equivalent to the size of a farm in Quebec or Ontario, and definitely smaller than any farm in Saskatchewan.

As it stands, the Indian Act restricts individuals from using their land deeds for collateral for funding purposes, so this restricts individual initiatives in business.

The schooling that our people receive contradicts the philosophies that we are taught at home. When we attempt to form meaningful co-operatives, our Canadian-American-European learned standards get in the way and confuse our innate ideologies.

Self-government is a phrase that sounds like a fairy tale when you face the reality of the Indian Act. It can be changed, however. The Tobique Women's Group influenced changes. We hope that the First Nations of Canada will also take a real look at the situation the Original People are in as we enter our 600th year under colonialism.

We can do something about this situation.

We can change the world.

Chapter 34

The Eagle Has Landed: Native Women, Leadership, and Community Development

Sylvia Maracle

Sylvia Maracle (Mohawk) is an Aboriginal Elder from the Tyendinaga Mohawk Territory who has worked extensively as a community organizer, provincially and nationally. Recognized as a primary shaper of culture-based management principles, she has served as the executive director of the Ontario Federation of Indian Friendships Centres (OFFC), vice president of the National Association of Friendship Centres (NAFC), president of the Native Women's Resource Centre (NWRC), and as a founding member of the Native Studies PhD Council at Trent University. She lectures and writes about a range of issues, including urban development, women's issues, education, health and wellness, the role of women in Aboriginal self-government, and the cultural revitalization of her people.

When I was a student in the early 1970s, a special teacher came to the Native Canadian Centre of Toronto. I will never forget what he said. Hopi Elder Thomas Banyaca shared a prophecy with us that day that I have since seen come alive. He came to tell us about the future of the Indigenous peoples of the Americas. In one powerful statement he made, he said that when the eagle landed on the Moon, the people would recover. Elder Banyaca's statement came directly from the Hopi prophecies. We were all astonished—the Apollo program had just landed its lunar module the *Eagle* on the Moon in 1969. The statement, "The *Eagle* has landed," thus foreshadowed major change in our communities.

In my lifetime, we have moved from people with crippling problems to communities that are slowly healing and reshaping our future. I have witnessed tremendous community development over the last thirty-five years, and much of it has been led by women. In this essay, I want to explore some of the ways in which urban Aboriginal women have developed the institutions that have helped to bring our people together to heal.

Birth of the Aboriginal Healing Movement

Thirty-five years ago, Aboriginal communities were struggling with rampant addictions, low education levels, poor housing, few employment opportunities and numerous family stresses. We had people whose lives had been profoundly scarred by the violence of residential school, training schools, adoption and other child and family service interventions, people who were apologetic for who they were. We had internalized the many forms of violence we experienced with colonization and had learned to express it laterally, against one another. Internalized colonization also meant we were not able to appreciate the value of our cultures or to see their application as vibrant and vital forms of community development. As communities, we lacked cohesiveness. We needed a vision.

Since that time, I have seen Native peoples make remarkable changes as they began the powerful movement towards cultural revitalization. Native peoples have taken up the consuming desire to ask the questions, "Who am I? Where have I come from? Where am I going? What are my responsibilities?" I believe that Aboriginal women were the first ones to wake up to this process, and the first to take up their responsibilities.

I recall attending a conference entitled "Rève-Toi!" (Wake up!) that was hosted by the Quebec Native Women's Association in the early 1970s. I remember watching women wake up to the call and begin to see what it was they wanted. Whether their vision was a Friendship Centre, a Native women's centre, a shelter or a dance troupe, they were willing to work for it. In doing so, they encouraged the painters and craftspeople, the dreamers and the teachers and the clans to recover their vision and culture. This took place in urban and rural settings, but many Native women had moved into urban centres by the 1970s.

It's important to consider why so many Aboriginal women found themselves in urban settings. First Nations women may have come because they weren't part of families that were popular. A number of Aboriginal women were victimized by the violence in their communities and were therefore forced to leave. Some had to leave when they married out and found themselves disenfranchised of their Indian status and band membership. Others left because they were not able to live with the very aggressive application of band policies that marginalized them as women in their communities, for example, in housing. There were also women who came to urban centres so their children could be educated. Many Métis and other non-status Aboriginal women came from communities that were never provided with a land base and were dispersed into the cities. For all of these reasons and more, Aboriginal women were forced to leave their communities, but they took their identities with them, as women, as clans, as Nations. And so, even though so many had no choice but to become urban, and some endured terrible experiences in the process, the creativity of these women turned hardship into opportunity. They knew that their families needed places to belong in urban settings as Native people, and so they created the very organizations that could help address their survival.

The beginnings of most of these organizations were very humble. No sooner were Native women established in urban settings than they would offer their homes for hospitality and even shelter for newcomers. From there, small gathering places were set up informally in somebody's garage or in a church basement. These places, funded by bake sales and the proceeds from selling beadwork or raffling quilts, and surviving on the volunteer work of community women, gradually grew into the first Friendship Centres. Sometimes Native women did it alone, and sometimes these centres were created through networks with other non-profit community groups or government agencies.

Their services started with tea and talk, and ultimately grew into sophisticated counselling and referral agencies. They gradually grew into the role of community development centres, attracting other Native women who were able to envision, and ultimately create, community-based agencies to look at specific needs in the areas of housing, employment and addictions treatment, to name a few. Many women provided important economic support to themselves and their families as they began to earn salaries in Aboriginal community organizations. These emerging organizations were symbols of pride in our communities. Out of nothing but a dream, an idea, hard work and the creativity of community women, they became our social safety nets, cultural education centres and agents of change.

There is no evidence that the women who were involved in creating the early Friendship Centres ever thought that they would become social planning bodies, or social justice centres or house discussions about self-determination and self-governance. The women did not set out specifically to do these things, yet all of the actions we undertake today are the results of that early organizing and volunteering. Furthermore, women usually developed these community groups and organizations to support the well-being of the community before they undertook to develop community resources for themselves. It was not until the mid-1970s that organizations specifically for the support of women were developed.

Women's Creativity and Leadership

In our communities, there are people who have titles and there are people who are leaders. These are not necessarily the same people. Our leaders are not necessarily the ones who have taken on a title. Natural leaders are the ones who seem to get things done. They have a healthy vision, possess knowledge, are passionately committed and have a personal leadership style that promotes action. Early on in our development, it was these natural leaders who worked to change our communities, and these leaders were, in overwhelming numbers, women.

While all this community development was happening, I saw the men rushing to keep up. They were our leaders in the formal sense, but they were running to catch up to their people. Many were not necessarily as healthy as their people yet. We know that a large percentage of our people have been affected by addictions, residential school trauma, criminal justice contact, violence and racism. All of these contributed to our generally unhealthy communities. Many who had been appointed our leaders at the time came from these roots as well, and many tried to lay claim to the work that the women had done.

Why was it primarily men who were occupying formal positions of leadership? When the treaty parties came to us, the Europeans didn't bring their women. In turn, they didn't want to deal with the women who were the leaders of our families, clans, communities and Nations. Colonial government policies and laws, including the *Indian Act*, reinforced political practices that excluded women. This interference ensured that only men carried titles like chief, band councillor and band administrator until very recently. In following these *Indian Act* practices over the past century, we have internalized the belief that those who carry these titles are the natural leaders of our communities. Many of us know that this is not always true, but public policy and negotiations with government continue to support this system of leadership, and often to the exclusion of women. For these reasons, it has been women who have led the challenge to change discriminatory practices and to look at more responsible leadership processes. I've seen governments prop up systems that governments have always propped up and watched women respond. That kind of advocacy had to occur at the community level where women could build organizations with mandates to challenge the way things were and to create change.

Some of our current notions of leadership were formed during the time that women were totally excluded from politics. Our development as peoples has been characterized by this tension between formal male leadership and informal female leadership, and there have been too few opportunities to recognize and celebrate what our women have done or to explore the distinct qualities of our women's leadership.

How do women approach leadership? Our traditions tell us that we are not the same as men, nor should we try to use the same approaches they use. I learned this lesson from my grand-mother on a visit home from university in 1973. My grandmother had never been to school and was curious to know what I was learning. She had some seventy grandchildren and another thirty-two great-grandchildren, and at that point I was the only one who had gone to university. As she was one of the most magnificent people I knew, I wanted to prove that I was worthy of her question. I responded by saying that I was learning about women's liberation. It was the heyday of second-wave feminism and feminism was a hot topic, but my grandmother had no idea what I was talking about. When she asked me to explain what I meant by women's liberation, I replied that women wanted to be equal with their men. It was about equality, I thought. But when my grandfather translated these notions into Mohawk, my grandmother started laughing. She said something in Mohawk, and when I asked my grandfather to translate, he told me that her exact words were "Why would women want to lower themselves to be equal to men?"

I had intended to impress my grandmother with all my worldly knowledge, yet she humbled me with a few words, reminding me of how powerful we are as women and of the great respon-sibilities we carry for our people. To my grandmother, women were lowered to Mother Earth first, with the responsibility to create and nurture, and she believed it was our responsibility to complete creation. It is inevitable, therefore, that our recovery as peoples would be led by the women. This interaction with my grandmother helped me to understand the role of women in community development.

Real community development involves working hard, for long hours, without real compensa-tion. Our women worked in community development because they were waking up to their responsibilities, and they had the vision. They did the work for the children, their family and the generations to come. They did it because they saw people living in ways that were not acceptable. They did it because many of the cultural teachings encouraged them to do it. Early community development allowed women to express who they were. They may have been driven out of their home community, but they were able to create a sense of community elsewhere, and especially in urban areas, which provided an anonymity and safety that allowed our women to freely express their creativity and vision.

In addition to vision, the early community development also created relationships, working partnerships and opportunities for sharing. I think that in real community development, there is a tendency to share the dream as opposed to the power. This is perhaps one of the fundamental differences between women's and men's approaches to community development. I have come to believe that it is not the power that is the ultimate end, it is the dream, and that this is the way that Aboriginal women have worked. For example, once these women got these organizations going, they did a remarkable thing as leaders: they let someone else take over. I think that this is a tremendous approach. To hand over one's vision to the next leader, natural or titled, is a very empowering thing. That is not to say that organizations that were the reflection of their leader did not suffer in some way when the founder left. But the fact that most of these founders had the vision to let other women take over attests to the unique leadership styles of Aboriginal women.

As a result of women's participation, I have seen an urban leadership that has become increasingly accountable. It's really hard to not tell your sister, daughter, aunt, mother or best friend what you are up to. I think it's a lot easier than being elected to formal leadership, where perhaps 30 percent of the community votes by ballot and puts you in power. Whether it was a conscious, long-range thought or a realization of a prophecy, I saw changes in leadership take place and people become more credible. I saw women engaging in more inclusive community-development processes.

Women are now 52 percent of the Aboriginal population, yet we are not 52 percent of the elected leadership of formal Aboriginal political organizations. When I look at urban organizations, I see a better representation of women than what I see among the chiefs, band councillors and leadership in the political organizations. Urban areas have long received more women who have been forced to migrate, and so they have participated in greater numbers in the labour force and in decision-making positions in our urban organizations.

Women's creativity continues to challenge and periodically threaten the processes in some of our organizations today. In the 1970s, Native women referred to the various First Nations organizations as male dominated. Métis and other non-status women have also encountered male domination in their organizations. We now see the establishment of women's secretariats and councils within First Nations and Métis politics as a response to the desire for women's involvement. But whether these will become real expressions of community development and empowerment remains to be seen.

Moving On to the Future

In the future, I think we are going to see more women creating partnerships and opportunities for sharing. It will be good to see all those women with all their energies pooled together. And although our initial urban leaders are ageing, many of those women who created the Friendship Centres and the network of other urban Aboriginal organizations are still around. They have provided the leadership today with the seeds to continue community development, and they continue to watch what we do to nurture those seeds and help them grow.

As more Aboriginal women become formal leaders, will we lose sight of those behaviours that encouraged our resiliency, brightness and creativity? Will we become part and parcel of the process that will limit young women's thinking? There wasn't an old guard when we came along, so there was no one to tell us what could or could not be done. At the present moment, I try very hard as part of my responsibility to encourage the next generation.

I worry that, as women leaders, we may have been negligent as mentors. When we were starting out, we benefited from the presence of those natural leaders who took the time to involve us and engage us, while building all of the organizations that they built. Now that we are involved in maintaining, improving, strengthening and expanding these groups, we have found ourselves too busy to mentor. We have to make time to talk with young people, especially young women, and to help them reflect on and analyze the issues that shape our leadership role. The other side of mentoring, however, is that those who want to be mentored have to be patient, ask questions, believe and commit their time and energies.

I think that many young women are again champing at the bit in terms of community development and leadership. Our women continue to be the cutting edge of our development and the voice that challenges our inequity. One way we see them doing this is in challenging some of our cultural practices. For example, there are increasing numbers of young women taking up singing and drumming, even though they are often met with resistance. These are seen historically as activities for our young men, but young women are challenging that cultural norm. The more they are told that it is not appropriate, the more they embrace it.

I think in the future, we will see young women leading our development into a number of new areas. They may already be leading the way in terms of health care, seniors' programming, culture-based education and holistic programming, as well as in entertainment and information technology. And of course it is our younger people, both women and men, who are already show-ing natural leadership in the arts, literature, and music and dance, through dreaming and creating new visions of being Aboriginal in the twenty-first century.

To foster community development, we need to actively engage our young men in undoing some of the gender stereotypes that they have learned. It is not acceptable in a healing community to encourage young men to drum and learn the teachings and have young women stand back. It is not acceptable in a healing community to organize athletic activities for boys and young men and have the young women stand around and watch. These conditions and experiences will bring forth the next generation of natural leaders, who will challenge the traditions they are given. Our job as adults will be to create safe spaces for both genders to develop, places where they can have conversations about each other in order to understand what they're feeling and thinking.

We continue to be affected and to feel the repercussion of formal political developments. It was, in large part, Indian Affairs policy and legislation that encouraged women to organize as Native women in the 1970s. For a period, there were some common areas of concern for all Aboriginal women. However, as our leadership evolved, so did the issues that they had to confront. While all of us face racism, poverty and loss of land, government legislation controls our realities in such different ways that many of us have questioned whether or not First Nations, Métis and Inuit women share enough similar circumstances that can be dealt with through common approaches. This has led to the same kind of fractionalization within the Aboriginal women's community that we see in the Aboriginal political organizations. We find ourselves having to organize separately according to how Canada has classified us, as First Nations, Métis or Inuit. And yet while we may have to organize in ways that differ from one another, ultimately we continue to face many common experiences as Aboriginal women.

I wonder how much the development of women's committees within the First Nations, Métis and Inuit political organizations will further fractionalize us. It is certainly envisioned as a strength in redirecting and redesigning the organizations as they were developed in the late 1960s and early 1970s. And yet it will take strong leaders to sit and talk about how they feel and to look to a future beyond their grandchildren's grandchildren in a time when all of our organizations are threatened by competition for federal government resources.

Urban women face specific circumstances. First Nations like to say that they represent the interests of their urban members, but they never talk to us or consult with us. The *Corbiere* deci-sion[1] says that we have the right to be involved in the selection of leadership in our home First Nations. In reality, we are tolerated there, but not welcome. Furthermore, chiefs have claimed that they represent their people regardless of residency and without having to consult them. The *Corbiere* decision said yes to more representation and it also said that it was the right of the indi-vidual member of a First Nation to access services and professions where and how that individual chose to do so. To invoke our token involvement in the politics of our home communities, or to have our affairs governed exclusively from our home communities, may limit the creativity and the nurturing that has brought us this far. As urban women, we have to consider the impact of this representation on our development.

Full Circle

As the numbers of Aboriginal peoples on the healing path increase, there will be questions and challenges about what to do after the healing is completed. We are not used to living life to its fullest, but rather to healing and helping others. We will need to learn how to balance the numerous aspects of life that we juggle: academic and lived experience, traditional culture and new forms of cultural expression, professional and personal life, and nurturing others versus nurturing ourselves.

As I understand it, leaders were traditionally understood to be servants of the people. The next generation will have to integrate this cultural practice into daily organizational behaviour. At the same time, there will be a need for more political savvy. This will mean that leaders will have to be more aware of politics that are both internal and external in order to facilitate community growth and development.

The process of colonization reinforces the divisions that undermine the power of the circle and cause women to distance themselves from one another. This has especially been done through the imposition of the labels First Nations, Métis and Inuit. Our early natural leaders used their collective power and efforts to create community-controlled organizations. Since then, divisiveness has been heightened and has become more pronounced. Increasingly the fight for the future has become the fight for money. We focus on majority and minority power and use processes learned from the colonizers, not those roles and responsibilities we have learned to carry in our healing journey. These were not the values and practices of those women who created our early community organizations.

Our leaders will need to sit again with the eagle and all of our other teachers to reflect on what is important in our future, define what role they will play, identify shared dreams and then determine how this will be reflected in our organizations and communities. If we recognize and accept this visioning task, we will be much stronger in the next phase of community development.

There is no doubt that Aboriginal women are leading the way in recovering our health as peoples, implementing the prophecies, recreating communities and birthing new dreams. We are now living these responsibilities as formal and natural leaders. And when those original women who are still watching us ask, "What are these women doing with what we started?" we will have to acknowledge that there is still much to be done. There are entirely new challenges still to be met and many young voices still to be developed. With 50 percent of our population under the age of twenty-four and 40 percent under the age of sixteen, there is a huge population of young women coming forward.

I have no doubt that our power will continue. We will answer those original women by recognizing that we borrow from our children. We must commit ourselves to realizing those yet unmet prophecies and to being responsible leaders regardless of the structure of our organizations. We must promise that we will continue to dream. We must show those original women that the eagle has landed and that we have picked up our eagle feathers.

Note

1. The Assembly of First Nations has produced a document on the *Corbiere* decision, which reads: "In *Corbiere*, the Supreme Court of Canada ruled that denying the vote to members because they live off reserve is a form of discrimination. *Corbiere* determined that voting rights could not be discriminatory. By creating this new category of discrimination, many questions were raised about other rights for non-resident members." See "The Corbiere Decision: What It Means for First Nations," Assembly of First Nations, retrieved from: www.afn.ca.

Part 4 Cultural Representations and Body Politics

Men look at women. Women watch themselves being looked at. This determines not only most relations between men and women but also the relation of women to themselves.... Thus she turns herself into an object—and most particularly an object of vision: a sight.

—John Berger, quoted in *Ways of Seeing* (1972, p. 47)

Part 4 explores diverse representations of women in contemporary popular culture, and examines some key issues concerning women's bodies, such as health care and women's health movements, menstruation, sexuality, reproductive rights, violence, and beauty.

4a: Cultural Representation and the Creation of Desire

In this first section, we examine contemporary consumer culture, focusing on advertising, children's animated films, music, television, and women's magazines. We explore image consumption as an active, not merely passive, process and encourage you to question how particular values and assumptions are "naturalized" through popular culture, and how these can be challenged.

4b: Regulating Women's Bodies and Desires

We look closely in this section at the social regulation of girls' and women's sexed bodies and sexualities in contemporary image culture as well as in all important contexts of home, community, health care, and school.

4c: Beauty Projects: Conformity and Resistance

In this section, we examine historical and contemporary beauty ideals and their gendered and racialized implications. We look specifically at how feminists have analyzed body modification projects (including weight loss, eating problems, skin lightening or tanning, and cosmetic surgery) as ways that women seek to conform to cultural ideals as well as resist bodily abjection and social exclusion. We invite you to reflect on "looking relations" and challenge myths of fatness and aging.

4d: Politics of Women's Health: From Medicalization to Health Care Reform

Here you will be introduced to feminist critiques of the biomedical model of health, feminist-inspired social and women-centred models of health, and social determinants of health. We also consider particular health issues affecting diverse women, and we explore some of the challenges posed for women's health movements and activism in contemporary neo-liberal contexts in Canada and globally.

4e: Social Status and Reproductive Rights

This section encourages a broad understanding of reproductive rights, focusing on specific issues such as birth control, abortion, and compulsory sterilization. We introduce you to multiple ways in which women's reproductive rights have been denied or limited historically and in contemporary contexts in North America and other parts of the world. Readers also learn about women's active involvement in various reproductive rights movements.

4f: Violence against Women

This section examines the nature, extent, and forms of violence against women, analyzing in particular gendered and racialized violence targeting specific groups, including Aboriginal women. We expose and challenge common myths and misconceptions, present women's own narratives and analyses of their experiences of violence, and examine actions and movements involved in violence prevention.

4a Cultural Representation and the Creation of Desire

Supplement 19

Fast Facts about Sexualization and Marketing to Girls

Sharon Lamb, Lyn Mikel Brown, and Peggy Orenstein

Sharon Lamb is distinguished professor of mental health in the Department of Counseling and School Psychology at the University of Massachusetts Boston. Regarded as an expert commentator on girls, sexuality, and popular culture, she has published widely in the areas of sexual abuse, sexual development, the sexualization of girls, and media and marketers' packaging of girlhood and boyhood. She is also cited frequently in popular media such as Parenting, Working Mother, *and* Seventeen.

Lyn Mikel Brown is professor of education and human development at Colby College in Waterville, Maine. She is highly acclaimed for her work on the relational life of girls. Her co-authored book, Meeting at the Crossroads: Women's Psychology and Girls' Development, *a New York Times Notable Book of the Year, helped to redefine conventional understandings of female development. As co-creator of Hardy Girls Healthy Women (HGHW), she supports and encourages girls' healthy development, empowerment, and leadership.*

Peggy Orenstein is an internationally known writer, editor, and speaker about issues affecting girls and women. Her notable published books include the groundbreaking New York Times *bestseller* Schoolgirls: Young Women, Self-Esteem and the Confidence Gap *and the award-winning memoir* Waiting for Daisy: A Tale of Two Continents. *Orenstein's newest book* Cinderella Ate My Daughter, *from which we have excerpted some of the following facts, examines the underside of pop culture: the persistent ultra-feminine and hyper-sexual messages being sent to a new generation of young girls.*

Sparkle, Sweetie!

- In 2007, we spent a whopping $11.5 billion on clothing for seven- to fourteen-year-olds, up from $10.5 billion in 2004.
- Close to half of six- to nine-year-old girls regularly use lipstick or gloss, presumably with parental approval; the percentage of eight- to twelve-year-olds who regularly use mascara and eyeliner doubled between 2008 and 2010, to 18 and 15 percent, respectively.

- "Tween" girls now spend more than $40 million a month on beauty products. No wonder Nair, the depilatory maker, in 2007 released Nair Pretty, a fruit-scented line designed to make ten-year-olds conscious of their "unwanted" body hair.

Source: Adapted from Peggy Orenstein, *Cinderella Ate My Daughter: Dispatches from the Front Lines of the New Girlie-Girl Culture* (New York: HarperCollins, 2011), 82.

Written on a Bikini Underwear Set for Sizes 4 and up

P–perfect
O–off the hook
P–princess
S–stylin'
T–too cool for you
A–angel
R–rockin'

Source: Sharon Lamb and Lyn Mikel Brown, *Packaging Girlhood: Rescuing Our Daughters from Marketers' Schemes* (New York: St. Martin's Press, 2006), 15.

Chapter 35

Image-Based Culture: Advertising and Popular Culture

Sut Jhally

Sut Jhally, professor of communication at the University of Massachusetts, is a leading scholar on the role that advertising and popular culture play in processes of social control and identity construction. Jhally is the founder and executive director of the Media Education Foundation (MEF), a non-profit organization that produces and distributes documentary films to inspire critical reflection on the social, political, and cultural impact of American mass media. The author of many books and articles, and the producer and director of influential films on gender, sexuality and race, commercialization, violence, and politics, he is also an award-winning educator.

Because we live inside the consumer culture, and most of us have done so for most of our lives, it is sometimes difficult to locate the origins of our most cherished values and assumptions. They simply appear to be part of our natural world. It is a useful exercise, therefore, to examine how our culture has come to be defined and shaped in specific ways—to excavate the origins of our most celebrated rituals. For example, everyone in this culture knows "a diamond is forever." It is a meaning that is almost as "natural" as the link between roses and romantic love. However, diamonds (just like roses) did not always have this meaning. Before 1938 their value derived primarily from their worth as scarce stones (with the DeBeers cartel carefully controlling the market supply). In 1938 the New York advertising agency of N.W. Ayers was hired to change public attitudes toward diamonds—to transform them from a financial investment into a *symbol* of committed and everlasting love. In 1947 an Ayers advertising copywriter came up with the slogan "a diamond is forever" and the rest, as they say, is history. As an N.W. Ayers memorandum put it in 1959: "Since 1939 an entirely new generation of young people has grown to marriageable age. To the new generation, a diamond ring is considered a necessity for engagement to virtually everyone."[1]

This is a fairly dramatic example of how the institutional structure of the consumer society orients the culture (and its attitudes, values, and rituals) more and more toward the world of commodities. The marketplace (and its major ideological tool, advertising) is the major structuring institution of contemporary consumer society.

This, of course, was not always the case. In the agrarian-based society preceding industrial society, other institutions such as family, community, ethnicity, and religion were the dominant institutional mediators and creators of the cultural forms. Their influence waned in the transition to industrial society and then consumer society. The emerging institution of the marketplace occupied the cultural terrain left void by the evacuation of these older forms. Information about products seeped into public discourse. More specifically, public discourse soon became dominated by the "discourse through and about objects."[2]

At first, this discourse relied upon transmitting information about products alone, using the available means of textual communication offered by newspapers. As the possibility of more effective color illustration emerged and as magazines developed as competitors for advertising dollars, this "discourse" moved from being purely text-based. The further integration of first radio and then television into the advertising/media complex ensured that commercial communication would be characterized by the domination of *imagistic* modes of representation.

Again, because our world is so familiar, it is difficult to imagine the process through which the present conditions emerged. In this context, it is instructive to focus upon that period in our history that marks the transition point in the development of an image-saturated society—the 1920s. In that decade the advertising industry was faced with a curious problem—the need to sell increasing quantities of "nonessential" goods in a competitive marketplace using the potentialities offered by printing and color photography. Whereas the initial period of national advertising (from approximately the 1880s to the 1920s) had focused largely in a celebratory manner on the products themselves and had used text for "reason why" advertising (even if making the most outrageous claims), the 1920s saw the progressive integration of people (via visual representation) into the messages. [...]

While this period is instructive from the viewpoint of content, it is equally fascinating from the viewpoint of *form*; for while the possibilities of using visual imagery existed with the development of new technologies, there was no guarantee that the audience was sufficiently literate in visual imagery to properly decode the ever-more complex messages. Thus, the advertising industry had to educate as well as sell, and many of the ads of this period were a fascinating combination where the written (textual) material explained the visual material. The consumer society was literally being taught how to read the commercial messages. By the postwar period the education was complete and the function of written text moved away from explaining the visual and toward a more cryptic form where it appears as a "key" to the visual "puzzle."

In the contemporary world, messages about goods are all-pervasive—advertising has increasingly filled up the spaces of our daily existence. Our media are dominated by advertising images, public space has been taken over by "information" about products, and most of our sporting and cultural events are accompanied by the name of a corporate sponsor. There is even an attempt to get television commercials into the nation's high schools under the pretense of "free" news programming. As we head toward the twenty-first century, advertising is ubiquitous—it is the air that we breathe as we live our daily lives.

Advertising and the Good Life: Image and "Reality"

I have referred to advertising as being part of "a discourse through and about objects" because it does not merely tell us about things but of how things are connected to important domains of our lives. Fundamentally, advertising talks to us as individuals and addresses us about how we can become *happy*. The answers it provides are all oriented to the marketplace, through the purchase of goods or services. To understand the system of images that constitutes advertising we need to inquire into the definition of happiness and satisfaction in contemporary social life.

Quality of life surveys that ask people what they are seeking in life—what it is that makes them happy—report quite consistent results. The conditions that people are searching for—what they perceive will make them happy—are things such as having personal autonomy and control of one's life, self-esteem, a happy family life, loving relations, a relaxed, tension-free leisure time, and good friendships. The unifying theme of this list is that these things are not fundamentally connected to goods. It is primarily "social" life and not "material" life that seems to be the locus of perceived happiness. Commodities are only *weakly related* to these sources of satisfaction.[3]

A market society, however, is guided by the principle that satisfaction should be achieved via the marketplace, and through its institutions and structures it orients behavior in that direction. The data from the quality of life studies are not lost on advertisers. If goods themselves are not the locus of perceived happiness, then they need to be connected in some way with those things that are. Thus advertising promotes images of what the audience conceives of as "the good life": beer can be connected with anything from eroticism to male fraternity to the purity of the old West; food can be tied up with family relations or health; investment advice offers early retirements in tropical settings. The marketplace cannot directly offer the real thing, but it can offer visions of it connected with the purchase of products.

Advertising thus does not work by creating values and attitudes out of nothing but by drawing upon and rechanneling concerns that the target audience (and the culture) already shares. As one advertising executive put it: "Advertising doesn't always mirror how people are acting but how they're *dreaming*. In a sense what we're doing is wrapping up your emotions and selling them back to you." Advertising absorbs and fuses a variety of symbolic practices and discourses, [and] it appropriates and distills from an unbounded range of cultural references. In so doing, goods are knitted into the fabric of social life and cultural significance. As such, advertising is not simple manipulation, but what ad-maker Tony Schwartz calls "partipulation," with the audience participating in its own manipulation.

What are the consequences of such a system of images and goods? Given that the "real" sources of satisfaction cannot be provided by the purchase of commodities (merely the "image" of that source), it should not be surprising that happiness and contentment appear illusory in contemporary society. Recent social thinkers describe the contemporary scene as a "joyless economy,"[4] or as reflecting the "paradox of affluence."[5] It is not simply a matter of being "tricked" by the false blandishments of advertising. The problem is with the institutional structure of a market society that propels definition of satisfaction *through* the commodity/image system. The modern context, then, provides a curious satisfaction experience—one that William Leiss describes as "an ensemble of satisfactions and dissatisfactions" in which the consumption of commodities mediated by the image-system of advertising leads to consumer uncertainty and confusion.[6] The image-system of the marketplace reflects our desire and dreams, yet we have only the pleasure of the images to sustain us in our actual experience with goods.

The commodity image-system thus provides a particular vision of the world—a particular mode of self-validation that is integrally connected with what one *has* rather than what one *is*—a distinction often referred to as one between "having" and "being," with the latter now being defined through the former. As such, it constitutes a way of life that is defined and structured in quite specific political ways. Some commentators have even described advertising as part of a new *religious* system in which people construct their identities through the commodity form, and in which commodities are part of a supernatural magical world where anything is possible with the purchase of a product. The commodity as displayed in advertising plays a mixture of psychological, social, and physical roles in its relations with people. The object world interacts with the human world at the most basic and fundamental of levels, performing seemingly magical feats of enchantment and transformation, bringing instant happiness and gratification, capturing the forces of nature, and acting as a passport to hitherto untraveled domains and group relationships.[7]

In short, the advertising image-system constantly propels us toward things as means to satisfaction. In the sense that every ad says it is better to buy than not to buy, we can best regard advertising as a *propaganda* system for commodities. In the image-system as a whole, happiness lies at the end of a purchase. Moreover, this is not a minor propaganda system—it is all-pervasive. It should not surprise us then to discover that the problem that it poses—how to get more things for everyone (as that is the root to happiness)—guides our political debates. The goal of *economic growth* (on which the commodity vision is based) is an unquestioned and sacred proposition of the political culture. As the environmental costs of the strategy of unbridled economic growth become more obvious, it is clear we must, as a society, engage in debate concerning the nature of future economic growth. However, as long as the commodity image-system maintains its ubiquitous presence and influence, the possibilities of opening such a debate are remote. At the very moment we most desperately need to pose new questions within the political culture, the commodity image-system propels us with even greater certainty and persuasion along a path that, unless checked, is destined to end in disaster.

Moreover, this problem will be exponentially compounded in the twenty-first century, as more and more nations (both Third World and "presently existing socialist") reach for the magic of the marketplace to provide the panacea for happiness. [...] Transnational corporations are licking their lips at the new markets that Eastern Europe and China will provide for their products. Accompanying the products (indeed preceding them, preparing the way) will be the sophisticated messages of global advertising emerging from Madison Avenue. From a global perspective, again at the very moment that there needs to be informed debate about the direction and scope of industrial production, the commodity propaganda system is colonizing new areas and new media, and channeling debate into narrower confines.

The Spread of Image-Based Influence

While the commodity image-system is primarily about satisfaction, its influence and effect are not limited to that alone. I want to briefly consider four other areas in the contemporary world where the commodity system has its greatest impact. The first is in the area of gender identity. Many commercial messages use images and representations of men and women as central components of their strategy to both get attention and persuade. Of course, they do not use any gender images but images drawn from a narrow and quite concentrated pool. As Erving Goffman has shown, ads draw heavily upon the domain of gender display—not the way that men and women actually behave but the ways in which we think men and women behave.[8] It is because these conventions of gender display are so easily recognized by the audience that they figure so prominently in the image-system. Also, images having to do with gender strike at the core of individual identity; our understanding of ourselves as either male or female (socially defined within this society at this time) is central to our understanding of who we are. What better place to choose than an area of social life that can be communicated at a glance and that reaches into the core of individual identity?

However, we should not confuse these portrayals as true reflections of gender. In advertising, gender (especially for women) is defined almost exclusively along the lines of sexuality. The image-system thus distorts our perceptions and offers little that balances out the stress on sexuality. Advertisers, working within a "cluttered" environment in which there are more and more messages, must have a way to break through the attendant noise. Sexuality provides a resource that can be used to get attention and communicate instantly. Within this sexuality is also a powerful component of gender that again lends itself even easier to imagistic representation.

If only one or two advertisers used this strategy, then the image-system would not have the present distorted features. The problem is that the vast majority do so. The iconography of the culture, perhaps more than any previous society, seems to be obsessed with sexuality. The end result is that the commodity is part of an increasingly eroticized world—that we live in a culture that is more and more defined erotically through commodities.

Second, the image-system has spread its influence to the realm of electoral politics. Much has been written (mostly negatively) about the role that television advertising now plays within national electoral politics. The presidency seems most susceptible to "image-politics," as it is the office most reliant on television advertising. The social commentary on politics from this perspective has mostly concerned the manner in which the focus has shifted from discussion of real "issues" to a focus on symbolism and emotionally based imagery.

These debates are too important and complex to be discussed in any depth here, but there is a fundamental point to be made. The evidence suggests that George Bush won the 1988 presidential race because he ran a better ad and public relations campaign. Given the incredible swings in the polls over a relatively short period of time, when media information was the only thing that voters had to go on, it seems to be a conclusion with some substance. The implications of such a conclusion, though, have not really been explored the way they should. The fact that large numbers of people are changing their minds on who to vote for after seeing a thirty-second television commercial says a great deal about the nature of the political culture. It means that politics (for a significant portion of the electorate) is largely conducted on a symbolic realm and that a notion of politics that is based upon people having a coherent and deep vision of their relationship to the social world is no longer relevant. Politics is not about issues; it is about "feeling good" or "feeling bad" about a candidate—and all it takes to change this is a thirty-second commercial.

*****

Third, the commodity image-system is now implicated, due to changes in the way that toys are marketed, in the very structure and experience of children's play. With both children's television programming and commercials oriented around the sale of toys, writers such as Stephen Kline argue that the context within which kids play is now structured around marketing considerations. In consequence, "Children's imaginative play has become the target of marketing strategy, allowing marketers to define the limits of children's imaginations…. Play in fact has become highly ritualized—less an exploration and solidification of personal experiences and developing conceptual schema than a rearticulation of the fantasy world provided by market designers. Imaginative play has shifted one degree closer to mere imitation and assimilation." Further, the segmentation of the child audience in terms of both age and gender has led to a situation where parents find it difficult to play with their children because they do not share the marketing fantasy world that toy advertisers have created and where there is a growing divide between boys and girls at play. […]

Fourth, the visual image-system has colonized areas of life that were previously largely defined (although not solely) by auditory perception and experience. The 1980s has seen a change in the way that popular music commodities (records, tapes, compact discs) are marketed, with a music video becoming an indispensable component of an overall strategy. These videos are produced as commercials for musical commodities by the advertising industry, using techniques learned from the marketing of products. Viewing these videos, there often seems to be little link between the song and the visuals. In the sense that they are commercials for records, there of course does not have to be. Video makers are in the same position as ad makers in terms of trying to get attention for their message and making it visually pleasurable. It is little wonder then that representations involving sexuality figure so prominently (as in the case of regular product advertising). The visuals are chosen for their ability to sell.

Many people report that listening to a song after watching the video strongly affects the interpretation they give to it—the visual images are replayed in the imagination. In that sense, the surrounding commodity image-system works to fix—or at least to limit—the scope of imaginative interpretation. The realm of listening becomes subordinated to the realm of seeing, to the influence of commercial images. There is also evidence suggesting that the composition of popular music is affected by the new video context. People write songs or lines with the vital marketing tool in mind.

Speed and Fragmentation: Toward a Twenty-First Century Consciousness

In addition to issues connected with the colonization of the commodity image-system of other areas of social life (gender socialization, politics, children's play, popular cultural forms), there are also important broader issues connected with its relation to modes of perception and forms of consciousness within contemporary society. For instance, the commodity information-system has two basic characteristics: reliance on visual modes of representation and the increasing speed and rapidity of the images that constitute it. It is this second point that I wish to focus on here (I will return to the first point at the end of the [chapter]).

The visual images that dominate public space and public discourse are, in the video age, not static. They do not stand still for us to examine and linger over. They are here for a couple of seconds and then they are gone. Television advertising is the epitome of this speed-up. There is nothing mysterious in terms of how it arose. As commercial time slots declined from sixty seconds to thirty seconds (and recently to fifteen seconds and even shorter), advertisers responded by creating a new type of advertising—what is called the "vignette approach"—in which narrative and "reason-why" advertising are subsumed under a rapid succession of lifestyle images, meticulously timed with music, that directly sell feeling and emotion rather than products. As a commercial editor puts it of this new approach: "They're a wonderful way to pack in information: all those scenes and emotions—cut, cut, cut. Also they permit you a very freestyle approach—meaning that as long as you stay true to your basic vignette theme you can usually just drop one and shove in another. They're a dream to work with because the parts are sort of interchangeable."[9]

The speed-up is also a response by advertisers to two other factors: the increasing "clutter" of the commercial environment and the coming of age, in terms of disposable income, of a generation that grew up on television and commercials. The need for a commercial to stand out to a visually sophisticated audience drove the image-system to a greater frenzy of concentrated shorts. Again, sexuality became a key feature of the image-system within this.

The speed-up has two consequences. First, it has the effect of drawing the viewer into the message. One cannot watch these messages casually; they require undivided attention. Intensely pleasurable images, often sexual, are integrated into a flow of images. Watching has to be even more attentive to catch the brief shots of visual pleasure. The space "in between" the good parts can then be filled with other information, so that the commodity being advertised becomes a rich and complex sign.

Second, the speed-up has replaced narrative and rational response with images and emotional response. Speed and fragmentation are not particularly conducive to *thinking*. They induce *feeling*. The speed and fragmentation that characterize the commodity image-system may have a similar effect on the construction of consciousness. In one series of ads for MTV, a teenage boy or girl engages in a continuous monologue of events, characters, feelings, and emotions without any apparent connecting theme. As the video images mirror the fragmentation of thoughts, the ad ends with the plug: "Finally, a channel for the way you *think*." The generalization of this speed/fragmentation strategy to the entire domain of image culture may in fact mean that this is the form that thought increasingly is taking at the end of the twentieth century.

Political Implications: Education in an Image-Saturated Society

There really is not much to dispute in the analysis I have offered of the history, character, and consequences the commodity image-system may have. The real question concerning these issues has to do with the political implications that one may draw from this kind of approach. Put simply: Is there a problem with this situation, and if so what precisely is it? Further, what solutions may be offered?

*****

[…] I am convinced that a modern cultural politics must be conducted on the terrain of the image-system. […] Given that our understanding of reality is always socially constructed (that "ideology" is present in any system or situation), visual images are the central mode through which the modern world understands itself. Images are the dominant language of the modern world. We are stuck with them. Further, we have to acknowledge the pleasure that such images provide. This is not simply trickery or manipulation—the pleasure is substantive.

I would focus a cultural politics on two related strategies. First, the struggle to reconstruct the existence and meaning of the world of substance has to take place on the terrain of the image-system. In some progressive cultural politics the very techniques associated with the image-system are part of the problem—that is, images themselves are seen as the problem. A struggle over definitions of reality (what else is cultural politics?) needs to use other mediums of communication. I believe such a strategy surrenders the very terrain on which the most effective battles can be fought—the language of the contemporary world.[10]

The second aspect of the strategy centers less on revealing matters of substance (the underlying reality) than on opening up further the analysis of the contemporary image-system, in particular, *democratizing* the image-system. At present the "discourse through and about objects" is profoundly authoritarian—it reflects only a few narrow (mostly corporate) interests. The institutions of the world of substance must be engaged to open up the public discourse to new and varied (and dissenting) voices.

The other set of concerns are connected to issues of *literacy* in an image-saturated society. […] While we can read the images quite adequately (for the purposes of their creators) we do not know how to *produce* them. Such skills, or knowledge of the process, must be a prerequisite for functional literacy in the contemporary world. Basic course work in photography and video production should be required in all high schools. Moreover, while messages can be read adequately, most people do not understand *how* the language of images works. Just as knowledge of grammar is considered vital in learning foreign languages, so the grammar of images (how they work) needs to be integrated into the high school curriculum. "Visual literacy" courses should be taken right after the production courses.

Finally, information about the institutional context of the production and consumption of the image-system should be a prerequisite for literacy in the modern world. Advertisements, for example, are the only message forms that are not accompanied by credits in terms of who has produced them. In this sense, movies and television programs have a different status within the image-system in that at least *some* of their process of production is revealed. At minimum, we know that they are made by lots of people!

Ads, on the other hand, simply appear and disappear without any credits. A third set of courses could focus on the political economy of the media and advertising industries. Stripping away the veil of anonymity and mystery would by itself be of great value in demystifying the images that parade before our lives and through which we conceptualize the world and our role within it. As Noam Chomsky puts it (talking about the media in general) in his book *Necessary Illusions*: "Citizens of the democratic societies should undertake a course of intellectual self-defense to protect themselves from manipulation and control, and to lay the basis for meaningful democracy."[11] Such a course of action will not be easy, for the institutional structure of the image-system will work against it. However, the invigoration of democracy depends upon the struggle being engaged.

Notes

1. See Epstein (1982).
2. This is discussed more fully in Leiss, Kline, and Jhally (1986).
3. See Hirsch (1976).
4. Scitovsky (1976).
5. Hirsch (1976).
6. Leiss (1976).
7. See Jhally (1987) and Kavanaugh (1981).
8. Goffman (1979).
9. Quoted in Arlen (1981, p. 182).
10. For more on progressive cultural politics, see Angus and Jhally (1989, Introduction).
11. Chomsky (1989).

References

Angus, I., & Jhally, S. (1989). *Cultural politics in contemporary America.* New York: Routledge.
Arlen, M. (1981). *Thirty seconds.* New York: Penguin.
Chomsky, N. (1989). *Necessary illusions: Thought control in democratic societies.* Boston: South End.
Epstein, E. (1982). *The rise and fall of diamonds.* New York: Simon & Schuster.
Goffman, E. (1979). *Gender advertisements.* New York: Harper & Row.
Hirsch, F. (1976). *Social limits to growth.* Cambridge, MA: Harvard University Press.
Jhally, S. (1987). *The codes of advertising.* New York: St. Martin's.

Kavanaugh, J. (1981). *Following Christ in a consumer society*. New York: Orbis.

Kline, S. (1989). Limits to the imagination: Marketing and children's culture. In I. Angus & S. Jhally (Eds.), *Cultural politics in contemporary America*. New York: Routledge.

Leiss, W. (1976). *The limits to satisfaction*. Toronto: University of Toronto Press.

Leiss, W., Kline, S., & Jhally, S. (1986). *Social communication in advertising*. Toronto: Nelson.

Scitovsky, T. (1976). *The joyless economy*. New York: Oxford University Press.

Disney's Version of Girlhood

Sharon Lamb and Lyn Mikel Brown

Disney girls are women with Barbie doll bodies. And, like Barbie, one small size fits all. The form-fitting clothing of these heroines proves it. They have the exotic made-up faces of women and the gowns and midriff-baring (Jasmine in *Aladdin*) bikini tops (Ariel in *The Little Mermaid*) of women. Not real women, of course—they're too perfect—but the male fantasy version. They arch their backs (did they use the same template for the Victoria Secret bra ad as they did for *The Little Mermaid* and *Pocahontas* bursting out of the water scenes?), toss their hair, smile sweetly, and speak softly. They're pretty when they're angry. Let's face it, changing skin and hair color and adding some exotic clothing does not a woman of color make. The one exception to this is Lilo and her older sister in *Lilo and Stitch*. What a relief to see real girls' bodies, faces, and personalities. No surprise—they don't make the princess doll set.

Disney girls and women are gossips and chatterboxes. "Girls talk too much," Peter Pan complains after Wendy accosts him. Women in *The Little Mermaid* gossip around the washtub. Ursula the Sea Witch warns Ariel, "The men up there don't like a lot of chatter." In *Dumbo*, a mean-spirited female elephant announces to her friends, "Have I got a trunk full of dirt."

Disney girls mother and do the housework. And not only Snow White and Cinderella. Wendy mothers the Lost Boys, while the native woman in *Peter Pan* admonishes her, "No dance! Go gettum firewood" (adding a little racism to the mix). The little girl who catches Mowgli's eye in *The Jungle Book* sings, "I will have a handsome husband, and a daughter of my own. And I'll send her to fetch the water. I'll be cooking in the home." The soldiers in *Mulan* sing about a girl worth fighting for who cooks and waits at home.

Disney girls have lovely voices. From Snow White to Pocahontas, those girls can really warble. It's part of what makes them beautiful. They sing their desire and woes to animals and other nonhuman creatures because, and this is important:

Disney girls have no support systems. Except for Lilo who has her big sister, Disney girls don't have girlfriends and very little family. If they do, they leave them for princes or beasts or bandits (*Robin Hood*). Even after proving themselves, they find real honor with a husband (*Mulan*). They typically don't have mothers, and their fathers tend to be buffoons (*Beauty and the Beast*, *Aladdin*) or authoritarian jerks (*The Little Mermaid*).

Disney girls can't resist a mirror. Check out Tinker Bell measuring her hips in a hand mirror. She is clearly shocked at what she sees. Are they that wide? Dated, you say? Elastigirl, the mother in the Disney/Pixar movie *The Incredibles*, checks out her hips in a mirror in the same fashion. It seems that saving her family and the world just has to wait. Disney girls can make mirrors out of anything. Cinderella checks her hair in a wash bubble and later in a pond. Lady of *Lady and the Tramp* catches her image in a water bowl.

Disney girls are incomplete without a man. It is not only romance, it is romance in a reality that affirms male power. Male power is what Disney does best, and not just in the old Disney movies. Every Pixar movie to date is a male journey story. Yes, girls exist as primary characters in *A Bug's Life*, *The Incredibles*, *Finding Nemo*, and *Cars*, but the main character is male. Men provide the energy, the rules, and the hope for safety (*Mulan*, *Pocahontas*), while we're reminded with one-liners that girls are crybabies (*Chicken Little*) or need to be rescued (almost every movie). Disney girls will do anything to meet or be chosen by the man of their dreams. Ariel gives up her voice; Tinker Bell betrays Wendy; Cinderella's stepsisters fight over the prince and betray her. Disney is brilliant at retelling history and creating romance where none existed: between Pocahontas and John Smith or between Mulan and her officer. A girl can't have her own story or live a life of bravery unless, in the end, she assumes her rightful place. She is not a Disney girl unless she marries.

Powerful Disney women are evil and ugly. Except for the grandmother spirit in *Pocahontas*, who shows up again in *Brother Bear*, when adult women exist they are typically vengeful and jealous of the Disney girl. They are also powerful and ugly: wicked stepmothers and queens (*Snow White*, *Cinderella*), ugly monsters and witches (*The Little Mermaid*, *The Sword and the Stone*, *Monsters, Inc.*). They are cruel and vengeful (Cruella DeVille in *101 Dalmatians* and the Queen of Hearts in *Alice in Wonderland*). Female power is itself evil: "It's time Ursula took matters into her own tentacles!" It is pretty clear to any little kid watching that dark skin is associated with evil. Check out Ursula or the evil queen in *Snow White* at their villainous peak. And while women with power will meet their demise in the most horrible ways—a stake through the heart, a car accident—Disney girls who recognize male power are rewarded with a place in his world: "Here she stands, the girl of his dreams" (*Cinderella*).

Disney girls are innocent. Tarty female characters in Disney movies pop up in funny places, usually in groups to underscore the Disney girl's singular innocence or to affirm a character's manliness: the busty barmaids in *Beauty and the Beast*, the sexy harem dancers in *Aladdin*, the vampish muses in *Hercules*. They are the girls that male characters like to flirt with but won't marry.

Let's be fair. We have welcomed the feisty, clever, and brave Disney girl of recent years. Look how Ariel defies her father and follows her heart! Isn't it great that Beauty is also a bit of a nerd and defiantly rejects the big handsome lout who pursues her? Isn't Pocahontas fearless, and isn't her relationship with her grandmother wonderful? Mulan really proves girls can do everything a guy can and, in this case, better than any other guy. Who wouldn't want their daughter to have such presence of mind and such impact on the world around her? The problem is that so much of the courage and feistiness is either in pursuit of romance or later put aside for it. Beauty endures horrific abuse to change her man; Ariel gives up her voice for her man; Pocahontas's goal is saving her man as much as preserving her homeland; Mulan's amazing feats dissolve in the presence of romance. This feels like a bait and switch. Draw a girl in with promises of something different and then bring in the same old thing through the back door.

Source: Sharon Lamb and Lyn Mikel Brown, *Packaging Girlhood: Rescuing Our Daughters from Marketers' Schemes* (New York: St. Martin's Press, 2006), 67–70.

Supplement 21

Questions for Critical Viewing

Sharon Lamb and Lyn Mikel Brown

Whether you're watching old favourites or new movies, ask yourself the following questions about representations of girls, women, and gender relations.

1. Who does most of the rescuing, and who is being rescued?
2. Who is full of personality? Why can't a lead girl be the one with all the personality?
3. Is the best friend of the girl in the movie a real friend, or is she dropped as a character early on?
4. Who gets to drive the cool vehicles? The motorcycles and the ATVs?
5. Does there have to be a girl-meets-boy romantic ending? Can you think of another happily-ever-after scenario?
6. What does she wear at the end of the movie? A white gown? Why?
7. Are there girls that reflect your daughter's race, class, or sexual orientation? And why are so many people in this movie white and rich?
8. Are the partyers in the film stereotypically people of color?
9. Is there a gratuitous scene where the girl tries on clothes, goes shopping, or appears on a catwalk?
10. Do the parents have cool jobs (football coach, author, artist, rock-and-roll singer) or real ones?
11. Are feminist moms or businesswomen the enemy rather than a resource?
12. Who holds the powerful jobs? (Children Now reports that 71 percent of lawyers, 80 percent of CEOs, 92 percent of officials, and 80 percent of doctors on TV are men.)
13. What are the lead girl's interests, talents, skills, and hobbies?
14. Why do they make the mean girl so one-dimensionally mean?
15. Why are there so few women producers, writers, and directors? (When a program has at least one woman writer, a female director, or a female producer, the TV show or movie has 5 to 10 percent more female characters.)

Source: Sharon Lamb and Lyn Mikel Brown, *Packaging Girlhood: Rescuing Our Daughters from Marketers' Schemes* (New York: St. Martin's Press, 2006), 91–93.

Chapter 36

Ghetto Bitches, China Dolls, and Cha-Cha Divas: Race, Beauty, and the Tyranny of Tyra Banks

Jennifer L. Pozner

Jennifer Pozner is a media critic, lecturer, and founder of Women in Media and News *(WIMN), a media analysis, education, and advocacy organization. She also created and manages WIMN's* Voices, *a blog that brings together dozens of leading female journalists, media critics, and activists to discuss and analyze the coverage of women in media. Her work has appeared in numerous well-known outlets, including* Ms., Chicago Tribune, *and* Bitch: Feminist Response to Pop Culture, *as well as a variety of anthologies on women and popular culture. The following article is taken from* Reality Bites Back: The Troubling Truth about Guilty Pleasure TV, *the first book of its kind to explore underlying messages reality TV sends about gender, race, class, and sexuality.*

It's my number one passion in my life to stretch the definition of beauty. I listen to many heartbreaking stories of women who thought they would be happier if they looked different. I want every girl to appreciate the skin she's in.
> —Tyra Banks, apologizing for making girls don blackface on
> *America's Next Top Model*[1]

As executive producer, Tyra Banks claims *America's Next Top Model* aims to expand beauty standards, as she herself did as the first Black solo cover model for *GQ*, *Victoria's Secret*, and *Sports Illustrated*'s swimsuit edition. [Elsewhere I have] documented how she fails at this lofty goal regarding weight, size, and eating disorders. Does she do any better at exploding race-based beauty biases?

Sometimes, yes. She exhorts *ANTM* contestants to be confident and love themselves, flaws and all. Her methods may be devised to break most models' spirits for our viewing pleasure, but there's something to be said for casting diverse young women and at least telling them that they're gorgeous. In a TV landscape that has typically depicted girls of color as ugly when not ignoring them entirely, sometimes a slightly positive mixed message is as good as it gets. Better yet, every once in a while a truly subversive, dare I say *feminist*, moment can be found among *ANTM*'s emotional and cultural wreckage. Model Anchal Joseph, who emigrated to the United States from New Delhi when she was six years old, wore blue contacts to her cycle 7 audition. When the judges asked her why, she said she'd always wanted different colored eyes:

> *Tyra:*   Do you think there's something culturally in America or even in your own country that is telling you that a lighter eye is prettier?
>
> *Anchal:*   In India they do believe that lighter skin and lighter eyes are prettier. I actually want to beat that. Be like, "Hey, I'm dark, I'm beautiful, and I'm Indian, so I don't have to have light skin or have light-colored eyes to be beautiful."

After Anchal's baby browns were photographed au natural, the judges said she was so gorgeous she could be Miss World. Asked how she felt looking at her picture without the contacts, she replied:

> *Anchal:*   It makes me feel pretty.
>
> *Tyra:*   It does? Why's that?
>
> *Anchal:*   Because in a way I think I was hiding behind them. I'm glad. [At this she broke down in tears of self-acceptance—and we got to watch her psychological break-through.]
>
> *Tyra [to judge Nigel Barker]:* Nigel, you being Indian, how do you respond to that?
>
> *Nigel:*   You are beautiful the way you are. We are all unique in our own ways, and it's that uniqueness that makes people beautiful.

I'll never accuse Tyra Banks of having a tenth of Toni Morrison's wisdom. Still, I was impressed by the editing of Anchal's initial longing for societal affirmation, à la *The Bluest Eye*, followed by her eventual realization that her dark skin and brown eyes simply make her more authentically stunning.

China Dolls, Dragon Ladies, and Spicy Latinas

Such moments are exceptions on *ANTM*, which [...] set many of the templates for racial type-casting on network reality TV.

Of the 170 contestants cast by cycle 13, only five besides Anchal have been East or South Asian. The first, April Wilkner, half-Japanese and half-white, said that before she decided to model, "I never really thought about my ethnicity." *ANTM* made sure viewers could think of little else. They framed her as uncomfortable with her cultural identity, while confusing that identity by adorning her with symbols from a country unconnected to her heritage (Chinese lanterns placed on her head, a dragon painted on her chest).

Cut to the cycle 6 audition of Korean contestant Gina Choe, who said, "I think there's just not enough Asian models out there. I feel that I can break down that barrier, and I think it's my responsibility." Nice! You'd almost think the casting directors finally sought out an Asian American woman who was proud of her racial background.

Sadly, no. A moment later, she told us, "I'm not into Asian guys." From then until her elimination five weeks later, Gina was edited as if she was struggling with "an identity crisis," and stereotyped as an "exotic" fading flower who couldn't stand up for herself when attacked by her competitors. She was vilified on the show, on fan sites, and by culture critics as being a poor representative of her race for making statements such as "As a Korean person and as an American person, I'm just a little bit of both, and I don't know which one I am more of." What went unexplored was why *Top Model* thought it appropriate to make Gina feel she had to choose whether she was "more" tied to her ethnicity or her nationality—the subtext of which implies that a Korean American is not a "real" American, just as Anchal was asked about attitudes in her "own country."

Top Model has mixed and matched from various long-held stereotypes about Asian women in American movies, described in *The Asian Mystique* as including the cold and calculating "Dragon Lady" (traits assigned to ambivalent April) and the submissive "Lotus Flower … China Doll" (docile Gina).[2] Cycle 11 finally cast a truly proud Asian American woman … then promptly reduced her to the clichéd "Vixen/Sex Nymph." When we were first introduced to Sheena Sakai, a half-Japanese, half-Korean go-go dancer with a large rack and an even bigger swagger, she announced, "I'm gonna show you, America. You ain't ready for this yellow fever. One time for the Asians!" Sheena was recruited by a casting director who saw her working as a stuntwoman for the movie *Tropic Thunder*—but as is often the case on reality television, producers revealed only those details that reinforced the frame they'd chosen for her character. Since they wanted her as that season's resident "hootchie," her stunt work wasn't discussed on the show or mentioned on her CW bio. Instead, she was criticized as too sexy in every episode. Early on a judge sneered, "You look like Victoria's Secretions." Later, during a challenge in Amsterdam's red light district, where prostitutes pose in storefronts to entice customers, she was told she looked like she should be selling herself in that window, rather than modeling clothes.

Latina *Top Model* hopefuls have been consistently typecast as promiscuous sluts, "naturally" good dancers, or bursting with machisma and ready to throw down. Semifinalist Angelea didn't make cycle 12's final cut after she got into a fight and was written off as hot-tempered, "ghettofied," and easily provoked to violence.

Cycle 8 winner Jaslene "Cha-Cha Diva" Gonzalez, who spoke Spanish in her Cover Girl commercial, was called "spicy" and portrayed as a cross between "a drag queen" and Carmen Miranda. High school dropout Felicia "Fo" Porter, half-Mexican and half-Black, was used to reinforce the "Latinos are lazy" trope: The unemployed model said she auditioned for the show to save herself "the busy hassle of putting your pictures out to agencies and hoping to get a call back."

Other Latina models throughout the series have been called "fiery" as a compliment and "hootchie" as an insult. Second-cycle winner Yoanna House, named one of *Latina* magazine's "It Girls," notably avoided such typecasting. Since she is fair-skinned enough to pass for white, the show chose to erase her ethnicity, playing into the standard Hollywood convention that positions Caucasians as the "default" American. Most viewers were unaware that she was half-Mexican. Instead, media outlets from NPR and *Time Out Chicago* to *International Cosmetic News* refer to Jaslene as "the first Latina" to win the series, an assumption echoed by *ANTM*'s fans.[3]

Entitled Divas and Ghetto Bitches

African Americans are pigeonholed into similar categories on *ANTM*, which introduced the Angry Black Woman to reality TV before Omarosa was a glint in the eye of *The Apprentice* producer Mark Burnett. Season 1 brought us self-indulgent, catty Camille, the Black model everyone loved to hate. By season 3, Tyra took to pretending she's not an executive producer who casts for type. She warned eventual winner "Eva the Diva" to act sweet, because "I don't want to cast another Black bitch." But of course she did cast and edit Eva as the birch du jour—until week 8, when two white image consultants instructed her to doff the diva label by "showing your best possible manners."

The Violent Ghetto Girl (or as one model was described, the "ghetto Black Barbie") also looms large. During her third-season tryout, low-income single mom Tiffany Richardson, who got kicked out of high school for acting like "the Devil," said she wanted to be on *ANTM* to "soften up" because "I don't want to fight no mo." Uh-oh. The semifinalists went out to a bar, where a local "skank" poured a drink over Tiffany's head. She freaked out, yelled, "Bitch poured beer on my weave!" and hurled a glass at her. Bottles started flying, and they hightailed it out of there. A white model condemned violence; Tiffany retorted, "That's great, Martin Luther King. But I'm with Malcolm." Violence is "all I know," she said, because "nobody ever taught me to handle my problems without fighting."

Though she was "trying to change for the better," she got sent home to "the hood" by the end of the episode, calling herself a failure. But because she *always* wants to feature "another Black bitch"—especially of the ratings-generating "ghetto" variety—Banks brought Tiffany back for the fourth season, after she'd been through anger management classes. She made it to the seventh episode, where she couldn't read from a teleprompter, grumbled, "This is humiliating more and more each week," and was eliminated. This time, instead of calling herself a failure, she smiled, hugged the other models, and told them she'd be okay. This didn't sit well with Tyra, who prefers self-flagellation and depression from rejectees, especially when they're poor and Black. So, she took it upon herself to remind the girl of her place: "This should be serious to you!" Tiffany replied that looks can be deceiving, but she was "sick of crying about stuff that I cannot change. I'm sick of being disappointed, I'm sick of all of it." Now apparently clairvoyant, Tyra yelled that Tiffany wasn't really sick of disappointment, because if she were, "you would stand up and take control of your destiny!"

Tyra continued to criticize her "defeatist attitude" until Tiffany got choked up, saying, "I don't have a bad attitude. Maybe I am angry inside, I've been through stuff, so I'm angry, but—" But she couldn't finish, because Tyra cut her off with a neck-rolling, finger-pointing, top-of-her-lungs tirade:

> Be quiet. Tiffany! BE QUIET! STOP IT! I have never in my life yelled at a girl like this! When my mother yells like this it's because she loves me. I was rooting for you, we were all rooting for you! How dare you! Learn something from this! When you go to bed at night, you lay there and you take responsibility for yourself, because nobody's going to take responsibility for you. You rollin' your eyes and you act like it's because you've heard it all before—you've heard it all before—you don't know where the hell I came from, you have no idea what I've been through. But I'm not a victim. I grow from it and I learn. Take responsibility for yourself!

And with that, Tiffany was turned into *ANTM*'s symbol of the irresponsible ghetto chick who isn't willing to work hard to care for herself or her child. Such pop culture imagery builds on decades of inaccurate, scapegoating news reports dating back to the 1980s, which blamed so-called "welfare queens" (a phrase that became code for poor women of color, often young mothers) for the poverty, educational inequity, and violence that plagued their communities. According to this media mantra, these weren't systemic problems requiring institutional solutions, they simply stemmed from laziness, greed, and lack of discipline inherent among poor youth of color. (Black and Latina girls bore the added burden of being branded promiscuous and immoral, while young men of color were pathologized as "Super Predators").[4, a] Tyra's hissy

---

a.   To convince the public to roll back the social safety net for the poor, 1980s and 1990s conservatives waged a war in the media against poor women. In addition to the derogatory "welfare queen" said to be "popping out babies for checks," African Americans and Latinas in particular were labeled "immoral" "brood mares," and even called "public enemy number one" by ABC's Diane Sawyer. *Newsweek* senior editor Jonathan Alter went further, insisting

fit about Tiffany's supposed "victim" mentality and "defeatist attitude" was a revival of that sorry script. That she issued this verbal beatdown in the name of "love"—and treated the twenty-two-year-old as "ungrateful" for the chance to be used and shamed on national television—is deeply manipulative. That *Top Model* affects viewers' perceptions of young women of color is even worse. Parroting Tyra's rhetoric, a Television Without Pity commenter wrote, "Tiff *and others like her* can't be bothered to pick up a book? Read. Learn. Get good grades.... Tyra was right. Get off your ass Tiff and accept responsibility for yourself. Her granmama put a roof over her head and food on the table and yet Tiff can't be bothered to study and get good grades and pull herself out of poverty? Slackers disgust me" (emphasis mine).[5]

Uppity Black Girls Need Humble Pie

Faced with a strong Black woman who couldn't be shoehorned as an ignorant, angry, ghetto bitch, Tyra had only one more card to play: "Bourgie Snob." Meet Yaya DaCosta, cycle 3's Ivy League runner-up. An African Studies and International Relations student at Brown University, she spoke Portuguese and French, auditioned with her hair in braids, and intended "to represent a beauty that is Black." She was elegant, intelligent, and poised. Tyra was initially "impressed" with Yaya's education and "her Afro-centric vibe," which may be why she was one of the only girls in *ANTM*'s history to be allowed to wear her hair in a natural 'fro, saying it showed her pride as a strong Black woman.

Alas, the sisterlove was short lived. Yaya looked like a stunning "chocolate Barbarella" in photos, but Tyra said she didn't seem "modelesque" in person. "Think ... glamour, as opposed to natural," she instructed. A white stylist was brought on to tell her that her "Earth Mother" look would turn off advertisers: "If you go into a toothpaste ad, are you gonna go in a dashiki?" she sneered. "They'll see the big hair and they'll see the African print and it's like, oh my God!" Later, during judging, the stylist disparaged her "intensity to prove your sort of Africanness ... it's overbearing. It's just too much. It's sort of a layer on top of a layer." To her credit, the camera caught Tyra glaring, clearly pissed off. In contrast, Yaya wasn't allowed to be upset at this obviously racist swipe.[b] When she protested being stereotyped and turned into "a cliché," Tyra reprimanded her for "being very defensive, and it's not attractive," and made her apologize to a kente cloth hat. During evaluation, Tyra reiterated that "Yaya brings [a] superiority, condescending attitude" that is "so ugly."

From then on, they had their frame. Through the magic of editing, Yaya's education and elegance became pretentiousness: her eloquence was characterized as showing off. She took dazzling photographs and shined on the catwalk, yet for the rest of the competition Yaya was represented as an arrogant, Blacker-than-thou snob. She was chosen as fashion designers' favorite at client meetings, yet the judges condemned her as so stuck-up and hypersensitive that "no one will want to work with you." She made it to the finale, but lost because the judges didn't consider her "likable" enough.

Viewers tend to believe that the caricatures they've seen on reality TV match (or at least resemble) participants' real-life personalities, regardless of the truth or falseness of that person's portrayal. Yaya

---

that "every threat to the fabric of this country—from poverty to crime to homelessness—is connected to out-of-wedlock teen pregnancy." Riddled with inaccuracies, these reports nevertheless helped turn the tide of public opinion, enabling Democratic President Bill Clinton to pass a punitive welfare reform package in 1996 that resulted in hundreds of thousands of women and children falling deeper into poverty.

b.   Banks has regularly encouraged Black models to put up with blatant bigotry she herself would never stand for. For example, on an episode in Spain, a male model disparaged African American contestant Jaeda Young, saying he didn't like Black women and didn't want to kiss her in a commercial they had to film for Secret deodorant. Editing emphasized how shaken she was by his racism, which could have led to a denunciation of bias in the industry by the judges. Instead, they eliminated Jaeda for making "excuses" and having poor chemistry in her ad.

is a case in point. The image foisted on her by *ANTM*'s producers clung to her for five years and numerous film and TV jobs later. In 2009, when *Entertainment Weekly* reported that she landed a role on ABC's *Ugly Betty*, readers said they "hate Yaya with a passion," called her "arrogant," "pretentious," and "nasty," and wrote that "she needs a big piece of humble pie!" When a smart, self-possessed African American woman is said to "need humble pie," the message is that this "uppity" Black person just doesn't know her place.[6]

Curious George, Work It Out!

Some of the above tropes, like Tyra's tirade against Tiffany, require some unpacking to realize how they connect to a long history of attacks on women of color in politics and the media. But deep-seated beauty biases were all too clear in the representation of Kelle, an affluent African American gallery owner who called herself "a white girl with a really good tan." She came into the competition exuding confidence to the point of conceit, but a few weeks in Tyra's den of self-doubt changed all that.

Over numerous episodes, viewers were treated to multiple scenes in which Kelle sadly inspected herself in a mirror, pondering newly perceived flaws and telling the camera that she'd grown to believe the judges' appraisal of her. "I just see myself and I'm like, *Oh my God, I'm hideous!*" she sobbed. "I can't look at myself in the mirror anymore.... Every time I look in the mirror I'm crying." As one of her competitors explained, "Kelle came in this competition and she was like, 'Oh, oh, I'm beautiful!' and the judges have totally broke her!" After being told repeatedly that her face, and particularly her mouth, were not photogenic, she broke down in a fit of internalized racism. While Tyra made each girl reveal her deepest body insecurity, Kelle complained that she hated her profile. "It's like I have a protruding mouth. You know what I mean? I almost feel like I have a monkey mouth. I guess [it] can look like really, I don't know, primitive."

It's telling that the show chose to air that comment rather than leaving it on the cutting room floor with hundreds of not-ready-for-prime-time hours of tape. Yet such a statement could have been used as a teaching moment, to raise awareness of the historic dehumanization of Black women starting with imagery during slavery and progressing to contemporary ads that depict Black women as exotic, primal animals. So, did Tyra "I'm a proud, beautiful Black woman" Banks break it down for Kelle, and for the millions of young viewers who idolize the former Victoria's Secret supermodel? Did she tell Kelle to do some emotional work to reject the external messages she's gotten from a culture that tells Black women that they are low, ugly creatures? Or did she even spout one of her clichéd "Girl, your mouth is fierce!" Tyra-isms?

Fat chance. Rebuking racist imagery doesn't fly in advertiser-driven reality TV, and Banks's role as producer took precedence over any sense of social responsibility or ethnic solidarity. "We're gonna have to do some profile shots and analyze that.... I'd be like, 'Go, Curious George, work it out!'" *Top Model*'s diva-in-chief replied. "I'm glad you guys are so honest, you know what I mean? That's what it's about, that everybody understands that you're not perfect. And that this is a business of smoke and mirrors, and fooling people into thinking you look like something else."

Let's unpack, shall we? A Black teenager thinks she's hot until *ANTM*'s judges convince her she's an ugly ape. To make her feel better, Tyra calls her Curious George,[7,c] but assures her that with the "smoke and mirrors" of makeup, lighting, and camera angles she can "fool people" into

---

c.   Curious George, the inquisitive monkey of children's book and PBS Kids fame, has been interpreted by literacy and culture scholars as a slave narrative. In the original story, The Man with the Big Yellow Hat kidnaps George from the African jungle and brings him to America, where he gets thrown in jail, escapes, and ends up behind bars in a zoo.

thinking she's not so primitive after all. Kelle revealed what *ANTM* taught her in an episode titled, "The Girl Who Cries When She Looks in the Mirror":

> I've realized what it was. It's this part of my mouth. It's like an extra layer of fat or something. So it's like a snout.... I was in denial about my snout. And now I know, and so it's just hard to work.... [It makes me] very limited.

Black Models Gone "Wild"

*****

The depiction of African Americans as animals and/or savages dates back to pre-abolition newspapers and magazines, where political cartoons and crude artwork accompanied editorial copy justifying the ownership of, and denial of basic human rights for, "the Negro race." At the same time, print ads sold all manner of products using such imagery to mock and dehumanize Black men, women, and children. Historically such media images functioned as visual propaganda, working to convince whites that Black people were not quite human—laying the groundwork for rationalizing slavery before abolition, segregation during Jim Crow, and contemporary pro-eugenics arguments.[8]

Such imagery is no longer considered appropriate in most mainstream news outlets. But [...] the advertising industry continues to employ these themes, especially with female subjects.

Women's bodies have borne the brunt of this vile ideology in contemporary advertising, which continues to portray Black women as provocatively clothed, snarling-mouthed animals in jungles, deserts, and safaris. "Tame and timid? That goes against my instincts," says a Black woman smoking a Virginia Slims cigarette in skintight leopard-print pants and matching halter top. "The hunting's always good at Daffy's," reads the caption of an ad featuring a Black model crouched on a beach next to a lion, her leg tucked under her in the same position as the cat's. "Gather your ammunition (cash, check, Mastercard, or Visa) and aim straight for Daffy's. It's the best hunting with the best bargains around." Are we hunting the feline, or the human? The ad draws no distinction—they're both wildcats.[9] In a September 2009 *Harper's Bazaar* spread headlined "Wild Things," supermodel Naomi Campbell skips rope with monkeys, rides an elephant and an alligator, and races a cheetah while her own spotted dress trails like a tail in the wind.

[...] Daffy's ad and *Harper's* spread tread old ground. In 1985, supermodel Iman was photographed next to a cheetah, her head tilted in the same position as the animal, her body turned in a catlike contortion, and her hair wrapped in a cheetah-print scarf. That same year, Iman stalked down a Thierry Mugler runway in safari garb with a live monkey hanging on her shoulder(!), while two buff Black men in loincloths trailed behind her carrying a giant umbrella.

Such images in advertising and fashion code women of color as "primitive," with untamed sexuality both fearful and seductive. Taken to its (il)logical conclusion, this fetishized depiction culminates in images of Black women as dangerous creatures who must be literally deprived of their freedom. Naomi Campbell's "Wild Things" pictorial was shot by world-famous fashion photographer Jean-Paul Goude. Nearly thirty years ago, Goude produced an infamous image of singer Grace Jones on all fours, naked, oiled up, and snarling inside a cage, surrounded by raw meat. Above her head, a zoolike plaque cautioned: Do Not Feed the Animal. (A similar caged photo of Jones graced the cover of Goude's 1981 book, *Jungle Fever*.) Locking her up is the only way to prevent her dangerous sexuality from overwhelming everyone in her wake, the picture suggests. This and several other now-iconic images of Jones posing behind bars, in chains, and with whips were replicated by biracial (Cape Verdian and Italian) model Amber Rose in the September 2009 issue of *Complex* magazine. As journalist Claire Sulmers notes, "Though the photos were taken decades apart, the message is the same. These women are so wild they must be caged—they're sultry, snarling sex beasts."[10]

By dressing a group of models up as "sexy" "native" creatures for a beauty ad as soon as they arrived in South Africa, *ANTM* wasn't engaging in a harmless homage to the land they were visiting. The Lubriderm photo shoot illustrates how the advertising industry's long-held racial essentialism influences the depiction of people of color in product-placement-driven reality TV.

I'm sure some may question whether the episode was actually racist, since white models were also featured as wildlife in the Lubriderm challenge. Yes, it was. The shoot built on a preestablished ad-industry precedent in which the mere *concept* of Africa and Black Africans are conjured to "represent white humans' own more primitive past," writes scholar Lisa Wade, on *Sociological Images*. Wade was describing a 2008–09 ad campaign by "Wild Africa Cream" liqueur, packaged in a leopard-print bottle with *ubuntu* beads around the neck. In the ads, a seductively clothed Black woman has grown a leopard's arm; another sports a cheetah's tail. White women and men in other ads in the series also have nonhuman features. The tagline? "Unleash your wild side." Each ad featured a smoldering male or female model, Black or white, each with a leopard's ear, hand, or arm. In an accompanying radio spot, a man speaks of following a sexy woman, wondering, "Did a leopard escape from the zoo?" while a female voice purrs that the liqueur can help everyone find "a little wild in them."[11]

Since fashion and beauty advertisers have worked with *ANTM*'s producers to build the show's content around their products (and ideas), it's no surprise that *ANTM*'s South African animals shoot shares the "Africa connects us to our animal natures" reasoning of Wild Africa Cream's marketing gambit. It's also why the show would see no problem devoting several episodes to the process of convincing a beautiful (and formerly confident) Black teenager that her "monkey" "snout" makes her ugly.

Dehumanizing African American women in advertising and media carries very real consequences for the self-esteem of Black girls and women, as well as for larger society. When an entire class of people are seen as animals, it becomes harder to prevent violence against them and easier to justify denying them equal social, economic, and political rights. If only Tyra Banks were equipped to realize the impact her programming choices can have.

Tyra Banks: Fashion Victim Turned Fashion Perpetrator

[…] Culture analysts have wondered why a powerful Black model who seems to really want the best for young women of color would subject them to such demeaning double standards. "On camera, many of the black *ANTM* contestants talk about how thrilled they are to be in Tyra's presence; how her success as a black supermodel inspired them, helping them see themselves as beautiful for the first time," *Slate*'s J.E. Dahl writes, "but how does she repay their adoration? By trying to eradicate ethnic idiosyncrasies in their personality and appearance."[12]

Comics call her crazy, critics dismiss her as an opportunist, and her young fans fiercely defend her as the benevolent granter of young women's dreams. I have a different theory: I believe she has grown up mentally colonized by fashion and beauty advertisers, leaving her with something akin to Stockholm syndrome.[d]

---

d.   Stockholm syndrome is popularly defined as a psychological condition in which kidnap or abuse victims form attachments to and identify with their captors.

Tyra Banks is many things. She's someone who believes she's an advocate for girls, especially girls of color. Four years before *ANTM* debuted she founded T-Zone, a summer camp program focused on self-esteem and leadership skills. Yet, she's also the ultimate capitalist beauty industry success story. She grew up without money, but used her nearly naked body, and an incredible parade of wigs, to become a media mogul. In addition to serving as host and executive producer of *ANTM*, she filled both those roles on her daytime chatfest, *The Tyra Banks Show*, for five seasons. This helped her earn an estimated $30 million in 2009 alone, more money than any other woman on prime-time TV. Her increasing fiscal power has drawn comparisons to Oprah Winfrey, despite the intellectual chasm between them.[13]

Most of the rest of us learn to navigate the everyday struggles of adolescence—body image insecurities, emerging sexuality, interpersonal relationships, and personal identity—from our friends, family, and community, at the same time as we are influenced by the media images surrounding us. But those images, and their makers, *were* Tyra's dominant community. From age fifteen on, Banks was raised by the fashion and beauty industry and its advertisers. In loco parentis, they gave her fame and fortune beyond her wildest dreams—but always while pitting her against other women, requiring her to hide her natural hair, and reminding her that her value depended on being young and thin.

And so the cycle continues. As a curvy Black model who achieved many firsts, Banks fought against unfair race and gender barriers throughout her career. But like so many dysfunctional patterns, Tyra grew up to become the ultimate perpetrator of the ideology of the fashion and beauty advertisers who stunted her intellectual development and shaped her self-image, psychology, and values. In that context, why is anyone surprised that she is simultaneously

- hilariously narcissistic, as well as compassionate;
- wracked with internalized racism and sexism, while renouncing the concept of discrimination; and
- concerned with girls' self-esteem, while profiting from a show that reinforces unhealthy body standards and racial stereotypes?

When she quit *The Tyra Banks Show* in 2010, she announced that her intention was to focus her Bankable Productions company on films that "can promote positive images of women." I don't doubt Tyra's sincerity. But as *ANTM* illustrates, victims of advertiser-based Stockholm syndrome have an extremely skewed definition of what "positive" media imagery is and what it isn't.

The truth is, the best thing Tyra could do to help "more women and young girls" to "feel as fierce as we truly are" would be to take *ANTM* off the air—or drastically remodel its format.[14]

Notes

1. "Tyra Banks Apologizes over Bi-Racial Episode of 'ANTM,'" StyleList.com, Nov. 18, 2009. Oliver, Dana.
2. *The Asian Mystique: Dragon Ladies, Geisha Girls, & Our Fantasies of the Exotic Orient*, (New York: Public Affairs, 2006). Prasso, Sheridan. p. 87.
3. "Ethnic Magazine Editors Discuss Health, Hollywood Buzz," Sept. 12, 2007. National Public Radio. "Can She Stay on *Top*?" *Time out Chicago*, no. 163: Apr. 10–16, 2008. Ach, Kevin; "Hidden Potential; Reaching Consumers," *International Cosmetic News*, Mar. 1, 2008. Guilbault, Laure.

4. *Extra!*, the magazine published by media watch organization Fairness & Accuracy in Reporting, produced some of the most well-documented debunking of 1980s and 1990s news coverage scapegoating "welfare queens" and criminalizing youth of color. See: "Five Media Myths about Welfare," *Extra!* May/June, 1995; "Public Enemy Number One? Media's Welfare Debate Is a War on Poor Women," *Extra!* May/June, 1995. Jackson, Janine and Flanders, Laura; "Wild in Deceit: Why 'Teen Violence' Is Poverty Violence in Disguise," *Extra!* Mar./Apr., 1996. Males, Mike; "Superscapegoating: Teen 'Superpredators' Hype Set Stage for Draconian Legislation," *Extra!* Jan./Feb., 1998. Templeton, Robin; "The Smell of Success: After 10 Years of 'Welfare Reform,' Ignoring the Human Impact," *Extra!* Nov./Dec. 2006. deMause, Neil.

5. "Eartha Quake," the avatar of a member of the TelevisionWithoutPity.com fan community, left this comment in the discussion forum devoted to Tiffany during *ANTM*'s fourth season. Apr. 14, 2005.

6. "'Ugly Betty' recast: 'Top Model' Is Willi's Daughter!" EW.com, Aug. 11, 2009. Ausiello, Michael.

7. "The Resisting Monkey: 'Curious George,' Slave Captivity Narratives, and the Postcolonial Condition," *Ariel: A Review of International English Literature* 28, no. 1 (Jan. 1997): 69–83. Cummins, June.

8. See: *Ethnic Nations*, 1987, directed by Marlon Riggs; and the Jim Crow Museum of Racist Memorabilia at Ferris State University.

9. The Gender Ads Project. Lukas, Scott A., PhD. www.genderads.com/Gender_Ads.com. html.

10. "Caged Black Women: Grace Jones & Amber Rose," FashionBombDaily.com, Aug. 13, 2009. "Iman @ Thierry Mugler in 1985," MakeFetchHappen.blogspot com, Aug 22, 2008. "Why Photograph a Black Woman in a Cage?" Jezebel.com, Aug. 14, 2009. Sauers, Jenna.

11. "Africa Is Wild, and You Can Be Too," SociologicalImages.blogspot.com, July 5, 2009. Wade, Lisa. Also see http://wildafricacream.blogspot.com/search/label/ADVERTISING.

12. "Is Tyra Banks Racist? The Peculiar Politics of America's Next Top Model," Slate.com, May 18, 2006. Dahl, J.E.

13. "Prime-Time's Top-Earning Women," Forbes.com, Oct. 12, 2009. Rose, Lacey; "Who's the Next Oprah?" E! Online, Nov. 27, 2009. Gornstein, Leslie; "Tyra Banks on It," Forbes.com, July 3, 2006. Blakeley, Kiri.

14. "Tyra Banks to Leave Talk Show," Variety.com, Dec. 28, 2009; "Tyra Banks Says Goodbye to Talk Show," People.com, Dec. 28, 2009.

Supplement 22

Activist Insight:
Fun with Media Literacy

Jennifer L. Pozner

As a sophisticated media consumer, you probably already know this, but it bears repeating: Our democracy cannot thrive without critical, independent journalism; our culture cannot expand without creative, thought-provoking art. Currently, our profit-driven media climate fails to meet these basic needs.

If you're tempted to get all Debbie Downer right now ... don't.

Yes, reality TV can be toxic for women. And, yes, this would all be really depressing if there were nothing you could do about it. Luckily, there's a lot we can do individually and collectively to transform the way we experience media—and the institutions that create, produce, and distribute it. A vibrant, multifaceted media justice movement is emerging as a powerful force in America [... and there are] plenty of ways you can get involved in local and national efforts for systemic change.

But before you roll up your sleeves and get to work for healthier entertainment and news media, the first step is to become an active, critical media consumer. That process can be intense, but it can also be fun.

Backlash Bingo

Does your family watch *American Idol* or *Project Runway* together and judge from the couch? Is *America's Next Top Model* appointment TV for your sorority sisters? Do you and your friends gather around to laugh at whatever hot mess VH1 is pumping out this season or discuss, Facebook, and Tweet about the latest catfights on *The Real Housewives of ...* anywhere?

Are you a mom, dad, older sibling, or teacher uncomfortable that kids you care about watch these series uncritically, but you don't know how to have a productive conversation with them about the messages they're receiving from their favorite shows?

If you watch reality television with your friends, a rousing game of BACKLASH BINGO can add some extra fun to your group TV nights. This game can also be an enjoyable and engaging way to get kids identifying and talking about the ideas their favorite shows are selling them. (And, bonus: They won't look at you like you're wearing a ratty bathrobe, waving your first, and shouting "You kids stay away from my flat-screen!")

HERE'S HOW YOU PLAY:

STEP 1: On a night when you'd usually get together to watch a particular reality show, have a party at least an hour before airtime. Ask your friends, siblings, classmates, or kids—whoever normally watches TV—to list reality shows they see regularly. Talk about what usually happens on those shows, especially the one you're about to watch together.

STEP 2: Ask yourselves questions such as:

- Who are the stereotypical characters who tend to appear each season? (For example: "The Weeping Woman," "The Bitch," "The Skank," the "Ghetto Girl," etc.)
- What specific quotes and phrases pop up repeatedly, even though the shows are "unscripted"? (For example: "I'm not here to make friends!" or "The claws were *bound* to come out....")
- What kinds of situations regularly occur that wouldn't usually happen in real life? For example, everyone seems to think it's completely normal to sob about how desperately you want to marry someone you've only known for twelve days. Or, the only women of color in an entire community are exotic dancers, porn actresses, or violent divas itching for a fight. Or, in the middle of a conversation about something else entirely, one of your friends suddenly holds up or points to a specific eyeliner, cell phone, soda can, or laundry bottle, and starts spouting talking points about how it improves her life.

STEP 3: Photocopy the blank Backlash Bingo card [... included here], or DIY your own. Have enough cards for everyone in the group. Fill in the bingo squares with your answers to questions such as those above, and any others that come up as you brainstorm together. Write your answers in different squares; no one's card should be exactly alike.

STEP 4: Game play begins when you flip on the remote and settle in to watch your favorite reality show. As you watch, identify quotes, characters, and scenarios similar to the things you've predicted on your bingo card. As soon as you see something on your card, call it out so everyone knows you've X'd off a square. You'll be [...] identifying some problematic reality TV messages [... and] every "Single woman called 'loser'!" or "Model in blackface!" or "Blatant product placement!" that matches your card brings you closer to victory.

STEP 5: The winner is the first person to find enough reality TV tropes to cross off every square on your card. If no one completes the entire card, the victor is the person who IDs the most squares.

Critical Thinking: The Building Blocks of Media Literacy

Media literacy is our strongest weapon against propaganda and manipulation in today's profit-driven media culture. Advertisers and media producers want us to watch their offerings passively, to zone out and let their messages wash over us uncritically. Playing games like Backlash Bingo out of the most outrageous or inappropriate reality show content can help you retrain yourself into active viewership. We need to change how we've been conditioned to receive media messages. Smart, empowered viewers take notice of the ideas being sent through the dialogue and action of reality shows, examine the meaning embedded in their narratives, and note the production tricks used to convey those messages.

You don't need to divorce yourselves from *The Real Housewives*, shoot down *The Pick-up Artist*, or cancel your cable. Over the long haul, it's far more important to learn *how* to watch: that is, how to resist the lure of passive viewership and turn your critical filters on high. The following template from the Media Literacy Project (MLP) can help youth and adults deconstruct many forms of media, from TV, movies, and music videos to commercials for everything from cosmetics to politicians.

Contact WIMN:

- To schedule a Reality TV Bindo media literacy workshop
- To bring WIMN's full multimedia presentation on representations of gender, race and class in reality RV to your campus or community group
- Or for more information on women and the media

Women In Media & News   **347-564-5190**   **info@WIMNonline.org**

Deconstruction Questions

1. Whose message is this? Who created or paid for it? Why?
2. Who is the "target audience"? What is their age, ethnicity, class, profession, interests, etc.? What words, images, or sounds suggest this?

3. What is the "text" of the message? (What we actually see and/or hear: written or spoken words, photos, drawings, logos, design, music, sounds, etc.)
4. What is the "subtext" of the message? (What do you think is the hidden or unstated meaning?)
5. What kind of lifestyle is presented? Is it glamorized? How?
6. What values are expressed?
7. What "tools or persuasion" are used?
8. What positive messages are presented? What negative messages are presented?
9. What groups of people does this message empower? What groups does it disempower? How does this serve the media maker's interests?
10. What part of the story is not being told? How and where could you get more information about the untold stories?

Source: Excerpted from Jennifer L. Pozner, *Reality Bites Back: The Troubling Truth about Guilty Pleasure TV* (Berkeley, CA: Seal Press, 2010), 300–312.

Gender Play

Sharon Lamb and Lyn Mikel Brown

Toys "R" Us as Alien Culture

A saunter through Toys "R" Us or Wal-Mart will teach you most of what you need to know about kids' toys. Three things will be apparent: (1) boys' toys and girls' toys are in separate aisles; (2) boys' toys are action toys, and girls' are homemaking, nurturing, or fashion toys; (3) boys' toys are red, blue, black, and green, and girls' are pink and purple. The way toys are advertised and sold, you'd think boys and girls came from different planets. The truth of the matter is that if men are from Mars and women are from Venus, it's because they've been educated in the language, customs, and behaviors of these stereotyped pseudo-planets from birth—and a lot of this education has been through toys.

Since we're talking about planets, let's imagine we're aliens sent to Earth to gather information about human beings. We land in the girls' toys section of Toys "R" Us, Wal-Mart, or Target, thinking that what we see represents the people of this planet. Here is what we learn about these supposedly imaginative, industrious, and somewhat volatile earthlings:

- Humans are obsessed with pink.
- Humans nurture everything but especially babies, and they practice with baby dolls.
- Humans must look pretty and fashionable. They must also make everyone else look pretty and fashionable.
- Humans love jewelry and accessories, either to wear or to decorate with.
- Humans love to decorate houses.
- Humans clean, cook, and entertain.
- Wearing the right accessories is critically important.
- Humans shop.
- All humans are queens, brides, princesses, fairies, ballerinas, and mermaids, or they are sexy shopping divas, pop stars, and cheerleaders.
- Humans are really happy about all this.

Educational Toys

Toys "R" Us isn't for everyone. Although it is a multinational, multiconglomerate corporation with about sixteen hundred stores in twenty-eight countries, there are alternatives. But before you decide to avoid Wal-Mart, Target, and the like, remember that choosing "educational" doesn't always mean choosing gender equity. Our kids love the Discovery Store and other stores like it. It has all sorts of cool science stuff about space, the earth, biology, and technology. But check out the catalog. Below is a list by gender of what kids featured in the catalog are doing. Guess which is the boys' list and which is the girls' list.

LIST A

Helping mother cut flowers with "home florist system"
Eating a snack
Playing indoor golf
Playing with an interactive educational globe
Hanging with Mom
Flying a kite
Watching someone launch a rocket
Getting money from a play ATM machine
Making a pot on a pottery wheel
Watching a kid use a radio-controlled hovercraft

LIST B

Looking through a telescope with Dad
Chasing a radio-controlled jet
Holding the controls of a radio-controlled jet
Playing a football game
Playing basketball
Flying a kite
Launching a rocket
Launching a UFO
Launching an air-powered glider
Using a spy tool off a spy utility belt
Using a metal detector
Wearing a Night Vision Communicator
Using a voice convertor system
Playing with a chemistry set or forensic lab
Looking through a telescope alone
Performing a magic trick
Working a radio-controlled hovercraft
Flying a radio-controlled helicopter

Particularly offensive is the thought that girls' play will involve shopping and could make use of a toy ATM machine. Where's the science and discovery in that? Also offensive is that she is used as a prop to observe and admire the boy working the controls for the radio-controlled hovercraft and launching a rocket. The only gender-neutral toy that the Discovery catalog features is the kite. Don't we want girls to discover the world, too?

Source: Excerpted from Sharon Lamb and Lyn Mikel Brown, *Packaging Girlhood: Rescuing Our Daughters from Marketers' Schemes* (New York: St. Martin's Press, 2006), 212–221.

Supplement 24

If Men Could Menstruate:
A Political Fantasy

Gloria Steinem

Gloria Steinem is a celebrated and accomplished American feminist writer, lecturer, and activist who has been actively involved in social justice movements for over 40 years. She is an internationally recognized expert on a broad range of equality issues. She co-founded Ms. *magazine, helped to found* New York *magazine, published articles in* Esquire, The New York Times, *and women's magazines as well as for publications in other countries. Her books include the bestsellers* Revolution from Within: A Book of Self-Esteem *and* Outrageous Acts and Everyday Rebellions. *Her writing also appears in many anthologies and textbooks. She has been honoured with numerous awards for her activism and journalism career.*

A white minority of the world has spent centuries conning us into thinking that a white skin makes people superior—even though the only thing it really does is make them more subject to ultraviolet rays and to wrinkles. Male human beings have built whole cultures around the idea that penis envy is "natural" to women—though having such an unprotected organ might be said to make men vulnerable, and the power to give birth makes womb envy at least as logical.

In short, the characteristics of the powerful, whatever they may be, are thought to be better than the characteristics of the powerless—and logic has nothing to do with it.

What would happen, for instance, if suddenly, magically, men could menstruate and women could not?

The answer is clear—menstruation would become an enviable, boast-worthy, masculine event: Men would brag about how long and how much.

Boys would mark the onset of menses, that longed-for proof of manhood, with religious ritual and stag parties.

Congress would fund a National Institute of Dysmenorrhea to help stamp out monthly discomforts.

Sanitary supplies would be federally funded and free. (Of course, some men would still pay for the prestige of commercial brands such as John Wayne Tampons, Muhammad Ali's Rope-a-Dope Pads, Joe Namath Jock Shields—"For Those Light Bachelor Days," and Robert "Baretta" Blake Maxi-Pads.)

Military men, right-wing politicians, and religious fundamentalists would cite menstruation ("men-struation") as proof that only men could serve in the Army ("you have to give blood to take blood"), occupy political office ("Can women be aggressive without that steadfast cycle governed by the planet Mars?"), be priest and ministers ("How could a woman give her blood for our sins?") or rabbis ("without the monthly loss of impurities, women remain unclean").

Male radicals, left-wing politicians, mystics, however, would insist that women are equal, just different, and that any woman could enter their ranks if she were willing to self-inflict a major wound every month ("you MUST give blood for the revolution"), recognize the preeminence of menstrual issues, or subordinate her selfness to all men in their Cycle of Enlightenment. Street guys would brag ("I'm a three-pad man") or answer praise from a buddy ("Man, you lookin' good!") by giving fives and saying, "Yeah, man, I'm on the rag!" TV shows would treat the subject at length. ("Happy Days": Richie and Potsie try to convince Fonzie that he is still "The Fonz," though he has missed two periods in a row.) So would newspapers. (SHARK SCARE THREATENS MENSTRUATING MEN. JUDGE CITES MONTHLY STRESS IN PARDONING RAPIST.) And movies. (Newman and Redford in "Blood Brothers"!)

Men would convince women that intercourse was more pleasurable at "that time of the month." Lesbians would be said to fear blood and therefore life itself—though probably only because they needed a good menstruating man.

Of course, male intellectuals would offer the most moral and logical arguments. How could a woman master any discipline that demanded a sense of time, space, mathematics, or measurement, for instance, without that in-built gift for measuring the cycles of the moon and planets—and thus for measuring anything at all? In the rarefied fields of philosophy and religion, could women compensate for missing the rhythm of the universe? Or for their lack of symbolic death-and-resurrection every month?

Liberal males in every field would try to be kind: the fact that "these people" have no gift for measuring life or connecting to the universe, the liberals would explain, should be punishment enough.

And how would women be trained to react? One can imagine traditional women agreeing to all arguments with a staunch and smiling masochism. ("The ERA would force housewives to wound themselves every month": Phyllis Schlafly. "Your husband's blood is as sacred as that of Jesus—and so sexy, too!": Marabel Morgan.) Reformers and Queen Bees would try to imitate men, and pretend to have a monthly cycle. All feminists would explain endlessly that men, too, needed to be liberated from the false idea of Martian aggressiveness, just as women needed to escape the bonds of menses envy. Radical feminists would add that the oppression of the non-menstrual was the pattern for all other oppressions ("Vampires were our first freedom fighters!") Cultural feminists would develop a bloodless imagery in art and literature. Socialist feminists would insist that only under capitalism would men be able to monopolize menstrual blood....

In fact, if men could menstruate, the power justifications could probably go on forever.

If we let them.

Source: Gloria Steinem, "If Men Could Menstruate: A Political Fantasy," *Ms.* (October 1978), 110.

Chapter 37

The Cult of Virginity

Jessica Valenti

Jessica Valenti is a well-known American feminist writer, lecturer, and activist. Named one of the Top 100 Inspiring Women in the World by The Guardian, *she is the author of three books, including* The Purity Myth: How America's Obsession with Virginity Is Hurting Young Women, *which has been made into a documentary. Valenti is founder of feministing.com, a feminist online community, for which she has won various awards, including the 2011 Hillman Journalism Prize.*

He said it was men invented virginity not women. Father said it's like death: only a state in which others are left....

—William Faulkner, *The Sound and the Fury*

In the moments after I first had sex, my then-boyfriend—lying down next to me over his lint-covered blanket—grabbed a pen from his nightstand and drew a heart on the wall molding above his bed with our initials and the date inside. The only way you could see it was by lying flat on the bed with your head smashed up against the wall. Crooked necks aside, it was a sweet gesture, one that I'd forgotten about until I started writing this book.

The date seemed so important to us at the time, even though the event itself was hardly awe-inspiring. There was the expected fumbling, a joke about his fish-printed boxers, and ensuing condom difficulties. At one point, his best friend even called to see how things were going. I suppose romance and discretion are lost on sixteen-year-olds from Brooklyn. Yet we celebrated our "anniversary" every year until we broke up, when Josh left for college two years before me and met a girl with a lip ring.

I've often wondered what that date marks—the day I became a woman? Considering I still bought underwear in cutesy three-packs, and that I certainly hadn't mastered the art of speaking my mind, I've gotta go with no. Societal standards would have me believe that it was the day I became morally sullied, but I fail to see how anything that lasts less than five minutes can have such an indelible ethical impact—so it's not that, either.

Really, the only meaning it had (besides a little bit of pain and a lot of postcoital embarrassment) was the meaning that Josh and I ascribed to it. Or so I thought. I hadn't counted on the meaning my peers, my parents, and society would imbue it with on my behalf.

From that date on—in the small, incestuous world of high school friendships, nothing is a secret for long—I was a "sexually active teen," a term often used in tandem with phrases like "at risk," or alongside warnings about drug and alcohol use, regardless of how uncontroversial the sex itself may have been. Through the rest of high school, whenever I had a date, my peers assumed that I had had sex because my sexuality had been defined by that one moment when my virginity was lost. It meant that I was no longer discriminating, no longer "good." The perceived change in my social value wasn't lost on my parents, either; before I graduated high school, my mother found an empty condom wrapper in my bag and remarked that if I kept having sex, no one would want to marry me.[a]

I realize that my experience isn't necessarily representative of most women's—everyone has his or her own story—but there are common themes in so many young women's sexual journeys. Sometimes it's shame. Sometimes it's violence. Sometimes it's pleasure. And sometimes it's simply nothing to write home about.

The idea that virginity (or loss thereof) can profoundly affect women's lives is certainly nothing new. But what virginity is, what it was, and how it's being used now to punish women and roll back their rights is at the core of the purity myth. Because today, in a world where porn culture and reenergized abstinence movements collide, the moral panic myth about young women's supposed promiscuity is diverting attention from the real problem—that women are still being judged (sometimes to death) on something that doesn't really exist: virginity.

The Virginity Mystery

Before Hanne Blank wrote her book, *Virgin: The Untouched History*, she had a bit of a problem. Blank was answering teens' questions on Scarleteen[1]—a sex-education website she founded with writer Heather Corinna so that young people could access information about sex online, other than porn and Net Nanny—when she discovered that she kept hitting a roadblock when it came to the topic of virginity.

"One of the questions that kept coming up was 'I did such-and-such. Am I still a virgin?'" Blank told me in an interview. "They desperately wanted an authoritative answer."

But she just didn't have one. So Blank decided to spend some time in Harvard's medical school library to find a definitive answer for her young web browsers.

"I spent about a week looking through everything I could—medical dictionaries, encyclopedias, anatomies—trying to find some sort of diagnostic standard for virginity," Blank said.

The problem was, there was no standard. Either a book wouldn't mention virginity at all or it would provide a definition that wasn't medical, but subjective.

"Then it dawned on me—I'm in arguably one of the best medical libraries in the world, scouring their stacks, and I'm not finding anything close to a medical definition for virginity. And I thought, *That's really weird. That's just flat-out strange.*"

Blank said she found it odd mostly because everyone, including doctors, talks about virginity as if they know what it is—but no one ever bothers to mention the truth: "People have been talking authoritatively about virginity for thousands of years, yet we don't even have a working medical definition for it!"

Blank now refers to virginity as "the state of having not had partnered sex." But if virginity is simply the first time someone has sex, then what is sex? If it's just heterosexual intercourse, then we'd have to come to the fairly ridiculous conclusion that all lesbians and gay men are virgins, and that different kinds of intimacy, like oral sex, mean nothing. And even using the straight-intercourse model of sex as a gauge, we'd have to get into the down-and-dirty conversation of what constitutes penetration.[b]

---

a.   After years of denying she ever said such a thing, to her benefit, my mother finally sheepishly apologized.

b.   My college roommate Jen and I, I'm somewhat ashamed to admit, had a three pumps or more rule. Less than three pumps? You didn't have to count it as sex. We thought it was genius, as the three pump chumps, as we called them, were not necessarily the guys you wanted to remember.

Since I've become convinced that virginity is a sham being perpetrated against women, I decided to turn to other people to see how they "count" sex. Most say it's penetration. Some say it's oral sex. My closest friend, Kate, a lesbian, has the best answer to date (a rule I've followed since she shared it with me): It isn't sex unless you've had an orgasm. That's a pleasure-based, non-heteronormative way of marking intimacy if I've ever heard one. Of course, this way of defining sex isn't likely to be very popular among the straight-male sect, given that some would probably end up not counting for many of their partners.

But any way you cut it, virginity is just too subjective to pretend we can define it.

Laura Carpenter, a professor at Vanderbilt University and the author of *Virginity Lost: An Intimate Portrait of First Sexual Experiences*, told me that when she wrote her book, she was loath to even use the word "virginity," lest she propagate the notion that there's one concrete definition for it.[2]

"What is this thing, this social phenomenon? I think the emphasis put on virginity, particularly for women, causes a lot more harm than good," said Carpenter.[3]

This has much to do with the fact that "virgin" is almost always synonymous with "woman." Virgin sacrifices, popping cherries, white dresses, supposed vaginal tightness, you name it. Outside of the occasional reference to the male virgin in the form of a goofy movie about horny teenage boys, virginity is pretty much all about women. Even the dictionary definitions of "virgin" cite an "unmarried girl or woman" or a "religious woman, esp. a saint."[4] No such definition exists for men or boys.

It's this inextricable relationship between sexual purity and women—how we're either virgins or not virgins—that makes the very concept of virginity so dangerous and so necessary to do away with.

Admittedly, it would be hard to dismiss virginity as we know it altogether, considering the meaning it has in so many people's—especially women's—lives. When I suggest that virginity is a lie told to women, I don't aim to discount or make light of how important the current social idea of virginity is for some people. Culture, religion, and social beliefs influence the role that virginity and sexuality play in women's lives—sometimes very positively. So, to be clear, when I argue for an end to the idea of virginity, it's because I believe sexual intimacy should be honored and respected, but that it shouldn't be revered at the expense of women's well-being, or seen as such an integral part of female identity that we end up defining ourselves by our sexuality.

I also can't discount that no matter what personal meaning each woman gives virginity, it's people who have social and political influence who ultimately get to decide what virginity means—at least, as it affects women on a large scale.

Virginity: Commodity, Morality, or Farce?

It's hard to know when people started caring about virginity, but we do know that men, or male-led institutions, have always been the ones that get to define and assign value to virginity.

Blank posits that a long-standing historical interest in virginity is about establishing paternity (if a man marries a virgin, he can be reasonably sure the child she bears is his) and about using women's sexuality as a commodity. Either way, the notion has always been deeply entrenched in patriarchy and male ownership.

> Raising daughters of quality became another model of production, as valuable as breeding healthy sheep, weaving sturdy cloth, or bringing in a good harvest.... The gesture is now generally symbolic in the first world, but we nonetheless still observe the custom

of the father "giving" his daughter in marriage. Up until the last century or so, however, when laws were liberalized to allow women to stand as full citizens in their own right, this represented a literal transfer of property from a father's household to a husband's.[5]

That's why women who had sex were (and still are, at times) referred to as "damaged goods"—because they were literally just that: something to be owned, traded, bought, and sold.

But long gone are the days when women were property... or so we'd like to think. It's not just wedding traditions or outdated laws that name women's virginity as a commodity; women's virginity, our sexuality, is still assigned a value by a movement with more power and influence in American society than we'd probably like to admit.

I like to call this movement the virginity movement.[c] And it is a movement, indeed—with conservatives and evangelical Christians at the helm, and our government, school systems, and social institutions taking orders. Composed of antifeminist think tanks like the Independent Women's Forum and Concerned Women for America; abstinence-only "educators" and organizations; religious leaders; and legislators with regressive social values, the virginity movement is much more than just the same old sexism; it's a targeted and well-funded backlash that is rolling back women's rights using revamped and modernized definitions of purity, morality, and sexuality. Its goals are mired in old-school gender roles, and the tool it's using is young women's sexuality. (What better way to get people to pay attention to your case than to frame it in terms of teenage girls having, or not having, sex? It's salacious!)

And, like it or not, the members of the virginity movement are the people who are defining virginity—and, to a large extent, sexuality—in America. Now, instead of women's virginity being explicitly bought and sold with dowries and business deals, it's being defined as little more than a stand-in for actual morality.

It's genius, really. Shame women into being chaste and tell them that all they have to do to be "good" is not have sex. (Of course, chastity and purity, as defined by the virginity movement, are not just about abstaining sexually so much as they're about upholding a specific, passive model of womanhood. But more on this later.)

For women especially, virginity has become the easy answer—the morality quick fix. You can be vapid, stupid, and unethical, but so long as you've never had sex, you're a "good" (i.e., "moral") girl and therefore worthy of praise.

Present-day American society—whether through pop culture, religion, or institutions—conflates sexuality and morality constantly. Idolizing virginity as a stand-in for women's morality means that nothing else matters—not what we accomplish, not what we think, not what we care about and work for. Just if/how/whom we have sex with. That's all.

Just look at the women we venerate for not having sex: pageant queens who run on abstinence platforms, pop singers who share their virginal status, and religious women who "save themselves" for marriage. It's an interesting state of affairs when women have to simply do, well, *nothing* in order to be considered ethical role models. As Feministing.com commenter electron-Blue noted in response to the 2008 *New York Times Magazine* article "Students of Virginity," on abstinence clubs at Ivy League colleges, "There were a WHOLE LOTTA us not having sex at Harvard ... but none of us thought that was special enough to start a club about it, for pete's sake."[6]

But for plenty of women across the country, it *is* special. Staying "pure" and "innocent" is touted as the greatest thing we can do. However, equating this inaction with morality not only

---

c.   The "abstinence movement" would be accurate as would the "chastity movement." But neither quite captures how this obsession really is about virginity, virgins, and an almost too-enthusiastic focus on young women's sexuality. So the "virginity movement" seemed not only appropriate but also a bit needling. Which I enjoy.

is problematic because it continues to tie women's ethics to our bodies, but also is downright insulting because it suggests that women can't be moral actors. Instead, we're defined by what we don't do—our ethics are the ethics of passivity. (This model of ethics fits in perfectly with how the virginity movement defines the ideal woman.)

Proponents of chastity and abstinence, though, would have us believe that abstaining indeed requires strength and action. Janie Fredell, one of the students quoted in the above-mentioned *New York Times Magazine* piece, penned a college newspaper article claiming that virginity is "rooted ... in the notion of strength."

"It takes a strong woman to be abstinent, and that's the sort of woman I want to be," Fredell told the magazine.[7] Her rhetoric of strength is part of a growing trend among the conservative virginity-fetish sect, which is likely the result of virginity movement leaders seeing how questionable the "passive virgin" is in modern society. Now we're seeing virginity proponents assert their fortitude. Conservative messages aimed at young men even call on them to be "virginity warriors," driving home the message that it's men's responsibility to safeguard virginity for their female counterparts, simultaneously quashing any fears of feminization that boys may have surrounding abstinence.

Perhaps it's true that in our sex-saturated culture, it does take a certain amount of self-discipline to resist having sex, but restraint does not equal morality. And let's be honest: If this were simply about resisting peer pressure and being strong, then the women who have sex because they actively want to—as appalling as that idea might be to those who advocate abstinence—wouldn't be scorned. Because the "strength" involved in these women's choice would be about doing what they want despite pressure to the contrary, not about resisting the sex act itself. But women who have sex are often denigrated by those who revere virginity. As feminist blogger Jill Filipovic noted in response to Fredell:

> I appreciate and applaud the personal strength of individuals who decide abstinence is the best choice for them. But what I can't support is the constant attacks on sexually active young people. People who have sex do not feel a constant need to tell abstinent people that their human dignity has been compromised, or that they're dirty, or that they are secretly unhappy, or that they're headed for total life ruin.[8]

And that is exactly what young women are taught, thanks in no small part to conservative backlash. In 2005, for example, the evangelical Christian group Focus on the Family came out with a study reporting that having sex before the age of eighteen makes you more likely to end up poor and divorced.[9] Given that the median age for sexual initiation for all Americans—male and female—is seventeen, I wonder how shocked most women will be when they learn that they have a life of poverty-stricken spinsterhood to look forward to!

But it's not only abstinence education or conservative propaganda that are perpetuating this message; you need look no further than pop culture for stark examples of how young people—especially young women—are taught to use virginity as an easy ethical road map.

A 2007 episode of the MTV documentary series *True Life* featured celibate youth.[10] Among the teens choosing to abstain because of disease concerns and religious commitments was nineteen-year-old Kristin from Nashville, Tennessee. Kristin had cheated on her past boyfriends, and told the camera she'd decided to remain celibate until she feels she can be faithful to her current boyfriend. Clearly, Kristin's problem isn't sex—it's trust. But instead of dealing with the actual issues behind her relationship woes, this young woman was able to circumvent any real self-analysis by simply claiming to be abstinent. So long as she's chaste, she's good.

Or consider singer and reality television celebrity Jessica Simpson, who has made her career largely by playing on the sexy-virgin stereotype. Simpson, the daughter of a Baptist youth minister, started her singing career by touring Christian youth festivals and True Love Waits events. Even when she went mainstream, she publicly declared her virginity—stating that her father had given her a promise ring when she was twelve years old—and spoke of her intention to wait to have sex until marriage. Meanwhile, not surprisingly, Simpson was being marketed as a major sex symbol—all blond hair, breasts, and giggles. Especially giggles. Simpson's character (and I use the word "character" because it's hard to know what was actually her and not a finely honed image) was sold as the archetypal dumb blond. Thoughtless moments on *Newlyweds*, the MTV show that followed her short-lived marriage to singer Nick Lachey, became nationally known sound bites, such as Simpson's wondering aloud whether tuna was chicken or fish, since the can read "Chicken of the Sea."

Despite Simpson's public persona as an airhead (as recently as 2008, she was featured in a Macy's commercial as not understanding how to flick on a light switch), women are supposed to want to be her, not only because she's beautiful by conventional standards, but also because she adheres to the social structures that tell women that they exist purely for men: as a virgin, as a sex symbol, or, in Simpson's case, as both. It doesn't matter that Simpson reveals few of her actual thoughts or moral beliefs; it's enough that she's "pure," even if that purity means she's a bit of a dolt.

For those women who can't keep up the front as well as someone like Simpson, they suffer heaps of judgment—especially when they fall off the pedestal they're posed upon so perfectly. American pop culture, especially, has an interesting new trend of venerating and fetishizing "pure" young women—whether they're celebrities, beauty queens, or just everyday young women—simply to bask in their eventual fall.

And no one embodies the "perfect" young American woman like beauty queens. They're pretty, overwhelmingly white, thin, and eager to please.[d] And, of course, pageant queens are supposed to be as pure as pure can be. In fact, until 1999, the Miss America pageant had a "purity rule" that barred divorced women and those who had obtained abortions from entering the contest—lest they sully the competition, I suppose.[11]

So in 2006, when two of those "perfect" girls made the news for being in scandalous photos on the Internet, supposed promiscuity, or a combination thereof, Americans were transfixed.

First, twenty-year-old Miss USA Tara Conner was nearly stripped of her title after reports surfaced that she frequented nightclubs, drank, and dated. Hardly unusual behavior for a young woman, regardless of how many tiaras she may have.

The *New York Daily News* could barely contain its slut-shaming glee when it reported on the story: "'She really is a small-town girl. She just went wild when she came to the city,' one nightlife veteran said. 'Tara just couldn't handle herself. They were sneaking those [nightclub] guys in and out of the apartment'... Connor still brought boyfriends home.... Soon she broke up with her hometown fiancé and started dating around in the Manhattan nightclub world...."[12]

Instead of having her crown taken away, however, Conner was publicly "forgiven" by Miss USA co-owner Donald Trump, who appeared at a press conference to publicly declare he was giving the young woman a second chance.[13] In case you had any doubts about whether this controversy was all tied up with male ownership and approval, consider the fact that Trump later

---

d.   Who, after all, can maintain a pearly white perma-grin through humiliating bathing suit competitions and inane questions—all for scholarships that are paltry in comparison to the money spent on gowns and coaches—other than women looking for some serious validation?

reportedly considered giving his permission for Conner to pose for *Playboy* magazine. He played the role of dad, pimp, and owner, all rolled into one.[14]

Mere days later, Miss Nevada USA, twenty-two-year-old Katie Rees, was dethroned after pictures of her exposing one of her breasts and mooning the camera were uncovered.[15] When you're on a pedestal, you have a long way to fall.

And, of course, it's impossible to talk about tipped-over pedestals without mentioning pop singer Britney Spears. Spears, first made famous by her song "Baby One More Time" and its accompanying video, in which she appeared in a Catholic schoolgirl mini-uniform, was very much the American purity princess. She publicly declared her virginity and belief in abstinence before marriage, all the while being marketed—much like Simpson was—as a sex symbol. But unlike Simpson, Spears fell far from grace in the eyes of the American public. The most obvious indications of her decline were splashed across newspapers and entertainment weeklies worldwide—a breakdown during which she shaved her head in front of photographers, and various pictures of her drunk and sans panties. But Spears began distancing herself from the virgin ideal long before these incidents hit the tabloids.

First, Spears got some press for moving in with then-boyfriend and fellow pop star Justin Timberlake. But the sexist brouhaha began in earnest when Spears was no longer considered "attractive," because she started to gain weight, got pregnant, and no longer looked like a little girl. Pictures of her cellulite popped up on websites and gossip magazines nationwide, along with guesstimations about her weight and jokes about her stomach. Because "purity" isn't just about not having sex, it's about not being a woman—and instead being in a state of perpetual girlhood. [...]

Shaming young women for being sexual is nothing new, but it's curious to observe how the expectation of purity gets played out through the women who are supposed to epitomize the feminine ideal: the "desirable" virgin. After all, we rarely see women who aren't conventionally beautiful idolized for their abstinence. And no matter how "good" you are otherwise—even if you're an all-American beauty queen—if you're not virginal, you're shamed.

The desirable virgin is sexy but not sexual. She's young, white, and skinny. She's a cheerleader, a baby sitter; she's accessible and eager to please (remember those ethics of passivity!). She's never a woman of color. She's never a low-income girl or a fat girl. She's never disabled. "Virgin" is a designation for those who meet a certain standard of what women, especially younger women, are supposed to look like. As for how these young women are supposed to act? A blank slate is best.

Selling Virginity

Unfortunately, this morality model of virginity—in which women's morals and ethical ability are defined solely by their sexual status—isn't the only type the virginity movement is pushing. Viewing virginity as a commodity—as it was seen back in the days in which daughters were exchanged as property—lives on, just in less obvious ways (though, arguably, much more insidiously). Now fathers participate in purity balls and virginity pledges to maintain ownership over their daughters, even if it's only symbolic. Women's sexuality is still very much for sale.

Not so shockingly to those of us who do feminist and progressive political work, the conservative, religious right has been at the center of keeping women's bodies on the market. The backlash against women's rights over the past three decades has ranged from rolling back our reproductive rights to launching antisexuality scare-tactic campaigns—all part of a larger concerted effort desperately seeking a return to traditional gender roles. Make no mistake about it—these efforts are at the heart of the virginity movement and its goals.

And they've been successful. To a large extent, the virginity movement is the new authority on sexuality. It's in our schools, telling our children what sex is (dirty, wrong, and dangerous), and in our homes, creating legislation that violates women's privacy and bodies. [...]

In addition to promoting the virginity-as-morality model, the virginity movement is working hard to reaffirm virginity as something to be bought, sold, and owned. Sometimes these attempts transpire in more obvious ways than others.

Take, for example, Virginity Vouchers. Sold to abstinence educators as abstinence commitment cards to hand out to students, these vouchers, which look much like credit cards, feature a background image of a bride and groom with the words VIRGINITY VOUCHER: DON'T BUY THE LIE, SAVE SEX FOR MARRIAGE emblazoned across it. The Abstinence Clearinghouse, the largest and best-known abstinence education nonprofit organization in the country, sells the card on its website and makes no effort to hide the fact that this product is, quite literally, commodifying virginity:

> This "Virginity Voucher" is a hard plastic commitment card with a place on the back to sign their name. Created for both young men and women, this card can be kept in their wallet to remind them of their decision.[16]

Right along with their Mastercards and Visas!

Or consider another abstinence product: a gold rose pin handed out in schools and at Christian youth events. The pin is attached to a small card that reads, "You are like a beautiful rose. Each time you engage in pre-marital sex, a precious petal is stripped away. Don't leave your future husband holding a bare stem. Abstain."[17]

Do we really want to teach our daughters that without their virginity, they're nothing but a "bare stem"?

Abstinence-only education [...] which receives more than $178 million a year in federal funding, is chock full of lessons like these that tell students that female sexuality is a "gift," "precious," and something to "save."

A 2008 advertisement promoting Abstinence Awareness Week in Washington, D.C., told young women to "guard your diamond" alongside a picture of a tremendous gem covered in chains and a lock.[18]

And, of course, there are purity balls—the federally funded father/daughter dances where girls as young as age six pledge their virginity to their dads, who in turn pledge to hang on to said virginity until an appropriate husband comes along, to whom the fathers can transfer ownership of their daughters.

Not all of the virginity-for-sale messages are so overt, but all of them are sexist and all of them are dangerous. Why? Because if virginity is a gift, or something "worth saving," that means that those who don't save it are somehow lacking—or, even worse, sullied.

Sex-as-dirty and women-as-tainted messages are central to the virginity movement and are perpetuated [in the] most unfortunate of places—our schools. The primary perpetrator, abstinence-only education, has established programs across the country to tell young women that they're somehow spoiled by sex.

One popular classroom exercise, for example, employs Scotch Tape to demonstrate how pre-marital sex can make girls dirty.[e] A teacher holds up a clear strip of tape, adhesive side down, on the arm of a boy in the class, to symbolize his sexual relationship with the girl. The teacher rips

---

e.   Most classroom exercises focus on girls and their potential filthiness.

off the tape (signifying the breakup, apparently) and holds it up again for the class to look at. Students are meant to see that the strip of tape—the girl—has picked up all kinds of dirt and hair from the boy's arm and is no longer clean. Then, when the teacher tries to stick the same strip of tape to another boy's arm, he or she notes that it doesn't stick—they can't bond! To end things with a bang, the abstinence educator makes a remark about the girl's being "used" and therefore unable to have strong future relationships.[19]

In another popular exercise, abstinence teachers use candy to make their "dirty" points. These candy exercises often consist of teachers showing how the candy can't fit back into its wrapper after being chewed/sucked/eaten. Another program in Nevada even used its abstinence-only state funding to run public radio service ads that said girls will feel "dirty and cheap" after having sex. (The ads were later pulled due to listener outrage.[20]) The fact that these examples nearly always focus on girls is no coincidence. After all, our bodies are the ones that get objectified and pathologized, and it's our morality that's supposedly in jeopardy.

But sullied students across America shouldn't fret! The virginity movement has ensured that there's a way out of the dirt trap: Megan Landry of Houma, Louisiana, signed a "Pure Love Promise" commitment card when she was sixteen years old while attending Abbey Youth Fest, a Louisiana event for young Catholics. The card, which she signed, dated, and carried in her wallet, reads, "Believing that sex is sacred, I promise to God that I will save the gift of my sexuality from now until marriage. I choose to glorify God with my body and pursue a life of purity, trusting that the Lord is never outdone in generosity."[21]

As it turns out, Landry had already lost her virginity to a boyfriend when she was in the tenth grade, but she moved to sign the card anyway after hearing one of the event speakers, Jason Evert, author of *Pure Love*.

"[Evert] gave a talk about purity and saving yourself for marriage. He told us about how he had waited until he was married for sex, but his fiancée had already slept with someone. They both decided not to sleep with each other—he took a pledge and his girlfriend took a secondary virginity pledge. I just thought that was sooooo sweeeet," Landry wrote in an email to me.

The notion of secondary virginity—that you can regain your spiritual and emotional purity by pledging abstinence until marriage, no matter what your sexual history—first became popular in the mid-1980s among conservative Christian groups.[22] Also called born-again virginity, the notion is widespread in Christian programs for young people, abstinence-only education, and even pop culture.

Perhaps sensing that the number of teen virgins in the United States was diminishing, religious groups saw secondary virginity as their opportunity to (for lack of a better term) put more asses in the seats. What better way to increase the numbers of virginity pledges than to open up the process to everyone—even the promiscuous! It's possible that the virginity movement even recognized that the purity standard of not having intercourse was simply unrealistic, and saw how promoting a promise that focused on emotional and spiritual purity might woo those who felt ostracized by their virginityless status.

What I find interesting about secondary virginity is that while it may seem like an easy out, with its emphasis on emotional and spiritual purity, it actually takes a hardline approach to chastity and has the effect of increasing the obstacles to being pure. After all, to be a virgin, all you have to do is not have sex. But to fully embrace your secondary virginity, you must abstain not only from intercourse, but also from masturbation or even thinking about sex. And there's no more of this "anything but" nonsense, either—Love Matters, a teen abstinence program, tells those considering being secondary virgins to "avoid intense hugging," and that "anything beyond a brief, simple kiss can quickly become dangerous."[23]

Some groups even advise women to change the way they act and dress to convey their chastity appropriately. An article from Focus on the Family, "Pure Again," notes that "women find they want to try a different way of dressing—to show more respect for their own bodies."[24, f]

Despite efforts to link secondary virginity to teens' emotional and spiritual selves, the virginity movement's obsession with bodily purity is impossible to hide. Undercutting the movement's argument that purity is about spirituality is the fact that many of the secondary-virginity and chastity messages come from crisis pregnancy centers, groups that masquerade as medical clinics when their actual purpose is to convince young women not to have abortions. What could be more intimately tied with women's bodies and sexuality than pregnancy? And, let's face it, the language of secondary virginity isn't exactly subtle. On the website for A Pregnancy Resource Center of Northeast Ohio, an article titled "Take2" asks, "Have you already unwrapped the priceless gift of virginity and given it away? Do you now feel like 'second-hand goods' and no longer worthy to be cherished? Do you ever wish you could re-wrap it and give it only to your future husband or wife?"[25]

But not to worry, there's an answer! "Guess what? You can be abstinent again! You can't change the past, but you can change the future. You can decide today to commit to abstinence, wrapping a brand-new gift of virginity to present to your husband or wife on your wedding night."[26]

The message is clear: Without your "gift," you're "second-hand goods." (Or at least, if you're properly repentant, that's what you should feel like.)

Like most virginity pledges, the appeal of secondary virginity doesn't seem to last long. Landry, the secondary virginity-pledging teen from Louisiana, broke her pledge within the year:

> "As the months went by, I gradually stopped hanging out with my religious friends and got a serious boyfriend," she said. "About eight months after I signed the pledge, on New Year's Eve, I had no use for that card anymore. We dated for about one month before we had sex. After this relationship, I had no interest in abstinence and purity pledges. I was over it."

Landry is not alone in being "over it." Like first-time virginity pledgers, secondary virginity pledgers are likely to abandon their promise, and even more likely to not use contraception.[g]

Another young virginity pledger, Emily Seipel of Michigan, even told me that her high school virginity pledge was "an easy [way] to resist flesh sins when you're already a closeted lesbian." (Gay people don't exist in the virginity movement, remember?) Seipel, who is technically still a virgin by conventional standards, is far from alone. The purity that the virginity movement is working so hard for is more of an illusion than it would like to own up to. Teens who make these pledges often do so in front of church members, peers, parents, and community leaders, and oftentimes they have no real choice in the matter. It's not as if many twelve- to fourteen-year-olds are going to be self-assured enough to refuse to take a chastity vow. ("No thanks, Mom, I'd like to keep my sexual options open!") These pledges are little more than cultural farces created to make parents feel better about their children's coming of age. And, frankly, parents who buy into the purity myth need some hope; after all, mainstream media would have them believe that their daughters are going wild and are perhaps irredeemably tainted. [...]

---

f.   As with most things in the virginity movement, there's a lot of lip service when it comes to young men and secondary or born-again virginity, but the focus remains on women.

g.   Contraception is for "bad" girls who planned out sex, not girls who got caught in the heat of the moment. And, of course, many of these teens are taught that birth control doesn't work anyway, so why bother?

Whether they're pledges, bare stems, or Virginity Vouchers, the messages are clearly regressive. But virginity proponents are doing one heck of a job marketing them as "revolutionary" and "empowering." Appropriating feminist rhetoric to reinforce traditional gender roles is nothing if not brilliant.

Wendy Shalit, a writer and virginity guru whose first book, *A Return to Modesty: Discovering Lost Virtue*, was the topic of much debate when it was released in 2000, is a prime player in the "making abstinence cool" movement (or, as she calls it, the "modesty movement"). Shalit, who in 2007 penned another ode to chastity, *Girls Gone Mild: Young Women Reclaim Self-Respect and Find It's Not Bad to Be Good*, founded a website, the Modesty Zone,[27] and a blog, Modestly Yours,[28] which has twenty-one in-house bloggers. The site describes itself as "an informal community of young women who don't have a voice in the mainstream media."

"Whether you're a virgin waiting until marriage, or just against casual sex more generally, you can find a safe harbour here to share your ideals, interests, and goals for the future," it reads. The Modesty Zone features "Rebels of the Month" and slogans like "Be Daring, keep your shift on!" Of course, the core message of the modesty movement is still in plain view, as evidenced by the blog's tagline: "Modesty Zone: A site for good girls."

Some virginity-movement members are even resorting to using sex to sell their antisex message. A shirt being sold on the website of the Heritage Foundation, a conservative Christian organization, says, VIRGINS ARE HOT, and groups on Facebook dedicated to the same message call their own work "passion for purity."

What's most telling about all of these efforts, whether they're being executed via education, religion, or social imperatives, is that they're not working—at least, not in the ways the movement would like them to. Virginity pledges have proved ineffective time and time again; the same is true of abstinence-only education.[29] Blogs like Shalit's Modesty Zone have little web traffic,[30] and the purity groups on social-networking sites are dwarfed by groups like "This Is What a Feminist Looks Like" or even those as trivial as "If You Can't Differentiate Between 'Your' and 'You're' You Deserve to Die."

Despite its inability to keep women "pure," or to convince most Americans that abstinence is best, the virginity movement is strong, well funded, and everywhere. While there isn't a critical mass of young people who identify with this movement, that doesn't mean they aren't affected by it; these are the people who are teaching our kids about sex and teaching our daughters about morality. And what they're teaching them is wrong.

Abstinence-only classes are part of the reason why one in four young American women have a sexually transmitted infection (STI),[31] and are certainly to blame for the disturbing revelation that teens in Florida believe drinking a cap of bleach will prevent HIV, and a shot of Mountain Dew will stop pregnancy.[32] These are the organizations with billboards peppered across America's highways telling young women, WAIT FOR THE BLING and THE ULTIMATE WEDDING GIFT IS YOUR VIRGINITY.[33]

All of these messages—which position certain young women as the ideal, substitute sexual purity for real morality, and commodify virginity—are part of a larger effort to roll back all women's rights. The virginity movement is seeking a return to traditional gender roles, and focusing on purity is the vehicle toward that end.

When I emailed my high school ex to let him know about this book, I asked him about our first time and what he took away from the experience. Like mine, his memories were wrought with uncomfortable moments[h] and questions. He remembers writing the date above his bed as

---

h.   Like his trying to hold back by staring at a bottle of Drakkar Noir cologne and attempting to spell the name backward.

a way to add permanence to a fleeting moment. I was surprised to learn, however, that his views about women's sexuality weren't any more sophisticated than what I remembered them to be during our teenage years.

"No matter how sexually curious or 'ready' a girl is, she seems to be able to keep her wits about her a bit better than her male counterparts, so more is expected of [women], and rightly so," Josh wrote to me. This is an all-too-common assertion—the idea that women are somehow less sexual than men and are therefore the gatekeepers of sexual morals. It's a fundamental notion of the virginity movement, however, so I shouldn't have been so shocked to hear this line of reasoning being regurgitated by my former boyfriend. After all, the purity message is widespread. But it's one thing to hear the media use this type of language about Britney Spears; it was quite another to hear an ex-boyfriend use it about me. At the end of the day, though, it *is* about me—it's about all of us. However theoretically we'd like to discuss issues of virginity, purity, and women's moral value, the fact is, they affect all of us.

Notes

1. www.scarleteen.com.
2. Laura M. Carpenter, *Virginity Lost: An Intimate Portrait of First Sexual Experiences* (New York: New York University Press, November 2005).
3. Laura M. Carpenter, Interview with the author, March 2008.
4. Dictionary.com definition of "virgin," http://dictionary.reference.com.
5. Hanne Blank, *Virgin: The Untouched History* (New York: Bloomsbury USA, 2007), 29.
6. Feministing.com, "Ivy Hymens: Why Glorifying Virginity Is Bad for Women," March 31, 2008, www.feministing.com/archives/008913.html.
7. Randall Patterson, "Students of Virginity," *New York Times Magazine*, March 30, 2008.
8. Jill Filipovic, Response to "Chastity Clubs: Bringing the Hymens to Harvard Since 2001," *Feministe*, March 31, 2008, www.feministe.us/blog/archives/2008.
9. Advocates for Youth, "Myths & Facts about Sex Education," www.advocatesforyouth.org.
10. MTV, "True Life: I'm Celibate," July 2007, www.mtv.com/videos.
11. Denise Felder, "Miss America 'Purity Rule' Change Halted," September 14, 1999, www.ktvu.com/entertainment.
12. *New York Daily News*, "Miss USA Tara Conner Sex & Cocaine Shame," December 17, 2006, www.feministing.com/archives/006220.html.
13. Mark Coulton, "Trump Deals Disgraced Miss USA a New Hand," *The Age*, December 21, 2006, www.theage.com.au/news.
14. Page Six, "Duck and Cover," *New York Post*, January 4, 2007, www.nypost.com/seven/01042007/gossip/pagesix/duck_and_cover_pagesix_.htm.
15. Fox News, "Miss Nevada Katie Rees Fired over Raunchy Photos," December 22, 2006, www.foxnews.com.
16. Abstinence Clearinghouse, Online store, www.abstinence.net/store.
17. Feministing.com, "Shit … I'm Out of Petals," September 27, 2006, www.feministing.com/archives/005775.html.
18. Ultra Teen Choice, Abstinence Awareness Week advertisement, www.ultrateenchoice.org/.
19. Tyler LePard, "What Teenagers Learn (and Don't Learn) in Sex Ed," *RH Reality Check*, October 13, 2006, www.rhrealitycheck.org.

20. Sexuality Information and Education Council of the United States, "The Five Most Egregious Uses of Welfare's Title V Abstinence-Only-Until-Marriage-Funds."

21. Pure Love Club, Online store, www.chastity.com/store.

22. Carpenter, *Virginity Lost*, 40.

23. Love Matters, "Five Steps to Becoming a Secondary Virgin," www.lovematters.com/startover.htm.

24. Laurel Cornell, "Pure Again," www.focusonthefamily.com/lifechallenges.

25. A Pregnancy Resource Center of Northeast Ohio, "Take2 Renewed Virginity," www.pscstark.com/42.

26. Ibid.

27. www.modestyzone.net.

28. http://blogs.modestlyyours.net.

29. Janet Rosenbaum, "Reborn a Virgin: Adolescents' Retracting of Virginity Pledges and Sexual Histories," *American Journal of Public Health*, May 2, 2006.

30. Alexa: The Web Information Company, Web traffic data, www.alexa.com/data.

31. Centers for Disease Control and Prevention, 2008 National STD Prevention Conference press release, www.cdc.gov/stdconference/2008/media.

32. Feministing.com, "One More Reason for Comprehensive Sex Education," April 3, 2008, www.feministing.com/archives/008936.html.

33. Feministing.com, "If Your Hymen Could Be Gift-Wrapped, What Would the Bow Look Like?" December 28, 2007, www.feministing.com/archives/008311.html.

Chapter 38

Introduction to *Our Schools/Our Selves*

Jessica Yee

Jessica Yee is a self-described "multiracial Indigenous hip-hop feminist reproductive justice fighter." She is the founder and executive director of the trail-breaking Native Youth Sexual Health Network, an organization that connects Indigenous youth working in the area of sexual and reproductive health. Yee is currently the first chair of the National Aboriginal Youth Council at the Canadian Aboriginal AIDS Network, the first North American youth representative at MenEngage International Alliance for Gender Equality, and the North American co-chair for the Global Indigenous Youth Caucus at the United Nations Permanent Forum on Indigenous Issues. She has received numerous honours and recognition for her work, including the YWCA Young Woman of Distinction award and the Miziwe Biik Aboriginal Youth Entrepreneur Award for founding the Native Youth Sexual Health Network.

I have long wondered about the vast relationships between the sexual education youth of colour are receiving and the impact of colonization on their sexuality in general. As a First Nations young woman, I often hear about colonization and how it has gravely affected the state of our people for generations on a multitude of levels, but rarely do these discussions go anywhere near the topic of sexuality. In my discussions with other youth of colour, more often than not I hear the same things being said, and the same exasperating results of this widespread reluctance to make sexual health a priority for all of our youth.

So is it any wonder that when approaching the subject of sexual education youth of colour are receiving in Canada, it is quite difficult to explain what exactly I'm looking for, and to find any resources that concretely address these very issues? I'm not looking for materials on how to be inclusive when teaching sex ed, and I'm certainly not looking for another adult to tell us as youth how we need to behave sexually. The information that is frequently disseminated from communities of colour regarding our sexual health is almost always pervasive in nature, highly statistical, and seldom speaks to the true realities we are facing to be represented in those "risky" numbers in the first place.

What happened to us anyway? Why is it that so many communities of colour are disproportionately affected to the point where many of us feel that we are, yet again, raising the importance of equitable sex education alone?

Colonization has a lot to do with that, and here in Canada we need to remember just how many of us are suffering the intergenerational impacts of colonization and what exactly it has done to us. Colonization is more than Columbus coming over to discover the "New World" in 1492 and causing the genocidal effect that millions of Indigenous peoples throughout the world can still painfully feel. Colonization is still happening, and it didn't just happen to us as First Nations.

> Without taking full control of our lives, starting with our own bodies, we would simply be wards of the state.
>
> —Katsi Cook

Before the invention of clinics, anatomy textbooks, or sexual health websites, my own people were practising sexual education, living with the ideals of feminism, and utilizing theories of reproductive justice to live as a healthy, strong, autonomous nation.

We might not have called it sexual health, or labeled it with any sort of clinicized connotation, but we sure as hell have always believed in our rights over our own bodies, and how fundamental that is to our continued existence. I mean, what do people really think we used to do? Wait for the colonizers to come and teach us about sex?!

You would think, however, that we would get the recognition for starting the concepts and frameworks that many non-Native academic movers and shakers have been internationally hailed for, but alas, we do not. In fact my people have been so far removed from practising our authentic ways that a lot of us don't even want to identify with any of our former sex-positive existence.

Sex was upheld in our culture as not only a sacred and powerful part of human life, but as a very normal part of it, too. Sexual education began in the ancient huts, longhouses, and teepees of our ancestors, where young people would learn from selected family or community members all about their body, how to care for it, and the inviolability of their sex. Many of our ancestral teachings show us that many of our societies were matriarchal and this included healthy, educated decisions over matters of childbearing and sexuality. We have different ceremonies and traditions that we've been practising for centuries to back this up.

Our long history of genocidal oppression, whether through colonization, Christianization, residential/mission/boarding schools, or just blatant racism, has drastically severed the ties between us and how traditionally we might have received the knowledge that would enable us to make informed choices about our sexual health and relationships. The fact is that many of our communities are reluctant to go anywhere near the topic of sexual health because it is now viewed as "dirty," "wrong," or a "White man's thing."

We have also carried a long history of being sexually exploited, which can be seen anywhere from the early Pocahontas and Squaw days right up until the modern over-sexualization of "easy" Native women, which still permeates much of the media.

> The American ideal of sexuality appears to be rooted in the American ideal of masculinity. This idea has created cowboys and Indians, good guys and bad guys, punks and studs, tough guys and softies, butch and faggot, black and white. It is an ideal so paralytically infantile that it is virtually forbidden—as an unpatriotic act—that the American boy evolve into the complexity of manhood.
>
> —James Baldwin

We share this agonizing history with so many other communities of colour, whose Western world invaders (whether through forced Christianization or removal of nations into slavery) sought to take away one of our most powerful human abilities—our sexuality—and use it against us to control, destroy, colonize, and mould us into exactly what they wanted us to be. English, a confusing language that the dominant society here insists we still speak, has created binaries like gay and straight, supremacy and subservience, which many of our communities simply didn't subscribe to. We're more interested in the essence of our humanity.

It's definitely worth reflecting on how different things might be if our future generations know about where we came from and call on their ancestral roots to help them make it through these present-day oppressions that we face. I think our job now is to find practical ways to translate all of this into modern terms for our young people to use so they can recover what past generations may have lost, and re-assert themselves as the resilient, fierce, and knowledgeable young people who were, once upon a time, the most sacred in many of our cultures.

> Colonization and racism go hand in hand. Racism has provided justification for the subjugation of peoples.... Over time, racial stereotypes and societal rejection may be internalized by the colonized group.
>
> —Emma S. LaRocque

We also must dispel the myth that Canada is a "mosaic" of cultures where everyone gets along in perfect racial symbiosis—and this is something our youth today need to be talking more about. While there might be multiple ethnicities, races, and cultures represented in larger urban centres like Toronto, Vancouver, Edmonton, and Montreal (and this only represents four cities of the 10 provinces and three territories in all of Canada), we aren't usually discussing how and why this is happening in order to facilitate knowledge, respect, appreciation, and understanding. Toronto alone has more than 60,000 Aboriginal peoples according to the 2006 Stats Canada Census, but walking through the city streets, you might never know who and where they are.

Growing up in the sprawling diverse metropolis of Toronto I hear people of colour say that while we might have neighbourhoods like Chinatown and Little Italy, we don't really sit down and discuss our cultures with one another. We see our cultures represented mostly in festivals or conferences, while in actuality we have the ability to do more than that. It's not enough to simply look at the foods and colours of people if you want to know about their culture; you have to understand wholly where the people come from. It's about more than just their country of origin.

Examining cultural competency and sex education means using what we already have in our culture to empower our youth to lead healthy, strong lives, while intersecting it with our present-day realities. SEX is still such a taboo topic in our society, when in fact it is the foundation of all humanity and is related to every social issue on some level. While we look to other existential issues to problem-solve the various challenges our communities are facing, the time has come to bring it back to the basics and strengthen our identities right from the ground up.

Rather than continuing to allow people outside our communities to dictate to us how to be "healthy," not actually involving us as youth on any sustainable level when working "for youth," and rarely disseminating anything in a culturally competent way, I decided to go directly to the source itself. For this issue of *Our Schools/Our Selves*, I asked youth of colour about their experiences with sex education and if colonization, in its many forms, affects how they view sexuality.

In this issue we hear from youth in words that are unfiltered, powerful, truthful, raw, radically self-aware, and painful on a wide spectrum of topics they needed to share. We hear first accounts of being a newcomer to the country and the frighteningly new methods of sex education. We listen to the tales of being gay in a culture that condemns it today, but so many years ago accepted homosexuality. We are inspired by the many youth change agents who are putting forward the gifts and strengths they carry, confronting their history of colonization, and breaking new ground to continue the fight.

What I really heard while putting all of these tales together was a loud, resounding cry from many youth that they are ready and willing to talk about sex, and while 90% of the drama in their own communities had to do with sex, they felt that existing hierarchies, power structures, and authority figures stood in the way and incapacitated them from making positive change. It is fair to say that we are already paying the price for the inadequacy in organizations, institutions, and society in general to actualize youth leadership when it comes to sex education.

> Peer education means that young people gain more from an experience when they are actively involved … [and] is a core premise of peer education and youth development. Research also suggests that programs for youth which are developed through a partnership of youth and adults may be highly effective in building youth people's skills and reducing their sexual risk-taking behaviors.
> —Advocates for Youth, Peer Education, Youth Development,
> and Youth-Adult Partnerships

The Merriam-Webster dictionary defines self-determination as "free choice of one's own acts without external compulsion, and especially as the freedom of the people of a given territory to determine their own political status or independence from their current state." It is essential that youth of colour are given the right to self-determination when we talk about sexual education, and that we listen carefully to how we can support them to realize this in their own lives. If we believe in autonomy, sovereignty, and self-government over our own bodies, youth must also be allowed these rights. How this plays out, looks, and works will vary greatly from youth to youth, reality to reality, and community to community.

I believe what it boils down to is not only the importance of our right to self-determination, but knowing and reclaiming our history. While today's youth were not alive when the initial colonization happened, we are alive now, and indeed it's still happening. We may not have been able to choose what our ethnicity was going to be, but we can own it now and stand as allies with other communities of colour. We can work together in our common struggle for the autonomy to live as our authentic selves in the face of oppression and bigotry. We need to celebrate our rich heritages in peaceful solidarity so we all survive, while together honouring the ancestors who lived so courageously to give us those few bits of raw culture we cling to today.

Education is the key to effecting positive change. Equitable and intersectional sex education—this is how we are going to take back our self-determination and put it out there as it once was, strong, sexy, powerful, and, most of all, unapologetic of who we are.

Activist Insight:
The New Sex Ed

Asian Communities for Reproductive Justice

Introducing Asian Communities for Reproductive Justice (ACRJ)

ACRJ promotes and protects reproductive justice through organizing, building leadership capacity, developing alliances and education to achieve community and systemic change.

What Is Reproductive Justice?

We believe reproductive justice exists when all people have the social, political, and economic power and resources to make healthy decisions about our gender, bodies, sexuality, and families for ourselves and our communities. Reproductive justice aims to transform power inequities and create long-term systemic change, and therefore relies on the leadership of communities most impacted by reproductive oppression. The reproductive justice framework recognizes that all individuals are part of families and communities and that our strategies must lift up entire communities in order to support individuals.

Introducing the New Sex Ed: Empowered Youth Strengthening Communities!

The New Sex Ed is a collaborative creation of the SexEd! Strategic Cohort, a movement-building vehicle of EMERJ (Expanding the Movement for Empowerment and Reproductive Justice). The five groups in SexEd! are all doing cutting-edge work on sexuality education in diverse communities across the country: Asian Communities for Reproductive Justice, California Latinas for Reproductive Justice, Colorado Organization for Latina Opportunity and Reproductive Rights, Illinois Caucus for Adolescent Health, and SPARK Reproductive Justice Now.

Why Do We Need It?

The growing awareness that abstinence-only education is a failed strategy creates an opportunity for us to demand the kind of sexuality education that will provide young people in all communities [with] the information, skills, and support they need to thrive. Comprehensive sexuality education (CSE) is useful, but we can do more to include the experiences and needs of communities of color, immigrant communities, LGBTQ communities, and others who have traditionally been left out of CSE programs and policies.

What Does It Provide?

The New Sex Ed has lots of tools and strategies that are holistic, grounded in our communities, and engages those whose experiences and realities are often overlooked. It is a resource for building a new movement for sexuality education in this country that is relevant to all people in all communities. Imagine that!

What Can You Do with It?

Use it, share it with your allies, and please let us know what worked and didn't work for you and your communities. Together we can work toward making sure that all of our communities have the support and resources they need to thrive!

Sexuality Education Justice (SEJ) Framework

Developed collaboratively by the SexEd! Strategic Cohort: Asian Communities for Reproductive Justice, California Latinas for Reproductive Justice, Colorado Organization for Latina Opportunity and Reproductive Rights, Illinois Caucus for Adolescent Health, and SPARK Reproductive Justice Now.

What We Want: Our Vision

- We want sexuality education that has a *holistic* view of sexuality and sexual health, including positive body image, self-esteem, gender identity, sexual orientation, and communication and decision-making in relationships, and for sexuality to be seen as a part of life.
- We want sexuality education that goes *beyond a deficit-based disease and pregnancy prevention framework* to recognize and celebrate sexuality as a natural part of human development.
- We want *attention, commitment, and resources* that focus on promoting overall sexual health of all people, including marginalized communities—people of color, LGBTQ folks, people with disabilities, immigrants.
- Sexuality education is about *equity*, and we want quality sexuality education for all students and all people.
- Sexuality education is a *core part of people's lives*, not an extra issue that we work on.
- What we want is sexuality education JUSTICE.

The Problem

- Abstinence-only education doesn't work, and even "comprehensive" sexuality education can be a *narrow, one-size-fits-all approach* that doesn't build on the strengths, histories, and experiences of young people, families, and communities.
- Some students get better sexuality education than others. In many cases, this is because some schools have more money and resources: *It's an issue of equity.*

- Educators, parents, and others who provide information about sexuality do not have tools to teach sexuality education that is *holistic, non-deficit based, and is relevant to our families, communities, and cultures.*

The Solution: SEJ

Sexuality Education Justice is holistic.

- It addresses the *needs and realities of all people*—including people of color, Indigenous people, immigrants and English language learners, people with disabilities, LGBTQ people, people of faith, and people of all ages and genders—and is based on the lived experiences and cultural norms of these diverse groups of people.
- It incorporates *social, cultural, and economic support* for pregnant and parenting youth, including directly addressing stigma and demonization of young people of color.
- It addresses *cultural and societal myths, stereotypes, and barriers* (e.g., shame and guilt) around sexuality and positive sexuality.
- It's having the *power and resources* to make informed decisions about our gender, body, sexuality, relationships, and well-being.

Why Do We Need SEJ?

- Sexuality education *impacts everyone*, not just the majority. So our approaches must resonate with all communities.
- Sexuality education must *support, not demonize*, communities that are "left out," e.g., those whose power to make decisions about their bodies is compromised by existing approaches to sexuality education, like communities of color, LGBT communities, teen parents, etc.
- Sexuality education must *build on the wisdom and experience of our communities*, and speak to the needs of our communities, in order to benefit our communities.

How Do We Achieve SEJ?

By building on community strengths:

- *Youth* can engage in peer education, leadership development, and organizing to ensure that they and their peers are gaining the knowledge and power they need to make informed decisions about sex and sexuality.
- *Parents* can break the silence and fear around talking about sexuality with their children if they have the tools they need to do so. Parents care about what their children are learning, they want to develop trust with their children, and they are willing to stand up for what is best for their families.
- *Organizations* can ensure that the communities they serve have the culturally relevant support and resources that allow all people to make the best decisions for themselves regarding their gender, bodies, sexuality, and relationships through providing direct services, developing tools, advocating for policies, and organizing for change.

Source: Excerpted from Asian Communities for Reproductive Justice, retrieved from http://reproductivejustice.org/ and http://reproductivejustice.org/assets/docs/ACRJ-SEJ-Framework.pdf

Chapter 39

Sugar and Spice and Something More Than Nice? Queer Girls and Transformations of Social Exclusion

Marnina Gonick

Marnina Gonick holds the Canada Research Chair in Gender at Mount Saint Vincent University in Nova Scotia. Her research areas of interest include girl studies, identity, feminist cultural studies, gender and school, and feminist qualitative research, and she has published a number of texts and articles on these topics. Recent books include Between Femininities: Ambivalence, Identity, and the Education of Girls *and* Young Femininity: Girlhood, Power, and Social Change.

Are Queer girls, girls? [...]

Far too often when the category "girl" is named, in the media, in feminist research, in education, sociology, and psychology discourses, and in popular culture amongst other sites, it is white, middle-class, and heterosexual girls whose experiences are referenced. If we understand "girl" as a category that is socially produced rather than as a naturally occurring biological and developmental phase in the life course, then this narrow view presents a problem in the way it restricts possible meanings of girlhood. But, the question "Are Queer girls, girls?" suggests even more may be involved than the already complicated project of creating more inclusive categories. It also demands that we look again at the intersecting discourses of femininity, age, agency, and sexuality and the social and cultural practices that constitute "girl" as category. It asks us to consider the institutionalized norms that regulate the boundaries of the category as well as girls' responses to them. Queering the category girl, therefore, is about more than simply adding Queer girls into an always already existing social category. Rather, it is a stance that allows us to both ask how girls become girls and to investigate the implications for those whose social, cultural, sexual, and aesthetic practices position them outside the normative meanings of the term.

There is no question that there are severe consequences for those living outside normative gender/sex categories. This article explores some of these consequences, including what Deborah Britzman (1997) [...] calls the "cognitive dissonance" of Queer youth. "Most persons who eventually identify themselves as homosexuals require a change in the meaning of the cognitive category *homosexual* before they can place themselves in that category" (cited in Britzman, 1997: 194). The very signifiers of queerness must, according to Britzman, be rearticulated in ways that are pleasurable, interesting, and erotic. As well as the everyday practices that produce this cognitive dissonance, I am interested in the efforts girls use to re-signify Queer identities.

Theorizing Intersectionality and Queer Youth

Just as the categories "girl" and "woman" are not singular, the category of Queer girls [comprises] a wide range of racialized, class, ethnic, and linguistic backgrounds. Included are people with and without disabilities and people who negotiate a range of gender identities and expressions of sexuality. Queer girls experience marginalization and oppression on the basis of sexuality and other markers of social difference, but they may also occupy positions of privilege on a range of other grounds. An approach that uses intersectionality to understand identity and theorize oppression looks at the complexity and contradictory ways people are located in relation to positions of dominance and marginality. Therefore, in considering the exclusionary practices that Queer girls encounter in their daily lives, related systems of power and privilege, such as white supremacy, patriarchy, and the capitalist system, need to be integrated into the analysis.

An intersectional analysis makes the connections between homophobia, power, and privilege, allowing for an analysis of the ways in which sexed, gendered, raced, and classed social positions intersect in shaping experiences of structural, political, physical, and representational exclusion against Queer youth. An intersectional focus highlights the need to account for multiple grounds of identity when exploring how the social world is constructed and experienced. For example, Kumashiro (2001) shows how the ways in which discourses of healthy gayness are constructed around "being out" may have different implications for youth of colour than for some white youth. Those who do not come out in those ways deemed "healthy" by the broader gay community may be construed or construe themselves in negative terms. He suggests that these norms may pose a problem for youth of colour, who may not "be out" to their families because of the ways gayness may be attached to meanings of whiteness in their communities. While they may not find support for their sexuality in their families and communities, Queer youth of colour may rely and depend on these same social spheres for support and survival strategies for the racism they encounter, including within the gay community. Thus, "being out" in the ways advocated in discourses of gay rights is not necessarily always a workable option.

An intersectional analysis is also important in considering intervention strategies. As Snider (1996: 296) suggests, programmes need to be designed in such a way that youth are not being asked to address homophobia separately from racism, thereby forcing them to choose potential involvement in the Queer community over involvement in their families' communities. To do otherwise is to ask Queer youth to hierarchize oppressions. [...]

Exclusionary Practices at Work

Researchers are producing a wealth of studies documenting the social consequences of challenging normative categories of sex/gender. Such consequences include high rates of suicide, depression, low self-esteem, drug use, and psychological trauma from abandonment (Kroll and Warneke, 1995).

Sexual violence is not an uncommon experience for Queer youth with Duncan (1990) reporting that such incidents were even higher for lesbians than for heterosexuals. One way of accounting for this is to consider the ways in which sexual violence and the threat of violence has often been used as a means of regulating and controlling women's sexuality and sexual expressions. The complex interactions of gender, race, and sexuality are also a feature of this violence. As Martinez (1998) suggests for Latina women, the double stereotypes of "sexually deprived lesbian" and the "ho-Latina woman" are often in play in this violence. Other stereotypes, such as the "sexually loose" Black or the "exotic" Asian woman, may also be at work. Interestingly, the Human Rights Watch Report (2001) suggests that in schools, it is lesbians who identify as or are perceived to be "butch" who are punished more for violating gender norms. There is a perception that lesbians who are "femme" are punished less by their peers, largely because the harassment takes the form of boys wanting to "watch" and then "join" the girls. Girls perceive this harassment not only as an invasion of their privacy but also as an implicit threat of sexual violence. One of the trans-sexual youth in Wyss's study (2004) reports being explicitly threatened by "guys who wanted to have sex with me and [... tried] to force themselves on me" (2004: 717). Others reported being raped, sometimes more than once.

> [The boys would] drag me into the bathroom and like humiliate me and try to find out what I was.... I was totally like sexually assaulted by them.... People talk about how they were harassed in high school. And what they mean is they got raped.... And it's bad to have things yelled at you because what that carries with it is the *threat* of something happening to you that is worse, you know? And it is humiliating to get yelled at and looked and stared at and spit at. *All* these things happened to me at that school. (2004: 718)

When adults downplay or ignore this type of harassment, they use a "boys will be boys" type of argument, downplaying the harassment as merely an expression of desire rather than a threat of violence (Human Rights Watch, 2001: 51). Trans-sexual youth push the boundaries of gender non-conformity even further, which also exposes them to more harassment and violence than other Queer youth. For example, Wyss suggests that many trans-girls who have tried cross-dressing in high school have been ridiculed, ostracized, and physically assaulted by their peers (Wyss, 2004: 710).

Social services is another area where exclusionary practices are at work. For example, Queer youth in out-of-home care settings have reported data that suggest this population receives less services, are more readily labelled as difficult, experience verbal harassment and physical violence regularly, are moved more often (multiple placements), are more likely to be separated from their siblings, experience high rates of homelessness, are not often reunited with their families, and have a more difficult time attending community-based educational programmes and accessing medical and mental health services than their heterosexual counterparts (Dame, 2004). Linda Dame (2004) recounts a chilling story of a case she encountered as a social worker with the province of Manitoba. She was told that the 15-year-old youth in question was considered the most difficult child in the system and when she first met "him" he was in the Crisis Stabilization Unit for his own safety. According to Dame, "I had reviewed the file before I visited the CSU, so I already know that this boy was in fact a transgendered male-to-female young woman and that she, not he, had been subjected to incredibly ridiculous and abusive case planning strategies for many years, if not throughout her entire young life. No note in the file referred to her transgenderism, and all notes referred to her as male and used her original male name, even though she had changed it years previous.... The staff in the treatment home where she lived routinely ridiculed her and ignored the Child Advocate's Office direction to respect her chosen name, even after she launched a formal complaint" (2004: 2). The province of Manitoba spent over a quarter of a million dollars in two years housing this one teenager, who has since run away from Winnipeg.

In Canada, as O'Brien argues, "grave inequities in the treatment of lesbian, gay and bisexual youth by group homes and youth shelters" not only exist, but are reinforced as "pathological" and "deviant" through professional discourse (1994: 37). Verbal and/or physical harassment usually not tolerated by child-care workers may be ignored or even encouraged when it is directed at Queer youth. A common theme is the stance by group homes and foster placements that openly Queer youth could not be placed in their programme because other residents would beat them up. This open discrimination is passed as an acceptable reason for denying placement of a Queer youth in a home (Dame, 2004).

As suggested above, the experience of violence has also been linked to high rates of Queer youth suicide. A 1995 study concluded that Canada has one of the highest youth suicide rates in the world (Kroll and Warneke, 1995) and an earlier study indicates that Indigenous Canadians have the highest suicide rate of any racial group in the world (York, 1990). This, combined with the statistic that Queer youth are six times more likely to attempt suicide, led Kroll and Warneke (1995) to suggest that suicide may appear as the only viable option in a situation where the lack of acceptance, experiences of discrimination, violence, stigmatization, and fear of rejection are predominant features of social life.

A Word of Caution on Discourses of "at Risk"

*****

[...] "At risk" discourse has been useful in the bid to secure resources for groups of Queer youth that have been virtually ignored and/or demonized in the public sphere as a threat to social security and the future of national interests. This includes those "at risk" for suicide, depression, low self-esteem, homelessness, dropping out of school, teen pregnancy, substance abuse, criminal activity, and violence. This designation has been a useful one for making the case for developing programming and services specific to Queer youth's needs relating to their higher-than-average rates of suicide, harassment, and experiences as victims of violence (U.S. Dept. of Health and Human Services, 1989). In this regard, the "at risk" discourse provides an alternative framework for conceptualizing the relationship between young people and the social structures shaping their lives. In a time such as the current one, where neo-liberal social policies severely curtail the allocation of resources to support the welfare state, and where the individual is made solely responsible for the direction and outcome of his or her life, the "at risk" discourse makes an alternative suggestion. It makes the case for social responsibility in providing the social services and resources such as education required to support Queer youth.

[...] Some commentators have pointed out how the "at risk" designation poses certain problematic limitations on understanding the experiences of Queer youth. As a highly racialized and classed discourse, "at risk" is often used as a euphemism for talking about social fears and anxieties that are projected onto young people of colour and/or working-class youth. It is also used as a rationale for increased adult surveillance and regulation of marginalized youth. It is possible that through this discourse, the individualization of responsibility for social problems is rendered stronger. In this case, programmes and services for youth considered "at risk" are designed to enhance the individual's "choice" making or problem management skills. Encountering problems is thus considered a feature of poor decision making and risk management. The discourse hides structural barriers such as discrimination and limited access to job markets due to economic restructuring that marginalized youth encounter limiting their "choices."

Talburt (2004: 119) warns of another danger of reliance on the "at risk" discourse to address the needs of Queer youth. She suggests that this reinforces the associations of "gay" with "problem."

Harbeck (1995: 127) cautions that an extreme and sole focus on suicide may replace one negative representation for another. Young people who are exploring their sexual identities may conclude that suicide is the consequence of being Queer. [...] Cornel West (1996) underscores the importance of thinking about difference as a source of strength, rather than merely as a set of obstacles and impediments. By interrogating the meanings that get produced by the categories "at risk" and "healthy," as well as by examining the power relations involved in labeling, there may be a greater acknowledgment of the different kinds of victimization and risk as well as a focus on young women's agency in order to move beyond simplistic assertions of who and what an "at risk" victim is. In what follows, I explore some of the exclusionary practices Queer youth encounter in schools, the media, and in access to public space.

Exclusionary Practices at School

In her article, "What Is this Thing Called Love? New Discourses for Understanding Gay and Lesbian Youth," Deborah Britzman (1997) provides an interesting entry into how to think about the experiences of Queer youth in schools. Building on Martin and Hetrick's analysis (1988), Britzman outlines four related kinds of isolation affecting queer youth: (1) cognitive isolation, where knowledge, practices, and histories of Queer people are unavailable; (2) social isolation, where Queer youth suffer from social rejection by heterosexual youth and adults and are isolated from each other; (3) emotional isolation, where being open about one's sexuality is viewed as a hostile act, while being closeted labels one as anti-social; and (4) aesthetic isolation, where Queer youth must rearticulate received representations of heterosexuality with their own meanings while imaginatively constructing Queer aesthetics and style. Britzman quotes Joseph Beam (1991), who describes this process as "making ourselves from scratch," and Michelle Cliff (1980), who suggests this kind of identity work is about "claiming an identity they taught me to despise." Within the context of schools, where identity making is a central, although not always clearly articulated, feature of educational agendas, we can investigate the relationship between these four kinds of isolation by examining issues such as curriculum materials, social relations between peers, between students and teachers, and school policies.

The National Education Association (NEA) Report, "Making the Grade" (1999) shows how few school districts have policies that protect students and teachers from harassment and discrimination, provide staff with workshops and training, support curriculum that includes the lives and contributions of Queer people, and encourage the formation of groups such as gay–straight alliances. Similar results were published in the National School Climate Survey conducted by the Gay, Lesbian, and Straight Education Network (GLSEN) in 2001. Writing about the Canadian context, an EGALE Report clearly states that much of the negativity Queer youth face begins in elementary schools (Boodram, 2003: 12). These include a range of incidents, such as harassment from peers and teachers, being called derogatory names, beatings, rape, and occasionally murder. The response of Queer youth is often to skip school or drop out. Savin-Williams (1994) reports that Queer youth are more than four times as likely as their peers to skip whole days of school out of fear, and approximately 28 percent of lesbian and gay youth drop out of high school before graduating.

The Human Rights Watch Report (2001) includes an interview with one young woman, who says that several months of verbal threats and other harassment culminated in physical violence. "I got hit in the back of the head with an ice scraper." By that time, she said she was so used to being harassed that "I didn't even turn around to see who it was" (2001: 42).

Queer youth of colour are more likely than white youth to report teachers as a source of harassment. And teachers are also more likely to single out students who violate gender norms than others (Human Rights Watch Report, 2001: 52). In one example cited in the report, a very young transgender student had a circle of friends who managed to protect her from her peers, but could not protect her from the teachers. Upset with her behavior, her teachers began to humiliate and embarrass her, telling her to "quit acting like a girl" (2001: 61). Thus, as Russell and Truong (2001) suggest, the forms of victimization and discrimination experienced by Queer youth of colour and white Queer youth, as well as those young people who push the boundaries of gender expression, may be different and of varying magnitudes. However, what is clear is that if teachers are perpetuating the problem rather than assisting to resolve it, it is unlikely that young people will turn to school officials for help when they are harassed. As one of the girls interviewed in the Human Rights Watch Report says, "we know not to say anything—it's like, unless you've been raped the administration doesn't want to know about it. They'll just say you're lying" (2001: 52).

There is a double bind of inhabiting a Queer position in schools. On the one hand, there is an incredible resistance to including Queer content in the curriculum. Yet, Queer people are subjected to the trauma and violence of publicly sanctioned pejoratives and are negatively marked within school spaces. As Loutzenheiser and MacIntosh (2004: 152) put it, "what is invisible and markedly absent from curriculum is often rendered visible and saturated with meaning outside of classrooms."

School curricula often exclude representations of Queer people in areas where it is directly relevant, such as discussions of sexuality, family life, and human rights. In addition, Queer people and issues are often ignored within the broader school curriculum, in subjects such as history, literature, and arts where, for example, heterosexual relationships are considered worth mentioning as relevant to a consideration of an historic figure's accomplishments or an author's work. According to Fisher (1999), crucial resources such as general information about Queer sexualities, coming out, same-sex relationships, and safe-sex practices are often not carried by school libraries or counselors. In fact, schools may deliberately prohibit such materials from the premises.

A recent court case in British Columbia offers an example. In 1998, the court overturned the Surrey School Board's decision to ban the use of resources from lesbian and gay organizations and books dealing with same-sex parenting from their schools. The resolution to ban the materials was initiated by conservative parents with the support of an organization called The Conservative Citizens Research Institute. Likewise, the case to overturn the ban was brought to court by members of EGALE BC, a parent, a student, and the author of one of the banned books. Madame Justice Saunders overturned the two School Board resolutions. She stated that the one prohibiting the use of materials from lesbian and gay organizations was made without jurisdiction, was unclear, and was made without relevant considerations such as the educational value of the resources being banned. She also ruled that the resolution prohibiting the use of the books was substantially influenced by religious considerations and contravened provisions in the British Columbia School Act prohibiting religion or overt religious influence in the conduct of schools.

The issue is one with far-reaching consequences for inclusivity in schools. Surrey is by no means the only Canadian school district in which these debates have surfaced. In 1997, for example, the Calgary Public School Board also banned books that they claimed promoted homosexuality. A spokesperson for a parents' group said that "a major concern is that a lot of the stories describe people who 'come out' as homosexual, which [the parents' group] finds inappropriate" (qtd. in Fisher, 1999).

Where school libraries do carry books about Queer identities, they are often shelved alongside texts on sexual dysfunction, child abuse, prostitution, and other socially stigmatized practices. Once found, a student may experience further complications accessing these materials. For example, parental permission may be required to take these books out of the library and there remains the stigma of carrying such books to the librarian's desk and the fear of exposure. These social practices are the remnants of the historic associations between homosexuality with forms of pathology and disease; the assumption of homosexuality as being unnatural; the stigma and illegalities of Queer practices; and the notion of homosexuality as contagious, where knowledge can infect innocent and unsuspecting youth.

Loutzenheiser and MacIntosh (2004: 154) argue that social change requires providing the means to interrogate power relations or the role of school cultures in limiting expressions of sexual and gender identities. They suggest further that inclusivity in and of itself is not enough to produce real change. As with anti-racist, anti-sexist, and multicultural discourses, there continues to be the danger that inclusivity borne of hetero-normative social institutions and motivations often results in assimilationist smoothing over of real difference and a covering up of larger ideological mechanisms of oppression.

This dynamic is visible in other everyday social practices within schools. For example, there continues to be a double standard for what is considered appropriate behaviour for same-sex couples in schools as opposed to their heterosexual peers. The assumption is still that couples attending school dances will be male-female and that any public displays of affection will also be between opposite-sex couples. In some parts of the U.S. some rather extreme situations have developed due to the Christian Right movement's influence on school policy and government funding to schools. In one instance, students, with the backing of the American Civil Liberties Union, sued their Texas high school for the right to hold Gay–Straight Alliance (GSA) meetings, having been denied permission to do so by the school administration. The GSA was finally allowed to meet, but there were significant restrictions due to the Abstinence Only Curriculum policy shaped by Christian fundamentalism, which restricts all information on birth control and sex education beyond abstinence and sex within heterosexual marriage. As part of the settlement, youth were allowed to attend GSA meetings only with their parents' permission and they were not allowed to talk about sex at all. In fact, all discussion around sexuality had to comply with the restrictive eight-point abstinence-only-until-marriage definition. As Burns and Torre (2005) note, forcing a gay-positive student group to forward the notion that sex outside of marriage is harmful to self and society, constitutes an actual harm to youth who identify as LGBT, and/or who challenge the institution and definition of marriage. Thus, while the existence of the GSA group might constitute a sign of inclusivity, the conditions of its existence and the restrictions on what can be spoken there only reproduce hetero-normative power relations.

Exclusionary Practices in Access to Public Space

Access to public space is related to questions of visibility, recognition, and inclusion in public life. Recently, discourses have emerged in some communities that link "quality of life" to increased police and everyday surveillance. In New York City, for example, Mayor Giuliani gained political acclaim for "cleaning" up the streets of the city. The effect of this campaign, according to members of the city's Audre Lorde Center for LGBT and People of Color Communities, has been a marginalizing and criminalizing of those communities seen as threats to the "moral fibre" of the society. As a result, there has been a shrinking of public spaces due to the "re-development" of meeting places used by Queer people, and the diminishing of immigrant communities' workplaces through the outlawing of street vendors. Thus, public spaces have been privatized in raced, classed, and sexed ways. Similar scenarios face youth on the streets, with an estimated 40 percent of homeless young people in major U.S. cities being lesbian and gay (Orion Center, 1986). Service providers working with this population report that as many as two-thirds have "discharged" themselves from out-of-home care—often for many of the same reasons that youth not in care leave home, including physical and sexual abuse and conflict over sexual identity (Clatts et al., 1998: 195). In Toronto and other large Canadian cities, where a portion of young people living in the streets are Queer youth who have been kicked out of their parents' homes or have run away to escape homophobia, abuse, and discrimination in their families and communities, moves have been made to criminalize "squeegee kids," using the rationale of rendering the city safer for others. In the process, however, what is eliminated is one of the few ways entrepreneurial youths living in the streets can earn a little money. Unquestioned in this process is why certain people and communities—the poor, people of colour, and Queer people—have come to be seen as more threatening than others and thus more susceptible to police surveillance. Homeless youth are also likely to be more prone to attracting police attention because there are few shelters that will accept youth residents and of those that exist, many are supported by religious organizations intolerant of sexual minorities. According to Dame (2004: 15), transgendered youth are particularly discriminated against in emergency shelters and are often stripped of their gender-identifying clothing and forced to stay as a member of their biological gender as opposed to their gender of choice. Thus, many may prefer the streets even if it means more encounters with the police. This includes the issue of the particular ways Queer youth of colour are stopped and frisked, as well as the ways transgender and trans-sexual women are targeted by the police on the assumption that they are all involved in sex work (Gore et al., 2001). The question of safety and protection for some becomes the issue of surveillance, harassment, and abuse for others.

Exclusionary Practices in the Media

The media is one of the sites where there has been increasing visibility and a trend towards more positive representations of Queer people and issues. Images of gay life are more prevalent in North America than in previous decades, and as a result young people are able to associate themselves with "alternative" sexual and gender categories at younger and younger ages (Human Rights Watch, 2001). Queer youth can read about or watch marches, protest demonstrations, gay and lesbian films, weddings, court cases, and, if fluent in the "codes of closet," read obituaries of people who are Queer. However, the representation of Queer bodies in television shows such as *Queer as Folk*, *Queer Eye for the Straight Guy*, *Will and Grace*, *Xena the Warrior Princess*, *Buffy the Vampire Slayer*, and the Canadian show *Kids in the Hall* (and *Kids'* Scott Thompson's *My Fabulous Gay Wedding*), are usually limited to the white, middle class, urban, wealthy and able bodied. The content of these shows also do not tend to take up questions of violence or to seriously address homophobic oppression. Nonetheless, the importance to young people of seeing positive images of Queer people is apparent in this interview excerpt with Dena Underwood, a young African American lesbian. "I remember watching television and seeing a lot of stereotypical Black gay men but not very many lesbians. And I remember watching *The Women of Brewster Place*, on television and being excited that there were lesbians like in this movie and, that's really it" (qtd. in Spain, 2001).

In news coverage, positive representations as well as serious coverage of news stories on homophobic violence, is rather limited. Gore et al. (2001: 260) show how media coverage of violence against Queer people—especially transgender people—usually relies on hetero-normative representations and analyses. They further argue that their analysis shows that violence against male-to-female persons is not taken very seriously. Mendez (1996) reaches a similar conclusion in his discussion of media representation of Queer violence in intimate relationships. For example, he cites a *New York Times* article that included an interview with a survivor and was a sensitively written piece. However, the headline demonstrated that the news media remains a problematic site. It read "gays can bash each other too." As Mendez points out, using the term "bash," which is commonly associated with homophobic violence, limits the way in which this phenomenon is understood, including the implication that there is mutuality in cases of gay domestic violence.

Access to public media spaces for the communication of issues and vital information for Queer youth also remains an issue. For example, the Calgary City Council has recently decided that a review be done on billboard advertising policies in the city. The review is the result of some complaints to the city objecting to a billboard advertising a telephone support line for Queer youth. The billboards, as well as signs in buses and malls, were sponsored by the Gay and Lesbian Community Services Association.

Thinking through Responses to Exclusionary Practices

Critical race theory (CRT) offers some interesting and useful insights on the paradoxical nature of using, working within, and rejecting a reliance on the courts or schools in the struggle for equality. These insights have also been paralleled by developments within Queer theory. The limitations of the rhetoric in liberal civil rights discourse, as well as the versions of these discourses that have been used in other policy arenas such as multicultural education policies, has included its reliance on colour-blind discourses that rely on assimilation as its end goal. CRT explodes the notion of colour blindness or race neutrality, just as Queer theory explodes heteronormativity and sexual sameness. Within Queer theory, Sedgwick's (1990) conceptualization of the terms of "minoritizing" versus "universalizing" has been extremely influential for thinking about the question of the meaning of sexuality and the process of creating social change. Minoritizing approaches frame the question of homosexuality as being relevant only to a small, distinct, relatively fixed homosexual minority. According to Britzman (1997), this approach shuts out the fact that identity is a social relation—that both homosexuality and heterosexuality are constituted in relation to each other. It is an approach that deems homosexuality as a separate and discreet category relevant only to homosexuals. In contrast, a universalizing approach views the divide between heterosexual and homosexual as a construction and "as an issue of continuing, determinative importance in the lives of people across the spectrum of sexualities" (Sedgwick, cited in Britzman, 1997: 203). Britzman argues that if programmes and interventions are to be effective in working with all youth, they must take a universalizing view. The question enabled by this approach, Sedgwick states, is: "In whose lives is homo/heterosexual definition an issue of continuing centrality and difficulty?" (1990: 40). The power of this question, Britzman suggests, is that everyone is implicated. "It theoretically insists upon the recognition that the quality of lives of Gays and Lesbians has everything to do with the quality of lives of heterosexuals" (1997: 203). Implicating everyone has the potential to disrupt the discourses that produce normalizing and regulative criteria for bodies, genders, social relations, and affectivity.

Interventions that will effectively address exclusionary practices need to do more than merely hope and plan for assimilation and acceptance on the basis of an argument built around sameness. Rather, programmes designed to create social change, as well as the programmes to support Queer girls in surviving the discrimination and harassment they encounter, will need to recognize, accept, and celebrate radical difference and combat the ideological and structural features of hierarchical social relations producing oppression. Thus, effective interventions need to be designed around the concept of expanding the options for expressing, living, and embodying a diverse range of sexualities and sexual identities. [...]

Girls' Lived Responses

In this last section, I would like to focus on the ways in which Queer girls have organized and resisted the pervasive experience of social exclusion, including violence, harassment, and abuse. They have been a driving force for many of the positive political and cultural changes in recent years. As I discussed earlier, central to these changes is attributing Queer identities with positive and powerful meanings so that they may be lived that way as well. One young lesbian in Ussher and Mooney-Somers' study (2000: 194) describes her feelings:

> I love being a dyke it's sometimes I sit down like when I have time for me self in the flat like this and I scream and I think oh my god I'm a lesbian you know. It just hits me now and it's fab. It's fab since I've come out I can't relate to the person that I was before it was like two different people and I just sit down and I think who the fuck was that.

Beginning in 1996, youth activists in California have held Queer Youth Lobby Day, an event designed to bring political attention to the issues and concerns of Queer youth. In 1999, youth played a critical role in securing the enactment of California's Student Safety and Violence Prevention Act of 2000. In the same year, students in Naperville, Illinois, called on their district's school board to include protection against discrimination on the basis of sexual orientation policies (Human Rights Watch Report, 2001).

One of the more widespread developments, initiated by students, is the formation of Gay–Straight Alliance groups in their schools. These groups provide peer support, information about issues related to sexuality and gender identity, and work towards building community and a more inclusive school environment. One young woman interviewed in the Human Rights Watch Report (2001: 110) says, "we held a safe schools workshop. It was a wicked good experience. We talked about gay issues, what we can do to improve schools, things like that. We have a case in our main entrance with a large rainbow flag. We have lots of fliers posted telling students where you can go giving information on programs like NAGLY [the North Shore Alliance of Gay and Lesbian Youth].... We're going to try to put up pictures of us at Youth Pride. None of our fliers have gotten ripped down. We're not asking for complete understanding, just acceptance." The effects of such groups in schools are sometimes widespread. According to one young woman who was co-founder of a GSA in her school, "there has been change in the general atmosphere of the school. There is an enormous awareness of what homophobia is, and that there are homosexual and bisexual students" (qtd. in Blumenfeld, 1995: 221). She adds that, since the creation of the GSA, teachers have attended workshops to manage their own homophobia and that of their students, and are learning how to help students who are struggling with issues of sexual identity. "People are now willing to interrupt homophobic jokes and slurs and now include sexual orientation when talking about diversity" (qtd. in Blumenfeld, 1995: 221).

As previously mentioned, however, not all attempts to organize these groups are welcomed by school administrators and teachers. For example, in September 2000, students prevailed over hostile school boards in California and Utah that attempted to deny them the right to form Gay–

Straight Alliance groups, in violation of the federal Equal Access Act. California's Orange Unified School District settled a lawsuit with El Modena High School students, permitting their group to meet on school grounds and use the school's public address system to announce club meetings. Salt Lake City's School Board voted, in the same month, to permit student non-curricular groups to meet on school grounds, reversing a 1995 decision that had abolished all non-curricular clubs in an effort to prevent students from forming an Alliance group (Human Rights Watch, 2001).

Within their schools, Queer girls have also challenged hetero-normative cultural practices such as school proms. One young woman, who was the first in her high school to bring a same-sex date to the biggest social event in her school, says, "I'm glad I did it for a lot of the closeted people at school. I think it was important for everyone to see that we could do it, and it wasn't a big deal" (qtd. in Blumenfeld, 1995: 221).

Queer girls have also responded by becoming politically active outside their schools. Some participate in state organizations such as Commissions on Gay and Lesbian Youth set up by state governors in response to the growing concern over suicide amongst LGBT youth (Blumenfeld, 1995). Others participate as youth representatives in demonstrations and marches, such as the historic March for Lesbian, Gay, and Bi Equal Rights and Liberation, which took place April 25, 1993, in Washington and local Gay, Lesbian, and Bi parades. One young woman who was at the Washington March says, "At fourteen, I felt like an outcast because of my bisexual feelings. I decided to be as different as possible. I joined the punk rock scene and became politically active. I went to gay marches, including the gay rights march in Washington D.C. They helped a lot because most of the time I have had to hold back being bisexual, but there I could just relax. I realized that there a lot more people who are gay than let on" (qtd. in Gray, Phillips, and Forney, 1998: 130). Queer youth are also joining and creating groups focused on culture as a site of resistance. One such group is the international organization Lesbian Avengers. According to Ussher and Mooney-Somers (2000), who interviewed girls in a UK London-based group, this is a non-violent, direct action organization, whose central premise is high-profile, media-friendly, "sexy" action to raise awareness of lesbians. They argue that becoming a member of this group provides a positive social identity, a sense of group solidarity, a source of role models, friendship, and common goals. [...]

*****

Conclusion

Excluded from the category "girl," from institutional sites including schools, from the media and public spaces, Queer girls encounter an inordinate amount of violence that may take many different forms, including actual harm to their bodies, misrepresentations or absence of representations of their lives, psychic and spiritual damage. This exclusion has been met by systematic failure, with few exceptions on the part of the public school systems, legal systems, the media, and social services. Through acts of commission and omission, Queer girls' rights to safety and security have been violated. And yet, despite these hardships, it would be a mistake to represent these young women as merely passive victims to a system that has neglected to recognize them. They have also refused the positions of marginalization afforded them by an indifferent and hostile society. They have joined organizations, and when there were none to join, they created them. They work with others to create changes in the places they live, in their families, their schools, and in their wider communities. They have refused to be rendered invisible or to accept the negative stereotypes thrust upon them. Instead, they have worked to produce positive self-identifications and representations and to create the social conditions that will open up new possibilities for living life as Queer people.

References

Beam, Joseph. "Introduction," in Essex Hempel, ed., *Brother to Brother: New Writing by Gay Black Men*. Los Angeles: Alyson Publications, 1991.

Blumenfeld, Warren. "Gay/Straight" Alliances: Transforming Pain to Pride," in Gerald Unks, ed., *The Gay Teen*. New York: Routledge, 1995: 113–121.

Boodram, Chris. *Building the Links: The Intersection of Race and Sexual Orientation*. Ottawa: Egale, 2003.

Britzman, Deborah. "What Is This Thing Called Love? New Discourses for Understanding Gay and Lesbian Youth," in Suzanne deCastell and Mary Bryson, eds., *Radical In<ter>ventions: Identity, Politics, and Difference/s in Educational Praxis*. Albany: SUNY Press, 1997.

Burns, April, and Maria Helena Torre. "Revolutionary Sexualities." *Feminism & Psychology*, 15.1 (2005): 21–26.

Clatts, Michael, et al. "Correlates and Distribution of HIV Risk Behaviours among Homeless Youths in New York City: Implications for Prevention and Policy." *Child Welfare*, 77.2 (1998): 195–207.

Cliff, Michelle. *Claiming an Identity They Taught Me to Despise*. Watertown, MA: Persephone Press, 1980.

Dame, Linda. "Live through This: The Experiences of Queer Youth in Care in Manitoba." *The Canadian Online Journal of Queer Studies in Education*, 1.1 (2004), http://jqstudies.oise.uto-ronto.ca/journal/viewarticle.php?id=2andlayout=html.

Duncan, David. "Prevalence of Sexual Assault Victimization Among Heterosexual and Gay/Lesbian University Students." *Psychological Reports*, 66 (1990): 65–66.

Fisher, John. *Reaching out: A Report on Lesbian, Gay, and Bi-sexual Youth Issues in Canada*. Ottawa: United Church of Canada, 1999.

Gay, Lesbian, and Straight Education Network. *School-Related Experiences of LGBT Youth of Color: Findings from the 2003 National School Climate Survey*. 2003. www.glsen.org.

Gore, Dayo, Tamara Jones Folayan, and Joo-Hyun Kang. "Organizing at the Intersections: A Roundtable Discussion of Police Brutality through the Lens of Race, Class, and Sexual Identities," in Andrea McArdle and Tanya Erzen, eds., *Zero Tolerance*. New York: New York City Press, 2001: 251–269.

Gray, Heather, Samantha Phillips, and Ellen Forney. *Real Girl/Real World: Tools for Finding Your True Self*. Seattle: Seal Press, 1998.

Harbeck, Karen M. "Invisible No More: Addressing the Needs of Lesbian, Gay, and Bisexual Youth and Their Advocates," in Gerald Unks, ed., *The Gay Teen*. New York: Routledge, 1995: 125–133.

Human Rights Watch. *Hatred in the Hallways: Violence and Discrimination against Lesbian, Gay, Bisexual, and Transgender Students in U.S. Schools*. New York: Human Rights Watch, 2001.

Kroll, Ian, and Lorne Warneke. *The Dynamics of Sexual Orientation and Adolescent Suicide: A Comprehensive Review and Developmental Perspective*. Calgary: University of Calgary, 1995.

Kumashiro, Kevin. "Queer Students of Color and Antiracist, Antiheterosexist Education: Paradoxes of Identity and Activism," in Kevin Kumashiro, ed., *Troubling Intersections of Race and Sexuality*. New York: Rowman and Littlefield, 2001: 1–25.

Loutzenheiser, Lisa, and Lori MacIntosh. "Citizenships, Sexualities, and Education." *Theory into Practice*, 43.2 (2004): 151–158.

Martin, A. Damien, and Emery Hetrick. "The Stigmatization of the Gay and Lesbian Adolescent." *Journal of Homosexuality*, 15.1–2 (1998): 163–183.

Martinez, Dorie Gilbert. "Mujer, Latina, Lesbiana: Notes on the Multidimensionality of Economic and Sociopolitical Injustice." *Journal of Gay and Lesbian Social Services*, 8.3 (1998): 99–112.

Mendez, Juan. "Serving Gays and Lesbians of Color Who Are Survivors of Domestic Violence." *Journal of Gay and Lesbian Social Services*, 4.1 (1996): 53–59.

National Education Association. "Making the Grade for All Students." *NEA Today*, 17.4 (1999). National Education Association.

O'Brien, Carol-Anne. "The Social Organization of the Treatment of Lesbian, Gay, and Bisexual Youth in Group Homes and Youth Shelters." *Canadian Review of Social Policy*, 34 (1994): 37–57.

Orion Center. *Survey of Street Youth*. Seattle, WA, 1986.

Russell, Stephen, and Nhan Truong. "Adolescent Sexual Orientation, Race and Ethnicity, and School Environments: A National Study of Sexual Minority Youth of Color," in Kevin Kumashiro, ed., *Troubling Intersections of Race and Sexuality*. New York: Rowman and Littlefield, 2001: 113–130.

Savin-Williams, Ritch C. "Verbal and Physical Abuse as Stressors in the Lives of Lesbian, Gay Male, and Bi-Sexual Youth." *Journal of Consulting and Clinical Psychology*, 62 (1994): 261–269.

Sedgwick, Eve. *Epistemology of the Closet*. Berkeley: University of California Press, 1990.

Snider, Kathryn. "Race and Sexual Orientation: The (Im)possibility of these Intersections in Educational Policy." *Harvard Educational Review*, 66.2 (1996): 292–302.

Spain, Chy Ryan. "An Interview with Dena Underwood," in Kevin Kumashiro, ed., *Troubling Intersections of Race and Sexuality*. New York: Rowman and Littlefield, 2001: 55–60.

Talburt, Susan. "Constructions of LGBT Youth: Opening up Subject Positions." *Theory into Practice*, 43.2 (2004): 116–121.

US Department of Health and Human Services. "Gay Male and Lesbian Youth Suicide," in *Report of the Secretary's Task Force on Youth Suicide*. Washington: U.S. Dept. of Health and Human Services, 1989.

Ussher, Jane, and Julie Mooney-Somers. "Negotiating Desire and Sexual Subjectivity: Narratives of Young Lesbian Avengers." *Sexualities*, 3.2 (2000): 183–200.

West, Cornel. *Race Matters*. Boston: Beacon Press, 2001.

West, Cornel, and Michael Lerner. *Jews and Blacks: A Dialogue on Race, Religion, and Culture in America*. New York: Plume Books, 1996.

Wyss, Shannon. "This Was My Hell": The Violence Experienced by Gender Non-conforming Youth in U.S. High Schools." *International Journal of Qualitative Studies in Education*, 17.5 (2004): 731–735.

York, Geoffrey. *The Dispossessed: Life and Death in Native Canada*. London: Vintage U.K., 1990.

Chapter 40

Exacting Beauty:
Exploring Women's Body Projects
and Problems in the 21st Century

Carla Rice

Carla Rice is Canada Research Chair in Care, Gender and Relationships at University of Guelph, a position she recently assumed after serving as associate professor in gender and women's studies at Trent University. A leader in the field of body image and of fat, disability, and embodiment studies in Canada, she is a founding member and former director of innovative initiatives such as the National Eating Disorder Information Centre, the Body Image Project at Women's College Hospital in Toronto, and Hersize: A Weight Prejudice Action Group. Her research explores cultural representations and narratives of body and identity. She recently founded Project Re•Vision, a participatory mobile media lab that works with communities to challenge stereotypes. In addition to Critical Terrain, *other notable books include the forthcoming* Becoming Women: The Search for Self in Image Culture.

Introduction

For girls coming of age in consumerist, individualist, and media-driven cultures, the body has become an important identity project. While the body has come to be a key medium of self-making, many girls and women also experience it as a significant obstacle and a source of distress. Studies conducted in many wealthy nations show how girls as young as six already express dissatisfaction with their bodies (Gardner, Friedman, and Jackson, 1999; Irving, 2000; Ricciardelli and McCabe, 2001; Shapiro, Newcomb, and Burns Loeb, 1997). More and more adolescents in the Western world suffer from eating problems. This includes a shocking 27 percent of Canadian middle-school girls, who report disordered eating practices (Jones et al., 2001). Sixty percent of those in grades 7 and 8 have tried dieting to lose weight (McVey et al., 2002). Worldwide, millions of women worry about their image, believing that appearance shapes their self-esteem, social status, and life chances (Etcoff et al., 2004). This has come to the point that 15 percent of women in one study said they would sacrifice five years of their life to achieve their weight goal (Garner, 1997). A psychologically sophisticated, highly profitable, globalizing beauty/dieting industry has colonized and capitalized on women's most intimate worries and wishes about their bodies to sell a dizzying array of products to expanding consumer markets. As a result, millions are affected by a growing global trade in harmful skin-lightening products and by mounting fears about a global obesity epidemic that is said to threaten public health.

In this chapter, I will explore how the female body has become both a site of constraint and possibility for girls and women living in the West and (increasingly) around the world. I use the material culture of beauty and body histories of close to 100 Canadian women to show how women's new freedom to play with appearance during the 20th century has been accompanied by ever more exacting beauty standards at the beginning of the 21st. Drawing on cultural representations and women's personal experiences, I explore the ways in which pressure to control the body has intensified and diversified for girls growing up today in a contemporary Canadian context. I expand this analysis beyond the borders of Canada and the confines of adolescence to show how a transnational and intergenerational multi-billion-dollar beauty business has tapped into, and taken advantage of, expanding markets of female consumers—from "tweens" to seniors, from women living in the global North to those in the global South. I examine how, in the opening years of the 21st century, girls and women have come to see different body sites—including weight, skin, hair, and breasts—as significant body projects and problems.

To show how beauty culture shapes women's body images, I draw on two primary sources: first, the material culture of beauty; and second, body histories of close to 100 Canadian women from diverse backgrounds. By the "material culture of beauty," I mean cultural objects such as mirrors, cosmetics, fashion magazines, photographs, and film that illuminate changing ideologies of beauty and show how women have perceived their bodies in the past and the present. Detailing developments in the material culture of beauty over the 20th century demonstrates how our visual and commercial culture has encouraged women's discovery of their images and display of their bodies (Brumberg, 1998). Drawing from my own research on adult women's body histories, I use narratives by ordinary women of varying body sizes and ethnic and racial backgrounds, with and without disabilities and physical differences, to reveal the ways in which cultural images have shaped their body image [...] (Rice, 2003). By combining the material culture of beauty with individuals' narratives of embodiment, I hope to explain contemporary body projects and problems from the vantage point of diverse women.

History of Beauty Culture and Women's Body Projects

In Western culture, women are identified socially with our bodies (Odette, 1994). How the culture values or devalues our physical features, sizes, and capacities has a significant impact on our sense of body and self. Yet how do girls and women internalize cultural images? How do they use these images to shape their identities and sense of themselves? Why have feminists come to see cultural representations as a site of struggle for girls and women? To answer these questions, I briefly outline feminist theory on cultural representations, and I offer a feminist account of the history of beauty culture. [...]

In explaining why the body [is] so important to women's identity, French feminist Simone de Beauvoir famously wrote that, "one is not born, but becomes a woman" (de Beauvoir, 1974:249). She argued that women's bodies are central to this process; through media, schools, medical systems, and beauty culture we learn how to fashion our bodies to "create" our gender. [...] Feminist critics have long been interested in cultural representations of female bodies because women looking at these often have had a hard time recognizing themselves (Hearne, 2007). When they looked at images, women quickly came to see that they were "objects" of men's gaze. As cultural critic John Berger (1980) said of the ways that women have been depicted in Western art and advertising: "women are to-be-looked-at" and men do the looking. [...]

It can be difficult to develop a critical perspective of the gendered looking relations that Berger describes because we live inside them. Values and assumptions that are "naturalized" in art, advertising, and popular culture can be hard to question. Immersed as we are in these conventions, they simply appear as "normal." If you have doubts about Berger's feminist analysis, try the following experiment: choose an image of a nude from a traditional European painting and then change the white woman into a white man or a man or woman of colour in your mind's eye or in your drawing of a reproduction. What does this do to your assumptions and judgments about the figure in the picture?

By remaking classical nudes in this way, modern-day Japanese "appropriation" artist Yasumasa Morimura invites us to think about the complexity of the relationship between the viewer and the visual text (Yasumasa Morimura, 2008). He alters his face and body features through makeup, costume, props, and digital image manipulation to insert himself in place of the idealized female figures in some of the most famous European paintings such as Da Vinci's *Mona Lisa* and Manet's *Olympia*. By putting himself, as a Japanese man, in place of iconic beauty "ideals," he draws our attention to gendered and racialized looking relations, challenging Western conventions of seeing female bodies as objects "to be looked at" and especially of seeing *white* women's bodies as desirable objects. These looking relations, which are pervasive throughout the history of Western art, continue in contemporary commercial culture. When women look at media, we learn to identify with actual or imagined spectators looking at the ideal woman depicted in the image. In this way, we become conscious of potential or actual others looking at us. As feminists have noted, these looking relations are not only inequitable; in teaching us to value certain bodies and traits and devalue others, they also are highly evaluative.

For most of us, mirrors are the oldest and most ubiquitous image-making technologies in our day-to-day lives. When reflecting surfaces became a staple of stores and homes from the late 19th century on, images of their bodies became more accessible to women and girls (Brumberg 1998). As cultural historians have shown, prior to the Victorian period only the wealthy could afford mirrors. In the 16th century, for example, a small glass mirror framed in precious metals and jewels cost the equivalent of a luxury car in today's currency (Melchior-Bonnet, 2001). Technological advancements in the 19th century saw massive increases in mirror production and their installation in public and private spaces. The new department stores, such as Eaton's in Canada and Macy's in the United States, used reflecting surfaces to inundate interiors with light (O'Brien and Szeman, 2004). Retailers hoped this would incite consumer desire and encourage spending. [...]

At the same time, mirrors became permanent fixtures of middle-class homes, especially in bathrooms and bedrooms, as well as portable accessories for many girls and women. We know that a woman gazing at herself in the mirror is a common theme in art, advertising, and popular culture. While "being looked at" has been coded as female throughout Western cultural history (Hearne, 2007), a majority of Western women began to subject their bodies' features to greater scrutiny only with the introduction of affordable image technologies—first mirrors, then photography and film. From its status as precious item to commonplace object, the mirror has come to occupy an important place in our imaginations. Amplifying our awareness of our bodies as images, mirrors and other image technologies have made sight, not touch, a primary sense through which we experience our physical selves (Rice, 2003).

Within contemporary image culture, appearance is portrayed as paramount to women. Yet in the 19th century, beauty was believed to derive from inner qualities such as character, morality, and spirituality. [...] To [...] orient female buyers toward consumption of cosmetics [...] marketers [...] heightened women's image consciousness by reminding them of the critical gaze of others. For example, one ad warns women "Strangers' eyes, keen and critical—can you meet them proudly, confidently, without fear?" Another claims, "Your husband's eyes ... more searching than your mirror."[1] Positioned as objects of an outsider's gaze, female viewers of commercial culture were, for the first time, invited to see themselves as recipients of evaluative looks.

Historically, skin became women's first body project as they learned the power of complexion to advance or undermine their social inclusion. From ancient times, pallor was associated with high social status; women at work outdoors were tanned and aged faster, whereas women of high social status were not obliged to work in the fields but stayed indoors and were pale-skinned. To be fair (in the sense of colour of skin and hair) was to be fair (in the sense of beauty)— and beauty of person was strongly associated with beauty of soul. During the 17th, 18th, and (especially) the 19th century, this superiority of white over dark was scientifically proclaimed, as white Europeans needed a convincing justification for slavery and colonization. Their oppression of persons of colour contradicted emerging political theories grounded in principals of human rights (Schiebinger, 1993). Scientists constructed a hierarchy of races based on physical traits such as skin colour and bone structure to rationalize the continued disenfranchisement of racialized peoples.

As a result, women of every hue attempted to improve their social standing through skin whitening, the most popular cosmetic of the 19th century (Brumberg, 1998). In period advertisements, skin whiteners for white women promised to enhance their complexion while products for black women pledged to remove their dark skin. For instance, one "face bleach" ad claims to "turn the skin of a black or brown person four or five shades lighter, and a mulatto person perfectly white" (*St. Louis Palladium*, 1901, cited in Rooks, 1996). According to Black feminist scholar Noliwe Rooks (1996), these ads persuaded African American women to purchase products by presenting dark skin as an ugly imperfection and by suggesting that skin lightening would promote women's class mobility and social acceptance in colourist, white supremacist society.

Surprisingly, while large corporations today control cosmetics markets, ordinary women were industry innovators. Canadian working-class farm girl Elizabeth Arden, poor Jewish immigrant Helena Rubinstein, and African American domestic servant and daughter of slaves Madame C.J. Walker became successful entrepreneurs (Peiss, 1998). Feminist social historian Kathy Peiss suggests that these socially marginalized women built their businesses by attracting other women to act as sales agents, and by using stories of their own struggles to attract customers (Peiss, 1998). Early entrepreneurs brought to advertising the idea that women could improve their social situation through personal transformation. Madame C.J. Walker, who is credited with popularizing the "hot" comb for straightening hair, sold such products as Black women's "passport to prosperity" (Rooks, 1996:65). She saw Black women's beauty in a political light—as a "vindication of black womanhood" demeaned by slavery and as a pathway to prosperity and respectability denied by white society (Peiss, 1998; Rooks, 1996). Many Black feminist and critical race scholars have debated whether Madame C.J. Walker preyed on African American women's feelings of inferiority or promoted pro-Black beauty through dignifying their beauty practices (Byrd and Tharps, 2001; Rooks, 1996; Russell, Wilson, and Hall, 1992). Yet in her advertisements, personal letters, and public talks, Walker clearly did not seek to embody white ideals. Instead, beauty was a way to challenge widespread stereotypes of Black women as unfeminine and unattractive, and in so doing, to raise Black women's self-confidence and contribute to their collective advancement.

By the 1920s, the beauty business mushroomed into a mass market overtaken by male manufacturers (Peiss, 1998). [...] Drawing from the social permissiveness of the period, advertisers connected women's cosmetic use with greater individuality, mobility, and modernity. The caption of [one] ad exclaims "The Lovely Rebel Who fought for Youth and Won!" and [another] reads "Be as MODERN as you like—for you can still be lovely." While marketers sold makeup as a means for women to assert autonomy and resist outmoded gender expectations, by the end of the 1930s, messages increasingly equated beauty with a woman's "true femininity." For example, in one ad entitled "Beauty Lost—Beauty Regained," readers are told how a "lovely lady who goes to pieces" recovers her mental health by "regaining her lost youth." Beauty ads now encouraged women's investment in appearance in the name of their emotional well-being and psychological health. When image became intertwined with a woman's identity, personality, and psychology in this way, modifying the body became, for many, a principal method of caring for the self. In this way, a woman's appearance came to be read as a prime measure of her self-esteem, feminine essence, and mental health.

Throughout the 1930s and 1940s, medical professionals and marketers encouraged middle-class mothers to invest energy in their own and their daughters' appearance in the name of physi-cal and emotional health (Brumberg, 1998). In one period ad, mothers are told that keeping their daughters' complexion clear is "a mother's duty" and in another that girls "are never too young" to begin their beauty routines. During World War II, beauty became a means for women to sup-port the war effort, with ad copy announcing that "beauty is a duty," that "fit" bodies increased women's productivity while "lovely" faces enhanced troop morale. [...]

It was not until the 1950s that cosmetics companies first targeted teenage girls—who had started to hold part-time jobs and had their own disposable income—with ads designed to appeal to their sense of generational distinctiveness and romantic desires. With copy encouraging read-ers to get "The 'natural' look men look for," ads for *Seventeen Cosmetics* spoke to girls' romantic desires to fit with prevailing heterosexual scripts by reinforcing their wish to attract an admiring male gaze.

In today's media, explicit reference to an evaluative other is no longer necessary. Take a look at a recent *Cosmo*, *Vogue*, or other fashion magazine. Let's explore the looking relations surrounding the image of the model on the cover. As you study the cover photo, ask yourself the following questions: *Who is the woman on the cover looking at? Who does she think is looking at her?* As dis-cussed earlier, feminists have long argued that women within Western art and advertising have been positioned as recipients of an implicit male gaze. Yet as you explore looking relations sur-rounding the picture, your analysis might suggest that the cover image operates not only as an object of vision for *male* but also for *female* audiences. As viewers, we might imagine ourselves to be a male or female spectator looking at the model with envy or desire. Alternately, we might imagine ourselves to be the beautiful, sexy model looking back with confidence, desire, or the conviction of our own desirability at the male and female spectators who are looking at us. In either case, through this complex relay of looks, the model becomes an object of desire for imag-ined spectators *who want her* and for those *who want to be like her*.

*****

Today's Body Projects

To gain insight into women's body image formation, I undertook a research project investigat-ing diverse women's experiences of their bodies. The women who participated in this study, from all walks of life and living in Canada, are among the first generation to come of age in a world replete with image technologies of mirrors, cameras, TV, and computers. While experiences varied depending on race, ethnicity, and physical ability, most women I spoke to also told [of] how their degree of body dissatisfaction increased between ages 9 to 16 when all encountered mounting pressures to appear desirable. Participants confronted the "predicament of puberty"—the growing gap between their changing bodies and the idealized images promoted in our culture—when others commented on their physical development and differences. Coming of age in consumerist, image-oriented society, many dealt with the disparity between their perceived differences (in ability, colour, ethnicity, size, and physical development) and cultural ideals of desirability by imagining their "best possible" body and self. In addition, all tried to navigate the "predicament of puberty" by envisioning and adopting diverse body alteration practices—from dieting, hair relaxing, to eating disorders and cosmetic surgery—that would enable them to amend the differences and embody their desired image.

Messages in today's magazines echo efforts of women in my study to close the gap between their body differences and desirable ideals. Fashion magazines are vehicles for delivering messages of the beauty business to female consumers; a primary purpose is to enlist readers into image enhancement through continuous consumption. [...] Rather than advocating one ideal, magazines try to democratize beauty by convincing readers that they can achieve their "best bodies." This message enables girls' and women's expression of individuality and celebration of difference. Yet it also portrays body modification as critical to self-expression. In addition, it pulls diverse audiences into preoccupation with perpetual body improvement and purchase of products.

In many ways, trendy TV shows like *America's Next Top Model*, *Search for the Next Pussy Cat Doll*, and *Girlicious* likewise instruct girls and young women that they can bridge the gap between their bodily difference and images of desirability by re-visioning their differences as desirable. Yet such shows frequently reinforce the idea that the greatest power a young woman can wield is her sexual sway over men. They thus present beauty makeovers as the ticket to success. Despite purporting to represent diversity, such shows still promote a narrow notion of beauty and encourage constant body modification through consumption to achieve the desirable look.

Beauty pageants in which contestants are women with disabilities are yet another example of the idea of re-visioning differences as desirable, within narrow confines. *Miss Ability* is a reality TV beauty contest from the Netherlands that started in 2006; contestants have to display a "handicap visible to the eye." [...] The winner of the first pageant, crowned by the Dutch Prime Minister, was a young woman named Roos who wears a cervical collar due to an acquired disability affecting her neck. The cervical collar is the only indication she has any physical disability or difference and is not an average model. Roos manages her disability by using the cervical collar sometimes and lying prone sometimes, yet images often depict her as very desirable and sexual. While it can't be ignored that she is disabled, the nature of her disability is socially acceptable—no dribbling, sudden movements, speech impairments, or any deviance from social protocols that make people uncomfortable. Thus, the winner is someone the non-disabled population can relate to in fundamental ways. She can look "normal," albeit for very brief periods; she is seen as sexually desirable; and she meets expectations of what is feminine. Even in a forum where it's supposedly "celebrated," disability must remain invisible (Rice, Lenooy, and Odette, 2007). It is interesting to note that due to the show's surprisingly high ratings in the Netherlands, broadcasters have snapped up the rights to remake *Miss Ability* in Britain, France, Germany, and the U.S. (Sherwin, 2006).

As a result of these cultural meanings given to notions of difference and desirability, many girls and women come to relate to their bodies as self-making projects (Beausoleil, 1994, 1999). Girls and women have come to see different body sites—skin, weight, hair, and breasts—as personal problems. For example, 90 percent of women interviewed in my study saw themselves as over- or underweight; close to 80 percent believed their breasts were too big or small; 31 percent believed their skin was too dark; and 27 percent disliked their hair colour and texture (Rice, 2003). This suggests that, despite celebrations of difference currently popular throughout image culture, pressure to control and re-shape the body is intensifying and diversifying for contemporary young women coming of age in a "body-centric" culture. I now turn to explore each of these body projects in greater detail.

The Weight Project

In contemporary Western culture, we learn to value a certain size as part of the body beautiful. For example, the thin female body is associated with health, wealth, sexiness, self-discipline, and success. Despite growing dialogue about body acceptance, fat is seen as unattractive, not physically or emotionally healthy, downwardly mobile, and lacking in body- and self-control. In addition, today's magazines seem to criticize women's bodies whatever their weight. Headlines such as "Battle of the Bones," "Celebrities' Secret Weight Loss Surgery," and "Stars' Worst and Best Beach Bodies" regularly invite readers' critical evaluation of famous female bodies and encourage widespread comparison and competition based on looks and size. [...]

While celebration and stigmatization of fat have fluctuated in different times among different cultures, concerns about medical and moral risks of being overweight have intensified over the last century (Stearns, 1997). In North America today, two competing frames shape dialogue on obesity. Is it an "epidemic" or is it a "myth" (Campos, 2004; Lawrence, 2004; Rice, 2007)? The first frame—the epidemic of obesity—dominates public discussion and debate. Global and national public health institutions have fuelled fear of fat by interpreting obesity as an escalating epidemic that threatens the health and fitness of populations and nations (Raine, 2004; World Health Organization, 2000, 2003). [...] Beyond health problems, an increasing number of social problems are being blamed on fat, from global warming (Jacobson and McLay, 2006) to America's vulnerability to terrorist attacks (Associated Press, 2006).

Despite the ubiquity of such moralistic medical messages, there is considerable uncertainty and controversy within obesity research about the causes, health consequences, measures, and treatment of obesity (Cogan and Ernsberger, 1999; Jutel, 2006). In response to these critical questions, concerned scientists and social scientists recently have developed an alternative perspective on the "obesity epidemic" that shifts our attention away from stemming the epidemic of fat folk to examining the emergence of an idea—obesity as a dangerous disease—that has captured our cultural imagination (Campos, 2004; Gard and Wright, 2005; Sobal and Maurer, 1999). This view does not dismiss health concerns raised by doctors, governments, or others but instead invites us to question obesity researchers' assumptions and interests, and to explore why our society has become so alarmed about fat (Oliver, 2006).

For instance, some critics argue that framing fat as a dangerous disease not only denies and distorts empirical uncertainty within obesity research but also masks deeper cultural anxieties at work in this message (Gard and Wright, 2005; Jutel, 2006). Epidemiologists now suggest that rising weights in our society may be related to people's biology combined with obesity-causing environments (Brownell and Horgen, 2004; Raine, 2004). In addition, we simply do not know the health consequences of obesity. We know that the relationship between health and weight is a U-shaped curve, meaning that health risks increase at extreme under- and overweight (Ross, 2005). While high weight is associated with hypertension and heart disease, this association does not mean [there is a] causal relationship—in other words, there is no evidence that being fat in itself causes these health problems (Cogan and Ernsberger, 1999). To date, there are no safe, proven treatments for excess weight (Ernsberger and Koletsky, 1999). The most common treatments such as dieting, pills, and surgery all have health risks and consequences (Bennett and Gurin, 1983).

Finally, weight measures such as Body Mass Index or BMI (weight in kilos divided by the square of height in metres) have also been called into question. While BMI was originally meant as a screening tool (to tell if someone is at risk for developing a health problem), it is now widely misused as a diagnostic tool (to tell if someone needs to lose weight) (Ikeda, Crawford, and Woodward-Lopez, 2006; Jutel, 2006). BMI categories have been applied inappropriately to people of all ages, ethnicities, genders, and athletic abilities (Fairburn and Brownell, 2002; Ikeda Crawford, and Woodward-Lopez, 2006). Kate Harding (2008) developed the *BMI Illustrated Categories Slide Show* to demonstrate the body sizes that fit BMI categories and to get us to think critically about them. Watch the slide show to judge for yourself whether you think these categories are skewed (http://kateharding.net/bmi-illustrated/).

Some scholars have written about "the obesity epidemic" as a moral panic, arguing that misplaced morality and ideological assumptions underlie our "war on fat" (Gard and Wright, 2005; Oliver, 2006). They argue that, despite serious debate among obesity experts about the culpability of bad habits such as overeating or inactivity in causing obesity, the causes of and solutions for obesity invariably come back to people's health practices. Not only does this view ignore empirical uncertainty about causes of weight gain, but it blames individuals by ignoring contexts such as poverty or weight prejudice that constrain their options for eating or activity.

Recent history shows that obesity epidemic discourses have emerged today as dominant partly because they dovetailed with earlier state-sponsored efforts designed to improve the health, fitness, and competitiveness of nations. From the late 1960s onwards, many Western governments, including Canada, initiated public education campaigns that advocated greater physical activity to prevent fatness and promote fitness in citizens (Bauman et al., 2004; MacNeill, 1999). In response to growing concerns about excessive consumption and the sedentary lifestyles of Canadians, Prime Minister Pierre Elliott Trudeau launched the ParticipACTION Campaign in the early 1970s (Rootman and Edwards, 2004). It famously compared the fitness levels of a 30-year-old Canadian with a 60-year-old Swede. (To view this ad, see the ParticipACTION Archive Project.) Many of these ads (see Figures 40.1 and 40.2) imagined the ideal Canadian citizen as a thin, fit, white, able-bodied male. They further raised the spectre of the unfit, feminized, underdeveloped, and Third-World "other," who threatened Canada's competitiveness on the global economic stage. Signifying the future health and prosperity of nations, children were targeted as a group needing special attention.

However, the effectiveness of interventions that link fatness prevention to fitness promotion has never been established. Studies show that fat kids are less likely to be physically active and more likely to have eating problems. *Yet research has not revealed whether overeating and underexercising increases overweight or whether being fat increases their susceptibility to problem eating and inactivity* (Boutelle et al., 2002). Some women in my research suggest that ParticipACTION ads disseminated throughout the 1970s and 1980s heightened their fear of fat and instilled the belief that their big bodies were "bad." By linking thinness with fitness and positioning fat as opposite to fit, ParticipACTION's popular "FitFat" ad conveyed that fatness and fitness could *not* coincide in the same body (see Figure 40.3).

Figure 40.1

Figure 40.2

Those perceived as fat in childhood describe how the demanding physical education programs introduced into schools during this period often dissuaded them from participating in physical activity altogether. Adults' enforcement of restrictive diets in an attempt to regulate their weights also resulted in long-term struggles with food, including compulsive, binge, and secretive eating (Rice 2007, 2009a). In other words, fatness prevention efforts contributed to producing the very behaviours and bodies that proponents were attempting to prevent!

Figure 40.3

FIT FAT
August 1970

Ebbe Marquardsen welcomes Peter Elson (former Executive Director of the Ontario Public Health Association) as the first member of the ParticipACTION Network (1984).

I remember this feeling of dread when the ["FitFat"] ad came on TV. Once my father and I were watching, I remember a man's voice saying, "This year fat's not where it's at." This made me so self-conscious.... (Maude, 27, white Canadian, blind from adolescence)

I wasn't doing very well in ParticipACTION or Canada Fitness. I hated gym class. I didn't like being tested in front of everybody.... (Yolanda, 23, Dutch-Indonesian Canadian)

Although ParticipACTION ended in 2001, the Canadian federal government recently re-launched the campaign to stem rising levels of obesity, once again focusing on kids as a high-risk group (Canadian Press, 2007). With a renewed focus on fatness prevention through fitness promotion, efforts to stem today's obesity epidemic may be leading a new cohort of large kids to adopt problem eating and inactivity, possibly contributing to their future problems with weight. This raises some critical questions for developing feminist-informed health and physical education policies and programs: *What do you think a fat-friendly and girl-friendly physical education curriculum would look like? What about a physical education program that affirmed the capacities of kids with different bodies, including those with physical differences or disabilities? If you had the task of designing a feminist health promotion campaign, what messages would you want to convey in order to promote girls' and young women's health?*

Framing fatness as undesirable and diseased implies that fat has become "abject." Adopted from the work of philosopher Julia Kristeva, the concept of "the abject" refers to body parts or processes associated in our culture with incapacity, vulnerability, uncleanliness, unattractiveness, and undesirability (Kristeva, 1982, 1991). The abject is feared and rejected because it resists our drive to master and control our bodies. Treating physical features or functions as abject reminds people of our connections with nature, vulnerability to disease, and inevitable death. One way to understand the abject is to see it as the opposite of the ideal—the young, sexy, self-contained, hard body. Media images continually play on our fears of abjection and desire to embody ideals by showing us "rejected" "before" and "perfected" "after" pictures of women who undergo body makeovers (Covino, 2004). [...]

Women I interviewed described beginning demanding dieting and disordered eating as a way of amending the abject fat body. Whether they started secretive eating in childhood to resist adult imposition of restrictive diets, or later adopted "disordered" eating to amend size differences, it is noteworthy that *all* participants perceived as fat eventually took up problem eating practices.

> At least I felt normal enough and desirable enough [when bulimic] that I could actually contemplate a sexual relationship. I could actually let go of protecting myself and enter into a relationship. (Gayle, 29, English and Métis Canadian, size difference from childhood)

> The times I have felt love are times my body has been the most socially acceptable [through starving and purging]. It makes me profoundly sad that the only ways of accessing those feelings are through having a conventional body. (Sylvie, 36, Italian-Scottish Canadian, size difference from childhood)

Other women talked of taking up "disordered" eating during adolescence once they encountered increased pressures to appear desirable. When women perceived as too fat, plain, unattractive, or ethnically different were positioned as "other than female" in the passage to womanhood, these women adopted problem eating to escape their labelling as deviant.

While weight restriction became a way of life for many I interviewed, research offers contradictory evidence about the race and class of those with disordered eating and dieting concerns. Many racialized women indicate that images of an attractive body spanned a broader range of sizes in their communities than in mainstream contexts. Yet those I interviewed grew up during a time when communities of colour comprised less than 5 percent of the Canadian population. For this reason, most recall being one of only a few children within their communities and schools identified as an ethnoracial "minority." Subjected to racial "other"ing and to isolation within social and cultural landscapes of childhood, many lacked a cultural or community context in which to develop a critical consciousness about racist beauty ideals or to imagine an alternative body aesthetic (Poran, 2002). In addition, with stereotypical images of starving African bodies circulating in Western media throughout the 1970s (especially through children's charity commercials), thinness also became abject, especially for racialized women bearing the trait. As a result, many were caught between stigmatizing stereotypes of starving racialized bodies in the mainstream media and sexist pressures to conform to conflicting beauty ideals within the dominant culture and their own cultural communities.

> A girl at school said I looked like starving kids in the World Vision commercial. That was the most hurtful thing anybody ever said to me. I thought, "I should be bigger and more normal because I look like those poster kids." (Rhonda, 32, West Indian Canadian)

The Skin Project

As a result of Western colonization and widespread sexism, many cultures associate light skin with beauty, and this fuels and is fuelled by a profitable business in skin-whitening products. While some feminists have suggested that skin whitening is a practice relegated to our racist past (Brumberg, 1998; Peiss, 1998), they are missing the rapidly growing global trade in skin-lightening products. Feminist critical race scholar Amina Mire (2005) has called this phenomenon "the globalization of white western beauty ideals." (If you doubt Mire's claim, do an Internet search for "skin lightening." It will yield over a million links!) In the West, many cosmetics companies market skin lightening to aging white women by associating light skin with youth and beauty. The aging process in ads frequently is framed as a pathological condition that can be mitigated through measures such as bleaching out "age spots." Globally, cosmetics companies also sell skin-whitening products to women of colour, often covertly via the Internet in order to avoid public scrutiny or state regulation of their commodities and campaigns (Mire, 2005). This is partially because many products contain unsafe chemicals such as hydroquinone and mercury, which inhibit the skin's melanin formation and which are toxic. The dangers of mercury poisoning due to skin lighteners—neurological, kidney, and psychiatric damage—are well known. However, the hazards of hydroquinone, which has been shown to be disfiguring in high doses and to cause cancer in laboratory studies, are less well documented. [...]

In Africa and other regions of the global South, skin whitening is traditionally associated with white colonial oppression, when waves of European conquerors instituted economic, political, and cultural hierarchies based on language and skin colour. Because women who practice skin-lightening were and are harshly judged as suffering from an "inferiority complex" due to colonization, many engage in the practice covertly (Mire, 2005). Companies thus rely on covert advertising to mitigate women's secret shame about their perceived physical deficiencies, as well as their need to conceal such practices in order to avoid condemnation. Companies selling covertly also avoid scrutiny of injurious stereotypes used in product campaigns. In some campaigns, explicitly racist advertisements associate dark skin with "diseases" and "deformities" such as "hyperpigmentation," "melasma," and other "pigmentation pathologies." In contrast, they typically associate light skin with youth, beauty, and empowerment. In its Internet ads, L'Oreal, a leading manufacturer and marketer of skin-whiteners such as *Bi-White* and *White Perfect*, references the inferiority of dark skin and the superiority of light complexions. *Bi-White* features an Asian woman unzipping her darker skin. (See the ad at http://www.vichy.com/gb/biwhite.) Directed mainly to Asian women consumers, the ad uses medical language to suggest that Asian bodies produce too much melanin, which *Bi-White* will block. As Mire (2005) writes, darkness is associated with falseness, dirtiness, ugliness, and disease. Lightness is seen as true, clean, healthy, and beautiful.

There is a growing trend for many Western-owned cosmetics corporations to rely less on covert Internet marketing and more on splashy TV and print campaigns to reach customers in Asia (Timmons, 2007). Since 1978, Hindustan Lever Limited, a subsidiary of the Western corporation Unilever, has sold its skin-whitening products to millions of women around the world (Melwani, 2007). *Fair & Lovely*, one of Hindustan Lever's best-known beauty brands, is marketed in over 38 countries and currently monopolizes a majority share of the skin-lightening market in India (Leistikow, 2003). One industry spokesperson recently stated that fairness creams are half of the skin-care market in India, and that 60 to 65 percent of Indian women use these products on a daily basis (Timmons, 2007). Ads for *Fair & Lovely* frequently feature depressed young women with few prospects who gain brighter futures by attaining their dream job or desired boy-friend after becoming much fairer (Hossain, n.d.). Other commercials show shy young women who take charge of their lives and transform themselves into "modern" independent beauties. Appealing to women's dual aspirations for desirability and economic equality, ads feature taglines such as *Fair & Lovely: The Power of Beauty* and *Fair & Lovely: For Complete Fairness* (Timmons, 2007). (See ads at http://www.youtube.com/watch?v=KIUQ5hbRHXk&NR=1.) [...]

Globally, racialized women are fed a persuasive beauty myth: that fairness is glamorous and that lighter skin is the ticket to getting ahead in life. Of course, cosmetics corporations deny that the promise of fairness has anything to do with colonial and gender relations or with the idealiza-tion of white Western looks (Melwani, 2007; Timmons, 2007). Ironically, Western psychologists and psychiatrists have framed skin whitening and other risky body modification practices as signs of mental illness, unconnected to colonial or other oppressive histories and legacies. Historically, in response to these discourses, feminists have spoken about women who adopt extreme body modification practices as "victims" of a powerful beauty system. They have analyzed how sexist, racist, and consumerist interests push women into appearance alteration to cure distresses and dissatisfactions created by oppressive forces (Bordo, 1993; Morgan, 1991). More recently, other feminist writers have contended that women are not cultural dupes of the beauty system but "secret agents" who rightly reject body otherness and strategically alter their appearance in their own best interests (Davis, 1995). Consideration of women's accounts about body modification suggests to me that appearance alteration encapsulates both feminist positions—that women's attempts at bodily transformation signify their capitulation to oppressive ideals *and* opposition to harmful abjection (Rice, 2009b). Within a social world intolerant of sexual ambiguity, ethnic variation, and physical difference, "amending the abject" may be one of our few chances for eco-nomic mobility, social acceptance, and emotional health (Covino, 2004).

Seen in this light, skin modification may be one of few options for racialized women who feel caught between the colonizing effects of white supremacy and their desires for feminine beauty and social acceptance. In the narratives of women I interviewed, as with fat women, some racial-ized women aspired to a light ideal to escape being seen as "other." Many spoke of avoiding sunlight, wearing light concealer, and using skin lightening in an effort to evade demeaning racist and sexist comments and/or to create a more desirable image.

*****

> We have a family friend who is a lot darker than we are. She bought *Fair & Lovely* and when everyone found out, they used to say "Oh, she uses *Fair & Lovely*." The fact that we talked about it is mean. The fact that she feels she has to use it is terrible. (Preeta, 29, South Asian Canadian)

Any exploration of skin lightening among racialized women raises important questions about the skin-altering practices of white women, especially those engaged in the current trend of tan-ning. Many white women are well aware of the cultural associations of dark skin with devalued status. Yet in a cultural context, where race is read off multiple body sites (skin colour, facial fea-tures, hair texture, etc.), tanned skin may be viewed as a temporary, detachable adornment rather than an essential feature that signifies someone's racial status (Ahmed, 1998).

Ironically, white women often see skin *darkening* as a beauty project. After World War I, tan-ning became a statement about high social status; a tan proclaimed the leisure to lie out in the sun and the money to go to tropical beaches in mid-winter. White women who tan can thus connect their bronzed skin to health, wealth, status, and attractiveness, secure in the knowledge that they still are seen as white and regardless of the health implications (increased risk of skin cancers, premature skin aging). Yet exploration of tanning too generates more interesting questions: *Why is there a greater emphasis placed on white women's attainment of a sun-kissed, sexy glow while racialized women feel pressured to aspire to the glow of fairness? Is bronzed skin a sign of a white woman's class status, suggesting her access to leisure time and vacation money? Is the obsession with fairness simply a bad case of a "colonial hangover," or is it an example of a Western cultural imperialism that uses global media to spread white beauty ideals? What are other possible roots of, and reasons for, women's differing skin projects?*

*****

The Hair Project

Within a racial hierarchy of beauty, Black women encounter complex messages about hair due to deeply entrenched associations of long, flowing hair with social mobility and idealized femininity (Byrd and Tharps, 2001). An estimated 80 percent of African American women in the U.S. straighten their hair (Swee, Klontz, and Lambert, 2000). In 1993, the World Rio Corporation marketed a hair-straightening product on its late-night infomercials that targeted these women. In these ads, "good" hair was equated with a straightened hair and "bad" hair with curly locks. Once again, ads used the familiar format of abject "before" and ideal "after" shots featuring women who had been given a complete makeover. As Black feminist scholar Noliwe Rooks (1996) notes, women in the "before" shots were without makeup, jewelry, or other accessories. They looked unhappy and their hair was wild, unstyled, and unkempt, almost made to look "primitive." The "after" shots featured women who had a complete beauty makeover, including designer clothes, makeup, and a fashionable hairstyle. While manufacturers claimed Rio had low levels of acid, it actually contained harsh chemicals. Many women (and some men) who used it experienced hair loss, burns, blisters, and sores on their scalps. Of 340,000 people who purchased the product, over 3,000 filed complaints, the largest number ever received in the United States for a cosmetic product (Swee, Klontz, and Lambert, 2000).

In the infomercials, women were repeatedly told that Rio would deliver them from the "bondage of chemically treated hair." Rio sold itself as a product that would enhance Black women's self-worth, freedom, and social mobility. It sent the message that they could escape sexist and racist oppression through relaxing their hair. Marketers used this message because it resonates with consumers. Many Black women in my study explained how they used hair relaxers, not because they desired whiteness, but because they wanted to avoid racial "other"ing, as well as aspiring to desirability, acceptability, and an enhanced sense of self.

> In high school, people would say, "What are you?" I realized if I blow dry my hair to get it straight I might not identify as anything separate…. The less I try to visually look like some stereotypes from the media or their beliefs, the less I am singled out. (Ada, 27, Trinidadian Canadian African and Chinese)

*****

In case you think stigmatization of natural hair is a thing of the past, consider this: in October 2007, *Glamour* magazine developed a presentation called "The dos and don'ts of corporate fashion" that showed an African American woman sporting an Afro with a caption reading "Say no to the 'fro" (Dorning, 2007). The presenter told a women's luncheon at a Wall Street law firm that black female attorneys should avoid wearing "political" hairstyles like dreadlocks or Afros because these styles were seen as unattractive and unprofessional. (To read *Glamour* magazine's account of the event, go to: http://www.glamour.com/news/articles/2007/10/leive_letter.) Members of the audience were justifiably upset with the replay of negative stereotypes about "natural" hair as overly political, unfeminine, and unprofessional. Not only do these attitudes have an impact on Black girls' and women's beauty perceptions and practices, but they also are linked to blocked educational and economic opportunities. Like the racialized women in my study, African Canadian girls report witnessing or experiencing racial harassment in schools due to others' perceptions of their hair. In addition, some school boards in the U.S. have suspended African American students for wearing braids, beads, cornrows, dreadlocks, and other "extreme" hairstyles seen as making an overly strong political or cultural statement (Rooks, 2001). Black women have even been fired from jobs in major corporations for styling their hair in dreadlocks and braids. Because of the ways in which Black women's hair may be seen as connoting disruptive or oppositional identities, those with offending styles are banished, thus undermining their rights to represent themselves in preferred ways in public spaces (Rooks, 2001).

The Breast Project

I want to turn to breasts as a final site of modification. It is difficult to get an accurate read on how many Canadian women seek breast augmentation or reduction every year because the Canadian government does not keep track of cosmetic surgery procedures (Canadian Broadcasting Corporation, 2008). Nor do many women, especially young women, have easy access to unbiased information about the negative health consequences of breast implants. However, it is estimated that 100,000 to 200,000 Canadian women have implants, and that most have or will have complications requiring additional surgery and/or implant removal (Tweed, 2003), due to rupture, deflation, and leakage, which occurs in three-quarters of recipients (Brown et al., 2000). In addition, anywhere from 25 percent to 100 percent of women with implants suffer from capsular contracture, where scar tissue forms around the implant (because it is a foreign body), causing implanted breasts to become hard, painful, misshapen, or lopsided (Tweed, 2003). In a recent study into the long-term health risks of implants, researchers have found that, compared to other recipients of plastic surgery, women with breast implants are twice as likely to die from brain cancer, three times as likely to die from lung cancer, and four times as likely to kill themselves (Brinton et al., 2001). There may also be a link between silicone gel implants and autoimmune diseases such as fibromyalgia (Brown, 2001).

In our makeover culture, the mainstream media increasingly promotes cosmetic surgery as a preferred solution to girls' body image problems. Given the health risks associated with implants, it is particularly distressing that breast augmentation and other cosmetic surgeries are advocated as reasonable solutions to young women's body dissatisfaction resulting from harassment. For example, an article in *The Globe and Mail* (MacDonald, 2001) presents cosmetic breast and eye surgeries as the only viable responses for young women to the emotional effects of racist and sexist body-related comments. By promoting individualized responses like cosmetic surgery to others' rejection, the article ignores possible systemic solutions to body image concerns—for example, stopping the harassment (Larkin and Rice, 2005).

*****

In the absence of institutional policies addressing harassment or of the political will to enforce policies where they exist, the drive for young women to seek out individualized solutions such as altering their perceived defects through surgery begins to make sense. As feminist cultural theorist Susan Bordo (1999) has noted, consumer culture depends on the continual creation and proliferation of female "defects." By making us feel bad about our bodies while pumping us with our own sense of choice, freedom, and agency, we are primed to purchase solutions offered by the beauty and cosmetic medical industries. Women in my own study sought breast augmentation and reduction surgeries to avert harassing looks and hurtful comments, and to free themselves from stressful efforts to conceal their breast size and shape.

*****

[Before my implants] I felt so uncomfortable hiding my breasts. I used to take off my bra, get under the covers, make sure it was dark so you couldn't see. I wouldn't let him touch the smaller one. If he did touch it, then he'd be "How come one's smaller?" (Maya, 22, Jamaican Canadian, disability from late childhood)

In general, cultural meanings given to girls' and women's bodies that circulate in their everyday social lives play a primary role in constructing their bodies (including weight, skin, hair, and breasts) as problem sites that need to be corrected. Women respond to these messages through diverse body modification projects that range from dieting and disordered eating to skin lightening and cosmetic surgery. Moving beyond these individual solutions, I take up a few examples of feminist responses to oppressive beauty ideals in the context of my concluding comments.

Conclusion

Women report two responses to beauty standards: changing their bodies, which can lead to harmful body image problems and risky body alteration practices; or changing their situations, which can lead to improved body self-images. Of course, most of us navigate between both solutions; we try changing certain aspects of our bodies to fit into our environments and altering aspects of our environments to enhance our sense of "fit" and belonging. In my research, many women learned to redirect their energy into creating life circumstances where self-worth was based on things other than appearance. Significantly, a woman's capacity to alter her environment emerged in each narrative as key to her greater control and ownership of image.

Beyond individuals' improvisational efforts to affirm their bodies and identities, other critical ways that women might change their situations is through changing their institutional and image environments. For instance, feminist-informed health and social policy might better serve girls and women (and boys and men) by shifting focus from changing people's bodies to altering aspects of social and cultural worlds that impede their options for eating, activity, and other aspects of embodiment. A "body equity" approach in schools, health care settings, and other institutional sites that would advocate the acceptance of diverse bodies could work to stop stereotyping and stigma based on size, disability, or other physical differences (Rice and Russell, 2002). The primary objective of a feminist "body ethics" would be to move away from current cultural practices of enforcing body norms and toward more creative endeavours of exploring physical abilities and possibilities unique to different bodies.

Of course, feminists committed to changing our image environments have developed and continue to offer critical analyses of cultural messages and counter-images that challenge conventional views. For many activists and artists, this has meant creating representations that celebrate bodily differences or that dare to depict the abject. In various times and across diverse spaces, feminist cultural production (in books, plays, and visual arts) has worked to disrupt dominant ways of portraying bodies. One example is the development of "fat drag," live performances that poke fun at our cultural stereotypes about fat. Another is theatre that explores Black women's relationship to beauty. A third is art activism that uncovers and critiques the under- and misrepresentation of women in the art world. Feminists have shown how limitations of resources, space, and opportunity, rather than lack of courage or creativity, have constrained women artists and activists from imagining new possibilities for representations.

In closing, women do not modify their bodies because they are mindless dupes of sexist, racist, and classist media culture. Rather, they respond to oppressive ideals and evaluative others by seeking a "best possible" body and self. I see women's greater focus on appearance as signs neither of their victimization nor of their emancipation in consumer culture, but as their best attempts to navigate an image system in which bodies have become critical markers of identity and value. Yet our solutions to the hegemonic image system have come at a high cost, intensifying and diversifying our body projects and problems into the 21st century.

Note

1. Unless otherwise noted in a citation, all historical advertisements discussed in this chapter were retrieved from Ad Access On-Line Project, Duke University, at http://scriptorium.lib. duke.edu/adaccess.

References

Ahmed, S. 1998. Animated borders: Skin, colour, and tanning, in *Vital signs: Feminist reconfigurations of the bio/logical body*, M. Shildrick and J. Price, eds., 45–65. Edinburgh: Edinburgh Univ. Press.

Associated Press. 2006. Surgeon General: Obesity epidemic will dwarf terrorism threat. *LiveScience.com*, March 2. http://www.livescience.com/health/ap_060302_obesity.html. Retrieved April 15, 2008.

Bauman, A., et al. 2004. ParticipACTION: This mouse roared, but did it get the cheese? *Canadian Journal of Public Health* 95(S2):S14–S19.

Beausoleil, N. 1994. Makeup in everyday life: An inquiry into the practices of urban American women of diverse backgrounds, in *Many mirrors: Body image and social relations*, N. Sault, ed., 33–57. New Brunswick, NJ: Rutgers Univ. Press.

Beausoleil, N. 1999. Afterword, in *That body image thing: Young women speak out*, S. Torres, ed., 106–110. Ottawa: CRIAW/ICREF.

Bennett, W., and J. Gurin. 1983. *The dieter's dilemma: Eating less and weighing more*. New York: Basic Books.

Berger, J. 1980. *Ways of seeing*. Harmondsworth, England: Penguin Books.

Bordo, S. 1993. *Unbearable weight: Feminism, Western culture, and the body*. Los Angeles: Univ. of California Press.

Bordo, S. 1999. *Twilight zones: The hidden life of cultural images from Plato to O.J.* Berkeley: Univ. of California Press.

Boutelle, K., et al. 2002. Weight control behaviors among obese, overweight, and non-overweight adolescents. *Journal of Pediatric Psychology* 27(6):531–540.

Brinton, L., et al. 2001. Mortality among augmentation mammoplasty patients. *Epidemiology* 12:321–326.

Brown, L. 2001. Silicone gel breast implant rupture, extracapsular silicone, and health status in a population of women. *Journal of Rheumatology* 28:996–1103.

Brown, L., et al. 2000. Prevalence of rupture of silicone gel breast implants in a population of women in Birmingham, Alabama. *American Journal of Roentgenology* 175:1–8.

Brownell, K., and K. Horgen. 2004. *Food fight*. New York: Contemporary Books.

Brumberg, J. 1998. *The body project: An intimate history of American girls*. New York: Vintage Books.

Byrd, A., and L. Tharps. 2001. *Hair story: Untangling the roots of black hair in America*. New York: St. Martin's Griffen.

Campos, P. 2004. *The obesity myth*. New York: Gotham Books.

Canadian Broadcasting Corporation. 2008. Cosmetic surgery: Balancing risk. *CBC News in Depth: Health*, April 10. http://www.cbc.ca/news/background/health/cosmetic-surgery.html. Retrieved April 19, 2008.

Canadian Press. 2007. $5M to bring back ParticipACTION exercise program. *CBCnews.ca*, February 19. http://www.cbc.ca/health/story/2007/02/19/participaction.html. Retrieved April 17, 2008.

Cogan, J., and P. Ernsberger. 1999. Dieting, weight, and health: Reconceptualizing research and policy. *Journal of Social Issues* 55(2):187–205.

Covino, D. 2004. *Amending the abject body: Aesthetic makeovers in medicine and culture*. Albany: State Univ. of New York Press.

Davis, K. 1995. *Reshaping the female body: The dilemma of cosmetic surgery*. New York: Routledge.

de Beauvoir, S. 1974. *The second sex*, 2d ed., tr. H.M. Parshley. New York: Vintage Books.

Dorning, A. 2007. Black hair dos and don'ts: *Glamour Magazine* can't shake fallout from bad hair advice. *ABC News Online*, October 10. http://abcnews.go.com/US/story?id=3710971&page=1. Retrieved April 19, 2008.

Ernsberger, P., and R. Koletsky. 1999. Biomedical rationale for a wellness approach to obesity: An alternative to a focus on weight loss. *Journal of Social Issues* 55(2):221–259.

Etcoff, N., et al. 2004. *The real truth about beauty: Findings of the global study on women, beauty, and well-being*. Unpublished report commissioned by Dove, Unilever Corporation, London, September.

Fairburn, C., and K. Brownell, eds. 2002. *Eating disorders and obesity: A comprehensive handbook*, 2d ed. New York: Guilford Press.

Gard, M., and J. Wright. 2005. *Obesity epidemic: Science, morality, and ideology*. New York: Taylor and Francis.

Gardner, R., B. Friedman, and N. Jackson. 1999. Body size estimations, body dissatisfaction, and ideal size preferences in children six through sixteen. *Journal of Youth and Adolescence* 28:603–618.

Garner, D. 1997. The 1997 body image survey results. *Psychology Today* 30:30–64.

Harding, K. 2008. BMI illustrated categories project. http://kateharding.net/bmi-illustrated/. Retrieved April 14, 2008.

Hearne, A. 2007. Shake yo' tail feathers: Watching and performing gender. Lecture, January 11, Women's Studies 100, An Introduction to Women's Studies. Trent University, Peterborough, ON.

Hossain, A. n.d. The color complex: Is the fixation really fair? *Sapna Magazine.* http://www.sapnamagazine.com/index.php?option=com_content&task=view&id=121&Itemid=30. Retrieved April 18, 2008.

Ikeda, J., P. Crawford, and G. Woodward-Lopez. 2006. BMI screening in schools: Helpful or harmful. *Health Education Research* 21(6):761–769.

Irving, L. 2000. Promoting size acceptance in elementary school children: The EDAP puppet program. *Eating Disorders* 8:221–232.

Jacobson, S., and L. McLay. 2006. The economic impact of obesity on automobile fuel consumption. *The Engineering Economist* 51(4):307–323.

Jones, J., et al. 2001. Disordered eating attitudes and behaviours in teenaged girls: A school-based study. *Canadian Medical Association Journal* 165(50): 547–552.

Jutel, A. 2006. The emergence of overweight as a disease entity: Measuring up normality. *Social Science and Medicine* 63:2268–2276.

Kristeva, J. 1982. *Powers of horror: An essay on abjection,* tr. L. Roudiez. New York: Columbia Univ. Press.

Kristeva, J. 1991. *Strangers to ourselves,* tr. L. Roudiez. New York: Columbia Univ. Press.

Larkin, J., and C. Rice. 2005. Beyond "healthy eating" and "healthy weights": Harassment and the health curriculum in middle schools. *Body Image* 2:219–232.

Lawrence, R. 2004. Reframing obesity: The evolution of news discourse on a public health issue. *Harvard International Journal of Press-Politics* 9(3):56–75.

Leistikow, N. 2003. Indian women criticize "Fair and Lovely" ideal. *Women's E-News,* April 28. http://www.womensenews.org/article.cfm/dyn/aid/1308/context/archive. Retrieved April 18, 2008.

MacDonald, G. 2001. Girls under the knife. *The Globe and Mail,* January 15, R1, R25.

MacNeill, M. 1999. Social marketing, gender, and the science of fitness: A case study of ParticipACTION campaigns, in *Sport and gender in Canada,* P. White and K. Young, eds., 215–231. Toronto: Oxford Univ. Press.

McVey, G., et al. 2002. Risk and protective factors associated with disordered eating during early adolescence. *Journal of Early Adolescence* 22:76–96.

Melchior-Bonnet, S. 2001. *The mirror: A history,* tr. K. Jewett. New York: Routledge.

Melwani, L. 2007. The white complex: What's behind the Indian prejudice for fair skin? *Little India,* August 18. http://www.littleindia.com/news/134/ARTICLE/1828/2007-08-18.html. Retrieved April 18, 2008.

Mire, A. 2005. Pigmentation and empire: The emerging skin-whitening industry. *Counterpunch Magazine Online,* July 28. http://www.counterpunch.org/mire07282005.html. Retrieved April 18.

Morgan, M. 1991. Women and the knife: Cosmetic surgery and the colonization of women's bodies. *Hypatia* 6:25–53.

O'Brien, S., and I. Szeman, I. 2004. *Popular culture: A user's guide.* Toronto: Nelson Education.

Odette, F. 1994. Body beautiful/Body perfect: Where do women with disabilities fit in? *Canadian Woman Studies/les cahiers de la femme* 14(3): 41–43.

Oliver, E. 2006. *Fat politics: The real story behind America's obesity epidemic.* New York: Oxford Univ. Press.

ParticipACTION Archive Project. http://www.usask.ca/archives/participaction/english/home. html. Retrieved June 26, 2008.

Peiss, K. 1998. *Hope in a jar: The making of America's beauty culture*. New York: Henry Holt.

Poran, M. 2002. Denying diversity: Perceptions of beauty and social comparison processes among Latino, Black, and white women. *Sex Roles* 47(1/2):65–81.

Raine, K. 2004. *Overweight and obesity in Canada: A population health perspective*. Ottawa: Canadian Institute for Health Information.

Ricciardelli, L., and M. McCabe. 2001. Children's body image concerns and eating disturbances: A review of the literature. *Clinical Psychology Review* 21:325–344.

Rice, C. 2003. Becoming women: Body image, identity, and difference in the passage to womanhood. Unpublished Women's Studies PhD dissertation, York University, Toronto.

Rice, C. 2007. Becoming "the fat girl": Acquisition of an unfit identity. *Women's Studies International Forum* 30(2):158–174.

Rice, C. 2009a. Imagining the other? Ethical challenges of researching and writing women's embodied lives. *Feminism & Psychology* 19(2):245–266.

Rice, C. 2009b. How big girls become fat girls: The cultural production of problem eating and physical inactivity, in *Critical feminist perspectives on eating disorders: An international reader*, H. Malson and M. Burns, eds., 97–109. London: Psychology Press.

Rice, C., L. Lenooy, and F. Odette. 2007. Talking about body image, identity, and difference. Envisioning New Meanings of Disability and Difference Project Workshop, November 26, Women's College Research Institute, Toronto.

Rice, C., and V. Russell. 2002. *Embodying equity: Body image as an equity issue*. Toronto: Green Dragon Press.

Rooks, N. 1996. *Hair raising: Beauty, culture, and African-American women*. New Brunswick, NJ: Rutgers Univ. Press.

Rooks, N. 2001. Wearing your race wrong: Hair, drama, and the politics of representation for African American women at play on a battlefield, in *Recovering the black female body: Self representations by African American women*, M. Bennett and V. Dickerson, eds., 279–295. New Brunswick, NJ: Rutgers Univ. Press.

Rootman, I., and P. Edwards. 2004. The best laid schemes of mice and men … ParticipACTION's legacy and the future of physical activity promotion in Canada. *Canadian Journal of Public Health* 95(S2):S37–S44.

Ross, B. 2005. Fat or fiction: Weighing the obesity epidemic, in *Obesity epidemic: Science, morality, and ideology*, M. Gard and J. Wright, eds., 86–106. New York: Taylor and Francis.

Russell, K., M. Wilson, and R. Hall. 1992. *The color complex: The politics of skin color among African Americans*. New York: Anchor Books.

Schiebinger, L. 1993. *Nature's body: Gender and the making of modern science*. Boston: Beacon Press.

Shapiro, S., M. Newcomb, and T. Burns Loeb. 1997. Fear of fat, disregulated-restrained eating, and body-esteem: Prevalence and gender differences among eight- to ten-year-old children. *Journal of Clinical Child Psychology* 26:358–365.

Sherwin, A. 2006. Reality TV puts disabled women in beauty show. *The Times Online*, December 27. http://www.timesonline.co.uk/tol/news/world/europe/article1068730.ece. Retrieved April 12, 2008.

Sobal, J., and D. Maurer, eds. 1999. *Interpreting weight: The social management of fatness and thinness*. New York: Walter de Gruyter.

Stearns, P. 1997. *Fat history: Bodies and beauty in the modern West*. New York: New York Univ. Press.

Swee, W., K. Klontz, and L. Lambert. 2000. A nationwide outbreak of alopecia associated with the use of hair-relaxing formulation. *Archives of Dermatology* 136:1104–1108.

Timmons, H. 2007. Telling India's modern women they have power, *New York Times Online*, May 30. http://www.nytimes.com/2007/05/30/business/media/30adco.html?ex=1181620800&en=201bcdec2fbde98d&ei=5070&emc=eta1. Retrieved April 19, 2008.

Tweed, A. 2003. *Health care utilization among women who have undergone breast implant surgery.* Vancouver: British Columbia Centre of Excellence for Women's Health.

World Health Organization. 2000. *Obesity: Preventing and managing the global epidemic.* Geneva, Switzerland: World Health Organization.

World Health Organization. 2003. Controlling the global obesity epidemic. Geneva, Switzerland. http://www.who.int/nutrition/topics/obesity/en/index.html. Retrieved April 30, 2006.

Yasumasa Morimura. 2008. Self-portrait as art history. http://www.assemblylanguage.com/images/Morimura.html. Retrieved June 26, 2008.

Chapter 41

Fat and Fabulous:
Resisting Constructions of Female Body Ideals

Kathleen LeBesco

Kathleen LeBesco is professor and Distinguished Chair of Communication Arts at Mary-mount Manhattan College in New York City. She is the author of Revolting Bodies? The Struggle to Redefine Fat Identity, *co-editor of a number of anthologies, including* Bodies out of Bounds: Fatness and Transgression, *and is currently working on a new book about food and class politics.*

"You can never be too rich or too thin." The linking of economic status and body size in this popular adage is far from coincidental. In fact, the unprecedented abundance of food resources in much of the Western world and the accompanying shift from the manual labor of the industrial age to the more sedentary bodies of the flourishing service and information economies have made it easier than ever before to be fat.

However, cultural ideals of beauty tend to follow from that which is difficult to attain in a given context. In a world where our jobs require little physical exertion, where media are best enjoyed while immobile, and where overprocessed fast food is increasingly convenient and ubiquitous, it is then unsurprising that the aesthetic ideal for women—a lean, gym-toned physique—signifies a clear departure from the logic of the culture itself. While there is certainly much profit to be made in the fattening process, there are even greater returns when fat and average-sized women are made to feel anxious and ashamed about their bodies. Diet and fitness industries prey upon the very insecurities that they help to create, reaping billions of dollars in annual revenue as a result.

It is vital to remember, in the face of professionally cultivated body shame, that spending one's money on diet products and, more generally, buying into diet rhetoric means allowing that shame to thrive unchecked. For many fat women, the only way to avoid derision by peers is to submit to the notion that there is something wrong with them and to confess a drive for change. Women who claim "fat pride" and inhabit their culturally scorned bodies comfortably get little refuge from the critical, discriminatory glare of those around them. On the other hand, those who internalize the perception that they would be incomparably improved if they could only lose weight—whether or not they actually do diet—are granted a bit of breathing space. Those women who fail to take up their own body as a project, who instead direct their attention to more pressing social and political projects, are given more than a slap on the wrist. They are pushed to the margins of society, *abjected*, making the objectification faced by their slimmer sisters look like a dream state.

Electronic and print media are some of the most notorious carriers of punishing messages about women's bodies. Fashion magazines aimed at young women showcase spreads featuring near-skeletal models and ads for diet products and flaw-masking cosmetics alongside articles about female empowerment—the bait and switch, indeed. Lad magazines aimed at young men so radically alter images of the actresses on their covers, thinning them down to peg-leg proportions, that the stars themselves (Kate Winslet, for example) complain.

Few genres of television programming feature women of average or even ample size, and when fat women do show up, they're often portrayed one-dimensionally as unhappy and lovelorn or zany comic figures (Mimi from *The Drew Carey Show*, for one). "Real" fat women appear on television in daytime talk shows, where they either capitulate to audience consensus that they're deeply flawed, or where they are roundly mocked for taking pleasure in their own bodies. Entertainment television reports also devote significant attention to the weight gain of actresses, real women whose bodily dimensions are the stuff of much public speculation. In recent years, numerous women inhabiting what many of us would consider conventionally beautiful bodies have been flayed in entertainment media for "betraying" the public by gaining a few pounds, including Alicia Silverstone, Kathleen Turner, Catherine Zeta-Jones, and others. Mainstream film treads similar ground, with few exceptions highlighting slender beauties as leading ladies and relegating their fatter counterparts to second-banana status. Even films that portend to take aim at fat-phobia and looks-ism like the Farrelly brothers' *Shallow Hal* end up reinscribing notions that beauty comes in a size six and that fat jokes pandering to the lowest common denominator are comedic gold.

One should not get carried away in pointing fingers at the media for promoting narrow body ideals, however, without examining how everyday talk about bodies—the kind that each one of us participate in—reinforces cultural prejudices against fat people. At a pool party, I recently overheard the following conversation about a middle-aged woman at the far end of the pool dressed in a fairly ample bikini and tank-top coverup whose large belly and fleshy hips made her an unusual wearer of a bikini-style swimsuit. The onlookers, both women, exchanged goofy smiles, and the first exclaimed, "Brave woman!" to which the second muttered, "More like CRAZY! What makes her think the public wants to see her big gut?" Even in a private chat, such conversational censure functions to police bodies that fail to correspond to bigoted standards. Similarly, when women describe their experience of having an "off" day as "having a fat day," fat is irrevocably positioned negatively. For mainstream body ideals to change, we must not only create and support more complex, sophisticated media representations of fat characters, but we must take responsibility in our own speech for how we present fat bodies.

This issue of responsibility rears its head quite frequently in discussions of whether fat women deserve to be treated respectfully, despite their differences from currently idealized body types. A fat body, like a lesbian body, a Black body, or a disabled body, is marked as "different" from what our culture idealizes. Racism and able-ism remain discouragingly prevalent in the North American context, though most people recognize that one does not choose one's race or disability. In contrast, battles over whether sexuality is an inherent orientation or instead a "lifestyle" choice continue to inform the decisions of many as to how homosexuals should be treated. The jury still seems to be out on fat people, as well, with many hoping that the identification of a "fat gene" will let fat folk off the hook, show that they're not responsible for their culturally maligned position, and augur some respect. Still other fat activists argue that regardless of the extent to which one is culpable (through eating and exercise habits) in one's own fatness, respectful treatment is *always* warranted.

Rather than despairing over the apparently maligned position of fat women in mainstream Western culture, one could look to the work of fat acceptance activists and culture workers for a blueprint to the anti-diet revolution. Groups like the radical Fat Underground from the 1970s and the more assimilationist National Association to Advance Fat Acceptance have labored to change our understandings of and responses to fatness. Less formal networks of fat women have collaborated on public actions like an ice cream eat-in in front of a Jenny Craig diet center and a scale-smashing in Seattle that seek in a highly visible manner to show their dissatisfaction with our culture's regard for them. Others use the Internet as a forum for hashing out more acceptable and sometimes celebratory meanings for fat women's bodies. Even corporate media have seen fit to show us complex fat female heroines; Emmy-winner Camryn Manheim of *The Practice* sets many hearts aflutter! Whatever the location, these forms of resistance demonstrate that female body ideals are being contested in profound ways.

In stepping up to the challenge of resisting mainstream notions of what a woman's body should be, we need to guard against the tendency to claim innocent intentions. To cave in to the rhetoric that "we can't help being fat, thus we shouldn't be treated poorly" is to allow our emotional safety to exist at the expense [of] our dignity and subjectivity. Never have I heard a Jewish woman defend herself from anti-Semitism by claiming "I was born this way, and I can't do anything about it—so leave me alone." To do so would be to undermine her agency and her faith. I believe that we need to encourage women to inhabit their bodies comfortably, whatever their size and shape, and to understand that it doesn't really matter how a body got to be the way it is for it to be respected. In this way, women can begin to abandon their "body projects" and give up the fantasies of what their lives would be like if only they were thin, and live *today*.

Chapter 42

Body Beautiful/Body Perfect: Where Do Women with Disabilities Fit in?

Francine Odette

Francine Odette is an educator, writer, community organizer, and activist. Odette has spent over 20 years advocating for the rights of girls and women with disabilities and has worked as a consultant, adviser, and researcher on numerous projects involving women in the education, arts, health, and work sectors. In 2008, she was awarded the YWCA Women of Distinction Award.

When I decided to write about the issue of body image and its impact on women with disabilities, the challenge brought with it a chance to explore the link between fat oppression and the experiences of women with disabilities. Unfortunately, little research has been conducted on this issue as it affects the lives of women with disabilities. This may reflect the belief that the lived experiences of many women with disabilities are not important or perceived as valid by mainstream researchers.

I do not represent the experiences of all women with disabilities regarding the issues of body image and self-perceptions; however, over the years I have listened to the stories of many women who have a range of disabilities. These women's disabilities include being non-verbal, [having difficulty with] mobility, deafness, hard of hearing, and/or visual impairments. Many of these women spoke of their lives and how they have begun to deal with some of their concerns. While recognizing that the issues for women with disabilities may vary from those of non-disabled women, our lives, experiences, and fears are very similar.

Women are identified socially with our bodies. For women living in Western culture, thinness is often equated with health and success. We are taught early to be conscious of our body shape, size, weight, and physical attributes. The current cultural "norm" or ideal is unattainable for most women. Fat women, women with disabilities, women from particular racial or ethnic groups or with non-heterosexual orientation, and other women who do not conform to the prescribed norm of social desirability are often viewed as having experiences and attributes somewhat different from that of other women in this culture and as a result are often isolated.

Women with disabilities living in this society are not exempt from the influence of messages that attempt to dictate what is desirable and what is not in a woman. These messages are often internalized, and have an impact on how we see ourselves. The further we see ourselves from the popular standard of beauty, the more likely our self-image will suffer. We may experience a greater need to gain control over our bodies, either by our own efforts of restrictive eating and exercising, or the intrusive procedures performed by those deemed to be the "experts"—the medical profession.

We form images of ourselves early in infancy and these are confirmed or altered by the responses, or evaluations, made by others in our lives. Based on physical judgments, women with disabilities hear various messages from family, friends, and society at large about our perceived inability to participate in the roles that are usually expected of women. Society believes that lack of physical attractiveness, as defined by the dominant culture, hampers our ability to be intimate. These misperceptions hamper our ability to get beyond our physical differences, perpetuate body-image dissatisfaction, and contribute to eating problems.

Within this culture, having a disability is viewed negatively. This nation is supported by the fact that the lives of women with different disabilities are not reflected in the media. We are invisible. However, when our lives are spoken of, they are distorted through romantic or bizarre portrayals of child-like dependency, monster-like anger, or super-human feats. This increases the discomfort of others when in contact with women with disabilities, which in turn perpetuates the sense of "otherness" that women with disabilities may feel.

As women and individuals with disabilities, the messages that we receive often indicate the lack of role expectations for us. For young girls with disabilities, the invisibility of our lives becomes reinforced by the fact that popular advertising suggests the "normal" body is that which is desirable. Once these messages become internalized and reinforced, young girls and women with disabilities may try to compensate for their disabilities by striving to look as close to the nondisabled "norm" as possible. Similar to many non-disabled women's experiences, some girls and women with different disabilities may try to hide their bodies or change how their bodies look. Comfort and health may be sacrificed as we attempt to move closer to the realm of what the "normal" body appears to be by manipulating our bodies through continuous dieting, plucking, shaving, cutting, and constricting.

Medicalizing Our Bodies

Much feminist theory has been focused on identifying the reality that within Western culture, women's bodies are objectified for the purposes of male pleasure and domination. As a result, women's perceptions of themselves and their bodies become distorted. We are taught to mistrust our own experience and judgment about the notion of desirability and acceptance. These qualities are defined by the dominant culture. They are socially and economically defined by those in power—white, able-bodied, heterosexual men. Within this context, the body becomes a commodity with which one may bargain in order to obtain more desirable opportunities, for example, work or security (Szekely).

Feminist analysis identifies women's alienation from themselves and their bodies as a result of the objectification of the female body. However, a great deal of feminist analysis may not be reflective of all women's experience. The way in which women's bodies are portrayed as commodities in the media may not be a reality for many women labelled "disabled." In reflecting societal beliefs regarding disability, our bodies become objectified for the purposes of domination, but within a different context.

Traditionally, disability, whether it is visible or invisible, has tended to be viewed as something that is undesirable. Whether we are born with our disability or acquire it later, our bodies become objectified as part of the medical process. Medical examinations are often undertaken by groups of male doctors who, despite their aura of "professionalism," are still perceived by the patient as a group of anonymous men. Regular routines such as dressing ourselves or other activities are observed by doctors while on their "rounds," as this is seen as an excellent training for new doctors.

Many of us recount our experiences of having to display our bodies to groups of male doctors in the guise of "medical treatment" without prior knowledge or consent. We may have been asked to strip, walk back and forth in front of complete strangers so that they can get a better view of what the physical "problem" is, or to manually manipulate our limbs to determine flexibility and dexterity. Today, pictures or videos are taken of us and used as educational tools for future doctors, with little thought given to our needs to have control over what happens to our bodies or who sees us. While the medical profession attempts to maintain control over our bodies, some women with disabilities may attempt to regain control through dieting, bingeing, or other methods of body mutilation.

Some disabled women speak of having numerous surgeries conducted with the hope of a "cure," when, in reality, the surgeries result in increased pain, discomfort, and [an] altered physical state of one's body. The concept of body image as it impacts young girls and women with disabilities is crucial, especially when one looks at instances where the functioning of certain body parts must change and be altered, resulting in scars, diminished sensation, or radically changing the physical state, for example, amputation, mastectomies. A common theme emerges between intrusive medical intervention and popular methods of cosmetic surgery; the perceived need to change or alter the "imperfect" body. For many women with disabilities the message is clear—the way our bodies are now is neither acceptable nor desirable. To be non-disabled is the "ideal" and along with that comes the additional expectations for the quest of the "perfect body."

Body image, self-image, and esteem are often linked with the perceptions held by society, family, and friends. Disability is often seen as a "deficit" and women with disabilities must address the reality that the "ideal" imposed by the dominant culture regarding women's bodies is neither part of our experience nor within our reach. As women with disabilities, some of us experience difficulty in having others identify us as "female."

Disability and "differentness" results in many of us living our lives from the margins of society. As women with disabilities, we must begin to challenge the perceptions of "body beautiful" along with the perceptions held by some non-disabled feminists who resist the "body beautiful" but ignore or affirm the notion of the "body perfect." Disability challenges all notions of perfection and beauty as defined by popular, dominant culture. We must reclaim what has been traditionally viewed as "negative" and accentuate the reality that "differentness" carries with it exciting and creative opportunities for change. A lot can be learned by the experiences of women with different disabilities, as we begin the process of reclaiming and embracing our "differences." This includes both a celebration of our range of sizes and shapes and abilities.

References

Szekely, Eva. *Never Too Thin*. Toronto: The Women's Press, 1988.

Chapter 43

"We Need a Theoretical Base": Cynthia Rich, Women's Studies, and Ageism: An Interview

Valerie Barnes Lipscomb

Valerie Lipscomb is an assistant professor of English at the University of South Florida. She completed her PhD at the University of South Florida, with concentrations in modern literature and teaching composition. Her research investigates the performance of age in modern drama. She is the recipient of a number of research and teaching awards.

Cynthia Rich is an activist who has been exposing ageism against old women for more than 25 years. She co-authored the trailblazing essay collection *Look Me in the Eye: Old Women, Aging, and Ageism* with her partner Barbara Macdonald in 1983. [...] Another expansion of that edition was published in 2001 after Macdonald's death at age 86, so that the essays span more than 20 years of analysis and activism, addressing society's pervasive ageism from a feminist perspective. Rich lives in San Diego, where she is a co-founder of The Old Women's Project. According to the project website, the group "works to make visible how old women are directly affected by all issues of social justice, and to combat the ageist attitudes that ignore, trivialize or demean us. We are a group of old women who use actions of various kinds to achieve this goal. We welcome women of all ages who wish to join in our actions" (The Old Women's Project, 2005). During a telephone conversation, Rich commented on relationships between Women's Studies, ageism against old women, and activism. [...]

VBL: Some of the comments on ageism on The Old Women's Project website are similar to those included in essays and speeches you and Barbara Macdonald wrote 20 years ago. Have perceptions of old age changed in society at large? Is the battle any different now as the general population ages?

CR: That's an excellent place to start. We're living out the world that Barbara projected for us in 1980 in her essay "Exploitation by Compassion" (Macdonald 2001). There are so many more old women now, and the corporations, the drug companies, the nursing facilities, the retirement homes have moved right in to reap the profits. But it also turns out that they can make money by actively promoting a fear and loathing around women's aging. Now 30-year-olds are just horrified by their first wrinkle, and it's become a major industry to make younger women see my

72-year-old body as hideous. Will it matter that the baby boomers are aging? Well, there may be more of us old women every day, but if numbers translated into power, women and people of color would rule the world. I don't put faith in numbers.

VBL: What direction do you believe academics should take, especially Women's Studies and age studies scholars?

CR: I want to say that any change in approach, in attitudes, needs to start in academia; we need a theoretical base. The women who set off the women's movement in the '70s and '80s will be moving into old age in large numbers—they could make a difference—but there's no theoretical analysis, no base for what they're encountering. Without a theoretical foundation that Women's Studies can provide us, women have no idea how to think about our aging and our organizing. They're struggling. Longtime feminists such as Ellen Goodman, Geraldine Ferraro, and Pat Schroeder tried to organize a voters' movement called Granny Voters, around their concern for their grandchildren. Granny Voters? These are strong feminists who never would have called themselves Mommy Voters, who never would have ignored the sexism they encountered or fed the stereotype that all women are mothers.

*****

They want to act, and they want to act as old women, but they have no theoretical base. I'm counting on academia, particularly Women's Studies, to provide them with one.

VBL: One theory of aging that many scholars have found useful is Kathleen Woodward's (*Aging and Its Discontents* 1991) mirror stage of old age. [...] The old person sees herself in the mirror and, instead of seeing an integrated self reflected, feels an alienation from the image of this aged body. Old people say they don't feel any different from when they were young adults, but they cannot believe that their bodies are so different from how they feel. They experience distancing from their bodies and a sense that their bodies are betraying them.

CR: That alienation from the body comes from the fact not only that we weren't always old, but also that we were ageist when we were young. We shared society's revulsion of aging flesh. We internalized the ageism. Our bodies are changing all our lives. We should always be standing in front of the mirror, saying, "I can't believe this is my body." At age 20, we should be in disbelief that it's the same body we had at age 5. It's so marked when we're old because we've internalized that physical revulsion that's not dissimilar to the physical revulsion that other marginalized people have experienced—people of color, the disabled, lesbians and gays, Jews. All marginalized people have heard at one time or another that it's "natural" for others to find them physically repulsive. That's key. There's a mechanism that connects all types of marginalization with a contempt for the physical body. Ageism is not different from other "isms"; we put it into the category of natural—naturally, younger people don't want to associate with old women. Not long ago, people thought it was natural for men not to want to associate with women outside of the home, or for white people not to associate with people of color. [...]

VBL: It's essential to recognize that ageism is in the same category as racism and sexism, but it differs in that during the life course, we all move from the unmarked to the marked position, from privilege to discrimination. That has a great deal to do with our resistance toward acknowledging ageism, including the resistance of scholars to address the issue. It seems that you've been delivering this same message on ageism for many years to the academic community, and too many of us still don't get it.

*****

As the baby boom ages, perhaps as larger numbers of those active in Women's Studies face ageism themselves, they will develop an interest and understanding.

CR: Women's Studies is most able to see that this is not just a "problem of the elderly"; we need to clearly see the world of difference between how old men and old women are treated—beyond the issue of their pocketbooks, which is huge. Old men who are especially frail and powerless are seen *as if* they are women, just as gay men sometimes are treated contemptuously *as if* they are women. But the world is run by old white men. The experiences are incredibly different. Here's an example. When newspaper publisher Katherine Graham died, Michael Bechloss, a liberal historian in his 50s, was speaking of his experience with her, and he literally said, "Everybody talks about her as an 84-year-old woman. I did not see her as an 84-year-old woman. She wasn't ossified" (Bechloss 2001). That says worlds about the differences between attitudes toward old men and old women—who would say that if Daniel Schorr (who's 90) or Mike Wallace (in his 80s) or Dan Rather died? And this is a liberal guy talking.

VBL: The example that strikes me is the obituary of columnist Ann Landers. You've noted that the story announcing her death on *NBC Nightly News* began, "A great-grandmother who ..." (2002). That had nothing to do with her accomplishments and would never have been applied to a man. The media simply do not point out that an accomplished old man is a grandfather, let alone foreground his place in the family. Moreover, you've pointed out that this is exactly the type of description applied to younger women in the 1950s: "A mother of two," etc. And you believe that drawing this analogy with attitudes toward younger women before the second wave can be an effective classroom technique.

CR: Yes, that's a crucial piece of feminist theory. Since the second-wave feminists began as young women, they didn't know old women existed, so that attitudes toward old women now are exactly the same as the earlier attitudes toward younger women. They've been frozen in time. It's an important piece of understanding, particularly to introduce students to issues of ageism in Women's Studies. Make clear to them how feminism really made a difference in the overt contempt for women that was mixed with an exaggerated, false respect and protection, and how it's the same for old women today. If we just point out old women's issues, that's a yawn for students. We have to connect these issues to the ones that younger women faced not so long ago. Connect how younger women in the '50s were patronized, seen as submissive and dependent, childlike, with how old women are treated now. Young women who spoke up were called "uppity," and still now, old women who speak up are called "feisty." Younger women weren't seen as terribly bright, not anyone you'd want to have a long conversation with, just as old women continue to be viewed now. It used to be that a few younger women would be complimented by being told, "Oh, you think just like a man." Well, the other day in Ben and Jerry's, I was told I couldn't be a senior because I was smiling; seniors were always grumpy. This happens all the time. I'm told, "I'd never guess you were 72," and that's supposed to be the highest compliment you can give someone.

In the classroom, the blatant contempt for old women needs not to be danced around, but needs to be brought out with outrage, to get it across that these are *women*. In fact, this represents one-third to one-half of our lives as women. In the 1960s and 1970s, we deconstructed "woman"—we need to help students deconstruct "old woman." Teachers need to use powerful presentation techniques, such as a *Vogue* article I have entitled, "How Old Do You Look?" (Green 2003), with an illustration of an old woman's hand made to look exactly like a chicken's claw. And that type of attitude is everywhere. We can do a scholarly analysis of birthday cards—the cards that inform me as an old woman just how disgusting and hideous I am. Then I'm chastised that I don't have a sense of humor when I object, the same comments we used to hear about sexist or racist jokes.

*****

And finally—I'm leaning heavily on Barbara [Macdonald] here—they need to see that there's a false power women gain by being young. What little power she gets—and it's a false one—she gets for every year that she distances herself from me in age. The price is that every succeeding year she loses power. The 30-year-old loses power by not being 20, the 40-year-old by not being 30, and so on. We can see it clearly in movies and TV—we already know that the male actors age and continue to win roles and build prestige and are coupled with young women, while the female actors age and disappear after 30. The same system that sees old women as hideous and boring starts to discard women at earlier and earlier ages, at 30. There are ways to make the issue of old women integral to any approach of feminism.

*****

VBL: You noted in the latest edition of *Look Me in the Eye* that you were aware of now being older than Barbara was when she wrote the essay, "Look Me in the Eye." While reading this edition, I was aware that many of the essays are now at least 20 years old, so that you now are about the age Barbara Macdonald was when you assembled the first edition. How does this perspective affect your reaction to your own aging?

CR: I am just so grateful to have had that opportunity to observe ageism and analyze it with Barbara over 20 years, so that now when I encounter it directly, it's still painful, but it's not as bad. At least I have what so many old women don't have, and that's an analysis of the truly bizarre things that people say and do. I ran into a young man in his 30s; we had been activists together, and after we had brought each other up to date about our political work, he said goodbye and added, "I'm so glad you're still up and around!" I realized at that moment that he saw me not as a political colleague, but as a wrinkled old woman about to keel over. The constant message is that we are nothing but our bodies, and our bodies are disgusting. Another example: When I went to visit a younger friend in the hospital, another woman in her 30s was there, talking about someone who was about 10 years younger than I. She said, "Well, she's somewhat elderly, but she's nice." I am standing there with my white hair, and I'm invisible. It's amazing the contempt for old women is so pervasive that nobody really notices it. They think it's natural. We have to remember when contempt for people of color, contempt for gays, felt just that natural. We're still working to combat that contempt in many corners, but we haven't even made a start with ageism. People don't even know it when they see it. For me personally, it's not as big a problem with people I know well because we've confronted it, but out in the world, it's still unexamined.

VBL: I think [that] readers would be interested in learning more about your current work with The Old Women's Project. How was it conceived, and how has it been received?

CR: The Old Women's Project began in 2001 as an idea cooked up around my kitchen table by Mannie Garza, Janice Keaffaber, and me as a way to honor Barbara, who had recently died. She was, after all, the first to name ageism as a central feminist issue as opposed to a problem of the elderly. She was the first to claim the word "old" as a political act. And the project allowed the three of us to confront the ageism we ourselves were encountering in our 60s and 70s. We aren't activists working specifically on old women's issues; Medicare and Social Security are essential women's issues, of course, but what I want to do is to change attitudes, to get at the root of ageism. We want to make visible the fact that old women are directly, personally affected by all issues of social justice. Our first action was to organize a large demonstration for low-cost housing on International Women's Day 2001. We brought together all sorts of groups, showing that old women are at one end of that issue of a lifetime of women's unpaid and low-paid work. That action and follow-up lobbying launched the low-cost housing movement in San Diego. We work to foster that spirit of connecting women, emphasizing actions that show how old women are impacted by every kind of issue.

VBL: The photos of the giant puppet you use in demonstrations are particularly impressive.

CR: The puppet is huge; it's a Kathe Kollwitz self-portrait. We chose her because she looks multiethnic, and we gave her long, white, braided multiethnic hair. She's very popular wherever she goes and her name is POWER, an acronym for Pissed Old Woman Engendering Revolution. People also love the bright T-shirts we have saying, "Old Women Are Your Future." Women have shown us that they're hungry for all-women's actions—I like to say, "even though that's so twentieth century." Our actions have brought together anywhere from 12 to 400 women—usually 50 to 100 at a time. We're respected in San Diego's progressive community because we do a lot of coalition work. It's helpful that we make it clear how old women are impacted by what we're working on in coalition. We're not just do-gooders helping others; we have a vested interest in the cause. We're looking to help progressive people see old women in a new light. We definitely don't call ourselves grannies. The grandma thing does away with a sense of equality and reduces old women to their roles within the family.

VBL: It seems to me that you're accomplishing a great deal through this coalition work. You can show how women are connected regardless of age, how they're affected by the same issues at various ages; at the same time, you're able to reach and educate a population who may ignore anything that is treated as only an old woman's issue.

*****

CR: I've been an activist for almost 50 years, and coalitions work. We focus on people on the bottom—and that means we're always working with women—whether they're low-wage home health care workers and janitors or those in need of low-cost housing. We show that these are old women's issues. As we say, "*No* living wage equals homeless old age." It's essential that whatever group we identify with, we hold firm to that identity, but we also must make connections to other issues, not out of the goodness of our hearts, but because the connections are real. For example, old women are affected both by policies of the "war on drugs" and by its results, which fill prisons instead of offering rehabilitation, because guess who has to raise the children of parents who are addicted or in prison? Old women. We hope other activists will see more and more the importance of not being single-issue. Single-issue politics are wrong for these times; these times are much too serious for that.

VBL: [...] Unless the issue concerns the healthy, carefree, empty-nester who is pictured on retirement brochures, the [media] coverage is aimed at a younger audience, asking what in the world we shall do about this burden of old people, as if they are helpless and generally worthless.

CR: If we're to address these social issues effectively, old women must be treated as human beings, as equals. And once more, the situations place women under intolerable stress because the younger women are expected to be caretakers. As Barbara foretold in "Exploitation by Compassion" (Macdonald 2001), the response to the challenges of increased longevity, maintaining independence, and providing health care is, "Don't you have a daughter to take care of you?" (1983); Barbara was analyzing that many years ago. No one's dealing with these social issues ahead of time, and it's going to get harder.

I want to add that what I've been talking about is white mainstream society, in part because it would be arrogant of me to speak about attitudes toward age in different ethnicities, and because the issues are different in different communities. But I address white dominant society first and foremost because these ageist attitudes have a huge impact on women of color. I'll quote Harriet Jackson-Lyons, an old African-American woman who has been organizing to get women who are raising their grandchildren the same rights and income that foster parents receive. This powerful woman talks about her experience organizing: "Ageism has been one of our biggest obstacles with politicians and agencies, convincing them that we do not want cookies, boat rides, trips to the mall. Being old does not mean that we cannot think. We are being respected more and more. Now they don't call me 'dearie' anymore" (Boston Women's Fund 2001, 91). I think that's a really valuable quotation. Otherwise, I think ageism can be seen as a bourgeois, frivolous, white women's issue, when it really cuts across all ethnicities and classes. Our saying used to be, "All issues are women's issues," and it's also true that all issues are old women's issues.

References

Bechloss, Michael. 2001. *PBS News Hour with Tim Lehrer.* 17 July. Alexandria, VA: PBS Broadcasting Corporation.

Boston Women's Fund. 2001. "Annual Report." Boston: Boston Women's Fund.

Granny Voters. 2004. Retrieved 12 October from http://www.grannyvoter.org.

Green, Penelope. 2003. "My Hands." *Vogue.* August: 296–7.

Macdonald, Barbara. 2001. "Exploitation by Compassion." In *Look Me in the Eye: Old Women, Aging, and Ageism,* new expanded edition (originally published in 1983), eds. Barbara Macdonald and Cynthia Rich, 43–52. Minneapolis: Spinsters Ink.

Macdonald, Barbara, and Cynthia Rich. 1983. *Look Me in the Eye: Old Women, Aging, and Ageism.* Minneapolis: Spinsters Ink.

NBC Nightly News. 2002. 23 June. New York: NBC Broadcasting Corporation.

Old Women's Project, The. 2005. Available at www.oldwomensproject.org.

Woodward, Kathleen. 1991. *Aging and Its Discontents*. Bloomington: Indiana University Press.

The Beast of Beauty:
Toxic Ingredients in Cosmetics

Chemicals that cause serious health problems are called "toxic." We don't often think of cosmetics, such as makeup and shampoo, as sources of exposure to toxic chemicals that may increase the risk of breast cancer and other health problems. Studies show that some cosmetic ingredients may be toxic. For example, some chemicals in cosmetics act like the hormone estrogen in our bodies; most breast tumours depend on estrogen to grow.

How Is Canada Regulating Cosmetics?

The sale of cosmetics is regulated under the *Food and Drug Act* and the *Cosmetic Regulations* under the Minister of Health. However, ingredients in cosmetics are mostly regulated by the cosmetic industry and not the government. Changes to the *Cosmetic Regulations* require that all cosmetics have an ingredients list on the label. Health Canada also has a list of over 500 prohibited and restricted cosmetic ingredients called the cosmetic ingredient "Hotlist."

If a cosmetic contains a Hotlist ingredient, Health Canada may advise the makers to:

- remove the ingredient;
- reduce the concentration of the ingredient;
- consider marketing the product as a drug;
- provide evidence that the product is safe for its intended use;
- confirm that the product is labelled properly;
- confirm that the product is sold in a child-resistant package.

Some strengths of the regulations:

- When cosmetic labels list ingredients, people can refer to the Hotlist to find out if their cosmetics contain restricted or prohibited ingredients.
- An ingredient is usually added to the Hotlist if it poses a health risk.

Some weaknesses of the regulations:

- Ingredients in cosmetics are not reviewed for safety before they are put on the shelves. Companies are required to send an ingredients list to Health Canada only ten days after the product goes on the market.
- Warning labels are not required for cosmetics that contain chemicals associated with cancer.

- The Hotlist does not always consider the long-term, low-dose health effects of cosmetic ingredients.
- It does not acknowledge that some combinations of chemicals may be more toxic than each one separately.

The chemicals listed below are classified as one or more of the following: established human carcinogen, possible human carcinogen, may increase the risk for cancer, skin cancer risk, may be a human reproductive or developmental toxin and/or an endocrine (hormonal) system disruptor.

Attention: The Hotlist Changes
For updates, consult the Hotlist on Health Canada's website:
www.hc-sc.gc.ca/cps-spc/perspn/cosmet/prohibited_e.html

Ingredients of Top Concern	Usually found in	On the Hotlist?
Coal tar dyes	• Hair dyes	Yes (with exceptions)
Formaldehyde	• Nail treatments	Yes
Parabens (ex. methylparaben, propylparaben)	• Many cosmetics	No
Phthalates (ex. dibutyl phthalate, DBP, dibutyl ester, Di(2-ethylhexyl) phlatate, DEHP)	• Nail polish • Nail treatments • Fragrances • Perfumes	No
Toluene	• Nail polish • Nail treatments	Yes
Alpha-hydroxy Acids (AHA)	• Facial cleanser • Skin cream • Moisturizer • Bar soap	Yes (with exceptions)

Take action!

Inform yourself about the products you use:

- Find out if the products you use are safe by searching the online database called Skin Deep from Environmental Working Group, which lists the ingredients and degrees of safety of thousands of popular cosmetics: www.ewg.org/reports/skindeep/.
- Check cosmetic ingredient labels and become familiar with Health Canada's "Hotlist."

Try to limit your use of cosmetics, in particular:

- dark hair dyes;
- nail treatments, polishes, and removers;

- products containing synthetic fragrances;
- perfumes.

Write to the government and encourage:

- a "Safelist"—cosmetic ingredients we can be sure are safe to use;
- warning labels on all cosmetics that contain chemicals associated with cancer;
- Health Canada to review the safety of cosmetic ingredients before they are sold;
- strengthening cosmetic ingredient regulations to ensure that toxic chemicals are eliminated or tightly restricted.

For more information, visit Breast Cancer Action Montreal: www.bcam.gc.ca.

Source: Adapted from Madeleine Bird, "The Beast of Beauty: Toxic Ingredients in Cosmetics." (Montreal: Breast Cancer Action Montreal and the McGill Centre for Research and Teaching on Women, 2005).

4d Politics of Women's Health: From Medicalization to Health Care Reform

Chapter 44

Introduction to *Women and Health: Power, Technology, Inequality, and Conflict in a Gendered World*

Kathryn S. Ratcliff

Kathryn S. Ratcliff is assistant professor of sociology at the University of Connecticut and adjunct assistant professor in the Department of Community Medicine, University of Connecticut Health Center. The recipient of awards for teaching and mentorship, she has also written a number of books and articles on women, health, and technology, including Women and Health: Power, Technology, Inequality, and Conflict in a Gendered World, *from which we have taken the following selection.*

The topic of women's health is a cornucopia of questions. Why is so little known about women's health? What birth control is available and is it safe? Is premenstrual syndrome (PMS) real? What are the risk factors for heart disease, and why have doctors ignored the symptoms and incidence of heart disease in women? Why do doctors dismiss other symptoms women report and say it is "all in their heads"? What do midwives do, and why aren't more midwives active in childbirth? Why are so many unnecessary hysterectomies, episiotomies, and cesarean sections performed on women? How did small breasts become a disease?

This anthology provides a sociological framework for discussing these questions. [...] An adequate sociological answer to a birth control safety question is not a simple listing of currently available methods with their safety and effectiveness data. Rather, the answer requires considering concepts such as power, to understand who controls the choices available; race and class discrimination, to understand who is offered what choices, how coercive that offering is, and why some people see birth control less as individual freedom from unwanted pregnancy and more as a way for society to control unwanted population; and structural incentives, to understand both the motivation of pharmaceutical-company decision makers and the reasons for potential biases in the data on safety and effectiveness.

[...] We argue that women's health and health care are fundamentally influenced by (1) the dominance of the biomedical model, which emphasizes finding a pathology, locating disease in the individual, seeking biological causes, and focusing on cure rather than prevention; (2) the technological favoritism in society, science, and medicine, which encourages new, fancy, specialized, and often untested solutions over less invasive ones; (3) the increasing for-profit intrusions into health and health care, which have encouraged some remedies more for profit than for health, and have redefined the incentive structure for caregivers; and (4) the gender-, race-, and class-based organization of society.

Each of these factors has parallels in understanding men's health as well, but understanding women's health also requires a woman-centered examination of the fourth theme, which asserts that the organization of society has different consequences for women. The powerful position of men in society, the male-centered assumptions about women; the gendered division of labor in society; the relative economic poverty of women; and the long-standing patterns of sexism, racism, and other systems of oppression affect women's health and health care in ways different from their effects on men's health and health care. For example, the reasons why our country spends billions of dollars on drug testing are partly understood by examining the influence of the biomedical model, the for-profit sector, and our love of technology. Yet these factors do not explain an important pattern in drug testing: For decades the conclusions about safety and effectiveness were based on male-only samples. Women were excluded from test groups or from analysis; women were "the Other." If we are to understand the faulty logic producing this lopsided knowledge, we need to understand the gender-based organization of society.

*****

Each of these four themes deserves some orienting comments here.

The Biomedical Model

The biomedical model has been the reigning paradigm in medical science and practice since the seventeenth century (Engel 1988). It is a complex, subtle, and intellectually invasive model that has focused popular attention, research grants, training curricula, medical reimbursement, and health care on certain aspects of health, and at the same time has neglected other aspects of health. What kinds of health care providers are available, why medical histories are done as they are, why doctors talk so little about prevention—we can understand these patterns in the context of a biomedical model. The biomedical model has taught us to see the physical body in a particular way, to ask a particular set of questions about disease, health, and health care, and not to ask other questions.

The biomedical model begins by defining health as the absence of disease. [...] To promote health, the biomedical model works to eliminate disease. To do so, professional health care providers learn to screen for and diagnose disease, and prescribe an appropriate cure, likely to be a pharmaceutical prescription or a surgical solution. With screening, diagnosis, and cure as the focus of the health care system, attention to *prevention* is neglected. Thus, we spend more time and money detecting and curing cancer than we do preventing it; we invest in fetal surgery rather than understanding the causes of infertility; we build expensive neonatal intensive care units rather than providing prenatal care to at-risk pregnant women; we provide hip replacements for elderly women who fall rather than making architectural changes to their homes, providing walkers, or teaching them balancing techniques. Prevention is largely relegated to the less prestigious and less well-funded field of public health.

Focusing on screening and diagnosing disease privileges *pathology*. When doctors are observing a natural and usually healthy process, their minds are trained to be vigilant to possible pathology. "Healthy and normal" are not typical words in their vocabulary (Kapsalis 1997:72). Childbirth is an excellent example. While nearly all births are the uncomplicated unfolding of the natural process of pregnancy, doctors refer to pregnancy as a disease, and to childbirth as the most dangerous day in a child's life, to be considered normal only in retrospect. A doctor's mindset anticipates that something might go wrong, so he or she constantly monitors the woman for problems and is ready to respond with drugs for inducing labor, or with surgery by performing a cesarean section. Sitting and waiting, as a midwife would, and supporting the natural process by reducing the woman's fear, making her more comfortable, or proposing a body position more conducive to successful contractions, are not the behaviors for which a doctor is trained. The doctor is trained to distrust the natural process, and to come to its rescue. This medicalization of a natural process takes control away from women and puts it in the hands of doctors. What was "women birthing" children has become "doctors delivering" them.

In its mission to eliminate disease, the biomedical model not only privileges cure over prevention and pathology over healthy processes, but it also privileges objective and technical approaches over subjective ones. The technical emphasis is seen in the biomedical model's implicit assumption of the body as a machine:

> The Cartesian model of the body as a machine operates to make the physician a technician, or mechanic. The body breaks down and needs repair; it can be repaired in the hospital as a car is in the shop; once "fixed," a person can be returned to the community. The earliest models in medicine were largely mechanical; later models worked more with chemistry, and newer, more sophisticated medical writing describes computerlike programming, but the basic point remains the same. Problems in the body are technical problems requiring technical solutions, whether it is a mechanical repair, a chemical rebalancing, or a "debugging" of the system. (Rothman 1991:34–35)

Any examination of the typical medical school curriculum shows this age-old model of body as machine still being taught, with courses that emphasize mastery of technical skills and knowledge, not mastery of the art of interviewing a patient. [...]

By focusing attention on the technical aspects of the problem, the body-as-machine metaphor ignores the subjective experience accompanying the disease. Often referred to as "the illness," this subjective experience includes the meanings a person attaches to the disease. Thus, a woman who has a mastectomy because of breast cancer, or a hysterectomy because of uterine cancer, grapples not just with the physical loss of a body part, but may grieve the loss of the breast or uterus as symbolically important to her sense of self and sexuality. The technical focus ignores this.

This body-as-machine metaphor also places boundaries on the object of concern, requiring that the doctor examine and treat only the individual. The model assumes that the disease is located in the individual and that the sole focus there is thus appropriate. The role of the family in successful treatment is often ignored, as is the context of the disease. Thus, in caring for women who have suffered domestic abuse, doctors record that an injury has occurred and may list the immediate cause—"blow to head by stick with nail in it" (Warshaw 1989:512; [...]). However, they often neglect to record the health threat, the abusive husband. In fact, they tend to fix the injuries (repair the machine) and then send the woman back to the same environment.

Criticisms of the Biomedical Model

Sociologists, feminists, and others critique the biomedical model as limited, and they propose alternative models, variously called sociocultural, sociomedical, or psychosocial models. These models see health in a broader context. Rather than focusing on physical causes as the biomedical model does (the classic biomedical model talked of one specific biological cause for each disease), these models incorporate social, psychological, cultural, economic, and political causes for disease. Thus, rather than stopping with the stick and nail in the preceding example, the sociomedical model would not only note the abusive husband as an immediate instrument of the injury, but trace the cause back to a patriarchal society that has privileged men and condoned such behavior as an appropriate method to control women. Stress, social support or its absence, poverty, discrimination, mass media influences (e.g., emaciated role models and diet advertisements), the neighborhood, community and ethnic context, and the power of corporations in producing an unhealthy situation (e.g., the tobacco industry targeting women) are important candidates in these alternative explanatory models.

The sociomedical perspective argues that diseases are social constructions. Although the biomedical model sees the naming of disease as the result of the objective discovery of physical conditions, the sociomedical model argues that social structure and culture shape our beliefs about our bodies and our health. What diseases get "discovered" and named, and what explanations of bodily processes and diseases are accepted, are not objective matters—they are shaped by society. Dominant beliefs once allowed lesbianism to be classified as a disease with symptoms including hostility, weakness, and an inability to face the responsibilities of adulthood. Similarly, masturbation was once accepted as a disease, causing one to become a physical, moral, and mental wreck (Freund and McGuire 1995:194). Changes in the political climate have caused these constructs to be discarded. But the politics of disease naming are still with us. A political battle raged within the American Psychiatric Association when the PMS diagnosis was proposed. Lobbying, picketing, and petitioning were all part of the process of arriving at a majority vote that this is a medical condition. [...]

Diseases are often defined by the biomedical model as statistical deviations from the norm on a measurable biological variable, be it anatomical, hormonal, neurophysiological, genetic, or biochemical. Such a designation has the ring of objectivity, until one examines who decides what variables have "harmful variation." When is such variation simply a part of the diversity of human experience with no health consequences? Is having breasts that are "abnormally" small a disease? Plastic surgeons have defined them as such, labeling this condition "micromastia," a deviation on a biological variable of breast size. But what makes this a disease? The power of the plastic surgeons to declare it so. [...]

Technological Favoritism

*****

With the biomedical model accepted as the dominant paradigm, the training of medical researchers and medical students emphasizes technical proficiency. That such training occurs in highly specialized hospitals that have the latest technology further supports technology. Doctors-in-training are likely to choose the more valued and rewarded specialties taught by the leading professors at their schools. Specialty medicine begets more technology.

Feminists have extensively researched and criticized the training of doctors and their workplace practices. The education of specialists in obstetrics-gynecology has come under close scrutiny by feminists because women have so much contact with this specialty. Obstetrician-gynecologists are specialists who provide generalist care for women in their reproductive years and beyond, serving as their primary care physicians. As surgical specialists, obstetrician-gynecologists tend to provide surgical solutions to problems. They are, for instance, more likely to deliver by cesarean section than are generalists (Kasper 1985). The surgical mentality of obstetrician-gynecologists conflicts with the health needs of women who typically come with everyday nonsurgical problems. Because surgery is a major avenue for advancement in the profession (Guillemin 1981), "the situation is ripe for the proliferation of unnecessary operations" (Scully 1994:139–140).

Doctors are also influenced to use high-tech procedures due to factors in their work context. For example, because of the perceived threat of malpractice suits as well as the growing complexity of the body of medical knowledge, doctors tend to practice defensive medicine, which calls for more extensive diagnostic tests. The patient often undergoes a barrage of tests, many routine and most low in informational payoff, because the doctor is seeking documented evidence confirming the wisdom of treatment decisions that were made on the basis of limited information.

Tests, along with drugs, devices, and procedures, are in ample supply because, despite an evaluation system formidable in appearance, we have, at best, a severely flawed method of determining the effectiveness and safety of health care innovations. New technologies are supposed to be evaluated at many levels. The most basic level is represented by the direct health care provider. However, although doctors are taught to be competent users of the latest medical innovations, they are not taught to be critical consumers or evaluators of such innovations. Their bias in favor of high-tech treatments is combined with limited training in research methodology. Furthermore, many technologies receive no evaluation whatever, are widely used prior to any systematic assessment (Banta and Behney 1981; McKinlay 1981), or are used despite negative evaluations. The electronic fetal monitor (Kunisch 1989), ultrasound (National Institute of Child Health and Human Development et al. 1984), intrauterine devices (IUDs) (Ruzek 1980:337), oral contraceptives (Corea 1985), and diethylstilbestrol (DES) (Mintz 1985) are among the technologies that have been used despite being poorly, belatedly, or negatively evaluated. Negative evaluations sometimes include strong cautionary statements, yet use of the technology persists or even increases (Ratcliff 1989:188).

Additionally, a problem in the evaluation system is the fact that evaluators are often interested parties. Evaluations of drugs are often based on industry-supplied data or on industry-funded research. The Dalkon Shield [...] was accepted in the clinical community based on the research of a professor who benefitted financially from the commercial success of the Shield. In this case, there was not just the *appearance* of potential bias in the research—the bias was real. A major design flaw in his evaluation model allowed women who were using the Shield to simultaneously use contraceptive foam. Therapies thus combined cannot lead to research conclusions about the effectiveness of one of them.

*****

[...] The easy availability of technology has greatly altered the health care experience. Technology is used when it is not necessary and even when alternatives exist. When in use, technology provides compelling information that distances the caregiver from the client. One doctor, speaking of intensive care units (ICUs), says, "Call to mind an ICU with monitors blinking and beeping, and remember how all eyes (even family members') go to the monitors—and away from the patient. It requires effort *not* to watch the monitors" (Cassell 1986:192). Referring to electronic fetal monitors (EFMs), another doctor notes how monitoring has dehumanized obstetrics: "We cannot divert our eyes or ears from the E[F]M's alluring LEDs [light-emitting diodes], beeps, and stylus-chattering graphs. We no longer listen to, talk with, gaze upon, or touch our patient" (Munsick 1979:410). Some have argued that we have ended up with a health care system that values machine information more than that obtained by mere humans (Banta and Gelijns 1987). The machine, not the physician (and certainly not the patient), ends up dictating the treatment (Crawshaw 1983).

The use of technology raises many issues. For feminists, equity is a central issue. "Technology has everything to do with who benefits and who suffers, whose opportunities increase and whose decrease, who creates and who accommodates" (Bush 1983:163). Basic access questions emerge because women are denied a technology for reasons of class (they cannot afford it) or moral judgment (they are not "appropriate" recipients because of their lesbianism, unmarried status, or poor education). More complex issues have emerged with the development of some technologies, such as prenatal testing procedures. These technologies, which may lead to the decision not to have a particular type of baby, have raised serious ethical concerns about who decides "who shall inhabit the earth" (Hubbard 1990). [...]

For-Profit Intrusion in Health Care

American medicine has long been an industry shaped by the profit and income orientations of key participants who have developed and promoted various technologies, including devices, procedures, and pharmaceuticals (Relman 1980), sometimes with little regard for the health of those using the technology. The Dalkon Shield [...] and the electronic fetal monitor are clear examples. The Shield was promoted because it was an incredibly inexpensive product that could bring large profits to the Robins company. The EFM, useful in the high-risk pregnancies it was developed for, became routine in the delivery room because a company saw profits and ignored the negative consequences of the EFM for low-risk women (Kunisch 1989).

In recent years, major organizational changes have altered and intensified the for-profit aspect of the health care system: Multistate chains of hospitals have emerged; health care institutions have adopted business orientations that stress economic returns and diminish service, and have increasingly put decision making into the hands of people concerned with the bottom line; and managed care has become the typical insurance-provider arrangement.

These trends further compromise health care because they provide incentives or guidelines for care that shape the quality and nature of the health care we receive. [...]

Whether or not a treatment is provided, how aggressively it is marketed, and how readily the diagnosis is accepted are questions asked and answered on a balance sheet. IVF clinics provide expensive and largely ineffective treatment for infertile, well-to-do couples. They are promoted as profit centers for hospitals and clinics, and they thrive in an unregulated environment in which the health costs and benefits of IVF are not carefully evaluated.

The growth of managed care is relatively new, but already consumers have voiced concerns about the priorities in medical care decision making. Consumers have loudly protested drive-through deliveries and outpatient mastectomy procedures. The form of for-profit influences is changing, such that overtreatment may become less of a problem, and undertreatment may become a major problem for all—not just for women with inadequate insurance or none at all. The enduring questions in this for-profit climate are: Who is making decisions? On what basis? And who is looking out for our health, not just the bottom line?

The Gender-, Race-, and Class-Based Organization of Society, Health, Health Research, and Health Care

The fourth theme [...] is the gender-, race-, and class-based organization of society. Although this fourth theme focuses on gender as a ubiquitous system of oppression, understanding women and health requires an examination of other systems of oppression: racism, classism, ageism, and discrimination against lesbians and women with disabilities. (See Bayne-Smith 1996 and Adams 1995 for an overview of ethnicity and health.)

The organization of society influences women's health, health research, and health care. For example, the androcentric assumptions, gendered power differences, and pervasive sexism of our patriarchal society are replicated within the health domain. Statements made to rationalize the exclusion of women from medical research (men are the norm; women are the "other"); the words used to justify hysterectomies ("women have outlived their ovaries"); or the concern with women as vectors and vessels, not as victims, of AIDS do not come from the biomedical model. They come from a culture that permits a view of women as less valuable than men, and useful primarily as reproductive vessels.

First, the organization of society affects how healthy women are. Simply put, women's health is compromised by their status in society. Poverty, the lack of power, racial discrimination, the gendered division of labor, and the devaluing of women all affect a woman's health. Women are exposed to different occupational conditions than men are, encounter more violence in the home, and have an increased risk of various health problems due to their relatively greater impoverishment.

Second, the gender-, race-, and class-based organization of society affects health research, which is largely done by men; researchers' cultural ideas about women shape their research. Some research excludes women because they are seen as reproductive beings, forever in a potentially pregnant state; other research includes women, but interprets the findings about women in stereotypical ways (women are dependent, emotional, and need to fulfill a biological destiny). Women with less power have been used as guinea pigs or ignored. Puerto Rican and poor women were subjects in early trials of drugs and devices that were dangerous (e.g., the Dalkon Shield, and birth control pills); and poor African American women were subjected to painful and experimental genital surgical techniques (Scully 1994). Lesbian women and women with disabilities, their problems deemed unimportant, have been little researched.

Third, the organization of society has influenced health care. The current stratification of health care practitioners by gender and ethnicity is dramatic, though changing. Doctors are predominately male and nurses female. Less well-paid health care workers are also primarily female, and often from minority ethnic groups. Within the medical profession, women are disproportionately in particular fields, such as family medicine and pediatrics. Furthermore, female health care providers encounter sexism and racism in training and on the job. [...]

Female patients in the health care system have less power than male patients due to their gender, and communication is likely to be less satisfactory for female patients. Ethnic minority female patients and those who are poor, lesbian, or disabled have even less power. Research shows that health care providers treat female and male patients differently, interpret the reporting of symptoms in a gendered way, are more likely to dismiss a woman's symptoms as psychological, request tests based in part on the patients' gender, and diagnose differently for men and women. For instance, women and men reporting angina (chest pain associated with heart disease) to a doctor are often treated differently. Men have typical angina, whereas women don't. Only if women present symptoms that are just like men's are they treated the same as men. [...]

The gendering of health care has been a particular problem in obstetrics and gynecology. Reviews of obstetrical texts indicate a persistently paternalistic and sometimes condescending attitude toward the female patient (Scully 1994:107), and gynecologists have been characterized as treating women "as though they were children" (Scully 1994:19).

References

Adams, Diane L., ed. 1995. *Health Issues for Women of Color: A Cultural Diversity Perspective*. Thousand Oaks, CA: Sage Publications.

Banta, H. David, and Clyde J. Behney. 1981. "Policy formulation and technology assessment." *Milbank Memorial Fund Quarterly* 59:445–479.

Banta, H. David, and Annetine Gelijns. 1987. "Health care costs: Technology and policy." Pp. 252–274 in *Health Care and Its Costs*, ed. Carl J. Schramm. New York: W.W. Norton.

Bayne-Smith, Marcia, ed. 1996. *Race, Gender, and Health*. Thousand Oaks, CA: Sage Publications.

Bush, Corlann Gee. 1983. "Women and the assessment of technology: To think, to be; to unthink, to free." Pp. 151–170 in *Machina ex Dea: Feminist Perspectives on Technology*, ed. Joan Rothschild. New York: Pergamon Press.

Cassell, Eric J. 1986. "The changing concept of the ideal physician." *Daedalus* 115:185–208.

Corea, Gena. 1985. *The Hidden Malpractice*. New York: Harper and Row.

Crawshaw, Ralph. 1983. "Technical zeal or therapeutic purpose: How to decide?" *JAMA* 250:857–859.

Engel, George L. 1988. "How much longer must medicine's science be bound by a seventeenth-century world view?" Pp. 113–136 in *The Task of Medicine*, ed. Kerr L. White. Menlo Park, CA: The Henry J. Kaiser Family Foundation.

Freund, Peter E.S., and Meredith B. McGuire. 1995. *Health, Illness, and the Social Body*, 2d ed. Englewood Cliffs, NJ: Prentice Hall.

Guillemin, Jeanne. 1981. "Babies by cesarean: Who chooses, who controls?" *Hastings Center Report* 11:15–18.

Hubbard, Ruth. 1990. *The Politics of Women's Biology*. New Brunswick: Rutgers University Press.

Kapsalis, Terri. 1997. *Public Privates: Performing Gynecology from Both Ends of the Speculum*. Durham: Duke University Press.

Kasper, Anne S. 1985. "Hysterectomy as social process." *Women and Health* 10:109–127.

Kunisch, Judith R. 1989. "Electronic fetal monitors: Marketing forces and the resulting controversy." Pp. 41–60 in *Healing Technology: Feminist Perspectives*, ed. Kathryn Strother Ratcliff, Myra Marx Ferree, Gail O. Mellow, Barbara Drygulski Wright, Glenda D. Price, Kim Yanoshik, and Margie S. Freston. Ann Arbor: The University of Michigan Press.

McKinlay, John B. 1981. "From 'promising report' to 'standard procedure': Seven stages in the career of a medical innovation." *Milbank Memorial Fund Quarterly* 59:374–411.

Mintz, Morton. 1985. *At Any Cost: Corporate Greed, Women, and the Dalkon Shield*. New York: Pantheon Books.

Munsick, Robert. 1979. "Comment on 'A controlled trial of the differential effects on interpartum fetal monitoring' by Haverkamp and others." *American Journal of Obstetrics and Gynecology* 134:409–411.

National Institute of Child Health and Human Development, Office of Medical Applications of Research, Division of Research Resources, and Food and Drug Administration. 1984. "Diagnostic Ultrasound Imaging in Pregnancy. Report of a Consensus Conference." Washington, DC: U.S. Government Printing Office.

Ratcliff, Kathryn Strother. 1989. "Health technologies for women: Whose health? Whose technology?" Pp. 173–198 in *Healing Technology: Feminist Perspectives*, ed. Kathryn Strother Ratcliff, Myra Marx

Ferree, Gail O. Mellow, Barbara Drygulski Wright, Glenda D. Price, Kim Yanoshik, and Margie S. Freston. Ann Arbor: University of Michigan Press.

Relman, Arnold. 1980. "The new medical-industrial complex." *NEJM* 303:963–970.

Rothman, Barbara Katz. 1991. *In Labor: Women and Power in the Birthplace.* New York: W.W. Norton.

Ruzek, Sheryl Burt, 1980. "Medical responses to women's health activities: Conflict, accommodation, and co-optation." Pp. 335–354 in *Research in the Sociology of Health Care: Volume I: Professional Control of Health Services and Challenges to Such Control,* ed. Julius A. Roth. Greenwich, Connecticut: JAI Press.

Scully, Diana. 1994. *Men Who Control Women's Health: The Miseducation of Obstetrician-Gynecologists.* New York: Teachers College Press.

Warshaw, Carole. 1989. "Limitations of the medical model in the care of battered women." *Gender & Society* 3:506–517.

Supplement 27

Activist Insight:
Our Bodies, Ourselves

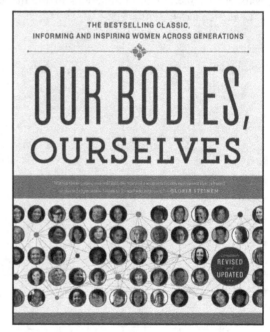

1973   2011

In 1969, as the women's movement was gaining momentum and influence in the Boston area and elsewhere around the country, twelve women met during a women's liberation conference. In a workshop on "women and their bodies," they talked about their own experiences with doctors and shared their knowledge about their bodies. Eventually they decided to form the Doctor's Group, the forerunner to the Boston Women's Health Book Collective, to research and discuss what they were learning about themselves, their bodies, health, and women.

The fruit of their discussions and research was a course booklet entitled *Women and Their Bodies*, a stapled newsprint edition published in 1970. The booklet, which put women's health in a radically new political and social context, became an underground success. In 1973 Simon & Schuster published an expanded edition, renamed *Our Bodies, Ourselves*.

OBOS introduced these key ideas into the public discourse on women's health:

- That women, as informed health consumers, are catalysts for social change
- That women can become their own health experts, particularly through discussing issues of health and sexuality with each other
- That health consumers have a right to know about controversies surrounding medical practices and about where consensus among medical experts may be forming
- That women comprise the largest segment of health workers, health consumers, and health decision-makers for their families and communities, but are underrepresented in positions of influence and policy making
- That a pathology/disease approach to normal life events (birthing, menopause, aging, death) is not an effective way in which to consider health or structure a health system

Today OBOS provides clear, truthful information about health, sexuality, and reproduction from a feminist and consumer perspective. We vigorously advocate for women's health by challenging the institutions and systems that block women from full control over our bodies and devalue our lives. Our long-standing commitment to serve only in the public interest and our bridge-building capacity are our hallmarks. We remain one of the few women's health groups in the U.S. that doesn't accept funds from pharmaceutical companies and that tries to be scrupulous about conflict of interest.

Source: Adapted from "About Us," Our Bodies, Ourselves website (2012), retrieved from www.ourbodies-ourselves.org

Chapter 45

Racism, Women's Health, and Reproductive Freedom

Carolyn Egan and Linda Gardner

Carolyn Egan is a long-time socialist feminist activist, well known for her leadership in the Ontario Coalition for Abortion Clinics (OCAC) and in trade union movements in Canada. A counsellor at the Toronto Birth Control and V.D. Information Centre, Egan has served as president of the Steelworkers Toronto Area Council and as president of the Immigrant Women's Health Centre. She has published numerous popular and academic articles on race, class, reproductive rights, and women's health issues. Egan has won several awards in recognition of her work.

Linda Gardner is a reproductive rights and HIV/AIDS activist who has played a critical role in developing HIV services sensitive to the needs and interests of women with HIV living in Ontario. She is the former chair of CATIE, a clearinghouse for knowledge and resources about HIV and hepatitis C, and the former diversity and community access coordinator at Women's College Hospital in Toronto, a hospital dedicated to advancing women's health research and practice.

> Of all the forms of inequality, injustice in health is the most shocking and inhumane.
> —Martin Luther King, Jr.

Unfortunately, there has been very little written on racism and women's health in Canada. We hope that this essay will be a useful contribution to the body of knowledge available, and will lead to more work being done on the topic. In the article we intend to […] review the findings of the research that is available that deals with the experiences of women of colour in the health care system, and examine the intersection of race, class, and gender. […]

Racism has long been present in health care in this country. In Alberta between 1928 and 1972, 2,844 people were forcibly sterilized through the province's sexual sterilization act. Under this legislation, a eugenics board approved the operation if reproduction involved the risk of "hereditary taint." Sixty-four percent of those sterilized were women, 20 percent were less than sixteen years old. They were, for the most part, poor and working class. The racism of its application is obvious. First Nations and Métis people represented 2.5 percent of the population, but accounted for 25 percent of the sterilizations in the law's later years.[1] Both Alberta and British Columbia had such laws in effect, and it is believed that hundreds of such operations were carried out in Ontario as well.

We believe that racism still permeates every facet of Canadian society, and medical services are no exception. A recent study, "Immigrant, Refugee, and Racial Minority Women and Health Care Needs," carried out by the Women's Bureau of the Ontario Ministry of Health, documents the health care experiences of minority women in Ontario. Researchers interviewed both individuals and groups of women in six regions: Ottawa, Thunder Bay, London, Windsor, Sudbury, and Toronto. These women outlined the situations they faced and the racism they experienced. The document concludes, "The most critical finding of this community consultation process was that immigrant, racial minority, and refugee women are discriminated against by the Ontario health care system."[2]

There are well over one million women who could be defined as immigrant, refugee, or racial minority in Ontario, at least one quarter of the female population of the province. There is, of course, an enormous range of difference in class, language abilities, racial, and ethnic backgrounds among these women, and therefore care has to be taken when making generalizations. The document does not differentiate between women of colour, and other immigrant and refugee women, which is unfortunate for our purposes. We know that the majority of immigrants to Canada today are from non-European countries.

You will see from the comments of the women themselves that they perceive their health is being jeopardized because of the racism and discrimination they face. Racial barriers were clearly identified in the study. Many of the respondents observed that those who are racially different are seen as inferior by white, Canadian health care providers. Women spoke of how they were treated disrespectfully and in a discriminatory manner. Structural barriers were outlined by the women, including the lack of access to language training and ghettoization in low-paying jobs, which restricts the time to access health services. Racism, limited language and literacy levels, combined with a lack of economic opportunities, inhibited the ability of respondents to use medical services, which has a huge impact on women's health.

Through no fault of their own, there is a lack of knowledge among immigrant and refugee women of health care practices that are available, such us Pap tests or breast screening. Very little effort is made in Ontario to make this information accessible in a racially sensitive manner, or in languages other than English or French. There is a lack of adequate translation and interpreter services, which creates real barriers and can greatly increase a sense of anxiety, alienation, and isolation. This can prevent women from using available services, and ensures that their needs remain unaddressed.

In Thunder Bay participants talked directly about their experience with racial discrimination and stereotyping by health care providers. Public health units were seen to be having a difficult time relating to them. Little effort has been made to develop programs and outreach initiatives, which were appropriate and responsive to minority women's needs. They spoke of how childbirth education programs were not reaching women. Concerns were also raised about the high number of Cesarean births and the over-medication of women involved in the study.

In Ottawa, women described a "softer but more pervasive" form of discrimination. Women spoke of a lack of understanding about their reality and the situations they were describing, as they spoke to health care providers. They felt very reticent to express concerns or feelings about their health, which contributed to stress and mental health problems. Health professionals were often dismissive, treating women as though they were stupid. The women spoke of a lack of trust, and felt no confidentiality in their interactions with health care providers. They felt that their experiences were devalued by the health care system.

In Sudbury women identified a particular need for information on gynecological care, pre- and postnatal services. Women underutilized Pap tests and breast exams because of the lack of outreach to their communities. They were being denied basic health services because of who they are. Many physicians were not aware of conditions such as sickle cell anemia, which can have devastating effects on women of colour.

The authors of the study told us that women's reactions ranged from "polite disappointment to outright anger." The report documented that immigrant, refugee, and racial minority women have obvious health care needs, but they make use of health care services at a significantly lower rate than other women. This is clearly due to the barriers they encounter, which are not only the biases of individual providers, but systemic barriers integrated into the health care delivery system itself. As the study states, "This contradiction is due in large measure to … racial, linguistic, gender and class barriers embedded within the system, their needs are not being met by existing programs and services … many areas of the health care delivery system are simply inappropriate for or insensitive to the needs of minority women."[3] Unfortunately, we were not provided with a breakdown on the racial backgrounds of the women interviewed, how long they have been in Canada, or differences among the cities targeted. But the interviews make it clear that immigrant women and refugees, the majority of whom today are women of colour, experience the health care system differently than white women because of the racism embedded within it.

An earlier study by the Immigrant Women's Health Centre (IWHC) in Toronto showed similar findings. The centre was established in 1975 and provides medical and educational services to women from a variety of communities. It also organizes around the health needs of immigrant women and women of colour. It is a multilingual, multiracial collective with a central focus on sexual health. The counsellors are members of the communities that the centre serves. They deal with birth control, pregnancy, childbirth, abortion, sexually transmitted diseases, and other gynecological issues, as well as stress management, nutrition, and patient's rights. The centre was started because of the racism that women encounter in mainstream health services, and the need for health care geared to meet their needs. It established specific outreach services, such as the Black Youth Hotline, a mobile unit, and has responded to the needs of the Tamil community and other recent immigrants to Toronto.

The IWHC conducted a study with the women who were using its mobile health unit, which visited work sites between January 1984 and August 1985. The study focused on working women between the ages of twenty-five and forty-five, including women from the West Indian, Vietnamese, Chinese, and Spanish communities. Many of the women spoke very little English, did not have previous Canadian job experience, and were forced to work in low-paying jobs, often with unhealthy working conditions. They were often not able to find medical services that they could access and that were sensitive to their needs.

In the study, a health care worker at the IWHC said, "They … are often taken advantage of without knowing what recourse to take. The implications for reproductive health, let alone reproductive rights, are limited. Unattended gynecological ailments, such as STDs, vaginal infections, information on breast examination, Pap tests, and stress-related infections are seen at the Centre. The women are prey to poor quality health services because of their economic, cultural, and political status in society."[4] Mainstream health care did not provide for these women, and this put their health at serious risk.

We don't have data on the numbers of women from each community that participated in the study, [but] we do know that today the majority of the women who are seen at the IWHC clinics are women of colour. The study reached 1,500 working women at twelve workplaces. Using information gathered in a 1983 community health survey, done by the City of Toronto health department, they compared the preventative health practices of women in the IWHC target group to those of other women in the city. They were asked questions about Pap tests, breast examination by physician, and breast self-examination. The findings showed that only 43 percent of women in the IWHC target group had a Pap test in the year prior to the interview, compared to 65 percent of other women. It was also found that women were even less likely to have had a Pap test if they worked in semi-skilled or unskilled occupations. "The overall pattern suggests that women in the communities served by the IWHC, who worked in semi-skilled and unskilled jobs are at more risk of having undetected cervical dysplasia than women in any other groups."[5] In terms of breast examination by a physician, a similar pattern emerged in both number and percentage of women who had this performed in the year prior to the interviews. This was the case not because the women had no concern about their health care needs, but because they had difficulty accessing services because of racism and systemic barriers.

The women seen by the IWHC tend to be concentrated in jobs where they work in assembly or product fabrication, as dishwashers, cleaners, cafeteria workers, waitresses, or domestic workers. The work makes women unable to take time off for routine health care. Treatable health problems, such as cervical or breast cancer, go undetected, jeopardizing chances of survival. Other health problems also go undiagnosed. For example, a woman with untreated high blood pressure is four times more likely to develop kidney disease. Women of colour face discrimination in employment, which makes it more likely that they will work in low-paying jobs, which do not allow easy access to medical services. They are denied health care that white, middle-class women take for granted.

In terms of reproductive issues, the study states, "women face a lack of options on family planning due to their economic condition and this has a direct relation to the measure of control they have or they don't have over their bodies. All of these must be taken into account: how the issue of birth control, pregnancy, abortion, etc., really affect women who work two jobs, who lack a facility in English, or who encounter racism in the society.... Women often seek abortions ... because their material conditions, i.e., housing, employment, lack of daycare, low salary jobs, have dictated to them how many children they may have at any given time in their reproductive life."[6] The intersection of race, class, and gender is very clear in the lives of the women interviewed in this study, and strongly impacts on how they experience health care in this country.

The racism that women of colour confront in the health care system is not confined to Ontario. In a study that specifically deals with the Chinese community in Vancouver, British Columbia, the rate of cervical cancer was also found to be much higher.[7] A significant number of Chinese women in their late forties through late sixties were being diagnosed with cervical cancer in a province that was said to be leading the world in Pap test screening. This was significantly higher than the general population. We do not know the class background of the women, but it is likely that they are poor or working class. Again it was a question of systemic racism, and the lack of appropriate community programs. Many Chinese women also found it unacceptable to be examined by male doctors, and this was not being taken into account by health providers.

There were a number of structural barriers. Pap screening was a provincial responsibility, but there was a very real absence of creative thinking or support for changes in the program that would make it more accessible to specific communities. Also, the Ministry of Health lacked a funding mechanism to allow for more accessible programs.

Women from the Chinese community took up the issue themselves. A Pap smear campaign was highlighted in the Chinese media, featured at community health fairs, and training was provided for volunteers and health professionals from the community. An evening program was launched providing women with information and services in their own language and women doctors from their own community. Chinese women developed their own solutions to a critical problem, which was being ignored by the medical community.

Interestingly Statistics Canada reported in 1996 that recent immigrants report less health problems of a chronic nature than people born in Canada, but the longer they are resident, the greater the incidence of chronic health problems. "The difference is particularly marked for recent immigrants from non-European regions, who now account for most of the immigration flow.... The evidence suggests that health status of immigrants weakens the longer they stay in Canada," said Edward Ng, an analyst for Statistics Canada.[8] The health status of people of colour deteriorates at a greater rate than white immigrants the longer they are in the country.

It is clear that government cutbacks are having an impact on the health care of the most vulnerable in Canadian society. Insufficient nutrition, emotional stress, isolation, poverty, and job or family pressures are contributing factors to the situation. Women of colour, because of the systemic racism that exists in the delivery of health care, and the class position that many of them occupy, are even more at risk.

We want to mention one last study that gives a national overview. At the fourth conference and biennial general meeting of the National Organization of Immigrant and Visible Minority Women, a document entitled "Political Participation for Change: Immigrant and Visible Minority Women in Action" was produced and examined a number of important issues confronting minority women. Health care was one of the concerns addressed. The document states, "The biological makeup of women and their role in society as child-bearers, mothers, nurturers, wives and sexual partners is an important component of life and calls for unique health care needs ... immigrant women with linguistic and cultural barriers are often denied and deprived of information and access to various options on reproductive health care services." This document identified sexually transmitted diseases, infertility, and unintended pregnancies as areas that had to be addressed. "With the advancement in reproductive technologies, women have options to control pregnancy with a variety of birth control measures or even to terminate their pregnancies. Even though these options are relatively accessible through mainstream health care services, immigrant and visible minority women's access to information on birth control options, information regarding their right to access these birth control options, and their awareness of making informed decisions in controlling pregnancy is severely limited because of language and cultural barriers. Other barriers also exist that prevent immigrant and visible minority women from accessing appropriate birth control options. These include cultural insensitivity, lack of cross cultural awareness or even racism."[9] This indicates that the conclusions of the Ontario study cited earlier in this essay—that women of colour face racial barriers in the health care system—appear to be applicable nationally.

*****

Notes

1. Janice Tibbets, *The Ottawa Citizen*, June 12, 1995.
2. *Immigrant, Refugee, and Racial Minority Women and Health Care Needs: Report of Community Consultations*, Women's Health Bureau, Ontario Ministry of Health (August 1993), 17.
3. *Immigrant, Refugee, and Racial Minority Women and Health Care Needs: Report of Community Consultations*, Women's Health Bureau, Ontario Ministry of Health (August 1993), iii.
4. *Immigrant Women's Health Centre, Annual Report* (1986), 8.

5. *Immigrant Women's Health Centre: Mobile Health Unit Project. Preventative Health Care for Immigrant Women* (September 1995), 6.
6. *Immigrant Women's Health Care: Mobile Health Unit Project. Preventative Health Care for Immigrant Women* (September 1995), 7.
7. *What Women Prescribe: Report and Recommendations*, from the National Symposium, Women in Partnership: Working toward Inclusive, Gender-Sensitive Health Policies, Canadian Advisory Council on the Status of Women (May 1995), 68–69.
8. Edward Ng, "Immigrants Healthier Than People Born Here," *Toronto Star* (April 2, 1996).
9. *Political Participation for Change: Immigrant and Visible Minority Women in Action*, Fourth National Conference and Biennial General Meeting of the National Organization of Immigrant and Visible Minority Women of Canada (March 1995), 38.

Chapter 46

Women, Disability, and the Right to Health

Paula C. Pinto

Paula Pinto is an activist and academic with a PhD in sociology from York University, Canada, and a master's degree in family studies from the University of Wisconsin-Madison, US. In her roles as a researcher at the Center for Administration and Public Policy in Lisbon, and as an invited faculty at the Technical University of Lisbon and the New University of Lisbon in Portugal, she has contributed greatly to the field of disability rights in Portugal and internationally. She is a research associate at Disability Rights Promotion International, a Canadian-based organization that is working to establish a monitoring system to address disability discrimination globally, and the author of a number of articles on disability, inclusion, and citizenship and human rights.

Introduction

Few studies have examined intersections of gender and disability, especially in their implications for women. In fact, both the disability and feminist movements have been criticized for ignoring the issues facing disabled women (Begum 1992; Gerschick 2000; Lloyd 2001; Morris 1993; Traustadottir 1990). Disability analyses are typically gender-blind, portraying disabled people as a homogeneous group. Therefore, the distinct ways in which gender affects the lives of women and men with disabilities are rarely investigated or discussed; in practice, however, disability studies have mostly echoed male-centric perspectives while the specific realities and concerns of disabled women have remained obscured. Disability has also been largely disregarded in feminist thought, even after relationships between gender and other forms of oppression such as race and class were acknowledged and investigated. In short, the particular needs and perspectives of women with disabilities are hardly reflected in either the disability or the feminist literatures.

The present chapter sets out to overcome this double marginalization by examining how gender and disability intersect to shape disabled women's health experiences. Naturally, with Nasa Begum (1992), I recognize that women with disabilities are themselves a diverse group and in this sense, multiple identities related to race, age, sexuality, and class are likely to compound or alleviate the forms of oppression they are subjected to. While addressing the complexity of all these interactions is beyond the scope of this chapter, it remains important not to overlook their significance.

In gendering disability and health, I want to avoid the pitfall of talking about disabled women experiencing a "double disadvantage." As pointed out by Jenny Morris (1993), this is neither truthful nor useful and leads to social constructs of these women as "passive victims of oppression" (p. 63). Feminist research on disabled women, on the contrary, must be empowering. By placing "women's subjective reality at its core" (p. 63), research must expose the prejudice that permeates social relations involving disabled women. At the same time it must recognize "the source of strength, celebration, or liberation" (p. 63) that disabled women find in their struggle to transform demeaning images of their lives. In an attempt to apply these principles here, the arguments throughout this chapter will be illustrated with stories of disabled women, including quotations from a pilot project in which I have been involved conducted with women with disabilities in Ontario, Canada. The decision to frame arguments in the language of human rights, with particular reference to the right to health, is also a deliberate intent to emphasize the humanness that fundamentally underlies disabled women's health experiences and needs—in other words, it highlights that what women with disabilities demand is nothing less than what all human beings are entitled to just by nature of their membership in the human family. Moreover, it is what the Canadian government (and many others all over the world) have subscribed and legally committed to under international human rights law.

BOX 46.1: The Right to the Highest Attainable Standard of Health

The international human rights system comprises a number of legally binding instruments enacted under the patronage of the United Nations and other international organizations. The right to the highest attainable standard of health, commonly known as the *right to health*, is codified in several of them including:

- the Covenant on Economic, Social, and Cultural Rights (CESCR),
- the Convention on the Rights of the Child (CRC),
- the Convention on the Elimination of Discrimination Against Women (CEDAW).

Canada is signatory to all of these Treaties, thus subscribing to a broad conception of the right to health that encompasses access to timely and appropriate health care and also involves the underlying pre-conditions for a healthy life, such as access to safe drinking water and adequate sanitation, proper nutrition and housing, to mention just a few. Under current human rights law the international community recognizes to everyone a right to health which involves the right to access without discrimination the resources and conditions that enable each individual to enjoy "the highest attainable standard of health conducive to living a life with dignity."

Source: United Nations, *Covenant on Economic, Social, and Cultural Rights* (2000).

According to recent official statistics (Office for Disability Issues 2004) 2 million females in Canada have a disability, compared to 1.6 million men. The experience of disability is thus more common among women than among men. The gap is particularly wide among seniors, as females tend to live longer than males and are therefore more likely to develop age-related chronic conditions that lead to disability. In addition, women are overrepresented among adults who have severe to very severe conditions (Office for Disability Issues 2004). Disabled women are thus likely to face distinct and unique challenges. It therefore becomes crucial to understand how the simultaneous experience of disability and gender (Lloyd 2001) affects women's lives.

Table 46.1: Quick Facts: Adults with Disabilities (age 15 and over) in Canada

	Adults with Disabilities		All Adults
	Females	Males	
	1,893,440	1,526,900	
Percentage of total population	15.7%	13.4%	
Adults with severe to very severe disability	42.4%	39%	
Average household income	$49,976	$50,770	$67,027
Achieved less than high school education	35%	38%	25.3%
Percentage in employment	40.3%	47.6%	74.9%

Source: Adapted from Statistics Canada, *A Profile of Disability in Canada, 2001—Tables,* 2001 Participation and Activity Limitation Survey, Catalogue no. 89-579-XIE (Ottawa: Government of Canada, 2002).

This paper will explore this theme by addressing four main topics: (1) access to health care and wellness; (2) sexual and reproductive rights; (3) gender-based violence; and (4) poverty. Unsurprisingly, these are important topics for any discussion about women's health in general. In fact, as Carol Gill (1997) pointed out, "the needs and concerns of women with disability are less exotic than many non-disabled people might think" (p. 1). Certainly, some health issues for disabled women are amplified or given a particular emphasis because of the unique features that surround the experience of disability in our culture; nevertheless, in essence, they remain basic women's health issues.

Defining Disability and Gender

Before we can address the intersections of disability and gender, we need to define what we mean by those concepts. Essentially, two broad models have shaped understandings of disability in Western societies. Traditional conceptions define disability as "a personal tragedy," the consequence of individual impairments and functional incapacities. Giving rise to actions aimed at repairing or eliminating individual impairments through therapeutic interventions, this approach became known as the "medical model" of disability. Over the last two decades, however, a vast number of disability scholars, who are many of them persons with disability (Barnes 1990; Finkelstein 1980; Oliver 1983, 1996; Rioux and Valentine 2006), have been calling attention to the ways in which social, economic, and political structures, processes, and institutions disadvantage, oppress, and *disable* some members of the human family. By placing the problem outside the person and in society, this approach became known as the "social model" of disability. It is also the paradigm that informs the present chapter. [...]

Much like disability, gender is socially construed through social and economic processes, practices, and relations. These relations are fundamentally unequal, marked by unequal access for women and men to material and non-material resources (Sen, George, and Östlin 2002). Gender norms, values, and expectations become entrenched in particular roles, attributes, and responsibilities that are distinctly assigned to women and men in the family and in society. Given the fundamental inequalities that signal the roles and relations between women and men, gender is, above all, a powerful form of stratification that both influences and is influenced by all other physical and social markers such as class, race, sexual orientation, and disability.

In short, both disability and gender are *socio-political realities*, and as such they need to be understood in the context of social relations of power and control. In Western societies, disability status and female gender are usually associated with greater vulnerability and powerlessness, and therefore women with disabilities are potentially at greater risk than disabled men of facing discrimination and having their human rights violated.

Access to Health Care and Well-being

Gender inequities are widespread within health care systems globally. They may involve differential access to health care resources by women and men as well as discrepancies in the way the system responds to their health needs. These disparities tend to reflect broader and more profound socio-economic inequalities that distinguish the lives of women and men in most societies. Drawing on data from the Canadian Community Health Survey—CCHS 2000–01—a Government of Canada report, "Advancing the Inclusion of Persons with Disabilities," shows that working-age women with disabilities are less able to get the health care they need than women without disabilities or even disabled men (Office for Disability Issues 2004). The survey also shows that for people with disabilities, lack of access to needed health care is associated with lower mental health, a condition that more women than men are likely to experience.

Disabled women's discrimination in the health care system is pervasive. Despite women's numerical supremacy, rehabilitation medicine has traditionally focused on the needs of men—the soldiers, the male workers, or athletes who had acquired disabilities (Gill 1997; Morrow 2000; Tuck and Wallace 2000). Therefore, conditions that mostly affect women, such as, for instance, Chronic Fatigue Syndrome, continue to be less investigated and are less understood than those that typically affect men (i.e., spinal cord injury). Because disabled women's lives have been rendered invisible, the examination of how different disabilities impact general female health conditions and needs has also been neglected (Frazee, Gilmour, and Mikytiuk 2006; Gill 1997; Morrow 2000). Not surprisingly, then, in several studies (Frazee et al. 2006; Masuda 1999; Morrow 2000; Odette et al. 2003) women with disabilities have identified a lack of information on issues so diverse such as routine health care, nutrition, and safe sex as a barrier to health and wellness.

While many disabled women go without needed care, women's experiences in clinical encounters have also been problematic. In health settings, as Gill (1997) explains, disabled women are not just rendered invisible, they are often de-gendered and dehumanized too, viewed only from the prism of their disability or impairment. [...]

*****

[...] For many disabled women, medical practices rather than being supportive are often oppressive—women find themselves stigmatized and ripped of any privacy and dignity, as when, for instance, they are required to appear undressed in front of a group of health providers who examine them as if they were "a scientific experiment" (Frazee et al. 2006).

The professional gaze that may assume forms of "public stripping" (Gill 1997) is certainly not an exclusive experience of women with disabilities, but "gender exacerbates the power difference between doctor and patient, making resistance or refusal to participate more difficult" (Frazee et al. 2006). Moreover, due to prevailing normative standards and representations of the female body, even beyond medical settings disabled women are caught between the intense "visibility" of their different bodies and the "invisibility" of their selves, desires, and needs as women and human beings.

As Hilde Zitzelsberger (2005) has found in her qualitative study of women with physical disabilities and differences, this paradoxical experience constantly challenges disabled women's ability to build healthy lives and identities. For instance, Hope, a woman Zitzelsberger (2005) interviewed, noted:

> So the focus was on being physically visible. Not emotionally being visible because a person could stare at me and see my crutches, but they would not go any further than that. They would not go and think that I could be visible in many different ways. I could be visible as a woman that could have a relationship, as a woman that could be a friend to someone, as a woman that could be seen in a workplace, as a woman that could be a mother one day. (p. 394)

In addition to experiencing heightened in/visibility (Zitzelsberger 2005), disabled women's access to health and wellness is further compromised by physical barriers and obstacles inscribed in the way health care is organized and delivered, which often does not take into account their varying needs and characteristics (Gill 1997). Stairs and narrow doors, inaccessible medical equipment (making routine exams difficult or impossible), lack of staff to assist with transfers and communication, and tight scheduling (limiting time available to understand needs, explain procedures, and build reciprocal trust) are some of the most common obstacles disabled women have to put up with in their encounters with the health care system (Gill 1997; Odette et al. 2003). But it is the increasingly unpredictable access to medical services that women most fear. As Shirley Masuda (1999) found in her study, in the present climate of fiscal restraint disabled women are experiencing the deterioration in health care and are concerned that financial policies will continue to affect the provision of care for them. One woman summarized: "Threatened cutbacks are very distressing. We live in fear of pain. Do they replace joints or do we have to pay?" (p. 9). In sum, disabled women are facing stigmatization and discrimination in the health care system, and their medical needs are not being adequately met. This represents a clear violation of their right to the highest attainable standard of health and a serious threat to their dignity and well-being.

Sexual and Reproductive Rights

Sexual and reproductive rights are of critical importance to all women, yet among those with disabilities, the term acquires a new and broader meaning. Non-disabled feminists fight sexist ideologies that reduce the lives of women to the role of mothers and nurturers; their arguments tend to focus on women's right to be free from unwanted pregnancy. But for disabled women, who have been sterilized without consent and denied the opportunity to mothering, the right to become pregnant and have a child—including a disabled child—and the right to refuse forced sterilization are equally or even more important (Kallianes and Rubenfeld 1997).

Social representations of the sexuality of disabled women are filled with contradictions. Construed as dependent, "eternal children," women with disabilities are often presumed to be asexual beings, with no desires, no sexual needs nor capacities. As such, they are not seen as in need of information about birth control, sexuality, and child bearing (Traustadottir 1990). But at the same time, efforts have always been made to block disabled women from participation in the sexual sphere. Historically, the reproductive abilities of disabled women, particularly those with learning disabilities, have been tightly controlled through institutionalization, forced sterilization, and social control. Many have lost custody of their children in divorce and others have had their children removed from their care by welfare agencies (Gill 1997; Kallianes and Rubenfeld 1997; O'Toole 2002; Traustadottir 1990). Therefore, for disabled women the choice of child-bearing is a political act that defies the social oppression they have been subjected to (Morris 1995). They claim the right to be recognized as sexual, whether in lesbian or heterosexual relationships, and the power to control their fertility and to child-bear if they so decide. They also demand access to necessary resources in support of their parenting role (DAWN Ontario, n.d.b). Yet they struggle to find sensitive and informed health providers to help them fully achieve these rights (Gill 1997; Kallianes and Rubenfeld 1997).

Little research has been conducted on the sexual health of disabled women (Basson 1998; Gill 1997). Health providers receive insufficient training about disability and many fail to assess and adequately respond to women's concerns and needs. Providers' attitudes are often shaped by popular beliefs that portray women with disabilities as not sexually active and, in consequence, disabled women may not receive appropriate medical care (Barile 2003; Riddel et al. 2003). This may have devastating consequences for their health.

Figure 46.1: Percentage of Women Who Had a Pap Smear Test Less Than Two Years Ago

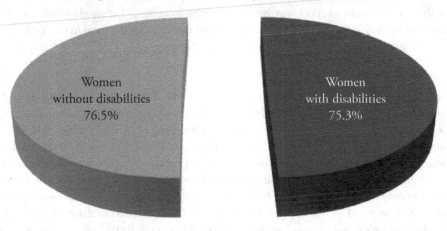

Source: Canadian Community Health Survey (2000/01), Cycle 1, statistics computed by the chapter author.

Figure 46.2: Percentage of Women Who Had a Mammogram Less Than Two Years Ago

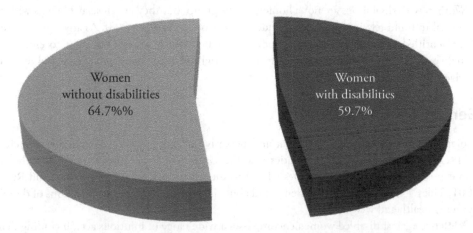

Source: Canadian Community Health Survey (2000/01), Cycle 1, statistics computed by the chapter author.

Lack of knowledge about disability and its interacting effects with women's sexual and reproductive health may also reinforce disablist attitudes on the part of health providers, as Irene, a woman interviewed by Lipson and Rogers (2000), has experienced. She recounted:

> Well, they told me I couldn't get pregnant first off, because of hemorrhaging. He didn't think that the hips, my pelvic area, and my lower back would support the weight of a child. And they didn't feel confident that with all the pelvic and hip fractures that I would be able to accommodate birth. And then after I got pregnant, they tried to tell me that I shouldn't keep him because he'd be brain damaged from all the Prozac and the drugs they were giving me. And I said I didn't care; he was a gift. (p. 18)

Despite the anxieties of health providers, Irene's baby was born healthy and without any known disabilities. Yet her story powerfully speaks of the many barriers facing disabled mothers—in particular, society's fears that they can only produce defective babies, and the increasing acceptance (inclusive within the women's movement) of selective abortion (the abortion of fetuses identified as disabled), which is seen by disabled people as an indication of how their lives are devalued in our society.

*****

As with other areas of health, barriers to appropriate sexual and reproductive care for women with disabilities further include the physical inaccessibility of many medical facilities and equipments (Barile 2003), which prevent them from being assessed and receiving care. Different disabilities require different things: for those with physical impairments, it is important that physicians' offices, examination tables, and other screening technologies are accessible; for those who are blind, deaf, or deal with learning disabilities, the lack of alternative formats to convey information may become an excluding barrier. But for all, finding responsive, sensitive providers is critical (Kallianes and Rubenfeld 1997; Riddel et al. 2003). Reports of disabled women being abused during clinical assessments have been collected (Thomas 2001). Access to gynecological care may be particularly constrained for women who have experienced sexual trauma. For these women, the consequences of not finding practitioners sensitive to their needs may even involve avoidance of treatment (Riddel et al. 2003).

Women with disabilities are not a homogeneous group, but they are all sexual beings with the potential to build relationships that include sexual aspects (Basson 1998). As any other women, all are entitled to basic sexual and reproductive rights, which involve the right to enjoy their sexuality, the right to decide to child-bear, and the right to access appropriate care and resources to give birth and raise their children.

Gender-Based Violence

Violence against women is a persistent and pervasive phenomenon in contemporary societies (WHO 2005). Women with disabilities face the same risks as all other women, but they are also exposed to specific vulnerabilities related to their disability (Nosek, Howland, and Rintala 2001; Tilley 1998). The issue of violence and abuse is therefore central for discussions of disabled women's health and well-being.

Violence against disabled women encompasses a wide range of injurious acts, including deliberate physical, psychological, or sexual maltreatment or abuse, as well as more passive forms of neglect such as denial of food or medical care (DAWN Ontario n.d.a). Verbal abuse, intimidation, social isolation and confinement, economic deprivation or exploitation, have also been described as typical forms of abuse of disabled women (Mays 2006). As in the non-disabled community, most of the abusive acts are perpetrated by men who tend to be close and well known to their victims (Mays 2006; WHO 2005).

A number of factors have been identified as contributing to disabled women's increased vulnerability to violence and abuse. First, it has been suggested that an increased dependency on a variety of people to provide assistance with daily activities greatly increases opportunities for abuse (DAWN Ontario n.d.a; Nosek, Howland et al. 2001; Nosek, Foley et al. 2001; Tilley 1998). Receiving care often involves intimate and emotional contact, and many women have experienced violence at the hands of their caregivers, including spouses and boyfriends, personal assistants, physicians, and therapists. Abuse from caregivers has been reported to involve inappropriate touch, physically rough treatment, refusal to respect women's choices, or even stealing their money and property (Nosek, Foley, et al. 2001). In one study a woman shared, "The orthotist told me he had to put his finger in my vagina to be sure the (artificial) leg fit right" (Nosek, Foley et al. 2001). Dependency on perpetrators for daily survival activities accentuates the vulnerability of women with disabilities, who may feel compelled to tolerate acts of abuse; as this other woman in the same study confided, "The father of a girlfriend kissed and fondled me. This was in exchange for helping me up and down steps and the like ..." (p. 184). Finally, low self-esteem and systematic denial of their human rights are said to produce feelings of powerlessness and over-compliance among many disabled women (Nosek, Howland et al. 2001; Nosek, Foley et al. 2001), diminishing their ability to escape abusive relationships.

A feminist approach, however, must go beyond acknowledging disabled women's vulnerabilities, or it will do little to challenge their stigmatization and marginalization (Mays 2006). Rather, it must be able to place analyses of violence in the broader context of the oppressive relations of disablism and sexism that encircle the lives of many of these women. It must stress that abuse of disabled women is strongly linked to gendered inequalities in power, and the historical, social, and material conditions that perpetuate and reinforce the subordinate position of people with disabilities in our society. For disabled women, these translate into limited economic opportunities and lack of independence, persisting demeaning images, stereotypes, and gender norms [...] (Mays 2006) with potentially devastating consequences for women's health and well-being.

Consequences may be even harsher because a woman with disability may find it particularly difficult to leave a situation of abuse and find adequate support—neither disability-related programs nor existing services for victims of abuse are adequately prepared to respond to disabled women's needs in this area. While disability workers have traditionally disregarded issues of violence and abuse among their clients, many women's shelters do not accommodate women who are in wheelchairs or who need assistance with daily care and medication (Nosek, Howland et al. 2001; Nosek, Foley et al. 2001). Disabled women may also fear they will not be heard or believed when they speak out. A study conducted in Sydney, Australia, indeed showed that women with learning disabilities face numerous barriers when reporting to the police, including prevailing stereotypes that portray them as sexually promiscuous and unable to provide credible accounts, and lack of time of police officers to engage and effectively communicate with victims (Keilty and Connelly 2001). Similar barriers are likely to be faced in other contexts by women experiencing different disabilities, further contributing to their social isolation and reinforcing assumptions in abusers that disabled women are "easy preys" (Nosek, Howland et al. 2001). Not surprisingly then, research has also found that disabled women experience abuse and violence for significantly longer periods of time than women without disabilities (Nosek, Howland, et al. 2001). For some, suicide might be the only possible escape (DAWN Ontario n.d.a).

*****

Poverty

All of the barriers to health and well-being highlighted so far are further compounded by disabled women's lack of adequate income. Research in the general population has shown that, on average, people with better income enjoy better health. Among the population with a disability, a strong relationship between income and health has also been found. Disabled women are more likely than men to experience economic deprivation and thus are at higher risk for ill health, too (Office for Disability Issues 2004).

The problematic income situation of women with disabilities is linked to all the other issues they face, particularly the discrimination they experience in the labour market and the welfare system. Official statistics in Canada show that people with disabilities are over three times more likely to be out of the labour force than adults without disabilities, disabled women being the least likely group to be employed (Office for Disability Issues 2004).

Women who are able to access work receive the lowest median hourly wage ($13.75), below that of non-disabled women ($14.00) and disabled men ($17.99) (Office of Disability Issues 2004). Thus, 16% of women with disabilities are found to have after-tax household incomes below Statistics Canada's low-income cut-off, defined as comprising people living in "straitened conditions."

The rate of low income is often related to the source of one's income. In the current disability income system, disabled women are particularly disadvantaged (Jongbloed 1998). Programs linked to labour force attachment, such as employment insurance or workers' compensation, usually offer better benefits than social assistance, but women with disabilities are more likely to have government transfers as their primary source of income. It has been recognized that the great majority (70%) of those on social assistance live in low-income households (Office for Disability Issues 2004), thus disabled women face an increased risk of poverty. Even if they do receive benefits based on employment earnings, women experience discrimination because they tend to have been paid less than men and are more likely to have taken time off or worked part-time, due to their traditional domestic roles. Yet, restrictions imposed on welfare programs over the last decade discourage many of them from exploring the possibility of a job to supplement their income for fear of losing their meagre, but secure, disability benefits (Jongbloed 1998; Masuda 1998).

In fact, women are experiencing increased difficulties in accessing the benefits and services they need, which makes their lives ever more difficult (Masuda 1998). Cuts in home care and homemaking services, for instance, are leaving many disabled women with basic daily needs unmet. Reduced availability and repair of required technical devices, and less help for child care impact disabled women's ability to live independent lives and perform family roles. Cuts to staff in hospital and institutions jeopardize the quality of care to them, especially those who need extra help. All of these have negative consequences for women's health and well-being (Masuda 1998).

Without an adequate income, disabled women become socially isolated (Schur 2004). Many cannot access a secure place to live, nor buy healthy food. Adults with disabilities are twice as likely as those without disabilities to have experienced food insecurity, a risk particularly high among lone mothers. In fact, more than one in every three lone mothers with disabilities runs out of money for food at least once a year (Office for Disability Issues 2004). Their health, and that of their children, is certainly impacted; their human rights and dignity further eroded.

Conclusion

Women with disabilities are an understudied and underserved group. Like other women, their lives are constricted by social and economic disadvantages that undermine their dignity as human beings and their capacity for self-determination. Because of prevailing sexist and disablist ideologies, they experience high poverty rates, severe ratios of violence and abuse, and systematic denial of their sexual, reproductive, and health rights. All these affect their physical and mental health and well-being.

More research is needed to fully understand the interconnections of gender and disability and their health impacts on disabled women. Integrated approaches that combine insights from feminist and critical disability theories can be very useful to uncover structures and social relations of power and control that constrain disabled women's lives. Bringing together women with disabilities, researchers, and social activists, such efforts are elemental not only to an understanding of the inequalities facing disabled women, but also to political processes aiming at ending their discrimination and advancing their human rights.

References

Barile, M. (2003). *Access to Breast Cancer Screening Programs for Women with Disabilities.* Montreal: Action des Femmes Handicapées de Montreal.

Barnes, C. (1990). *Cabbage Syndrome: The Social Construction of Dependence.* Lewes: Falmer Press.

Basson, R. (1998). Sexual Health of Women with Disabilities. *Canadian Medical Association Journal* 159(4): 359–362.

Begum, N. (1992). Disabled Women and the Feminist Agenda. *Feminist Agenda* 40: 70–84.

DAWN Ontario (n.d.) (a). *Family Violence against Women with Disabilities.* Retrieved from: dawn.thot.net/violence_wwd.html.

DAWN Ontario (n.d.) (b). *Women with Disabilities and Reproductive Rights: Plain Language Fact Sheet.* Retrieved from: dawn.thot.net/wwd_reproductive_rights.html.

Finkelstein, V. (1980). *Attitudes and Disabled People.* New York: World Rehabilitation Fund.

Frazee, C., J. Gilmour, and R. Mikytiuk (2006). Now You See Her, Now You Don't: How Law Shapes Disabled Women's Experience of Exposure, Surveillance, and Assessment in the Clinical Encounter. In D. Pothier and R. Devlin (eds.), *Critical Disability Theory: Essays in Philosophy, Politics, Policy, and Law* (pp. 223–247). Vancouver: UBC Press.

Gerschick, T. (2000). Toward a Theory of Disability and Gender. *Signs: Journal of Women in Culture and Society* 25(4): 1263–1268.

Gill, C. (1997). *Last Sisters: Health Issues of Women with Disabilities.* Retrieved from: dawn.thot.net/cgill-pub.htm#top.

Jongbloed, L. (1998). Disability Income: The Experiences of Women with Multiple Sclerosis. *Canadian Journal of Occupational Therapy* 65(4): 193–201.

Kallianes, V., and P. Rubenfeld (1997). Disabled Women and Reproductive Rights. *Disability & Society* 12(2): 203–221.

Keilty, J., and G. Connelly (2001). Making a Statement: An Exploratory Study of Barriers Facing Women with an Intellectual Disability When Making a Statement about Sexual Assault to the Police. *Disability & Society* 16(2): 273–291.

Lipson, J.G., and J.G. Rogers (2000). Pregnancy, Birth, and Disability: Women's Health Care Experiences. *Health Care for Women International* 21: 11–26.

Lloyd, M. (2001). The Politics of Disability and Feminism: Discord or Synthesis? *Sociology* 35(3): 715–728.

Masuda, S. (1998). *The Impact of Block Funding on Women with Disabilities.* DAWN Canada (DisAbled Women's Network Canada). Ottawa: Status of Women Canada.

Masuda, S. (1999). *Women with Disabilities: We Know What We Need to Be Healthy!* Vancouver: British Columbia Centre of Excellence for Women's Health and DAWN Canada: DisAbled Women's Network Canada.

Mays, J.M. (2006). Feminist Disability Theory: Domestic Violence against Women with a Disability. *Disability & Society* 21(2): 147–158.

Morris, J. (1993). Feminism and Disability. *Feminist Review* 43(Spring): 57–70.

Morris, J. (1995). Creating a Space for Absent Voices: Disabled Women's Experience of Receiving Assistance with Daily Living Activities. *Feminist Review* 51(Autumn): 68–93.

Morrow, M. (2000). *The Challenges of Change: The Midlife Health Needs of Women with Disabilities.* Vancouver: British Columbia Centre of Excellence for Women's Health.

Nosek, M.A., C.C. Foley, R.B. Hughes, and C.A. Howland. (2001). Vulnerabilities for Abuse among Women with Disabilities. *Sexuality and Disability* 19(3): 177–189.

Nosek, M.A., C. Howland, and I. Rintala. (2001). National Study of Women with Physical Disabilities: Final Report. *Sexuality and Disability* 19(1): 5–39.

Odette, F., K.K. Yoshida, P. Israel, A. Li, D. Ullman, A. Colontonio et al. (2003). Barriers to Wellness Activities for Canadian Women with Physical Disabilities. *Health Care for Women International* 24: 125–134.

Office for Disability Issues. (2004). *Advancing the Inclusion of Persons with Disabilities: A Government of Canada Report.* Ottawa: Social Development Canada.

Oliver, M. (1983). *Social Work with Disabled People.* Basingstoke: Macmillan.

Oliver, M. (1996). *Understanding Disability: From Theory to Practice.* London: Macmillan.

O'Toole, C.J. (2002). Sex, Disability, and Motherhood: Access to Sexuality for Disabled Mothers. *Disability Studies Quarterly* 22(4): 81–101.

Riddel, L., K. Greenberg, J. Meister, and J. Kornelsen. (2003). *We're Women Too: Identifying Barriers to Gynaecological and Breast Health Care for Women with Disabilities.* Vancouver: British Columbia Centre of Excellence for Women's Health.

Rioux, M.H., and F. Valentine. (2006). Does Theory Matter? Exploring the Nexus between Disability, Human Rights, and Public Policy. In D. Pothier and R. Devlin (eds.), *Critical Disability Theory: Essays in Philosophy, Politics, Policy, and Law* (pp. 47–69). Vancouver: UBC Press.

Schur, L. (2004). Is There Still a "Double Handicap"? Economic, Social, and Political Disparities Experienced by Women with Disabilities. In B.G. Smith and B. Hutchison (eds.), *Gendering Disability* (pp. 253–271). New Brunswick, NJ: Rutgers University Press.

Sen, G., A. George, and P. Östlin. (2002). Engendering Health Equity: A Review of Research and Policy. In G. Sen, A. George, and P. Östlin (eds.), *Engendering International Health: The Challenge of Equity* (pp. 1–33). Cambridge, MA: The MTI Press.

Thomas, C. (2001). Medicine, Gender, and Disability: Disabled Women's Health Care Encounters. *Health Care for Women International* 22: 245–262.

Tilley, C.M. (1998). Health Care for Women with Physical Disabilities: Literature Review. *Sexuality and Disability* 16(2): 87–102.

Traustadottir, R. (1990). *Obstacles to Equality: The Double Discrimination of Women with Disabilities.* Retrieved from: dawn.thot.net/disability.htm.

Tuck, I., and D. Wallace. (2000). Chronic Fatigue Syndrome: A Women's Dilemma. *Health Care for Women International* 21: 457–466.

WHO. (2005). *Multi-country Study on Women's Health and Domestic Violence against Women: Summary Report of Initial Results on Prevalence, Health Outcomes, and Women's Responses.* Geneva: World Health Organization.

Zitzelsberger, H. (2005). (In)visibility: Accounts of Embodiment of Women with Physical Disabilities and Differences. *Disability & Society* 20(4): 389–403.

Understanding the
Social Determinants of Health

There are many definitions of the social determinants of health. Here are two influential ones:

Social determinants of health are the economic and social conditions that influence the health of individuals, communities, and jurisdictions as a whole. Social determinants of health determine whether individuals stay healthy or become ill (a narrow definition of health). Social determinants of health also determine the extent to which a person possesses the physical, social, and personal resources to identify and achieve personal aspirations, satisfy needs, and cope with the environment (a broader definition of health). Social determinants of health are about the quantity and quality of a variety of resources that a society makes available to its members.

Source: Dennis Raphael, ed., *Social Determinants of Health: Canadian Perspectives* (Toronto: Canadian Scholars' Press Inc., 2004), 1.

The social determinants of health are the conditions in which people are born, grow, live, work, and age, including the health system. These circumstances are shaped by the distribution of money, power, and resources at global, national, and local levels, which are themselves influenced by policy choices. The social determinants of health are mostly responsible for health inequities—the unfair and avoidable differences in health status seen within and between countries.

Source: World Health Organization, "Social determinants of health," retrieved from http://www.who.int/social_determinants/en/

Fast Facts on the Social Determinants of Health

- Poverty, social exclusion, poor housing, and poor health systems are among the main social causes of ill health.
- Differences in the quality of life within and between countries affect how long people live. A child born in Japan has a chance of living 43 years longer than a child born in Sierra Leone.
- The probability of a man dying between the ages of 15 and 60 is 8.2 percent in Sweden, 48.5 percent in the Russian Federation, and 84.5 percent in Lesotho.
- In Australia, there is a 20-year gap in life expectancy between Australian Aboriginal and Torres Strait Islander peoples, and the Australian average.
- Low- and middle-income countries account for 85 percent of the world's road deaths.

General Socio-economic, Cultural, and Environmental Conditions

- In 2002, nearly 11 million children died before reaching their fifth birthday—98 percent of these deaths were in developing countries.
- Inequality in income is increasing in countries that account for more than 80 percent of the world's population.
- Few governments have explicit policies for tackling socially determined health inequalities.

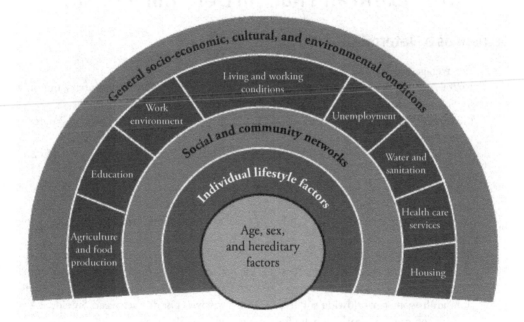

Source: World Health Organization, "FACT FILE: Social Determinants of Health," retrieved from http://www.who.int/features/factfiles/sdh/01_en.html

Supplement 29

How Sexism and Racism Determine Health

Sexism as a Determinant of Health

- On average, women live six to eight years longer than men globally.
- In 2007, women's life expectancy at birth was more than 80 years in 35 countries, but only 54 years in the WHO African region.
- Girls are far more likely than boys to suffer sexual violence (any sexual abuse: 8.7 percent boys; 25.3 percent girls globally).
- Road traffic injuries are the leading cause of death among adolescent girls in *high- and middle-income countries*.
- Pregnancy-related complications, especially due to unsafe abortions, are a leading cause of death among girls aged 15–19 years in developing countries.
- Ninety-nine percent of the half a million maternal deaths every year occur in developing countries.
- For women in their reproductive years (15–44), HIV/AIDS is the leading cause of death and disease worldwide, while unsafe sex is the main risk factor in developing countries.
- Women are more susceptible to depression and anxiety than men. An estimated 73 million adult women worldwide suffer a major depressive episode each year. Suicide is the seventh top cause of death globally for women aged 20–59 years.
- Breast cancer is the leading cancer killer among women aged 20–59 years in high-income countries.
- Globally, cardiovascular disease, often thought to be a "male" problem, is the leading killer of women.

Source: Adapted from World Health Organization, "Factsheet no. 334, Women's Health," retrieved from http://www.who.int/mediacentre/factsheets/fs334/en/index.html

Racism as a Determinant of Health

- Black women are significantly less likely than white women to receive minimum expected therapy for breast cancer.
- First Nations adults in Canada have a 20.8 percent higher rate of cancer than the general Canadian population.
- African Americans are significantly less likely to receive major colorectal treatment for their cancer, follow-up treatment, or chemotherapy.

- Blacks are less likely to receive surgical treatment than whites, and they are likely to die sooner than whites.
- Members of visible minorities were less likely to have been admitted to hospital, tested for prostate-specific antigen, administered a mammogram, or given a Pap test; members of visible minorities were less likely than white people to have had a mammogram or Pap test.
- In the United States, non-whites are treated by lower-quality surgeons, quality being measured by risk-adjusted mortality rates.
- Minority patients were less likely than whites to have pain recorded even after adjustment for language differences.
- In settings with predominantly racial and ethnic minority patients, 62 percent of those patients were undertreated by WHO standards, and they were three times more likely to be under-medicated than patients seen in non-minority settings.
- Many Aboriginal peoples face racism and discrimination on a day-to-day basis. Cultural discontinuity, including loss of Indigenous languages, has been associated with higher rates of depression, alcoholism, suicide, and violence, and as having a greater impact on youth.
- A history of racial discrimination, social exclusion, and poverty can combine with mistrust and fear to deter members of racialized groups and Aboriginal communities from accessing services and getting culturally appropriate care.

Source: Adapted from Elizabeth Anne McGibbon and Josephine B. Etowa, *Anti-racist Health Care Practice* (Toronto: Canadian Scholars' Press Inc., 2009), 54–58.

Chapter 47

HIV/AIDS, Globalization, and the International Women's Movement

Sisonke Msimang

Sisonke Msimang, until rcently, was the self-described "non-executive director" of the Open Society Initiative for Southern Africa (OSISA). She is an activist and policy analyst who has worked with international organizations such as African Gender Institute (AGI), the United Nations Women's Development Fund (UNIFEM), and UNAIDS in the areas of HIV/AIDS, maternal health, international development, and women's health. Msimang has published numerous book chapters and articles on gender, HIV/AIDS, and human rights, including in the Southern African feminist journal AGENDA and Oxfam's Gender and Development.

HIV/AIDS and Globalization

Globalization has been described as "the drive towards an economic system dominated by supra-national trade and banking institutions that are not accountable to democratic processes or national governments" (Globalization Guide, www.Globalizationguide.org/01.html). It is characterised by an increase in cross-border economic, social, and technological exchange under conditions of (extreme) capitalism. As human bodies move across borders in search of new economic and educational opportunities, or in search of lives free from political conflict and violence, they bring with them dreams and aspirations. Sometimes, they carry the virus that causes AIDS, and often, they meet the virus at their destinations.

As corporations increasingly patrol the planet, looking for new markets, and natural and human resources to exploit, they set up and abandon economic infrastructure—opening and closing factories, establishing hostels. In so doing, they create peripheral communities, hoping to benefit from employment and the presence of new populations where previously there were none. And when they move on, once they have found a cheaper place to go, they leave in their wake communities that are extremely susceptible to HIV/AIDS.

This is because the virus follows vulnerability, crosses borders with ease, and finds itself at home where there is conflict, hunger, and poverty. The virus is particularly comfortable where wealth and poverty co-exist—it thrives on inequality. It is not surprising, then, that Southern Africa provides an excellent case study of the collusion between globalising processes and HIV/AIDS.

The economy of the region has been defined in the last two centuries by mining: gold and diamonds. In an era of plummeting gold prices, and an increasing shift towards the service industry, Southern Africa is shedding thousands of jobs. Yet the last century of globalization has provided a solid platform for the current AIDS crisis.

If there was a recipe for creating an AIDS epidemic in Southern Africa, it would read as follows: "Steal some land and subjugate its people. Take some men from rural areas and put them in hostels far away from home, in different countries if need be. Build excellent roads. Ensure that the communities surrounding the men are impoverished so that a ring of sex workers develops around each mining town. Add HIV. Now take some miners and send them home for holidays to their rural, uninfected wives. Add a few girlfriends in communities along the road home.

"Add liberal amounts of patriarchy, both home-grown and of the colonial variety. Ensure that women have no right to determine the conditions under which sex will take place. Make sure that they have no access to credit, education, or any of the measures that would give them options to leave unhappy unions, or dream of lives in which men are not the centre of their activities. Shake well and watch an epidemic explode."

There's an optional part of the recipe, which adds an extra spice to the pot: African countries on average spend four times more on debt servicing than they do on health. Throw in a bit of World Bank propaganda, some loans from the IMF and beat well. Voilà. We have icing on the cake.

As the gap between the rich countries of the North and the poor countries of the South grows, we are beginning to see serious differences in the ways that states can afford to take care of their citizens. Access to technology, drugs, and strong social safety nets in the North mean that HIV/AIDS is a manageable chronic illness in most developed countries. Yet there are pockets of poor, immigrant, gay, and otherwise marginalised communities within these countries, where HIV prevalence is on the rise. An analysis of the complex intersections between inequalities tells us that it is not enough to belong to a rich country—that alone does not protect you from vulnerability to HIV infection, nor does it guarantee treatment. Where you sit in relation to the state is equally important—whether you are a woman, a poor woman, a black woman, an educated woman, a lesbian, a woman with a disability who is assumed not to be having sex, an immigrant who is not entitled to many of the social security benefits of citizens. All these factors determine your vulnerability to HIV/AIDS.

Now what does this mean for a 25-year-old woman living in Soweto? Jabu works as a security guard at a shopping centre in Johannesburg. Every day she spends two hours travelling to work because of the distances the architects of apartheid set up between city centres and the townships that serviced them. Jabu is grateful to have a job. Her two little ones are in KwaZulu Natal with their grandmother until Jabu can get a stable job. She is on a month-to-month contract with the security company. She watches expensive cars all day, protecting their owners' investments while they work. The company doesn't want to take her on as staff so each month she faces the uncertainty of not having a job the next month. Joining a union is not an option—she's not technically a staff member and she can't afford to make trouble. Jabu's boyfriend Thabo drives a taxi. Their relationship saves her cash because he drives her to and from work every day—a saving of almost one third of her salary each month. She has another boyfriend at work, who often buys her lunch. She has to be careful that Thabo doesn't find out.

In addition to race, class, and gender, Jabu's life is fundamentally shaped by the forces of globalization—where she works and how secure that work is, where her children live, even how she arrives at work. These factors all influence her vulnerability to HIV infection.

HIV/AIDS and Feminism

During the last eight years of my work on sexual and reproductive rights, my focus has been primarily on HIV and AIDS. For me, the pandemic brings into stark relief the fact that states have failed to provide their citizens with the basic rights enshrined in the declaration of human rights.

Twenty years ago, AIDS was known as Gay-Related Immune Disease—so associated was it with gay men. Today, the face of AIDS has changed. It looks like mine. It is now black, female, and extremely young. In some parts of sub-Saharan Africa, girls aged 15–19 are six times more likely than their male counterparts to be HIV-positive. Something is very wrong.

In the next 10 years, the epidemic will explode in Asia and in Central and Eastern Europe as well as in Latin America. The pandemic will have profound effects on the burden of reproductive work that women do, and this in turn will have far-reaching consequences for the participation of women in politics, the economic sector, and other sectors of society. The very maintenance of the household, the work that feminist economists like Marilyn Waring, Diane Elson, and others tell us keeps the world running, may no longer be possible.

As older women are increasingly called upon to care for children, and as life expectancy shrinks to the forties and fifties, in Africa we face the prospect of a generation without grandparents, and an imminent orphan and vulnerable children crisis that will effectively leave kids to take care of kids. As the orphan crisis deepens, child abuse is on the rise. Girls without families to protect them are engaging in survival sex to feed themselves and their siblings, and we are told that communities will "cope." There is a myth of coping that pervades the development discourse on AIDS. What it really means is that women will do it. What it translates into is that families split up, girls hook for money and food, and a vicious cycle is born.

While there is some feminist analysis of the AIDS epidemic, we have not yet heard a rallying cry from the women's movement. A recent article by Noeleen Heyzer, UNIFEM's executive director, begins to formulate some arguments about why, in the context of AIDS, women can no longer wait for equality with men (www.csmonitor.com/2002/0718/p13s02-coop.html). Dr. Heyzer points out that it takes 24 buckets of water a day to care for a person living with AIDS—to clean sheets fouled by diarrhoea and vomit, to prepare water for bathing (sometimes several times a day), to wash dishes and prepare food. For women who must walk miles, and still do all the other chores that always need doing, the burden becomes unbearable.

This past spring in New York, I was asked to speak to a group at a high school in Brooklyn about HIV/AIDS and violence against women in the South African context. They were an intelligent group, well versed in feminism. I was not the only presenter. A young American woman who had worked with *Ms. Magazine* talked about pop culture, and the politics of wearing jeans and letting your G-string show. I left the meeting feeling disconcerted. I had made my presentation and received a few awkward questions about men in Africa. I cringed on behalf of my brothers because I certainly was not trying to demonise them, but the students were feeding into a larger narrative of the familiar discourse of black male laziness, deviancy, and sexual aggression that I was careful to point out to them. Aside from that, they found little else to talk about.

On the other hand, the woman from the US struck a chord with them. They talked about eating disorders and the media, about Britney Spears and Janet Jackson. It was fascinating. Having lived in the US, I was able to follow and engage, but my interests as an African feminist do not lie in this subject matter. It was a clear example of how far apart we, as feminists, sometimes are from one another.

Contexts vary, and of course the issues that are central in the global North will be different from those of Southern feminists. And amongst us there will be differences. I understood where the high school students were coming from. Indigenous feminism must be rooted in what matters most to women at a local level. At a global level within feminism, however, I fear that we may be in danger of replicating the G-strings versus AIDS conversation. I am worried by the relative silence from our Northern sisters about a pandemic that is claiming so many lives.

A Way Forward

In the context of HIV/AIDS, it is no longer enough to frame our conversations solely in terms of race, class, and gender. These are primary markers of identity, but increasingly, we need more. We need to look at where women are located spatially in relation to centres of political, social, and economic power. We need also to examine how where we live—rural, urban, North, or South—intersects with poverty and gender. We also need to think about how the experience of poverty interacts with, and not just intersects with, gender. Culture is another factor that deserves attention.

We are beginning to see dangerous patriarchal responses to the epidemic from virginity tests to decrees about female chastity from leaders. In part this is simply an extension of deeply rooted myths about female sexuality. However, with HIV/AIDS, it can also be attributed to the fact that in many cases women are the first to receive news of their sero-positive status. This is often during pre-natal screening, or when babies are born sick. Bringing home the "news" that there is HIV in the family often means being identified as the person who caused the infection in the first place. We know that, in the vast majority of cases, this is simply not true.

The Treatment Action Campaign (TAC), a movement begun by and for people living with HIV/AIDS in South Africa, has managed to mobilise national and international support for the idea of universal access to drugs for people with AIDS. The group began their campaign by using pregnant women as their rallying cry. The right to nevirapine for pregnant women opened the door for TAC's broader claims about the rights of all people with HIV/AIDS to HIV medication. The campaign has been hugely successful. TAC encouraged the South African government to take the pharmaceutical industry to court and the government won, paving the way for a win at the World Trade Organization. Companies' patent rights can no longer supersede the rights of human beings to access life-saving medicines.

TAC's strategy needs to be vigorously debated and analysed by feminists. TAC did not use arguments about reproductive and sexual rights. They simply said, "It is unfair for the government not to give drugs to pregnant women so they can save their babies' lives." It was a classic "woman as the vessel" argument. TAC's interest was not in women's rights—but in the rights of people living with HIV/AIDS, some of whom happen to be women. The campaign's success was largely based on the notion that the average South African found it difficult to accept that "innocent" babies would die because of government policy. This requires some serious feminist interrogation. TAC has since been pushed by gender activists within the movement to ensure that the drugs do not stop when the baby is born.

Gender activists to date have struggled to get their voices heard in the doctor-dominated AIDS world. The mainstream women's movement needs to get on board and face up to the challenge of HIV/AIDS. AWID's "Globalise This" campaign provides an opportunity to highlight the HIV/AIDS epidemic and the threat it poses to women.

At precisely the moment when we need international solidarity to focus on the impact of AIDS on poor women's lives, and their need to be able to control their lives and their bodies, we have to oppose the US administration's cutbacks on funding for essential reproductive health services. We are also still waiting for the G8 to enact their long-standing commitment to spend 0.7 per cent of GDP on overseas development assistance each year. How likely is it that they will ever reach this target if they focus instead on supporting the war against Iraq?

Our sisters in the North need to develop a consciousness about the fight against AIDS as a feminist fight. We need civil society and feminist voices in developing countries to challenge their governments to tackle HIV/AIDS as a health issue, as a human rights issue, and as a sexual and reproductive rights issue. If we lose this fight, it will have profound effects on the lives of girls and women into the next century.

Chapter 48

The Women Are Coming: The Abortion Caravan

Judy Rebick

Judy Rebick is one of Canada's best-known feminists and political commentators. The CAW-Sam Gindin Chair Emerita in Social Justice and Democracy at Ryerson University, she is a former president of the National Action Committee on the Status of Women, and is the founding publisher of the progressive independent news and discussion site, rabble.ca. She makes regular appearances on television and radio, contributes frequently to newspapers and magazines, and has authored several books, including Transforming Power: From the Personal to the Political, *and* Ten Thousand Roses: The Making of a Feminist Revolution, *from which the following chapter is drawn.*

If men could get pregnant, abortion would be a sacrament.

—Florynce R. Kennedy[1]

The first national action of the women's movement in Canada was the 1970 abortion caravan. Seventeen members of the Vancouver Women's Caucus, one of the earliest women's liberation groups, decided to travel to Ottawa to protest the abortion law that had been passed by Parliament in 1969.

Up until 1969, abortion was illegal. Many women risked going to backstreet abortionists, who were rarely doctors, or tried to terminate a pregnancy themselves. Many pharmacists stocked slippery elm, which a woman would insert into her cervix, hoping for a miscarriage. Some desperate women douched with Lysol, threw themselves down stairs or, in the mythology of the pro-choice movement, inserted a coat hanger into their vaginas. One of the strongest arguments for legal abortion was the number of women resorting to these drastic measures. According to one estimate, 33,000 illegal abortions were performed in Canada in 1959 alone. A botched abortion was the number one reason for hospital emergency admissions of young women in those years. But instead of making abortion completely legal, the 1969 law limited abortions to accredited hospitals and allowed them to be performed only when approved by a therapeutic abortion committee of four doctors, for reasons associated with the woman's health. That meant a woman often needed a letter from a psychiatrist to get a legal abortion.

The abortion caravan women set off from Vancouver with the goal of arriving in Ottawa in time for Mother's Day. They stopped in cities and towns along the way for meetings and protest rallies, getting extraordinary press coverage everywhere they went. In 1970 women's liberation was news.

As the first unified action of the women's movement, the abortion caravan revealed some of the differences emerging among feminists. Most of the travelling Vancouver women were active in the New Left and the anti-war movement. They had some political disagreements among them-selves, but they managed to work together well until they hit Toronto, where socialist feminists and radical feminists had just experienced a split.

The caravan arrived in Ottawa to much excitement on Friday, May 8. More women arrived from Toronto and Montreal the next morning. On Saturday afternoon, 300 women and men marched on Parliament Hill and then held a meeting inside the Parliament Buildings. Angry that no representative of the government would meet with them, about 150 of the demonstrators headed to Prime Minister Pierre Elliott Trudeau's residence on Sussex Drive. Trudeau was not in town that weekend, but demonstrators managed to leave a coffin representing all the women who had died from illegal abortions at his doorstep. On the Monday, about 30 women chained themselves to their chairs in the galleries in the House of Commons, in tribute to the British suf-fragists who had chained themselves at Parliament to get the vote a century before.

Feminists saw Trudeaumania as sexist enthusiasm over the bachelor prime minister. For his part, Trudeau had little patience for the challenges coming from radical young women. Some of the abortion caravan women managed to meet with him months later in a Vancouver hotel. They made an impression. Maude Barlow, then Trudeau's adviser on women's issues, remembers that when she asked the prime minister to meet with representatives of the National Action Commit-tee on the Status of Women, he responded, "Are those the same wild, wild women that I met with last year? If so, it may be counterproductive."

In Conversation: Betsy Meadley Wood, Ellen Woodsworth, Bonnie Beckman, Margo Dunn, Marcy Cohen, and Jackie Larkin

Betsy Meadley Wood: The Vancouver Women's Caucus didn't last long, but it was the best group ever. It came out of Simon Fraser University. Ellen Woodsworth came from the University of British Columbia, but we were mostly from SFU. Driving to and from work is how I got into the women's caucus. I heard someone talking about it on the radio, and I thought, Wow! I lived in West Vancouver at the time, and all the women there were getting their tranquilizers and sleeping pills and wake-me-up pills. The NDP didn't even have a women's committee at the time. And here was this fantastic group that had everything together and was moving.

On Thanksgiving weekend of '69, we held the first western conference on women's liberation. There were about 100 women there. The Vancouver Women's Caucus put forward the idea of a women's cavalcade to Ottawa.

Ellen Woodsworth: We'd been having incredible discussions about what issue we could take up to mobilize all kinds of women, and abortion seemed like the right one.

Margo Dunn: We decided on a caravan because it was linked a bit to the On to Ottawa Trek of unemployed people in 1935.

Marcy Cohen: At that point the law was interpreted in such a way that you had to say you were not together emotionally to get an abortion. You had to go to a psychiatrist. A law doesn't mean much unless you change the climate.

Jackie Larkin: It didn't take long to arrive at the slogan "Free Abortion on Demand." If you are going to take on an issue, you are going to go all the way.

Betsy: Doctors wouldn't talk to you about abortion in those days. You would ask them, and they would look the other way.

Marcy: My first commitment was more abstract. I was a student radical and I wanted to make a difference and take the world on. It didn't really matter what issue. I remember coming to Vancouver from Calgary and not fitting in, and then the women's movement happened and it was an explosion. I could think and I could express myself and I was a person.

Bonnie Beckman: I was so new to it. I had been involved in some political stuff, but men controlled it. Women's liberation, what was that? I found this group and came away with a clear concept of what was being said. My impression was that the first thing we were going to do was repeal the abortion law. When we finished that, we were going to get 24-hour daycare. And when we finished that, we were going to get equal wages for work of equal value.

I had dropped out of high school and travelled around the world, and when I got back to Vancouver, I found all of this brewing. It was really exciting.

Ellen: We wanted liberation. We were just women strategizing with each other. Talking about patriarchy, talking about capitalism, talking about how we could mobilize women. I was secretly and in a positive way reading lesbian literature, which I couldn't share with anyone. But I knew this was going to open up. Abortion wasn't my issue personally, but there was momentum on it.

Bonnie: I had been trying to get a tubal ligation, and the doctors wouldn't let me have it. So my issue wasn't abortion, either. It was trying to come together in something that gave us a common language. The abortion issue lent itself very easily to a focused mobilization. As we radicalized, we were thinking what had big control over our lives—men, the media, advertising and the state. Abortion was a great example of something you could go after the state on. All we had to do was change the law.

Margo: Abortion is the issue that has mobilized more women than any other. I feel as strongly now about it at the age of 60 as I did in my twenties.

Betsy: When the Women's Caucus started out, there were four things we stood for: equal pay, child care, abortion clinics, and birth control. When I went to the Women's Caucus, I didn't go because of abortion. I went for equal pay. But no matter what our primary issue was, everyone worked on preparing for the abortion caravan. Seventeen women from Vancouver made the trip.

Bonnie: We travelled in two cars and a van. Before we left, someone painted "Smash capitalism" on the van. We got to Kamloops and met in a church basement. There was a big debate. Some people wanted the slogan off the truck and other people were defending it, and the discussion went on and on. I hadn't participated in all the ideological discussions of the women's movement. I put my sleeping bag off in a comer and went to sleep.

Betsy: The slogan had never been talked about in the group, but there it was. I just about died. "Smash capitalism" is fine, but that wasn't the time or place for it. I felt we could gain a lot of support, and "smash capitalism" could cause us to lose people. The debate continued as we travelled.

We got fantastic publicity. We had sent out our poster, which was fabulous, to every paper across the country along with our schedule. Everywhere we went there was publicity waiting for us. In Calgary, I opened up the paper and I couldn't believe it. It seemed to me that the paper was all about reproduction, and before the caravan you wouldn't have seen that. That's how fast it changed.

Ellen: I don't think any social movement since the thirties had planned something on such a national scale. We were consciously using the media and trying to figure out how to get other women to join the campaign and build on it.

Marcy: We had guerrilla theatre portraying a backstreet abortion all the way across, too.

It was a better time economically. I was a student assistant, but I stopped working and did the caravan full time, without pay, of course. It was much easier to survive in those days.

Jackie: I was a national organizer for the Waffle in Ottawa at the time. They released me and let me work on the caravan. There was a strong cross-country connection of socialists, students, women, and anti-war activists. They were the framework for what happened.

Margo: We sent letters to women's groups across the country, telling them we were coming. Could they find us a place to stay and give us a little dinner, something simple like chili? So everywhere we went we'd stay in United Church basements and there'd be chili. It was chili all the way.

Bonnie: As we entered a town, we'd sit on the back of the van with our banners and really make an entrance.

Margo: The van had a coffin on top, which we had our luggage stowed in. The plan was ultimately to deliver the coffin to Sussex Drive.

Every day we had this routine: drive 300 miles, do guerrilla theatre, eat, and have a public meeting. We collectively decided who would deal with the media. Some women were experienced with the media and some hadn't done it before, and we rotated. It was very feminist, the entire internal organization. The public meeting would inevitably wind up with wrenching horror stories and tears. I still remember some of the stories. The meetings would go later than we'd planned. And then we'd go back to where we were staying and argue about taking "Smash capitalism" off the van and about whether or not we should be smoking dope on the caravan. Before we left Vancouver, we'd had a meeting with a radical lawyer who told us all the things we could get arrested for. We were ready to be arrested once we got to Ottawa. We had bail ready.

Ellen: It wasn't until we reached Ottawa that we really confirmed what we were going to do.

Marcy: I know we'd already had an idea of going into the House of Commons because I brought a mini-skirt to wear. We had tensions among ourselves about what we were going to do in the Ottawa action, and we also discussed this with women along the way. In Toronto, feminists were definitely positioned on different sides. People weren't talking to each other, and it galvanized the differences we had internally. I remember feeling that there was a lot of difficulty in Toronto, and later when we got to Ottawa.

The Ottawa women's group almost all came out of the left of the NDP and the student movement, so they were less ideological. We used to think of the Toronto women as too heavy, too ideologically intense. They were the heavy women's liberationists.

Ellen: We had one meeting organized at the University of Toronto, and people were not friendly to us. It was a whole different feeling than going through small towns and cities, where we had a real sense of exhilaration. In Toronto, women were icy cold, fighting each other, unclear if they were going to come to Ottawa and take this risk with us.

Marcy: We had to pander to the socialist feminists, exaggerating our internal differences so that the socialist feminists in Toronto would go with us.

Margo: When we arrived in Ottawa, we went to a meeting at a school with 200 women. That was Friday night.

Jackie: The demonstration happened Saturday. Women from Montreal and Toronto arrived on Saturday morning. The decision to go to Trudeau's house happened spontaneously.

Marcy: We had had a lot of demonstrations in Vancouver where we had taken over the streets, so at first the Ottawa demonstration seemed fairly tame. We were on the sidewalks, and we pushed people to take over the streets.

Betsy: And then the speeches were over and wham, people were saying, "On to Trudeau's house!'"

Margo: Before the demonstration, there was a big meeting in the Railway Room in the Parliament Buildings. I remember I had the tools of an illegal abortion in my bag: a garden hose, a hanger, and a can of Drano. A security guard opened my purse, looked in, and waved me through. Grace MacInnis spoke at the meeting.[2] Henry Morgentaler spoke and was hissed for not being radical enough. Doris Powers, a woman from Toronto who was involved in an anti-poverty group, spoke too. I think it was her speech that kicked things over the edge. We were furious when we got out onto the streets.

Betsy: We had agreed that if John Munro, the minister of health; Trudeau; and John Turner, the minister of justice, wouldn't meet with us, we would issue a declaration of war against the Canadian government for May 11, 1970, at 3 P.M., the day after Mother's Day. I think Trudeau was off at some meeting and Munro had gone to Europe.

Jackie: None of the ministers showed up. When we got to Trudeau's house, there were only two RCMP guys there. They didn't know what to do with us, so we just sat down on the grass.

Marcy: We had linked arms because we expected to be stopped, but they didn't stop us, so we just kept going.

Betsy: The RCMP came and asked each of us if we were the spokesperson for the group, and we answered, "There are no leaders here."

Margo: There were all the angry poor women from the Just Society Movement, a Toronto anti-poverty group. I remember women saying, "We are going to stay here till Trudeau comes back." Gwen Hauser read a poem, and I gave the implements of illegal abortion to Gordon Gibson, Trudeau's staff assistant at the time, who had shown up. I remember people didn't know who he was.

Margo: We could have gotten into Trudeau's house if we had been prepared to break a window.

Marcy: But then we would have gotten arrested. So we went back to the school where we were meeting to plan Monday's action at the Parliament Buildings. There had started to be some scuffling on the lawn at Trudeau's, and we didn't want that. About 200 women came back to the school with us.

Jackie: The idea was to have a quick meeting and then have a party.

Betsy: We were going to have a debate about Monday's action, but the debate didn't happen. This is where Marcy and I parted company for a couple of years. Even teenagers who came with the women from Toronto could go into the Parliament Buildings, but only three of us from Vancouver could go in, and I wasn't going to be one of them. Finally Mary Trew stood up and said, "Is this a plan to keep Betsy out?" and a woman said, "Yes." The reason given was to protect me. If we were charged by the police, there would be trips back and forth to Ottawa, and since I had four kids, I couldn't afford it, or so they said.

Marcy: We were all part of the decision. It was torturous, and there was a lot of discussion as to who could hold the position of the group. There was a feeling that some people had a different philosophy from the rest of the group about how we should be arguing our position on abortion and how to deal with the police or a trial.

Ellen: Our differences were not only over the "Smash capitalism" slogan and dope smoking. We were debating whether we were for the right to abortion only, or whether we were fighting to smash a system.

Margo: I was one of the people who also wanted to go inside, and I didn't have any of the jeopardies that we had defined—women who were not citizens or had criminal records, anything that would make their case more difficult than others if they were nabbed. It narrowed down in my mind to who had been in the leadership. And to me that meant Marcy, Ellen, and Betsy. But there were these differences. There were lifestyle issues, issues around clothes, etcetera, and it was so important that the three women who might go to court be united. So I remember voting for someone other than Betsy.

Marcy: I had a lot of guilt about it. I knew that my feelings came from the experience of being in Toronto and seeing the divisions between the socialist feminists and the radical feminists. Seeing Betsy gravitate to the radical feminists made me decide that if we were going to be at risk, we had to make sure we could carry the struggle. There was a continual struggle in terms of our differences, and if we were going to carry through what we had started, then we had to be solid and not risk breaking apart.

Ellen: We assumed that we were going to be arrested and that we would be in a political battle with the courts and with the media, and we wanted people to not be fighting each other too. We wanted to be able to continue mobilizing for women's liberation in Canada.

Betsy: The only division I saw was that this was not the place for "Smash capitalism" if you wanted to smash capitalism. Abortion was such a great thing for bringing people together, and that was what we should stick to. I felt we were safe. I wasn't afraid of going into the building because there was no way they were ever going to arrest us. But as sisters, everyone else was making up my mind for me.

Jackie: I think a lot of what went on was the political immaturity of the movement. If we go out on an abortion demonstration today, we don't worry about the politics of who is speaking; we get a broad cross-section of people. In those days the big issue was, did you have the right politics behind what you said? Here's an example. About a month after the abortion caravan, I was in Toronto, and Peggy Morton, a Toronto socialist feminist, sat on the steps of a co-op with me and said, "You know, we made a really big mistake when we went into the House of Commons," and I said "Oh, yeah?" and she said, "We should have been saying, 'Victory to the NLF.'"[3] It's exactly the same issue. If you are supporting abortion rights, then really you are in favour of smashing capitalism: that's what you guys argued then. Or if you are really going to support abortion, you have to be a socialist feminist. It's bullshit, but that's what we were arguing.

Marcy: I don't agree that we were arguing that.

Bonnie: I think there was a generation gap happening, because Betsy was almost 20 years older than the rest of us. For me, this was very much about the way I wanted to change the world. Betsy, you came at it from a single-issue point of view, but you should have been participating. We wouldn't have been there if it hadn't been for you. But those were the times we lived in.

Margo: In the big meeting, there was a three-hour discussion about whether we should chain ourselves to the chairs in the parliamentary gallery. I remember someone saying we should chain ourselves like the suffragists did.

Marcy: I remember all this talking and talking and talking, and then suddenly it was Monday morning. We had borrowed a lot of things to get us ready to set off.

Jackie: I remember digging through people's cupboards in co-ops, trying to find nylons. We had to go out and buy gloves and purses.

Ellen: We strategized about who would go into which gallery and who would start the chant. If one person was taken out, what would we do? Go limp?

Jackie: I remember going up the elevator in the Parliament Buildings, and no one looking at one another.

Marcy: Standing in the line with all these people you knew, but everyone looked different because we were dressed up … our other selves.

Margo: There were three or four men from Ottawa who were beards for some of the women.[4] I think there were 35 or 36 who went inside. There was also a demonstration outside that was supposed to act as a camouflage.

Jackie: My chant didn't work in the end. My memory is that for half of the women who went in, the chains didn't hold.

Ellen: We also had to figure out how to get those goddamn chains out of our purses quietly. We tried not to be noisy or obvious, but we were listening to the MPs trashing some men in Vancouver who were marching across the border in Blaine to protest the war in Cambodia. Many of these men were our friends and lovers, so things started to move really fast back and forth across the gallery, and then it was pandemonium, people looking up and saying, "What's going on here?" They couldn't figure out where the shouting was coming from. Some people started to be dragged away. We went limp and they would try to drag us and we would go limp again. It took them quite a while.

Margo: There was a text, written collectively, we were going to read. One person was supposed to start, and then the next person would continue in the next gallery. That was the plan, but it didn't work out that way.

Jackie: The police took our chains. They didn't arrest us, but 10 women were taken down to the police station and then released.

Margo: Meanwhile outside, about 200 women wearing black headscarves walked two by two around the eternal flame. Our heads were bowed in mourning for the women who continued to die because of lack of access to safe abortion. At 3 P.M., we threw off the black scarves to reveal red ones and charged up the steps to begin the first action of the "war." We set fire to a placard containing the text of the law. Soon the women who had been in the House ran out to join us. We were surprised, but thrilled, that no one was arrested. The caravan shut down the House of Commons for 45 minutes, and we got tons of media coverage.

A few weeks later, back in Vancouver, the Vancouver Women's Caucus had a meeting with Trudeau. We met him at the Bayshore Inn. He had phoned from his plane to say he wanted to talk to us, and we only had three hours' notice to get women down there. We activated our phone trees. We got to the room in the Bayshore before Trudeau did. We discussed making him sit on the floor, but thought we wouldn't get away with it. We didn't want him sitting in the middle of the room, though, so we moved his chair off-centre. When he got there, we were relentless—it was great. And there was a lot of press.

Bonnie: I remember saying, "Look, we want this abortion law repealed," and he said, "Well, go and get the people to vote for it. You have the right to have it, but go and do the job." He wasn't against it. He said, "Go and convince people."

Marcy: The thing I remember about him was his arrogance. I remember him saying that if you needed an abortion and you had money, you could go to the States.

Ellen: And we were shouting, "Just society, just for the rich."

Notes

1. Florynce Kennedy was the first African American woman to graduate from Columbia Law School. She was a flamboyant civil rights and feminist activist in the United States, well known for her quotable quotes. This one comes from a 1973 speech.

2. Grace MacInnis was the only female member of Parliament at this time. She represented the NDP from Vancouver Kingsway.
3. National Liberation Front in North Vietnam. The radical slogan in the anti-Vietnam War movement was "Victory to the NLF," whereas the unifying slogan was "Stop the War."
4. Men who escorted the women to cover their true purpose.

Chapter 49

Sterilization and Abortion

Betsy Hartmann

Betsy Hartmann is director of the Population and Development Program, and professor of development studies at Hampshire College in Massachusetts. A long-standing activist in the international women's health movement, she speaks and consults on international population, development, environment, and security issues. She is the author of both fiction and non-fiction pieces about important national and global issues. The following piece is from her feminist classic, Reproductive Rights and Wrongs: The Global Politics of Population Control.

Sterilization and abortion are the most controversial of birth control methods—sterilization because of its permanence, abortion because it terminates pregnancy. While arguments rage over the ethics of both methods, this does not prevent their widespread use by women all over the world. This chapter looks at the crucial question of why these methods are chosen, and who makes the choice.

Barren Policies

*****

If some excesses appear, don't blame me.... You must consider it something like a war. There could be a certain amount of misfiring out of enthusiasm. There has been pressure to show results. Whether you like it or not, there will be a few dead people.
—Dr. D.N. Pai, Harvard-educated director of family planning in Bombay,
commenting on his plans for compulsory sterilization
(*New York Times*, 1976)[1]

Today sterilization is the world's most widespread form of birth control, accounting for over a third of contraceptive use worldwide, and almost half in developing countries. Female sterilization is much more common than male—by 1992 an estimated 140 million women of reproductive age had been sterilized, as opposed to 42 million men. Female to male sterilization ratios are higher in developing countries than in developed ones.[2] The concentration on female sterilization raises troubling concerns, since it is a more complicated and riskier operation than vasectomy and can take longer to recover from.

The most common complications of female sterilization are anesthesia-related problems, internal injury, and infection, and there may be long-term side effects such as heavier menstrual periods or lower back pain. The mortality rate probably differs significantly depending on where the operation is done. According to *Population Reports*, in the U.S. the rate is approximately one death in every 70,000 procedures, but it is likely to be much higher in mass-sterilization camps and clinics in countries like India and Bangladesh. Nevertheless, new female surgical methods are often billed as easy and safe—Planned Parenthood, for example, calls the "minilap" technique "Band-Aid surgery"—although they all require a high degree of technical competence.[3]

By contrast, male sterilization (vasectomy) is relatively risk-free, yet it is common in only four countries: the United States, Great Britain, India, and China. The mortality rate from vasectomy is virtually zero in the United States, though in those Third World countries where vasectomies are performed in large "fairs" or "camps" under less than sanitary conditions, deaths from infection are not unknown. Bangladesh and India in particular have poor records in this regard.[4]

*****

Although vasectomy is much safer than female sterilization, there are many prejudices against it. Many men fear vasectomy will somehow affect their virility and potency, while many doctors find female sterilization more "interesting," not the least because they receive higher fees for it than for vasectomy. Most family planning programs ignore male responsibility for contraception—and hence vasectomy—an attitude that reflects the basic unequal power relationship between the sexes. Nevertheless, there are examples of successful vasectomy programs, where a real effort has been made to educate and communicate with men.[5]

Because of its permanence, sterilization has frequently been employed as a method of population control. However, there is considerable debate over its demographic effectiveness. Couples who opt for *voluntary* sterilization (in the true sense of the word) tend to have completed their family size, and in many cases already have more children than would be commensurate with a reduced rate of population growth. Thus a number of population agencies favor birth-spacing methods, such as the IUD and hormonal methods, which appeal to younger couples, who ideally will have fewer children, farther between, with a more pronounced impact on birth rates.[6] Of course, there is a way to make sterilization more demographically effective—that is, to make it *involuntary*—through targeting people who have not completed their family size by means of incentives/disincentives or force.

The United States has played a major role in the introduction of sterilization into Third World family planning programs. In a 1977 interview Dr. R.T. Ravenholt made his now famous statement that the United States was seeking to provide the means by which one quarter of the world's fertile women could be voluntarily sterilized.[7] The U.S. Agency for International Development (AID) funds the Program for International Education in Gynecology and Obstetrics (PIEGO), which brings foreign medical personnel to the United States to learn sterilization techniques along with population indoctrination. In the mid-seventies, the PIEGO center at Washington University Medical School in St. Louis was closed after a community coalition challenged its medical and ethical standards and population control bias.[8] AID also funds the greater part of the Association for Voluntary Surgical Contraception's (AVSC—formerly Association for Voluntary Sterilization or AVS) international program budget.

AVSC, formerly linked with the eugenics movement, works in over sixty countries. [...] Both AID and AVSC insist that they support only *voluntary* sterilization programs, and ones in which other contraceptive methods are also offered in order to ensure freedom of choice. But both have worked in and often actively supported incentive-based programs, for example, in Sri Lanka and Bangladesh. And they tend to push *female* sterilization, as is presently occurring in Kenya, where AVSC, with AID assistance, has rapidly expanded female sterilization sites.[9] [...]

Incentives are not the only means of restricting individual choice in sterilization programs. As the following Latin American case studies reveal, there are other important social dimensions to the problem.

La Operación: Sterilization in Latin America

The history of U.S. involvement in sterilization abroad began on the Caribbean island of Puerto Rico. In the 1930s, as poverty and unemployment fueled social unrest, U.S. colonial officials labeled overpopulation as a main cause of the "Puerto Rican problem," conveniently ignoring their own role in generating the economic crisis. After the United States seized control of the island from the Spanish in 1898, U.S. sugar interests quickly moved in, evicting farmers and cattle ranchers to make way for large plantations. By 1925, less than 2 percent of the population owned 80 percent of the land, and 70 percent of the people were landless.[10]

In the 1940s, in another wave from the mainland, U.S. manufacturing industries began to locate in Puerto Rico, attracted by tax-free investment incentives and the prospect of cheap labor. Women were an important part of that cheap labor force, and sterilization was perceived as a way to help "free" them for employment, as opposed to, for example, providing good child-care facilities.

Both private agencies, including the International Planned Parenthood Federation (IPPF), and the Puerto Rican government, with United States government funds, encouraged women to accept sterilization by providing it at minimal or no cost. By 1968 one third of women of childbearing age had been sterilized on the island, the highest percentage anywhere in the world at that time.[11]

Many women undergoing *la operación*, as it is commonly called in Puerto Rico, were no doubt eager for birth control, but, as Rosalind Petchesky points out, their choice of sterilization was voluntary only in a narrow sense. Not only were many women unaware that the operation was permanent, but other forms of contraception were either unavailable or prohibitively expensive. [...]

Despite the claims of the Malthusians, sterilization and population control did nothing to solve the island's problems. Puerto Rico now faces a serious HIV epidemic [...], as well as an epidemic of violence, substance abuse, and unemployment. The island's environment has been badly damaged, not by population pressures, but by pollution from U.S. chemical plants. "Today few illusions exist that population control policies will solve the island's environmental, economic or social problems," writes Dr. Helen Rodriguez-Trias, long-time health activist and former president of the American Public Health Association. "Women still struggle for family planning, safe abortions and health care, but resist pressures to end their reproductive lives prematurely."[12]

In the early 1980s Colombia was the scene of Latin America's most vigorous sterilization drive. Female sterilization was the second most popular family planning method after the pill, not surprising since these were the two methods most heavily promoted. Sterilizations were largely promoted and performed by the private Profamilia family planning organization, supported by AID, AVSC, and IPPF, among others. Profamilia's executive director, Dr. Miguel Trias, famous on the population scene, has lectured the U.S. Congress on the dire consequences of rapid population growth. Miguel Trias justified his organization's accent on female sterilization on the basis that its side effects are "negligible," the cost to the acceptor is "extremely low," and "its irreversibility puts the patient safely beyond any possible social, religious, or marital conflict."[13]

In Colombia, where illegal abortion rates are high and complications common, sterilization is also presented as an antidote to abortion. "If we reduced our surgery program," said Dr. Trias, "we would stimulate an epidemic of illegal abortions."[14]

Do such factors form a solid foundation for a voluntary sterilization program? As in Puerto Rico, Colombian women were not outright coerced into sterilization, but their acceptance must be viewed in context. The view that the side effects of the operation were negligible meant that women were not well counseled about them. According to a British researcher who visited Colombia, "The information given about the operation is very brief; no mention is made about possible side effects or problems. The main emphasis is the economic advantages to be gained by having fewer children."[15]

Because sterilization was heavily subsidized, the cost to the acceptor was low, but this raises the question of whether the poor would have preferred other methods, if they were available and low cost as well. [...]

Not-so-subtle pressures were sometimes exerted on women to undergo the operation, especially right after giving birth. The British researcher found that women in state hospitals were told that if they consented to sterilization after delivery, they could stay in the hospital for three days instead of the normal twenty-four hours, "a great temptation to an exhausted woman with other children at home."[16]

As for abortion, is sterilization really the cure? As Dr. Helen Rodriguez-Trias points out, "Abortion is a principle cause of maternal mortality in Colombia, but instead of providing safe, legal abortion, the population people promote sterilization."[17] This is not to argue that sterilization should be eliminated from the Colombian family planning program, but its aggressive promotion raises serious questions.

The phenomenon of sterilization regret, long unrecognized and understudied, is starting to command attention. A 1985 WHO study of sterilized women in India, Colombia, Nigeria, the Philippines, and the United Kingdom found that from 1 to 6 percent of women regretted having the operation in the twelve-month follow-up interview. (One would expect the percentage to rise as women's circumstances change, children die, etc.) The highest figures were in Colombia and India. A 1987 survey in Mexico found that over 10 percent of women who had been sterilized would not have the operation again if they had a choice.[18] Sterilization's irreversibility, instead of placing the patient safely beyond conflict, thus may instead engender deep conflict, if the decision, made in haste or under pressure, leads later to regret.

*****

India: Something Like a War

The continuum between restriction of choice and outright physical compulsion is dramatically exposed in India. From the introduction of targets and incentives in the mid-1960s to the mass vasectomy camps of the early 1970s, India's family planning program, one of the first and largest in the world, consistently treated the poor recipients of its services as second-class citizens. Lack of respect translated into lack of results. Despite massive infusions of foreign and national funds, India's birth rate has come down much more slowly than anticipated.[19]

Then, in 1975, Prime Minister Indira Gandhi declared Emergency Rule. Encouraged by her son Sanjay, she decided to take action once and for all to solve the country's population problem.

Civil liberties were suspended in 1975, and in 1976 a variety of laws and regulations on sterilization were enacted, as the central government put pressure on the states to meet sterilization quotas. Public employees' salaries were made contingent on the number of acceptors they brought
for sterilization. Fines and imprisonment threatened couples who failed to be sterilized after three
children, and food rations and other government services were withheld from the unsterilized.

In some cases, state governments resorted to brute force, with police raids to round up "eligible" men for forcible sterilization. In at least one case, *all* the young men of one village were
sterilized.[20] It was the poor who were most often the victims of both the regulations and police
violence, since the wealthy were able to buy their way out either with bribes or substitution of
poor men in their places.

In the last six months of 1976, 6.5 million people were sterilized, four times the rate of any
previous period. Meanwhile hundreds, if not thousands, died from infections associated with the
operation, and in riots and protests against the program.[21]

Although the compulsory sterilization campaign received critical coverage in the foreign press,
many members of the population establishment were slow to condemn it. When World Bank
President Robert McNamara visited India during Emergency Rule, he paid tribute to "the political will and determination shown by the leadership at the highest level in intensifying the family
planning drive with a rare courage of conviction." Paul Ehrlich, author of *The Population Bomb*,
criticized the United States for not supporting a proposal for mandatory sterilization of all Indian
men with three or more children: "We should have volunteered logistic support in the form of
helicopters, vehicles and surgical instruments. We should have sent doctors.... Coercion? Perhaps, but coercion in a good cause." The UNFPA's Dr. Joep van Arendonk, who went personally
to India in 1976 to investigate the situation, still maintains that compulsory sterilization did not
exist "except for a few abuses."[22]

These "few abuses," however, were enough to bring down Indira Gandhi's government in 1977
in a dramatic electoral defeat. There followed a predictable backlash against family planning: The
number of sterilizations dropped to 900,000 that year.

Today India's sterilization program is back in full swing. Although direct coercion is rare, other
forms of pressures are brought to bear on the poor.

Carrying out research in rural South India, demographers John and Pat Caldwell and P.H.
Reddy saw some of these pressures first hand. Although the rural elite preferred to use the
IUD, poor villagers were offered no other birth control alternative but sterilization in the
belief that they were too ignorant to cope with anything else and that their fertility had to be
controlled at all costs. [...]

Such pressure is also exerted on India's tribal minorities, even those who are in danger of
extinction. While visiting a Rabha tribal village in the Indian state of West Bengal in 1982, I
witnessed a government development officer putting pressure on village leaders to send women
"10 to 15 at a time" to the hospital to be sterilized. I later learned that the entire Rabha tribe only
numbers 2,500 people, out of a total population of over 55 million in West Bengal.

Added to these pressures is the inducement of incentives—a woman receives the equivalent
of $22 for submitting to sterilization, a man $15.[23] This differential reflects the government's
policy of concentrating on female sterilization after the politically costly vasectomy abuses during
Emergency Rule. As analyst Alaka Basu explains: "What better way than to turn to another target
group—that of women—which lacked the individual and group capability to protest and which
in any case was beginning to display a demand for some form of birth control even if tubectomy
was still not its first preference?"[24] In 1989–90, female sterilizations accounted for over 90 per-

cent of total sterilizations.[25]

More than 70 percent of the sterilizations are performed in camps, where hygienic standards are appalling. In the autumn of 1985 India was rocked by yet another sterilization scandal: in a Maharashtran sterilization camp one woman died and seventeen others were in serious condition after being given an antidiabetic drug mistaken for a pain killer. During the sterilization operation itself, the woman who died had screamed with pain since the anesthetic had not taken effect. The doctors had paid no attention. "The family planning program is beginning to resemble a giant, over-developed and hyperactive limb growing out of an inefficient health system which is incapable of supervising and controlling it," commented an editorial in a prominent Indian weekly.[26] A [...] documentary on India's population program, *Something Like a War*, produced by Dheepa Dhanraj for British television, provides graphic footage of the shocking conditions within sterilization clinics and the heavy-handed methods used by local elites to recruit "acceptors."

The Indian government's capitulation to an IMF structural adjustment agenda in the early 1990s is now leading to an intensification of the population control program. Observers believe external pressure is behind the government's decision to cut health expenditures while dramatically increasing funds for family planning. The UNFPA and AID meanwhile have substantially raised their contributions to the program. The government has set an (impossible) target of reducing the crude rate from 30.5 to 26.7 by 1995.[27] It aims to build a "population control movement by the people" in which local village leaders will be the "kingpins," increasing the risks of abuse.[28]

In New Delhi, a huge population clock has been set up at a central intersection, registering every new birth in order to alarm passersby—of course, it fails to register the number of children who die each day from malnutrition and simple diseases, or women who die in childbirth. In India, as in Bangladesh, primary health care has been seriously undermined by the sterilization program.[29]

Is there no alternative? One wonders what would happen if the Indian government simply took the sensible and humane step of providing decent health and voluntary family planning services to its people, as well as education and employment opportunities, instead of herding poor women like cattle into sterilization camps. Not only might human suffering be greatly alleviated, but the birth rate might actually come down.

The United States Parallel

Today sterilization is the most widely used method of birth control in the United States,[30] but, as in many parts of the Third World, sterilization "choice" often takes place in a restrictive context. This is especially the case for poor white, black, Hispanic, and Native American women who lack access to other birth control methods and/or who are the victims of racially motivated designs to limit their numbers. Their choice was further restricted in 1977 when public funding of abortion was virtually eliminated, although sterilization continues to be covered in Medicaid programs for up to 90 percent of the cost.[31]

*****

Compulsory sterilization also has a long history in the United States, with the focus on the [intellectually disabled], prison inmates, and ethnic minorities. In the famous Relf case in the early 1970s, when two young black teenagers in Alabama were sterilized without their consent or knowledge, a federal district court found that there was uncontroverted evidence in the record that minors and other incompetents have been sterilized with federal funds and that an indefinite number of poor people have been improperly coerced into accepting a sterilization operation under the threat that various federally supported welfare benefits would be withdrawn unless they submitted to irreversible sterilization.[32]

In 1976 the U.S. General Accounting Office revealed that the federally funded Indian Health Service had sterilized 3,000 Native American women in a four-year period using consent forms "not in compliance ... with regulations."[33]

These and other abuses led feminists and health activists to campaign for more stringent sterilization regulations in the United States. The first victory was won in New York City in 1975, when stricter guidelines were enacted, which later formed the basis of federal sterilization reform. These include more rigorous informed consent procedures, a thirty-day waiting period between consent and the actual operation, a prohibition on hysterectomies for sterilization purposes, and a moratorium on federally funded sterilizations of minors, the involuntarily institutionalized, and the legally incompetent.[34]

*****

There is a place for sterilization, without pressure or incentives, with full knowledge and informed consent. In the right hands it can be a powerful tool of reproductive freedom. In the wrong hands it is an intrusive act of physical violence, no matter how clean the surgeon's gloves or the consciences of the donors from abroad.

A Woman's Right to Her Life

*****

Despite the controversy surrounding it, abortion should not be viewed in isolation from other contraceptive methods, since it is ideally a complement to them. No contraceptive method is entirely effective. The backup of safe abortion—the termination of a pregnancy by extracting the fetus—provides an important insurance against contraceptive failure and allows women to use safer but sometimes less effective methods such as barrier contraceptives and natural family planning. If all women were guaranteed access to safe, cheap, legal abortion, the profile of contraceptive use might very well shift from riskier but more effective varieties.

Denying women the right to abortion makes women bear all the hardship and blame for unwanted pregnancies, ignoring the fact that men bear responsibility too, and that many unwanted pregnancies result from unwanted intercourse. For many women, and especially for the young, an unwanted pregnancy can alter irrevocably the course of their lives, closing off options, forcing them into marriages they do not want, or making them raise a child without social and material support. No woman wants an abortion if she can help it, but sometimes it is the only way out.

BOX 49.1: Quinacrine: Population Controller's Dream May Become Woman's Nightmare

The most zealous population controllers have long wanted a cheaper and "easier" form of female sterilization, and now many think they have found the answer to their dreams: quinacrine sterilization pellets. Developed in the 1920s, the drug quinacrine was first used to treat malaria and now has a variety of other medical applications. After initial research in Chile in the 1970s, quinacrine pellets were developed as a sterilizing agent. Inserted into the top of a woman's womb, the pellets dissolve and cause a low-level inflammation. This produces scar tissue at the ends of the fallopian tubes, preventing the passage of the egg into the uterus.

Both the WHO and the USFDA have refused to approve large-scale human trials of quinacrine sterilization until animal toxicology studies, conducted according to accepted standards, have been carried out. Quinacrine risks include a possible link with cancer, ectopic pregnancy, uterine complications leading to hysterectomy, and vaginal burning and irritation. Nevertheless, two North Carolina-based population agencies, Family Health International (FHI) and the Center for Research on Population and Security, have supported testing on women. The Center provides free quinacrine pellets to government health agencies and researchers, while FHI has funded research in Chile and two small studies of U.S. women, and is planning a new clinical trial in Vietnam. To date 80,000 women have received quinacrine in eleven countries: Bangladesh, Chile, Costa Rica, Croatia, Egypt, India, Indonesia, Iran, Pakistan, Venezuela, and 30,000 in Vietnam alone.[35]

Within the population community there is mounting controversy over quinacrine, with AVSC taking a leading role in exposing its possible dangers. In late 1993 AVSC issued a highly critical report of a Vietnamese study of quinacrine that had been published in the British medical journal, the *Lancet*. The study's glowing account of quinacrine use by 31,781 Vietnamese women was not only based on seriously flawed statistical techniques but dubious assumptions. Quinacrine "represents our most cost-effective way of lowering maternal mortality," the study states, using the same false logic applied to sterilization in Bangladesh and elsewhere.[36]

Lowering population growth is the underlying agenda, and there are already allegations of coercive use of quinacrine in Vietnam's heavy-handed population program. In 1993 the Vietnamese publication *The Woman* exposed the case of 100 women on the Hoa Binh rubber plantation, who had quinacrine inserted into their uteruses without their knowledge when they thought they were having routine IUD checks.[37] As AVSC notes, "The potential for coercion and abuse in the context of demographic goals may be of greater concern than the medical risk from side effects and long-term health consequences of quinacrine itself."[38]

The drug's chief advocates claim that quinacrine "would increase the prevalence of sterilization in economically depressed regions" because "it can be delivered by any health personnel already trained in IUD insertion." They openly condone its use by physicians as a sterilization agent "under the legal use of an approved drug for an unapproved use." Quinacrine is a common treatment for malaria and giardia, and is thus easily available to doctors. Where malpractice suits are prevalent, they urge that informed consent forms be signed by patients. So much for respecting basic regulatory procedures![39]

Legal abortion performed within the first three months of pregnancy is relatively safe, with a lower death rate than from the use of oral contraceptives or even from a simple tonsillectomy.[40] Nevertheless, it is not entirely risk-free, and possible complications, especially infection, are likely to be higher where antiseptic conditions are not maintained.

*****

The controversy surrounding abortion is a relatively recent phenomenon. In most societies, abortion has been used for centuries as a common fertility control method, tolerated implicitly, if not explicitly, by social custom and law. Traditional European, British, and U.S. common law, for example, allowed abortion before "quickening," the noticeable movement of the fetus, which usually occurs during the fifth month of pregnancy. Even the Catholic Church was relatively tolerant of early abortion—not until 1869 did Pope Pius IX declare all abortion to be murder.[41]

Historically, society's view of abortion has reflected changing perceptions of the medical profession and the role of women. In the United States, for example, as medical practice became more institutionalized in the late nineteenth century, doctors sought to secure a monopoly over the practice of medicine and medical technology through an attack on irregular practitioners, such as midwives and women healers, who provided abortion services. At the same time Victorian morality was gaining ground: middle-class women were relegated back to the home, where their main mission in life was to produce children. Abortion became criminalized, separated from its original context of birth control.[42]

Today, as a conservative backlash sweeps many countries, women are once again being told that their place is at home with their families, though "home" is hardly the safe refuge it is made out to be. Denying women access to abortion is part of that process; even where abortion is legal, women are made to feel it is a crime. There are many people, of course, who have sincere moral and religious objections to abortion, but it is important to point out that not all of them are Right to Lifers. Many feel that, although they would not choose abortion personally, it must be up to each individual woman to make that choice.[43]

On the international stage, the U.S. government led the attack against abortion in the 1980s, despite its legality in the United States. Under the Reagan and Bush administrations, all foreign nongovernmental organizations that received funds originating from AID had to sign an infamous clause certifying that they would not perform or actively promote abortion as a family planning method. This extended to counseling and referral services as well. A "gag rule" within the U.S. also prevented publicly funded family planning clinics from even counseling women about abortion. The Reagan and Bush administrations' attack on abortion resembled the German book burning of the 1930s and reflected a deep political cynicism. In order to win the domestic antiabortion vote, the White House and conservative Congressmen were willing to deny Third World women access to desperately needed safe abortion facilities.

*****

In many countries, illegal abortion is a leading cause of death for women in their childbearing years. Could it not be said that denying women the right to safe abortion is itself a form of murder?

*****

Population "Quality" Control

Today the abortion issue has taken on a new dimension with the development of reproductive tech-nologies—amniocentesis, ultrasound, chorionic villus sampling—that can identify the fetus's sex and certain genetic defects such as Down Syndrome and spina bifida in the early stages of pregnancy.

Sex-selective abortion of girls is not only a serious problem in China, but in India too, espe-cially in the north and west. Sex-selective abortion, mainly in private clinics, has reached what some observers term "epidemic proportions"—even poor villagers are saving up money for amniocentesis and ultrasound. Sex selection must be seen in the context of "son preference" and the widespread oppression of Indian women of all classes.

The women who decide to undergo it usually do so because they are under intense pressure them-selves, threatened by the ongoing hostility of their in-laws or the prospect of divorce if they bear yet another daughter or fail to conceive a son. Rising dowry demands, largely as a result of growing consumerism, are a major factor—many families can simply not afford to pay for the marriage of their daughters if it means buying the prospective groom a refrigerator, motorcycle, or TV.[44]

Traditional son preference and female neglect, coupled with the spread of a smaller-family norm and sex-selection technology, are leading to a serious decline in the sex ratio. In 1991 there were an estimated 929 women for every 1,000 men in the Indian population, the lowest level in this century. The average obscures differences between states—the north tends to have worse ratios than the south, but in only one state, Kerala, does the number of women exceed that of men.[45]

Direct female infanticide is also a serious problem in some locations. A study of Salem District in Tamil Nadu state found a high incidence of infanticide related to the growth of consumerism, high dowry demands, and the internalization of the small-family norm as the road to prosperity. According to the authors, "When the strong preference for sons and negativism about daughters impinges on the strongly internalized small-family norm, the daughters are eliminated! ... The internalization of the small-family norm ... is itself one of the sources of female infanticide."[46] These findings raise serious questions about the wisdom of Information, Education, and Com-munication (IEC) programs promoting the two-child family as the happy, prosperous family in a context of deep-rooted male bias and rampant materialism.

*****

Although instances of sex selection are not unknown in Western countries, amniocentesis and other new reproductive technologies are more typically used to identify genetic defects, with the expectation that women will abort any defective fetuses. These technologies pose very difficult ethical dilemmas.

As women with disabilities have pointed out, the decision to abort a disabled child is influ-enced by a number of factors besides purely personal ones. In a society like the United States, for example, where the media sells an image of health that only the affluent young can hope to fulfill, fears about raising a disabled child may be way out of proportion to the facts, or far greater than they would be in a more compassionate environment. As one disabled woman describes:

> There is tremendous pressure upon us to have "perfect" babies. Do we want a world of
> "perfect people?" I really wonder what are the human costs of attempts to control our
> differences, our vulnerability. I believe that if women are to maintain our "choice" we
> must include *the choice to have a disabled child*.[47]

The new reproductive technologies and medical advances in prenatal and neonatal care are bringing the issue of eugenics back into the population arena.

In the last analysis, today's controversy over abortion is misplaced. Whether or not abortion should occur is really not the issue. It will occur, no matter how many bombs are thrown at abortion clinics, how many times the Pope condemns it, or how widely other forms of contraception are distributed. Unwanted pregnancies may decline, but they will not vanish altogether.

Instead, the vital issues regarding abortion are these:

- whether it is legal, safe, and accessible, or illegal, dangerous, and out of reach geographically or financially.
- whether it is abused as an instrument of population quantity or quality control, or used as a tool of reproductive choice.
- Properly performed, abortion is a woman's safety net and one of the most important reproductive rights of all.

Notes

1. Henry Kamm, "Indian State Is Leader in Forced Sterilization," *New York Times*, 13 August 1976. Dr. Pai is still active in international sterilization circles.
2. See Mahmoud Fahmy Fathalla, "Fertility Control Technology," p. 226, for percentages and "Voluntary Female Sterilization: Number One and Growing," *Population Reports*, Series C, no. 10 (November 1990); and "Vasectomy: New Opportunities," *Population Reports*, Series D, no. 5 (March 1992), for latest figures.
3. Mortality rate from *Population Reports*, Series C, no. 10. "Band-Aid surgery" from Rosalind Petchesky, "'Reproductive Choice' in the Contemporary United States." Sterilization may have a long-term effect on menstruation, leading to heavier periods in some women, though the evidence is not conclusive one way or the other. See, for example, Coralie Sunanda Ray, "The Long-Term Menstrual Side Effects Associated with Tubal Sterilization, a Literature Review and Case-Control Study with Special Reference to Women in South Asia," unpublished dissertation, London School of Hygiene and Tropical Medicine, September 1983, and "Menstrual Function Following Tubal Sterilization," *AVS Medical Bulletin*, vol. 2, no. 1 (February 1981).
4. "Vasectomy—Safe and Simple," *Population Reports*, Series D, no. 4 (November–December 1983).
5. Ibid. Also see special issue on vasectomy, *Studies in Family Planning*, vol. 14, no. 3 (March 1983).
6. George Zeidenstein, former president of the Population Council, expressed this view in a letter to the author. Also see Alaka M. Basu, "Family Planning and the Emergency: An Unanticipated Consequence," *Economic and Political Weekly*, vol. 20, no. 10 (9 March 1985).
7. Ravenholt quoted in Paul Wagman, "U.S. Goal: Sterilize Millions of World's Women," *St. Louis Post-Dispatch*, 22 April 1977.
8. Ad Hoc Committee to End the Sterilization Program, "Documentation of the Ejection of the PIEGO Program from Washington University Medical School," n.d. Also personal communications with those involved.

9. See first edition of this book for more details of Sri Lankan case. On Kenya, see *Population Reports*, Series C, no. 10, pp. 12–13. "I would like to spread the gospel of tubal ligation to my friends and others," *Population Reports* quotes a Kenyan woman.

10. See James W. Wessman, "Neo-Malthusian Ideology and Colonial Capitalism: Population Dynamics in Southwestern Puerto Rico," in Karen L. Michaelson, ed., *And the Poor Get Children* (New York: Monthly Review Press, 1981). See also chapter on Puerto Rico in Bonnie Mass, *Population Target: The Political Economy of Population Control in Latin America* (Toronto: Women's Press, 1976).

11. Helen Rodriguez-Trias, "The Women's Health Movement: Women Take Power," in Victor W. Sidel and Ruth Sidel, *Reforming Medicine: Lessons of the Last Quarter Century* (New York: Pantheon Books, 1984).

12. Helen Rodriguez-Trias, "Puerto Rico, Where Sterilization of Women Became 'La Operación,'" *Political Environments*, no. 1 (Spring 1994).

13. Dr. Trias's comments from U.S. Congress, House, *Population and Development in Latin America and the Caribbean*. Hearing before the Subcommittee on Inter-American Affairs of the Committee on Foreign Affairs, 97th Cong., 2d sess., 8 September 1982, p. 52.

14. Trias quoted in Alan Riding, "Battleground in Colombia: Birth Control," *New York Times*, 5 September 1984.

15. Ruth Holly, "Population Control in Colombia," paper prepared for the International Contraception, Abortion, and Sterilization Campaign, London, 1981.

16. Holly, "Population Control in Colombia."

17. Personal interview, February 1984.

18. "Mental Health and Female Sterilization: A Follow-up, Report of a WHO Collaborative Prospective Study," *Journal of Biosocial Science*, vol. 17, no. 1 (January 1985). On Mexico, see Terezita de Barbieri, "Gender and Population Policies: Some Reflections," *Reproductive Health Matters*, no. 1 (May 1993).

19. See Marika Vicziany, "Coercion in a Soft State: The Family-Planning Program of India. Part I: The Myth of Voluntarism," *Pacific Affairs* , vol. 55, no. 3 (1982), pp. 373–402, and "Part II: The Sources of Coercion," *Pacific Affairs*, vol. 55, no. 4 (1982–83), pp. 557–92, for excellent analysis of the program's assumptions and failures in its early stages. For a more recent overview, see T.K. Sundari Ravindran, "Women and the Politics of Population and Development in India," *Reproductive Health Matters*, vol. 1 (1993), pp. 26–38.

20. See "Entire Village Sterilized," *India Now* (August 1978).

21. Information on forced sterilization in India from Debabar Banerji, "Political Economy of Population Control in India," in Lars Bondestam and Staffan Bergström, eds., *Poverty and Population Control* (London: Academic Press, 1980); Davidson R. Gwatkin, "Political Will and Family Planning: The Implications of India's Emergency Experience," *Population and Development Review*, vol. 5, no. 1 (March 1979); "Delhi to Penalize Couples for Not Limiting Births," *New York Times*, 26 February 1976.

22. McNamara quote from Government of India, Department of Family Planning, *Centre Calling*, vol. XI (11 November 1976), cited in Banerji, "Political Economy of Population Control in India." Ehrlich quote from 1983 edition of *The Population Bomb*, cited in John Tierney, "Fanisi's Choice," *Science*, vol. 86 (January–February 1986), p. 42. Van Arendonk quote from personal interview, February 1984. An article published by the Population Crisis Committee, instead of condemning the program, states: "For a coercive program to work, a hugely expanded commitment of administrative and financial resources will be necessary.

The world will be watching India's policy closely to see if, and how, state governments follow up their new legislation with bigger budgets and more effective action." See Kaval Gulhati, "Compulsory Sterilization: The Change in India's Population Policy," *Science*, vol. 195 (25 March 1977), pp. 1300–05.

23. "In India, Birth Control Focus Shifts to Women," *New York Times*, 7 March 1982.

24. Basu, "Family Planning and the Emergency."

25. Ravindran, "Women and the Politics of Population."

26. "A Family Planning Story," *Economic and Political Weekly*, vol. 20, no. 40 (5 October 1985), p. 1668.

27. Ravindran, "Women and the Politics of Population."

28. Government of India, Planning Commission, *Fifth Five Year Plan, 1992–97*, vol. II, New Delhi, p. 337.

29. For the effect on health services, see Ravindran, "Women and the Politics of Population."

30. *Population Reports*, Series C, no. 10.

31. See Petchesky, "'Reproductive Choice' in the Contemporary United States."

32. Quoted in Rosalind P. Petchesky, "Reproduction, Ethics, and Public Policy: The Federal Sterilization Regulations," *Hastings Center Report* (October 1979).

33. Quoted in ibid.

34. Ibid. These regulations, however, have not been strictly enforced, and groups such as the Committee for Abortion Rights and Against Sterilization Abuse (CARASA) and the National Women's Health Network are now working to ensure that they meet with compliance.

35. General information on quinacrine from Fawn Vrazo, "Sterilization Method Raises Hopes, Fears," *Philadelphia Inquirer*, 2 December 1993; Judy Norsigian of the Boston Women's Health Book Collective; "Controversy over Quinacrine Sterilization Pellet," *Political Environments*, no. 1 (Spring 1994); and AVSC, "AVSC Technical Statement: Quinacrine Pellets for Nonsurgical Female Sterilization" (New York: September 1993).

36. Do Trong Hieu et al., "31,781 Cases of Non-surgical Female Sterilization with Quinacrine Pellets in Vietnam," *Lancet*, vol. 342 (24 July 1993). AVSC critique referenced above.

37. Cited in reply from Vietnam Insight to Southeast Asia Discussion List, "Women Subjected to Sterilization against Will," electronic mail, 3 September 1993.

38. AVSC, "AVSC Technical Statement," p. 7.

39. E. Kessel, J. Zipper, D.T. Hieu, B. Mullick, and S.D. Mumford, "Quinacrine Pellet Method of Non-surgical Female Sterilization," Proceedings of VIIIth World Congress on Human Reproduction and IVth World Congress on Fallopian Tube in Health and Disease, Bali, Indonesia, April 1993, to be published in *Advances in Human Reproduction* (page proofs).

40. See Congress of the United States, Office of Technology Assessment, *World Population and Fertility Planning Technologies* (Washington: U.S. Government Printing Office, February 1982), p. 89; and Malcolm Potts, Peter Diggory, and John Peel, *Abortion* (Cambridge: Cambridge University Press, 1977), p. 211.

41. Barbara Seaman and Gideon Seaman, *Women and the Crisis in Sex Hormones* (New York: Bantam Books, 1978).

42. K. Kaufmann, "Abortion, a Woman's Matter: An Explanation of Who Controls Abortion and How and Why They Do It," in Rita Arditti et al., eds., *Test-Tube Women: What Future for Motherhood* (London: Pandora Press, 1984).

43. For a discussion of the basic values underlying the abortion debate, see Kristin Luker, *Abortion and the Politics of Motherhood* (Berkeley: University of California Press, 1984).

44. Ravindra Rukmini Pandharinath, "Fighting Female Foeticide: A Long Way to Go," *The Lawyers* (India) (August 1991). Also see S.H. Venkatramani, "Born to Die," *India Today* (15 June 1986); Viola Roggencamp, "Abortion of a Special Kind: Male Sex Selection in India," in Arditti et al., eds., *Test-Tube Women*; and Radhika Balakrishnan, "The Social Context of Sex Selection and the Politics of Abortion in India," in Gita Sen and Rachel C. Snow, eds., *Power and Decision: The Social Control of Reproduction* (Cambridge: Harvard University Press, 1994).

45. Government of India, *Census of India 1991*, New Delhi. On discrimination against girls, see Malini Karkal, "Invisibility of the Girl Child in India," *The Indian Journal of Social Work*, vol. 52, no. 1 (January 1991).

46. R. Venkatachalam and Viji Srinivasan, *Female Infanticide* (New Delhi: Har-Anand Publications, 1993), p. 55.

47. Marsha Saxton, "Born and Unborn: The Implications of Reproductive Technologies for People with Disabilities," in Arditti et al., eds., *Test-Tube Women*, p. 306. See also Anne Finger, "Claiming All of Our Bodies: Reproductive Rights and Disability," in same volume; Gena Corea, *The Mother Machine* (New York: Harper and Row, 1985); and Barbara Katz Rothman, *The Tentative Pregnancy* (New York: Viking Press, 1986).

Large Numbers of Natives Were Sterilized by Province

Brian Savage

How many Native people were sterilized over the years as part of the province's systematic long-term program of forced genetic—and racial—purification established by the Alberta Eugenics Board?

The answer so far is not known but University of Lethbridge professor Tony Hall suggests thousands and cites a text called *Our Own Master Race*, written by Professor Angus McLaren, who wrote, "In the last years of the Board's activities, Indians and Métis, who represented only 2.5 percent of Alberta's population, accounted for over 25 percent of those sterilized."

The province is now mired in compensation and damage claims from those survivors and could well face lawsuits by those who feel the offered compensation figures are not enough.

Hall is surprised that there has not been a bigger outcry from Alberta Natives over what he calls "eugenicsgate."

"We're seeing an era here where the Assembly of First Nations is basically playing most of its cards behind closed doors, a play by the rules ethos, a Liberal party insider ethos.

"I think there are a lot of issues that are important and central to Indian country that aren't being aired in public because the national leadership is not of the activist school."

Hall feels the numbers of Alberta Natives may be much higher than the published figures suggest.

"I suspect that the statistics from the Alberta Eugenics Board are part of a much larger phenomena in Indian country."

Hall says similar accounts have been uncovered in the U.S. and such programs may actually extend beyond the border of Alberta. He feels that the more publicity such covert practices receive in the media the better it may be to bring forward those whose voices have not been heard so far.

Stories told to Hall about two large hospitals in Edmonton where large numbers of Native patients were sent, and where "experiments" may have taken place may have a basis in fact but still need public corroboration.

"We know for instance that educators had their own approach to assimilation in the fifties and sixties through the boarding schools and the legislatures had a similar kind of preoccupation that came to fruition in the White Paper, that was going to eliminate all the legal infrastructure of Indian identity and status. It doesn't seem surprising to expect that there was a similar kind of philosophy that took root here and there in the medical community," says the university lecturer.

"We know of the Alberta government's role in passing the Eugenics Act but there hasn't been very much focus on the role of the College of Surgeons and Physicians, in other words the professional body overseeing this work.

"There doesn't seem to be a lot of soul-searching or grappling with the idea of how the professional authorities overseeing this allowed it to happen."

Though condemned today, eugenics, the deliberate genetic manipulation of a population, was once widely hailed as a scientific breakthrough.

Says Hall, "Eugenics was not a preoccupation of the right. Tommy Douglas was a proponent of it, so was Nellie McClung. You can't pin this on one school or another.

"But after World War II and the big eugenics experiment in Germany most jurisdictions dropped their flirtation with eugenics, like Scandinavia.

"Alberta really sticks out on the continent as an area where it continued, and if you look at this phenomena it started as an approach to racial purification, by the time it ends it really is sort of ethnically based."

That transformation from a questionable, discredited scientific experimental exercise into legislated practice is what disturbs Hall.

"What is it about Alberta?" he asks. "It's not only about Indian politicians not pressing questions but it's about the society in general. Why is there so little curiosity into something so deeply a part of the social, political and intellectual culture of this province?

"You can see (Premier) Klein playing on the idea that because this supposedly happened a long time ago, and is not going on now, it has nothing to do with contemporary Alberta."

Hall wonders how such thinking can be accepted by Alberta Natives.

The compensation package announced by Alberta Justice Minister Jon Havelock stands at $48 million for 500 claimants but other victims are seeking legal redress through lawyers for amounts well above the proposed $150,000.

The government has also been criticized for the creation of a special panel to review the payments. Pam Barret, leader of the New Democrats, called the creation of the panel as a "sneaky" and "cynical" effort to get victims to settle out of court while lawyer Jon Faulds, representing a number of claimants suing the government, condemned the Klein government in the *Edmonton Journal* for allowing victims to appear at hearings regarding compensation without legal guidance.

Originally, the government had tried to pass Bill 26, which would have curtailed any legal action against the government over compensation. After a firestorm of public criticism the Klein government withdrew the bill. That bill called for minimum compensation payments of $5000 to each victim.

Note to readers: In 1995 Leilani Muir successfully sued the Province of Alberta for wrongful sterilization. Since then, over 700 victims of the Alberta Sterilization Act have sued the province.

Source: Brian Savage, "Large Numbers of Natives Were Sterilized," *Alberta Native News* (June 1988).

Chapter 50

A Primer on Reproductive Justice and Social Change

What Is Reproductive Justice?
Loretta Ross

> *Loretta Ross is a founder and the national coordinator of the SisterSong Women of Color Reproductive Health Collective. Her areas of expertise are reproductive rights, human rights, women's issues, diversity issues, hate groups, and bias crimes.*

Reproductive Justice is the complete physical, mental, spiritual, political, social, and economic well-being of women and girls, based on the full achievement and protection of women's human rights. This definition, as outlined by Asian Communities for Reproductive Justice (ACRJ), offers a new perspective on reproductive issues advocacy, pointing out that for Indigenous women and women of color, it is important to fight equally for (1) the right to have a child; (2) the right not to have a child; and (3) the right to parent the children we have, as well as to control our birthing options, such as midwifery. We also fight for the necessary enabling conditions to realize these rights. [...]

The Reproductive Justice framework analyzes how the ability of any woman to determine her own reproductive destiny is linked directly to the conditions in her community—and these conditions are not just a matter of individual choice and access. Reproductive Justice addresses the social reality of inequality, specifically, the inequality of opportunities that we have to control our reproductive destiny. Moving beyond a demand for privacy and respect for individual decision making to include the social supports necessary for our individual decisions to be optimally realized, this framework also includes obligations from our government for protecting women's human rights. Our options for making choices have to be safe, affordable, and accessible, three minimal cornerstones of government support for all individual life decisions.

One of the key problems addressed by Reproductive Justice is the isolation of abortion from other social justice issues that concern communities of color: issues of economic justice, the environment, immigrants' rights, disability rights, discrimination based on race and sexual orientation, and a host of other community-centered concerns. These issues directly affect an individual woman's decision-making process. By shifting the focus to reproductive oppression—the control and exploitation of women, girls, and individuals through our bodies, sexuality, labor, and reproduction—rather than a narrow focus on protecting the legal right to abortion, SisterSong Women of Color Reproductive Health Collective is developing a more inclusive vision of how to build a new movement.

Because reproductive oppression affects women's lives in multiple ways, a multi-pronged approach is needed to fight this exploitation and advance the well-being of women and girls. There are three main frameworks for fighting reproductive oppression defined by ACRJ:

1. Reproductive Health, which deals with service delivery
2. Reproductive Rights, which addresses legal issues, and
3. Reproductive Justice, which focuses on movement building.

Although these frameworks are distinct in their approaches, they work together to provide a comprehensive solution. Ultimately, as in any movement, all three components—service, advocacy, and organizing—are crucial.

*****

Reproductive Justice focuses on organizing women, girls, and their communities to challenge structural power inequalities in a comprehensive and transformative process of empowerment. [...]

[...] We have to address directly the inequitable distribution of power and resources within the movement, holding our allies and ourselves responsible for constructing principled, collaborative relationships that end the exploitation and competition within our movement. We also have to build the social, political, and economic power of low-income women, Indigenous women, women of color, and their communities so that they are full participating partners in building this new movement. This requires integrating grassroots issues and constituencies that are multi-racial, multi-generational, and multi-class into the national policy arena, as well as into the organizations that represent the movement.

SisterSong is building a network of allied social justice and human rights organizations that integrate the reproductive justice analysis into their work. We are using strategies of self-help and empowerment so that women who receive our services understand they are vital emerging leaders in determining the scope and direction of the Reproductive Justice and social justice movements.

Resources

In order to find out more about Reproductive Justice, please visit the following websites:

- www.sistersong.net
- www.forwardtogether.org

Conditions of Reproductive Justice
Rickie Solinger

Rickie Solinger is a well-known independent scholar and curator. She is the author of numerous books and articles about reproductive, welfare, and prison politics, including the award-winning Wake Up Little Susie: Single Pregnancy and Race before Roe v. Wade *and* Beggars and Choosers: How the Politics of Choice Shapes Abortion,

Adoption, and Welfare in the United States. *She curates travelling art exhibits associated with the themes of her books, which seek to engage viewers and challenge widely held stereotypes and misconceptions.*

Reproductive Justice Recognizes Women's Right to Reproduce as a Foundational Human Right

The right to be recognized as a legitimate reproducer regardless of race, religion, sexual orientation, economic status, age, immigrant status, citizenship status, ability/disability status, and status as an incarcerated woman encompasses the following:

Women's right to manage their reproductive capacity

1. The right to decide whether or not to become a mother and when
2. The right to primary culturally competent preventive health care
3. The right to accurate information about sexuality and reproduction
4. The right to accurate contraceptive information
5. The right and access to safe, respectful, and affordable contraceptive materials and services
6. The right to abortion and access to full information about safe, respectful, affordable abortion services
7. The right to and equal access to the benefits of and information about the potential risks of reproductive technology

Women's right to adequate information, resources, services, and personal safety while pregnant

1. The right and access to safe, respectful, and affordable medical care during and after pregnancy, including treatment for HIV/AIDS, drug and alcohol addiction, and other chronic conditions, including the right to seek medical care during pregnancy without fear of criminal prosecution or medical interventions against the pregnant woman's will
2. The right of incarcerated women to safe and respectful care during and after pregnancy, including the right to give birth in a safe, respectful, medically appropriate environment
3. The right and access to economic security, including the right to earn a living wage
4. The right to physical safety, including the right to adequate housing and structural protections against rape and sexual violence
5. The right to practise religion or not, freely and safely, so that authorities cannot coerce women to undergo medical interventions that conflict with their religious convictions
6. The right to be pregnant in an environmentally safe context
7. The right to decide among birthing options and access to those services

A woman's right to be the parent of her child

1. The right to economic resources sufficient to be a parent, including the right to earn a living wage

2. The right to education and training in preparation for earning a living wage
3. The right to decide whether or not to be the parent of the child one gives birth to
4. The right to parent in a physically and environmentally safe context
5. The right to leave from work to care for newborns or others in need of care
6. The right to affordable, high-quality child care

10 Reasons to Rethink Overpopulation
Population and Development Program at Hampshire College

The Population and Development Program (PopDev) is a progressive research and advocacy think tank that works with grassroots environmental justice, reproductive freedom, and peace organizations to build a space where these social movements can come together to promote positive change. PopDev creates activist tools, publications, and educational resources for organizers, students, policy-makers, and journalists.

A central requirement for reproductive justice is not only for women to have the right not to have children, but to also exercise the right to have children. Women have been denied this right through population control programs that care more about reducing birth rates than empowering women to have control over their reproductive health and rights. The ideology that informed the programs has not gone away, and below are 10 reasons why rethinking overpopulation is vital to creating the global understanding and solidarity needed to advance women's reproductive and sexual rights.

1. The population "explosion" is over. Although world population is still growing and is expected to reach 9 billion by the year 2050, the era of rapid growth is over. With increasing education, urbanization, and women's work outside the home, birth rates have fallen in almost every part of the world and now average 2.7 births per woman.
2. The focus on population masks the complex causes of poverty and inequality. A narrow focus on human numbers obscures the way different economic and political systems operate to perpetuate poverty and inequality. It places the blame on the people with the least amount of resources and power rather than on corrupt governments and rich elites.
3. Hunger is not the result of "too many mouths" to feed. Global food production has consistently outpaced population growth. People go hungry because they do not have the land on which to grow food or the money with which to buy it.
4. Population growth is not the driving force behind environmental degradation. Blaming environmental degradation on overpopulation lets the real culprits off the hook. The richest fifth of the world's people consume 66 times as many resources as the poorest fifth. The U.S., with a low fertility rate, is the largest emitter of greenhouse gases responsible for global warming.
5. Population pressure is not a root cause of political insecurity and conflict. Especially since 9/11, conflict in the Middle East has been linked to a "youth bulge" of too many young men whose numbers supposedly make them prone to violence. Blaming population pressure for instability takes the onus off powerful actors and political choices.
6. Population control targets women's fertility and restricts reproductive rights. All women should have access to high-quality, voluntary reproductive health services, including safe

birth control and abortion. In contrast, population control programs try to drive down birth rates through coercive social policies and the aggressive promotion of sterilization or long-acting contraceptives that can threaten women's health.

7. Population control programs have a negative effect on basic health care. Under pressure from international population agencies, many poor countries made population control a higher priority than primary health care from the 1970s on. Reducing fertility was considered more important than preventing and treating debilitating diseases like malaria, improving maternal and child health, and addressing malnutrition.

8. Population alarmism encourages apocalyptic thinking that legitimizes human rights abuses. Dire predictions of population-induced mass famine and environmental collapse have long been popular in the U.S. Population funding appeals still play on such fears even though they have not been borne out in reality. This sense of emergency leads to an elitist moral relativism, in which "we" know best and "our" rights are more worthy than "theirs."

9. Threatening images of overpopulation reinforce racial and ethnic stereotypes and scapegoat immigrants and other vulnerable communities. Negative media images of starving African babies, poor, pregnant women of color, and hordes of dangerous Third World men drive home the message that "those people" outnumber "us." Fear of overpopulation in the Third World often translates into fear of increasing immigration to the West, and thereby people of color becoming the majority.

10. Conventional views of overpopulation stand in the way of greater global understanding and solidarity. Fears of overpopulation are deeply divisive and harmful. In order to protect and advance reproductive rights in a hostile climate, we urgently need to work together across borders of gender, race, class, and nationality. Rethinking population helps open the way.

Supplement 31

Reproductive Rights around the World

Contraception

Unmet need, 2007

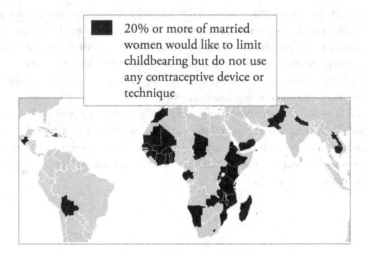

20% or more of married women would like to limit childbearing but do not use any contraceptive device or technique

Types of contraception

Proportion of married or "in union" women worldwide using each method, late 1990s or latest available data

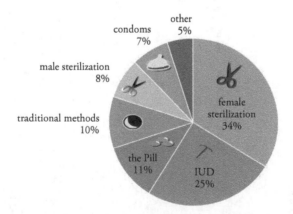

other 5%

condoms 7%

male sterilization 8%

traditional methods 10%

female sterilization 34%

the Pill 11%

IUD 25%

Abortion

Unsafe abortions

Estimated percentages that are unsafe within each region, 2003

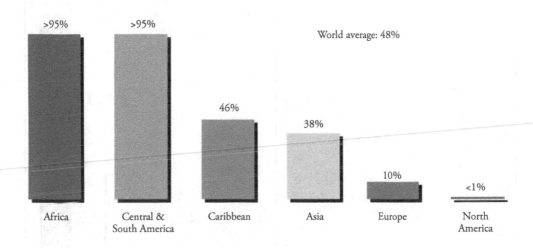

Deaths from unsafe abortions

Percentage of total deaths by region, 2003

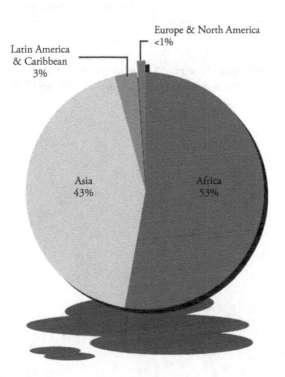

Maternal Mortality

Race and mother-death in the U.S.

Maternal deaths per 100,000 births, 2003

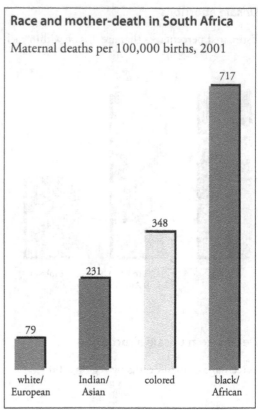

Race and mother-death in South Africa

Maternal deaths per 100,000 births, 2001

Source: Excerpted from Joni Seager, "Plate no. 10 (Contraception)," "Plate no. 11 (Abortion)," and "Plate no. 12 (Maternal Mortality)," *The Penguin Atlas of Women in the World,* 4th ed. (New York: Penguin Books, 2009), 36, 39, 41.

Chapter 51

The Ultimate Rape Victim

Jane Doe

The woman known as Jane Doe is an internationally recognized anti-rape writer, lecturer, and arts and culture worker. She successfully sued the Toronto Police for negligence and gender discrimination in the investigation of her rape, and subsequently changed Canadian law. In her acclaimed book, The Story of Jane Doe: A Book about Rape, *she positions sexual assault within the context of equity issues and integrates issues of race, immigration, colonialism, queer-phobia, and sex work into her analysis. The Jane Doe case is widely cited in Canadian law textbooks and studied in law schools internationally.*

I don't really know how to be a raped woman. I didn't in 1986 and I don't today. I just have never completely figured it out. Being a raped woman has come to define me in some ways, but I struggle still to understand and define it personally, as opposed to the stereotypes. But I own those too. Trauma and despair have been mine. Depression and pain have marked me. Yet there is more. And less.

A raped woman is framed socially and within the law as something broken. Neither Madonna nor whore, but somewhere in between. The carrier of bad luck. There is a general but grudging acceptance that it isn't really her fault, but if she had done something else, gone in another direction, not had that drink or worn that dress or smiled that way, it might never have happened. And thank God it wasn't me or anyone I love. If it had to happen to someone, thank-you-God it was her.

Raped women make other people uncomfortable. Try talking about your rape with friends, at a dinner party or with family. The subject jump-starts every socialized and biological instinct to protect, to seek revenge, to contain, to minimize or to deny that the human psyche stores. The nature of these responses requires the woman to carefully select, when, to whom and how she will recount her experience. Or to decide if she should or can recount it at all. Ever.

Raped women are fallen women. Pushed really, but the shame is on them. A stain like original sin, not of their making but never to be removed or forgotten. Raped women cannot display their rage or joy or sexuality. They cannot be glamorous or successful or funny. They certainly cannot be agents of social and political change.

There are many reasons for this present and historical construction of the woman who has been raped. They are as intricate as political systems, as revered as sacraments.

*****

I have never allowed anyone to refer to me as a "rape victim." Certainly for the time that buddy held a knife to my throat I was his victim and I cannot deny that. But every time that term is used to define me, I feel I am returned to that moment, that night of terror and helplessness. Nor am I fond of the label "survivor." Like everyone else, I was already surviving the normal pain and hardships of life before I was raped, thank you very much. "Okay. So what do we call you?" you ask. Call me a woman. Call me a woman who has been raped. Call me a woman who has been raped by a man.

Rape victims are supposed to be helpless. We require assistance and must play a passive role while the good men, the police, lawyers and judges, punish the one, isolated bad man who committed the crime. Mass media reflect on and report their version of the raped or beaten woman as victim. Rape victims are othered, viewed as less than normal, unraped people. The term, its use and purpose, is not particular to the legal system and its players or the media. It is commonly used by members of the medical and helping professions as well, and by feminists.

A more appropriate language to describe these crimes of violence was developed by feminists during the seventies and eighties but has been all but forgotten. Look at terms like "wife assault," "partner assault," "domestic violence" and "family abuse." Statistics overwhelmingly support the fact that these crimes are committed by men against women and children. And yet the language we use is gender-neutral. Listening to it, one could logically assume that the wife or partner had assaulted herself, that the children of the family were fighting with or abusing each other and that the violence referred to was homegrown as opposed to imported.

Not so long ago, women working in rape crisis centres and shelters developed language that identified the nature and perpetrator of the crime. Meaning men. Rape is about men. "Male violence" and "violence against women" were the terms we used. After a few years of this, and as we began to work with legal, social and government systems in the hope of effecting change, after we accepted their money to pay our wages and signed on the dotted line of institutional bureaucracy, we were requested to alter our language, to cut back on the perceived "rhetoric" so as not to alienate or hurt the feelings of the men who were sensitive to our issues (and signed our cheques). The long-term effect has been the un-gendering of sexual assault. But what is its cause? What are its other components? How does it end? Who benefits? Why do men rape?

If rape hadn't existed by now, we would have invented it. The rape of women has immense economic, social and legal advantages that are seldom articulated. Put plainly, rape works. It is a tool of sexism, and like racism, it exists because it "works." Stay with me, don't go away, this gets interesting. As a white woman who is anti-racist, I work hard to understand the causes and effects of racism. I understand that I benefit socially and economically from racism, especially the systemic, institutionalized, polite form that Canada has perfected.

As a white woman, I am more employable, better paid and less fetishized than Native women or women of colour. My menfolk are not incarcerated or stopped by police at the same rate. My children are not taunted, bullied or subjected to discriminatory treatment based solely on their skin colour. I can move a little more freely, hold my head a little higher, because I am not a visible container for racial intolerance. In these ways I enjoy privilege based on my racial origin. This acknowledgement does not by itself make me a racist. It helps me to understand racism and how it works.

Similarly, men benefit in systemic and obvious ways from a society that is inherently sexist. Men earn more than women, hold more positions of power, are not responsible for the unpaid work of mothering, walk freely and are free to walk alone. They need not worry about unwanted pregnancies, body image, aging and financial security with anywhere near the same intensity as women. They do not consciously fear the stranger rapist or feel compelled to monitor the actions of strange women around them. They are not taught at a very early age that there is a damned good chance they will experience a form of male violence staved off only by their lifelong vigilance and the curtailing of certain actions, pleasures and freedoms they might otherwise enjoy.[1]

In Canada, the government statistics are that one in four men would rape if given the opportunity. This is unacceptable, frightening, outrageously high. But let's flip that stat for a moment and look at the inverse proposition: three out of four men would not rape. Indeed there are many more good men than bad. Where are they? What are they doing to address the rapes of their mothers, daughters, sisters and wives? How do I differentiate them from the bad guys? Sure, they're against rape, but do they understand the ways in which it maintains their privileged status as males? If rape is an extreme tool of sexism used to maintain the male status quo, doesn't it work for all men?

In lectures I have given, this is where good men redden, their brows furrow and they start to disengage. They don't understand and they ask what they can do, what they should do, but mostly they want to go home. At another time—and appropriately so—I might have said, "Read a book. Don't expect me to take responsibility for your consciousness-raising." But this is what I say here: It's hard to be a man. I shouldn't like to try it.

Men are still socialized from a very young age that to be emotional, delicate or tender is to be a girl, and that that is the worst they can be. They must not cry or play with nurture-based toys or wear pastels. They are overwhelmed with male images that drive cars, leave the house for the majority of the day, and return only to mete out discipline and to enjoy the labour of the more home-based female parent. Traditional family values do not require that men prepare food, clean, organize, schedule or provide health care at the same level as women or at all. Their leisure pursuits are sports or technology-based, their literacy level is lower than girls', their demonstrative signs of affection limited.

Our baby boys, whom we love and cherish and who are born to us free from malice or ill will, are conditioned to understand human sexuality as singular to their individual wants and needs, to translate "bitch" and "ho" as labels of both affection and contempt, to mistrust anything that "bleeds for five days every month and doesn't die," and to appreciate "gay," "faggot" and "queer" as variations of the greatest, most final insult of all.

A good friend of mine, a man who is sweet, smart and pro-feminist, has pointed out in more than one conversation about the meaning of life that his instinct, his motivation, is to follow his dick. To be true to it. I have challenged him on this, suggested that perhaps these are not quite the words he is reaching for when he discusses his life. But he stands firm, and I retreat, fearful that he really means what I think he means. Fearful that I really do—or don't—understand men and the cultural divide that distances them from me.

Every few decades and recently so, the tired sociological saw that men are biologically predetermined to rape is dressed up and trotted out to explain the eternal and rising incidence of the crime.[2] Women are cautioned to govern themselves accordingly given that the boys simply can't help it. The books, articles, columns that tooth the saw are well received and become the subject of circular logic and debate. What I cannot understand, am fascinated by, is that men themselves do not rebel against such a limited definition of their ethos and are not insulted by their group equation to molluscs and amphibian life.

Good men don't do it. Our men don't do it. What to make of the fact that 75 to 80 per cent of reported rapes are committed by men known to the women involved. The woman has no problem making an identification. The lighting is fine. She can provide you with her rapist's address and any other identifying information you could imagine. Some you could not. There is no need for a profile, criminal, geographic or artistic. Computer experts, criminologists, DNA and forensic scientists are not called in. They will not be part of the investigation into a crime that escalates yearly and has the lowest reporting rate of all violent crimes. That job goes to the uniformed officer who catches the 911 call or takes the report at the station. That officer has received a maximum of five days' training in a workshop called Family Violence, which blends the rape and sexual assault of adult women with similar crimes of violence committed against youth and children. The training is delivered by other police officers. A rape victim may talk about how well her assault was investigated, she might chide (never challenge) or horrify the cadets to attention with her story. The necessity for adequate diversity training to assist these young men in sexual-assault investigation—which cops themselves will tell you is the most murky and difficult crime to investigate—is ignored. Directives to increase the numbers of women and non-white police force applicants have failed or fallen far short of their projected marks.

Instead, increasingly significant portions of police budgets are designated for the purchase, maintenance and upgrading of computer technology to investigate and solve crime. VICAP and VICLAS, the systems used in Canada and the United States, are compatible with European and other international policing instruments. They are effective in dealing with international espionage, corporate and white-collar crimes, and auto, credit card or jewellery theft rings. And that's a good thing. Their efficacy in infiltrating prostitution, sex trade, pornography and child abuse networks is heralded by law enforcement officers. I'm sure they have been helpful in other violent crimes. But if you have not been raped by a stranger or an "anger retaliatory rapist" (who constitute only 25 per cent of the rapist population), your crime will not be compatible with computer technology. These tools and the information they store are based on faulty conclusions about empirical evidence. Which means they can be as racist and as sexist as the agents who design and interpret them. Only now they get to call profiling "science," so it acquires a whole new, if undeserved, credibility.

In the majority of rape cases, consent is the issue. The accused has agreed that there was sexual intercourse but it was, he swears, consensual. If the woman involved has prior activity that registers on the VICLAS system, it is used against her in a court of law. For instance, if the woman involved was raped before or if she did time for a crime she did or did not commit. If in the past she was apprehended by police under the Mental Health Act,[3] if she was hospitalized for postpartum depression or protested against government policies resulting in police apprehension, or if she whored to pay for college or drugs, fled her country of origin because of police abuse or was part of a Native roadblock, it will show up in a VICLAS search. (If you don't believe that this kind of information is collected and stored and available for some to access, take the time to file an Access to Information Act application on yourself. There is probably a file with your name on it.) Next, an "expert" witness will be hired to testify that you are a slut, addict, terrorist, deviant or other form of miscreant, and your rapist is free to rape you again or otherwise complicate your life. Actually, it probably won't even get as far as the expert-witness scenario because the rapist's lawyer can ask questions to elicit the information himself, or he can get it through his own computer search and not even have to pay for expert medical testimony.

One of the things we need if we are to encourage women to report is increased and ongoing training and education on rape and other crimes of violence committed against women by men, delivered by women who are professionals in the area, meaning women who work in shelters and rape crisis centres. This will only happen through police policy and operational changes in law enforcement practices. Changes that will also benefit policing. Changes that women have been suggesting globally. For decades.

Women who work in anti-violence, who write about it and educate others and have first hand experience of it, are the experts in the field of rape—not some Eliot Ness clone or computer nerd with a PhD. Hire us. And by the way, we will expect to be paid for our work.[4] The escalating focus on "stranger danger" by police through the media and with the assistance of so-called victim's rights groups has worked to maintain a climate of fear that ensures a large degree of control over how and where women live. Current warnings issued by police to alert communities of a serial rapist are fear-based and hysterical in language and nature. Instead of factual warnings that give us information about the dangerous men in our midst, they issue "don'ts" directed toward women, the people most at risk: The don'ts include:

> Don't go out alone. Don't go out alone at night. Don't go out alone or at night unless accompanied by someone (male). Don't open the windows. Don't open the doors. Lock the windows and doors. Don't talk to strangers (men). Don't assist strangers (men). Don't take shortcuts. Alternate your daily routine and routes to work or school. Don't take elevators by yourself (or with strange men). Monitor the motions of the men around you. Don't ride the bus alone. Don't get off the bus alone. Leave your lights on. Don't use underground parking. Don't park on the street. Walk in pairs. Walk on the road. Walk down the middle of the road. Carry a cellphone. Don't struggle. Don't resist. Don't fight back. Don't arm yourself. Eat grass.

Hey! We already don't do those things! Tell us something we don't know. Give us adequate information that does not interfere with your investigation. Give us dates, times, locations, any description you might have, and let us work in community to craft solutions and to support you and each other.

And stop using the fear of strange men to deflect the bigger problems of sexual assault, beatings and other inhumane atrocities committed against us by men we know.

A lot of women have told me that they think it would be "worse" to be raped by a stranger than by a man you know. Personally, I think that in the larger sexual-assault lottery, I lucked out by being raped by a stranger. For one thing, I was not assaulted by someone I loved or trusted or otherwise chose to let into my life. I did not have to deal with that level of emotional betrayal. For another, there was never any question of consent or introducing my past sexual history during the rapist's trial. Oh, his lawyer would have done it—in fact, there is even a pamphlet called "Whack the Sexual Assault Complainant at Preliminary Hearing," which advises defence lawyers on how to get women's past sexual history introduced at trial. Defence lawyer Michael Edelson wrote (originally in an article published in a professional journal called *Lawyers Weekly* in May 1988):

> You have to go in there as defence counsel and whack the complainant hard … get all the medical evidence; get the Children's Aid Society records … and you've got to attack with all you've got so that he or she will say, "I'm not coming back."

The fact that I was raped by a stranger who was a serial offender with a history of identical crimes actually worked in my favour in court. It predisposed the police and the courts to believe that I was telling the truth and not making a false allegation. As a result, there was no legal basis to introduce my sexual history. (I did not dream that it or my medical and family histories would become issues in my civil trial twelve years later. In fact, if I had known it would come to that, I probably would not have proceeded.)

It is easier (but not a foregone conclusion) for the courts to establish lack of consent if the rapist is a stranger. The justice system is less likely to think or believe that you agreed to sex and then changed your mind or just made the whole thing up to get attention. It should be relatively safe to assume that if a strange guy has a knife at your throat, the issue of consent is not to be debated.[5]

Mind you, if you change the picture just a bit and make the man with the knife at your throat your husband, boyfriend or date, well maybe he thought you liked it that way because he'd done it before and you didn't call the police that time, or it was just a little fantasy so he's not guilty. Not really. If he doesn't have a weapon but hurts you with his hands or threatens to, drops something in your drink or withholds money or food or shelter unless you succumb, then your consent does become the issue. The only issue that matters. The fact that you had prior sexual relations with him (or others), had been sexually assaulted before, consumed drinks or drugs that night (or ever), the very fact that you knew him can be used against you in a court of law to raise doubt about your consent and to determine that he is not guilty.

And they wonder why more women don't report....

Notes

1. Again, the incidence of male-on-male violence is high and rising. Young men today, especially youth of colour, think twice about walking alone at night. Their mothers certainly worry about it. The subject I am addressing, however, is the rape and sexual assault of adult women by adult men, and how that works as a tool of sexism.
2. *A Natural History of Rape: Biological Basis of Sexual Coercion*, by Randy Thornhill and Craig T. Palmer (2000), is the most recent manifesto of this sort.
3. The Mental Health Act gives police the authority to arrest and incarcerate individuals they deem to be mentally ill who are held (but not charged) until the diagnosis is confirmed. The record of the arrest is permanent.
4. The point of payment for work done by professional women who consult with police departments on rape or wife assault is one of the hottest hot-button issues I have encountered in my work as Jane Doe. Even other women working in the area take issue with it, claiming it will further alienate police. Since 1975 anti-violence workers in Toronto have left their paid work to sit on panels and committees or go to meetings with police without financial reimbursement for wages and time lost. And to no effect. Would consultants on helicopter use and purchase or stun-gun efficacy in crime fighting work for free? Should they? The practice of not paying people for their work results in that work being undervalued or ignored. Not to mention poverty.
5. The film *The Accused*, starring Jodie Foster and based on a true story, is an example of the courts believing that a woman consented to a gang rape by strangers, even though she was sure she did not. We need not go as far as Hollywood to find examples. In Canada see *Regina v. Wald, Hockett and Girt*, Alberta Court of Appeal and *Regina v. Sansregret*, Supreme Court of Canada.

Chapter 52

Factsheet: Violence against Women and Girls

Marika Morris and the Canadian Research Institute for the Advancement of Women (CRIAW)

Marika Morris is the former research coordinator for the Canadian Research Institute for the Advancement of Women (CRIAW) and former lecturer in the School of Canadian Studies at Carleton University. She is now serving as senior policy adviser with Public Safety Canada.

The Canadian Research Institute for the Advancement of Women (CRIAW) provides tools and resources to support researchers and organizations in advancing social justice and equality for all women. CRIAW focuses on generating and promoting urgently needed feminist research, and on making it available for public advocacy and education. Recent projects include Intersectional Feminist Frameworks, which aims to promote inclusiveness in research, and FemNorthNet, which seeks to engage women living in northern communities in research on their experiences and needs due to economic restructuring.

What Is Violence against Women?

Violence can be physical (such as punching, kicking, choking, stabbing, mutilating, disabling, murdering), sexual (such as rape, any unwanted touching or act of a sexual nature, forced prostitution), verbal/psychological (such as threats to harm the children, destruction of favourite clothes or photographs, repeated insults meant to demean and erode self-esteem, forced isolation from friends and relatives, threats of further violence or deportation if the woman attempts to leave), stalking (such as persistent and unwanted attention, following and spying, monitoring of mail or conversations), financial (such as taking away a woman's wages or other income, limiting or forbidding access to the family income), and other forms of control and abuse of power. Violence against women is about the control and coercion of women. It is a significant problem in Canada and around the world, also including female genital mutilation, child marriage, dowry-related murder, honour killings, female infanticide, and trafficking in women. Mass rapes and enslavement of women are also used as an instrument of war and genocide.

- Half of Canadian women have survived at least one incident of sexual or physical violence.[1]
- Over a quarter (29%) of Canadian women have been assaulted by a spouse.[2] Forty-five percent of women assaulted by a male partner suffered physical injury. Injuries

included bruising, cuts, scratches, burns, broken bones, fractures, internal injuries, and miscarriages.[3]

- In Canada, four out of five people murdered by their spouses are women murdered by men.[4] In 1998, 67 women were killed by a current or ex-spouse, boyfriend or ex-boyfriend. That's one to two women per week. In six out of 10 spousal murders, police were already aware that violence characterized the relationship.[5]

- Girl children are targets of abuse within the family more so than are boys. Four out of five victims of family-related sexual assaults (79%) are girls, and over half (55%) of physical assaults of children by family members are against girls.[6] In 1997, fathers accounted for 97% of sexual assaults and 71% of physical assaults of children by parents.[7]

- Only 10% of sexual assaults on women are reported to the police.[8] Extrapolating from these data, there are 509,860 reported and unreported sexual assaults in Canada per year.[9] That's 1,397 per day; which means that every minute of every day, a woman or child in Canada is being sexually assaulted. Very often, sexual assaults are repeated on the same woman or child by the same offender.

- Ninety-eight percent of sex offenders are men and 82% of the survivors of these assaults are girls and women.[10]

- Forty-three percent of women in one study reported at least one incident of unwanted sexual touching, forced or attempted forced sexual intercourse, or being forced to perform other acts of a sexual nature before the age of 16.[11] The majority of these cases were at the level of unwanted sexual touching, usually repeated incidents by the same offender.

- Sexual assaults often occur in contexts in which the abuser is in a position of trust in relation to the person assaulted, such as a husband, father, other relative, doctor, coach, religious adviser, teacher, friend, employer, or date.

- A minimum of 1 million Canadian children have witnessed violence against their mothers by their fathers or father figures. In 52% of these cases, the mother feared for her life, and in 61%, the mother sustained physical injuries.[12] Children who witness violence against their mothers often exhibit signs of post-traumatic stress disorder, and their social skills and school achievement are adversely affected.[13]

- Fear of violence also limits many women's lives. Forty-two percent of women, compared with 10% of men, feel "totally unsafe" walking in their own neighbourhood after dark, which in Canadian winters can begin at 3:30 p.m., even earlier in the North. Over a third (37%) of women, compared with one in 10 men, are worried about being in their own homes alone in the evening or night.[14]

- In Canada, a man who beats and rapes his female partner can stay in his own home while the woman and children must sometimes move from shelter to shelter, disrupting their lives, work, or schooling. In a 1993 survey, 295,000 abused Canadian women had no access to counselling or housing services.[15]

Who Is Most Likely to Be Abused?

All women are vulnerable to violence, but some are more vulnerable than others.

- Around the world, as many as one woman in every four is physically or sexually abused during pregnancy, usually by her partner.[16] In Canada, 21% of women abused by a partner were assaulted during pregnancy, and 40% reported that the abuse began during pregnancy.[17] Abuse often begins or worsens during pregnancy, when a woman is most vulnerable and most dependent on her partner's support.[18]

- Young women and female children are highly vulnerable to sexual assault. In 1997, people under 18 were 24% of the population, but represented 60% of all sexual assault victims and one fifth (19%) of physical assault victims.[19] Of sexual offences against kids under 12, the ages at which boys are most likely to be sexually assaulted, girl victims outnumber boys by two to one.[20] Women under 25 are also at greatest risk of being killed by their male partners.[21]

- A DisAbled Women's Network survey found that 40% of women with disabilities have been raped, abused, or assaulted. More than half (53%) of women who had been disabled from birth or early childhood had been abused.[22] Women with disabilities may also be physically, sexually, or financially abused by people who aid in their care. Less than two-thirds of shelters for abused women report being accessible to women with disabilities.[23] However, women with disabilities report that only one in 10 who sought help from women's shelters were accommodated.[24]

- Research repeatedly shows that a vast majority of Aboriginal women have been assaulted, and that the chance of an Aboriginal child growing up without a single first-hand experience of abuse or alcoholism is tiny. Violence may have begun while at residential school or by parents whose souls were damaged by the residential school experience of rape, physical abuse, and cultural genocide. Violence continues into adulthood, ranging from 48% to up to 90% of Aboriginal women being assaulted at the hands of their partners, depending on the community in which they live. Aboriginal women also experience racially motivated attacks and are harassed on the streets by the public and police more so than non-Aboriginal women.[25]

- Violence against women crosses socio-economic lines.[26] However, low-income women may be more often trapped in abusive relationships because of a lack of financial resources for housing and income support. For Inuit women and others, "The virtual absence of alternative housing arrangements often forces women and children to stay in dangerous and potentially deadly situations."[27]

- In addition to racist violence, women who are of minority racial, ethnocultural, or linguistic groups also suffer violence at the hands of their intimate partners. However, their access to the justice system and to services is not the same. Only 57% of Canadian shelters offered services that were sensitive to cultural differences.[28] Women who have difficulty speaking the official language where they live face enormous barriers in accessing services and dealing with the justice system. When services and the justice system fail, women find it even more difficult to escape abuse.

- Women working in certain occupations are also more vulnerable to violence. For example, foreign domestic workers work for low wages, isolated in private homes, and are vulnerable to threats of deportation if they complain of physical or sexual abuse. They are often unaware of their legal rights or of services. Other occupations in which women are very vulnerable to workplace violence are health care workers and women in the military. All women in subordinate positions are vulnerable to sexual harassment in the workplace, and women in male-dominated occupations may be subject to workplaces that are hostile toward women. Women working in the sex trade are at enormous risk of sexual and physical assault, ongoing abuse, and murder. They receive the least amount of support due to the stigma surrounding prostitution, and the belief that prostitution is a "lifestyle" decision. This ignores the fact that almost all young women who end up in the sex trade are fleeing abusive homes, and that economic options for young women on their own are minimal.[29]

> **BOX 52.1: Violence in Lesbian Relationships**
>
> A small study found that 20% of lesbians had experienced some form of emotional/psycho-logical or physical violence in a relationship with a woman. Eleven percent had experienced physical violence, and 2% had been sexually assaulted in the relationship. The statistics are much lower than in male–female relationships, but it nevertheless remains an important issue, particularly because lesbians may not feel they can seek help from social services, police, or the courts because of the stigma and discrimination around sexual orientation.[30]

Why Not Talk about Violence against Men, Spousal Violence, or Just Violence?

- Males commit the overwhelming majority of all violent crimes, and usually against women or girls. In 1996, half (48%) of all violent crimes committed in Canada involved a male perpetrator against a female victim. Thirty-nine percent of violent crimes involved males attacking other males, while 7% were female assailants of other females and 6% were girls or women against boys or men.[31]
- To call violence against women "spousal assault" obscures the fact that most of the violence is perpetrated by men against intimate female partners, and as men tend to be physically stronger than women, more women end up in hospital, or dead, as a result of the violence.
- More than half of all reported physical assaults on adult women are by family members, half by their spouses. Only 14% of assaults on men are committed by family members, 8% by their male or female intimate partners.[32] A similar pattern emerges for people under 18: Boys are more likely to get into fights with acquaintances and strangers, while girls are more likely to be physically and sexually assaulted by family members.[33] The fact of being harmed and controlled on a continual basis by someone who is supposed to love you is the deepest betrayal of trust, and carries an enormous long-term psychological impact. It is significantly different in character than other types of assaults such as one-time, isolated conflicts with strangers.
- Any kind of violence is wrong, be it against men, women, or children. The idea is not to paint men as villains, but to try to understand the root causes of violence and how to prevent it. If we are afraid to look at the clear gender relationship in violence, and what it tells us about the issue and potential solutions, we will simply perpetuate the problem for generations to come.

Is Violence Biological in Men? Is There Anything We Can Do about It?

- If violence were a biological imperative in men, all men would be violent, and they are not. Many men are decent, loving, responsible, and respectful people who do not harm women. To understand the problem, we must understand the various factors involved in the socialization of boys. Many boys are goaded into proving their "masculinity" through acts of violence and a lack of compassion. Violent role models for boys, such as wrestlers, boxers, war heroes, action figures, outnumber peaceful, responsible, and caring ones. Weak, insecure men sometimes feel they have to control others, especially women, in order to be a "real man."
- Violence is learned from male role models early in life. Women experiencing violence by male partners are three times as likely to state that their male partners witnessed their own

mothers being beaten by their fathers than are women who experience no violence from their male partners.[34]

- We can see from evaluations of programs for men who batter that it is not simply a question of "anger management." Although the majority of men (53% to 85%) who complete such programs remain physically non-violent for up to two years after treatment, many continue other types of threatening or coercive behaviour toward their partners. The most effective programs don't just deal with anger management but focus on women's equality and non-violent male gender roles.[35]
- In almost half (45%) of wife assault cases in which the police intervened, male violence ceased or decreased following the intervention.[36] Where there are consequences for male violence, violence is reduced.

BOX 52.2: Problems with Measuring Violence Can Lead to an Underestimation of Violence against Women

The controversial findings of Statistics Canada's 1999 General Social Survey (GSS) seem to contradict previous Stats Can surveys on violence. Because it uses the Conflict Tactics Scale or similar survey questions—which measure the number of hits but ignore context such as who started the violence, whether violence was used as an act of aggression or self-defence, who has the power in the relationship, or who ended up dead or in hospital as a result of the violence—it comes to the conclusion that women and men are equally violent in intimate relationships. When you dig deeper into the survey, Statistics Canada admits that men use more serious types of violence, women are assaulted much more often, women suffer greater injury and are five times more likely to need medical attention, more than one third of assaulted women feared for their lives (38%) versus 7% of assaulted men, and the violence has deeper long-term consequences for women than men, including depression, anxiety, lower self-esteem, being fearful for themselves and their children: In fact, 22% of men who say they were assaulted said the violence did not have much impact on them at all, compared with a tiny proportion of women.[37] Even the type of emotional abuse is different: The survey finds men and women equally emotionally abusive, but the only two measures that were actually even for women and men were about jealousy and demanding to know where the other person was. On all other measures (trying to limit contact with family and friends, name-calling, threats to harm someone close to the other person, damaging or destroying property, preventing the other person from having access to the family income) men outscored women.[38] Every time you see a study that says men and women are equally violent, ask questions about the context and effects of the violence. According to Health Canada, the Conflict Tactics Scale and similar measures are not an accurate reflection of what is happening between men and women in the home.[39] They are a tool used by the right to deny that violence against women is a problem.

The GSS measures violence in current relationships and in the past five years, whereas Statistics Canada's more comprehensive 1993 Violence against Women Survey measures violence since age 16. Neither survey includes Canada's North or Aboriginal reserves, where we know that violence is prevalent, nor does it include people who do not speak English or French well, women in transition homes, or those without phones. Statistics Canada admits that the GSS is an underestimation of current violence because people with a violent partner who may be monitoring their phone calls would be afraid to disclose the violence to an unknown interviewer.[40] Interviewer effect is also important: A woman may be less likely to disclose intimate violence to a male interviewer, but this factor does not seem to have been taken into account for the GSS.

Are Women Becoming Just as Violent as Men?

- Some people think violence committed by girls and women is skyrocketing because the media reports "100% increases" in rates of crimes committed by female young offenders. It is important to go beyond media sensationalism. Male youths account for four out of five cases of youth crimes, and the majority of the crimes for both sexes are property offences.[41]
- When you see a story about a percentage increase in female violence, remember that the number is going from very few incidents to few incidents. An increase of one incident to two is an increase of 100%.
- Now that there are a variety of role models for girls, including violent action heroes, it is not surprising that some girls as well as boys may be seeing violence as a way to solve their problems and make them feel powerful.

Why Don't We Have Shelters for Battered Men?

- Shelters for abused women did not come from the government. They began informally with groups of women running a type of "underground network," sheltering abused women in their own homes because they knew women who were being assaulted and who had nowhere to go. Later, women endured ridicule and skepticism when they argued for the need for shelters. Finally, after years of lobbying and documenting abuse, the first shelters were established.
- On just a single day in April 1998, over 6,100 women and children were staying in 422 shelters across Canada that offer refuge from violence in the home. About 48% were women and 52% were the children of these women. About three-quarters of the children were under the age of 10.[42] Staff of shelters are generally very low paid and work many draining, unpaid hours. The rest of the work is done by volunteers.
- If there were a need for shelters for abused men, people concerned would organize them the way women organized for shelters in the 1970s.
- A shelter for battered men opened in Britain, but was closed for lack of use.[43]

BOX 52.3

Governments may talk about equality, but their housing, income, employment, education, criminal justice, immigration, health, home care, and child care policies help keep women trapped in abusive relationships. Governments could become a part of the solution, but at this time, they are actively and lethally perpetuating the problem.

Why Do Some Women Stay in Violent Relationships?

- *Fear:* Women are sometimes murdered or severely assaulted when trying to leave or after having left their violent partner. Between 1974 and 1992, six times as many women were killed by their husbands while separating than while co-residing.[44] A woman may think it's better to be where she can keep an eye on him than be stalked and killed. She may believe the abuser's threats that he will kill her and their children if she leaves, and in some cases, she will be right. Although police forces and the justice system have improved since the early 1980s concerning violence against women, they still provide inadequate protection of women from known abusers. The justice system also provides less protection for some women than others, such as the incident in Winnipeg in which two Métis women, fearing assault from a known abuser who was breaking a restraining order to keep away, were found dead after police ignored their five 911 calls made over a period of eight hours.[45]

- *Lack of resources, no place to go:* In Canada, women earn less money than men for work requiring similar skill levels, and make up the majority of the poor. Many women stay in abusive relationships because they simply have no place else to go in the context of a shortage of affordable housing, lower wages for women, and waiting lists for subsidized child care that impede women from finding paid employment and/or training/education to support herself and her kids.

- *Violence is just a part of life:* A woman may have grown up watching her mother being beaten, and received the message that violence is just a part of relationships.[46] An abuser may use sadomasochistic videos and gravitate toward violent movies and friends, so the woman is surrounded by cultural messages that violence against women is not only okay, but normal and desirable.

- *Love, loyalty:* Abusive men often come across at the beginning as very romantic and charming. Violence is often followed by a "honeymoon period" in which the man is apologetic, buys gifts and/or swears it will never happen again, and that the abuse is due to the tough time he's going through and needs the woman he loves to stick by him. This is the man she fell in love with, had kids with, promised to live with forever "for better or for worse." It is not an easy bond to break.

- *Low self-esteem:* A woman may have been battered and raped for so long that she starts to believe the abuser when he says she is worthless, good for nothing, will never make it on her own, or deserves it. With every incident of physical, sexual, and psychological violence, a little more of her soul is destroyed.

- *Embarrassment/shame:* Some women think they are to blame for the violence, that if they were more capable they would be able to "save" their marriages or help their violent husbands. Leaving the relationship is a shameful admission of failure. Particularly in communities and networks where there is little or no support for abused women, and in which people are told not to "air their dirty laundry" in public, women may want to avoid the stigma that would fall on them and their children.

- *Lack of support:* She may have already spoken to neighbours who didn't want to become involved, clergy or family members who told her to stick with her husband no matter what, police who didn't do anything, a court that gave her abusive partner a suspended sentence, or a psychiatrist or psychologist who blamed the abuse on her.

- *Immigration sponsorship and other ties:* If the woman is dependent on the abusive partner for staying in Canada, or she doesn't speak either official language well, or is dependent on the abuser for personal care for an illness or disability, it becomes almost impossible to leave.

- A cross-cultural study found that most abused women use active strategies to maximize their safety and that of their children. Some resist the abuse and fight back, some flee, others try to keep the peace by capitulating to their partner's demands. What may seem to be a lack of response to abuse may in fact be a strategic assessment of ensuring her own and her children's survival.[47]

> **BOX 52.4**
>
> Women do not lie about sexual assault any more than anyone might lie about having been robbed or other criminal acts committed against them. In fact, one quarter of sexually assaulted women never tell anyone at all about the assault. Reporting sexual assault can be almost as traumatic as the sexual assault itself. Women and girls need to be supported and believed.

Why Don't Women Always Report Sexual Assault?

- Some women and girls don't recognize date or marital rape as sexual assault, a criminal offence.
- Some feel responsible in some way for the assault as a result of believing myths that women who are sexually assaulted "deserve it."
- Some fear not being believed, being ridiculed, being alienated from the group to which they and the offender might belong (family, place of worship, school, etc.), and shame at having been violated—not wanting anyone to know.
- Some fear retribution and further violence by the offender if they tell.
- Many lack faith in an ineffectual and racist police and justice system: In 1997–98, there were 7,629 sexual assault trials in adult criminal courts. Only 1,533 resulted in a prison sentence. Over two-thirds (39%) of convicted sex offenders were given probation as the harshest sentence. A judge recently ruled a repeat sexual offender not guilty of sexual assault partly because his 17-year-old victim, who was wearing a T-shirt and shorts in summer, was not dressed in "bonnet and crinolines" and was not a virgin.[48] Many women simply do not want to deal with the Stone Age attitudes of some police officers and judges, and want to put the assault behind them instead of reliving the abuse during lengthy trials in front of total strangers, particularly because the outcome is likely to be unsatisfactory.

What Consequences Does Violence against Women Have on Women and Society?

On society:

- The physical and sexual abuse of girls and women costs the Canadian economy $4.2 billion each year, factoring into account social services, criminal justice, lost employment days, and health care interventions.[49] Nearly 90% of the financial cost is borne by government—your tax dollars. Your taxes go into cleaning up the mess that abusers leave behind.
- Children who witness violence against their mothers are significantly more likely to develop aggressive behaviour (bullying, fighting), emotional disturbances (depression, continual fear, anxiety), criminal activity (destroying property, theft, and vandalism), and experience negative effects on social and academic development. The majority of inmates in federal prisons with some history of committing violence against family members witnessed violence as children.[50]

Immediate consequences for women:

- *Death:* Worldwide, an estimated 40% to over 70% of homicides of women are committed by intimate partners, often in the context of an abusive relationship.[51] Only a small proportion of men who are murdered are killed by their female partners, and in such cases the women usually are defending themselves or retaliating against abusive men.[52]
- *Injury/permanent disability:* Violence is a major cause of injury to women, ranging from cuts and bruises to permanent disability and death. In Canada 43% of women injured by their partners had to receive medical care, and 50% of those injured had to take time off from work.[53]
- Unwanted pregnancy/abortion
- Sexually transmitted infections, HIV/AIDS
- Emotional trauma

Long-term consequences for women:

- Women who have experienced physical or sexual abuse as kids or adults are at greater risk of health problems, such as injury, chronic pain, gastrointestinal disorders, anxiety, and clinical depression. Violence also undermines health by increasing self-destructive behaviours, such as smoking and substance abuse. The influence of abuse can persist long after the abuse has stopped.[54] Over their lifetimes, survivors of abuse average more surgeries, physician and pharmacy visits, hospital stays, and mental health consultations than other women, even after accounting for other factors affecting health care use, and discounting emergency room visits.[55]
- *Suicide:* Women who have been sexually assaulted and/or battered are significantly more likely than other women to commit suicide.[56]

Political Will

Over the past 20 years, governments have commissioned or funded literally hundreds of studies about violence against women. A high-profile example at the federal level alone is the $10 million travelling commission, the Canadian Panel on Violence against Women, which issued a national action plan with over 100 recommendations in 1993. The women's movement has also been busy with documentation of the problem and the charting of effective solutions, as it is on the front line of mopping up the blood every day. Government has taken no action on the majority of the recommendations in these hundreds of reports, particularly in the areas of economic equality and housing, which are fundamental necessities for women escaping abuse.

What you can do:

- Support organizations that advocate and provide services for abused women.
- Challenge newspapers, radio, or TV stations when they misinform the public about violence against women. Challenge attitudes, practices, and policies that promote the development of violent tendencies in boys, excuse violence in men, or show a lack of respect toward women. *Equality between women and men is key to ending violence against women.*
- Discuss this issue with friends, relatives, neighbours, co-workers, and your local media. Challenge your workplace, school, place of worship, book club, or any group to which

you belong to take three specific steps to reduce violence against women and to help abused women and children. The National Clearinghouse on Family Violence may have discussion resources you can use in Women's Health and Freedom from Violence: Practical Tools. Phone: 1-800-267-1291; website: www.phac-aspc.gc.ca/ncfv-cnivf

• Contact your political representatives and ask them what specific measures they will undertake to reduce/eliminate violence against women. Pay attention to structural policies that keep women trapped in abusive relationships, such as lack of affordable housing, lack of well-paying employment, lack of child care, underfunding of services to help abused women and children, and criminal justice reform. If the representative simply lists past actions, remember that initiatives governments have already taken do not come anywhere close to addressing the magnitude of the problem. Ask for specific commitments to implement particular recommendations of the many studies of the past two decades. Set a target date for action and follow up to see if the representative has kept his or her word.

A revised version of this factsheet is in preparation and will be available in 2012 from CRIAW-ICREF at http://criaw-icref.ca.

Notes

1. Statistics Canada, "The Violence against Women Survey," *The Daily*, November 18, 1993.
2. Statistics Canada, *Family Violence in Canada* (Ottawa: Minister of Industry, 1999) p. 18. The data are from Statistics Canada's 1993 Violence against Women Survey of 12,300 Canadian women aged 18 or over. The survey underestimates the amount of violence against women as it did not cover Canada's northern territories, where violence is prevalent. According to 1997 police reports cited on p. 15 of the same study, "spousal violence" accounts for one in five of all violent offences in the Yukon and Northwest Territories (now the Yukon, NWT, and Nunavut).
3. Statistics Canada, *Family Violence in Canada*, p. 12.
4. Statistics Canada, "Homicide Statistics 1998," *The Daily*, October 7, 1999.
5. Statistics Canada, "Homicide Statistics 1998."
6. Statistics Canada, *Family Violence in Canada*, p. 6.
7. Ibid.
8. Ontario Women's Directorate, "Dispelling the Myths about Sexual Assault." Factsheet posted at www.gov.on.ca/ owd/resources/sexual_assault_dispel_myths/sexassa.htm. Toronto: Queen's Printer for Ontario, 1998.
9. In 1998, 179 police forces in six provinces participating in Statistics Canada's Revised Uniform Crime Reporting Survey reported 25,493 sexual assaults. As the RCMP and other police forces do not participate, the survey covers less than half (48%) of the national volume of reported crime. Therefore, a conservative estimate for a national figure of reported sexual assaults would be 50,986, which represents 10% of 509,986.
10. Statistics Canada, "Sex Offenders," *Juristat* 19(3) March 1999, p. 1. *Juristat* is a publication of Statistics Canada's Canadian Centre for Justice Statistics.
11. Data from the Women's Safety Project, a survey of 420 randomly selected women living in Toronto. Reported in Canadian Panel on Violence against Women, *Changing the Landscape: Ending Violence—Achieving Equality* (Ottawa: Minister of Supply and Services, 1993).

12. Statistics Canada, *Family Violence in Canada*, p. 30.

13. Cathy Trainor, "Canada's Shelters for Abused Women," *Juristat* 19(6) June 1999, p. 7.

14. Statistics Canada, *Women in Canada: A Statistical Report* (Ottawa: Minister of Industry, 1995) p. 115.

15. Trainor, "Canada's Shelters for Abused Women," p. 7.

16. Lori Heise, Mary Ellsberg, and Megan Gottemoeller, "Ending Violence against Women," *Population Reports*, Series L, no. 11. Baltimore: Johns Hopkins University School of Public Health, Population Information Program, December 1999.

17. Statistics Canada, *Family Violence in Canada*.

18. B. Lent, "Obstetrical Issues in Wife Abuse," *Canadian Journal of Obstetrics/Gynaecology & Women's Health Care* 4(5) 1992, pp. 330–33, as cited in Canadian Panel on Violence against Women, *Changing the Landscape*, p. 34.

19. Statistics Canada, *Family Violence in Canada*, p. 27.

20. Statistics Canada, "Sex Offenders," p. 1.

21. Statistics Canada, *Family Violence in Canada*.

22. Jillian Ridington, *Beating the Odds: Violence and Women with Disabilities* (Vancouver: Dis-Abled Women's Network, 1989), pp. 1, 6.

23. Trainor, "Canada's Shelters for Abused Women."

24. Ridington, *Beating the Odds*, pp. 1, 6.

25. Canadian Panel on Violence against Women, *Changing the Landscape*. See chapters prepared by the Aboriginal Circle, pp. 101–190.

26. Statistics Canada, *Family Violence in Canada*, p. 19.

27. Pauktuutit Inuit Women's Association, *Inuit Women: The Housing Crisis and Violence*. (Ottawa: Pauktuutit, c. 1995), p. 1. Prepared for Canada Mortgage and Housing Corporation.

28. Trainor, "Canada's Shelters for Abused Women."

29. Canadian Panel on Violence against Women, *Changing the Landscape*, pp. 41–44.

30. Health Canada, *Abuse in Lesbian Relationships: Information and Resources* (Ottawa: Health Canada, 1998).

31. Derek Janhevich, "Violence Committed by Strangers," *Juristat* 18(9) June 1999, p. 9.

32. Statistics Canada, *Family Violence in Canada*, p. 27.

33. Ibid., p. 28.

34. Karen Rodgers, "Wife Assault: The Findings of a National Survey," *Juristat* 14(9) 1994, pp. 1–21.

35. Heise, Ellsberg, and Gottemoeller, "Ending Violence against Women."

36. Rodgers, "Wife Assault." Although male violence stops or decreases in half the cases where there is police intervention, it is important to note that in 40% of cases there was no change in men's behaviour following intervention, and in 10% of cases, male violence increased. An effective criminal justice response is an important element in dealing with male violence against women, but it cannot be the only response.

37. Statistics Canada, *Family Violence in Canada: A Statistical Profile 2000* (Ottawa: Minister of Industry, 2000), pp. 12, 14, 18.

38. Ibid., p. 17.

39. Health Canada, *Husband Abuse: An Overview of Research and Perspectives* (Ottawa: Health Canada, 1999), pp. 8–11.

40. Statistics Canada, *Family Violence in Canada: 2000*, p. 14.

41. Statistics Canada, "Youth Violent Crime 1998," *The Daily*, Dec. 21, 1999.

42. Statistics Canada, "Shelters for Abused Women," *The Daily*, June 11, 1999.
43. Health Canada, *Husband Abuse*, p. 21.
44. Rebecca Kong, "Criminal Harassment," *Juristat* 16(12) 1996.
45. The Drum: Manitoba's Source for Aboriginal News, retrieved from: http://collection.nlc-bnc.ca/100/201/300/first_perspective/2001/04-18/drum5.html.
46. Those who witness their fathers committing violence against their mothers are significantly more likely to become victims or perpetrators of this kind of violence in adulthood. P. Jaffe, D. Wolfe, and S. Kaye Wilson, *Children of Battered Women* (Newbury Park, CA: Sage, 1990), p. 50.
47. Heise, Ellsberg, and Gottemoeller, "Ending Violence against Women."
48. This decision was overturned by the Supreme Court of Canada in 1999, but the judge in question and others like him are still sitting on the bench presiding over sexual assault cases.
49. L. Greaves, O. Hankivsky, and J. Kingston-Riechters, *Selected Estimates of the Costs of Violence against Women* (London, Ontario: Centre for Research on Violence against Women and Children, 1995).
50. Statistics Canada, *Family Violence in Canada*, p. 31.
51. Heise, Ellsberg, and Gottemoeller, "Ending Violence against Women."
52. P.H. Smith, K.E. Moracco, and J.D. Butts, "Partner Homicide in Context: A Population-Based Perspective," *Homicide Studies* 2(4) 1998, pp. 400–421.
53. Rodgers, "Wife Assault."
54. Heise, Ellsberg, and Gottemoeller, "Ending Violence against Women."
55. Ibid.
56. Ibid.

Chapter 53

Their Spirits Live within Us: Aboriginal Women in Downtown Eastside Vancouver Emerging into Visibility

Dara Culhane

Dara Culhane is an associate professor of anthropology at Simon Fraser University in British Columbia. Her scholarship focuses on historical and contemporary relations between Aboriginal peoples and the Canadian nation-state, the politics of Indigenous women's health, collaborative research methodologies, and urban studies. She has authored important books on these themes and received several awards in recognition of her leadership, scholarship, and activism. Culhane served as deputy director of social and cultural research for the Royal Commission on Aboriginal Peoples.

We are Aboriginal women. Givers of life. We are mothers, sisters, daughters, aunties, and grandmothers. Not just prostitutes and drug addicts. Not welfare cheats. We stand on our mother earth and we demand respect. We are not there to be beaten, abused, murdered, ignored.
— From a flyer distributed at Downtown Eastside Women's Memorial March, February 14, 2001, Vancouver, British Columbia, Canada

Anyone passing through inner-city Vancouver on foot, on a bus, or in a car cannot help but *see*, in a literal sense, the concentration of Aboriginal peoples here. For most urban Canadians, and visitors from elsewhere, this is an unusual and often surprising visual experience on which they feel compelled to remark. Even so, many representations of this and other inner-city neighborhoods in western Canada are characterized by a marked *invisibility* of Aboriginal peoples, and women in particular.[1] This essay describes both the construction of this invisibility in public culture, and an event that symbolizes Aboriginal women's active resistance to these acts of erasure.

Academic, professional, public, and popular discourses deploy a plethora of identifying labels and categorizations that obscure and depoliticize the embodied nature of colonialism that evidences itself in inner-city Vancouver, Canada. The annual Valentine's Day Women's Memorial March gives political expression to a complex process through which Aboriginal women here are struggling to change the language, metaphors, and images through which they come to be (re) known as they emerge into public visibility. [...]

The intersection of Main and Hastings streets—known locally as "Pain and Wastings"—marks the heart of Vancouver's inner-city neighborhood: the Downtown Eastside. Since 1997, when the

City of Vancouver Health Department declared a public health emergency in response to reports that HIV infection rates among residents exceeded those anywhere else in the "developed" world, Downtown Eastside Vancouver has become a focal point in emerging local, national, and international debates about the causes of, and solutions to, widespread practices of intravenous injection of illicit drugs and the spread of HIV/AIDS. Public health and law enforcement authorities, in an effort to respond to these "twin epidemics," have treated the Downtown Eastside as a containment zone, rather than as an enforcement zone: few, if any, arrests are made for simple possession or trafficking of small quantities of illegal drugs, or for soliciting for the purposes of prostitution.[2] An open, publicly visible street market in illicit drugs and commercial sex has mushroomed.

Predictably, national and international media, as well as a surfeit of both well-intentioned and/or brashly self-promoting artists, writers, and researchers, have been drawn as moths to flames to document, analyze, represent, treat, and market the dramatic and photogenic spectacle of social suffering in this neighborhood. [...]

On one day of the year, though, for at least a few hours, the scene at Main and Hastings is dramatically altered. In 1991, Aboriginal and non-Aboriginal women's organizations in inner-city Vancouver declared February 14 a day of remembrance to honor neighborhood women who have been murdered or who have disappeared. In the Downtown Eastside, Valentine's Day has been transformed into an occasion to protest against racism, poverty, and violence against women, and to celebrate resistance, solidarity, and survival. In this struggle, visibility and recognition are inseparable from the goals of material survival: these women are engaged in a struggle to stay alive and to change the material and symbolic conditions of existence for women who come after them.

Media spectacles of sex, drugs, crime, violence, murder, and disease have brought Downtown Eastside Vancouver into living rooms around the world.[3] Yet this overexposure is at the same time constitutive of a "regime of disappearance." I borrow this term from Goode and Maskovsky, who have coined it to describe a neo-liberal mode of governance that selectively marginalizes and/or erases categories of people through strategies of representation that include silences, blind spots, and displacements that have both material and symbolic effects.[4]

[...] Recognition of the burden of social suffering carried by Aboriginal peoples in this neighborhood—and in Canada as a whole—elicits profound discomfort within a liberal, democratic nation-state like Canada, evidencing as it does the *continuing* effects of settler colonialism, its ideological and material foundations, and its ongoing reproduction.

The city of Vancouver was built on land owned and occupied by the Coast Salish peoples for at least 10,000 years. In 1923 the last Aboriginal village was relocated across Burrard Inlet to a reserve north of the new city. Aboriginal peoples from Coast Salish and many other First Nations have maintained a continual presence in what is now called the Downtown Eastside, and in recent years the numbers of Aboriginal peoples living here have increased significantly to current estimates of around 5,000, representing about one-third of the total population of the neighborhood.[5] It is important to note that not all Aboriginal peoples in the City of Vancouver live in the Downtown Eastside.[6] However, while about 10 percent of the Canadian population as a whole is Aboriginal, they are disproportionately located in the poorest neighborhoods of Canadian cities, at the bottom of the socioeconomic hierarchy.[7]

In the Downtown Eastside, as elsewhere, while much *public* space has been taken over by police, drug dealers and users, sex workers and pimps, pawn shops and street fences, the majority of residents of the neighborhood are none of the above.[8] The Downtown Eastside is one of the poorest neighborhoods in Canada, where average annual incomes hover far below the national poverty line at around $12,000 (Cdn).[9] Approximately 16,000 people now live in the Downtown Eastside and estimates are that around 6,000 are active drug users.[10] Some are people suffering from mental illness who have been "deinstitutionalized," but the majority are people too poor to live anywhere else in Canada's highest-rent city.[11] While poverty is frequently noted as a characteristic of the inner city, it is most often presented in the form of a naturalized, inevitable backdrop against which exoticized practices of drug addiction and commercial sex are played out. Dominant explanatory discourses tend towards pathologizing or medicalizing poverty. That is, poverty is identified as the *outcome* of drug addiction, which itself is increasingly explained as a "chronic relapsing mental illness." Poverty is rarely analyzed as a causal condition that gives illicit drug use and sex work their particular public character and devastating consequences in this place, at this time. Illicit drug use and the exchange of sex for material benefit are, after all, not limited to the Downtown Eastside and other impoverished inner-city locales. Rather, denizens of wealthier neighborhoods engage in these practices as well. They do so in private homes, brothels, and escort agencies. There, wealth serves to conceal and privatize what, here, poverty reveals to the public gaze.

A less publicized aspect of Vancouver's HIV/AIDS crisis is that infection rates are significantly higher among women than among men, and about twice as high among both male and female Aboriginal intravenous drug users than among non-Aboriginals.[12] Aboriginal women are seroconverting at higher rates than any other designated population in Canada in general, and in Vancouver in particular. [...] While neither HIV/AIDS nor IV drug use are restricted to impoverished and marginalized communities, it is the case, across the globe, that the burden of these epidemics is disproportionately borne by those with the least economic and political power.[13]

*****

A study conducted in 2000 estimated that 70 percent of street prostitutes working in the most dangerous and lowest paying "tracks" in the Downtown Eastside were Aboriginal women under the age of 26, and most are mothers.[14] In the racialized hierarchy of Vancouver's sex trade, non-Aboriginal women who work on the street have access to somewhat safer and higher-earning areas of Downtown Centre, Downtown South, and the West End. Others work through escort agencies and massage parlors. Researchers, sex workers, and advocates alike agree that men who seek out women working the "low track," in Vancouver and elsewhere, are buying licence to commit violence, to degrade, and to demean women considered disposable by "Johns" and by society as a whole. Few non-Aboriginal analysts or advocates, however, acknowledge the *specific* vulnerability and overexposure of Aboriginal women to sexual exploitation, violence, and murder that has historically, and continues contemporarily, to be a fact of Canadian life.

The most dramatic example of both the material and symbolic location of Aboriginal women in Downtown Eastside Vancouver and their representation in public culture is the story of the "Missing and Murdered Women." Since 1983 at least 61 women from Downtown Eastside Vancouver have been officially listed as "missing persons." When their relatives and friends began trying to alert police and other authorities to this, they were ignored. Then-mayor of Vancouver, Philip Owen, responded to the families' appeals to the police to investigate these disappearances by saying that public monies would not be spent running a "location service for prostitutes." As the numbers of missing women grew, and as academics, advocates, and journalists became involved and joined forces with women's families, "Vancouver's Missing Women" became a public issue, and the possibility that a serial killer was preying on the neighborhood captured widespread attention. [...]

In February 2002 Robert William Pickton, a pig farmer from suburban Port Coquitlam, was arrested. He has since been charged with 15 counts of first-degree murder, making this the largest serial killer investigation in Canadian history. International media have flocked to Vancouver to film court proceedings and the massive, multimillion-dollar search for evidence currently being conducted utilizing state-of-the-art technology at the Pickton farm. It has become a reality-based version of the popular television dramatic series, *CSI: Crime Scene Investigation*. Families of the missing and murdered women and their supporters maintain a vigil at the Pickton farm, standing as witnesses. Aboriginal women conduct healing ceremonies, insisting on inclusive—*not exclusive*—recognition that so many of the women whose body parts or DNA might be found were or are Aboriginal.

In comparison to depictions of illness and hopelessness, less attention is paid by media, politicians, and the public to the strength and courage of many people in the Downtown Eastside who struggle daily to maintain and create community, to initiate and support change, to survive. The Downtown Eastside is an active and activist neighborhood with a long tradition of labor and anti-poverty organizing. In the 1970s and 1980s feminist organizations whose work has focused on developing spaces for women, such as drop-in centers, social housing, shelters, and transition houses that are safe from public and private violence, gained in numbers and influence. Aboriginal women have long been a part of leftist anti-poverty and feminist anti-violence political movements, but beginning in the early 1990s they began to take significant leadership as organized Aboriginal voices per se in the Downtown Eastside. Their numbers had increased locally, and the Aboriginal movement—and Aboriginal women's movement specifically—gained more prominence nationally and provincially.[15] Urban Aboriginal political recognition also advanced at this time in the form of inclusion of Aboriginal individuals and representatives on citizens' advisory and community participation panels. Aboriginal women, particularly older women no longer using drugs and/or alcohol, have emerged as community organizers, ritual specialists, spiritual icons, and political leaders in the neighborhood.

The feeling that the issues particular to women in the Downtown Eastside—specifically poverty, racism, violence against sex workers, HIV/AIDS, and addiction—are given insufficient attention by other Aboriginal and non-Aboriginal organizations is cited as a reason for holding the annual Valentine's Day marches. By organizing their own events on a specific day, Downtown Eastside women activists mark their difference from other feminist anti-violence groups, and from mainstream Aboriginal organizations.[16] The main social and political movements in the neighborhood—Aboriginal, women's, anti-poverty, and community development movements for the most part, each including several highly politicized factions—coexist in uneasy coalitions fraught by conflict but moved to collective action such as the Valentine's Day March by shared, though diverse, visions of social justice. [...]

The Valentine's Day March changes somewhat each year, but the particular event I will focus on is the 2001 March. The day began at noon with a gathering in the auditorium of the Carnegie Community Centre. The people gathered were mostly, but not exclusively, women of a variety of ages, dressed in fashions from trendy, to punk, to understated but very expensive leather, to pickings from donations from free clothing bins. Many, but not all, were Aboriginal. Gathered too were young Asian women, white women of all ages, a few African Canadian women, and a handful of men of different ages and races. Most of the dignitaries on stage and all of the singers, drummers, and speakers to come were Aboriginal women. The program at the Carnegie Centre began, as community gatherings usually do now, with an offer of thanks to the Coast Salish First Nations upon whose unceded land the ceremonies were about to take place. This was followed by prayers, drumming, and smudging led by elderly Aboriginal women. A round of speeches ensued. Most of the speakers were middle-aged or elderly Aboriginal women, many of whom were leading community activists. Some were employed in social service agencies, but most were self-described "Volunteer Queens" and women called "Street Moms" who simply live in the community. They talk. They help. They cook. They run AA and NA meetings. They look after children and old people. They conduct healing circles. They try to keep young people off the street.

A representative from an Aboriginal women's organization narrated how European patriarchal values and structures were superimposed on Indigenous societies, displacing women from the positions of respect they held traditionally. Another talked about the Indian Act and how registered Indian women who married non-Indian men were denied legal status and prohibited from living on reserves. Since 1985 most of these women and their children have been eligible for reinstatement, but conditions on reserves, which include competition over distribution of scarce resources, and sometimes longstanding conflicts within and between families, have made returning to reserves more a disappointment than a reality for many. Homophobia, fear of HIV and those who are infected and lack of services for them, and high rates of domestic violence and abuse in some First Nations communities, as well as employment and education opportunities and more possibilities for diverse lifestyles in the city, also play a role in creating an urban population made up predominantly of women and youth. Not all the women who live in the Downtown Eastside are from reserves, though. There are Métis women, non-status women, people whose families have lived off-reserve for more than a generation or two, and many young people who grew up in the foster care system or were "adopted out" and have more questions than assumptions about their Aboriginal identity and their relationships to reserve-based communities.

Another speaker criticized the existing Aboriginal health and social services and accused them of paying insufficient attention to the needs of Aboriginal peoples in the Downtown Eastside. As evidence of the inadequacy of existing services she cited lack of treatment facilities for drug and alcohol recovery, absence of follow-up care or resources for people coming out of treatment, lack of safe and secure housing, discriminatory child apprehension practices, and slow police responses to calls about domestic or street violence. She blamed lack of jobs and below-subsistence welfare rates for driving young women into the sex trade and young men into the drug trade. She concluded with a critique of those people she calls "poverty pimps" and demanded that staffing of neighborhood social services be culturally proportionate to clientele: "If half your clients are Native people," she said "Then I want to see half your staff Native too!"[17] Her speech was angry, emotional, and at times hard to follow. Reading the transcript carefully, however, revealed an anticolonial analysis, Indigenous explanations of addiction in Aboriginal women's lives, and a list of policy and treatment recommendations that have been repeated in more professional and restricted language in well-financed study after well-financed study.

The speeches continued. Multigenerational kinship groups stood together behind their speakers. Mothers, grandmothers, great-grandmothers, and aunties related their own histories, lamented the loss of children to drugs and alcohol, and pointed proudly to those who have survived.

*****

For the last few years, the Valentine's Day Memorial March has focused on the "Missing and Murdered Women," now the subject of international media attention. The Carnegie Centre Auditorium was decorated with red hearts, each one bearing the name of a disappeared woman. Individuals, adopting a tactic made famous by the Madres of the Plaza dey Mayo in Argentina, carried pictures of their missing relatives.

The gathering in the auditorium drew to a close with a prayer and a two-minute silence in honor of the dead, and the crowd filed out of the Carnegie Centre, led by Aboriginal women in button blankets and shawls, singing songs and beating drums. Joining hands and linking arms, they formed a circle anchored on each of the four corners of Main and Hastings, stopped traffic of all kinds, disrupted popular images, and demanded recognition. Contingents assembled around their various banners, and the annual Valentine's Day Women's Memorial March began.

The marchers wound their way down Hastings Street, detouring through alleys and parks. Women stopped to smudge outside notorious bars, strip clubs, in alleyways, in parking lots, and beside dumpsters where women's bodies have been found. They read the names of women who had died, told how they died, and listed their relations: mother of ____, sister of ____, daughter of ____, friend of ____. In this way they inscribed these women's lives on land, and in place. It is appropriate that there is so much focus on mourning and death. Perpetual, repetitive, relentless experiences of tragic loss permeate the lives of individuals and families in this community. The representational politics surrounding the missing women mark an important moment for Aboriginal and non-Aboriginal women. The strongest criticism of the police—and, by proxy, of the public—has been that they ignored early reports because the women were prostitutes, addicts, Aboriginal. And that this is wrong, that these women have equality rights of some sort, that they are as human as anyone else, and that their families' grief is as important as any other family's grief. "These women are *mothers, sisters, aunts.* They are *human beings,*" a speaker proclaimed.

By politicizing the issue of the Missing and Murdered Women in particular, and rallying considerable support across class, gender, racial, and neighborhood divides, the families of the missing women and their supporters have claimed a space of dignity for the poorest and most marginalized women in Canada and have achieved some degree of victory in setting the terms and conditions under which a previously invisible population has entered into public discourse. The sad irony is, of course, that the recognition and respect now accorded the Missing and Murdered Women in death was often denied them in life.

*****

Material conditions for Aboriginal women in Downtown Eastside Vancouver have worsened considerably during the last two years. British Columbians elected an extreme right-wing party—ironically named the Liberals—to form the provincial government. Welfare reform policies adopted from the United States have been implemented that have reduced benefits and services to single mothers, unemployed youth, and disabled people. HIV infection rates continue to increase, with Aboriginal youth between the ages of 17 and 25 constituting the "highest risk group." Homelessness is increasing, and anecdotal reports, observations, and research data demonstrate that the numbers of young Aboriginal women arriving in the inner city is on the rise.

Nevertheless, Aboriginal women continue to resist and to envision change. A group called Breaking the Silence advocates for safe housing and health and social services for neighborhood women. [...] The Valentine's Day Women's Memorial March in 2003 was large, well attended, sorrowful, and celebratory.[18] A woman speaking on behalf of the Aboriginal Women's Action Network addressed the gathering and said: "We've shown the world that we won't stand by while our women are murdered and disappeared. We demand justice for the missing and murdered women of all nations. And we won't tolerate it that our young women are still pushed onto the street by poverty and racism. This is our land and we belong here. We have a right to justice and a decent life. We are not going anywhere."[19]

Notes

1. For statistical overview of Aboriginal populations in Canadian inner cities, see Carol LaPrairie, *Aboriginal Over-representation in the Criminal Justice System: A Tale of Nine Cities* (Ottawa: Department of Justice, 2001). For a discussion of "invisibility" of urban Aboriginal peoples in mainstream Canadian culture, see Evelyn J. Peters, "Subversive Spaces: First Nations Women and the City," *Environment and Planning D: Society and Space* 16 (1998): 665–85. For analysis of routinized violence against inner-city Aboriginal women in Canada, see Sherene Razack, "Gendered Racial Violence and Spatialized Justice: The Murder of Pamela George," *Canadian Journal of Law and Society* 15:2 (2000): 91–130. For a case study of mental health and substance abuse issues among inner-city Aboriginal populations in Canada, see Kahá:wi Jacobs and Kathryn Gill, "Substance Abuse in an Urban Aboriginal Population: Social, Legal, and Psychological Consequences," *Journal of Ethnicity in Substance Abuse* 1:1 (2002): 7–25.

2. In Canada, prostitution—that is, the exchange of sexual services for money—is not illegal. However, soliciting for the purposes of prostitution is illegal.

3. Beverly A. Pitman, "Re-mediating the Spaces of Reality Television: *America's Most Wanted* and the Case of Vancouver's Missing Women," *Environment and Planning A* 334 (2002): 167–84.

4. Judith Goode and Jeff Maskovsky, eds., *The New Poverty Studies: The Ethnography of Power, Politics, and Impoverished People in the United States* (New York: New York University Press, 2001).

5. For a discussion of current census and other demographic data, and for a recently published article that signals the beginnings of a movement into academic visibility of Aboriginal women in Downtown Eastside Vancouver, see Celia Benoit et al., "In Search of a Healing Place: Aboriginal Women in Vancouver's Downtown Eastside," *Social Science and Medicine* 56:6 (2003): 821–33.

6. Reliable demographic data is hard to establish in this milieu, but estimates can provide an overview sketch. In 1998–99, hoping to obtain a more accurate estimate of the Aboriginal population of the city of Vancouver, the Vancouver/Richmond Health Board commissioned a "Capture/Recapture Study" based on Census Canada 1996 figures. This study, entitled *Healing Ways*, estimated a total population of 28,000 Aboriginal peoples living in the city of Vancouver. Of these, approximately 5,000 (17 percent) reside in the Downtown Eastside; 14,000 (50 percent) live in the adjacent neighborhoods of Northeast, East, and Southeast Vancouver; with the remaining 9,000 (33 percent) scattered throughout other neighborhoods. Over 50 percent of urban Aboriginal households in Vancouver are headed by women, and these are concentrated in the sectors of East Vancouver, where the majority of Aboriginal peoples live. *Healing Ways: Aboriginal Health and Service Review* (Vancouver: Vancouver/Richmond Health Board, 1999), 102.

7. For analysis of the systemic nature of current poverty and economic marginalization among Aboriginal peoples in Canada, see Joan Kendall, "Circles of Disadvantage: Aboriginal Poverty and Underdevelopment in Canada," *American Review of Canadian Studies* 31:1/2 (2001): 43–59.

8. Phillipe Bourgois, "Understanding Inner-City Poverty: Resistance and Self-Destruction under U.S. Apartheid," in *Exotic No More: Anthropology on the Front Lines*, ed. Jeremy Mac-Clancy (Chicago: University of Chicago Press, 2002), 15–32.

9. *Downtown Eastside Community Monitoring Report*, Population Statistics, Census Canada 1996 (Vancouver: City of Vancouver, 2000).

10. *Downtown Eastside Community Monitoring Report.*

11. Vancouver/Richmond Health Board, *Healing Ways.*

12. Patricia Spittal et al., "Risk Factors for Elevated HIV Incidence Rates among Female Injection Drug Users in Vancouver," *Canadian Medical Association Journal* 166:7 (2002): 894–99. See also Susan Ship and Laurel Norton, "'It's Hard to Be a Woman': First Nations Women Living with HIV/AIDS," *Native Social Work Journal* 3:1 (2000): 69–85.

13. Sally Zierler and Nancy Krieger, "Reframing Women's Risk: Social Inequalities and HIV Infection," *Annual Review of Public Health* 18 (1997): 401–36.

14. Sue Currie, "Assessing the Violence against Street Involved Women in the Downtown Eastside/Strathcona Community," Report for the Ministry of Women's Equality (Province of British Columbia, 2000).

15. For analyses of the Aboriginal Women's Movement in Canada, see Jo-Ann Fiske, "The Womb Is to the Nation as the Heart Is to the Body: Ethnopolitical Discourses of the Canadian Indigenous Women's Movement," *Studies in Political Economy* 51 (Fall 1996): 65–96; Native Women's Association of Canada, *Hear Their Stories: 40 Aboriginal Women Speak* (Ottawa: The Association, 1997); Winona Stevenson, "Colonialism and First Nations Women in Canada," in *Scratching the Surface: Canadian Anti-racist Feminist Thought*, ed. Enakshi Dua and Angela Robertson (Toronto: Women's Press, 1999).

16. Since the "Montreal Massacre" of December 6, 1989, when a man burst into an engineering class at L'Ecole Polytechnique at the Université de Montréal, in Montréal, Québec, yelling that he "hated feminists" and gunned down 14 female students, activists in the movement against violence against women mobilize on December 6 every year. The anti-rape movement holds "Take Back the Night" marches in October each year. Trade union- and left-wing-affiliated women focus on International Women's Day on March 8.

17. Dara Culhane, Fieldnotes, February 14, 2001.

18. For discussion and examples of Aboriginal women's activities surrounding health and health care, see Connie Deiter and Linda Otway, "Sharing Our Stories on Promoting Health and Community Healing: An Aboriginal Women's Health Project," Prairie Women's Health Centre (Winnipeg: Prairie Women's Health Centre, 2001).

19. Culhane, Fieldnotes.

Ten Things Men Can Do to Prevent Gender Violence

Jackson Katz

Jackson Katz is a leading anti-sexist male activist. An internationally recognized educator, public speaker, author, and filmmaker, he is known for his groundbreaking work in the field of gender violence-prevention education with men and boys, particularly in the cultures of sports, professional athletics, and the military. He helped to create educational videos for college and high school students, including the well-known Tough Guise: Violence, Media, and the Crisis in Masculinity *(2000).*

1. Approach gender violence as a *men's* issue involving men of all ages and socioeconomic, racial, and ethnic backgrounds. View men not only as perpetrators or possible offenders, but as empowered bystanders who can confront abusive peers.
2. If a brother, friend, classmate, or teammate is abusing his female partner—or is disrespectful or abusive to girls and women in general—don't look the other way. If you feel comfortable doing so, try to talk to him about it. Urge him to seek help. Or it you don't know what to do, consult a friend, a parent, a professor, or a counselor. *Don't remain silent.*
3. Have the courage to look inward. Question your own attitudes. Don't be defensive when something you do or say ends up hurting someone else. Try hard to understand how your own attitudes and actions might inadvertently perpetuate sexism and violence, and work toward changing them.
4. If you suspect that a woman close to you is being abused or has been sexually assaulted, gently ask if you can help.
5. If you are emotionally, psychologically, physically, or sexually abusive to women, or have been the past, seek professional help *now*.
6. Be an ally to women who are working to end all forms of gender violence. Support the work of campus-based women's centers. Attend "Take Back the Night" rallies and other public events. Raise money for community-based rape crisis centers and battered women's shelters. If you belong to a team or fraternity, or another student group, organize a fundraiser.
7. Recognize and speak out against homophobia and gay-bashing. Discrimination and violence against lesbians and gays are wrong in and of themselves. This abuse also has direct links to sexism—e.g., the sexual orientation of men who speak out against sexism is often questioned, a conscious or unconscious strategy intended to silence them. This is a key reason few men do speak out.
8. Attend programs, take courses, watch films, and read articles and books about multicultural masculinities, gender inequality, and the root causes of gender violence. Educate

yourself and others about how larger social forces affect the conflicts between individual men and women.

9. Don't fund sexism. Refuse to purchase any magazine, rent any video, subscribe to any Web site, or buy any music that portrays girls or women in a sexually degrading or abusive manner. Protest sexism in the media.

10. Mentor and teach young boys about how to be men in ways that don't involve degrading or abusing girls and women. Volunteer to work with gender violence-prevention programs, including anti-sexist men's programs. Lead by example.

Source: Jackson Katz, "10 Things Men Can Do to Prevent Gender Violence," retrieved from http://www.jacksonkatz.com/wmcd.html

Part 5 Gendering Work, Globalization, and Activism

If women are to "clean up the mess," they have a right to challenge the people and institutions which create the problems.
> —Peggy Antrobus, quoted in Joni Seager, "What's the Problem Here?"
> in *Earth Follies: Coming to Feminist Terms with the Global Environmental Crisis*
> (1993, p. 7)

Part 5 examines the changing nature of gender relations in our increasingly globalized world. We introduce to gendered and racialized understandings of globalization and globalization's unequal gendered and racialized distribution of costs and benefits within and between countries in the economic North and South. We also look at women's movements organizing for gender and economic justice within and across communities, cultures, and borders.

5a: Women and Global Restructuring

This section introduces you to feminist analyses of globalization, neo-liberalism, and structural adjustment policies, highlighting their differential impacts on women and other marginalized social groups within and between the economic North and South. We examine in particular the effects of globalization on "Third World" women's migration, labour, economic security, and health. We also begin to consider some of the ways in which women are attempting to secure their economic and social rights.

5b: The "New Economy": On (Not) Getting By in North America

Here we focus on how neo-liberalism and economic restructuring are impacting women's paid and unpaid work and economic security in Canada and the United States. Restructuring, the rolling back of the welfare state, and liberalized trade are shown to increase the precarious nature of women's employment and responsibilities for social reproduction, and to deepen the feminization and racialization of poverty.

5c: Poverty, Homelessness, and Social Welfare in Canada

This section focuses on women's experiences of poverty and homelessness in the context of the neo-liberal dismantling of the welfare state and the criminalization of poor women in Canada, especially since the 1990s. We highlight poverty and homelessness in urban and rural settings and in northern Canada. We also explore some analyses, proposals, and actions of contemporary anti-poverty activists.

Supplement 33

What Is Neo-liberal Globalization?

Alison Jaggar

Alison Jaggar is professor of philosophy and women and gender studies at the University of Colorado in Boulder. Her areas of interest include contemporary social, moral, and political philosophy from a feminist perspective and gendered aspects of global justice. She has published numerous works on these topics, including Just Methods: An Interdisciplinary Feminist Reader, Abortion: Three Perspectives, *and the forthcoming* Global Gender Justice.

Interpreted broadly, the term "globalization" refers to any system of transcontinental travel and trade. However, contemporary globalization is distinguished by its integration of many local and national economies into a single global market, regulated by the World Trade Organization. This treaty organization was established in 1995 to determine the rules for global trade. WTO rules supersede the national law of any signatory nation and are rationalized by a distinctive version of liberal political theory, namely, neo-liberalism.

Although its name suggests that it is something novel, "neo-liberalism" in fact marks a retreat from the liberal social democracy of the years following World War II. It moves back toward the non-redistributive laissez faire liberalism of the seventeenth and eighteenth centuries, which held that the main function of government was to make the world safe and predictable for the participants in a market economy. Following are some main tenets of contemporary neo-liberalism.

"Free" Trade

Neo-liberalism promotes the free flow of both traded goods and of capital. However, not only does it not require the free flow of labour, the third crucial factor of production, but it also seeks actively to control that flow. Although immigration from poorer to wealthier countries is currently at record levels, much of it is achieved in the teeth of draconian border controls that often cost would-be immigrants their lives.

Opposition to Government Regulation

Neo-liberalism opposes government regulation of such aspects of production as wages, working conditions and environmental protections. Indeed, legislation intended to protect workers, consumers or the environment may be challenged as an unfair barrier to trade.

Refusal of Responsibility for Social Welfare

Neo-liberalism presses governments to abandon the social welfare responsibilities that they have assumed over the twentieth century, such as providing allowances for housing, health care, education, disability and unemployment.

Resource Privatization

The final feature of contemporary neo-liberalism is its push to bring all economically exploitable resources into private ownership. Public services are turned into profit-making enterprises, sometimes sold to foreign investors, and natural resources such as minerals, forests, water and land are opened up for commercial exploitation in the global market.

Source: Adapted from Alison Jaggar, "Vulnerable Women and Neoliberal Globalization: Debt Burden Undermines Women's Health in the Global South," *Theoretical Medicine* 23 (2002): 425, 426.

Chapter 54

Women and Globalization

Shawn Meghan Burn

Shawn Meghan Burn is professor in the Department of Psychology and Child Development at California Polytechnic State University. She researches gender issues, environment sustainability behaviour, group dynamics, and stigma and prejudice. She is also a program consultant for the university's sexual assault prevention program. She has written numerous texts and articles on human behaviour, as well as books on international women's issues, including Women across Cultures: A Global Perspective, *now in its third printing.*

Global economic and trade policies are not "gender neutral." The failure of governments and intergovernmental organizations to formulate and evaluate trade policies from a gender perspective has exacerbated women's economic inequity.
—Women's Environment and Development Organization (2009)

This chapter discusses the ways that globalization has reshaped women's lives worldwide. You will learn how the growing trend toward a world economy impacts women. By the year 2000, it was increasingly likely that the goods consumed by people in one country were grown, produced, or assembled in a multitude of other countries. Americans dine on fruit grown in Central America and wear clothes assembled in Vietnam or the Dominican Republic. Russians wear American-brand clothes manufactured in developing countries. South Africans smoke American cigarettes and drink Coca-Cola. Europe is dotted with Pizza Huts and Starbucks. An economic crisis in one country affects the economies of other countries. These are examples of globalization. *Economic globalization* refers to the integration and rapid interaction of economies through production, trade, and financial transactions by banks and multinational corporations, with an increased role for the World Bank and the International Monetary Fund, as well as the World Trade Organization (WTO) (Moghadam, 1999). *Cultural globalization* refers to the transnational migration of people, information, and consumer culture.

Critics of globalization are alarmed by the fact that the costs and benefits of globalization are not evenly distributed across nations. For example, more affluent northern governments provide subsidies to their farmers so that they can afford to sell their products for less in the global market. Farmers from southern countries where subsidies are unavailable are unable to compete and become poorer. Northern governments also frequently impose tariffs and import limits on goods from other countries. This keeps "cheaper" goods out of the home market and protects the profits of corporations in the home country. Liberalized trade agreements have eroded workers' rights and unionization. Environmental sustainability is compromised when poor countries, desperate for a piece of the global economic pie, let transnational corporations exploit or pollute their natural resources. Protests at world trade meetings are frequent, large, and often dramatic.

The Effects of Globalization on Women

The economic shifts that come with globalization create some jobs for women in their own countries, particularly low-paid jobs in the fresh export produce sector, the export clothing sector, and the outsourced service sector (UNIFEM, 2009). For example, Colombian women might package flowers for export to northern nations, Honduran women might sew clothing for export to northern nations, and Indian women might work in a service call center answering calls from people in northern nations.

[...] Employment has the potential to increase women's power and status, so you might expect that the creation of jobs for women is a positive benefit of globalization. There is some truth in this. For example, Lim (1990) found that women in developing countries often cite the benefits of employment, such as the ability to earn independent income and spend it on desired purchases; the ability to save for marriage or education; the ability to help support their families and "repay" their debt to parents; the opportunity to delay marriage and childbearing and to exercise personal choice of a marriage partner; and the opportunity to enjoy some personal freedom, the companionship of other women, and to experience more of what life has to offer, such as a "widening of horizons." [...]

Figure 54.1: Effects of Globalization on Women's Labor

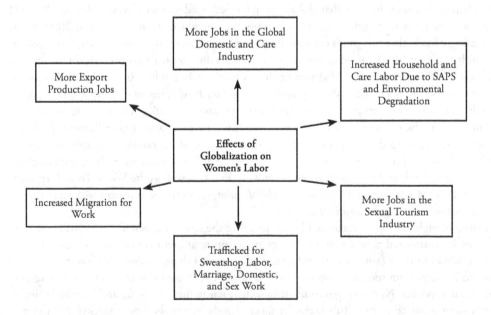

However, whether paid employment benefits a woman depends on whether she has control over the money she makes, whether her wages are sufficient to escape poverty, whether she is still responsible for the majority of household and care labor, and the work conditions. As will become apparent [...], many of the jobs created by globalization for women are poorly paid with little job security and offer difficult work conditions. Many of the jobs are domestic and care labor jobs that replicate traditional gendered roles and may allow more affluent women to participate more equally in labor force while confining migrant women to low-status, gendered roles.

Globalization has affected women in other ways, besides creating jobs. One effect of special concern is how economic recessions and crises affect women. The integration of world economies results in a global economic *system* where the economy of one country or region is linked to others. This means that economic recessions and collapses in one country or region trigger economic problems in others. Research indicates that the effects of these economic downturns are disproportionately borne by women and, within a country, disproportionately affect women from certain ethnicities, classes, castes, and regions (Gunewardena and Kingsolver, 2007). For example, according to the World Bank, women in 33 developing countries, half of them in sub-Saharan Africa, are more vulnerable to effects from a world economic crisis (World Bank, 2009).

These negative effects of globalization on women first became apparent during the 1980s. During the decade's financial crisis, Southern Hemisphere commodity prices dropped, interest rates rose, and many developing nations could not make payments on their development loans. Debtor countries in Africa and Latin America were forced to ask for more money from the International Monetary Fund (IMF; the UN's international banking agency), and from wealthy northern countries. The new loans were made contingent upon a series of reforms (often called *structural adjustment programs*, or SAPs). The lenders said that without reforms, debt would continue to grow and economic development would be hindered. The reforms emphasized earning foreign exchange to service the debt by making it easier to attract international capital and transnational corporations. Production for domestic use was discouraged and production of cash crops and goods for exports was encouraged. To increase the amount they could pay on their loans, governments were pushed to cut budgets for social services, schools, hospitals, nutrition programs, public transportation, and utilities.[1] Ostensibly to deal with the economic crisis, there was also a shift [...] to policies based on neo-liberal capitalism (Moghadam, 2005). In a nutshell, neo-liberalism emphasizes free-market corporate capitalism, balanced government budgets, and the reduction of government services. This further fueled industrialized nations' emphasis on SAPs, reducing government spending and increasing austerity measures in developing nations.

Economic recessions and SAPs that lead to cuts in wages and social services, and rises in the costs of basic goods and services, have a greater impact on women because women are normally responsible for providing food, water, and health care for family members (Blumberg, 1995; Chang, 2000; Lorentzen and Turpin, 1996; Mosse, 1993). For example, women's unpaid labor increases as government services are cut and women must provide more care for children, elderly parents, and the sick (Chang, 2000; Desai, 2002). Women struggle to feed their families because the prices of household goods, especially food, rise as government subsidies are removed to save the government money. Food prices also rise from the globalization of the food industry. Food is less available because of reduced subsistence farming (for family consumption) as farmland is converted to commercial use. Women have less money due to high rates of unemployment and inflation.

Economic recessions also mean that in their desperation for cash, southern countries compromise environmental sustainability. To look attractive as sites for transnational factories (needed for jobs and cash), governments often relax environmental laws. [...] This largely impacts women, who must travel farther for water and have less access to arable land to grow food for their families. Women in poor, urban neighborhoods find their communities polluted by toxic chemical wastes and human wastes (Desai, 2002). In short, the costs of economic adjustment and change fall heavily on the shoulders of women already burdened by poverty.

Although globalization sometimes increases women's paid employment, which can benefit women, many of the jobs created for women by globalization are not secure jobs—their availability depends on consumption patterns in northern countries and whether their country provides the most favorable conditions for corporate profit. This means that if demand for consumer products falls in northern countries or corporations can relocate to another country where labor regulation is weaker, the jobs disappear. In times of economic downturns and transitions, women are often the first to lose their jobs. This is especially true in developing nations where women tend to work in the informal sector, or for transnational corporations in factories or services. [...]

Globalization has also led to dramatic increases in women's migration to other countries for work, a topic covered at length later in this chapter. When women are unable to sustain their families, they may have no viable option but to leave their families and migrate for work (Chang, 2000). Migration can benefit women and their families by reducing their poverty. It can allow women to escape patriarchal societies and abusive marriages. It can also promote gender role change—women abroad sometimes play a role in promoting gender equality back home (UNFPA, 2006). However, in many cases migrant women end up in vulnerable types of employment marked by low pay and poor working conditions, and prejudice against migrants prevents their full and equal participation in the host country. [...]

Women's Work in the Transnational Factory

In the global economy, knowledge-intensive aspects of the production process often remain in Western countries, but labor-intensive activities are subcontracted to factories in developing countries where cheap female labor is abundant (Naples, 2002; Stearns, 1998). The United States was the first to relocate labor-intensive factory work such as garment-making and production of footwear and electronics to lower-wage sites in the Caribbean, East Asia, and Latin America (United Nations, 1999). *Free trade zones (FTZs)*, or *export processing zones (EPZs)*, were established in many cash-hungry southern nations to attract transnational factories. The ILO [International Labour Organization] defines EPZs as "industrial zones with special incentives set up to attract foreign investors, in which imported materials undergo some degree of processing before being re-exported" but "imported material" also include electronic data entry facilities and call centers (International Labour Organization, 2007). In these zones, companies are generally exempt from labor, health and safety, and environmental laws and pay few, if any, taxes. [...]

As neo-liberalism gained hold, women in developing nations came to be viewed as sources of cheap labor that would lower the costs of production and consequently increase profits. Women dominate employment in most EPZs and are [an] important part of *global supply chains* where different pieces of production are spread across geographic locations (UNIFEM, 2009). For example, many EPZ factories in Central America (which are often called *maquiladoras* or *maquilas*) assemble clothing; other parts of production are done elsewhere. Women constitute over 75 percent of the workers in EPZs in Cape Verde, El Salvador, Honduras, Nicaragua, Jamaica, Bangladesh, and Sri Lanka (Boyenge, 2007; UNIFEM, 2009). [...]

Women are the preferred labor supply because they can be hired for lower pay with no benefits, job guarantees, or social security (UNIFEM, 2009). In developing countries, they are treated by transnational corporations as a flexible, low-paid labor force that can be drawn in or dropped as needed (UNIFEM, 2009). Women's [presumed] manual dexterity and docility [...], their desperation for work and lack of awareness about their rights, and their seemingly limitless supply have made them the choice factory workers of transnational corporations worldwide. Some theorists argue that women's low-wage labor for transnational corporations fuels global production and is at the heart of corporate profits (Fuentes & Ehrenreich, 1983; Salzinger, 2003).

BOX 54.1: Conditions at the Meitai Plastics and Electronics Factory

"We feel like we are serving prison sentences."
—Meitai factory worker making Microsoft keyboards

The Taiwanese-owned Meitai Plastics & Electronics Factory in Dongguang City in Guangdong, China, employs two thousand workers (75 percent women aged 18–25) and produces computer equipment for U.S. companies Dell, Lenovo, Microsoft, and IBM. Workers are prohibited from talking, listening to music, raising their heads, and putting their hands in their pockets. The young workers sit on hard wooden stools twelve hours a day, seven days a week as 500 computer keyboards an hour move down the assembly line (one every 7.2 seconds). Workers are allowed just 1.1 seconds to snap each key into place, repeating the same operation 3,250 times an hour, 35,750 times a day, 250,250 times a week and over one million times a month. Workers are fined for being one minute late, for not trimming their fingernails—which could impede the work, and for stepping on the grass. Workers are searched on the way in and out of the factory. Workers who hand out flyers or discuss factory conditions with outsiders are fired. Employees are required to live on-site in crowded dorms (10–12 workers share an 11 × 20 room) and have only a bucket with which to wash. On average they work 74 hours a week with only two days off a month. They are locked into the compound four days a week. Although they earn 76 cents an hour, this drops to 41 cents an hour after room and board are paid. These wages are below the Chinese minimum wage and are not a living wage.

Source: The National Labor Committee, "High Tech Misery in China" (2009), retrieved from http://www.nlcnet.org/reports.php?id=613

Women's Sweatshop Labor

Unfortunately, many factories in EPZs, are little more than *sweatshops*—businesses that do not provide a living wage, require excessively long work hours, and provide poor working conditions with many health and safety hazards. In sweatshops, mistreatment of women workers (such as verbal, physical, and sexual harassment) is common and those who speak out, organize, or attempt to unionize for better conditions are quickly shut down. In some sweatshops, such as those in the United States, Turkey, and Jordan, the workers are primarily impoverished migrant women (some illegal migrants) who tolerate abuses because their families are dependent on their meager income, because they fear immigration authorities, or because they are indentured to recruiters. The odds are good that the majority of your clothes, shoes, toys, and electronics were created with women's sweatshop labor in countries such as Bangladesh, Burma, China, the Dominican Republic, Haiti, Honduras, Indonesia, Guatemala, Malaysia, Mexico, Nicaragua, the Philippines, and Vietnam. (See Box 54.1 for a report on a factory in a Chinese EPZ.)

It is common for proponents of EPZs to say that these jobs benefit women by reducing their poverty and that the women are better off than they would be without the jobs. However, in most cases the wages are insufficient to escape poverty. Take, for example, the Salvadoran women working for the Korean-owned Youngone maquila in Olocuilta, La Paz, El Salvador, who sew jackets for the American company North Face. They are paid 94 cents for every $165 jacket and during the busy season work up to 91 hours a week. Due to soaring food costs they cannot afford milk and basic necessities for their children. It is estimated that if North Face required that the subcontractors pay the women $1.49 an hour (enough to make a difference in their standard of living), it would increase the direct labor costs to produce the jacket by only 68 cents, just four-tenths of 1 percent of the retail price of the jacket (National Labor Committee, 2008). Similarly, at the Korean-owned Nicotex maquila in Mixco, Guatemala, women sew garments for American apparel companies like Lane Bryant and JC Penney. The mostly indigenous women workers in their mid-twenties work a 64- to 69-hour work week. According to the U.S. State Department and National Labor Committee investigations, wages in Guatemalan EPZs are not enough to meet basic subsistence needs (National Labor Committee, 2008). In Nicaragua, the average worker in an EPZ makes 300 cordobas a month but needs 4,800 cordobas for groceries (ICFTU, 2006).

*****

Activism to Stop Sweatshop Labor

Although it is sometimes said that owners of transnational factories operating in EPZs prefer female workers because they are cheap and docile, they regularly attempt to organize themselves to advocate for a living wage, reasonable work hours, and safe working conditions. As Louie (2001) put it, they transform themselves from sweatshop workers to sweatshop warriors. Strikes and efforts to organize for better work conditions and pay are common, but are often swiftly and harshly punished, and collective bargaining agreements remain rare in EPZs (ICFTU, 2006). Organizers are fired, threatened with dismissal, intimidated in a variety of ways, and blacklisted such that they can't find work elsewhere. Strikes are shut down quickly, often with police help. When unions are formed, companies often close factories and move to friendlier locations. Governments often participate in the suppression of labor organizing because of competition with other economically struggling countries for foreign investment. They feel they need the jobs and foreign currency to pay off loans and know that transnational corporations will move their operations to other countries that do not enforce labor regulations.

Establishing a set of global norms and standards by which all corporations must abide by is one key to stopping corporate abuse of women's rights, livelihoods, and the environment (WEDO, 2009). Sweatshops are inconsistent with workers' human rights as defined by the ILO, and ILO conventions on labor human rights are routinely violated in many EPZs. [...] International free trade agreements such as GATT (General Agreement on Tariffs and Trade), NAFTA (North American Free Trade Agreement), and CAFTA (Central American Free Trade Agreement) have aggravated poor labor conditions by making it easier for corporations to ask for and receive exemptions from laws that ostensibly interfere with free trade.

Ideally, international trade agreements would require compliance with International Labour Organization core labor rights conventions and the Universal Declaration of Human Rights. This would ensure a level playing field such that companies and countries honoring workers' rights will not be at a competitive disadvantage. Some have also suggested that the World Trade Organization play a role in enforcement of these international labor standards in EPZs (Moran, 2002; WEDO, 2009). Several bills have been introduced in the U.S. Congress to encourage compliance with ILO standards. The Decent Working Conditions and Fair Competition Act would have prohibited the import, export, and sale of goods made with sweatshop labor (it was supported by then-Senator Hillary Clinton and Barack Obama). The legislation would have required the Federal Trade Commission to investigate complaints and fine offenders and would have used the Homeland Security department for some aspects of enforcement. So far this bill and similar ones have died in committee and have not come up for a vote.

Nongovernmental organizations have played a key role in documenting abuses, organizing workers, mobilizing shareholders and consumers to exert pressure on corporations to clean up their act, and creating standards of conduct for corporations. For example, the Clean Clothes Campaign, based in the Netherlands, offers guidelines on what companies can do to better assess, implement, and verify compliance with labor standards in their supply chains, and eliminate abuses where and when they arise. The Maquila Solidarity Network (MSN) is a labor and women's rights organization that supports the efforts of workers in global supply chains to win improved wages and working conditions and a better quality of life. They work with women's and labor rights organizations in Mexico, Central America, and Asia, through corporate campaigning and engagement, networking and coalition building, and policy advocacy. Some NGOs, like Green America, encourage northern consumers to avoid buying sweatshop-made items, and to push local businesses (including campus stores) and sports teams to avoid sweatshop products. They also recommend that consumers write their favorite retailers and ask questions about labor practices in their supply chains. Those owning stocks are asked to vote in support of shareholder resolutions requiring the company to improve its labor policies.

Activist groups are sometimes successful in exacting change from corporations. Many corporations have adopted their own corporate social responsibility arrangements in response to activism, but evidence is mixed on their success (UNIFEM, 2009). For example, in the 1990s, a number of NGO investigations revealed sweatshop conditions and labor rights violations in Nike's supply chain, where women comprise 80 to 90 percent of workers. Following activism, including consumer boycotts, Nike became the first in its industry to disclose its subcontracted factory locations. It also instituted a Code of Conduct to address minimum wages, freedom of association, and gender and maternity discrimination, and employed independent monitors to assess code compliance (WEDO, 2007). Although Nike has made progress, problems remain at many Nike subcontractors. [...]

Lawsuits are another avenue for change, but many women lack the legal literacy, legal systems are not yet developed to support these types of complaints, and lawsuits require money and legal expertise often unavailable to affected women. However, in a victory for sweatshop activists, in 2004 the last of three lawsuits brought in 1999 by Sweatshop Watch, Global Exchange, Asian Law Caucus, Unite, and Saipan garment workers against dozens of U.S. big-name retailers and Saipan garment factories was settled (Bas, Benjamin, and Chang, 2004). The suits alleged violations of U.S. labor laws and international human rights standards in Saipan, an island in the U.S. Commonwealth of the Northern Mariana Islands. This island is home to a $1 billion garment industry, employing more than 10,000 workers, almost all young women from China, the Philippines, Thailand, Vietnam, and Bangladesh. Recruited with promises of high pay and quality work in the United States, the workers labored in sweatshop conditions to repay recruitment fees of up to $7,000. The retailers were also charged with misleading advertising by using the "Made in the U.S.A" label and promoting their goods as sweatshop-free. The companies agreed to improve work conditions, to pay $20 million in back wages (the largest award to date in an international human rights case), and to create a monitoring system to prevent labor abuses in Saipan factories (Bas et al., 2004; Collier and Strasburg, 2002). Increased public attention to sweatshops on Saipan has also led to greater enforcement of labor laws by the U.S. government (Bas et al., 2004). [...]

The Global Economy and Women's Migration

*****

It is estimated that worldwide, there are over 47 million legal and illegal women migrants (UNFPA, 2006). Scholars now speak of the "feminization of migration" because in many countries, female immigrants outnumber male immigrants (UNFPA, 2006). This section focuses on how globalization makes economic survival difficult in some countries and how this leads poor women to migrate to more affluent countries, where there is a strong demand for low-wage workers.[2] Many leave children behind in the care of family members, They typically send anywhere from half to nearly all of what they earn home to their families (*remittances*) and send a higher proportion of their earnings than men do (Ehrenreich and Hochschild, 2002). Governments in some countries, such as Sri Lanka, Vietnam, and the Philippines, encourage women to migrate because the money sent home contributes to the economy and reduces poverty (Chang, 2000; Ehrenreich and Hochschild, 2002; Parrenas 2008). For example, the largest sources of foreign currency in the Philippines are remittances sent home from migrant women (Parrenas, 2008).

The work that women migrants do in the global economy is often a reflection of traditional gender roles, and migrant women tend to work in traditionally "female" occupations marked by low wages and poor working conditions (UNFPA, 2006). They are the janitors, maids, and nannies, "hostesses" and "entertainers" (sex workers), nurses, and home health workers. Ironically, globalization and migration push women into wage labor that could conceivably result in economic independence and increased status, but at the same time, the type of work they tend to do reaffirms traditional gender roles (Parrenas, 2008). Women also sometimes migrate to become brides where there are shortages of women due to son preference or migration, or shortages of women that will accept traditional gender-role arrangements.

Women migrants are among the most vulnerable to human rights abuses (UNFPA, 2006). Migrant recruitment agencies often enable poor women to migrate to become domestic or care laborers, factory workers, or brides, but leave them in a position of indenture (*debt bondage*) as they work to pay off the fees (Parrenas, 2008). Criminal networks not only traffic drugs and guns, they use deception, coercion, and violence to traffic women for prostitution, domestic work, and sweatshop labor in what the United Nations calls the "dark underside" of globalization (UNFPA, 2006). During transit, women and girl migrants are often at risk for sexual harassment and abuse (UNFPA, 2006). Once they arrive, they often face multiple discriminations due to gender, race, class, and religion (UNFPA, 2006). Language, cultural barriers, and economic desperation interfere with migrant working women asserting their rights as women and workers and accessing services in cases of abuse. Undocumented workers without legal work papers and those who live where they work (like many nannies and domestics) are more likely to be exploited and to be physically or sexually abused since they face deportation or homelessness if they go to authorities.

Migrating for Domestic and Care Work

The globalization of domestic and care work is exemplified by the migration of southern women to northern nations. Domestic service and care work is one of the largest fields of employment for female migrants; there are literally millions of migrant women domestic and care workers. Approximately 1.5 million women domestic workers, primarily from Indonesia, Sri Lanka, and the Philippines, work in Saudi Arabia alone (Human Rights Watch, 2008; UNFPA, 2006). Domestic and care work is neither socially nor intellectually fulfilling but is chosen for economic reasons (Parrenas, 2001).

The increased demand for these workers in affluent countries is partly due to the entry of educated women in northern countries into the workforce (UNFPA, 2006). As middle- and upper-class women enter the professional workforce and have less time to devote to household labor, they seek help with the traditional household duties typically done by women. For the most part, men have not provided this help. Indeed, research indicates that women's entry into the workforce has barely impacted the amount of child care and household labor performed by men (Ehrenreich and Hochschild, 2002; UNFPA, 2006). Not only have men not taken up much of the "slack," but in many industrialized nations like the United States, governments do not provide or subsidize child care, after-school care, or paid maternity and family leave, thus leaving employed women few choices but to turn to migrant domestics. Worldwide, migrant domestics are also common in the homes of the most affluent families with stay-at-home wives and mothers (Anderson, 2002). Many, if not most, migrant women domestics have children and migrate as a means to support them. They express guilt and remorse about leaving their own homes and children to care for the households and children of others (Hochschild, 2002). [...]

While many domestic workers enjoy decent work conditions, others endure a range of abuses, including nonpayment of salaries, forced confinement, food deprivation, excessive workload, and instances of severe psychological, physical, and sexual abuse (Human Rights Watch, 2006, 2008). [...] Because domestic work is done in the home, unfair work conditions are not visible and subject to regulation (UNFPA, 2006). Most abuses occur in countries like Kuwait, Saudi Arabia, and United Arab Emirates, where domestic workers are not protected under law. Practices include taking women's passports upon arrival and law enforcement agencies' refusal to investigate or prosecute abuses, resulting in the return of domestic workers to their employers (UNFPA, 2006; Human Rights Watch, 2007). Some women and girls are trafficked into domestic service (VOA News, 2009).

In addition to human rights organizations like Human Rights Watch, a number of migrant workers' organizations work to expose abuses, fight for workers' rights, and assist victims of abuse. These include the British organization Kalayaan, RESPECT in Costa Rica, the Caribbean Female Household Workers Federation, and, in the United States, the Break the Chain Campaign for Migrant Domestic Worker Rights. Activists and the UN would like to see more labor laws and codes protecting migrant domestics' rights, criminal laws and penalties for abuses, accessible complaint mechanisms, and better resources for identifying and assisting victims. They also call upon the "labor-sending" countries to use diplomacy to improve conditions and to improve services at embassies and consular offices that would enable workers to leave abusive situations (Human Rights Watch, 2006). The UN calls upon affected countries to ratify and enforce the ILO's International Convention on the Rights of All Migrant Workers and Their Families.

Migrating to Marry

Another example of women migrating due to poverty is the phenomenon of *mail-order and Internet brides*. Women in poor economic circumstances are marketed as brides to American, European, and Asian men seeking traditional marriages and to Asian men who seek wives due to "bride deficits" caused by migration or son preference. For example, prenatal sex-selection and infanticide in some areas of India have led to a shortage of women. Villagers often turn to brokers to arrange for marriages between Indian men and Nepalese and Bangladeshi girls and women (UNFPA, 2006). Women are willing to migrate for marriage because they have few economic options. Sometimes they are under the impression that men in other countries will make better husbands and are less traditional than men in their country. Some are forced: girls as young as 13 (mainly from Asia and Eastern Europe) are trafficked as mail-order brides (UNICEF, 2009). In most cases these girls and women are powerless and isolated and at risk of violence.

There are thousands of commercial organizations that arrange introduction and broker marriages with foreign men. By the 1990s, international marriage agencies marketing women from the Philippines, India, Thailand, Eastern Europe, and Russia were established throughout Europe, the United States, Japan, and Australia. For a fee, potential customers can peruse hundreds of Internet mail-order bride sites and catalogues complete with photos and brief biographies. Some companies have package tours to countries like Russia and the Philippines to meet prospective brides. No firm statistics exist on the practice. However, in the United States alone, it is estimated that more than 500 international matchmaking services operate, annually arranging 9,500 to 14,000 marriages between American men and foreign women, mostly from the Philippines and former Soviet Union (Lindee, 2007).

There is some evidence that mail-order and Internet wives are more susceptible to domestic violence, but governments typically do not collect specific data on violence against this group of women (Lindee, 2007; Sassen, 2002). Imbalances in power, cultural differences, linguistic barriers, mail-order brides' lack of social and support networks, and the marketing of mail-order brides as submissive and deferential, likely increase risk (Lindee, 2007; UNFPA, 2006). In one famous U.S. case, Indle King, a 39-year-old man with a history of domestic violence, murdered his wife of two years, Anastasia, a 20-year-old mail-order bride from Kyrgystan. It was later discovered that Indle, while planning Anastasia's murder, was already seeking another mail-order wife. Some also argue that international marriage brokers participate in human trafficking (Barry, 1995; Lindee, 2007). Not only do they generally treat women as commodities to be "sold" to men, but some international marriage brokers are little more than covers for sexual tourism operations and, in extreme cases, covers for prostitution rings that traffic recently immigrated mail-order brides (Lindee, 2007).

Nongovernmental women's organizations act to protect mail-order and Internet brides from abuse. For example, in the United States, the Tahirih Justice Center played a key role in getting the U.S. Congress to draft and pass the International Marriage Broker Regulation Act of 2005. Signed into law by President G.W. Bush in 2006, the act requires international marriage brokers to obtain criminal histories on their male clients, including any records from the National Sex Offender Public Registry, and provide a report to foreign women in their native language. It also requires that prospective brides receive an information packet with domestic violence resources. Gabriela, a Philippines-American women's organization, the Coalition against Trafficking in Women, and the Global Alliance against Trafficking in Women (GATW), also work on this issue. Domestic violence shelters in regions where mail-order and Internet brides are more common are also adapting their services to help those who experience domestic violence.

Women and Girls' Labor in the Global Sex Trade

Women have engaged in sex work for centuries, but globalization has shaped the economics and practice of sex work in some remarkable ways.

Sexual Tourism

Easy global travel has changed the global sexual landscape, and travel for sexual purposes has grown with globalization. Sex work connected to tourism is known as *sexual tourism*. Sexual tourism is another effect of globalization and is made possible by a globalized system of communication and transportation (Cabezas, 2002). It arises out of a globalized economy that makes sex work one of the only ways for some women to earn a living wage and is fed by men from industrialized nations who draw on a racialized ideology where foreign females are thought [to] be more submissive and available than women in their own countries (Enloe, 1989). Sexual tourism is based on inequalities of power based on race, gender, class, and nationality (Brennan, 2004). Governments that need the money brought by international tourism are willing to encourage, or at least ignore, sexual tourism; it is their way of getting their piece of the global economic pie. Sexual tourism is yet another example of how the effects of globalization are not gender-neutral.

Sexual tourists are the hundreds of thousands of men who travel to other countries for sex holidays. Sex tourists come primarily from Australia, Canada, France, Germany, Japan, Kuwait, New Zealand, Norway, Qatar, Saudi Arabia, Sweden, the United Kingdom, and the United States (Seager, 1997). Their main destinations are Brazil, Cambodia, Costa Rica, Cuba, the Dominican Republic, India, Indonesia, Hungary, Kenya, Morocco, the Philippines, and Thailand. Thailand is one of the largest markets. Driven mostly by Australian, European, and American tourists, the number of prostitutes in Thailand ranges from 800,000 to 2 million, 20 percent of whom are 18 or younger (Guzder, 2009).

The nature of sex work in the global tourism industry varies based on region. For example, research in Sousa, Dominican Republic, suggests that some women perceive sex work as a possible stepping-stone to marriage to a foreigner and migration to a better life in another country (Brennan, 2002, 2004; Cabezas, 2002). Some Dominican sex workers attempt to persuade European tourists to send them money or marry them. They keep in touch with clients through global communications such as telephones, faxes, wire transfers, and the Internet (Brennan, 2002, 2004; Cabezas, 2002). In contrast, in the so-called "sexual Disneyland" of Bangkok, Thailand, sexual tourists can find [...] opportunities for sex with children (Guzder, 2009). [...]

Sex Trafficking

The majority of sex workers are forced by economic and, often, by single motherhood, into prostitution, but it is economics, not others, that forced them. In stark contrast are the millions of sex workers coerced or tricked, and even sold into sexual slavery and taken away from their home countries. They are part of the multi-billion-dollar *sex trafficking* industry. Sexual trafficking is a form of *human trafficking*, the acquisition of people by improper means such as force, fraud, or deception, with the aim of exploiting them (UNODC, 2009). Trafficking can be intra-regional (within a country or region) or trans-regional (across regions). Trafficking criminals target and exploit desperate people who are simply seeking a better life and orphaned and poverty-stricken children. Women and girls comprise 80 percent of victims (UNODC, 2009). [...]

Sex trafficking occurs all over the world, even in the United States, where an estimated 50,000 women are trafficked into the country each year (Seager, 2009). Here's just a sampling: Nepalese women and girls are trafficked to India; Bangladeshi women and girls are trafficked to Pakistan; Burmese women and girls are trafficked from Burma, Laos, and Cambodia to Thailand; women and children from East Asia, Southeast Asia, Eastern Europe, Russia, South America, and Latin America are trafficked to Japan; Nigerian and Balkan women (from Croatia, Bosnia-Herzegovina, Moldova, Yugoslavia, Kosovo, Macedonia, and Albania) are trafficked to Europe and Israel (Bales, 2002; Ebbe and Das, 2007; Seager, 2009; United States Department of State, 2009). [...]

Figure 54.2: Situations Women and Girls Are Trafficked Into

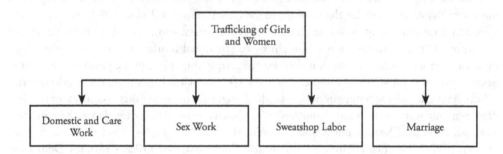

Trafficking agents, both women and men, are common. Agents use the offer of work to entice poor women to illegally immigrate to other countries. Women might be told they will work as maids, waitresses, or entertainers. Sometimes they are lured through false marriage offers. Upon arrival, however, their agent or "fiancé" sells them to a brothel or "club." Poverty-stricken parents may even sell their daughters to brothel brokers and agents, in most cases believing that the girls will work as maids, waitresses, or dishwashers, but sometimes understanding the work will be as a prostitute (Bales, 2002). According to Human Rights Watch, the recruiters often take advantage of families known to have financial difficulties. Debt bondage is not uncommon as women and girls are forced to continue in prostitution through the use of unlawful "debt" purportedly incurred through their transportation or recruitment (United States Department of State, 2009). They must first repay with interest the money given to their family or agent at the time of recruitment. This debt mounts as they are charged for food, shelter, and clothing. Should they try to leave the brothel without paying their debt, they are likely to experience physical punishment by the brothel owner or the police. To keep them there, they are threatened with harm to their parents and with being arrested as illegal immigrants. Lack of familiarity with the local language or dialect puts them at a further disadvantage. Because trafficked women are often in the country illegally, law enforcement agencies respond to them as lawbreakers rather than as victims. To make things worse, they may be prosecuted for illegally leaving their own country should they attempt to return home.

Women forced into prostitution are exposed to significant health risks in the forms of violence and disease (Bales, 2002; Human Rights Watch, 1995; Pyne, 1995). Rapes and beatings are used to ensure compliance. Multiple daily clients, and the occasional sadistic client, inflict more pain. In brothels, women are exposed to sexually transmitted diseases, such as HIV/AIDS, because they are not allowed to negotiate the terms of sex and are forced to have sex with as many as 20 clients a day. Sex-trafficked women and girls face especially high risks of HIV infection. For example, HIV prevalence of 38 percent has been found among sex-trafficked females who have been repatriated to Nepal; up to half of the women and girls trafficked to Mumbai, India, have tested HIV-positive (UNAIDS, 2008). Although condoms may be available to clients, the client typically has the choice of whether or not to use them. The case of Lin Lin, a young woman from Burma (Myanmar), is described in Box 54.2 and illustrates these points.

BOX 54.2: Forced Prostitution: The Case of Lin Lin

Lin Lin was thirteen years old when she was recruited by an agent for work in Thailand. Her financially destitute father took 12,000 baht (equal to $480) from the agent with the understanding that his daughter would pay the loan back out of her earnings. The agent took Lin Lin to Bangkok, and three days later she was taken to the Ran Dee Prom brothel. Lin Lin did not know what was going on until a man came into her room and started touching her breasts and body and then forced her to have sex. For the next two years, Lin Lin worked in various parts of Thailand in four different brothels.

The owners told her she would have to keep prostituting herself until she paid off her father's debt. Her clients paid the owner 100 baht ($4) each time. If she refused a client's requests, she was slapped and threatened by the owner. On January 18, 1993, the Crime Suppression Division of the Thai police raided the brothel, and she was taken to a shelter run by a local nongovernmental organization. She was fifteen years old and tested positive for HIV.

Source: H.H. Pyne, "AIDS and Gender Violence: The Enslavement of Burmese Women in the Thai Sex Industry," in *Women's Rights, Human Rights: International Feminist Perspectives,* eds. J. Peters and A. Wolper (New York: Routledge, 1995), 215–223.

Stopping human trafficking is difficult because demand is high and there is a steady supply of potential victims to feed it—a supply sustained by poverty, ignorance, organized crime, and government and police tolerance and corruption. Some suggest that the only way to reduce demand is through the apprehension and prosecution of perpetrators—this will require a big commitment from governments worldwide. Reduction of supply will only be accomplished through a lessening of poverty, educating potential victims, and the dismantling of criminal trafficking networks. Trafficking is also difficult to eradicate because it is based on prejudice against women, minorities, and lower socioeconomic groups (Ebbe and Das, 2007).

Due to globalization and sophisticated criminal networks, international cooperation is essential. The Protocol to Prevent, Suppress, and Punish Trafficking in Persons, especially Women and Children, was adopted by the UN General Assembly in 2003 and by 2009 had been ratified by 132 member nations (UN Treaty Collection, 2009). It is the first global legally binding instrument with an agreed definition on trafficking in persons. Objectives of the Protocol are to prevent and combat the trafficking of women and children; to protect and assist the victims of trafficking; and to promote cooperation among governments to achieve these objectives. [...]

There are many NGOs working on the issue. Human rights NGOs like Human Rights Watch and Amnesty International investigate the trafficking of women and girls and compile data that are useful in advocacy efforts. They pressure governments to bring their countries into compliance with international trafficking treaties. Donor countries are advised to use every opportunity to raise the issue of trafficking publicly and in official meetings. The Coalition against Trafficking in Women-International (CATW), a GRSO that works with NGOs all over the world, was founded in 1988. CATW was the first international nongovernmental organization to focus on human trafficking, especially sex trafficking of women and girls. They have many programs, projects, and campaigns. The GRSO the Global Fund for Women has awarded over $3 million to 300 groups in 71 countries, which work to prevent or stop trafficking and offer services and counseling to survivors. GROs like Shakti Samuha in Kathmandu, Nepal, help survivors. Shakti Samuhu established the first shelter run by and for trafficking survivors in South Asia. NGOs such a Shared Hope International, with outreach efforts in the United States, India, Nepal, and Jamaica, and Safe House for Women in Yugoslavia, rescue women and provide them with medical treatment and counseling. Finally, sex worker NGOs such as MODEMU in the Dominican Republic and Zi Teng in Hong Kong, work to advocate for the rights and welfare of sex workers (Cabezas, 2002; Lim, 2008). They seek to legitimize sex work as a profession where sex workers are not abused, persecuted, or exploited and have decent work conditions.

Conclusion

In this chapter you learned that globalization has had mixed effects for women and girls. Although it has increased women's paid employment and consequently benefited some women, the costs of economic adjustment are also often disproportionately borne by women—especially women who are already poor. Such women are hit harder by economic downturns and are more likely to directly experience the effects of environmental degradation. Because they have few economic choices, they can be exploited in the global labor marketplace and by human traffickers. This is another example of how women's disadvantage arises out of material, economic forces. Globalization has also created a number of violations of women's human rights. We need to ask, as Hochschild (2002) suggested, what kind of a world globalization has created when working in a sweatshop, sex work, migration to work as a domestic, and becoming a mail-order bride are rational economic choices. These may appear to be individual choices, but they are not really free—they are the result of economic globalization. This chapter also illustrates intersectionality because how globalization affects women depends on their race, region, and socioeconomic class. It further illustrates the connectedness of women everywhere.

[...] This chapter illustrates the global women's studies theme of activism and empowerment. Once again, we saw that where there are gendered wrongs, there are people working for women's rights. The "silver lining" of the globalization "cloud" is that in many cases globalization has inadvertently led to women's empowerment as women organize to combat its negative effects. Globalization can expose women to ideas and influences that inspire them to question and challenge gender inequality where they live. It opens up new spaces for resistance such as cross-border networks and transnational activism (Lim, 2008). Fueled by the dynamic of globalization itself, women all over the world fight the negative effects of globalization and use the transnational political stage to press for social, economic, environmental, and political justice (Cabezas, 2002; Desai, 2007a, 2007b). Transnational networks of activists play an increasing role in international and regional politics and may have progressive effects on policies regarding women, human rights, and the environment (Karides, 2002; Keck and Sikkink, 1998). They can expose injustices in an international arena. This is globalization from below, rather than from above. They use electronic communication and international and regional conferences to share information and expand political participation.

*****

Notes

1. In northern countries like the U.S., recessions and neo-liberal economic policies also lead to cuts in services and subsidies, cuts that disproportionately affect poor women and children.
2. Women also migrate to escape war, violence, and persecution (there are approximately 6 million women refugees). See http://www.unhcr.org/pages/49c3646c1d9.html.

References

Anderson, B. 2002. Just another job? The commodification of domestic labor. In *Global woman: Nannies, maids, and sex workers in the new economy*, edited by B. Ehrenreich and A.R. Hochschild. New York: Metropolitan Books.

Bales, K. 2002. Because she looks like a child. In *Global woman: Nannies, maids, and sex workers in the new economy*, edited by B. Ehrenreich and A.R. Hochschild. New York: Metropolitan Books.

Barry, K. 1995. *The prostitution of sexuality.* New York: New York University Press.

Bas, N.F., M. Benjamin, and J.C. Chang. 2004. Saipan sweatshop lawsuit ends with important gains for workers and lessons for activists. http://www.cleanclothes .org/ about-us/ 617-saipan-sweatshop-lawsuit-ends-with-important-ga.

Blumberg, R.L. 1995. Gender, microenterprise, performance, and power: Case studies from the Dominican Republic, Ecuador, Guatemala, and Swaziland. In *Women in the Latin American development process*, edited by C.E. Bose and E. Acosta-Belen. Philadelphia: Temple University Press.

Boyenge, J.S. 2007. *ILO database on export processing zones (Revised).* Geneva: International Labour Organization.

Brennan, D. 2002. Selling sex for visas: Sex tourism as a stepping stone to international migration. In *Global woman: Nannies, maids, and sex workers in the new economy*, edited by B. Ehrenreich and A.R. Hochschild. New York: Metropolitan Books.

Brennan, D. 2004. *Transnational desires and sex tourism in the Dominican Republic: What's love got to do with it?* Durham, NC: Duke University Press.

Cabezas, A.L. 2002. Tourism, sex work, and women's rights in the Dominican Republic. In *Globalization and human rights*, edited by A. Brysk. Berkeley: University of California Press.

Chang, G. 2000. *Disposable domestics.* Cambridge, MA: South End Press.

Collier, R., and J. Strasburg. 2002. Clothiers fold on sweatshop lawsuit. *San Francisco Chronicle*, September 7, Al.

Desai, M. 2002. Transnational solidarity: Women's agency, structural adjustment, and globalization. In *Women's activism and globalization: Linking local struggles and transnational politics*, edited by A. Naples and M. Desai. New York: Routledge.

Desai, M. 2007a. The messy relationship between feminisms and globalizations. *Gender and Society,* 21, no. 6, 797–804.

Desai, M. 2007b. The perils and possibilities of transnational feminism. *Women's Studies Quarterly,* 35, 333–337.

Ebbe, O.N.I., and D.K. Das. 2007. *Global trafficking in women and children.* Boca Raton, FL: Taylor & Francis.

Ehrenreich, B., and A.R. Hochschild (Eds.). 2002. *Global woman: Nannies, maids, and sex workers in the new economy.* New York: Metropolitan Books.

Enloe, C. 1989. *Bananas, beaches, and bases: Making feminist sense of international relations.* Berkeley: University of California Press.

Fuentes, A., and B. Ehrenreich. 1983. *Women in the global factory.* Boston, MA: South End Press.

Gunewardena, N., and A. Kingsolver. 2007. Introduction. In *The gender of globalization: Women navigating cultural and economic marginalities,* edited by N. Gunewardena and A. Kingsolver. Santa Fe, NM: School for Advanced Research Press.

Guzder, D. 2009. Thailand: The world's sex capital. *Untold stories: Dispatches from the Pulitzer Center on Crisis Reporting.* http://pulitzercenter.trypepad.com/untold_stories/2009/08/thailand-flesh-market.html#more.

Hochschild, A.R 2002. Love and gold. In *Global woman: Nannies, maids, and sex workers in the new economy,* edited by B. Ehrenreich and A.R. Hochschild. New York: Metropolitan Books.

Human Rights Watch. 1995. *The Human Rights Watch global report on women's human rights.* New York: Human Rights Watch.

Human Rights Watch. 2006. *Swept under the rug: Abuses against domestic workers around the world.* http://www.hrw.org/en/reports/2006/07/27swept-under-rug-0.

Human Rights Watch. 2007. *Exported and exposed: Abuse against Sri Lankan domestic workers in Saudi Arabia, Kuwait, Lebanon, and the United Arab Emirates.* http://www.hrw.org/en/reports/2007/11/13/exported-and-exposed-1.

Human Rights Watch. 2008. *"As if I am not human": Abuses against Asia domestic workers in Saudi Arabia.* http://www.hrw.org/en/reports/2008/07/07if-i-am-not-human-0.

ICFTU (International Confederation of Trade Unions). 2006. *Annual survey of violations of trade union rights 2006.* Brussels, Belgium: Author.

International Labour Organization. 2007. *What are EPZs?* http://ilo.org/public/english/dialogue/sector/themes/epz.htm.

Karides, M. 2002. Linking local efforts with global struggle: Trinidad's national union of domestic employees. In *Women's activism and globalization: Linking local struggles and transnational politics,* edited by N.A. Naples and M. Desai. New York: Routledge.

Keck, M.E., and K. Sikkink. 1998. *Activists beyond borders: Transnational advocacy networks in international politics.* Ithaca, NY: Cornell University Press.

Lim, G. 2008. *Invisible trade II: Secrets of the sex industry in Singapore.* Singapore: Monsoon Books.

Lim, L.Y.C. 1990. Women's work in export factories: The politics of a cause. In *Persistent inequalities,* edited by I. Tinker. Oxford: Oxford University Press.

Lindee, K.M. 2007. Love, honor, or control: Domestic, violence, trafficking, and the question of how to regulate the mail-order bride industry. *Columbia Journal of Gender & Law,* 16, 551–602.

Lorentzen, L.A., and J. Turpin. 1996. Introduction: The gendered new world order. In *The gendered new world,* edited by J. Turpin and L.A. Lorentzen. New York: Routledge.

Louie, M.C.Y. 2001, *Sweatshop warriors*. Cambridge, MA: South End Press.

Moghadam, V.M. 1999. Gender and globalization: Female labor and women's mobilization. *Journal of World Systems Research*, 5, 367–388.

Moghadam, V.M. 2005. *Globalizing women: Transnational feminist networks*. Baltimore, MD: Johns Hopkins University Press.

Moran, T.H. 2002. *Beyond Sweatshops: Foreign direct investment and globalization in developing countries*. Washington, DC: Brookings Institution Press.

Mosse, J.C. 1993. *Half the world, half a chance: An introduction to gender and development*. Oxford: Oxfam.

Naples, N.A. 2002. Changing the terms: Community activism, globalization, and the dilemmas of transnational praxis. In *Women's activism and globalization: Linking local struggles and transnational politics*, edited by N.A. Naples and M. Desai. New York: Routledge.

National Labor Committee. 2008. *Women exploiting women: Women in the U.S. are purchasing clothing sewn by women who are exploited in Guatemala*. http://www.nlcnet.org/reports.php?id=614.

National Labor Committee. 2009. *High-tech misery in China*. http://www.nlcnet.org/reports.php?id=613.

Parrenas, R.S. 2001. *Servants of globalization: Women, migration, and domestic work*. Stanford, CA: Stanford University Press.

Parrenas, R.S. 2008. *The force of domesticity: Filipina migrants and globalization*. New York: New York University Press.

Pyne, H.H. 1995. AIDS and gender violence: The enslavement of Burmese women in the Thai sex industry. In *Women's rights, human rights: International feminist perspectives*, edited by J. Peters and A. Wolper. New York: Routledge.

Salzinger, L. 2003. *Genders in production: Making workers in Mexico's global factories*. Berkeley: University of California Press.

Sassen, S. 2002. Global cities and survival circuits. In *Global women: Nannies, maids, and sex workers in the new economy*, edited by B. Ehrenreich and A.R. Hochschild. New York: Metropolitan Books.

Seager, J. 1997. *The state of the world atlas: New revised second edition*. London: Penguin.

Seager, J. 2009. *The Penguin atlas of women of the world*, 4th ed. New York: Penguin.

Stearns, J. 1998. *Gender and international relations: An introduction*. New Brunswick, NJ: Rutgers University Press.

UN (United Nations). 1999. *World survey on the role of women in development: Globalization, gender, and work*. New York: Author.

UNAIDS. 2008. *2008 report on the global AIDS epidemic*. Geneva: UNAIDS.

UNFPA (United Nations Population Fund). 2006. *State of the world population 2006: A Passage to hope—women and international migration*. http://www.unfpa.org/swp/2006/.

UNICEF (United Nations Children's Fund). 2009. *Child trafficking*. http://www.unicef.org/protection /index_exploitation.html.

UNIFEM (United Nations Development Fund for Women). 2009. *Progress of the world's women 2008/2009: Who answers to women? Gender and accountability*. http://www.unifem.org/progress/2008.

United States Department of State. 2009. *Trafficking in persons report*. http://www.state.gov/g/tip/rls.tiprpt/2009/.

UNODC (United Nations Office of Drugs and Crime). 2009. *Global report on trafficking in persons.* United Nations Office of Drugs and Crime. http://www.unodc.org/documents/human_trafficking.

UN Treaty Collection. 2009. *Protocol to Prevent, Suppress, and Punish Trafficking Persons, Especially Women and Children, Supplementing the United Nations Convention against Transnational Organized Crime.* http://treates.un.org/Pages/ViewDetails.aspx?src=TREATY&mtdsg_no=XVIII-12-a&chapter=18&lang=en.

VOA News. 2009. *Trafficking in women and girls.* August 8. http://www.voanews.com/uspolicy/2009-08-10-voal.cfm.

WEDO. 2007. *Challenging Nike to deliver on worker rights.* http://www.wedo.org/tag/corporate-campaigns.

WEDO. 2009. *Corporate accountability.* http://www.wedo.org/category/learn/campaigns/corporate-accountability/policy-advocacy.

World Bank. 2009. *Gender in agricultural sourcebook.* Washington, DC: Author.

The IMF: Violating Women since 1945

Christine Ahn and Kavita Ramdas

Christine Ahn is a policy analyst with expertise in globalization, militarism, women's rights, and philanthropy. She is the editor of Shafted: Free Trade and America's Working Poor *and contributor to* The Revolution Will Not be Funded. *She has addressed U.S. Congress, the United Nations, and the National Human Rights Commission in South Korea and has been interviewed on CNN, Al-Jazeera, National Public Radio, and Voice of America. Ahn is currently the senior research and policy analyst at the Global Fund for Women, senior fellow with the Oakland Institute, and a consultant to the Grassroots Global Justice Alliance.*

Kavita Ramdas is a visiting scholar at Stanford University's Center on Democracy, Development and the Rule of Law and the Center for Philanthropy and Civil Society. From 1996 to 2010 she served as president and CEO of the Global Fund for Women, the largest grant-making foundation in the world focused exclusively on supporting international women's human rights. Ramdas currently serves as a member of Princeton University's Board of Trustees, the Board of Trustees of Mount Holyoke College, and the Advisory Panel to the Global Development Program of the Bill and Melinda Gates Foundation.

As Dominique Strauss-Kahn, head of the world's most powerful financial institution, the International Monetary Fund (IMF), spends a few nights in Rikers Island prison awaiting a hearing, the world is learning a lot about his history of treating women as expendable sex objects. Strauss-Kahn has been charged with rape and forced imprisonment of a 32-year-old Guinean hotel worker at a $3,000-a-night luxury hotel in New York.

While the media dissects the attempted rape of a young African woman and begins to dig out more information about Strauss-Kahn's past indiscretions, we couldn't help but see this situation through the feminist lens of the "personal is political."

For many in the developing world, the IMF and its draconian policies of structural adjustment have systematically "raped" the earth and the poor and violated the human rights of women. It appears that the personal disregard and disrespect for women demonstrated by the man at the highest levels of leadership within the IMF is quite consistent with the gender bias inherent in the IMF's institutional policies and practice.

Systematic Violation of Women's Human Rights

The IMF and the World Bank were established in the aftermath of World War II to promote international trade and monetary cooperation by giving governments loans in times of severe budget crises. Although 184 countries make up the IMF's membership, only five countries—France, Germany, Japan, Britain, and the United States—control 50 percent of the votes, which are allocated according to each country's contribution.

The IMF has earned its villainous reputation in the Global South because in exchange for loans, governments must accept a range of austerity measures known as structural adjustment programs (SAPs). A typical IMF package encourages export promotion over local production for local consumption. It also pushes for lower tariffs and cuts in government programs such as welfare and education. Instead of reducing poverty, the trillion dollars of loans issued by the IMF have deepened poverty, especially for women who make up 70 percent of the world's poor.

IMF-mandated government cutbacks in social welfare spending have often been achieved by cutting public sector jobs, which disproportionately impact women. Women hold most of the lower-skilled public sector jobs, and they are often the first to be cut. Also, as social programs like caregiving are slashed, women are expected to take on additional domestic responsibilities that further limit their access to education or other jobs.

In exchange for borrowing $5.8 billion from the IMF and World Bank, Tanzania agreed to impose fees for health services, which led to fewer women seeking hospital deliveries or post-natal care and, naturally, higher rates of maternal death. In Zambia, the imposition of SAPs led to a significant drop in girls' enrollment in schools and a spike in "survival or subsistence sex" as a way for young women to continue their educations.

But IMF's austerity measures don't just apply to poor African countries. In 1997, South Korea received $57 billion in loans in exchange for IMF conditionalities that forced the government to introduce "labor market flexibility," which outlined steps for the government to compress wages, fire "surplus workers," and cut government spending on programs and infrastructure. When the financial crisis hit, seven Korean women were laid off for every one Korean man. In a sick twist, the Korean government launched a "get your husband energized" campaign encouraging women to support depressed male partners while they cooked, cleaned, and cared for everyone.

Nearly 15 years later, the scenario is grim for South Korean workers, especially women. Of all OECD countries, Koreans work the longest hours: 90 percent of men and 77 percent of women work over 40 hours a week. According to economist Martin Hart-Landsberg, in 2000, 40 percent of Korean workers were irregular workers; by 2008, 60 percent worked in the informal economy. The Korean Women Working Academy reports that today 70 percent of Korean women workers are temporary laborers.

Selling Mother Earth

IMF policies have also raped the earth by dictating that governments privatize the natural resources most people depend on for their survival: water, land, forests, and fisheries. SAPs have also forced developing countries to stop growing staple foods for domestic consumption and instead focus on growing cash crops, like cut flowers and coffee for export to volatile global markets. These policies have destroyed the livelihoods of small-scale subsistence farmers, the majority of whom are women.

"IMF adjustment programs forced poor countries to abandon policies that protected their farmers and their agricultural production and markets," says Henk Hobbelink of GRAIN, an international organization that promotes sustainable agriculture and biodiversity. "As a result, many countries became dependent on food imports, as local farmers could not compete with the subsidized products from the North. This is one of the main factors in the current food crisis, for which the IMF is directly to blame."

In the Democratic Republic of Congo (DRC), IMF loans have paved the way for the privatization of the country's mines by transnational corporations and local elites, which has forcibly displaced thousands of Congolese people in a context where women and girls experience obscenely high levels of sexual slavery and rape in the eastern provinces. According to Gender Action, the World Bank and IMF have made loans to the DRC to restructure the mining sector, which translates into laying off tens of thousands of workers, including women and girls who depend on the mining operations for their livelihoods. Furthermore, as the land becomes mined and privatized, women and girls responsible for gathering water and firewood must walk even further, making them more susceptible to violent crimes.

We Are Over It

- Women's rights activists around the globe are consistently dumbfounded by how such violations of women's bodies are routinely dismissed as minor transgressions. Strauss-Kahn, one of the world's most powerful politicians whose decisions affected millions across the globe, was known for being a "womanizer" who often forced himself on younger, junior women in subordinate positions where they were vulnerable to his far greater power, influence, and clout. Yet none of his colleagues or fellow Socialist Party members took these reports seriously, colluding in a consensus shared even by his wife that the violation of women's bodily integrity is not in any sense a genuine violation of human rights.

Why else would the world tolerate the unearthly news that 48 Congolese women are raped every hour with deadening inaction? Eve Ensler speaks for us all when she writes, "I am over a world that could allow, has allowed, continues to allow 400,000 women, 2,300 women, or one woman to be raped anywhere, anytime of any day in the Congo. The women of Congo are over it too."

We live in a world where millions of women don't speak their truth, don't tell their dark stories, don't reveal their horror lived every day just because they were born women. They don't do it for the same reasons that the women in the Congo articulate—they are tired of not being heard. They are tired of men like Strauss-Kahn, powerful and in suits, believing that they can rape a black woman in a hotel room, just because they feel like it. They are tired of the police not believing them or arresting them for being sex workers. They are tired of hospitals not having rape kits. They are tired of reporting rape and being charged for adultery in Iran, Pakistan, and Saudi Arabia.

Fighting Back

For each one of them, and for those of us who have spent many years investing in the tenacity of women's movements across the globe, the courage and gumption of the young Guinean immigrant shines like the torch held by Lady Liberty herself. This young woman makes you believe we can change this reality. She refused to be intimidated. She stood up for herself. She fought to free herself—twice—from the violent grip of the man attacking her. She didn't care who he was—she knew she was violated and she reported it straight to the hotel staff, who went straight to the New York police, who went straight to JFK to pluck Strauss-Kahn from his first-class Air France seat.

In a world where it often feels as though wealth and power can buy anything, the courage of a young woman and the people who stood by her took our breath away. These stubborn, ethical acts of working-class people in New York City reminded us that women have the right to say "no." It reminded us that "no" does not mean "yes" as the Yale fraternities would have us believe, and, most importantly, that no one, regardless of their position or their gender, should be above the law. A wise woman judge further drove home the point about how critically important it is to value women's bodies when she denied Strauss-Kahn bail, citing his long history of abusing women.

Strauss-Kahn sits in his Rikers Island cell. It would be a great thing if his trial succeeds in ending the world's tolerance for those who discriminate and abuse women. We cannot tolerate it one second longer. We cannot tolerate it at the personal level, we must refuse to condone it at the professional level, and we must challenge it every time it we see it in the policies of global institutions like the International Monetary Fund.

Source: Christine Ahn and Kavita Ramdas, "The IMF: Violating Women Since 1945," in *Foreign Policy in Focus* (2011), retrieved from http://www.fpif.org/articles/the_imf_violating_women_since_1945

Chapter 55

Women behind the Labels: Worker Testimonies from Central America

STITCH and the Maquila Solidarity Network

STITCH is an independent, non-profit women's solidarity network that supports women workers in Central America and immigrant workers in the United States to plan and carry out labour organizing campaigns. By adopting a feminist perspective, STITCH seeks to sustain unions and women's and workers' rights through leadership development, training programs, and exchanges that increase women's organizing skills and build ties between workers and activists.

The Maquila Solidarity Network (MSN) is a labour and women's rights organization that supports the efforts of workers in global supply chains to win improved wages and working conditions, and therefore a better quality of life for themselves and their families. MSN works alongside women's and labour rights organizations in Mexico, Central America, and Asia to strengthen their capacity to challenge the negative impacts of globalization on workers in the global garment industry.

Introduction

The women whose stories appear [here] are pioneer union organizers. They are the women behind the clothing labels and food brands that have inspired campaigns against sweatshops across North America. They are emerging leaders of a growing movement of strong and committed women determined to improve conditions for themselves and their co-workers. They want jobs, yes, but dignified jobs, and wages that allow them to provide for themselves and their families.

The Maquilas

Marie [and others] have worked in Central America's maquiladora garment factories, making brand-name apparel for the North American market. They organized workers in an industry with almost no unions and even fewer collective bargaining agreements.

Maquiladoras, also known as maquilas, are factories that assemble goods for export. In Central America, the majority of maquilas assemble clothing, almost all of which is exported to North America.

Guatemala and Honduras each have approximately 300 maquiladora factories. Yet, as of August 2000, there are only 10 maquilas with signed collective agreements in Honduras and none in Guatemala.

Countless studies of Central America's maquiladoras have documented inhumane working conditions; verbal, physical, and sexual abuse of women workers; and vehement union-busting tactics of employers. Reports of sweatshop abuses have generated citizen outcry in Central America and a growing anti-sweatshop movement in North America.

Companies have flocked to Central America not just for so-called cheap labour, but also because here they can operate with impunity. They face almost no regulation from local governments dependent on foreign investment to create employment, and little opposition from the local labor movement weakened by years of violent repression.

The workers' stories reveal the human reality behind the statistics: how it feels to work a 16-hour shift in a crowded factory, the unrelenting pressure to produce more in less time, the continual harassment by supervisors, harassment that turns to repression when workers begin to organize to defend their rights.

*****

The interviews also reveal a less visible aspect of the maquila—how organizing experiences have changed women's lives.

For the first time, these women took on positions of leadership, and, in some cases, began to demand their rights at home as well as at work. Long after the initial campaigns were over, and in spite of the setbacks, the women who tell their stories continue to organize for change, in other factories, in their personal lives, and in the broader union and social movement.

*****

The Women behind the Labels

Too often, the media, and even the anti-sweatshop movement, present the women behind the labels and brands as helpless victims. We hope these stories of Central American women working for change will help challenge that notion.

The women who speak through the pages of *Women behind the Labels* share stories of organizing against all odds for better wages and working conditions, but also for justice, respect, and a better future for themselves and their children.

At some point, each of the women decides she can no longer accept the inhumane conditions forced upon her and her family and fellow workers. [...]

The interviews were carried out by Marion Traub-Werner in October–December of 1998.

*****

If you don't learn to defend yourself, you're in real trouble.

—Marie Mejia

Marie Mejia is the lead organizer for the International Textile, Garment and Leather Workers Federation (ITGLWF)[1] maquila organizing project in Guatemala. For the past two years she has spent close to seven days a week going from house to house and maquila to maquila talking to workers about the benefits of organizing. Marie speaks from experience—as a former maquila worker, teenage domestic worker, and child laborer on coffee plantations.

The oldest of seven from a Mayan indigenous family in the western province of San Marcos, Marie has lived several lifetimes in her 26 years. She started working at the age of 12. At 15, she left home to work in Mexico in order to help her family. That experience left her fiercely independent—a characteristic embodied in her determined step, her perfect posture, and her resolute voice.

Hearing about the interviews I was doing, Marie approached me one day and asked to participate. "You should really interview me," she said. "I have worked in just about every job there is." During the interview, I barely had to ask any questions. For two hours, Marie led me through an emotional journey, one she had not shared with many people. Later, she played the tapes for her siblings as a way of explaining to them what it was like for her to come of age away from them, her parents, and her country.

Marion: What is your family like?

Marie: I am the oldest of seven. I left school when I was 12. I went with my father to cut coffee outside of Tapachula in Mexico. When we arrived at the finca, the coffee harvest was over. The only work for women was collecting garbage, while the men worked clearing brush in the mountains. I helped my father clear brush even though they said it was "men's work." One day my father was bitten by a scorpion while working, and from then on he wouldn't let me do that work.

After a while there wasn't work for women or men. That's when I decided to go to Tapachula to get a job as a domestic worker. My father accompanied me to the house. I remember how he cried when the señora took me inside and closed the door. I could see him outside, just standing there. I only lasted two months in that first house. I was desperate to see my mother and father. I knew that if my father had reacted that way, my mother was sure to be feeling even worse. I went home for two months, and then had to return to Tapachula. That was in 1988.

I found work at another house, earning 80 pesos [U.S.$32] a month. But I didn't like it. I had problems with the grandfather who lived there. He was always watching me. Once he pushed me into my room and locked me in. I found out later that he had raped all the maids that had come to work there. That's when I left. I worked at that house for five months.

At the next house I earned 150 pesos [U.S.$60] a month. It was only about three blocks from where I worked before. By that time, I was 16. I never went hungry in that house. Never. I had food and my own room, and nobody tried to come in. But I had to work very hard. The house was huge, with something like five bathrooms and a big patio. I worked there for six years, until I ran into problems after the señor divorced and remarried. After living nine months with his new wife, I had to leave. She said I was paid too much for the amount of work that there was to do. Can you imagine? I did everything—washed and ironed their clothes, made their food, went to the market, mopped and scrubbed the floors. Everything. I would get up at 6:00 in the morning and be rushing all day until 10:00 or 10:30 at night when I finally could stop working.

Marion: Are your parents ladino² or indigenous?

Marie: They are indigenous. They speak Mam,³ but my father never permitted us to learn to speak that dialect. When he was little, he didn't learn to speak Spanish, and had a lot of problems because of it. My mother still wears traditional dress. I did too when I was little, but I stopped when I was working in Tapachula.

Marion: And in Tapachula, did you earn enough to help out your parents or just to support yourself?

Marie: When I started I was earning 80 pesos a month. I kept 20 pesos for myself and gave the rest to my father, who used to come to Tapachula every month. Later, when I earned 150 pesos a month, I gave my father 120 and kept 30 for myself. And with those 30 pesos, I had to buy soap, shampoo, deodorant, towels, and all of that. It wasn't much, but I always tried to find a way to make the money last, because I was working there to help my family.

Marion: How did you learn to sew?

Marie: When I was having problems with the last señora, I started thinking about finding another kind of work. So I asked the señor if he would give me permission to study sewing for one hour a day.

My next job was working in a tailor shop. I earned very little, 10 pesos [U.S.$3.50] for each piece of clothing I finished. I made one piece a day, which meant I had only 10 pesos to pay for a room, food, and transportation. That was not enough, so I decided to look for work in a house again.

At the next house where I worked I earned good money, but I had to do the work of two. In the morning I made breakfast for the girls and took them to school. Then I made breakfast for the señora and her husband, the doctor. After that, I would go to the market, wash and iron the clothes, and clean the house. When the girls got back from school, I took them to ballet. I looked after those two girls as if they were my own; it was a huge responsibility. The girls had rooms of their own with separate bathrooms. Lots of clothes. Sheets for the bed. Everything had to be washed, and of course there was no washing machine.

The man who lived next door tried to warn me that the señora was bad, but I thought she was alright. I learned how wrong I was. I had just returned from going to visit my family when she accused me of stealing. She started going through my clothes. She even searched my underwear, which I think is what hurt me the most. The señora called the police and they came and took me to the station. The police commander said he would let me go if I would go out with him. I told him that he better arrest me, because I would never go out with him. He disgusted me.

I went to my old boss for help. He went the very next morning to a government official and got the charges dropped.

That was the last time I worked in a house. I decided to rent a small room and started working as a food vendor, making 30 pesos [U.S.$4.70] a day. There were a lot of problems with that job too, but the good thing about the job was that the vendors were organized and I started to learn about unions. In 1996, I left Tapachula for good and came here to Guatemala.

Marion: Is that when you started working in the maquila?

Marie: Yes. My uncle suggested that since I liked sewing, I should try working in the maquila. So my brother and I went looking for work all along Avenida Petapa [the main industrial road]. At the Daimi factory we asked if there were any openings. I told them I was an operator, that I had experience. They hired both of us right away.

I had never worked in a factory and didn't know what to expect. But it didn't take long before I started to see how badly they treated people, how they yelled at them. A Korean supervisor named Señora Lee was the worst. You wouldn't believe how she mistreated people. She screamed at people in front of everyone. Her favorite phrases were: "Do you want to work? Yes or No?" Or, "Why don't you look for another job if you don't want to work?" And, "You are useless. You aren't worth a salary." When she yelled at the workers, most of the women would cry.

I was afraid that Señora Lee would yell at me, but the woman she scolded the most on our line was our line supervisor, Carmen. Who knows what she had against her? Señora Lee would throw pieces of clothing in her face. When she finally managed to get Carmen suspended, a few of us tried to stop the line. We couldn't do it because some of the workers refused to join us.

My pay for the first two weeks at Daimi was 90 quetzales [U.S.$15]. Oh, it made me want to cry. Every day I had to pay for four bus trips and food, and then to receive only 90 quetzales. It made me very angry, but I couldn't quit because my sister had just left her husband and we needed the money. The most I ever earned at Daimi was 365 quetzales [U.S.$60] for two weeks' work and that included all my overtime hours.

I didn't complain about the wages because I didn't know how much I was entitled to. At that point I didn't even know what the minimum wage was.

Marion: What were the hours like?

Marie: Long. We had to be at work at 7:00 in the morning, and then supposedly we'd be able to leave at 4:40 in the afternoon. But almost every day we had to work overtime until at least 7:40 p.m. The Koreans would stand in front of the door and not let anybody out. They would stand there and shout, "You, overtime." They'd even grab you and haul you inside. It didn't matter whether you wanted to work or not. They wouldn't let you out.

I worked all day sitting on a little stool, with only one short break for lunch. By the end of a 12-hour day, my body really hurt. And then there were the night shifts. Sometimes we would have to stay all night and maybe take a break to sleep three or four hours on the floor next to the machine. If I was doing pants, I would take a bunch down and cover myself so I wouldn't get too cold. In the morning, I would fold them back up like nothing had happened. They would give you breakfast in the morning and tell you to get to work. You have to learn to defend yourself during those all-nighters. It can be dangerous. Men and women stay together in a small area, and there have been cases of women being raped.

Marion: How did you find out about the union?

Marie: A young guy in the factory came and told me about Juan Jose, a student who was working as an organizer with the ITGLWF. I think he'd heard me complain about how little we got paid. He told me that there was a way to fix the situation. When I asked how, he told me that there were some students who wanted to help improve conditions in the maquilas, but that things would only improve if we wanted them to change. He asked if he could give Juan Jose my address, and I said yes.

That next Sunday Juan Jose came to my house. He explained how they worked, and that we needed to organize to improve conditions in all the factories. If we didn't, then the bosses would always treat our people this way. I told him I wanted to get involved; at that point my brother didn't want to. He didn't believe it could work.

I started going to meetings. We'd look over the lists of workers to identify people we might be able to recruit. Over time, I was able to recruit a number of people from my line.

Soon the owners started getting suspicious. They started watching us. About that time, there were several waves of firings. That was in 1997. I hardly knew anyone who was fired in the first round. I knew one person that was fired in the second. Then I was fired in the third round.

By then, I was one of the older workers. I was 24. Most of the workers were young people, 14, 15, and 18 years old. The bosses exploited them, yelled at them, hit them, made them work double shifts, and paid them less than the older workers. When workers are young, they don't complain when they are not paid properly. The owners hire young people because they often don't know their rights.

Marion: How many workers were employed at Daimi?

Marie: There were about 400 workers. We had five production lines, plus the people working in cutting, ironing, packing, buttons, and in the warehouse.

Marion: What happened with the organizing effort in Daimi before and after you were fired?

Marie: I was only able to talk with people on my line. You know more about people on your own line: what they're like, if they get along, if they stay when there is overtime, how they react if they are forced to stay extra hours, things like that.

Seven people on my line were with me. That's why the supervisors broke up the line. They moved some workers to other lines, and then fired the rest. The firings did the most damage.

We worked so hard to get the workers at Daimi to stand up for themselves. But despite all the problems in the factory, many workers wouldn't join with the union. Perhaps they were afraid. Some would even hide from us. Of course some did join, but many did not. I was very sad when they fired me. Still, the struggle continued inside the factory.

After I was fired, there were just a few union supporters left. Three of them, two girls and my brother—who had gotten active by then—placed an injunction on the factory. Then one of the girls quit, which left only my brother and the other girl.

The supervisors started really harassing my brother. When he showed up for work, they wouldn't give him anything to do. He just had to stay sitting in the office. They would try to scare him. Then they offered him money, but he didn't take it. They harassed him like that for about three days and then more or less left him in peace. They let him work on a line, but wouldn't give him any overtime. That meant he could only earn the minimum wage.

It was a difficult experience for my brother; it really affected him. He worked so hard to get people to support the struggle at Daimi. He'd get home at 10:00 at night after going with the organizers to visit the workers. But instead of supporting the union, people often made fun of it. Of course that made the owner feel good.

One night, the supervisors shut my brother inside the factory. When I called the factory to ask if my brother was there, they told me he wasn't. I called back later and they admitted he was there, but said I couldn't speak with him because they were "fixing a problem." I was desperate. I didn't know what to do. I couldn't say anything to my uncle because he's with the military and wouldn't have supported the union. My brother was stuck there alone with management in the factory most of the night. He finally called at 1:00 in the morning and I went to the bus stop to wait for him. My sister came along. She was very angry with me. She blamed me for what had happened. A couple [of] days later, my brother quit his job.

Marion: Does the factory still exist?

Marie: Yes, it exists. They changed the name and fired a supervisor, the Korean woman who was really bad. But the bad conditions and hiring of minors continues. And of course, some of the workers who were fired during the campaign still haven't gotten their severance pay.

That factory cost us a lot. The only thing we achieved was to scare the owner and maybe get a message to some of the workers. Some of them did begin to realize that organizing was a good thing.

Marion: What did you do after you were fired?

Marie: I looked for other work. I got a job in the same factory where my sister worked, Modas Montañas, also Korean-owned. They make pants from nylon. The wages were a bit better, but the conditions were really bad. We had to drink tap water, from dirty, greasy cups. The bathrooms didn't have doors, and the men made a hole in the wall that separated the bathrooms so they could look [at] us while we were using the bathroom.

There was tons of work. Eleven hundred pieces a day wasn't considered a lot. When we were forced to stay all night, they gave us food that made us sick. I got parasites while I was there.

The material we sewed was like little cat hairs. You'd have it all over your face and in your pores. Both my sister and I started to get throat infections.

The only good thing was that I managed to get permission to study on Saturdays. The director of personnel said I could work half-days on Saturdays and then go to class. He actually encouraged me to do it and said that I was very intelligent.

It was around that time that the coordinator of the ITGLWF's organizing project in Guatemala City asked me to come and work in the office. I wasn't sure about leaving because there are things about the maquila that I liked. You can learn a lot working in the maquila.

Marion: What do you learn?

Marie: You learn how to defend yourself. You learn to be strong. If not, everyone yells at you. The mechanic, the supervisor, the chief of production, the assistant, the operator behind you and the one in front of you, the inspectors.... The whole world yells at you. If you don't learn how to defend yourself, you're really in trouble. That kind of experience builds character. You learn how to stand up to people and tell them they don't have the right to yell at you.

What I like is that you can see the product of your work. You can see exactly what you've made. It's right up there on the board in front, that you're producing 100 pieces each hour. Then in the afternoon you can see that you've finished, say, 1,500 pieces and you can be proud of what you and your compañeros have accomplished. That's the good part of the maquila. Of course the bad part is the mistreatment, the low salaries, and the bad conditions.

Right from the beginning, I loved to sew. I make my own clothes, although less so now because I don't have a machine. But I decided to leave the maquila to work with the organizing project because I wanted to learn new things, for example, more about worker rights.

Here I'm learning about the conditions in other maquilas. We find that conditions are pretty much the same everywhere. Workers don't get paid well, they are treated badly, and their rights are violated.

Of course there are differences. In some maquilas workers are treated really badly, while in others conditions are slightly better. Another thing I've learned is that workers don't know what the minimum wage is or how much they are being paid for overtime. Some don't even know they are being robbed.

The most important thing I have learned is how to organize workers. It's funny, but if I hadn't been hired at Daimi, I probably would still be working in a maquila.

Notes

1. The International Textile, Garment and Leather Workers' Federation (ITGLWF) is an International Trade Secretariat bringing together 250 organizations associated with the apparel and textile industries in 130 countries, with a combined membership of 10 million workers.
2. Ladino or ladina refers to someone who is of mixed heritage. Indigenous people who wear western clothing are often referred to as ladino. The ladino ethnicity is considered one of the four broad ethnic categories in the country; the other ethnicities are Maya, Garifuna and Xineo.
3. One of the Mayan dialects.

Supplement 35

Structural Adjustment Programs Work for Elites and Impoverish the Rest

Global Exchange

Global Exchange is an international human rights organization committed to promoting social, economic, and environmental justice at a local and national level around the world.

How—and why—do the structural adjustment programs (SAPs) that the IMF and World Bank impose create conditions that multinational corporations desire and that devastate most people in the southern countries? A look at some common SAP conditions shows how economic "advice" is used to maintain the interests of the wealthy at the expense of continued suffering for the bulk of the people.

IMF/World Bank Condition	Impact on Elite (Corporations, Investors, Wealthy)	Impact on Poor
Cut Social Spending: Reduce expenditures on health, education, etc.	More debts repaid, including to World Bank and IMF	Increased school fees force parents to pull children—usually girls—from school; literacy rates go down Poorly educated generation not equipped for skilled jobs Higher fees for medical service mean less treatment, more suffering, needless deaths Women, already overburdened, must provide health care and caretaking for family members

Shrink Government: **Reduce budget expense by trimming payroll and programs**	Fewer government employees means less capacity to monitor businesses' adherence to labor, environmental, and financial regulations Frees up cash for debt service	Massive layoffs in countries where government is often the largest employer Makes people desperate to work at any wage
Cut Subsidies for Basic Goods: **Reduce government expenditures supporting reduced cost of bread, petroleum, etc.**	Frees up more money for debt payments	Raises cost of items needed to survive Most frequent flashpoint for civil unrest
Re-orient Economies from Subsistence to Exports: **Give incentives for farmers to produce cash crops (coffee, cotton, etc.) for foreign markets rather than food for domestic ones; encourage manufacturing to focus on simple assembly (often clothing) for export rather than manufacturing for own country; encourage extraction of valuable mineral resources**	Produces hard currency to pay off more debts Law of supply and demand pushes down price of commodities as more countries produce more, meaning guaranteed supply of low-cost products to export markets Local competition eliminated for multinational corporations Increased availability of low-cost labor	Law of supply and demand pushes down price of commodities as more countries produce more, meaning local producers often lose money Best lands devoted to cash crops; poorer land used for food crops, leading to soil erosion Food security threatened Women often relegated to gathering all food for family while men work for cash Makes country more dependent on imported food and manufactured goods Forests and mineral resources (oil, copper, etc.) over-exploited, leading to environmental destruction and displacement

Source: Global Exchange and 50 Years is Enough, "Structural Adjustment Programs Work for Elites and Impoverish the Rest," in *World Bank/IMF Factsheet* (2011), retrieved from http://www.globalexchange.org/campaigns/wbimf/facts.html

Chapter 56

The Gendered Politics and Violence of Structural Adjustment: A View from Jamaica

Faye V. Harrison

Faye V. Harrison is a professor of anthropology and African-American studies at the University of Florida-Gainesville. She is an executive member and past chair of the International Union of Anthropological and Ethnological Sciences' Commission on the Anthropology of Women. An award-winning social/political anthropologist interested in culture, politics, and political economy as they relate to various forms of social inequality, she has published extensively about a range of topics, including structural adjustment policies, poverty, the informal economy, political violence, the social construction of race, and gendered and racialized inequalities as global human rights issues.

An Ethnographic Window on a Crisis

"The ghetto not'ing but a sad shantytown now." This is what one of my friends and informants sadly remarked to me upon my 1992 visit to "Oceanview," a pseudonym for an impoverished slum neighborhood with a roughly 74 percent formal unemployment rate in the downtown district of the Kingston Metropolitan Area. Times were so hard that the tenements had deteriorated beyond repair. The conspicuous physical decline was a marker of the deepened socioeconomic austerity accompanying what some critics (e.g., *Race & Class* 1992) now consider to be the "recolonization" of Jamaica by "the new conquistadors"—the policies and programs that the International Monetary Fund (IMF), the World Bank, and the Reagan and Bush administrations of the United States government designed to "adjust" and "stabilize" the country's revived export-oriented economy. These strategies for delivering third world societies from collapsing economies are informed by a development ideology that euphemizes the widening social disparities that have been the outcome of policies imposing an unbearable degree of austerity on living conditions. Hence, these policies have sacrificed ordinary people's—especially the poor's—basic needs in health care, housing, education, social services, and employment for those of free enterprise and free trade.

Since 1978, I have observed and conversed with Oceanview residents about the social, economic, and political conditions shaping their lived experiences and struggles for survival in this neighborhood (e.g., Harrison 1987a, b, 1988, 1991a, b). The late 1970s was a time of economic hardship and political turbulence, a time when the People's National Party's (PNP) democratic socialist path to economic development and social transformation was vehemently contested, blocked, and destabilized by political opponents both within and without the country and by the concerted economic force of an international recession, quadrupled oil prices, and a massive flight of both domestic and foreign capital. Life was certainly hard then, but, as one resident commented, "Cho, mahn [sic]; tings worse now." Despite the bright promises of political and economic "deliverance" made by the Jamaica Labour Party (JLP) and its major backer, the Reagan and later Bush administrations of the U.S. government, the 1980s and early 1990s—under the leadership of a much more conservative PNP—brought only a deepened poverty to the folk who people the streets and alleys of slum and shantytown neighborhoods like Oceanview. This deepening poverty is reflected, for example, in a serious decline in the conditions of public health. The implementation of structural adjustment policies has brought about alarming reductions in government health-care expenditures and promoted the privatization of more costly and less accessible medical care (Phillips 1994, 137). Those most heavily burdened by the impact of these deteriorating social conditions and capital-centered policies are women (Antrobus 1989) who serve as the major "social shock absorbers" (Sparr 1992, 31; 1994), mediating the crisis at the local level of households and neighborhoods. Nearly 50 percent of all Kingston's households are female-headed, giving women the major responsibilities for making ends meet out of virtually nothing (Deere et al. 1990, 52–53). Concentrated in the informal sector of the economy, these women, along with their children, are most vulnerable to the consequences of malnutrition, hunger, and poor health: rising levels of morbidity and mortality (Phillips 1994, 142; Pan American Health Organization/World Health Organization 1992).

To appreciate and understand the effects, contradictions, and meanings that constitute the reality of a structurally adjusted pattern of production and trade, we must examine the everyday experiences, practices, discourses, and common sense of real people, particularly those encouraged to wait—and wait—for social and economic benefits to trickle down. In the interest of an ethnographically grounded view of Jamaica's current economic predicament, I present the case of Mrs. Beulah Brown, an admirable woman whose life story I collected over several years, to help elucidate the impact the ongoing crisis has on the everyday lives of ordinary Jamaicans, particularly poor urban women and those who depend most on them. A longtime household head and informal-sector worker like so many other Jamaican women, Mrs. Brown was once a community health aide with a government program that provided much-needed health services to a population to which such care would not have been available otherwise. Mrs. Brown would not have gotten or held that job for the years that she did without "the right political connections," something, unfortunately, that too few poor people ever obtain. Although visible benefits from membership in the local PNP group may have set her apart from most of her neighbors, the centrality of patronage-clientelism in local and national politics makes a former political client's experience an insightful window on the constraints and vulnerabilities built into Jamaica's political and economic policies.

Highlights from Mrs. Brown's life story lead us to the more encompassing story of postcolonial Jamaica's experience with debt, export-led development, and structural adjustment, and their combined impact on women workers as well as on neighborhood-level negotiations of crisis.

A Hard-Working Woman's Story within a Story

In the 1970s Beulah Brown, then a middle-aged woman responsible for a two-generation household and extended family, worked as a community health aide under the combined aegis of a government public health program and a local urban redevelopment agency, two projects that owed their existence to the social-policy orientation of the reformist PNP administration. Mrs. Brown had begun her employment history as a worker in a factory manufacturing undergarments. However, she preferred household-based self-employment over the stringent regimentation of factory work. A woman with strong civic consciousness and organizing skills, she had worked her way into the leadership of the PNP group within the neighborhood and wider political division. By the late 1970s, she was no longer an officer; however, her membership in the party was still active.

Mrs. Brown was so effective at working with patients and exhibiting good citizenship that she was widely recognized and addressed as "Nurse Brown," the term "nurse" being a title of utmost respect. When Mrs. Brown made her daily rounds, she did more than expected of a health aide. She treated her patients as whole persons with a range of basic needs she felt obligated to help meet. To this end, she saw to it that they had nutritional food to eat, clean clothes to wear, and neat and orderly rooms in which to live. She was especially devoted to the elderly, but she also invested considerable energy in young mothers who were often merely children themselves. She shared her experiences and wisdom with them, admonishing them to eat healthy foods, read good books, and, given her religious worldview, "pray to the Lord Jesus Christ" so that their babies' characters and personalities would be positively influenced while still in the womb.

When I initially met her, Mrs. Brown was responsible for caring for her elderly father, her handicapped sister, her sister's three daughters, and her own two daughters. At earlier times she had even minded a young niece who eventually joined her other siblings and mother, another of Mrs. Brown's sisters, in Canada. Despite many hardships, Beulah managed her household well enough to see to it that the children were fed, clothed, and schooled. Indeed, one of her nieces, Claudia, is now a nurse in New York City, and—"by the grace of God"—her eldest daughter, Cherry, is a graduate of the University of the West Indies. Unfortunately, Marie, the daughter who still remains at home, had difficulty getting and keeping wage work, whether in an office or factory, so she decided to make and sell children's clothes so she could work at home while minding her children. Despite the economic uncertainty of informal sector work, Marie appreciates its flexibility and the freedom from the "downpressive" (oppressive) industrial surveillance about which a number of former factory workers in Oceanview complain.

Because the community health aide job did not bring in enough income to support the household, Mrs. Brown found ways to augment her income. Mainly she made dresses, a skill and talent she had cultivated over most of her life. Years ago she had even had a small shop in Port Antonio that catered to locals as well as foreign tourists. That was before she gave up everything—her shop and her husband—to return home to Kingston to care for relatives who were going through some hard times. Besides her dressmaking enterprise, Mrs. Brown also baked and sold meat patties, bought and sold cheese, and sold ice from the deep freezer she had purchased with remittances from her twin sister in England and help from her church. Through political party connections gained through her earlier activism in the local PNP group, she also saw to it that her sister got a job cleaning streets in the government Crash Programme. Although her family managed better than most of their neighbors, survival was still an everyday struggle.

In the mid-1980s, Mrs. Brown lost her health aide job. The Community Health Aide Program suffered massive losses due to the retrenchment in public-sector employment stipulated by the structural-adjustment and stabilization measures imposed by the IMF and World Bank. Luckily, the layoff came around the time when the girls she had raised were coming of age and could work to support themselves and their families. By 1988, the household was made up of only Beulah, her second daughter, Marie, and Marie's three small children. Everyone else had moved on to independent residences in Kingston or emigrated to the U.S. and Canada to live with relatives, "a foreign," overseas. This dispersal relieved the household of considerable financial pressure, but to make ends meet, Beulah still had to intensify her informal means of generating income. She did more dressmaking and added baking wedding and birthday cakes to her list of money-making activities.

No matter how much work she did, she never seemed to be able to do more than barely make ends meet. With the devaluation of the Jamaican dollar and the removal of subsidies on basic consumer items like food, the costs of living had increased dramatically. What more could she do to keep pace with the inflationary trend designed to make Jamaican exports more competitive on the international market? She knew that she would never resort to the desperate illicit measures some of her neighbors had taken by "tiefing" ("thiefing") or dealing drugs. She simply refused to sell her soul to the devil for some of the "blood money" obtainable from the activities of local gangs—now called posses—that move from Kingston to the U.S. and back trafficking in substances like crack cocaine. Increasingly, especially with political patronage becoming more scarce, drug trafficking has become an important source of local subsistence and small-scale investment. However, the price paid for a life of crime is too high. She lamented that too many "youts" (youths) involved in the drug economy make the return trip home to Jamaica enclosed in deathly wooden crates.

Like most Caribbean people, Mrs. Brown has long belonged to and actively participated in an international family network extending from Jamaica to Great Britain, Canada, and the U.S. (Basch et al. 1994). Her sisters abroad had often invited her to visit them, and they had also encouraged her to migrate so that she, too, could benefit from better opportunities. Before the mid-1980s, Mrs. Brown had been determined to remain at home caring for her family. Moreover, she loved her country, her church, and her party, and she wanted to help shape the direction of Jamaica's future. She strongly felt that someone had to remain in Jamaica to keep it going on the right course. Everyone couldn't migrate. "My home is here in Jamaica," she insisted adamantly.

These were her strong feelings *before* structural adjustment hit the heart of her home: her refrigerator, deep freezer, and kitchen table. In 1990 alone, the cost of chicken—a desirable entree to accompany rice and peas on Sunday—went up three times. The cost of even more basic staples also rose, making items such as fresh milk, cornmeal, and tomatoes (whose price increased 140 percent) more and more unaffordable for many people (Statistical Institute of Jamaica 1991).

Between 1987 and 1992, Mrs. Brown travelled abroad twice for extended visits with relatives in England, Canada, and the U.S. While away for nearly a year at a time, she "did a likkle babysitting and ting" to earn money that she was able to save for her own purposes. Her family treated her "like a queen," buying her gifts ("good camera, TV, radio, and ting"), not letting her spend her own money for living expenses, and paying for her air transportation from point to point along her international itinerary. The savings she managed to send and bring back home were key to her Oceanview household's survival. Her transnational family network, and the geographical mobility it offered, allowed her to increase her earnings by taking advantage of the marked wage differential between Jamaica and the countries where her relatives live (Ho 1993, 33). This particular financial advantage has led even middle-class Jamaican women to tolerate an otherwise embarrassing and humiliating decline in social status to work as nannies and domestic helpers in North American homes. International migration within the Caribbean region, as well as between it and major metropoles, has been a traditional survival strategy among Jamaicans since nineteenth-century post-emancipation society.

Harsh circumstances forced Mrs. Brown to join the larger wave of female emigrants from the Caribbean who, since the late 1960s, have outnumbered their male counterparts (Deere et al. 1990, 76; Ho 1993, 33). Thus far, Mrs. Brown has remained a "visitor," but she acknowledges the possibility and perhaps even the probability that someday soon she will join her sisters as a permanent resident abroad. Meanwhile, she continues to take care of business at home by informally generating and allocating resources within the kinship-mediated transnational social field within which her local life is embedded.

Mrs. Brown's story and many others similar to it are symptomatic of the current age of globalization, marked by a deepening crisis that policies such as structural adjustment and its complementary export-led development strategy attempt to manage in favor of the mobility and accumulation of transnational capital. Mrs. Brown's story, however, is only a story within a story about the dramatic plot-thickening details of Jamaica's nonlinear struggle for development and decolonization. Let us now place Beulah Brown's lived experience in a broader context, and in so doing, illuminate the forces and conditions that differentially affect Jamaica's hard-working women, particularly those who work in the informal sector and free trade zone. As we shall see, their dilemmas and struggles are closely interrelated.

Once upon a Time: Dilemmas of Development

Deep into Debt

Postcolonial Jamaica, like many other third world and southern hemisphere countries, is beset by a serious case of debt bondage. Jamaica is embroiled in a crisis that can be traced back to the economic turmoil of the mild-1970s. By 1980, when the conservative JLP ousted the democratic socialist PNP from power, Jamaica's debt had doubled due to the extensive borrowing undertaken to absorb the impact the receding international economy was having on the country, to offset massive capital flight (a domestic and international panic response to the PNP's move to the left), and to underwrite state-initiated development projects. To stabilize and reinvigorate the collapsed economy, the JLP administration, with the support and guidance of the Reagan administration, relied on the IMF and the World Bank for massive loans to redress its critical balance of payments and fiscal deficits. Consequently, the country's indebtedness grew by leaps and bounds. As a result, Jamaica now owes more than U.S. $4 billion. Its debt servicing exceeds what it receives in loans and grants (Ferguson 1992, 62), and it devours 40 percent of the foreign exchange it earns from its exports, which are supposed to jump start the economy into a pattern of sustained development. The development strategy pursued since 1980—one that privileges private-sector export production—has been underwritten by these relations of indebtedness. The IMF, World Bank, and the U.S. government's Caribbean Basin Initiative (CBI) and USAID have delimited terms for Jamaica's economic restructuring that further integrate the island into a global hierarchy of free-trade relations. This global hierarchy is not only class- and racially biased (Köhler 1978); it is also fundamentally gendered (Antrobus 1989; Enloe 1989; Sparr 1994).

The Path to Economic Growth and Social Crisis

The debt-constrained, export-led, and free trade–based development path that the Jamaican economy is following has failed to deliver the masses of Jamaican people from the dilemmas of persistent poverty and underdevelopment. Benefits from this development strategy have not trickled down the socioeconomic ladder. However, what have trickled down are the adverse effects of drastic austerity measures, which are the strings attached to aid from the IMF and World Bank. These strings stipulate that the government de-nationalize or privatize public sectors of the economy, cut back social services and public employment, devalue the Jamaican dollar, impose restraints on wages, liberalize imports, and remove subsidies and price controls on food and other consumer goods (Antrobus 1989, 20). These measures, along with the stipulated focus on export production, have resulted in increased unemployment, a decline in real wages for those fortunate enough to have regular incomes, a dramatic rise in the costs of living, and, with these, an increase in malnutrition and hunger, a general deterioration in public health, and an escalating incidence of drug abuse and violence—including violence against women (Antrobus 1989, 23). [...] Those bearing the heaviest burden in coping with today's social and economic austerity are women, a large proportion of whom have the responsibility—whether they are formally employed or not—to support households and family networks (Bolles 1991).

Although it has sacrificed ordinary people's basic needs, the debt bondage and free trade strategy has successfully restored "the military and economic foundations of U.S. superiority ... incorporating the Caribbean Basin countries into the U.S. military-industrial complex" (Deere et al. 1990, 157). A central aspect of the CBI has been the increased sale of U.S. exports to the Caribbean (McAfee 1991, 43). Exports from the Caribbean that receive duty-free entry into the U.S. market are produced in foreign and, to a considerable extent, U.S.-controlled free-trade zones where items (usually those of apparel and electronics) are assembled from raw materials and capital goods imported from the U.S. In other words, the Caribbean has become an offshore site for branch plants that are not generating the backward linkages and horizontal integration necessary for stimulating the domestic sectors of Jamaica's economy.

Gender Inequality in Globalization

Transnational capital has appropriated the enterprising freedom to repatriate profits without any enforced obligations to invest in the host country's future; it has enjoyed the freedom to employ workers, to a great extent female, whose labor has been politically, legally, and culturally constructed to be cheap and expendable. As Enloe (1989, 160–163) argues, economic globalization depends upon laws and cultural presumptions about femininity, sexuality, and marriage that help to lower women's wages and benefits. For instance, transnational garment production has taken advantage of and reinforced the patriarchal assumptions that activities such as sewing are "natural" women's tasks requiring no special skill, training, or compensation; that jobs defined as skilled belong to men, who deserve to be remunerated for their special physical strength and training; that women are not the major breadwinners in their households and families and are really supported by their fathers or husbands (Safa 1994); and finally that women's needs should not direct the policies and practices of business management and development specialists.

The profitability, capital mobility, and structural power (Wolf 1990) constitutive of globalization are fundamentally gendered phenomena marked by a masculinist logic. Present-day strategies to adjust, stabilize, and facilitate capital accumulation implicate constructions of femininity and masculinity that, in effect, legitimate the superexploitation of the productive and reproductive labor of women, with women of color bearing the heaviest burdens (see Enloe 1989; Deere et al. 1990; Antrobus 1989) and being the most vulnerable targets of structural violence—the symbolic, psychological, and physical assaults against human subjectivities, physical bodies, and sociocultural integrity that emanate from situations and institutions structured in social, political, and economic dominance (Köhler 1978).

*****

End of Story within a Story—for Now

Tired from feeling the weight of her 63 years, especially the past 10 of them, Mrs. Brown complained to me about the prohibitive costs of living and the unjust formula being used to devalue the Jamaican dollar so as to make the economy more penetrable for foreign investment. "And all at the people's expense!" As we waited at the airport for my departure time, she remarked that she didn't know how she could have made it through all her trials and tribulations if it weren't for the grace of God who gave her industry, creativity, and a loving family as gifts; her church, upon which she had always been able to depend for both spiritual guidance and material aid; and Blessed Sacrament School, its PTA, and the various other activities and community services based on the grounds of that strategic local sanctuary from political warfare and economic desperation. [...]

*****

I am back home now, but I can't help but think—and worry—about Beulah and Oceanview in light of the global restructuring that affects life in the Caribbean as well as in the U.S., where the implementation of first world versions of structural adjustment are being felt and confronted. The economic restructuring occurring in the U.S. is only a variation on a wider structural adjustment theme reverberating across the globe. Policies implemented in the U.S. resemble the austerity measures the IMF and World Bank are imposing on "developing" nations: cutbacks in social spending and public investments in housing, education, and health care; deregulation of airline, trucking, banking, finance, and broadcasting industries; corporate union-busting; currency devaluation; divestment of public enterprises; the increasing privatization of public services; and dramatic alterations of the tax system, shifting the tax burden away from wealthy individuals and large corporations (Sparr 1992, 30–31).

Probing the political and moral economy of poverty in "the field" (cf. D'Amico-Samuels 1991) has led me to reconceptualize analytical units and boundaries in ways that discern and utilize points of articulation and conjuncture between, for instance, Beulah Brown and myself, and Jamaica and the U.S., for a deeper, more broadly situated, and more personally grounded understanding of structural adjustment's gendered assaults—its invidious structural violence.

References

Antrobus, Peggy. 1989. Crisis, Challenge, and the Experiences of Caribbean Women. *Caribbean Quarterly* 35(1&2):17–28.

Basch, Linda, Nina Glick Schiller, and Cristina Szanton Blanc. 1994. *Nations Unbound. Transnational Projects, Postcolonial Predicaments, and Deterritorialized Nation-States*. Langhorne, PA:

Gordon and Breach Science Publishers.

Bolles, A. Lynn. 1991. Surviving Manley and Seaga: Case Studies of Women's Responses to Structural Adjustment Policies. *Review of Radical Political Economy* 23(3&4):20–36.

D'Amico-Samuels, Deborah. 1991. Undoing Fieldwork: Personal, Political, Theoretical, and Methodological Implications. In *Decolonizing Anthropology: Moving Further toward an Anthropology for Liberation*. Ed. Faye V. Harrison. Washington, D.C.: American Anthropological Association.

Deere, Carmen Diana, et al. 1990. *In the Shadows of the Sun: Caribbean Development Alternatives and U.S. Policy*. Boulder: Westview Press.

Enloe, Cynthia. 1989. *Bananas, Beaches, and Bases: Making Feminist Sense of International Politics*. Berkeley: University of California Press.

Ferguson, James. 1992. Jamaica: Stories of Poverty. *Race & Class* 34(1):61–72.

Harrison, Faye V. 1987a. Crime, Class, and Politics in Jamaica. *TransAfrica Forum* 5(1):29–38.

Harrison, Faye V. 1987b. Gangs, Grassroots Politics, and the Crisis of Dependent Capitalism in Jamaica. In *Perspectives in U.S. Marxist Anthropology*. Ed. David Hakken and Hanna Lessinger. Boulder: Westview Press.

Harrison, Faye V. 1988. The Politics of Social Outlawry in Urban Jamaica. *Urban Anthropology and Studies in Cultural Systems and World Economic Development* 17(2&3):259–277.

Harrison, Faye V. 1991a. Ethnography as Politics. In *Decolonizing Anthropology: Moving Further toward an Anthropology for Liberation*. Ed. Faye V. Harrison. Washington, D.C.: American Anthropological Association.

Harrison, Faye V. 1991b. Women in Jamaica's Urban Informal Economy: Insights from a Kingston Slum. In *Third World Women and the Politics of Feminism*. Ed. Chandra T. Mohanty et al. Bloomington: Indiana University Press.

Ho, Christine G.T. 1993. The Internationalization of Kinship and the Feminization of Caribbean Migration: The Case of Afro-Trinidadian Immigrants in Los Angeles. *Human Organization* 52(1):32–40.

Köhler, Gernot. 1978. Global Apartheid. *World Order Models Project*. Working Paper no. 7. New York: Institute for World Order.

McAfee, Kathy. 1991. *Storm Signals: Structural Adjustment and Development Alternatives in the Caribbean*. Boston: South End Press.

Pan American Health Organization/World Health Organization. 1992. *The Health of Women in the English-Speaking Caribbean*.

Phillips, Daphene. 1994. The IMF, Structural Adjustment, and Health in the Caribbean: Policy Change in Health Care in Trinidad and Tobago. *Twenty-first Century Policy Review* 2(1&2):129–149.

Race & Class. 1992. *The New Conquistadors* 34(1) (July–Sept.):1–114.

Safa, Helen. 1994. *The Myth of the Male Breadwinner: Women and Industrialization in the Caribbean*. Boulder: Westview Press.

Sparr, Pamela. 1992. How We Got into This Mess and Ways to Get Out. *Ms.* March/April, 130.

Sparr, Pamela, ed. 1994. *Mortgaging Women's Lives: Feminist Critiques of Structural Adjustment*. London: Zed Books.

Statistical Institute of Jamaica. 1991. *Statistical Yearbook of Jamaica*. Kingston: Statistical Institute of Jamaica.

Wolf, Eric. 1990. Distinguished Lecture: Facing Power—Old Insights, New Questions. *American Anthropologist* 92(3):586–596.

Chapter 57

Fruits of Injustice:
Women in the Post-NAFTA Food System

Deborah Barndt

Deborah Barndt is associate professor in environmental studies and coordinator of the Community Arts Program at York University. Her award-winning research and teaching bring together her multiple talents as an academic, photographer, popular educator, and activist. Working for many years with social justice movements in Canada, the United States, and Central America, she has become a leading scholar and educator on the global food system, and on community arts and popular education. Her publications include Tangled Routes: Women, Work, and Globalization on the Tomato Trail.

Precious Human Cargo

As we approached the Toronto airport in the still-dark dawn, I asked Irena which terminal her plane was leaving from. I expected her to say Terminal Three, which is the main departure point for international flights and by far the most elegant, with sky-lit boutiques and chic restaurants. When she said "Terminal One," I questioned her, especially as the sign for Terminal One said "Cargo." "But I'm going as cargo!" she jokingly explained.

I was well aware of the Foreign Agricultural Resource Management Services, known as the FARMS program, established in 1974, which brings Jamaican and Mexican farm-workers such as Irena to Canada every summer to pick our fruit and vegetables.

I knew it was considered the "crème de la crème" of migrant worker schemes, selecting the heartiest who tolerate a few months of backbreaking work in our fields, 12 hours a day, six and half days a week, because they can make more in an hour here than they make in Mexico in a day. And while I knew that they are brought en masse by plane in the spring and sent home en masse in the fall, no reading or interviews prepared me for the sight I faced as we entered Terminal One that day: a sea of brown and black bodies, primarily men, in massive line-ups, pushing carts bursting with boxes of appliances they were taking home. Security guards surrounded this precious human cargo, moving less freely than goods now move across borders in the post-NAFTA context. I imagined lighter-skinned Mexican professionals boarding planes in Terminal Three, briefcases in hand, having just completed a new trade deal with Canadian-based companies, or even middle-class and upper-class students now availing themselves of increased exchanges among North American universities.

For the past seven years, I have been involved in a unique cross-border research project involving feminist academics and activists in Mexico, the United States, and Canada, that has taken advantage of this deepening economic and cultural integration of the continent, and the privilege of university research monies to move academics and graduate students across borders much more easily than Irena can move. We have been mapping the journey of the corporate tomato from a Mexican agribusiness to a Canadian supermarket and U.S.-based fast-food restaurant as a device for examining globalization from above (the corporate agendas) and globalization from below (the stories of lowest-waged women workers in these sectors). We met Irena during this tracing of the tomato's trail, discovering a piece of the story that did not fit into any straight line or simple South–North axis. While most people are aware that our winter tomatoes are planted, picked, and packed by Mexican workers, few realize that our locally produced summer tomatoes are also brought to us by Mexican hands, borrowed for the summer as cheap labour. This is one of the less visible stories of trade within the new global economy.

One of the environmental activists advocating for the human rights of Indigenous migrant workers in the Mexican fields calls the tomatoes they pick the "fruits of injustice." We began to realize that not only have the tomatoes become increasingly commodified in the neoliberal industrialized food system, but the most marginalized workers are also commodities in this new trade game. In fact, tomatoes—a highly perishable, delicate fruit and one of the winners for Mexico in the NAFTA reshuffle—are often treated better than the workers.

In this article, I will focus exclusively on the Mexican women workers in the tomato food chain,[1] and primarily those who would never dream of boarding a plane for Canada, but move in and out of seasonal production processes, key actors in the deepening agro-export economy of post-NAFTA Mexico. Their stories will reveal the increasing participation of young women, the deepening exploitation of Indigenous women, the worsening working and living conditions among workers in chemically dependent agribusinesses, and the triple workloads of women who combine salaried work, subsistence farming, and domestic labour to meet the survival needs of their families. While Canadian women workers in the tomato chain also experience increasing inequities, Mexican women are clearly the most marginalized and invisibilized.

Interlocking Analysis of Power

The increasingly globalized food system builds on and perpetuates deeply rooted inequalities of race and ethnicity, class, gender, age, urban-rural, and marital status. As we followed the tangled routes of women workers along the tomato trail, we evolved an interlocking analysis that took into account five key dimensions of power that emerged as the most salient to understanding hierarchies within this food chain.

Figure 57.1 locates our gender analysis first within a context of North–South asymmetries, and in the case of the food system, the dynamic that the South (ever more dependent on agro-exports for foreign exchange) increasingly produces for consumption in the North. We do not want to perpetuate a simplistic North–South analysis. We recognize its limitations by revealing the dynamics within Mexico whereby southern impoverished regions feed cheap migrant labour to the richer industrial North of that country. As a result, disintegrating rural communities are sucked into the demands of an increasingly urban Mexico. Poor Indigenous *campesinos* [small-scale farmers or farm workers] are now salaried labour serving the food needs of a wealthier *mestizo* [mixed-race Mexican] population as well as consumers in the North. In the continental food system, this North–South axis has allowed us to compare the similarities and differences between women who plant, pick, and pack tomatoes in Mexico and those who scan and bag, or slice and serve tomatoes in Canadian retail and fast-food industries.

Figure 57.1

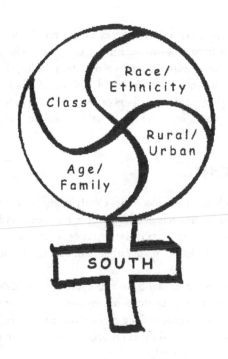

Class: There are clearly different socio-economic statuses among women in the food system, even among the lower-waged workers in each sector that we are studying here and in each of the three NAFTA countries. Each company constructs its own hierarchy of workers, sometimes, though not always, related to educational level, but usually defined by skill levels, disparate wage levels, and working conditions.

Race/ethnicity: Also interacting with class and gender are race and ethnicity, shifting in meaning from one place and time to another. In Mexico ethnic differences are perhaps most pronounced between the Indigenous workers that the agribusiness brings by truck to pick tomatoes under the hot sun and the more skilled and privileged *mestiza* women they bring in buses to pack tomatoes in the more protected packing plant.

Age and family status: The interrelated factors of age, marital status, and generational family roles are clearly significant in the Mexican agricultural context, where the workforce is predominantly young and female (a relatively recent phenomenon based on necessity but challenging patriarchal practices). The family wage has become critical, too, as family members combine their salaries as well as unsalaried work for subsistence production to survive a deepening economic crisis.

Rural/urban: In the context of food and agriculture, the rural–urban dynamic is central. Development strategies in both Mexico and Canada have favoured urban dwellers, but still depend on rural workers to feed populations of the burgeoning cities. Mexican *campesinos* are migrating to both rural and urban areas in Mexico, and the survival of most families depends on the migration of some family member(s) to the U.S. or Canada, even if temporarily, as in the case of Irena.

It is almost impossible to describe the above dimensions of power in isolation. The stories of women in the tomato chain reveal the complex interaction between these categories of identity and power and thus enrich our understanding of gender and women's experience as plural, diverse, and constantly changing.

*****

Profiles of Women in Three Contexts

I will introduce [several] women who work for Empaque Santa Rosa, the Mexican agribusiness at the production end of the tomato chain. The differences among the Indigenous and *mestiza* workers, the pickers and the packers, will challenge any notion we might harbour in the North of a singular or monolithic Mexican woman worker.

Picking and Packing for the North: Mexican Women Agricultural Workers

Job categories and divisions of tasks within tomato production have evolved over decades (indeed centuries) to reflect and reinforce institutionalized classism, sexism, racism, and ageism. According to Sara Lara, the restructuring and technologization of tomato production during the 1990s—promoted by neoliberal trade policies—has not changed the sexual division of labour, but has, in fact, exploited it even further. By employing greater numbers of women, companies contract skilled but devalued labour that is not only qualitatively but quantitatively flexible (Lara 1998: 210). […]

A Moving Maquila: The "Company Girls"

The packing plant is one of the places where entrenched gender ideologies clearly reign. Women are considered both more responsible and more delicate in their handling of the tomatoes; and because the appearance of the product is so critical to tomato exporters, there is at least some recognition of this work as a skill, even if managers consider it innate rather than part of female socialization, as Lara argues it is (Lara 1998: 208).

Women who sort and pack tomatoes for Santa Rosa are drawn from two sources: local girls living in the town and mostly young women hired permanently by the company and moved from site to site, harvest to harvest. The latter are the most privileged, and are clearly "company girls," a kind of "moving maquila." They provide the flexible labour and the skills needed by Santa Rosa at the important stage of sorting and packing tomatoes for export.

*****

Yolanda, Sorter

> I'm 21, and have been working for Santa Rosa for six years. My father was a manager at the packing plant in Sinaloa, and I began working there during school vacations. I liked packing work better than school. The atmosphere is different, it's more fun, and you can make money.
>
> I came here from Sinaloa, and share an apartment with my mother, sister, and brother-in-law. He works in the Santa Rosa office and gets special living expenses. I earn almost 1,000 pesos ($200) a week. I'm saving money for a house I'm building back in Sinaloa.

Many young women Yolanda's age see this as temporary work, a good way to make some money, travel, and perhaps find a husband, so that they can then get on to the "real" business of settling down and raising their own families. Older women, who do not marry and leave the job, have become virtually wedded to the company, with no time or space for creating their own lives. They move from harvest to harvest, like swallows, returning annually to their hometown.

None of the sorters or packers are Indigenous but rather are lighter-skinned *mestizas*. They are the women who are in greatest contact with the company management. The most privileged, in fact, seem to be women with close connections to men who have administrative jobs with Santa Rosa, such as Yolanda's brother.

There is, however, a hierarchy of skills and of treatment between the two main jobs of sorting and packing, with the packers being the more privileged. [...]

*****

Male workers in the packing plant are still the most privileged, however. Most *cargadores* or carriers (who move boxes), for example, make up to 1,200 pesos a week, or 240 dollars, while packers average 600–900 a week ($120–$180).

*****

Factories in the Fields: Hi-Tech Greenhouse Production

The future of tomato production in Mexico appears to be in greenhouses, which allow year-round production and almost total control of key factors like climate, technology, and labour.

Greenhouse production can be seen as the epitome of the "maquila" model, which, since NAFTA, has now moved from the northern border to be applied to businesses throughout Mexico. Maquila industries are characterized by four dimensions: feminizing the labour force, highly segmenting skill categories (majority unskilled), lowering real wages, and introducing a non-union orientation (Carillo cited in Kopinak 1997: 13). The only Mexican inputs are the land, the sun (the company saves on electricity and heating), and the workers. And like most maquilas, 100 per cent of the produce is for export (10 per cent going to Canada, but most to the U.S.).

Only in recent years has it become culturally acceptable for young women in patriarchal rural communities to enter the paid labour force at all, and then only out of necessity. Most young people have taken these jobs because there is nothing else available and because their income is needed for the family wage.

Greenhouse work offers a new form of employment that combines planting and packing, and in terms of wages and status, falls somewhere between the fieldworkers and the packers at the larger plants. For women, there are basically two different kinds of roles: working in the green-houses planting and picking tomatoes, or working in the packing house in a more sophisticated process that combines selecting and packing.

*****

Yvonne, Greenhouse Packer

Yvonne works in the enormous packing house. In her three years working at the greenhouse, the 20-year-old has witnessed the move into hi-tech packing. The pressure that the comput-erized process on the lines creates within and among the workers is palpable. The French manager's strategy has worked on people like Yvonne, who has succumbed to the competi-tive dynamic:

> I was depressed at first because they would tell me "You're below the quota." I would be ashamed, because this means you're not worth anything. So I was very tense, concerned about getting faster, so they'd have a better impression of me.

Yvonne's efforts to keep up with the new technology and to prove herself a productive worker also reveal the internalization of new work values. "Good workers" are being shaped in Mexico by the combination of controlling technology and foreign management. Yet sexism reigns as once again the male workers are paid more: "If we make 100, men make 175," explains Yvonne.

Into the Fields

The women workers who are closest to the land, the plants, and the tomatoes themselves are also the lowest paid and least skilled in the hierarchy outlined here. They are the most exposed to the hot sun and the rain, as well as the pesticides sprayed incessantly in the fields. Two stories here will reveal two major sources of tomato field workers: local *campesinos* and Indigenous migrants from the South.

Tomasa, Local Fieldworker

As an older woman (68 years old), Tomasa is perhaps not a typical fieldworker. But her story reflects many important characteristics of migrant labour in Mexico. First, her personal history growing up as a *mestizo campesino* girl in the countryside reveals the deeply rooted sexism that produces and reproduces the gendered division of labour in the agricultural sector. Second, like many other peasant families, she and her husband combine subsistence farming with salaried work for agribusiness. Finally, her story reveals the family wage economy, which is the major strategy of survival for poor Mexicans.

> We raised ourselves, that is, my father died when I was two and so my mother was left alone to raise us. She had to work to feed us. As a child, I played around the house, but when I was eight or nine, my mother put me to work—sweeping, fetching water from a faraway stream. When I became older, I helped grind and mix the cornmeal to make tortillas.
>
> My kids helped me with the housework and they still help. Two of my sons have gone to work in the U.S. and send money back. My other sons work in the lumber business, cutting pine trees nearby. The women don't work in the field; they stay at home with their family. I'm the only one who runs around like a fried chili, picking tomatoes! My youngest daughter stays at home, and has food ready for us when we return from the fields.

The unpaid domestic work that keeps Mexican *campesino* families alive is not accounted for in any of the official calculations. Tomasa, in fact, works a triple day: as a salaried worker for agribusiness, as a subsistence farmer on their family *milpa* (literally, cornfield or family plot), and as the cook and caretaker of her family.

*****

If gender discrimination is entrenched in the tasks offered women workers and in their double or triple days, racism is manifested particularly against the Indigenous migrant workers who are brought in packed trucks by contractors, without certainty of getting work, and with even worse living and working conditions than local *campesinos*. Housed in deplorable huts, without water, electricity, stores, or transport, they come as families to work in the fields and move from harvest to harvest. The women bear the brunt of this lack of infrastructure—cooking and washing, taking care of kids (even while working in the field), and dealing with their own exhaustion and the poor health engendered by the conditions of extreme poverty. Because their own regions offer even less opportunity, they are forced to suffer these jobs and the racist treatment built into them (Lara 1994: 41).

Reyna, Indigenous Migrant Farm Worker

> We're from Guerrero. Contractors came to our town to find people to work here. After we finish our contract, they take us back in trucks.
>
> Some women carry their children on their backs while they're working, because they don't have anyone who can take care of them.
>
> We earn 28 pesos a day. It's never enough to save anything. Sometimes the children need shoes and it's not enough. They give us some clothes, because 28 pesos is nothing. There's no union and no vacations.

While children are paid the daily rate, it is often the case that their parents, especially mothers, will rush to fill their own quota, so they can help their children complete theirs. This dynamic makes the fieldwork much more intense and more like piecework (Barrón [personal communication]). Mothers must also carry their babies on their backs as they work in the fields. In breast-feeding her child, Reyna passed the pesticides from the plants on her hands, which then got into his mouth, and almost poisoned him. Indigenous women, as well as men and children, are clearly in the most precarious position of all who bring us the corporate tomato.

In the stories above, the multiple strategies for survival become clearer. Women are key protagonists for their families, in their triple functions: as salaried workers (with varying status and wage levels), as subsistence farmers (when they have access to land), and as domestic labourers (with a wide range of living conditions, from the horrific camps of Indigenous migrants to the better equipped but transient homes of the mobile packers). But no one woman's story can be understood in isolation from her family's story, nor separately from her ethnicity, age, marital status, and experience. Globalizing agribusinesses such as Santa Rosa have built their workforces on these historically entrenched inequalities and differences.

Tangled Roots and Routes

The interlocking dimensions of power are even more complex than I was able to reveal here, however, and are constantly changing. The cases of Canadian supermarket cashiers and fast-food workers also demonstrate the growing phenomenon of flexible labour strategies with women bearing the brunt of part-time work schedules. One shift in the Mexican labour force, for example, has been toward younger and younger workers; in a context of oversupply, 15–24 is the new ideal age, so a woman's career as a salaried agricultural worker may be finished before she reaches the age of 30. Deepening impoverishment in the countryside has meant that a *campesino* family now needs five rather than three members of the family working in order to eke out their collective subsistence.

Epilogue

The continental economic integration promoted by neoliberal trade policies and agreements such as NAFTA has also pushed groups working for social and environmental justice to consider the connections between workers in the border-crossing production of food and other goods. There have been spaces within our collaborative research project [where] women workers have read each other's stories and expressed solidarity with their sisters responsible for moving the tomato along its trail from South to North.

*****

Note

1. The stories of women in three different sectors—the agribusiness workers as well as Canadian supermarket cashiers and fast-food workers are featured in my book, *Tangled Routes: Women, Work, and Globalization on the Tomato Trail.*

References

Barrón, Antonieta. (2000). Personal communication. Miami, March.

Kopinak, Kathy. (1997). *Desert Capitalism: What Are the Maquiladoras?* Montreal: Black Rose Books.

Lara, Sara. (1994). "La Flexibilidad del Mercado del Trabajo Rural." *Revista Mexicana de Sociologia 54* (1) (January–February): 41.

Lara, Sara. (1998). *Nuevas Experiences Productiva y Nuevas Formas de Organizacion Flexibile del Trabajo en la Agricatura Mexicana.* Mexico City: Pablos.

5b The "New Economy": On (Not) Getting By in North America

Chapter 58

Nickel-and-Dimed: On (Not) Getting By in America

Barbara Ehrenreich

Barbara Ehrenreich is a highly influential American feminist journalist, author, and activist. Beginning her professional life with a PhD in cell biology, she traded the sciences for social criticism, focusing especially on women's rights, economic justice, peace and war, health and illness. She has written extensively for leading magazines and newspapers like the New York Times, Time Magazine, Harper's Magazine, The Nation, *and* The Progressive, *and she has also published 20 books. Ehrenreich extended the article excerpted below into a full-length book,* Nickel and Dimed: On (Not) Getting By in America, *which became a* New York Times *bestseller.*

At the beginning of June 1998 I leave behind everything that normally soothes the ego and sustains the body—home, career, companion, reputation, ATM card—for a plunge into the low-wage workforce. There, I become another, occupationally much diminished "Barbara Ehrenreich"—depicted on job-application forms as a divorced homemaker whose sole work experience consists of housekeeping in a few private homes. I am terrified, at the beginning, of being unmasked for what I am: a middle-class journalist setting out to explore the world that welfare mothers are entering, at the rate of approximately 50,000 a month, as welfare reform kicks in. Happily, though, my fears turn out to be entirely unwarranted: during a month of poverty and toil, my name goes unnoticed and for the most part unuttered. In this parallel universe where my father never got out of the mines and I never got through college, I am "baby," "honey," "blondie," and, most commonly, "girl."

My first task is to find a place to live. I figure that if I can earn $7 an hour—which, from the want ads, seems doable—I can afford to spend $500 on rent, or maybe, with severe economies, $600. In the Key West area, where I live, this pretty much confines me to flophouses and trailer homes. [...]

So I decide to make the common trade-off between affordability and convenience, and go for a $500-a-month efficiency thirty miles up a two-lane highway from the employment opportunities of Key West, meaning forty-five minutes if there's no road construction and I don't get caught behind some sun-dazed Canadian tourists. [...]

[...] My aim is nothing so mistily subjective as to "experience poverty" or find out how it "really feels" to be a long-term low-wage worker. I've had enough unchosen encounters with poverty and the world of low-wage work to know it's not a place you want to visit for touristic purposes; it just smells too much like fear. And with all my real-life assets—bank account, IRA, health insurance, multiroom home—waiting indulgently in the background, I am, of course, thoroughly insulated from the terrors that afflict the genuinely poor.

No, this is a purely objective, scientific sort of mission. The humanitarian rationale for welfare reform—as opposed to the more punitive and stingy impulses that may actually have motivated it—is that work will lift poor women out of poverty while simultaneously inflating their self-esteem and hence their future value in the labor market. Thus, whatever the hassles involved in finding child care, transportation, etc., the transition from welfare to work will end happily, in greater prosperity for all. Now there are many problems with this comforting prediction, such as the fact that the economy will inevitably undergo a downturn, eliminating many jobs. Even without a downturn, the influx of a million former welfare recipients into the low-wage labor market could depress wages by as much as 11.9 percent, according to the Economic Policy Institute (EPI) in Washington, D.C.

But is it really possible to make a living on the kinds of jobs currently available to unskilled people? Mathematically, the answer is no, as can be shown by taking $6 to $7 an hour, perhaps subtracting a dollar or two an hour for child care, multiplying by 160 hours a month, and comparing the result to the prevailing rents. According to the National Coalition for the Homeless, for example, in 1998 it took, on average nationwide, an hourly wage of $8.89 to afford a one-bedroom apartment, and the Preamble Center for Public Policy estimates that the odds against a typical welfare recipient's landing a job at such a "living wage" are about 97 to 1. If these numbers are right, low-wage work is not a solution to poverty and possibly not even to homelessness.

*****

On the morning of my first full day of job searching, I take a red pen to the want ads, which are auspiciously numerous. Everyone in Key West's booming "hospitality industry" seems to be looking for someone like me—trainable, flexible, and with suitably humble expectations as to pay. I know I possess certain traits that might be advantageous—I'm white and, I like to think, well-spoken and poised—but I decide on two rules: One, I cannot use any skills derived from my education or usual work—not that there are a lot of want ads for satirical essayists anyway.

Two, I have to take the best-paid job that is offered me and of course do my best to hold it; no Marxist rants or sneaking off to read novels in the ladies' room. [...]

So I put on what I take to be a respectful-looking outfit of ironed Bermuda shorts and scooped-neck T-shirt and set out for a tour of the local hotels and supermarkets. Best Western, Econo Lodge, and HoJo's all let me fill out application forms, and these are, to my relief, interested in little more than whether I am a legal resident of the United States and have committed any felonies. My next stop is Winn-Dixie, the supermarket, which turns out to have a particularly onerous application process, featuring a fifteen-minute "interview" by computer since, apparently, no human on the premises is deemed capable of representing the corporate point of view. I am conducted to a large room decorated with posters illustrating how to look "professional" (it helps to be white and, if female, permed) and warning of the slick promises that union organizers might try to tempt me with. The interview is multiple choice: Do I have anything, such as child-care problems, that might make it hard for me to get to work on time? Do I think safety on the job is the responsibility of management? Then, popping up cunningly out of the blue: How many dollars' worth of stolen goods have I purchased in the last year? Would I turn in a fellow employee if I caught him stealing? Finally, "Are you an honest person?"

Apparently, I ace the interview, because I am told that all I have to do is show up in some doctor's office tomorrow for a urine test. This seems to be a fairly general rule: if you want to stack Cheerio boxes or vacuum hotel rooms in chemically fascist America, you have to be willing to squat down and pee in front of some health worker (who has no doubt had to do the same thing herself). The wages Winn-Dixie is offering—$6 and a couple of dimes to start with—are not enough, I decide, to compensate for this indignity.

I lunch at Wendy's, where $4.99 gets you unlimited refills at the Mexican part of the Superbar, a comforting surfeit of refried beans and "cheese sauce." A teenage employee, seeing me studying the want ads, kindly offers me an application form, which I fill out, though here, too, the pay is just $6 and change an hour. Then it's off for a round of the locally owned inns and guesthouses. At "The Palms," let's call it, a bouncy manager actually takes me around to see the rooms and meet the existing housekeepers, who, I note with satisfaction, look pretty much like me—faded ex-hippie types in shorts with long hair pulled back in braids. Mostly, though, no one speaks to me or even looks at me except to proffer an application form. At my last stop, a palatial B&B, I wait twenty minutes to meet "Max," only to be told that there are no jobs now but there should be one soon, since "nobody lasts more than a couple weeks." (Because none of the people I talked to knew I was a reporter, I have changed their names to protect their privacy and, in some cases, perhaps, their jobs.)

Three days go by like this, and, to my chagrin, no one out of the approximately twenty places I've applied calls me for an interview. I had been vain enough to worry about coming across as too educated for the jobs I sought, but no one even seems interested in finding out how overqualified I am. Only later will I realize that the want ads are not a reliable measure of the actual jobs available at any particular time. They are, as I should have guessed from Max's comment, the employers' insurance policy against the relentless turnover of the low-wage workforce. Most of the big hotels run ads almost continually, just to build a supply of applicants to replace the current workers as they drift away or are fired, so finding a job is just a matter of being at the right place at the right time and flexible enough to take whatever is being offered that day. This finally happens to me at one of the big discount hotel chains, where I go, as usual, for housekeeping and am sent, instead, to try out as a waitress at the attached "family restaurant," a dismal spot with a counter and about thirty tables that looks out on a parking garage and features such tempting fare as "Pollish [sic] sausage and BBQ sauce" on 95-degree days. [...]

So begins my career at the Hearthside, I shall call it, one small profit center within a global discount hotel chain, where for two weeks I work from 2:00 till 10:00 P.M. for $2.43 an hour plus tips. In some futile bid for gentility, the management has barred employees from using the front door, so my first day I enter through the kitchen, where a red-faced man with shoulder-length blond hair is throwing frozen steaks against the wall and yelling, "Fuck this shit!" "That's just Jack," explains Gail, the wiry middle-aged waitress who is assigned to train me. "He's on the rag again"—a condition occasioned, in this instance, by the fact that the cook on the morning shift had forgotten to thaw out the steaks. For the next eight hours, I run after the agile Gail, absorbing bits of instruction along with fragments of personal tragedy. All food must be trayed, and the reason she's so tired today is that she woke up in a cold sweat thinking of her boyfriend, who killed himself recently in an upstate prison. No refills on lemonade. And the reason he was in prison is that a few DUIs caught up with him, that's all, could have happened to anyone. Carry the creamers to the table in a monkey bowl, never in your hand. And after he was gone she spent several months living in her truck, peeing in a plastic pee bottle and reading by candlelight at night, but you can't live in a truck in the summer, since you need to have the windows down, which means anything can get in, from mosquitoes on up.

At least Gail puts to rest any fears I had of appearing overqualified. From the first day on, I find that of all the things I have left behind, such as home and identity, what I miss the most is competence. Not that I have ever felt utterly competent in the writing business, in which one day's success augers nothing at all for the next. But in my writing life, I at least have some notion of procedure: do the research, make the outline, rough out a draft, etc. As a server, though, I am beset by requests like bees: more iced tea here, ketchup over there, a to-go box for table fourteen, and where are the high chairs, anyway? Of the twenty-seven tables, up to six are usually mine at any time, though on slow afternoons or if Gail is off, I sometimes have the whole place to myself. There is the touch-screen computer-ordering system to master, which is, I suppose, meant to minimize server–cook contact, but in practice requires constant verbal fine-tuning: "That's gravy on the mashed, okay! None on the meatloaf," and so forth—while the cook scowls as if I were inventing these refinements just to torment him. Plus, something I had forgotten in the years since I was eighteen: about a third of a server's job is "side work" that's invisible to customers—sweeping, scrubbing, slicing, refilling, and restocking. If it isn't all done, every little bit of it, you're going to face the 6:00 P.M. dinner rush defenseless and probably go down in flames. I screw up dozens of times at the beginning, sustained in my shame entirely by Gail's support— "It's okay, baby, everyone does that sometime"—because, to my total surprise and despite the scientific detachment I am doing my best to maintain, I care.

*****

After a few days at the Hearthside, I feel the service ethic kick in like a shot of oxytocin, the nurturance hormone. The plurality of my customers are hard-working locals—truck drivers, construction workers, even housekeepers from the attached hotel—and I want them to have the closest to a "fine dining" experience that the grubby circumstances will allow. No "you guys" for me; everyone over twelve is "sir" or "ma'am." I ply them with iced tea and coffee refills; I return, mid-meal, to inquire how everything is; I doll up their salads with chopped raw mushrooms, summer squash slices, or whatever bits of produce I can find that have survived their sojourn in the cold-storage room mold-free.

*****

I could drift along like this, in some dreamy proletarian idyll, except for two things. One is management. If I have kept this subject on the margins thus far it is because I still flinch to think that I spent all those weeks under the surveillance of men (and later women) whose job it was to monitor my behavior for signs of sloth, theft, drug abuse, or worse. Not that managers and especially "assistant managers" in low-wage settings like this are exactly the class enemy. In the restaurant business, they are mostly former cooks or servers, still capable of pinch-hitting in the kitchen or on the floor, just as in hotels they are likely to be former clerks, and paid a salary of only about $400 a week. But everyone knows they have crossed over to the other side, which is, crudely put, corporate as opposed to human. Cooks want to prepare tasty meals; servers want to serve them graciously; but managers are there for only one reason—to make sure that money is made for some theoretical entity that exists far away in Chicago or New York, if a corporation can be said to have a physical existence at all. Reflecting on her career, Gail tells me ruefully that she had sworn, years ago, never to work for a corporation again. "They don't cut you no slack. You give and you give, and they take."

Managers can sit—for hours at a time if they want—but it's their job to see that no one else ever does, even when there's nothing to do, and this is why, for servers, slow times can be as exhausting as rushes. You start dragging out each little chore, because if the manager on duty catches you in an idle moment, he will give you something far nastier to do. So I wipe, I clean, I consolidate ketchup bottles and recheck the cheesecake supply, even tour the tables to make sure the customer evaluation forms are all standing perkily in their places—wondering all the time how many calories I burn in these strictly theatrical exercises. When, on a particularly dead afternoon, Stu [the assistant manager] finds me glancing at a *USA Today* a customer has left behind, he assigns me to vacuum the entire floor with the broken vacuum cleaner that has a handle only two feet long, and the only way to do that without incurring orthopedic damage is to proceed from spot to spot on your knees.

On my first Friday at the Hearthside there is a "mandatory meeting for all restaurant employees," which I attend, eager for insight into our overall marketing strategy and the niche (your basic Ohio cuisine with a tropical twist?) we aim to inhabit. But there is no "we" at this meeting. Phillip, our top manager except for an occasional "consultant" sent out by corporate headquarters, opens it with a sneer: "The break room—it's disgusting. Butts in the ashtrays, newspapers lying around, crumbs." This windowless little room, which also houses the time clock for the entire hotel, is where we stash our bags and civilian clothes and take our half-hour meal breaks. But a break room is not a right, he tells us. It can be taken away. We should also know that the lockers in the break room and whatever is in them can be searched at any time. Then comes gossip; there has been gossip; gossip (which seems to mean employees talking among themselves) must stop. Off-duty employees are henceforth barred from eating at the restaurant, because "other servers gather around them and gossip." When Phillip has exhausted his agenda of rebukes, Joan complains about the condition of the ladies' room and I throw in my two bits about the vacuum cleaner. But I don't see any backup coming from my fellow servers, each of whom has subsided into her own personal funk. [...]

*****

The other problem, in addition to the less-than-nurturing management style, is that this job shows no sign of being financially viable. You might imagine, from a comfortable distance, that people who live, year in and year out, on $6 to $10 an hour have discovered some survival stratagems unknown to the middle class. But no. It's not hard to get my co-workers to talk about their living situations, because housing, in almost every case, is the principal source of disruption in their lives, the first thing they fill you in on when they arrive for their shifts. After a week, I have compiled the following survey:

- Gail is sharing a room in a well-known downtown flophouse for which she and a roommate pay about $250 a week. Her roommate, a male friend, has begun hitting on her, driving her nuts, but the rent would be impossible alone.
- Claude, the Haitian cook, is desperate to get out of the two-room apartment he shares with his girlfriend and two other, unrelated, people. As far as I can determine, the other Haitian men (most of whom only speak Creole) live in similarly crowded situations.
- Annette, a twenty-year-old server who is six months pregnant and has been abandoned by her boyfriend, lives with her mother, a postal clerk.

- Marianne and her boyfriend are paying $170 a week for a one-person trailer.
- Jack, who is, at $10 an hour, the wealthiest of us, lives in the trailer he owns, paying only the $400-a-month lot fee.
- The other white cook, Andy, lives on his dry-docked boat, which, as far as I can tell from his loving descriptions, can't be more than twenty feet long. He offers to take me out on it, once it's repaired, but the offer comes with inquiries as to my marital status, so I do not follow up on it.
- Tina and her husband are paying $60 a night for a double room in a Days Inn. This is because they have no car and the Days Inn is within walking distance of the Hearthside. When Marianne, one of the breakfast servers, is tossed out of her trailer for subletting (which is against the trailer-park rules), she leaves her boyfriend and moves in with Tina and her husband.
- Joan, who had fooled me with her numerous and tasteful outfits (hostesses wear their own clothes), lives in a van she parks behind a shopping center at night and showers in Tina's motel room. The clothes are from thrift shops.

It strikes me, in my middle-class solipsism, that there is gross improvidence in some of these arrangements. When Gail and I are wrapping silverware in napkins—the only task for which we are permitted to sit—she tells me she is thinking of escaping from her roommate by moving into the Days Inn herself. I am astounded: How can she even think of paying between $40 and $60 a day? But if I was afraid of sounding like a social worker, I come out just sounding like a fool. She squints at me in disbelief, "And where am I supposed to get a month's rent and a month's deposit for an apartment?" I'd been feeling pretty smug about my $500 efficiency, but of course it was made possible only by the $1,300 I had allotted myself for start-up costs when I began my low-wage life: $1,000 for the first month's rent and deposit, $100 for initial groceries and cash in my pocket, $200 stuffed away for emergencies. In poverty, as in certain propositions in physics, starting conditions are everything.

There are no secret economies that nourish the poor; on the contrary, there are a host of special costs. If you can't put up the two months' rent you need to secure an apartment, you end up paying through the nose for a room by the week. If you have only a room, with a hot plate at best, you can't save by cooking up huge lentil stews that can be frozen for the week ahead. You eat fast food, or the hot dogs and styrofoam cups of soup that can be microwaved in a convenience store. If you have no money for health insurance […] you go without routine care or prescription drugs and end up paying the price. Gail, for example, was fine until she ran out of money for estrogen pills. She is supposed to be on the company plan by now, but they claim to have lost her application form and need to begin the paperwork all over again. So she spends $9 per migraine pill to control the headaches she wouldn't have, she insists, if her estrogen supplements were covered. Similarly, Marianne's boyfriend lost his job as a roofer because he missed so much time after getting a cut on his foot for which he couldn't afford the prescribed antibiotic.

My own situation, when I sit down to assess it after two weeks of work, would not be much better if this were my actual life. The seductive thing about waitressing is that you don't have to wait for payday to feel a few bills in your pocket, and my tips usually cover meals and gas, plus something left over to stuff into the kitchen drawer I use as a bank. But as the tourist business slows in the summer heat, I sometimes leave work with only $20 in tips (the gross is higher, but servers share about 15 percent of their tips with the busboys and bartenders). With wages included, this amounts to about the minimum wage of $5.15 an hour. Although the sum in the drawer is piling up, at the present rate of accumulation it will be more than $100 short of my rent when the end of the month comes around. Nor can I see any expenses to cut. True, I haven't gone the lentil-stew route yet, but that's because I don't have a large cooking pot, pot holders, or a ladle to stir with (which cost about $30 at Kmart, less at thrift stores), not to mention onions, carrots, and the indispensable bay leaf. I do make my lunch almost every day—usually some slow-burning, high-protein combo like frozen chicken patties with melted cheese on top and canned pinto beans on the side. Dinner is at the Hearthside, which offers its employees a choice of BLT, fish sandwich, or hamburger for only $2. The burger lasts longest, especially if it's heaped with gut-puckering jalapenos, but by midnight my stomach is growling again.

So unless I want to start using my car as a residence, I have to find a second, or alternative, job. I call all the hotels where I filled out housekeeping applications weeks ago—the Hyatt, Holiday Inn, Econo Lodge, HoJo's, Best Western, plus a half dozen or so locally run guesthouses. Nothing. Then I start making the rounds again, wasting whole mornings waiting for some assistant manager to show up, even dipping into places so creepy that the front-desk clerk greets you from behind bulletproof glass and sells pints of liquor over the counter. But either someone has exposed my real-life housekeeping habits—which are, shall we say, mellow—or I am at the wrong end of some infallible ethnic equation: most, but by no means all, of the working housekeepers I see on my job searches are African Americans, Spanish-speaking, or immigrants from the Central European post-Communist world, whereas servers are almost invariably white and monolingually English-speaking. When I finally get a positive response, I have been identified once again as server material. Jerry's, which is part of a well-known national family restaurant chain and physically attached here to another budget hotel chain, is ready to use me at once. The prospect is both exciting and terrifying, because, with about the same number of tables and counter seats, Jerry's attracts three or four times the volume of customers as the gloomy old Hearthside.

*****

Management at Jerry's is generally calmer and more "professional" than at the Hearthside, with two exceptions. One is Joy, a plump, blowsy woman in her early thirties, who once kindly devoted several minutes to instructing me in the correct one-handed method of carrying trays but whose moods change disconcertingly from shift to shift and even within one. Then there's B.J., a.k.a. B.J.-the-bitch, whose contribution is to stand by the kitchen counter and yell, "Nita, your order's up, move it!" or, "Barbara, didn't you see you've got another table out there? Come on, girl!" Among other things, she is hated for having replaced the whipped-cream squirt cans with big plastic whipped-cream-filled baggies that have to be squeezed with both hands—because, reportedly, she saw or thought she saw employees trying to inhale the propellant gas from the squirt cans, in the hope that it might be nitrous oxide. On my third night, she pulls me aside abruptly and brings her face so close that it looks as if she's planning to butt me with her forehead. But instead of saying, "You're fired," she says, "You're doing fine." The only trouble is I'm spending time chatting with customers: "That's how they're getting you." Furthermore I am letting them "run me," which means harassment by sequential demands: you bring the ketchup and they decide they want extra Thousand Island; you bring that and they announce they now need a side of fries; and so on into distraction. Finally she tells me not to take her wrong. She tries to say things in a nice way, but you get into a mode, you know, because everything has to move so fast.

I mumble thanks for the advice, feeling like I've just been stripped naked by the crazed enforcer of some ancient sumptuary law: No chatting for you, girl. No fancy service ethic allowed for the serfs. Chatting with customers is for the beautiful young college-educated servers in the down-town carpaccio joints, the kids who can make $70 to $100 a night. What had I been thinking? My job is to move orders from tables to kitchen and then trays from kitchen to tables. Customers are, in fact, the major obstacle to the smooth transformation of information into food and food into money—they are, in short, the enemy. And the painful thing is that I'm beginning to see it this way myself. [...]

*****

I make friends, over time, with the other "girls" who work my shift: Nita, the tattooed twenty-something who taunts us by going around saying brightly, "Have we started making money yet?" Ellen, whose teenage son cooks on the graveyard shift and who once managed a restaurant in Massachusetts but won't try out for management here because she prefers being a "common worker" and not "ordering people around." Easy-going fiftyish Lucy, with the raucous laugh, who limps toward the end of the shift because of something that has gone wrong with her leg, the exact nature of which cannot be determined without health insurance. We talk about the usual girl things—men, children, and the sinister allure of Jerry's chocolate peanut-butter cream pie—though no one, I notice, ever brings up anything potentially expensive, like shopping or movies. As at the Hearthside, the only recreation ever referred to is partying, which requires little more than some beer, a joint, and a few close friends. Still, no one here is homeless, or cops to it anyway, thanks usually to a working husband or boyfriend. All in all, we form a reliable mutual-support group: If one of us is feeling sick or overwhelmed, another one will "bev" a table or even carry trays for her. If one of us is off sneaking a cigarette or a pee, the others will do their best to conceal her absence from the enforcers of corporate rationality.

*****

I make the decision to move closer to Key West. First, because of the drive. Second and third, also because of the drive: gas is eating up $4 to $5 a day, and although Jerry's is as high-volume as you can get, the tips average only 10 percent, and not just for a newbie like me. Between the base pay of $2.15 an hour and the obligation to share tips with the busboys and dishwashers, we're averaging only about $7.50 an hour. Then there is the $30 I had to spend on the regulation tan slacks worn by Jerry's servers—a setback it could take weeks to absorb. (I had combed the town's two downscale department stores hoping for something cheaper but decided in the end that these marked-down Dockers, originally $49, were more likely to survive a daily washing.) Of my fellow servers, everyone who lacks a working husband or boyfriend seems to have a second job: Nita does something at a computer eight hours a day; another welds. Without the forty-five-minute commute, I can picture myself working two jobs and having the time to shower between them.

So I take the $500 deposit I have coming from my landlord, the $400 I have earned toward the next month's rent, plus the $200 reserved for emergencies, and use the $1,100 to pay the rent and deposit on trailer number 46 in the Overseas Trailer Park, a mile from the cluster of budget hotels that constitute Key West's version of an industrial park. Number 46 is about eight feet in width and shaped like a barbell inside, with a narrow region—because of the sink and the stove—separating the bedroom from what might optimistically be called the "living" area, with its two-person table and half-sized couch. The bathroom is so small my knees rub against the shower stall when I sit on the toilet, and you can't just leap out of the bed, you have to climb down to the foot of it in order to find a patch of floor space to stand on. Outside, I am within a few yards of a liquor store, a bar that advertises "free beer tomorrow," a convenience store, and a Burger King—but no supermarket or, alas, laundromat. By reputation, the Overseas park is a nest of crime and crack, and I am hoping at least for some vibrant, multicultural street life. But desolation rules night and day, except for a thin stream of pedestrian traffic heading for their jobs at the Sheraton or 7-Eleven. There are not exactly people here but what amounts to canned labor, being preserved from the heat between shifts.

In line with my reduced living conditions, a new form of ugliness arises at Jerry's. First we are confronted—via an announcement on the computers through which we input orders—with the new rule that the hotel bar is henceforth off-limits to restaurant employees. The culprit, I learn through the grapevine, is the ultra-efficient gal who trained me—another trailer-home dweller and a mother of three. Something had set her off one morning, so she slipped out for a nip and returned to the floor impaired. This mostly hurts Ellen, whose habit it is to free her hair from its rubber band and drop by the bar for a couple of Zins before heading home at the end of the shift, but all of us feel the chill. Then the next day, when I go for straws, for the first time I find the dry-storage room locked. Ted, the portly assistant manager who opens it for me, explains that he caught one of the dishwashers attempting to steal something, and, unfortunately, the miscreant will be with us until a replacement can be found—hence the locked door. I neglect to ask what he had been trying to steal, but Ted tells me who he is—the kid with the buzz cut and the earring. You know, he's back there right now.

*****

[…] When my month-long plunge into poverty is almost over, I finally land my dream job—housekeeping. I do this by walking into the personnel office of the only place I figure I might have some credibility, the hotel attached to Jerry's, and confiding urgently that I have to have a second job if I am to pay my rent and, no, it couldn't be front-desk clerk. "All right," the personnel lady fairly spits, "So it's housekeeping," and she marches me back to meet Maria, the housekeeping manager, a tiny, frenetic Hispanic woman who greets me as "babe" and hands me a pamphlet emphasizing the need for a positive attitude. The hours are nine in the morning till whenever, the pay is $6.10 an hour, and there's one week of vacation a year. I don't have to ask about health insurance once I meet Carlotta, the middle-aged African-American woman who will be training me. Carla, as she tells me to call her, is missing all of her top front teeth.

On that first day of housekeeping and last day of my entire project—although I don't yet know it's the last—Carla is in a foul mood. We have been given nineteen rooms to clean, most of them "checkouts," as opposed to "stayovers," that require the whole enchilada of bed-stripping, vacuuming, and bathroom-scrubbing. When one of the rooms that had been listed as a stay-over turns out to be a checkout, Carla calls Maria to complain, but of course to no avail. "So make up the motherfucker," Carla orders me, and I do the beds while she sloshes around the bathroom. For four hours without a break I strip and remake beds, taking about four and a half minutes per queen-sized bed, which I could get down to three if there were any reason to. We try to avoid vacuuming by picking up the larger specks by hand, but often there is nothing to do but drag the monstrous vacuum cleaner—it weighs about thirty pounds—off our cart and try to wrestle it around the floor. Sometimes Carla hands me the squirt bottle of "BAM" (an acronym for something that begins, ominously, with "butyric"; the rest has been worn off the label) and lets me do the bathrooms. No service ethic challenges me here to new heights of performance. I just concentrate on removing the pubic hairs from the bathtubs, or at least the dark ones that I can see.

*****

When I request permission to leave at about 3:30, another housekeeper warns me that no one has so far succeeded in combining housekeeping at the hotel with serving at Jerry's: "Some kid did it once for five days, and you're no kid." With that helpful information in mind, I rush back to number 46, down four Advils (the name brand this time), shower, stooping to fit into the stall, and attempt to compose myself for the oncoming shift. So much for what Marx termed the "reproduction of labor power," meaning the things a worker has to do just so she'll be ready to work again. The only unforeseen obstacle to that smooth transition from job to job is that my tan Jerry's slacks, which had looked reasonably clean by 40-watt bulb last night when I handwashed my Hawaiian shirt, prove by daylight to be mottled with ketchup and ranch-dressing stains. I spend most of my hour-long break between jobs attempting to remove the edible portions with a sponge and then drying the slacks over the hood of my car in the sun.

[…] At eight, Ellen and I grab a snack together standing at the mephitic end of the kitchen counter, but I can only manage two or three mozzarella sticks and lunch had been a mere handful of McNuggets. I am not tired at all, I assure myself, though it may be that there is simply no more "I" left to do the tiredness monitoring. What I would see, if I were more alert to the situation, is that the forces of destruction are already massing against me. There is only one cook on duty, a young man named Jesus ("Hay-Sue," that is) and he is new to the job. And there is Joy, who shows up to take over in the middle of the shift, wearing high heels and a long, clingy white dress and fuming as if she'd just been stood up in some cocktail bar.

Then it comes, the perfect storm. Four of my tables fill up at once. Four tables is nothing for me now, but only so long as they are obligingly staggered. As I bev table 27, tables 25, 28, and 24 are watching enviously. As I bev 25, 24 glowers because their bevs haven't even been ordered. Twenty-eight is four yuppyish types, meaning everything on the side and agonizing instructions as to the chicken Caesars. Twenty-five is a middle-aged black couple, who complain, with some justice, that the iced tea isn't fresh and the tabletop is sticky. But table 24 is the meteorological event of the century: ten British tourists who seem to have made the decision to absorb the American experience entirely by mouth. Here everyone has at least two drinks—iced tea and milk shake, Michelob and water (with lemon slice, please)—and a huge promiscuous orgy of breakfast specials, mozz sticks, chicken strips, quesadillas, burgers with cheese and without, sides of hash browns with cheddar, with onions, with gravy, seasoned fries, plain fries, banana splits. Poor Jesus! Poor me! Because when I arrive with their first tray of food—after three prior trips just to refill bevs—Princess Di refuses to eat her chicken strips with her pancake-and-sausage special, since, as she now reveals, the strips were meant to be an appetizer. Maybe the others would have accepted their meals, but Di, who is deep into her third Michelob, insists that everything else go back while they work on their "starters." […]

Much of what happened next is lost in the fog of war. Jesus starts going under. The little printer on the counter in front of him is spewing out orders faster than he can rip them off, much less produce the meals. Even the invincible Ellen is ashen from stress. I bring table 24 their reheated main courses, which they immediately reject as either too cold or fossilized by the microwave. When I return to the kitchen with their trays (three trays in three trips), Joy confronts me with arms akimbo: "What is this?" She means the food—the plates of rejected pancakes, hash browns in assorted flavors, toasts, burgers, sausages, eggs. "Uh, scrambled with cheddar," I try, "and that's …" "NO," she screams in my face. "Is it a traditional, a super-scramble, an eye-opener?" I pretend to study my check for a clue, but entropy has been up to its tricks, not only on the plates but in my head, and I have to admit that the original order is beyond reconstruction. "You don't know an eye-opener from a traditional?" she demands in outrage. All I know, in fact, is that my legs have lost interest in the current venture and have announced their intention to fold. I am saved by a yuppie (mercifully not one of mine) who chooses this moment to charge into the kitchen to bellow that his food is twenty-five minutes late. Joy screams at him to get the hell out of her kitchen, please, and then turns on Jesus in a fury, hurling an empty tray across the room for emphasis.

I leave. I don't walk out, I just leave. I don't finish my side work or pick up my credit-card tips, if any, at the cash register or, of course, ask Joy's permission to go. And the surprising thing is that you *can* walk out without permission, that the door opens, that the thick tropical night air parts to let me pass, that my car is still parked where I left it. There is no vindication in this exit, no fuck-you surge of relief, just an overwhelming, dank sense of failure pressing down on me and the entire parking lot. [...]

In one month, I had earned approximately $1,040 and spent $517 on food, gas, toiletries, laundry, phone, and utilities. If I had remained in my $500 efficiency, I would have been able to pay the rent and have $22 left over (which is $78 less than the cash I had in my pocket at the start of the month). During this time I bought no clothing except for the required slacks and no prescription drugs or medical care (I did finally buy some vitamin B to compensate for the lack of vegetables in my diet). Perhaps I could have saved a little on food if I had gotten to a supermarket more often, instead of convenience stores, but it should be noted that I lost almost four pounds in four weeks, on a diet weighted heavily toward burgers and fries.

How former welfare recipients and single mothers will (and do) survive in the low-wage workforce, I cannot imagine. Maybe they will figure out how to condense their lives—including child-raising, laundry, romance, and meals—into the couple of hours between full-time jobs. Maybe they will take up residence in their vehicles, if they have one. All I know is that I couldn't hold two jobs and I couldn't make enough money to live on with one. And I had advantages unthinkable to many of the long-term poor—health, stamina, a working car, and no children to care for and support. Certainly nothing in my experience contradicts the conclusion of Kathryn Edin and Laura Lein, in their recent book *Making Ends Meet: How Single Mothers Survive Welfare and Low-Wage Work*, that low-wage work actually involves more hardship and deprivation than life at the mercy of the welfare state. In the coming months and years, economic conditions for the working poor are bound to worsen, even without the almost inevitable recession. As mentioned earlier, the influx of former welfare recipients into the low-skilled workforce will have a depressing effect on both wages and the number of jobs available. A general economic downturn will only enhance these effects, and the working poor will of course be facing it without the slight, but nonetheless often saving, protection of welfare as a backup.

The thinking behind welfare reform was that even the humblest jobs are morally uplifting and psychologically buoying. In reality they are likely to be fraught with insult and stress. But I did discover one redeeming feature of the most abject low-wage work—the camaraderie of people who are, in almost all cases, far too smart and funny and caring for the work they do and the wages they're paid. The hope, of course, is that someday these people will come to know what they're worth, and take appropriate action.

Chapter 59

Factsheet: Women and Restructuring in Canada

Deborah Stienstra

Deborah Stienstra is professor in disability studies at the University of Manitoba. She has worked with various national organizations, including the Canadian Research Institute for the Advancement of Women, the Council of Canadians with Disabilities, the National Action Committee on the Status of Women, the Feminist Alliance for International Action, and the Canadian Voice of Women for Peace. Her research focuses on the impacts of economic and social restructuring on women and people with disabilities; the intersections between disability, race/ethnicity, and Aboriginality; and the experiences of people with disabilities in end of life and cancer care. Her publications include a forthcoming book called About Canada: Disability Rights.

Over the past three decades, Canada's economy has undergone significant restructuring by private companies and governments. This has caused tremendous changes for some communities, families, and individual lives. Women experience the effects of this restructuring in ways that directly increase their responsibilities and negatively affect their communities, families, and well-being. Restructuring affects particular groups of women more than others and in different ways. Think of seniors, recent immigrant women, single-parent mothers, and women with disabilities. They live with more serious effects of restructuring.

Lots of changes related to restructuring are happening right now or about to happen. Some signals are the significant downturn in the global economy in 2009, increased government involvement to address this, and the emerging public spending cuts to reduce deficits. Who is affected by these actions and how? This factsheet outlines some of the key issues for women in Canada as a result of restructuring and some actions women can take to address these issues.

*****

What Is Restructuring?

Restructuring is a process of change that has been happening in Canada and across the world for the past decades. It has its roots "in multiple sources, including globalized pressures on social spending, altered labor force realities, changing demographics and family relations, challenges over appropriate sites for government intervention, new reliance on public-private partnerships, and renewed roles for the voluntary or third sector."[1] The global economic downturn in 2009 intensified these changes and made a new wave of restructuring likely.

These changes are most often described in economic terms—companies downsize their workforce, governments try to reduce deficits and debts by eliminating or restricting public programs, and selling public or crown companies to private companies through privatization. Yet as feminist writers remind us, restructuring is changing the market, our governments as well as our communities, families, and social movements.[2]

*****

What Are The Issues for Women?

Restructuring has impacts on both women and men, and the impacts are often more intensely experienced by those who have been marginalized in Canadian society as a result of gender, race, immigrant status, disability, or poverty. Using tools like intersectional feminist frameworks[3] and sex- and gender-based analysis,[4] we begin to see more precisely who is affected by which actions and what the longer-term impacts are of these changes.

In this factsheet we ask which women are affected most by the changes to the Canadian economy and society over the past decades, and which are most likely to be affected by the changes as a result of the recent economic downturn. Not surprisingly we find that single-parent mothers, women with disabilities, racialized women, recent immigrants, and poor women face increased intensified negative effects from both ongoing restructuring and the recent downturn.

We look specifically at [two] areas of restructuring and the effects on women:

- changing labour markets
- restructuring government programs [...]

We want to answer three questions:

- Where are the women?
- What are the effects of restructuring and the recession on women?
- Which women are most affected?

1. Changing Labour Markets

Where are the women?

Today women make up almost half (47%) of Canada's labour force, much more than in the mid-1970s when they were just over one-third (37%) of the workforce. Most women (about three-quarters) work full-time and have historically. But women are much more likely than men to work part-time. Seven in 10 part-time employees are women and this has been consistent since the 1970s. As well, more women than men, and especially young women, are likely to hold more than one job at a time.[5]

Women continue to be concentrated in service-related occupations, administrative work, and teaching. Two-thirds of all employed women are found in these areas.[6] Racialized women are three times more likely than other women to be employed in manufacturing jobs.[7]

Women's hourly wage is 84% of men, but the gap was significantly reduced among unionized women and men where women earn 94% of men's rate.[8] The gender gap is higher for full-time women between 25 and 54, with women earning 76 cents for each dollar men earned.[9]

Women without children systematically earn more than women with children. The gap is even greater for single-parent mothers.[10] In 2006, single-parent families headed by women had average earnings of $30,598 while father-led single-parent families had average earnings of $47,943 per year.[11]

Average earnings for immigrant workers are falling further behind that of Canadian-born workers, with average immigrant women's earnings plummeting from 85 cents for each dollar [earned by] Canadian-born women in 1980 to 56 cents in 2006.[12] Recent immigrant women who live in poverty are also likely to be racialized, have a university education, and live in the large urban areas of Toronto and Vancouver.[13]

One reason for lower earnings by racialized women, or those Statistics Canada calls "visible minority women," is that they are less likely to be employed even though they are better educated than other Canadian women. In 2000 their earnings were about 10% less than other Canadian women.[14] By 2005, this had grown to a 15% gap, as the average income of visible minority women was significantly below that of other women ($23,369 vs $27,673).[15]

Women with disabilities earn considerably less than women without disabilities and men with or without disabilities. Specifically, in 2006 women with disabilities earned approximately $11,000 per year less than men with disabilities. Women with disabilities who are unionized have better wages than women with disabilities who are not ($35,677 and $21,983), although they remain lower than men's.[16]

Aboriginal women are generally less likely than their non-Aboriginal counterparts to be part of the paid workforce and the unemployment rates are twice the rate for non-Aboriginal women.[17] Aboriginal women and men have lower than average incomes and less of an income gap between them. New findings show that with increasing education, Aboriginal women close the income gap with non-Aboriginal women.[18]

While these statistics illustrate the issues for different groups of women in the labour force, we do not have statistics to tell us about women who fit in more than one group, including Aboriginal women with disabilities or racialized women who are single parents. This is a significant gap in what we can know about women's situations.

What Are the Effects of Restructuring and Recession on Women?

Four key issues emerge for women as a result of restructuring:

a) Impact on Women's Jobs and Income

There has been an increase in precarious or insecure work. Precarious work, including part-time, temporary, and multiple jobs, makes up approximately 40% of women's employment, compared to 30% of men's.[19] This type of work is normally low paid, with few or no benefits. When women lose these jobs, they may not be eligible for Employment Insurance (EI). Only 39% of unemployed women are receiving Employment Insurance benefits (2008) replacing just 55% of their usual earnings when they are out of work.[20] Women in the provinces hardest hit by the 2009 recession have not benefited from Employment Insurance benefits. Only one in three women and men in Ontario and the Western provinces received EI benefits.[21]

b) Impact on Women's Well-being

The negative impacts of restructuring on some women's jobs, income, and families is closely linked to women's well-being. When women face changes in their work life, it has ripple effects throughout their lives. Women with children who need to find childcare in order to spend more time in paid labour face challenges finding quality childcare. Plus, they have to juggle that expense. For single-parent mothers, the presence of young children shapes their employment and therefore their income.[22] During the recession of the 1990s lone-parent mothers experienced a significant decline in their employment that was not the same for mothers of two-parent families.[23] Working-age women with disabilities noted that their life satisfaction is significantly affected by stress related to work, health, and finances.[24]

c) Impact on Families

During the most recent economic downturn, there has been a significant loss in men's jobs, especially in the manufacturing and natural resources industries like the boom-and-bust oil and gas industries and the forestry industry. Women have had to take on responsibility for more of the family income in heterosexual families, and more women over 55 are working, largely full-time, an increase of 5% since October 2008.[25]

d) Impact on Communities

During economic downturns, there is an increased demand for services, yet often fewer resources to deliver these. Unlike most economic sectors, the non-profit sector typically sees an increase in the demand for services during an economic downturn, especially front-line organizations working in human and social services.[26]

*****

2. Restructuring Government Programs

Where are the women?

Government programs are a significant source of income for women, especially for senior women, disabled women, and single-parent mothers. Government program transfers are a larger part of women's income than men's. This reliance on transfer programs is most significant for senior women. Government transfer programs account for over half (55%) the income of senior women. These programs provide only 15% of income for women between 55 and 64 and less than that for other age groups.[27]

Old Age Security (OAS) and Guaranteed Income Supplements (GIS) make up the single largest component of government transfer benefits received by women. The next largest were the Canada and Quebec Pension Plans, Child Tax benefits, social assistance benefits, and Employment Insurance payouts.[28]

Lone-parent families headed by women rely on government transfer payments for a relatively large share of their income. Government transfer programs accounted for over a quarter (27%) of all income for women-led lone-parent families in 2003. This compares with 11% of all income for male-headed lone-parent families and just 6% of that for two-parent families with children.[29] Many single-parent families led by women rely on social assistance as their main source of income.[30]

Employment Insurance is an increasingly important source of income for women, especially the special benefits. In 2008/9 twice as many women received the special EI benefits (maternity, parental, sickness, and compassionate care) than men (345,600 women vs 168,900 men). Yet during the same year, women made up only 38% of those receiving regular benefits (603,900 women and 1,038,600 men). In 2008/9, 36% of all female EI beneficiaries were receiving either maternity or parental benefits.[31] In 1997 the rules to qualify for EI benefits were significantly changed to the numbers of hours rather than weeks worked. Given that women work fewer hours than men, and are more likely to have precarious work without job security, the changes will have greater meaning for women.

It will mean fewer women will qualify to get EI during this economic downturn than during the 1980s recession. Under the old program of Unemployment Insurance, at the time of the last recession, in the late 1980s, almost 83% of unemployed women and 85% of unemployed men got benefits. Coverage dropped dramatically after the rules were changed. By 2008, only 39% of unemployed women and 45% of unemployed men were receiving Employment Insurance benefits, replacing just 55% of their usual earnings when they are out of work. In some parts of the country, coverage is much lower than that.[32]

Working-age people with disabilities were over three times as likely to receive government transfers in 2006 as adults without disabilities. Over 55% of women with disabilities had government transfers as a source of personal income while only 47% of men with disabilities did.[33] Many people with disabilities rely on provincial social assistance programs, or government disability benefit programs. The Canada Pension Plan Disability (CPP-D) is the major disability insurance program in Canada.[34] Several provinces have particular disability benefits programs, including Alberta (AISH), Ontario (ODSP), and BC, but none of the statistics available include a gender breakdown for the users.

*****

Women are also significant users of public services, including home care and disability supports programs and transportation. Although the statistics on home care usage are quite old, they illustrate that in 1996/97 at least 2.5% of Canadians over the age of 18 used homecare, most notably seniors and people with chronic illness.[35] As well, we know that the majority of long-term care home residents are women, both seniors and those under 65 who need continuing care.[36] Women with disabilities are more likely than men with disabilities to receive help from formal and informal providers for daily activities (67.4% versus 47.9%).[37]

Women are also in a majority of public service workers and thus are affected as workers by changes to government programs. They remain concentrated in the service sector workforce. In the health services, 80% of the workforce are women, although they remain clustered in the nursing professions; dental assistants, hygienists, and therapists; dietitians and nutritionists; and audiologists and speech-language pathologists.[38] Many other women work in the health services sector as personal care workers, cooks, cleaners, laundry and clerical workers.[39]

What Are the Effects of Restructuring and Recession on Women?

a) Eliminating and Reducing Public Services

As the number of claims to government programs increase and the funds become more limited, governments often choose to eliminate programs or reduce or restrict who can receive those programs.

The Employment Insurance program was radically changed for women in 1997 by linking eligibility to hours rather than weeks worked. Women in part-time and precarious work were affected most. Recent government changes intended to address the economic downturn in 2009 primarily targeted those who had been in relatively stable jobs before they were laid off. This has meant that many women have fallen through the cracks. For women, the increase in the number of EI beneficiaries just matched the increase in the number of unemployed.[40]

More recently, at least two provincial governments have changed or restricted eligibility to some measures under social assistance programs that will especially affect people with disabilities. For example, the Ontario 2010 budget eliminated the special diet allowance for people on social assistance and replaced it with a health supplement, which is medically assessed and will only assist those with severe medical needs.[41] In the 2010 British Columbia budget, similar cuts were made to the range of medical equipment and supplies funded by the government. Eligibility for the monthly nutritional supplement was also tightened, including applicants now having to demonstrate they have at least two symptoms rather than one under the existing criteria.[42]

In 2002, the British Columbia government made dramatic cuts to legal aid services, primarily in the areas of family and poverty law. These cuts had the biggest effect on women who rely on legal aid to assist in divorce and custody disputes, as well as appeals related to welfare, Employment Insurance benefits, or housing.[43]

*****

b) Privatizing Government Services

Another way for governments to reduce expenditures on public programs has been to sell or transfer a service to a private, for-profit entity, without the same degree of public accountability or regulation.

The City of Vancouver privatized its bus services in 2008, which has [a] significant and disproportionate impact on women, poor people, people with disabilities, and seniors who rely extensively on public transportation. The Bus Riders Union in Vancouver argues that "[w]omen are a majority of these bus riders. Many women, particularly women of colour, need public transit because they are concentrated in low-wage, night shift, temporary, part-time work, and have a lot of family responsibilities. They need reliable, affordable, and 24-hour public transit. As Trans-Link privatizes transit services, women have to deal with high fares, poor service, and barriers to [their] ability to get around."[44]

The parallel public transportation system for people with disabilities, HandyDart, was also privatized in October 2008. Before the first year under the new company was over, the drivers held a 10-week strike because of conflict with the employer about wages and benefits.[45] As a result of the contracting out of this service, the regional transportation has no authority to require binding arbitration or force a return to work.

British Columbia also undertook a massive privatization of public health services since 2003. At least 8,500 public sector jobs were eliminated in the health support services, and housekeeping services in 32 hospitals in the Lower Mainland and southern Vancouver Island were privatized.[46] The majority of the workers who lost their jobs and gained the privatized jobs were working-class women. In addition, many of these were women of colour from immigrant and non-immigrant backgrounds. A study of this shift illustrated that incomes for the privatized workers were very low, often below the poverty line, and working conditions were harsh. Contracting out not only endangers the health of these workers, but the well-being of their families and the patients they serve.[47]

c) Downsizing Public Service Employment

Cuts to the British Columbia public service illustrate some of the significant impacts on women and their economic security. A 2005 report suggested three-quarters of the job cuts to health care, support services, education, and other areas of public service were jobs held by women.[48]

d) Impact on Women's Well-being

All of these changes as a result of restructuring affect women's health and well-being. As public services are reduced, families are often left with the ongoing responsibility for care that remains. When services are provided in the home, such as home care, there is often an assumption that families, meaning primarily women, will provide support to fill any gaps. This increases stress, anxiety, and exhaustion for informal care providers.[49] Increased difficult conditions in a privatized service environment can also increase the negative impacts on women's health and well-being.[50]

*****

Notes

1. Susan Prentice, "High Stakes: The "Investable" Child and the Economic Reframing of Childcare," *Signs: Journal of Women in Culture and Society* (34) 2009: 701.
2. Isabella Bakker and Rachel Silvey, eds., *Beyond States and Markets: The Challenges of Social Reproduction* (London and New York: Routledge, 2008); Marianne H. Marchand and Anne S. Runyan, eds., *Gender and Global Restructuring: Sightings, Sights, and Resistances* (New York: Routledge, 2000); Isabella Bakker, ed., Introduction to *Rethinking Restructuring: Gender and Change in Canada* (Toronto: University of Toronto Press, 1996), pp. 3–25.
3. Marika Morris and Benita Bunjun, *Using Intersectional Feminist Frameworks in Research: A Resource for Embracing the Complexities of Women's Lives* (Ottawa: Canadian Research Institute for the Advancement of Women, 2007).
4. Barbara Clow, Ann Pederson, Margaret Haworth-Brockman, and Jennifer Bernier, *Rising to the Challenge: Sex and Gender-Based Analysis for Health Planning, Policy, and Research in Canada* (Halifax: Atlantic Centre of Excellence for Women's Health, 2009).
5. Statistics Canada, *Women in Canada: A Gender-Based Statistical Report* (5th ed.) (Ottawa: Minister of Industry, 2005).
6. Ibid.
7. Ibid.
8. Statistics Canada, *Economic Fact Sheet* (Ottawa: Minister of Industry, 2010).
9. Statistics Canada, "Census of Population, 2006," http://www12.statcan.ca/census-recensement/2006/as-sa/97-563/table/t7-eng.cfm.
10. Xuelin Zhang, Statistics Canada, *Earnings of Women with and without Children* (Ottawa: Minister of Industry, 2009).
11. Ibid.
12. Ibid.
13. Dominque Fleury, *A Study of Poverty and Working Poverty among Recent Immigrants to Canada* (Ottawa: Human Resources and Social Development Canada, 2007).
14. Statistics Canada, *Women in Canada: A Gender-Based Statistical Report* (5th ed.).

15. Canadian Association of Social Workers, *Comparing Women's Income in 2000 and 2005: Improvements and Disappointments* (Ottawa: CASW, 2009).

16. Human Resources and Skills Development Canada, *Federal Disability Report: Advancing the Inclusion of People with Disabilities* (Gatineau: HRSDC, 2009), p. 38.

17. Statistics Canada, *Women in Canada: A Gender-Based Statistical Report* (5th ed.).

18. Daniel Wilson and David MacDonald, *The Income Gap between Aboriginal Peoples and the Rest of Canada* (Ottawa: Canadian Centre for Policy Alternatives, 2010).

19. Monica Townson, *Women's Poverty and the Recession* (Ottawa: Canadian Centre for Policy Alternatives, 2009), p. 18.

20. Ibid., p. 7.

21. Ibid., p. 7.

22. Statistics Canada, *Women in Canada: Work Chapter Updates* (Ottawa: Minister of Industry, 2006).

23. Statistics Canada, *Women in Canada: A Gender-Based Statistical Report* (5th ed.).

24. Susan Crompton, *Living with Disability Series: Life Satisfaction of Working-Age Women with Disabilities* (Ottawa: Minister of Industry, 2010).

25. Yuquian Lu and Rene Morissette, "Women's Participation and Economic Downturns," *Perspectives*, Statistics Canada (May 2010): 18–22; Trish Hennessy and Armine Yalnizyan, *Canada's "He-cession"—Men Bearing Brunt of Rising Unemployment* (Ottawa: Canadian Centre for Policy Alternatives, Behind the Numbers (10)4, July 2009).

26. Lynne Toupin, *Managing People through Turbulent Times* (HR Council for the Voluntary & Non-profit Sector, Trends & Issues, January 2009).

27. Statistics Canada, *Women in Canada: A Gender-Based Statistical Report* (5th ed.).

28. Ibid.

29. Ibid.

30. Townson, *Women's Poverty and the Recession*; Peter Dunn and Lea Caragata, *Preliminary SLID findings* (Toronto: Lone Mothers: Building Social Inclusion, 2007).

31. Statistics Canada, *Women in Canada: A Gender-Based Statistical Report* (5th ed.).

32. Caledon Institute of Social Policy, *Canada's Shrunken Safety Net: Employment Insurance in the Great Recession* (Ottawa: Caledon Institute of Social Policy, Caledon Commentary, April 2009), p. 1.

33. Human Resources and Skills Development Canada (HRSDC).

34. Michael J. Prince, *Canadians Need a Medium-Term Sickness/Disability Income Benefit* (Ottawa: Caledon Institute of Social Policy, 2008).

35. Health Canada, "Health Care in Canada 1999: An Overview," http://www.hc-sc.gc.ca/hcs-sss/pubs/home-domicile/1999-home-domicile/situation-eng.php#a6.

36. Pat Armstrong, Madeline Boscoe, Barbara Clow, Karen R. Grant, Margaret Haworth-Brockman, Beth E. Jackson, Ann Pederson, Morgan Seeley, and Jane Springer, *A Place to Call Home: Long-Term Care in Canada* (Black Point, NS: Fernwood, 2009), p. 34.

37. HRSDC.

38. Canadian Institute for Health Information, *Canada's Health Care Providers, 2007* (Ottawa: CIHI, 2007), p. 60.

39. Pat Armstrong, Hugh Armstrong, and Krista Scott-Dixon, *Critical to Care: The Invisible Women in Health Services* (Toronto: University of Toronto Press, 2008).

40. Andrew Jackson and Sylvain Schetagne, *Is EI Working for Canada's Unemployed? Analyzing the Great Recession* (Ottawa: Canadian Center for Policy Alternatives, Alternative Federal Budget 2010, Technical Paper, April 2010).

41. Laurie Monsebraaten, "Anti-poverty Advocates Decry Loss of Food Help," *The Star*, March 25, 2010.

42. B.C. Coalition of People with Disabilities, "March 2010 Medical Funding Cuts," http://www.bccpd.bc.ca/cutstomedical.htm.

43. Alison Brewin, *Women's Employment in B.C.: Effects of Government Downsizing and Policy Changes* (Vancouver: Canadian Centre for Policy Alternatives, B.C. Commentary (8)1, 2005); Sylvia Fuller and Lindsay Stephens, *Women's Employment in B.C.: Effects of Government Downsizing and Policy Changes* (Vancouver: Canadian Centre for Policy Alternatives, B.C. Commentary (8)1, 2005).

44. Bus Riders Union, "Women in Transit: Transit Is a Woman's Right," http://bru.vcn.bc.ca/women-in-transit.

45. Matthew Burrows, "HandyDart Strike Leaves Disabled Passengers Out in the Cold," *Straight.com, Vancouver's Online Source*, November 26, 2009, http://www.straight.com/article-272034/vancouver/disabled-left-out-cold.

46. Jane Stinson, Nancy Pollak, and Marcy Cohen, *The Pains of Privatization: How Contracting out Hurts Health Support Workers, Their Families, and Health Care* (Vancouver: Canadian Centre for Policy Alternatives, 2005).

47. Ibid., p. 5.

48. Fuller and Stevens, *Women's Employment in B.C.*

49. Denyse Côté, Eric Gagnon, Claude Gilbert, Nancy Guberman, Francine Saillant, Nicole Thivierge, and Marielle Tremblay, *The Impact of the Shift to Ambulatory Care and of Social Economic Policies on Quebec Women* (Ottawa: Status of Women Canada, 1998).

50. Stinson et al., *The Pains of Privatization*.

Chapter 60

Provisioning:
Thinking about All of Women's Work

Sheila Neysmith, Marge Reitsma-Street, Stephanie Baker Collins, and Elaine Porter

Sheila Neysmith is associate dean of research, professor of social work, and RBC Chair in Applied Social Work Research at the University of Toronto. Her work focuses on feminist theory and praxis, specifically how knowledge is constructed and used in professional practice and in the development of programs and policies.

Marge Reitsma-Street is professor in the Studies in Policy and Practice Program at the University of Victoria. Educated as a social worker with a doctorate in social policy, her current research interests and activist work centre on poverty, welfare, women's provisioning work, and community organizations.

Stephanie Baker Collins is professor in the Faculty of Social Work at the University of Toronto. A major focus of her research is the impact of public policy on the lives of marginalized groups, including those who live in poverty and/or on social assistance and those who are homeless.

Elaine Porter is professor in the Department of Sociology at Laurentian University. Her areas of interest span from the sociology of childhood and the family to life course studies and gerontology.

Working together, these researchers have recently co-authored a new book on women's work, Beyond Caring to Provisioning Labour: A 21st Century Perspective on Women's Work.

Local and transnational firms search for flexible workforces, cheaper goods, and more consumers and profits. Women in Canada and elsewhere find they are expected to respond to rising demand for flexible part-time, contract, and insecure jobs. At the same time they must also meet the demand for consistent contributions to parenting, household, mutual aid, and community work. "Women's work is never done" expresses the reality for all too many women, especially poor women. Invisibility adds to the tyranny of this endless work. Much of what women do is not considered work or not counted as valuable.

Seeing, counting, and valuing all the work women do is an important way to resist the invisibility yet endlessness of women's work. This article presents several ways of conceptualizing and accounting for the work women do. Each of these approaches highlights aspects of women's labour. Each comes from different disciplinary practices and addresses concerns that have arisen in that tradition, while uncovering other problems. The article ends by proposing the concept of provisioning as a way to think about all the work that women do in more nuanced, complex ways, which attends to the time, purpose, diversity, claims, and possible entitlements. The concept of provisioning, used to date by some feminist economists (Nelson), may open up a more comprehensive understanding of what women actually do to acquire resources for meeting the responsibilities they carry for the well-being of themselves and others, and for imagining different policy and practice possibilities. Our research intends to examine the multiple dimensions, costs, and implications of provisioning in ways that extend the contributions that have been made to understand the paid, unpaid, caring, and volunteer labour performed by women.

Paid Employment

Paid employment is the way that individuals and households are expected to acquire the resources they need to purchase the necessities of life. The majority of poor women have for centuries engaged in farm or market employment to bring money into the household. In the past few decades, however, girls and women of all classes are increasingly expected to do paid work in addition to fulfilling traditional female work expectations. Today, welfare policy, pension policy, daycare policies, and virtually all social and educational policies and benefits are designed to ensure that women participate in paid employment, promise rewards if they do, and make life difficult if they do not.

Yet paid employment is but one avenue used for achieving the goal of acquiring resources for life's necessities. There has been considerable research carried out in the '90s that documents the multiple income strategies used by those who live in low-income households (Barndt; Goode and Maskovsky; Razavi). When considering this data it is important to remember that such strategies are commonly used in high-income households—it is just that the latter have more choice, more options available to them. For low-income households, like their high-income counterparts, patterns of employment changed during the '80s and '90s under the powerful regulation of a new economic discourse of global economy, local restructuring, and the need for a flexible workforce that allows industry to quickly respond to changing international conditions (Beneria, Flora et al.). In many countries, Canada being no exception, this process was marked by massive layoffs across many different types of employment sectors (Cohen). New hires were for jobs that were contract. This was key to ensuring that the workforce was flexible, but it also marked the end to the ideas of a stable job or a career ladder—key assumptions in post-WWII labour market policies (Bakker). People became contingent workers, moving from contract to contract as firms adapted a just-in-time approach to inventories. Although this new labour force has been billed as particularly attractive to women, giving them some time and work location flexibility (Gardiner), as well as work/non-work options, the majority of these jobs are dead-end, as well as short-term. Thus, frequently women are faced with the additional work of constantly looking for new contract jobs and reorganizing their caring responsibilities (de Wolff).

The speed and scope of globalization, it is argued, was possible because of the advent of information technology, which meant that even if workers were not mobile, their labour was. This did mean that those with certain technical skills could command good salaries, but, as in the "old economy," information technology also spun off bad jobs—many of which were taken up by women (Anderson). Another result was that certain types of work could now be done in the home. The advantages of this need to be counterbalanced against the costs that women carry in terms of balancing yet another type of work carried out in the home, along with its attendant isolation and lack of benefits. Not surprisingly, the incomes women make continue to be low, while sources and amount of income are unstable (Luxton; Saraswati). The expectations placed on women to be employed, and the insecurity of the types of jobs available to them, are important for understanding why women negotiate responsibilities and build community in the ways that they do.

*****

Household and Domestic Work

The household and domestic work done by women has been the site of a rich and diverse scholarship, as well as political debates (Matthews; Porter and Kauppi). Some took the form of documenting the tasks done, the time devoted to these tasks, the skills required to do them, their value when translated into monetary terms, and their contribution to GDP. The sheer amount and dollar worth of this work is no longer questioned. However, a reservation frequently noted, even by those promoting a research approach that documents the dollar value of unpaid work, is that the labour market value of such work is low (Waring). Thus, the translations, while high in terms of hours, are consistently low in terms of the monetary market worth of the work. The critique arising from this debate is what is pertinent to this paper. Namely, work that is associated with the household, the private realm, is undervalued.

Another thread in domestic work scholarship stems from its historic connection with labour policies and immigration regulations designed to bring into Canada people, mainly women, who are able to fulfill the local demand for domestic servants (Anderson). Historically, in the Canadian context, these women came disproportionately from the Caribbean and, more recently, from South Asia. Such domestic work policies are one arena within which anti-racist critiques have developed. Through such policies and practices Canada traffics in a global care chain of women migrants whose wages are important sources of foreign exchange to their home economies and whose labour meets the domestic demands of Canadian households. Feminist scholars as well as childcare advocates have connected this to Canada's lack of a national childcare policy (Arat-Koc; McWatt and Neysmith).

Caring Work

Since Janet Finch and Dulcie Groves published their much-quoted volume, *A Labour of Love: Women, Work, and Caring* in 1983, research and theory on caring labour have expanded (Armstrong and Armstrong). The literature now addresses the range of activities, working conditions, relationships, tasks, and difficulties when caring labour is performed by paid and unpaid carers in households and community (Neysmith; Perrons).

One of the initial distinctions about caring work is still fundamental to current debates, namely, they argued that a distinction needs to be made between caring for and caring about. Caring *for* speaks to physical and concrete activities, including feeding, cleaning, and attending to needs of others, while caring *about* captures the relational and emotional work. The importance of this distinction lies in the challenge it raises for assumptions that equate the expectation that women will care for others if they care about them. It is this assumption that undergirds social policies and practices that centre women as responsible for ensuring the care of dependants. At the same time the state, as well as men, eschew such responsibilities, while reaping the benefits of putting their time, energy, and capital resources elsewhere. This critique is not limited to Canada. It has proved to be an important lens when examining a range of social policies whether these are in progressive countries, such as Sweden, or welfare laggards, such as the U.S. (Gottfried and Reese). The provision of services to children and old people has been particularly critiqued by feminists for their gender bias about caring labour.

*****

Two aspects from this rich body of literature we find particularly useful: (1) Caring research has highlighted the importance of social relations in the production of quality care work. Whether paid or unpaid, the work is accomplished through social relationships. If, as Foucault argued, such relations are the capillaries of power, research on caring suggests that they are also the arteries of care. Feminist scholars have taken pains to point out that these arteries are not exclusively embodied in female kin, which, as noted above, seems to be an assumption in current social policies around care of dependants. Political scientist Nancy Fraser's universal caregiver model elucidated what a gender neutral policy might look like. (2) The examination of caring labour has exposed assumptions about definitions of time. Most jobs are defined in terms of hours of work and frequently are paid accordingly. "Time is money" is a colloquialism that highlights the connection between the two in industrialized society. The clash has been documented in development literature (Adam), frequently invoking the idea that adherence to clock time is an indicator of progress while other concepts of time are remnants of old cultural practices. In Canada the time clash is visible in home-care services, where the care work has been broken down into a series of tasks. For instance, a bath is allocated 20 minutes. The in-joke status of this referent in home-care circles works as humour because everyone knows that giving a bath, its very possibility, and the time required to accomplish it is dependent upon the quality of the caregiver–care recipient relationship. Clock time and caring work are not necessarily compatible. They may not always be contradictory, but to bind the two together into a job description conflates the market economy with what some have called the "other economy" of caring (Donath).

Volunteer and Community Work

These terms are considered together because they are frequently conflated. Volunteering is considered an important avenue for making a contribution to one's community. In 1997 Statistics Canada released an important document that estimated the amount of time that Canadians contributed to various types of volunteering. The results supported those found in earlier, less systematic studies, namely, that the patterns between men and women differed; higher-income groups undertook voluntary work that was quite different from that of lower-income Canadians, older people volunteered more than people of working age, among others. The critique of the survey was that it only captured formally structured volunteer activities (Neysmith and Reitsma-Street 2000). People who work irregular hours, have childcare responsibilities, work multiple jobs in order to make ends meet, who are recent immigrants, etc., seldom belong to formal volunteer organizations. They also frequently do not define the volunteer work that they do as volunteer work. The language does not capture how they see this work.

In research done by the authors of this paper, even when participants clearly understood that the work they were doing could be classified as volunteer work, the amount of work was consistently underestimated (Reitsma-Street and Neysmith). The authors emerged from this foray into volunteer work with the concern that the concept rendered invisible much of the work that women in poor communities were doing. As a result, such work would never appear on surveys such as that done by Statistics Canada. Indeed, these women would fall into that category of not doing volunteer work and, by default, not contributing to community well-being. Thus once again a concept, and the tools used to operationalize it, fail to capture an important dimension of women's lives.

[…] The point to be made here is that whatever the debates about how to identify community, who belongs, or where the boundaries are drawn, community does not exist without people making it happen. Women, poor and wealthy, put much time, energy, and resources into their community work. They care for and about others beyond the household based on a collective, historical sense of what is important to preserve and struggle for.

The Third Shift

This term is frequently invoked to capture the multiple work demands that women juggle (Hochschild). It stands in counterpoint to definitions that categorize people as being in the labour force (employed or unemployed) or not. Women might work one shift a day in a paid job and another shift at home, but at any given time while visibly in any of these named options, at the same time they are caring for children, elderly members of the family, maintaining an irregular contract job, and participating in community work. The scope and time commitments, as well as the organization of these different aspects of a woman's life, also change over time. Thus, the word "shift" captures the dynamics as well as the flow and shuffling of work demands. The work and its conditions in one shift affect that of others. Furthermore, the work is not sequenced. Frequently shifts are occurring at the same time, making different demands and requiring different sets of skills.

The term captures the dimension that some of the other concepts do not. For instance, very different and multiple types of activities can be occurring within one unit of time. Research and theorizing about work need to account for this. Secondly, there is work involved in negotiating among the demands made of women within and between the different shifts.

Provisioning

[…] Provisioning is a concept we are introducing into research on women, poverty, and communities to see if it opens new doors to thinking comprehensively yet succinctly about all the work women do. Provisioning refers to the multiple tasks, time required, and relational dimensions of women's work in the context of the purposes for which the work is done. Debates on provisioning aim to explicate how the work women do is valued, and by whom, and what impact these value decisions have on claims for the resources required to perform adequate provisioning for households, community, and society.

The following short case summary captures some of the multi-dimensionality of women's work that demands description, interpretation, and explanation. The woman, named Ms. A, has been employed and aims to get a job again. She is continuously engaged in household and caring work, and wishes to give back volunteer work to the communities that have helped her. Her current limited financial resources constrain her options and make it necessary for her to take far more time and energy to garner resources for herself, her children, and others that she cares for.

Her poverty increases the difficulty of all the work she, and the many other poor women like her, do. As the case highlights, living in poverty also increases the invisibility of the work of women like Ms. A because it robs them of a language for describing this work with words that are valued.

Ms. A is in her 30s and [the] mother of three children. She left her last husband following years of abuse and now claims welfare. She had been an educational assistant before and wants to do similar work after upgrading her education. She is also seeing a counsellor about the abuse and her addictions because "I've got to be able to function properly." For the past year her children had to live with relatives, but she sees them "all the time," and she visits the relatives and workers who are taking care for her children. With the help of an agency working with abused women, she recently became eligible for a place in public housing and now has more space so her eldest child can live with her half time. Ms. A receives a single person's shelter allowance and monthly welfare of just over $500 per month as if she is single and employable and as if "her kids still do not count" even though she directly provides for them part of the time.

It is a "long climb back," she says, to establish a household. She spends careful, anxious hours trying to figure out what she is eligible for and negotiating with her various counsellors and welfare workers—eight in the last year—as well as teachers, parents, and volunteers from various churches and food banks. It takes skill to do "what is needed to be done": to get adequate food and clothing for herself and the children; to find furniture for the bedrooms; to obtain medical care coverage for her children; to accompany her son to a friend's birthday party and watch her daughter play ball on the street as "that doesn't cost anything"; to find free dental care. She is paying for a phone that she can't afford but needs so she can call her children, welfare and various workers, and pursue leads to paid work.

Besides setting up a new household and working to get her children back to live with her full-time, Ms. A is finishing high school. She is also thinking about the future, and trying to put money away for her children so they can have the opportunity to do "whatever they're gifted at." Yet, she worries that she cannot provide. She hears "the clock is ticking" and is worried that she may be one of those in British Columbia who will be cut off welfare because of the two-year limits in the new laws and she won't find a job that pays enough to provide for herself or her children. Thus she wonders if it is right to have children if she cannot afford them, stating "If I don't have enough food for them, and I can't support them that way, then I wonder if I'm doing the right thing. But we've really gotten really close again. And you know they want to come around so it's kind of a drag." Ms. A also hopes to volunteer at a thrift shop for women and for another organization that helped her over the years, as she says, "I'd like to give some back, you know."

In our research we are using the concept of provisioning in furthering the goal of exposing and documenting the complexity and sheer amount of different types of work that women like Ms. A do on a daily basis (Neysmith and Reitsma-Street 2003). We define provisioning as the work of securing resources and providing the necessities of life to those for whom one has relationships of responsibility. This definition speaks to a range of specific activities that are never finished, must be performed regularly, and require energy and attention. Provisioning includes paid employment and unpaid household and caring work. It takes place in the three spheres of market, household, and community, and shifts between them. Provisioning activities cannot be isolated or separated from the context of social relationships in diverse times and spaces because provisioning consists of those daily activities performed to ensure the survival and well-being of oneself and others. Both the activities and the relationships may be voluntary or prescribed. The point is that the activities are necessary: without them, people would not survive.

Preliminary analysis (Neysmith, Reitsma-Street, Aronson, Baker Collins, and Porter) of 67 qualitative interviews conducted with women living on low or insecure incomes in five communities indicate women engage in a complex pattern of provisioning for a variety of relationships using a range of activities, including:

- domestic household services;
- caring labour especially for kin, but also ex-spouses, friends, and others;
- employment and bartering;
- claims making for services from family, agencies, and the state;
- innovative, manipulative, and illegal pursuits, including not telling the truth and creating stories to account for poverty;
- creation of time as a resource through multi-tasking and using time rather than money as a resource.

A key finding is women on low, insecure incomes face many contradictions and nearly impossible situations as they try to provide. They report they could not fulfill their provisioning obligations without the support of informal community and formal state resources. The community and others, however, also become a site of obligations and responsibility for provisioning as well. [...]

Concluding Comments

Dominant understandings of women's work are limited to the two solitudes of family and the market. If it occurs in the former, it is named caring; if in the latter, it is employment. Theories of social networks that are depicted as pathways to connect the two solitudes and build social capital have been limited to formal engagement in organized voluntary activities or leisure activities such as sport. Feminists have critiqued such gender-blind depictions of work and social capital (Rankin). Missed were, for example, the networks that women develop to meet the multiple demands of caring for children. These are face-to-face relationships of relative equality that foster trust as well as forming the basis for collective action.

However, the private/public split continues to mark both research and theory about the many types of work that women do. Within such discourses Ms. A is silenced. Because she at this moment is not the primary caregiver of her children, and not holding a full-time job, she gets categorized as "not working" on both counts. Yet her days are filled with the work of provisioning for herself with part-time employment and welfare assistance, attending to the multiple tasks that need to be done before the children come home, reciprocating in kind some of the resources made available to her by others, and planning for the future of those for whom she has responsibility.

We argue that the concept of provisioning is more robust than other available terms for revealing aspects of the work performed by Ms. A and all women. Articulating the community and policy implications of provisioning has a particular urgency to those who live in the midst of the increasing poverty, instability, regulations, and penalties that accompany decreases in public support in Canada and elsewhere (Goode and Maskovsky; Luxton; Neysmith). Frequently employment and dependant-care policies have actually pitted differentially located groups of women against each other (Fraser). The concept of provisioning is useful in laying out the dynamics of the options and strategies used by women to secure resources for themselves and others. Women who live on limited, insecure incomes need a more solid conceptual basis that makes visible all the work they do, and values it. Without provisioning, women cannot provide for themselves and others, nor accumulate what is required to sustain households and community in the future.

References

Adam, B. "The Gendered Time Politics of Globalization: Of Shadowlands and Elusive Justice." *Feminist Review* 70 (2002): 3–29.

Anderson, B. *Doing the Dirty Work? The Global Politics of Domestic Labour.* London: Zed Books, 2000.

Arat-Koc, S. *Caregivers Break the Silence: A Participatory Action Research on the Abuse and Violence, Including the Impact of Family Separation, Experienced by Women in the Live-in Caregiver Program.* Toronto: Intercede, 2001.

Armstrong, P., and H. Armstrong. "Thinking It through: Women, Work, and Caring in the New Millennium." *Caring for/Caring about: Women, Home Care, and Unpaid Caregiving.* Eds. Karen R. Grant, Carol Amaratunga, Pat Armstrong, Madeline Boscoe, Ann Pederson, and Kay Wilson. Aurora: Garamond Press, 2004. 5–44.

Bakker, I., Ed. *Rethinking Restructuring: Gender and Change in Canada.* Toronto: University of Toronto Press, 1996.

Barndt, D. *Tangled Roots: Women, Work, and Globalization on the Tomato Trail.* Aurora: Garamond, 2002.

Beneria, I., M. Flora et al. "Introduction: Globalization and Gender." *Feminist Economics* 16 (3) (2000): vii–xviii.

Cohen, M., Ed. *Training the Excluded for Work: Access and Equity for Women, Immigrants, First Nations, Youth, and People with Low Income.* Vancouver: University of British Columbia Press, 2003.

de Wolff, A. "The Face of Globalization: Women Working Poor in Canada." *Canadian Woman Studies/les cahiers de la femme* 20 (3) (2000): 54–59.

Donath, S. "The Other Economy: A Suggestion for a Distinctively Feminist Economics." *Feminist Economics* 6 (1) (2000): 115–125.

Finch, J., and D. Groves, Eds. *A Labour of Love: Women, Work, and Caring.* London: Routledge and Kegan Paul, 1983.

Fraser, N. *Justice Interruptus: Critical Reflections on the "Postsocialist" Condition.* New York: Routledge, 1997.

Gardiner, J. *Gender, Care, and Economics.* London: Macmillan, 1997.

Goode, J., and J. Maskovsky, Eds. (2002). *The New Poverty Studies.* New York: New York University Press, 2002.

Gottfried, H., and L. Reese. "Gender, Policy, Politics, and Work: Feminist Comparative and Transnational Research." *Review of Policy Research* 20 (1) (2003): 3–20.

Hochschild, A.R. *The Time Bind: When Work Becomes Home and Home Becomes Work.* New York: Metropolitan Books, 1997.

Luxton, M. *Getting by in Hard Times: Gendered Labour at Home and on the Job.* Toronto: University of Toronto Press, 2001.

Matthews, G. *"Just a Housewife": The Rise and Fall of Domesticity in America.* New York: Oxford University Press, 1987.

McWatt, S., and S. Neysmith. "Enter the Filipino Nanny." *Women's Caring* (Rev. Ed). Eds. C. Baines, P. Evans, and S. Neysmith. Toronto: Oxford University Press, 1998.

Nelson, J. "Labour, Gender, and the Economic/Social Divide." *International Labour Review* 137 (1) (1998): 33–46.

Neysmith, S., Ed. *Restructuring Caring Labour: Discourse, State Practice, and Everyday Life.* Toronto: Oxford University Press, 2000.

Neysmith, S., and M. Reitsma-Street. "Valuing Unpaid Work in the Third Sector: The Case of Community Resource Centres." *Canadian Public Policy* 26 (3) (2000): 331–346.

Neysmith, S., and M. Reitsma-Street. "Provisioning: The Practical and Strategic Work of Women and Their Communities in the New Economy." Paper presented at the 11th Canadian Social Welfare Policy Conference, June 16, 2003, Ottawa, Canada.

Neysmith, S., M. Reitsma-Street, J. Aronson, S. Baker Collins, and E. Porter. "Redefining Boundaries and Crossing Borders: Implications of Women's Provisioning Work in Community." Paper presented at the Global Social Work Congress. Adelaide, Australia, October 3, 2004.

Perrons, D. "Care, Paid Work, and Leisure: Rounding the Triangle." *Feminist Economics* 6 (1) (2000): 105–114.

Porter, E., and C. Kauppi. "Women's Work Is (Almost) Never Done ... (by Anyone Else)." *Changing Lives: Women in Northern Ontario.* Eds. M. Kechnie and M. Reitsma-Street. Toronto: Dundurn Press, 1996. 162–173.

Rankin, K. "Social Capital, Microfinance, and the Politics of Development." *Feminist Economics* 8 (1) (2002): 1–24.

Razavi, S., Ed. *Shifting Burdens: Gender and Agrarian Change under Neoliberalism.* Bloomfield, CT: Kumarian Press, 2002.

Reitsma-Street, M., and S. Neysmith. "Restructuring and Community Work: The Case of Community Resource Centres for Families in Poor Urban Neighbourhoods." *Restructuring Caring Labour: Discourse, State Practice, and Everyday Life.* Ed. S. Neysmith. Toronto: Oxford University Press, 2000. 142–163.

Saraswati, J. "Poverty and Visible Minority Women in Canada." *Canadian Woman Studies/les cahiers de la femme* 20 (3) (2000): 49–53.

Statistics Canada. *Caring Canadians, Involved Canadians: Highlights from the 1997 National Survey of Giving, Volunteering, and Participating.* Cat. no. 71-542XIE. August 1997.

Waring, M. *Counting for Nothing: What Men Value and What Women Are Worth.* Wellington: Allen and Unwin, 1988.

5c Poverty, Homelessness, and Social Welfare in Canada

Chapter 61

Poverty in Canada

Ann Duffy and Nancy Mandell

Ann Duffy is professor in the Department of Sociology at Brock University. Working from a feminist political economy perspective, she straddles sociology and labour studies, researching issues such as part-time employment, unemployment, unpaid work, families, and violence. She has co-authored and co-edited important volumes on gender, work, families, family violence, and Canadian society, and she is co-editor of a recent collection of essays called The Shifting Landscape of Work.

Nancy Mandell is professor in the Department of Sociology at York University, where she also taught women's studies for many years. She publishes on a range of topics, including midlife women's experiences of intimacy and family, violence against women, the feminization of poverty, and academic–community research partnerships. Her contributions to women's studies have been immense, and she is editor of the classic Canadian introductory text, Feminist Issues: Race, Class, and Sexuality, *now in its 5th edition.*

Poverty Today

*****

Poverty is one of the great unresolved and often overlooked social issues confronting Canadians. Although Canada numbers among the wealthiest countries in the world, many of its citizens, especially children, people with disabilities, and single mothers, are unable to escape the debilitating effects of impoverishment. Despite periods of strong economic growth, many sectors of the population have been left behind. Now, [after the economic crisis of 2008–09], their economic marginalization is likely to become even more harrowing.

Evidence of the poverty problem is everywhere. In virtually every small town and city, the persistent appeals from food banks speak to the hunger in our midst. In March 2008, 704,414 Canadians used a food bank at least once, and fully one-third of food banks reported difficulty meeting the demand for their services (Food Banks Canada, 2008; Pasma, 2008). Since 1997, food bank use has increased 6 percent. In Ontario in 2008, the use of food banks was up 13 percent from a year earlier, and 230 Ryerson University students were using the university's food bank each week, up 30 percent from the preceding year (Findlay, 2008; McGrath, 1998; Wallace, 2008). Considered at their inception in the 1980s as a short-term form of assistance, they have become permanent fixtures in our communities. Harsh economic times underscore their significance (Food Banks Canada, 2008).

Food bank clients include students, seniors, families, workers, and welfare recipients. In 2008, one in seven of those using food banks in Canada had paid employment, but their wages were too low to cover their living expenses. Nearly one in four food bank clients is a child. Half of food bank users rely on social assistance, underscoring the inability of welfare payments to meet numerous families' basic requirements (Food Banks Canada, 2008).

Equally grim reminders of poverty can be found during any walk through the inner core of Canada's major cities. There, huddled on hot air gratings or squatting in bus shelters, it is easy to find some of the estimated 200,000 to 300,000 Canadians who are homeless for at least part of the year (CBC News, 2007). In 2007, an estimated 1,020 shelters provided 26,872 beds on a regular basis, up 22 percent from 2006 (Human Resources and Social Development Canada [HRSDC], 2008c; Wellesley Institute, 2008). These statistics only hint at the dimensions of the problem. In Vancouver between April and December 2007, homeless shelters turned away more than 40,000 people (Bula, 2008). [...]

The homeless are only the most visible symptom of Canada's poverty. Behind closed doors are hundreds of thousands more poor Canadians, some relying on social assistance or disability income, some depending on minimum wage employment, and all struggling to keep going in a society that too often ignores their plight. [...]

It is hard to draw a line between the poor and the nonpoor. After all, polls suggest that as many as half of Canadians fear they would fall into poverty if they missed one or two paycheques, and between 2002 and 2006, more than one in five Canadians between the ages of 18 and 60 had experienced low income for at least one year (CBC News, 2007; HRSDC, 2008a: 27). To sort out the murkiness surrounding poverty, government agencies, social researchers, and advocacy groups have proposed a number of definitions of poverty. To date, despite these efforts, Canada has not arrived at an "official" designation (Broadbent, 2005; Fellegi, 1997; Sarlo, 2008; Smith, 2008). Yet, the definition of poverty has broad implications. Employing a stricter or more lenient definition to count the poor may, at the stroke of a pen, dramatically reduce or increase the number of poor. For governments that are seeking to respond to pressures for budget reform, "reduction by redefinition" is a tempting alternative.

Keeping in mind the ongoing definitional debates, the best-known and most widely used poverty measure in Canada is that of Statistics Canada. It establishes "low-income cut-offs" (LICOs) below which people are considered to live in "straitened circumstances." The cut-offs are based on the idea that poor families must spend 20 percent more than the average family of a similar size on the necessities of food, shelter, and clothing. Since the average Canadian family spent about 43 percent of its after-tax income on food, clothing, and shelter in 1992, poor families must spend at least 63 percent of their income on these necessities. Since 1992, the government has used the Consumer Price Index to adjust the income cut-offs for inflation. Today, the low-income cut-off typically refers to income after taxes, since taxes may significantly reduce available funds. Income cut-offs vary by household size and the size of the community in which one resides, so there are 35 low-income cut-offs. For example, a single person living in Toronto in 2006 who earned less than $17,500 was considered "poor" by the Statistics Canada definition, while a two-person family living on less than $13,989 after taxes in a rural area would be deemed poor. The ultimate result is a gauge of *relative* poverty because it establishes a poverty rate by comparing individuals and families relative to the average (Canadian Council on Social Development [CCSD], 2008a; HRSDC, 2008a).

*****

The poor constitute a heterogeneous category. They are not all on welfare. Many poor Canadians are employed, but their wages are so low that they do not exceed the LICO. Nonetheless, with few exceptions, if you are among the 1.7 million Canadians (including almost half a million children) relying on welfare, you are probably surviving on income significantly below the LICO (CCSD, 2008c). Thus, in 2007, the annual welfare income for a lone parent with one child living in Ontario was 75 percent of the LICO. A couple with two children living on welfare in Quebec received 64 percent of the LICO. A single employable person in New Brunswick received just 19 percent of the LICO (National Council of Welfare, 2008: 44–45). Moreover, over the past two decades, the value of welfare benefits has steadily declined in some jurisdictions. [...]

In addition to the poor who rely solely on welfare, many others are poor because they earn so little. Some 44 percent of poor households have at least one working adult, and in Ontario in 2008, 70 percent of children living in poverty had a parent who was working in the paid labour force (Monsebraaten, 2008b: A4; Torjman, 2008). Welfare recipients who work receive monthly "earnings exemptions" allowing them to keep part of their earned income. Exemption rules vary by jurisdiction, the employability of the person, and the size of his or her family. In some provinces, earnings exemptions include work-related expenses, such as child-care costs. Although the provincial and territorial governments' stated intention is to reduce welfare rolls, and despite the already low level of welfare support, some policies on earnings exemptions make it difficult for welfare recipients to take on paid work. [...]

*****

Our portrait of poverty in Canada today is sobering. Economic growth caused the poverty rate to fall between 2000 and 2006, but one in 10 Canadians, including more than a million children under the age of 18, still live below the LICO. Some categories of Canadians contain a disproportionately high percentage of low-income people. Thus, nearly a third of lone-parent families headed by women are low income, as are 29 percent of unattached individuals between the ages of 45 and 64 (Statistics Canada, 2008a: 87; Statistics Canada, 2006a). [...] [Twenty-nine] percent of Aboriginal Canadians living off reserve and 25 percent of recent immigrants are poor, as are nearly a third of people with work-limiting disabilities. Furthermore, the rate of *persistent* poverty for people in the categories just listed is more than four times as high as for other categories of Canadians (HRSDC, 2008a: 23–28). These are 2006 figures. The sharp economic downturn of 2008–09 undoubtedly made the situation worse.

The Feminization of Poverty

Under identifiable circumstances, Canadian women are at high risk of slipping into poverty. In fact, many scholars talk about the "feminization of poverty" insofar as women are more likely to be poor than men in many countries (Goldberg, 1990; Nelson 2006; Pearce, 1978). Nor is this a new problem. Deserted, widowed, and orphaned women have long populated the ranks of the poor in disproportionate number (Katz, 1975: 60; Simmons, 1986).

While the reasons behind women's impoverishment are complex, they have much to do with traditional gender ideology, inequities in the labour force, family law issues, and the way we typically respond to marriage breakdown. Historically, people have expected women to devote their lives to unpaid duties as wives and mothers. Although many women worked for pay, rules against the employment of married women, and the peripheralization, stigmatization, and low pay scales for "women's jobs" reinforced the idea that women's proper place was really in the home (Duffy and Pupo, 1992: 13–40; Statistics Canada 2006a).

This idea came under attack in the twentieth century. The women's movement, increased opportunities for higher education, and the reduction in family size made possible by the legalization of contraception helped to undermine the traditional sexual division of labour. In addition, many Canadian families found it difficult to live off the income of a single breadwinner. The failure of wages to keep pace with inflation, increased taxation, high unemployment, skyrocketing housing costs, and the loss of high-paying manufacturing jobs made the male-breadwinner family increasingly anachronistic. Today, about two-thirds of women with children under the age of three are in the paid labour force (Statistics Canada, 2006a: 105).

However, significant gender differences in work and family life persist. Many mothers continue to take time away from paid employment when their children are young and/or balance family and paid work with part-time or self-employed work (Cranford et al., 2006). Unless they are well-to-do, women who marry, have children, and assume primary responsibility for domestic work and childcare run the risk [of] impoverishment in the event of divorce or early widowhood—even if they maintain a consistent presence in the part-time labour force (as more than a fifth of adult Canadian women do) (Statistics Canada, 2006a: 109; 2006b). Employment in traditional low-paid women's occupations and taking time off to care for young children can result in economic disaster when a marriage ends in divorce or when women face years of widowhood. Being a recent immigrant, disabled, or a member of a visible minority increases the chance of becoming poor.

Specifically, according to [one measure], 35 percent of Canadian single-parent mothers were poor in 2006 compared with 12 percent of single-parent fathers (HRSDC, 2008a: 31). In the first year after divorce, women's household income drops by an average of between 20 to 40 percent, depending on family size. Three years post-divorce, women's income remains on average significantly below their income during the marriage and well below their ex-husband's current income. Women typically assume primary custody of the children. Further, despite numerous efforts, the enforcement of child support payments from noncustodial parents remains plagued with difficulties. Although many women have made considerable advances in the labour market, divorce patterns still contribute to the feminization of poverty (Ambert, 2005). Despite the needs of single mothers, welfare policy has done little to improve their situation. For example, in Ontario, able-bodied single welfare mothers of school-age children are required to sign up for some form of state-orchestrated employment. In Alberta, new regulations restrict both eligibility for support and amount of welfare payments while mandating that welfare recipients participate in job training programs. Unfortunately, these efforts have tended to address the problems of single mothers inadequately—particularly the need for reliable, low-cost child-care and the inadequacy of women's jobs in low-wage, low-skill work (Breitkreuz, 2005). Compounding their plight, single mothers on welfare must also confront the persistent stereotypes that cast them as less worthy of social support than, say, low-income, two-parent families. People often stigmatize single mothers who receive social assistance as promiscuous and irresponsible (Goar, 2008).

Growing old provides no guarantee of relief, even though policy initiatives in the 1980s and 1990s removed much of the poverty burden for the elderly. Unattached women over the age of

64—typically widowed, divorced, or separated—face high poverty rates. A recent study found that five years after her husband dies, a woman's income declines on average by more than 15 percent. Meanwhile, a man who loses his spouse experiences a nearly 6 percent *increase* in income. Some 3.6 percent more women than men experience poverty five years after the death of their spouse (Statistics Canada, 2006b). Elderly women are particularly at risk of poverty because they are less likely to receive income from occupational pension plans, the Canada/Quebec Pension Plan, and investments. Work interruptions to take care of family responsibilities, work in low-paying jobs with meagre benefits, and part-time and contractual work thus contribute to low income even in one's retirement years (Gaszo, 2005: 59; McDonald, 1997; Statistics Canada, 2006a). [...]

Immigrant, homeless, minority, and Aboriginal women and those with disabilities are at above-average risk of poverty. For example, Aboriginal women between the ages of 25 and 54 earn a median income on average $8,000 below that of non-Aboriginal women, even though they tend to have larger families and are more likely to be single parents (National Council of Welfare, 2007: 23). Visible-minority and immigrant women are also disadvantaged because they frequently find that racial and ethnic discrimination, along with language difficulties and inadequate government policy, translate into long hours of low-wage work, high rates of unemployment, and low income (Statistics Canada, 2006a: 225, 228, 249, 252, 254). Age intensifies the inequality. Elderly women who are recent immigrants earn incomes below those of their Canadian-born counterparts and rely more on government transfer payments (Statistics Canada, 2006a: 211–38). Aboriginal and visible minority women are also overrepresented among homeless women. A recent Toronto survey found that more than one-quarter of homeless women belong to a visible minority group and one in five are Aboriginal (Bacquie, 2008; Street Health Report, 2007).

Finally, disability exacts an added toll on many women's lives. Although most adults with disabilities live on low income, women with disabilities are generally worse off than men with disabilities are. For example, women with mild and moderate disabilities have an employment rate approximately 10 percent lower than that of their male counterparts (Statistics Canada, 2006a: 294). Women with disabilities over the age of 14 earn on average $17,200 annually, compared with $26,900 for men with disabilities. Thus, 6 percent more women with disabilities than men with disabilities earn incomes below the LICO, and the gender gap grows with age (Statistics Canada, 2006a: 296–97).

*****

The Changing Face of Poverty

The percentage of Canadians living below the LICO fell between 1980 and 2006 (Statistics Canada, 2008b). However, income among the richest one-fifth of Canadians has grown even faster, so the gap between the rich and poor in Canada has grown larger (HRSDC, 2008a: i–ii; HRSDC, 2008b; Statistics Canada, 2007).

The fortunes of the poor fluctuate with the overall health of the economy, but social policy has also made for significant change. Canada's seniors remain the outstanding success story. Improvements in their economic situation demonstrate that poverty is reversible. In the 1960s, the plight of impoverished seniors made headlines when newspapers reported that some seniors were reduced to eating cat food to survive. The creation of the federal Guaranteed Income Supplement in 1967 for low-income seniors, the Canada/Quebec Pension Plan in 1966, and provincial supplements caused a dramatic shift. In 1980, more than one in three seniors were living below the LICO but by 2006, this figure stood at just 5.4 percent (CCSD, 2003; National Council of Welfare, 1999; Statistics Canada, 2008a: 87).

Policy initiatives have also helped child poverty rates. The Canada Child Tax Benefit (1998) helps low-income families with children. In 2003, the plan added a Child Disability Benefit. While these programs have not lifted many families out of poverty, they have reduced the depth of poverty for many (Torjman, 2008: 14). Some provinces have tackled the problem too. In 2004, Quebec became the first jurisdiction in Canada to embark on an official anti-poverty strategy and it has succeeded in dramatically reducing its child poverty rates (Torjman, 2008: 1). [...]

Canadian Poverty in International Context

Canadians often take pride in the fact that the level of social inequality in Canada is lower than that in the United States (CCSD, 2008b). In the United States, the top 1 percent of Americans enjoys 38 percent of the nation's wealth, and the bottom 40 percent just 1 percent. The bottom 20 percent of U.S. income earners not only have more debt than assets, their incomes have barely grown in real terms since the mid-1970s (Canada and the World Backgrounder, 2004). Poverty rates reflect these patterns. In 2002, when Canada's poverty rate was about 10 percent, in the United States it reached 17 percent. Furthermore, 31 percent of the U.S. poor were victims of persistent poverty (five years or more) in contrast to 24 percent of the Canadian poor (Statistics Canada, 2005a). Similarly, the U.S. child poverty rate was 7 percent higher than the Canadian rate.

However, when we compare Canada to countries other than the United States, we find less reason for pride. Canada ranks 18th of 30 industrialized countries in terms of income inequality—certainly well ahead of the United States in 27th place, but behind France, Hungary, Germany, Australia, and South Korea (Monsebraaten, 2008a). In Sweden, only about 6 percent of the population and fewer than 3 percent of children are considered poor (Canada and the World Backgrounder, 2005). In recent years, Finland and Belgium have substantially reduced poverty among lone-parent families, and Germany and the United Kingdom have substantially reduced the percentage of persistently poor people (Picot and Myles, 2005). In almost all of these success stories, the governments have allocated significant resources to addressing poverty.

Struggling with Poverty: The Personal Experience

Being poor has always meant more than getting by at some arbitrary level of income, and understanding poverty demands more than a statistical overview (Burman, 1988). Poverty often affects people's lives, their sense of self, and their most important relationships with others. Although the toll of poverty is most apparent in the lives of children, few adults survive impoverishment unscathed. For children and their families, poverty still generally translates into inadequate housing in unsafe areas (Statistics Canada, 2006c). In Calgary, Edmonton, Vancouver, and Toronto, as well as on remote reserves, poor children are likely to live with substandard heating, too little hot water, improper ventilation, generally unsafe conditions (exposed wiring and electrical outlets, and so on), and too little space in which to play and study. Even inadequate housing in large metropolitan areas may gobble up social assistance benefits, leaving little for other necessities, let alone emergencies. Housing problems are frequently compounded by neighbourhoods plagued with high rates of crime and vandalism, inadequate play facilities, high levels of pollution, and hazardous traffic (Baxter, 1988, 1993; Doolittle, 2008; Goar, 2008; McMurtry and Curling, 2008; Raphael, 2007; Welsh, 2008).

Poor families often lack the income to maintain a nutritious diet. High housing costs and the spectre of homelessness mean that food budgets are stretched to the limit. The result may be ill health and frequent hospitalization, even among infants. While Canada's food banks and soup kitchens provide a stopgap solution for many families, many poor children get by on too little food or food with high fat and sugar content (Statistics Canada, 2008c). The homeless are frequently plagued by health problems, including malnourishment, chronic respiratory and ear infections, gastrointestinal disorders, sexually transmitted disease, and chronic infections. The psychological health of the poor also reflects the painful social and emotional environment in which they live. The pressure of poverty contributes to family breakdown and dislocation. Life often becomes unpredictable. Being poor means not knowing whether you will be able to continue living in your home, whether you will retain custody of your children, whether your children will have to change schools and make new friends. In these and numerous other ways, the foundations of one's life may be shattered. Living with profound uncertainty inevitably takes a toll on self-confidence and hopefulness (Hurtig, 1999; Neal, 2004).

Evidence shows that poor families are more subject than other families to violence, including woman abuse and child abuse and neglect (Goar, 2008; Gelles and Cornell, 1990: 14–15; Statistics Canada, 2005b). Growing up poor often means coping with parents who are struggling with fear, anger, frustration, isolation, and despair. Many poor adults and children cope with courage, resourcefulness, and a sense of humour, and many poor children grow up with positive adult role models and a strong sense of family loyalty. However, the adults in most poor children's lives are also often not only deeply troubled by their economic conditions but also vulnerable to abuse and exploitation. Poverty typically means more than doing without. It means feeling cut off from the mainstream. With few exceptions, the lives and experiences of the poor are not reflected sympathetically on television or in the movies. Advertisements in magazines and on subway trains underscore the insufficiencies of their lifestyle. Mothers must scramble to make sure their children have the money to "fit in." As one mother said, "Another thing that comes out [of the monthly budget] that's very important is the children's milk money for school, and their pizza and hot dog money every week, because they won't be ostracized. I won't have other children saying they're too poor to get those." However, meeting these needs means that "sometimes I can afford [heating] oil, sometimes I can't" (Power, 2005: 652).

Many poor people report that dealing with the social assistance apparatus compounds feelings of stigmatization and vulnerability. Even when welfare workers are helpful and supportive, the relationship between worker and client is structured to erode the autonomy, power, and privacy of the poor. The negativity of some welfare workers makes a bad situation worse. One single mother comments, "Every time I come back from there I cry. They make you feel so low, they make you feel like you're worthless, and they think they're God because of what they give you. And they give you nothing. They don't" (Power, 2005: 649). [...] Home visits by welfare workers, personal questions from workers, and the constant fear of being "reported to welfare" for not following the rules tend to undermine clients' sense of personal power and self-confidence.

The negative reaction of the public to welfare recipients complicates problems with the welfare apparatus. Commonly, property owners will not rent to people on welfare, and women on welfare may find themselves labelled as desperate and sexually available. Degradation becomes part of everyday experience: "And then the taxi driver is looking at you, 'Oh, not another charity case'" (McIntyre et al., 2003: 324). Most commonly, the social assistance recipient has to confront the still widespread belief that people on welfare cheat (Blackwell, 2003: 107–08).

Informed by the historical notion that many of the poor are not deserving or should be punished for their plight, popular attitudes toward the provision of adequate social assistance remain ambivalent and uninformed.

Despite the enormous pressure to "get back on your feet," endless roadblocks exist on the path to getting off welfare. For many single mothers, adequate child-care support is a major obstacle to employment: "The daycare she went to when she was a baby, every day they called. I had just started this job and every day, I swear, every day they were calling me that something was wrong with her. I'd come in, walk in at 9:00, by 10:00 she's got a rash, or pink eye or something and then I had to leave" (Mason, 2003: 50). A Toronto single mother of three recounts that when her youngest child started Grade 1, she took a part-time job to improve their economic situation. However, her extra income immediately caused her subsidized rent to double. After taxes and employment-related expenses, she found she had not improved her family's economic situation at all (Monsebraaten, 2008b: A4).

What Can We Do about Poverty?

Several points are clear from the above discussion. Poverty is a significant social issue across Canada and in all likelihood is about to worsen. The victims of poverty include the most vulnerable Canadians. Poverty is rooted in the economic and political systems. While some individuals, such as teenage parents and high school dropouts, may have made poor decisions, their impoverishment can be traced to the low minimum wage, the decline in manufacturing employment, the growth in nonstandard employment in the service sector, and the weak response from federal, provincial and territorial, and municipal governments to the inequities in our midst. Finally, we have seen that innovative and generous social policies can reduce the number of poor people and the negative outcomes of poverty.

References

Ambert, A. (2005). "Divorce: Facts, Causes, and Consequences." Vanier Institute of the Family. On the World Wide Web at http://www.vifamily.ca/library/cft/divorce_05.html.

Bacquie, S. (2008). "Homeless Women in Canada." section 15.ca. On the World Wide Web at http://section15.ca/features/news/2008/08/22/homelessness/.

Baxter, Sheila. (1988). *No Way to Live: Poor Women Speak Out.* Vancouver: New Star Books.

Baxter, Sheila. (1993). *A Child Is Not a Toy: Voices of Children in Poverty.* Vancouver: New Star Books.

Blackwell, J. (2003). "The Welfare State Rewards Laziness." In J. Blackwell, M. Smith, and J. Sorenson, eds., *The Culture of Prejudice* (pp. 107–12). Toronto: Broadview Press.

Breitkreuz, Rhonda. (2005). "Engendering Citizenship? A Critical Feminist Analysis of Canadian Welfare-to-Work Policies and the Employment Experiences of Lone Mothers." *Journal of Sociology and Social Welfare,* 32 (2): 147–65.

Broadbent, Ed. (2005). "Addressing Child Poverty." *Perception,* 27 (3&4): 9.

Bula, F. (2008). "Shelters Turned away Homeless 40,000 Times in Nine Months." *Vancouver Sun* May 22. On the World Wide Web at http://www.canada.com/vancouversun/news/story.html?id+0f7602e2-1444-4cb8-9fc5-34.

Burman, Patrick. (1988). *Killing Time, Losing Ground: Experiences of Unemployment.* Toronto: Wall & Thompson.

Canada and the World Backgrounder. (2004). "Survival of the Richest" 70 (1): 17–23.

Canada and the World Backgrounder. (2005). "Poor Families Equal Poor Children" 40 (5): 23–27.

Canadian Council on Social Development. (2003). "Census Shows Growing Polarization of Income in Canada." On the World Wide Web at http://www.ccsd.ca/pr/2003/censusincome.htm.

Canadian Council on Social Development. (2008a). "CCSD's Stats & Facts: Labour Market—Earnings." On the World Wide Web at http://www.ccsd.ca.

Canadian Council on Social Development. (2008b). "Growing up in North America: The Economic Well-being of Children in Canada, the United States, and Mexico." On the World Wide Web at http://www.ccsd.ca.

Canadian Council on Social Development. (2008c). "Stats & Facts: Economic Security—Poverty." On the World Wide Web at http://www.ccsd.ca.

CBC News. (2007). "Homelessness 'Chronic' in Canada: Study." On the World Wide Web at http://www.cbc.ca/canada/story/2007/06/26/shelter.html.

Cranford, C.J., L. Vosko, and N. Zukewich. 2006. "The Gender of Precarious Employment in Canada." In V. Shalla, ed., *Working in a Global Era: Canadian Perspectives* (pp. 99–119). Toronto: Canadian Scholars' Press.

Doolittle, R. (2008). "Agencies Brace for Crime Wave." *Toronto Star* 27 December: A17.

Duffy, Ann, and Norene Pupo. (1992). *Part-Time Paradox: Connecting Gender, Work, and Family*. Toronto: McClelland & Stewart.

Fellegi, I.P. (1997). *On Poverty and Low Income*. Ottawa: Statistics Canada. On the World Wide Web at http://www.statcan.gc.ca/pub/13f0027x/13f0027x19999001-eng.htm.

Findlay, S. (2008). "Food Bank Use Soars 13%." *Sun Media* 3 December. On the World Wide Web at http://cnews.canoe.ca/CNEWS/Canada/2008/12/03/pf-7615691.html.

Food Banks Canada. (2008). *Hunger Count 2008: Food Bank Use in Canada*. Toronto: Food Banks Canada.

Gazso, Amber. (2005). "The Poverty of Unattached Senior Women and the Canadian Retirement Income System: A Matter of Blame or Contradiction?" *Journal of Sociology and Social Welfare*, 32 (2): 41–62.

Gelles, Richard J., and Claire P. Cornell. (1990). *Intimate Violence in Families*, 2nd ed. Newbury Park, CA: Sage.

Goar, C. (2008). "Abuse Follows in Poverty's Wake." *Toronto Star* 14 November: AA6.

Goldberg, Gertrude Schaffner. (1990). "Canada: Bordering on the Feminization of Poverty." In Gertrude Schaffner Goldberg and Eleanor Kremen, eds., *The Feminization of Poverty: Only in America?* (pp. 59–90). New York: Praeger.

Human Resources and Social Development Canada. (2008a). "Low Income in Canada: 2000–2006 Using the Market Basket Measure—Final Report." On the World Wide Web at http://www.hrsdc.gc.ca/en/publications_resources/research/index.shtml.

Human Resources and Social Development Canada. (2008b). "Well-being in Canada: Financial Security—Income Distribution." On the World Wide Web at http://www4.hrsdc.gc.ca/.

Human Resources and Social Development Canada. (2008c). "Well-being in Canada: Housing—Homeless Shelters and Beds." On the World Wide Web at http://www4.hrsdc.gc.ca/.

Hurtig, Mel. (1999). *Pay the Rent or Feed the Kids: The Tragedy and Disgrace of Poverty in Canada*. Toronto: McClelland & Stewart.

Katz, Michael B. (1975). *The People of Hamilton, Canada West: Family and Class in a Mid-Nineteenth-Century City*. Cambridge, MA: Harvard University Press.

Mason, Robin. (2003). "Listening to Lone Mothers: Paid Work, Family Life, and Childcare in Canada." *Journal of Children and Poverty*, 9 (1): 41–54.

McDonald, Lynn. 1997. "The Invisible Poor: Canada's Retired Widows." *Canadian Journal of Aging*, 16 (3): 553–83.

McGrath, Paul. (1998). "Food Banks Part of Life on Campus." *Toronto Star* 23 February: F1, F2.

McIntyre, Lynn, Suzanne Officer, and Lynne M. Robinson. (2003). "Feeling Poor: The Felt Experience of Low-Income Lone Mothers." *Affilia*, 18 (3): 316–31.

McMurtry, R., and A. Curling. (2008). "Roots of Violence Grow in Toxic Soil of Social Exclusion." *Toronto Star* 15 November: AA6.

Monsebraaten, L. (2008a). "Income Gap Growing Wider." *Toronto Star* 21 October: A4.

Monsebraaten, L. (2008b). "Having a Job, but Losing Ground." *Toronto Star* 2 April: A4.

National Council of Welfare. (1999). *Poverty Profile* 1997. Ottawa: Minister of Public Works and Government Services Canada.

National Council of Welfare. (2007). *First Nations, Métis and Inuit Children and Youth: Time to Act*. Ottawa: Ministry of Supply and Services.

National Council of Welfare. (2008). *Welfare Incomes, 2006 and 2007*. Ottawa: NCW.

Neal, Rusty. (2004). *Voices: Women, Poverty, and Homelessness in Canada*. Ottawa: The National Anti-Poverty Organization's Study on Homelessness.

Nelson, Adie. (2006). *Gender in Canada*, 3rd ed. Toronto: Pearson Prentice Hall.

Pasma, C. (2008). *Toward a Guaranteed Liveable Income: A CPJ backgrounder on GLI*. Ottawa: Citizens for Public Justice.

Pearce, Diana. (1978). "The Feminization of Poverty: Women, Work, and Welfare." *Urban and Social Change Review*, 11 (February): 28–36.

Picot, Garnett, and John Myles. (2005). *Income Inequality and Low Income in Canada: An International Perspective*. Ottawa: Minister of Industry. Statistics Canada, Catalogue no. 11F0019MIE.

Power, Elaine M. (2005). "The Unfreedom of Being Other: Canadian Lone Mothers' Experiences of Poverty and 'Life on the Cheque.'" *Sociology*, 39 (4): 643–60.

Raphael, D. (2007). *Poverty and Policy in Canada*. Toronto: Canadian Scholars' Press.

Sarlo, C. (2008). "Measuring Poverty in Canada." *Fraser Forum*. Vancouver: Fraser Institute.

Simmons, Christina. (1986). "'Helping the Poorer Sisters': The Women of the Jost Mission, Halifax, 1905–1945." In Veronica Strong-Boag and Anita Clair Fellman, eds., *Rethinking Canada: The Promise of Women's History*. Toronto: Copp Clark Pitman.

Smith, J. (2008). "Definition of Poverty Stalls Federal Committee." *Toronto Star* 16 April. On the World Wide Web at http://www.thestar.com/printArticle/414057.

Statistics Canada. (2005a). "Study: Trends in Income Inequality in Canada from an International Perspective." *The Daily* 10 February. On the World Wide Web at http://www.statcan.gc.ca/daily/.

Statistics Canada. (2005b). "National Longitudinal Survey of Children and Youth: Home environment, income and child behaviour." *The Daily* February 21. On the World Wide Web at http://www.statcan.ca.gc.ca/daily/.

Statistics Canada. (2006a). *Women in Canada: A Gender-Based Statistical Report*, 5th ed. Ottawa: Ministry of Supply and Services.

Statistics Canada. (2006b). "Study: The Death of a Spouse and the Impact on income." *The Daily* 10 July. On the World Wide Web at http://www.statcan.gc.ca/daily/.

Statistics Canada. (2006c). "Study: Neighbourhood Characteristics and the Distribution of Crime in Regina." *The Daily* 2 November. On the World Wide Web at http://www.statcan.gc.ca/daily/.

Statistics Canada. (2007). "Study: Income Inequality and Redistribution." *The Daily* 11 May. On the World Wide Web at http://www.statcan.gc.ca/daily/.

Statistics Canada. (2008a). *Income in Canada 2006*. Ottawa: Minister of Industry. Catalogue no. 75-202-X.

Statistics Canada. (2008b). "Income of Canadians." *The Daily* 5 May. On the World Wide Web at http://www.statcan.gc.ca/daily/.

Statistics Canada. (2008c). "Study: Impact of Neighbourhood Income on Child Obesity." *The Daily* 18 February. On the World Wide Web at http://www.statcan.gc.ca/daily/.

Street Health Report. (2007). *Research Bulletin #2: Women & Homelessness*. Toronto: Ontario Women's Health Network.

Torjman, S. (2008). *Poverty Policy*. Ottawa: Caledon Institute of Social Policy.

Wallace, K. (2008). "Students Flood Food Bank." *Toronto Star* 19 November: A13.

Wellesley Institute. (2008). "Housing Insecurity at Record Levels." On the World Wide Web at http://wellesleyinstitute.com/node/1601/.

Welsh, M. (2008). "Poorest Areas Also Most Polluted, Report Shows." *Toronto Star* 27 November: A6.

Chapter 62

The Leaner, Meaner Welfare Machine: The Ontario Conservative Government's Ideological and Material Attack on Single Mothers

Margaret Hillyard Little

Margaret Hillyard Little is an anti-poverty activist and professor in the departments of Gender Studies and Political Studies at Queen's University. Her research focuses on the experiences of single mothers and abused women on welfare in Canada, neo-liberal welfare reform, and retraining initiatives for women on welfare. Recently she has also been exploring discourses of motherhood in "second wave" feminism in Canada. She has written two books, including No Car, No Radio, No Liquor Permit: The Moral Regulation of Single Mothers in Ontario, 1920–1997, *which won the Floyd S. Chalmers Book Award.*

Marcey is recently divorced and trying to raise her 10-year-old son on welfare. She is anxious because the government has recently cut her welfare cheque by 22 percent. As a result, more than one-fifth of her income has disappeared overnight. She pleads with her landlord to lower the rent because she knows that she cannot feed her child *and* pay her rent. He agrees to lower the rent—provided she has sex with him occasionally. Because she refuses, she is forced to look for another place to rent, worrying about how she can pay first and last months' rent and move her belongings—all on a reduced welfare cheque (Interview 6, Kenora, February 25, 1999).

Katrina recently left her violent boyfriend when she was seven months pregnant. She applied for welfare and was told that she was eligible provided she went to three job sites per day looking for work. She traipsed up and down the streets of her small town with swollen ankles, inquiring about employment when she was obviously very pregnant and traumatized by the recent violence in her life. She suspects that her baby was born a month early because of this stress (Interview 4, Greater Toronto Area, May 1998). Belinda recently discovered that her welfare cheque was cancelled because they are investigating her for welfare fraud. Apparently someone has called the welfare fraud telephone line and reported that she is living with a spouse. She has no partner, but she is becoming friendly with a co-worker at her part-time job at the donut shop. They just talk while they're working—she hasn't even gone on a date. She suspects her ex-boyfriend of calling the welfare fraud line, but she does not know because all fraud complaints are anonymous (Interview 3, North Bay, January 28, 1999).

These are all true accounts of the lives of single mothers that reflect the impact of three major changes to welfare under the Conservative government in Ontario. While single mothers have always been harassed, forced to prove themselves deserving in order to receive welfare, this chapter will demonstrate how this level of scrutiny or moral regulation has greatly intensified under the Ontario Conservative government. This research is based on one-on-one interviews I have conducted with more than 30 workfare recipients across the province, interviews with anti-poverty activists, and 200 focus group interviews conducted by members of Ontario Workfare Watch, a non-profit organization established to monitor welfare changes across Ontario. I have conducted this type of research for more than a decade so I was surprised to find myself so overwhelmed by this recent trek across the province. Although I knew about the dismantling of our social programs, these interviews forced me to come face to face with the devastating results of these policy changes. You, too, will be shocked and alarmed when you read about the everyday struggles of single mothers who are simply trying to feed and care for their children as best they can.

The Historical and National Context

The poor have always been condemned in our society. Since the creation of the Elizabethan Poor Laws in the 1700s, our governments have divided between the worthy and unworthy poor. The Poor Laws required the poor to complete a work test in order to be eligible for public charity. If you were strong enough to cut a cord of wood, you were generally considered ineligible for government help and expected to find your own work despite the massive unemployment and social upheaval that was occurring during the industrial revolution. If you were deemed worthy, you were given a few scanty provisions such as food and coal or you were eligible to live in a poorhouse, a disease-infested public home for the old, the sick, and single mothers.

With the creation of the modern welfare state in the early 20th century we incorporated these same basic premises about poverty into our so-called modern welfare programs. Initially governments helped only poor widows and deserted mothers who proved to be both financially and morally deserving. These women would receive a penurious welfare cheque on which it was simply not enough to live. It was expected that these women would top up their welfare cheques with some part-time work that would not interfere with the time needed to care for their children, Eventually, governments expanded their welfare programs to include other types of single parents, such as divorced, unwed, and even single fathers. But every single parent had to prove continuously that they were both financially and morally deserving in order to receive government aid. Welfare administrators would scrutinize the cleanliness of the homes, the sleeping arrangements, the number and types of visitors to the homes, the dress and manner of the parent, the school records of the children, and many other aspects of daily life. All of this intense scrutiny was conducted in order to determine an applicant's worthiness. And once the welfare cheque was granted, home visits by welfare administrators continued in order to ensure that the recipient maintained a frugal and moral life.

But this is all in the past, you say. What does this have to do with today's poor single mothers? Although the moral regulation of poor single mothers has changed over time, it has persisted in new forms throughout the history of welfare. Today, single mothers still have to prove themselves both financially and morally deserving in order to receive welfare. And during the era of the Ontario Conservative government, there are more and more rules to determine just who is and who is not a worthy single mother.

The Ontario Conservative government is not the only guilty party when it comes to the moral regulation of poor single mothers. The federal government has made this possible when it dismantled the Canada Assistance Plan (CAP) and replaced it with the Canada Health and Social

Transfer [CHST] in 1996. The CAP, established in 1966, provided unlimited cost-shared federal funding for welfare and promised to eradicate many of the punitive features of earlier welfare policies. In order to receive this federal grant, welfare programs had to meet three conditions: (1) benefits based solely on financial need; (2) all provincial residence requirements eradicated; and (3) an appeal board established in each province to protect recipients' rights.

While these CAP conditions had a number of limitations, they still helped to guarantee the poor a certain level of financial security (Little, 1999 Spring). The first condition is important to highlight for the purposes of this chapter. This stipulation prohibited workfare and other employment-tied welfare programs. Regardless of the reason for a citizen's impoverishment, regardless of the citizen's employment history, she or he was eligible for welfare simply because of poverty. Also, regardless of the moral character of an applicant, she or he was eligible for welfare provided she or he could prove economic need.

Despite the limitations of the CAP, it provided much more support to the poor than the CHST. With the CHST there is no federal funding specifically designated for welfare programs. Instead, each province receives a lump sum to spend on education, health, and welfare; each province can choose just how much to spend in each of these three areas. Given the popularity of health and education, provincial governments have begun to concentrate spending in these areas at the expense of welfare programs.

Under the CHST the federal government has erased almost all national standards for welfare. Poor Canadians no longer have a right to welfare based on economic need. Now the provinces can establish their own eligibility requirements. This change permits not only workfare but also any other eligibility criteria that the provincial and municipal governments wish to implement. It also allows provincial and municipal governments to refuse to grant a person welfare for any reason deemed appropriate. This has opened the door for a number of employment-tied welfare programs. We have now returned to the work test of the Elizabethan Poor Laws. It is not enough to be poor. You now must also prove that you are deserving. The implication is that you are responsible for the fact that you do not have a job during a time of high unemployment.

The Importance of Moral Regulation

To best understand how changes to Ontario welfare policy under the Ontario Conservative government have affected single mothers I use the moral regulation approach [...] (Corrigan & Sayer, 1985). [...]

There are five aspects of moral regulation, which makes it a useful concept for my own work on welfare. First, it highlights certain moral processes in society. The government and various social organizations are involved in processes to create and perpetuate certain power inequities, be they class, race, gender, sexual inequities, or others. But while these organizations are creating and maintaining these inequities, they are also creating and maintaining a certain moral order— a certain set of rules and regulations that establish what is moral and immoral. Second, this process of moral regulation is not static, but rather continuous. Once the rules and regulations are established, they need to be maintained. When these rules and regulations are challenged, the government and social organizations will reestablish or modify them. Third, the public must accept this process of moral regulation. If the public does not agree with these moral codes, they can challenge these rules—they can vote for a different political party, run for political office, participate in a political protest, or even attempt to overthrow the government. Consequently the government needs legitimacy of the public to maintain its moral rules and regulations. Fourth, this process or moral regulation will meet resistance. These moral codes are usually not accepted by all. The government does not have absolute power to impose these moral codes. I want to highlight this aspect of moral regulation because it is sometimes confused with social control. Social control implies that those who make and administer the regulations are all-powerful and do not meet with resistance. Instead, moral regulation scholars insist that this set of moral rules and regulations can and will be challenged. Fifth, the relationship between the regulator and the regulated is beneficial to both. Even in the most unequal relationships created by moral codes, both parties have something to gain from this relationship. The regulated, or the weaker party, often needs the regulator, or the stronger party, for money, food, and shelter. But the regulator also needs the regulated to establish his or her status, to ensure his or her moral superiority. In the case of welfare, the poor need the welfare worker in order to receive their welfare cheques and survive. But at the same time, the welfare worker needs the poor in order to continue to have a job and status in society. Otherwise, the welfare worker will be without work and she or he will end up applying for welfare! (See Piven & Cloward, 1971.)

*****

Application of Moral Regulation to Ontario Welfare Policy

The current welfare policy of Ontario is an excellent example of moral regulation at work. There are three policy changes under the Conservative government that have helped to perpetuate the notion that poor single mothers are morally undeserving. Both the welfare rate cuts and the implementation of workfare ensure that welfare is extremely stingy and punitive to its recipients. These two measures help to ensure that the current welfare policy meets the needs of capitalists. Today capitalists in this increasingly globalized market economy are competing with companies all over the world. Local capitalists require workers who will work for lower wages and less benefits. When the local welfare policy is made more stingy and punitive, making it almost impossible to survive on welfare, it encourages the poor to compete with workers for any jobs available. This in turn allows local capitalists to reduce wages and benefits to workers because they know there is a desperate group of poor citizens who are willing to work for less. Whereas the first two policy changes meet the current needs of intensified capitalism, the third policy change reinforces certain moral codes of society. This third policy change, the heightened policing of welfare fraud, blatantly encourages the public to believe that all the poor are immoral cheaters who must be constantly investigated.

These welfare changes have had a dramatic impact on single mothers' lives. Not only is it increasingly difficult for single mothers to feed, clothe, and shelter their children, but it is almost impossible for them to insist that they are morally deserving of all the respect and dignity other citizens enjoy.

Welfare Rate Cuts

One of the most dramatic changes to welfare policy in Ontario occurred in 1995 when all able-bodied welfare recipients had their cheques reduced by 21.6 percent. In the entire history of welfare this was an unprecedented cut. While all welfare recipients have found this extremely difficult, single mothers have been particularly hurt by the cuts. With child-care responsibilities these mothers have fewer opportunities to top up their scanty welfare cheques by finding employment. [...]

The National Council of Welfare reported that single mothers have fallen further and further below the poverty line as a result of the Ontario welfare rate cuts. In 1995 single mothers in Ontario were $8,488 below the poverty line. After the welfare rate cuts they were $9,852 below the poverty line. In fact, the number of single mothers living on incomes less than *one half* of the poverty line jumped from 10.2 percent to 12.2 percent as a result of the welfare rate cuts (National Council of Welfare, 1995, 1996).

The everyday lives of single mothers have dramatically worsened. Single mothers whom I have interviewed told me that they have attempted suicide, reduced their food consumption to one meal a day, sold almost all their household furniture, moved in with abusive ex-partners—all in an attempt to survive the welfare rate cuts.

Given that food is one of the largest non-fixed items in many single mothers' budgets, this is where women are making huge sacrifices. Two-thirds of food bank recipients on welfare report going without food at least one day per month. Most of them report that they go without food one day a week or more. Twenty-one of the 30 single mothers whom I have recently interviewed across Ontario admit that they are eating less than three meals a day. One Aboriginal single mother said, "I always wondered how vegetarians survive—now I know. I never see meat anymore. Tonight's supper is popcorn and a stale muffin I got on sale" (Interview 1, Kenora, February 25, 1999).

*****

Many of the single mothers I interviewed were desperate to prove to me just how creative they were to provide food for their children. One mother opened up every kitchen cupboard at the beginning of the interview to show me that she had lots of food to feed her children, including food from the local food bank (Interview 12, Greater Toronto Area, May 1998).

Another single mother confided that she has a vegetable garden at a friend's house and she cans, freezes, and hides this food at her parent's home (Interview 6, Kenora, February 25, 1999).

Another woman went immediately to the grocery store after I handed her the honorarium at the end of the interview, stating that she had not gone grocery shopping in two months (Interview 10, Kenora, February 24, 1999).

In more than a decade of conducting interviews with single mothers, I have never seen them so desperate to prove to me that they are deserving and faithfully feeding their children.

*****

Even a telephone becomes a luxury for poor single mothers in the aftermath of the welfare rate cut. A recent survey of single mothers in Toronto found that as many as 27 percent of them had went without telephone service some time during the last two years (Ontario Workfare Watch, 1999).

Telephones fulfill three very important functions for single mothers. First, they link a mother to emergency services, which are particularly important when you are raising children on your own. Second, they are essential for seeking employment opportunities, which is an obligation for many on welfare. Third, they link a single mother, who is often isolated in her own home, to family and friends.

Housing has become an enormous concern for single mothers since the welfare rate cuts. Without stable housing, life is thrown into a constant upheaval and is reduced to a desperate scramble to find shelter, temporary, permanent, good or bad. Health suffers and damages the ability to make any long-term plans. Changes to welfare and tenant protection laws in Ontario have resulted in many people hanging on to their housing precariously, being forced into sub-standard accommodation or, worse, losing their housing altogether. Welfare benefits are paid in two parts: a shelter allowance plus a basic needs benefit that is supposed to cover all non-shelter costs. Maximum shelter allowances are far below the median rents actually paid by tenant house-holds across Ontario.

While shelter allowances have been frozen, rents have continued to rise, shrinking the number of affordable units, putting thousands more people at risk of homelessness. These housing changes have dramatically affected single mothers. A number of single mothers interviewed had their electricity, gas, or telephones cut off. Others have been evicted and have moved themselves and their children into shelters. All of this has placed enormous stress upon poor single mothers, for once a single mother loses her housing, she is reported to the Children's Aid Society and she lives in fear that she will lose her child or children.

*****

Certainly my research supports the general belief that low-income women experience high degrees of violence and that this violence escalates when they become even more vulnerable. During my recent interviews, single mothers explained that they had experienced more difficul-ties with ex-partners, employers, and landlords. The Ontario shelter movement has reported that since the welfare rate cut, more women are returning to abusive partners in order to feed and clothe their children (Ontario Association of Interval and Transition Houses, 1997).

One Aboriginal woman told about her difficult decision to permit her abusive ex-partner to rejoin her and her son in their home. "With him here this month it's been such a change for me. I eat more often—I only ate once a day since the welfare rate cuts. I sleep better, I worry less. I have support" (Interview 12, Kenora, February 24, 1999).

*****

In more than one community, single mothers have complained that landlords have attempted to exchange sex for lower rents. "He [the landlord] told me that if I had sex with him he would take off $150 a month for rent," explained one single mother (Interview 6, Kenora, February 25, 1999).

*****

In one single mother's case, her ex-partner claimed that she had received $2,000 in child sup-port and immediately her welfare cheque was cut off. According to this mother, her ex-partner had threatened her with a knife and had previous charges, including assaulting two police officers. "I don't want to have to deal with him at all. Yet, here I was—being faced with welfare problems when I was in a shelter because he claimed he had given me money I'd never seen.... I was pretty stressed about that; they were even talking about charging me with fraud." She currently has $50 per month deducted from her cheque because of this support payment the welfare department claims she received. Once she charges her ex-partner with violence, the welfare department will stop deducting this money, but for several months she has been both financially and emotionally distressed because of this situation (Interview 4, Greater Toronto Area, May 1998).

Most welfare recipients are attempting to top up their miserable welfare cheques in whatever way they can. Because of child-care responsibilities, few single moms are able to find work to top up their welfare cheques. Only one single mother I interviewed reported any type of underground employment, which would have enhanced the welfare cheque. This woman, in a snowbound northern Ontario town, shared one pair of boots between herself and her son as they delivered newspapers.

Instead of doing underground employment, many women have increased the amount of caring work they do. Some women have moved in with their parent(s) and are caring for them in exchange for cheap rent. Others visit the home of their parent(s) or other family members and care for them in exchange for groceries or other necessities.

This welfare cut has severely reduced a single mother's economic independence. Where the welfare cheque in the past often meant a release from oppressive personal relationships, this is increasingly no longer the case. Instead, single mothers have had to once again rely upon abusive ex-partners, harassing landlords, or demanding family members—all in an effort to feed, clothe, and shelter their children.

Workfare

From the introduction of welfare for single mothers in 1920 up until the arrival of the Ontario Conservative government, single mothers were considered a distinct category of welfare recipients whose primary responsibility was the care of their children. As a result, single mothers were not expected to look for full-time work. Instead, they were only encouraged to take work that did not interfere with their primary duty as mothers of the next generation. With the introduction of workfare, the Ontario Conservative government has dramatically altered the nature of welfare for single mothers. Now, all single mothers with school-aged children are expected to be participating in the workforce to the same degree as single men and women. In other words, single mothers are no longer fully recognized for their child-care responsibilities. Instead, they are treated very similarly to all other welfare recipients.

Treating single mothers with school-aged children as if they were *single* with no dependants creates enormous hardship for these mothers. [...]

*****

Interviews with anti-poverty advocates revealed that "inadequate job searches" are the most common reasons given for cutting people off welfare. "I'm hearing about this all the time now. You can't appeal 'inadequate job searches' so it is an easy way to reduce the welfare case load," explains Lana Mitchell, a single mother and long-time coordinator of Low Income Peoples Involvement, an anti-poverty group in North Bay (Interview, North Bay, January 28, 1999). Consequently, welfare recipients feel enormous pressure to conduct these job searches despite how futile they know the search to be.

Retraining and educational upgrading has been severely restricted under workfare. Welfare support for post-secondary education was abolished in 1996: Now any education and training approved under Ontario Works must be short term and directed only at the fastest possible entry to the labour market. This has frustrated many of the single mothers interviewed. Some of them have attempted to remain in university or college and scrape by on the Ontario Student Aid Program, but this requires them to carry huge debts that are much larger than the average student loan. Others have had to drop out of post-secondary education as a result of this policy change.

It is the Community Participation component that is the new aspect of this policy. This is what is publicly understood as workfare, unpaid work in return for welfare. Workfare recipients in this stream can be required to work up to 70 hours per month in a not-for-profit or public sector workplace.

A number of single mothers work part-time, but this only leads to further problems with the workfare administration. One mother's situation exemplified the difficulties of part-time employment: "I'll make too much money one month and they'll cut me off welfare and then the next month I'll make much less and I have to re-apply all over. I'm always running back and forth from the donut shop to the welfare office with these $90 pay stubs. They don't pay for the transportation to get down to the welfare office every two weeks" [Interview 1, Kenora, February 25, 1999].

*****

Community participants are not considered real workers. Although they are eligible for Workers' Compensation, the Employment Standards Act or Employment Insurance does not cover them. Also, it remains unclear whether workfare participants will be protected by the Ontario Human Rights Code, which protects workers against discrimination, including sexual and other harassment. [...]

*****

Workfare participants cannot simply quit a placement. If you refuse an offer of employment, a community placement, or if you refuse to look for work, you are no longer eligible for welfare. If you are considered to not be making enough effort in this regard, you receive a warning and your case is refused within 30 days. If after the first warning you are still considered to not be making enough effort, your cheque is suspended for three months. Three months is a very long time when you have no other source of income or assets. After suspension you must re-apply and meet the requirements all over again in order to attempt to receive welfare benefits (Ontario Ministry of Community and Social Services, 2000).

The entire premise of workfare is that welfare recipients are lazy and require a "push" or incentive in order for them to find work. Nothing could be further from the truth. The reality is that most welfare recipients are on welfare for a very short time. The average amount of time a single employable person is on welfare is approximately one year. Single mothers average approximately three years even though they have small children. The largest study of welfare recipients in Ontario found that excluding those who were already working, going to school, were ill or had a disability, or reported that they had unavoidable child-care responsibilities, *three quarters* of single mothers were already looking for work (Ornstein, 1995). According to another study, 15 percent of single mothers were already doing volunteer work before workfare was implemented (Ontario Workfare Watch, 1999). [...]

For the most part, these retraining and workfare schemes do not provide adequate child care; it is up to the single mother to find her own childcare. One mother was granted child care for only one of her three children. Another mother was told to find child care for her three-month-old baby. Another mother had to pay $40 per week out of her welfare cheque to finance her own child care while she participated in workfare (Ontario Workfare Watch, 1999).

All of these examples are against the stated regulations of workfare. They demonstrate that there is little recognition that parenting is the first concern of most single mothers. Instead, single mothers are blamed if they are not able to participate in retraining and workfare schemes. Money is deducted from their welfare cheques or they are told that they are ineligible for welfare at all—unless they participate in these programs. At the same time, single mothers are blamed if their children "act up at school" for lack of attention at home. This brings us back to a long history of contradictory expectations for single mothers on welfare. We have always expected single mothers on welfare to financially provide for their children. But at the same time we also expect these single mothers to adequately care for their children. Financial provision and mothering are contradictory expectations that are often impossible to meet. Workfare only exacerbates this contradiction, making women's unpaid caring work even more demanding and more invisible than it has been in the past.

Welfare Fraud

The Ontario Conservative government has established a number of mechanisms to "stamp out" fraud. Several anti-fraud measures will be examined below to explore how single mothers, in particular, have been constructed as morally suspicious.

A number of new verification procedures have been created. Today, welfare workers can demand literally hundreds of different pieces of information, depending on the circumstances of the case, and they can refuse, delay, or cancel welfare payments if this information is not provided. People are often told to provide information that they cannot possibly obtain, or to provide it within impossibly short periods of time. This documentation includes their Social Insurance Number, OHIP number, proof of identity and birth date, complete information on income and assets, medical reports, information on budgetary requirements (lease, rent receipts, etc.), school attendance, employment activities, and status in Canada. Other documentation can, and is, demanded of people regularly. The information requirements frequently go well beyond what is required to establish a person's eligibility, suggesting that workers can use their discretion about what documentation must be provided.

Welfare recipients are often asked to provide such documentation within 10 working days or less. This is often difficult for single mothers who have to find child-care arrangements and additional transportation money to provide this information. And sometimes the documentation is very costly. For example, one single mother from North Bay said that her welfare worker had demanded that she provide monthly statements of her bankbook and those of her four children for the last three years. When she went to the bank to get these necessary documents the bank official said it would cost $120 per hour to provide this documentation. Another single mother had to produce evidence that she had given up her car 15 years ago (Interview 1, Kingston, May 1999). Many women stated that they have been forced to locate violent ex-partners in order to obtain some of the necessary documentation (AWARE & the Single Mothers Support Network, 1999, p. 5). These are extremely intensive measures, which stigmatize those on welfare, encouraging the belief that welfare recipients are often thieves who must be caught. [...]

Immigrant and Aboriginal women have more difficulty obtaining the necessary documents for their welfare workers. Aboriginal women have to appeal to the Department of Indian and Northern Development to receive sworn documents. Birth certificates are not always available for Aboriginal or immigrant women, and the substitute documents require lengthy processing time. Also, people in smaller reserve communities tend not to have bank accounts, therefore they are unable to provide the required bank statements. All of these exceptions require extra negotiation with the welfare caseworker (Interview 5, Kenora, February 26, 1999). [...]

In 1995 the Ontario Conservative government opened its provincial welfare fraud telephone [line]. Granting anonymity to the person who calls to report welfare fraud raises some interesting questions. If someone calls the police department to report noise or other bylaw violations, your name, address, and telephone number must be given. As a rule these identification details are given to the person you have complained about. In the case of welfare fraud, the caller does not have to take any responsibility for his or her actions due to the cloak of anonymity. The recipient will never be told who provoked an investigation into her case. It is also interesting to note who takes advantage of and who is most often the scapegoat of these circumstances. According to welfare fraud evidence, single mothers are most often the targets of those who call the welfare office to report fraud. In the Ontario 1999 welfare fraud report, spouse-in-the-house issues were the second most common reason for people to call the welfare fraud telephone line. Also, according to interviews I conducted with anti-poverty advocates and community legal workers, it is generally believed that ex-partners are amongst the most likely people to call the welfare fraud line to report on single mothers' activities (Ontario Ministry of Community and Social Services, 1998a).

The Ontario Conservative government has also dramatically changed its position on single mothers' spousal relationship. From 1987 until 1995, Ontario had the most progressive legislation in Canada regarding spousal relations. During this period, single mothers were permitted to live with a partner for up to three years before the government considered the couple common law and deducted the financial resources of the spouse from the welfare cheque. In August 1995 as part of an "anti-fraud" initiative, the Ontario Conservative government announced that single mothers [on welfare] would no longer be permitted to live with a spouse.

The impact of the Ontario Conservative government's anti-fraud campaign against single mothers in spousal relationships has been devastating. During the first eight months of this new amendment, more than 10,000 recipients were deemed ineligible under the new definition and cut off welfare, 89 percent of whom were women (*Falkiner et al., v. Her Majesty the Queen*). A number of women have been falsely accused of cohabiting with former spouses when these men have relocated to other countries, are dead, or are imprisoned. Some have been cut off assistance without a hearing, which would have demonstrated their innocence. In all cases, a single mother is considered guilty until she proves herself innocent—until she demonstrates that she is not in a spousal relationship. As many single mothers have realized, providing evidence that you are not in a spousal relationship is, indeed, a challenge (Little & Morrison, 1999).

Those single mothers who have remained on welfare have experienced more extensive and intrusive investigation into their lives. When a man moves into their home, they must fill out a questionnaire to determine whether the man is a boarder or a spouse. The 11-page questionnaire reveals that the definition of spouse is broad, encompassing an economic, social, and familial relationship. The questionnaire includes the following questions:

14)   Do you and your co-resident have common friends?

15b)   Do other people invite the two of you over together?

18)   Do you and your co-resident spend spare time at home together?

24b)   Does your co-resident ever do your laundry (or the children's)?

27)   Who takes care of you and your co-resident when either of you are ill?

35a)   Does your co-resident attend your children's birthday parties? (Ontario Ministry of Community and Social Services, 1995 October)

Such a questionnaire could hardly be more intrusive. And what makes it particularly insidious is that there is no rule regarding how many questions need to be answered in the affirmative in order to be declared in a spousal relationship. Even if the recipient succeeds in persuading the welfare worker that her co-resident is not a spouse, her status remains in question. According to the Ontario regulations, the same investigation will be carried out annually as long as the living arrangement continues.

*****

Community legal workers and welfare recipients spoke at length about how this change in spousal definition has deeply affected the lives of single mothers. In North Bay one mother was accused of being in a spousal relationship because her boarder drove her children to school. In another case, the mother and father had never lived together, but the son was 18 years old and physically disabled. The father came over to help shower the child because the petite-framed mother could no longer do this on her own. This sharing of parental responsibility was considered evidence of a spousal relationship (Interview 3, North Bay, January 28, 1999). Another woman hides her engagement ring from her welfare worker because she is afraid this will be considered evidence that she is in a spousal relationship (Interview 5, North Bay, January 1999). The welfare department called one woman's house in Kenora and accused her of hanging men's clothes on her clothesline. "This was true, they were my son's and they were only out there for a couple hours," she explained (Interview 10, Kenora, February 1999). [...]

As well as implementing more mechanisms to "catch" welfare cheaters, the Ontario government has also dramatically increased the severity of the punishments. The Ontario Works Act permits recipients to be fined a maximum of $5,000 or six months' imprisonment if someone receives workfare payments that he or she is not entitled to. The new legislation punishes those who obstruct or knowingly give false information to a welfare worker. [...]

The impact of being accused of welfare fraud is incredibly damaging. One single mother in North Bay wept when she recounted her story of being wrongly charged with welfare fraud. She was charged for "undeclared income" and explained that she had received a welfare cheque when she had obtained full-time employment (ironically, her job was at the local welfare office). "I didn't even open up the cheque, I sent it right back, and I kept telling them to cancel my benefits," she explained. Then one day the police came to the welfare office where she was working and charged her with welfare fraud. The next day she woke up to find her name, address, and the fact that she had been charged with welfare fraud in the local newspaper and on the local radio station every half an hour for a whole day. "North Bay is a small community. My kids didn't want to go to school because they were bothered by other kids about it." Even though the charges were eventually dropped, this woman fears that she will never find employment again in North Bay. [...] (Interview 2, North Bay, January 1999).

The impact of welfare fraud charges is even more disturbing when one realizes that there is no evidence to support the government's obsession with welfare fraud. According to the most recent Ontario government welfare fraud report, there were 747 welfare fraud convictions of a 238,042 case load in 1998 to 1999, which means a welfare fraud rate of 0.3 percent. Of the more than 49,000 recipients suspected of fraud (as a result of complaints from [the] fraud line, information from welfare staff, information sharing with other governmental departments), more than two thirds were found to have no fraud or error. So the vast majority of those suspected of fraud are not cheating the system (Ontario Ministry of Community and Social Services, January 2000).

It is important to remember that welfare recipients, who violate technical rules, knowingly or otherwise, remain very poor as very few such cases involve significant amounts of money. Because the rules are many, complicated, and largely unknown to recipients, it is very possible for the most scrupulous person to break a regulation. Given that welfare payments are so inadequate, an important study from the U.S. suggests that most people on welfare supplement their welfare incomes in some manner (Edin & Lein, 1997). In my interviews all of the men admitted to receiving either gifts in kind or cash under the table to supplement their welfare cheques. The women interviewed did not have the same access to cash for work under the table, but they spoke instead of ways they hid additional food or resources from welfare workers. As one woman explained during my first interviews with single mothers more than a decade ago, "That's called abuse, but we call it survival" (Little, 1998).

*****

Conclusion

These dramatic changes to the Ontario welfare policy have devastated the lives of poor single mothers. Because they are assumed to be undeserving, their benefits and other support services have been slashed. Because they are assumed to be lazy, there are coercive measures enforced to make sure that they are constantly looking for employment or participating in job-related activities. And because they are assumed to be cheaters, single mothers are constantly scrutinized by government workers, neighbours, landlords, teachers, and family. This is a highly intrusive, punitive welfare state that does not begin to treat its citizens with dignity or recognize their real needs. This results in a loss of both material and moral power for poor single mothers. Single mothers have lost material resources—now many of them are constantly anxious about their ability to provide food, shelter, and clothing for their children. But as well, single mothers have lost moral ground. The government has convinced the public that many single mothers are not deserving of public help. As a result, there is little public outcry about the many mean-spirited investigative procedures that the government now uses to determine who is and who is not deserving of welfare. These material and ideological changes not only affect single mothers, they affect all women. When welfare programs are miserly, punitive, and demeaning in nature, it affects the choices all women can make about their lives. It discourages women from leaving abusive partners and harassing employers in an attempt to create a new and brighter future. We must all open our eyes and take stock of what our welfare policies are doing to single mothers and their children for the results will have a lasting impact on the next generation.

References

AWARE & the Single Mothers Support Network. (November 1999). Workfare or Work Fair: Perspectives on Ontario Works from Single Mothers. Kingston.

Corrigan, P., & Sayer, D. (1985). *The great arch: English state formation as cultural revolution.* Oxford: Basil Blackwell.

Edin, K., & Lein, L. (1997). *Making ends meet: How single mothers survive welfare and low-wage work.* New York: Russell Sage Foundation.

Falkiner et al. v. Her Majesty the Queen in right of Ontario as represented by the Ministry of Community and Social Services, Court File no. 810/95 (Ontario Court [General Division] Divisional Court), Affidavit of Robert Fulton, October 25, 1995 as cited in Mosher, "Managing the Disentitlement of Women," in Sheila M. Neysmith (Ed.), *Restructuring caring labour: Discourse, state practice, and everyday life* (Toronto: Oxford University Press, 2000), p. 34.

Little, M. (1998). *No car, no radio, no liquor permit: The moral regulation of single mothers in Ontario, 1920–1997*. Toronto: Oxford University Press.

Little, M. (1999, Spring). The limits of Canadian democracy: The citizenship rights of poor women. *Canadian Review of Social Policy*, 43, 59, 76.

Little, M., & Morrison, L. (1999). The pecker detectors are back: Changes to the spousal definition in Ontario welfare policy. *Journal of Canadian Studies*, 34, 2, 110–136.

National Council of Welfare. (1995, 1996). *Poverty profile*. Ottawa: National Council of Welfare.

Ontario Association of Interval and Transition Houses. (1997). *Some impacts of the Ontario Works Act on survivors of violence against women*.

Ontario Ministry of Community and Social Services. (1995, October). *Residing with a spouse*. Family benefits policy guidelines 0203, 05.

Ontario Ministry of Community and Social Services. (1998b, November 13). "Government anti-fraud initiatives save $100 million." News release, Toronto.

Ontario Ministry of Community and Social Services. (2000, January). "Welfare fraud control report, 1998–99." Toronto.

Ontario Ministry of Community and Social Services. (2000, May 5). "Nearly a half a million people move off welfare in Ontario." Press release.

Ontario Workfare Watch, Interim Report. (1999, April 30). *Broken promises: Welfare reform in Ontario*. Retrieved from: www.welfarewatch.toronto.on.ca/promises/report.htm.

Ornstein, M. (1995). *A profile of social assistance recipients in Ontario*. Toronto: Institute for Social Research, York University.

Piven, F.F., & Cloward, R.A. (1971). *Regulating the poor: The functions of public welfare*. New York: Pantheon Books.

Hidden Homelessness

Raising the Roof

Raising the Roof is a non-profit Canadian organization that provides national leadership on long-term solutions to the crisis of homelessness through partnership and collaboration with diverse stakeholders, investing in local communities, and public education. The organization's vision is that all members of Canadian society have access to a safe and stable home, together with the supports they need to achieve their potential.

10 Facts about the Hidden Homeless

1. Every community in Canada has homeless people, even if you don't see them on the street.
2. Most homeless people don't live on the street. More than 80% of Canada's homeless are improperly housed or on the verge of eviction. Many are sleeping in temporary beds at a friend's or relative's home, in church basements, at a welfare motel, in abandoned buildings and vehicles, and in other places away from the public eye.
3. About one in seven users of shelters across Canada is a child. Compared to children with permanent homes, homeless children suffer more from lack of educational opportunities, health issues, and injuries.
4. As women generally earn less than men, women are more vulnerable to becoming homeless.
5. Newcomers to the rental housing market, especially young people, immigrants, and refugees, are often obliged to rent housing that they cannot afford. They are often one paycheck away from eviction.
6. Many seniors face eviction due to fixed incomes and increasing rents and taxes.
7. Our young people also make up the hidden homeless. Many homeless youth are living in shelters or bunking in with friends—many are fleeing abusive situations.
8. The working poor, often single parents with young children, end up living in crowded housing as they are unable to afford a decent place to live while feeding and clothing their children.
9. The hidden homeless are at risk of long-term physical and emotional harm. The longer anyone remains homeless, the greater the social and economic costs.
10. As a society we all pay for the tragedy of homelessness.

10 Things You Can Do to Help

1. Volunteer with and contribute to the work of a charity or community group in your town or city that is working to assist the homeless and create housing.
2. Start an innovative project like a local rent or utility bank to assist low-income families and individuals.
3. Ask your municipality to allow homeowners to create apartments or second suites in their homes. These can be the least expensive form of rental accommodation and can help families become homeowners.
4. Organize a Raising the Roof Toque Campaign in your community or workplace.
5. Support the work of Raising the Roof by making a donation.
6. Invite speakers on homelessness and housing to meetings of your local school council, religious group, labour union, or business council.
7. Start or join an organization that is working on long-term solutions to homelessness.
8. Advocate for more affordable housing in your community and across the nation.
9. Secure support services to help people maintain their housing.
10. Get community support for affordable housing in your area. Get the manual *Yes in My Back Yard* from the Community Choice Coalition.

Source: Raising the Roof, "Hidden Homeless Campaign," retrieved from http://www.raisingtheroof.org/ Our-Programs/Hidden-Homeless-Campaign.aspx#10FactsAboutHiddenHomeless

Chapter 63

Research Bulletin no. 2:
Women and Homelessness

Street Health and Sistering

Street Health is a non-profit, community-based agency that works to improve the health and well-being of homeless and under-housed individuals in the southeast part of Toronto by addressing the social determinants of health through programs, services, education, and advocacy.

Sistering is a non-profit, community-based women's agency serving homeless, marginalized, and low-income women in Toronto. The organization focuses on program and service delivery to increase women's control over their lives, and advocacy to change the social conditions that put women at risk.

I will not live on a park bench anymore, or in a tent like I was doing. They should have a lot more housing for us. Because it's terrible.

—Heather, 48, nine years homeless

Homelessness Has a Life-Threatening Impact on Women's Health

Homeless women are not healthy and they are not safe. Alarming rates of violence, pain, mental distress, and serious physical health conditions were commonly reported in a recent survey of homeless women in Toronto by Street Health. Yet despite their poor health and extreme vulnerability, homeless women cannot access the health care, social services, and supports they urgently need. They face major barriers to health care, adequate housing, and other essential social services.

Patterns of Homelessness

You can't get out of poverty, no matter how you try. Nothing works together. They have systems, but they don't work together. Believe me, I have tried every possible way, but you can't. For three years I've been going around in a circle. And I can't get out of it. I'm very resourceful, I'm intelligent, and I'm not lazy. I'm sure people give up, but I keep going.

—Survey Respondent

BOX 63.1: Women in Our Survey

In total, we surveyed 97 people who identified as female.

- The average age was 42 years, with an age range of 19 to 66
- 26% identified as belonging to a racialized group[1]
- 21% identified as Aboriginal[2]
- 91% were Canadian citizens, 6% were landed immigrants, 2% had temporary status
- 81% identified as heterosexual and 16% identified as lesbian, bisexual, or trans
- 44% had completed high school and of those, 18% had a college or university degree

---

For women in Toronto, homelessness is not a short-term crisis.

- Women in the study had been homeless an average of three years

Homeless women live in extreme poverty. Although few women cited formal employment as a source of income, only half receive government income supports.

- 42% reported that they lived on $2,400 or less per year
- 10% are employed: 2% work full-time, 5% work part-time, and 3% reported doing casual or piece work
- 7% reported income from sex work and 3% from panhandling
- 23% reported receiving Ontario Works benefits, 24% reported receiving Ontario Disability Support Program benefits, and 5% reported receiving a government pension

Women become homeless and remain homeless due to poverty and because there is a lack of safe, afford-able, and supportive housing.

Women gave the following main reasons for becoming homeless[3]:

- Not being able to afford the rent (33%)
- Eviction (33%)
- Family or relationship breakdown (24%)
- Poor housing conditions (12%)
- Lack of safety (18%)

Women gave the following main reasons for why they remained homeless:

- Cost of rent is too high or lack of income (65%)
- Lack of suitable housing (unsafe or poor conditions, bad landlords) (25%)
- Physical and mental health conditions (33%)

The Daily Lives of Homeless Women: Difficult, Dangerous, and Stressful

> I never used to have memory loss, where I would have three hours of not remembering what's happened to me in a day, and it's not drug induced. It's not alcohol induced. Just exhaustion, because you don't know "Where am I going to sleep tonight?" Or I'm at some house and I can't go to sleep because I don't know what's going to happen from minute to minute. You're sleeping with one eye open. I had clumps of hair coming out.
>
> —Survey Respondent

Homeless women do not get enough shelter, sleep, or food.

- 50% said they had not been able to access a shelter bed at least once in the past year, on average 24 times
- 35% reported getting less than six hours of sleep each night
- 43% reported going hungry at least one day per week

Homeless women have difficulty taking care of basic health needs and hygiene routines.

- 34% reported difficulty getting their clothes washed
- 27% reported difficulty finding a place to bathe
- 33% reported difficulty finding a place to use the bathroom
- 32% found it difficult to obtain pads and tampons

> It's so hard, so hard. I almost gave up so many times—I almost did. It's so nice when someone treats you like a human being. If I don't get a home soon, I'll end up at the mental hospital. Being homeless is driving me crazy.
>
> —Survey Respondent

Homeless women are exposed to high levels of violence.

- 37% had been physically assaulted in the past year
- 21% had been sexually assaulted or raped one or more times in the past year

Homeless women live with extreme pain, exhaustion, and constant stress.

- 20% reported that they are usually in severe pain
- 68% reported living with extreme fatigue
- 58% experienced high levels of stress on a daily basis

Homeless women experience serious mental distress.

In the past year:

- 58% said they had experienced trouble understanding, concentrating, or remembering
- 68% experienced serious depression
- 64% experienced serious anxiety or tension
- 12% had tried to commit suicide

The circumstances and living conditions of homelessness are both a barrier and a threat to women's health. Lack of access to healthy food and sleep impacts physical health, psychological well-being, and energy levels. Personal hygiene was a critical and constant issue for homeless women. The inability to maintain personal hygiene not only has an impact on physical health, but also seriously impacts feelings of self-worth and undermines women's ability to maintain their dignity while homeless.

The staggering levels of violence experienced by women who are homeless reveal the vulnerable position that poverty puts women in and the lack of safety homeless women must live with every day. Violence has a broad range of negative physical and psychological effects. The high levels of pain reported by women suggest that many have injuries, disabilities, or medical conditions that are not being diagnosed or treated.

The stress reported by women can compromise the immune system over long periods of time and makes them more susceptible to a range of other health conditions. High rates of depression, anxiety, and suicide attempt are a reflection of the extremely harsh reality of homeless women's lives and the lack of hope that many homeless women experience.

> When people are homeless, they're already in a crisis. Why are they putting them out to sleep on the street at night when it's a lot more dangerous? Almost always they come in and say "I've been raped." Stop it. Let them sleep indoors.
>
> —Susan, 45, one year homeless

Health Status: The Health of Homeless Women Is Alarming

> Well, I have a heart problem. So I usually have a lot of chest pains. Right now I can't hold down a job because I can't do much. It's too strenuous for me to do anything because I get tired too quickly and my chest gets very congested where I can't breathe. And I have a lot of stomach pains and just yesterday I got an x-ray for my spine. I got spinal pain.
>
> —Survey Respondent

Homelessness is a life-threatening condition for women. Women who are homeless live with high rates of chronic physical health conditions, acute illnesses, and mental health issues. Women in our study reported high rates of a number of serious health conditions and have much worse health than women in the general Canadian population. Other research has shown that homeless women aged 18 to 44 are 10 times more likely to die than women of the same ages who had homes.[4]

Eighty-four percent of homeless women reported having at least one serious physical health condition.[5]

Homeless women in our study had significantly higher rates for almost all physical health conditions where comparable data for women in the general population was available. For example, our results show that homeless women are:

- five times as likely to have heart disease
- three times as likely to have asthma
- two and a half times as likely to have arthritis or rheumatism
- four times as likely to have diabetes

Table 63.1: Chronic or Ongoing Physical Health Conditions

Homeless women in our survey compared with women in the general Canadian population

	Homeless General	Women Population
Arthritis or rheumatism*	50%	20%[6]
Allergies other than food allergies*	50%	31%[6]
Migraines*	43%	15%[6]
Liver disease*	26%	10%[7]
Asthma*	33%	10%[6]
Problem walking, lost limb, other physical handicap	33%	n/a
Chronic obstructive pulmonary disease (COPD)*	29%	1%
Hepatitis C	24%	n/a
Anemia	23%	n/a
Stomach or intestinal ulcers*	23%	3%[6]
Heart disease*	20%	4%[6]
High blood pressure	20%	16%[6]
Diabetes*	16%	4%[6]
Epilepsy	10%	n/a
Inactive or latent tuberculosis	9%	n/a
Heart attack in lifetime	8%	n/a
Stroke in lifetime	6%	n/a
Cancer	4%	1%[6]
Fetal alcohol spectrum disorder	4%	n/a
Congestive heart failure	2%	n/a
Hepatitis B	2%	n/a
HIV-positive	1%	n/a
AIDS	1%	n/a

*statistically significant difference
n/a = data not available

> I'm supposed to be on a special diet and I can't at the shelter have the things I'm supposed to eat. I'm lactose-intolerant and I'm supposed to have high-protein food. And you don't really have much of choice.
>
> – Survey Respondent

There are also some acute health issues that homeless women commonly experience. These issues are related to the unique and difficult living circumstances of homelessness, which include violence and injury, crowding, and prolonged exposure to the elements.

Table 63.2: Acute or Episodic Physical Health Issues Reported by Women in the Past Year

	%
Foot problems	43%
Bed bug bites	25%
Pneumonia	24%
Seizure	13%
Skin infection, skin sores, or ulcers	13%

Fifty-five Percent of Homeless Women Reported Having a Mental Health Diagnosis

Although more than half of all homeless women had received a diagnosis for a mental health issue at some point in their lifetime, the most common mental health diagnoses were depression and anxiety. This does not support the stereotype of the mentally ill homeless person who suffers from psychosis and wants to live on the street.

Table 63.3: Mental Health Conditions

Most common mental health diagnoses reported by homeless women in our survey	%
Depression	29%
Anxiety	19%
Post-traumatic stress disorder	10%
Bipolar (manic depressive)	10%
Addiction to drugs or alcohol	6%
Schizophrenia	4%

Mental health problems do not directly cause homelessness. People with mental health issues can become homeless when they lack income stability and appropriate supports. Many of the factors that compromise mental health, such as instability, social isolation, and violence are also part of the daily reality of homelessness. For people who experience mental health problems, these problems may worsen or be amplified by the everyday traumas experienced due to homelessness.

Compared to homeless men, homeless women in our survey are:

- 10 times more likely to be sexually assaulted
- More likely to have serious physical health problems
- Twice as likely to have received a mental health diagnosis

Access to Health Care: Health Care Services Are Not Meeting Homeless Women's Needs

> It's discrimination. They do treat you differently because you're homeless. Who the hell are you? You're nobody. You don't have a place to stay, you're nobody.
>
> —Survey Respondent

Many homeless women do not have a stable source of primary health care. They have far worse access to family doctors than women in the general population.

- 29% have no regular source of health care or use the emergency department as their usual source of care
- 56% do not have a family doctor (compared with only 10% of women in the general Canadian population)

Hospitals are a frequently used source of health care for homeless women.

- 61% had visited a hospital emergency department in the past year, on average four times
- 24% had been hospitalized at least one night

Homeless women have many unmet health care needs, including post-natal care and access to substance use programs.

- 14% said they have had a baby while homeless; of those, 23% had been discharged from the hospital after giving birth without having any place to go
- 21% of women who used alcohol or drugs had tried to access detox or treatment in the past year, but were not able to

Homeless women have poor access to medications and important preventive health care services.

- 42% did not have a drug benefit card
- 60% had not been able to obtain needed prescription medications in the past year
- 38% of women over age 40 had never had a mammogram
- 59% of all women had not had a Pap test in the past year

Homeless women face discrimination by health care providers when attempting to access health care.

- 47% said they had been judged unfairly or treated with disrespect by a health care provider in the past year
- The most common reasons women felt they were discriminated against were because they were homeless (cited by 71%), because of their use of drugs or alcohol (48%), because of their gender (26%), and because of their race/ethnic background (21%)

Many women can't follow health care advice because of their difficult living circumstances and because of poverty.

- 42% said that they had not been able to follow their health care provider's advice or treatment plan in the past year; of those, 83% said that their living situation wouldn't allow it or it was too difficult to do and 23% said that the advice or treatment plan cost too much

Access to a stable primary health care provider who knows your medical history and with whom you feel comfortable is very important, especially for women who may have been traumatized in the past by figures of authority. At best, poor treatment by health care providers means that many homeless women do not have their health problems adequately addressed. At worst, some homeless women are being retraumatized in the process of seeking help for their health issues.

Good health requires more than a doctor's visit yet health advice or treatment plans can be difficult to follow when homeless. For example, having to take medications with food would be difficult for the many women in our survey who reported high rates of hunger.

> Just because we're homeless, we're still people. You know, you can work nine to five, you can work a 40-hour week and still be homeless.
>
> —Lorrie, 42, four months homeless

BOX 63.2: Women's Homelessness—A Common Occurrence

The women who were surveyed for this study are among the more visibly homeless. In addition to people who use shelters or sleep outside or in places not intended for human habitation, homelessness also includes a continuum of people who are less visibly homeless but who live in poor housing or overcrowded conditions and people with low incomes who are at risk of becoming homeless. Homeless women are often less visibly homeless than men because they are more likely to double up with friends or relatives or move between temporary situations. This type of homelessness is often referred to as "hidden" homelessness.

Solutions

> If people were housed, they could take care of their medical problems more easily. There's all these condominiums going up all the time. Can they put up housing for the homeless, like just a couple, okay?
>
> —Survey Respondent

Homelessness has a devastating impact on women's health and well-being. Immediate action is needed to address poverty and the lack of safe, affordable housing that underlie homelessness and the distressing rates of illness, violence, and mental distress experienced by homeless women. The recommendations below are aimed at improving the health of homeless women and eliminating homelessness.

Income

> Welfare doesn't give you enough money to survive, to get out of it. I was on welfare, I was living in a room for $510 and they gave me $520 in welfare. I never managed to survive for a month without not having food for a few days.
>
> —Survey Respondent

The women in our survey live in extreme poverty: 42% live on less than $200 per month. Our survey found that women become homeless and stay homeless largely because of poverty. Income is a major determinant of health and was cited throughout the study as a barrier that prevented women from accessing health care and maintaining good health. Ensuring that women have adequate incomes will improve their health and reduce homelessness.

1. The Ministry of Community and Social Services should *raise benefit levels* for Ontario Works and the Ontario Disability Support Program by at least 40% (to reinstate the 23% cut made in the 1990s and adjusted to reflect a current minimum standard of living), then index and adjust rates annually to meet this minimum standard of living.
2. The Ontario Ministry of Labour should *raise the minimum wage rate* to $10 an hour immediately, then index and adjust the wage annually to meet a minimum standard of living.

Housing

> I want a door that locks, that's secure and safe. I can work with anything as long as it's got that—I can make it home.
>
> —Survey Respondent

Women need housing in order to stabilize their lives and be healthy. Ensuring that women have access to affordable and safe housing in neighbourhoods where they feel comfortable will both reduce the number of homeless women and prevent more women from becoming homeless. Many homeless women have physical and mental health issues, indicating a strong need for supportive housing to help address their specific needs.

3. The City of Toronto and Toronto Central Local Health Integration Network, with adequate funding from the governments of Canada and Ontario, should increase the availability of *women-only supportive housing* designed to accommodate women with physical and mental health needs, as well as harm-reduction housing, which supports women with alcohol and other substance-use issues.
4. The City of Toronto, with adequate funding from the governments of Canada and Ontario, should *increase the availability of affordable and adequate housing* in Toronto. This should include the construction of new affordable homes, improvements to sub-standard existing social housing to make it safer for women, and rent supplements that follow the individual rather than the housing unit.
5. The City of Toronto Department of Shelter, Support, and Housing Administration should give *women who have children high priority on the social housing wait list*, whether they live with these children or not, to prevent women from losing custody of their children because they lack adequate housing, and to assist women in regaining custody of their children.

Child Care

> The hardest part [about being homeless] for me is thinking about my son and where he's at....
>
> —Survey Respondent

> As a single mother I have had to struggle for both me and my child. Yes, I've worked and I'm a hard worker. But sometimes it just doesn't pay the rent.
>
> —Survey Respondent

Although our survey captures predominantly the experiences of women living in single-adult shelters, the experience of being a low-income parent came up frequently throughout the survey. Few women cited formal employment as a source of income, and other research has shown that women with children are less likely to work after they become homeless.[8] A universal system of publicly funded early childhood education and care for all children and families is needed. In the short term, adequate child care supports will reduce homelessness for women and their children by increasing women's access to education, training, and employment.

6. The Ministry of Children and Youth Services and the City of Toronto should increase the number of *subsidized day care spaces* for low-income parents and *extend the period of childcare subsidy* for women looking for employment.
7. The Ministry of Children and Youth Services should adequately fund existing community-based advocacy programs and create additional ones to *support low-income parents who need help to navigate the child welfare system*. This could include a support group for parents needing to understand child welfare practices, as well as supportive accompaniment to legal appointments and court appearances.

Health Care

> I believe the health care system could use some changes. I think they need to implement more social workers and take an interest in the mental well-being of people.
>
> —Survey Respondent

> It's like a walk-in clinic for [the] homeless at the community health centre. They care. Even the secretaries—there's thousands of patients and you walk in and they know your name, you know? Never ask you—"Oh, can I have your health card?" again. No, you just go on in.
>
> —Survey Respondent

Homelessness has a devastating impact on women's health. Eighty-four percent of the women in our survey reported having at least one serious physical health condition, which is significantly higher than their male counterparts, 70% of whom reported the same. Although our study did not interview women at Violence against Women shelters, it is clear from our findings that violence is an issue for many homeless women, regardless of where they access services.

Despite their poor health status, homeless women cannot access the health care they need. They often receive health care advice they are unable to follow because of their living circumstances and they often face discrimination from health care providers. There is an immediate need to address the barriers in the health care system for women.

8. The Ontario Ministry of Health and Long-Term Care and Toronto Central Local Health Integration Networks should adequately fund and *expand comprehensive, multidisciplinary, low-barrier models of health care*, such as family health teams and community health centres. These services should: provide easy access for homeless women through practices such as unscheduled walk-in hours and no health card requirements; include expanded community health work such as outreach, harm reduction, case management, and counselling; and offer services during evenings and on weekends.

9. The Ontario Ministry of Health and Long-Term Care and Toronto Central Local Health Integration Network should provide funding to *increase the number of women-only drug and alcohol detox beds* in Toronto, as well as residential treatment options for women with addictions. This should include detox beds that are medically supervised.

10. The Ontario Ministry of Health and Long-Term Care should develop education and training programs to increase awareness and capacity among health care providers to enable them to provide *trauma-informed service delivery*, which takes into account knowledge about the physical and emotional impact of trauma and incorporates appropriate strategies for providing services.

11. The Ontario Ministry of Health and Long-Term Care, Toronto Central Local Health Integration Network and Toronto Public Health should collaborate to establish hospital/ community, multidisciplinary models of practice that *provide pre-/post-natal and well baby care specifically for homeless and low-income women*. Dedicated nurse specialists should coordinate these models of shared care within hospitals and on an outreach basis at shelters and community-based clinics.

Until income, housing security, and other broad social causes and amplifiers of homelessness for women are adequately addressed, there is an immediate need to improve emergency services for women who are homeless.

Shelters and Drop-ins

> You are not in control of yourself anymore. At the shelter I am at now it's difficult because we have to get up five days a week at 7 and at 9:30 we have to be out of the shelter, but then we have to be back at 3 o'clock in the afternoon.
>
> —Survey Respondent

The living conditions of homeless women are a major contributing factor to their poor health and well-being. One of the reasons for this is a shortage of services and programs for homeless women in Toronto. Of the approximately 2,500 single-adult shelter beds in the city, only about 725 are for women.[9] It is evident from our study findings that there is a connection between lack of access to shelter and the victimization of women. Many women in the study expressed the need for more flexibility and control over daily routines in shelters, as well as the need for more emotional and social support. Allowing for more autonomy and reducing social isolation are key to enabling homeless women to participate more fully in society.

Racialized women were underrepresented in our sample compared with the population and with poverty rates in Toronto, which are disproportionately racialized. This raises questions as to where these women are accessing support.

12. The City of Toronto and the federal government's Homelessness Partnering Strategy should provide adequate funding to ensure that *community-based meal programs can expand their hours year-round, and increase the quantity and quality of food served* so that women who are homeless have access to three nutritious meals a day, seven days a week.

13. The City of Toronto and the federal government's Homelessness Partnering Strategy should provide adequate funding so that drop-ins can *expand the number and hours of service of women-only drop-ins year-round*, so that women who are homeless always have a safe, indoor space to connect with other people. Drop-ins should be funded to provide skills training as well as activities that decrease isolation and help women connect with each other and to their communities. This could include peer-support groups, community gardens, and cooking cooperatives. It should also include nighttime drop-ins for women who do not use shelters or who work at night, so that they too have a safe space to spend time and access other services.

14. The City of Toronto should provide adequate funding *to improve and enforce shelter standards* to address issues such as overcrowding, safety, and nutrition. Provide *additional women-only shelters and adapt existing shelters* so that they are more flexible, less institutional, and designed to better support the well-being of women and accommodate their health needs, including more shelters with private rooms. This should also include more shelters that operate from a harm-reduction philosophy, as well as harm-reduction shelter programs like the Seaton House Annex program for men. The three-month maximum stay policy should be eliminated at shelters where it still exists.

I can't do much because I'm always short of breath, I have to sit down. I don't sleep very often. And living in a shelter, to be honest with you, is not healthy at all. It's not the best place to be…. The place is infested with bugs. I got bitten three times.

—Kathy, 37, two years homeless

15. The Ontario Ministry of Health and Long-Term Care and the Toronto Central Local Health Integration Network should partner with experienced community-based organizations to increase the number of *community-based caseworkers* who can assist homeless women in navigating various aspects of the health and social service systems, [and] to provide support such as accompaniment to doctor's appointments and negotiating with landlords.

16. The Ministry of Citizenship and Immigration should *extend provincial funding for Violence against Women* programs and services at all shelters, drop-ins, and community-based agencies serving women at the same level as Violence against Women shelters to enable them to also provide trauma counselling and support services for women.

17. In an effort to make homeless services more accessible to immigrant and racialized women, the City of Toronto and the federal government's Homelessness Partnering Strategy should fund and require drop-ins and shelters to:

- create language-specific staff positions
- fully implement anti-oppression and cultural competency into their practices
- expand or create service partnerships with immigrant settlement services
- develop outreach programs to reach hidden homeless women who are not accessing services, many of whom are racialized and immigrant women

Notes

1. Respondents were asked to identify which racial or cultural groups they belonged to and could choose more than one.
2. Aboriginal peoples made up a much higher percentage of our sample when compared to the percentage they represent in the general population of Toronto. In the 2001 Census for the City of Toronto, only 0.5% of women identified as Aboriginal. This is consistent with findings from other homeless research across Canada, which have also found that Aboriginal peoples are vastly overrepresented among the homeless.
3. In cases like this, respondents were able to choose more than one answer and totals may add up to more than 100%.
4. A.M. Cheung and S.W. Hwang, Risk of death among homeless women: A cohort study and review of the literature, *Canadian Medical Association Journal* 170(8) (2004): 1243–1247.
5. A "serious physical health condition" was defined as any of 22 serious conditions, including: cardiovascular and respiratory diseases, hepatitis and other liver diseases, gastrointestinal ulcers, diabetes, anemia, epilepsy, cancer, and HIV/AIDS.
6. *Source:* Statistics Canada, *Canadian Community Health Survey (CCHS) Cycle 3.1* (2005). This analysis is based on Statistics Canada's *Canadian Community Health Survey, Cycle 3.1* (2005), Public Use Microdata File, which contains anonymized data. All computations on these microdata were prepared by Street Health and the responsibility for the use and interpretation of these data is entirely that of the authors.
7. Canadian Liver Foundation, telephone communication, May 22, 2008, Toronto.
8. Ann Decter, *Lost in the Shuffle: The Impact of Homelessness on Children's Education in Toronto* (Toronto: Community Social Planning Council of Toronto, 2007).
9. City of Toronto, *Toronto Shelter, Support & Housing Administration. Guide to Services for People Who Are Homeless '08* (Toronto: City of Toronto, 2008).

Supplement 37

Rural Women and Poverty

In 2002 the Rural Women and Poverty Action Committee, with the support of Women Today of Huron, conducted a participatory action research study with rural women living in poverty in Grey, Bruce, and Huron counties. Thirty-five diverse women, including women on Ontario Works and those dealing with abuse, attended two workshops to speak of their experience of rural poverty. Women in this study said they are poor because:

- There are no jobs or job opportunities for women to use the good skills they have. Most of the higher-paying jobs are reserved for men, while women are forced into low-paying jobs that leave them in poverty.
- They experience sudden loss of unemployment, loss of health or disability issues, abuse, divorce/separation that propel them quickly from middle class to poverty.
- There is little access to education or retraining in rural communities.
- They are economically dependent on men in rural communities.
- They care for their children and this work is not valued or compensated.
- They live on farms and the farm takes everything they have.
- Social assistance and Disability Pensions are not adequate to keep women out of poverty.

Women in this study reported that Ontario Works is a dead-end for women in this rural community, noting that the system is a maze, lifetime bans are threatening, there are constant audits of women, and women cannot get ahead. The women in this study recommended an evaluation of Ontario Works to get a true picture of what is happening to women and children in rural areas to inform changes that will make Ontario Works work for women.

Source: Colleen Purdon, *Women Abuse and Ontario Works in a Rural Community: Rural Women Speak about Their Experiences with Ontario Works: Final Report* (Goderich, ON: Women Today of Huron, 2003), 19.

Chapter 64

The Little Voices of Nunavut:
A Study of Women's Homelessness North of 60

Qulliit Nunavut Status of Women Council

The Qulliit Nunavut Status of Women Council works to advance women's equal participation in society by promoting changes in social, legal, and economic structures that hinder women. The Council is part of a pan-territorial steering committee of service providers and women's advocacy organizations that is currently conducting research on homelessness among northern women. The Nunavut Qulliit Nunavut Status of Women Council took responsibility for the Nunavut component of this project. What follows are excerpts from its 2007 report.

Defining Homelessness

There is broad consensus in the literature that homelessness in general, and among women in particular, represents a continuum of circumstances. These include living on the street, seeking refuge in shelters, sleeping in the homes of friends or relatives, accepting shelter in return for sexual favours, remaining in households in which they and/or their children are subjected to various types of abuse, staying in accommodation that is unsafe and/or overcrowded, and paying for accommodation at the expense of other livelihood needs (such as food, clothing, and health care).

- *Visible or absolute homelessness* includes women who stay in emergency hostels and shelters and those who sleep rough in places considered unfit for human habitation, such as doorways, vehicles, and abandoned buildings
- *Relative homelessness* applies to those living in spaces that do not meet basic health and safety standards, including [spaces that lack] protection from elements, security of tenure, personal safety, and affordability
- *Hidden homelessness* includes women who are temporarily staying with friends or family or are staying with a man only in order to obtain shelter, and those living in households where they are subject to family conflict or violence
- At risk of becoming homeless can include those who are one step away from eviction, bankruptcy, or family separation

Although the number of women living on the street is increasing in many parts of Canada, street homelessness is not representative of most women's experiences. Definitions that focus on "absolute" or "visible" homelessness therefore leave most homeless women, especially those with children, out of homelessness counts and media portrayals of the issue. Women are more likely than men to be single parents, to work in low-paying and non-permanent employment, to take on care-giving roles when family members become incapacitated, [and] to suffer a dramatic decrease (averaging 33%) in household income in the case of separation or divorce. As well, domestic violence creates a need for housing that cannot be anticipated months in advance. In other words, women are dramatically impacted by "short-term changes and transitions which are often not captured by general affordability or adequacy measures" and are therefore "often overlooked in programmatic responses to homelessness" (Centre for Equality Rights in Accommodation, 2002).

Many women can often cycle through the various stages of homelessness described above. For example, 2.2 million adult women in Canada could be defined as at risk of homelessness because of poverty. All it takes is a small change in their circumstances (e.g., losing their employment, becoming ill) to throw them into hidden homelessness (i.e., staying with friends or family or anyone who will provide shelter). If this situation becomes untenable (e.g., they are no longer welcome, [or] they are experiencing abuse), they can end up in a shelter if one is available or on the streets (absolute homelessness). If they return to an abusive situation simply in order to have shelter for themselves and their children, they are then back in a hidden homelessness situation. Or, if they are able to access appropriate and sufficient resources, they may be able to find accommodation again, but will remain at risk of homelessness. The stories in *A Study of Women's Homelessness North of 60* provide many different examples of how women move in and out of the various stages of homelessness.

Theme Anthology no. 1: Every Woman Is Potentially at Risk

> There is not much distance from where you are to finding yourself on the other side of the fence.

This quote from one of the interviewees captures accurately how much of a reality homelessness has become for countless northern women. Homelessness in Nunavut has a very different reality than the circumstances generally found in southern Canada. The structure of small communities in this sparsely populated territory creates a sense of desperation when it comes to finding affordable housing, while other Nunavummiut are constantly at risk of losing their homes. The threat of homelessness exists for a broad range of women, from the unemployed, to members of the workforce who have no subsidized housing or don't earn enough to pay market rents, to Government of Nunavut employees who are in precarious possession of staff housing.

> I just can't afford the high cost of living and rent here. The housing situation is really desperate. That stress is what drives families apart and then other relatives are taking sides. Family is pitted against family all the time.

Theme Anthology no. 2: Partners' Behaviour and Circumstances

> I put up with sexual abuse from my common law because leaving him leaves my children with no father. I didn't want them to suffer for mistakes they didn't even make.

A woman's intimate partner often plays a large role in the occurrence of homelessness in all areas of the country. The situation for northern women is unique, however.

The vast majority of the women interviewed have been victims of violence, or exposed to high levels of violence when moving from place to place. Several of the women became homeless when they made the decision to flee an abusive family member, most often their intimate partners. When asked what they believe is causing women's homelessness, the interviewees have been very forthcoming in noting violence as a serious problem requiring immediate intervention in the North.

> You go with this man even though you don't want to. You don't love him, you don't like him, but he has a bed to sleep on. You have no choice but to follow him because you need a place to sleep. It makes you sick inside, makes you lose your mind.

Theme Anthology no. 3: Forced Eviction and Relocating to Another Community

> I fled from my violent husband from my home community. I couldn't stand the violence. Women are always running from their communities.

Forced eviction from social housing units was a reality for many of the women interviewed. A primary reason for eviction is that the male lists a unit under his name, exclusive of his female counterpart. If the relationship ends, becomes abusive, or if the woman becomes widowed, she is expected to evacuate her home. The vast majority of women who have shared stories of eviction have been forced out of their homes because of their partners' actions. Tenant damage is also another reason women become evicted from public housing.

> I got evicted on more than one occasion—three times actually. The first time it was because my first husband passed away and his name was on the lease. They made me leave. Another time my ex-boyfriend was vandalizing and his name was on the lease so we got kicked out. My family members are homeless too and have been for many years. I had a brother who was homeless. Bills ran up and he ended up moving to Yellowknife. He didn't want to come back because there is no housing over here. He would have waited for many years and he did not want that. His body was found in a cardboard box. My sister down in Ontario, she can't come back because she is ill, and the housing will be too long too and she don't want to come back because over here there is lots of drugs and alcohol. I also have another brother who is homeless in Calgary. I don't want Inuit to go through this. It's hard. It affects too many families of all cases.

Theme Anthology no. 4: Lack of an Adequate Support System

> I haven't eaten a meal in over a week. I just feel so uncomfortable to do that at my brother's. If you are uncomfortable where you are staying, you feel like you're in the way of them. They want to help you but they are still pushing you away, making you feel uncomfortable.

Inuit women who are homeless in Nunavut survive because of the values that are placed on maintaining family ties and sharing. Fifty-four percent of Inuit currently live in overcrowded conditions, and 38.7% of them are considered in core need. This statistic is so high because the desperate lack of housing options forces these women to turn to friends and family. Women are often coming with more than just their own mouth to feed, and families can only provide so much. Three or four generations of families often huddle under one roof, which becomes a breeding ground for frustration. Women are forced to sleep in shifts, and if they are lucky enough to have a room, it is shared with several others. They have no privacy, and their tenure is based on the circumstances of others. If the home becomes violent and unbearable, the absence of alternative housing leaves the women feeling trapped. They often feel as though they are a burden to their families and end up moving from home to home, stripping them of stability. This also creates difficulty for women to maintain employment or access existing government programs if they do not have the security of a roof over their heads.

> I am going through that right now. My son and I are living with my brother and his family and it's a one-bedroom. It's really crowded, so then we start arguing and fighting. Everybody goes all over the place, so when it gets tense I have to find somewhere else to stay for the night. I won't go home for days. I just go from home to home, couch to couch, friends to friends. I'm so tired of that.

Theme Anthology no. 5: Personal Wellness and Capacity

> I've thought about hiring someone to beat me up just so I can stay at the women's shelter. I know it sounds crazy, but that's what desperation does to your mind when you have no place to go.

Another determinant of homelessness in Nunavut women involves wellness and capacity. A woman's potential for improving her position in life is often inhibited by her health and/or her perception of her own personal abilities.

> I don't think that it's because we're Inuk, but that most of us don't have the education to get good paying jobs to afford the high cost of rent up here. I know Inuit people don't have all these diplomas that people want, but we do have the skills to do it. We just need the opportunity, the chance.

Women often find themselves suffering from physical and emotional exhaustion, including feelings of disempowerment, which trap them in a cycle from which they can find no respite. Being incapable of sheltering/protecting themselves and their children results in feelings of worthlessness, eventually taxing every other area of their lives. They are stripped of all esteem, and poor health negatively infringes upon their capacity to better their situations. Many of the women interviewed stated that they have experienced a complete loss of identity, with no remaining sense of a culture that brought such a great sense of pride to their forebears.

Theme Anthology no. 6: Community Institutions and Structures

> Students get housing right way, people coming in, government employees coming in. And they keep those houses open, even if they don't have staff to put in them. It's always the people that are from here that are homeless.

The structure of communities in Nunavut is what makes this homeless epidemic so unique. On the surface, many people fail to understand how things operate because it is so vastly dissimilar from southern Canadian communities. Iqaluit is currently the largest community in Nunavut, with a population of under 7,000, while the other 24 communities have significantly fewer people. The dynamics involved with the operation of our current institutions are often overlooked when examining our homeless situation.

Major issues include a lack of services and resources and the ineffectiveness of many existing services (partly because privacy and confidentiality are not respected). A harsh climate, the structure of family and intimate relationships in isolated conditions, issues of racism, and a vast northern terrain complicate communication and connectedness between Nunavut communities. Also critical is the high cost of living. Quite a large gap exists between the employed and unemployed, and if you are not benefiting from a Government of Nunavut salary, it is virtually impossible to get ahead. As of 2004, almost 50% of Nunavummiut were income-support clients (data supplied by the Department of Health and Social Services), which clearly illustrates the problematic economy currently in place.

> We owned our own home together; it was under both of our names and I don't think it was right to put his name under the home because it was a program for me and now that we are separated because I have no job. But I'm very educated. I'm fighting so hard for my home. I was born and raised here. My ex just laughs at everybody, the whole community, he's got no respect for elders. I'm just all over, trying to find work and so on. It's so hard to put my life back together when I don't even have a place to call home.

Theme Anthology no. 7: Cost of Living and Business Sector Practices

> The government is great at putting programs on. I can take all sorts of programs, but where's the jobs?

Cost of living is another unique circumstance of northern life. "It just doesn't make sense that the minimum wage is $8 an hour (or about $1,280 a month) when a one-bedroom apartment in Iqaluit can cost anywhere between $900–$1,600 per month" ("Most Nunavut Homeless," *Nunatsiaq News*, October 5, 2001). The cost of heating, electricity, and water is so high that many residents cannot afford to maintain accommodations without subsidy. According to Jackson, for example, (2006:15), the cost of supplying a gallon of water to a household is about the same as a gallon of gasoline.

> Can't afford to live here. The rent is too high and there's just not enough public housing. Affordable housing would solve a lot of problems here. I have been a house mother for the last 5 years and unemployed for 5 years, and I'm a surviving child of parents that went to residential school, and I have been healing on my own with the help of our wellness center and the programs they offer.

Theme Anthology no. 8: Societal Indifference/Punitiveness toward the Homeless (Including Racism)

> There is no feeling worse than to be homeless, to be unloved, and to think that nobody in the community wants you....

Regardless of where you live in Canada, the homeless tend to be negatively stigmatized by other members of society. Homeless people are often judged and mistreated based on the stereotypes of what a homeless person is. The situation in Nunavut is no exception.

> A generation of Nunavummiut are growing up in desperate situations, where people value life less than they did in the past. Previously, Inuit had stable homes where traditions could be passed on. [...] Now, the poor of Nunavut can't afford a permanent family home to provide stability. I see it as the absolute destruction of a culture. ("Homeless Shelter on the Rocks," *Nunatsiaq News*, March 11, 2005)

This sentiment is shared by many, as the Inuit way of life has become confused and eroded since they were forced into southern models of life.

The vast majority of women believe it would be more beneficial to go back to their traditional way of living. It was expressed in numerous interviews that "Qallunaat [non-Inuit people] are taking over our land." While most women maintain that they feel no prejudice toward White people, they feel the "White way of life" does not fit their traditional lifestyle and has further complicated their living situation. Women have also stated that "Qallunaat get houses faster," and "If I were a Qallunaaq, I'd probably have a house." Several of the women suggested [that] by simply looking at the homes owned by Inuit versus [those] of Qallunaat, ... the message is clear as [to] who is valued the most. This gap continues to increase, suggesting a systematic failure. The government ought to implement strategies to help northern constituents help themselves, rather than displacing them in nontraditional "southern" models, which have proven unsuccessful.

> Qallunaats are running the show here. They get houses immediately. Nunavut used to be more community-oriented. Everyone helped each other out. We need to help everybody out like our ancestors did. Go back to Inuit culture. We need to go back to the traditional way of life.

Theme Anthology no. 9: Climate/Weather

> In the wintertime, it's cold right to the bone.

Although homelessness is a global issue, Inuit women face unique challenges that call for different solutions in the North. Homelessness tends to be invisible in Nunavut—people are not living on the street as you often see in southern cities because the harsh weather prevents them from doing so. On the most frigid days of the year, the climate can reach 60 below zero, forcing penniless women to pile into local establishments, hoping to make a cup of coffee span the day, or gathering at a friend or family member's already overcrowded home. The northern climate, combined with lack of available housing, is why homelessness in Nunavut shows itself in the average number of people per dwelling. With no homeless shelters for women anywhere in the territory, women are left relying on family to house them from the cold.

> Winter is so much harder. Existing buildings that aren't in use can be used to give women shelter from the cold at least. So many ladies are left out in the cold with no income when they separate from their partners. They have no income, no home, no hope of getting another house. I see so many situations like that and that's why everyone's house is so overcrowded.

References

Centre for Equality Rights in Accommodation. (2002). *Housing in Canada: Barriers to Equality*. Toronto: Centre for Equality Rights in Accommodation.

"Homeless shelter on the rocks." (March 11, 2005). *Nunatsiaq News*. Iqaluit, Nunavut.

Jackson, P. (2006). *Information Sharing on Homelessness in the North*. National Secretariat on Homelessness. Unpublished document.

"Most Nunavut homeless suffer in silence." (October 5, 2001). *Nunatsiaq News*. Iqaluit, Nunavut.

Part 6 Organizing for Change

More than ever, our societies need women with a vision of the future.
—Rigoberta Menchú Tum, Nobel Peace Laureate, quoted in
"Appeal of the Nobel Peace Prize Laureates for the Children of
the World: International Decade for a Culture of Peace and
Non-Violence for the Children of the World (2001–2010)" (1999)

The final section of the text explores movements of women organizing for gender and economic justice within and across communities, cultures, and borders. The focus is primarily, though not exclusively, on contemporary neo-liberal times.

6a: Women's Movements in Canada

This section begins with an overview of historical and contemporary women's movements in Canada, and then takes up specific sites of struggle through activism by older women, younger women, and through broad coalitions of differently located women.

6b: Transnational Feminism: Challenges and Possibilities

We wind up this text with a section that examines the promise and pitfalls of organizing across national borders in transnational or global feminist movements. While problematizing historical notions of global "sisterhood," the articles emphasize the importance of transnational alliances that challenge the logic of neo-liberalism and global capitalism and work to secure women's economic, social, and cultural rights.

Supplement 38

Activist Insight:
History Shows the Importance of Breaking Silence

Paulette Senior

Paulette Senior is chief executive officer of the YWCA Canada, the largest and oldest women's multi-service organization in the country. An advocate for women's rights for over two decades, she has a rich background of involvement in community development and social justice issues. At the YWCA she works to raise awareness of gender issues, and leads the development of programs that support the economic and social empowerment of girls and women. Her contributions have been recognized through many awards, including the African Canadian Achievement Award and the Margot Franssen Leadership Award.

[....] "Breaking the silence" echoed through the women's movement of the 1970s and 1980s. It was a catch-phrase and an act of liberation. Women courageously took painful personal experiences public, sharing stories that exploded into public awareness and the public discourse as social issues demanding action. Women spoke out about violence and intimidation, about unsafe abortions, about rape. Lives hung in the balance. We took back the night, broke the silence, and vowed, "Never again." And we broke the silence for everyone, not just women and girls. Women named incest and child sexual abuse, lifting veils of secrecy, betrayal, and deceit that continue to unravel to this day, from the Truth and Reconciliation Commision on residential schools to the impenetrable mysteries of the Vatican.

Silence is not our friend. Silence is peril.

We need to keep hearing stories, keep listening to women. I've travelled to Iqaluit regularly over the last few years, working on development of YWCA Agvvik in Nunavut. Those visits have taught me that we cannot be silent about women's lives in northern Canada. We need to hear more about women's voices from the North, to hear what they have to say about the need for housing, for culturally appropriate services, for an end to violence, abuse, and poverty.

Last summer, a photo of two young boys asleep outside the NorthMart store in Iqaluit at 6 a.m. on a sunny morning was taken by someone passing by and sent to the local news media. The photo went viral, appearing across the country to shock and outrage. A follow-up interview in the *Globe and Mail* with the mother of one of the boys received less attention. "I thought I was doing them good by staying with their father. I finally realized I was abusing them, too, by letting them watch their father verbally, physically, mentally abuse me," said the 31-year-old mother of five. "When that started happening, my son, who was four or five years old, would walk out the door and not come home for a while.... It's a pattern I want to break." Without that mother's story, there are two boys inexplicably asleep on hard ground. With it, we know women in the North need more options when abuse starts, for themselves and their children. Women's stories and women's voices are essential to public awareness and to social development.

Speaking out and speaking up has been integral to change for women and girls in Canada since before women had the right to vote, hold public office, or own property after marriage. Since before women were legally "persons." To echo Nellie McClung, often quoted in these days of breaking barriers and disrupting silences, "Never retract, never explain, never apologize—get the thing done and let them howl." With pressure mounting to reduce reproductive choice and controls on guns, it is all too clear that, if we don't maintain a strong public presence of progressive women's voices, gains can be rolled back.

Feminism is woven into the fabric of life in North America as surely as Lisa Simpson plays saxophone and Oprah was key to Barack Obama becoming president. Our governor-general, Michaëlle Jean, clearly articulated feminist principles when she said, "Empower women and you will see a decrease in poverty, illiteracy, disease, and violence."

Women in Canada will not be pushed back to the days before women's shelters, access to safe abortion, and Charter protections, but shutting up will neither sustain us nor move us forward. Every gain that improved women's lives required speaking out, acting up, taking challenges to the courts—sometimes all of these and much more. In times like these, silence puts the rights of future generations at risk. Silence will not protect us or the next generation. Speaking out and struggling for change can.

Source: Paulette Senior, "History Shows the Importance of Breaking Silence," in *Speaking Truth to Power: A Reader on Canadian Women's Inequality Today*, eds. Trish Hennessey and Ed Finn (Ottawa: Canadian Centre for Policy Alternatives, 2010), 95–98.

Chapter 65

The Women's Movement in Canada

Jacquetta Newman and Linda White

Jacquetta Newman is associate professor of political science at King's University College at the University of Western Ontario, where she teaches courses on Canadian politics, women and politics, and comparative politics. Her research focuses on the politics of women's movements and other social movements, political identity formation, citizenship, and collective action. She is co-author of Women, Politics, and Public Policy: The Political Struggles of Canadian Women, *one chapter of which is excerpted below.*

Linda White is associate professor of political science at the University of Toronto, where she is also affiliated with the School of Public Policy and Governance, and the Centre for the Study of the United States. Her areas of research include comparative social and family policy (especially child care, early childhood education, and maternity and parental leave), comparative welfare states, and Canadian politics. Her publications include co-authorship of the book Women, Politics, and Public Policy: The Political Struggles of Canadian Women, *from which the following selection is taken.*

*****

Waves Eroding the Shores of Male Domination: Women's Struggles, Politics, and Movements

*****

It was not until the late nineteenth century that a self-conscious women's movement with an explicitly feminist orientation appeared as a distinct entity in Britain and North America. This we identify as feminism's first wave. Its most obvious feature was a demand for the right to vote, but it also involved more fundamental challenges to the denial of women's autonomy, including efforts to effect social change by campaigning for reproductive control and better working conditions in female trades. The second wave is associated with the emergence of the modern women's liberation movement at the end of the 1960s. It was a reaction to the perceived middle-class, institutionally focused liberalism of the first wave suffragists and to the inequality women experienced in the civil rights, student, and new left movements of the 1960s. It stressed a more "personal" politics recognizing the structurally limited nature of women's lives, protesting inequality in the family, and claiming control over women's bodies through sexual emancipation. There was continuity between the two waves since, for many women, the struggle continued to involve demands for access to political decision making and issues of workplace and economic rights. As with second wave feminism, third wave feminism presents a reaction to its precursor, in particular the monolithic and unrepresentative conception of womanhood or sisterhood. The third wave stresses the differing identities of women and recognition of the complex webs of oppression many women experience. It also requires recognition that many other women, not only Western, white, middle-class, educated women and not all of them feminists, have been explicitly involved in actions to achieve an end to their oppression.

*****

When we look at the women's movement we see a diverse movement with a rich history, constructed on growing understandings of the experiences of women and the need for action to bring about social change. It is not especially cohesive, homogeneous, or given to espousing one specific goal but has developed as women have elaborated strategies to end women's oppression and make their lives better.

The Canadian Women's Movement

*****

The First Wave: Political and Civil Rights

[…] From the earliest days, Canadian women have been involved in productive and remunerative work outside and inside the home. Widows and single women found ways of supporting themselves, ranging from teaching to domestic service to prostitution. For the majority of married women, domestic work such as farm work, weaving, sewing, taking in laundry, or looking after boarders was intrinsic to the family income. […]

However, practical realities are one thing but social norms another. While women had a stake in and worked hard in early Canada, traditional views of the division of the sexes and sexual inequality were maintained. Women were not seen as public persons in their own right in either the legal or political sphere. The assumption was that a husband had the right to control his wife's person and a father his daughter's until marriage. In rape cases, redress was not for the victim but for the father or husband because, to put it crudely, his goods had been spoiled (Prentice et al. 1988, 84).

*****

With our early twenty-first century values, it is not surprising that we consider the first wave of the women's movement quite conservative, accepting as it did the position of women in the private sphere. This was the nature of the "social" feminism or "maternal" feminism characteristic of the first wave in Canada. The majority of the women activists who emerged in this period largely accepted the private/public division (Brooks 2000; Prentice et al. 1988; Valverde 1991). In the last quarter of the nineteenth century, Canada was experiencing many social changes that affected Canadian families. Growing industrialization, immigration, urbanization, and imperial decline all had an effect on Canadian society. One result of the disruption, it was argued, was an increase in public drunkenness. Drunkenness became associated with a number of socially unacceptable behaviours—increased domestic violence, prostitution, desertion, and alcoholism—that threatened the family structure. Women's organizations focused their energies on the moral issues surrounding the family and the perceived threat to its maintenance. Underlying their arguments for a greater role in dealing with these issues was the belief that because of women's position in the private world, characterized by maternal graces and morality, they would bring virtue and morality to decisions made in the public sphere.

Charity was the significant feature of first wave feminism in Canada. Women's organizations focusing on good works flourished, some associated with churches and others more secular. These associations, clubs, and groups functioned to bring together and create networks of women barred from public political and economic work. They also provided space for women to work for social reform, as many saw themselves as members of a reform movement committed to raising the standard as well as the quality of life in Canada. This reformist impulse in turn brought them to political action for suffrage and the right to political participation. As campaigns for social reform expanded, particularly those dealing with temperance and prostitution, women found that more political leverage was required to achieve action from national and provincial legislatures. An obvious way to create political pressure was the vote.

*****

There is a significant upper-middle-class flavour to the social feminism discussed above. Not all women had the ability to pursue charity: some received charity themselves, and others could be considered victims of the zeal of charitable social reformers. Many middle- and lower-class women were essential to the family income and in some cases provided the only source of income. For example, middle- and lower-class women continued to work on farms, in domestic service, and as teachers, laundresses, or boarding house operators. In addition, with the growth in manufacturing, more and more women became employed as home workers paid by the piece. This work was rarely recognized publicly and was open to abuse. Women workers were also abused in industrial work outside the home, predominantly in the textile industry, where hierarchical work relations in factories put women below male workers and their remuneration was barely a living wage (Prentice et al. 1988, 125–7).

Working women were suspicious of upper-middle-class women and their zeal for social reform, particularly prohibition, seeing their efforts as attempts at class domination (Prentice et al. 1988). Support for suffrage among working women emerged out of the belief that women should be on a more equal footing with men, but their primary concerns related to surviving in the working world and obtaining better wages and better work opportunities.

The obvious route for the collective organization of working women was through unionization. Some women did become involved and in a few cases formed their own women's unions and associations. While women have historically participated in union mobilizations supporting both male and female worker demands, some union activities in the early twentieth century took on a female character. For example, women were the predominant participants in the strike by Bell Telephone operators in 1907 and in the Eaton's factory strike of 1912 (Prentice et al. 1988, 130). However, women's union militancy was limited for a number of reasons: (1) it was difficult to organize women scattered among small shops or in home-based manufacturing; (2) unionization efforts tended to focus on organizing skilled male workers; (3) male unionists were often suspicious of and hostile toward women in the labour force, accusing them of taking men's jobs and keeping wages low; and (4) domestic obligations limited women's freedom to attend union meetings.

There was another, smaller group in the first wave movement, women concerned with equal rights generally. This group demanded not only political rights but also political, economic, and social equality. Their push for suffrage and political rights was based on "arguments of simple justice" and "a viewpoint that stressed how much women resembled men, and how unjust it was that they should have fewer rights" (Prentice et al. 1988, 169). However, like working and union women, equity feminists were a marginal presence in a movement dominated by the more mainstream social reforming social feminists.

By the first decades of the twentieth century, a number of groups of women were struggling for women's rights. An organization of interest to us in this period is the National Council of Women (NCW). The NCW was a national network of women's organizations that formally advocated voting rights for women. It was formed in 1893 as a national umbrella organization with a membership made up of a diverse range of women's organizations that chose to affiliate. It had a fairly broad focus, advocating not only for suffrage and temperance through prohibition but also for better working conditions for female domestic and factory employees, the rights of married women to property, and measures related to public health (Burt 1994; Prentice et al. 1988). Although dominated by upper-middle-class urban social feminists, the NCW offered a setting where social and equal rights views could coexist and cooperate. However, tensions existed in a number of areas. Arguments arose between social feminists and more radical feminists regarding the militancy or lack of militancy of the suffrage campaigns. Further tensions arose around class divisions. There were significant rural/urban differences between Western Canada and the East. And the movement remained white and predominantly Anglo-Saxon.

However, the coalitional nature of the movement and the mix of feminisms reflected in it resulted in some interesting qualities that the movement would expand on and develop once the surge of the early twentieth century ended. First, suffrage was not the only focus of the Canadian movement; it was not the "obsessive goal" that it was in other countries. Second, while the NCW could act as a voice for many Canadian women and did play an important role, the movement did not present a single unified face. Its strength lay in its diversity. Third, unlike the British and, to a lesser extent, US movements, the Canadian struggle for suffrage focused on the less militant and less violent activities of petitioning, lobbying public appeals and education, and using private connections with politicians (Prentice et al. 1988). This was a result of social feminists dominating the movement. It remained for the most part non-violent and less militant, shying away from hunger strikes and attacks on property and politicians. Consequently, even when the movement lost a unifying focus and much of its surge when suffrage was achieved and when significant irreparable cracks appeared in the coalition as a result of disagreements over World War I (1914–18), it did not disappear.

*****

With World War II (1939–45), many [...] social norms began to change more rapidly. Large numbers of women entered the labour force, answering the growing call for workers in industries supporting the war effort. [...] The war-related labour shortage also led to the creation of women's paramilitary organizations and their admittance into the armed forces after 1942. Women's entry into public life en masse did not result in equality: women continued to be placed in subordinate positions, and traditional attitudes tended to prevail. However, women's public participation and their portrayal as public women (for example, the "emancipated" Rosie the riveter) created a context that worked to undermine the traditional norms of the private housewife, mother, and daughter. [...]

The Second Wave Hits the Beach: Personal Feminist Politics

The second wave of the women's movement is often categorized as a "new" social movement, one of the movements that emerged out of the political and social protests of the late 1960s. These movements were characterized as a new form of protest, which emphasized spontaneity and imagination in political action and an anti-bureaucratic and anti-institutional view of organization. The women's liberation stream of the second wave emerged as young women reacted to their experiences of being marginalized by male colleagues in the student, new left, and peace movements and the hippie counterculture, movements characterized by the progressive language of liberation and equality. In their reaction to such treatment, these women rejected the traditional political structures and ideologies put forward by these movements with regard to the role of women.

The second wave movement represented a new generation of women, and the analysis and aims expressed were much more secular and radical than the Christian morality of social feminism. It encompassed a wide variety of goals and groups, and while, as Sandra Burt (1994, 215) argues, the distinctions between them are not completely clear-cut, a number of visions can be identified. Equal rights feminism appeared dominant in English Canada, with a focus on attaining equal access for women to education, employment, and political representation. Socialist feminists were active, arguing for the overthrow of both class and gender divisions and working to build links between private and public production undertaken by women. Radical feminists also emerged, arguing that "the personal is political" and that women were oppressed by a naturalized system of patriarchy perpetuated in the everyday practices of women's lives (Burt 1994). The second wave also saw the appearance of many small women's groups that voiced the concerns of specific women's identities. These groups represented aboriginal women, Inuit women, black women, lesbians, farm women, immigrant and refugee women, and so on.

*****

The transition from the first to the second wave was a response to the changing nature of Canadian society, to the developing views and understandings of women's oppression (based on and responding to those developed in the first wave), and to the women's movement's relationship to the protest movements of the 1960s. The organizational network of women's groups was much more developed in the second wave than it had been in the first, but the first wave and the interwave period had created the base on which the second could build and expand. [...]

*****

A growing number of women were employed outside the home and enrolled in post-secondary education, yet a double standard applied to these women, and the subordinate position forced on them was all too apparent. Young women who entered post-secondary education institutions found that the concerns, experiences, and history of women were not represented in the curriculum. They found that their ability to achieve their ambitions was limited once they graduated compared to those of men. Not the least of their problems was a general assumption that they attended university to find good husbands—the infamous "MRS" degree. In the workforce, although most of the women employed in wartime industry went back to the home at the end of the war, the number of women at work, both single and married, soon began to rise steadily. By 1967 the total number of women at work equaled the number employed at the height of the war effort (Wilson 1991). Many of these women found that while work was available to them and federal legal guarantees for equal pay had been legislated in 1956, they were unlikely to advance in their careers as their male colleagues did, and as a whole, they continued to be paid significantly less than men.

In short, the social norms governing the position and appropriate behaviour of women were vastly different from women's realities, and the gap between norm and reality made women's lives very difficult. This led to a growing disenchantment that found its way into the editorial pages of Canada's major women's magazine of the time, *Chatelaine*, and made Betty Friedan's *The Feminine Mystique* (published in 1963) a bestseller. Women came to recognize that the language of equality prevalent in the period of affluence following World War II did not really apply to them. While they had become legal "persons" in 1929, they were not individual citizens. Their role in society was still defined by their position as mothers and wives based on their sex, not by their existence as equal public individuals, which would require them and their work to be equally valued.

Formal access to rights was clearly not enough to guarantee women's equality. Women's subordination was maintained throughout society, in political institutions, the workplace, schools, churches, clubs, and so on. Women's lives remained structurally and culturally limited, and the way to change this was to make the inequalities in both the public and the private spheres transparent. For women, there was no distinction between private and public: they had to overcome subordination in all spheres of their lives. Consequently, the personal became political, the private public, and old and new feminisms were brought together.

The result was a mobilization of women across the country to change their situation across a broad spectrum of political, economic, and cultural structures. Politically, women pressed for better representation at all levels of government and the bureaucracy and greater sensitivity to women's needs in decision making. In education, women pushed for curricula more appropriate for girls and women, equal opportunity in educational advancement, and the establishment of women's studies at the university level. In the workplace, women demanded equal pay for equal work, equality in career advancement, and an end to workplace sexual harassment. Both inside and outside mainstream politics, issues of sexuality, a women's right to control her own body, birth control, violence against women, domestic violence, pornography, and rape became lightning rods for women's activism. The focus was also on the cultural, as women sought to change the social norms around the naturalized subordinate place accorded to them in the media, in language, and in society in general.

Closely associated with this was the practice of consciousness-raising. Consciousness-raising brought small groups of women together to share their experiences of men, work, sex and sexuality, and so on. These sessions allowed participants to informally identify their oppression and better understand its roots. Consciousness-raising groups fostered a sense of shared experience, anger, and ultimately empowerment. Women came to understand that their personal grievances were political. As women transformed their anger into political action, consciousness-raising groups became a significant part of grassroots organizing. Informal consciousness-raising groups brought women to formal organizations. [...]

The importance of consciousness-raising groups in bringing women into the movement and in creating "womanspace" should not be underestimated. [...] The creation of womanspace and "womanculture" was a key feature of radical feminism's vision of a woman's politics that reclaimed an identity connecting and celebrating womanhood. Throughout the second wave period, women established women-centred services—from rape crisis centres, health centres, abortion and contraception services, safe houses for battered and homeless women, centres for single mothers, women's studies programs, magazines, journals, art galleries, cultural centres, and publishing companies run for and by women. These vibrant grassroots efforts came to illustrate the second wave's feminist character of "women doing it for themselves."

As in the first wave, there were significant disputes and divisions within the second wave movement. Radical, Marxist, and socialist feminists, and those who identified with the women's liberation movement, held anti-hierarchical and anti-institutional views, while liberal feminist groups maintained a "commitment to the ordinary political process, a belief in the welfare state, a belief in the efficiency of state action in general to remedy injustices" (Vickers 1992, 40).

In addition, the relationship between English Canadian and French Canadian feminists was often tenuous; French Canadian feminism's association with Quebec nationalism, while both advantageous and disadvantageous for the Quebec movement, resulted in breaks in the relationship with English Canadian feminists, particularly during constitutional discussions regarding the position of Quebec in Canada. Disputes also emerged throughout the 1970s between the growing number of groups of minority women and the white middle-class–dominated movement.

*****

The Royal Commission on the Status of Women and the National Action Committee (NAC)

In Canada, governments facing controversial issues often establish a royal commission or inquiry as a convenient way of appearing to address an issue without actually taking action through policy. Nonetheless, in the late 1960s it was difficult for women to obtain even this symbolic action. As Monique Begin (1992, 26), secretary to the commission when it was finally established, observes, "women did not represent ... a constituency on the political agenda of the Canadian State." Many events and women came together to force the establishment of the Royal Commission on the Status of Women. Canada had recently undergone a national evaluation of its identity with the Royal Commission on Bilingualism and Biculturalism, which tabled its reports in 1965 and 1967. In addition, English Canadian women's groups were impressed by the US Commission on the Status of Women (1961–3), headed by former First Lady Eleanor Roosevelt (Begin 1992). The timing was also opportune because the Liberal government of the time was a minority government, with the New Democratic Party (NDP) holding the balance of power. However, even with pressure from the newly allied CEW [Committee for the Equality of Women] and FFQ [Fédération des femmes du Québec], women in the media, and female members of Parliament such as Liberal cabinet minister Judy LaMarsh and NDP member Grace MacInnis, it still took a threat of mobilizing large violent protests by two million women on Parliament Hill to compel the government to commit to a commission. [...]

On 16 February 1967, the government of Lester Pearson established the Royal Commission on the Status of Women (RCSW). Its mandate was wide-ranging: "to inquire into and report upon the status of women in Canada, and to recommend what steps might be taken by the Federal Government to ensure for women equal opportunities with men in all aspects of Canadian society." This included the "laws and practices under federal jurisdiction concerning the political rights of women," the present and potential role of women in the labour force, marriage and divorce, taxation issues, and immigration and citizenship laws (RCSW 1970, ix).

The reaction of Canadian women was stunning. In response to brochures distributed in supermarkets and libraries, the commission received 468 briefs and "1000 letters of opinion" (RCSW 1970, ix). During hearings across Canada in 1968, some 890 witnesses appeared. In addition, 40 special studies were commissioned and published separately. The final report, released in September 1970, listed 167 recommendations and covered issues of economics, education, the law, reproductive control, child care, the needs of aboriginal, Inuit, and minority women, and women's representation in public life. The report itself represented a lengthy analysis of the structural nature of women's inequality in Canada and a blueprint for its alleviation.

We spend time reviewing the RCSW because it was such a central event in Canadian second wave feminism. More than 30 years after its release, it remains an unfulfilled dream of what Canadian women need to ensure their equality. When it was released, it was, as one *Toronto Star* journalist described it, a ticking time bomb and a persuasive call to revolution (Begin 1992, 22). Government action on the report was at best slow and in some areas— national daycare and abortion most obviously—non-existent. However, for women's groups, the inquiry process illustrated what the mobilization of Canadian women could do, and the process of preparing briefs and making recommendations helped to spread feminist ideals among Canadian women's groups.

Significantly, it provided a target and a set of goals for women's organizing and confirmed that the personal grievances of many women were indeed political. The recommendations of the RCSW stood as a tangible list on which women's groups could focus their mobilizing efforts. They were also a set of criteria against which government action and inaction could be measured. One important feature was recommendation 155, which called on the federal government to fund women's groups and thus facilitate their access to public life (RCSW 1970, 49). Finally, the document outlined a relationship of Canadian women to the state framed in the logic that state action could remedy injustices through public policy choices based on a belief in social and political rights. As such, it fit comfortably with the language and activity of liberal feminists.

*****

The RCSW marks a point at which many of the segments of the movement and streams of feminist thought came together around a common set of goals. This coalition was given an organizational identity in 1972 with the establishment of the National Action Committee on the Status of Women, which was intended to pressure government and ensure that the recommendations of the RCSW were implemented. As Jill Vickers, Pauline Rankin, and Christine Appelle (1993) describe it, NAC was a "parliament of women," bringing both "reformist" liberal feminists and radical feminists into a coalition, even if tenuous.

*****

Member groups include women operating local women's centres and shelters, minority and aboriginal women, academic and business women, and women from the trade union movement. NAC'S priorities in 2005 were wide ranging, listing poverty, child care, violence against women, participation in governance and international institutions, protection of the rights of indigenous,

immigrant, and refugee women, anti-racism, anti-homophobia, rights in health education, training, employment, housing, reproductive autonomy, and environmental issues (http://www.nac-
cca.ca/about/about_e.htm). [...]

[...] Initially, NAC focused on lobbying efforts and establishing a close working relationship with the state. This worked well, as the booming Canadian economy allowed the
Liberal government of Pierre Trudeau to maintain a "spirit of generosity and openness"
(Begin 1997, 17) and to increase spending in support of women's initiatives. However, circumstances changed in the latter half of the 1970s as the economy took a downturn. Faced
with stagflation in the economy and a significant increase in demands from a diversifying
women's movement, governments became much more hostile. Ironically, Begin (1997, 17)
identifies 1975, the International Year of the Woman, as the start of the change: "it was
the last year in which women perceived a pro-active cooperation between women's groups
and government." While legal and legislative changes were achieved after this point, such
changes were commonly achieved in conflict with governments rather than in cooperation.
Tellingly, many of these achievements were gained through the courts rather than through
government. NAC [now defunct, a victim of government cuts and backlash] adapted to the
changing climate by adopting a more confrontational approach and working much more
through the court system and less so through the government.

Women and the Charter of Rights and Freedoms

The next focus of mass mobilization for the women's movement in Canada was the repatriation
and reform of the Canadian constitution in the early 1980s. While women mobilized around
the possibility of attaining constitutionally guaranteed equality rights, they were also motivated
by the need to protect the rights of aboriginal women, employment rights, economic rights,
reproductive rights, and rights within the family. Across Canada, women closely followed, discussed, and researched the constitutional proposals and their position within them. This activity intensified when the federal government unilaterally brought forward its proposals, which
included a Charter of Rights containing equality provisions that women's groups found too
weak (Dobrowolsky 2000). In parliamentary hearings on the proposal, women's groups such as
NAC, the Canadian Advisory Committee on the Status of Women, the National Association
of Women and the Law, and the Canadian Abortion Rights Action League took similar stands
regarding explicit mention of women's equality, but they also raised the broader issues of women's
representation on the Supreme Court and in Parliament, education and reproductive rights, the
status of aboriginal women, and discrimination on the basis of marital status, sexual orientation,
and political belief. There were some exceptions: the Fédération des femmes du Québec chose not
to appear, and groups representing aboriginal women, namely the Native Women's Association
of Canada and Indian Rights for Indian Women, speaking from the position of being in both
Canadian society and aboriginal society, were much more critical of the broader constitutional
proposals (Dobrowolsky 2000). The response of the parliamentary committee was supportive of
the positions outlined by women's groups because it fit with the government's interest in having
emphasis placed on the Charter in its constitutional package. As a result, some of the women's
movement's demands were met, particularly those around equality guarantees. Other demands,
however, were left out. [...]

*****

The combined efforts of the movement had influenced the process of constitutional change, with most of the movement's demands for equality rights in section 15 met. [...] Section 15(1) of the Constitution Act of 1982 (part 1 of which constitutes the Canadian Charter of Rights and Freedoms) sets out explicit equality rights stating, "every individual is equal before and under the law and has the right to the equal protection and equal benefit of the law without discrimination and, in particular, without discrimination based on race, national or ethnic origin, colour, religion, sex, age or mental or physical disability" (http://laws.justicte.gc.ca/en/charter//). [...]

Constitutional guarantees of equal rights opened up a new avenue for pressing women's concerns. Women's groups started in earnest to press the courts to interpret the section 15 provisions to mean "equality of result" as a means of ending systemic discrimination. Groups such as the National Association of Women and the Law and the Women's Legal Education and Action Fund became much more prominent in the movement.

Agreement on a liberal interpretation of equality rights was not unanimous, however. Many women remained committed to working on issues outside the courts, focusing less on the abstract language of constitutional rights and more on the reality of their everyday lives. [...]

Within the labour force, issues of pay equity, discrimination in promotion, and the relegation of women to the badly paid pink ghetto of "women's work" were significant. But concerns were not limited to pay and achieving a "living wage" for women. They also included the culture of the workplace, such as sexualized dress codes for such women workers as secretaries, cashiers, nurses, and flight attendants, which often highlighted their sexuality to the detriment of comfort and job efficiency, and, even more disturbing, the acceptance of sexual harassment on the job. Outside of the labour force, women pressed for recognition of their unpaid work in the home. Some of these grievances could and would be pursued through legal structures, but others required concerted work by women through unions, informally in the workplace, and in grassroots networks of women.

The effort to change the culture regarding sexual harassment and domestic work was indicative of the movement's demand that the inequality and politics of the private sphere had to be recognized. This extended to battles regarding reproductive autonomy, the accessibility of contraception, and abortion. Again, these battles took place on a number of fronts. In the legal and legislative spheres, they were fought as issues of freedom of choice, discrimination because of pregnancy, and the right to "security of person." In local communities, they were addressed by organizations such as Planned Parenthood and women's health clinics.

Much of this effort concerned the recognition and protection of women's autonomous control over their selves. As a result, one of the major issues during this period was violence against women. At the beginning of the twenty-first century, the idea that violence against women is unacceptable is a "no-brainer." However, that has not always been the case, and it can be argued that one of the successes of the second wave movement was the change in public attitudes and norms regarding domestic violence. In demanding amendments to the Criminal Code and pursuing charges and protections through the courts, women's groups were able to change the structures governing violent behaviour. They also made changes by providing services for abused and assaulted women through networks of shelters and rape crisis centres. Slowly, general social attitudes changed regarding the acceptability of violence against women. However, the large number of cash-strapped and over-subscribed shelters and rape crisis centres testifies to the fact that such violence is far from eradicated. [...]

These problems remain difficult to solve. However, the women's movement continued to address them through a number of avenues, including courts, government, and community action. [...]

Backlash: The Tide Goes Out on the Second Wave

The demands that the women's movement put forward required significant changes in society. Thus, it was not surprising that resistance and counter-movements would emerge. In 1964 a new women's group appeared on the scene, not an unusual happening since groups were popping up all across Canada. However, what set this group apart was its message. REAL Women—Realistic, Equal, Active, for Life—promoted an anti-feminist vision focused on preserving the "traditional family" from the changing nature of Canadian society and the feminist agenda. Members saw their mandate as advocating for legislative and legal protection of the "Judeo-Christian" understanding of marriage, the central role of women in the home, and the rights of the fetus. REAL Women and provincial organizations, such as the Alberta Federation of Women United for Families, claimed to represent a large silent majority of Canadians who were not feminists (MacIvor 1996). By the end of the 1980s, the group had found a willing ally in the Conservative government in Ottawa, which was generally hostile to the demands of women's and feminist groups. The emergence of REAL Women as a national actor marked the arrival of the backlash against feminism in Canada. The tide was turning against the second wave.

What is remarkable is how successful both the government and the media were in redefining the image of Canadian feminism: the movement was no longer seen to be about women's social and political equality but as just one of many "special interests" making unreasonable demands on the greater society. The image of feminist politics was transformed from that of equality-seeking to the seeking of greater advantage and superior treatment—in other words, inequality-seeking. For governments facing difficult economic times, this transformation made it that much easier to cut funding to women's programs and causes.

The cuts and vilification were felt across the movement, and the mainstream movement discovered that even legal opportunities could backfire. Those involved in the counter-movement against feminism, such as REAL Women, found that the Charter and its equality provisions could be used to oppose affirmative action, pregnancy leaves, the right of a pregnant woman to choose abortion without the father's consent, and similar policies and could even be used to support the rights of those accused of sexual assault against those of the victim (Mandel 1992, 258).

*****

[…] As the Canadian state embraced neo-conservatism, Canadians became increasingly ambivalent about feminism, government funds and support were cut, and more and more women identified themselves as "I'm not a feminist but …," the movement became ever more frustrated and defensive.

"I'll Be a Post-feminist in the Post-patriarchy": The Third Wave?

[…] By the 1980s philosophical currents were emerging that pointed to much more complex understandings of what defines womanhood. While many of these new writings were criticized as being too abstract and academic, they were not without influence in the movement. Faced with decreasing support from the state and greater society, feminism appeared to become much more self-reflexive and introspective and took on a much more cultural thrust.

That the focus should become cultural to a much greater extent is not surprising. Feminism had become increasingly concerned with working out the complexity and multiplicity of what "woman" meant as an identity. Third wave feminism emerged as aboriginal women, women of colour, poor women, lesbians, and young women pointed out that their personal experiences were derived from intersecting and reinforcing identities rather than from a homogeneous category of woman. They emphasized the complexities and ambiguities of people's lives, illustrating the conflicts between equality and sameness. The third wave was built on concepts of difference rather than sameness and particularity rather than universality (Arneil 1999, 87). Third wave feminism became about gaining control and re-appropriating all possible identities available to women and celebrating all of those empowered selves. This project to appropriate and celebrate identities and challenge systemic oppression in the social norms made culture a significant sphere of conflict. Thus, while the political face of the movement appeared to decline, its activities could still be subsumed under the mantle of the movement.

*****

[...] The fragmented and self-reflexive nature of the third wave certainly raises questions about the movement as a political project. Arneil (1999, 187–8) sets a hopeful note: "the third wave is washing over all feminists as they are forced to grapple seriously with the central issues of women's perspective, and its implications for previous formulations of politics, history and knowledge." Can a politics be found in this world of plural identity in which seemingly contradictory grievances around sameness and difference are brought together? For Arneil (1999, 189–90) and third wave feminists, the third wave addresses this conundrum by adding "a new dimension to a process already underway. More than anything else, the new generation feminists are calling for a new understanding of the 'personal is political.'"

Conclusion: Women and Social Movement Politics: The Power of Small-P Politics

*****

[...] It is important at this point to note the success of the women's movement through the twentieth century in bringing the politics of women's existences into the open and making their oppression transparent. The movement has been most successful in achieving its demands for legal recognition of equality. It also has had success in influencing the policy decisions of the state, although as demonstrated during the 1980s and 1990s, the level of success in that regard depends on the broader economic and social context.

[...] It is easy to pronounce either that the women's movement has met its goals or that it is dead, much as *Time* magazine announced in June 1998. However, such a view represents a belief that the activities that take place in social and cultural life are not fully political. Studies have largely been confined to a narrowly and conventionally defined idea of politics. [...]

In the first wave, women's local organizing resulted in policy changes regarding regulation of alcohol and prostitution. While these policies and the vision of many social feminists were overly harsh towards particular classes of women, they did assert that women had a role in determining the public good. In the second wave, women's efforts to establish rape crisis centres, shelters for abused women, counselling groups, and contraceptive and family planning services were also driven by an understanding of the public good. All of these activities were connected to public policy—by making transparent the services women required, providing models for service provision, and often becoming the structures through which policy was applied by state funding. Even in a limited definition of politics, these activities are political when viewed this way.

*****

At the beginning at the twenty-first century, we can look back and observe that the twentieth century was tumultuous for Canadian women, even revolutionary. Yet, as the wave metaphor reminds us, women have not experienced a steady progression forward. Instead, progress has come in a series of steps forward, and then back, like waves eroding a shoreline.

References

Arneil, Barbara. 1999. *Politics and feminism*. Oxford: Blackwell.

Begin, Monique. 1992. "The Royal Commission on the Status of Women in Canada: Twenty years later." In Constance Backhouse and David H. Flaherty (Eds), *Challenging times: The Women's Movement in Canada and the United States*, 21–38. Montreal and Kingston: McGill-Queen's University Press.

Begin, Monique. 1997. "The Canadian government and the commission's report." In Caroline Andrew and Sanda Rodgers (Eds), *Women and the Canadian state*, 13–26. Montreal: McGill-Queen's University Press.

Brooks, Stephen. 2000. *Canadian democracy: An introduction*. 2nd ed. Don Mills, ON: Oxford University Press.

Burt, Sandra. 1994. "The women's movement: Working to transform public life." In James P. Bickerton and Alain-G. Gagnon (Eds), *Canadian politics*, 207–23. 2nd ed. Peterborough, ON: Broadview Press.

Dobrowolsky, Alexandra. 2000. *The politics of pragmatism: Women, representation, and constitutionalism in Canada*. Don Mills, ON: Oxford University Press.

Friedan, Betty. 1963. *The feminine mystique*. New York: Dell.

MacIvor, Heather. 1996. *Women and politics in Canada*. Peterborough, ON: Broadview Press.

Mandel, Michael. 1992. *The Charter of Rights and the legalization of politics in Canada*. Toronto: Thompson Educational Publishing.

Prentice, Alison, Paula Bourne, Gail Cuthbert Brandt, Beth Light, Wendy Mitchinson, and Naomi Black. 1988. *Canadian women: A history*. Toronto: Harcourt Brace Jovanovich.

RCSW (Royal Commission on the Status of Women in Canada). 1970. *Report of the Royal Commission on the Status of Women in Canada*. Ottawa: Information Canada.

Valverde, Marianna. 1991. *The age of light, soap, and water: Moral reform in English Canada 1885–1925*. Toronto: McClelland and Stewart.

Vickers, Jill. 1992. "The intellectual origins of the women's movements in Canada." In Constance Backhouse and David H. Flaherty (Eds), *Challenging times: The women's movement in Canada and the United States*, 39–60. Montreal and Kingston: McGill-Queen's University Press.

Vickers, Jill, Pauline Rankin, and Christine Appelle. 1993. *Politics as if women mattered: A political analysis of the National Action Committee on the Status of Women*. Toronto: University of Toronto Press.

Wilson, Susannah. 1991. *Women, families, and work*. 3rd ed. Toronto: McGraw-Hill Ryerson.

Chapter 66

2,000 Good Reasons to March

Fédération des femmes du Québec

Fédération des femmes du Québec (FFQ) is a feminist organization founded in the 1960s that brings together individuals and groups with the goal of promoting and defending the interests and rights of women, and fighting against all forms of violence, discrimination, marginalization, and exclusion toward women. The FFQ is especially well known for organizing the highly successful Bread and Roses March in Canada in 1995, and for initiating the World March of Women, which took place in over 150 countries in 2000.

The idea to hold a world march of women in the year 2000 was born out of the experience of the Women's March against Poverty, which took place in Québec in 1995. This march, initiated by the Fédération des femmes du Québec (FFQ), was hugely successful. Fifteen thousand people greeted the 850 women who marched for 10 days to win nine demands related to economic justice. The entire Québec women's movement mobilized for the march, as did many other segments of the population. The presence of women from countries of the South in that march reminded us of the importance of global solidarity-building.

The Beijing Conference later that year proved that women everywhere are struggling for equality, development, and peace more than ever before. It was in Beijing that we made our first proposal to organize an international women's march. The International Preparatory Meeting for the World March was held in Montreal, Québec, Canada, on October 16–18, 1998; 140 delegates from 65 countries adopted the platform of world demands stated here and developed a plan of action for the World March of Women in the Year 2000.

The World March of Women in the Year 2000 is an action to improve women's living conditions. More precisely, the specific demands centre on the issues of poverty and violence against women. The international meeting held in October 1998 was only one of countless initiatives from civil society where women reaffirmed their determination to eradicate poverty and violence against women, with the conviction that this change must come from a large-scale mobilization of women around the world.

We Are Counting on the Presence of Thousands, Hopefully Millions, of Women in the Streets in the Year 2000!

We, the women of the world, are marching against the poverty that crushes four billion people on our planet, most of whom are women.

We are also marching to protest violence against women because this is a fundamental negation of human rights.

Against neoliberal capitalism that turns human beings, especially women, into an increasingly disposable, interchangeable, and exploitable commodity. Against the subordination of individual and collective rights to the dictates of financial markets. Against the progressive disappearance of political power in the face of rising economic power.

Against the complicit silence of international financial institutions that sprang up after the Second World War (International Monetary Fund, World Bank, World Trade Organization) and other international and regional institutions: they perpetuate the exploitation of peoples by imposing structural adjustment programs in the South, deficit fighting and social program cutbacks in the North, and by concocting trade and other kinds of agreements such as the Multinational Agreement on Investment.

Against patriarchal ideology, still largely dominant today, under which violence against women continues to be a universal fact of life: spousal violence, sexual abuse, genital mutilation, homophobic and racist attacks, systematic rape in wartime, etc.

Against all wars. Against threats to the planet's survival and to a healthy environment.

Against all forms of violence against women, adolescent girls, and children. Against all forms of violence perpetrated against the most vulnerable women in society.

We are marching against poverty and for sharing of wealth, against violence against women, and for the control and respect of our bodies.

What Kind of a World Do We Live In?

We live in a world where, at the turn of the millennium, profound disparities still exist between North and South, rich and poor, women and men, human beings and Nature.

We live in a world where unrestricted globalization of markets, coupled with unbridled speculation, are giving rise to extreme poverty. A total of 1.3 billion people, of whom 70 percent are women and children, live in abject poverty. It is a world that is hungry, a world where the richest 20 percent possess 83 percent of the planet's revenue.

We live in a world where the State is neglecting its responsibilities and obligations due to the dictatorship of the market. It is a world where institutions such as the World Bank and the International Monetary Fund impose their rules on governments through structural adjustment policies.

We live in a world where discrimination against women is the main source of gender inequality. It is a world where, since time immemorial, women have contributed to humanity's development without their work being truly acknowledged. Thus, although women actually supply two-thirds of work hours, they only receive one-tenth of world revenue. Since the earliest times, the economy, no matter what kind, has been largely based on women's work, whether paid or unpaid, visible or invisible.

We live in a world where violence against women continues to be a universal reality. Conjugal violence, sexual aggression, genital mutilation, rape in wartime are the plight of thousands of women. Racism and homophobia add to the bleak picture.

What Kind of World Do We Want to Live In?

Women from all over the world are marching so that in the third millennium, their fundamental freedoms, indissociable from their human rights and undeniably universal in nature, are implemented once and for all. They are determined in their belief that all human rights are interdependent and that the values of equality, justice, peace, and solidarity will predominate.

Women from all over the world are marching in the knowledge that they have a responsibility to participate in political, economic, cultural, and social life.

Women from all over the world are marching against all forms of violence and discrimination to which they are subjected.

Women from all over the world are marching to consolidate actions, based on principles of cooperation and sharing, aimed at instituting crucial changes.

Women are marching in affirmation of their desire to live in a better world.

Our Demands

Central to the purpose of the World March are the demands to end poverty and violence against women (drafted at the International Preparatory Meeting in October, 1998).

TO ELIMINATE POVERTY, WE DEMAND:

1. That all States adopt a legal framework and strategies aimed at eliminating poverty.

    States must implement national anti-poverty policies, programs, action plans, and projects, including specific measures to eliminate women's poverty and to ensure their economic and social independence through the exercise of their right to:

    • Education;
    • Employment, with statutory protection for work in the home and in the informal sectors of the economy;
    • Pay equity and equality at the national and international levels;
    • Association and unionization;
    • Property and control of safe water;
    • Decent housing;
    • Health care and social protection;
    • Culture;
    • Life-long income security;
    • Natural and economic resources (credit, property, vocational training, technologies);
    • Full citizenship, including in particular recognition of civil identity and access to relevant documents (identity card); and
    • Minimum social wage.

    States must guarantee, as a fundamental right, the production and distribution of food to ensure food security for their populations.

    States must develop incentives to promote the sharing of family responsibilities (education and care of children and domestic tasks) and provide concrete support to families such as daycare adapted to parents' work schedules, community kitchens, programs to assist children with their school work, etc.

    States must promote women's access to decision-making positions. They must make provisions to ensure women's equal participation in decision-making political bodies.

    States must ratify and observe the labour standards of the International Labour Office (ILO). They must enforce observance of national labour standards in free trade zones.

    States and international organizations should take measures to counter and prevent corruption.

All acts, pieces of legislation, regulations, and positions taken by governments will be assessed in the light of indicators such as the human poverty index (HPI), introduced in the Human Development Report 1997; the human development index (HDI), put forth by the United Nations Development Program; the gender-related development index (including an indicator on the representation of women in positions of power) discussed in the Human Development Report 1995, and Convention 169 of the International Labour Organization particularly as it concerns Indigenous and tribal peoples' rights.

2. The urgent implementation of measures such as:

   • The Tobin tax. [In 1972, to stem rising speculation, James Tobin, economist and adviser to President Kennedy of the United States, proposed that a small tax of 0.1 percent to 0.5 percent be imposed on each speculative transaction. The World March has chosen to target the Tobin tax in particular for its immediate impact on speculation because this tax would generate a significant world fund, and because it is an attainable objective in the short term.] Revenue from the tax would be paid into a special fund:
     – Earmarked for social development;
     – Managed democratically by the international community as a whole;
     – According to criteria respecting fundamental human rights and democracy;
     – With equal representation of women and men; and
     – To which women (who represent 70 percent of the 1.3 billion people living in extreme poverty) would have preferred access;
   • Investment of 0.7 percent of the rich countries' Gross National Product (GNP) in aid for developing countries;
   • Adequate financing and democratization of United Nations programs that are essential to defend women's and children's fundamental rights; for example, UNIFEM (UN women's program), UNDP (United Nations Development Program) and UNICEF (program for children);
   • An end to structural adjustment programs;
   • An end to cutbacks in social budgets and public services; and
   • Rejection of the proposed Multilateral Agreement on Investment (MAI).

3. Cancellation of the debt of all Third World countries, taking into account the principles of responsibility, transparency of information, and accountability.
   We demand the immediate cancellation of the debt of the 53 poorest countries on the planet, in support of the objectives of the Jubilee 2000 campaign.
   In the longer term, we demand cancellation of the debt of all Third World countries and the setting up of a mechanism to monitor debt write-off, ensuring that this money is employed to eliminate poverty and further the well-being of people most affected by structural adjustment programs, the majority of whom are women and girls.

4. The implementation of the 20/20 formula between donor countries and the recipients of international aid. (In this scheme, 20 percent of the sum contributed by the donor country must be allocated to social development and 20 percent of the receiving government's spending must be used for social programs.)

5. A non-monolithic world political organization, with authority over the economy and egalitarian and democratic representation of all countries on earth and equal representation of

women and men. This organization must have real decision-making power and authority to act in order to implement a world economic system that is fair, participatory, and where solidarity plays a key role. The following measures must be instituted immediately:

- A World Council for Economic and Financial Security, which would be in charge of redefining the rules for a new international financial system based on the fair and equitable distribution of the planet's wealth. It would also focus on increasing the well-being, based on social justice, of the world population, particularly women, who make up over half that population. Gender parity should be observed in the composition of the Council's membership. Membership should also be [composed] of representatives of the civil society (for example NGOs, unions, etc.), and should reflect parity of representation between countries from the North and South;
- Any ratification of trade conventions and agreements should be subordinated to individual and collective fundamental human rights. Trade should be subordinated to human rights, not the other way around;
- The elimination of tax havens;
- The end of banking secrecy;
- Redistribution of wealth by the seven richest countries; and
- A protocol to ensure application of the International Covenant on Economic, Social, and Cultural Rights.

6. That the embargoes and blockades—principally affecting women and children—imposed by the major powers on many countries, be lifted.

TO ELIMINATE ALL FORMS OF VIOLENCE AGAINST WOMEN, WE DEMAND:

1. That governments claiming to be defenders of human rights condemn any authority—political, religious, economic, or cultural—that controls women and girls, and denounce any regime that violates their fundamental rights.
2. That States recognize, in their statutes and actions, that all forms of violence against women are violations of fundamental human rights and cannot be justified by any custom, religion, cultural practice, or political power. Therefore, all states must recognize a woman's right to determine her own destiny, and to exercise control over her body and reproductive functions.
3. That States implement action plans, effective policies, and programs equipped with adequate financial and other means to end all forms of violence against women. States should take all possible steps to end patriarchal values and sensitize the society towards democratization of the family structure.

    These action plans must include the following elements in particular: prevention; public education; punishment; "treatment" for attackers; research and statistics on all forms of violence against women; assistance and protection for victims; campaigns against pornography, procuring, and sexual assault, including child rape; non-sexist education; end to the process of homogenization of culture and the commodification of women in media to suit the needs of the market; easier access to the criminal justice system; and training programs for judges and police.
4. That the United Nations bring extraordinary pressure to bear on member states to ratify without reservation and implement the conventions and covenants relating to the rights of

women and children, in particular, the International Covenant on Civil and Political Rights, the Convention on the Elimination of All Forms of Discrimination against Women, the Convention on the Rights of the Child, the International Convention on the Elimination of All Forms of Racial Discrimination, the International Convention on the Protection of the Rights of All Migrant Workers and Their Families.

That the United Nations pressure governments to respect human rights and resolve conflicts.

That States harmonize their national laws with these international human rights instruments as well as the Universal Declaration of Human Rights, the Declaration on the Elimination of Violence against Women, the Cairo and Vienna Declarations, and the Beijing Declaration and Platform for Action.

5. That, as soon as possible, protocols be adopted (and implementation mechanisms be established):

   • To the International Convention on the Elimination of All Forms of Discrimination against Women; and
   • To the Convention on the Rights of the Child.

   These protocols will enable individuals and groups to bring complaints against their governments. They are a means to apply international pressure on governments to force them to implement the rights set out in these covenants and conventions. Provision must be made for appropriate sanctions against non-compliant States.

6. That mechanisms be established to implement the 1949 Convention for the Suppression of the Traffic in Persons and of the Exploitation of the Prostitution of Others, taking into account recent relevant documents such as the two resolutions of the United Nations General Assembly (1996) concerning trafficking in women and girls and violence against migrant women.

7. That States recognize the jurisdiction of the International Criminal Court and conform in particular to the provisions defining rape and sexual abuse as war crimes and crimes against humanity.
   That the United Nations end all forms of intervention, aggression, and military occupation.

8. That all States adopt and implement disarmament policies with respect to conventional, nuclear, and biological weapons. That all countries ratify the Convention against Land Mines.

9. That the right to asylum for women victims of sexist discrimination and persecution and sexual violence be adopted as soon possible. Also, that the United Nations assure the right of refugees to return to their homeland.

   The next two demands were supported by the majority of women present at the meeting on the condition of a country-by-country adoption process. Some delegates were not in a position to be able to commit to defending publicly these demands in their country. They remain an integral part of the World March of Women in the year 2000.

10. That, based on the principle of equality of all persons, the United Nations and States of the international community recognize formally that a person's sexual orientation should

not bar them from the full exercise of the rights set out in the following international instruments: the Universal Declaration of Human Rights, the International Covenant on Civil and Political Rights, the International Covenant on Economic, Social, and Cultural Rights, and the International Convention on the Elimination of All forms of Discrimination against Women.

11. That the right to asylum for victims of discrimination and persecution based on sexual orientation be adopted as soon as possible.

Activist Insight:
Messages of Hope for Young Aboriginal Women

Priscilla Settee

Priscilla Settee (Cree) is associate professor in the Department of Native Studies at the University of Saskatchewan and a member of the Cumberland House Cree First Nations from northern Saskatchewan. The recipient of the Saskatechewan Council for International Co-operation's Global Citizens Award, she has worked with local and international Indigenous communities. She is on the parent council of Saskatoon's only Aboriginal high school, Oskayak, and is a member of the Iskwewak group, which focuses on disappeared and missing Indigenous women. Her research interests include Indigenous knowledge systems, Indigenous women, Indigenous foods and food sovereignty, and the impact of globalization on Indigenous peoples. Among her publications is a recently edited collection of Indigenous women's stories, The Strength of Women, Âhkamêyimowak.

The other night I went to see the movie *Dirt*, an amazing story about hope, commitment, and environmental protection. I came away from the movie inspired, uplifted, and hopeful. I went home and turned on the television to watch the nightly news, where my optimism was quickly dashed by the images and stories on "the news."

I tell this story because, even though I am aware of the power of the media to establish a public psyche, this incident became even more powerful for me personally. The feelings went from extreme highs to extreme lows, and I wondered how many people fall victim to the power of the media. As someone who is engaged in the energizing work of community activism, I know how important it is to maintain a sense of hope and balance and to create and broadcast the stories of hope, especially in these times of Gulf of Mexico disasters, murdered and missing Aboriginal women, high unemployment, fires that destroy public housing, hunger, poverty, and the haunting faces of street people. We need to claim our spaces to tell our stories of hope.

My work as a university professor teaching and learning alongside my students is one way of claiming our space in publicly funded places. I believe that education cannot be just about reading books, but about reading the community one lives in. So every term I require that students do at least one community project as part of their course requirement. They can produce a radio show at Saskatoon's independent radio station. They can learn about the informal educational organizations, such as the Federation of Saskatchewan Indian Nations, the Métis Nation of Saskatchewan, the Treaty Commission, OXFAM International, the Saskatchewan Indian Cultural Centre, Saskatoon's Aboriginal high school, Oskayak, the United Nations Permanent Forum on

Indigenous Peoples, as well as many community-based civil society non-Indigenous organizations, locally and internationally. In each of these centres may be found human stories of struggle, accomplishment, and social change.

Some 20 students from my Native Women's class did interviews with their favourite heroine's work: Métis and Treaty Indian women who are making important contributions to different Saskatchewan communities. People like Winona LaDuke, Lindsay "Eekwoll" Knight, and Rita Bouvier, to name a few.

Winona is from the White Earth Anishnabe community in northern Minnesota. If you are not familiar with Winona's work, go to the White Earth Land Recovery Project website or the Honour the Earth website. Here you will read about amazing community transformation around land recovery, food production, and putting renewable energy (wind/solar) production back in the hands of the people.

Rita Bouvier, poet extraordinaire and social change agent, has spent most of her life as an educator, including working on labour issues as an executive for the Saskatchewan Teachers' Federation.

Eekwol is an amazing young Cree hip-hop artist, whose lyrics hit hard. She is a rising musician and has a huge following of young people who are inspired by her powerful message of the good life, social change, and the empowerment of youth, especially young Indigenous women.

Another year, my Native Women's class organized the International Women's Day inner city celebration event. They developed a program of music, speeches, raised money, cooked food, and organized door prizes and gifts for speakers. They outdid themselves and were grateful for the opportunity to take their learning out of the classroom and into the community.

I believe in action education and education for social change. Higher and formal learning should not just be about reading books and writing well; those are good goals in themselves, but, considering the sorry state of the world and the environment, students must learn to be so much more of the solution—the solution to undoing manmade wars, gross inequalities, racism, and poverty.

As a First Nations woman, I harbour a rage about the grim statistics that face our communities: structural unemployment, 600 Aboriginal women missing and murdered, epidemic suicide rates, gang violence among our youth, and armies of children in the care of social services. I want my students, Indigenous and non-Indigenous, to understand their role and challenges of becoming social change agents, perhaps teaching future generations, perhaps being policy writers, becoming elected leaders, parents, and simply engaged citizens.

Prior generations have left this world in a mess for our youth. We watch helplessly as the images of the oil spill in the Gulf of Mexico are splashed across our television screens; we are horrified when we see people being killed for bringing boatloads of humanitarian aid to the Gaza Strip. I use every opportunity to impress on students that their research, writing, and course work must make a difference in the community, that research just for the sake of getting a mark/grade is not a goal that I promote.

The status quo is not an option. In the spaces that we have carved out for ourselves, each of us must create a sense of hope for humanity, which for the most part is being dumbed down by the media. We must reclaim and recreate the media, the message, and wake up the sleeping masses. I recall this memorable statement: "No one is a passenger on this Earthship; we are all crew."

Source: Priscilla Settee, "Messages of Hope for Young Aboriginal Women," in *Speaking Truth to Power: A Reader on Canadian Women's Inequality Today*, eds. Trish Hennessey and Ed Finn (Ottawa: Canadian Centre for Policy Alternatives, 2010), 99–102.

Chapter 67

The Future of Feminism

Judy Rebick

Judy Rebick is one of Canada's best-known feminists and political commentators. The CAW-Sam Gindin Chair Emerita in Social Justice and Democracy at Ryerson University, she is a former president of the National Action Committee on the Status of Women, and is the founding publisher of the online magazine rabble.ca. She makes regular appearances on television and radio, and has authored many articles and several books, including Ten Thousand Roses: The Making of a Feminist Revolution *and* Transforming Power: From the Personal to the Political.

In 1970 Canadian second-wave feminism emerged in its full glory in interaction with the state through the Royal Commission on the Status of Women and the Abortion Caravan; its subsequent development focused increasingly on the state. Thus, it is not surprising that the rise of neoliberalism, or corporate globalization, with its turn away from the social programs so essential to feminist organizing, resulted in a serious decline of the women's movement.

Second-wave feminism in Canada may not be dead, but it has lost its influence and visibility. [...] Many groups from second-wave feminism still remain and continue to do important work. For example, the recent push for a national child care campaign was led in large part by the same women who began the struggle in the 1960s and continued it through every broken promise. But like all social movements, the women's movement ebbs and flows, and today we are in more of an ebb than a flow.

Many women call themselves third-wave feminists. By "third wave" they mean a set of ideas that they see as quite different from those of the second wave. They are clearer from the outset on the intersection of various forms of domination, class, race, sex, and gender. They focus more on sexuality, although that is probably more a function of youth than of political difference. They have adopted the LGBT (Lesbian, Gay, Bisexual, Transgendered) approach to sexual orientation and see second wavers as transphobic. They are more focused on cultural interventions than on political and social interventions. In many ways, their development reflects the turn away from the state as a site of struggle. [...] I think third wavers do some interesting and important work, but they have not yet reached out to a wider layer of women in a way that is required to create a broad social movement.

My generation never called itself second wave. That was just a way for academics to distinguish between the two huge upsurges of women. The first wave won women the vote; the second gained them reproductive, economic, and legal rights. Feminist activism continued between the first and second waves, of course, and it perseveres today, but I don't yet see a mass movement dealing with gender issues. On the other hand, I think the division between generations exists in part because my generation has not made enough space for young women. The world is very different for young women today, and they should be in the lead of defining what a new feminism will look like.

Much conventional wisdom addresses the decline of the women's movement in Canada. Many blame it on identity politics. If feminists had only focused on what united women, they say, instead of on what divided them, the women's movement would have remained strong. It is true that the cross-class alliance of the women's movement was an important part of its power.

That there were a handful of women in positions of authority to promote the feminist agenda was critical to our success. But feminism would have betrayed its vision, and therefore lost its purpose, if it had continued to marginalize the poorest and most oppressed women to favour those more privileged.

In fact, the organizing of women of colour and their insistence that the women's movement belonged to them too breathed new life into a feminism that was co-opted by its own success at the end of the 1980s. As neoliberal globalization increased the gap between rich and poor, the challenge of maintaining a common vision among women became much greater. The global backlash against feminism and, in Canada, the federal state's funding cuts to women's groups made dealing with these difficulties even harder. The women's movement in Canada worked hard to find new ways to unite across differences. Today, the security state and the war on terror are further isolating already marginalized religious minorities and communities of colour.

[…] Gender itself is becoming a contested notion under neoliberalism. As Janine Brodie says so eloquently […]:

> Since then, however, the issue of gender equality has been progressively erased from official policy discourses and practices. This disappearance of gender coincides with the implementation of neoliberal governing practices in Canada and most advanced liberal democracies. Although the scope and degree of neoliberal policy reform vary widely among these states, neoliberalism has greatly influenced the framing of citizenship claims as well as relationships between the state and both the private sector (the economy and civil society) and the private sphere (the individual and the family) (Brodie, 1997; Clarke, 2004b). In the process, we have been submerged in a politics that seeks to reform and transform the irredeemably gendered subjects of the post-war welfare state into genderless and self-sufficient market actors. (Brodie, 2007: 165)

Carol Shields said it more poetically in her book *Unless* (2002: 99, emphasis in original): "*But we've come so far*; that's the thinking. So far compared with fifty or a hundred years ago. Well, no, we've arrived at the new millennium and we haven't 'arrived' at all. We've been sent over to the side pocket of the snooker table and made to disappear."

As gender disappears, and class and race divisions among women grow, it is increasingly difficult for women to self-identify as a group. It was that identification, captured in the phrase "sisterhood is powerful," that was so central to second-wave feminism. Women are still hungry for that identification and gender solidarity, but the ground for it has shifted.

In English Canada, we spent many years struggling with the differences among women. The efforts of marginalized women to be heard in feminism have been central to its development. Young feminists begin with the understanding of difference that took us many years of blood, sweat, and mostly tears to develop. But somehow, in creating a new comprehension of feminism that, in the words of bell hooks (quoted in Lewis, n.d.), embraced the "recognition of difference without attaching privilege to difference," we have stopped seeing what women have in common, feeding into the neoliberal drive to eliminate gender as a category.

The Quebec women's movement evolved quite differently from that of English Canada. The later arrival of neoliberalism in Quebec meant that the women's movement continued to grow and make gains well into the late 1990s, most significantly a truly universal child care program. The social service cuts that so devastated the women's movement in most provinces were not as great in Quebec. On the other hand, the struggles around racism that so defined the women's movement in English Canada in the late '80s and the 1990s have not played out in the same way in Quebec, in part because of the influence of the national question. So the Quebec women's movement has not achieved the diversity of its English-Canadian counterpart. Nevertheless, the more general impact of neoliberalism is also manifest in Quebec.

Despite our differences, women today continue to face common problems. Feminists fought for universal child care and for men to assume their full share of child rearing, but neither battle has yet been won. The reality today is that most women are working longer hours outside the home than they used to but are still taking primary responsibility within it. Whether they are pressured to overwork so as to advance in their profession or whether they are obliged to hold two or three part-time jobs, most women struggle with the crushing burden of paid work combined with the still excessive demands of labour in the home.

Although I agree that we need to regender our understanding of the state, [...] I also believe that we must revisit the attention to the "private" sphere that was much more pronounced in the early years of the second wave. Women's equality will be possible only in a world that accepts nurturing and caring as important roles for both men and women. Gloria Steinem has said that her generation of feminists made it possible for women to do what men traditionally did; now it is time for the opposite to occur. Men who wish to spend more time with their children and enjoy their lives will be our allies in challenging a society that values career and money alone. Yet such men are still few and far between. Even in countries where government policy encourages men to take parental leave, [...] the uptake is small.

We need a strategy that includes child care, a shorter work week, and improved parental leave for both men and women. But most of all, women must decide to stop carrying such an unfair share of the work of society. But as we learned in the second wave, the first step is to speak the name of the problem. In the 1960s, Betty Friedan (1963) spoke about the "problem with no name," thus sparking so much of the original second-wave activism. Today that problem is too much work, too much pressure, too little time. It's a problem that women share with men but suffer from much more. This problem is not about the state but about women's continuing predominance in the private sphere. A different kind of struggle is required, one that focuses much more on education and new kinds of relationships than it does on engaging with the state.

Another continuing and related problem is the intractable hold of men on power. Second-wave feminists put on armour to enter the battlefields created by patriarchy. To challenge the way in which power is practised, we need to challenge the men who hold it. In the 2005 Montreal roundtable to discuss my book about the Canadian women's movement, *Ten Thousand Roses*, journalist and filmmaker Francine Pelletier described the problem of the invisible glass ceiling. She said that although men initially welcome women into the workplace, they subsequently become uncomfortable with their presence and seek to marginalize them. It is difficult to name the problem because the men talk the talk of women's equality. Many young women in the audience nodded their heads in agreement. "It's so confusing," one young woman who works for an

NGO told me. "We have strong feminists on our board, so how could our workplace be sexist? But it is. Women in leadership positions are always marginalized."

Both problems come from the fact that my generation of feminists failed to achieve its goal: to overturn the patriarchy. The system of male domination remains intact and is reinforced through male culture in the workplace, in politics, and in still too many families. This culture is not perpetrated solely by men. Many women in positions of power adopt the same methods of control as do their male colleagues. Our notions of leadership, for example, are still very masculinized. And certainly, the fact that so little value is placed on raising children or on caring for family, friends, and community is a sign that though, economically, we have moved radically from the family wage that allowed a male breadwinner to support a woman at home, in cultural terms, we have not moved very far at all.

At the beginning of the second wave, we were openly and actively challenging that male culture, but as our influence increased, we focused more and more on demands for reform and less and less on the deeper cultural and structural changes that would threaten patriarchy. Too many of us accepted a place within the patriarchal structures. In a 2004 interview I conducted with Frances Lankin, now the CEO of Toronto's United Way, she explained what happened to her feminist process once she became a minister in the Bob Rae government:

> I came into government having worked in a consensus model, and we tried to work in government that way. But, I had to move quickly to match the style of that world—very top-down, directive, and not consensus oriented. People who knew me didn't understand how I could do it, but I did. I made it work and paid a price for that inside. I've found myself a lot in my life having to work in ways that I don't like. You get a strong training when you work in a male way of doing things, and it sometimes takes over how you are as a person. I sometimes wish I could have worked more in a women's collective and had more balance. I think this is why I've been successful in a man's world.
>
> I take pride in that but not in thinking that I've changed things to make it easier for women coming along. I think there's a lot of work for women to do to change the way in which institutions are run.

The pressure, as described by Lankin, to succeed as a woman in a traditionally male role almost always trumps the desire to change the way things are done to make room for other women. For one thing, all the hegemonic pressures push women in that direction; for another, we have no blueprint of any kind for making changes to deeply engrained hierarchical structures. The more power that resides in an organization, the harder it is to change.

How do we play the game but change the rules? As the poet Audre Lorde (1984: 110) so famously said, "The master's tools will never dismantle the master's house." But neither can we make change exclusively from the outside. The success of the second wave was in its ability to work both inside and outside the system: as some writers have put it, in and against the state. Once you are inside a system, however, the pressure to conform is tremendous. Feminists of my generation started as kick-ass radicals but were slowly co-opted. Italian philosopher Antonio Gramsci (1971: 389–90) called this hegemony, the way that capitalism maintains its ideological hold.

We need to explore new ways of decision making that entail cooperation rather than domination, inclusion rather than elitism, and new kinds of leadership that involve empowering others rather than aggrandizing ourselves. We tried to do this in the second wave but generally failed. In my view we internalized too many patriarchal ways of operating to successfully create nonhierarchical organizations. Instead, as Jo Freeman states in her brilliant essay, "The Tyranny of Structurelessness" (1972–73), we created informal power that was even more inaccessible to marginalized women than the formal structures of power themselves. Today we have the benefit of much more work, both academic and practical, in making decisions differently in realms ranging from popular education to participatory democracy. We know much more about creating egalitarian structures. Speaking truth to power, it turns out, is not enough. We must change the very nature of power.

A lot of young activists, seeing the dangers of co-option and the corruption of the existing political structures, choose to work completely outside of those structures. Young women ask me what I think of the impact of cyber feminism, for example. On the net you can communicate with large numbers of like-minded thinkers, developing ideas, debating issues, and even organizing protests. But unless we find ways to reach out to others who are not hooked into our networks, it is hard for me to see how we will effect change.

The World March of Women defined the priority of today's women's movement as fighting poverty and violence. Dealing with female poverty means dealing with neoliberalism. [...] With little or no discussion, welfare moms became part of the undeserving poor, and raising children was accorded even less economic and social value than it has had traditionally. When discussing why she should be a feminist, a young university professor recently asked me, "What's in it for me?" When you have access to privilege in a society that is so unequal, what's in it for you is the feeling that you are making a contribution to overcoming that inequity. Many people do see that need when it comes to solidarity with women and men in the developing countries but not so much within their own. The pressure, both financial and emotional, on poor women today is terrible. Racialized poor women or women in the sex trades face even greater marginalization and degradation. The horror that hundreds of Aboriginal women have disappeared, not only from Vancouver's Downtown Eastside but also across the country, illustrates that authorities still consider some women's lives to be dispensable.

Feminist strategies for protecting and empowering women have saved thousands of lives, and attitudes that blamed women for the violence directed against them have changed radically. Yet male violence continues almost unabated, in Canada as elsewhere. Although improving laws and their application is critical, that won't eliminate male violence. A new feminism needs to debate strategies for ending violence against women. My own view is that these discussions must include men. Men have been active in combating male violence through the all-male White Ribbon Campaign. Anti-violence feminists have been quite critical of that campaign, maintaining that it often takes up the space and financing desperately needed by women's groups. It is certainly irritating that when you Google "violence against women," the White Ribbon Campaign comes up near the top. However, what I have in mind is not a male group that combats violence but a mixed discussion on the issue.

If we are to end violence against women, we must better understand how masculinization takes place and how it can be changed. From an early age, boys are still socialized to be aggressive, dominating, and competitive. There are few positive male role models in popular education. Boys still learn how to be men from patriarchal and often violent males, such as the heroes of team sports, action movies, and video games. And feminist men have to play a critical role in speaking out for a new masculinity that isn't based on the oppression of women.

Many young women identify as third-wave feminists. I see them as similar to the small group of women in the early and mid-1960s who identified as feminists. Years before the movement arose, women such as Simone de Beauvoir, Betty Friedan, and Doris Anderson were writing about the issues that would spawn it. Similarly, third-wave feminists are redefining feminism in new ways that focus on sexuality, the intersection of various forms of oppression, and the beauty myth. Not surprisingly, some of their ideas are a reaction to the excesses or absences of the generation before. They have also been heavily influenced by the postmodernism that has swept women's studies over the last number of years. To this old socialist feminist, the idea that intervening in strictly cultural arenas can change the world is highly idealistic and problematic. Without addressing the material reality of women, whether work time, child care, or violence, feminism will not find an echo among masses of women.

Nevertheless, sexuality and body image are central issues for feminism today. Several years ago, I had an e-mail conversation with Candice Steenburgen, a third-wave feminist academic, about sex. She told me, "We have no script about what equal sexual relationships look like." Second-wave feminists did challenge the male domination in relationships. However, though some individuals worked through their own relationships, we never really developed an understanding of what a new kind of equal relationship, whether heterosexual or lesbian, could be.

In her recent series about women and sex, Francine Pelletier (2005) reveals an incredibly broad diversity of women's sexual experience. She says that although women appear to have a lot of sexual agency today, you find something else when you dig deeper. She doesn't quite have the words to describe the lingering self-hatred that seems to remain from centuries of oppression and is fuelled by a massive industry designed to make us feel inadequate. We aren't thin enough, sexy enough, beautiful enough. We're too tall, too short, too loud, too quiet, too aggressive, too timid. What has changed is that no one now tells us we are too smart. Instead, the pressure today is to be smart, accomplished, *and* beautiful. And that pressure goes beyond youth with a terrifying explosion of cosmetic surgery.

As second-wave feminism began as a peace movement in Canada with the formation of the formidable Voice of Women (VOW), so peace must remain a central element of feminism. As VOW has always understood, women have the strongest interest in ending war. This is not solely because, increasingly, women and children suffer most from war and because mass rapes have become a generalized instrument of war. It is also because war is a central prop to patriarchy. A world in which women hold equal power with men will be a world in which war is no longer either a method of domination or a method of dispute resolution. And ecofeminism, an important part of the second wave, has taken on even more significance in this day and age. As Sandra Delaronde put it during the 2005 Winnipeg roundtable on *Ten Thousand Roses*, "Second-wave feminism was focused on us as women and improving our status vis-à-vis men. Perhaps third wave feminism is about changing the world" (author's notes).

Indeed, most young feminists are more active in the global justice movement than in the women's movement. As a socialist feminist, I have always understood that women's equality can never be achieved in a capitalist system that is based on entrenched inequality. However, capitalism is not the only system of domination and inequality. The interlocking systems of capitalism, patriarchy, and colonialism produce the inequalities and injustice we seek to correct. Unless we challenge all those systems of domination, we will take two steps backward for every step forward. And the struggle to end this domination involves continuing engagement with the state but not in the almost exclusive focus that carne to represent second-wave feminism. The personal is political too.

References

Brodie, Janine. 2007. "Putting Gender Back In: Women and Social Policy Reform in Canada." In Yasmin Abu-Laban, ed., *Gendering the Nation State: Canadian and Comparative Perspectives*. Vancouver: UBC Press, 2007. p. 165.

Freeman, Jo. 1972–73. "The Tyranny of Structurelessness." *Berkeley Journal of Sociology* 17: 151–65.

Friedan, Betty. 1963. *The Feminine Mystique*. New York: Random House.

Gramsci, Antonio. 1971. *Selections from the Prison Notebooks*. Edited by Q. Hoare and G.N. Smith. New York: International Publishers.

Lewis, Jone Johnson. n.d. "Women Voices: Quotations by Women—bell hooks." Available at http://womenshistory.about.com/library/qu/blquhook.htm.

Lorde, Audre. 1984. *Sister Outsider: Essays and Speeches*. Freedom, CA: Crossing Press.

Pelletier, Francine. 2005. "Sex, Truth, and Videotape." CBC Broadcast, Virage Productions.

Shields, Carol. 2002. *Unless: A Novel*. London and New York: Random House Canada.

RebELLEs:
Manifesto of the Pan-Canadian
Young Feminist Gathering

This manifesto was adopted at the Pan-Canadian Young Feminist Gathering "Waves of Resistance," Montreal, October 13, 2008.

We are the young RebELLEs who have answered a feminist call and we are proud to call ourselves feminists. We recognize that there are multiple interpretations of feminism and we celebrate and integrate this diversity. We are committed to the continual expansion of the plurality of our voices. We are committed to an ongoing process of critical self-reflection to inform and transform our movement. We acknowledge the historical exclusion of "Othered" women by the majority Western feminist movement. We strive to learn from the past, honour the struggles of our fore-mothers, and continue to dream for the future. We value the allies of feminism who support us in our fight for equity and justice.

We are women of diverse abilities, ethnicities, origins, sexualities, identities, class backgrounds, ages, and races. Among us are employed, underemployed, and unemployed women, mothers, students, dropouts, artists, musicians, and women in the sex trade. We state that transfolks, two-spirited, and intersexed people are integral to our movement and recognize and respect gender fluidity and support the right to self-identify. Our women-only spaces include everyone who self-identifies and lives as a woman in society.

We are told that feminism is over and outdated. If this were true then we wouldn't need to denounce the fact that:

In reality, many of the demands of our feminist mothers and grandmothers remain unmet. Women continue to be the victims of sexual violence. Our communities are haunted by the silence that follows these assaults. Throughout Canada, in spite of our right to it, access to abortion services remains insufficient. Across Canada as well, colonized, marginalized, racialized, and disabled women are coerced and/or forced to undergo unwanted or uninformed abortions, forced to use contraception, and are subjected to forced sterilization. The hyper-sexualization of women in the media has taught us to view women as sexual objects rather than complete human beings. Getting off, lesbianism and being queer are taboo and a woman's choice to seek sexual pleasure is seen as negative. Our identities are eroded as we are taught, from the time we are children, and through television and magazines, that how we should look, dress, and act is determined by our sex. Violence is normalized, sexual abuse eroticized. Our sexual health education is inadequate and our reproductive rights are disrespected. Our needs are not being met.

In reality, women still represent the majority of the underprivileged. Our government steals children from poor and Aboriginal women. Capitalism exploits working-class women and confines middle- and upper-class women to "consumer" roles. We are told that equality has been achieved, but still the wage gap persists. Immigrant women are denied acknowledgement of their academic credentials and are forced to endure intolerable work environments in order to stay on Canadian soil. We lack affordable and accessible childcare. Women remain underpaid, underappreciated, and undervalued in the work force. We have gained the right to vote, yet gender-based discrimination keeps women virtually underrepresented in political office.

In this globalized world, we must construct international feminist solidarity. The actions of Canadian political and economic elites harm women around the world, and in a way that is specifically gender-related. War, genocide, and militarization are characterized by the use of rape as a war weapon, femicide, and the sexual exploitation of thousands of our sisters. Free trade contributes to women's increasing social, economic, and cultural insecurity. In response to Canadian imperialism, we will globalize our feminist solidarity.

In this so-called post-feminist world, our roles in society are still defined by traditional views on gender. Religious and political forces aimed at maintaining the pillars of power in our society silence us from voicing our rights. We denounce the current rise of right-wing ideology in Canadian society and the steps backward in women's rights that this has caused. We are being stripped of rights for which those who came before us fought hard. Geography marginalizes women, with remote, northern, and rural women lacking access to basic services. Showing solidarity with our sisters means trying to understand all of the issues we face—including race, class, and gender—and standing together against oppression.

Finally, we denounce the dismissal of the feminist movement as redundant. Our struggle is not over. We will be post-feminists when we have post-patriarchy.

Feminists Unite!

DOWN WITH the colonial legacy of genocide and assimilation of Aboriginal peoples, particularly of Aboriginal women
DOWN WITH the sexism and racism of the Indian Act
DOWN WITH dishonoured treaties
DOWN WITH assimilation
DOWN WITH racial profiling
DOWN WITH Canada's fake multicultural policy
DOWN WITH warmongers and military power
DOWN WITH racist child welfare policies
DOWN WITH stereotypes in the media
DOWN WITH genocide and femicide
DOWN WITH stealing women and children
DOWN WITH COLONIALISM

RebELLEs AGAINST banks for hijacking the world
RebELLEs AGAINST drug companies for institutionalizing women's health
RebELLEs AGAINST public spaces that don't accommodate all bodies
RebELLEs AGAINST development that destroys nature
RebELLEs AGAINST the class system that keeps us impoverished and deprives us of safe, affordable housing
RebELLEs AGAINST the state that forces other countries to adopt the capitalist system

RebELLEs AGAINST the devaluation of women's paid and unpaid work
RebELLEs AGAINST corporations for making money off our backs
RebELLEs AGAINST the advertisers who destroy our self-esteem and then sell it back to us
RebELLEs AGAINST CAPITALISM

RISE AGAINST the industries that cause us to hate our bodies and our sexuality
RISE AGAINST heterosexism that makes it seem that there is only one way of living, loving, and being sexual
RISE AGAINST the socialization of children in gender binaries, race categories, and colonial crasures
RISE AGAINST the education that reinforces the heteronormative nuclear family
RISE AGAINST the religious Right and its influence on State policy and legislation
RISE AGAINST rape and violence against women
RISE AGAINST the objectification and control of women's bodies
RISE AGAINST all anti-choice bills, laws, and strategies
RISE AGAINST the sexual division of labour
RISE AGAINST poverty and women's economic disadvantage and dependency
RISE AGAINST income-support programs based on family status instead of individual status
RISE AGAINST masculinists, their false claims, and demagogic arguments
RISE AGAINST sexual exploitation
RISE AGAINST PATRIARCHY

Source: Excerpted from RebELLEs, "Home" and "Manifesto of the Pan-Canadian Young Feminist Gathering" (2010), retrieved from http://www.rebelles.org/en/manifesto

6b Transnational Feminism: Challenges and Possibilities

Supplement 41

The World Conferences on Women

The International Women's Year was 1975, and the first world conference on women convened in Mexico City to examine the problems of continuing inequality for women and to propose solutions. The next 10 years became the United Nations Decade for Women, which focused on women's advancement and global dialogue about gender equality. That conference was followed by three other world conferences. The UN's most recent update in 2005 points to the ongoing need for nations to continue to work to improve women's lives. The four conferences are described below.

FIRST WORLD CONFERENCE ON WOMEN

Mexico City, 19 June–2 July 1975

At this meeting, the process was launched and three objectives were identified in relation to equality, peace, and development for the Decade:

*   Full gender equality and the elimination of gender discrimination
*   The integration and full participation of women in development
*   An increased contribution by women toward strengthening world peace

The conference urged governments to formulate national strategies, targets, and priorities. It led to the establishment of the International Research and Training Institute for the Advancement of Women (INSTRAW) and the United Nations Development Fund for Women (UNIFEM), which serve as an institutional framework for research, training, and operational activities in the area of women and development. At this conference, held in Mexico City, women played a highly visible role. Of the 133 delegations from member states, 113 were headed by women. Women also organized the International Women's Year Tribune, which attracted some 4,000 participants, and a parallel forum of nongovernmental organizations that signaled the opening up of the United Nations to nongovernmental organizations, enabling women's voices to be heard in the organization's policy-making process.

SECOND WORLD CONFERENCE ON WOMEN

Copenhagen, 14–30 July 1980

This conference recognized that there was a disparity between women's guaranteed rights and their capacity to exercise them. Participants identified three spheres in which measures for equality, development, and peace were needed:

- Equal access to education
- Equal access to employment opportunities
- Equal access to adequate health care services

THIRD WORLD CONFERENCE ON WOMEN

Nairobi, 15–26 June 1985

The data presented by the United Nations to the delegations of member states revealed that the improvements observed had benefited only a limited number of women. Thus, the Nairobi Conference was mandated to seek new ways of overcoming obstacles for achieving the objectives of the decade: equality, development, and peace.

Three basic categories were established to measure the progress achieved:

- Constitutional and legal measures
- Equality in social participation
- Equality in political participation and decision making

The Nairobi Conference recognized that gender equality was not an isolated issue, but encompassed all areas of human activity. It was necessary for women to participate in all spheres, not only in those relating to gender.

FOURTH WORLD CONFERENCE ON WOMEN

Beijing, 4–15 September 1995

The Beijing Declaration and Platform for Action were adopted at the Fourth World Conference on Women by the representatives of 189 countries. The platform reflects the new international commitment to achieving the goals of equality, development, and peace for women throughout the world. It also strengthens the commitments made during the United Nations Decade for Women, 1976–1985, which culminated in the Nairobi Conference, as well as related commitments undertaken during the cycle of United Nations world conferences held in the 1990s.

The 12 critical areas of concern in the Platform for Action are as follows:

1. Women and poverty
2. Education and training of women
3. Women and health
4. Violence against women
5. Women and armed conflict
6. Women and the economy
7. Women in power and decision making
8. Institutional mechanisms for the advancement of women
9. Human rights of women
10. Women and the media
11. Women and the environment
12. The girl child

The Platform for Action sets out strategic objectives and explains the measures that should be adopted by governments, the international community, nongovernmental organizations, and the private sector.

Source: United Nations, "Outcomes on Gender and Equality," retrieved from http://www.un.org/en/development/devagenda/gender.shtml

Chapter 68

The Evolution of Transnational Feminisms: Consensus, Conflict, and New Dynamics

Aili Mari Tripp

Aili Mari Tripp is president of the African Studies Association, and professor of political science and gender and women's studies at the University of Wisconsin-Madison, where she is also director of the Center for Research on Gender and Women. She teaches and researches in the fields of women and politics, global feminism, African and comparative politics, and gender studies in an international context. She has authored and edited many articles and books, including Global Feminism: Transnational Women's Activism, Organizing, and Human Rights *(excerpted below).*

In the past two decades, we have witnessed the evolution of an international consensus around particular norms regarding women's rights. This rights-based consensus combines development and human rights interests, engages advocates within and outside transnational women's groups, and has been very much a product of global dialogue and interaction. Much of this consensus has been reflected in the various international agreements and treaties, including the 1979 Convention on the Elimination of All Forms of Discrimination against Women, the 1995 United Nations Beijing Platform of Action, the 1996 International Labour Organization Convention on Homeworkers, the 1999 UN Jomtien Resolution on Education for All, and the 2000 UN Security Council Resolution 1325 on the participation of women in peace-building. These and other international decisions indicate increasing international recognition of women's rights and interest in changing women's status and removing key impediments to women's advancement in almost every arena.

The impetus in these international forums has been truly transnational, with non-Western and Western countries alike contributing to the growth of this consensus. The consensus represents an important convergence of feminisms and women's rights advocacy worldwide. Regardless of the common perception in the West that ideas regarding the emancipation of women have spread from the West outward into other parts of the world, this chapter argues that, in fact, the influences have always been multidirectional, and that the current consensus is a product of parallel feminist movements globally that have learned from one another but have often had quite independent trajectories and sources of movement.

Today's global consensus is far from absolute. There remains polarization around issues such as lesbian rights, abortion, trafficking in women, and sex work. There is disagreement over the importance of other issues, such as militarization and global economic inequalities. These differences can be found within countries as well as across various transnational divides. Slowly, however, the debates around these issues are changing even in regions that have been very resistant to incorporating these concerns into a women's rights agenda. [...]

At the same time, there exist very serious challenges to this consensus from the Vatican and Islamic countries such as Saudi Arabia and Iran. The United States under the Bush administration has similarly worked against this consensus through policies like the gag rule and withdrawal of support to the United Nations Population Fund (UNPFA). On January 22, 2001, U.S. president George W. Bush imposed what is known as the "Global Gag Rule," which restricts foreign nongovernmental organizations (NGOs) that receive U.S. family planning funds from using their own, non-U.S. funds to provide legal abortion services, lobby their own governments for abortion law reform, or provide accurate medical counseling or referrals regarding abortion. [...]

*****

This chapter offers a framework for understanding how local women's movements around the world responded to broader national political, economic, and cultural trends and events, as well as how they influenced and were influenced by global women's movements over the course of a long history of global development. The national contexts of these movements affected the possibilities for change at any given time, as well as their choice of strategies, timing, and priorities. I suggest that many of the challenges in forging transnational linkages among these movements are a product of a difficulty in fully appreciating these differences, even when the goals have intersected. This has resulted, for example, in Western scholars often defining the global movement with respect to the first and second waves of feminism in the West as though these phases occurred universally and as though Western movements were the precursors to similar movements in other parts of the world. Looking through the prism of the history of transnational feminism, instead one sees national and local trajectories always featured significantly, creating regional waves of feminism with their own dynamics and pace that did not necessarily correspond to Western trends. In more recent years, for example, the momentum for feminist mobilization has picked up in non-Western countries, whereas activism in Western countries has declined relative to them, as well as in absolute terms.

First Wave of Transnational Mobilization (1880–1930)

During the first wave of *international* women's mobilization (1880–1930), many organizations focused on issues of peace, suffrage, temperance, equal access to education and industrial training, equal pay for equal work, and labor legislation, but also on social welfare and religious concerns. The year 1868 marks the formation of the first transnational women's organization, the Association Internationale des Femmes, in Geneva to address issues of suffrage and secular education (Adams 2004). Between the years 1880 and 1900, the global mobilization of women expanded with the formation of new transnational women's organizations around a wide range of issues and in a variety of contexts. For example, although transnational influences were also evident, the suffrage movement in Japan in the 1880s emerged in response to a domestic popular rights movement; in China the suffrage movement of the early 1900s was part of an anti-Qing movement that demanded political rights for women. In both countries, the struggle for the right to vote was coupled with campaigns to get women elected into office. Later in the 1920s in Japan, suffragists like Ichikawa Fusae saw the struggle for the right to vote as more than just a means of getting legislation passed to benefit women and children, as women's suffrage had been framed in the United States. For her and other Japanese feminists, the women's vote would allow women to assert themselves on a wide range of issues affecting society. The 1920s suffrage movements in Japan and India were, according to Ellen DuBois, more feminist and vigorous than any other such movements in that period worldwide (DuBois 2000, 541–549). Similarly, the Chilean Women's Civic Party, formed in 1922, advocated suffrage for women but saw it in a broader context of obtaining civil, political, and economic equality with men (Pernet 2000, 671).

[...] Other international women's organizations established in this period included the World Women's Christian Temperance Union (founded in 1883), the International Congress of Women (1888), the International Council of Women (1888), the General Federation of Women's Clubs (1889), which was one of the world's largest and oldest women's volunteer service organizations, the World Young Women's Christian Association (1894), and the International Women's Suffrage Alliance (1904) (Boulding 1977, 188). These particular transnational organizations were based in the West, and their leadership was almost entirely Western, although there were exceptions right from the beginning. The International Congress of Women's founding meeting in 1888 had delegates not only from Europe but also from India. The Women's Christian Temperance Union chapters that were formed in China, Japan, India, Korea, and Burma in the 1880s became an important focal point for the suffrage movement in these countries (DuBois 2000, 547).

One of the first major transnational struggles of women was over the right to vote, which started in the Pacific and Europe and quickly spread worldwide with decolonization. New Zealand and Australia were the first countries that granted women this right, in 1893 and 1902, respectively. Finland was the first country in Europe to grant voting rights to women, in 1906; Canada was the first in North America (1918), with the United States following two years later; Ecuador was the first in Latin America (1928), as were Sri Lanka in Asia (1931) and Senegal in Africa (1945). After World War II, many countries granted women universal suffrage along with men as part of the process of creating newly independent nations, since by then the inclusion of women as voters had been institutionalized within new nations (Ramirez, Soysal, and Shanahan 1997, 736).

Ramirez and coauthors show how suffrage movements were only partially national struggles; they were part of transnational movements drawing on universal aspirations that use the resources of various kinds of international organizations. They appealed to global principles that transcended national boundaries. However, it is important to recognize that transnational influences were being absorbed by local movements in distinctive ways and that the inspiration and form the movements took were shaped by national events and trends. Moreover, the suffrage movement was not the only transnational movement in this period. In 1910 the International Women's Congress in Latin America met in Buenos Aires with delegates from Peru, Paraguay, Uruguay, and Argentina; their focus was on women's education and civil and political rights as well as divorce. [...]

*****

Winning the right to vote for women in Europe and North America had taken the momentum out of many women's rights movements in these countries, but for the rest of the world, major women's rights movements were gearing up. Women in Pacific Rim countries, for example, met in 1928 in Honolulu to establish a women's rights network, and out of these early meetings the Pan-Pacific Women's Association was formed in 1930. In 1935 a coalition of women's rights organizations brought the treaty to the League of Nations, which voted to further study the issue.

*****

In the decades under colonial rule in Asia and Africa, transnational activism was characterized by efforts by some Western women to work with colonized women in the areas of education, health, political representation, and legal status. These initiatives were complicated by the fact that they were frequently closely entwined with the colonial project of modernization and the missionary project of promoting Christian beliefs, values, and lifestyle. At times these initiatives were welcomed by local activists and contributed to their own efforts to eradicate various practices. [...]

*****

Women from the colonial countries themselves varied in orientation, as Kumari Jayawardena (1995) has shown in the case of South Asia. Some colonial feminists thoroughly supported the imperial project and were bent on carrying out their civilizing mission, whereas others were social reformers who did not challenge colonialism but did not actively support it either. Although few in number, there were individual Western women's rights advocates who actively supported the cause of third world independence. Similar variance in colonial women activists was found in Africa (Callaway 1987; Denzer 1992; Jayawardena 1995; Labode 1993; Ranchod-Nilsson 1992; Strobel 1991; Tripp 2002).

Second Wave of Transnational Mobilization (1945–1975)

After World War II, a new wave of international gender-based mobilization took off as women became active in efforts to secure independence for their countries and resist colonialism. Organizations that had a European and North American focus became more international in scope. The membership of the International Council of Women (ICW) jumped from having 78 percent of its affiliate councils based in Europe and the United States in 1938 to having only 47 percent of its membership from these countries by 1963.

Many women's movements worldwide sprang up in this period quite independent of women's movements in the West, contrary to claims that they originated in feminist movements in North America and Europe (e.g., Keck and Sikkink 1998, 168). In Africa, as Margaret C. Snyder (2003) has argued, the African women's movement evolved from its own independent base with its own intrinsic philosophy and distinct goals. It was not a carbon copy of Western movements and in fact predated the second-wave movement in the West. Its beginnings were African, rooted mostly in the fight for independence. DuBois (2000), Jayawardena (1986), Lavrin (1995), Pernet (2000), and others have shown much the same in the case of women's rights movements throughout Asia, Latin America, Africa, and the Middle East. In their local struggles for equal rights, women in these regions developed their own feminisms distinct from Western feminisms.

After World War II, the UN Commission on the Status of Women [CSW], established in 1945, became a focal point of international advocacy and for the promotion of women's rights in all spheres. It was largely a product of efforts of Latin American women suffragists. The 1950s was not a period of "doldrums" for feminism in Latin America but rather the decade in which many Latin American countries extended the franchise to women, and activists there were energized and internationally engaged. Nonetheless, when the CSW began, its fifteen members came primarily from Western countries. Today it has forty-five members, including thirteen from African states, eleven from Asian states, four from Eastern European states, nine from Latin American and Caribbean states, and eight from Western European and other states. The makeup of the

CSW not only reflects global demographics and changes in the structure of the UN that took place after independence but also suggests a geopolitical realignment that has resulted from shifting dynamics within transnational women's movements globally, giving more voice and legitimacy to the global South.

Third Wave of Transnational Women's Mobilization (1985–)

Although influences from the global South had always been in evidence throughout the two earlier waves of mobilization (1880–1930 and 1945–1975), it was not until the third wave of transnational women's activism (1985 to present) that the South began to challenge in a concerted fashion the ideological dominance of the North in framing the international women's agenda. This coincided with a major expansion of transnational mobilization.

The 1970s were a period of ferment in the West. Large numbers of organizations formed around feminist principles with the rise of "second-wave feminism" In the United States and Europe. Women's movements and broader social movements increasingly interacted with and influenced one another. New international organizations and networks, such as Women's International Network (WIN), International Feminist Network, and International Women's Information and Communication Service, emerged and were focused on women's health, reproductive rights, peace, human rights, poverty, prostitution, and violence against women. But many of the established international groups in the 1970s were led by white, middle-class women from the North, and the majority of their funding came from North America and the United States (Stienstra 1994, 100–101). This became an increasing source of tension.

Early Challenges to Northern Dominance: Women in Development Agendas

The UN conferences became a venue in which various North–South tensions were played out. Many of the conflicts focused on the objections by women in the South to the northern women's emphasis on the primacy of feminism and on relations between men and women. Many women from the South, for example, accused women from the North of coming to the UN women's conference in Mexico in 1975 presuming that a specific feminist orientation would provide a common framework for action. Gloria Steinem had drawn up a feminist manifesto without any input from women in the South, which seemed to many third world women to be a subtle form of cultural imperialism. Women from the South tended to focus on how women's problems were defined by global inequality, imperialism, and other political concerns that were not seen as gender-specific. At this first UN conference on women, and even more so at the Copenhagen conference (1980) that followed, women from the South challenged northern women to see development issues as women's concerns.

*****

Third world networks of activists and scholars, like Development Alternatives with Women for a New Era (DAWN) formed in 1984 in the Caribbean, Latin America, and South Asia, pushed for an agenda that incorporated women's concerns in development strategies, policies, and theories. These concerns became integral to the efforts of the United Nations Development Fund for Women (UNIFEM), which supported women's projects and women's participation in mainstream development programs (Pietilä 2002, 37, 38). The formation of many third world–based

international networks—like DAWN and Women Living under Muslim Laws in the mid-1980s
and Women in Law and Development in Africa (WILDAF) in 1990—represented the beginning
of the shift in the center of gravity in global women's mobilization dynamics. These organizations
were not just coexisting alongside organizations based in the North, but claimed a leadership role
in transnational women's movements (Bunch 2001, 380).

Shifting Momentum

By 1985 at the UN Nairobi conference, the earlier North–South tensions over agenda priorities
had subsided. Feminist activists in the North had come to accept the importance of global
development concerns as relevant to women, and women in the South became more willing to
focus on gender equality (Snyder and Tadesse 1995). More than 60 percent of the attendees in
Nairobi were from the South. It was at this point that the overall feminist center of gravity began
to move from the North to the South.

Transnational networks were formed around violence against women as early as 1974, with
the creation of Isis. By the 1990s, violence against women had gained in importance as a major
issue around which activists forged networks and alliances around the world. By the end of the
century, it had become the most important international women's issue and the most dynamic
human rights concern globally (Keck and Sikkink 1998, 166).

Women's organizations had been working on issues of state violence against women in the
1970s and 1980s. The 1981 feminist Encounter for Latin America and the Caribbean in
Bogotá held a Day to Resist Violence against Women, which led to annual commemorations
throughout Latin America and eventually to the global campaign Sixteen Days of Activism
against Gender Violence. Transnational networks focused on violence began to emerge at the
UN Women's Conference in Copenhagen in 1980 and in Nairobi in 1985. Regional groups
formed in Asia, Latin America, and elsewhere, and global networks formed around particular
issues such as the trafficking of women. At the UN conference in Nairobi, understandings of
violence against women were broadened from domestic violence and rape to violence against
women caused by economic deprivation, structural adjustment, environmental degradation,
war, and political repression.

The 1993 World Conference on Human Rights in Vienna marked a turning point: it represented
a major success in bringing the women's rights agenda into the human rights agenda. Foundations
made funding available in this area of women and human rights, and new organizations emerged,
like the Global Campaign on Women's Human Rights organized by the Center for Women's Global
Leadership (Keck and Sikkink 1998, 181). New international conventions adopted these concerns.
The phrase "violence against women" was first used by the Organization of American States when
it adopted the Inter-American Convention on the Prevention, Punishment, and Eradication of
Violence against Women in 1994. It was the culmination of years of work by women's activists.

There was also a new awareness that emerged around the use of rape in civil war in former
Yugoslavia that could then be used to highlight the use of rape in other conflicts as well. In part,
as Charlotte Bunch explained, the unities came from a realization that while everyone shared
these problems, no one had a monopoly on the solutions, thus laying a better basis for discussion. Violence against women was absorbed into the language of human rights, which already
had gained acceptance as a legal norm (Bunch and Fried 1996). Particular experiences of violence, for example, sati, dowry deaths, and female genital cutting, were treated as examples of
violence against women rather than as "exotic practices signifying the primitive nature of national

cultures," as they had been characterized in UN conferences in Mexico and Copenhagen. The inclusivity of the movement was key to its success, Weldon argues (2004).

By the beginning of the twenty-first century, the two strands within the global women's movements had come together: human rights issues and sustainable development concerns. They merged into what is referred to as the "rights-based approach." Human rights is seen as the central focus of sustainable human development: it offers the means, the ends, and a framework for assessing sustainable development and for guaranteeing a full array of rights that went well beyond those found in legislation and constitutions. This rights-based orientation had a more expansive reach beyond the approaches to development that emphasized donor or NGO assistance and local participation by adding to these concerns another level of action. The rights-based advocacy approach stressed the need for coalitions of NGOs and local activists and other actors to lobby governments, corporations, international financial institutions, and other global and domestic actors to create the necessary political, economic, and human rights conditions for equality, sustainable human development, and social justice.

This new universalism faced challenges when it came into conflict with defenders of cultural practices who regarded women's rights as secondary to ethnic, religious, clan, and other such particularistic practices and beliefs. [...]

By the time of the UN's Fourth World Conference on Women in Beijing in 1995, there was considerable unity around the framing of "women's rights as human rights" and opposition to violence against women, which helped further bridge northern and southern interests. The gap between the North and South was closing. Thus, in the third-wave debates around human rights and development, women's movements in the South were especially important in expanding definitions of what women's concerns included and in looking at the broader global political and economic forces that influence women's status. They pointed to changing factors that shaped gender relations, ranging from colonialism during the struggles for independence, to poverty, militarization, and democratization both in newly independent states and in the former colonial powers, to contemporary issues of globalization that institutionalize inequality through international debt, structural adjustment policies, and unequal trade relations.

In sum, the changing global dynamics in women's mobilization can be traced to the initial challenges to Western dominance around the time of the 1975 Mexico conference. The 1985 Nairobi conference marked a major turning point in North–South dynamics as new third world networks emerged. The impetus generated by the 1995 UN Beijing conference produced a new rights-based approach blending sustainable development and human rights concerns in the twenty-first century. Today, the shift in momentum from North to South is evident in three ways: in the types of issues being put on the table; in the kinds of organizations championing these agendas, including informal networks; and in the extent to which women's rights is perceived as a universal goal rather than as a Western feminist project.

Changing Agendas and Actors

In the past decade, many of the specific initiatives pertaining to women's rights have come from the global South. For example, a key demand of many women's movements is equal representation of women in legislative bodies, local government, and other decision-making bodies. In various African countries like South Africa, Namibia, Uganda, Kenya, and Sierra Leone, there are 50/50 movements advocating that women claim half of all parliamentary seats. International and regional bodies, including the Inter-Parliamentary Union, the Beijing conference on women, the Southern African Development Community, the Socialist International, and the Organization of

American States, have been debating the use of quotas to promote women's parliamentary representation. More than eighty countries have adopted some form of quotas to improve the selection of female candidates running for office, and another twenty have launched quota debates over the past ten years (Krook 2004). [...]

Another area that has generated considerable momentum in the South has been the adoption of "gender budgets," or attempts to make the gender implications of national spending priorities more explicit and ultimately more fair. After the UN women's conference in Beijing (1995), many countries adopted women's budgets patterned along the lines of South Africa's 1994 budget exercise and the budgets of federal and state governments in Australia, which were adopted as early as 1984. By 2000, gender-sensitive budget initiatives were underway in eighteen countries in four regions. Gender budget initiatives are generally coordinated by the ministry of finance and involve collaboration among NGOs and the legislature. The gender budgeting process involves analysis of existing budgets to determine the differential gender impact on women, men, girls, and boys, and making recommendations for future budgets to improve the way in which funds are allocated (Budlender 2000). [...]

Women's economic activity also gained recognition as new women's entrepreneurial organizations linked economic empowerment and access to credit to social empowerment issues, including access to health care, literacy, and housing, opposing domestic violence, and other such issues. Feminist economists and activists struggled to make policymakers understand that key economic indicators like the gross domestic product and gross national product do not account for women's unpaid labor in the home and the community. Such labor includes care work of the family, voluntary work, subsistence agricultural labor, and self-employed or subcontracted labor in informal markets, all of which are important to the economy in many developing countries. Were such labor to be accounted for, they argued, economic reform, welfare, labor, and other such policies would be shaped in fundamentally different ways. Policies should respond not only to the demands of the market, which is only a portion of the economy, but also to the needs and priorities of those involved in unpaid labor, informal labor markets, and other forms of "hidden" labor, they argued. These new understandings of women's labor began to reconfigure the way many policymakers thought of the market, as well as notions of value, efficiency, and productivity.

Another aspect of gendered globalization is the flow of labor across borders. In December 2000, 121 countries signed the UN Convention against Transnational Organized Crime to States, and more than eighty countries signed one of its supplementary protocols—the Protocol to Prevent, Suppress, and Punish Trafficking in Persons, Especially Women and Children— which was aimed at undermining international crime networks and fighting the trafficking of people, especially women. Trafficking includes the recruitment, transportation, transfer, holding, and receipt of people through coercion, abduction, fraud, or deception. It also refers to the abuse of power to exploit someone through prostitution, sexual exploitation, forced labor, slavery, servitude, or other such means. The protocol was the result of years of extensive lobbying by coalitions, alliances, and organizations of women's rights, anti-trafficking, human rights, and migrants' groups, many of which had very different views on prostitution and its relation to trafficking (Sullivan 2003).

One of the main strategies that has developed to foster women's empowerment in poor countries is the provision of microcredit and the means to a living, generally through self-employment. The Self Employed Women's Association (SEWA), based in Ahmedabad, India, adopts a holistic approach to women's empowerment, serving as a model globally. SEWA was formed in 1972, drawing inspiration from the thinking of the Indian nationalist leader and pacifist

Mahatma Gandhi. It is an advocacy organization and at the same time a movement of poor, self-employed women workers themselves. Such women workers are part of the larger sector of nonsalaried unprotected labor that makes up 93 percent of all workers in India. SEWA not only has pressed the Indian government to provide training programs and other services for this sector and lobbied for better legislation for self-employed workers in India but also has taken its campaign onto the global arena. It was a leading force in mobilizing international pressure to get the International Labour Organization's Home Work Convention (1996) adopted.

*****

Causes of the Shift in Momentum

Several factors have contributed to the shift in momentum in women's mobilization from the global North to the South. In the United States, for example, there is a growing complacency about the necessity of improving women's status and a greater need to defend gains already made. The demise of the labor movement, a deficit in the numbers of women activists holding political office, especially at the national level, a lack of femocrats in government positions, and the general strengthening of the position of conservative political forces have all contributed to a situation where the United States is falling behind in many key areas. [...]

In contrast, we have witnessed in the global South the vigorous use of transnational coalitions and networks, along with international treaties, platforms, and conferences to push new women's rights agendas. Intense regional networking in Latin America, Africa, and Asia around particular issues (trafficking, land reform, education, peace building, reproductive rights, violence against women, electoral quotas) has helped define these concerns and develop strategies to address them. Feminists in state and international policymaking positions have supported movement initiatives in these areas.

Some of the elements of this global shift have regional dimensions. Active or nascent women's movements have emerged in Africa, creating new energy around women's issues. The increased influence of femocrats within state institutions as in Latin America, coupled with the NGOization or professionalization of women's activism, have provided sustained interest in women's concerns that had been primarily the domain of women's movements in the 1970s and 1980s. New donor interest in supporting gender concerns as part of effective use of development aid has also contributed to the new momentum found in the global South.

The educational levels of women have changed dramatically around the world since the 1970s. The gender gap in literacy and school enrollment closed by half between 1970 and 1990. The gap between female enrollment at the tertiary level jumped from less than half the male rate in 1970 to 70 percent by 1990 (UNDP 1995, 33–34). This meant that the numbers of women with the necessary skills to lead national organizations and to hold decision-making positions increased dramatically, which had implications for women's participation in international forums. As Moghadam has observed, "Transnational feminist networks have emerged in the context of a growing population of educated, employed, mobile and politically aware women around the world" (2000, 79).

After the 1990s, the expanded use of the Internet, e-mail, faxes, and other forms of communication greatly facilitated networking globally. Governments were increasingly eager to demonstrate that they had modernized and were seeking to adhere to the emerging international norms regarding women. They had committed themselves to many international and regional treaties and conventions regarding women's status and needed to show progress in at least some of the goals ratified there. All these factors contributed to the shifting dynamics in transnational mobilization around women's rights that increasingly placed the momentum in the South.

Another factor contributing to the shift in the global momentum in advocacy for women's rights relates to the dynamics within the women's movements in the United States and Europe. In European and U.S. women's movement organizations there is surprisingly little discussion of how their countries' policies and economic practices affect women in other parts of the world. This is especially striking because the policies of the global North are a key subject of discussion in women's movements in the global South. The locus of global economic and political power resides in the industrially developed countries, and what happens in them has worldwide implications. There has yet to emerge a full appreciation of the way in which the policies of the North affect the South, and the interconnections between our mutual fates and futures. With a few important exceptions (e.g., political representation for women in Iraq and Afghanistan and development policy in Scandinavia), there is relatively little lobbying of the governments in the North by U.S. and European women's organizations to address concerns of women in the South, especially regarding global inequalities and the role of international financial institutions like the World Bank and International Monetary Fund.

*****

Conclusions

This chapter has traced some of the changes in momentum at a transnational level and explored the consequences of these changes. It has evaluated the need to address these issues at a time when bilateral and multilateral aid is shrinking, and to consider the difficulties posed by continuing North–South gaps in approach and concerns. Even though feminists in North America and Europe have seemed to dominate transnational movements at particular moments, such as the early UN conferences on women in the 1970s, the closer one looks at particular movements, the more one finds that the influences on both agenda and organizations have always been multidirectional, even going back to the late 1800s. But one also finds that despite their transnational dimensions, women's movements define themselves and their vision of feminism with respect to local conditions. Non-Western countries continue to actively define their own agendas and have, in fact, claimed much of the momentum of feminist and women's rights advocacy globally, as movements in the global North have declined or become complacent or merely parochial. Global feminism is not a new phenomenon, but it is a more South-centered movement than ever before. This presents new challenges, of course, but there are also opportunities for women worldwide. The rights-centered approach to development offers a new and potentially powerful basis for cooperation. It is now up to feminist organizations in the global North to become more active participants in this worldwide movement.

References

Adams, Melinda. 2004. "Renegotiating the Boundaries of Political Action: Transnational Actors, Women's Organizations, and the State in Cameroon." Ph.D. diss., University of Wisconsin-Madison.

Boulding, Elise. 1977. *Women in the Twentieth Century World.* New York: Halsted Press.

Budlender, Debbie. 2000. "The Political Economy of Women's Budgets in the South." *World Development* 28: 1365–1378.

Bunch, Charlotte. 2001. "International Networking for Women's Human Rights." In Michael Edwards and John Gaventa, eds., *Global Citizen Action*, 217–229. Boulder, Colo.: Lynne Rienner.

Bunch, Charlotte, and Susana Fried. 1996. "Beijing '95: Moving Women's Human Rights from Margin to Center." *Signs*, August, 200–204.

Callaway, Helen. 1987. *Gender, Culture, and Empire: European Women in Colonial Nigeria.* Urbana: University of Illinois Press.

Denzer, LaRay. 1992. "Domestic Science Training in Colonial Yorubaland." In Karen Hansen, ed., *African Encounters with Domesticity*, 116–139. New Brunswick, N.J.: Rutgers University Press.

DuBois, Ellen. 2000. "Woman Suffrage: The View from the Pacific." *Pacific Historical Review* 69: 539–551.

Jayawardena, Kumari. 1986. *Feminism and Nationalism in the Third World.* London: Zed Books.

Jayawardena, Kumari. 1995. *The White Woman's Other Burden: Western Women and South Asia during British Rule.* New York: Routledge.

Keck, Margaret E., and Kathryn Sikkink. 1998. *Activists beyond Borders: Advocacy Networks in International Politics.* Ithaca, N.Y.: Cornell University Press.

Krook, Mona. 2004. "Reforming Representation: The Diffusion of Candidate Gender Quotas Worldwide." Paper presented at the meeting of the International Studies Association, Montreal, Canada.

Labode, Modupe. 1993. "From Heathen Kraal to Christian Home: Anglican Mission Education and African Christian Girls, 1850–1900." In Fiona Bowie, Deborah Kirkwood, and Shirley Ardener, eds., *Women and Missions: Past and Present—Anthropological and Historical Perceptions*, 126–144. Oxford: Berg.

Lavrin, Asuncion. 1995. *Women, Feminism, and Social Change in Argentina, Chile, and Uruguay, 1890–1940.* Lincoln: University of Nebraska Press.

Moghadam, Valentine M. 2000. "Transnational Feminist Networks: Collective Action in an Era of Globalization." *International Sociology* 15, no. 1: 57–85.

Pernet, Corinne A. 2000. "Chilean Feminists, the International Women's Movement, and Suffrage, 1915–1950." *Pacific Historical Review* 69: 663–688.

Pietilä, Hilkka. 2002. *Engendering the Global Agenda: The Story of Women and the United Nations.* Development Dossier, UN/Non-government Liaison Service, Geneva.

Ramirez, Francisco O., Yasemin Soysal, and Suzanne Shanahan. 1997. "The Changing Logic of Political Citizenship: Cross-National Acquisition of Women's Suffrage Rights, 1890 to 1990." *American Sociological Review* 67: 735–745.

Ranchod-Nilsson, Sita. 1992. "'Educating Eve': The Women's Club Movement and Political Consciousness among Rural African Women in Southern Rhodesia, 1950–1980." In Karen Hansen, eds., *African Encounters with Domesticity*, 195–217. New Brunswick, N.J.: Rutgers University Press.

Snyder, Margaret C. 2003. "African Contributions to the Global Women's Movement." Paper presented to "National Feminisms, Transnational Arenas, Universal Human Rights," Havens Center Colloquium Series, Madison, Wisconsin, April 14.

Snyder, Margaret C., and Mary Tadesse. 1995. *African Women and Development: A History.* London: Zed Books.

Stienstra, Deborah. 1994. *Women's Movements and International Organizations*. New York: St. Martin's Press.

Strobel, Margaret. 1991. *European Women and the Second British Empire*. Bloomington: Indiana University Press.

Sullivan, Barbara. 2003. "Trafficking in Women: Feminism and New International Law." *International Feminist Journal of Politics* 5, no. 1: 67–91.

Tripp, Aili Mari. 2002. "Women's Mobilization in Uganda (1945–1962): Nonracial Ideologies within Colonial-African-Asian Encounters." *International Journal of African Historical Studies* 35: 1–22.

UNDP. 1995. *Human Development Report 1995*. New York: Oxford University Press.

Weldon, S. Laurel. 2004. "Inclusion, Solidarity, and Transnational Social Movements: The Global Movement against Gender Violence." Paper presented at the annual meeting of the American Political Science Association, Chicago, September 4.

Supplement 42

Feminism without Borders

Building on the long history of feminist activism, in recent years, women around the world have developed new transnational grassroots organizations to help them face the challenges of the 21st century. DAWN and AWID are two such organizations.

Development Alternatives with Women for a New Era (DAWN)

Development Alternatives with Women for a New Era (DAWN) is a network of feminist scholars, researchers, and activists from the economic South working for economic and gender justice and sustainable and democratic development. DAWN provides a forum for feminist research, analyses, and advocacy on global issues (economic, social, and political) affecting the livelihoods, living standards, rights and development prospects of women, especially poor and marginalized women, in regions of the South.

DAWN envisions processes of economic and social development that are geared to enabling human rights and freedoms. DAWN draws strength from, and is committed to further empowering, the women's movement in the South. Its various activities include:

- developing and disseminating analyses of the economic, social, cultural, and political processes which cause and perpetuate inequalities of gender, class, race, and other forms of unfair social ordering and discrimination;
- engaging in global and regional inter-governmental and non-governmental forums and processes to challenge and change mainstream thinking, policy, and practice which hurt poor women in the South;
- co-sponsoring global civil society initiatives aimed at achieving sustainable, equitable, and gender-just social, economic, and political development;
- contributing to selected reform initiatives instituted in response to feminist or civil society demands for global institutional or policy changes; and
- providing training in analysis and advocacy skills to young feminists from the South who are engaged (or interested) in working on global issues covered by the four DAWN themes.

Since the founding of DAWN in 1984, the network has been recognized as a significant agent in the development of south feminist analyses in gender and development and a key participant in the global feminist/women's movements. A political and ideological "south" location-position remains vitally relevant in the era of globalization.

Source: Development Alternatives with Women for a New Era, "What We Do," retrieved from http://www.dawnnet.org/about.php?page=us

Association for Women's Rights in Development (AWID)

The Association for Women's Rights in Development (AWID) is an international, feminist, membership organization committed to achieving gender equality, sustainable development, and women's human rights. A dynamic network of women and men around the world, AWID members are researchers, academics, students, educators, activists, business people, policy-makers, development practitioners, funders, and more.

AWID's mission is to strengthen the voice, impact, and influence of women's rights advocates, organizations, and movements internationally to effectively advance the rights of women.

AWID believes that women's rights are not only necessary in and of themselves, but that they are central to ending the challenges the world faces today. Eradicating poverty, building peace, effectively tackling the HIV and AIDS pandemics, to name just a few—no lasting solutions to these issues are possible without a strategy that puts women's rights at the centre. AWID works to build a world where women's rights have been achieved and where all people enjoy their human rights.

Source: Association for Women's Rights in Development, retrieved from http://www.awid.org/

Gender Power at the United Nations

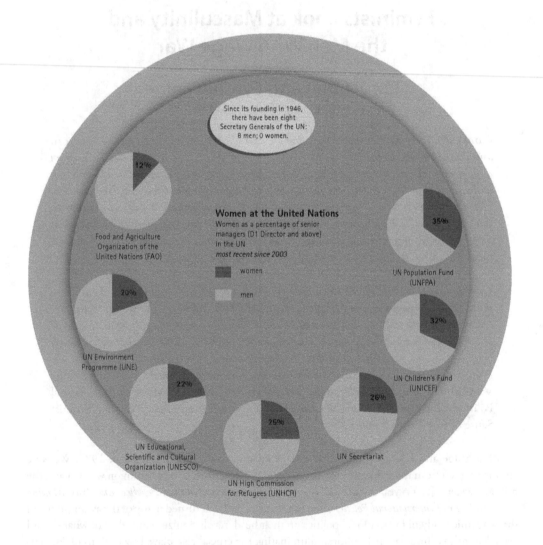

Since its founding in 1946, there have been eight Secretary Generals of the UN: 8 men; 0 women.

Women at the United Nations
Women as a percentage of senior managers (D1 Director and above) in the UN
most recent since 2003

- women
- men

Food and Agriculture Organization of the United Nations (FAO) — 12%

UN Environment Programme (UNE) — 20%

UN Educational, Scientific and Cultural Organization (UNESCO) — 22%

UN High Commission for Refugees (UNHCR) — 25%

UN Secretariat — 26%

UN Children's Fund (UNICEF) — 32%

UN Population Fund (UNFPA) — 35%

Source: Joni Seager, *The Penguin Atlas of Women in the World*, 4th ed. (New York: Penguin Books, 2009), 93.

Chapter 69

A Conversation with Cynthia Enloe: Feminists Look at Masculinity and the Men Who Wage War

Carol Cohn and Cynthia Enloe

Carol Cohn is the director and a founding member of the Consortium on Gender, Security, and Human Rights at the University of Massachusetts. She is a leading scholar focusing on a range of gender and security topics, including gender integration issues in the US military, weapons of mass destruction, and the gender dimensions of contemporary armed conflicts. Her recent work looks at gender mainstreaming in international peace and security institutions. She publishes widely in both academic and policy arenas, and conducts consultations and workshops on gender mainstreaming and organizational change for various organizations, including the UN Department of Peacekeeping Operations.

Cynthia Enloe is research professor in the Departments of International Development, Community, and Environment and Women's Studies at Clark University in Massachusetts. Her excellence in both teaching and research has been recognized with many awards. A prolific publisher, her research focuses on the interactions of feminism, women, militarized culture, war, politics, and globalized economics in countries such as Japan, Iraq, the US, Britain, the Philippines, Canada, Chile, and Turkey. She is the author of 12 books, including Nimo's War, Emma's War: Making Feminist Sense of the Iraq War, The Morning After: Sexual Politics at the End of the Cold War, *and* Bananas, Beaches, and Bases: Making Feminist Sense of International Politics.

Cynthia Enloe and I (Carol Cohn) first met in Finland in the frigid January of 1987. We were among women from more than twenty countries who had gathered for a forum on women and the military system. [...] A year later the U.S. edition of Cynthia's *Bananas, Beaches, and Bases: Making Feminist Sense of International Politics* came out (Enloe 1990).[1] It turned many of the assumptions in the academic study of international politics on their head, revolutionizing our ideas of what should even "count" as "international politics," illuminating the crucial role played by notions of "masculinity" and "femininity" in international relationships, and sparking a vibrant project of feminist critique, research, and theorizing in the study of international relations.[2]

As colleagues in the small world of feminist international relations theorists, we have had many occasions since 1987 to discuss our overlapping interests in militaries, masculinities, international organizations, and gendered conceptions of security. In the spring of 2002, we sat down at my kitchen table to explore the directions feminist analysis of international politics might take in the changed, and unchanged, post-September 11 world.

Carol Cohn (CC): Cynthia, what do you think we still don't know enough about in the realm of international politics?

Cynthia Enloe (CE): Like you, I, of course, see the "international" as embedded in the national and in the local. And, like you, I also see—or, better, have been taught by other feminists to see—the "political" in many spaces that others imagine are purely economic, or cultural, or private. With those provisos, I think we really don't know enough about how masculinity operates; but to carry on that exploration, we have to be at least women's studies–informed. This is not masculinity studies.

CC: Because understanding the dynamics of masculinity requires being curious about the complex workings of femininity?

CE: Yes, I really believe that. I think more and more about marriages, about particular masculinities—especially of the sort that states think they need—about how they're being confirmed by women in their roles as wives. Those women, of course, are not always willing to fulfill the state's needs! Your own classic article about the American male intellectuals who designed cold war nuclear strategies is so revealing about the ways in which certain forms of masculinity get confirmed by certain highly deflective modes of discourse (Cohn 1987, 1993). You were surrounded by men and operating as a sort of mole in a hypermasculinized subculture. But looking back, do you think it mattered that you were a *feminist* scholar doing this research on cold warrior discourse?

CC: When I was there, I tried very hard to shed my analytic lenses—even though we all know this is never completely possible—and to just pay careful attention to what was happening around me. What was clearly important, however, from day one, was that I was a *female* scholar. For example, I think many men were much more willing to talk with me, to answer my "dumb," naive questions with great openness, both because of a kind of genuinely chivalrous generosity and because it was in a sense "normal" for a female to be asking such basic questions. Also, it was relatively easy for me personally to deal with being in the "nonexpert" position. A male colleague who also did interviews with powerful nuclear decision makers told me somewhat ruefully that he and the men he was interviewing would sometimes get into a kind of competitive "who's-the-bigger-expert-here?" deadlock. It was probably quite productive that my relationships with these men did not provoke that kind of dynamic in either one of us!

CE: Yes, delving into masculinized cultures does turn the usually maddening presumptions about the "naive little lady" into an advantage—it was easier, though, for me to carry this off back in the days when I used to wear sleeveless sundresses!

I also want to know how the genderings of institutional cultures work inside international aid organizations. I want a feminist analysis of Doctors without Borders, Oxfam, the International Red Cross. This is part of my current interest in what it takes to genuinely *de*militarize a society—and, the intimately connected question, how do postwar societies manage to reestablish masculinized privilege in their political cultures? These peace-building groups become crucial in any demilitarizing processes. For instance, feminists inside Oxfam UK are asking *both* what Oxfam's postconflict operations' impacts are on local women *and* what are the politics of femininity and masculinity inside Oxfam itself. Suzanne Williams, a British feminist and a longtime staffer inside Oxfam UK, asked me to come up to Oxford last spring for a noontime conversation with about fifty Oxfam staff people. I remember thinking, "Oh, this is my chance.'" So I asked, "Okay, group, I don't know enough about Oxfam, so tell me what's the most masculinized of all Oxfam's departments?" They thought a minute, whispered among themselves, and then came up with their answer: the Emergency Aid Department. Why? Because their staff handles water pipes. If you're the ones delivering water to refugee camps, you get the Land Rover first; you're doing the heavy lifting; your daily work is surrounded by the aura of urgency; you're doing a job that calls for technical expertise. Put it altogether and laying water pipes in the Congo or East Timor becomes a distinctly "manly" enterprise. Now it's important to remember, the Oxfam water pipes guys are noncombatant, antimilitarist men, providing essential humanitarian aid to people who have been driven out of their homes and into refugee camps in wartime. A bit later, I asked these smart, worldly, dedicated folks, "Okay, so what's the least masculinized department in Oxfam?" One woman sort of chuckled and ventured, "development education." Everybody in the room sort of nodded, "yeah, yeah." "So, that means it's the most feminized?" "Well, I don't think about it that way, but yes."

CC: You know, in my research at the UN, I've heard the Third Committee of the General Assembly—that's the committee that works on social, humanitarian, and cultural issues—referred to in-house as the "ladies' committee."[3] On the other hand, the Security Council remains an overwhelmingly male and masculinized preserve, although there have been some very important contributions from women ambassadors in the last few years.

CE: The "ladies' committee" … good grief! What you're now uncovering inside the UN makes me all the more convinced that we need to launch explicitly feminist investigations of institutional political cultures. Let's have a feminist analysis of the two International War Crimes Tribunals at the Hague and in Arusha—I wonder if the two are identical? We have Carla Del Ponte (Swiss) coming right after Louise Arbour (Canadian), two women chief prosecutors. That is pretty amazing! If we really took them seriously, not just as "remarkable women," what would we reveal about this fledgling new world order—and about what it will take to make the brand new UN International Criminal Court work for women? Could it be that we're on the verge of creating, through the international war crimes tribunals, institutions that are less masculinized than the UN Secretariat, the WTO, the World Bank, or the IMP—how could we *tell*?

CC: That's a really provocative and important question. And I think that the feminist questions you've proposed for monitoring postwar demilitarization are an extremely useful example of how to approach it.[4] So once we get feminist analyses of international institutional political cultures, what do we have?

CE: A lot more realistic notion of how the world operates. That translates into a far more accurate causal explanation for patriarchy's global malleability.

*****

CC: [...] You are quite purposeful about using the term *patriarchy*. Tell me why?

CE: Well, I can remember the first time I ever heard *patriarchy* used—it terrified me. *(Laughter)* It sounded so ideological, heavy, and—I don't know—all the things that at that age I wasn't. It was Jean Grossholz who used it. Jean was mobilizing people behind the scenes at the first Wellesley conference on women and development, which turned into one of the very early special issues of *Signs*. I think it was 1980. I remember Jean going around and saying to people during coffee breaks, "We *have* to talk about patriarchy." And I thought, "Oh no, not patriarchy—I don't know what patriarchy is, and furthermore, it's not the kind of language I use!" Today I can't imagine trying to think seriously about the constructions of power and the systems by which power is both perpetuated and implemented *without* talking about patriarchy.

When I use *patriarchy* I try to be very clear and to give lots of examples. I try to remember what I was like when I heard Jean use this, and I remember how scary it sounded, right? It certainly sounds scary to many academics and policy makers today who don't want to be seen as an out-there feminist. I can understand why they would much rather use *gender hierarchies* (that's if they're really tough), or maybe just *gender divisions of labor*, or simply *discrimination*, or *inequality*.

In my teaching and writing, I try to be as precise and as concrete as I can be, which requires an endless curiosity! *Patriarchy* is not a sledgehammer being swung around a raving feminist head. It is a tool; it sheds light at the same time as it reveals patterns of causality.

CC: But let me pursue that a little. If you say "Is X patriarchal?" for people familiar with the term, normally the response would be, "Well, of course—find something that isn't!"

CE: Yeah, right.

CC: But what they might mean is simply that men are on top, men are in power. So saying "It's a patriarchy" wouldn't really shed light on the institution. The term is, for lots of people, a thought-stopper. So why does it seem like such a thought-*opening* question to you?

CE: Because it means you have to ask about the daily operations of both masculinity and femininity in relationship to each other. It is not men-on-top that makes something patriarchal. It's men who are recognized and claim a certain form of masculinity, for the sake of being more valued, more "serious," and "the protectors of/and controllers of those people who are less masculine" that makes any organization, any community, any society patriarchal. It's never automatic; it's rarely self-perpetuating. It takes daily tending. It takes decisions—even if those are masked as "tradition." It relies on many women finding patriarchal relationships comfortable, sometimes rewarding. And you and I in our own work have found women who would much rather not rock the patriarchal boat—often for good reasons. Patriarchal structures and cultures have proved to be so adaptable! That's what's prompted me to watch them over time—the British House of Commons, textile companies, the Israeli military, Chilean political parties, Bosnia's and Afghanistan's new governments.

CC: In the two institutions in which I've most recently done work, the word *patriarchy* is never used, but *gender* is all over the place. In the U.S. military, it is *gender integration*. At the UN, it is *gender balance* and *gender mainstreaming*. Although many people see *gender* as a more neutral, less inflammatory word than *patriarchy*, in these institutional cultures, *gender* is apparently often just as alienating and thought-stopping a term, evoking/representing "political correctness." The other thing that strikes me is that, in these institutions where attention to gender has been mandated, it remains an extremely opaque word. At the UN, for example, everyone is supposed to integrate a "gender perspective" in their programs, but many people simply don't have a real clue what that means. And the training that might make it clearer has been in short supply. But all of that is really about the practical effects of using specific words rather than the actual conceptual or analytic difference between *patriarchy* and a term such as *gender system*.

CE: And I have kept using *patriarchy* because it reminds us that we're investigating power.

*****

CC: Cynthia, one thing that everyone who knows you comments on is that you are amazingly generous to your feminist colleagues and graduate students. Why are you?

CE: Oh, a lot of people are.

CC: But you are to a remarkable degree. Why?

CE: Because I think we're all in this together. Because I know that 95 percent of everything I know, I know because somebody else has done the work. I'm totally dependent on other people feeling confident enough, empowered enough, energized enough, and funded enough that they can do the work that will help make me smarter. Also, I actually want to have a lively set of experiences with people. It makes academic life more fun; it makes it more interesting; it's worth doing it. I'm not the sort who wants to go to a log cabin in the woods and think my own shallow thoughts by myself. This means it really matters to me to change institutions, to change the cultures in our departments, in ways that give people who are coming along, just like other people did for me, a sense that, together, you can change cultures; you don't have to buy into it. I think about institutional cultures a lot. I think they're changeable, though it's surprising what one has to figure out in order to make those transformations stick. This is why the host of women's caucuses we've all created in so many professional associations, and all the new feminist journals we've launched with their formats and processes self-consciously crafted and nurtured, are so significant. Each and every one of them, I think, are feminist experiments in creating healthier professional institutions—in the process, we're trying to transform the very meanings of "professionalism" and "career."

*****

CC: [...] Did the events of September 11 change what you want to be thinking about?

CE: I don't think I'm knowledgeable enough yet to think very clearly about the actual men who took part. I would have to think about where masculinity comes into it, and the way in which masculinity gets mobilized. *Frontline* on PBS has had some very slow, thoughtful, jigsaw-puzzle kinds of biographies of two or three of the men, and I found them very helpful. To be honest, I—this doesn't mean other people shouldn't be interested—but I myself am not *very* enlivened in my own curiosity about men or women, but especially men, who engage in what is now defined as terrorism. I think I'm quite determined not to be seduced into thinking that those men are more interesting than men who look much more conventional, much more institutionalized, more rational, and *seemingly* nonviolent. There is a temptation—and this is simply the strength of narration—to find Timothy McVeigh or Mohammed Atta much more intellectually engaging than a person who usually goes nameless, for example, who flies—or designs—a B-52 bomber. Curiosity about the rank-and-file terrorist so often distracts us from asking where power really lies. [...]

September 11 engaged my emotions, a sense of horror, and a sense of worry about people I knew in New York. But the terrorists who hijacked those three planes? They aren't the main objects of my curiosity, because I think they are more the symptom than the cause. And I think ultimately they are nowhere near as capable of affecting our ideas, our lives, the structures and cultures in which we live, as a lot of other people who look not very narratively interesting. I'm pretty interested in bland people, people whose blandness is part of what's interesting about them—the rank-and-file men in conventional armies, the women who work as secretaries in aerospace corporations. Or Kenneth Lay, the CEO of Enron; nobody till last winter thought he was as interesting as Timothy McVeigh. I'm interested in Kenneth Lay and the culture he and his colleagues helped create that destroyed everybody's pensions. So, yes, I put up a bit of an intellectual firewall between my curiosity and certain popular—and state-crafted—diversionary narratives. When reporters phone to talk about, for instance, women terrorists, I try to lead them to consider other, more politically fruitful puzzles.

*****

CC: What other questions did your feminist curiosity turn to as being really important questions to ask—not just in relation to the events of September 11, but everything that has come after?

CE: Looking at U.S. society, I became intrigued with the gendered sprouting of American flags. Thinking about them pushed me to think about, on the one side, private emotions, particularly grief, grief for people whom you don't know, and, on the other side, constructions, reconstructions, and perpetuations of a militarized nation. The connection can only be fathomed if one asks feminist questions. Back in that October I happened to be talking to a woman at a campus social gathering. A staff woman came up to say "hi." She had on her lapel one of those jeweled American flags. I didn't look at it and grimace—it would be terrible if I had. Still, she immediately said, "Oh, you know I'm wearing this not to say anything political, but I had to find some way to express my sadness, and my feelings of solidarity with the people who've lost so much." I was very embarrassed that she felt she had to explain her wearing the flag pin to me. Did I come across as judgmental?

Later I thought that maybe especially people who don't have much power—certainly many women who are in staff-support positions in universities don't have much power to shape the expression of ideas and meanings—maybe they have to search for a way to make a public expression of grief that won't be misinterpreted—that somebody else won't co-opt, expropriate, exploit. Women are in that position so often, and so are a lot of men without power, but women are in that position so often because—and this comes back to patriarchal cultures—because their *ideas* about grief are not taken very seriously. Their *expressions* of grief are treated as important symbolically, but not their ideas about grief, and certainly not their ideas about the relationship of grieving to public policy. So in that circumstance, how does a woman reduce her complex ideas to a pin she wants to wear on her lapel?

CC: How have your reflections on the relations between grief and patriotism shaped your approach in your public talks since September 11?

CE: I try to talk about grieving, about the multiple forms of security, what feminists have taught us about "national" and "security." I try to describe other countries where people see as strange what Americans take to be normal.

CC: Such as?

CE: The presumption that the military as an institution is the bulwark of "national security"—it's not just a U.S. idea, but it's such a distinctively American late-twentieth-, early twenty-first-century presumption. It certainly is not, however, a Canadian presumption, not an Italian presumption, not a German or Japanese presumption. And then I try to suggest how asking *feminist* questions helps me make sense of things that otherwise are very puzzling. I want to present feminist questions as a tool. And usually I'll try to get them to talk about the images they've seen of Afghan women, and did they know that there are Afghan feminists, and why does it seem so hard to take on board the idea of an Afghan feminist organizing, strategizing, analyzing.

CC: What did you think of the "women's week" in presidential politics, when Laura Bush was out talking about Afghan women?

CE: You know, in some ways, I found it very embarrassing, absolutely insulting. It was not Laura Bush's or even George Bush's message. It was White House strategist Karen Hughes's message, her effort to close the gender gap between Democrats and Republicans.

CC: Yet in some ways, it seemed to work for them. I was struck by all the women who supported U.S. military action, *because* of the condition of Afghan women—something that was news to many of them.

CE: You know, when researching *Bananas*, I became fascinated with the World's Fairs in the 1870s, '80s, and '90s. One of the things that promoted the value of Americans' colonization of the Philippines was expressed in the tableaus that were put up on the midway in the World's Fairs. The "benighted woman," usually carrying a heavy burden, was put there to make the Americans in Chicago going through the midway think, "Oh, that's terrible." The oppression of women, for at least the last 150 years, has been used as a measure of how enlightened a society is, without much deeper commitment to deprivileging masculinity. That's why you have to have a feminist understanding of orientalism.

CC: No one could ever accuse me of being an optimist, but let me push this. Now that the position of women has been publicly inserted in national security discourse, now that it has been rhetorically marked as a supposed concern of male national political elites (no matter what their motivation), do you think there is even the slightest chance that that new discursive legitimacy of talking about "women" and "national security" in the same breath can be used as a wedge for political good?

CE: Here's my sense—but we're all going to have to keep watching this. If Afghan women, like Kosovar women, Bosnian women, and East Timorese women, manage to make serious gains in demasculinizing the reconstructed Afghan society, it will not be because of tokenist, exploitative discourse maneuvers by Bush and Blair and others. It will be because, first, Afghan women themselves are organized. Second, because there has been so much serious, feminist-savvy, detailed work going on inside international groups such as Oxfam, Human Rights Watch, and Amnesty, as well as inside UN agencies—UNDPKO [UN Department of Peacekeeping Operations], UNICEF [United Nations Children's Fund], and the UNHCR [Office of the United Nations High Commissioner for Refugees]. Most of us in our research and teaching barely know all the things that you […] and others are trying to teach us about how feminists have made dents in the masculinist operations of international and local institutions operating in Afghanistan and other "postconflict zones."

CC: My wondering if there could be any positive impact comes from my conversations with NGO activists about Resolution 1325, the UN Security Council's landmark resolution on women, peace, and security, passed in 2000. While the Security Council may have anticipated simply another thematic debate, women's NGOs ran with it; they publicized it, printed and distributed copies of it, and got the word out to women's activist groups in many different countries. So now, 1325 has an active constituency who monitor and push for its implementation. Women's groups are really using it as a tool. For example, in the resolution, the council committed to consult with women's organizations when on field missions. So on the council mission to Kosovo, the women got to meet with the council members and present them [with] a letter critiquing the UN mission's Gender Unit and pass on information they wanted the council to have—although the meeting *did* end up occurring at 11 P.M. in a diplomat's hotel room! Another example—before Lakhdar Brahimi, the UN's special representative to Afghanistan, left New York to start talks about an interim Afghan government, women's NGOs provided him with a list of Afghan women's NGOs they felt he should consult with—and he did. And 1325 isn't just having an impact on UN activities; women are also using it to put pressure on their own governments. I spoke with a woman from the Russian Committees of Soldiers' Mothers, for example, who told me that when they first got the resolution in the mail, they looked, thought, "Oh, just another Security Council resolution," and didn't bother to read it. But later, someone looked—and they've found it to be a gold mine. "Now," she says, "when we go to talk to political or military leaders, we take it with us. And because the Russian leadership is now very concerned about their international legitimacy, they feel that they have to listen to us, because that's what the resolution says."

CE: But that's not a high-tech aerial bombing campaign that's improving women's lives.

CC: Right. But is there the least possibility now of a parallel move? Despite the motivations of the Bush government, could this opening of rhetorical space for talking about women's lives and "national security" in the same breath be seized upon by women activists for ends that go far beyond the intentions of Bush's policy advisors and speechwriters?

CE: It's really risky for anyone who's trying to understand cause and effect to imagine that the military campaign strategists who were desperate for international legitimacy and thus grasped on to whatever they could—and girls being denied schooling happened to work very nicely, thank you—had that as their strategic objective. Maybe sometimes it's a risk that it's worth feminists taking. After all, we aren't served up many chances to get our foot in the patriarchal door. Still, so many feminist studies of imperialism, colonization, World's Fairs, warfare, the global spread-ings of Christian missionary work, and capitalist markets are here to provide us with a blinking yellow cautionary light: that is, when on occasion women's liberation is wielded instrumentally by any masculinized elite as a rationale-of-convenience for their actions, we should be on high alert; they'll put it back on the shelf just as soon as it no longer serves their longer-range purpose.

CC: So, in those weeks after September 11 and before the bombing started, what did you say when you were asked for a feminist response to the question "What should 'we' do now?"

CE: I didn't have it all worked out—I found myself saying, well, first of all, let's really think about what is the *appropriate* response, and what, in the long term, is the most useful response. [...] Feminists have taught us to be very, very careful before we adopt a response to grief, loss, and anger that is a *state* response, especially a militarized state response.
What did you say during those weeks?

CC: My starting place was that we needed to analyze *why* military violence seemed like a good response—or why it seemed so impossible not to strike back. We can't take it as self-evident.
I've been very influenced by working with Sara Ruddick on a "feminist ethical perspective on weapons of mass destruction" (Cohn and Ruddick 2004). She has written that the efficacy of violence is overrated, while its costs are consistently underestimated—although I actually believe that more than she does at this point! Anyway, I think that response to September 11 is really a prime example. The seemingly "self-evident" (to a lot of people) need to strike back is partly based on the assumption that it will "work," that it will be the most effective form of response. People assume that military violence will, in general, work a lot better than a negoti-ated political solution or a response based on the enforcement of national or international law or on economic actions.
I think that assumption needs to be examined, challenged. Even if you see the question of whether to use military force as a strategic, pragmatic question, apart from moral consideration, I am not at all sure that it *is* an effective response to terrorists or the causes of terrorism—even from a purely U.S. perspective. What I am sure of is that the human costs will be enormous, including the spread of further violence, and that in the long run the political consequences both for the United States and for many Arab women will be quite damaging.
I think one reason it's so hard politically to even examine the assumption that "striking back" is the best option is that ideas about masculinity are so intricately and invisibly interwoven with ideas about national security. So-called realist strategic dictums for state behavior sound a lot like dictums for hegemonic masculinity.

CE: You mean, "We have to do something."

CC: And, "The risks of inaction [read 'passivity'] are far greater than the risks of action," and "We have to show we are strong," and "We have to show them they can't push us around," and "We aren't going to take this lying down," and "We can't let them think we are wimps."

CE: "It's our honor." Americans in the early twenty-first century have created what seems to me to be a deadly combination for themselves (ourselves!)—possessing such disproportionate power combined with a cultural sense of being vulnerable. It gives me the shivers.

CC: But I think the problem is more than the sense of being vulnerable. It is the refusal to acknowledge the *inevitability* of our vulnerability. After all, vulnerability is a fact of human and political life. The attempt to deny its inevitability is what has led to the development of weapons of mass destruction "as deterrents," to massive investments in "national missile defense" and other baroque weapons technology, while we refuse to make serious investments in dealing with the worldwide HIV epidemic, or starvation, or poverty around the world. It has led to U.S. partnerships with oppressive regimes and multiple military attacks on other nations—and another being talked about by the Bush administration even as we speak! And all of these, of course, are part of what creates the desperation and anger that are the seeds of terrorism.

My fantasy is that if we acknowledged the impossibility of making ourselves invulnerable, of constructing Reagan's Plexiglass shield, we would have to have policies that fostered and strengthened good will and interdependence, that invested in making the planet a livable place for people in all countries, that aimed at disarmament instead of weapons "advancement" and proliferation. And my fear is that we won't acknowledge it, because these assumptions about strength and weakness, and vulnerability, are simultaneously engaged at the very personal, identity level but also built right into beliefs about national security and into national security doctrine—as though they reflected "objective reality" and in no way stemmed from deeply felt and held identities.

So stopping to try to disentangle emotions and assumptions about violence and its efficacy was the starting place for me. Ultimately, I want to ask what it will take to change the discourse, to alter the meanings of strength and justice in the international political arena.

CE: You know, having conversations like the one we've been having makes me more convinced than ever of the necessity of crafting, and teaching others to craft, a feminist curiosity. And I guess that my conviction comes from our being at a very particular moment in world politics and feminist politics; we're living in a world where American militarized policy carries more clout—disproportionate clout—than ever in world history, while we're also living at a time when feminists in the United States are more conscious than ever that we'll only be able to understand the world if we take seriously the insights of women from Finland to Fiji!

Notes

1. See also Enloe 1993, 2001–2.
2. There is now a feminist Theory and Gender Studies section in the International Studies Association. The journal launched by its members, the *International Feminist Journal of Politics*, is an excellent location for exploring some of this new scholarship.
3. The other five committees of the General Assembly are the First Committee (disarmament and international security), the Second (economic and financial), the Fourth (special political and decolonization), the Fifth (administrative and budgetary), and the Sixth (legal). The Web site http://www.peacewomen.org has a very useful guide to the UN system.
4. Cynthia proposed these at "A Dialogue between Academics, Activists, and UN Officials" on women, peace, and security, held at the UN on April 11, 2002. The April 11 event was part of a larger continuing NGO-academic-UN dialogue project being organized by Sheri Gibbing at the Women's International League for Peace and Freedom (WILPF), which Carol has been working on. In addition to Cynthia and Carol, other participants in the April 11 session on Security Council Resolution 1325 included Jennifer Klot (then senior governance

adviser at UNIFEM [UN Development Fund for Women], now at the Social Science Research Council [SSRC]), Ann Tickner (director of international studies, University of Southern California), Maha Muna (then at the Women's Commission for Refugee Women and Children, now at UNIFEM), and Iris Marion Young (professor of political science, University of Chicago). For an edited transcript, see http://www.peacewomen.org. See also Enloe 2002.

References

Cockburn, Cynthia, and Dubravka Zarkov, eds. 2002. *The Postwar Moment: Militaries, Masculinities, and International Peacekeeping.* London: Lawrence & Wishart.

Cohn, Carol. 1987. "Sex and Death in the Rational World of Defense Intellectuals." *Signs: Journal of Women in Culture and Society*, 12(4):687–718.

Cohn, Carol. 1993. "Wars, Wimps, and Women: Talking Gender and Thinking War." In *Gendering War Talk*, ed. Miriam Cooke and Angela Woollacott, 227–46. Princeton, N.J.: Princeton University Press.

Cohn, Carol, and Sara Ruddick. 2004. "A Feminist Ethical Perspective on Weapons of Mass Destruction." In *Ethics and Weapons of Mass Destruction*, ed. Sohail Hashmi and Phillip Valera. Cambridge: Cambridge University Press. Available on-line at http://www.ksg.harvard.edu/wappp/research/cohn.htm.

Enloe, Cynthia. 1990. *Banana, Beaches, and Bases: Making Feminist Sense of International Politics.* Berkeley: University of California Press.

Enloe, Cynthia. 1993. *The Morning After: Sexual Politics at the End of the Cold War.* Berkeley: University of California Press.

Enloe, Cynthia. 2001–2. "Sneak Attack: The Militarization of U.S. Culture." *Ms. Magazine*, December–January, 15.

Enloe, Cynthia. 2002. "Demilitarization—or More of the Same? Feminist Questions to Ask in the Postwar Moment." In Cockburn and Zarkov 2002, 22–32.

Global Women's Strike/
Huelga Mundial de Mujeres

Invest in Caring, Not Killing

Women and girls do two-thirds of the world's work, most of it unwaged. [More than] $1 trillion/ year is spent on the military worldwide, more than half by the U.S. Ten percent of this would provide the essentials of life for all: water, sanitation, basic health, nutrition, literacy, and a minimum income.

The Global Women's Strike is a grassroots network with national coordinations in a number of countries. Invest in caring, not killing is our strategy for change. We campaign for the return of military budgets to the community, beginning with women, the main carers in every country of people and the planet. Women, and men who support our goals, take action together on 8 March, International Women's Day, and throughout the year. We work to ensure that power relations among us are addressed, and that each of our struggles is backed by our collective power.

Women from different sectors are involved: women of colour, Indigenous and rural women, mothers, women in waged work, lesbian, bisexual women, and TT women, sex workers, religious activists, women with disabilities, older and younger women....

Global Women's Strike Demands

- *Payment for all caring work* in wages, pensions, land, and other resources. What is more valuable than raising children and caring for others? Invest in life and welfare, not military budgets or prisons.
- *Pay equity* for all, women and men, in the global market.
- *Food security* for breastfeeding mothers, paid maternity leave, and maternity breaks. Stop penalizing us for being women.
- *Don't pay "Third World debt."* We owe nothing, they owe us.
- *Accessible clean water, health care, housing, transport, literacy.*
- *Non-polluting energy and technology*, which shortens the hours we work. We all need cookers, fridges, washing machines, computers, and time off!
- *Protection and asylum* from all violence and persecution, including by family members and people in positions of authority.
- Freedom of movement. Capital travels freely. Why not people?

Source: Adapted from Global Women's Strike/Huelga Mundial de Mujeres, retrieved from http://www. globalwomenstrike.net/

Copyright Acknowledgements